CEDU쎄듀는 A Comprehensive English eDUcation(종합적 영어교육)의 약자입니다.

펴낸이 김기훈 I 김진희
펴낸곳 (주)쎄듀 I 서울특별시 강남구 논현로 305 (역삼동)
발행일 2020년 9월 8일 1쇄
내용문의 www.cedubook.com
구입문의 콘텐츠 마케팅 사업본부
Tel. 02-6241-2007
Fax. 02-2058-0209
등록번호 제 22-2472호
ISBN 978-89-6806-195-0

절대평가 수능대비
수능 영어
정복의 첫걸음

첫단추
독해유형편

저자

김기훈 現 ㈜쎄듀 대표이사
現 메가스터디 영어영역 대표강사
前 서울특별시 교육청 외국어 교육정책자문위원회 위원
저서 천일문 / 천일문 Training Book / 천일문 GRAMMAR
첫단추 BASIC / 쎄듀 본영어 / 어휘끝 / 어법끝 / 문법의 골든룰 101
절대평가 PLAN A / 리딩 플랫폼 / ALL씀 서술형 / 독해비
Reading Relay / The 리딩플레이어 / 빈칸백서 / 오답백서
첫단추 / 파워업 / 수능영어 절대유형 / 수능실감 등

쎄듀 영어교육연구센터
쎄듀 영어교육센터는 영어 콘텐츠에 대한 전문지식과 경험을 바탕으로
최고의 교육 콘텐츠를 만들고자 최선의 노력을 다하는 전문가 집단입니다.
오혜정 수석연구원

검토위원
허경원 서울대 영어영문학과 졸업
저서 쎄듀 문법을 알아야 독해가 된다 / 능률교육 리딩튜터
신사고 리스닝엔탑 / 신사고 Writing Salad

개발에 도움을 주신 분
장정근 선생님 (대성고)

마케팅 콘텐츠 마케팅 사업본부
영업 문병구
제작 정승호
인디자인 편집 올댓에디팅
표지 디자인 윤혜영
내지 디자인 홍단
영문교열 Eric Scheusner

이 책을 내며

'첫단추를 잘 끼워야 한다' 이 말은 '시작'의 중요성을 강조한 말입니다. 첫단추를 잘못 끼우면 그 단추를 풀고 다시 채우는 데는 두 배의 노력이 들지만, 만약 제대로 끼운다면 나머지는 손쉽게 채울 수 있습니다. 〈첫단추 Button up 독해유형편〉은 예비 고1~고2 학생들이 제대로 된 시작을 할 수 있도록 돕기 위해 기획되었습니다. 이 책은 〈첫단추 독해 모의고사〉의 개정판으로, 쉬운 수능 시대에서도 유지되는 기존 수능 영어의 틀을 양질의 문제를 통해 완벽하게 학습할 수 있도록 준비했습니다.

이 책의 특징은 다음과 같습니다.

첫째, 수능의 기초를 잡아줍니다.
이 책은 수능 모의고사를 처음 접하는 학생이 알아야 할 기초적인 내용을 담은 준비편, 본격적으로 수능에 출제되는 유형을 학습할 수 있는 유형편, 실제 시험에 대비할 수 있는 실전편으로 구성되어 있습니다. 세 단계를 통해 수능이 무엇인지, 수능에는 어떤 문제가 나오는지, 수능에 어떻게 대비해야 하는지에 대한 해답을 얻을 수 있습니다.

둘째, 문제 유형별 자세한 해결 전략을 제시합니다.
수능에는 유형이 반복되어 출제되므로 유형별 학습을 통해 훈련하는 것이 가장 좋습니다. 이 책에서는 수능에 출제되는 유형을 최근 다시 등장하는 '함의 추론'을 포함하여 18가지로 나눠 제시하며, 각 유형의 해결 전략을 스스로도 도출해볼 수 있도록 구성했습니다. 대표 문제를 통해 각 유형별 해결 전략을 익힌 후, 챕터마다 제공되는 미니 모의고사와 독해 모의고사, 실전 모의고사까지 풀고 나면 수능 모의고사에 대한 자신감이 생길 것입니다.

셋째, 모든 지문을 철저히 분석하여 담았습니다.
길고 복잡한 구조의 문장도 읽고 바로 해석하도록 도와주는 직독직해와 구문 분석, 지문의 흐름을 도식화하여 보여주는 지문 Flow, 꼼꼼한 정답과 오답 풀이로 혼자서도 학습이 가능하도록 구성하였습니다.

수능은 단기간에 끝낼 수 있는 것이 아니라 장기간에 걸쳐 쌓은 실력으로 승부해야 하는 시험입니다. 따라서 실제 수능을 보기 전까지 계속 치러지는 모의고사는 중요한 준비 과정이며, 결코 소홀히 해서는 안 됩니다. 쎄듀 첫단추 독해유형편은 수능 모의고사를 대비하는 모든 학생들에게 꼭 필요한 교재가 되어왔으며, 계속해서 수능의 첫단추를 채우려는 모든 학생들의 든든한 동반자가 되기를 바랍니다.

저자

이 책의 구성과 특징

이 책은 다음과 같이 구성되어 있습니다.

1 준비부터 확실히! **준비편**

수능의 첫단추를 제대로 끼우세요.

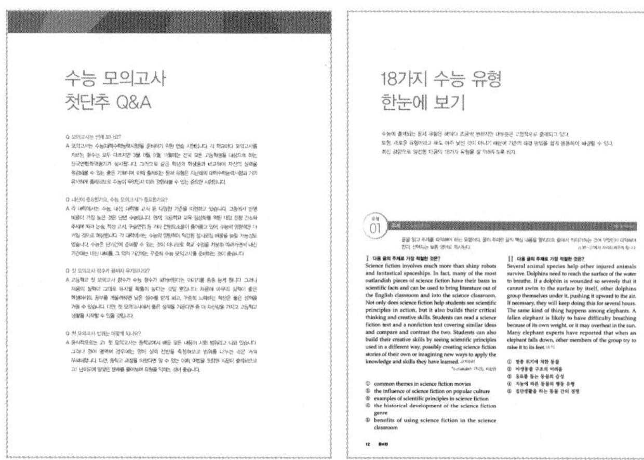

| **수능 첫단추 Q&A**에서 수능 모의고사를 처음 접하는 학생들의 궁금증을 해결해 드립니다.

| 수능 모의고사에 어떤 문제가 나오는지 궁금하다면 **18가지 수능 유형 한눈에 보기**에서 엿보세요.

2 수능 유형과의 첫 만남! **유형편**

모의고사에 출제되는 최신 유형으로 공부하세요.

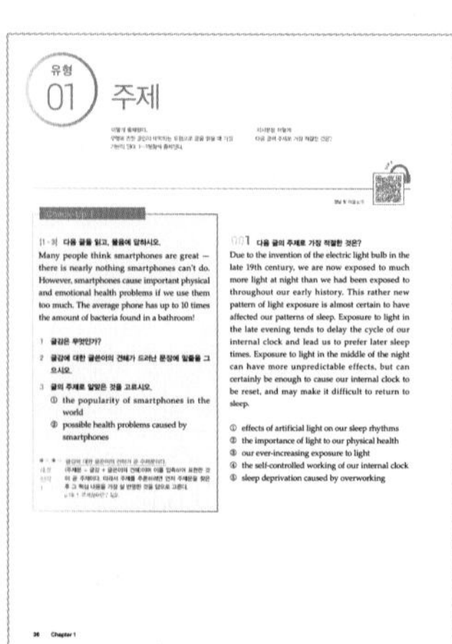

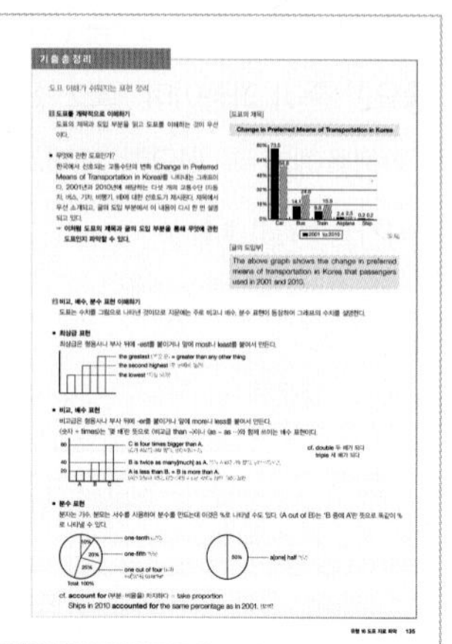

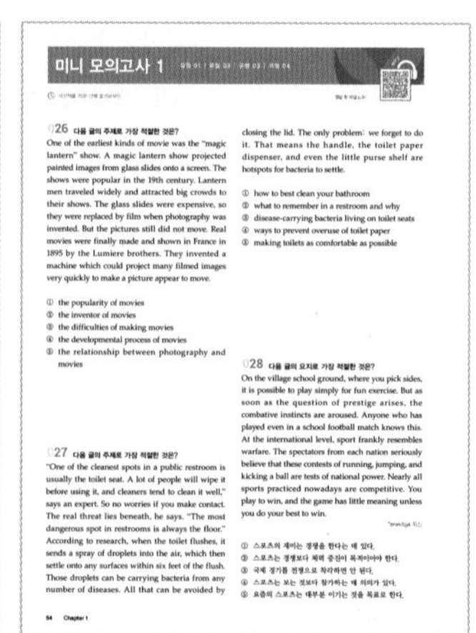

| **Check-Up**을 통해 문제풀이에 꼭 필요한 개념을 스스로 발견할 수 있습니다. 여기서 도출된 **해결 전략**을 **대표 문제**에 적용하면서 풀어보세요.

| **기출총정리**는 철저한 기출 분석을 통해 학생들에게 필요한 개념을 정리한 코너입니다.

| **실전적용독해**와 **미니 모의고사**를 통해 각 유형을 충분히 학습할 수 있습니다. 앞에서 배운 내용을 적용해서 주어진 시간 내에 풀 수 있도록 연습하세요.

3 실력 최종 검토! **실전편**

지금까지 쌓은 나의 실력을 점검해 보세요.

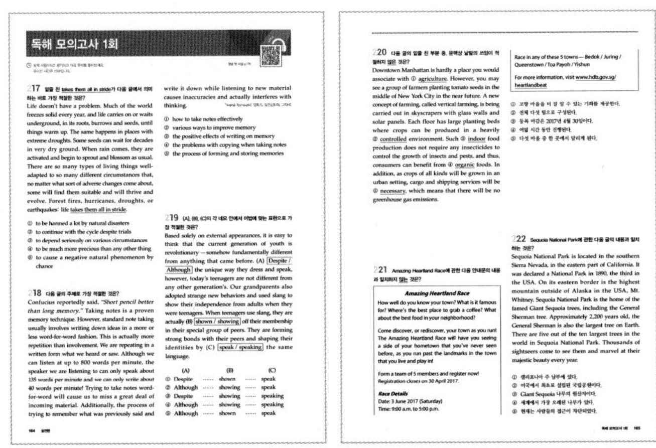

| **독해 모의고사**를 통해 최종적으로 자신의 실력을 점검해보세요. 실제 시험을 본다고 생각하고 풀어보세요.

4 꼼꼼하고 친절하게! **정답 및 해설**

자세하고 똑똑한 설명으로 모든 지문을 완벽히 학습하세요.

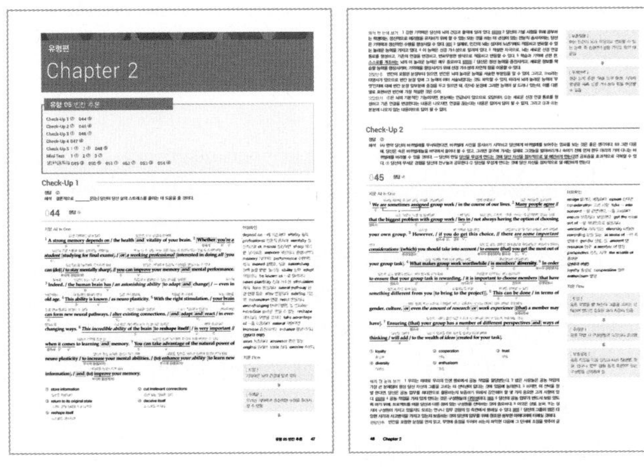

| 모든 문장이 자세하게 분석된 지문 All in One으로 직독직해를 연습하고 구문을 파악하세요. 또한, 꼼꼼하고 친절한 정답과 오답 풀이로 정답률을 높이세요.

5 무료 **부가서비스**

어휘리스트, 어휘테스트, 어휘 출제 프로그램, MP3

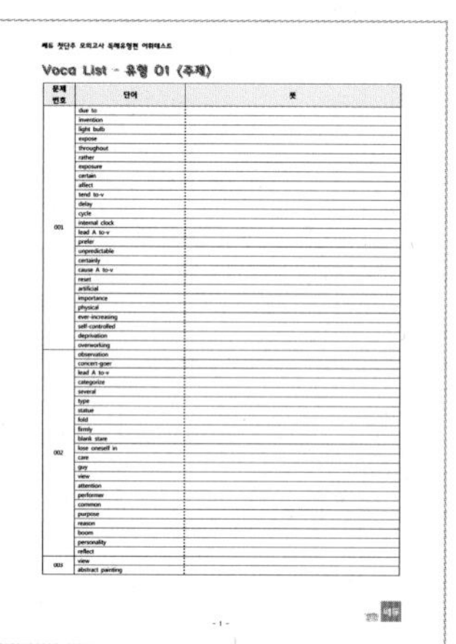

교재에 나온 어휘를 모두 정리한 어휘리스트로 단어를 암기하고, 어휘테스트로 확인해 보세요. www.cedubook.com에서 무료로 다운로드 받으실 수 있습니다.

일러두기

S 주어 (S-S': 주절의 주어-종속절의 주어) **V 동사** **C 보어**
O 목적어 (IO 간접목적어, DO 직접목적어, O-O' 주절의 목적어-종속절의 목적어)

- 끊어 읽기 표시(/, //)는 문장구조와 자연스러운 우리말을 고려한 의미 단위(sense group)별로 끊어서 나타낸 것입니다.
- 일반적인 어구의 끊어 읽기는 /로 표시하되, 중문과 복문을 구성하는 절과 절의 구별은 //로 표시합니다. 다만, 더 큰 절 내의 부속절은 /로 표시합니다.
- 수식어구는 [ ]로 표시하며 수식 받는 선행사는 이탤릭체로 표시합니다.
- ( )안의 단어 또는 구는 생략된 어구를 나타냅니다.

음성 파일을 어떻게 활용해야 하나요?

1 **듣기 실력 향상을 위한 연습**
문제만 먼저 읽고 지문 없이 음성을 들으며 글의 핵심내용을 파악해 보세요. 문제의 답과 연관되는 부분을 파악하며 메모하는 습관을 기르는 것도 듣기 실력 향상에 도움이 됩니다.

2 **Shadow Reading**
Shadow Reading이란, 원어민의 음성을 들으며 그림자처럼 따라 읽는 것을 말합니다. 이는 발음과 톤 교정에 효과적입니다.

3 **복습**
책 없이 MP3만을 들으며 지문의 내용을 복습해 보세요. 음성 파일을 들어도 파악이 잘 안 되는 부분들은 다시 한 번 학습하세요.

CONTENTS

준비편

모든 일의 시작에는 준비가 필요합니다.
'준비편'을 통해 모의고사에 대한 궁금증을 풀어보고,
모의고사에는 어떤 문제 유형이 출제되는지 익혀두세요.
본격적인 내용은 이어지는 '유형편'에서 배우게 됩니다.

수능 모의고사 첫단추 Q&A

18가지 수능 유형 한눈에 보기

수능 모의고사 첫단추 Q&A

Q 모의고사는 언제 보나요?

A 모의고사는 수능(대학수학능력시험)을 준비하기 위한 연습 시험입니다. 각 학교마다 모의고사를 치르는 횟수는 모두 다르지만 3월, 6월, 9월, 11월에는 전국 모든 고등학생을 대상으로 하는 전국연합학력평가가 실시됩니다. 그러므로 같은 학년의 학생들과 비교하여 자신의 실력을 점검해볼 수 있는 좋은 기회이며, 이때 출제되는 문제 유형은 지난해의 대학수학능력시험과 거의 유사하게 출제되므로 수능이 무엇인지 미리 경험해볼 수 있는 중요한 시험입니다.

Q 내신이 중요한가요, 수능 모의고사가 중요한가요?

A 각 대학에서는 수능, 내신, 대학별 고사 등 다양한 기준을 마련하고 있습니다. 그중에서 반영 비율이 가장 높은 것은 단연 수능입니다. 현재, 고등학교 교육 정상화를 위한 대입 전형 간소화 추세에 따라 논술, 적성 고사, 구술면접 등 기타 전형요소들이 줄어들고 있어, 수능의 영향력은 더 커질 것으로 예상됩니다. 각 대학에서는 수능의 영향력이 막강한 정시모집 비율을 늘릴 가능성도 있습니다. 수능은 단기간에 준비할 수 있는 것이 아니므로 학교 수업을 차분히 따라가면서 내신 기간에는 내신 대비를, 그 외의 기간에는 꾸준히 수능 모의고사를 준비하는 것이 좋습니다.

Q 첫 모의고사 점수가 끝까지 유지되나요?

A 고등학교 첫 모의고사 점수가 수능 점수가 되어버린다는 이야기를 종종 듣게 됩니다. 그러나 처음의 실력이 그대로 유지될 확률이 높다는 것일 뿐입니다. 처음에 아무리 실력이 좋은 학생이라도 공부를 게을리하면 낮은 점수를 받게 되고, 꾸준히 노력하는 학생은 좋은 성적을 거둘 수 있습니다. 다만, 첫 모의고사에서 좋은 성적을 거둔다면 좀 더 자신감을 가지고 고등학교 생활을 시작할 수 있을 것입니다.

Q 첫 모의고사 범위는 어떻게 되나요?

A 공식적으로는 고1 첫 모의고사는 중학교에서 배운 모든 내용이 시험 범위라고 나와 있습니다. 그러나 영어 영역의 경우에는 영어 실력 전반을 측정하므로 범위를 나누는 것은 거의 무의미합니다. 다만, 중학교 과정을 마쳤다면 알 수 있는 어휘, 어법을 포함한 지문이 출제되므로 고1 난이도에 알맞은 문제를 풀어보며 유형을 익히는 것이 좋습니다.

Q 모의고사는 어떻게 준비해야 하나요?

A 모의고사는 어디까지나 자신의 실력을 점검하기 위한 시험입니다. 내신처럼 성적이 기록되어 대학 입시에 바로 반영되는 시험은 아니지만, 꾸준히 다양한 문제를 풀어보면서 차분히 준비하는 것이 좋습니다.

1. 기출 문제 및 다양한 문제를 풀어봅니다.

많은 문제를 풀어보는 것만큼 좋은 시험 대비 방법은 없습니다. 특히 기출 문제는 실제 수능이나 전국연합학력 평가가 어떻게 출제되는지 보여주는 가장 정확한 자료입니다. 모든 문제는 EBSi 사이트의 '입시정보'란에서 무료로 다운받을 수 있으며 (www.ebsi.co.kr), 수능 출제기관인 한국교육과정평가원에서 시행하는 시험은 평가원 사이트 (kice.re.kr)에서도 다운받을 수 있습니다. 쎄듀 첫단추 시리즈는 이 중 가장 대표적인 기출 문제를 엄선하여 유형별로 자세한 해결 전략을 제시하고 있습니다.

2. 틀렸던 문제들을 중점적으로 공부합니다.

문제를 많이 풀어보는 것보다 한 번 풀어본 문제를 확실히 이해하고 넘어가는 것이 더 중요합니다. 모든 문제를 다시 살펴보면서 몰랐던 어휘나 해석하기 어려운 구문 등을 표시해두고 해설과 해석을 참고하여 확실히 암기하고 이해하도록 합니다. 적어도, 틀린 문제와 헷갈리는 문제는 따로 표시를 해두고 반드시 다시 풀어보면서 자신이 부족한 점을 보완하도록 합니다.

Q 곧 모의고사를 봅니다. 주의할 점은 없나요?

A 모의고사는 실제 수능처럼 하루 동안 전 영역의 시험을 보게 되므로 긴 시간 동안 집중력을 유지하면서 많은 문제를 풀 수 있어야 합니다. 또한, 실제로 모의고사를 보게 되면 시간이 모자라 당황하는 경우가 많습니다. 영어 영역은 70분간 총 45문제를 풀게 되는데, 검토와 답안지 작성을 위해서 3~5분의 시간이 필요하므로 평소에도 실제 모의고사를 보는 것처럼 시간 관리 연습을 하는 것이 좋습니다.

18가지 수능 유형 한눈에 보기

수능에 출제되는 문제 유형은 해마다 조금씩 변하지만 대부분은 고정적으로 출제되고 있다.
또한, 새로운 유형이라고 해도 아주 낯선 것이 아니기 때문에 기존의 해결 방법을 쉽게 응용하여 해결할 수 있다.
최신 경향으로 엄선한 다음의 18가지 유형을 잘 익혀두도록 하자.

주제 1~2문제/28문제

정답 및 해설 p.2

글을 읽고 주제를 파악해야 하는 유형이다. 글의 주제란 글의 핵심 내용을 말하므로 글에서 이야기하는 것이 무엇인지 파악해야 한다. 선택지는 보통 영어로 제시된다.

p.36~37에서 자세히 배우게 됩니다.

I 다음 글의 주제로 가장 적절한 것은?

Science fiction involves much more than shiny robots and fantastical spaceships. In fact, many of the most outlandish pieces of science fiction have their basis in scientific facts and can be used to bring literature out of the English classroom and into the science classroom. Not only does science fiction help students see scientific principles in action, but it also builds their critical thinking and creative skills. Students can read a science fiction text and a nonfiction text covering similar ideas and compare and contrast the two. Students can also build their creative skills by seeing scientific principles used in a different way, possibly creating science fiction stories of their own or imagining new ways to apply the knowledge and skills they have learned. [모의응용]

*outlandish 기이한, 이상한

① common themes in science fiction movies
② the influence of science fiction on popular culture
③ examples of scientific principles in science fiction
④ the historical development of the science fiction genre
⑤ benefits of using science fiction in the science classroom

II 다음 글의 주제로 가장 적절한 것은?

Several animal species help other injured animals survive. Dolphins need to reach the surface of the water to breathe. If a dolphin is wounded so severely that it cannot swim to the surface by itself, other dolphins group themselves under it, pushing it upward to the air. If necessary, they will keep doing this for several hours. The same kind of thing happens among elephants. A fallen elephant is likely to have difficulty breathing because of its own weight, or it may overheat in the sun. Many elephant experts have reported that when an elephant falls down, other members of the group try to raise it to its feet. [모의]

① 멸종 위기에 처한 동물
② 야생동물 구조의 어려움
③ 동료를 돕는 동물의 습성
④ 지능에 따른 동물의 행동 유형
⑤ 집단생활을 하는 동물 간의 경쟁

유형 02 요지, 주장 2문제/28문제

정답 및 해설 p.3

글의 요지, 필자의 주장, 글이 시사하는 바를 묻는 다양한 지시문으로 출제되지만 모두 글의 핵심 내용인 '요지'를 파악해야 풀 수 있는 유형이다. 선택지는 보통 우리말로 제시되지만, 영어 속담이나 격언이 출제되기도 한다.

p.40~42에서 자세히 배우게 됩니다.

I 다음 글의 요지로 가장 적절한 것은?

The initial stages of a relationship are usually relatively conflict-free. But later, there is often conflict. To many, conflict within a relationship means that the relationship itself is in trouble; the absence of conflict is considered the standard we should all strive for. As it turns out, conflict is not only unavoidable but actually crucial for the long-term success of a relationship. Think of conflict as a form of vaccine. Immunization involves injecting a small amount of a disease into the body. This lets the body learn the disease's weaknesses and prepares the body for real illness. Likewise, minor conflicts help our relationship develop defenses; they immunize the relationship and help partners deal with major gridlocks when they arise. [모의응용]

*gridlock 교착 상태

① 심리적인 안정이 질병에 대한 면역력을 강화시킨다.
② 분쟁 조정을 위해 제 3자의 객관적 조언이 필요하다.
③ 장기적인 관점에서 갈등은 관계 유지에 도움이 된다.
④ 성공적인 관계를 규정하는 기준은 사람마다 다르다.
⑤ 학습 시 단기적 목표와 장기적 목표를 각각 수립해야 한다.

II 다음 글에서 필자가 주장하는 바로 가장 적절한 것은?

The Internet is wonderful in so many different ways. It has transformed the way we live. We can contact people instantly, wherever they are. We can plan things together, without ever needing to meet. We have access to a world of information at the click of a mouse. On the other hand, the Internet glues us to our computer monitors and isolates us from our fellow human beings. We now send an e-mail to someone, rather than call them up or walk ten yards to the next office to say hello. We need to create a balance between the World Wide Web and the real wide world we live in. Turn your computer off for one day a week, leave your laptop at home, get out into the real world, and live your life. [모의응용]

① 과장된 인터넷 상업 광고를 조심하라.
② 신속한 정보 전달을 위해 인터넷을 사용하라.
③ 인터넷 사용을 줄여 현실 세계와 균형을 유지하라.
④ 학습 효과를 높이기 위해 인터넷 강의를 수강하라.
⑤ 인터넷 화상 통화를 활용하여 불필요한 모임을 줄여라.

유형 03 제목 1~2문제/28문제

정답 및 해설 p.3

글을 읽고 영어로 된 알맞은 제목을 고르는 유형이다. 글의 요지를 파악한 다음, 글의 내용과 특징을 가장 잘 드러내는 제목을 정답으로 고른다.

p.46~47에서 자세히 배우게 됩니다.

I 다음 글의 제목으로 가장 적절한 것은?

In 2000, the government in Glasgow, Scotland, happened upon a remarkable crime prevention strategy. Officials hired a team to beautify the city by installing a series of blue lights in various noticeable locations. In theory, blue lights are more attractive and calming than the yellow and white lights that illuminate much of the city at night, and indeed the blue lights seemed to cast a soothing glow. Months passed and researchers noticed a striking trend: The locations with blue lights experienced a dramatic decline in criminal activity. The blue lights in Glasgow, which mimicked the lights of police cars, seemed to imply that the police were always watching. The lights were never designed to reduce crime, but that's exactly what they appeared to be doing. [모의응용]

① Turn Lights Off for Our Planet
② Blue Makes People Feel Lonely
③ Colorful Lights Lifting Your Spirits
④ An Unexpected Outcome from Blue Lights
⑤ Cleaner Streets Lead to Lower Crime Rates

II 다음 글의 제목으로 가장 적절한 것은?

You might have heard stories of expert intuition: for example, the physician who makes a complex diagnosis after a single glance at a patient. Expert intuition strikes us as magical, but it is not. Indeed, each of us performs feats of intuitive expertise many times each day. Most of us are highly-skilled in detecting anger in the first word of a telephone call and recognize as we enter a room that we were the subject of the conversation. Our everyday intuitive abilities are no less amazing than the striking insights of a physician — only more common. [모의응용]

① Don't Make a Phone Call in Anger!
② Intuitive Expertise: Not Only for Experts
③ Collect More Evidence, Be More Intelligent
④ Intuition: A Magician's Basic Qualification
⑤ Intuition Will Never Beat Experience

유형 04 글의 목적 파악 1문제/28문제

정답 및 해설 p.4

글을 쓴 목적을 파악하는 문제이다. 주로 편지글, 광고문 등의 실용문이 출제된다. 최근에는 구체적인 목적을 묻는 문제가 주로 출제되므로 세부 내용까지 이해해야 한다.

p.50~51에서 자세히 배우게 됩니다.

I 다음 글의 목적으로 가장 적절한 것은?

Dear Mrs. Coling,
My name is Susan Harris, and I am writing on behalf of the students at Lockwood High School. Many students at the school have been working on a project about the youth unemployment problem in Lockwood. You are invited to attend a special presentation that will be held at our school auditorium on April 16th. At the presentation, students will propose a variety of ideas for developing employment opportunities for the youth within the community. As you are a famous figure in the community, we would be honored by your attendance. We look forward to seeing you there.
Sincerely,
Susan Harris

[모의응용]

① 학생들이 준비한 발표회 참석을 부탁하려고
② 학생들을 위한 특별 강연을 해 준 것에 감사하려고
③ 청년 실업 문제의 해결 방안에 관한 강연을 의뢰하려고
④ 학생들의 발표회에 대한 재정적 지원을 요청하려고
⑤ 학생들의 프로젝트 심사 결과를 알리려고

II 다음 글의 목적으로 가장 적절한 것은?

Two years ago, Green County Library decided to stay open until 8 p.m. every Thursday. This was to make library services available to people for whom evening was the only convenient time to visit. However, visitor numbers have not shown a strong demand for the later hours, and library officials have determined that staff time would be more effectively utilized by adjusting operating hours. So, I have to inform you that hours of operation at Green County Library will change starting October 8, 2015. Operating hours on Thursdays will return to normal, from 9 a.m. to 6 p.m. All normal library services will still be available during those hours. Additionally, the shift will allow Green County Library to improve and increase services to the community. [모의응용]

① 도서관 휴관일 변경을 안내하려고
② 독서 프로그램 수강생을 모집하려고
③ 도서관 연장 운영의 중단을 공지하려고
④ 대출 기간 내 도서 반납을 당부하려고
⑤ 공사로 인한 도서관 이용 제한을 알리려고

유형 05 빈칸 추론 3~4문제/28문제

정답 및 해설 p.4

글에 주어진 빈칸을 완성하는 유형이다. 글의 내용에 근거하여 빠진 정보를 추론해야 한다. 빈칸을 포함한 문장은 대개 주제문이거나 핵심 내용을 담고 있으므로 항상 글의 요지를 파악한 후 빈칸의 내용을 추론하도록 한다.

p.62~65에서 자세히 배우게 됩니다.

I 다음 빈칸에 들어갈 말로 가장 적절한 것은?

In small towns, the same workman makes chairs and doors and tables, and often the same person builds houses. And it is, of course, impossible for a man of many trades to be skilled in all of them. In large cities, on the other hand, because many people make demands on each trade, one trade alone — very often even less than a whole trade — is enough to support a man. For instance, one man makes shoes for men, and another for women. And there are places even where one man earns a living by only stitching shoes, another by cutting them out, and another by sewing the uppers together. Such skilled workers may use simple tools, but their __________ results in more efficient and productive work. [모의응용]

*trade 일; 거래

① specialization ② criticism ③ competition
④ diligence ⑤ imagination

II 다음 빈칸에 들어갈 말로 가장 적절한 것은?

People have ______________________. For example, a person might buy a bottle of water, but after reading an article on possible risks of plastic bottles, that same person might avoid an identical bottle of water the next day. When a year later this same person flies to an antiplastics conference and crashes in the desert, a plastic bottle of water might suddenly become one of the most valuable things in the universe — to that person, at that time, and in that place. This person shows a preference for one thing over another and demonstrates a ranking and ordering of values with every choice and every action. [모의]

① economic freedom of choice
② smart strategies on consumption
③ different reactions to natural disasters
④ their own ways of saving the environment
⑤ changing values depending on the situation

유형 06 함의 추론 1문제/28문제

정답 및 해설 p.5

밑줄 친 어구의 문맥상 의미를 찾아야 하는 유형이다. 글의 핵심 내용을 파악한 뒤 밑줄 친 어구의 의미의 근거를 찾고 제시된 영어 선택지 중에서 고른다.

p.70에서 자세히 배우게 됩니다.

I 밑줄 친 "rise to the bait"가 다음 글에서 의미하는 바로 가장 적절한 것은?

We all know that tempers are one of the first things lost in many arguments. It's easy to say one should keep cool, but how do you do it? The point to remember is that sometimes in arguments the other person is trying to get you to be angry. They may be saying things that are intentionally designed to annoy you. They know that if they get you to lose your cool you'll say something that sounds foolish; you'll simply get angry and then it will be impossible for you to win the argument. So don't fall for it. A remark may be made to cause your anger, but responding with a cool answer that focuses on the issue raised is likely to be most effective. Indeed, any attentive listener will admire the fact that you didn't "rise to the bait." [모의]

① stay calm
② blame yourself
③ lose your temper
④ listen to the audience
⑤ apologize for your behavior

유형 07 요약문 완성 1문제/28문제

정답 및 해설 p.6

주어진 글을 읽고 요약문의 빈칸을 완성하는 유형이다. 요약문은 글의 핵심 내용이라 할 수 있으므로 우선 글의 요지를 파악해야 하며, 이것을 근거로 요약문의 빈칸에 들어갈 말을 추론한다.

p.72~74에서 자세히 배우게 됩니다.

I 다음 글의 내용을 한 문장으로 요약하고자 한다. 빈칸 (A), (B)에 들어갈 말로 가장 적절한 것은?

An American hardware manufacturer was invited to introduce its products to a distributor in Germany. To make the best possible impression, the company sent its most promising young executive, Fred Wagner, who spoke fluent German. When Fred first met his German hosts, he shook hands firmly, greeted everyone in German, and even remembered to bow the head slightly, which is the German custom. Fred, a very effective public speaker, began his presentation with a few humorous jokes to set a relaxed atmosphere. However, he felt that his presentation was not very well received. Even though Fred thought he had done his cultural homework, he made one particular error. His jokes were viewed as too informal and unprofessional in a German business setting. [모의응용]

*distributor 배급 업체

↓

This story shows that using ____(A)____ in a business setting can be considered ____(B)____ in Germany.

	(A)		(B)
①	humor	……	essential
②	humor	……	inappropriate
③	gestures	……	essential
④	gestures	……	inappropriate
⑤	first names	……	useful

II 다음 글의 내용을 한 문장으로 요약하고자 한다. 빈칸 (A)와 (B)에 들어갈 말로 가장 적절한 것은?

Timothy Wilson did an experiment in which he gave students a choice of five different art posters, and then later surveyed them to see if they still liked their choices. People who were told to consciously examine their choices were least happy with their posters weeks later. People who looked at the poster briefly and then chose later were happiest. Another researcher produced the same results in the real world with a study set in a furniture store. Furniture selection is one of the most cognitively demanding choices any consumer makes. The people who made their furniture choices after less conscious examination were happier than those who made their purchase after a lot of careful examination.

[모의응용]

↓

According to experiments, people who think more ____(A)____ about what to choose feel less ____(B)____ with their choices.

	(A)		(B)
①	carefully	……	satisfied
②	positively	……	disappointed
③	critically	……	annoyed
④	negatively	……	disappointed
⑤	briefly	……	satisfied

유형 08 무관한 문장 찾기 1~2문제/28문제

정답 및 해설 p.6

글의 흐름과 무관한 문장 하나를 골라내는 유형이다. 글의 주제에서 벗어난 문장을 찾도록 한다.

p.84~85에서 자세히 배우게 됩니다.

I 다음 글에서 전체 흐름과 관계 없는 문장은?

Asians and many Native American cultures view silence as an important and appropriate part of social interaction. ① Speakers from these cultures often take a few moments of silence before offering a response to another speaker. ② Silence causes division and separation, creating serious problems in relationships. ③ Such initial silence conveys the listener's respect for the speaker: it indicates that the listener has heard the speaker's words and is giving them due thought. ④ Silence is viewed as a time to learn, to think about, and to review what the speaker has said. ⑤ In cultures that prize silence, responding too quickly after speakers have finished their turns is interpreted as having devoted inadequate attention and consideration to the speakers' words and thoughts. [모의응용]

II 다음 글에서 전체 흐름과 관계 없는 문장은?

A snowy owl's ears are not visible from the outside, but it has incredible hearing. The feathers on a snowy owl's face guide sounds to its ears, giving it the ability to hear things humans cannot. ① Each of its ears is a different size, and one is higher than the other. ② The different size and location of each ear helps the owl distinguish between sounds. ③ It can hear at the same time the distant hoofbeats of a large deer, the flap of a bird's wings above it, and the digging of a small animal below it. ④ In fact, it has excellent vision both in the dark and at a distance. ⑤ After choosing which sound interests it most, the snowy owl moves its head like a large circular antenna to pick up the best reception. [모의응용]

*hoofbeats 발굽소리

유형 09 글의 순서 배열 1~2문제/28문제

정답 및 해설 p.7

주어진 글 다음에 이어지는 (A), (B), (C) 세 개의 문단을 알맞은 순서대로 배열하는 유형이다. 논리적 순서대로 글의 흐름이 자연스럽게 이어지는지 확인하도록 한다.

p.88~89에서 자세히 배우게 됩니다.

I 주어진 글 다음에 이어질 글의 순서로 가장 적절한 것은?

> One of the most essential decisions any of us can make is how we invest our time.

(A) During this period, people worked for more than eighty hours a week in factories. But some spent their few precious free hours reading books or getting involved in politics instead of visiting pubs.

(B) Of course, how we invest time is not our decision alone to make. Many factors determine what we should do either because we are members of the human race, or because we belong to a certain culture and society.

(C) Nevertheless, there is room for personal choice, and control over time is to a certain extent in our hands. Even in the most oppressive period of the Industrial Revolution, people didn't give up their free will when it came to time. [모의응용]

*oppressive 억압적인

① (A) – (C) – (B)　② (B) – (A) – (C)
③ (B) – (C) – (A)　④ (C) – (A) – (B)
⑤ (C) – (B) – (A)

II 주어진 글 다음에 이어질 글의 순서로 가장 적절한 것은?

> It is said that in ancient Athens the followers of Plato gathered one day to ask themselves the following question: "What is a human being?"

(A) Holding it in his hand, he shouted "Look! I present you with a human being." After the stir had passed, the philosophers tried again. A human being, they said, is a featherless biped with broad nails.

(B) This curious story from the history of early philosophy shows the kinds of difficulties philosophers face when attempting to give abstract, general definitions.

(C) After a great deal of thought, they came up with the following answer: "a human being is a featherless biped." Everybody seemed content with this definition until a philosopher burst into the lecture hall with a live featherless chicken. [모의응용]

*biped 두 발 동물

① (A) – (C) – (B)　② (B) – (A) – (C)
③ (B) – (C) – (A)　④ (C) – (A) – (B)
⑤ (C) – (B) – (A)

문장 삽입 1~2문제/28문제

정답 및 해설 p.8

주어진 문장을 적절한 곳에 넣어 글을 완성하는 유형이다. 흐름이 끊기거나 논리적 비약이 생기는 부분을 찾아서 주어진 문장을 넣은 후, 내용이 자연스럽게 이어지는지 읽어본다.

p.92~93에서 자세히 배우게 됩니다.

I 글의 흐름으로 보아, 주어진 문장이 들어가기에 가장 적절한 곳은?

But there will be times in your life when there is no one around to stand up and cheer you on.

It's great to have people in your life who believe in you and cheer you on. (①) They are truly interested in what you are trying to achieve and support you in all of your goals and efforts. (②) Each of us needs people in our lives who encourage us so that we can feel confident in our capabilities and move forward toward our goals. (③) When this happens, don't get depressed. (④) Instead, become your own cheerleader. (⑤) Give yourself a motivational pep talk because nobody knows your strengths and talents better than you and no one can motivate you better than you. [모의]

*pep talk 격려의 말

II 글의 흐름으로 보아, 주어진 문장이 들어가기에 가장 적절한 곳은?

However, the actual chance of being attacked by a shark is very small.

Fear of sharks has kept many pool swimmers from testing the ocean water. (①) Especially, the movie *Jaws*, featuring a series of shark attacks in a small beach community, provided vivid images that convinced many people to avoid the ocean. (②) You take a greater risk while driving to and from the beach. (③) According to the International Shark Attack File, the low number of shark attacks indicates that these big fish do not feed on humans by nature. (④) Most shark attacks are simply due to mistaken identity. (⑤) In 2007, there were 71 reported shark attacks on humans worldwide and only one death, which is significantly lower than the 2007 death rate for bee stings and snake bites. [모의응용]

정답 및 해설 p.8

200~300단어 이상인 지문에 2~3개의 문제가 주어진다. 장문 유형은 약간씩의 변화가 있어 왔고 앞으로도 그럴 것으로 예측된다. 그러나 완전히 생소한 유형이 등장할 가능성은 낮으므로 기존 유형의 해법을 최대한 잘 적용시킨다.

p.104~106에서 자세히 배우게 됩니다.

I 다음 글을 읽고, 물음에 답하시오.

(A)

A fourteen-year-old girl named Victoria had always loved to sing. She often tried out for school musicals, but never for one of the leading roles. The spotlight didn't attract her, and she preferred to blend into the chorus. Then (a) she was faced with a serious challenge.

(B)

Then, Victoria decided to give it a try. The musical, *Into the Woods*, offered a number of great roles. She tried out for the part of the fairy godmother. To her surprise, she won the part — and the nerves set in immediately. She would have to sing soprano, which was several notes above her range. The script even called for (b) her to be hanging six feet above the stage at one point!

(C)

Victoria was determined, however. She trained every day for months to prepare for the moment when the whole audience would focus entirely on (c) her. On the big day, despite her fears, Victoria played her role to perfection. With her mother sitting proudly in the audience, Victoria felt delighted.

(D)

The annual school musical at Victoria's school would be held in a few months. Victoria's mother had an important meeting on that day. She promised (d) she would skip the meeting if Victoria landed a leading role. She wanted Victoria to know that she believed in (e) her. She also wanted Victoria to believe in herself. What she said made Victoria fall deep into thought for a while.

[모의응용]

i) 주어진 글 (A)에 이어질 내용을 순서에 맞게 배열한 것으로 가장 적절한 것은?

① (B) – (D) – (C)　② (C) – (B) – (D)
③ (C) – (D) – (B)　④ (D) – (B) – (C)
⑤ (D) – (C) – (B)

ii) 밑줄 친 (a)~(e) 중에서 가리키는 대상이 나머지 넷과 다른 것은?

① (a)　② (b)　③ (c)
④ (d)　⑤ (e)

iii) 윗글의 Victoria에 관한 내용으로 적절하지 않은 것은?

① 코러스단에 섞이는 것을 선호했다.
② 뮤지컬 'Into the Woods'에서 배역을 맡았다.
③ 자기 음역보다 높게 소프라노로 노래해야 했다.
④ 두려움 때문에 무대에서 실수를 했다.
⑤ 엄마의 말을 듣고 한동안 깊은 생각에 잠겼다.

II 다음 글을 읽고, 물음에 답하시오.

Last year, Roberta Vinci had a tennis match with No.1 - ranked Serena Williams in the U.S. Open. No one thought Vinci would win, but she did. In an interview after the match, Vinci said she did not think it was possible, so she tried not to think about winning. "In my mind I said, 'Hit the ball and run. Don't think, just run.' And then I won."
Vinci's attitude stands strongly against today's culture where we emphasize positivity too much. If you are feeling like something is impossible, then you are told that you are just not thinking positively enough. However, if you really believe that something is impossible, or that you won't succeed, then trying to convince yourself otherwise can increase your anxiety, and actually doesn't help at all. Therefore, sometimes the best way to accomplish a difficult objective is to stop thinking that it is possible, and just take things one step at a time. Remember, focusing too much on the ________ can prevent you from achieving the thing you want. Forget about it. Just hit the ball, and run.

[모의응용]

i) 윗글의 제목으로 가장 적절한 것은?

① The Power of Positive Thinking
② Stop Thinking, Be in the Moment
③ Keep Your Original Plan on Track
④ Physical Activity Reduces Anxiety
⑤ Want to Succeed? Learn from Mistakes!

ii) 윗글의 빈칸에 들어갈 말로 가장 적절한 것은?

① goal　② effort　③ fame
④ luck　⑤ pleasure

유형 12 심경, 분위기 파악 1문제/28문제

정답 및 해설 p.9

글을 읽고 글의 등장인물이 느끼는 심경, 글에서 느껴지는 분위기를 추론해보는 유형이다. 소설과 같은 문학 작품이 주로 출제되며 글의 종합적 감상 능력을 측정한다.

p.110~111에서 자세히 배우게 됩니다.

I 다음 글에 드러난 'I'의 심경으로 가장 적절한 것은?

Sunset was late in coming. It had been a hot sunny day and the air was heavy and still. I saw a large fountain in the middle of the town square, but there was no water. The square was empty except for a black cat staring at me with a scary, sharp look. The shops were closed, and there was no one about. I started to grow anxious as it got dark. I walked over to a cafe and sat down at a table, putting my bag on the seat beside me. The cafe was empty except for two rough-looking men at a table next to the window. They observed me threateningly and suddenly started to approach me. I really wanted to escape. [모의응용]

① fearful ② pleased
③ relieved ④ curious
⑤ indifferent

II 다음 글의 상황에 나타난 분위기로 가장 적절한 것은?

Grandfather said, "Viola, won't you have a glass?" Viola glanced at Mother and then said, "No, no, Mr. Tate, I couldn't —." He ignored her and put a glass into her hands and then another into SanJuanna's hands. They all stood and raised their glasses in celebration. We imitated them with glasses of milk, laughing. Father spoke. "To our good health, to our continuing prosperity, and, on this grand occasion, to Grandfather and his scientific accomplishment. I must admit that there were times when I wondered about the way you spend your time, but you have proven it to be all worthwhile. We are a proud family tonight!" Harry started up a chorus of "For He's a Jolly Good Fellow" and then led them all in giving three cheers. [모의응용]

① calm and peaceful ② festive and exciting
③ sad and sorrowful ④ dangerous and urgent
⑤ solemn and sacred

유형 13 지칭 대상 파악 1문제/28문제

정답 및 해설 p.10

여러 대명사 중 다른 대상을 가리키는 것을 고르거나 밑줄 친 어구의 함축적 의미를 추론하는 유형이다. 최근에는 대명사가 가리키는 대상이 다른 것을 고르는 문제만 출제되고 있다.

p.122~123에서 자세히 배우게 됩니다.

I 밑줄 친 <u>he[his]</u>가 가리키는 대상이 나머지 넷과 <u>다른</u> 것은?

An elderly carpenter was ready to retire. He told his boss of his plans to be with ① <u>his</u> family. He would miss the paycheck each week, but he wanted to retire. The boss was sorry to see his good worker go and asked if ② <u>he</u> could build just one more house as a personal favor. The carpenter said yes, but ③ <u>his</u> heart was not in his work. He used poor materials and didn't put much time or effort into his last work. It was an unfortunate way to end his lifelong career. When ④ <u>he</u> finished his work, his boss came to check out the house. Then ⑤ <u>he</u> handed the front-door key to the worker and said, "This is your house, my gift to you." [모의응용]

II 밑줄 친 부분이 가리키는 대상이 나머지 넷과 <u>다른</u> 것은?

Carol was new to the United States. A friend called to invite ① <u>her</u> to lunch. She offered to pick her up on the corner of 34th Street and Fifth Avenue at 11:30 a.m. When Carol arrived, ② <u>she</u> noticed a sign above her head. It said, "No Standing." Carol didn't know what to do. She started walking back and forth on the street. When her friend arrived, she couldn't wait to get into ③ <u>her</u> car. She excitedly explained that it was a bad idea to meet at that corner because people aren't allowed to stand there. ④ <u>Her</u> friend said, "What? Of course you can." "No," ⑤ <u>she</u> said, "the sign says 'No Standing'." Her friend burst into laughter. "That just means we can't park there." [모의응용]

유형 14 세부 내용 파악 1문제/28문제

정답 및 해설 p.11

선택지의 내용이 글의 내용과 일치하는지 아닌지를 판단하는 유형이다. 널리 알려져 있지 않은 인물이나 동식물, 사물을 소개하는 글이 주로 출제된다.

p.126~127에서 자세히 배우게 됩니다.

I Nauru에 관한 다음 글의 내용과 일치하지 않는 것은?

Nauru is an island country in the southwestern Pacific Ocean. It is located about 800 miles to the northeast of the Solomon Islands; its closest neighbor is the island of Banaba, some 200 miles to the east. Nauru has no official capital, but government buildings are located in Yaren. With a population of about 10,000, Nauru is the smallest country in the South Pacific and the third smallest country by area in the world. The native people of Nauru consist of 12 tribes, as symbolized by the 12-pointed star on the Nauru flag, and are believed to be a mixture of Micronesian, Polynesian, and Melanesian. Their native language is Nauruan, but English is widely spoken as it is used for government and business purposes. [모의]

① 솔로몬 제도로부터 북동쪽에 위치해 있다.
② 공식 수도는 없으나 Yaren에 정부 건물이 있다.
③ 면적이 세계에서 세 번째로 작은 국가이다.
④ 원주민은 12개의 부족으로 구성되어 있다.
⑤ 모국어가 있어 다른 언어는 사용하지 않는다.

II short-horned lizard에 관한 다음 글의 내용과 일치하는 것은?

Short-horned lizards are small, flat, round lizards that have short, stubby horns. They are found in the deserts and semi-arid environments of North and Central America. During hot weather, they are most active during the morning hours and less active in the afternoon. Short-horned lizards prefer soft, sandy soils, near rocks where they can blend in with the background. Their color varies from red-brown to yellow-grey, depending on their surroundings, since their color provides them with camouflage. Their underside is white or light gray, without spots. When threatened, they are capable of blowing their bodies up to twice their normal size. And if this proves insufficient, they shoot blood from their eyes to confuse their predators. The blood can travel a distance of up to three feet. [모의응용]

*semi-arid 반건조 기후의

① 날씨가 더울 때는 오후에 가장 활동적이다.
② 바닥에 딱 붙어 몸을 숨길 수 있는 딱딱한 토양을 선호한다.
③ 몸의 아랫면에 흰색이나 밝은 회색의 반점이 있다.
④ 몸을 평소 크기의 3배까지 부풀릴 수 있다.
⑤ 눈에서 피를 쏘아 포식자를 교란시킨다.

유형 15 실용 자료 파악 2문제/28문제

정답 및 해설 p.11

실용문을 읽고 선택지의 내용이 세부 내용과 일치하는지 아닌지를 파악하는 유형이다. 실용문으로는 주로 안내문, 공고문 등이 제시된다.

p.130~131에서 자세히 배우게 됩니다.

I Night at the Museum에 관한 다음 안내문의 내용과 일치하는 것은?

Night at the Museum

Have you ever imagined sleeping with Egyptian sculptures or waking up beside mummies? Come to "Night at the Museum"! You can spend a night exploring the museum after dark!

Date & Time
Every third weekend of the month
(Saturday 6:30 p.m. to Sunday 7:30 a.m.)
Admission(Price)
8- to 13-year-olds only ($40 per child)
Including
Materials for activities, overnight accommodations, breakfast
(Note: Food will not be provided until breakfast, so you should bring snacks.)

Booking Information
- Book tickets online through the "Night at the Museum" page on the museum website.
- You must sign up as a member on the museum website to book tickets.
- Refunds can only be given up to two weeks before the event.

[모의응용]

① 매주 주말에 진행된다.
② 8세 이상이면 누구나 참여할 수 있다.
③ 음식 반입이 불가능하다.
④ 박물관 웹사이트 회원 가입 없이 티켓 예약이 가능하다.
⑤ 행사 2주전까지만 환불이 가능하다.

유형 16 도표 자료 파악 1문제/28문제

정답 및 해설 p.12

도표를 설명하는 글을 읽고 도표가 의미하는 바를 잘못 설명한 문장을 고르는 유형이다. 숫자 표현, 비교 표현 등을 익혀두어야 실수가 없다.

p.134에서 자세히 배우게 됩니다.

I 다음 도표의 내용과 일치하지 않는 것은?

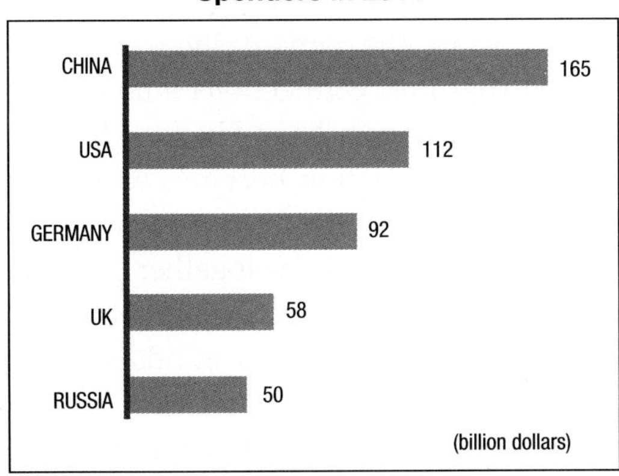

The above graph shows the world's top international tourism spenders in 2014. ① China was at the top of the list with a total of 165 billion dollars. ② The United States of America (USA), the world's second largest spender, spent more than twice as much as Russia on international tourism. ③ Germany, which spent 20 billion dollars less than the USA, took third place. ④ The United Kingdom (UK) spent 58 billion dollars, which was less than half of the amount spent by the USA. ⑤ Of the five countries, Russia spent the smallest amount of money on international tourism. [모의응용]

유형 17 어법성 판단 1문제/28문제

정답 및 해설 p.12

기본적인 어법 지식을 묻는 유형이다. 두 가지 형태가 출제되는데 하나는 어법에 맞는 표현을 고르는 문제이고, 다른 하나는 어법상 틀린 것을 고르는 문제이다.

p.148~149에서 자세히 배우게 됩니다.

I (A), (B), (C)의 각 네모 안에서 어법에 맞는 표현으로 가장 적절한 것은?

A lot of customers buy products only after they are made aware that the products are available in the market. Let's say a product, even if it has been out there for a while, is not (A) [advertising / advertised]. Then what might happen? Not knowing that the product exists, customers would probably not buy it even if the product may have worked for (B) [it / them]. Advertising also helps people find the best for themselves. When they are made aware of a whole range of goods, they are able to compare them and make purchases so that they get (C) [that / what] they desire with their hard-earned money. Thus, advertising has become a necessity in everybody's daily life. [모의]

	(A)		(B)		(C)
①	advertising	……	it	……	that
②	advertising	……	them	……	what
③	advertised	……	them	……	what
④	advertised	……	it	……	what
⑤	advertised	……	them	……	that

II 다음 글의 밑줄 친 부분 중, 어법상 틀린 것은?

Foraging is a means of searching for wild food resources. This is a method ① <u>that</u> has been used for a long time and is possibly the oldest method of finding food, tracing back to thousands of years ago. In the past, people commonly foraged for food in forests, riversides, caves, and virtually any place where food could possibly ② <u>be found</u>. Most of the foods foraged ③ <u>were</u> root crops, weeds, and shrubs. These days, foraging is becoming popular once again. People in today's fast-paced society ④ <u>engaging in</u> this either for necessity or for entertainment. Whatever the purpose may be, people are now slowly but surely getting acquainted with foraging. More and more people are finding it quite a fulfilling task and very ⑤ <u>beneficial</u>. [모의응용]

*forage 식량을 찾아다니다

유형 18 어휘 추론 1문제/28문제

정답 및 해설 p.13

문맥 속 어휘의 이해를 묻는 유형이다. 혼동되는 두 개의 어휘 중 문맥상 적절한 표현을 고르는 유형 또는 글에서 밑줄 친 단어의 쓰임이 적절한지 판단하는 유형으로 1문항이 출제된다. 평소 다양한 어휘 지식을 쌓아 놓아야 한다.

p.152~153에서 자세히 배우게 됩니다.

I (A), (B), (C)의 각 네모 안에서 문맥에 맞는 낱말로 가장 적절한 것은?

Feeling and emotion are crucial for everyday decision making. The neuroscientist Antonio Damasio studied people who were perfectly normal in every way except for brain injuries that damaged their emotional systems. As a result, they were (A) [able / unable] to make decisions or function effectively in the world. While they could describe exactly how they should have been functioning, they couldn't determine where to live, what to eat, or what products to buy and use. This finding (B) [contradicts / supports] the common belief that decision making is the heart of rational, logical thought. But modern research shows that the affective system provides critical (C) [assistance / interference] to your decision making by helping you make rapid selections between good and bad, reducing the number of things to be considered. [모의응용]

	(A)		(B)		(C)
①	able	……	contradicts	……	assistance
②	unable	……	contradicts	……	assistance
③	unable	……	contradicts	……	interference
④	unable	……	supports	……	interference
⑤	able	……	supports	……	interference

II 다음 글의 밑줄 친 부분 중, 문맥상 낱말의 쓰임이 적절하지 <u>않은</u> 것은?

When people share the same daily, weekly, monthly, and seasonal rhythms, connections among them form faster and stay stronger. They trust each other more deeply, and ① <u>coordination</u> becomes easier. After all, they are ② <u>frequently</u> doing the same things and working on the same problems together. In fact, several organizations use regular meetings to maintain strong bonds and reinforce a ③ <u>shared</u> mindset. A CEO of a food company talks about his short daily meeting with his team. He explains, "The rhythm that frequency generates allows relationships to ④ <u>weaken</u>, personal habits to be understood, and stressors to be identified. All of this ⑤ <u>helps</u> the members of the team understand not only their roles but also how they can get the best out of one another." [모의응용]

Q. 수능 유형은 변한다?

A. 수능에 출제되는 유형은 매년 조금씩 변한다. 하지만 앞에서 소개한 모든 문제 유형을 제대로 소화한다면 새로운 유형이 나오더라도 충분히 풀 수 있는 정도이다. 다음 문제들은 과거에는 많이 출제되었지만 최근에는 거의 출제되지 않는 유형이다. 글의 일부만 이해해도 정답을 고를 수 있거나, 단순한 어휘 지식으로 풀리는 문제는 변별력이 없어 결국 새로운 유형으로 교체된다는 것을 알 수 있다.

Old **다음 One Hand Reach의 그림에 대한 글의 내용 중 밑줄 친 낱말의 쓰임이 적절하지 <u>않은</u> 것은?**

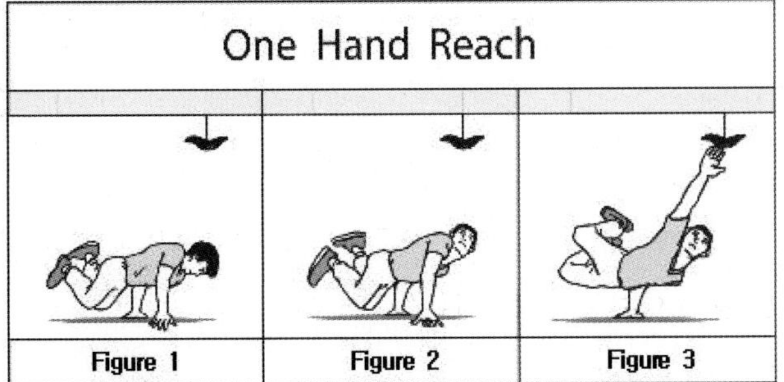

One Hand Reach is one of the traditional games played by people in Alaska. While playing the game, the player should balance only on one or two hands. The target should be within the reach of the player's ① <u>hand</u>. The player begins by keeping his feet ② <u>off</u> the floor as shown in Figure 1. Then, to measure the distance, he looks ③ <u>down</u> at the target hanging from the ceiling as in Figure 2. Finally, he ④ <u>stretches</u> one of his hands towards the target as shown in Figure 3. If he ⑤ <u>touches</u> it while balancing on the other hand, the player succeeds. [모의]

▶ 글을 읽고 그림과 일치하지 않거나 문맥상 적절하지 않은 어휘를 고르는 문제이나, 2010년 수능 이후 최근에는 출제되지 않고 있다.

Old **밑줄 친 <u>them(they)</u>이 가리키는 것으로 가장 적절한 것은?**

It is said that the Chinese first made <u>them</u> in the 800s, filling bamboo sticks with gunpowder and exploding them at the New Year with the hope that the sound would scare away evil spirits. People say that Marco Polo brought <u>them</u> back to Europe. Their loud sounds and various colored lights were described as "bombs bursting in the air." Today <u>they</u> are a key part of celebrating national holidays and cultural events. [모의]

① 폭죽 ② 연 ③ 피리
④ 풍선 ⑤ 활

▶ 대명사가 가리키는 것을 묻는 문제이며 해당 대명사가 모두 같은 것을 가리키므로 난도가 낮은 편이다. 최근에는 여러 대명사 중 다른 대상을 가리키는 것을 고르는 유형으로만 출제되고 있다.

유형편

지금부터는 수능 모의고사에 출제되는 문제를 총 18가지 유형으로 나눠서 각각의 해결 전략을 알아보게 됩니다. 대표 문제를 풀어보면서 유형을 익힌 후에, 배운 내용을 적용해서 실전 문제를 풀어보세요. 또한, 한 챕터가 끝날 때마다 나오는 미니 모의고사를 풀어보면서 자신의 실력을 점검해 보세요.

Chapter 1

Chapter 2

Chapter 3

Chapter 4

Chapter 5

Chapter 6

Chapter 1

특강 글의 핵심 내용 파악하기

유형 01 주제

유형 02 요지, 주장

유형 03 제목

유형 04 글의 목적 파악

미니 모의고사 1

특강

글의 핵심 내용 파악하기

글을 읽을 때는 우선 글쓴이가 무엇을 이야기하고 있는가를 따져봐야 한다.
이것을 '글의 핵심 내용을 파악한다'라고 한다. 수능에 출제되는 문제의 반 이상은 글의 핵심 내용을 파악해야 풀 수 있는 만큼 이것은 글을 읽는 데 기본이 되며, 매우 중요하다.

1 주제문이란?

하나의 글에는 하나의 생각이 담겨 있다. 글쓴이는 말하려는 핵심 내용을 한두 문장에 표현하는데, 이를 주제문이라고 한다. 주제문에는 글의 소재(글감)와 그에 대한 글쓴이의 견해가 담겨 있으므로 주제문에서 주제와 요지를 추론할 수 있다.

주제문 = 글감 + 글감에 대한 글쓴이의 견해 / 주장 / 태도
(Topic Sentence = Topic + Opinion / Argument / Attitude about Topic)

주제문: Rice is one of the most important food crops in Asia.

주제·요지 추론

요지: 쌀은 아시아에서 중요한 작물이다.
주제: 아시아에서의 쌀의 중요성(the importance of rice in Asia)

주제문에서 글감인 '쌀'에 대해 '아시아에서 중요한 작물이다'라는 글쓴이의 견해가 드러나므로 요지와 주제를 위와 같이 추론할 수 있다. 이처럼 글쓴이의 견해를 풀어서 표현한 것은 '요지'이고, 이를 압축한 어구는 '주제'이다.

예시1 주제문: We should use different expressions in different social situations.
요지: 상황에 맞는 표현을 사용해야 한다.
주제: 상황에 맞는 표현 사용의 필요성

예시2 주제문: Everyone needs cultural awareness when they meet people from other backgrounds.
요지: 다른 배경을 가진 사람들을 만날 때는 문화적 인식이 필요하다.
주제: the necessity of cultural awareness

Mini Test

정답 및 해설 p.14

1 다음 주제문을 읽고, 알맞은 주제를 고르시오.

Good readers follow specific steps in order to achieve accurate understanding.

① 정확한 이해를 위한 독서법　　② 독서를 통한 이해력 신장

2 다음 주제문을 읽고, 알맞은 요지를 고르시오.

We might never learn about others' personalities if they do not meet our standards for physical attractiveness.

① 외모보다는 성격이 더 중요하다.　　② 외모로 성격을 판단하는 경우가 많다.

2 주제문의 성격

❶ 포괄적이다

주제문은 글 전체의 내용을 아우르므로 단락에서 가장 포괄적인 문장이다. 즉 주제문은 나머지 문장들보다 상위 개념이다. 상위 개념이란 쉽게 말해 '곤충'처럼 개미, 벌 등을 포괄하는 더 일반적이고 넓은 개념을 말한다. (곤충⊃개미, 벌)

Sweets, dead worms, and fruit are the ant's favorite foods.
(단것, 죽은 벌레, 과일은 개미가 가장 좋아하는 음식이다.)
Some ants eat other ants and even their own eggs.
(어떤 개미들은 다른 개미나 심지어 자신의 알을 먹기도 한다.)

위의 두 문장은 모두 개미가 먹는 음식에 관한 내용이다. sweets, dead worms, fruit, other ants, their own eggs는 모두 '개미가 먹는 음식'이라는 상위 개념으로 묶을 수 있다. 따라서 이 두 문장을 포괄하는 일반적인 진술, 즉 주제문은 다음과 같다.

Ants have a varied diet.
(개미는 다양한 음식을 먹는다.)

❷ 보충설명이 필요하다

포괄적이라는 것은 바꿔 말하면 '구체적이지 않다'는 것이다. 위의 예에서 볼 수 있듯이, 주제문만으로는 개미가 어떠한 다양한 음식을 먹는 것인지 알 수 없고 막연하다. 글을 이루는 나머지 문장들, 즉 주제문을 뒷받침하는 보충설명(Supporting Details)을 통해 구체적인 음식이 제시되어야 주제문을 온전히 이해할 수 있다.

다음의 예도 마찬가지이다.

We should know that crying is not as beneficial as we think.
(우리는 우는 것이 생각만큼 이롭지는 않다는 것을 알아야 한다.)

위의 주제문만 보면 왜 우는 것이 이롭지 않다고 주장하는 것인지 명확히 알 수 없다. 그렇게 주장하는 근거에 해당하는 설명이 뒤따라야 한다.

보충설명 예시

1. Scientists say two thirds of women feel no better after crying.
   여성의 2/3는 울고 나서도 전혀 기분이 나아지지 않음.
2. In fact, 9 percent of people say that crying makes them feel even more depressed and upset.
   9퍼센트의 사람들은 울고 나서 더 기분이 안 좋아짐.

정답 및 해설 p.14

3 다음은 하나의 글에서 발췌한 문장이다. 주제문(Topic Sentence)이면 T, 주제문을 뒷받침하는 보충설명(Supporting Details)이면 D를 고르시오.

(1) Statistics can help us learn more about people. (T / D)

(2) We can also use statistics to help us make decisions about the things we do. (T / D)

(3) There are many ways in which we can use statistics to help us. (T / D)

3 주제문의 단서

❶ 포괄적 의미의 어구가 있다

주제문에는 구체적으로 무엇을 뜻하는지가 애매한 포괄적 의미의 어구가 있고, 그 구체적인 내용은 글의 다른 문장들에 의해 보충설명(support)된다.

Promising advances have been made in the area of human genetics. [모의]
(전망 있는 진보들이 인류 유전학 분야에서 이루어져 왔다.)

→ 구체적으로 어떤 전망 있는 진보들이 이루어져 왔는지가 애매하다. 나머지 문장들에 의해 보충설명되어야 한다.

In most cases, sound reaches the ear through the air; but air is not the only medium through which sound is carried. [모의]
(대부분의 경우, 소리는 공기를 통해 귀에 도달하지만, 공기는 소리가 전달되는 유일한 매개체가 아니다.)

→ 공기가 소리를 전달하는 유일한 매개체가 아니라면 어떤 매개체들이 있다는 것인지가 애매하다. 공기 이외의 다른 매개체들(e.g. 물, 흙, 기타 고체들)이 뒤이어 소개되어야 할 것이다.

❷ 주장을 나타내는 표현이 있다

주제문은 흔히 글쓴이의 견해를 나타내므로 should, have to, must, important, necessary, vital, critical 등의 '~해야 한다' 혹은 '중요하다' 등의 강한 주장 표현이 포함되거나 (부정)명령문으로 표현된다. 때로는 '~하는 것은 유감이다' 혹은 can, may 등이 쓰여 주장이 완곡하게 표현되기도 하는데, 그 주장의 근거로서 글의 나머지 문장들이 주제문을 뒷받침한다는 점은 같다.

Doctors should identify root causes of disease to come up with a personalized treatment. [수능응용]
(의사들은 개인에게 적합한 치료법을 내놓기 위해 병의 근본적인 원인을 식별해내야 한다.)

→ should처럼 '~해야 한다'라는 표현에 글쓴이의 강한 주장이 직접적으로 드러난다.

It is important to be mindful about every single aspect of purchasing food. Try not to race through your shopping. [수능]
(식품 구매의 매 단계마다에 신경을 쓰는 것이 중요하다. 쇼핑을 하면서 서두르지 마라.)

→ '중요하다'라는 표현과 부정명령문에 '식품 구매 시에는 ~해야 한다'는 글쓴이의 견해가 잘 드러나 있다.

Believe it or not, someone's hairstyle can be one of the easiest types of nonverbal communication. [모의]
(믿거나 말거나, 머리 스타일은 비언어적인 의사소통의 가장 쉬운 유형 중 하나일 수 있다.)

→ can처럼 '~일 수 있다'라는 표현에 글쓴이의 주장이 완곡하게 드러나 있다.

❸ 앞의 내용을 반박하는 어구 뒤에 온다

일반적으로 but, however 등의 연결어 뒤에는 글쓴이가 전하고자 하는 핵심 내용이 언급된다.

> Most people have a vase or two in a cupboard, but lots of things around your own home can be turned into stylish containers for a flower arrangement. [수능]
> (대부분의 사람들이 수납장에 한두 개의 꽃병을 가지고 있다. 그러나 당신 자신의 집 여기저기에 있는 많은 것들이 꽃다발의 멋진 용기가 될 수 있다.)

→ 반박의 연결어 but 뒤에 나오는 '꽃병 대신 집안 곳곳에 있는 것들을 이용하여 꽃을 멋지게 꽂을 수 있다'는 것이 글쓴이가 전하려는 핵심 내용이다.

> While most experts say eight hours of sleep is ideal, the truth is it all depends on how you feel. Some people do well with seven hours or less, while others require nine or more to be at their best. [모의]
> (대부분의 전문가들이 여덟 시간의 수면이 이상적이라고 말하지만, 사실 그것은 전적으로 당신이 어떻게 느끼느냐에 달려 있다. 어떤 사람들은 일곱 시간 혹은 그 미만으로도 잘 지내지만, 다른 사람들은 최상의 상태에 있기 위해 아홉 시간 또는 그 이상을 필요로 한다.)

→ '~이지만' 또는 '~인 반면에'라는 의미의 연결어 While이 이끄는 절에 일반적인 통념(Myth)을 소개한 후, 이에 대한 반박으로 뒤이어 나오는 사실(Truth)이 글쓴이의 견해에 해당하는 주제문이다.

❹ 전체 내용을 요약하거나 결론을 내린다

보통 글의 마지막 부분에 위치하며, therefore, thus, so, in short, clearly 등의 연결어로 시작하는 경우가 많다. 연구(Study) 및 조사(Research), 실험(Experiment)에 관한 글은 그 결과 및 결과의 시사점에 해당하는 문장이 주제문인 경우가 많다.

> Therefore, to apologize sincerely, we must first listen attentively to how the other person really feels about what happened — not simply assert what we think happened. [수능]
> (그러므로 진심으로 사과하기 위해서는 벌어진 일이라고 우리가 생각하는 것을 단순히 주장하는 게 아니라 상대방이 벌어진 일에 대해 정말로 어떻게 느끼는지에 대해 먼저 주의 깊게 들어야 한다.)

→ Therefore(그러므로) 뒤에 나오는 문장이 앞부분에서 전개된 구체적인 설명의 전체 내용을 포괄적으로 정리 요약한 문장으로서 주제문이다.

> They found that the authors who heavily mentioned social roles in their life stories lived, on average, five years longer than those who did not. [모의]
> (그들은 자신들의 신상 이야기에서 사회적 역할을 비중 있게 언급한 작가들이 그렇지 않은 작가들보다 평균적으로 5년 더 오래산다는 것을 발견했다.)

→ 연구를 통하여 발견한(found) 내용으로서 결과를 말하고 있으므로 주제문에 해당한다.

❺ 질문이나 문제 제기에 대한 답변 및 해결책에 해당한다

질문이나 문제를 제기한 경우 그것은 주로 주제를 시사하며, 질문의 답이나 문제의 해결책을 나타내는 문장이 주제문이다.

> How should parents introduce their kids to pocket money? Whatever your decision, make clear why your children get pocket money and what it means. [모의]
> (부모들은 자녀들에게 용돈을 어떻게 소개해야 하는가? 당신의 결정이 무엇이든지 간에, 당신의 자녀들이 왜 용돈을 받는지 그리고 그것이 무엇을 의미하는지를 명확히 해라.)

→ 질문에 주제(자녀에게 용돈을 소개하는 방법)가 시사되어 있고, 이에 대한 답변에 해당하는 문장이 주제문이다.

글을 이루고 있는 모든 문장은 하나의 생각을 일관되게 표현하기 위한 각자의 역할이 있다. 주제문(Topic Sentence)은 글의 핵심 내용을 포괄적으로 표현하며, 이를 뒷받침하기 위해 보충설명(Supporting Details)이 필요하다.

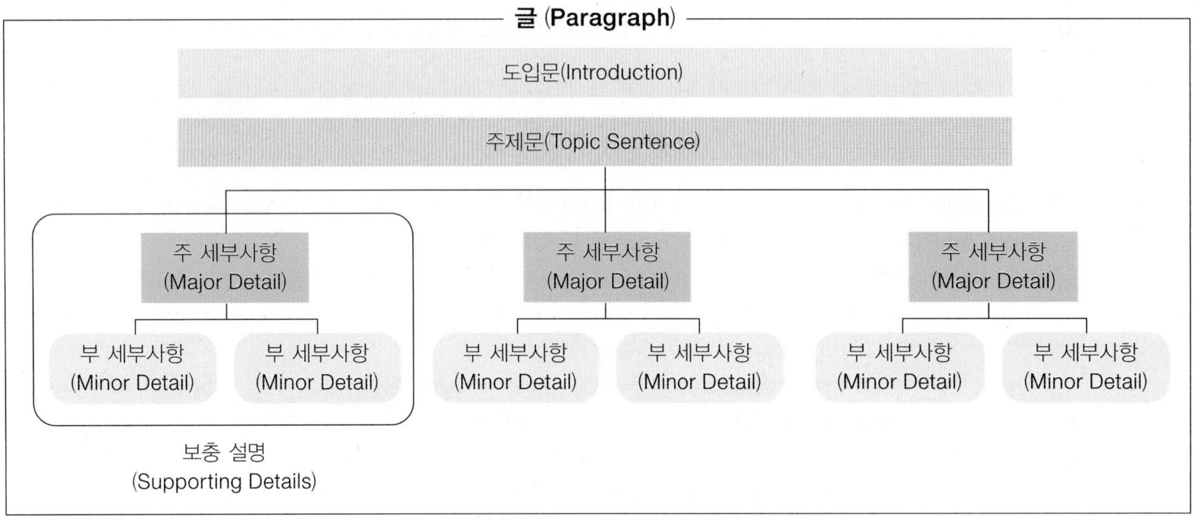

글의 흐름을 더 자연스럽게 하고 이해를 돕기 위해 주제문 앞에 도입문(Introduction)이 오는 경우가 많은데, 주로 글감과 연관되는 내용이다. 보충설명 문장들은 모두 주제문을 뒷받침하지만, 각 문장이 글에서 똑같은 중요성을 지니고 있는 것은 아니다. 핵심 내용을 직접적으로 뒷받침하는 주 세부사항(Major Details)은 글에 반드시 포함되어야 한다. 반면에 주 세부사항의 추가 정보를 담고 있는 부 세부사항(Minor Details)은 반드시 필요한 것은 아니다.

예시 다음 글에서 각각의 문장이 어떤 역할을 하는지 파악하고 글의 구조를 도식으로 이해해 보자.
① Many people keep a diary when young, but give it up before long. ② However, keeping a diary has many benefits. ③ First, you may learn a lot about yourself. ④ You can express your deepest feelings and thoughts. ⑤ A diary makes you a better writer, too. ⑥ You can record new words and ideas. ⑦ Just a few minutes a day with your diary improves your writing skills. ⑧ Finally, a diary is good for your mental health. ⑨ Stress is reduced when you write. ⑩ Your diary gives you time to be quiet and to be a friend to yourself.

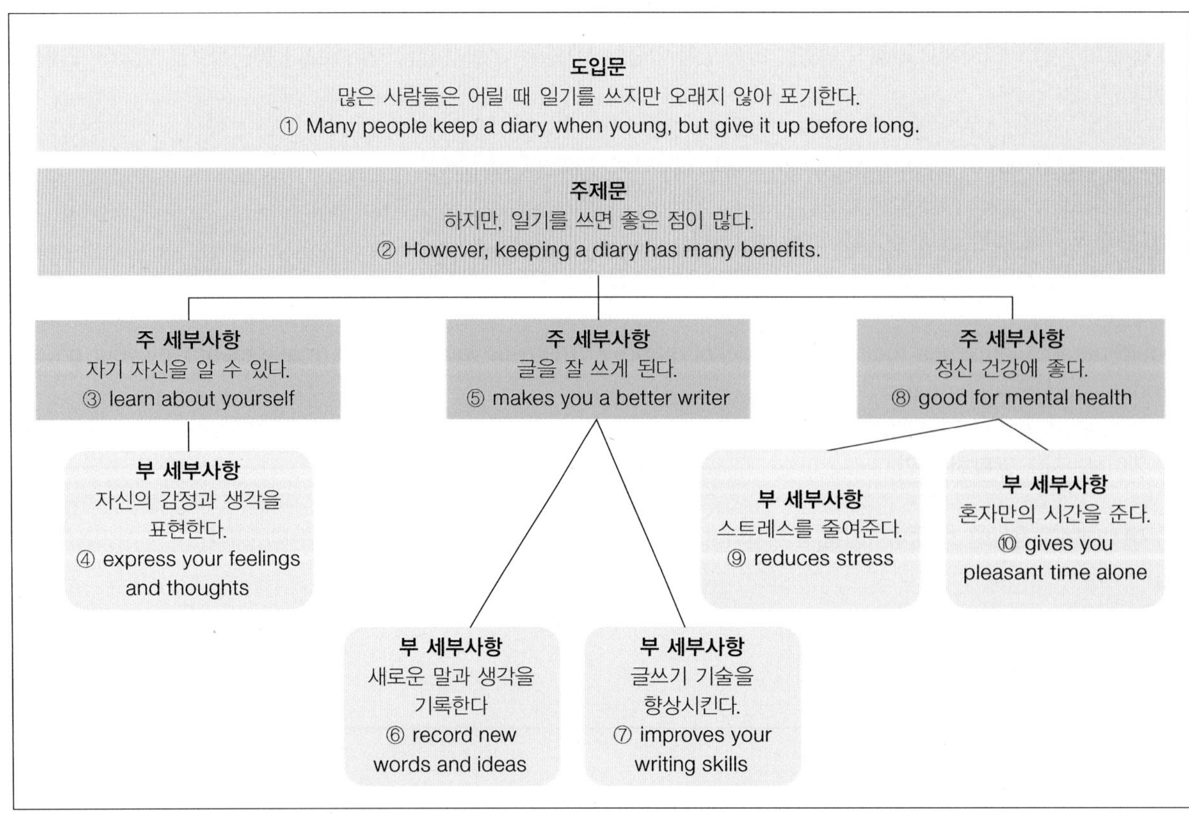

● 다음 글을 읽고, 주제문을 고르시오.

4 ① In most situations, social proof is very useful. ② The restaurant with the fullest parking lot usually does have the best food. ③ You will make fewer mistakes in life by paying attention to what others are doing than by ignoring them. ④ For example, when you are driving down the expressway and all the cars in front of you start changing lanes, those drivers probably know something you don't know. ⑤ If you ignore the drivers, you may end up hitting something. [모의응용]

5 ① Healthy kids turn off the TV or computer and go play outdoors. ② Wherever possible, children should ride a bike or walk to school. ③ A recent study found that less than 90 minutes of daily exercise makes kids more likely to develop major illnesses. ④ For health and wellbeing, kids should get more than an hour and a half of moderate exercise every day. ⑤ Moderate exercise is any exercise like walking quickly, climbing stairs, or riding a bike.

6 ① If you are looking to build muscle, it can be very tempting to really push your body beyond its limits. ② Many people seem to agree that exercise should be painful. ③ But is this really the truth of the matter? ④ In reality, fatigue and pain are your body's ways of saying that it is in danger and is being overworked. ⑤ While a good workout should offer pressure and challenges, it should absolutely never be painful. [모의응용]

● 다음 글에서 각 문장의 역할을 파악한 후, 알맞은 글의 구조를 [보기] 중에서 고르시오.

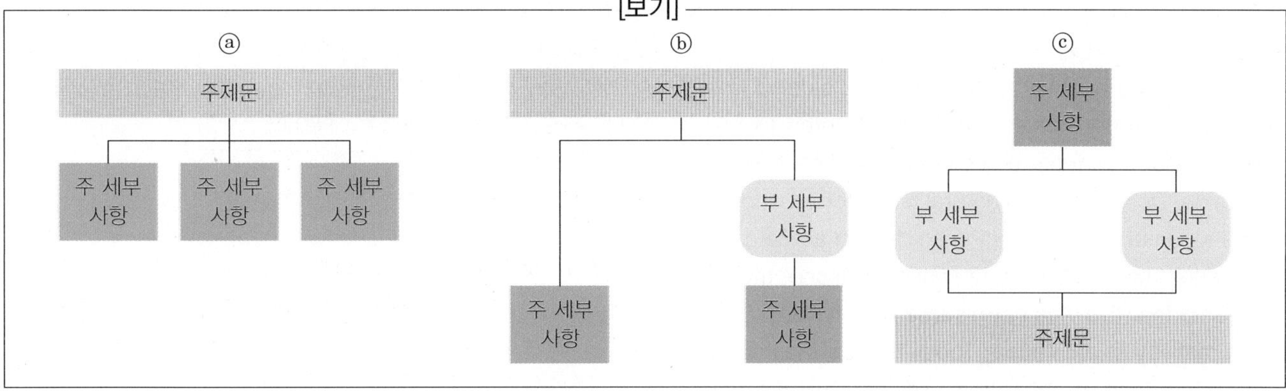

7 Many insects don't live through the cold winter, but others have come up with clever plans to survive until spring. For example, some flies stay in corners of a warm house over the winter, so it's unlikely to see them flying outside. Certain honeybees pack together in a small space and move their wings quickly to produce heat, so that they can keep warm. Some mosquitoes, like frogs, sleep through the winter cold. [모의응용]

8 As children get older and become teenagers, they often get their own way and get in trouble. For example, they often want to stay out late. They say that their friends are allowed to do so. If children are to be brought up properly, however, their parents must be careful not to be too generous. [모의]

5 주제문이 없는 경우

글에 뚜렷한 주제문이 없는 경우도 더러 있다. 특히 일화나 이야기 글에서 그러하며, 설명문이나 논설문에서도 그런 경우가 있다. 이때는 다음과 같은 방법으로 핵심 내용을 파악해 본다.

❶ 공통되는 내용을 종합한다

주제문이 없는 글이라도 하나의 글은 하나의 핵심 내용을 갖는다. 그러므로 각 문장에서 공통되는 내용을 종합하여 숨어 있는 핵심 내용을 파악하도록 한다.

★ 주제문이 없는 글

① It is considered very rude to use your hands to eat, unless it is some type of finger-food such as pizza or fried chicken. ② It is important that you should not chew with your mouth open, nor talk while there is food in your mouth. ③ Some people think it is rude if you rest your elbows on the table while eating a meal. ④ They also think it is important to wait until everyone is served before you start eating your meal. ⑤ Lastly, if you don't finish everything on your plate, it is often a sign that you did not particularly like the food. [모의응용]

① 손으로 먹는 것은 교양 없는 행동이다.
② 음식을 먹으면서 입을 벌리거나 말하지 않는다.
③ 식탁에 팔꿈치를 올리고 식사하는 것은 무례하다.
④ 모든 이에게 음식이 다 왔을 때 식사를 시작한다.
⑤ 음식을 남기면 음식이 그리 좋지 않다는 표시이다.

식사 예절 (Dining Etiquette)

이 글에는 뚜렷한 주제문이 없지만, 각 문장이 모두 '식사 예절 (Dining Etiquette)'에 관한 내용이므로 이것을 핵심 내용으로 볼 수 있다.

❷ 일화나 이야기 글은 사건이나 상황을 파악하고 교훈이나 시사점을 생각해 본다

누군가 경험한 일을 이야기체로 서술한 글에는 주제문이 없는 경우가 많다. 이때는 글의 사건이나 상황을 종합하여 추론한다. 특히 사건이나 상황의 결과가 시사하는 점 혹은 교훈이 무엇인지를 생각해 본다.

★ 주제문이 없는 이야기 글

My son, Sean, had a talent for art, which he studied from childhood on. When he was eleven, he wanted to take Japanese lessons so that he could read Japanese books on animation. Despite Sean's natural talent for art and animation, I focused on his debating ability and advised him to prepare for law school. But he wouldn't accept my advice. He said that this was not his true way. He wanted to use his creativity in animation. Today he has created his own animated cartoon characters. They are used on the backpacks that he has designed for a famous luggage company. [모의]

예술과 애니메이션에 재능이 있던 아들이 법대를 가라는 필자의 충고에도 불구하고 애니메이션 분야의 길을 선택하여 고유의 애니메이션 캐릭터를 만들어 냈다는 내용이다.

다른 사람의 충고보다는 자신의 길을 추구하는 것이 성공의 비법임을 시사한다.

요약문을 완성시키는 문제라면 다음과 같은 요약문을 완성시킬 수 있다.

In order to succeed, you <u>should pursue</u> your own course in life, sometimes <u>ignoring</u> other people's advice.

(성공하기 위해서는 다른 사람들의 충고를 가끔은 **<u>무시하면서</u>** 자신의 인생행로를 **<u>추구해야 한다</u>**.)

● 다음 글을 읽고, 주제문을 고르시오.

9 Little kids enjoy playing on the swings and slides at the park. Older children can play little league baseball or other team sports on the park's field. Teenagers like to play football on the grass. Adults can take walks, and seniors often enjoy sitting on the park benches and feeding the birds.

① The park is a pleasant place for everyone.

② The park is really important for city residents.

10 Some children are serious and responsible. Others mature at university or while gaining experience on their first job. Other folks need even longer, and some people grow old but never really grow up.

① It's important to become mature at some point in life.

② It seems that people mature at different rates.

11 People who enjoy blues, jazz, classical, and folk are more likely to be creative. On the other hand, those who like pop, country, and religious music tend to be trusting of others and hardworking. People who prefer rock and heavy metal tend to be physically active and adventurous. [모의]

① A person's favorite music may actually say quite a lot about him.

② Music affects our mood and even changes the way we perceive the world.

● 다음 글의 내용을 한 문장으로 요약하고자 한다. 빈칸 (A)와 (B)에 들어갈 말로 가장 적절한 것은?

12 On a Sunday evening many years ago, we were driving from New York City to Princeton, as we had been doing every week for a long time. We saw an unusual sight: a car on fire by the side of the road. When we reached the same spot of the road the following Sunday, another car was burning there. But this time, we found that we were less surprised than we had been on the first occasion. This was now "the place where cars catch fire." [모의응용]

⬇

The ____(A)____ of the same kind of accident ____(B)____ the surprise of watching it.

	(A)		(B)
①	repetition	……	reduced
②	repetition	……	increased
③	prevention	……	revealed
④	prevention	……	reduced
⑤	analysis	……	increased

유형 01 주제

이렇게 출제된다.
무엇에 관한 글인지 파악하는 유형으로 글을 읽을 때 가장 기본이 된다. 1~2문항씩 출제된다.

지시문은 이렇게
다음 글의 주제로 가장 적절한 것은?

정답 및 해설 p.15

Check-Up 1

[1 - 3] 다음 글을 읽고, 물음에 답하시오.

Many people think smartphones are great — there is nearly nothing smartphones can't do. However, smartphones cause important physical and emotional health problems if we use them too much. The average phone has up to 10 times the amount of bacteria found in a bathroom!

1 **글감은 무엇인가?**

2 **글감에 대한 글쓴이의 견해가 드러난 문장에 밑줄을 그으시오.**

3 **글의 주제로 알맞은 것을 고르시오.**

① the popularity of smartphones in the world
② possible health problems caused by smartphones

해결 전략 1 **글감에 대한 글쓴이의 견해가 곧 주제문이다.**
〈주제문 = 글감 + 글쓴이의 견해〉이며 이를 압축하여 표현한 것이 곧 주제이다. 따라서 주제를 추론하려면 먼저 주제문을 찾은 후 그 핵심 내용을 가장 잘 반영한 것을 답으로 고른다.
p.28 1. 주제문이란? 참조

001 다음 글의 주제로 가장 적절한 것은?

Due to the invention of the electric light bulb in the late 19th century, we are now exposed to much more light at night than we had been exposed to throughout our early history. This rather new pattern of light exposure is almost certain to have affected our patterns of sleep. Exposure to light in the late evening tends to delay the cycle of our internal clock and lead us to prefer later sleep times. Exposure to light in the middle of the night can have more unpredictable effects, but can certainly be enough to cause our internal clock to be reset, and may make it difficult to return to sleep.

① effects of artificial light on our sleep rhythms
② the importance of light to our physical health
③ our ever-increasing exposure to light
④ the self-controlled working of our internal clock
⑤ sleep deprivation caused by overworking

Check-Up 2

다음 중 나머지를 포괄하는 문장을 고르시오.

① Collecting plants or animals can teach children about the natural world.
② Collecting stamps shows children cultures or historical events of a country.
③ Collecting can open new worlds for children.

글에서 가장 포괄적인 문장이 주제문이다.

해결 전략 2 주제문은 글에서 말하려는 내용을 모두 아우르는 포괄적인 어구를 이용하여 표현한 것이다. 따라서 글 전체의 내용을 모두 포괄하는 상위 개념인 문장에서 주제를 추론할 수 있다.
p.29 2. 주제문의 성격 참조

Check-Up 3

(A), (B)를 종합하여 알맞은 주제를 고르시오.

(A) Dolphins support each other in times of need, swimming underneath injured dolphins and holding them above the surface so they may breathe.
(B) Fallen elephants are likely to have difficulty breathing, so when one falls, others try to pick it up.

① examples of animals helping injured animals
② animals seeking aid from stronger animals

공통되는 내용을 종합하여 주제를 도출한다.

해결 전략 3 주제문이 없거나 불분명한 글도 있는데, 이때도 분명 말하려는 핵심은 하나이다. 각 문장에서 공통되는 내용을 찾아내 종합적이고 포괄적인 내용의 주제로 바꾼다. 특히 일화나 이야기 글인 경우는 글의 사건이나 상황을 종합적으로 파악하고 사건이나 상황의 결과가 시사하는 점 및 교훈에도 집중한다.
p.34 5. 주제문이 없는 경우 참조

002 다음 글의 주제로 가장 적절한 것은?

People love going to concerts. I do, too. My observations as a long-time concert-goer led me to try to categorize concert-goers into several types. One of the types, "The Statue," never wants to seem like he's enjoying anything. He stands with his arms folded firmly and a blank stare towards the stage. We can also see people who have truly lost themselves in the music, as they throw their hands in the air like they just don't care what anyone thinks. I would call this group "The Fish-Out-Of-Water" type. The next type is "The Girl-On-Shoulders." This person sits on the shoulders of a guy at the concert, probably because they are too far back from the stage or because they want a better view or because they just want to get the attention of the performer.

① common purposes of concert-goers
② reasons people love concerts
③ the boom of the concert business
④ different types of people at concerts
⑤ how personality is reflected in choice of music

003 다음 글의 주제로 가장 적절한 것은?

When you view an abstract painting, don't search for recognizable images from your world. Instead, try to enter the artist's world and feel what the artist was feeling. Take a step back and view the painting from a distance. Note the impact it has on you. Ask yourself what emotions the colors, shapes, and lines suggest. Move closer and examine the brushstrokes, the texture of the paint, and the arrangement of the details. See how all the parts relate to each other. Relax and give the painting time. The longer you look, the more meaningful the painting will become.

① 예술가의 심리　② 추상화의 역사
③ 추상화 감상법　④ 현대미술의 특징
⑤ 미술관 관람 예절

기출총정리

주제 선택지로 자주 등장하는 표현

다음은 주제 유형에 출제된 기출 영문 선택지를 빈출 순으로 정리한 것이다. '~의 중요성' 등 견해를 밝히는 것이 가장 많았지만 '원인, 결과, 방법' 등을 설명하는 선택지도 많았다. 의미를 잘 익혀두자.

1 중요성 / 필요성

the importance of traditional culture	전통 문화**의 중요성**
the significance of maintaining physical health	신체 건강을 유지하는 것**의 중요성**
the necessity of teaching cultural differences	문화 차이를 가르치는 것**의 필요성**

2 원인

various **causes of** tears	눈물**의** 다양한 **원인**
factors that affect the occurrence of natural disasters	자연 재해 발생**에 영향을 미치는 요인들**

3 결과

effects of laughter on pain	웃음**이** 고통에 미치는 **영향**
the influence of good manners	좋은 예의범절**의 영향**
the outcome[consequence] of reckless behaviors	무모한 행동**의 결과**
impacts of falling circulations of papers	줄어드는 신문 발행 부수**의 영향**

4 방법

how to deal with others' emotions	타인의 감정에 대처하**는 법**
ways to promote critical thinking	비판적 사고를 키우**는 방법**
tips for selecting dairy foods	유제품을 고르**는 요령**
efforts to overcome a poor economy	불경기를 극복하**려는 노력**

5 장단점

the advantage[benefit] of slow walking	천천히 걷기**의 이점[장점]**
the danger of gaining weight	살찌는 것**의 위험성**
negative aspects of disguising the head of insects	곤충의 머리를 위장하는 것**의 부정적 측면**
the side effects of selling personal information	개인 정보를 파는 것**의 부작용**

6 비교 / 대조

a comparison of popular jobs	인기 있는 직업들**의 비교**
the pros and cons of our imperfect memories	우리의 불완전한 기억들**에 대한 찬반양론**

7 기타

the characteristics of Korean food	한국 음식**의 특징**
the value of social interactions	사회적 상호작용**의 가치**
the purpose of education	교육**의 목적**
the function of the budget	예산**의 기능**
the proper procedure of a survey	설문조사**의 올바른 절차**

실전적용독해

정답 및 해설 p.17

3문제를 4분 안에 풀어보세요.

004 다음 글의 주제로 가장 적절한 것은?

In the hottest days of summer, appetites and energy are weakened by heat and humidity. This is when it seems like an ice cream cone or a popsicle is the perfect thing. But a theory from oriental medicine tells us that eating cold foods is not the answer. Instead, one should eat "hot" foods to beat the heat. The most popular traditional summer food in Korea is *samgyetang*. It's a young chicken stuffed with rice and boiled in soup with garlic and ginseng. These ingredients have powerful warming energy that invigorates the body and stimulates the mind. These kinds of "hot" foods replace the nutrients we lose through excessive sweating, and keep us feeling healthy and strong.

*popsicle 아이스바 **invigorate 기운 나게 하다

① the ingredients of *samgyetang*
② various healthy diets
③ korean foods around the world
④ a recipe for better health
⑤ a hot meal to survive the heat

005 다음 글의 주제로 가장 적절한 것은?

Why are people sports fans? Sports fans receive support by connecting with other fans at a stadium or in their day-to-day life. This support allows the fans to cope with threats to their identity, such as bad outcomes during a game, opposing fans, and poor performance of the team in the short-term, as well as difficult life circumstances in the long-term. Moreover, attachment or identification with one's favorite team is most likely to lead to the benefits of fandom. The social-psychological benefits of being a sports fan include lower levels of loneliness and stress during sporting events, a sense of belonging to a larger community, and better psychological functioning.

*fandom: 팬 층, 팬인 것

① the absence of sportsmanship in sports
② the importance of fans in sports events
③ the recent increasing popularity of sports
④ the emotional gains from being a sports fan
⑤ what makes fans remain loyal to their team

006 다음 글의 주제로 가장 적절한 것은?

The gifts we are born with and those we work to develop throughout our lives vary in form and function. Some we find use for every day, while others are only of value in specific circumstances. Many times we overlook opportunities to share our unique gifts with others. It is fear of criticism or the paralyzing weight of uncertainty that holds us back. Ultimately, we doubt that our innate talents and practiced skills can truly add to others' lives, but it is the world as a whole that benefits when we willingly share our gifts. This is because every gift lying hidden in your soul has the potential to fill a need in someone else's life. Your natural ability to soothe hurt, inspire compassion, organize, or think outside the box can be a boon to someone in need.

*boon 요긴한 것

① benefits of pursuing one's gifts
② the form and function of our gifts
③ effective ways to use one's gifts
④ the importance of developing our talents
⑤ the necessity of sharing one's gifts with others

VOCAbulary 어휘확인

004 **appetite** 식욕 **humidity** 습도 **theory** 이론 **oriental medicine** 동양의학 **stuff A with B** A를 B로 채우다 **boil** 끓이다 **ginseng** 인삼 **ingredient** 재료, 성분 **stimulate** 자극하다 **replace** 대체하다 **nutrient** 영양분 **excessive** 지나친 **sweating** 발한 005 **cope with** ~에 대처하다 **threat** 위협 **identity** 정체성 **outcome** 결과 **opposing** 상대편의 **performance** 성적, 성과 **in the short-term** 단기적으로(↔ **in the long-term** 장기적으로) **circumstances** 상황, 환경 **moreover** 더욱이, 또한 **attachment** 애착 **identification** 동일시, 일체화 **lead to** ~로 이끌다 **social-psychological** 사회심리학의 **functioning** 기능, 작용 006 **gift** 재능; 선물 **overlook** 간과하다 **criticism** 비판 **hold A back** A를 저지하다 **paralyze** 무력하게 만들다 **uncertainty** 불확실성 **ultimately** 궁극적으로 **innate** 선천적인, 타고난 **soothe** 달래다 **compassion** 동정심 **in need** 어려움에 처한

유형 02 요지, 주장

이렇게 출제된다.
글쓴이가 전달하려는 핵심 내용이나 주장을 파악하는 유형이다. 논설문이나 수필을 중심으로 2문항씩 출제되며 선택지가 속담이나 교훈을 묻는 형태로 출제되기도 한다.

지시문은 이렇게
다음 글의 요지로 가장 적절한 것은?
다음 글에서 필자가 주장하는 바로 가장 적절한 것은?
다음 글이 시사하는 바로 가장 적절한 것은?
다음 글이 주는 교훈으로 가장 적절한 것은?

정답 및 해설 p.19

Check-Up 1

다음 중 글쓴이의 주장이 가장 잘 드러난 문장을 고르시오.

① One of the biggest problems people encounter when starting a new plan is that motivation rapidly decreases because of ambitious goals. ② Attempting to do too much too fast is worse than doing nothing at all. ③ You should set small but specific goals along the way.

해결 전략 1 주제문을 찾아 요지를 파악한다.
글의 요지는 곧 글쓴이의 주장을 말한다. 따라서 주장의 표현이 담긴 문장을 찾아 그 문장이 나머지 문장들에 의해 뒷받침되고 있는지를 파악하도록 한다.
p.30 3. 주제문의 단서 참조

007 다음 글의 요지로 가장 적절한 것은?

If you've ever heard someone say, or have said to yourself, something like "If I could remember information like I remember song lyrics, I'd be the smartest person in the world," then you have already experienced what I claim about how music influences us. Why is it that many students feel they can adequately learn information if it is in lyrical form? I believe that hearing information musically is catchier for the listener and makes learning less of a nuisance and more of a fun activity. By altering our mindset, music can transform how we absorb knowledge and look at the world.

① 공부를 할 때는 익숙한 노래를 듣는 것이 좋다.
② 공부를 하면서 음악을 듣는 것은 좋지 않다.
③ 음악은 공부에서 오는 스트레스를 줄여줄 수 있다.
④ 우리는 음악을 지식 습득의 도구로 사용할 수 있다.
⑤ 사람에 따라 똑같은 음악을 다양하게 해석한다.

Check-Up 2

다음 중 글쓴이의 주장이 드러난 문장을 찾으시오.

① Listening to music can be more relaxing than sleeping.

② The police said three people were injured in the accident.

해결 전략 2

주장은 다양한 표현으로 나타날 수 있다.

should, must, 명령문만 찾아서는 해결력을 갖출 수 없다. 글쓴이의 견해·주장은 can, will, may 등의 조동사로 완곡하게 표현될 수도 있고 it's desirable ~ (~하는 것이 바람직하다), Why not ~? (어째서 ~하지 않는가 = ~하는 게 어떤가?), it's a shame ~ (~은 유감스럽다 = ~하지 말아야 한다) 등의 다양한 표현으로 나타날 수 있음을 명심하자. '주장'은 개인의 주관적인 견해(opinion)를 밝히는 것이며, 누구도 부인할 수 없는 사실(fact)과는 구별된다.

p.30 3. 주제문의 단서 참조

008 다음 글의 요지로 가장 적절한 것은?

Suppose a person is tired of the city — the smog and the hurry — and he decides to get away for a while. He gets into his car and travels away toward freedom and relaxation. Along the way, he pulls over to the side of the road to enjoy the quiet beauty of a country scene. What does he see? Billboards! One billboard shows giant dice dripping dirty motor oil; another billboard displays huge slices of bread falling on a giant plate; still another shows pastel toilet tissue, spelling out the name of the product he should buy. These and numerous other billboards are ugly replacements for the trees and fields, rivers, lakes, deserts, hills, and mountains he is seeking. These ugly things spoil his enjoyment of natural roadside beauty.

① 도시를 이따금씩 떠나 있는 것은 재충전이 된다.
② 크고 눈에 띄는 옥외 광고판은 여행의 활력소이다.
③ 옥외 광고판을 통해 인기 있는 제품을 알 수 있다.
④ 옥외 광고판은 자연과 조화를 이루는 것이 좋다.
⑤ 옥외 광고판은 자연 풍경의 아름다움을 해친다.

Check-Up 3

해결 전략 3

글의 내용을 종합적으로 이해하자.

모든 글에 주제문이 드러나 있는 것은 아니다. 뚜렷한 주제문이 보이지 않을 때는 각 문장에서 공통적으로 다루는 내용을 가장 잘 종합하였고 글쓴이가 말하려고 하는 바가 무엇인지를 가장 잘 나타낸 선택지를 고르도록 한다.

p.34 5. 주제문이 없는 경우 참조

009 다음 글에서 필자가 주장하는 바로 가장 적절한 것은?

Small rural schools face closure and sending students to other larger schools. Population decrease in rural areas may have contributed to the closure of some smaller schools. But more frequently, it is just bad judgment by those who associate fewer schools with efficiency of management. As size increases, it is more difficult to personalize and individualize education, or to pay attention to problems in students' growth. In this respect, a teacher serving a few students is not a waste; instead, it is a benefit that should motivate parents to choose such schools. Keeping schools running in rural communities is an effective way to attract adult workers to develop strong economies in less-developed areas of the country.

① 학급의 크기를 줄여 교육의 질을 높여야 한다.
② 학교별 보조금을 규모에 따라 차등 지급해야 한다.
③ 시골 소학교들에 대한 보조금 지원을 늘려야 한다.
④ 학생별 특성에 맞게 커리큘럼을 다양화해야 한다.
⑤ 시골 소학교들을 폐쇄하는 대신 장점을 살려야 한다.

Check-Up 4

글의 결과나 결말이 시사하는 점을 파악하고 알맞은 영어 속담이나 격언을 선택한다.

해결 전략 4

이야기 글이나 수필과 같은 종류의 글이 나오면 교훈이나 시사점을 묻는 경우가 많은데, 이때는 글의 사건이나 상황을 종합적으로 파악하고, 사건이나 상황의 결과가 시사하는 점이나 교훈에 집중한다.

p.34 5. 주제문이 없는 경우 참조

이때 선택지로 속담이나 격언이 주어지기도 하므로 영어속담이나 격언을 그 숨은 뜻까지 정확히 알고 있어야 한다.

p.44, 45 기출총정리 참조

010 다음 글이 시사하는 바로 가장 적절한 것은?

The English poet Coleridge wrote in *The Rime of the Ancient Mariner*, "water, water everywhere but not a drop to drink." It means that one can be in the middle of the ocean and still die of thirst. The Saudi Arabians have a similar problem. Sand is essential for building and many other industries. The Saudis are surrounded by deserts full of sand, but it's the wrong kind of sand for building and industry. So the Saudis have to import river sand from Scotland. It's strange that a desert nation has to buy its sand from Europe.

① All that glitters is not gold.
② Rome wasn't built in a day.
③ Blood is thicker than water.
④ Kill two birds with one stone.
⑤ A bird in the hand is worth two in the bush.

011 다음 글이 시사하는 바로 가장 적절한 것은?

A jeweler's friend wanted a special present for his fiancée. So, the jeweler picked out a $500 necklace that he was willing to let his friend have for $250. But when the jeweler quoted the $250 price, his friend's face fell, and he began backing away from the deal because he wanted something "really nice." When the jeweler realized what had happened, he called his friend and asked him to come back. This time, the jeweler introduced the new piece at its regular $500 price. His friend liked it enough to buy it on the spot. But before any money was exchanged, the jeweler told him that, as a wedding gift, he would drop the price to $250. This time, rather than finding the $250 sales price offensive, he was overjoyed to have it.

① 친한 사이라도 돈거래는 안 하는 것이 좋다.
② 상대방의 호의는 되도록 거절하지 말아야 한다.
③ 값비싼 물건은 그 값어치를 하게 마련이다.
④ 사람들은 가격으로 물건의 가치를 판단한다.
⑤ 선물은 가격보다 정성을 깃들이는 것이 좋다.

실전적용독해

3문제를 4분 안에 풀어보세요.

정답 및 해설 p.23

012 다음 글의 요지로 가장 적절한 것은?

Parents often have high expectations of future career success for their children, and they believe that academic success is most strongly linked to it. But those expectations can be useless if children don't have the basic tools to succeed in life. Values like honesty, patience, and responsibility are essential to be an effective member of society. Those are far more important in the long run than A's on student report cards. Solid values rather than academic studies are the best gifts that parents can give and will have the greatest effect on future success.

① 성공을 위한 초석인 학업에 매진하라.
② 지나친 기대는 아이에게 부담을 준다.
③ 아이의 실수에 관대한 자세를 취하라.
④ 삶의 가치관 형성이 성적보다 중요하다.
⑤ 성공을 위해서는 인내의 시간이 필요하다.

013 다음 글의 요지로 가장 적절한 것은?

Diversity is a wonderful thing — diversity of culture, people, geography, history, and lifestyle all makes the world a fascinating place. Schools, by their very nature, are diverse organizations, but in this period of rapid educational evolution they are becoming more and more diverse in terms of what is being taught, how it is taught and assessed, who is teaching, and who is learning. Our educational curriculum encourages diversity and aims to be flexible; that is a good thing because students learn in different ways. Providing a diverse range of learning experiences and allowing students to explore and inquire make school learning programs today very different from those of the past.

① 시대에 맞는 학교 교육이 필요하다.
② 다양성을 융통성 있게 가르쳐야 한다.
③ 교육과정 선택은 학생에 의해 이루어져야 한다.
④ 학교 커리큘럼은 상황에 따라 변화해야 한다.
⑤ 다양화되는 오늘날의 교육은 환영받을 만하다.

014 다음 글에서 필자가 주장하는 바로 가장 적절한 것은?

I edit a lot of job applications to help my students. Mostly I shorten them. I try not to change word choice or do something that would take away from the writer's original voice. It's a shame, but I see many small but critical errors — misspellings, grammatical errors (including lack of capital letters), and extremely casual writing in formal circumstances. This is something which must stop if you ever hope to get a job in the real world. Recruiters find the lack of capital letters combined with overall carelessness completely irritating. And let's face it, they do the hiring. I want every person to solemnly swear that they will never send another email full of errors. I can hear the protests now — we cannot be perfect, can we? Don't forget! It's precisely this type of behavior that comes back and bites you.

① 구직용 자기소개서는 전문가의 검토를 받아야 한다.
② 구직 서류는 간단명료하게 작성하는 것이 좋다.
③ 서류 작성 시 용도에 맞는 문체를 선택해야 한다.
④ 지나친 완벽주의는 구직 활동에 좋지 않은 영향을 준다.
⑤ 구직 서류 작성 시 실수를 저지르지 않아야 한다.

VOCAbulary 어휘확인

012 **expectation** 기대 **academic** 학업의 **link** 관련되다 **responsibility** 책임감 **essential** 필수적인 **effective** 효과적인 **in the long run** 긴 안목으로 보면, 결국은 **solid** 견고한, 단단한 **have an effect on** ~에 영향을 미치다
013 **diversity** 다양성 **geography** 지리 **fascinating** 매혹적인 **evolution** 진화 **in terms of ~** 면에서 **assess** 평가하다 **curriculum** 교육과정 **aim** 목표로 하다 **flexible** 융통성 있는 **range** 범위 **inquire** 질문하다 014 **edit** (원고를) 손질하다, 교정보다 **job application** 취업 지원서 **take away from** ~로부터 벗어나다 **critical** 중대한, 결정적인 **misspelling** 오타 **casual** 격식이 없는 **formal** 공식적인 **recruiter** 신인 모집자 **combined with** ~와 결합된 **carelessness** 부주의 **irritating** 짜증나게 하는 **solemnly** 엄숙하게, 진지하게 **swear** 맹세하다 **protest** 항의, 이의

기출총정리

영어 속담의 숨은 뜻

요지를 묻는 글에서 선택지가 속담이나 격언으로 주어질 때는 그 숨은 뜻까지 알고 있어야 한다. 우리말에도 유사한 속담이 있는 경우가 많으므로 비교해서 알아두자.

- A bad workman blames his tools.
  (서투른 일꾼이 연장만 탓한다.)
  숨은 뜻: 실력 없는 사람일수록 핑계를 댄다.
  우리말 속담: 서투른 목수 연장 탓한다.

- Many hands make light work.
- Two heads are better than one.
  (많은 손이 일을 가볍게 만든다.)
  (한 사람이 하는 것보다는 두 사람이 하는 것이 낫다.)
  숨은 뜻: 서로 힘을 합치면 일이 쉬워진다.
  우리말 속담: 백지장도 맞들면 낫다.

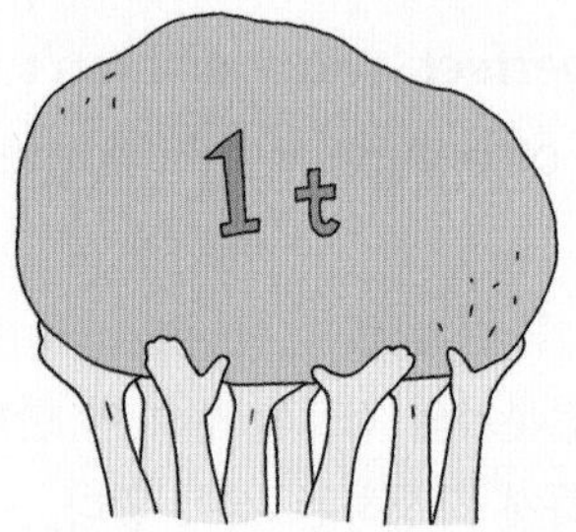

- Birds of a feather flock together.
  (깃털이 같은 새끼리 모인다.)
  숨은 뜻: 끼리끼리 모인다. / 유유상종.
  우리말 속담: 가재는 게 편이다.

- Too many cooks spoil the broth.
  (요리사가 너무 많으면 수프를 망친다.)
  숨은 뜻: 간섭하는 사람이 많으면 일을 망칠 수 있다.
  우리말 속담: 사공이 많으면 배가 산으로 간다.

- You reap what you sow.
  (씨앗을 뿌린 것을 거둔다.)
  숨은 뜻: 좋든 나쁘든 심은 대로 거둔다.
  우리말 속담: 콩 심은 데 콩 나고 팥 심은 데 팥 난다.

- Actions speak louder than words.
  (행동은 말보다 더 큰 소리로 말한다.)
  숨은 뜻: 말보다 행동이 중요하다.

- A stitch in time saves nine.
  (제때의 한 땀이 아홉 땀의 수고를 던다.)
  숨은 뜻: 적절한 때에 조치를 취해야 나중의 수고를 덜 수 있다.
  우리말 속담: 호미로 막을 일 가래로 막는다.

- Old habits die hard.
  (오랜 습관은 쉽게 사라지지 않는다.)
  숨은 뜻: 몸에 밴 습관은 고치기 힘들다.
  우리말 속담: 세 살 버릇 여든까지 간다.

- Honesty is the best policy.
  (정직이 최상의 방책이다.)

- Strike while the iron is hot.
- Make hay while the sun shines.
  (쇠는 뜨거울 때 쳐라.)
  (해가 비칠 때 건초를 말려라.)
  숨은 뜻: 좋은 때[기회]를 놓치지 마라.
  우리말 속담: 쇠뿔도 단김에 빼라.

- Barking dogs seldom bite.
  (짖는 개는 좀처럼 물지 않는다.)
  숨은 뜻: 내용이 없을수록 겉만 번지르르하다.
  우리말 속담: 빈 수레가 요란하다.

- It is no use crying over spilt milk.
  (엎질러진 우유를 보고 울어봐야 소용없다.)
  숨은 뜻: 이미 벌어진 일은 돌이킬 수 없다.
  우리말 속담: 이미 엎질러진 물이다.

- Look before you leap.
  (뛰기 전에 보아라.)
  숨은 뜻: 항상 신중해라.
  우리말 속담: 돌다리도 두드려 보고 건너라. / 아는 길도 물어 가라.

- Kill two birds with one stone.
  (한 개의 돌로 두 마리의 새를 잡는다.)
  숨은 뜻: 한 번에 두 가지를 얻는다.
  우리말 속담: 일석이조. / 꿩 먹고 알 먹기.

- A big fish in a little pond.
  (작은 연못 안의 큰 물고기.)
  숨은 뜻: 세상을 넓게 보지 못하고 자기가 잘난 줄 안다.
  우리말 속담: 우물 안 개구리.

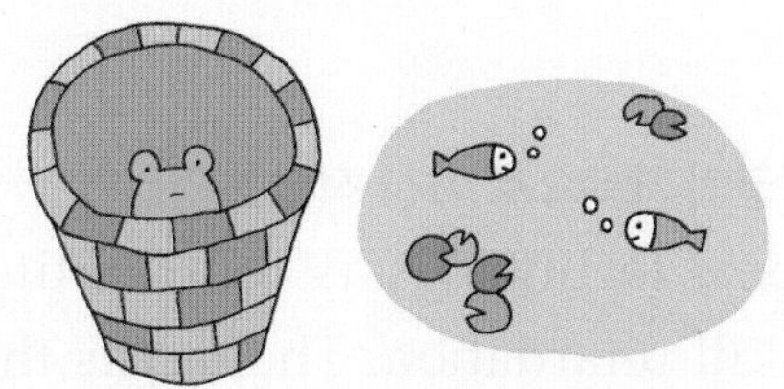

- Don't count your chickens before they hatch.
  (병아리가 부화될 때까지 병아리를 세지 마라.)
  숨은 뜻: 뭔가 벌어지기 전에 헛된 꿈부터 꾸지 마라.
  우리말 속담: 김칫국부터 마신다.

- The grass is always greener on the other side of the fence.
  (울타리 저편의 잔디가 항상 더 푸르다.)
  숨은 뜻: 자기 것보다는 남의 것이 더 좋아 보인다.
  우리말 속담: 남의 떡이 커 보인다.

- The pot calls the kettle black.
  (솥이 주전자보고 검다고 한다.)
  숨은 뜻: 자신의 결점은 모르고 남의 작은 잘못을 탓한다.
  우리말 속담: 똥 묻은 개가 겨 묻은 개 나무란다.

- Little drops of water make the mighty ocean.
  (작은 물방울들이 큰 바다를 이룬다.)
  숨은 뜻: 작은 것이라도 모이면 큰 것을 이룬다.
  우리말 속담: 티끌 모아 태산이다.

- Out of the frying pan into the fire.
  (프라이팬에서 나와 불 속으로 뛰어든다.)
  숨은 뜻: 상황이 점점 악화된다.
  우리말 속담: 갈수록 태산이다. / 설상가상.

- A little knowledge is dangerous.
  (얕은 지식은 위험하다.)
  숨은 뜻: 어설프게 아는 것은 위험하다.
  우리말 속담: 선무당이 사람 잡는다.

- What's learned in the cradle is carried to the grave.
  (요람에서 배운 것이 무덤까지 간다.)
  숨은 뜻: 어려서 익힌 습관은 없애기 힘들다.
  우리말 속담: 세 살 버릇 여든 간다.

- A burnt child dreads the fire.
  (불에 덴 아이는 불을 무서워한다.)
  숨은 뜻: 쓰라린 경험은 잊혀지지 않는다.
  우리말 속담: 자라 보고 놀란 가슴 솥뚜껑 보고 놀란다.

- Don't judge a book by its cover.
- You can't tell a book by its cover.
  (표지만 보고 책을 판단하지 말라.)
  숨은 뜻: 겉모습으로 사람을 판단하지 말라.

- Familiarity breeds contempt.
  (잘 알면 무례해지기[무시하기] 쉽다.)
  숨은 뜻: 친할수록 예의를 지켜야 한다.

- Slow and steady wins the race.
  (느려도 꾸준하면 이길 수 있다.)
  숨은 뜻: 성실함이 무엇보다 중요하다.

유형 03 제목

이렇게 출제된다.
글의 핵심 내용을 함축하며 동시에 글의 간판이 되는 제목을 고르는 유형이다. 약 1~2문항씩 출제된다.

지시문은 이렇게
다음 글의 제목으로 가장 적절한 것은?

정답 및 해설 p.25

Check-Up 1

다음은 어떤 글의 주제문이다. 주제문의 내용을 가장 잘 반영한 제목을 고르시오.

A wide range of evidence shows that contact with nature enhances children's education, personal and social skills, and health and wellbeing.

① How to Make Education Work
② Nature: What Children Need

해결 전략 1 **글의 주제나 요지를 파악한다.**
제목은 글의 핵심 내용을 압축적으로 표현한 것이다. 글의 핵심 내용을 담고 있는 것은 주제문이므로, 제목 문제를 풀 때도 주제문을 우선적으로 찾아 이를 가장 잘 반영한 것을 정답으로 고른다.
p.28 1. 주제문이란? 참조

015 다음 글의 제목으로 가장 적절한 것은?

I believe some technology is contributing to the spread of skill retardation. The fact is that we're collectively getting worse at most things — math, literacy, being able to read maps, hands-on skills, and even using our memory. Young people in particular are already proving to be the least skilled generation ever, and a lot of companies recognize this, which is why they're increasingly reluctant to hire young graduates. Even my wife, who's a primary school teacher, is often telling me about the growing number of kids she sees who lack basic skills and knowledge. This extends to social skills, too. Young people are becoming less skilled at basic human communication, handling conflicts, and even dating or meeting people.

*retardation 지체, 지연, 방해

① The Continual Advancement of Technology
② Where Technology Cannot Beat Humans
③ Technology Is Making the Young Stupid
④ A New Generation of Technology Loving Kids
⑤ What Distinguishes Skilled and Unskilled People

Check-Up 2

내용을 종합하거나 사건, 상황이 시사하는 점을 생각해 본다.

해결 전략 2

뚜렷한 주제문이 없는 글일 때는 앞에 제시된 주제와 요지의 경우와 마찬가지 방법으로 추론한다.

p.34 5. 주제문이 없는 경우 참조

Check-Up 3

제목은 읽는 이의 호기심을 자극한다.

해결 전략 3

제목은 글의 핵심을 나타내면서도 읽는 이의 호기심을 자극하는 기능을 한다. 즉 제목만 보아도 글의 내용이 궁금하여 읽게 만드는 것이다. 글의 주제와 유사하기 때문에 주제를 그대로 제목으로 쓸 수도 있고 요지를 포함하기도 하지만, 훨씬 더 다양한 스타일로 표현될 수 있음을 기억하고, 기출의 예를 통해 잘 익혀두자.

p.48 기출총정리 참조

016 다음 글의 제목으로 가장 적절한 것은?

BottleRocket is a recycling service that supplies users — mostly college students — with cardboard bins to fill with bottles. Users then request pickups when their bins are full, and when enough users are ready for pickup in an area, they collect the bins and drop them off at a recycling center. Users can choose how to be rewarded, such as earning $5 per bin. "I like the idea, since college kids obviously have lots of cans and bottles to recycle, but they are too lazy to go out and recycle themselves," said a student who uses BottleRocket's services. The company is still expanding, and may be able to recycle electronics, such as old smartphones, and clothing in the future, the founder said.

① Recycling: A Principle of a Healthy Society
② A New Recycling Service Appeals to Users
③ Volunteers for a Better World
④ College Students Turn to Starting their Own Businesses
⑤ A New Way of Being Connected with People Online

017 다음 글의 제목으로 가장 적절한 것은?

Music surrounds us every day, coming to us from car radios, elevator speakers, the little voices of singing children, and countless other sources. However, music has value beyond entertainment. There is evidence that rhythm and sound have an effect on our senses and, in turn, influence muscle control. Studies also suggest that music can stimulate some neurons. When we hear or feel an outside source of rhythm such as music, our bodies naturally try to match our own rhythms to the beat. The beats per minute of a piece of music stimulate the body and brain in various ways. For example, 60 beats per minute is good before bed because it helps to return the body's natural rhythm to a calm state. One hundred beats per minute is best to help with attention to a task, etc.

*neuron 뉴런, 신경 세포

① The Importance of Music in Entertainment
② Music: A New Tool for Mental Growth
③ Does Music Really Make Us Feel Good?
④ Is Music Entertainment or Art?
⑤ How Music Affects Our Body and Brain

기출총정리

제목 이해하기

제목은 압축적이고 상징적이므로 다양한 형태로 쓰인다. 영문 제목과 글의 내용을 연결하면서 어떤 표현이 가능한지 잘 이해해 보도록 하자.

1 의문사가 쓰인 제목

제목에 쓰인 의문사를 보고 핵심 내용을 알 수 있다. 예를 들어 why는 '이유'를, how는 '방법'을 나타낸다.

- **What**'s Behind a Brilliant Smile
  (무엇이 빛나는 미소 뒤에 숨어 있는가)
  글의 내용: 빛나는 미소를 위해 필요한 조건인 치아에 대한 설명
- **Who** First Made Buffalo Wings
  (누가 처음으로 버팔로윙을 만들었는가)
  글의 내용: 버팔로윙의 유래
- **How** to Make Your Own Weekly Schedule
  (주간 계획을 어떻게 세워야 하는가)
  글의 내용: 주간 계획을 세우는 방법
- **Why** Women Cry More Than Men
  (왜 여자는 남자보다 더 많이 우는가)
  글의 내용: 여자가 남자보다 더 많이 우는 이유

2 동격 표현이 쓰인 제목

콤마나 콜론은 앞뒤 내용이 서로 동격(A = B)임을 나타낸다. 흔히 글감과 그에 대한 글쓴이의 견해로 구성되어 있다.

- Cowboys, Great Cooks
  (카우보이는 훌륭한 요리사)
  글의 내용: 카우보이는 요리를 잘한다.
- Translators: Still Imperfect Devices
  (번역기는 아직 불완전한 기계)
  글의 내용: 번역기는 여러 가지 문제로 아직 완벽하지 않다.
- Anticipation: A Way to Avoid Fear
  (예상은 두려움을 피하는 방법)
  글의 내용: 먼저 예측하는 시간을 가짐으로써 두려움을 줄일 수 있다.
- Biofuels: The Right Answer for Global Warming?
  (생물연료는 지구 온난화에 대한 옳은 답인가?)
  글의 내용: 생물연료 개발이 환경오염을 해결해 주는지에 대한 신중한 고려가 필요하다.

3 문장 형태의 제목

문장 형태의 제목에는 주로 요지가 담겨 있다.

- Weekends Make You More Productive
  (주말은 당신을 더 생산적으로 만들어준다.)
- Still Spending? Start to Save!
  (← Are you still spending? You should start to save.)
  (아직도 소비하고 있나요? 저축을 시작하세요!)
- Say Goodbye to Your Bad Feelings!
  (당신의 나쁜 감정들과 이별하세요!)
- No Water before Meals
  (← You shouldn't drink water before eating a meal.)
  (식사 전에 물을 마시지 마세요.)

4 매력적인 제목

제목은 글의 핵심 내용을 짧은 구나 문장에 담아내면서도 글을 읽고 싶도록 흥미를 끄는 것이어야 한다. 위에 제시된 몇몇 예에서 알 수 있듯이 제목은 다양한 방법으로 표현된다.

- 요지를 포함한 제목

- **Why Is Tuesday the Most Productive Day?**
  (왜 화요일이 가장 생산적인 날인가?)
  글의 내용: 화요일이 가장 생산적인 날인 이유에 대한 설명
- **Are Dolphins Really Our Friends?**
  (돌고래는 정말로 우리의 친구일까?)
  글의 내용: 돌고래가 사람에게 이로운 예와 해로운 예를 모두 포함

- 표현을 달리한 제목

글의 요지를 호기심을 유발하거나 강조하는 방향으로 말바꿈하거나, 의문문 형태로 바꿔 쓰기도 한다.

- One of the ways to identify your values is to look at what frustrates or upsets you.
  ⇨ **Negative Feelings: Clues to Your Values**
  (부정적인 감정들은 당신의 가치관에 대한 단서들)
  - anger, mad, frustrated, upset, annoyed = **negative feelings**
- Last month, Comet 17P/Holmes suddenly grew 400,000 times brighter than normal. However, no one expected the comet to get especially bright.
  ⇨ **The Unusual Brightness of a Comet**
  (흔치 않은 혜성의 빛남)
  - 400,000 times brighter = **brightness**
    than normal, no one expected = **unusual**
- So never ever let yourself get thirsty because you are making your brain shrink and become restless and forgetful.
  ⇨ **Does Your Brain Get Enough Water**?
  (당신의 뇌는 충분한 물을 얻고 있나요?)
  물을 많이 마시라는 요지를 직접적으로 기술하지 않고 의문문으로 돌려 말해 호기심을 유발함.
- Therefore, music should not be present where careful mental work is required.
  ⇨ **Music: Friend or Enemy for Work**?
  (음악은 일에 있어 친구일까 적일까?)
  요지는 집중이 필요한 일을 할 때는 음악이 없어야 한다는 것이지만 호기심을 자극하기 위해 or를 사용한 의문형으로 나타냄.

정답 및 해설 p.28

3문제를 4분 안에 풀어보세요.

018 다음 글의 제목으로 가장 적절한 것은?

The growth of the Internet has caused a revolution in the news media that is obvious in several ways. Younger people especially like to reproduce their own news, choosing from the Internet's millions of blogs, UCC videos, and newspaper sites. People want their news to be relevant to their personal interests, and they discard everything else. Another characteristic of today's news is its focus on analysis and opinion. People want to know more than what's happening and where it's taking place. That is, they want to know what the events mean to other people and how the events will impact them in their own lives.

① The Power of the Media
② What People Want These Days
③ The Role of Youth in the Media
④ The Decreasing Quality of News
⑤ The Changing Character of News

019 다음 글의 제목으로 가장 적절한 것은?

There are around 45,000 surnames, or family names, in England today. But this wasn't always the case. In fact, in England's early history, only the nobility had two names. Common people used only a personal name or nickname. In villages and in the country, surnames were unnecessary as everyone knew who "John" or "Mary" was. But in 1066, William from France conquered England and ruled that everyone should have a surname. With surnames, it would be easier to keep records of people and to collect taxes based on those records. This meant that everyone had to choose a second name that would be passed on from fathers to their sons and daughters.

① The Value of the Surname
② Common Names in England
③ The Origin of Family Names
④ The Great Conqueror, William
⑤ The Function of Family Names

020 다음 글의 제목으로 가장 적절한 것은?

I started an organization to provide decent clothing for foster care teens last August 2016. We serve about 42 teens every month. We are not a typical charity. The clothes are not used, worn-out, or dirty. We provide new underwear, socks, and other essentials to as many teens as possible, and everything is brand-new. As for me, success is making a difference and helping others who have often been forgotten about. We have been able to motivate our community members by bringing awareness to this issue. Teens in foster care deserve to shop with dignity, choose new clothing and accessories, and receive the necessary hygiene essentials. Teens leave our shop with confidence and raised self-esteem.

*foster care 위탁 양육 **hygiene 위생

① A New Trend in Shopping for Clothing
② Clothing Items Favored by Stylish Teens
③ What Success Means to Most Teenagers
④ A Shop with More Fashion Choices for Teens
⑤ An Organization for Helping Needy Teens

VOCAbulary 어휘확인

018 revolution 혁명 obvious 뻔한, 명백한 reproduce 재생산하다 be relevant to ~와 관련되어 있다 discard 버리다 characteristic 특징 analysis 분석 take place 일어나다, 개최되다 019 surname 성(姓)(= family name, second name) nobility 귀족 common 보통의; 흔한 conquer 정복하다 rule 결정을 내리다 keep a record of ~을 기록하다 tax 세금 based on ~을 토대로 하여 pass on (to) (~에게) 넘겨주다 020 decent (상황에) 적절한 charity 자선 단체 worn-out 닳아 해진 essentials 필수품 motivate 동기 부여하다 awareness 인식 deserve to-v ~할 가치가 있다 dignity 위엄, 품위 confidence 자신감 self-esteem 자존감

유형 04 글의 목적 파악

이렇게 출제된다.
필자가 글을 쓴 의도를 파악하는 유형이다. 1문항씩 출제되며 실용문(편지글, 광고문 등)의 출제 비중이 높다.

지시문은 이렇게
다음 글의 목적으로 가장 적절한 것은?

정답 및 해설 p.30

Check-Up 1

1 다음 글을 읽고, 글쓴이가 글을 쓴 의도가 가장 잘 드러나는 문장을 고르시오.

① Starting June 1st, we'll be offering our regular customers check-ups of vehicles for free. ② Thus, we're inviting you to bring your car into our shop. ③ The service will last till June 30th, from 8:00 a.m. to 3:00 p.m., Monday through Friday.

2 021 지문을 읽고, 글쓴이가 글을 쓴 의도가 가장 잘 드러나는 문장을 찾아 밑줄을 그으시오.

해결 전략 1

글을 쓴 의도가 가장 잘 드러나는 문장을 찾는다.

글쓴이는 글의 의도를 가장 잘 드러낼 글의 형식과 표현을 골라 사용한다. 예를 들어 편지글에서 '나는 이러한 이유로 편지를 쓴다' 또는 광고문에서 '이런 경우라면 우리 제품을 사용하라'라는 말은 글쓴이의 의도를 드러내는 표현이다. 이와 같은 표현을 익혀 글의 목적이 드러나는 부분을 찾을 수 있도록 하자.

021 다음 글의 목적으로 가장 적절한 것은?

Dear Dorothy,

I hope you're having a good morning. Personally, I feel terrible about ruining your lovely lunch yesterday by arguing with Celia about Will Ladislaw. You certainly did everything you could to save the situation, and I apologize for ignoring good taste and old friendships in pursuing a "discussion" that was completely inappropriate. I talked to Celia first thing this morning and attempted to fix things with her, but I feel a great deal worse about what I did to you. The lunch was delicious, and the first two hours were delightful. I hope you will someday be able to forgive me for ruining the last half an hour.

Your friend,

Judy

① 친구들과의 모임 약속을 전달하려고
② 친구와 다툼이 있었던 것을 고백하려고
③ 담장을 망가뜨린 것을 항의하려고
④ 오찬 모임을 망친 것을 사과하려고
⑤ 모임에 늦게 도착하게 된 사정을 설명하려고

Check-Up 2

[3 - 4] 다음 글을 읽고, 물음에 답하시오.

I have won the Big Dream Scholarship for Redwood University! This was possible because you wrote that recommendation letter. Your recommendation must have persuaded the scholarship committee to take a chance on me. I cannot thank you enough for your help.

3 글을 쓴 목적으로 가장 적절한 것을 고르시오.

① 대학 장학금을 타게 된 것을 알리려고

② 추천서를 써 준 것에 대해 감사하려고

4 글쓴이가 글을 쓴 실제 의도가 드러나는 부분을 찾아 밑줄을 그으시오.

5 022 지문을 읽고, 글의 실제 목적이 드러나는 부분을 찾아 밑줄을 그으시오.

해결 전략 2 **글쓴이의 진짜 의도를 파악하라.**

'고맙지만 사양하겠다'라는 말은 감사가 아니라 거절을 나타낸다. 이와 마찬가지로 글을 쓸 때도 의례적인 말이나 상황 설명 다음에 본론을 꺼내는 경우가 많다. 따라서 글을 끝까지 읽고 글쓴이의 진짜 의도가 무엇인지 파악하는 것이 중요하다.

예시 1) As your tenant, I always pay my rent on time and am very happy with the house. However, I am extremely disappointed by your recent decision to increase my rent.
(세입자로서 저는 늘 제때 임대료를 지급하고 있고 집에도 매우 만족하고 있습니다. 하지만 저는 최근 임대료를 올리기로 하신 결정에 매우 실망했습니다.)

☞ 의례적인 인사말 이후 However로 내용을 전환하여 글을 쓴 실제 목적을 드러내고 있다.

예시 2) No money or time for a college degree?
Sylvan is your solution.
(대학 학위를 딸 돈이나 시간이 없으십니까? Sylvan이 해결해 드리겠습니다.)

☞ 사람의 이목을 끄는 문구로 시작하지만, Sylvan이라는 학위 취득 프로그램에 대한 광고문이다.

022 다음 글의 목적으로 가장 적절한 것은?

Dear Ms. Dallas,

I very much enjoy working for Stegner Publishing, and you in particular have been most helpful in introducing me to people and showing me around. When I was interviewed for the job, Mr. Oliver consistently used the term "production editor," and the job duties he listed were those generally associated with the position of production editor. In my three weeks on the job, however, I have done nothing but copyediting. After speaking to you yesterday and discovering that this was not just a training stage but my permanent position, I suspect there has been a misunderstanding. I would like to meet with you and Mr. Oliver sometime soon to see if we can resolve this situation.

Sincerely,

Adam Gillum

① 일을 그만둠을 통보하려고

② 정식 직원 채용 여부에 대해 문의하려고

③ 담당 업무와 관련하여 만남을 제안하려고

④ 직속상관이 누구인지 명확히 문의하려고

⑤ 출판사 전체 일의 흐름에 대해 문의하려고

기출총정리

글의 목적을 콕콕 찍어내는 법

1 글의 목적을 나타내는 표현을 알아두자.

가장 자주 출제되는 글의 목적은 '알림, 홍보, 안내, 권유' 등이다. 선택지가 영어로 제시되는 경우도 많으므로 글의 목적을 나타내는 다음 표현을 익혀두자.

- to inform 알리려고[알려주려고]
- to promote 홍보하려고
- to guide[show] 안내하려고
- to recommend 권유[추천]하려고
- to request 요청하려고
- to encourage 장려[독려]하려고
- to introduce 소개하려고
- to inquire 문의하려고
- to explain 설명하려고
- to request 부탁[요청]하려고
- to advise 조언하려고
- to complain 항의하려고
- to confirm 확인하려고
- to advertise 광고하려고
- to celebrate 축하하려고
- to suggest 제안하려고

2 글의 핵심 내용을 이해하자.

최근에는 단순히 '항의하는지, 광고하는지'를 묻는 것이 아니라 '무엇을 항의하는지, 어떤 상품을 광고하는지'와 같이 좀 더 구체적인 내용을 파악해야 하는 문제가 출제되고 있다. 따라서 요지를 파악하듯이 글의 핵심 내용을 정확히 이해하는 것이 중요하다.

[단순한 목적] → [구체적인 목적]
① 항의하려고 → 직원의 불친절한 태도에 대해 항의하려고
② 권유하려고 → 수면 관련 세미나 등록을 권유하려고
③ 문의하려고 → 여행 일정에 대해 문의하려고
④ 요청하려고 → 장학금 수여식 참석을 요청하려고
⑤ 감사하려고 → 교사의 세심한 학생 지도에 감사하려고

Mini Test

정답 및 해설 p.32

● **다음을 읽고, 글의 목적으로 가장 적절한 것을 고르시오.**

1 Writers aged over thirteen from all countries are encouraged to enter the East India Press Short Story Writing Contest. You should submit your story by March 1, 2017. [모의]
① 단편 소설 공모전을 안내하기 위해
② 백일장 심사를 부탁하기 위해

2 Here is a special lecture for beginners that breaks the codes and provides quite a few examples that can be seen in the influential daily economic newspapers. [모의]
① to confirm ② to promote

3 When I received my bank statement, I discovered that you charged my card twice. I would be grateful if you could resolve this matter quickly. [모의]
① 신용카드 결제 오류의 해결을 요청하려고
② 신용카드 발급 가능 여부를 확인하려고

4 I wanted to be the editor of the school paper, but the teacher in charge picked another student. I was disappointed, but I kept writing and now I'm a columnist in a newspaper. So never give up! You are great, and that's all that matters! [모의]
① to encourage ② to inquire

5 Your contribution has helped so much, but the need is still great. Together we are transforming lives and building brighter futures, but without you, it wouldn't be possible. [모의]
① 기부에 대해 감사하려고
② 지속적인 기부를 요청하려고

실전적용독해

3문제를 4분 안에 풀어보세요.

정답 및 해설 p.32

023 다음 글의 목적으로 가장 적절한 것은?

Dear Mrs. Green,

We were so sorry to learn that you have been hospitalized. I have already stopped your newspaper and mail delivery for the time being. Since I had a copy of your house key, I went in to make sure all the faucets were off and the windows shut (except for leaving one upstairs and one downstairs open an inch for air). I've been going in at night and turning on a few lights so it doesn't look empty. I wasn't sure you were up to a phone call, but I thought you'd want to know that the house is being looked after. We are all hoping and praying for your speedy recovery. In the meantime, if there is anything you'd like us to do, please don't hesitate to call.

With best wishes,

Randy Lahey

① 병문안 가지 못함을 사과하려고
② 보안을 더 철저히 할 것을 당부하려고
③ 빈집 관리를 하고 있음을 알리려고
④ 집 관리 관련 세부 내용을 문의하려고
⑤ 전화 연락을 해달라고 요청하려고

024 다음 글의 목적으로 가장 적절한 것은?

We received and read your manuscript with surprise and delight. It is the first time we have reviewed such a brilliant book in the 67-year history of this publishing house. Every one of our editors was similarly impressed, and we discussed your manuscript eagerly for quite some time. After several meetings we agreed that if we were to publish your book, we could never match its standard. Any books that we publish in the future will surely be nothing in comparison to yours. Therefore, to our great regret, we must return this astonishing work to you and beg your forgiveness for our decision.

① 출판 일정을 의논하려고
② 원고 투고를 장려하려고
③ 책의 출판을 거절하려고
④ 원고 집필을 의뢰하려고
⑤ 훌륭한 원고를 칭찬하려고

025 다음 글의 목적으로 가장 적절한 것은?

The Internet may be a writer's best resource, but at my old age of 90, computers are far too much trouble. My stiff fingers cannot work the mouse or the keyboard. But I could not have written this book without the Internet's resources, nor without the help of some fantastic people. My sincere gratitude goes to Tanika Hasley, the Internet expert, and to Deanne Warrick, who inspired me to write the book in the first place. Also to my publisher, Patricia Law, for her encouragement and support. And of course it would be a mistake not to mention my wonderful and supportive family. I couldn't have done it without you all.

① to give thanks for help
② to offer a job in publishing
③ to praise the work of a poet
④ to request computer repairs
⑤ to complain about a deadline

VOCAbulary 어휘확인

023 hospitalize 입원하다 faucet 수도꼭지 be up to ~을 감당할 수 있다, ~할 만큼 좋다 look after ~을 돌보다 recovery 회복 in the meantime 그동안 hesitate 주저하다 024 manuscript (책 등의) 원고 brilliant 훌륭한 publishing house 출판사 impressed 감명을 받은 eagerly 열심히 match (필요에) 맞추다 standard 수준[기준] in comparison to ~와 비교해 볼 때 to one's regret 유감스럽게도 astonishing 정말 놀라운 beg 간청[애원]하다 forgiveness 용서 025 resource 자원; 자료 stiff 굳은, 뻣뻣한 sincere 진심 어린 gratitude 감사 expert 전문가 inspire 고무하다 in the first place 애초에, 먼저 publisher 출판업자; 출판사 encouragement 격려 support 지지, 지원 cf. supportive 힘을 주는

미니 모의고사 1

유형 01 | 유형 02 | 유형 03 | 유형 04

18문제를 25분 안에 풀어보세요.

정답 및 해설 p.34

026 다음 글의 주제로 가장 적절한 것은?

One of the earliest kinds of movie was the "magic lantern" show. A magic lantern show projected painted images from glass slides onto a screen. The shows were popular in the 19th century. Lantern men traveled widely and attracted big crowds to their shows. The glass slides were expensive, so they were replaced by film when photography was invented. But the pictures still did not move. Real movies were finally made and shown in France in 1895 by the Lumiere brothers. They invented a machine which could project many filmed images very quickly to make a picture appear to move.

① the popularity of movies
② the inventor of movies
③ the difficulties of making movies
④ the developmental process of movies
⑤ the relationship between photography and movies

027 다음 글의 주제로 가장 적절한 것은?

"One of the cleanest spots in a public restroom is usually the toilet seat. A lot of people will wipe it before using it, and cleaners tend to clean it well," says an expert. So no worries if you make contact. The real threat lies beneath, he says. "The most dangerous spot in restrooms is always the floor." According to research, when the toilet flushes, it sends a spray of droplets into the air, which then settle onto any surfaces within six feet of the flush. Those droplets can be carrying bacteria from any number of diseases. All that can be avoided by closing the lid. The only problem: we forget to do it. That means the handle, the toilet paper dispenser, and even the little purse shelf are hotspots for bacteria to settle.

① how to best clean your bathroom
② what to remember in a restroom and why
③ disease-carrying bacteria living on toilet seats
④ ways to prevent overuse of toilet paper
⑤ making toilets as comfortable as possible

028 다음 글의 요지로 가장 적절한 것은?

On the village school ground, where you pick sides, it is possible to play simply for fun exercise. But as soon as the question of prestige arises, the combative instincts are aroused. Anyone who has played even in a school football match knows this. At the international level, sport frankly resembles warfare. The spectators from each nation seriously believe that these contests of running, jumping, and kicking a ball are tests of national power. Nearly all sports practiced nowadays are competitive. You play to win, and the game has little meaning unless you do your best to win.

*prestige 위신

① 스포츠의 재미는 경쟁을 한다는 데 있다.
② 스포츠는 경쟁보다 체력 증진이 목적이어야 한다.
③ 국제 경기를 전쟁으로 착각하면 안 된다.
④ 스포츠는 보는 것보다 참가하는 데 의의가 있다.
⑤ 요즘의 스포츠는 대부분 이기는 것을 목표로 한다.

029 다음 글의 목적으로 가장 적절한 것은?

On May 19, I bought a $1,200 TV in your store after shopping around for several days. Your salesman told me I could have it delivered by train to my home, for just $12. This seemed like a reasonable offer, so I agreed, and paid the fee. Two days later, I got a call from the railway station, 80 kilometers away, to tell me a delivery had arrived for me. But they said that I owed $24 for shipping. Furthermore, they said a truck could ship my TV from the station to my home for an additional $12. You can imagine how I felt! I will be waiting for your reply.

① 늑장 배달에 대해 항의하려고
② 직원의 친절에 대해 감사하려고
③ 물품 대금 지급 연기를 신청하려고
④ 배달 비용 추가에 대해 항의하려고
⑤ 물품 손상에 대한 배상을 청구하려고

030 다음 글의 제목으로 가장 적절한 것은?

Many people believe that they are unaffected by advertising. They may say that they have complete freedom of choice when shopping. They may also say that they use only their common sense and intelligence when they choose what to buy. But advertising is a very powerful force in modern society. Companies spend billions on advertising as they compete fiercely for our money. Can you really believe they are throwing all that money away? Advertisements are everywhere. You can't escape them no matter how hard you try. People who think that ads have no influence on their decisions when shopping are just fooling themselves. Just look at the brands in your kitchen and bathroom.

① Overspending on Advertising
② The Foolish Behaviors of Shoppers
③ The Powerful Effects of Advertising
④ Freedom in Choosing Goods to Buy
⑤ Escaping the Influence of Advertising

031 다음 글의 제목으로 가장 적절한 것은?

Whether you are planning a lunch for 50 or a wedding for 500, Amberly Manor is the ideal place for you. The Manor is famed for its five-star service, excellent food, and unique and magnificent design. Our ballroom is the best in the city, as it is easily divided into separate rooms for smaller functions. The Manor's highly-trained chefs, waiters, and managers ensure that your every need is provided for. No detail will be overlooked, and we welcome special requests of any nature. We will work together with you to create your perfect event and make sure you leave Amberly Manor with great memories to last a lifetime.

① Why Use a Dining Service?
② Host Your Event at Our Place
③ An Invitation to Our Wedding Party
④ How to Make Valuable Memories
⑤ How to Plan a Party Successfully

032 다음 글의 요지로 가장 적절한 것은?

The dishwasher is spouting water. The flood is spreading across the kitchen floor. You think to yourself, "if I had washed the dishes by hand, this wouldn't be happening." When things go wrong, we look to lay blame, and often we look in the mirror. Psychologists find that many of us fall victim to the "everything is my fault" approach to life. Two things we often overlook are how little we directly control a situation and how little value there is in spending our time blaming ourselves. These thoughts do not fix the problem. Blame is about the past; a plan of action to fix a problem is about the future.

① 과거를 돌아보는 것은 미래 설계에 중요하다.
② 일이 잘못되면 책임 소재부터 따져야 한다.
③ 자신이 한 일에 책임질 줄 아는 자세가 필요하다.
④ 문제 발생 시 자책하지 말고 해결을 해야 한다.
⑤ 인생을 가치 있게 살려면 현재를 열심히 살아야 한다.

033 다음 글의 주제로 가장 적절한 것은?

Millions of tons of clothing are tossed into garbage landfills each year. They rot and produce methane gas. A major source of discarded clothes in landfills is the "fast fashion" industry. "Fast fashion" is the modern trend towards low cost, low quality, and quickly changing fashion. We don't care if the shoes are worn out soon or if the clothes are poorly made. Instead, we just want the latest "look." We then discard the clothes and they go into a landfill. However, consumers must learn that cheap and fast fashion comes at a very high cost to the environment. Buy less and pay more for clothing that lasts.

*methane gas 메탄가스

① the problem with fast fashion
② the size of the fashion industry
③ problems with garbage landfills
④ the high speed of change in fashion
⑤ advantages of low-cost clothing

034 다음 글의 주제로 가장 적절한 것은?

When we are speaking, it's not always possible to say exactly what we want to say. Few speakers possess a wide vocabulary, and even those that do often lack the level of control necessary to choose the perfect word in the heat of the moment. That is because there is no sure way to prepare for what to say next as we are speaking. Words pop into our heads and come out of our mouths in a careless way. In writing, however, we have more time to write what we want to say correctly. Much more editing is possible. Writers can work for hours on a single paragraph just to get it "right."

① how to speak carefully
② factors to be considered in speech
③ why it's difficult to write
④ the difference between speaking and writing
⑤ the necessity for accurate use of vocabulary

035 다음 글의 제목으로 가장 적절한 것은?

More and more people are suffering from shoulder pain. There are a few steps that can be taken to cure an aching shoulder, but experts agree that the best strategy is prevention. One important part of the prevention strategy is to build muscle strength and flexibility. But it's even more important to select the right bag and carry it properly. When you travel, carry light bags with wheels. If you must carry a backpack or book bag for school, you should stand up straight and keep the pack high on your back. Don't carry the pack, nor any other heavy bags, over one shoulder.

① What to Pack for Traveling
② Stress: The Enemy of Health
③ Keeping Good Body Posture
④ Prevention: The Best Cure for Shoulder Pain
⑤ The Benefits of Traveling Light

036 다음 글의 제목으로 가장 적절한 것은?

With today's Internet and satellite technologies, it is easy for military leaders in far-away headquarters to communicate with their armies. Of course, this wasn't always the case. Armies of the past had to find other methods of getting messages safely and quickly through enemy lines. One of those ways was by pigeon. This is because pigeons have an amazing ability to find their homes at high speed across great distances. The pigeons used for this sort of communication were usually kept in cages at military camps. Then, when the birds were released with messages tied to their legs, they would fly to headquarters, where the messages could be read.

① Pigeons as Messengers
② Safe Handling of Wild Birds
③ Sending Messages in the Army
④ Pigeons' Instinct to Return Home
⑤ The Communication Forms of Today

037 다음 글의 주제로 가장 적절한 것은?

Like the human eye, a fish eye has a pupil, a lens, and optic nerves leading to the brain. But in most fish, the eyes are placed on opposite sides of the head, so they can see different images with each eye. This location of their eyes gives them a very wide field of vision — up to 360 degrees. This is much wider than the human field of vision, and it's especially useful under the water, where predators can attack from any direction at any time. But this is not the only interesting feature. Because they live in water, fish have no eyelids, whereas we need them to keep our eyes moist.

*pupil 동공, 눈동자 **eyelid 눈꺼풀

① a fish's wide field of vision
② unique features of a fish's eyes
③ similarities between fish eyes and human eyes
④ the range of colors that a fish can see
⑤ advantages of a fish's wide field of view

038 다음 글의 목적으로 가장 적절한 것은?

I am a poor college student who can't afford a car, so I rely heavily on my bike. As mass transit in my hometown suffers from construction and gas prices remain astronomical, biking should be the best way to get around. But wherever I go, biking is unnecessarily difficult. Bikes are prohibited on sidewalks, yet bike lanes are scarce. I think I'm putting my life in the hands of distracted drivers every time I bike in the street. Portland is moving forward. It is reaping the economic and environmental benefits of embracing cycling. I expect Mayor Jackson to change his mind about cycling and create bike lanes, install bike racks, and urge residents to switch from horsepower to pedal power.

*astronomical (양·가격 등이) 천문학적인, 어마어마한

① 자전거 활성화 정책을 촉구하려고
② 다른 도시의 모범 사례를 제시하려고
③ 자전거 시설의 교체를 건의하려고
④ 운전자의 부주의를 상기시키려고
⑤ 자전거의 위험성을 지적하려고

039 다음 글의 요지로 가장 적절한 것은?

I live a thousand miles away from my daughter. But thanks to the Internet, we have been together all day. Despite the distance, I know all about her life and what she is going through. She had her wisdom teeth pulled out this morning. If we had not been able to talk, I would have been so worried. But we've been online, chatting, since she got home from the clinic. I'm so glad that I can talk to her so easily. And though she is in pain and bleeding, she gets comfort from feeling so close to me. How wonderful it is that we can so easily keep in touch with our loved ones!

① 특히 몸이 아플 때 가족의 필요성을 느끼게 된다.
② 가족의 사랑은 무엇과도 바꿀 수 없이 소중하다.
③ 인터넷 덕분에 멀리 있는 가족과 연락이 용이하다.
④ 외국에 나가서야 비로소 가족의 소중함을 알게 된다.
⑤ 멀리 떨어진 가족과 연락하는 것을 게을리하면 안 된다.

040 다음 글의 주제로 가장 적절한 것은?

Hula is a traditional Hawaiian dance set to special chants and music that combines flowing movement with unique facial expressions. When *hula* began, it was a form of worship. Prince Lot Kapúaiwa kept the *hula* alive in Hawaii at a time when there was less and less interest in it. The prince was noted for his energy and strong will. One of his interests was to promote and preserve Hawaiian culture, especially the *hula*. He did this by holding *hula* performances at his cottage. To many, the *hula* represents the Hawaiians' view of the world. In appreciation of Prince Lot's efforts to preserve Hawaiian culture, the Prince Lot Hula Festival was established in 1978. Each year, *hula* schools come to the festival to perform in Honolulu. This festival also includes other Hawaiian activities and exhibits.

① ways to perform the *hula*
② the diversity of Hawaiian culture
③ the uniqueness of Hawaiian dances
④ the importance of keeping traditions
⑤ the origin of the Prince Lot Hula Festival

041 다음 글의 요지로 가장 적절한 것은?

In the worlds of science and technology, precise measurement is critical to success in research and product development. Although most of us in everyday life don't perform experiments or design high-tech products, a great many people insist on using unnecessary precision. When you ask them for the time, they'll say "9:59" instead of "about 10:00." And they will tell you they have a "15.1-inch screen" on their PC instead of a "15-inch screen." These people have convinced themselves that tiny variations are important. I understand that precision is crucial in scientific investigations, but it's not in everyday life. After all, you can't sense the difference between 9:59 and 10:00. "Close" is usually good enough.

① 과학 실험에서는 정확한 측정이 중요하다.
② 현대 사회에서는 시간 개념이 정확해야 한다.
③ 일상생활에서는 정확성을 너무 따질 필요가 없다.
④ 전문용어와 일상용어는 구분해서 사용해야 한다.
⑤ 제품을 개발할 때는 항상 품질을 우선시해야 한다.

042 다음 글에서 필자가 주장하는 바로 가장 적절한 것은?

Day after day, news programs report the results of opinion polls. Although the polls usually have to do with the political scene, they sometimes cover social or economic issues. Lots of people listen with interest to poll results. They are fascinated that the results are reported with extraordinary precision. And they tend to believe that the authority figure reporting the results is objective and knowledgeable. In fact, the reality is often much different. So, when you hear the result of an opinion poll, you should take it with a grain of salt. The people writing the questions might be biased, or the sample population might not reflect the population as a whole. Furthermore, polls are frequently used by news organizations simply as filler — something to grab the viewers' interest, regardless of quality. These and other potential problems make polls unreliable.

*filler (중요하지는 않으며 시간이나 공간을) 채우기 위한 것

① 여론 조사의 정확성을 높이자.
② 여론 조사를 공정하게 시행하자.
③ 여론 조사 결과를 과신하지 말자.
④ 여론 조사에 대한 사람들의 관심도를 높이자.
⑤ 여론 조사에 대한 사람들의 불신을 해소하자.

043 다음 글의 요지로 가장 적절한 것은?

Today, college students tend to identify college education with preparing them for their jobs and for contributing to their growth in working as part of a team, communicating effectively, and applying knowledge. A college education, however, has value beyond delivering job skills. College students enroll because they want to develop as whole people. Whichever majors they choose, they also participate in athletics, leadership programs, student government, and service work. Most of them also want much more than a job after school. Whether they are studying to become therapists who heal injuries, or digital communications majors who improve online experiences, students pursue a degree because they want to live fulfilling, well-rounded lives and make the world a better place. Colleges and universities have the resources, the expertise, and the structures in place to provide a more satisfying and fulfilling full-course meal of a college degree.

① 대학 교육의 목적은 시대의 요구에 따라야 한다.
② 대학은 직업 준비 프로그램의 다양화에 힘써야 한다.
③ 대학 교육의 가치는 직업 생활 준비 그 이상에 있다.
④ 대학 교육의 초점은 사회생활 준비에 맞춰져야 한다.
⑤ 전인 교육은 대학이 아니라 개인의 노력에 달려 있다.

Chapter 2

유형 05 빈칸 추론

유형 06 함의 추론

유형 07 요약문 완성

미니 모의고사 2

유형 05 빈칸 추론

이렇게 출제된다.

빈칸에 적절한 단어, 어구 또는 문장을 넣어 지문을 완성하는 유형이다. 2014학년도 수능까지는 빈칸이 두 개인 문제도 출제되었으나 빈칸 추론 유형의 문항 개수가 줄어서 출제되지 않을 가능성도 있다. 3~4문항씩 출제되며, 다른 유형에 비해 3점짜리 고난도 문항이 많이 출제된다.

지시문은 이렇게

다음 글의 빈칸에 들어갈 말로 가장 적절한 것은?
다음 글의 빈칸 (A), (B)에 들어갈 말로 가장 적절한 것은?

정답 및 해설 p.47

Check-Up 1

다음 문장을 읽고, 빈칸을 추론하려면 지문을 읽으면서 어떤 내용을 찾아야 하는지 고르시오.

In conclusion, ________________ can help you reduce the stress in your life.

① 스트레스를 줄여야 하는 이유
② 스트레스를 줄이는 데 도움이 되는 것

해결 전략 1 **빈칸을 포함한 문장부터 먼저 읽어라.**
빈칸을 포함한 문장을 먼저 읽고 무엇에 중점을 두고 읽어야 하는지 파악한 후 그 단서를 찾아 읽어 내려가면 좀 더 빨리 그리고 정확하게 원하는 정보를 찾을 수 있다.

044 **다음 글의 빈칸에 들어갈 말로 가장 적절한 것은?**

A strong memory depends on the health and vitality of your brain. Whether you're a student studying for final exams, or a working professional interested in doing all you can to stay mentally sharp, you can improve your memory and mental performance. Indeed, the human brain has an astonishing ability to adapt and change — even in old age. This ability is known as neuro plasticity. With the right stimulation, your brain can form new neural pathways, alter existing connections, and adapt and react in ever-changing ways. This incredible ability of the brain to ________________ is very important when it comes to learning and memory. You can take advantage of the natural power of neuro plasticity to increase your mental abilities, enhance your ability to learn new information, and improve your memory.

*neuro plasticity 신경 가소성

① store information
② cut irrelevant connections
③ return to its original state
④ deceive itself
⑤ reshape itself

Check-Up 2

다음 두 문장 (A), (B)를 종합하여 아래 빈칸에 적절한 말을 고르시오.

(A) If you are frightened of roaches, it is a good idea to start staring at pictures of roaches and watch movies that show you some roaches.

(B) Next, you can try sweeping dead roaches off your floor, and then eventually look at one or two crawling cockroaches first before actually stepping on them or killing them.

↓

You can overcome your phobias effectively if you ______________________.

① share your terrifying experiences with your friends

② gradually make yourself less sensitive to what scares you

해결 전략 2 **빈칸을 추론할 수 있는 단서를 찾아라.**
빈칸의 단서는 반드시 글 안에 존재한다. 이때 단서와 빈칸은 동일한 어구일 수도 있지만 거의 대부분 말 바꿈이 이루어진다. 특히 빈칸이 포함된 문장은 대개 글의 주제문이며, 빈칸의 단서는 이를 뒷받침하는 세부사항에서 찾을 수 있으므로, 이 경우에는 세부사항을 포괄적으로 표현한 것이 빈칸에 들어갈 말이 된다.
p.64 기출총정리 참조

045 다음 글의 빈칸에 들어갈 말로 가장 적절한 것은?

We are sometimes assigned group work in the course of our lives. Many people agree that the biggest problem with group work lies in not always having the option of choosing your own group. However, if you do get this choice, there are some important considerations you should take into account to ensure you get the most out of your group task. What makes group work worthwhile is members' ____________. In order to ensure that your group task is rewarding, it is important to choose members that have something different from you to bring to the project. This can be done in terms of gender, culture, or even the amount of research or work experience a member may have. Ensuring your group has a number of different perspectives and ways of thinking will add to the wealth of ideas created for your task.

① loyalty ② cooperation ③ trust
④ diversity ⑤ enthusiasm

Check-Up 3

다음 두 문장이 같은 맥락이 되도록 빈칸에 적절한 말을 고르시오.

In other words, collaborating produces better results.

↑

Research shows that almost 90 percent of the time, people in ____________ environments outperform people in competitive environments.

① cooperative ② independent

해결 전략 3 **글의 주제문을 찾아라.**
빈칸 문장은 주제문이 아닌 세부사항에 해당할 수도 있는데, 이때 주제문은 빈칸 추론에 있어 결정적인 단서가 된다.

046 다음 글의 빈칸에 들어갈 말로 가장 적절한 것은?

Domesticated animals are those that live with humans. At one point, they were all wild animals, but that is no longer the case. Over thousands of years, domestic animals have undergone distinct changes, like becoming smaller compared to wild animals of related species. However, the most remarkable transformation is that they have come to rely on humans for survival. For example, wolves know how to find shelter and hunt for food, and can tell the difference between enemies and friends. The dog is related to the wolf, but the domesticated one's ________________ has disappeared. It expects humans to provide all of its needs. It can't live a good life without human help. To a greater or lesser degree, the same is true for cats and farm animals.

① survival skill ② hunting instinct
③ physical strength ④ ability to multiply
⑤ dependence on nature

Check-Up 4

두 개의 빈칸이 있는 유형도 크게 다르지 않다!

해결 전략 4

빈칸이 글의 초반과 후반에 각각 하나씩 제시되는데, 주로 하나는 주제문에 제시되고 다른 하나는 세부사항에 제시되거나, 또는 둘 다 각기 다른 세부사항에 하나씩 제시되곤 한다. 빈칸이 주제에 있으면 글에 제시된 세부사항을 포괄하는 단어를 찾으면 되고, 빈칸이 세부사항에 있으면 그 세부사항을 압축시킨 핵심 단어를 찾으면 된다.

047 다음 글의 빈칸 (A), (B)에 들어갈 말로 가장 적절한 것은?

Some people miss out on lots of fun, mind-expanding activities because of the "always do your best" mentality. You don't need to be one of them. Adjust your perception. Realize that it's okay to be an ______(A)______ pianist if playing the piano makes you feel good. And it's okay to be an average golfer if you like to play golf. And it's okay to be a mediocre artist if you enjoy painting. If there's something you enjoy, just do it and forget "their" standards. If you like doing it, concern with how well you do it and with the evaluations of others should be ______(B)______.

*mediocre 보통밖에 안 되는

	(A)		(B)
①	exceptional	……	important
②	exceptional	……	trivial
③	excellent	……	unnecessary
④	unexceptional	……	irrelevant
⑤	unexceptional	……	essential

기출총정리

빈칸 추론, 말 바꾸기

빈칸을 추론할 수 있는 단서를 찾았다면 이와 유사한 의미의 선택지를 찾아야 한다.
빈칸의 내용과 추론의 단서가 서로 어떤 연관성이 있는지 알아두도록 하자.

1 단서: **Taking time off** recharges your batteries so you can sprint forward when you return to work. [모의]

Rest is important.

▶ 본문의 Taking time off(휴식을 취하는 것)를 유의어인 Rest(휴식)로 말 바꿈하였다.

2 단서: **The more** you can do this, the stronger an option will be. [모의]

The best way to find a good idea is **to have a lot of ideas**.

▶ 본문의 The more(더 많이)를 유의어인 a lot of로 말 바꿈하였다.

3 단서: **Each brings their own culture** with them and changes the entire area into one **big melting pot**. [모의]

The Olympics gives a good chance of **sharing cultures**.

▶ 본문의 Each brings their own culture(각각은 그들 자신의 문화를 가져온다)와 big melting pot(많은 사람과 문화가 섞여 있는 용광로가 된다)의 표현을 종합한 상위 개념은 sharing cultures(문화를 공유하는 것)이다.

4 단서: We would suggest that you **don't burden your readers** with messages that are **too long** or **include unnecessary information**. [모의]

One of them is to keep your messages **brief**.

▶ 본문의 too long(너무 긴), unnecessary information(불필요한 정보)을 피하라고 했으므로 반의어 brief(간단한)로 말 바꿈하였다.

Check-Up 5

[1 - 2] 다음 두 문장을 읽고, 물음에 답하시오.

(A) Exercise is one of the easiest ways of improving both your physical and mental health.

(B) A little regular exercise can make you feel more energetic throughout the day, sleep better at night, have sharper memories, and feel more relaxed and positive about yourself and your life.

1 (A)와 (B)를 토대로 다음 문장을 완성하시오.

(B)는 (A)의 (① 예시 ② 반박)이다.

2 (A)와 (B)를 이어주는 연결어로 가장 적절한 것을 고르시오.

① For example ② However

빈칸 앞뒤 문장의 논리적 관계를 파악하라.

해결전략 1

연결어는 글의 흐름이 자연스럽도록 문장과 문장을 긴밀히 이어주는 역할을 한다. 예를 들어, 'I think. I am.'이라는 두 문장은 '원인과 결과'의 관계이므로 연결어 therefore를 넣어서 읽으면 '나는 생각한다. 그러므로 나는 존재한다.'라는 의미가 더욱 잘 드러난다. 이처럼 적절한 연결어를 찾으려면 먼저 빈칸 앞뒤 문장의 논리적 관계를 파악한 후 이에 알맞은 연결어를 넣어 자연스러운지 읽어본다.

p.66, 67 기출총정리 참조

048 다음 글의 빈칸 (A), (B)에 들어갈 말로 가장 적절한 것은?

Organisms of different species can interact in many ways. They can compete, or they can be long-term partners helping each other survive. They can also form one of the links in a food chain. ____(A)____, one of them can eat the other. In ecology, a food chain is a series of organisms that eat one another so that energy and nutrients flow from one to the next. ____(B)____, if you had a hamburger for lunch, you might be part of a food chain that flows like this: grass → cow → human. What if you had lettuce on your hamburger? In that case, you're also part of a food chain that goes like this: lettuce → human.

	(A)		(B)
①	However	……	In short
②	Fortunately	……	For example
③	However	……	Similarly
④	That is	……	On the other hand
⑤	That is	……	For example

기출총정리

빈출 연결어 완벽 정리

연결어 가운데 수능에 가장 자주 출제되는 것을 엄선했다. 다음에 제시된 연결어를 반드시 알아두자.

1 결과를 나타내는 연결어

▪ therefore (그러므로)
▪ thus (이렇게, 이와 같이)
▪ as a result (그 결과)
▪ consequently (그 결과, 따라서)
▪ hence (그런 고로)
▪ accordingly (그런 이유로, 그래서)

예시 1 Many voters think wealthy politicians will not understand the problems of the average worker. **Therefore**, the politicians try to show they are just "average people." [모의]
(많은 유권자들은 부유한 정치인은 평범한 노동자의 문제를 이해하지 못할 거라고 생각한다. **그러므로** 정치인들은 자신들이 그냥 '평범한 사람들'이라는 것을 보여주려고 노력한다.)

2 예시를 나타내는 연결어

▪ for example (예를 들어)
▪ for instance (예를 들어)

예시 2 Sometimes, people use expressions that sound like invitations but which are not real invitations. **For instance**, someone may say, "You should come over for a meal sometime." or "Let's get together for lunch soon." [모의]
(때때로 사람들은 초대처럼 들리지만 진정한 초대가 아닌 표현을 사용한다. **예를 들어**, 누군가가 "언제 식사 한번 하러 오세요." 혹은 "조만간 점심식사 같이 해요."라고 말할지도 모른다.)

3 역접, 대조를 나타내는 연결어

▪ however (하지만, 그러나)
▪ in[by] contrast (이와 대조적으로)
▪ on the other hand (반면에)
▪ on the contrary (반대로)
▪ otherwise (그렇지 않으면)
▪ conversely (정반대로, 역으로)
▪ nevertheless (그럼에도 불구하고)
▪ in spite of that (그럼에도 불구하고)
▪ yet (그렇지만, 그런데도)

예시 3 Many people think that nothing is better than a nap after a big meal. **However**, taking a nap isn't a good idea at all. [모의]
(많은 사람들이 배부른 식사 후의 낮잠보다 더 좋은 것은 없다고 생각한다. **그러나** 낮잠을 자는 것은 결코 좋은 생각이 아니다.)

4 첨가, 부연을 나타내는 연결어

▪ in addition (게다가, 더욱이)
▪ also (또한)
▪ besides (게다가, 그 외에)
▪ moreover (게다가, 더욱이)
▪ furthermore (게다가, 더욱이)

예시 4 If people slept eight hours, they would be more alert and productive at work. **In addition**, they would have fewer accidents, and make the world a safer place. [모의]
(사람들이 8시간을 잔다면, 그들은 일을 할 때 더 정신이 초롱초롱하고 생산적일 것이다. **게다가** 그들은 사고를 덜 당하여 세상을 보다 더 안전한 장소로 만들 것이다.)

5 강조를 나타내는 연결어

▪ indeed (정말로, 참으로)
▪ in fact (사실상)

cf. in fact는 대조나 반박을 나타내기도 한다.
I thought she was wrong. **In fact**, she was right.
(나는 그녀가 틀렸다고 생각했다. **사실은** 그녀가 옳았다.)

예시 5 Keeping a proper sense of distance between people is important. **Indeed**, we are likely to get more hurt from being too familiar than from complete ignorance of the other party. [모의응용]
(사람들 간에 적절한 거리감을 유지하는 것은 중요하다. **정말로** 우리는 상대방을 전혀 모르는 것으로부터보다 너무 친숙한 것으로부터 더 많이 상처받는 경향이 있다.)

6 유사성을 나타내는 연결어

▪ similarly (유사하게)
▪ likewise (마찬가지로)

서로 비교한 결과, 유사함을 나타낸다.

예시 6 A coin in a pool will seem to tremble because water bends the path of the light. **Similarly**, stars twinkle because their light has to pass through Earth's atmosphere. [모의응용]
(수영장 속의 동전은 물이 빛의 경로를 굴절시키기 때문에 떨고 있는 것처럼 보일 것이다. **이와 유사하게** 별들은 그들의 빛이 지구의 대기를 통과해 지나가야 하기 때문에 반짝인다.)

7 환언에 쓰이는 연결어

▪ in other words (다시[바꿔] 말해, 즉)
▪ that is (to say) (즉, 말하자면)

예시 7 Planning a trip to a foreign destination can at first seem difficult. However, arranging things in advance will enable you to avoid costly and dangerous mistakes. **In other words**, preparation determines success. [모의응용]
(해외 목적지로의 여행을 계획하는 것은 처음에는 어렵게 보일 수 있다. 그러나 일들을 미리 준비하는 것은 당신이 비용이 많이 들고 위험한 실수를 피할 수 있게 해줄 것이다. **다시 말해**, 준비가 성공을 결정한다.)

8 결론을 내리는 연결어

▪ in conclusion (끝으로, 결론적으로, 요는)
▪ in short (한마디로 말하면, 요컨대)
▪ in brief (요컨대, 간단히 말해서)

9 기타 연결어

▪ instead (그 대신에, 그보다도)
▪ above all (무엇보다도, 특히)
▪ meanwhile (한편)

Mini Test

정답 및 해설 p.51

● **빈칸에 알맞은 연결어를 고르시오.**

1 Failure may be due to lack of ability or to lack of motivation. Success, ____________, requires a high degree of motivation working with a high degree of ability. [모의]
① on the other hand
② in addition

2 Most of the time when someone drives somewhere in a vehicle, an accident like a car crash does not occur. But to be safe, drivers and passengers should always fasten their safety belts. ____________, you should always wear and use safety gear in the laboratory — whether you are conducting an experiment or just observing. [모의]
① Instead ② Likewise

3 Does parents' physical touch communicate their love to the teenager? The answer is yes and no. It all depends on when, where, and how. ________________, a hug may be embarrassing if it's done when a teenager is with his friends. It may cause the teenager to push the parent away or say, "Stop it." [모의]
① Therefore ② For instance

정답 및 해설 p.51

6문제를 8분 안에 풀어보세요.

049 다음 글의 빈칸에 들어갈 말로 가장 적절한 것은?

If you were to go into a café where the coffee is great, and the atmosphere and staff are friendly and inviting, would you go back? For most people, the answer would be yes. It is precisely for this reason that cafés have prospered almost everywhere. However, the best thing about café culture nowadays is that you do not have to be social in a café. Often, cafés provide shared public spaces where coffee lovers can enjoy their drink in peace, do some reading, or bring their laptop and do some work without caring what others think of them. There is, therefore, a paradox that while being alone, you are ____________ being social. After all, you are in a café surrounded with people, making the taboo of being alone socially acceptable.

① accidentally ② fortunately
③ simultaneously ④ intentionally
⑤ accordingly

050 다음 글의 빈칸에 들어갈 말로 가장 적절한 것은?

White elephants are extremely rare and have long been regarded as divine in South-East Asia. Although they are often depicted as pure white, their skin is usually a soft reddish-brown that turns light pink when wet. To keep a white elephant, one must spend a lot of money to feed it special food and to serve the many pilgrims who come to pray to it. Long ago, if a king was not pleased with a palace official, he gave the official a white elephant. Nobody could refuse a gift from the king. But an elephant was of no use for the official and the cost of caring for it caused financial ruin. This is the origin of the modern idiom, "white elephant," which means ____________.

① a useful and beautiful gift
② a symbol of one's wealth
③ a symbol of disliking someone
④ a very large object in a museum
⑤ a useless and expensive burden

051 다음 글의 빈칸에 들어갈 말로 가장 적절한 것은?

If worries about lack of time stem from the sense that time is highly valuable, then one of the best things we can do to reduce this sense of pressure may be to give our time away. Indeed, new research suggests that giving time away to help others can actually alleviate feelings of time pressure. Some companies provide their employees with opportunities to volunteer their time to help others, potentially reducing feelings of time stress and burnout. And Google has encouraged employees to use 20 percent of their time on their own personal projects. Although some of these projects have resulted in profit, the greatest benefit of giving this free time might lie in reducing employees' sense that ____________.

*alleviate 완화하다

① their time is scarce
② they are so stressed
③ they have to help others
④ they are wasting their time
⑤ they are not given free time

VOCAbulary 어휘확인

049 atmosphere 분위기 inviting 매력적인, 마음을 끄는 precisely 바로, 정확하게 prosper 번성하다 paradox 역설 simultaneously 동시에 surround 둘러싸다 taboo 금기 acceptable 받아들일 수 있는 050 extremely 극도로 rare 희귀한 regard A as B A를 B로 여기다 divine 신성한 depict 묘사하다 reddish 불그스름한 pilgrim 순례자 be of no use 쓸모없다 financial 재정의 ruin 파산 idiom 관용구, 숙어 burden 짐 051 lack 부족, 결핍 stem from ~에서 생겨나다 give away 기부하다[선물로 주다] volunteer 자진하여 하다, 지원하다 potentially 어쩌면, 가능성이 있게 burnout 극도의 피로(감) lie (생각, 특질, 문제 등이)있다, 발견되다; 눕다 scarce 부족한, 드문

052 다음 글의 빈칸 (A), (B)에 들어갈 말로 가장 적절한 것은?

The great thing about adjectives is that you don't need to memorize the antonyms. All you need is a negative particle (e.g. not) that you can apply to an adjective in conversation. ___(A)___, you can say "That man is not fat" instead of "That man is skinny," though the two do not sound exactly alike. You'll pick up the antonyms over time as you learn more and more words. ___(B)___, you don't need to memorize thousands of nouns. If you don't know the word for "washing machine" for example, you could say "the thing I wash my clothes in." "Thing" is a very handy word to know. Arm yourself with enough basic language and you'll no longer need to struggle to find the best word for what you want to say.

*antonyms 반의어

	(A)		(B)
①	However	……	Likewise
②	For example	……	Likewise
③	That is	……	However
④	In other words	……	On the other hand
⑤	Indeed	……	On the other hand

053 다음 글의 빈칸 (A), (B)에 들어갈 말로 가장 적절한 것은?

The Sherpa people, of whom there are approximately 150,000, mainly live in the mountainous regions of eastern Nepal. Natural born mountaineers, they live at higher altitudes than any other humans. Prior to contact with Europeans, they were yak herders and traders in the Himalayas. ___(A)___, the arrival of western explorers changed the Sherpa lifestyle forever. On early British expeditions, the Sherpas earned high praise for their mountain skills. They were dedicated, honest, sincere, and strong. ___(B)___, they became an essential part of all Himalayan expeditions. Their work as guides and partners on mountain expeditions improved their standard of living and became the basis of their economy. Himalayan expeditions are now the most important part of Sherpa culture.

*yak herders 야크(티베트산 들소)를 모는 목동

	(A)		(B)
①	In fact	……	Instead
②	That is	……	However
③	However	……	As a result
④	Otherwise	……	For example
⑤	For example	……	Therefore

054 다음 글의 빈칸 (A), (B)에 들어갈 말로 가장 적절한 것은?

What we see in the world is not an objective view of reality but a view of reality based on our predispositions. Some have argued that the key to successful communication in a relationship is taking advantage of this process by finding someone who looks at things the same way you do. ___(A)___, find someone who sees the world the same way you do, and you will find someone who will see a relationship the same way you do. Despite the logic behind the theory, in reality, relationship success does not depend on seeing things the same way. ___(B)___, respect of the other person's view is far more important than constant agreement with it.

*predisposition 성향, 경향

	(A)		(B)
①	As a result	……	On the other hand
②	In addition	……	Likewise
③	However	……	For example
④	In other words	……	Instead
⑤	Therefore	……	Moreover

VOCAbulary 어휘확인

052 adjective 형용사 pick up (정보를) 알게 되다 noun 명사 handy 유용한, 편리한 arm 무장하다 basic 기본의 struggle 애쓰다, 노력하다
053 approximately 대략, 거의 mountainous 산악의 natural born 타고난 mountaineer 등산가 altitude (해발) 고도 prior to A A에 앞서 trader 상인 expedition 원정 dedicated 헌신적인 sincere 진심 어린 essential 필수적인 standard of living 생활수준 basis 기초 054 objective 객관적인 take advantage of ~을 이용하다 despite ~에도 불구하고 logic 논리 theory 이론 constant 끊임없는

유형 06 함의 추론

이렇게 출제된다.

밑줄 친 어구의 함축적 의미를 추론하는 유형이다.
한동안 출제되지 않다가 최근 다시 1문항씩 출제되고 있다.

지시문은 이렇게

밑줄 친 "There is no there there"이
다음 글에서 의미하는 바로 가장 적절한 것은?
밑줄 친 information blinded가
다음 글에서 의미하는 바로 가장 적절한 것은?

정답 및 해설 p.56

Check-Up 1

055 지문을 읽고, 밑줄 친 어구 중에서 a Snooky가 함축적으로 의미하는 바를 고르시오.

① 결정을 내리는 사람의 감정 상태
② 사람들에게 조언하는 역할

해결 전략 1 밑줄 친 어구의 함축 의미를 추론할 단서를 찾아라.
밑줄 친 어구는 표면적으로 봐서는 알기 힘든 어구나 비유적인 표현이 주로 등장한다. 따라서 문맥적 의미를 유추할 수 있는 단서를 글 안에서 찾아야 한다.

해결 TIP "글의 전체적인 주제나 요지를 파악하라."
밑줄 친 어구는 글의 요지와 관련된 내용이 함축된 경우가 많으므로, 글에 제시된 주제문이나 뒷받침 문장 등의 내용이 밑줄 친 어구와 어떻게 연관되어 있는지를 파악한다.

055 밑줄 친 pull a Snooky first가 다음 글에서 의미하는 바로 가장 적절한 것은?

People's emotional states can completely alter their thinking, decisions, and interactions. Your friend Snooky may be convinced by an argument you are making if she happens to be anxious that day, but unaffected if she happens to be relaxed. Under different emotional states, people are prepared to attend to particular cues. This principle is important to keep in mind. It explains, for example, why fear campaigns can be useless in a certain time and place, yet effective in another. Thus if you attempt to give advice effectively to others — to a player who keeps winning, a patient who has just received an awful diagnosis, or a client in the midst of fighting with friends — you need to pull a Snooky first.

① reveal yourself to them immediately
② figure out what their feelings are now
③ obtain their personal information quickly
④ consider what Snooky has done for them
⑤ think about them not emotionally but reasonably

실전적용독해

3문제를 4분 안에 풀어보세요.

정답 및 해설 p.57

056 밑줄 친 to bear fruit가 다음 글에서 의미하는 바로 가장 적절한 것은??

A rewarding part of dog ownership is successfully training your dog. Training is an excellent way to bond with your dog and will help you build a good relationship with it. Teaching your dog to sit is a great step to start with your training. If you're to have your dog sit as you wish, you need to hold a tasty treat, with him in a standing position. Keeping the treat near your dog's nose, move your hand in an arc over his head. As the dog raises his head to follow the treat, his bottom will go on the floor. The instant he sits, praise him and give him the treat. Practice this a number of times in short but regular sessions. You can now add the cue word 'sit' as he goes to sit. Training your dog this way for a few days should allow your efforts to bear fruit.

① take a pleasant walk with your dog
② become best friends with your dog
③ make your dog sit whenever you want
④ train your dog effectively outdoors
⑤ order your dog not to move his position

057 밑줄 친 something beyond price가 다음 글에서 의미하는 바로 가장 적절한 것은?

A wise woman who was hiking in the mountains found a precious stone in a stream. The next day she met another hiker who was hungry, and the wise woman opened her bag to share her food. Seeing the precious stone, the hungry hiker asked the woman if he could have it. She gave it to him without hesitation. The man left, pleased with his good fortune. He knew the stone was worth enough to give him comfort and security for a lifetime. But a few days later he came back to return the stone to the wise woman. He said: "I know how valuable the stone is, but I give it back in the hope that you can give me something beyond price. Give me what you have within you that instantly enabled you to give me the stone in the first place."

① the same luck that she has
② a more precious stone hidden in her bag
③ all the money and jewelry she has collected so far
④ the warm heart willing to give up her priceless thing
⑤ the courage that makes her hike alone in the mountain

058 밑줄 친 falling into that same trap이 다음 글에서 의미하는 바로 가장 적절한 것은?

There are some people who say, "I'm my own person. It doesn't matter what others think." Yet they feel disappointed when others don't treat them politely, fail to respect their time, or ignore their information. These same people complain when they don't get the job they want or the salary they expect. They don't understand why the best employees hate to work for them. Other people's motivations remain a mystery to them. Gaining support and acceptance from others always seems like a hit-or-miss situation when they're leading the effort. Before falling into that same trap, consider this: other people's perceptions create their reality. Your own facts, intentions, and motives do not. People can't see how you think and what you intend. Always be aware of how your actions look to other people.

*hit-or-miss 운에 맡기는, 되는대로 하는

① getting angry at your poor results
② thinking about not others but yourself
③ looking at the bright side of your reality
④ spending too much time on team projects
⑤ giving up recognizing others' accomplishments

VOCAbulary 어휘확인

056 rewarding 보람 있는 ownership 소유 bond 유대감을 형성하다; 유대 treat 간식; 만족[기쁨]을 주는 것 arc 둥근[활] 모양 bottom 엉덩이; 맨 아랫부분 the instant ~하자마자 praise 칭찬하다 session 기간, 시간; 활동
057 stream 개울, 시내 hesitation 주저, 망설임 comfort 편안함 security (미래를 위한) 보장, 안정; 보안 instantly 즉시 enable ~을 할 수 있게 하다 058 politely 정중하게, 예의 바르게 motivation 동기(=motive) acceptance 승인, 동의 trap 함정, 덫 perception 인식; 지각, 자각 be aware of ~을 인지하다[알다]

유형 07 요약문 완성

이렇게 출제된다.
글의 내용을 한 문장으로 요약한 것이 주어지고 그 문장의 빈칸을 완성하는 유형이다. 1문항씩 출제되며 논설문, 설명문뿐만 아니라 실험문이나 교훈을 담은 일화도 출제된다.

지시문은 이렇게
다음 글의 내용을 한 문장으로 요약하고자 한다. 빈칸 (A)와 (B)에 들어갈 말로 가장 적절한 것은?

정답 및 해설 p.59

Check-Up 1

059 지문의 요약문과 선택지를 먼저 읽고, 글의 내용으로 짐작할 수 있으면 ○ 그렇지 않으면 ×를 고르시오.

의사 결정에 있어서 선택의 의미에 대한 내용일 것이다. (○ / ×)

해결 전략 1 요약문과 선택지를 먼저 읽고 글의 내용을 짐작한다.
요약문은 글 전체를 한 문장으로 압축한 것으로 글의 핵심 내용을 담고 있다. 따라서 본문을 읽기 전에 요약문과 선택지를 먼저 읽으면 그 내용을 일부 짐작할 수 있는 것이 있어 훨씬 유리하다.

059 다음 글의 내용을 한 문장으로 요약하고자 한다. 빈칸 (A)와 (B)에 들어갈 말로 가장 적절한 것은?

Good decision-making is a skill that comes easily to some people, not so easily to others. Choices are confusing. Choices can make you anxious. They can cost you peace of mind, even after you've made the decision. In order to be a good decision-maker, you should first learn to accept that you can't have it all. Decisions force us to close the door on other possibilities, small ones and big ones. You can't order every delicious dish on the menu. And there will be paths not taken, careers not chosen, experiences not encountered. Also, more thinking is not always better thinking. It's often good to think through your decisions. But don't overdo it. Many good decisions can be made based as much on intuition as on precise assessment of endless data.

↓

Making a choice means willingly ____(A)____ other options, and more time spent on it does not always ____(B)____ a good one.

	(A)		(B)
①	taking	……	change
②	taking	……	lead to
③	taking	……	follow
④	losing	……	lead to
⑤	losing	……	change

Check-Up 2

다음 글에서 반복되는 표현을 찾아 밑줄 긋고, 아래 요약문에 들어갈 말로 그와 유사한 표현을 고르시오.

The smell of vanilla helps people relax. Cinnamon and apple smells remind many people of their homes.

⬇

________ can change the way you feel.

① Scents ② Tastes

글의 핵심어나 그와 관련된 표현이 요약문의 빈칸에 들어간다.

해결 전략 2

핵심어는 글 전체에서 가장 중요한 말로서 대개 반복되거나 글의 주제와 연관되므로 요약문에도 포함되는 경우가 많다. 그러므로 핵심어에 해당하거나 그와 관련된 동의어, 반의어 표현이 선택지에 있다면 우선적으로 요약문의 빈칸에 넣어 보고 글의 내용을 제대로 반영하고 있는지 판단한다.

060 다음 글의 내용을 한 문장으로 요약하고자 한다. 빈칸 (A)와 (B)에 들어갈 말로 가장 적절한 것은?

As a driver, you will encounter both green and red lights. Most of us don't give this a second thought, because the greens and reds average out over time and we're all in the same boat. In other words, most of us don't take it personally. But there are unfortunate souls who have fallen into the trap of perceiving every red light as a personal insult or sign of their lack of control. They respond by driving recklessly, stepping on the accelerator pedal to speed through the intersection before the yellow light turns red. This is a silly way to drive and no way to navigate your life. Red lights are not barriers to your progress; they are your cue to relax, breathe, step back from responsibility, and think.

⬇

Many of the things troubled individuals view as ____(A)____, such as red lights, are in fact opportunities giving them a chance to ____(B)____ themselves.

	(A)		(B)
①	conveniences	……	evaluate
②	conveniences	……	save
③	obstacles	……	protect
④	obstacles	……	express
⑤	obstacles	……	refresh

Check-Up 3

다음 글에서 밑줄 친 표현을 압축적으로 나타낸 단어를 골라 주어진 요약문을 완성하시오.

Humans and dolphins both spend the majority of their time around others of their own species.

Like humans, dolphins are ________ animals.

① intelligent ② social

지문의 내용을 압축적으로 나타낸 표현을 찾아라.

해결 전략 3

요약문의 빈칸에는 핵심어 외에도 지문에 등장한 어구나 내용을 압축적으로 나타낸 표현이 들어간다. 요약문의 빈칸에 들어갈 내용을 지문에서 찾고 이를 가장 잘 압축한 표현이 선택지에 있다면 빈칸에 넣어 읽어보고 자연스러운지 확인한다.

061 **다음 글의 내용을 한 문장으로 요약하고자 한다. 빈칸 (A)와 (B)에 들어갈 말로 가장 적절한 것은?**

The words "travel" and "vacation" are often used interchangeably, but careful examination indicates some differences between the two. Vacation implies an escape from your everyday life — from your work and duties — while travel may offer the opportunity to become totally lost in a different culture. Two types of journeys occur during travel. The outer journey describes the physical experience of travel: where you went, what you saw, and what you did. The inner journey is characterized by your interpretation of the experience. It describes what you learned, and how it changed your perspective on life.

Unlike the mere escape from ___(A)___ of vacation, travel involves both a real physical journey and an important ___(B)___ one.

	(A)		(B)
①	place	……	psychological
②	place	……	mental
③	routine	……	social
④	routine	……	geographical
⑤	routine	……	personal

실전적용독해

정답 및 해설 p.62

2문제를 2분 40초 안에 풀어보세요.

062 다음 글의 내용을 한 문장으로 요약하고자 한다. 빈칸 (A)와 (B)에 들어갈 말로 가장 적절한 것은?

What you do before sleep influences the quality of your sleep. Researchers have identified a variety of practices and habits that can help us maximize the hours we spend sleeping. Invest a little time before you get into your bed. Then you will wake up refreshed the next day. Ease the change from wake time to sleep time with a period of relaxing activities an hour or so before bed. Take a bath (the rise, then fall in body temperature promotes drowsiness), read a book, watch television, or practice relaxation exercises. Avoid stressful, stimulating activities — doing work, discussing emotional issues. They can cause the body to release a stress hormone which is associated with increasing alertness.

↓

> The activities you choose before bedtime ___(A)___ the quality of your sleep, so choose ___(B)___ ones to wake up feeling refreshed.

	(A)		(B)
①	describe	······	favorite
②	describe	······	learning
③	affect	······	additional
④	affect	······	light
⑤	affect	······	flexible

063 다음 글의 내용을 한 문장으로 요약하고자 한다. 빈칸 (A)와 (B)에 들어갈 말로 가장 적절한 것은?

Do you have "No" power or do you have no power? Becoming successful requires learning how to respectfully refuse people's unreasonable requests. If being agreeable has become a habit, you can begin reversing it by taking this step to "No" power. From now on, when people ask you to do something, take time to make your decision. If the other person tries to pressure you, simply say, "Fine, if you have to have an answer right now, it's no." Then get away from this person so you can think this through in private. Delaying your answer and removing yourself from their sphere of influence prevents bullies from mentally crowding you. You are giving yourself some space so you can think about the issue and determine whether saying yes is in your best interests.

↓

> By not giving others a ___(A)___ answer, you can avoid being ___(B)___ by them.

	(A)		(B)
①	negative	······	distracted
②	negative	······	refused
③	prompt	······	detected
④	prompt	······	manipulated
⑤	prompt	······	hindered

VOCAbulary 어휘확인

062 quality 질(質) identify 발견하다, 찾다 invest 투자하다 ease 덜어 주다 promote 촉진하다 drowsiness 졸음 relaxation 휴식 stimulating 자극적인 release 방출하다 hormone 호르몬 be associated with ~와 연관[관련]되다 alertness 각성도, 빈틈없음 063 respectfully 정중하게 unreasonable 불합리한 agreeable 동의하는 reverse 반전시키다 take (a) step 조치를 취하다 get away from ~에서 멀리 떨어지다 sphere 영역 bully (약자를) 괴롭히는 사람 crowd (생각이 마음속에) 밀려오다 prompt 즉각적인 manipulate 조종하다

미니 모의고사 2 유형 05 | 유형 06 | 유형 07

18문제를 25분 안에 풀어보세요.

정답 및 해설 p.64

064 다음 글의 빈칸 (A), (B)에 들어갈 말로 가장 적절한 것은?

Zoos have a long and varied history dating back over 5,000 years to the exotic animal collections of Egyptian pharaohs. Despite their popularity, in recent decades, conflict has emerged over the traditional zoo. Some people believe zoos encourage the general public to appreciate and respect the animal world. ____(A)____, they say zoos can protect animals against diseases and natural enemies, and be a shelter for threatened animals. ____(B)____, others claim that it is cruel to keep animals in zoos. These people argue that the small, unnatural houses cause unnecessary stress and suffering. They say zoos must create environments which look like the natural homes of the animals.

	(A)		(B)
①	Moreover	……	For example
②	However	……	Moreover
③	Therefore	……	For example
④	For instance	……	In contrast
⑤	Moreover	……	In contrast

065 다음 글의 빈칸에 들어갈 말로 가장 적절한 것은?

Large or useful data files need not be genuinely complex. In science, we seek explanations that are "natural" in this way because they tend to be more reliable and to connect to other useful ideas. We abhor long lists of exceptions and special cases. Consider, for example, the goal of theoretical physics. In theoretical physics, we try to summarize the results of a great number of observations and experiments in terms of a few powerful laws. We try, in other words, to produce the shortest possible program that outputs the world. In that precise sense, it's a quest for ____________.

*abhor 혐오하다

① truth
② laws
③ precision
④ complexity
⑤ simplicity

066 다음 글의 빈칸에 들어갈 말로 가장 적절한 것은?

Science-fiction TV series and movies like *Star Wars* may be entertaining, but they ____________________. Spaceships on these shows all travel faster than the speed of light, but it's physically impossible to do that. Similarly, the acceleration of such spaceships would be so extreme as to break apart nearly any vessel, making the impossible journeys unsurvivable even in theory. Also, the way in which the stars pass by the windows of the spaceships is unnatural. If the spaceships were really traveling at the speed of light, the stars would appear as a bright light show, spreading out in a rainbow of colors. But, in those movies, they appear small and still, just like they do to us down here on earth.

① are also realistic
② violate key laws of physics
③ are old-fashioned and boring
④ can be dangerous to children
⑤ are difficult for us to understand

067 다음 글의 내용을 한 문장으로 요약하고자 한다. 빈칸 (A)와 (B)에 들어갈 말로 가장 적절한 것은?

A research finding related to timed math testing was posted on a blog: "Timed math tests can discourage students, leading to math anxiety and a long-term fear of the subject." The brief statement started a debate on the merits of timed testing. The debate divided the audience in half. One side argued that timed testing was valuable because there are real deadlines in life and careers — and real consequences to missing them. Others felt that timed testing causes a kind of fear in children, damaging students' ability to think and hurting deeper learning. Despite the disagreement, many teachers felt that timed tests are an important step on the road to mathematical fluency, as they improve speed and lay a foundation for complex problem solving. To many teachers, not preparing students for real-life situations with timed testing felt like "setting the kids up for failure."

⬇

> Despite all the ____(A)____ about math anxiety, the majority of teachers agree on the ____(B)____ of timed math testing.

	(A)		(B)
①	criticisms	……	defects
②	merits	……	benefits
③	merits	……	uselessness
④	concerns	……	necessity
⑤	concerns	……	weaknesses

068 다음 글의 빈칸 (A), (B)에 들어갈 말로 가장 적절한 것은?

It's hard to imagine a life free from the worries of money and debt. Spending money without increasing debt is like a zero-sum game. So, if you want to spend more on education, you have to spend less on entertainment. ____(A)____, if you want a career, you have to sacrifice family time. If you want more family life, you have to make sacrifices at work. ____(B)____, time is not like money, which disappears as you spend it. The way you spend your time is a measure of efficiency, not quantity. When you use your time better, you can do more and balance both the work and family sides of your life.

*zero-sum game 제로섬 게임(승자의 득점과 패자의 실점을 합치면 0이 되는 게임)

	(A)		(B)
①	In fact	……	Similarly
②	Instead	……	Furthermore
③	Likewise	……	However
④	Likewise	……	In other words
⑤	Instead	……	Otherwise

069 밑줄 친 Adopt the technique이 다음 글에서 의미하는 바로 가장 적절한 것은?

Visualization is a skill that most people use to accomplish their goals, and they usually turn to the sense of sight to create images in their minds. However, there are four other senses that are powerful visualizing tools. To visualize yourself more powerfully, supplement your images with the senses of hearing, smell, touch, and taste. You can dramatically increase the impact of visualization by using the maximum number of senses. If you're working to improve your golf game, you can visualize yourself better with various senses such as hearing your driver hit the ball straight or touching the dew-covered grass. It will help achieve your goal more effectively. The importance of visualization cannot be downplayed. Adopt the technique and you will become equipped with powerful forces in your life.

① Doubt the power of visualization
② Use as many senses as possible
③ Work hard to accomplish your goal
④ Visualize yourself with your friends
⑤ Focus on what you have in mind now

070 다음 글의 빈칸에 들어갈 말로 가장 적절한 것은?

How and when do secrets, and the revelation of secrets, give rise to shame and embarrassment? Sometimes the causes of shame are open secrets. Open secrets are things that everyone knows but still pretends to be secret. And so one has to live with the publicity of this open secret. Shame is the feeling that often accompanies the public revelation of a secret that is considered morally wrong in some way. But one only feels shame about actions that __________________. Someone may exclaim: "Shame on you for using that language!" But if we do not feel that our language was inappropriate or blameworthy, then we need not feel shame. In other words, one feels shame when judged by other people for a fault that one agrees is a fault.

① are against social rules
② one accepts as faults
③ are blamed by others
④ one cannot hide well
⑤ are threats to one's safety

071 다음 글의 내용을 한 문장으로 요약하고자 한다. 빈칸 (A)와 (B)에 들어갈 말로 가장 적절한 것은?

"A rolling stone gathers no moss" is a well-known saying in both America and Japan. For Americans, a rolling stone means someone who is free-spirited and always moving. That kind of person is usually considered cool because they aren't tied down by the constraints that hold most of us back. Moss represents the bad things about staying in one place and getting old. The Japanese, on the other hand, see a rolling stone as a person who fails to keep a steady job, someone who avoids responsibilities and has no cares. As for moss, it represents the kind of wisdom or wealth that grows only in peace and stillness and would never be found on a rolling stone.

↓

America and Japan share the same proverb, but it has different ____(A)____ because of each culture's ____(B)____ rolling stones and moss.

	(A)		(B)
①	uses	……	experience with
②	forms	……	thoughts about
③	origins	……	focus on
④	meanings	……	viewpoint on
⑤	purposes	……	attitude about

072 다음 글의 내용을 한 문장으로 요약하고자 한다. 빈칸 (A)와 (B)에 들어갈 말로 가장 적절한 것은?

An egg cream is a refreshing cold drink that originated in New York City soda shops about a hundred years ago. It's made of milk, flavored syrup, and soda water. It contains neither eggs nor cream, but it's called an egg cream nevertheless. That's just the way it is. Likewise, people are not always predictable, instruction manuals are sometimes unclear, and fast food may or may not be served fast. It's important to recognize and accept that things won't always make sense. That's really okay because both the logical and the nonsensical are threads in the same rich tapestry that we call life.

↓

We need to ____(A)____ the fact that the world does not always operate ____(B)____.

*tapestry 태피스트리(여러 가지 색실로 그림을 짜 넣은 직물)

	(A)		(B)
①	accept	……	rationally
②	reject	……	legally
③	accept	……	sensitively
④	dispute	……	legally
⑤	reject	……	rationally

073 다음 글의 빈칸에 들어갈 말로 가장 적절한 것은?

It is vital that young people ________________ ______________. More specifically, they must have the right to decide if, when, how much, and by whom they want to be taught. Furthermore, they must be allowed to decide whether they want to go to university or not, and for how long. For those who do attend university, it's best that they are allowed to determine their own course of study. This is a freedom that is protected in all advanced societies. Freedom to choose one's own education is an important part of freedom of thought. Therefore, it is a right that we must protect in order to guarantee the future success of our society.

① obtain a high level of education
② think whatever they want to think
③ learn to be strong through hardship
④ control and direct their own learning
⑤ lead an independent life from their parents

074 다음 글의 빈칸 (A), (B)에 들어갈 말로 가장 적절한 것은?

No one is surprised that the sunny warmth of summer makes people happy, but the influence of weather doesn't stop there. Rainy weather makes us introspective and thoughtful, which in turn ____(A)____ our memory. In one study, people more accurately remembered the features of a store on rainy days. More surprising still is the relationship between changes in weather and depression, and various kinds of accidents. The association between warmth and human kindness is more than a metaphor; recent studies have shown that people find strangers more ____(B)____ when holding a cup of hot coffee. The warmth-kindness metaphor extends to social exclusion: people literally feel colder when they've been socially isolated.

	(A)		(B)
①	worsens	……	familiar
②	worsens	……	likeable
③	resets	……	familiar
④	enhances	……	likeable
⑤	enhances	……	threatening

075 다음 글의 빈칸 (A), (B)에 들어갈 말로 가장 적절한 것은?

One of the reasons the violin is difficult to learn to play is that its fingerboard contains no visual aids to help the beginner acquire competence in fingering. Unlike the guitar, ____(A)____, the violin has no frets, that is, no small metal bars or bumps to guide the fingers. Therefore, the beginner must learn exact positions and literally feel his or her way, unaided, from position to position up the fingerboard of the instrument. Until the learner develops skill, many notes are painfully out of tune. Even when skill increases, the player may still sound poor unless he or she has a good ear. ____(B)____, not only does the beginner suffer, he or she can also torture those listening, as many a patient parent or sacrificial sibling can tell you.

*fret 프렛(현악기의 지판을 구분하는 작은 돌기)

	(A)		(B)
①	instead	……	Thus
②	as a result	……	Moreover
③	as a result	……	Likewise
④	for instance	……	Likewise
⑤	for instance	……	Thus

076 다음 글의 빈칸에 들어갈 말로 가장 적절한 것은?

It has long been known that dolphins are among the smartest creatures on Earth, possessing sophisticated communication skills and the capacity for true learning. But their uniqueness among species doesn't end there. Dolphins are social creatures and can establish strong social bonds. They will stay with injured or ill individuals, even helping them to breathe by bringing them to the surface if needed. This tendency does not appear ________________. The dolphin Moko in New Zealand has been observed guiding a female whale together with her calf out of shallow water where they had been stranded several times. They have also been seen protecting swimmers from sharks by moving in circles around the swimmers or swimming toward sharks to make them go away.

① to be an inborn characteristic
② to be limited to their own species
③ in emergency circumstances
④ in moving individually
⑤ to last throughout their whole lives

077 다음 글의 내용을 한 문장으로 요약하고자 한다. 빈칸 (A)와 (B)에 들어갈 말로 가장 적절한 것은?

Father Jim Scott, who has been an academic administrator for most of his career, believes it is his habit of directing his focus outward instead of inward that has consistently landed him in leadership roles. He tells a story about a young man who came to ask for advice before embarking on his career. Father Jim responded, "My advice to you is very simple. No matter whom you meet, no matter where you meet them, always presume that they're much better than you are. When I look around, the most devastating Achilles' heel that I see people suffering from is that they take themselves too seriously. While it's very important to take others seriously, don't take yourself that seriously." It is this constant attention to the "realness" of others that makes for an ideal leader.

⬇

The keys to leadership are genuine ____(A)____ and real interest in and ____(B)____ others.

	(A)		(B)
①	confidence	……	curiosity about
②	confidence	……	guidance for
③	modesty	……	protection of
④	modesty	……	respect for
⑤	modesty	……	openness toward

078 밑줄 친 turn into a sharp hawk가 다음 글에서 의미하는 바로 가장 적절한 것은?

In a sports game, coaches should be cautious that youth participation does not become work for children. The outcome of the game should not be more important than the process of learning sport and other lessons. In today's youth sport setting, however, young athletes may be worrying more about who will win instead of enjoying themselves and the sport. Following a game, many coaches tend to turn into a sharp hawk. So children who made mistakes or thought they didn't perform well are reluctant to talk with them, since the young players know they're supposed to be criticized for what they did. But criticism can create high levels of stress, leading to burnout. Positive reinforcement should be provided, regardless of the outcome. It has a greater effect on children's learning in sports than criticism.

① analyze the game through technology
② focus on searching for the best player
③ have children practice harder than before
④ be eager to find fault with young players
⑤ be forced to develop new skills for children

079 다음 글의 빈칸에 들어갈 말로 가장 적절한 것은?

As parents, we all get a lot of well-meaning advice on how to raise our children. Usually it centers on the techniques of child control that have been used by others with success. But ____________________________. One parent may offer the time-honored advice to spank your child on his behind. That will make him listen! Maybe. Then again, you may have the type of child who does not respond to physical punishment. There are such children. If that is the case, you may as well go out and spank your car tire. Understanding what makes your child different from other children should be the first step toward understanding his developmental needs, on which you can start to build a sound relationship with your child.

① it's important to apply them step by step
② using a little violence sometimes works
③ someone else's child is not your child
④ it usually hurts more than cures the relationship
⑤ techniques not based on a sound theory promise failure

080 밑줄 친 your simple act가 다음 글에서 의미하는 바로 가장 적절한 것은?

Do you think observing people in an experiment can interfere with the behavior that is being studied? Suppose employees are asked to take a personality test as part of research on job satisfaction. The employees knowing that their answers will be checked by their boss may deliberately distort their test responses because they do not want to reveal personal tendencies. For another example, consider research to investigate the effects of jet engine noise on the efficiency of airline mechanics. If the mechanics are aware that they are part of a psychological research study, they may deliberately work faster or slower than they would on a normal workday when they were not being observed. It is inferred, therefore, that your simple act can vary how people behave.

① keeping an eye on people
② making an effort to change
③ distorting opinions deliberately
④ sticking to the original attitude
⑤ getting rid of personal tendencies

081 다음 글의 내용을 한 문장으로 요약하고자 한다. 빈칸 (A)와 (B)에 들어갈 말로 가장 적절한 것은?

In order to lead, one must first learn to follow. The first step to become a leader is to become a sincere follower first. The crown of a leader attracts many individuals as it seems to represent power and control over others. These are only the cheap thoughts of a person who seeks to establish control over others, however. Remember, these are the people who are weak. True leaders know the value of responsibilities and duties. A true leader never controls, but instead supports; never overpowers, but instead gives power; never demands obedience except from himself. Strong men find a way to control their minds, because the most difficult and rewarding battle is the battle with yourself; and leaders are already winners in their own noticeable way.

⬇

True leadership comes from the power of controlling ____(A)____, and from the ____(B)____ that the leader is the one who has to follow.

	(A)		(B)
①	others	……	superstition
②	others	……	belief
③	others	……	recognition
④	oneself	……	suspicion
⑤	oneself	……	awareness

Chapter 3

유형 08 무관한 문장 찾기

이렇게 출제된다.
주어진 글에서 글의 흐름과 무관한 문장 하나를 골라내는 유형이다. 글의 주제에서 벗어난 문장을 찾아야 한다. 1~2문항씩 출제된다.

지시문은 이렇게
다음 글에서 전체 흐름과 관계 없는 문장은?

정답 및 해설 p.78

Check-Up 1

082 지문의 첫 두 문장을 읽고, 글의 주제를 추론하시오.

① 콘서트에 참석한 후 보고서를 쓰는 방법
② 콘서트에 가기 전 확인해야 하는 예절

해결 전략 1 글의 첫 부분을 읽고 이어질 내용을 예상하라.
무관한 문장을 고르는 문제로 출제되는 글의 첫 한두 문장, 즉 선택지 번호가 달려 있지 않은 부분은 대개 주제문이거나 주제를 소개하는 도입 내용이다. 따라서 그 부분을 읽고 주제를 추론한 뒤, 그것을 뒷받침하지 않는 문장을 고르면 된다.

082 **다음 글에서 전체 흐름과 관계 없는 문장은?**

An important element of a music course is, often, attending a musical performance — such as a concert or an opera — and then writing a report. Before you go to a concert, you need to review concert etiquette. ① If possible, arrive at the concert hall at least fifteen minutes before the performance, so that you can relax and read the program notes. ② Bear in mind, too, that at many concert halls, latecomers aren't allowed to take their seats until some break in the music occurs. ③ When you're late, however, you can still ask for a refund as long as you arrive before the concert is completely finished. ④ During the performance, absolute silence helps the performers to concentrate and increases the emotional intensity of the musical experience. ⑤ Performers can be distracted by talking, coughing, humming, or occasional noises — which will also distract and annoy other audience members.

Check-Up 2

다음 문장은 어떤 글의 주제문이다. (A), (B)가 이 주제문을 뒷받침하면 ○, 아니면 ×를 고르시오.

Too much exposure to the sun is unhealthy.

(A) Repeated and long-term exposure to too much sun over a number of years can cause damage to skin. (○ / ×)

(B) The effects of sun exposure have been greatly exaggerated by doctors and the media. (○ / ×)

해결 전략 2 주제와 관련되지만 초점이 다른 문장에 현혹되지 마라.

전체 흐름과 무관한 문장이라 하더라도 글의 주제와 부분적으로는 관련이 있는 것이 출제된다. 예를 들어 '햇볕과다 노출에 의한 건강상의 위험'이 주제라고 할 때, '햇볕 노출 영향의 지나친 과장'은 '햇볕 노출'이라는 핵심어가 포함되어 혼동을 유발하지만 주제와 무관하다. 실제 기출 문제들의 오답을 분석해 보면 핵심어를 포함하고 있는 것이 대부분이므로 주의해야 한다.

p.86 기출총정리 참조

해결 TIP "글에는 통일성이 있어야 한다."

단락 내의 모든 문장은 단 한 가지의 주제를 적절하게 뒷받침해야 한다. 이를 일컬어 '글에 통일성이 있다'라고 한다. 만약 주제와 무관한 문장이 들어 있다면 그 단락은 통일성이 없는 것이다.

083 다음 글에서 전체 흐름과 관계 없는 문장은?

News that many of us are consuming twice the recommended amount of salt is serious cause for concern. ① An expert says the biggest problem is that people are failing to realize just how much salt they are adding to their food, either while cooking or at the table. ② People are also consuming hidden salt in some of our most common foods, including breads, processed meats, soups, sauces, and salty snacks. ③ They tend to consume about the same amount of salt no matter where they live, and this amount hasn't changed much in decades. ④ The easiest and most effective way to reduce salt intake is to boost the amount of fresh foods we consume and cut back on processed food. ⑤ Recent changes to food labelling have been helpful, but easily accessible information on recommended daily salt intake is still badly needed.

기출총정리

무관한 문장은 글의 통일성을 저해한다.

글의 통일성을 해치는 무관한 문장은 주제와 관련된 것처럼 보이지만 실제로는 주제와 전혀 다른 내용을 담고 있다. 실제로 기출에 어떤 예들이 나왔는지 알아보자.

1

주제문: Consider how often you shift position in your chair when you are studying or sitting in a lecture.
흐름과 유관한 문장: Our ability to recognize and respond to discomfort is critical for preventing physical damage to the body.
흐름과 무관한 문장: Movement or noise in the classroom may distract the students from their work. [모의]

☞ 흐름과 무관한 문장은 교실(classroom)에서의 움직임과 소음이 공부에 미치는 나쁜 영향에 대한 내용으로, 주제문의 chair, studying, lecture와 관련돼 보이지만 무관하다.

2

주제문: Clark's nutcrackers in North America survive by their remarkable memory.
흐름과 유관한 문장: It hides at least 30,000 nuts in up to 5,000 small places each year, yet it is able to remember the location of about 75 percent of its hiding places.
흐름과 무관한 문장: The bird uses its powerful bill to twist open cones of pine trees and remove the nuts. [모의응용]

☞ 글의 주제가 견과를 숨겨 놓은 수많은 장소를 거의 다 기억하는 산갈가마귀의 놀라운 기억력에 대한 내용임을 알 수 있다. 무관한 문장 안에 '견과(nuts)'가 있어 관련되어 보이지만, 견과를 먹을 때 부리를 이용한다는 내용이므로 글의 흐름과 무관하다.

3

주제문: When you are in danger and feel afraid, your body automatically produces a chemical, called adrenalin, in your blood.
흐름과 유관한 문장: However, when you are absolutely terrified, your body can produce too much adrenalin, which causes your muscles to become so hard that you cannot move at all.
흐름과 무관한 문장: That's why you do exercise to build up your muscles. [모의응용]

☞ 이 글은 우리가 위험한 상황에 처했을 때 우리 몸은 아드레날린을 분비하는 데 너무 많이 분비되면 근육을 딱딱하게 만든다는 내용이다. 무관한 문장은 '근육'이란 단어가 포함되어 있어 언뜻 관련되어 보일 수 있지만 근육을 키우기 위해서는 운동을 해야 한다는 내용이므로 글의 흐름과는 무관하다.

4

주제문: Your knees take a great deal of stress every day, and you need to take good care of them.
흐름과 유관한 문장: To increase your knee strength, you should boost the surrounding muscles, which act as a support system.
흐름과 무관한 문장: The next time you go out walking or jogging, remember how hard your heart and lungs are working for you. [모의]

☞ 무릎 관리를 주제로 하는 글임을 알 수 있다. 유관한 문장은 무릎 주변의 근육 강화 운동을 소개하고 있어 주제를 잘 뒷받침하지만, 무관한 문장은 '운동'이라는 것만 관련될 뿐 심장과 폐에 관한 내용이므로 글의 전체 흐름과 무관하다.

Mini Test

정답 및 해설 p.80

● **나머지 문장과 관련이 없는 한 문장을 고르시오.**

1 When you take a bite and begin to chew your food, it becomes smaller, softer, and easier to swallow. ① Your lips close to stop food from falling from your mouth and your teeth crunch your food into smaller pieces. ② Nutrients from the digested food in the stomach can be absorbed directly into the blood. ③ As your food moves around, it becomes coated in saliva, which helps to break down some ingredients of food into smaller pieces. [모의]

*saliva 침, 타액

2 A Scottish company developed a new security device called an "electronic sniffer dog." ① The device uses lasers to identify explosive materials in gases in the air. ② Many dogs are trained to sniff and detect explosive materials in passengers' luggage. ③ The machine looks similar to the metal detectors now used at airports. [모의]

*sniffer (냄새) 탐지기

실전적용독해

3문제를 4분 안에 풀어보세요.

정답 및 해설 p.80

084 다음 글에서 전체 흐름과 관계 없는 문장은?

Health-conscious people generally prefer green tea to black tea, possibly because green tea has undergone less processing. But recent studies have found that black tea is just as good for you as its green cousin. ① The studies show that black tea can prevent many illnesses and diseases just like green tea can. ② For example, drinking black tea can lower the risk of stroke, a serious concern for anyone over forty. ③ It can reduce the risk of heart disease, too. ④ However, an estimated 17 million people die of strokes and heart attacks every year. ⑤ Furthermore, drinking just one cup a day significantly improves the function of the blood vessels.

*stroke 뇌졸중

085 다음 글에서 전체 흐름과 관계 없는 문장은?

Voting matters both to the health of the political system and to the people who participate in it. It's a way to make your voice heard as a citizen and to show you care about your community. ① When you think about it like that, it's not surprising that voters tend to be community-minded in many ways besides just politics. ② According to statistics, voters are known to be more engaged in volunteering. ③ Voters are classified into several groups according to their reasons to participate. ④ They are also more informed about local affairs. ⑤ Especially, they are more concerned about their communities and have a greater sense of their ability to impact the world around them.

086 다음 글에서 전체 흐름과 관계 없는 문장은?

Most of us consume caffeine every day, but how much do we really know about its effect on our body? ① This natural substance with a bitter taste stimulates the central nervous system, making you feel more alert. ② In moderate doses, it can actually offer health benefits, helping to boost memory, concentration, and mental health. ③ If someone drinks five cups of decaffeinated coffee, the dose of caffeine could reach the level of a cup of caffeinated coffee. ④ And caffeine in particular has been associated with a possible decrease in the risk of getting Alzheimer's disease and certain cancers. ⑤ But caffeine overuse can cause anxiety, restlessness, and a rapid heart rate.

*central nervous system 중추신경계

VOCAbulary 어휘확인

084 **health-conscious** 건강에 특별한 관심이 있는 **undergo** 겪다 **processing** 공정(工程); 처리 **lower** ~을 낮추다 **estimated** 추정되는 **heart attack** 심장마비 **significantly** 크게 **blood vessel** 혈관 085 **voting** 투표 **political** 정치적인 **voter** 투표자, 유권자 **statistics** 통계, 통계학 **be engaged in** ~에 종사하다 **classify** 분류하다 **affair** 사건, 일 **concerned** 관심 있는 086 **consume** 섭취하다 **caffeine** 카페인 **substance** 물질 **bitter** (맛이) 쓴 **stimulate** 자극하다 **alert** 정신이 초롱초롱한 **moderate** 보통의 **dose** (약의) 복용량 **boost** 증진시키다; 신장시키다 **decaffeinated** 카페인을 제거한 (↔ **caffeinated**) **overuse** 남용(하다) **restlessness** 초조 **heart rate** 심장박동 수

유형 09 글의 순서 배열

이렇게 출제된다.
주어진 글에 이어질 문장들의 순서를 배열하는 유형이다.
뒤바뀐 문장들의 순서를 논리적 흐름에 맞게 바로잡아야 한다.
1~2문항씩 출제된다.

지시문은 이렇게
주어진 글 다음에 이어질 글의 순서로 가장 적절한 것은?

정답 및 해설 p.82

Check-Up 1

[1 - 2] 다음 글을 읽고, 물음에 답하시오.

Leonardo da Vinci lived in a period called the Renaissance. (A) He became a great artist of (B) that period because he was much more than a painter. ____(C)____, he was a scientist, an inventor, an architect, a musician, and a mathematician.

1 밑줄 친 (A), (B)가 가리키는 것을 쓰시오.

(A) ____________________

(B) ____________________

2 빈칸 (C)에 들어갈 알맞은 연결어를 고르시오.

① For example ② However

해결 전략 1 **글의 흐름이나 순서를 알려주는 여러 가지 표현을 근거로 글을 배열한다.**
연결어, 대명사, 한정어 등의 쓰임을 보고 글의 순서를 판단할 수 있다.
p.90 기출총정리 참조

087 주어진 글 다음에 이어질 글의 순서로 가장 적절한 것은?

Do you feel sleepy during the day? If so, are you sure it's really sleepiness rather than just being tired?

(A) On the other hand, when we are tired, we may feel fatigued but still remain relatively alert. It is a good idea to try to save all your sleep for night time, so if you feel mildly sleepy during the day, do your best to fight it.

(B) For example, exercising at lunchtime can be a good idea. Getting out in the daylight is also very important because natural light helps keep us alert. Coffee and energy drinks can also give us a "boost" during times of low energy.

(C) They are different things, and it's important to distinguish one from the other. When we feel sleepy, it is a conscious struggle to remain awake.

① (A) – (C) – (B) ② (B) – (A) – (C)
③ (B) – (C) – (A) ④ (C) – (A) – (B)
⑤ (C) – (B) – (A)

Check-Up 2

[3 - 4] 다음 글을 읽고, 물음에 답하시오.

(A) The earth has only so much fresh water for us to drink and use. Don't let the water tap run unnecessarily, and turn it off firmly.

(B) When you don't let the water tap run and you make sure to turn it off firmly, you're helping to conserve water.

3 (A), (B)에서 공통되는 내용을 찾아 밑줄을 그으시오.

4 (A), (B)의 순서로 알맞은 것을 고르시오.

① (A) – (B) ② (B) – (A)

해결 전략 2

내용 전개상 자연스럽게 연결되는 순서로 배열한다.

지문 중에는 연결어, 대명사 등의 단서가 거의 없는 글들도 있다. 이런 글들은 글의 자연스러운 의미 흐름에 의거하여 답을 해야 한다. 예를 들어, 한 단락의 뒷부분에 언급된 내용이 다음 단락의 앞부분으로 이어지는 것이 자연스럽다. 또한 시간 전개상 문제가 먼저 발생한 뒤에 해결 내용이 나오는 것이 자연스럽고, 사건과 사건 사이에 인과관계 등의 요인이 있어 자연스러운 순서를 판단할 수 있기도 하다.

해결 TIP

"글의 순서를 정한 뒤에는 그 순서에 따라 글을 다시 빠르게 읽어 본다."

글의 순서를 정한 뒤에는 되도록 그 순서대로 글을 다시 한 번 빠르게 읽어보며 글의 흐름이 자연스러운지 확인한다.

088 주어진 글 다음에 이어질 글의 순서로 가장 적절한 것은?

Archimedes was a famous ancient Greek scientist. A legend says that he was the first to use the sun's rays to start a fire.

(A) Knowing that something had to be done, he hatched a plan. Archimedes took out a mirror and held it up to the sun. He knew the rays of the sun would reflect off the glass onto the Roman ships.

(B) He did it to defend his country against Rome. Rome had come by sea to invade, and Roman ships were about to attack Syracuse, Archimedes' home city.

(C) After a while, the intense heat of the sun's rays reflected by Archimedes' mirror caused a ship to catch fire. The whole fleet was burned, and Syracuse was saved.

*fleet 함대

① (A) – (C) – (B) ② (B) – (A) – (C)
③ (B) – (C) – (A) ④ (C) – (A) – (B)
⑤ (C) – (B) – (A)

기출총정리

글의 순서를 알려주는 연결 고리

1 지시적인 표현을 찾아 글의 순서를 배열한다

연결어, 대명사, 한정어 등이 글의 순서를 알려주는 단서가 된다.

Natural disasters such as fires, floods, and hurricanes happen every year, somewhere in the world.

세상에는 여러 종류의 자연재해가 있다.

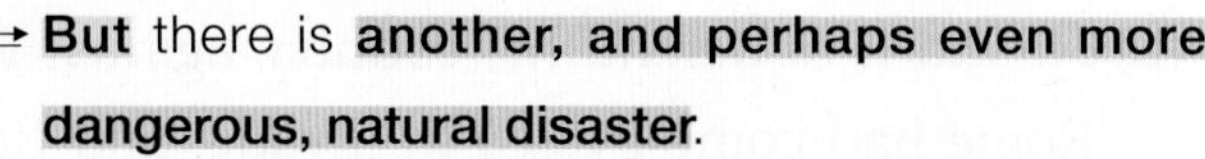

But there is **another, and perhaps even more dangerous, natural disaster**.

그러나 더욱 위험한 자연재해가 있다.

☞ 연결어 But으로 내용이 전환된다. 앞에서 Natural disasters가 언급되었으므로 natural disaster 앞에 한정어 another가 쓰였다.

It is a tsunami, a huge wave that can cause terrible damage and destruction. [모의]

그것은 쓰나미이다. 쓰나미는 엄청난 파괴력을 가진 거대한 파도이다.

☞ 대명사 It은 앞 문장의 another ~ natural disaster를 받는다.

2 각 문장이 내용상 유기적으로 연결되도록 순서를 배열한다

한 단락의 뒷부분에 언급된 내용은 다음 단락의 앞부분에서 이어지는 경우가 많다.

When you move to a big city, **it's hard to get to know people**.

큰 도시로 이사하면 사람들을 알아가는 게 어렵다.

☞ 이사 후 사람들과 알고 지내는 것이 어렵다는 내용이 나왔으므로 이웃과 잘 지내는 방법에 관한 내용이 이어져야 자연스럽다.

One of the best ways to get along with your neighbors is by joining a block association. It is an organization of ordinary citizens. **What kinds of activities do they do**?

이럴 때는 지역 모임에 가입하는 것이 좋다. 그들이 하는 활동은 무엇일까?

Their common activities are tree and flower planting, clean-up days, and group picnics. Some associations work together with the police to help protect their neighborhoods from crime.

그들은 수목 가꾸기부터 치안 유지까지 다양한 활동을 한다.

☞ 앞 단락이 '그들은 무슨 활동을 하는가'라는 질문으로 끝났으므로, 뒤에는 그들이 하는 활동을 소개하는 것이 자연스럽다.

If your area doesn't have a block association, talk to your neighbors about starting one. [모의]

만약 사는 지역에 지역 모임이 없다면, 새로 만들어라.

☞ 앞의 내용은 모두 지역 모임에 참여하라는 내용이므로 만약 지역 모임이 없다면 만들어 보라는 내용은 마지막에 나오는 것이 자연스럽다.

실전적용독해

2문제를 2분 40초 안에 풀어보세요.

정답 및 해설 p.84

089 주어진 글 다음에 이어질 글의 순서로 가장 적절한 것은?

> HIV is a virus that attacks the immune system, which is our body's natural defence against illness. The virus destroys a type of white blood cell in the immune system called a T-helper cell, and makes copies of itself inside these cells. T-helper cells are also referred to as CD4 cells.

(A) This means someone living with HIV, who is not receiving treatment, will find it harder and harder to fight off infections and diseases.

(B) As HIV destroys more CD4 cells and makes more copies of itself, it gradually breaks down a person's immune system.

(C) After 10 or 15 years, if HIV is left untreated, the immune system may be so severely damaged it can no longer defend itself at all.

*the immune system 면역 체계
**T-helper cell 보조 T 림프구

① (A) – (C) – (B)
② (B) – (A) – (C)
③ (B) – (C) – (A)
④ (C) – (A) – (B)
⑤ (C) – (B) – (A)

090 주어진 글 다음에 이어질 글의 순서로 가장 적절한 것은?

> We are individuals, responsible for our own judgments and in possession of our own free will, but nonetheless we are part of something larger.

(A) Your awareness of these responsibilities creates your value system. The exact details of this will depend on your upbringing and your culture, but if your belief is strong, it will sustain you and your close friends in the face of life's challenges.

(B) Some may call it the collective unconscious. Others may label it "spirit" or "life force." But whatever your word of choice, you gain confidence from knowing that we are not isolated from one another.

(C) Furthermore, this feeling of connectedness implies certain responsibilities. If we are all part of a larger picture, then we must not harm others because we will be harming ourselves. We must not exploit because we will be exploiting ourselves.

① (A) – (C) – (B)
② (B) – (A) – (C)
③ (B) – (C) – (A)
④ (C) – (A) – (B)
⑤ (C) – (B) – (A)

VOCAbulary 어휘 확인

089 **HIV** 에이즈 바이러스(= human immunodeficiency virus) **virus** 바이러스 **defence** 방어 cf. **defend** 방어하다 **white blood cell** 백혈구 **refer to A as B** A를 B로 부르다 **CD4** 보조 T 림프구 등의 표면에 있는 항원 **treatment** 치료 **fight off** ~와 싸워 물리치다 **infection** 감염 **break down** 파괴하다 **untreated** 치료를 받지 않는 **090** **individual** 개인 **possession** 소유, 재산 **free will** 자유 의지 **awareness** 인식, 인지 **upbringing** 양육 **sustain** 지탱하다 **in the face of** ~에 직면하여 **collective** 집단적인 **unconscious** 무의식 **label** (…을) ~로 부르다 **isolate** 고립시키다 **connectedness** 유대감, 소속 의식 **imply** 내포하다 **exploit** 착취하다

유형 10 문장 삽입

이렇게 출제된다.
주어진 문장을 적절한 곳에 넣어 글을 완성하는 유형이다.
글의 흐름이 끊기거나 논리적 비약이 생기는 곳을 찾아야 한다.
1~2문항씩 출제된다.

지시문은 이렇게
글의 흐름으로 보아, 주어진 문장이 들어가기에 가장 적절한 곳은?

정답 및 해설 p.85

Check-Up 1

091 지문의 주어진 문장을 읽고, 예상할 수 있는 것을 모두 고르시오.

① 문장에 however가 있으므로 이 문장 앞에는 이와 대립, 반대되는 내용이 나온다.
② 앞부분에는 '어떤 것을 운으로 생각한다'는 내용이 나온다.
③ 뒷부분에는 '운이라고 생각하지 않는다'는 필자의 주장에 대한 설명이 나온다.

해결 전략 1
주어진 문장을 읽은 후, 연결어나 지시어 등을 활용하여 판단하라.
주어진 문장에는 보통 앞뒤의 내용을 알려주는 단서가 있으므로 주어진 문장을 먼저 읽는다. 연결어의 논리적 전후관계를 이용하여 문장의 위치를 파악한다.

연결어뿐만 아니라 정관사, 인칭대명사, 지시어 등도 글의 흐름을 알려주므로 이것들을 통해서도 주어진 문장의 제 위치를 찾을 수 있다.
p.94 기출총정리 참조

091 글의 흐름으로 보아, 주어진 문장이 들어가기에 가장 적절한 곳은?

I don't believe it's luck, however.

I wish people "Good Luck!", but I only have a limited belief in luck. Instead, I believe we make our own luck. (①) Two people could be given the same situation with the same resources and create completely different outcomes. (②) Some might regard it as "lucky" or use luck as an excuse, saying "I'm just unlucky," or "She's luckier than me." (③) Rather it's attitude: how you choose to look at the world and interact within it. (④) Your attitude and how you view the world is everything in life, and it's up to you. (⑤) As every moment of every day provides you with choices about how to approach life, you are in charge, and you can either complain and run away or greet opportunity and embrace it with joy.

Check-Up 2

[1 - 2] 다음 글을 읽고, 물음에 답하시오.

Things which hold gravity pull things towards themselves. (Ⓐ) For example, Jupiter is so big that all of the other planets could fit inside of it. (Ⓑ) Thus, it has stronger gravity than all the other planets

1 위의 Ⓐ, Ⓑ 중 글의 흐름이 끊기는 부분을 고르시오.

2 위 글에 논리적 비약이 없기 위해 1의 답에 들어가야 할 내용을 고르시오.

① 크기가 큰 행성이 있다.

② 물체가 클수록 중력이 세다.

해결 전략 2 **흐름이 끊기는 부분을 찾아라.**
주어진 문장의 제 위치를 찾는 유형은 다시 말해 글의 흐름이 끊기는 부분을 고르는 문제 유형이다. 주어진 문장으로 예상하는 것이 여의치 않을 때는, 글의 흐름상 반드시 필요한 내용이 빠져 있거나 갑자기 글의 흐름이 바뀌어 논리적 비약이 있는 부분을 찾는다.

해결 TIP **"주어진 문장이 필요한 곳을 찾아라."**
논리적인 글은 한 문장 한 문장이 톱니바퀴처럼 유기적으로 잘 연결되어 있다. 따라서 연결이 어색한 부분이 있다면 그 자리가 바로 주어진 문장이 들어가야 할 자리이다.

092 글의 흐름으로 보아, 주어진 문장이 들어가기에 가장 적절한 곳은?

> That is, we are fluent enough if we're able to use the target language to learn more of the target language.

A lot of people are under the impression that to be fluent in another language means that you speak it as well as, or almost as well as, your native language. (①) However, I have my own definition of fluency in a language. (②) For example, if you don't know the word for *tail* in your target language but you know how to describe *the long body part behind a dog or cat*, then you've demonstrated a high level of fluency. (③) That's it. Does it seem tough? (④) Try it with some basic words in your target language to find out if you are fluent or not. (⑤) You'll quickly see what fluency is all about.

기출총정리

글의 흐름을 알려주는 연결 고리

1 앞에 나온 어구를 다시 언급할 때 쓰는 한정어

부정관사(a, an) 외의 한정어는 주로 앞에 나온 명사를 다시 언급할 때 쓰인다. 예를 들어, He has a pool at home.이라는 문장이 나온 뒤에 명사 a pool을 다시 언급하려면 The pool is big. / His pool is three meters wide.와 같이 정관사 the나 기타 한정어(his, my, this, that, some, any, another 등)를 붙여 쓴다.

예 1) **Water** is pumped into the field around the bank. Farmers walk into **the water** and plant small rice plants in the field. [모의]

물이 둑 주위의 논으로 펌프질하여 보내진다. 농부들은 **그 물** 속으로 걸어 들어가 논에 모를 심는다.

☞ 앞 문장에 언급된 Water를 다음 문장에서 the water로 받고 있다. 이처럼 정관사는 보통 앞에서 언급된 명사라는 것을 알려준다.

예 2) Ancient people used **foods as medicine.** The ancient Egyptians recommended **garlic** for headaches. **Another important food** in traditional medicine is **grapes.** [모의]

고대인들은 **식품을 약으로** 사용했다. 고대 이집트인들은 두통에 **마늘**을 추천했다. 전통적인 약재로 **중요한 또 다른 식품**은 **포도**이다.

foods as medicine
garlic (약으로 쓰인 식품 1)
Another important food
grapes (약으로 쓰인 식품 2)

☞ 앞에서 언급된 foods 중 또 하나의 예를 Another important food로 받고 있다.

2 지칭하는 대상을 찾아야 하는 대명사

대명사는 명사를 대신한다. 따라서 대명사를 포함한 문장의 앞뒤에는 대명사가 지칭하는 내용이 있어야 한다.
예를 들어 That's what I want.라는 문장 앞에는 대명사 That이 가리키는 내용이 나와야 한다.

예 3) Fire-fighting may seem like **a simple job. Just find a fire, aim the fire hose, and spray**. In fact, dealing with a burning building involves much more than **that**. [모의]

화재 진압은 **간단한** 일처럼 보일지도 모른다. **그저 화재를 발견하고, 소방호스를 겨눈 다음, 물을 뿌린다**. 사실 화재가 난 건물을 다루는 일은 **그것**보다 훨씬 많은 일을 수반한다.

☞ that은 앞에 언급된 a simple job, 이것을 구체적으로 설명한 다음 문장(Just find ~ and spray.)을 받는다.

3 논리적 흐름을 보여주는 연결어

연결어는 문장 간의 논리적인 흐름을 드러내므로 앞뒤 내용을 예상할 수 있도록 도와준다. 예를 들어 '그래서 우리는 TV를 사기로 결정했다'라는 문장 앞에는 '가격이 저렴했다 / 디자인이 예뻤다 / 여윳돈이 생겼다' 등 TV를 사게 된 '이유'가 언급되었을 것이다.

예 4) **Softer borders** between countries in the EU have boosted crossings by car, bus, and train. **Also**, **low-cost airline flights** are speeding up the trend. [모의]

EU 소속 국가들 간의 **보다 더 유연해진 국경**은 자동차, 버스, 기차에 의한 횡단을 촉진시켜 왔다. **또한 저가 항공 비행기들**이 그러한 경향을 가속화시키고 있다.

Softer borders
(국가 간 교통 왕래가 늘어난 이유 1)
Also
low-cost airline flights
(국가 간 교통 왕래가 늘어난 이유 2)

☞ 추가를 나타내는 연결어 Also가 쓰였으므로 앞뒤에는 대등한 내용이 이어질 것을 알 수 있다.

실전적용독해

3문제를 4분 안에 풀어보세요.

정답 및 해설 p.87

093 글의 흐름으로 보아, 주어진 문장이 들어가기에 가장 적절한 곳은?

> However, they cannot move their eyes as mammals do.

With their huge eyes and quiet, watchful behavior, owls are among the greatest hunters of the forest. (①) During the daytime, when they are not hunting, they keep their eyes half-shut. (②) But when the sun goes down, they can see far better than almost any other animal. (③) They open their eyes wide to let in as much light as possible and become skillful hunters. (④) Instead, they rely on turning their heads almost 180 degrees to find their prey. (⑤) As soon as they find it, they swiftly catch it with a swoop of their silent wings.

*swoop 급강하, 일격

094 글의 흐름으로 보아, 주어진 문장이 들어가기에 가장 적절한 곳은?

> A schedule like this should be made for each subject that focuses on different priorities.

Every person is born with a particular potential which is unique to him. (①) People are of different types and not all of them are brilliant students. (②) Therefore, how to prepare for exams is a big question. (③) First of all, before starting with their studies, students should design their own timetable which describes all the material that has to be covered and tells them how much needs to be studied each day. (④) Tough subjects and the ones in which a student is weak should be given more hours, and easier ones should be given less hours with sufficient intervals between each subject. (⑤) It's very important that these breaks be included in the timetable itself.

095 글의 흐름으로 보아, 주어진 문장이 들어가기에 가장 적절한 곳은?

> Although substitution can extend our mineral supplies, it is not a cure-all for resource shortages.

The substitution of more abundant materials for scarce minerals is an important goal of manufacturing. (①) The search for substitutes is driven in part by economics: one effective way to cut production costs is to substitute an inexpensive or abundant material for an expensive or scarce one. (②) As a result, plastics, ceramic composites, and glass fibers have been substituted for scarcer materials in many industries. (③) Earlier in the 20th century, tin was a critical metal for the can-making industry; since then, plastic, glass, and aluminum have been substituted for tin. (④) There are certain minerals for which no known substitutes exist on Earth. (⑤) For example, no substance having the unique properties of platinum has yet been found.

*ceramic composite 세라믹 조성물(합성물)

VOCAbulary 어휘확인

093 **mammal** 포유동물 **watchful** 주의 깊은 **shut** (눈이) 감긴 **prey** 먹이 **swiftly** 빨리, 신속히 094 **priority** 우선 순위 **particular** 특정한 **potential** 잠재력 **describe** 설명하다 **cover** 다루다, 포함하다 **tough** 어려운, 힘든 **sufficient** 충분한 **interval** 간격 **break** 휴식 (시간) 095 **substitution** 대체 cf. **substitute** 대체물; 대체하다 **mineral** 광물(질) **supply** 비축[공급](량) **cure-all** 만병통치약 **abundant** 풍부한 **scarce** 희박한, 드문 **manufacturing** 제조업 **property** 성질, 특성 **platinum** 백금

미니 모의고사 3

유형 08 | 유형 09 | 유형 10

18문제를 25분 안에 풀어보세요.

정답 및 해설 p.89

096 다음 글에서 전체 흐름과 관계 없는 문장은?

One of the benefits you get from travel is that you can experience history in the places you visit. You can read about history in a book, but you can feel it when you see it in person. Many places offer more than meets the eye. ① For example, Breckenridge, Colorado, is known for its ski resort, but this former Victorian mining town has done a great job of preserving Victorian homes. ② Many of them have been modernized by the young housewives who desire them. ③ Boston is an exciting party town, but you can also evoke the American Revolution by walking the Freedom Trail. ④ A walk through the Coliseum in Rome will transport you back to the days of the Roman Empire. ⑤ It may be impressive in pictures, but it's overwhelming when you see it in real life.

097 글의 흐름으로 보아, 주어진 문장이 들어가기에 가장 적절한 곳은?

> But an interesting fact is that, despite its low population, Australia is ethnically diverse.

Australia is the only island that is also a continent, but that's far from the only interesting fact about it. (①) It is around 77 times bigger than South Korea, but has only 20 million people, whereas South Korea has more than twice that number. (②) Not surprisingly, Australia is the least densely populated continent on Earth excluding Antarctica. (③) For example, most Australian people have British ancestry, which is a result of colonization during the late 18th and 19th centuries. (④) Other Australians include the Aborigines and people from around 120 different countries. (⑤) In particular, since the 1970s, a great number of migrants have come from Asia.

*Aborigine 오스트레일리아 원주민

098 주어진 글 다음에 이어질 글의 순서로 가장 적절한 것은?

> Quicksand is an area of sand that has been mixed with too much water. In movies, it behaves like a liquid and sucks people down and kills them.

(A) Stay calm. Move as little as possible, spread your arms, and lean back just as if you were trying to float on your back in a swimming pool. This will increase your body's surface area and make you stop sinking.

(B) But the truth about quicksand is that it isn't really dangerous. You just need to keep your wits about you. If you accidentally step in quicksand and begin to sink, don't panic.

(C) When you have stopped, you can gently swim using only your arms to get out of the quicksand. Of course you'll be a complete mess afterward, but otherwise no harm will have been done.

*quicksand 유사(流砂, 바람이나 흐르는 물에 의하여 흘러내리는 모래)

① (A) – (C) – (B)　② (B) – (A) – (C)
③ (B) – (C) – (A)　④ (C) – (A) – (B)
⑤ (C) – (B) – (A)

099 다음 글에서 전체 흐름과 관계 없는 문장은?

People love to sit in hot tubs to relieve tense muscles, but hot baths are not recommended for everyone. In fact, for some people, a hot bath can be a very dangerous thing. ① As hot water increases the heart rate, a hot tub can be dangerous for people with high blood pressure. ② Therefore, you should get some exercise every day to reduce blood pressure in a healthy way. ③ Body temperature also increases in hot water, which can lead to loss of essential body fluids. ④ Furthermore, when body temperature rises, blood sugar burns faster. ⑤ This can be very risky for people who have diabetes.

*diabetes 당뇨병

100 글의 흐름으로 보아, 주어진 문장이 들어가기에 가장 적절한 곳은?

> Still, there are things that parents and other caregivers can do in order to encourage babies to put their needs into words.

Every baby is different and will develop language skills at its own rate. (①) While some are speaking in full sentences by 18 months, others of that age are nowhere near ready. (②) There is no magic method that will guarantee a child's ability to talk early. (③) Talking to babies is important, preferably without using "baby talk." (④) Babies learn to talk from listening to others, so adults who are careful with their speech will help their children to communicate effectively, too. (⑤) It is especially helpful to talk in a friendly, conversational manner — pointing out things that you see and describing activities as you go about your day.

101 주어진 글 다음에 이어질 글의 순서로 가장 적절한 것은?

Hurricane winds may not reach the same speeds as the winds in tornados, but hurricanes cause far more damage.

(A) A tornado is narrow at its base and usually only covers a small area of less than a kilometer across. In comparison, a hurricane can measure up to 1,500 kilometers wide at its base.

(B) On the other hand, hurricanes can last for many days and travel thousands of kilometers over the sea. Also, when they reach land, it is typically near a large coastal city where there are many buildings to destroy.

(C) Another reason is that a tornado lasts an hour at the most. Furthermore, the average tornado forms in the relatively unpopulated areas of the Midwestern United States, and it usually doesn't travel very far.

① (A) – (B) – (C) ② (A) – (C) – (B)
③ (B) – (C) – (A) ④ (C) – (A) – (B)
⑤ (C) – (B) – (A)

102 글의 흐름으로 보아, 주어진 문장이 들어가기에 가장 적절한 곳은?

When the clouds get too heavy, the water is released.

The water cycle is how Earth's water recycles itself. Whether flowing in a river, melting from a glacier, or washing ashore on a sandy beach, Earth's water is constantly in motion. The water cycle describes exactly how it is recycled. First, the sun evaporates water from Earth's surface. (①) This water vapor rises to the sky and forms clouds. (②) Then it returns to Earth in the form of rain or snow. (③) This can sink into the ground and get filtered by sand and rock. (④) It also runs off the surface of Earth into rivers, lakes, and oceans. (⑤) There, the sun evaporates the water, and the whole cycle begins again.

*evaporate (물 등을) 증발시키다

103 다음 글에서 전체 흐름과 관계 없는 문장은?

There are many uses for the solid, see-through substance that we know as glass, and without it, the world around us would be a very different place. ① Glass made into windows allows us to see the outdoors from indoors, and brings natural light into buildings. ② The very thin glass used in electric light bulbs lets rays of light pass through. ③ Bottles, jars, vases, and containers made of clear or colored glass let us view their contents. ④ Also, glass bottles should be separated by color to be recycled. ⑤ Glass used to make eyeglasses helps people with poor eyesight to see the world normally.

104 주어진 글 다음에 이어질 글의 순서로 가장 적절한 것은?

Up until the early 19th century, wristwatches were considered "uncool."

(A) Millions of soldiers were given a wristwatch at that time, something more accessible than a pocket watch while they were in uniform. These "trench watches" the soldiers carried during battle gave watches in general a masculine reputation.

(B) In the Western world, pocket watches were a masculine status symbol, while wristwatches were considered feminine and impractical.

(C) That attitude began to change as soldiers discovered wristwatches were far more practical on the battlefield than a pocket watch, though changes were small until World War I.

*trench 참호, 군인용

① (A) – (B) – (C) ② (B) – (A) – (C)
③ (B) – (C) – (A) ④ (C) – (A) – (B)
⑤ (C) – (B) – (A)

105 다음 글에서 전체 흐름과 관계 없는 문장은?

Nowadays, more and more mothers with young children work outside the home. This represents a huge shift in the distribution of the workforce and has a real impact on the lives of many women and families. ① Our country has been slow to acknowledge this, and has done little to improve working mothers' lives. ② The biggest problem is the lack of affordable childcare facilities. ③ Day-care centers are few, their fees are high, and many mothers don't have relatives to take care of children. ④ On the other hand, it is true that fathers do more to help with childcare. ⑤ Childcare in this country is far from satisfactory for working mothers.

106 글의 흐름으로 보아, 주어진 문장이 들어가기에 가장 적절한 곳은?

But you may find signs that are just as strong about what *not* to do.

We often try to avoid following in a parent's footsteps. (①) But, actually, it's a great idea to study the example of your ancestors, as revealed in the stories of how they spent their lives. (②) You may find clues to what to do based on shared talents or interests. (③) There may be a compelling reason why so many medical school students have a parent who's a doctor or why farmers or firefighters run in some families. (④) If your mother despised sitting in an office all day, you might think twice about business school. (⑤) On the other hand, if your uncle wore out early as a construction worker, a desk job might not look too bad.

107 주어진 글 다음에 이어질 글의 순서로 가장 적절한 것은?

> Toxic gases produced by factories and fumes from motor vehicles cause air pollution, which has terrible consequences.

(A) This corrosive liquid is strong enough to erode almost any surface over time. It eats away at stone, marble, and other building materials.

(B) As a result, it has caused great damage to ancient marble buildings. In India, for example, the white marble surface of the famed Taj Mahal is being destroyed. Sadly, there is little that can be done to prevent this destruction unless the source of the problem is removed.

(C) Not only does it cause lung damage and skin problems in humans, but it also damages buildings. This is because acid rain is the result of toxic air pollution mixed with moisture in clouds.

*corrosive 부식성의

① (A) – (C) – (B)　② (B) – (A) – (C)
③ (B) – (C) – (A)　④ (C) – (A) – (B)
⑤ (C) – (B) – (A)

108 다음 글에서 전체 흐름과 관계 없는 문장은?

When you, the leader, delegate responsibility to others, not only the organization but also you benefit. ① In the process, you develop leadership skills and abilities in your people and enhance their initiative, creativity, and competence. ② You build their confidence and self-esteem and let them flex their own leadership muscles. ③ The key to leadership is not to focus on making other people follow, but on making yourself the kind of person they want to follow. ④ When people at every level feel they are trusted and empowered to act, the entire organization is able to move decisively and respond quickly to changing situations. ⑤ As a result, your image may be enhanced: instead of being judged on your individual performance, you are judged by the magnified effectiveness of the team or organization you lead.

*delegate (권한·책임 등을) 위임하다 **flex (준비 운동으로) 몸을 풀다

109 주어진 글 다음에 이어질 글의 순서로 가장 적절한 것은?

> Waste dumping is an enormous problem for cities, but some brilliant solutions have been devised.

(A) Most of these eventually end up in junkyards alongside other wrecked cars and old appliances. There, they are flattened before they are sent to a steel mill for recycling.

(B) Take the issue of abandoned vehicles as an example. Because old vehicles are difficult to dispose of, many people simply walk away from them. In New York alone, around 40,000 cars are left on the streets every year.

(C) After the flattening process, extra scrap metal is mixed with concrete and made into bricks. These are very popular in the building industry because of their great strength.

*steel mill 철강 공장

① (A) – (C) – (B)　② (B) – (A) – (C)
③ (B) – (C) – (A)　④ (C) – (A) – (B)
⑤ (C) – (B) – (A)

110 글의 흐름으로 보아, 주어진 문장이 들어가기에 가장 적절한 곳은?

> Previous generations did not have to give health and fitness building activities much thought — they were part of their daily lives.

All-around health and fitness is seldom achieved through practicing specific team sports, such as basketball and football. (①) And while some alternative sports do promote health and fitness, such as cycling, swimming, jogging, and strength training, American culture has resisted recognizing these activities as true sports for children. (②) This is unfortunate. (③) Parents should encourage their children to participate in these activities. (④) There was no choice but to walk to work or school, carry groceries, work in the fields, do chores manually rather than by machine, and eat diets high in complex carbohydrates. (⑤) All this has changed, however, and most of us now have to make a conscious effort to get the exercise our bodies need.

*carbohydrate 탄수화물

111 다음 글에서 전체 흐름과 관계 없는 문장은?

It's been said that we only use 10 percent of our brain. ① Keeping the brain strong and sharp isn't a goal just for seniors; it's something we should strive for throughout our lives. ② Exercise your brain regularly and thoroughly, and you can virtually guarantee that cognitive function will remain in top form into your seventies, eighties, and beyond. ③ It also provides the opportunity to learn about the underlying causes of cognitive loss in aging individuals. ④ Numerous studies have shown that people who lead lives with little mental stimulation experience greater cognitive loss as they age. ⑤ Their memory fades and they have trouble performing simple mental tasks that come easily to those who "exercise" their brain often.

112 글의 흐름으로 보아, 주어진 문장이 들어가기에 가장 적절한 곳은?

Instead, we focus on how pleasing the food is to our palate.

Do you ever stop to think that the food we eat is merely fuel to keep our body functioning healthily? In many ways, it's no different from purchasing gasoline to run our automobiles. (①) Unfortunately, our taste buds have become a pleasure gauge rather than a quality gauge. (②) We no longer look for the taste that is healthy. (③) Food and drinks have become things of pleasure and are no longer viewed just as a source of needed fuel. (④) But choosing unhealthy foods to eat throughout the day is an extraordinarily unhealthy behavior. (⑤) There is nothing wrong with enjoying a meal, but you should keep in mind what your body really needs at the same time.

*palate 구미, 미각 **taste bud (혀의) 미뢰

113 주어진 글 다음에 이어질 글의 순서로 가장 적절한 것은?

People have always looked for ways to preserve food. Preservation methods like smoking, salting, pickling, and drying have been used for thousands of years.

(A) It was made of wood and had a shelf for a block of ice. This was quite an improvement because the ice was kept cold for much longer and a more stable temperature was achieved. Then, after electricity was invented, the modern refrigerator became part of every home.

(B) But since it was discovered that cold temperatures lengthen the life of fresh foods, people have worked to find better techniques of cold preservation. The earliest of these techniques relied on what nature had to offer.

(C) The ancient Romans collected ice and snow for food preservation. This worked fairly well and remained the common practice for some time, but it was far from convenient. Hundreds of years later, the icebox was invented.

① (A) – (B) – (C)　　② (A) – (C) – (B)
③ (B) – (A) – (C)　　④ (B) – (C) – (A)
⑤ (C) – (A) – (B)

Chapter 4

장문 독해

이렇게 출제된다.
200~300단어가 넘는 지문이 주어지며 5문항이 출제된다. 장문 유형에 포함된 문제는 약간씩 변화가 있었고 앞으로도 그럴 가능성이 있을 것으로 예측된다. 하지만 완전히 생소한 유형이 등장하는 것은 아니므로 비슷한 기존 유형의 해결 방법을 적용시키면 된다.

지시문은 이렇게
주어진 글 (A)에 이어질 내용을 순서에 맞게 배열한 것으로 가장 적절한 것은?
밑줄 친 (a)~(e) 중에서 가리키는 대상이 나머지 넷과 다른 것은?
위 글의 내용과 일치하지 않는 것은?
위 글의 제목으로 가장 적절한 것은?
위 글의 빈칸에 들어갈 말로 가장 적절한 것은?

MP3

정답 및 해설 p.102

Check-Up 1

[1 - 4] 다음 문제를 해결하기에 가장 적절한 풀이 방법을 (A)~(D) 중에서 고르시오.

1 위 글의 내용과 일치하는 것은?

2 빈칸에 들어갈 말로 가장 적절한 것은?

3 밑줄 친 부분이 의미하는 바로 가장 적절한 것은?

4 글의 순서로 가장 적절한 것은?

(A) 글의 핵심 내용을 파악한다.
(B) 각 문단의 앞뒤를 읽고 내용상 자연스럽게 이어지는지 확인한다.
(C) 글의 전체 맥락에서 추론의 단서가 되는 표현을 찾는다.
(D) 선택지를 읽고 순서대로 본문과 대조한다.

해결 TIP **"문제 유형에 따라 알맞은 풀이 방법을 적용하여 풀어라."**
장문 유형에 포함된 각각의 문제는 앞에서 학습한 유형과 유사하다. 따라서 해당 유형의 풀이 방법을 적용하여 풀도록 한다.

해결 TIP **"문제부터 읽어라."**
하나의 지문을 읽고 2~3개의 문제를 해결해야 하는 장문 유형을 풀 때는 문제부터 읽는다. 문제에 따라 적절한 해결 방법을 적용하여 지문을 읽게 되면 보다 정확한 풀이와 시간 절약이 가능하게 되기 때문이다.

Check-Up 2

[114 - 116] 다음 글을 읽고, 물음에 답하시오.

(A)

Roy was a nine-year-old boy like any other, full of hope and curiosity. But you'd never find him running around with the other children. That was because Roy was a sick child, ill with the deadly disease called leukemia. Though the disease had been getting better, there was always the chance of it getting worse again at any moment. But the little one did not once complain or weep over the cruel hand given to (a) <u>him</u> by fate. He merely sat at his favorite window, watching the children at play. His silence was heart-breaking to his parents, Mathew and Susan. Susan found his calm acceptance more unbearable. *leukemia 백혈병

(B)

One day, as Susan sat watching her son enjoy the evening play of the children, she suddenly saw (b) <u>him</u> laugh loudly. With a sudden thrill of joy, Susan rushed to see the cause of Roy's unusual excitement. A little boy, hardly 2 years old, was pushing (c) <u>his</u> nose up at Roy. Surprisingly, Roy was also making funny gestures at the little guy, who copied every action of Roy's. This went on for some time, making Susan extremely happy — happy that Roy was finally laughing!

(C)

"Darling, why don't you watch television or play computer games?" she would say; and the answer would be, "No, Mummy, not interested." Sometimes Mathew would sit with (d) <u>him</u> and try to get to know him, to find out what would make (e) <u>him</u> laugh. Though Roy would smile a little to make his parents happy, he never laughed, nor did he ask for anything.

(D)

That night, she shared her tiny piece of happiness with Mathew, who was also overjoyed. He took Roy onto his lap and sang, "My little Roy saw a tiny boy and was filled with joy." Their faces were shining with joy as they held their son in their arms.

글의 순서 배열

문제별 해결 전략 1

글의 순서는 각 문단을 읽고 내용상 자연스럽게 이어지는지 파악하여 배열한다. 이때 각 문단에 사용된 연결어, 대명사, 한정어 등의 쓰임이 단서가 되기도 한다.

p.88 09. 글의 순서 배열 참조

114 주어진 글 (A)에 이어질 내용을 순서에 맞게 배열한 것으로 가장 적절한 것은?

① (B) – (C) – (D)
② (B) – (D) – (C)
③ (C) – (B) – (D)
④ (C) – (D) – (B)
⑤ (D) – (C) – (B)

지칭 대상 파악

문제별 해결 전략 2

지칭 대상이 다른 하나를 고르는 문제이므로 각각의 대명사가 가리키는 대상을 찾아본다. 알맞은 순서대로 글을 읽으면서 밑줄 친 대명사의 앞뒤에서 그 대상을 찾는다.

p.122 13. 지칭 대상 파악 참조

115 밑줄 친 (a)~(e) 중에서 가리키는 대상이 나머지 넷과 <u>다른</u> 것은?

① (a) ② (b) ③ (c) ④ (d) ⑤ (e)

세부 내용 파악

문제별 해결 전략 3

글과 선택지의 내용이 일치하는지 판단하는 문제이다. 글의 내용이 선택지 내용과 일치하는지 묻는 문제는 반드시 지문에서 근거를 찾아 확인한다. 확인한 내용은 선택지 옆에 O, × 등으로 표시해 놓는 것이 좋다.

p.126 14. 세부 내용 파악 참조

116 위 글의 내용과 일치하지 <u>않는</u> 것은?

① Roy는 백혈병으로 병이 호전되고 있었다.
② Roy는 아픈 것에 대해 전혀 불평하지 않았다.
③ 부모는 Roy가 고요히 지내는 것에 안심했다.
④ Roy는 꼬마를 만나 즐거운 시간을 보냈다.
⑤ Roy는 TV와 컴퓨터 게임에 흥미가 없었다.

[117 - 118] 다음 글을 읽고, 물음에 답하시오.

Digital footprints are online portfolios of who we are, what we do, and by association, what we know. They are a guaranteed by-product of life in a connected world. So if you ever get online or use social media, you create a digital footprint. Every time you get on a website, click on a link, post a picture, or update a status, it is tracked. People can go online to any search engine, such as Google, or any social media site and learn about you. Everything that you think is ____________ isn't. But why should you care? Does it really matter that someone can look up all of this stuff? Actually, this can affect your life in major ways. It can cause you not to get a job, or even not to get into the college that you want. A 2009 survey found that 70% of 275 U.S. recruiters said they have rejected candidates based on information they found online that conflicted with company standards. You could have an extremely impressive resume showing all of the community work you have done, but if your digital footprint shows a different side of your personality, you may never achieve your dream. Hopefully, you will be aware of your digital footprint and how it can affect you.

문제별 해결 전략 4

실험 결과나 시사점을 압축적으로 표현한 부분이 보통 주제문이다.

글이 실험, 조사, 연구 등과 관련된 내용인 경우, 결과나 시사점을 한 마디로 줄인 표현이 제목이 된다. 가설과 실험 내용이 무엇인지 주의 깊게 살펴보고, 그것을 통해 얻어낸 결론이나 시사점이 무엇인지 파악한다.

p.46 03. 제목 참고

117 위 글의 제목으로 가장 적절한 것은?

① Do Not Look Up Others' Digital Footprints
② Searching Online Portfolios: An Invasion of Privacy
③ Be Cautious about What You Post Online
④ Advantages and Disadvantages of Digital Footprints
⑤ Spam Mailers: Digital Footprint Trackers

문제별 해결 전략 5

빈칸 추론

빈칸 문장부터 읽고 무엇을 찾아 읽어 내려가야 할지 파악한 후, 나머지 부분에서 단서를 찾아라.

앞에서 이미 출제된 문제가 제목 등 대의를 묻는 것일 경우, 그다음 문제는 대개가 이와 겹치지 않도록 출제하는 것이 일반적이므로 빈칸이 주어지는 문장은 직접적으로 주제를 드러내기보다는 주제문을 뒷받침하는 세부사항 중 하나에 주어지는 경우가 많다.

p.62 05. 빈칸 추론 참조

118 위 글의 빈칸에 들어갈 말로 가장 적절한 것은?

① necessary
② improper
③ appropriate
④ private
⑤ satisfactory

실전적용독해

7문제를 9분 20초 안에 풀어보세요.

정답 및 해설 p.105

[119 - 121] 다음 글을 읽고, 물음에 답하시오.

(A)

I've watched Kevin with admiration as he has strived to meet goals others might think impossible. At nineteen, he decided to try his hand at competitive powerlifting. This wasn't a natural choice for a former cyclist, but (a) <u>he</u> was determined to break the national record for dead lifts.

*dead lift (기계를 쓰지 않고) 바로 들어올리기

(B)

After several years of weight training, he entered a competition to see how (b) <u>he</u> stacked up against others. We arose at 5:00 a.m. and drove three hours to Fresno for a formal meet. The gym was filled with weight lifters who'd been competing for years. I was worried (c) <u>he</u> would be disappointed with his performance.

(C)

But Kevin blew away both the federation's state and national records by lifting 590 pounds — this was 50 pounds more than the previous record holder. Was he lucky? Of course he was lucky. All the cards lined up for him that day. But (d) <u>he</u> would never have succeeded unless he had put tremendous effort behind his goals.

(D)

Kevin identified the best trainer in northern California and drove two hours each way, several times a week, to learn from (e) <u>him</u>. Kevin read everything he could about the sport, carefully crafted a diet to build more muscle, and spent hours training at the gym.

119 주어진 글 (A)에 이어질 내용을 순서에 맞게 배열한 것으로 가장 적절한 것은

① (B) – (D) – (C)
② (C) – (B) – (D)
③ (C) – (D) – (B)
④ (D) – (B) – (C)
⑤ (D) – (C) – (B)

120 밑줄 친 (a)~(e) 중에서 가리키는 대상이 나머지 넷과 다른 것은?

① (a) ② (b) ③ (c) ④ (d) ⑤ (e)

121 위 글의 Kevin에 관한 내용과 일치하지 <u>않는</u> 것은?

① 19살에 역도 선수가 되려고 결심했다.
② 한때 사이클 선수였다.
③ 훈련 없이 경기에 참가했다.
④ 신기록으로 우승했다.
⑤ 역도에 관한 책을 읽었다.

VOCAbulary 어휘확인

119~121 admiration 감탄 strive to ~을 얻으려고 노력하다 try one's hand at ~을 시도해 보다 competitive 경쟁을 하는 powerlifting 역도 former 예전의 stack up (against) (~와) 견줄 만하다 arise (잠자리에서) 일어나다; 생기다 formal 공식적인; 격식을 차린 blow away ~을 수월하게 이기다 federation 연맹[연합] previous 이전의 put effort 노력을 들이다 tremendous 엄청난

[122 - 123] 다음 글을 읽고, 물음에 답하시오.

Life can be hard — running around all the time and never feeling like you actually get anything you really want done. Habits can help. They've helped me to get more organized and find more time in my day. Habits are things that become part of your life without you even thinking about them, and because they don't take up any brain space, they tend to give you more time without you even realizing it. When you brush your teeth each day, do you think about not doing it at all, or do you just do it? After all, we all brush our teeth every morning and evening — it takes a few minutes and then is done. We don't find a way to avoid it, as we know it needs to be done, and we know what time and when in our day we should do it. It has become so ________________ to do that we just do it. It's become a habit. If we can make lots of positive things in our life a habit like this, so that they become second nature, then we can help ourselves, and our lives will run more smoothly each and every day.

122 위 글의 제목으로 가장 적절한 것은?

① Habits Create Who We Are
② Life Is Full of the Unexpected
③ Tips to Get Organized in Your Study
④ The Difficulty of Removing Bad Habits
⑤ Habit: A Helper in Managing Our Life

123 빈칸에 들어갈 말로 가장 적절한 것은?

① hard　② meaningless
③ special　④ practical
⑤ simple

VOCAbulary 어휘확인

122~123 **run around** 돌아다니다 **get organized** 조직화되다 **take up** 차지하다 **tend to-v** ~하는 경향이 있다 **avoid** 피하다 **positive** 긍정적인 **nature** 천성 **smoothly** 순조롭게, 평탄하게

[124 - 125] 다음 글을 읽고, 물음에 답하시오.

Many of us have grown up being told that we are in control of our own fate — that we have ultimate control over whether we succeed or not. While some may still hold onto this notion, it is often the root of depression and sense of failure when we don't succeed in life. In order for a country to be rich, you need a good system of economics and government, and an established infrastructure, among other factors. However, being a "rich" country doesn't mean that its citizens are happy. Societies where the people focus on money-related goals tend to have high rates of depression. What can be said about this situation?

All of the successful and "rich" countries in the world have a culture focused on success, and that leaves people ___________ for personal or business failure. Constant innovation is often a top priority in such a social atmosphere. Engineers and those in technical fields drive innovation, and it is often these workers that suffer from a great sense of failure from being unable to advance. Remember, failure is natural and to be expected. Life is not just about succeeding. You still have to go on if you're met with difficulties on your journey.

124 위 글의 제목으로 가장 적절한 것은?

① What Makes a Country Financially Successful
② Successful Nations Create Successful People
③ The Obsession of Modern Man with Success
④ Cultural Pressure to Succeed Brings People Down
⑤ Innovation as a Shortcut to Economic Success

125 위 글의 빈칸에 들어갈 말로 가장 적절한 것은?

① unnoticed ② eager
③ respected ④ unprepared
⑤ ignorant

VOCAbulary 어휘 확인

124~125 fate 운명 ultimate 궁극적인, 최후의 notion 개념, 관념 depression 우울증 government 정부 established 확립된 infrastructure 사회 기반 시설 factor 요인, 인자 rate 비율 unprepared 준비가 되지 않은 constant 끊임없는 innovation 혁신, 쇄신 priority 우선 사항 atmosphere 분위기 drive 추진시키다 suffer from ~으로 고통받다 advance 진보하다, 전진하다

유형 12 심경, 분위기 파악

이렇게 출제된다.
글을 종합적으로 이해하여 주인공의 심경이나 전반적인 글의 분위기를 파악하는 유형이다. 소설과 같은 문학 작품이나 일화를 지문으로 하여 둘 중 1문항이 출제된다. 선택지로 심경이나 분위기를 나타내는 형용사가 2개씩 제시되기도 한다.

지시문은 이렇게
다음 글에 드러난 필자의 심경으로[심경 변화로] 가장 적절한 것은?
다음 글의 상황에 나타난 분위기로 가장 적절한 것은?

정답 및 해설 p.109

Check-Up 1

1 다음 문장의 'I'가 자신이라고 생각하고 'I'의 심경을 짐작해 보자.

I found that everything was out of order. The window above the sink was broken, and hundreds of pieces of glass had made a mess on my kitchen floor. My legs were trembling so badly that I could hardly stand still.

① 쓸쓸한 ② 무서운 ③ 죄책감이 드는

2 'I'를 자신이라고 생각하고 126 지문을 읽어보자.

해결 전략 1
주인공의 심경과 직·간접적으로 관련된 어휘에 주목하라.
주인공의 심경이 글에 직접적으로 묘사되기도 하지만, 간접적으로 표현되는 경우도 많다. 예를 들어, 주인공이 중요한 시험을 앞두고 있는 상황에서 식은땀이 난다면 주인공의 심경으로 가장 적절한 것은 '초조한, 긴장한'일 것이다.
p.112 기출총정리 참조

해결 TIP
"분위기는 독자가 느끼는 감정이고, 심경은 글의 주인공이 느끼는 감정이다."
분위기와 심경 문제가 같은 것을 묻는다고 생각하기 쉽다. 하지만 분위기는 글을 읽는 독자가 느끼는 감정이고 심경은 글의 주인공이 처한 상황에서 어떤 감정을 느끼는지를 나타낸다. 예를 들어 '엄숙한 자리에서 실수로 넘어져 많은 사람들이 웃었다'는 내용에서 글의 분위기를 묻는다면 humorous, 주인공의 심경을 묻는다면 embarrassed가 정답으로 적절하다.

126 다음 글에 드러난 'I'의 심경으로 가장 적절한 것은?

Things went well for the first thirty seconds. I was able to greet my guests and Collin was nowhere in sight. After thirty-three seconds, however, he said he was bored and wanted me to read to him. I reminded him that he was supposed to be good. He angrily walked away. A minute later there was a crash from the next room. Collin, reaching for the cake in the middle of the dining room table, had knocked a coffeepot onto the floor. While I mopped up, Collin again complained that he didn't have anything to do. "Just go play," I said forcefully, trying to calm myself. I looked at my guests for sympathy. I got plenty. After a few minutes, Collin was again pulling my sleeve. I attempted to ignore him, so he threw himself on my lap, creating a scene again.

① proud and delighted
② calm and bored
③ disappointed and nervous
④ embarrassed and annoyed
⑤ expectant and hopeful

Check-Up 2

3 다음 어구에서 공통적으로 느껴지는 분위기로 가장 적절한 것을 고르시오.

a loud bang / flames / two more explosions / already sunk into the ocean

① 평화로운 ② 긴급한 ③ 재미있는

4 형용사, 부사와 같은 수식어구에 유의하여 127 지문을 머릿속에 그림을 그리듯이 읽으시오.

해결 전략 2

글의 분위기: 형용사, 부사 등을 중심으로 머릿속에 그림을 그리며 읽어라.

전체적인 맥락에서 글의 분위기를 파악해야 하므로 글의 상황을 머릿속에 그림을 그리듯 상상하며 읽는 것이 도움이 된다. 특히 형용사, 부사 등의 수식어구에 주목하여 글을 읽도록 한다. '걷는다'는 표현보다 '느리게 걷는다'는 표현이 느낌을 더 정확히 전달하기 때문이다.

127 다음 글의 상황에 나타난 분위기로 가장 적절한 것은?

Linda leaned over to admire the bouquet of peach-colored roses she had just bought. It was a smell she remembered from her childhood. Her mind wandered fancifully from the flowers to the wonderful smell of fresh bread coming from the bakery next door. Standing to the side of the entrance was an amateur juggler. With his wildly colored costume, he attracted an audience of children who giggled each time he made a mistake. She walked a bit closer, careful not to disturb the gathered children. She watched a few minutes, and found herself giggling too. He finished his performance with a bow toward Linda. She took a deep bow in return and handed him a rose.

① lonely ② sympathetic
③ depressing ④ mysterious
⑤ pleasant

기출총정리

심경·분위기 빈출 어휘

심경과 분위기를 묻는 문제의 선택지로는 다음과 같은 단어가 출제된다. 단어의 뜻과 그 느낌을 잘 익혀두자.

1 긍정적 느낌을 나타내는 어휘

- **joyful** 기쁜
- **joyous** 아주 기뻐하는; 기쁜
- **merry** 즐거운, 명랑한
- **delighted** 기쁜
- **thrilled** 신나는, 스릴 있는
- **amused** 재미있어하는
- **humorous** 웃긴, 익살스러운
- **lively** 활기찬, 생기 있는
- **festive** 활기찬, 즐거운
- **fantastic** 환상적인
- **fascinated** 매료[매혹]된
- **romantic** 낭만적인
- **hopeful** 희망적인
- **encouraged** 용기를 얻은
- **thankful** 감사하는
- **satisfied** 만족하는
- **confident** 자신 있는
- **harmonious** 조화로운
- **comfortable** 편안한
- **calm** 침착한, 차분한
- **relieved** 안심한
- **comforted** 위안을 받은
- **relaxed** 느긋한, 여유 있는
- **sympathetic** 동정적인, 동정 어린

2 부정적 느낌을 나타내는 어휘

- **shameful** 부끄러운, 창피한
- **terrified** 무서워하는
- **horrified** 공포에 질린
- **depressed** 낙담한, 우울한
- **frustrated** 좌절감을 느끼는
- **hopeless** 절망적인
- **gloomy** 우울한
- **embarrassed** 창피한, 당황한
- **indifferent** 무관심한
- **frightened** 겁이 난
- **annoyed** 화난, 짜증 난
- **envious** 부러워하는
- **monotonous** 단조로운
- **miserable** 비참한, 불행한
- **tragic** 비극적인
- **urgent** 긴박한
- **tense** 긴장되는
- **nervous** 긴장한, 초조한
- **anxious** 불안한, 걱정하는
- **concerned** 걱정스러운
- **discouraged** 낙심한
- **desperate** 간절한, 필사적인
- **confusing** 혼란스러운
- **mysterious** 기이한, 불가사의한
- **regretful** 후회하는
- **weird** 이상한, 기이한
- **guilty** 죄책감이 드는

Mini Test

정답 및 해설 p.110

● **다음을 읽고, 글에 드러난 주인공의 심경으로 가장 적절한 것을 고르시오.**

1 I was looking at living whales for the first time. I couldn't see the entire body of each whale — only their backs as they surfaced to blow. But that was enough to make me thrilled. I had never seen an animal that large in the wild. Words alone can't describe how this first sighting affected me. [모의]

① indifferent ② fascinated

2 Then, he pushed so many different commands. It was no good. He was bothered and couldn't stay calm. For some reason, he was getting consistent error messages. He couldn't understand what they meant. He shook his head in irritation. [모의]

① annoyed ② relieved

● **다음을 읽고, 글의 상황에 나타난 분위기로 가장 적절한 것을 고르시오.**

3 At last, without further warning, the creature came into view. He felt his pulse hammering in his throat. His thoughts seemed to be running a desperate race with each other. [모의]

① festive ② urgent

4 Three rescue workers trying to dig the trapped miners out were also killed when a wall of the mine exploded, burying them. They never saw or heard any sign of the miners, and all six men were considered missing and probably dead. All rescue efforts were eventually abandoned. [모의응용]

① tragic and discouraging
② scary and mysterious

실전적용독해

3문제를 4분 안에 풀어보세요.

정답 및 해설 p.111

128 다음 글의 상황에 나타난 분위기로 가장 적절한 것은?

The officers exited their patrol car and crossed the parking lot on foot. They approached the apartment with caution. Tennant whispered to his junior partner, Roscoe, "Get to the other side of the doorway and try the door." The younger officer moved quietly and quickly, as he had been trained to do. He gently turned the doorknob. It wasn't locked. "Now!" shouted Tennant. Together they burst into the apartment. A few seconds passed as they scanned the room. Then, a loud noise came from the back of the apartment, and Roscoe ran quickly toward the sound. Tennant shouted "No!" but seconds later, the young officer was lying on the floor, bleeding from a serious bullet wound to his shoulder.

① festive and noisy
② tense and urgent
③ hopeful and lively
④ strange and confusing
⑤ happy and harmonious

129 다음 글에 드러난 'I'의 심경으로 가장 적절한 것은?

A lady took my seat in church a while back. It's not that important really. She is a very nice lady, and a good friend, too. Any person should be comfortable sitting anywhere, so it's no big deal. I'm sure she didn't intend to take my seat. I love my seat. But I would never raise a fuss about a seat. She probably didn't intend anything personal by taking my seat. Actually, it was about three months ago when she took my seat. I really don't know why she took it, since I've never done anything to her. I've never taken her seat. But see! This is the way great social injustices begin: insensitive people taking other people's seats in church. People will just sit anywhere they please. And the next thing they'll do is take my parking place, too.

① pleasant ② regretful ③ excited
④ upset ⑤ lonely

130 다음 글에 드러난 필자의 심경 변화로 가장 적절한 것은?

One Friday afternoon, I was on my way from Los Angeles to Palm Springs. As I came to a stop behind a long line of cars, I glanced in my rear-view mirror to discover that the car behind me was not stopping. In fact, it was coming toward me with tremendous speed. I realized that the driver was not paying attention and that I was going to be hit hard. I closed my eyes, took a breath, and dropped my hands to my sides. Then I was hit with enormous force. When the movement and noise stopped, I opened my eyes. My car was compacted like an accordion, but I was fine. The police told me I was lucky I had relaxed, for muscle tension increases the likelihood of severe injury.

① frightened → relieved
② excited → disappointed
③ ashamed → proud
④ comfortable → anxious
⑤ curious → annoyed

VOCAbulary 어휘확인

128 patrol car 순찰차 approach 다가가다 with caution 조심스럽게 whisper 속삭이다 junior 후배, 부하 doorknob 손잡이 burst into ~로 갑자기 뛰어들다 scan 훑어보다 bleed 피를 흘리다 bullet wound 총상(총에 맞은 상처) 129 intend 의도하다, 작정하다 raise a fuss 요란을 피우다, 호들갑을 떨다 insensitive 무신경한, 둔감한 130 come to a stop 멈춰 서다 glance 흘낏 보다 rear-view mirror (자동차의) 백미러 tremendous 엄청난 take a breath 숨을 쉬다 enormous 막대한 movement 움직임 compact 압축하다; 다지다 accordion 아코디언 tension 긴장 likelihood 가능성 severe injury 중상(아주 심한 부상)

미니 모의고사 4 유형 11 | 유형 12

18문제를 25분 안에 풀어보세요.

정답 및 해설 p.113

131 다음 글에 드러난 George의 심경으로 가장 적절한 것은?

When George got to Belle's house, there had already been a visitor there before him. Ed Handby had come to the door and was calling Belle out of the house. George had wanted to ask this woman to come away with him and to be his wife, but when he saw her standing by the door with Ed, he lost his self-assurance and his face turned red. "You stay away from that kid," he yelled, and then, not knowing what else to say, turned to go away. "If I see you together again, I won't be able to control myself," he added. George had come to express his love, not to threaten, and now was angry with himself for losing his temper in front of everyone.

① satisfied ② frightened ③ pleased
④ jealous ⑤ hopeful

132 다음 글에 드러난 Warren의 심경 변화로 가장 적절한 것은?

Warren was a middle-aged professor. But the college faced a budget shortfall, and took the step of eliminating a number of its departments, including Warren's. For him, everything seemed to have been destroyed. Instead of giving up, however, Warren realized how much the world had to offer. He chose to focus on the opportunity set before him. Never before had he had the chance to start again, to decide what he wanted to do and where he wanted to do it. He wound up taking a year off from the world to live in a rural town. And how did he feel at the end of the year? "I've never been better."

① relaxed → frightened
② discouraged → satisfied
③ proud → ashamed
④ comfortable → anxious
⑤ curious → annoyed

[133 - 135] 다음 글을 읽고, 물음에 답하시오.

(A)

One day a young mother left her daughter Bonnie with their next-door neighbor while (a) she went to work. Later in the day, as Bonnie was playing on the neighbor's front lawn, a car came flying around the corner, out of control. It flew up onto the lawn and hit the little girl, knocking her into the street. By the time the police and the ambulance arrived, she had stopped breathing.

(B)

The doctors sat down with her and explained her daughter's injuries and what they had done to try to save her life. This didn't help the mother. The nurse sat down with (b) her and explained how they had done everything possible to save her little girl. The mother remained upset — so hurt that the staff thought they might have to treat this poor mother. Then the mother walked through the emergency room to the pay phone, to call her relatives.

(C)

One of the nurses at the hospital called the mother and shared this terrible news as gently as possible. Although the hospital offered to send someone to drive the mother in, (c) she insisted on making the long drive herself. Finally the mother walked into the hospital, emotionless until she saw her little girl lying lifelessly on the table. She completely broke down.

(D)

Seeing (d) her, the policeman who had been sitting there for almost four hours stood up. He had been the first to arrive on the scene, the one who had held little Bonnie in his arms. He walked up to this mother and told her what had happened, adding, "I just want you to know she was not alone." The mother was so grateful to hear that in her daughter's last moments on this earth, (e) she was held and loved. The mother finally felt consoled, knowing her daughter had felt love at the end of life, even if it was from a stranger.

133 주어진 글 (A)에 이어질 내용을 순서에 맞게 배열한 것으로 가장 적절한 것은?

① (B) – (D) – (C) ② (C) – (B) – (D)
③ (C) – (D) – (B) ④ (D) – (B) – (C)
⑤ (D) – (C) – (B)

134 밑줄 친 (a)~(e) 중에서 가리키는 대상이 나머지 넷과 다른 것은?

① (a) ② (b) ③ (c) ④ (d) ⑤ (e)

135 위 글의 내용과 일치하지 않는 것은?

① Bonnie는 이웃집에서 놀다가 차 사고를 당했다.
② 간호사가 사고 소식을 엄마에게 알렸다.
③ 엄마는 직접 운전해서 병원으로 왔다.
④ 간호사의 말이 엄마에게 위안을 주었다.
⑤ 경찰관은 사고를 당한 Bonnie를 안아 주었다.

[136 - 137] 다음 글을 읽고, 물음에 답하시오.

Everybody makes decisions all the time — some of them big, some of them small. We gain satisfaction not just from the outcome of the decision but also from the amount of time we spend considering *what-ifs*. What-ifs are all the possible things that might happen as a result of your actions, and there is no limit to them. But spending time thinking about every other imaginable scenario can ________ the value of a decision you have made. What-ifs do not help us create the best possible outcome for the decisions we have already made. Film director Blake Edwards' first experience in the movie business made him doubt himself. "Spending a great deal of time imagining what-ifs, I continuously changed my decisions to try to please the potential investors. Then they decided not to invest money in my project. That was when I sat down and thought about everything I had changed to please them." He eventually decided that if he was really going to make the movie, it had to be his movie, not theirs. Later, he said his movie came alive only when "I stopped thinking about what-ifs."

136 위 글의 제목으로 가장 적절한 것은?

① The Importance of Saving Time
② Living Today in Dangerous Situations
③ Considering Potential Investors in Projects
④ The Necessity of Supporting the Movie Industry
⑤ The Uselessness of Thinking about Other Possibilities

137 위 글의 빈칸에 들어갈 말로 가장 적절한 것은?

① replace
② indicate
③ weaken
④ calculate
⑤ imagine

138 다음 글의 상황에 나타난 분위기로 가장 적절한 것은?

With 30 seconds remaining, the Huskers will attempt a field goal. After a hard-fought game by both teams, the Huskers are behind by just one point. The ball is on the 35-yard line. Jeff's mind is racing, his heart is pounding, and his palms are sweating. He takes a deep breath, says a prayer, "God bless this kick," and waits for the snap. All goes well; he kicks the ball and watches in what seems like slow motion as the ball sails beautifully between the goal posts. The fans give each other hugs and high-fives as if they were on the field themselves. His teammates and TV crews bombard the boy.

*snap 스냅(공을 다리 사이로 패스하는 것)

① scary and mysterious
② sad and miserable
③ relieved and comforted
④ tense and festive
⑤ quiet and peaceful

139 다음 글에 드러난 필자의 심경 변화로 가장 적절한 것은?

My train was quickly approaching a crossing when suddenly a yellow school bus appeared ahead! This was a situation I had mentally prepared for but never believed would really happen. I slammed on the emergency brake, shut my eyes, prayed, and waited for the terrible crash. There was nothing else I could do. When the train finally stopped, I opened my eyes and saw the bus in front of the train. My prayers had been answered! If it had been any closer, it would have been a disaster. I got down from the train. The driver also got out of the bus and ran to give me a great big hug! Oh, we were both in tears!

*slam on (브레이크 등을) 급히 밟다

① gloomy → excited
② confident → disappointed
③ desperate → relieved
④ hopeful → discouraged
⑤ joyful → sorrowful

140 다음 글에 드러난 'I'의 심경 변화로 가장 적절한 것은?

Being a parent of a child with special needs produces a lot of conflicting emotions. I recall, for instance, a school concert in which my son was asked to be the flag-bearer during several songs. His face shone with pride as he tried to hold up the pole, and at first, my husband and I shared his emotions. We felt a warmth from knowing that he had a meaningful role in the concert and that he was enjoying a sense of accomplishment. Then, like a bolt of lightning, I was struck by the moving mouths of all the other fifth-graders. They sang all the songs and read all the music. Reminded of my son's limitations, I was no longer able to smile. My heart sank as I thought about his differences and saw him standing apart from his peers.

① pleased → annoyed
② sad → pleased
③ bored → excited
④ proud → sad
⑤ indifferent → interested

[141 - 143] 다음 글을 읽고, 물음에 답하시오.

(A)

I stared at the chessboard in disbelief. I was going to lose a tournament game to a player who was two years younger than I was. My opponent, Max, could put my king in mate in only three moves. I only hoped that (a) he didn't see the opportunity. No such luck.

*mate(= checkmate) ((체스)) 체크 메이트(킹이 붙잡히게 된 상황, 완전히 패배한 상황)

(B)

"You played a great game," Max said as (b) he caught up to me. "I especially liked the way you used your knights to attack. I think you could have had me," he said as he extended his hand toward me. For a second, I didn't know how to react. I looked up at my mom, and she just smiled. Then I turned to Max and proudly shook (c) his hand. "Thanks a lot, Max. It was a great game," I said. Already the sick feeling in my stomach was gone. "Maybe someday you can be the next Bobby Fischer!"

(C)

"Not everybody can be Bobby Fischer, Greg," my mom said. She knew how I always wanted to be like Bobby Fischer, the mysterious and brilliant chess champion. Fischer was the U.S. Chess Champion when he was only fourteen years old. I realized I was not going to be like (d) him. Tears started to well up in my eyes, and I started feeling sick. As we were getting ready to leave the competition room, I saw Max approaching me.

(D)

(e) He moved his bishop into position, setting up the end of the game. I looked sadly over at my mom who was standing at the side of the room. She knew the game was over but smiled and gave a thumbs-up sign anyway. Back at the chessboard, I made a few last meaningless moves to make the game official and walked away from the board as fast as I could — straight to my mom.

**bishop (체스) 비숍(체스의 말 중 하나)

141 주어진 글 (A)에 이어질 내용을 순서에 맞게 배열한 것으로 가장 적절한 것은?

① (B) – (D) – (C)
② (C) – (B) – (D)
③ (C) – (D) – (B)
④ (D) – (B) – (C)
⑤ (D) – (C) – (B)

142 밑줄 친 (a)~(e) 중에서 가리키는 대상이 나머지 넷과 다른 것은?

① (a) ② (b) ③ (c) ④ (d) ⑤ (e)

143 위 글의 'I'에 관한 내용과 일치하지 않는 것은?

① 체스 경기에서 Max에게 졌다.
② Fischer 같은 챔피언이 되고 싶었다.
③ 실망감에 눈물을 흘렸다.
④ Max를 찾아가 우승을 축하했다.
⑤ 경기가 끝난 후 곧장 어머니에게 달려갔다.

[144 - 145] 다음 글을 읽고, 물음에 답하시오.

Are you afraid even to imagine great things could happen in your life because you can't face the disappointment of seeing hopes go to pieces? A lot of people feel that way. But there's no need to be afraid of even the worst situation. Life may not be easy, but you can always make it better, especially if you remember, when life gives you lemons — make lemonade. Here's a good example, from the tough world of boxing. Gene Tunney was a talented heavyweight boxer, with knockout power in both hands. Unfortunately, he broke so many bones in his hands so many times that it looked like his career was over. Many fighters would have given up if they had been in Tunney's shoes. But Tunney didn't quit. He simply changed his entire approach to his sport. He altered his style, from that of a big-swinging aggressive fighter to that of a master of planning, thinking, and strategy. Tunney's new scientific style worked well, and he became the heavyweight boxing champion of the world in 1926. Like Tunney, you can adjust to what life throws at you. You don't need to give up when things don't work out the way you hope.

144 위 글의 제목으로 가장 적절한 것은?

① Keep Fighting: Failure Is Not the End
② Face Your Fears Head On to Find Yourself
③ Gene Tunney: Legend of Heavyweight Boxing
④ Who Can Avoid the Troubles of Life?
⑤ Better to Fail Than Never to Try

145 위 글의 Gene Tunney에 관한 내용과 일치하지 않는 것은?

① 재능 있는 헤비급 권투선수였다.
② 양손 펀치력이 매우 강했다.
③ 손뼈가 부러지는 부상을 여러 번 입었다.
④ 힘든 상황에서도 포기하지 않았다.
⑤ 부상 후 전략에 능한 코치가 되었다.

[146 - 148] 다음 글을 읽고, 물음에 답하시오.

(A)

It was a sunny day. I was covered with dust and dirt as I rolled on the ground, playing. Just another ordinary day in my second grade class. My teacher, Mrs. Robertson, waved at my mom from afar and then walked closer. "Mrs. Bit, can we talk for a second?" (a) she said, smiling. My mom walked into a room, and I waited outside, assuming that it would be great news. After a while, my mom came out of the room and looked at me. I felt immediately that something was wrong.

(B)

On our way home, I asked her what (b) she had said to her. "You're failing. She said that you're the only one failing in her class. She said she's pretty sure that you're not going to make it into third grade, I'm sorry," my mom said sadly. Those words she uttered ruined every piece of my childhood. I was only ten years old then.

(C)

I hesitated at first. But (c) she did everything to convince me, and it worked. I successfully led the group. From that moment, I learned to smile again. From time to time, I had to suffer from what I'd heard from my previous teacher, though. Some of my happiness was forever lost because of (d) her sharp words that day. Though I mostly believed in myself again, I had learned the true power of speech.

(D)

The failing grades and (e) her comparison of me with other students made me feel like I was nothing. No one believed in me, not even myself. Shortly afterwards I transferred to another school, where I met a new teacher. She was far from the one I'd had before. She sat beside me one time, and we talked. "I am planning a group activity and wondering if you could be a group leader," she said, cheerfully.

146 주어진 글 (A)에 이어질 내용을 순서에 맞게 배열한 것으로 가장 적절한 것은?

① (B) – (D) – (C) ② (C) – (B) – (D)
③ (C) – (D) – (B) ④ (D) – (B) – (C)
⑤ (D) – (C) – (B)

147 밑줄 친 (a)~(e) 중에서 가리키는 대상이 나머지 넷과 다른 것은?

① (a) ② (b) ③ (c) ④ (d) ⑤ (e)

148 위 글의 내용과 일치하는 것은?

① Robertson 선생님이 엄마에게 할 말을 미리 알고 있었다.
② Robertson 선생님은 내 성적이 곧 좋아질 거라고 격려했다.
③ 글쓴이는 성적이 뒤처진다고 해서 속상해하지는 않았다.
④ 글쓴이는 리더를 맡겠다고 선생님께 자원했다.
⑤ 글쓴이는 단체 활동을 성공적으로 이끌었다.

Chapter 5

유형 13 지칭 대상 파악
유형 14 세부 내용 파악
유형 15 실용 자료 파악
유형 16 도표 자료 파악
미니 모의고사 5

유형 13 지칭 대상 파악

이렇게 출제된다.
가리키는 대상이 나머지와 다른 대명사를 고르는 유형으로 대명사가 가리키는 것이 무엇인지를 알맞게 추론하여야 한다. 1문항씩 출제된다.

지시문은 이렇게
밑줄 친 부분이 가리키는 대상이 나머지 넷과 다른 것은?
밑줄 친 he가 가리키는 대상이 나머지 넷과 다른 것은?

정답 및 해설 p.124

Check-Up 1

1 다음 ①, ② 중 밑줄 친 they, their가 가리키는 대상을 고르시오.

① Lizards have five hundred thousand tiny ② hairs on the bottom of their feet, and they are the secret to their amazing climbing skills.

they: ________
their: ________

2 149 지문을 읽고 밑줄 친 각 부분이 가리키는 대상을 찾으시오.

해결 전략 **대명사가 가리키는 대상 찾기**
글에 등장하는 여러 대명사가 각각 가리키는 대상이 무엇인지 파악한다. 대명사는 주로 앞에 나온 명사를 대신하며 간혹 뒤에 나오는 명사를 대신하여 쓰이기도 한다. 이런 유형의 문제가 출제되는 글에서는 대명사가 대신할 수 있는 명사가 둘 이상 있는 경우가 대부분이므로 명사를 대입해서 해석했을 때 문맥이 자연스러운지를 판단해야 한다.
p.124 기출총정리 참조

149 밑줄 친 부분이 가리키는 대상이 나머지 넷과 다른 것은?

Two men were walking through a desert. At some point they had an argument, and one of them slapped ① the other in the face. The man was hurt, and he wrote in the sand: "TODAY MY BEST FRIEND SLAPPED ME IN THE FACE." Then they started walking again, until they found an oasis, where they decided to take a bath. There ② the one who had been slapped got stuck in some mud and started to drown. Luckily, ③ his friend saved him. This time ④ the man wrote on a stone: "TODAY MY BEST FRIEND SAVED MY LIFE." Out of curiosity, his friend asked him, "After I hurt you, you wrote in the sand, and now you write on a stone — why?" ⑤ He replied, "When someone hurts us, we should write it down in sand, where winds of forgiveness can erase it away. But, when someone does something good for us, we must write it in stone, where no wind can ever erase it."

▼ ▲ ▼ ▲ **"대명사가 가리키는 대상을 대입하여 읽어본다."**

해결 TIP

대명사는 명사를 대신한다. 따라서 이들이 가리키는 대상을 찾은 후에는 대명사 자리에 그 명사를 넣어 문맥이 자연스러운지 확인한다.

예시)

Trans fats are very dangerous, and ① they increase the total cholesterol level.
(트랜스 지방은 매우 위험하며, 그것들은 전체 콜레스테롤 수치를 높인다.)

① they는 Trans fats를 받는다.

다음 문장의 ② They 대신 Trans fats를 넣어서 읽어본다.

② They block up the blood vessels.
(그것들(트랜스 지방)은 혈관들을 막아버린다.)

문맥이 자연스러우므로 ①과 ②는 같은 대상을 지칭한다.

다음 문장도 같은 방식으로 읽어본다.

As a result, the bloodstream in ③ them is not smooth.
(그 결과 그것들(트랜스 지방) 속의 혈류가 부드럽지 않다.)

문맥이 자연스럽지 않다.

이때의 ③ them은 문맥상 앞 문장의 blood vessels를 대신한다. 따라서 ③은 ①, ②와는 다른 대상을 지칭한다.

150 **밑줄 친 부분이 가리키는 대상이 나머지 넷과 다른 것은?**

When Father was seventy he had cancer, and he was forced to stay in bed for half a year while his condition gradually got worse. Because of ① his age, surgery was not considered, and death became just a matter of time. Toward the end, for almost a month, we expected each day to be ② his last. My sisters, brother, and I took turns in caring for him in his last hours. The last time I visited Father the doctor told me ③ he would probably hold out for four or five more days, so I returned that night to my place to change my clothes. But when I got there the next morning, ④ he was announcing that he had just drawn his last breath. ⑤ He was said to be alert to the very end, giving detailed instructions about whom to notify of his death.

기출총정리

지칭 추론 해결 방법

1 대명사가 가리키는 대상을 찾아라.

여러 대명사 중 가리키는 대상이 다른 대명사를 고르는 문제는 각각의 대명사가 가리키는 바를 정확히 찾아야 한다.

대명사는 주로 앞뒤에 언급된 명사를 대신하여 쓰이므로 앞뒤에서 대명사의 성별과 수가 일치하는 것을 찾는다.

2 대명사가 가리키는 대상을 대입하여 읽어보라.

대명사가 가리키는 대상을 찾았다면 그 대상을 나머지 선택지에 있는 대명사 대신 넣어서 읽어보자. 문맥상 어색한 부분이 정답이다.

3 지칭 대상이 뒤에 있는 경우도 있다.

부사절에 쓰인 대명사의 경우, 뒤에 나오는 주절에 쓰인 대상을 받기도 하므로, 잘 살펴봐야 한다.

If **he** paid more attention in class, Luke would achieve better results.

If you want **them**, there are cookies on the table.

When **she** stops eating dinner, Jamie will take a walk.

Mini Test

정답 및 해설 p.125

● 밑줄 친 각 대명사가 가리키는 것을 〈보기〉에서 고르시오.

1 Dragons have the skin of a reptile, the body of an elephant, the head of a horse, and the tail of a lizard. (A) They are known to have many magical powers. One of (B) them is breathing fire. While in some stories dragons are good and wise, in others (C) they are evil monsters. [모의]

〈보기〉 ① dragons
② magical powers
③ some stories

(A): ________
(B): ________
(C): ________

2 A few years ago, while (A) they were setting up camp deep in the rain forest, Morgan and Sanz heard a party of chimpanzees vocalizing loudly in the distance. (B) They thought the chimpanzees were moving rapidly among trees. The chimpanzees were yelling louder, and (C) they seemed to be heading straight for the camp. [모의응용]

〈보기〉 ① Morgan and Sanz
② the chimpanzees
③ trees

(A): ________
(B): ________
(C): ________

실전적용독해

정답 및 해설 p.126

3문제를 4분 안에 풀어보세요.

151 밑줄 친 부분이 가리키는 대상이 나머지 넷과 다른 것은?

Working as a secretary at an international airport, my sister had an office next to the room where security temporarily holds suspects. One day a security officer was questioning ① a man when he was suddenly called away on another emergency. To the horror of my sister and her colleagues, ② he was left alone in the unlocked room. After a few minutes, the door opened and ③ he began to walk out. Gathering her courage, one of the secretaries yelled, "Get back in there, and don't you come out until you're told!" ④ He ran inside and shut the door loudly. When the security guard returned, the women reported what had happened. Without a word, ⑤ he walked into the room and released one frightened telephone repairman.

152 밑줄 친 him[his]이 가리키는 대상이 나머지 넷과 다른 것은?

Many Athenians felt that Socrates was dangerous and was deliberately going against the government. In 399 BC, when Socrates was 70 years old, one of them, Meletus, took ① him to court. Meletus claimed that Socrates was neglecting the Athenian gods, and introducing new gods of ② his own. Socrates was teaching the young men of Athens to behave badly, according to ③ him, encouraging them to turn against the authorities. True or not, these were very serious claims. Perhaps Socrates really did discourage ④ his students from following the state religion, and there is some evidence that he enjoyed demonstrating the flaws in Athenian democracy. That would have matched well with ⑤ his character. What is certainly true is that many Athenians believed the charges.

153 밑줄 친 부분이 가리키는 대상이 나머지 넷과 다른 것은?

When I begin to write I always find there is one character who refuses to come alive. There is nothing psychologically false about ① him, but it takes great effort to find words for him. All the technical skill I have acquired through the years has to be employed in making ② him appear alive to my readers. Sometimes I get a sour satisfaction when a famous reviewer praises ③ him as the best-written character in the story. I'm left wondering how ④ he could somehow be unable to see the complete awkwardness of this character. This character lies heavily on my mind whenever I start to work like an ill-digested meal on the stomach, robbing me of the pleasure of creation in any scene where ⑤ he is present.

VOCAbulary 어휘확인

151 security 보안 요원(= security officer, security guard) temporarily 임시로 hold (사람을) 유치하다 suspect 용의자 question 심문하다 release 풀어 주다 repairman 수리공 152 deliberately 의도적으로 go against ~에 저항하다 claim 주장하다; 주장 neglect 등한시하다; 방치하다 behave 행동하다 turn against ~에게 등을 돌리다 authorities 정부 discourage 막다 evidence 증거 demonstrate 입증하다 flaw 결함 democracy 민주주의 charge 고발; 요금 153 psychologically 심리학적으로 employ 쓰다, 소비하다 satisfaction 만족(감) awkwardness 어색함 ill-digested 제대로 소화되지 않은 rob A of B A에게 B를 빼앗다 scene 장면 present 존재하는

유형 14 세부 내용 파악

이렇게 출제된다.
글을 읽고 세부사항이 선택지의 내용과 일치하는지 파악하는 유형이다. 설명문, 전기 형식의 글에서 내용 일치 혹은 불일치를 묻는 문제가 1문항 출제된다.

지시문은 이렇게
Taiwan 기차 여행에 관한 다음 글의 내용과 일치하지 않는 것은?
American lobster에 관한 다음 글의 내용과 일치하지 않는 것은?
Wangari Maathai에 관한 다음 글의 내용과 일치하는 것은?

정답 및 해설 p.128

Check-Up 1

[1 - 3] traveler's palm에 관한 우리말 설명이 영문과 일치하면 ○, 아니면 ×를 고르시오.

1 The traveler's palm is a species of plant native to the island of Madagascar, which is off the coast of east Africa in the Indian Ocean.
마다가스카르 섬이 원산지인 식물이다. (○ / ×)

2 It has been given the name "traveler's palm" because its long stems with green leaves on the top of them extend out from the trunk like a giant hand fan.
이름은 줄기들이 큰 부채 모양으로 뻗은 모양과 관련이 있다. (○ / ×)

3 It thrives and grows best in full sun, so it requires a lot of light, especially when grown indoors.
햇빛이 많은 곳보다 그늘진 곳에서 더 잘 자란다. (○ / ×)

해결 전략 1 **선택지를 먼저 읽고 순서대로 본문과 대조하며 정답을 고른다.**
글과 선택지의 내용이 일치하는지 판단하는 문제이므로 선택지를 먼저 읽고 해당 내용이 나오는 곳을 찾아 빨리 읽어 내려가는 것이 효율적이다. 보통은 본문에서 설명된 순서대로 선택지가 제시되므로 해당하는 내용의 단서를 본문에서 찾도록 한다. 확인한 내용은 선택지 옆에 ○, × 등으로 표시해 놓는 것이 좋다.

154 **Taiwan 기차 여행에 관한 다음 글의 내용과 일치하지 않는 것은?**

Taiwan is an easy country to visit as an independent traveler, and this train tour gives a fine introduction to the best the country has to offer. Beginning with a full-day exploration of the capital city of Taipei, this 9 nights and 10 days tour takes full advantage of the country's excellent railway network. On your journey to Pingxi to experience the city's spectacular Lantern Festival — the biggest event of Taiwan's calendar year — you will make stops at numerous points of interest. Highlights include a stop in Neiwan for traditional Hakka cuisine and one in Tainan, the historic former capital. You'll also view an unforgettable sunrise from the Alishan Mountain Railway, which was originally built to transport logs from the forest but now carries thousands of tourists each year.

*cuisine 요리(법)

① Taipei 관광을 포함한다.
② 9박 10일 일정의 코스이다.
③ Pingxi에서 열리는 등불 축제에 간다.
④ Hakka와 Tainan 전통 요리를 맛본다.
⑤ 해돋이 관광을 포함한다.

Check-Up 2

선택지를 구성하는 원리를 알아두라.

해결 전략 2

내용 일치 문제는 선택지 구성의 특징을 알아두면 좀 더 쉽게 풀 수 있다. 오답 선택지는 주로 본문의 내용과 반대가 되는 표현을 사용하거나 일부 단어를 바꿔 만든다.

p.128 기출총정리 참조

Check-Up 3

지시문을 읽고 내용 '일치'인지 '불일치'인지 정확하게 파악하라.

해결 전략 3

선택지와 본문의 내용이 '일치'하는 것을 고르는 문제인지 '불일치'하는 것을 고르는 문제인지 반드시 확인한다. 지시문을 잘못 이해하면 아는 문제도 틀릴 수 있으니 주의한다.

155 American lobster에 관한 다음 글의 내용과 일치하지 않는 것은?

The American lobster is a large-bodied lobster, and a commercially targeted sea species. It reaches weights of at least 45 pounds (20 kg). Along with crabs and other lobsters, the American lobster has ten legs, and it is covered with a hard shell that provides it with some protection from other animals. The American lobster's front legs are modified into very large claws. The two claws are slightly different from each other, with one being stronger (used for crushing) while the other is sharper (used for cutting). During the day, American lobsters remain in hiding places along rocky ocean shores. During the evening hours and at night, individuals are much more active and search along the shore for a variety of foods, including rotting organic matter, and some algae.

*algae 해조류, 해초

① 상업적인 목적으로 이용된다.
② 적어도 20kg의 무게에 달한다.
③ 두 개의 똑같은 집게발을 가지고 있다.
④ 낮에는 암초에 몸을 숨긴 채로 있다.
⑤ 저녁과 밤 시간에 먹이를 찾아 활동한다.

156 Wangari Maathai에 관한 다음 글의 내용과 일치하는 것은?

Wangari Maathai was an internationally renowned Kenyan scientist. Having earned degrees from two U.S. colleges, she returned to Kenya and earned her PhD from the University of Nairobi, and then worked as a professor in their department of veterinary medicine. In 1976, Maathai began promoting a tree-planting program to save forests and provide firewood for Kenyan women. Soon known as the Green Belt Movement, the program led to the planting of millions of trees. In 1997, she ran unsuccessfully for president and for a seat in Parliament, but in December of 2002 she was elected to Parliament, and in 2003 she was appointed to the Ministry of Environment, Natural Resources, and Wildlife. She won the Nobel Peace Prize in 2004, with the Nobel committee praising "her contribution to environmentally-friendly development, democracy, and peace." She was the first African woman to win a Nobel Prize.

*veterinary medicine 수의학

① 미국에서 대학교수로 재직했다.
② 아프리카에서 수의사로 일했다.
③ 그린벨트 운동으로 알려진 사회운동을 전개했다.
④ 공직에 야망이 있었으나 뜻을 이루지 못했다.
⑤ 노벨상을 수상한 최초의 여성이다.

기출총정리

출제자의 정답·오답 구성 원리 살짝 넘보기

내용 일치 유형의 선택지는 다음과 같은 원리로 만들어진다.

1 본문 해석을 살짝 바꿔 정답으로 만든다.

- It is not native to Jamaica but was imported from West Africa around 1778, and was probably transported by slave ships. [모의]
  18세기경 자메이카에 들어왔다. (O)
  ☞ '1778년쯤'을 '18세기경'으로 바꿔서 표현했다.

- The fish use their light-producing organs to signal one another. [모의]
  물고기의 발광기관은 **의사소통**에 사용된다. (O)
  ☞ 물고기가 서로에게 신호를 보내는 것을 '의사소통'으로 바꿔서 표현했다.

- There she rode a horse along mountain cliffs to distant villages, looking for blind children for her school. [모의]
  직접 학생들을 **모집**하러 다녔다. (O)
  ☞ 그녀가 말을 타고 학교 학생들을 찾으러 다녔다고 했으므로 '직접' 학생들을 '모집'하러 다녔다는 것은 맞다.

2 반대의 내용을 오답으로 만든다.

- Its population is on the decline due to the harvesting of their beautiful shells. [모의]
  개체수가 점점 **늘어나는** 추세이다. (×)
  개체수가 점점 **줄어드는** 추세이다. (O)

- The Nile flooded every year, and they could get good harvests and wealth. [모의응용]
  매년 강이 범람하여 농사를 지을 수 **없었다**. (×)
  매년 강이 범람했고 그들은 **풍작**과 부를 얻을 수 있었다. (O)

3 일부 단어만 바꿔서 오답을 만든다.

- She gave up music in the 1970s because she was unable to make a living. [모의]
  생계를 유지할 수가 없어서 **1985년에** 음악을 그만두었다. (×)
  생계를 유지할 수가 없어서 **1970년대에** 음악을 그만 두었다. (O)

- Much of James's work deals with the contrast in values of Americans and Europeans. [모의]
  동서양의 가치관 차이가 주된 관심사였다. (×)
  미국인과 유럽인의 가치관 차이가 주된 관심사였다. (O)

4 잘못 해석하기 쉽거나 복잡한 구문이 있는 문장을 문제화한다.

- Even the biggest are **no more than** 6 inches long. [모의]
  크기는 평균 6인치 이상이다. (×)
  크기는 기껏해야 6인치이다. (O)
  ☞ 〈no more than〉은 only의 뜻으로 '겨우, 단지'라는 뜻이다. 가장 큰 것도 '겨우' 6인치이므로 커봤자 기껏 6인치라는 설명은 맞다.

- My classes **don't** begin **until** Monday morning. [모의]
  월요일 아침에는 수업이 없다. (×)
  월요일 아침에 수업이 시작된다. (O)
  ☞ 〈not A until B〉는 'B하기 전까지 A하지 않다', 즉 'B해서야 비로소 A하다'라는 뜻이다. 월요일 아침이 되어서야 비로소 수업이 시작된다는 의미이다.

- H. Mephisto is a kind of roundworm living deep underground on Earth. It only measures from 0.52 to 0.56 millimeters in length, which may sound small, but it is millions of times bigger than **the bacteria it feeds on**. [모의응용]
  자신보다 **몸집이 큰 박테리아**를 먹는다. (×)
  그것은 **그것이 먹고 사는 박테리아보다** 수백만 배 더 크다. (O)
  ☞ 밑줄 친 문장의 it은 모두 H. Mephisto를 가리킨다. 〈배수사 비교급 than …〉은 '…보다 몇 배 더 ~한/하게'를 의미하며, the bacteria와 it 사이에는 전치사 on의 목적어인 목적격 관계대명사 which나 that이 생략되었다.

5 서로 다른 두 가지 사항의 관련 내용을 바꿔 연결하여 오답으로 만든다.

- Warthogs have poor eyesight, but excellent senses of smell and hearing. [모의]
  시력은 좋지만 청력은 좋지 않다. (×)
  시력은 좋지 않지만 청력은 좋다. (O)
  ☞ 좋지 않은 것과 좋은 것을 잘못 연결하였다.

- When a young chambered nautilus first hatches from its egg, it is about an inch in diameter and has a shell with seven chambers. [모의]
  부화했을 때의 지름은 약 **7인치**이다. (×)
  부화했을 때의 지름은 약 **1인치**이다. (O)
  ☞ 지름이 7인치가 아니라 7개의 방이 있는 껍질을 지니고 있다.

실전적용독해

3문제를 4분 안에 풀어보세요.

정답 및 해설 p.130

157 hummingbirds에 관한 다음 글의 내용과 일치하는 것은?

Hummingbirds are very small birds which are native to the Americas and the western hemisphere. They were given the name "hummingbird" because of the easily recognizable humming sound their wings make when they fly. The bee hummingbird is the world's smallest bird. It is only five centimeters long and weighs about 1.8 grams, which is about the same weight as a penny. Most hummingbirds migrate north in the early spring and return south in the early fall. They have a lifespan of nine to twelve years. Hummingbirds are very curious and aggressive with each other. One of the best-known facts about hummingbirds is that they can fly backwards. No other bird in the world can do this.

① 가장 작은 것은 크기가 동전만 하다.
② 초봄부터 초가을까지는 남쪽에 산다.
③ 다 자라려면 9~12년이 걸린다.
④ 온순한 성격으로 떼 지어 다닌다.
⑤ 유일하게 뒤로 날 수 있는 새다.

158 voyageurs에 관한 다음 글의 내용과 일치하지 않는 것은?

The story of the voyageurs is a colorful feature of Canadian history that is celebrated to this day. Voyageur means "traveler" in French, and many of the voyageurs were of French descent. They were men who made their living in the 18th century transporting goods to distant parts of Canada by canoe. Among the goods they transported, the vast majority were furs that would be sold in the larger cities, such as Montreal. Voyageurs had to be strong and courageous, since they canoed through vast wilderness. They were also cheerful, optimistic, and fun-loving men with a sense of humor. But eventually the railroad replaced the canoe as the most efficient and inexpensive way to transport goods, and voyageurs soon disappeared.

*voyageur 보이저(캐나다의 뱃사공) **canoe 카누; 카누로 가다

① 대부분은 프랑스인의 후손들이다.
② 카누를 타고 캐나다에서 무역을 했다.
③ 거친 환경에서 생활하는 강인한 사람들이었다.
④ 성격이 활기차고 긍정적인 사람들이었다.
⑤ 카누가 철도를 대체하면서 호황을 누렸다.

159 George Eyser에 관한 다음 글의 내용과 일치하지 않는 것은?

George Eyser was born in Germany in 1870 and emigrated to the St. Louis area at age fourteen. Sometime during his adolescence, he lost his left leg after being hit by a train. He was outfitted with a wooden leg, which allowed him to run and jump. If you were German, gymnastics was part and parcel of the St. Louis community experience, and Eyser's lack of a left leg did not change this at all. Eyser's experience as a gymnast paid off. Even though the competitors in the 1904 Olympics were ranked as amateurs, Eyser dominated. He took gold medals on the parallel bars, vault, and in the rope climb.

*gymnastics 체조, 체육 **part and parcel 중요 부분, 요점

① 14세에 St. Louis로 이민 왔다.
② 열차 사고로 한쪽 다리를 잃었다.
③ 나무로 된 의족에 의지한 채 운동했다.
④ 체조가 인기 있던 지역에서 성장했다.
⑤ 쟁쟁한 프로 선수들을 이기고 금메달을 땄다.

VOCAbulary 어휘확인

157 **native** 원산(지)의 **hemisphere** (지구의) 반구 **recognizable** 쉽게 알 수 있는 **humming** 윙윙거리는 **penny** 페니(영국의 동전 단위) **migrate** 이동하다 **lifespan** 수명 **curious** 호기심이 강한 **aggressive** 공격적인 158 **descent** 혈통, 가문 **make one's living** 생계를 꾸리다 **transport** 수송하다; 수송 **vast** 엄청난[방대한] **majority** 다수 **courageous** 용감한 **wilderness** 황무지, 황야 **optimistic** 낙천적인 **railroad** 철도 **inexpensive** 저렴한, 비싸지 않은 159 **emigrate** 이민을 가다 **adolescence** 청소년기 **outfit** (복장·장비를) 갖추어 주다 **gymnastics** 체조, 체육 **part and parcel** 중요 부분 **gymnast** 체조 선수 **pay off** 성과를 올리다 **competitor** (시합) 참가자; 경쟁자 **rank** (등급·등위·순서를) 평가하다 **amateur** 아마추어 선수 **dominate** (경기에서) 압도하다; 지배하다 **parallel bars** 평행봉 **vault** ((체조)) 도마 **rope climb** 밧줄 타기

유형 15 실용 자료 파악

이렇게 출제된다.
실용문을 읽고 세부사항이 선택지의 내용과 일치하는지 파악하는 유형으로 약 2문항씩 출제된다. 실용문으로는 주로 안내문, 공고문 등이 제시된다.

지시문은 이렇게
다음 구인광고의 내용과 일치하지 않는 것은?
It's a Bug's World에 관한 다음 안내문의 내용과 일치하지 않는 것은?

정답 및 해설 p.132

Check-Up 1

[1 - 4] 다음 1~4의 내용 일치 여부 확인을 위해 읽어야 할 부분의 소제목을 골라 그 기호를 쓰시오.

Ⓐ **Activities**
Tree houses, jungle bridges, storytelling, boat trips, building animal houses, going down the slippery slope, and marsh walks

Ⓑ **Times**
• From the beginning of April through to the end of October
• From 10 a.m. to 5 p.m.

Ⓒ **Admission Rates**
Aged under 6 years …… Free
Aged 6-14 years …… $10.00
Aged 15-65 years …… $13.00
Aged over 65 years …… $7.50
• Group rates: $7.00 per person (group of 12 or more)

Ⓓ **Foods & Drinks**
You can bring your own food.
We have a restaurant and two refreshment stands.

1 보트 여행과 동물 집짓기 활동을 할 수 있다. (　　)
2 4월부터 10월까지 운영된다. (　　)
3 단체 요금을 적용받으면 1인당 7달러이다. (　　)
4 음식 반입이 허용되지 않는다. (　　)

해결 전략 1 **선택지와 소제목을 십분 활용한다.**
모든 문장을 샅샅이 읽을 필요가 없다. 실용문의 경우 이미 글에 소제목으로 내용이 잘 구분되어 있는 경우가 많으므로 선택지를 먼저 읽고 해당 소제목을 찾아 그 내용을 빠르게 훑어 확인한다.

해결 TIP **실용문은 구체적인 내용은 다를지라도 대개 비슷한 내용이 필수적으로 등장한다.**
이를테면, 행사 참가를 안내하는 안내문의 경우, 행사의 소개, 일시, 비용, 참가 대상, 등록, 추가 정보 등의 내용으로 구성되는데, 이러한 각 내용을 표현하는 어구들 역시 일정하게 정해져 있기 마련이다. 그러므로 실용문 대비를 위해서는 빈출 어구들을 미리 정리해 두는 것이 효과적이다.
p.132 기출총정리 참조

160 다음 구인광고의 내용과 일치하지 않는 것은?

Job Title: Temporary Assistant Teacher
Location: Henrico, VA, US
Organization Name: HCPS(Henrico County Public Schools)

Essential Duties
– Plan instructional activities for students
– Assess and maintain records of students' progress
– Utilize a variety of instructional strategies in order to promote student success

Minimum Qualifications
Bachelor's Degree required.

Additional Information
$83.84/per day
This vacancy is open until filled.

FOR SPECIFIC QUESTIONS ABOUT THIS POSITION PLEASE CONTACT HCPS at 804-795-7030.

How To Apply
To be considered for this position, please mail written references and college transcripts to:

Henrico County Public Schools
Department of Human Resources
P.O. Box 23120
3820 Nine Mile Road
Henrico, VA 23223-0420

① 임시 보조 교사를 구하는 것이다.
② 업무에는 학생 성적 평가가 포함된다.
③ 학사 학위 이상인 자가 지원 가능하다.
④ 마감일 없이 상시 지원 가능하다.
⑤ 제출 서류는 우편으로 우송해야 한다.

Check-Up 2

순서대로 풀어라.

해결 전략 2

선택지의 정오를 판단할 수 있는 지문 내의 단서는 선택지 순서와 대개 일치한다. 따라서 선택지의 순서대로 지문에서 단서를 찾아나가면 쉽게 일치/불일치 여부를 판별할 수 있다. 이때 절대 실수하지 않도록 주의해야 한다. 오답 선택지는 주로 본문의 내용과 반대되는 표현을 사용하거나 일부 단어를 바꿔 만든다. 또한 선택지가 본문에 명시되어 있지 않아 세어봐야 하거나 간단한 계산을 해야 할 경우에 유의한다.

p.132 기출총정리 참조

161 It's a Bug's World에 관한 다음 안내문의 내용과 일치하지 않는 것은?

It's a Bug's World

It's a Bug's World is turning Shortstown Village Hall into a jungle this April!

When: 22 April 2017 10:00 ~ 13:00
Where: Shortstown Village Hall, Shortstown, Bedford

This FREE informal, educational exhibition is an exciting opportunity to meet face to face with a wide variety of exotic insects and see for yourselves that, despite their reputation, they're not scary at all.

- Animal handling experiences available with their keepers
- Items for sale, such as animal equipment and other related, animal-themed goods
- Information and interactive activities to get you inspired
- Qualified and experienced keepers will answer your questions.

Parking is restricted at the Village Hall, and it is requested that local residents walk to the event.

① 3시간 동안 단 1회 진행되는 행사이다.
② 참가비는 무료이다.
③ 동물을 직접 만져 볼 수 있다.
④ 전문 사육사에게 사육 관련 내용을 질의할 수 있다.
⑤ 주차장이 따로 없어 주차는 불가능하다.

기출총정리

실용문에 꼭 나오는 필수 빈출 어구만 모았다!

1 각종 안내문, 공지문, 공고문 (행사, 모임, 대회, 전시 등)

1. 일정
hours, office hours (영업) 시간
duration, period 기간
times 기간
dates 날짜
event schedule 행사 일정

2. 활동
activities 활동
be held 열리다, 거행되다
experience 경험
highlights 하이라이트, 가장 좋은[흥미로운] 부분

3. 장소
location 장소, 위치

4. 등록 및 제출
register 등록하다 (registration, entry application 등록)
submit 제출하다 (submit in person 직접 제출하다 / submit via e-mail 이메일로 제출하다)
attend, participate 참가하다
participant 참가자 / applicant 지원자 / candidate 지원자, 후보자
application form 신청서 / recommendation 추천(서)
registration period 신청 기간
qualification 자격
submission period 제출 기한 / deadline 기한, 마감 일자
in advance 미리, 먼저
additional[detailed] information 부가적[자세한] 정보

2 기타 각종 서신, 이메일 등 (각종 실생활, 의식주, 여가활동 등 관련)

1. 여행
make a reservation for / reserve / book 예약하다
visa cost 비자 발급 비용
international airfare 국제선 항공료
travel insurance 여행자 보험

2. 숙박
accommodation 숙박, 거처
comforts, facilities 편의 시설
shuttle bus service 셔틀 버스 서비스
pick up 픽업하다, 마중가다
free welcome beverage 무료 환영 음료

3. 식(食)
food and drinks 음식물
refreshment 다과

4. 여가, 문화 활동
art museum 미술관 (exhibition 전시회)
hours of operation 개장 시간 (opening 개장 / closing 폐장)
guide and interpretation service 가이드 및 통역 서비스
parking 주차
check-out and return (도서관) 대출 및 반납
fully equipped 완비된, 다 갖춰진
available on a first-come basis 선착순 판매[이용]

5. 각종 지불 관련
cost 비용 / price 비용, 가격
entry fee 입장료 / admission[entrance] fee[rate] 입장료
general admission 일반 요금
group rates 단체 요금
discounted admission 할인 요금
special rates 특별 요금
senior citizen / elderly people 노인
children under ~ ~세 미만의 어린이
aged under[over] ~ ~세 이하[이상]의
low season discounts 비수기 할인
refundable 환불 가능한 (non-refundable 환불 불가능한)
off 할인되는 / bargain, discount 가격을 인하하다

6. 약
pill 알약 (tablet 정제 / ointment 연고)
take medicine 약을 복용하다 (medication 약, 투약(법))
apply medication 약[연고 등]을 바르다
external use 외용 (internal use 내복)
dose, dosage (보통 약의) 복용량, 투여량
instruction 지시, 지도
direct (의사가) 지시[지도]하다

실전적용독해

2문제를 2분 40초 안에 풀어보세요.

정답 및 해설 p.134

162 Kristin School IB World School에 관한 다음 안내문의 내용과 일치하는 것은?

> **Kristin School IB World School**
>
> A private, co-educational day school for grades K—13 (ages 4—18).
>
> Our mission:
> To provide our students with a superior all-round education and to prepare them to be responsible world citizens who think creatively, reason critically, communicate effectively, and learn enthusiastically throughout life.
>
> Located in Albany on Auckland's North Shore (30 minutes from downtown Auckland and 50 minutes from Auckland International Airport)
> Ratio of teaching staff to students: 1:10
> Percentage of international students: 3%
> Academic Year:
> Late January—first week of December
> Study breaks/holidays of 2—3 weeks each in April, July, and September.

① 공립학교로서 남녀 공학이다.
② Auckland 시내에서 30분 거리이다.
③ 한 반 평균 인원이 10명이다.
④ 학사 일정은 1월 초에서 12월 초이다.
⑤ 1년에 총 2~3주의 단기방학이 있다.

163 Take Me Away에 관한 다음 안내문의 내용과 일치하지 않는 것은?

> **Take Me Away**
> Throughout history, writers have created imaginary worlds. Now it's your turn to take us away to a land of make-believe.
>
> **Here's how**
> Create an imaginary world with distinct features and landmarks. Then write a short story or a poem set in this imaginary place. You can include an illustration of your imaginary world. Four winners will be selected by our guest judge. Winning entries will be published in the April issue of *Write Now*.
>
> **Rules to Know**
> - The contest is open to students in grades 5—12.
> - Poems should not exceed 400 words, and stories should be no longer than 800 words.
> - All entries must be postmarked by Dec. 20, 2017.
> - Mail contest entries to: *Write Now* Magazine "Take Me Away" 200 First Stamford Place, P.O. Box 1200 Stamford, CT 069-0024

① 판타지 장르의 글쓰기 대회 안내문이다.
② 선정된 글은 4월호 잡지에 실린다.
③ 4학년은 제출할 수 없다.
④ 모든 글은 400~800단어여야 한다.
⑤ 우편 발송을 해야 한다.

VOCAbulary 어휘확인

162 **private** 사립의 **co-educational** 남녀 공학의 **day school** 통학 학교(기숙학교와 대조적으로 학생들이 집에서 다니는 사립학교) **mission** 임무 **superior** 우수한 **all-round** 다방면의, 전반적인 **reason** 추론하다, 논하다 **critically** 비판[비평]적으로; 혹평하여 **enthusiastically** 열정적으로 **ratio** 비율 **academic year** 학년 163 **take A away (to B)** A를 (B로) 멀리 데리고 가다 **imaginary** 가상의 **make-believe** 상상, 환상 **landmark** 랜드마크(멀리서 보고 위치 파악에 도움이 되는 대형 건물 같은 것) **illustration** 삽화 **entry** 출품작; 입장 **issue** (잡지·신문 같은 정기 간행물의) 호; 주제 **open to A** A가 참여할 수 있는 **exceed** 초과하다 **postmark** 우편물의 소인을 찍다

유형 16 도표 자료 파악

이렇게 출제된다.
도표를 설명하는 지문의 내용이 도표와 일치하는지 묻는 유형이다. 1문항씩 출제되며 막대, 꺾은선, 파이 그래프 등 다양한 형태의 도표가 나온다.

지시문은 이렇게
다음 도표의 내용과 일치하지 않는 것[문장]은?

정답 및 해설 p.136

Check-Up 1

[1 - 2] 다음 문장을 읽고, 164번의 도표와 일치하면 O, 아니면 ×를 고르시오.

1 The number of immigrants to the U.S. rose dramatically between 1891 and 1901. (O / ×)

2 The number of immigrants to Canada surpassed the U.S. figures after 1910. (O / ×)

해결 전략 지문 내용을 도표에서 찾아 꼼꼼히 비교한다.
지문을 읽고 각 문장의 설명이 도표에 나타난 내용과 일치하는지 하나씩 확인한다. 확인한 내용은 선택지 번호 옆에 O, × 등으로 표시를 하면서 읽도록 하자.

해결 TIP "무엇에 관한 도표인지 파악하라."
도표의 제목과 지문의 도입 부분은 도표의 기본 정보를 담고 있으므로 먼저 읽으면 도표를 이해하는 데 도움이 된다.
p.135 기출총정리 1 참조

해결 TIP "비교, 증감 표현 등에 주의하자."
도표에서 문제화되는 부분은 대개 수치가 크게 변화하는 부분이거나 최고점, 최저점이다. 이를 나타내는 다양한 표현을 알아두자.
p.135, 136 기출총정리 2, 3 참조

164 다음 도표의 내용과 일치하지 않는 것은?

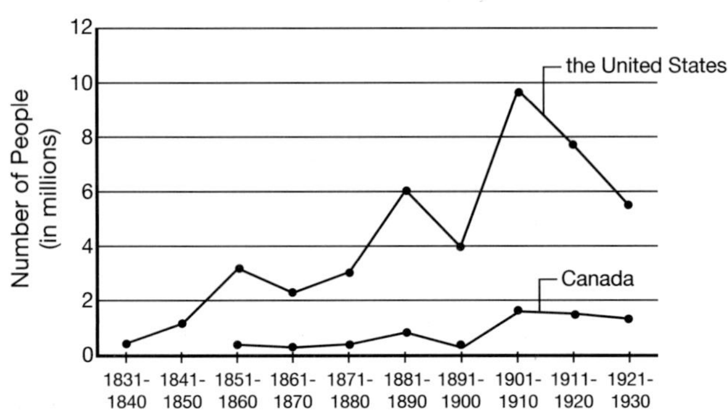

The chart above shows the immigration trends of the United States and Canada during the years 1831 — 1930. ① The number of immigrants to the U.S. reached its peak during the period from 1901 — 1910, which was the same with Canada. ② After 1910, the number of immigrants to the U.S. began to drop, falling to less than 6 million in the 1921 — 1930 period. ③ The number of immigrants to Canada was comparatively smaller than that of the U.S. in all periods, but it continued to increase until 1910, when it started to decline. ④ The number of immigrants to the U.S. when it reached its peak was more than five times bigger than that to Canada in its peak. ⑤ Canada never saw its number of immigrants go beyond 2 million during the given periods.

기출총정리

도표 이해가 쉬워지는 표현 정리

1 도표를 개략적으로 이해하기

도표의 제목과 도입 부분을 읽고 도표를 이해하는 것이 우선이다.

▪ 무엇에 관한 도표인가?

한국에서 선호되는 교통수단의 변화 (Change in Preferred Means of Transportation in Korea)를 나타내는 그래프이다. 2001년과 2010년에 해당하는 다섯 개의 교통수단 (자동차, 버스, 기차, 비행기, 배)에 대한 선호도가 제시된다. 제목에서 우선 소개되고, 글의 도입 부분에서 이 내용이 다시 한 번 설명되고 있다.

☞ **이처럼 도표의 제목과 글의 도입 부분을 통해 무엇에 관한 도표인지 파악할 수 있다.**

[도표의 제목]

Change in Preferred Means of Transportation in Korea

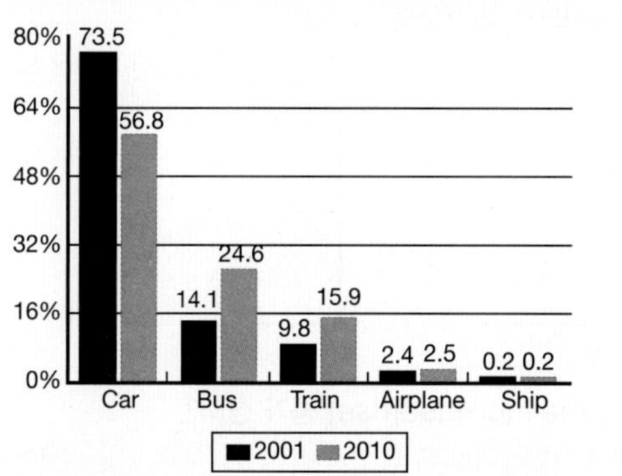

[모의]

[글의 도입부]

The above graph shows the change in preferred means of transportation in Korea that passengers used in 2001 and 2010.

2 비교, 배수, 분수 표현 이해하기

도표는 수치를 그림으로 나타낸 것이므로 지문에는 주로 비교나 배수, 분수 표현이 등장하여 그래프의 수치를 설명한다.

▪ **최상급 표현**

최상급은 형용사나 부사 뒤에 -est를 붙이거나 앞에 most나 least를 붙여서 만든다.

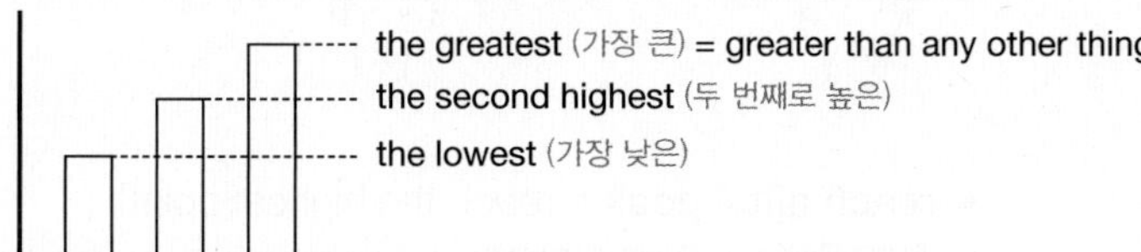

▪ **비교, 배수 표현**

비교급은 형용사나 부사 뒤에 -er를 붙이거나 앞에 more나 less를 붙여서 만든다.

〈숫자 + times〉는 '몇 배'란 뜻으로 〈비교급 than ~〉이나 〈as ~ as …〉와 함께 쓰이는 배수 표현이다.

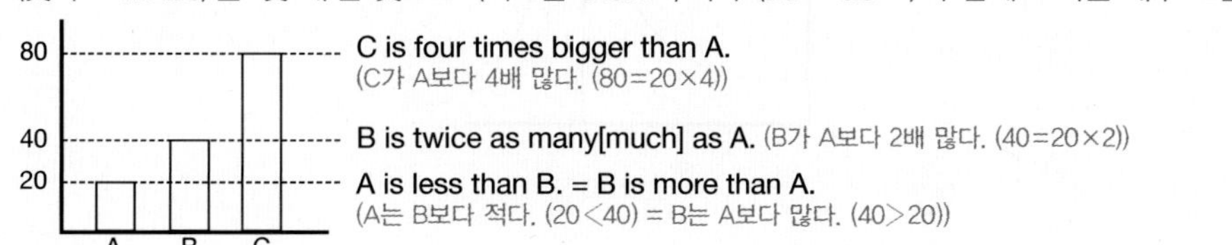

80
40
20
A
B
C
C is four times bigger than A.
(C가 A보다 4배 많다. (80=20×4))
B is twice as many[much] as A. (B가 A보다 2배 많다. (40=20×2))
A is less than B. = B is more than A.
(A는 B보다 적다. (20<40) = B는 A보다 많다. (40>20))

cf. double 두 배가 되다
triple 세 배가 되다

▪ **분수 표현**

분자는 기수, 분모는 서수를 사용하여 분수를 만드는데 이것은 %로 나타낼 수도 있다. 〈A out of B〉는 'B 중에 A'란 뜻으로 똑같이 %로 나타낼 수 있다.

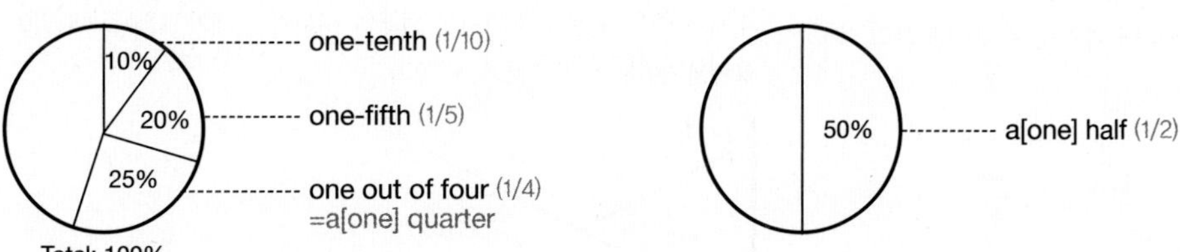

cf. **account for** (부분·비율을) 차지하다 = take proportion

Ships in 2010 **accounted for** the same percentage as in 2001. [모의]

3 증감 표현 이해하기

도표에서는 증감 표현이 문제화되는 경우가 많은데 부사를 이용한 표현이 자주 등장한다.

▪ **continuously increase** = continue to increase, showed a consistent increase
지속적으로 증가하다

그래프의 해당 구간이 한 번도 하락하지 않고 상승한 경우에 쓰는 표현이다.

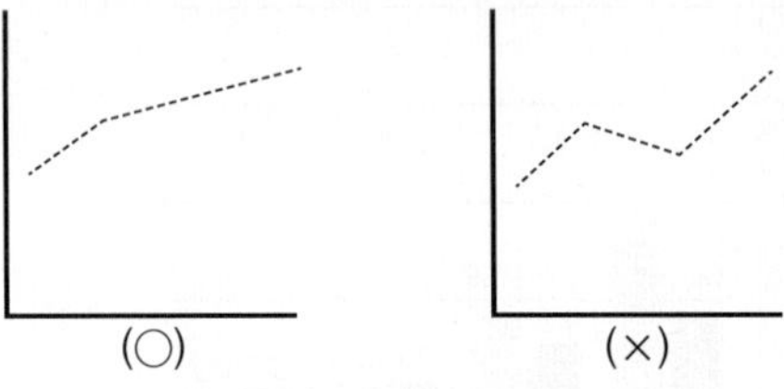

(○) (×)

cf. **on the increase[rise] 증가 상태인**

수치가 꾸준히는 아니더라도 전체적으로 증가세에 있을 경우에 쓴다.

▪ **steadily[continuously] decrease[decline]**
= show a decrease, generally decrease
서서히 줄어들다

그래프의 해당 구간이 한 번도 상승하지 않고 꾸준히 감소한 경우에 위와 같은 표현을 쓴다.

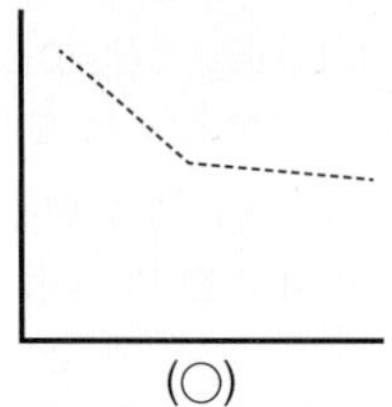

(○)

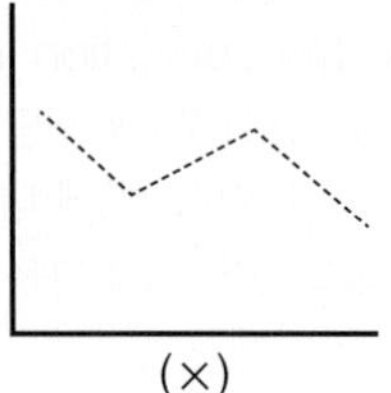

(×)

cf. **on the decrease 감소 상태인**

수치가 꾸준히는 아니더라도 전체적으로 감소세에 있을 경우에 쓴다.

▪ **rise dramatically[sharply, drastically]**
급격히 증가하다

그래프의 수치가 급격하게 증가한 부분이 있는 경우에 사용하는 표현이다. 왼쪽 도표의 C와 D 사이처럼 수치가 급격히 늘어난 경우에 쓴다.

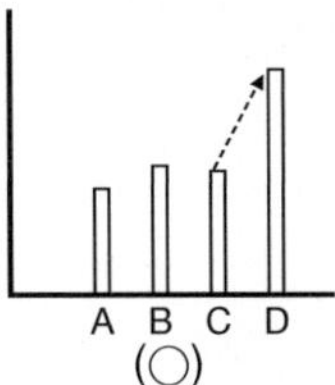

(○)

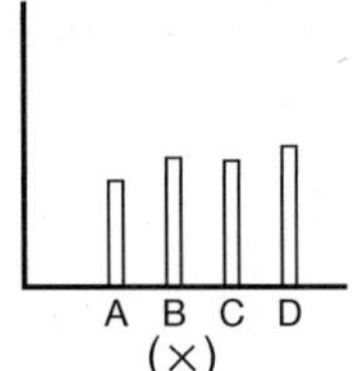

(×)

▪ **slightly more than**
약간 더 많은

두 수치의 차이가 다른 수치의 차이에 비해 상대적으로 매우 작을 때 사용하는 표현이다.

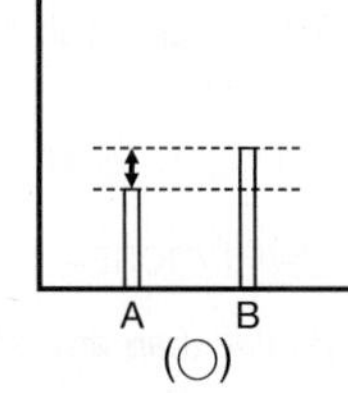

(○)

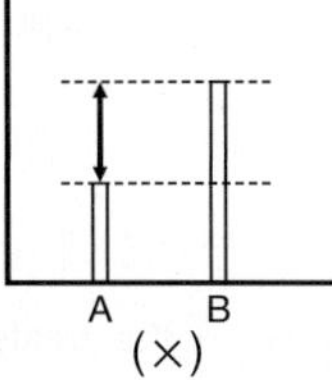

(×)

▪ **decrease the most**
가장 많이 줄다

수치 변화가 가장 큰 것은 C와 D 사이인데 이때 위와 같은 표현을 쓴다.

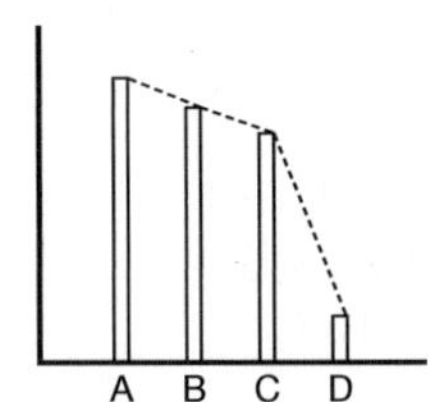

▪ **reach a[its] peak** = reach the highest[point]
최고점[최고 수준]에 다다르다

수치가 증가하다가 최고점에 다다랐을 때 위와 같은 표현을 쓴다.

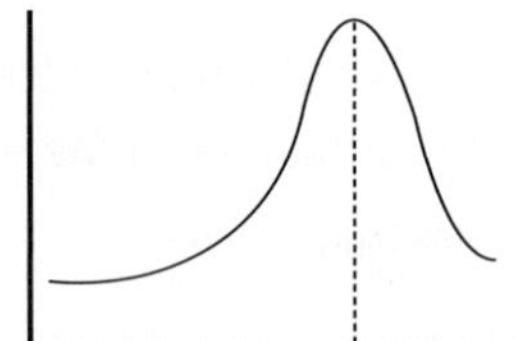

4 여러 개의 수치를 비교하기

▪ **surpass 능가하다, 뛰어넘다** = exceed **초과하다**

수치가 증가하면서 다른 수치를 뛰어넘었을 때 위와 같은 표현을 쓴다.

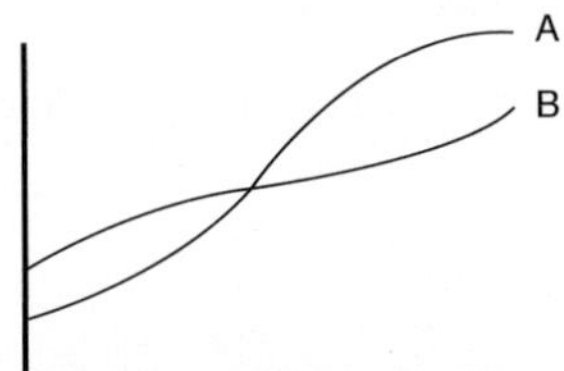

▪ **reverse 역전되다**

수치가 증가 또는 감소하면서 원래의 상황과 반대가 되었을 때 위와 같은 표현을 쓴다.

Mini Test

정답 및 해설 p.137

[1 - 8] 다음 문장이 도표와 일치하면 ○, 아니면 ×를 고르시오.

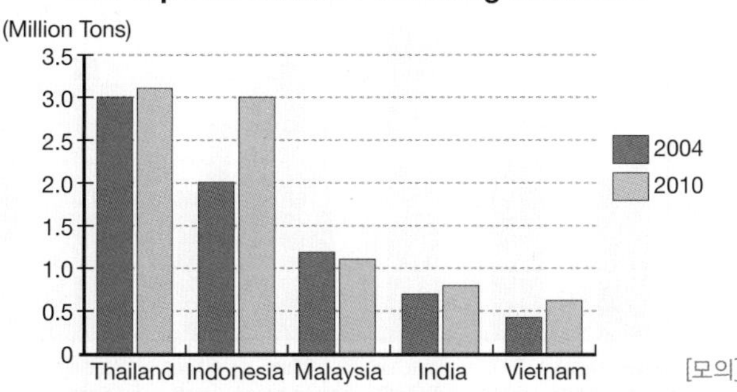

1 Of the five countries above, Thailand was the largest producer of rubber in both years. (○ / ×)

2 The amount of rubber produced by Thailand was larger than that of any other country in both years. (○ / ×)

3 Indonesia was the second largest producer of rubber only in 2010. (○ / ×)

4 Malaysia produced more rubber than India in both 2004 and 2010. (○ / ×)

5 India and Vietnam both showed a slight decrease in 2010 from 2004. (○ / ×)

6 As Malaysia's did in 2010, India's production also slightly declined. (○ / ×)

7 Vietnam produced the least amount of rubber among the five countries both in 2004 and 2010. (○ / ×)

8 The amount of rubber produced by Indonesia in 2004 was about three times as large as that of Vietnam in the same year. (○ / ×)

[9 - 12] 다음 도표를 보고 네모 안에서 알맞은 것을 고르시오.

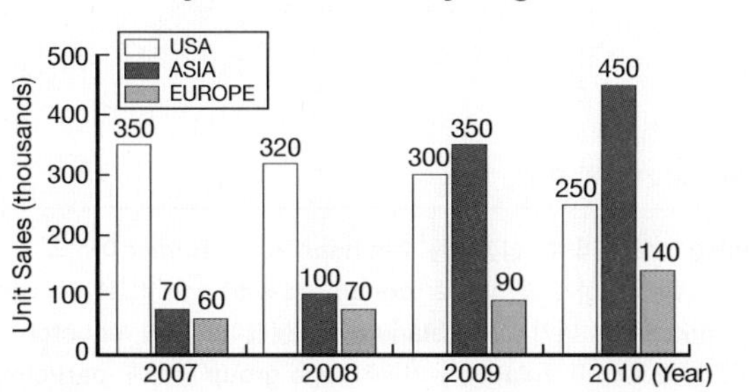

9 In 2007, hybrid car sales in these three regions were [the strongest / the weakest] in the U.S.A.

10 In 2009, hybrid car sales in Asia were [four times / five times] as high as they were in 2007.

11 Hybrid car sales in the U.S.A. decreased [steadily / suddenly] while those of Asia and Europe continuously increased.

12 In 2010, hybrid car sales in Asia [had doubled / had reached their peak], surpassing both the U.S.A. and Europe in sales.

[13 - 15] 다음 문장이 도표와 일치하면 ○, 아니면 ×를 고르시오.

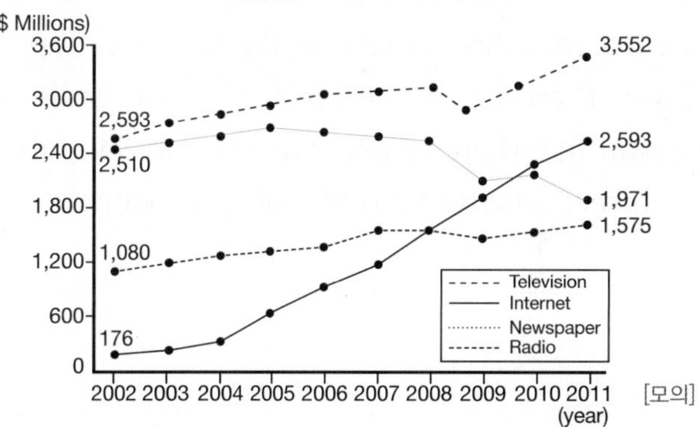

13 All the media's advertising revenues in 2011 had increased compared to the year of 2002. (○ / ×)

14 Television advertising revenue ranked the highest each year throughout the period between 2002 and 2011. (○ / ×)

15 In 2002, Internet advertising revenue was smaller than any other media's, but it surpassed Radio and Newspaper advertising revenue in 2011. (○ / ×)

실전적용독해

2문제를 2분 40초 안에 풀어보세요.

정답 및 해설 p.138

165 다음 도표의 내용과 일치하지 않는 문장은?

Exercise and Pulse Rate

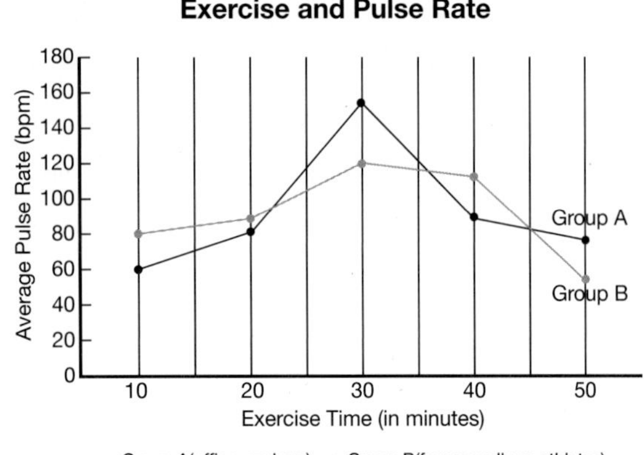

This graph compares the effects of exercise on the average heart rates of a group of office workers and another group of former college athletes. ① The heart rate of both groups was highest at 30 minutes of exercise. ② The rate of Group A was lower at 10 minutes than at 50 minutes. ③ Between 40 and 50 minutes, the pulse rate of Group B decreased more dramatically compared with Group A. ④ During the last five minutes of exercise, the rate of Group B was lower than that of Group A. ⑤ As a result, it can be said that there is more variation in the pulse rate of former athletes than that of office workers.

166 다음 도표의 내용과 일치하지 않는 문장은?

Children Involved in Selected Leisure Activities, Victoria, by Age

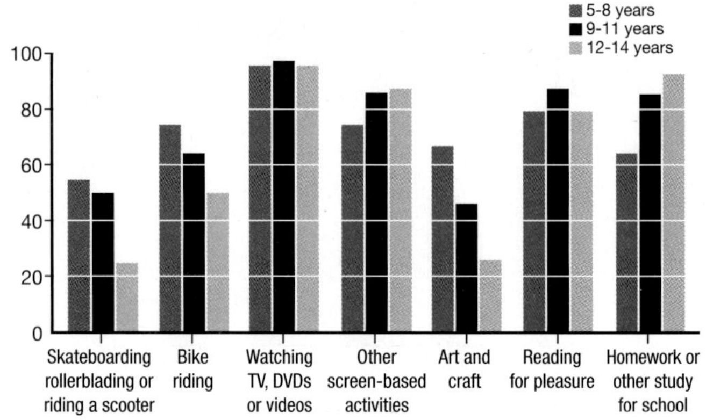

The above graph shows the preferred leisure activities of the children aged 5 — 14 in Victoria. ① It is clear from the data that quiet activities such as watching TV, DVDs, or videos, and homework or other study for school are more popular nowadays than active ones such as skateboarding, rollerblading, or riding a scooter. ② Reading for pleasure was relatively popular among all age groups, but most so for those 9 — 11 years old. ③ The leisure activities with the greatest differences between age groups were art and craft activities, where the participation rates were higher in the 5 — 8 year age group. ④ Homework and other study for school had lower participation rates in the 12 — 14 year age group. ⑤ Skateboarding was the least popular activity among the seven for the youngest age group.

VOCAbulary 어휘확인

165 **pulse rate** 맥박 수, 심장박동 수(= heart rate) **former** 이전의 **dramatically** 급격하게; 극적으로 **compared with** ~와 비교하여 **variation** 변화 166 **leisure** 여가 **rollerblading** 롤러블레이드 타기 **scooter** 스쿠터(소형 오토바이) **relatively** 비교적 **age group** 연령대 **participation** 참여, 참가

미니 모의고사 5

유형 13 | 유형 14 | 유형 15 | 유형 16

17문제를 24분 안에 풀어보세요

정답 및 해설 p.140

167 밑줄 친 he[He]가 가리키는 대상이 나머지 넷과 다른 것은?

Robert Baden-Powell was a lieutenant-general in the British Army, a writer, and a primary founder of the Boy Scout Movement. In 1899, during a war, ① he commanded a British military unit in the town of Mafeking, South Africa. Mafeking was surrounded by the enemy, and ② he lacked the troops to defend it. The situation was desperate, and ③ he needed help. An officer suggested that they employ local boys to assist them. ④ He gave the boys military-style training in groups and got them to work as watchers and messengers. Baden-Powell was impressed at the sight. When ⑤ he returned to England, he organized training camps for boys, and that was the beginning of the international Scout Movement.

*lieutenant-general 육군 중장

168 Poon Lim에 관한 다음 글의 내용과 일치하는 것은?

Poon Lim was a Chinese sailor who became world-famous after an amazing survival experience. He was working on a British merchant ship during World War II. The ship was on its way from Cape Town to Suriname. When the ship was bombed by German submarines, Poon Lim jumped as it burned and sank. He was in the sea for two hours when a lifeboat floated by. He climbed in and found water, food, and a flashlight. When supplies ran low, he relied on fishing and catching seabirds to eat and gathering rainwater to drink. Amazingly, he survived for 133 days on the ocean in that lifeboat. Eventually he was rescued near the coast of Brazil and returned to England as a great hero.

① 2차 대전 때 군인으로 참전했다.
② 배가 뒤집혀 바다에 표류했다.
③ 구명보트에서 물과 음식을 발견했다.
④ 바다에서 5달 넘게 생존했다.
⑤ 브라질 어선에 의해 구조되었다.

169 다음 도표의 내용과 일치하지 않는 문장은?

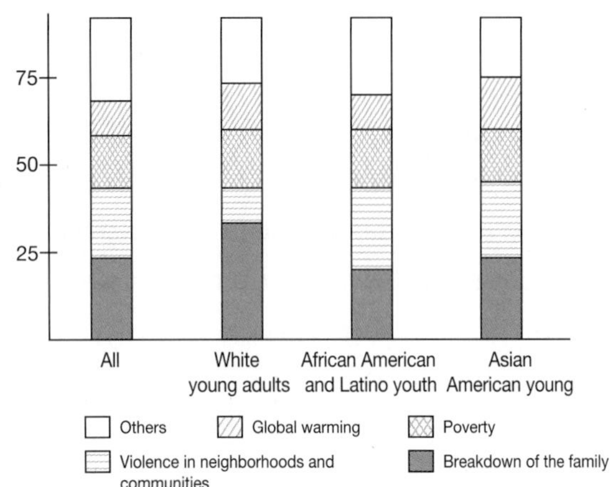

The above graph shows what young adults aged 16 — 22 feel are the primary issues impacting their lives. ① Twenty-four percent of the respondents consider the breakdown of the family to be the most pressing issue facing their generation today, but several significant differences among racial and ethnic groups do exist. ② White young adults named family breakdown as number one, followed by poverty and global warming. ③ African American and Latino youth, however, believed violence in their communities was the most pressing issue facing their generation, followed by poverty and global warming. ④ Asian American young adults, meanwhile, named family breakdown as the number-one issue, but they felt neighborhood violence was almost equally important. ⑤ Overall, though American young adults feel insecure related to poverty and global warming, they feel more insecure about their family relationships and community safety.

170 밑줄 친 it이 가리키는 대상이 나머지 넷과 다른 것은?

As one of the most-respected tests of intelligence, dedication, and strategic thinking, it is no surprise that many countries have claimed that they deserve the title of the birthplace of chess. But it is now generally agreed that the game had its origins in India, since ① it is mentioned in Indian literature dating from 500 BC. One thousand five hundred years later, ② it appeared in Spain. From there, ③ it quickly spread over the rest of Europe. In 1924, when the International Chess Federation was established in Paris, ④ it played a large part in spreading the popularity of the game of chess all over the world. Today, ⑤ it is one of the world's most popular games.

171 Mistletoe에 관한 다음 글의 내용과 일치하지 않는 것은?

Mistletoe grows on the branches or trunk of a tree and sends out roots that enter the tree and steal its food. But it is also capable of growing on its own — using photosynthesis. Some people have thought that Mistletoe had mystical powers, and down through the centuries it became associated with many myths and customs. In the Middle Ages, branches of mistletoe were hung from ceilings to defend against evil spirits. In Europe, they were placed over house and barn doors to prevent the entrance of witches. Kissing under the mistletoe was first associated with a Greek festival and later with early marriage practices. At Christmas time, a young lady standing under a ball of mistletoe could not refuse to be kissed. Such a kiss could mean deep romance or lasting friendship and goodwill.

*mistletoe 겨우살이(줄기를 크리스마스 장식에 쓰는 덩굴식물)
**photosynthesis 광합성

① 뿌리를 나무속에 박아 자라기도 한다.
② 광합성을 통해 스스로 자랄 수도 있다.
③ 많은 민간 풍습들과 연관이 있다.
④ 나쁜 기운을 쫓는 데 쓰이기도 했다.
⑤ 덩굴에 키스하는 크리스마스 풍습이 있다.

172 Modern Library에 관한 다음 안내문의 내용과 일치하는 것은?

Modern Library's collection of eight thousand items includes general histories of art and exhibition catalogues. All materials must be used or viewed in the library. We offer wireless access, color scanners, and onsite access to the library's resources.

Hours

Daily 10:00 a.m. — 5:00 p.m.
(Closed on national holidays; the library closes at 3:00 p.m. on Fridays before holiday weekends.)

Storytime

- Storytime is a special program offered for children ages three through seven.
- It is held Monday — Friday from 3:00 p.m. — 3:30 p.m. and Sundays at 2:00 p.m.
- Space is limited. First come, first served.

① 자료들을 외부로 가지고 나갈 수 있다.
② 유선으로만 온라인 자료에 접근이 가능하다.
③ 연휴가 낀 주말이 시작되기 전 금요일에는 열지 않는다.
④ 3세 아동은 Storytime에 참가할 수 없다.
⑤ Storytime 참가는 선착순이다.

173 밑줄 친 it[It]이 가리키는 대상이 나머지 넷과 다른 것은?

Meditation is a self-induced form of mind control that has been practiced for thousands of years. ① It started to gain popularity in the West in the 1960s, especially after The Beatles traveled to India to study and practice it. Basically, ② it involves sitting quietly, usually on the floor with your eyes closed, and focusing on a single image or sound in order to clear your mind. It's well known that regular practice of ③ it can lower blood pressure, increase feelings of wellbeing, and boost mental alertness. People who have incorporated ④ it into their daily routines claim that stress is significantly reduced. So little of ⑤ it remains that it can easily be dealt with, which leaves you relaxed and healthy.

*self-induced 자기 유도의

174 Nazca Lines에 관한 다음 글의 내용과 일치하지 <u>않는</u> 것은?

Dedicated as a UNESCO World Heritage Site in 1994, the Nazca Lines of South America are among the most fascinating historical objects found anywhere in the world. These gigantic lines were discovered in the 1930s by airplane pilots. Drawn in Peru's Nazca Desert more than 3,000 years ago, they depict such things as birds, monkeys, and abstract designs. Mysteriously, it is impossible to see the pictures if one is standing on the ground. One can only see them from the sky. It's hard to imagine how primitive people achieved such gigantic, detailed designs. Various theories have been proposed about the methods used to make the Nazca Lines, but there is no exact evidence to explain the reason why and how they were made.

*World Heritage Site 세계문화유산

① 1930년대에 비행기 조종사들이 발견했다.
② 동물과 기하학적 문양이 그려져 있다.
③ 지상에서는 그림의 일부만 볼 수 있다.
④ 거대할 뿐 아니라 정밀하게 그려졌다.
⑤ 만들어진 방법과 동기는 정확하지 않다.

175 다음 도표의 내용과 일치하지 <u>않는</u> 것은?

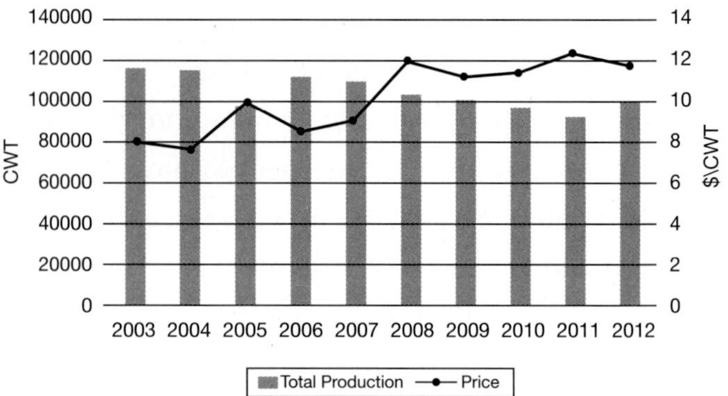

The figure above displays Canadian potato production and prices. The bar chart shows the production level in terms of thousands of hundredweights (CWT) and prices (dollars per hundredweight) over the years between 2003 and 2012. ① Potato production experienced the highest level in 2003 and the lowest level in 2011. ② Between 2006 and 2012, the total production generally decreased, though there were increases in 2006 and 2012. ③ The amount of potatoes produced in 2005 and in 2010 was similar, but the price was higher in 2005. ④ The prices fluctuated over time and experienced their highest level in 2011 and the lowest level in 2004. ⑤ In 2007 the price went up again and continued to rise in 2008, but came down a bit in 2009.

176 Greenville Symphony Orchestra에 관한 다음 안내문의 내용과 일치하는 것은?

> **GREENVILLE SYMPHONY ORCHESTRA**
> David S. Pollitt, Music Director
> MASTERWORKS SERIES
> Saturday, October 19, 8:00 p.m. and Sunday, October 20, 3:00 p.m., The Peace Center
>
> MOZART
> The Requiem in D minor
>
> MENDELSSOHN
> Violin Concerto in E Minor
> ROBERT McDUFFIE, *Violin*
>
> *Intermission*
>
> TCHAIKOVSKY
> Symphony No. 4 in F Minor
>
> Latecomers will not be admitted during the performance.

① 토요일 2회, 일요일 1회 공연이다.
② 모두 세 작곡가의 곡들이 연주된다.
③ Robert McDuffie가 오케스트라를 총 감독한다.
④ 중간 휴식시간 없이 공연이 계속된다.
⑤ 공연 시작 후 10분까지는 입장이 가능하다.

177 다음 도표의 내용과 일치하지 않는 것은?

Time Spent in Housework and Housework Tasks

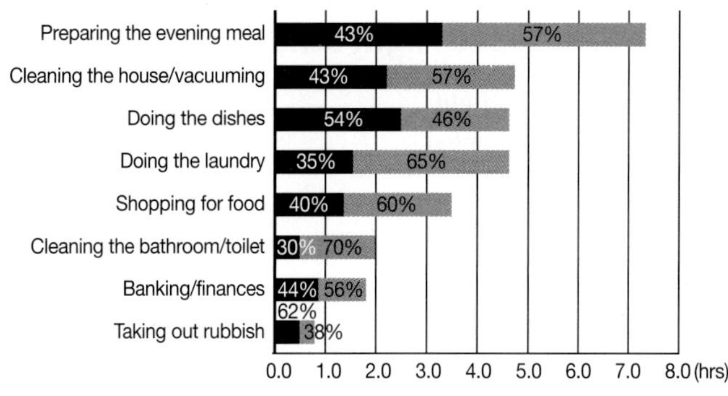

	Taking out rubbish	Banking/finances	Cleaning the bathroom/toilet	Shopping for food	Doing the laundry	Doing the dishes	Cleaning the house/vacuuming	Preparing the evening meal
■ Man(hrs)	0.5	0.8	0.6	1.4	1.6	2.5	2.1	3.2
■ Woman(hrs)	0.3	1.0	1.4	2.1	3.0	2.1	2.8	4.2

The above graph shows the average time spent by men and their partners in a range of routine household tasks in Australia. ① Although women tend to do most of the housework, the extent of men's participation varies according to task. ② The only tasks where men report that they do more than their partners are doing the dishes and taking out the rubbish. ③ For all other tasks, men's partners spend more time each week, with women spending much more time than men doing the laundry, cleaning the bathroom and toilet, and food shopping. ④ The biggest difference in the percentage share for men and women is shown in cleaning the house and vacuuming. ⑤ The graph also shows that preparing the evening meal was the most time-consuming task and taking out the rubbish was the least.

178 A380 Flight Schedule에 관한 다음 표의 내용과 일치하지 않는 것은?

A380 Flight Schedule

Route (from — to)	Flight number	Departure	Arrival	Days of operation
New York (JFK) — Seoul (Incheon)	K082	14:00	17:20+1	Tue, Thu, Sat (Daily from Sept. 1)
Seoul (Incheon) — New York (JFK)	K081	11:00	11:55	Tue, Sat (Daily from Sept. 1)
Los Angeles — Seoul (Incheon)	K018	12:30	17:30+1	Tue, Thu, Sat (Daily from Oct. 20)
Seoul (Incheon) — Los Angeles	K017	15:00	09:50	Tue, Sat (Daily from Oct. 20)

• Flight schedules and aircraft types are subject to change without notice.
• '+1' indicates arrival after one day.
• Departure gates close 20 minutes prior to scheduled departure.
• Passengers are allowed two pieces of checked baggage plus one carry-on per person.

① 10월 20일부터는 모두 매일 운항한다.
② K082는 일주일에 3일 운항 중이다.
③ K018은 서울에 오후 6시 30분에 도착한다.
④ 비행기 기종은 사전 안내 없이 변경될 수 있다.
⑤ 이륙 20분 전까지는 탑승을 완료해야 한다.

179 다음 도표의 내용과 일치하지 않는 것은?

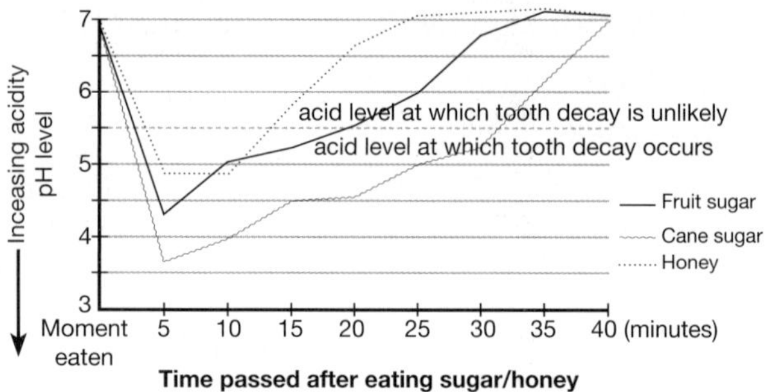

The above graph shows the level of acid in the mouth after eating sweet foods by comparing fruit sugar, cane sugar, and honey. Sweet foods cause pH to drop for a while, and the longer pH levels remain below 5.5, the greater the opportunity for tooth decay to occur. ① Honey seems to be the least risky substance because mouth acid returns to above pH 5.5 in under fifteen minutes. ② And fruit sugar takes about 20 minutes for it to go back to above pH 5.5. ③ In contrast, after eating cane sugar, pH levels do not rise above pH 5.5 until at least 35 minutes have passed. ④ By comparing fruit sugar, cane sugar, and honey, we find that cane sugar produces the greatest risk of the three. ⑤ The implications, then, are that honey or fruit sugar appear preferable to cane sugar.

*acid ((화학)) 산 cf. acidity 산성
**pH 피에이치, 페하(용액의 수소 이온 농도 지수)

180 Dr. TUMS의 복용에 관한 다음 유의 사항과 일치하지 <u>않는</u> 것은?

Dr. TUMS

Uses
for the relief of
- acid indigestion and sour stomach
- upset stomach with headache from overeating

Flavors
Dr. TUMS chewable tablets come in 4 flavors: cherry, lemon, strawberry, and tangerine.

Directions
Fully dissolve 2 tablets in 4 ounces of water before taking.
Adults and children 12 years and over: take 2 tablets every 4 hours. Do not exceed 8 tablets in 24 hours.
Adults 60 years old and over: take 2 tablets every 4 hours. Do not exceed 4 tablets in 24 hours.

Active Ingredients
1,000 milligrams of Calcium Carbonate per chewable tablet

Warnings
Do not use if you are allergic to aspirin or any other pain reliever.

*Calcium Carbonate 탄산칼슘

① 소화 불량이나 복통에 먹는 약이다.
② 다양한 맛으로 출시되고 있다.
③ 60세 이상 성인은 하루에 8알을 넘게 먹으면 안 된다.
④ 성인은 1회 섭취 시 2,000밀리그램의 탄산칼슘을 섭취한다.
⑤ 다른 진통제에 알레르기 증상이 있으면 복용해선 안 된다.

181 George Burns에 관한 다음 글의 내용과 일치하지 <u>않는</u> 것은?

George Burns was born in New York on January 20, 1896. He was a comedian best known for his long-running radio and television show with his wife Gracie Allen. When they first teamed up onstage to perform a comedy act in the 1930s, he had the experience and she was new to the business. George took the lead and had Gracie feed him the straight lines while he told all the jokes. The act was a disaster. The next night George took the straight lines and gave Gracie all the laugh lines. The rest is show business history. First onstage, then on radio, and then on TV, the real-life and stage couple played their roles perfectly. For George Burns, standing out of the spotlight in the act while his wife was the center of the show was simply a recognition of ability. "Gracie had a talent the audience loved. I had a talent the audience didn't. I knew how to write it, and she knew how to say it."

① 뉴욕 태생의 방송 코미디언이었다.
② 1930년대에 Gracie와 팀을 이루었다.
③ 무대에서는 부인이 더 조명을 받았다.
④ 부인보다 웃기는 데 재능이 많았다.
⑤ 쇼의 대본을 쓰는 재능이 있었다.

182 Cool Fitness에 관한 다음 광고문의 내용과 일치하지 않는 것은?

Cool Fitness

We provide a complete selection of cardio equipment, weight machines, and fitness classes. We also provide a comfortable facility for our members, whether they are just starting an exercise program or are at an advanced level.

- **Benefits**

All new members are given a personal training session with one of our trainers. These sessions are free to members. We are always available to provide instruction in the correct use of all of our equipment.

- **Activities**

Members regularly have the opportunity to participate in both charity and social events sponsored by the gym — building a sense of community that goes beyond exercise.

- **Hours**

Monday — Thursday	6:00 AM — 10:00 PM
Friday	7:00 AM — 9:00 PM
Saturday — Sunday	8:00 AM — 7:00 PM

*cardio 유산소 운동, 심장 (강화 운동)

① 운동을 처음 시작하는 사람들도 가입할 수 있다.
② 할인된 가격에 개인 훈련을 받을 수 있다.
③ 언제든지 기구 사용에 대한 지도를 받을 수 있다.
④ 원하면 사회봉사 활동에 참여할 수 있다.
⑤ 주말은 금요일보다 이용시간이 3시간 더 짧다.

183 The Animal Care Society 회원의 혜택에 관한 다음 안내문의 내용과 일치하지 않는 것은?

The Animal Care Society

Yes! I want to become a member of The Animal Care Society and join the fight to end animal cruelty wherever it occurs. It costs just $25 a year to be a member of the Society.

As a thank you for joining, you'll receive:

- A one-year subscription to our bimonthly magazine, *My Animals*
- A weekly newsletter about taking simple actions for animals
- Investigative reports from the animal protection field

You'll also get:

- Invitations to the events and special lectures held by the Society
- A personalized greeting card with a special message

Have a question about your ACS membership?
Write to us, email *animalcare@society.org*, or call 102-242-1200.

① 일 년에 25달러를 내면 회원이 될 수 있다.
② 일 년 동안 잡지를 무료로 구독할 수 있다.
③ 동물을 위한 조치에 관한 주간 뉴스레터를 받는다.
④ 동물 보호에 관한 조사 보고서를 받는다.
⑤ 정부 주관 행사에 초대받는다.

Chapter 6

유형 17 어법성 판단

유형 18 어휘 추론

미니 모의고사 6

유형 17 어법성 판단

이렇게 출제된다.

기본적인 문법사항의 이해를 묻는 유형이다. 둘 중 어법에 맞는 표현을 고르는 문제 혹은 밑줄 친 부분 중 어법상 틀린 표현을 고르는 문제가 1문항 출제된다.

지시문은 이렇게

(A), (B), (C)의 각 네모 안에서 어법에 맞는 표현으로 가장 적절한 것은?

다음 글의 밑줄 친 부분 중, 어법상 틀린 것은?

정답 및 해설 p.154

Check-Up 1

해결 전략 1 기본적인 문법사항을 익혀두자.

기본적인 문법사항을 알고 있는지 확인하기 위한 문제 유형이고 같은 사항이 반복 출제되는 경향을 보이므로 이를 숙지해 두어야 한다.

해결 전략 2 해당 문장만으로 정답을 파악한다.

어법 문제는 다른 유형과는 달리 전체 내용을 다 읽지 않고도 풀 수 있는 경우가 대부분이다. 선택지가 포함된 각각의 문장을 읽고 어법에 맞는 표현을 찾는다. 글의 전체 내용이나 요지에 신경 쓰기보다는 해당 문장만 읽고 정답을 고르면 시간을 좀 더 절약할 수 있다.

해결 TIP "네모 안의 표현에서 묻고 있는 문법사항을 파악한다."

예를 들어, 네모 안에 adequate와 adequately가 있다면 형용사와 부사를 구분하는 문제라는 것을 알 수 있다. 이렇게 미리 파악한 문법사항에 초점을 맞춰 문제를 푼다.

(A) 형용사와 부사의 구별: 형용사는 명사와 보어를 수식하고, 부사는 형용사, 동사, 부사 또는 전체 문장을 수식한다. (A)가 수식하는 것이 무엇인지를 확인한다.

(B) 수일치: 주어가 단수인지 복수인지를 확인한다.

(C) 능동·수동 구별: 의사가 질문을 'ask'하는 것인지 질문이 의사에게 'ask'되는 것인지를 확인한다.

184 **(A), (B), (C)의 각 네모 안에서 어법에 맞는 표현으로 가장 적절한 것은?**

Most adults need seven to eight hours of sleep per night, although some people need more or less sleep time to be (A) [adequate / adequately] rested. Not getting enough sleep or poor quality of sleep (B) [has / have] serious consequences. If you're getting enough sleep but still feel sleepy all the time, you could have a sleep disorder. Sleep disorders disrupt a person's ability to fall asleep or stay asleep. The first question sleep doctors (C) [ask / are asked] when new patients visit their sleep clinic is "Are you getting enough sleep?" That's a big question because doctors think a lot of patients are not. They're lacking sleep, either partially or occasionally or all the time.

	(A)		(B)		(C)
①	adequate	……	has	……	ask
②	adequate	……	have	……	are asked
③	adequately	……	has	……	ask
④	adequately	……	has	……	are asked
⑤	adequately	……	have	……	ask

Check-Up 2

"밑줄 친 부분에서 묻고 있는 문법사항을 파악한다."

해결 TIP

예를 들어, 밑줄 친 단어가 동사라면 주어에 수일치가 되었는지, 능동·수동 표현이 적절한지, 동사 자리가 맞는지 등을 확인한다.

① 빈출 표현의 쓰임: be used to v-ing, be used to-v, used to-v를 구분하여 올바르게 쓰였는지 확인한다.

② 보어의 형태: 동사의 보어 자리에는 (대)명사, 형용사 외에도 to-v, v-ing 등 다양한 형태가 올 수 있으므로, 밑줄 친 부분이 동사의 보어가 될 수 있는지를 파악한다.

③ 형용사를 보어로 취하는 동사: feel, look, sound, smell, taste 등은 형용사를 보어로 취하는 동사들이므로 부사가 보어 자리에 올 수 없다.

④ 관계대명사 what의 쓰임: 관계대명사 what은 선행사를 포함한다. 문맥을 살펴봤을 때 what이 이끄는 절이 앞의 a confidence를 수식한다. 즉 선행사가 문장에 명시되어 있으므로 관계대명사로는 선행사를 자체 내에 포함하지 않는 which나 that이 와야 한다.

⑤ 병렬 구조: 등위접속사 앞에서 문맥과 어법상 연결될 수 있는 것의 형태를 파악한 뒤, 연결된 형태가 문법적으로 대등한지 확인한다.

185 다음 글의 밑줄 친 부분 중, 어법상 틀린 것은?

Do you feel lonely or isolated among people? Learn to enjoy your own company! It might feel weird at first if you're used to ① being surrounded by other people. But, spending time alone can be really ② liberating. The freedom to be alone with your thoughts can be a great way to relax. Try and feel ③ comfortable with just yourself for company. Generally when we think of people we want to be around, they are people who have a confidence ④ what is attractive to others. Learning to be on your own and ⑤ like your own company is a step towards this kind of confidence.

실전적용독해

정답 및 해설 p.155

6문제를 8분 안에 풀어보세요.

186 (A), (B), (C)의 각 네모 안에서 어법에 맞는 표현으로 가장 적절한 것은?

When it comes to taking care of your heart, what you watch may be as important as what you eat or do. A study at the University of Maryland found that watching comedy is as good for your heart (A) [as / than] exercise. The study involved 40 adults, (B) [who / whose] hearts were monitored as they watched a sad movie and a funny movie. The funny movie increased blood flow while the sad movie decreased it. The researchers claimed that watching sad movies has a similar effect as doing math problems, while the effect of watching funny movies (C) [is / are] like aerobic exercise. So, if you want to do something good for your heart, make a point of watching comedy.

	(A)		(B)		(C)
①	as	……	who	……	is
②	as	……	whose	……	are
③	as	……	whose	……	is
④	than	……	whose	……	are
⑤	than	……	who	……	is

187 (A), (B), (C)의 각 네모 안에서 어법에 맞는 표현으로 가장 적절한 것은?

The moral of the story that life is short is this: take advantage of every day you are (A) [giving / given]. This phrasing is intentional, in that many of our elders suggested that each day (B) [be / was] taken as a gift and treated that way. A Latin aphorism has come into common usage: "carpe diem." Made famous by the movie *Dead Poets Society*, it is usually translated as "seize the day." The meaning of the original Latin, however, is closer to "harvesting" the day. Each day has an unharvested abundance of pleasure, enjoyment, and beauty that many younger people miss. A very common human failing is not taking advantage of life's pleasures and (C) [attendance / attending] to the very joy of being alive.

*aphorism 격언

	(A)		(B)		(C)
①	giving	……	be	……	attendance
②	giving	……	was	……	attendance
③	given	……	be	……	attending
④	given	……	was	……	attending
⑤	given	……	be	……	attendance

188 (A), (B), (C)의 각 네모 안에서 어법에 맞는 표현으로 가장 적절한 것은?

Jean-Paul Sartre's *The Imaginary* is a detailed essay about the nature of imagination. It is the result of more than a decade's work, over the course of (A) [what / which] Sartre researched and developed many ideas. These include, for example, the nature of philosophy and its relation to psychology. His theory of imagination is developed and (B) [defends / defended] partly through discussions and applications of these areas of his thought. As well as being interesting on its own, the work provides foundations for much of Sartre's later work on the human condition. His theories of freedom and bad faith, for example, and of the nature of literature, quietly (C) [draw / draws] on thoughts and themes emphasized in this book.

	(A)		(B)		(C)
①	what	……	defends	……	draw
②	what	……	defended	……	draws
③	which	……	defends	……	draw
④	which	……	defended	……	draws
⑤	which	……	defended	……	draw

VOCAbulary 어휘확인

186 when it comes to ~에 관한 한 monitor 관찰하다; 측정하다 aerobic 에어로빅 make a point of 반드시 ~하다 187 moral 교훈; 도덕 take advantage of ~을 이용하다 phrasing 말, 표현 intentional 의도적인 in that ~라는 점에서 harvest 수확하다 abundance 풍부 188 decade 10년 over the course of ~ 동안 philosophy 철학 psychology 심리학 application 응용 foundation 토대[기초] condition 조건; 상태 literature 문학

189 다음 글의 밑줄 친 부분 중, 어법상 틀린 것은?

A quiet, dark, and cool environment can help promote sound sleep. Why do you think bats choose caves for their daytime sleep? ① To achieve such an environment, lower the volume of outside noise with earplugs or a "white noise" appliance. Use heavy curtains, blackout shades, or an eye mask to block light, a powerful cue ② that tells the brain that it's time to wake up. Keep the temperature comfortably cool — between 60 and 75°F — and the room well ③ ventilate. And make sure your bedroom is equipped with a comfortable mattress and pillows. Also, if a pet regularly wakes you during the night, you may want to consider ④ keeping it out of your bedroom. Keeping computers, TVs, and work materials out of the room ⑤ strengthens the mental association between your bedroom and sleep.

*congregate 모이다

190 다음 글의 밑줄 친 부분 중, 어법상 틀린 것은?

If you walk into any classroom today, you will quickly notice that it is quite different from those of the past. For one thing, computers in the classroom are as common as blackboards once were. And this is true at all levels of education. Many universities require all students ① to have a powerful personal computer and high-speed Internet access. The situation at primary and secondary schools ② is changing swiftly, too. Now, children ③ are used to computer-based learning systems. At kindergartens, you are likely to see three- and four-year-olds ④ using computers. One company sells a computer for children as young as two that gives instructions and ⑤ ask questions in a friendly voice.

191 다음 글의 밑줄 친 부분 중, 어법상 틀린 것은?

Thanks to research by medical professionals and sports scientists, we know that fitness makes us healthier and ① improves the quality of our lives. But what level of fitness should we aim for, and how much time and effort should we devote to our personal workout routines? We all need to be ② fit enough to do ordinary work and maintain minimum health levels. But not all people do the same kind of work. Nor ③ do they do the same workout, because they need different levels of physical strength. Professional athletes need ④ much more exercise than teachers or office workers do to perform their jobs successfully. Thus, a fitness program ⑤ was designed for your needs will be enough to keep you fit for life.

VOCAbulary 어휘확인

189 promote 촉진하다 earplug 귀마개 white noise 백색소음, 잡음 appliance (가정용) 기기 blackout 암막; 정전 cue 단서, 신호 ventilate 환기하다 equip 장비를 갖추다 strengthen 강화하다 association 연관성
190 common 흔한 access 접속; 접근 primary school 초등학교 secondary school 중등학교 swiftly 빠르게 instruction 지시; 설명
191 professional 전문가; 전문적인 fitness 체력 단련 aim for ~을 목표로 하다 devote 쏟다, 바치다 fit 건강한

유형 18 어휘 추론

이렇게 출제된다.
문맥 속 어휘의 이해를 묻는 유형이다. 혼동되는 두 개의 어휘 중 문맥상 적절한 표현을 고르는 유형 또는 글에서 밑줄 친 단어의 쓰임이 적절한지 판단하는 유형으로 1문항이 출제된다.

지시문은 이렇게
(A), (B), (C)의 각 네모 안에서 문맥에 맞는 낱말로 가장 적절한 것은?
다음 글의 밑줄 친 부분 중, 문맥상 낱말의 쓰임이 적절하지 않은 것은?

정답 및 해설 p.160

Check-Up 1

해결 전략 1 **반의어, 유사 어휘, 파생어를 익혀두자.**
주로 반대 뜻 어휘가 출제되고 있는데, 간혹 철자나 발음이 유사한 어휘, 한 단어에서 파생된 어휘로 선택지가 구성되어 혼동을 준다. 따라서 평소 이런 어휘들을 잘 알아두어야 어려움 없이 문제를 풀 수 있다. 앞서 공부한 어휘들을 다시 한 번 점검하자.

해결 전략 2 **문맥에 적절한 단어를 고른다.**
먼저 해당 문장 내의 문맥에서 자연스러운 어휘를 고를 수 있는지 살펴본다. ▶ (B) 참조
단서가 부족하다면, 해당 문장 앞뒤의 문맥을 살펴 가장 자연스러운 어휘를 정답으로 고른다. ▶ (A), (C) 참조

(A) 앞 문장에서 인간은 사회적 동물이라고 설명하고 있으므로 우리가 연합(association) 속에서 생존하지 못할 것인지, 고립(isolation) 속에서 생존하지 못할 것인지 자연스러운 것을 고른다.

(B) 다른 정서적 반응과는 달리, 웃음은 전뇌에 걸쳐 다수 영역에 관여한다고 했으므로, 다른 정서적 반응이 뇌에서 제한적(limited)인지 무제한적(unlimited)인지 고른다.

(C) 앞에서 웃음이 두뇌에 좋다고 했으므로 농담을 듣고 자기 것으로 만드는 것이 학습과 창의력에 중요한 두뇌 영역을 활성화(activates)시킬지 마비(paralyzes)시킬지 중에서 고른다.

192 (A), (B), (C)의 각 네모 안에서 문맥에 맞는 낱말로 가장 적절한 것은?

Countless studies show that a life that's full of friends and fun comes with benefits to the brain. Humans are highly social animals. We're not meant to survive, let alone succeed, in (A) [association / isolation]. Relationships stimulate our brains — in fact, interacting with others may be the best kind of brain exercise. Moreover, laughter is especially good for your brain. You probably have heard that laughter is the best medicine, and that holds true for the brain as well as the body. Unlike other emotional responses, which are (B) [limited / unlimited] to specific areas of the brain, laughter engages multiple regions across the whole brain. Furthermore, listening to jokes and making your own (C) [activates / paralyzes] areas of the brain vital to learning and creativity. As psychologist Daniel Goleman notes in his book *Emotional Intelligence*, "Laughter seems to help people think more broadly and associate more freely."

	(A)		(B)		(C)
①	association	……	limited	……	activates
②	association	……	unlimited	……	activates
③	isolation	……	limited	……	paralyzes
④	isolation	……	limited	……	activates
⑤	isolation	……	unlimited	……	paralyzes

●●● 바로 앞뒤의 단어들과 자연스럽게 이어지는 단어를 고른다.

해결 전략 3

하나의 어구처럼 쓰이는 표현을 알고 있다면 선택지 앞뒤의 단어만 보고도 적절한 어휘를 고를 수 있다. 이때는 문맥을 확인하지 않고도 적절한 어휘인지 아닌지 구별할 수 있으므로 시간을 절약할 수 있다. 예를 들어 우리는 '버스를 탄다'라고는 하지만 '버스를 사용한다'라고는 하지 않는다. 이처럼 영어에도 사람들이 고정적으로 사용하는 표현이 있다. 다음과 같은 문제를 보자.

[dairy / daily] routine

둘 중 알맞은 단어를 고르려면 선택지 바로 뒤의 routine과 자연스럽게 이어지는지 확인해 본다. dairy routine이란 표현은 쓰이지 않지만 daily routine(매일 반복되는 일상)은 흔히 쓰이는 표현이다. 따라서 이러한 표현을 알고 있다면 쉽게 정답을 고를 수 있을 것이다. ▶ (A) 참조

(A) hold conferences가 적절한 표현인지 hand conferences가 적절한 표현인지 판단한다.

(B) it이 가리키는 것이 무엇인지 찾고, 앞뒤의 문맥을 살펴 그것을 예방하는(prevent)지 예측하는(predict)지 고른다.

(C) 그가 낮잠 덕분에 활기찬(lively) 태도로 일할 수 있는 것인지 살아 있는(live) 태도로 일할 수 있는 것인지 자연스러운 것을 고른다.

193 (A), (B), (C)의 각 네모 안에서 문맥에 맞는 낱말로 가장 적절한 것은?

Considering how exhausted many of us are after an eight-hour workday, it is impressive that Winston Churchill worked 16 hours a day, even into his seventies. How did he do it? Every morning until 11 o'clock, he worked in bed, even (A) [holding / handing] important conferences in his bedroom. After lunch, he slept for an hour, and in the evening he slept for two more hours before supper. It wasn't a cure for tiredness. He didn't need to cure it. Instead, he (B) [prevented / predicted] it. Thanks to his frequent naps, he was able to work with a (C) [live / lively] attitude and plenty of energy, until long past midnight.

	(A)		(B)		(C)
①	holding	……	prevented	……	live
②	holding	……	prevented	……	lively
③	holding	……	predicted	……	lively
④	handing	……	predicted	……	lively
⑤	handing	……	prevented	……	live

Check-Up 2

다음 문장의 밑줄 친 낱말이 문맥상 맞게 쓰였으면 ○, 아니면 ×를 고르시오.

Making an effort to communicate in another person's language shows your <u>disrespect</u> for that person. (○ / ×)

●●● 전체 내용을 파악하고 밑줄 친 어휘가 문맥에 적절한지 판단한다.

해결 전략 4

글의 전체적인 이해가 중요하다. 앞뒤 문맥을 세밀히 살펴 의미가 자연스러운지 확인해야 한다.

▼▼ "밑줄 친 어휘의 반의어를 떠올려 보라."

해결 TIP

어휘의 쓰임이 적절한지 적절하지 않은지 확신할 수 없을 때는 반의어를 떠올리고 바꿔 읽어보자. 문맥상 반의어로 바꿔야 자연스럽다면 그 부분이 정답이다.

194 다음 글의 밑줄 친 부분 중, 문맥상 낱말의 쓰임이 적절하지 <u>않은</u> 것은?

Consider the following situation: a bag that you will use just once to carry a purchase from a store to your home can ① <u>harm</u> the earth for hundreds of years to come. Nothing good can come from accepting plastic bags with purchases, unless you consider the ② <u>inconvenience</u> it affords you. Even if you make an effort to walk or cycle to a shop to reduce the environmental harm you might otherwise do by driving, a bunch of plastic bags can ③ <u>counter</u> the efforts. This is because even if you reuse and recycle the bags, the fact ④ <u>remains</u> that they are made from fossil fuels. It is impossible to remove all the carbon that was ⑤ <u>released</u> while manufacturing the plastic.

실전적용독해

5문제를 6분 40초 안에 풀어보세요.

정답 및 해설 p.162

195 (A), (B), (C)의 각 네모 안에서 문맥에 맞는 낱말로 가장 적절한 것은?

Pre-teens and teenagers are trying to understand the world and find their own selves, so this can be a very hard time for them. Parents can help by actively attempting to strengthen a teen's (A) [stable / unstable] self-confidence. Smiling at their children, holding eye contact while speaking, encouraging them during a difficult time or task, praising them for a job well done, asking for their opinion, and taking an interest in their interests are all ways that parents can help (B) [foster / undermine] their child's self-confidence. Parents should also be aware that their opinions and promises mean a great deal to their teens. (C) [Careful / Careless] remarks and promises are easy ways to ruin a teen's self-esteem, and should be avoided at all costs.

	(A)		(B)		(C)
①	stable	……	foster	……	Careful
②	stable	……	undermine	……	Careless
③	stable	……	undermine	……	Careful
④	unstable	……	foster	……	Careless
⑤	unstable	……	undermine	……	Careful

196 (A), (B), (C)의 각 네모 안에서 문맥에 맞는 낱말로 가장 적절한 것은?

When faced with many responsibilities, it is almost always helpful to make a schedule. However, it is important for each individual to choose the type of schedule that (A) [fills / fits] his or her circumstances best. Some students work better with a detailed schedule, whereas others work better with a brief list of things to do. Circumstances also (B) [include / influence] the type of schedule a student should make. There are on-campus students, commuting students, employed students, and night-class students, and each has different scheduling requirements. Every student should tailor the principles of schedule building to his or her personal circumstances, rather than (C) [adapt / adopt] some ideal model which fits hardly anybody.

	(A)		(B)		(C)
①	fills	……	include	……	adapt
②	fills	……	influence	……	adopt
③	fits	……	include	……	adapt
④	fits	……	influence	……	adapt
⑤	fits	……	influence	……	adopt

VOCAbulary 어휘확인

195 **pre-teen** 십대 초반 청소년 **teenager** 십대 **attempt** 시도하다 **self-confidence** 자신(감), 자기 과잉 **aware** 알고 있는 **remark** 발언, 말, 언급 **ruin** 망치다 **self-esteem** 자부심 **at all costs** 어떤 희생을 치르더라도
196 **circumstance** 상황 **whereas** ~인 반면에 **on-campus** 교내의 **commuting** 통학하는; 통근 **requirement** 요건 **tailor** (특정한 목적에) 맞추다; 재단사 **principle** 원칙

197 (A), (B), (C)의 각 네모 안에서 문맥에 맞는 낱말로 가장 적절한 것은?

It is important not to overlook the health of our hearing. By reducing the noises we hear to under ninety decibels or by taking simple precautions such as wearing ear plugs when working around loud equipment, we can (A) [prevent / protect] damage to our hearing. The drawbacks of hearing loss certainly (B) [lessen / outweigh] the inconveniences of prevention. The sense of hearing is important for survival and should be taken care of just as we take care of our lives. More and more advances are being (C) [determined / developed] every year to improve hearing problems, but they are expensive and do not always cure the problem. Prevention is the only one-hundred-percent cure for hearing impairments.

	(A)		(B)		(C)
①	prevent	……	lessen	……	determined
②	prevent	……	outweigh	……	determined
③	prevent	……	outweigh	……	developed
④	protect	……	lessen	……	developed
⑤	protect	……	outweigh	……	developed

198 다음 글의 밑줄 친 부분 중, 문맥상 낱말의 쓰임이 적절하지 않은 것은?

Most kids and teens are emotional at times, so it can be ① hard for parents to distinguish between normal behavior and cause for concern. Short-term (less than two weeks) sadness is usually not thought to be alarming. However, when feelings of sadness or hopelessness last, a larger problem may ② disappear. Kids who were once good students but now don't ③ care about their academic responsibilities may be depressed. Any child who talks about running away from home should be evaluated by a professional counselor. Those kids are calling out for help and are counting on those around them to take them ④ seriously. It is far better to seek assistance than to ⑤ ignore the symptoms of depression, which can have tragic consequences.

199 다음 글의 밑줄 친 부분 중, 문맥상 낱말의 쓰임이 적절하지 않은 것은?

Through their shared secrets, the time they spend alone, and the knowledge they gain, siblings learn to ① cooperate and get along together. With their learning and knowledge, siblings also build a personal history. That is not to say that brothers and sisters have ② identical histories. Each child in a family experiences life differently, relates differently to parents, and creates a different and ③ unique environment for the other. Yet there is a family ethos, as well as a pool of memory that transcends individual experiences and forms a ④ different past for siblings. The pull of memory and the rewards of sibling companionship ⑤ draw adult brothers and sisters to each other in spite of their differences.

*ethos 기풍, 정신

VOCAbulary 어휘 확인

197 overlook 간과하다 decibel 데시벨(음의 세기를 나타내는 단위) precaution 예방책 drawback 문제점, 결점 inconvenience 불편, 애로 impairment (신체적·정신적) 장애 198 distinguish 구별하다 behavior 행동 alarming 걱정스러운, 두려운 evaluate 평가하다 counselor 상담사 count on ~을 믿다, 의지하다, 기대다 assistance 도움, 지원 tragic 비극적인, 비극의 consequence (발생한 일의) 결과 199 sibling 형제자매 get along 사이좋게 지내다 relate to ~와 관계가 있다; ~와 관련되다 transcend 초월하다 companionship 우애, 우정

미니 모의고사 6 유형 17 | 유형 18

17문제를 24분 안에 풀어보세요.

정답 및 해설 p.166

200 (A), (B), (C)의 각 네모 안에서 어법에 맞는 표현으로 가장 적절한 것은?

Exploration was a driving force behind the success of human civilizations and our mastery of the environment. In fact, cultures such as the Vikings defined themselves primarily in terms of exploration. Nowadays, however, there are few areas of our planet that (A) [remain / remains] untouched and unexplored. Especially since the beginning of the great Age of Exploration in the early 15th century, explorers and scientists have been (B) [uncovering / uncovered] the secrets of remote mountains, deep forests, huge oceans, and the freezing polar regions. Curiosity and ambition led adventurers to go into the unknown and to put themselves in extreme danger. Because of those (C) [who / which] went before us, there are not so many mysteries left to discover on Earth.

	(A)		(B)		(C)
①	remain	……	uncovering	……	who
②	remain	……	uncovered	……	which
③	remains	……	uncovering	……	who
④	remains	……	uncovered	……	which
⑤	remain	……	uncovered	……	who

201 다음 글의 밑줄 친 부분 중, 어법상 틀린 것은?

Many ① who enjoy reading novels also enjoy watching movies that are based on those novels. Seeing a story ② come to life on the big screen can be, one might say, a novel experience. But if you read the book after seeing the movie, it will be impossible not ③ to see the movie's actors and settings in your mind's eye. That's a shame because part of the fun of reading is ④ that *you* get to imagine the details of the characters and settings. If much of that work already has been done for you, your reading experience will be less ⑤ actively and less enjoyable. Regardless of a novel's length, the movie script that is based on it will be between 90 and 120 pages — one page for each minute of shooting.

202 (A), (B), (C)의 각 네모 안에서 문맥에 맞는 낱말로 가장 적절한 것은?

The wisest of our elders knows to accept whatever may come, adapting to difficulties when they arise while never (A) [getting / losing] the sense of joy inherent to living in spite of problems. I like to call this outlook "happy in spite of." This (B) [contrasts / complies] with the viewpoint held by the majority, which I'd call "happy if only." In general, the outlook of the young says: "I would be happy if only I..." The statement can be completed in any numbers of ways: if I lose weight, find a mate, get healthy, get rich, and on and on. Researchers believe that such a "happy if only" attitude will do nothing but lead to (C) [disappointment / contentment].

	(A)		(B)		(C)
①	getting	……	contrasts	……	contentment
②	losing	……	contrasts	……	contentment
③	getting	……	complies	……	contentment
④	losing	……	contrasts	……	disappointment
⑤	getting	……	complies	……	disappointment

203 다음 글의 밑줄 친 부분 중, 문맥상 낱말의 쓰임이 적절하지 않은 것은?

Many fruits and vegetables experience rapid ① losses in their nutritional value when stored in a refrigerator for several days. This occurs partly because the produce has already spent a few days in transport and on store shelves ② before you buy it. Try the two following options. One, look for locally grown fresh produce — it has usually traveled ③ longer distances and thus still has most of its nutritional value. The second option is to use frozen produce. While frozen fruits and vegetables may seem to ④ lack the flavor and appeal of fresh produce, they are treated immediately with flash freezing after being picked, and this can ⑤ slow down the loss of vitamins and nutrients.

204 (A), (B), (C)의 각 네모 안에서 어법에 맞는 표현으로 가장 적절한 것은?

If you want to sound knowledgeable, you must learn the difference between visual effects and special effects. *Special effects* are created on the set. The wind, lightning, and rain machines that are used to (A) [simulate / simulating] a storm are tools of the special effects team. *Visual effects* are created off the set and then added in post-production. Visual effects people spend a lot of time talking about blue screens. When the studio (B) [wants / will want] to show Superman flying, they'll lift the actor in front of a screen that is literally blue, and then superimpose what they shoot against another background. Weather reporters use the same technique to show you the cloud patterns (C) [moved / moving] across the weather map. It's a technique that combines artistic sensibilities with great technical expertise and innovation.

*superimpose 겹쳐놓다, 덧붙이다

	(A)		(B)		(C)
①	simulate	……	wants	……	moved
②	simulate	……	wants	……	moving
③	simulate	……	will want	……	moving
④	simulating	……	wants	……	moved
⑤	simulating	……	will want	……	moving

205 (A), (B), (C)의 각 네모 안에서 문맥에 맞는 낱말로 가장 적절한 것은?

Individuals who travel across time zones or work the night shift typically have two symptoms. One is insomnia when they are trying to sleep at unfamiliar times, and the other is excessive sleepiness during the time when their internal clock says that they should be (A) [awake / asleep]. Half of all night shift workers regularly report (B) [nodding off / setting off] and falling asleep when they are at work. This should be seen as an important concern both for individuals and society, given that airline pilots, air traffic controllers, physicians, nurses, police, and other public safety workers are all employed in professions in which peak functioning during a night shift may be (C) [critical / optional].

	(A)		(B)		(C)
①	awake	……	nodding off	……	optional
②	awake	……	nodding off	……	critical
③	asleep	……	nodding off	……	critical
④	asleep	……	setting off	……	critical
⑤	asleep	……	setting off	……	optional

206 다음 글의 밑줄 친 부분 중, 문맥상 낱말의 쓰임이 적절하지 않은 것은?

We are ① <u>constantly</u> brainwashed to believe that more wealth will make us happier. We certainly need ② <u>sufficient</u> money in the current economic system and, as the comedian Woody Allen observed, "Money is better than poverty." It is, however, ③ <u>sensible</u> to take a step back occasionally. As the economist Adam Smith pointed out, if we want to escape from the trap of anxiety and ④ <u>independence</u> on money, we must look at ways to spend less rather than find ways to make more money. We can never earn enough to satisfy our ever-increasing needs. Only through ⑤ <u>frugality</u> can we learn how satisfying it is to be free from concern.

207 (A), (B), (C)의 각 네모 안에서 문맥에 맞는 낱말로 가장 적절한 것은?

Television is such a universal part of our lives that we seldom give it a second thought. However, if aliens came to Earth from outer space and watched TV for a day, they would be convinced that all humans are either very successful and attractive, or about to die by violence. Television (A) [affects / effects] us more than we know. We worry that the horrifying things that we see on television will happen to us. And we feel (B) [frustrated / exhausted] because the success that everyone seems to possess on television hasn't yet come to us. (C) [Suspect / Separate] the illusion from what you know is real. Let reality be your judge.

	(A)		(B)		(C)
①	affects	……	frustrated	……	Suspect
②	effects	……	frustrated	……	Suspect
③	affects	……	frustrated	……	Separate
④	effects	……	exhausted	……	Separate
⑤	affects	……	exhausted	……	Suspect

208 (A), (B), (C)의 각 네모 안에서 어법에 맞는 표현으로 가장 적절한 것은?

Various forms of writing have existed for thousands of years, and nowadays, being able to read and write is an essential skill. However, there was a time (A) [when / which] writing was very hard to do, because pens did not exist. Bird feathers, called quills, were used to (B) [write / writing] until the invention of the pen in the 18th century. The new pen had a metal point, called a nib, which was repeatedly dipped in ink while writing. The fountain pen was invented in the 19th century. It had a refillable ink supply and a steel nib. Gone were the days when writers had to stop writing every few words and (C) [dip / dipping] their pens in ink.

	(A)		(B)		(C)
①	when	……	write	……	dip
②	when	……	writing	……	dip
③	when	……	write	……	dipping
④	which	……	writing	……	dip
⑤	which	……	write	……	dipping

209 다음 글의 밑줄 친 부분 중, 어법상 틀린 것은?

First ① established in 1830 in the town center at Via Port'Alba 18, Italy, Antica Pizzeria Port'Alba is widely believed to be the world's first pizzeria. The restaurant replaced street vendors who would make pizza and bring it onto the street, keeping it ② warmly in small tin stoves. It soon became a well-known meeting place for men living on the street. Most patrons had little money, so the pizzas made ③ were usually simple. A payment system was developed that allowed customers to pay up to eight days after their meal. A resulting local joke was that a pizza from Port'Alba might be someone's last free meal if they ④ died before they paid. Some patrons created poetry ⑤ to honor the pizzas.

210 (A), (B), (C)의 각 네모 안에서 문맥에 맞는 낱말로 가장 적절한 것은?

If you drive, it's wise to learn a bit more about your car than simply how to park it. In fact, a lot of basic maintenance and many emergency repairs are actually quite simple. For example, it's not hard to learn how to change a flat tire. Your instruction manual in your car will tell you exactly what to do. Make sure you have the (A) [proper / prompt] tool, such as a wrench, to loosen the nuts. It is very important to loosen the nuts before using the jack to (B) [rise / raise] the car off the ground. When the flat tire is off the ground, remove the nuts completely and replace it with your spare tire. You must attach this tire (C) [tightly / strictly].

	(A)		(B)		(C)
①	proper	……	rise	……	tightly
②	proper	……	raise	……	strictly
③	proper	……	raise	……	tightly
④	prompt	……	rise	……	strictly
⑤	prompt	……	raise	……	tightly

211 (A), (B), (C)의 각 네모 안에서 문맥에 맞는 낱말로 가장 적절한 것은?

It's said that getting fewer than eight hours of sleep can seriously impact performance. However, recent research does not entirely (A) [support / deny] this claim. Studies have found that if eight-hour sleepers are restricted to less than six hours of sleep for a week, their performance drops. However, most of these studies have involved young, eight-hour sleepers. Further research has shown that younger and longer sleepers are more (B) [sensitive / sensory] to the effects of sleep loss. One of the few studies involving older people found that their performance after sleep loss was not significantly altered. Since they represent a large group of the sleep-deprived population, these findings indicate that our understanding of real-world sleep loss is far from (C) [complete / incomplete].

	(A)		(B)		(C)
①	support	……	sensitive	……	complete
②	support	……	sensory	……	incomplete
③	support	……	sensitive	……	incomplete
④	deny	……	sensory	……	complete
⑤	deny	……	sensitive	……	complete

212 (A), (B), (C)의 각 네모 안에서 어법에 맞는 표현으로 가장 적절한 것은?

Our mothers do so much for us throughout our lives that it is only natural we should want to thank them. In America, Mothers' Day is celebrated on the second Sunday of May. It is a day to acknowledge our mothers, and let them (A) [know / to know] our love and respect for them. Children at school are encouraged to make special cards and gifts. Stores fill with Mothers' Day cards, from those with funny messages to those with (B) [touched / touching] poems. Many families treat their mothers to special outings and restaurant meals. Mothers' Day is clearly important. But we also should not forget (C) [what / that] the greatest gift is. That is showing our love every day.

	(A)		(B)		(C)
①	know	……	touched	……	what
②	to know	……	touched	……	that
③	know	……	touching	……	what
④	to know	……	touching	……	what
⑤	to know	……	touching	……	that

213 다음 글의 밑줄 친 부분 중, 어법상 틀린 것은?

The new year has always served as a time of reflection, celebration, and starting over. But not every culture has chosen to celebrate the occasion at the same time of the year or in the same way. For example, in ancient Babylonia, more than 4,000 years ago, the beginning of a new year was always celebrated ① around the end of March. This is a natural time to celebrate the coming of a new year, as it is the beginning of spring when new crops ② are planted. ③ Like us, the Babylonians made New Year's resolutions. Of course, they didn't resolve to lose weight or quit ④ smoking. The most common resolution made by the Babylonians ⑤ were to return farming tools they had borrowed.

214 다음 글의 밑줄 친 부분 중, 어법상 틀린 것은?

It seems that the feeling of affection is universal among peoples all over the world, but different cultures have their own ways to express it. It's common in the West ① to greet friends and family by kissing. Kissing became an accepted part of greeting thanks to the French. They ended their dances with a kiss between partners. This custom soon spread ② throughout Europe, and is still a widely recognized expression of friendliness. On the other hand, ③ another cultures have different greetings. For example, some tribal South Americans show ④ how happy they are to see loved ones by weeping loudly. The crying is a way of ⑤ communicating love for them.

215 다음 글의 밑줄 친 부분 중, 문맥상 낱말의 쓰임이 적절하지 않은 것은?

Whether we would like to be or not, it is an undeniable fact that all of us are affected by our emotions. And when it comes to emotions, in most cases, a moderate level of emotional involvement intensifies communication and makes it more personal. However, too much emotional involvement can be an ① obstacle to communication. For example, too much anger can create an environment where ② reasonable discussion is impossible. Likewise, prejudice (automatically rejecting certain people or ideas), stereotyping (placing individuals into categories), and boredom all ③ hinder effective communication. Such emotions tend to create a blocked mind that is closed to new ideas, ④ accepting ideas that don't agree with one's world view. ⑤ Developing an open mind that is free from emotional bias is a lifelong process that begins with awareness of the problem.

216 (A), (B), (C)의 각 네모 안에서 문맥에 맞는 낱말로 가장 적절한 것은?

There are many illnesses and health problems that we must watch out for as we age, and among them, a stroke is one of the most terrifying for a variety of reasons. For one thing, most victims have no warning that they will suffer a fatal stroke. One out of three incidences of stroke results in (A) [sudden / predicted] death. Only the lucky few get any warning signs. Not even (B) [sensible / sensitive] eating and weight control can protect everyone from a stroke. The best way to (C) [prevent / preserve] a stroke is to see your doctor for regular checkups. This is especially important if there is a history of stroke in your family.

	(A)		(B)		(C)
①	sudden	……	sensible	……	prevent
②	sudden	……	sensitive	……	prevent
③	sudden	……	sensible	……	preserve
④	predicted	……	sensible	……	prevent
⑤	predicted	……	sensitive	……	preserve

실전편

이제 실제 시험을 치르는 마음으로 다음 모의고사를 풀어봅시다.
앞에서 배운 내용을 적용해 가면서 풀 뿐만 아니라 주어진 시간 내에 문제를 풀 수 있도록 시간 관리에도 중점을 두도록 합시다.

이어지는 모의고사는 총 3회로 구성되어 있으며 한 회의 모의고사는 18개의 각기 다른 유형의 문항으로 구성되어 있어, 실전에 등장하는 모든 유형을 골고루 접할 수 있습니다.

독해 모의고사 1회

독해 모의고사 2회

독해 모의고사 3회

독해 모의고사 1회

MP3

실제 시험이라고 생각하고 다음 문제를 풀어보세요.
주어진 시간은 25분입니다.

정답 및 해설 p.178

217 밑줄 친 takes them all in stride가 다음 글에서 의미하는 바로 가장 적절한 것은?

Life doesn't have a problem. Much of the world freezes solid every year, and life carries on or waits underground, in its roots, burrows and seeds, until things warm up. The same happens in places with extreme droughts. Some seeds can wait for decades in very dry ground. When rain comes, they are activated and begin to sprout and blossom as usual. There are so many types of living things well-adapted to so many different circumstances that, no matter what sort of adverse changes come about, some will find them suitable and will thrive and evolve. Forest fires, hurricanes, droughts, or earthquakes: life takes them all in stride.

① to be harmed a lot by natural disasters
② to continue with the cycle despite trials
③ to depend seriously on various circumstances
④ to be much more precious than any other thing
⑤ to cause a negative natural phenomenon by chance

218 다음 글의 주제로 가장 적절한 것은?

Confucius reportedly said, *"Short pencil better than long memory."* Taking notes is a proven memory technique. However, standard note taking usually involves writing down ideas in a more or less word-for-word fashion. This is actually more repetition than involvement. We are repeating in a written form what we heard or saw. Although we can listen at up to 800 words per minute, the speaker we are listening to can only speak about 135 words per minute and we can only write about 40 words per minute! Trying to take notes word-for-word will cause us to miss a great deal of incoming material. Additionally, the process of trying to remember what was previously said and write it down while listening to new material causes inaccuracies and actually interferes with thinking.

*word-for-word 정확히 말한[글자] 그대로

① how to take notes effectively
② various ways to improve memory
③ the positive effects of writing on memory
④ the problems with copying when taking notes
⑤ the process of forming and storing memories

219 (A), (B), (C)의 각 네모 안에서 어법에 맞는 표현으로 가장 적절한 것은?

Based solely on external appearances, it is easy to think that the current generation of youth is revolutionary — somehow fundamentally different from anything that came before. (A) [Despite / Although] the unique way they dress and speak, however, today's teenagers are not different from any other generation's. Our grandparents also adopted strange new behaviors and used slang to show their independence from adults when they were teenagers. When teenagers use slang, they are actually (B) [shown / showing] off their membership in their special group of peers. They are forming strong bonds with their peers and shaping their identities by (C) [speak / speaking] the same language.

	(A)		(B)		(C)
①	Despite	……	shown	……	speak
②	Although	……	showing	……	speak
③	Despite	……	showing	……	speaking
④	Although	……	showing	……	speaking
⑤	Although	……	shown	……	speak

220 다음 글의 밑줄 친 부분 중, 문맥상 낱말의 쓰임이 적절하지 않은 것은?

Downtown Manhattan is hardly a place you would associate with ① agriculture. However, you may see a group of farmers planting tomato seeds in the middle of New York City in the near future. A new concept of farming, called vertical farming, is being carried out in skyscrapers with glass walls and solar panels. Each floor has large planting beds where crops can be produced in a heavily ② controlled environment. Such ③ indoor food production does not require any insecticides to control the growth of insects and pests, and thus, consumers can benefit from ④ organic foods. In addition, as crops of all kinds will be grown in an urban setting, cargo and shipping services will be ⑤ necessary, which means that there will be no greenhouse gas emissions.

221 Amazing Heartland Race에 관한 다음 안내문의 내용과 일치하지 않는 것은?

Amazing Heartland Race

How well do you know your town? What is it famous for? Where's the best place to grab a coffee? What about the best food in your neighborhood?

Come discover, or rediscover, your town as you run! The Amazing Heartland Race will have you seeing a side of your hometown that you've never seen before, as you run past the landmarks in the town that you live and play in!

Form a team of 5 members and register now!
Registration closes on 30 April 2017.

Race Details
Date: 3 June 2017 (Saturday)
Time: 9:00 a.m. to 5:00 p.m.
Race in any of these 5 towns — Bedok / Juring / Queenstown / Toa Payoh / Yishun

For more information, visit www.hdb.gov.sg/heartlandbeat

① 고향 마을을 더 잘 알 수 있는 기회를 제공한다.
② 전체 다섯 팀으로 구성된다.
③ 등록 마감은 2017년 4월 30일이다.
④ 여덟 시간 동안 진행된다.
⑤ 다섯 마을 중 한 곳에서 달리게 된다.

222 Sequoia National Park에 관한 다음 글의 내용과 일치하는 것은?

Sequoia National Park is located in the southern Sierra Nevada, in the eastern part of California. It was declared a National Park in 1890, the third in the USA. On its eastern border is the highest mountain outside of Alaska in the USA, Mt. Whitney. Sequoia National Park is the home of the famed Giant Sequoia trees, including the General Sherman tree. Approximately 2,200 years old, the General Sherman is also the largest tree on Earth. There are five out of the ten largest trees in the world in Sequoia National Park. Thousands of sightseers come to see them and marvel at their majestic beauty every year.

① 캘리포니아 주 남부에 있다.
② 미국에서 최초로 설립된 국립공원이다.
③ Giant Sequoia 나무의 원산지이다.
④ 세계에서 가장 오래된 나무가 있다.
⑤ 현재는 사람들의 접근이 차단되었다.

223 다음 글의 상황에 나타난 분위기로 가장 적절한 것은?

Fourth Street was not far from the hotel and was at the heart of the central shopping area in downtown Binghamton. In the morning, it rained a lot. Kelly wondered whether she should visit the crowded shopping area. But by the time she had emerged from the hotel, cloudy skies were finally clearing and the sun was beginning to shine. The air was clear and inviting with the delicate scent of flowers and slightly wet tree leaves. The sun provided an accent to the conversation of people, making the afternoon walk breathtakingly attractive. As she walked, she passed countless stores, various restaurants, and some houses.

① fresh and lively
② busy and urgent
③ calm and lonely
④ funny and amusing
⑤ exciting and thrilling

[224 - 226] 다음 글의 빈칸에 들어갈 말로 가장 적절한 것을 고르시오.

224 A study has found that people who have ____________________.
For example, vegetarians are usually artistic and don't really like competitive sports or jobs. They tend to be thoughtful and caring, especially with animals, and they tend to embrace open-mindedness, different cultures, and new ideas. On the other hand, meat-eaters tend to be more active than vegetarians. They enjoy competitive sports, prefer careers in business, have a lot of ambition, and like to get things done quickly. They also tend to be more rigid in their thinking and more likely to embrace traditional viewpoints. Of course, these stereotypes are not absolute truths, but simply common observations.

① firm beliefs are not willing to change
② different viewpoints tend to have different appetites
③ a balanced diet tend to stay in shape
④ similar diets are likely to have similar personalities
⑤ eating problems are able to overcome them

225 If you resist giving away personal information about yourself to others, you might be giving yourself too much importance. If you look closely at what you might reveal, you will probably find that nothing is actually a great secret. Enjoyable close relationships are impossible to have unless you are prepared to reveal things about yourself. Of course, some thoughts and feelings are best left unspoken, especially in the office or with complete strangers. However, ____________________ is almost a guarantee that you will be lonely all your life. Thus, the next time someone shows an interest in your background, personal feelings, or opinions, you should take a risk; reveal something unique about yourself, and enjoy the reward of feeling good.

① distrusting people's motives
② revealing other people's secrets
③ being interested in a close relationship
④ avoiding getting along with strangers
⑤ refusing to share anything personal

226 Whether physical or not, punishment simply teaches children that if they break rules they will suffer negative consequences. Punishment does not necessarily teach children why the rules are in place, why the rules are important, or how they can best follow the rules. Punishment also does not teach children to be responsible or to take into account the thoughts, needs, or experiences of others. Discipline, on the other hand, always carries a lesson which helps children to understand what appropriate behaviors are and why they have become accepted in our society. Disciplining children is really a means of teaching children how to ____________ themselves.

① spoil ② define
③ punish ④ better
⑤ free

227 다음 글의 빈칸 (A), (B)에 들어갈 말로 가장 적절한 것은?

A pill to erase bad memories? This sounds like something out of a movie, but it may be closer to reality than you think. The drug, named "Propranolol," has the potential to heal painful memories. The drug breaks the link between the memory and its related emotions while the patient is thinking about the traumatic event. Then, the pain disappears. ____(A)____, critics of the drug insist that our memories make us human, and that painful events help us to become better people. ____(B)____, they are concerned that the drug will be used carelessly, to erase the normal feelings that come from everyday events like minor arguments and embarrassing situations.

(A)		(B)
① However	……	Also
② Similarly	……	Otherwise
③ Moreover	……	Instead
④ For example	……	Therefore
⑤ On the other hand	……	Nevertheless

228 다음 글에서 전체 흐름과 관계 없는 문장은?

Studies in American society show white teachers have lower expectations that their black students will graduate and go to college, and that lower expectations for black and Latino students are one possible explanation for observed achievement gaps. ① Meanwhile, black students receive suspensions at nearly four times the rate for white students. ② As solutions, many school systems have banned suspensions for subjective categories such as disobedience, and begun to rethink teacher training. ③ As a result, the costs for the new teacher training program have doubled. ④ At the same time, school districts have made a push to hire more teachers of color, motivated by findings showing that students of color do better in school if they have a teacher of the same race. ⑤ As one expert said, "Focus should be made on fostering a culture of equity and ensuring that all kids have access to high-quality teaching."

*suspension 정학 **equity 형평(성), 공평

229 글의 흐름으로 보아, 주어진 문장이 들어가기에 가장 적절한 곳은?

> However, there are times when aircraft are useful in getting food to people.

It should come as no surprise that the fastest way to transport food is by aircraft. (①) Also, it is the most expensive way to move food. (②) So between nearby countries, food is usually transported over land by truck or train. (③) Ships are usually used to transfer it between very distant countries because they are able to carry such large volumes. (④) Suppose there was a flood or an earthquake and people could not be reached by train or truck. (⑤) If food could not be transported by aircraft, those people might starve.

230 다음 글의 내용을 한 문장으로 요약하고자 한다. 빈칸 (A)와 (B)에 들어갈 말로 가장 적절한 것은?

To tolerate others, according to *The American Heritage Dictionary*, means, to recognize and respect them and their beliefs or practices, without necessarily agreeing or sympathizing with them. On the other hand, the word can mean to put up with others, though you may despise them, because some force, such as social norms, requires that you do so. It seems to me that people often pretend to use the first meaning of the word when they really have in mind the second meaning. In such cases, people are hypocritical when they use the word, and I do not admire them. They pretend to respect others, but in reality they are merely putting up with them. It is as though they are saying: Behave yourself, and I will be gracious enough to permit you to exist. Or, if you will accept my superiority, I will tolerate you.

⬇

> Contrary to its official meaning, a sense of ____(A)____ is often implied by the word "tolerate," which I find ____(B)____.

	(A)		(B)
①	modesty	……	admirable
②	modesty	……	unacceptable
③	unequalness	……	unacceptable
④	unequalness	……	admirable
⑤	balance	……	understandable

231 주어진 글 다음에 이어질 글의 순서로 가장 적절한 것은?

> Before you start a writing project, it's good to have a brainstorming session to get creative writing ideas. Sit, think, and write down every single idea that comes into your head.

(A) Your final copy should be double-spaced. Then, give it one last check before printing. Make sure your name and the title of your essay are written clearly on the first page.

(B) After you've finished the initial rough copy, review it carefully. Take some extra time at this stage to be really thorough. Think of better words and clearer sentences, and fix all obvious mistakes.

(C) When you are ready to start writing, just let your ideas flow, and don't worry too much about correct spelling or grammar. This is not the time to be a perfectionist.

① (A) − (B) − (C)　② (B) − (A) − (C)
③ (B) − (C) − (A)　④ (C) − (A) − (B)
⑤ (C) − (B) − (A)

[232 - 234] 다음 글을 읽고, 물음에 답하시오.

(A)

A man came home from work, late and exhausted — as usual. His little boy was still awake, sitting up in bed. Before going to sleep himself, the man sat down next to his son to say goodnight as he always did. "Daddy, how much money do you make an hour?" (a) he asked. "Your Daddy makes $20 an hour," the man replied, then sighed. "Now go to sleep."

(B)

The man got up, walked out, and closed the bedroom door. It had been another long day and the only thing he was looking forward to was sleep. But then (b) he thought maybe there was something his boy really needed that $10 for. He opened the bedroom door again. "I'm sorry, baby. It's been a long day, and I took my stress out on you. Here's that $10." "Oh, thank you, Daddy!" The little boy was delighted.

(C)

But the little boy wouldn't lie down. He sat up very straight near the edge of the bed, looked at his father, and politely asked a question. "Daddy, may I borrow $10?" The man looked annoyed. "Did you only want to know how much money I make so that you can squeeze some out of me? You already have enough toys and junk!" The little boy shook (c) his head and said, "Goodnight, Daddy."

(D)

Then, (d) he reached under his mattress and pulled out an envelope full of dollar bills. "Why did you ask for $10? You're rich already!" said the father. Again he was slightly annoyed, thinking that it had all been an act to get money for toys. "I didn't have enough yet, Daddy, but now I do," (e) he said. "I have $20 now. Can I buy an hour of your time?"

232 주어진 글 (A)에 이어질 내용을 순서에 맞게 배열한 것으로 가장 적절한 것은?

① (B) − (C) − (D)
② (C) − (B) − (D)
③ (C) − (D) − (B)
④ (D) − (B) − (C)
⑤ (D) − (C) − (B)

233 밑줄 친 (a)~(e) 중에서 가리키는 대상이 나머지 넷과 다른 것은?

① (a) ② (b) ③ (c) ④ (d) ⑤ (e)

234 위 글의 내용과 일치하는 것은?

① 아들은 장난감을 사기 위해 20달러가 필요했다.
② 아버지는 아들에게 돈의 소중함을 가르쳐 주었다.
③ 아들은 아버지의 스트레스를 덜어 주고 싶었다.
④ 아들은 아버지와 함께 시간을 보내고 싶었다.
⑤ 아버지는 용돈을 달라는 아들의 부탁을 흔쾌히 들어주었다.

독해 모의고사 2회

실제 시험이라고 생각하고 다음 문제를 풀어보세요.
주어진 시간은 25분입니다.

정답 및 해설 p.191

235 밑줄 친 her ability to scrutinize everything이 다음 글에서 의미하는 바로 가장 적절한 것은?

Could openness to other people's viewpoints cause you to lose your intellectual independence? Yes, but only if you accept their views unconditionally. As long as you test their ideas before accepting them, you will have nothing to fear. Take the example of Carol Tavris, a psychologist and a professor at Yale University. She began her work by considering the widespread belief that expressing anger openly makes us feel less angry. But she didn't stop there. She also considered opposing views and the correctness of related findings. Her conclusion that expressing anger tends to reinforce and even intensify it was the result of openness to all viewpoints plus her ability to scrutinize everything.

① discussing the matter with other experts
② blindly researching favorable opinions
③ considering others' views in a critical way
④ expressing openly that she could be wrong
⑤ making changes to the current environment

236 다음 글의 요지로 가장 적절한 것은?

If you ask your children to clean the kitchen, make sure they know what that means to you. Many parents get upset when their children do a terrible job with chores, even though they have never taken time for training. Taking time for training also does not mean children will do things as well as you would like. Improvement is a lifelong process. And, remember, the things you want them to do may not be a high priority for them until they become adults. Even though cleanliness and manners may not be a high priority for children, they still need to learn these qualities. Adults, however, need to remember that kids are kids.

① 부모는 자녀에게 솔선수범해야 한다.
② 가정교육을 위한 시간을 따로 마련해야 한다.
③ 아이들의 요구를 모두 들어줘서는 안 된다.
④ 자녀의 잘못된 행동에 일일이 화를 내서는 안 된다.
⑤ 가정교육 시 아이들에 대한 이해가 선행되어야 한다.

237 밑줄 친 it[its]가 가리키는 대상이 나머지 넷과 다른 것은?

Aquariums are popular around the world, and a wide variety of fish are kept domestically. Among them, the kissing gourami is popular because of ① its unusual habit of kissing other fish, plants, and various objects. ② It is exported to Japan, Europe, North America, and other parts of the world in great numbers. ③ It matures quickly, and rapidly gets too big for a small fish tank. Since ④ it likes to eat the slimy seaweed which grows on the inside of your aquarium, you don't need to clean the glass very often. It is very useful as a seaweed eater, helping to control ⑤ its growth.

*slimy 점액성의, 끈적끈적한

238 (A), (B), (C)의 각 네모 안에서 어법에 맞는 표현으로 가장 적절한 것은?

South Korean weather researchers expect this year's yellow dust season to be milder than those of recent years. Still, the dust caused the Korea Meteorological Administration to give warnings in Seoul and several other (A) [surrounding / surrounded] cities on Sunday. High levels of the yellow dust particles, which can cause breathing illness, remained in the air through Monday afternoon. Accordingly, KMA officials recommend that all outdoor activities (B) [are / be] canceled during yellow dust warnings, and that the young, old, and weak stay indoors. The dust typically comes from the Chinese and Mongolian deserts, potentially (C) [bring / bringing] along with it bacteria and industrial wastes.

*the Korea Meteorological Administration 한국기상청

	(A)		(B)		(C)
①	surrounding	……	are	……	bringing
②	surrounding	……	be	……	bringing
③	surrounding	……	be	……	bring
④	surrounded	……	are	……	bring
⑤	surrounded	……	be	……	bring

239 (A), (B), (C)의 각 네모 안에서 문맥에 맞는 낱말로 가장 적절한 것은?

"Stress causes illness!" If you want to stay physically and mentally healthy, avoid stressful events. This is a memorable message the majority of research and studies on stress have delivered to us. But such simple advice is just (A) [possible / impossible] to follow. Even if stressful events are dangerous, many — like the death of a loved one — are impossible to avoid. Moreover, any warning to avoid all stressful events is a prescription for staying away from opportunities as well as trouble. The notion that all stress makes you sick also (B) [reflects / ignores] a lot of what we know about people. It assumes we're all weak and passive in the face of difficulty. But what about human strength, initiative, and creativity? Many come through periods of stress with (C) [more / less] physical and mental strength than they had before.

	(A)		(B)		(C)
①	possible	……	ignores	……	more
②	possible	……	reflects	……	less
③	impossible	……	ignores	……	less
④	impossible	……	ignores	……	more
⑤	impossible	……	reflects	……	more

240 다음 도표의 내용과 일치하지 않는 문장은?

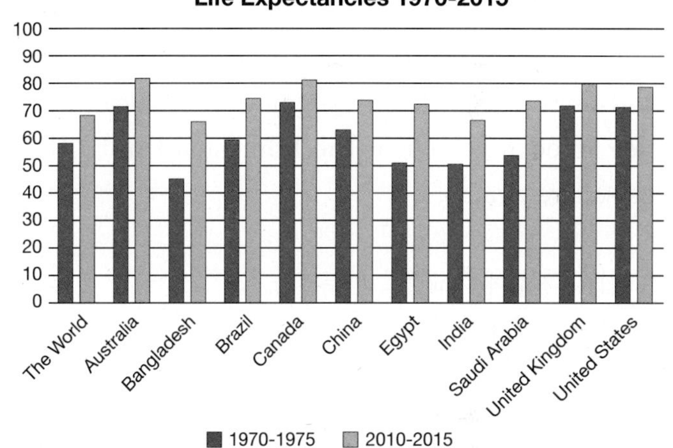

The graph above demonstrates the change in life expectancy between the periods 1970 — 1975 and 2010 — 2015. ① While four countries were below the worldwide average life expectancy in the 1970 — 1975 survey, only two countries remained below the average in the more recent survey. ② Australia, Canada, and the United Kingdom were the three countries that recorded the highest life expectancy in both surveys. ③ Among the four countries whose people lived more than 75 years on average in the more recent survey, the United States recorded the lowest average age. ④ The biggest increases were seen in Bangladesh, Egypt, and Saudi Arabia, all of which recorded an average of less than 50 in the earlier survey. ⑤ In contrast, countries that had recorded higher numbers made comparatively smaller increases during the last forty years than those with lower original numbers.

241 Emily Dickinson에 관한 다음 글의 내용과 일치하지 <u>않는</u> 것은?

Born on December 10, 1830 in Amherst, Massachusetts, Emily Dickinson left school as a teenager, eventually living a lonely life away from the company of others. There, she secretly created bundles of poetry and wrote hundreds of letters. Due to a discovery by her sister Lavinia, Dickinson's remarkable work was published after her death, and she is now considered one of the most important figures of American literature. Though the precise reasons for Dickinson's departure from school are unknown, it is said that her weak emotional state may have played a role in her father's decision to pull her from school. Emily and her sister Lavinia served as chief caregivers for their sick mother until she passed away in 1882. Neither Emily nor her sister ever married, and they lived together at the homestead until their respective deaths.

① 십 대 시절에 학교를 그만두었다.
② 한 농장에서 은둔의 삶을 살았다.
③ 작품이 여동생에 의해 발견되었다.
④ 사후에 작품이 출간되었다.
⑤ 병든 어머니를 돌보다가 사망하였다.

242 다음 글의 상황에 나타난 분위기로 가장 적절한 것은?

I make my way endlessly along an empty beach. I am aware that waves are crashing somewhere in the distance, but their sound is unclear and faint, as if I'm not really there. There's a light in the distance, but it seems the more I walk, the further away it gets from me. I finally give up, since I know I'll never reach it. The sun is almost gone, disappearing into a dark red sea. Low clouds are glowing as the sun sinks low. Behind them the dark shadow of an island appears. Its mountains seem like black giants in the sky. Suddenly everything melts into total darkness. There is not even a moon to show me the way now.

① calm and gentle
② joyful and festive
③ noisy and crowded
④ thrilling and exciting
⑤ hopeless and gloomy

[243-245] 다음 글의 빈칸에 들어갈 말로 가장 적절한 것을 고르시오.

243 It is a rare thing for cutting-edge technology to reach out and touch us on an emotional level, but when it does, the result can be brilliant and unexpected. For example, researchers in America and England have developed software that uses people's facial expressions to generate a work of art. People view a painting on a computer screen while a webcam records their faces. The computer can recognize an individual's emotions by analyzing eye and mouth movements. Each time the viewer's expression changes, the computer changes colors and brushstrokes to match the person's mood. The computer does all of this in real time, which means that ______________________.

① facial expressions change quickly
② using high-tech software is easy
③ its artwork is better than human artwork
④ the best colors are selected automatically
⑤ the viewer's emotions change the artwork

244 As social animals, a large portion of our lives revolves around guessing what others may be thinking or feeling. And we've developed several tricks for this. For example, many people believe that our eyes reveal the truth about how we are feeling: when we really like someone, we think that the person can probably tell that we do just by looking into our eyes. Now, scientists have proven it. They've found that our pupils ______________ ______________. Pupils are the little black circles in the middle of our eyes. They get bigger when you look at someone or something you like and smaller when you look at things you don't like.

*pupil 동공, 눈동자

① are unique like fingerprints
② move when we are telling lies
③ get smaller when we are angry
④ change size depending on our feelings
⑤ expand to let in more light when it's dark

245 Most people suffer some degree of anxiety when preparing for a test. This can be anything from a mild nervous feeling to a full panic attack. Whatever your level of anxiety, learning to reduce it is very important to study effectively for a test. Leave yourself ____________________________. Waiting until the night before a test to start studying is likely to increase your anxiety. You will be short of time, rushed, overwhelmed, and physically tired, with no time to ask questions or look up necessary information. Instead of waiting until the last minute, start studying as soon as a test is scheduled. With several days to prepare, you'll feel more relaxed.

① time to make plans
② plenty of time for studying
③ enough energy to start the work
④ a few places to study most efficiently
⑤ freedom to pursue your own study schedule

246 다음 글의 빈칸 (A), (B)에 들어갈 말로 가장 적절한 것은?

Many researchers and politicians make the unfortunate mistake of distinguishing between countries as "Western" or "Eastern." Although certain cultural characteristics are shared among "Western" and among "Eastern" countries, the same countries differ in many important areas. ____(A)____, religious differences within Europe itself probably mean that Southern Europe is more similar to much of Catholic South America than to Northern Europe. Samuel Huntington, a well-known political scientist, argued that it is better to speak of the "West" and the "Rest," where the distinction is based on economic activity and wealth. ____(B)____, with the rapid economic development of some of the non-West nations, this too will become increasingly irrelevant.

	(A)		(B)
①	In addition	……	However
②	In addition	……	Instead
③	In addition	……	Therefore
④	For example	……	However
⑤	For example	……	Therefore

247 다음 글에서 전체 흐름과 관계 없는 문장은?

A planet is a massive round object which orbits a star. They may be primarily made of gas, like Jupiter, or solid, like Earth or Mars. Some have rings or moons while others do not. The ancient Greeks were the first to map and name these objects. ① They called them "planets," which means "wanderers." ② Wanderers travel randomly from place to place and have no permanent home. ③ The Greeks believed that the planets wandered freely in the sky. ④ There are eight major planets and three minor planets in our solar system, and these planets orbit the sun. ⑤ However, modern science has proved that the planets have fixed orbits, and their movement can be predicted very accurately.

*moon 위성

248 글의 흐름으로 보아, 주어진 문장이 들어가기에 가장 적절한 곳은?

> But these hard-shelled reptiles don't need to run fast to survive.

Turtles are among the oldest creatures on Earth. (①) Land turtles are called tortoises, and their bodies are made to do everything very slowly. (②) Despite Aesop's famous story, the tortoise will never win a running race against a rabbit. (③) Its heavy and hard shell makes its body too stiff for running. (④) Tortoises can hide inside their shells when they are attacked by enemies. (⑤) Also, since most tortoises eat only vegetarian food, they don't need to run and catch animals for their dinner.

249 다음 글의 내용을 한 문장으로 요약하고자 한다. 빈칸 (A)와 (B)에 들어갈 말로 가장 적절한 것은?

Some people keep their rooms and workspaces in a spotless condition. For them, everything has a proper place, and they find it impossible to relax unless everything is exactly where it belongs. Others have rooms and desks in a state of complete chaos. They rarely give a second thought to where anything should be stored. But when these people need something, they can often find it straight away. Disorder does not always equal disorganization. It doesn't matter if other people think your room looks like a disaster area. If you can find everything when you need it, if you can keep things in fairly good condition, and if you feel comfortable in your space, then you are organized!

⬇

> Organization is not about how a space ____(A)____, but how it ____(B)____.

	(A)		(B)
①	looks	······	changes
②	looks	······	functions
③	looks	······	is cleaned
④	works	······	functions
⑤	works	······	changes

250 주어진 글 다음에 이어질 글의 순서로 가장 적절한 것은?

Stars consist mainly of hydrogen and helium, the two lightest elements in the universe.

(A) However, Earth is made up mostly of heavier elements, such as oxygen, silicon, and aluminum. The answer to where these elements came from is somewhat surprising. All of them were made by the stars billions of years ago.

(B) Those explosions fused the heavy elements into even heavier ones and threw them across vast distances. Those elements created new solar systems, including ours.

(C) Back then, when the stars were alive, enormous pressure and heat fused their light elements to produce heavier elements. As more and more of the stars were turned into heavy elements, the stars slowly ran out of energy and became unstable. Then, the stars exploded as they died.

*silicon 규소, 실리콘 **fuse 융합시키다

① (A) − (B) − (C)　② (A) − (C) − (B)
③ (B) − (A) − (C)　④ (B) − (C) − (A)
⑤ (C) − (B) − (A)

[251 - 252] 다음 글을 읽고, 물음에 답하시오.

"Take one pill three times a day for three days and you'll be fine," said the doctor. The patient did what the doctor said, and started to feel better. However, the pills contained no medicine. Then, why did the patient feel better? Most likely, it was due to the "placebo effect." In clinical tests, some people are given placebos instead of real medicine. A placebo appears to be medicine but is not. Scientists know very well the importance of mind over matter when it comes to medicine. Thousands of trials and studies have shown that between 50 and 75 percent of patients improve when treated with placebos. This is true for all problems, from minor allergies and burns to depression and cancer. One question: what type of placebo works best? The size and color of a pill does not seem to matter, but the type of treatment does. Injections, for example, produce greater placebo effects than pills do. But the biggest impact appears to come from ____________________. Doctors who show greater interest in their patients, and display greater confidence in their work, are responsible for more and stronger placebo effects.

*placebo effect 플라세보 효과
(위약 투여에 의한 심리 효과로 실제로 병이 호전되는 일)

251 위 글의 제목으로 가장 적절한 것은?

① Good Doctors Are Better Than Good Drugs
② Placebos: A Harmless Alternative to Traditional Medicine
③ The Placebo Effect: An Unscientific Myth
④ Placebos: What They Are and When They Work Best
⑤ Mind Over Matter: Take Control of Your Health

252 위 글의 빈칸에 들어갈 말로 가장 적절한 것은?

① the patient's age　② the doctor's behavior
③ physical appearance　④ family background
⑤ university education

독해 모의고사 3회

실제 시험이라고 생각하고 다음 문제를 풀어보세요.
주어진 시간은 25분입니다.

정답 및 해설 p.204

253 다음 글에서 필자가 주장하는 바로 가장 적절한 것은?

One of the most valuable lessons to learn in business is the concept of "lifetime value." This is what a customer is worth to you over the average period of time that he or she stays loyal to you. It is a tremendously helpful concept. Obviously, different customers have different values, but you can still make a reasonable guess. Let's assume you have a customer who buys his lunch from you three days a week. On average he spends £8 a day, which is £24 a week. We'll allow him six weeks of vacation, so that's £1,104 a year. If we assume that he stays with you for four years, then this equates to a total value of £4,416. This gives you a very different view on how you should treat him on a daily basis.

① 고객에 따른 맞춤 서비스를 개발해야 한다.
② 고객의 다양한 요구를 수용하는 것은 어렵다.
③ 단골 고객을 대상으로 한 할인 정책은 효과가 좋다.
④ 고객과의 관계를 장기적으로 유지하는 것이 중요하다.
⑤ 질 높은 서비스는 단골 고객을 만드는 지름길이다.

254 다음 글의 목적으로 가장 적절한 것은?

Are you swimming against the tide? Do you feel the need to escape from rules and tradition, to live life according to your own ideas and desires? No problem! We provide you with everything you need to design your environment in line with your own personal style. Live life to your own design! There is no limit to your freedom to determine your individual wall design. Whether you choose a pattern of shapes for the wallpaper in your child's room or decorate a modern kitchen with romantic flowery wallpaper — anything goes! Remember: exceptional wallpaper does not necessarily mean great expense; reasonably priced wall coverings can be used to create a unique and attractive wall. And for those with deeper pockets, our hand-made Luxury Wallpapers with beautiful bead detail will fit the bill.

① 좋은 가족 휴양지를 소개하려고
② 디자인 프로그램을 안내하려고
③ 저렴한 인테리어 방법을 알려주려고
④ 벽지 고르는 방법을 설명하려고
⑤ 다양한 벽지를 갖춘 상점을 광고하려고

255 밑줄 친 the same purpose가 다음 글에서 의미하는 바로 가장 적절한 것은?

A long time ago, Johann encountered his friend Hans in the forest and said, "Hans, I got that horse I wanted at a good price. I'm really lucky." In a second, however, Johann realized he had made a big mistake; he shouldn't have talked about his good luck out loud. Johann immediately ran to the nearest tree and started knocking on it. He believed that the gods lived in trees, and if they heard about any human happiness, they would cause problems. Johann, aware of what he had done in the listening forest, knocked on the wood to drive the gods away in the hope that his good fortune would suffer no reversal. Even when it was no longer a custom to literally "knock on wood," the phrase has remained to this day to fulfill <u>the same purpose</u>.

① helping friends in danger
② keeping good luck as it is
③ remembering your mistakes
④ believing trees to be their god
⑤ understanding your inner voice

256 (A), (B), (C)의 각 네모 안에서 어법에 맞는 표현으로 가장 적절한 것은?

It's very frustrating to lose or misplace things or (A) [waiting / to wait] for someone who is late. It's also bad when you fail to achieve a goal through lack of planning. At times like these, it can feel like your life is not under your control. But what's worse is that all these things are usually (B) [caused / causing] by mess and disorder. Depression, anxiety, anger, low self-esteem, and ruined relationships can also result. Mess and disorder are two forms of cancer that grow unnoticed until they become unmanageable. So get organized! It makes you (C) [control / to control] yourself and frees you to do the things you really enjoy.

	(A)		(B)		(C)
①	waiting	······	caused	······	control
②	waiting	······	causing	······	to control
③	to wait	······	caused	······	control
④	to wait	······	caused	······	to control
⑤	to wait	······	causing	······	control

257 다음 글의 밑줄 친 부분 중, 문맥상 낱말의 쓰임이 적절하지 <u>않은</u> 것은?

Language can strengthen social relationships as well as convey facts. Conversations between parents and children, or "small talk" between acquaintances, may not provide a lot of new information but are ① vital for forming bonds between individuals. Familiar legends and stories ② weaken a community's sense of history and values. Language can also highlight social distinctions. People speak ③ differently to friends, to those younger or older than themselves, and to employers. In some societies, rulers and elders are addressed with special titles that show ④ respect. People may also use words or dialects that are considered "prestigious" to make themselves appear ⑤ more cultured or important.

*dialect (어떤 사회·계급·직업의) 통용어, 은어; 방언

258 Pasadena Flea Market에 관한 다음 안내문의 내용과 일치하는 것은?

Welcome!
The Pasadena Flea Market features fascinating antiques and collectibles, thousands of tools, clothes, toys, and much more.

Location
The parking lots along the east side of campus and in our new lot located on the west side of campus at the corner of Hill and Del Mar

Show Time & Admission
The market is traditionally held on the first Sunday of the month from 8:00 a.m. ~ 3:00 p.m., and admission is FREE.

Note for Would-be Vendors
Due to the Market's popularity, all vending spaces are full and we maintain a waiting list. The waiting list is currently open. Please note that once on the waiting list, it can be several years before a space becomes available.

Parking Fee
Due to changes in campus policies, parking at the Flea Market is no longer free. Parking is now $2.00 for the day.

① 의류와 장난감은 판매되지 않는다.
② 시장은 대학 캠퍼스 운동장에서 열린다.
③ 시장은 매주 일요일마다 열린다.
④ 한 달 정도 대기하면 시장에서 물건을 팔 수 있다.
⑤ 주차장은 유료 이용으로 전환되었다.

259 Suzanne Collins에 관한 다음 글의 내용과 일치하지 않는 것은?

Suzanne Collins is the author of several novels for younger readers, including a best-selling series that began with 2008's *The Hunger Games*. With a college background in theater, she began her writing career in television. After spending several years writing kids' shows, she switched to writing novels for young readers, and published five novels in *The Underland Chronicles* series. She then wrote *The Hunger Games*, a tale of a teen girl forced to fight for her life in a dark and dangerous future U.S.A. Collins admits her stories are informed by the war experiences of her father, a veteran of the Vietnam War, and her childhood in a military family. Her skill at exciting storytelling is what made *The Hunger Games* popular, and what was intended as a novel for teenagers became a hit with readers of all ages.

① 대학에서 연극을 공부하였다.
② 방송 작가로 글쓰기를 시작하였다.
③ 상당 기간 동안, 어린이 프로그램을 썼다.
④ 첫 소설은 *The Hunger Games*이다.
⑤ 아버지의 전쟁 경험을 소설에 반영하기도 했다.

260 다음 글에 드러난 'I'의 심경 변화로 가장 적절한 것은?

I remember when we first arrived in Norway when we started our European Tour last year. When we got out of the airport, we were amazed at how clean the air smelled there. I was like a dog in a car sticking his head out the window and sniffing everything excitedly. It was so delicious. The difference is easy to notice. For those of you living in countries with clean air, don't take it for granted. It's lovely. I wish I could breathe in air like that all the time. I almost can't sleep thinking about what the long-term effects are of being in a place with poor air quality. How many years of our lives are we giving up?

① worried → relieved
② satisfied → hopeful
③ delighted → concerned
④ anxious → worried
⑤ curious → satisfied

[261 - 263] 다음 글의 빈칸에 들어갈 말로 가장 적절한 것을 고르시오.

261 People tend to show their ________________ unconsciously when they are speaking. While interviewing applicants for a scholarship, a university professor noted that students answered questions differently when asked about future plans. If they had achieved very high grades at school, they used the words "I am" and "I will." In contrast, relatively low-achieving students spoke in qualifiers, as in "Maybe I ...," "But I...," and "If I...," and filled their sentences with "Umms" and "Errrs." The students who used the words "I am" and "I will" had a strong belief that they would obtain their goals, while the others merely hoped to succeed but didn't believe they would make it.

① ambition ② self-belief
③ prejudices ④ sense of competition
⑤ desire for a scholarship

262 By the time you have reached adulthood, your brain has developed millions of neural pathways that help you process information quickly, solve familiar problems, and execute familiar tasks with a minimum of mental effort. But if you always stick to these well-worn paths, you are not giving your brain the stimulation it needs to keep growing and developing. You have to ______________________! Try taking a new route home from work or the grocery store, visiting new places on the weekend, or reading different kinds of books to keep your brain challenged with unexpected information and experiences. These activities break your routine and challenge you to use and develop new brain pathways.

① spare some time for exercise
② figure out ways to learn more efficiently
③ shake things up from time to time
④ stimulate your brain at a young age
⑤ respect your routine in order to develop

263 How can ______________________ affect the temperature of the planet? Believe it or not, studies show that it may be the biggest thing you can do. Going vegetarian, or at least cutting red meat out of your diet, is about stopping a practice that is doing tremendous damage to the entire earth. If you can't bring yourself to quit meat, try buying your animal products from local, small farms. Many small farms engage in carbon-offsetting programs to decrease any damage to the environment they make. By supporting local businesses that believe in environmentally friendly programs, you will be making it known that these factors matter and should be encouraged.

*carbon-offsetting 탄소 (배출량) 상쇄 (환경 보호 프로그램)

① starting small farms
② supporting local businesses
③ making animal products
④ changing your diet
⑤ protecting the environment

264 다음 글에서 전체 흐름과 관계 없는 문장은?

Mealtimes are more than just eating food; they are times to sit around the table together and talk. ① Children who eat meals together with their families are able to talk about important things or ask their parents questions. ② This is an important part of language development because it helps children improve their vocabularies to practice with more experienced speakers. ③ Furthermore, it's an opportunity for children to develop a sense for appropriate dinner conversation, a valuable social skill. ④ In this way, the ritual of preparing family meals fosters feelings of belonging, as well as teaching the importance of diet. ⑤ Parents can maximize the language benefit of family mealtimes by making it a point to foster interesting dinner conversation instead of watching TV.

265 글의 흐름으로 보아, 주어진 문장이 들어가기에 가장 적절한 곳은?

> In some cases, however, we may not know exactly what the result of our choice will be.

The interesting thing about stress is its true source. Throughout our lives, we receive, in a continuous series, rewards and punishments. (①) Through personal experiences over time, we learn which of our behaviors will earn rewards and which ones will create the negative feedback associated with punishment. (②) We adjust our lives on the basis of our perceptions of how to maximize rewards and minimize punishments. (③) We make a decision assuming it will have a positive outcome, but instead it may turn out badly. (④) When this happens, we must choose between the options of fight or flight. (⑤) At the same time, we must attend to the stress we are experiencing because our plans didn't work out as expected.

266 다음 글의 내용을 한 문장으로 요약하고자 한다. 빈칸 (A)와 (B)에 들어갈 말로 가장 적절한 것은?

Supermarket aisles are loaded with small-portion "diet packs" of snacks that will help you control your urges and hopefully eat less. But will buying such packs really help you reduce your consumption? To find out, researchers gave participants either two bags of potato chips or nine diet packs and asked them to watch TV. Before diving into their treats and TV, participants were weighed in front of a mirror to create a "dieting mind-set." The results revealed that participants given the diet bags ate twice as many chips as those given the large bags. The researchers speculated that the participants given the diet packs felt they didn't need to exercise as much self-control and thus ended up eating more.

⬇

> According to an experiment on diet packs, it turns out that diet foods ____(A)____ people to eat more because they feel less need to ____(B)____ themselves.

	(A)		(B)
①	forbid	……	enhance
②	forbid	……	relax
③	urge	……	defend
④	encourage	……	control
⑤	encourage	……	doubt

267 주어진 글 다음에 이어질 글의 순서로 가장 적절한 것은?

> Our relatively steady state of alertness over the course of a 16-hour day is due to what scientists call the circadian alerting system, a function of our internal biological clock.

(A) Only when the internal clock's alerting signal drops off does sleep load overcome this opposing force and allow for the start of sleep.

(B) The clock, which is responsible for controlling a large number of daily cycles, is found in a relatively small collection of neurons deep within the brain. Under normal conditions, the clock is closely matched to our sleep/wake cycle.

(C) When it is, the clock's alerting signal increases with every hour of wakefulness, opposing the sleep drive that is building at the same time.

*circadian (24시간을 주기로 변하는 생물체의) 생물학적 주기의

① (A) − (B) − (C)
② (B) − (A) − (C)
③ (B) − (C) − (A)
④ (C) − (A) − (B)
⑤ (C) − (B) − (A)

[268 - 270] 다음 글을 읽고, 물음에 답하시오.

(A)

Bette Graham Nesmith wasn't a great typist, which was unfortunate, because her job as an executive secretary at the Texas Bank and Trust required (a) her to do a lot of typing. This was at a time before word processors, when a single typing mistake could require starting the entire document over.

(B)

She tried to keep her typing trick a secret, but coworkers eventually caught on. People began asking (b) her to make bottles for them. Working nights and weekends, she turned her kitchen into a lab and her garage into a bottling plant. She recruited a chemistry teacher to help perfect the formula. She began selling hundreds of bottles a month — then thousands.

(C)

Graham called (c) her product *Mistake Out* but eventually changed the name to *Liquid Paper*. Over the course of twenty years, she turned her one-woman venture into a major company that sold more than 65,000 bottles of *Liquid Paper* every day. (d) She was eventually bought out by Gillette for nearly 50 million dollars, plus a royalty on every bottle sold.

(D)

While earning some overtime decorating bank windows at holiday time, Graham noted how the artist she was assisting corrected mistakes not by erasing but by painting over. This would serve as the inspiration for a major idea. Graham decided to put some white paint in a small bottle along with a tiny paintbrush to correct typing mistakes just like (e) she had done. The result was quite successful.

268 주어진 글 (A)에 이어질 내용을 순서에 맞게 배열한 것으로 가장 적절한 것은?

① (B) − (C) − (D)
② (B) − (D) − (C)
③ (C) − (B) − (D)
④ (D) − (B) − (C)
⑤ (D) − (C) − (B)

269 밑줄 친 (a)~(e) 중에서 가리키는 대상이 나머지 넷과 다른 것은?

① (a) ② (b) ③ (c) ④ (d) ⑤ (e)

270 위 글의 Graham에 관한 내용과 일치하지 않는 것은?

① 타자를 많이 쳐야 하는 업종에 종사했다.
② 오타 수정법을 알게 되어 동료들에게 널리 알렸다.
③ 더 완벽한 수정액을 만들기 위해 화학 교사를 고용했다.
④ 수정액을 개발한 뒤 5천만 불 이상의 돈을 벌었다.
⑤ 한 화가로부터 수정액에 관한 아이디어를 얻었다.

MEMO

MEMO

쎄듀런

1 구문

판매 1위 '천일문' 콘텐츠를 활용하여 정확하고 다양한 구문 학습

끊어읽기 | 해석하기 | 문장 구조 분석 | 해설·해석 제공 | 단어 스크램블링 | 영작하기

2 문법·서술형

쎄듀의 모든 문법 문항을 활용하여 내신까지 해결하는 정교한 문법 유형 제공

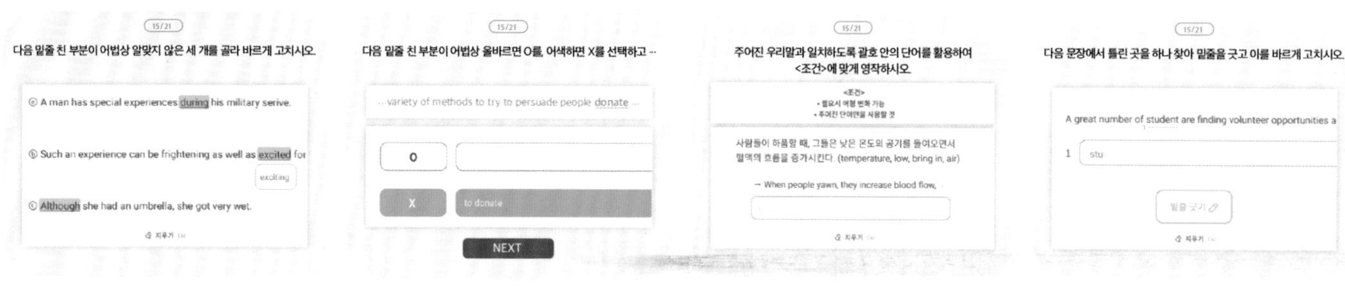

객관식과 주관식의 결합 | 문법 포인트별 학습 | 보기를 활용한 집합 문항 | 내신대비 서술형 | 어법+서술형 문제

3 어휘

초·중·고·공무원까지 방대한 어휘량을 제공하며 오프라인 TEST 인쇄도 가능

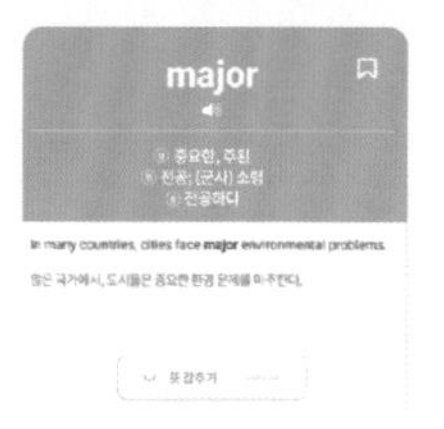

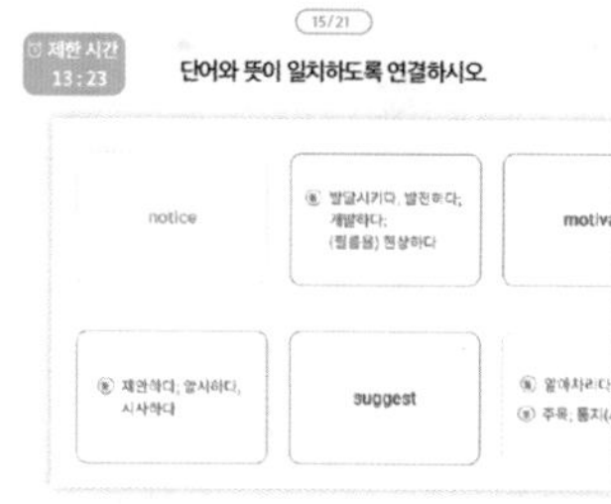

영단어 카드 학습 | 단어 ↔ 뜻 유형 | 예문 활용 유형 | 단어 매칭 게임

4 선생님 보유 문항 이용

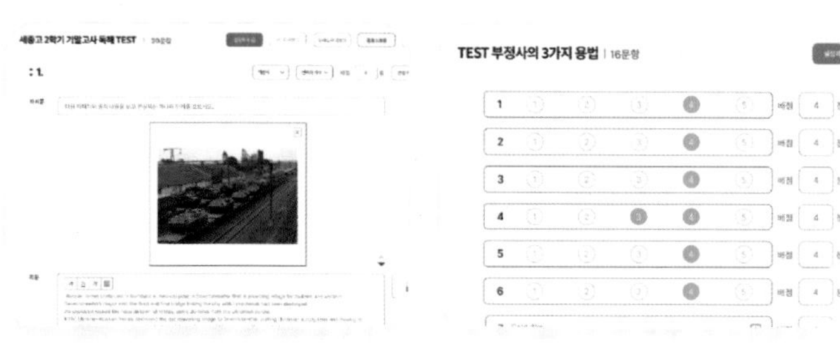

Online Test | OMR Test

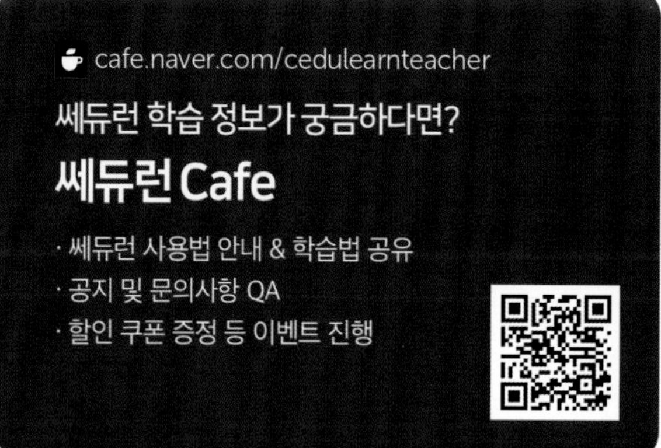
cafe.naver.com/cedulearnteacher
쎄듀런 학습 정보가 궁금하다면?
쎄듀런 Cafe
· 쎄듀런 사용법 안내 & 학습법 공유
· 공지 및 문의사항 QA
· 할인 쿠폰 증정 등 이벤트 진행

쎄듀 초·중등 커리큘럼

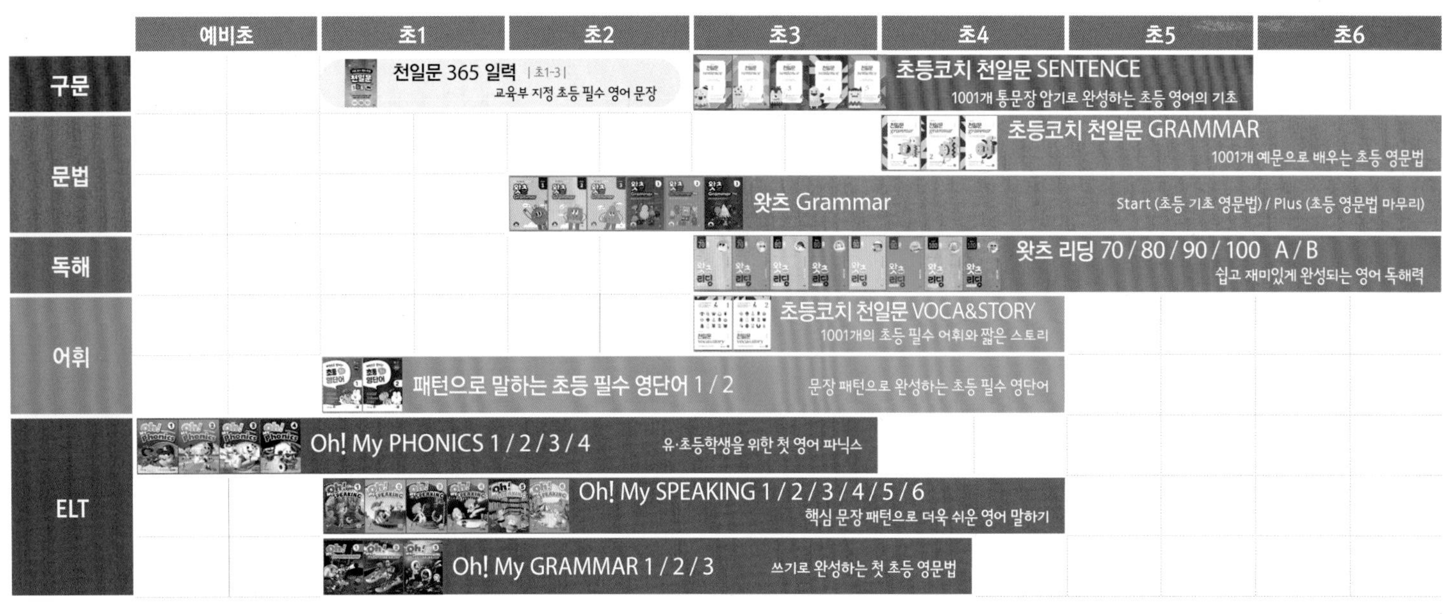

예비초 | 초1 | 초2 | 초3 | 초4 | 초5 | 초6

구문
- 천일문 365 일력 | 초1-3 | 교육부 지정 초등 필수 영어 문장
- 초등코치 천일문 SENTENCE — 1001개 통문장 암기로 완성하는 초등 영어의 기초

문법
- 초등코치 천일문 GRAMMAR — 1001개 예문으로 배우는 초등 영문법
- 왓츠 Grammar — Start (초등 기초 영문법) / Plus (초등 영문법 마무리)

독해
- 왓츠 리딩 70 / 80 / 90 / 100 A / B — 쉽고 재미있게 완성되는 영어 독해력

어휘
- 초등코치 천일문 VOCA&STORY — 1001개의 초등 필수 어휘와 짧은 스토리
- 패턴으로 말하는 초등 필수 영단어 1 / 2 — 문장 패턴으로 완성하는 초등 필수 영단어

ELT
- Oh! My PHONICS 1 / 2 / 3 / 4 — 유·초등학생을 위한 첫 영어 파닉스
- Oh! My SPEAKING 1 / 2 / 3 / 4 / 5 / 6 — 핵심 문장 패턴으로 더욱 쉬운 영어 말하기
- Oh! My GRAMMAR 1 / 2 / 3 — 쓰기로 완성하는 첫 초등 영문법

예비중 | 중1 | 중2 | 중3

구문
- 천일문 STARTER 1 / 2 — 중등 필수 구문 & 문법 총정리

문법
- 천일문 GRAMMAR LEVEL 1 / 2 / 3 — 예문 중심 문법 기본서
- GRAMMAR Q Starter 1, 2 / Intermediate 1, 2 / Advanced 1, 2 — 학기별 문법 기본서
- 잘 풀리는 영문법 1 / 2 / 3 — 문제 중심 문법 적용서
- GRAMMAR PIC 1 / 2 / 3 / 4 — 이해가 쉬운 도식화된 문법서
- 1센치 영문법 — 1권으로 핵심 문법 정리

문법+어법
- 첫단추 BASIC 문법·어법편 1 / 2 — 문법·어법의 기초

문법+쓰기
- EGU 영단어&품사 / 문장 형식 / 동사 써먹기 / 문법 써먹기 / 구문 써먹기 — 서술형 기초 세우기와 문법 다지기
- 올씀 1 기본 문장 PATTERN — 내신 서술형 기본 문장 학습

쓰기
- 거침없이 Writing LEVEL 1 / 2 / 3 — 중등 교과서 내신 기출 서술형
- 중학 영어 쓰작 1 / 2 / 3 — 중등 교과서 패턴 드릴 서술형

어휘
- 천일문 VOCA 중등 스타트/필수/마스터 — 2800개 중등 3개년 필수 어휘
- 어휘끝 중학 필수편 — 중학 필수어휘 1000개
- 어휘끝 중학 마스터편 — 고난도 중학어휘 +고등기초 어휘 1000개

독해
- ReadingGraphy LEVEL 1 / 2 / 3 / 4 — 중등 필수 구문까지 잡는 흥미로운 소재 독해
- Reading Relay Starter 1, 2 / Challenger 1, 2 / Master 1, 2 — 타교과 연계 배경 지식 독해
- READING Q Starter 1, 2 / Intermediate 1, 2 / Advanced 1, 2 — 예측/추론/요약 사고력 독해

독해전략
- 리딩 플랫폼 1 / 2 / 3 — 논픽션 지문 독해

독해유형
- Reading 16 LEVEL 1 / 2 / 3 — 수능 유형 맛보기 + 내신 대비
- 첫단추 BASIC 독해편 1 / 2 — 수능 유형 독해 입문

듣기
- Listening Q 유형편 / 1 / 2 / 3 — 유형별 듣기 전략 및 실전 대비
- 쎄듀 빠르게 중학영어듣기 모의고사 1 / 2 / 3 — 교육청 듣기평가 대비

절대평가 수능대비
수능 영어
정복의 첫걸음

첫단추

독해유형편

BUTTON UP

정답 및 해설

준비편

18가지 수능 유형 한눈에 보기

유형01 I ⑤ II ③	유형02 I ③ II ③	유형03 I ④ II ②	유형04 I ① II ③	유형05 I ① II ⑤	유형06 I ③
유형07 I ② II ①	유형08 I ② II ④	유형09 I ③ II ④	유형10 I ③ II ②	유형11 I ④ ④ ④ II ② ①	유형12 I ① II ②
유형13 I ⑤ II ③	유형14 I ⑤ II ⑤	유형15 I ⑤	유형16 I ④	유형17 I ③ II ④	유형18 I ② II ④

유형 01 주제

I 정답 ⑤

해석 한눈에 보기 공상 과학 소설은 반짝이는 로봇과 환상적인 우주선 그 이상의 더 많은 것을 포함한다. 주제문 **실제로, 대부분의 많은 기이한 공상 과학 소설 작품들은 과학적 사실에 기초를 두고 있으며 문학을 영어 교실에서 끌어내어 과학 교실로 가져오기 위해 사용될 수 있다.** 공상 과학 소설은 학생들이 과학적 원리들이 쓰이는 것을 볼 수 있도록 도움을 줄 뿐만 아니라 또한 학생들의 비판적 사고와 창의적 기술을 길러준다. 학생들은 비슷한 개념을 다루는 공상 과학 소설의 글과 논픽션의 글을 읽고, 그 둘을 비교하고 대조할 수 있다. 또한, 학생들은 아마도 스스로 과학 소설 이야기를 창조하거나 그들이 배운 지식과 기술을 적용하는 새로운 방법들을 상상하면서 다양한 방식으로 사용된 과학적 원리를 봄으로써 창의적 기술을 기를 수 있다.

① 공상 과학 영화의 공통적인 주제
② 인기 있는 문화에 대한 공상 과학 소설의 영향
③ 공상 과학 소설에 나타난 과학적 원리의 예
④ 공상 과학 소설 장르의 역사적 발전
⑤ 과학 교실에서 공상 과학 소설 사용의 이점

정답단추 이 글은 문학인 공상 과학 소설을 과학 교실에서 사용할 때 얻을 수 있는 다양한 이점에 대해서 설명하고 있어. 따라서 이 글의 주제로 가장 적절한 것은 ⑤야.

오답단서 ①, ②, ④는 글에서 언급한 science fiction을 이용해 만든 선택지일 뿐, 글의 내용과는 관련이 없어. ③도 글에 나온 science fiction과 scientific principles를 사용했지만, 과학적 원리의 예에 관한 글이 아니라서 오답이야.

어휘확인 science fiction 공상 과학 소설 involve 포함하다 shiny 반짝이는, 빛나는 fantastical 환상적인 spaceship 우주선 in fact 실제로; 사실은 outlandish 기이한, 이상한 piece 작품; 조각 basis 근거, 이유 scientific 과학의 literature 문학 principle 원리[원칙] in action 쓰이는, 작동을 하는 critical 비판적인 thinking 사고[생각] text 글; 본문 nonfiction 논픽션(소설이나 허구의 이야기가 아닌 전기·역사·사건 기록 따위) cover 다루다; 가리다 similar 비슷한 compare 비교하다 contrast 대조하다 possibly 아마 imagine 상상하다 apply 적용하다; 신청하다 knowledge 지식
〈선택지 어휘〉 common 공통의; 흔한 theme 주제 influence 영향 historical 역사적 development 발전, 발달 genre (예술 작품의) 장르 benefit 이점, 이득

눈에 보이는 핵심 구문

Not only does science fiction(S1) **help**(V1) students see scientific principles in action, // **but** it(S2) **also** builds(V2) their critical thinking and creative skills.

→ 「not only A but B ...」 구문이 사용된 문장으로 두 개의 절을 이어주고 있다. 부정어구 Not only가 문장의 앞으로 나오면서 주어와 동사가 도치된 문장이며 일반동사인 helps 대신 조동사 does가 주어 앞에 쓰였다. (= Science fiction not only helps students ~ skills.)

II 정답 ③

해석 한눈에 보기 주제문 **몇몇 동물 종(種)들은 다른 상처 입은 동물이 생존하도록 돕는다.** 돌고래는 숨쉬기 위해 수면에 도달해야 한다. 만약 돌고래가 너무 심하게 상처를 입어 혼자서 수면까지 헤엄칠 수 없다면, 다른 돌고래들이 그 상처 입은 돌고래 아래에서 무리를 지어 모여서 그 돌고래를 대기(물 밖)를 향해 위쪽으로 밀어 올린다. 만약 필요하면 돌고래들은 몇 시간 동안 이 일을 계속한다. 같은 종류의 일이 코끼리 사이에서도 일어난다. 코끼리가 쓰러지면 몸무게 때문에 호흡하는 데 어려움을 겪을 수 있고, 햇빛 아래에서 몸이 과열될 수 있다. 많은 코끼리 전문가들은 코끼리 한 마리가 쓰러지면, 무리의 다른 코끼리들이 그 코끼리를 일으켜 세우려 한다고 말했다.

정답단추 이 글은 몇몇 동물 종이 다른 다친 동물을 돕는다는 글로 첫 번째 문장에서 주제를 알 수 있으며, 돌고래와 코끼리를 그 예로 들고 있어. 따라서 이 글의 주제로 가장 적절한 것은 ③이야.

오답단서 ①, ②, ④, ⑤는 모두 글에서 언급한 '동물'을 가지고 만든 오답이야.

어휘확인 several (몇)몇의 species 종(種) injured 부상을 입은, 다친 survive 생존하다 wound 상처를 입히다 severely 심하게 by oneself 혼자, 스스로 group (무리를 지어) 모이다 upward 위쪽으로 향한 fallen (땅에) 쓰러진 be likely to-v ~할 것 같다 overheat 과열되다 expert 전문가

눈에 보이는 핵심 구문

If a dolphin(S') is wounded(V') **so** severely / **that** it(S") cannot swim(V") to the surface by itself, // other dolphins(S) group(V) themselves under it, / **pushing it upward to the air**(= as they push ~).

→ 「so + 형용사[부사] + that ...」 구문은 '너무 ~해서 …하다'라는 뜻으로 이때의 that은 결과를 나타내는 접속사이다. pushing ~ air는 동시동작을 나타내는 분사구문으로 as they push it ~ air.로 나타낼 수 있다.

유형 02 요지, 주장

I 정답 ③

해석 한눈에 보기 관계의 초기 단계들은 대개 비교적 갈등이 없다. 그러나 나중에 갈등은 종종 존재한다. 많은 사람들에게 관계 내에서의 갈등은 관계 자체가 곤경에 빠졌다는 것을 의미한다. 갈등이 없는 것이 우리 모두가 얻으려고 노력해야 하는 하는 기준으로 여겨진다. 주제문 밝혀진 바와 같이, 갈등은 피할 수 없을 뿐만 아니라, 실제로 관계의 장기적인 성공에 중요하다. 갈등을 백신의 한 유형으로 생각해라. 면역은 몸에 적은 양의 질병을 주입하는 것을 수반한다. 이것은 몸이 병의 약점을 배우도록 하고 실제 병에 대비해 몸을 준비시킨다. 마찬가지로, 사소한 갈등은 우리의 관계가 방어 능력을 키울 수 있도록 돕는다. 갈등은 관계에 면역성을 주고, 중대한 교착 상태가 발생했을 때 파트너들이 그것들을 처리하도록 도와준다.

정답단추 이 글은 관계에서 갈등이 없는 것이 좋을 것 같지만, 길게 보았을 때 관계에 도움이 된다는 점을 백신에 빗대어서 설명하고 있어. 따라서 이 글의 요지는 ③이야.

오답단서 ①, ②, ④, ⑤는 각각 글에서 언급된 disease, conflict, relationship, long-term을 가지고 만든 선택지로 글 전체 내용을 포괄하는 답이 될 수 없어.

어휘확인 initial 초기의 relationship 관계 relatively 비교적 conflict 갈등 free ~이 없는 within ~ 내에[안에] absence 없음; 결석 consider 여기다[생각하다]; 고려하다 standard 기준 strive for ~을 얻으려고 노력하다 turn out ~인 것으로 밝혀지다[드러나다] unavoidable 불가피한 crucial 중대한 long-term 장기적인 success 성공 form 유형, 종류 vaccine (예방) 백신 immunization 면역; 면제 cf. immunize 면역력을 갖게 하다 involve 수반[포함]하다 inject (액체를) 주입하다; 주사하다 amount 양; 총액 illness 병, 아픔 likewise 마찬가지로; 또한 minor 사소한, 작은(↔ major 중대한) develop 성장[발달]시키다 defense 방어 deal with ~을 처리하다; ~을 다루다 gridlock 교착 상태 arise 발생하다, 생기다

눈에 보이는 핵심 구문

This(S) **lets**(V_1) the body **learn** the disease's weaknesses / and prepares(V_2) the body for real illness.

⋯ 주어 This에 두 개의 동사 lets와 prepares가 and로 병렬 연결되어 있다. 사역동사 let의 목적격 보어 자리에 동사원형 learn이 쓰였다.

II 정답 ③

해석 한눈에 보기 인터넷은 아주 많은 다양한 면에서 놀랍다. 그것은 우리가 사는 방법을 변형시켜왔다. 우리는 사람들이 어디에 있든지 그들과 즉각 연락할 수 있다. 우리는 만날 필요조차 없이, 함께 계획들을 세울 수 있다. 우리는 마우스 클릭 한 번으로 정보의 세계에 접근한다. 반면에, 인터넷은 우리를 컴퓨터 화면에 붙잡아두고 동료 인간으로부터 격리시킨다. 우리는 이제 안부 인사를 하기 위해 전화를 걸거나 옆 사무실까지 100야드를 걸어가기보다는 이메일을 보낸다. 우리는 월드 와이드 웹과 우리가 살고 있는 실제 넓은 세상과의 균형을 만들어 낼 필요가 있다. 주제문 일주일에 하루 동안 당신의 컴퓨터를 끄고 당신의 노트북을 집에 남겨둔 후, 실제 세상 속으로 나와서 당신의 삶을 살아라.

정답단추 인터넷에는 여러 장점이 있지만, On the other hand부터는 인터넷이 우리를 현실 세계로부터 단절시킨다는 단점이 있음을 설명하고 있어. 그리고 마지막 문장 Turn ~ your life.에 필자의 주장이 나타나 있지. 따라서 정답은 ③이야.

오답단서 ①, ②, ④, ⑤ 모두 인터넷이라는 이 글의 핵심어를 사용했지만, 본문의 내용과는 거리가 멀어.

어휘확인 way 방법; 길 transform 변형시키다 instantly 즉각, 즉시 wherever 어디든지, 어디에나 have access to ~에 접근할 수 있다 information 정보 glue 붙이다; 접착제 monitor 화면, 모니터 isolate 격리하다, 고립시키다 fellow 동료; 친구 human being 인간 rather than ~보다는 call A up A에게 전화를 걸다 yard 야드(길이 단위); 마당 turn A off A를 끄다 laptop 노트북[휴대용 컴퓨터]

유형 03 제목

I 정답 ④

해석 한눈에 보기 2000년에 스코틀랜드의 글래스고 정부는 주목할 만한 범죄 예방 계획을 우연히 발견했다. 공무원들은 팀을 고용하여 일련의 파란색 전등을 다양한 눈에 띄는 장소에 설치함으로써 도시를 아름답게 했다. 이론상으로 파란색 전등은 밤에 도시의 상당 부분을 비추는 노란색과 흰색 전등보다 더 매력적이고 차분하며 정말로 그 파란색 전등들은 진정시키는 불빛을 발하는 듯했다. 몇 달이 지나서 연구원들은 두드러진 추세를 알아차렸는데, 파란색 전등이 있는 장소에서 범죄 활동의 극적인 감소를 겪었다(는 것이다). 글래스고의 파란색 전등은 경찰차의 전등을 흉내 내 경찰이 언제나 지켜보고 있음을 암시하는 듯했다. 그 전등은 결코 범죄를 줄이기 위해 설계되진 않았지만, 그것이 정확히 그들(전등)이 하는 것처럼 보이는 것이다.

① 우리 행성을 위해 불을 꺼라
② 파란색은 사람을 외롭게 한다
③ 당신의 기운을 돋우는 다채로운 불빛
④ 파란색 전등의 예상 밖의 결과
⑤ 더 깨끗한 거리가 더 낮은 범죄율로 이어지다

정답단추 글래스고 정부에서 도시를 가꾸기 위해 파란색 전등을 설치했는데, 본래 의도와는 달리 설치 장소의 범죄율이 감소했다는 점을 발견했다는 글이야. 이 내용을 종합했을 때, 본문의 제목으로 가장 적절한 것은 ④야.

오답단서 ①, ③은 본문의 핵심어인 lights를 이용해 오답을 유도하고 있어. ②는 전등의 색으로 언급된 blue를 사용한 오답이야. ⑤는 본문에서 언급된 적이 없어서 답이 될 수 없어.

어휘확인 happen upon ~을 우연히 발견하다 remarkable 주목할 만한, 놀라운 crime 범죄 cf. criminal 범죄의 prevention 예방 strategy 계획[전략] official 공무원; 공식적인 hire 고용하다 beautify 아름답게 하다 install 설치하다 a series of 일련의 various 다양한 noticeable 눈에 띄는; 뚜렷한 location 장소 theory 이론 attractive 매력적인 calming 진정시키는 illuminate (~에 불을) 비추다 indeed 정말 cast (빛을) 발하다; 출연자들 soothing 진정시키는 glow 불빛; 빛나다 researcher 연구원 notice ~을 알다; 주목 striking 두드러진, 눈에 띄는 trend 추세, 동향 dramatic 극적인 decline 감소 mimic ~을 흉내 내다[모방하다] imply 암시하다 exactly 정확히, 틀림없이 appear ~인 것 같다

〈선택지 어휘〉 planet 행성 unexpected 예상 밖의 outcome 결과 lead to-v ~로 이어지다 rate -율, 비율

눈에 보이는 핵심 구문

The blue lights in Glasgow,(S) / **which** mimicked the lights of police cars, / seemed(V) to imply // that the police(S') were always watching(V').

⋯ which ~ cars는 선행사 The blue lights를 보충 설명하는 관계사절이다. 선행사를 보충 설명하는 관계사절은 삽입되어 쓰이는 경우가 많다.

II 정답 ②

해석 한눈에 보기 당신은 예를 들어 환자를 한번 흘낏 본 후에 복잡한 진단을 내리는 의사 같은 전문가의 직관에 대한 이야기를 들어본 적이 있을 것이다. 전문가의 직관은 우리에게 마술 같은 인상을 주지만, 그것은 그렇지 않다. 사실 우리 각자

는 직관적 전문지식의 위업을 매일 여러 번 행한다. 우리 대부분은 전화 통화의 첫 단어 속에서 분노를 감지하는데 고도로 숙련되어 있으며 방에 들어갈 때 우리가 대화의 주제였다는 것을 알아챈다. 주제문 우리의 일상의 직관적 능력은 의사의 인상적인 통찰력에 못지않게 경이롭다. 단지 더 흔할 뿐이다.

① 화난 채로 전화 통화를 하지 마라!
② 직관적 전문지식은 전문가만을 위한 것이 아니다
③ 증거를 더 모아서 더 똑똑해져라
④ 직관: 마법사의 기본적인 자질
⑤ 직관은 결코 경험을 이기지 못할 것이다

정답단추 전문가에게만 있을 것 같은 직관적 전문지식이 사실은 우리에게도 있다는 글로 마지막 문장 Our everyday ~ more common.에 주제가 드러나 있어. 이를 가장 잘 압축한 제목은 ②야.

오답단서 ①은 본문에 나온 anger, a telephone call 등을 활용해 오답을 유도한 선택지야. ③은 이 글의 내용과 관련이 없어. ④, ⑤는 이 글의 핵심어인 intuition을 가지고 만든 선택지로 이 글의 내용과는 거리가 멀어.

어휘확인 expert 전문가 intuition 직관 cf. intuitive 직관적인, 직관력이 있는 physician 의사 complex 복잡한 diagnosis 진단 glance 흘낏 봄; 흘낏 보다 patient 환자 strike (~하다는) 인상을 주다; 치다 magical 마술적인 indeed 사실; 정말 perform 행하다 feat 위업 expertise 전문지식 highly-skilled 고도로 숙련된 detect 감지하다[알아내다] anger 분노, 화 recognize 알다 conversation 대화 ability 능력 striking 눈에 띄는 insight 통찰력
〈선택지 어휘〉 evidence 증거 intelligent 똑똑한 magician 마법사 basic 기본적인 qualification 자질[자격]

눈에 보이는 핵심 구문

Our everyday intuitive abilities (S) are (V) **no less** amazing **than** the striking insights of a physician — only more common.

··· 「A no less ~ than B」는 'A는 B에 못지않게 ~하다'로 해석한다. 'A는 B보다 덜 ~하지 않다'로 해석하지 않도록 유의한다.

유형 04 글의 목적 파악

I 정답 ①

해석 한눈에 보기 Coling 부인께,
제 이름은 Susan Harris이며 록우드 고등학교 학생들을 대신하여 씁니다. 학교의 많은 학생들은 록우드의 청년 실업 문제에 관한 프로젝트를 수행해 왔습니다. 4월 16일에 학교 강당에서 열리는 특별 발표회에 귀하를 초대합니다. 발표회에서 학생들은 우리 지역에 있는 청년들을 위한 고용 기회를 만들어 내기 위한 다양한 의견을 제안할 것입니다. 지역 사회의 유명한 인물 중 한 분으로서 귀하께서 참석해 주신다면 영광으로 생각할 것입니다. 그곳에서 귀하를 뵐 수 있기를 고대합니다.
Susan Harris 드림

정답단추 Susan이 이 편지글을 쓴 목적이 가장 잘 드러나는 문장을 찾아야 해. 글의 마지막 두 문장에서 Coling씨의 발표회 참석을 바란다고 있어. 따라서 이 글의 목적으로 가장 적절한 것은 ①이야.

오답단서 ③, ④는 글의 핵심어를 포함한 선택지이지만, 이 편지글의 궁극적인 목적이 아니라서 답이 될 수 없어. ②, ⑤는 이 글과 전혀 상관 없는 선택지야.

어휘확인 on behalf of ~을 대신하여 youth 청년; 어린 시절 unemployment 실업 attend 참석하다 cf. attendance 참석 presentation 발표회; 발표 hold (회의·시합 등을) 열다; 잡고 있다 auditorium 강당 propose 제안하다 a variety of 여러 가지의 develop 개발하다 employment 고용; 직장 opportunity 기회 within ~ 안에[내에] community 지역 사회; 주민 figure 인물; 수치 honored 영광으로 생각하여 look forward to ~을 고대하다 sincerely ~ 드림(편지를 맺는말로 이름 서명 전에 씀); 진심으로

II 정답 ③

해석 한눈에 보기 2년 전, 그린 자치주 도서관은 매주 목요일에는 저녁 8시까지 개방하기로 결정했습니다. 이것은 도서관을 방문하기에 저녁 시간이 유일하게 편리한 사람들에게 서비스가 가능하도록 하기 위한 것이었습니다. 그러나 그 늦은 시간에 방문객 숫자가 높은 수요를 보이지 않았고, 그래서 도서관 임원들은 운영 시간을 조정함으로써 직원 (근무) 시간을 좀 더 효율적으로 활용하기로 결정했습니다. 그래서 저는 여러분께 그린 자치주 도서관의 운영 시간이 2015년 10월 8일부터 변경될 것을 알려드리게 되었습니다. 목요일 운영시간은 정상적인 운영시간인 오전 9시부터 오후 6시까지로 되돌아갈 것입니다. 모든 정상적인 도서관 서비스는 이 운영시간 동안 계속 가능합니다. 또한, 이 변화는 그린 자치주 도서관이 지역사회에 대한 서비스를 개선하고 증가시키는 것을 가능하게 할 것입니다.

정답단추 이 글은 도서관 운영 시간과 관련된 안내문이야. 2년 전부터 목요일 운영 시간을 늘렸지만, 방문객 숫자가 그리 많지 않아서 운영시간을 조정하겠다는 내용이야. 글의 중간 So ~ 2015.와 그 다음 문장인 Operating ~ 6 p.m.을 통해 이 글의 직접적인 목적을 알 수 있어. 따라서 이 글의 목적은 도서관 연장 운영의 중단을 알린다는 ③이야.

오답단서 ①, ②, ④, ⑤ 모두 이 글에서 언급된 적이 없는 내용의 선택지라서 답이 될 수 없어.

어휘확인 county (영국·아일랜드·미국에서) 자치주[군] available 이용할 수 있는 convenient 편리한 visitor 방문객, 손님 demand 수요; 요구 official 임원; 공식적인 determine 결정하다 staff 직원 effectively 효과적으로 utilize 활용[이용]하다 adjust 조정하다 operate 운영하다; 작동하다 cf. operation 운영; 수술 inform 알리다 return 돌아가다[오다] normal 정상적인, 보통의 additionally 또한, 게다가 shift 변화; 이동하다 allow 가능하게 하다; 허락하다 increase 증가시키다 community 지역사회

눈에 보이는 핵심 구문

This (S) was (V) to make (v) library services (o) available (c) / to *people* [for whom evening was *the only convenient time* [to visit]]. (C)

··· to make ~ available은 명사 역할을 하는 to부정사구로 여기서 보어로 쓰였다.

유형 05 빈칸 추론

I 정답 ①

해석 한눈에 보기 작은 마을에서는 똑같은 직공이 의자와 문과 탁자를 만들고, 흔히 그 동일 인물이 집을 짓는다. 그리고 물론 여러 일에 종사하는 사람이 그 일 모두에 능숙하기는 불가능하다. 주제문 반면에 큰 도시에서는 많은 사람이 각각의 일을 필요로 해서, 온전한 일에 훨씬 미치지 못하는 일 하나만으로도 한 사람을 부양하기에 충분하다. 예를 들어 어떤 사람은 남성용 신발을 만들고, 다른 사람은 여성용 신발을 만든다. 그리고 어떤 사람은 신발에 바느질만 하고, 다른 사람은 그것을 잘라 내는 것으로, 또 다른 사람은 신발의 윗부분을 꿰매 붙이는 것으로 한 사람이 생계를 꾸리는 곳도 있다. 그런 숙련된 직공들은 간단한 도구를 사용할지도 모르지만, 그들의 전문화는 더 효율적이고 생산적인 작업을 초래한다.

① 전문화 ② 비판 ③ 경쟁
④ 근면 ⑤ 상상

정답단추 빈칸 문장을 먼저 읽으면, 더 효율적이고 생산적인 작업을 초래하는 것이 직공들의 '무엇'인지를 찾아야 함을 알 수 있어. 글의 앞부분에는 한 직공이 여러 일을 해서 모든 일에 능숙할 수 없다고 하고 있어. 그런데 In large cities부터는

신발 만드는 일을 예로 들어 한 가지 일을 세분해서 각 직공이 그 세분된 일만 하는 경우를 설명하고 있지. 이를 통해 작업의 효율성과 생산성을 높이는 것은 직공의 '전문화'임을 알 수 있어. 따라서 빈칸에 들어갈 말로는 ①이 가장 적절해.

오답단서 ②, ③, ④, ⑤ 모두 이 글의 내용과 무관한 내용이라 답이 될 수 없어.

어휘확인 workman 직공; 노동자 trade 일; 거래 skilled 능숙한, 숙련된 make demands on ~을 필요로 하다, ~을 요구하다 whole 온전한, 전체의 support 부양하다; 지지하다 for instance 예를 들어 earn a living 생계를 꾸리다 stitch 바느질하다; 바늘땀 sew 꿰매다; 바느질하다 upper (구두의) 윗부분; 더 위에 있는 tool 도구, 연장 result in ~을 초래하다, ~을 야기하다 efficient 효율적인; 유능한 productive 생산적인; 생산하는

〈선택지 어휘〉 specialization 전문화 criticism 비판 diligence 근면, 성실 imagination 상상

눈에 보이는 핵심 구문

And there are(V) *places*(S) even [where one man(S') earns(V') a living by only stitching shoes, another (**man earns a living**) by cutting them out, and another (**man earns a living**) by sewing the uppers together].

··· 이미 나온 어구인 man earns a living이 another 뒤에 각각 생략되어 문장을 간결하게 만들었다.

II 정답 ⑤

해석 한눈에 보기 주제문 사람들은 상황에 따라 변하는 가치관을 가지고 있다. 예를 들어, 어떤 사람이 물 한 병을 샀다고 하자. 그러나 플라스틱 병의 위험성에 관한 기사를 읽고 난 후, 다음 날에는 같은 사람이 똑같은 물병을 멀리할 수도 있다. 이 사람이 일 년 후 비행기를 타고 반(反) 플라스틱 회의에 가다가 사막에 추락한다면 플라스틱 병에 든 물 한 병이 그때 그곳에서는 그 사람에게 갑자기 세상에서 가장 귀중한 것이 될 수도 있다. 이 사람은 어느 하나를 다른 것보다 더 선호하는 성향을 보여주며, 매번 선택하고 행동할 때 가치에 순위와 순서를 매긴다는 것을 보여준다.

① 선택의 경제적 자유
② 영리한 소비 계획
③ 자연 재해에 대한 각기 다른 반응
④ 환경을 구하는 자신만의 방법
⑤ 상황에 따라 변하는 가치관

정답단추 빈칸 문장을 통해 사람들이 '무엇'을 가지고 있는지 찾아야 함을 알 수 있어. 플라스틱 병의 위험성에 관한 글을 읽고 이를 멀리하던 사람에게 비행기 추락으로 사막에 떨어졌을 때 플라스틱 병의 가치가 어떻게 달라질 수 있는지를 설명하고 있어. 이는 사람이 처한 환경에 따라 가치관이 변할 수 있음을 의미해. 따라서 빈칸에 들어갈 말로 가장 적절한 것은 ⑤야.

오답단서 ①, ②, ③, ④는 모두 이 글과 무관한 내용이라서 오답이야.

어휘확인 article 기사 risk 위험(성) identical 똑같은 anti- ~에 반대하는 conference 회의[학회] valuable 귀중한 cf. value 가치 universe 세계; 우주 preference 선호(도) demonstrate 보여주다; 입증하다 ranking 순위 order 순서

〈선택지 어휘〉 economic 경제의 freedom 자유 strategy 계획[전략] consumption 소비 reaction 반응 natural disaster 자연 재해 depending on ~에 따라 situation 상황

눈에 보이는 핵심 구문

For example, / a person(S) might buy(V) a bottle of water, // but **after reading an article on possible risks of plastic bottles**, ~.
= after the person reads an article ~

··· after reading ~ bottles는 의미를 명확히 하려고 접속사를 생략하지 않은 분사구문으로, 완전한 절로 고치면 after the person reads an article ~ bottles가 된다.

유형 06 함의 추론

I 정답 ③

해석 한눈에 보기 우리는 모두 많은 언쟁에서 가장 빨리 잃는 것 중 하나가 성질이라는 것을 안다. 냉정을 유지해야 한다고 말하는 것은 쉽지만, 어떻게 그렇게 하는가? 기억해야 할 요점은 때때로 언쟁에서 상대방이 당신을 화나게 하려고 애쓴다는 것이다. 그들은 당신을 화나게 하려고 의도적으로 계획한 것들을 말할 수도 있다. 그들은 만약 그들이 당신의 냉정을 잃게 한다면 당신이 무언가 어리석게 들리는 것을 말할 걸 아는데, 당신은 그저 화나게 될 것이고 당신이 그 언쟁에서 이기는 것을 불가능할 것이다. 그러니 그것에 넘어가지 마라. 한 발언이 당신의 화를 야기하게 말해질 수도 있지만, 제기된 문제에 초점을 맞춘 침착한 답변으로 응답하는 것은 가장 효과적일 가능성이 있다. 실제로, 어떤 세심한 청자도 당신이 "미끼를 물지" 않았다는 사실을 높게 평가할 것이다.

① 침착함을 유지하다
② 당신 자신을 책망하다
③ 화를 내다
④ 청중에게 귀를 기울이다
⑤ 당신의 행동에 대해 사과하다

정답단추 이 글은 언쟁에서 상대방이 당신을 화나게 하려고 하더라도, 화나게 되면 언쟁에서 이기는 것은 불가능할 것이니 그것에 넘어가지 말라는 내용이야. 따라서 밑줄 친 어구 "미끼를 물다"가 의미하는 바는 ③이야.

오답단서 ②, ⑤는 언쟁의 상황과 관련이 있는 반응이지만, 글의 요지인 '의도적으로 화나게 하는 것에 넘어가지 말라'는 것과 거리가 멀어. ①은 밑줄 친 부분과 반대되는 의미야.

어휘확인 temper 성질; 화, 짜증 cf. lose one's temper 화를 내다 argument 언쟁, 논쟁 keep cool 냉정을 유지하다(↔ lose one's cool 냉정을 잃다, 흥분하다) intentionally 의도적으로, 고의로 annoy 화나게 하다 foolish 어리석은 fall for ~에 넘어가다[속다] remark 발언, 말 issue 문제, 쟁점 raise (문제 등을) 제기하다; 들어 올리다 attentive 세심한, 주의 깊은; 경청하는 rise to the bait 미끼를 물다; 꾐에 빠지다 cf. bait 미끼

〈선택지 어휘〉 blame 비난하다

눈에 보이는 핵심 구문

The point(S) [to remember] is(V) **that** sometimes in arguments / the other person is trying / to **get you to be angry**.(C)

··· 「get A to-v (A가 v하게 하다)」에서 to-v의 수동태가 쓰였다.

Indeed, / any attentive listener will admire *the fact* / **that** you didn't "rise to the bait." (the fact = that절)

유형 07 요약문 완성

I 정답 ②

해석 한눈에 보기 미국의 한 하드웨어 제조업체가 독일의 배급 업체에 자사의 제품을 소개해달라는 초대를 받았다. 가능한 한 가장 좋은 인상을 주고 싶어서 그 회사는 독일어를 유창하게 하는 자사의 가장 유망한 젊은 경영 이사인 Fred Wagner를 보냈다. Fred가 자기를 초대한 독일인들을 처음 만났을 때 그는 굳게 악수를 했고 모두에게 독일어로 인사를 했으며 고개를 약간 숙여 인사하는 것까지도 잊지 않았는데, 그렇게 하는 것이 독일의 풍습이다. 매우 유능한 연설가인 Fred는 편안한 분위기를 만들려고 몇 가지 웃기는 농담으로 자신의 발표를 시작했다. 그러나 그는 자기의 발표가 그렇게 잘 받아들여지지 않았다고 느꼈다. 비록 Fred는 자신이 문화적 숙제를 했다고(문화에 대해 대비했다고) 생각했지만, 그는 한 가지 특정한 실수를 저질렀다. 그의 농담은 독일의 사업 상황에서 너무 격식을 차리지 않고 비전문적인 것으로 여겨졌다.

> 이 이야기는 사업 상황에서 (A) 유머를 사용하는 것이 독일에서는 (B) 부적절하게 여겨질 수 있다는 것을 보여준다.

(A) (B)
① 유머 …… 필수적으로
② 유머 …… 부적절하게
③ 몸짓 …… 필수적으로
④ 몸짓 …… 부적절하게
⑤ 이름들 …… 유용하게

정답단추 먼저 요약문을 읽으면 독일에서는 사업적인 자리에서 '이것'을 사용하는 것이 '어떻게' 받아들여질 수 있는 것에 대해 찾아야 함을 알 수 있어. 독일의 배급 업체를 대상으로 한 발표에서 Fred가 편안한 분위기를 조성하기 위해 몇 가지 웃기는 농담을 했는데 사실 독일 문화에서 사업 상황에서의 농담은 격식에서 벗어나고 전문가답지 못한 것으로 받아들여진다고 설명하고 있어. 따라서 (A)에는 humor(유머), (B)에는 inappropriate(부적절하게)가 들어가야 해.

오답단서 ①은 글의 내용과 반대되는 의미의 essential(필수적인) 때문에 답이 아님을 알 수 있어. ③과 ④는 gesture(몸짓)가 글의 핵심 내용과 관련이 없어서 오답이야. ⑤는 first names(이름들)와 useful(유용한) 모두 이 글에서 언급된 적이 없으므로 답이 될 수 없어.

어휘확인 hardware (컴퓨터) 하드웨어 manufacturer 제조업체[회사], 제조자 product 제품, 상품 distributor 배급 업체 impression 인상 promising 유망한 executive 경영 이사[간부] fluent 유창한 host (손님을 초대한) 주인 shake hands 악수하다 firmly 굳게, 확고히 bow (고개 숙여) 인사하다; 휘다 slightly 약간 custom 풍습, 관습 effective 유능한; 효과적인 public speaker 연설가 presentation 발표; 제시 humorous 재미있는 relaxed 편안한, 느긋한 atmosphere 분위기; 대기 even though 비록 ~일지라도 cultural 문화와 관련된, 문화의 particular 특정한 error 실수[오류] informal 격식에 얽매이지 않는, 편안한 unprofessional 비전문적인, 전문가답지 못한 business 사업 setting 환경[장소]
〈선택지 어휘〉 humor 유머 essential 필수적인 inappropriate 부적절한 first name (성이 아닌) 이름

눈에 보이는 핵심 구문

Fred(S), / a very effective public speaker, / began(V) his presentation / with a few humorous jokes / **to set** a relaxed atmosphere.
(Fred = a very effective public speaker; to set: 부사적 용법(목적))

··· a very effective public speaker는 Fred를 구체적으로 설명하는 동격인 명사구이다. to부정사구 to set ~ atmosphere는 목적의 뜻으로 쓰여 '~하기 위해서'라고 해석한다.

II 정답 ①

해석 한눈에 보기 Timothy Wilson은 학생들에게 다섯 개의 다른 미술 포스터의 선택권을 주는 실험을 했고, 그러고 나서 나중에 그들이 자신의 선택을 여전히 좋아하는지를 알아보기 위해 조사했다. 자신의 선택을 의식적으로 검토하라고 말을 들은 사람들은 몇 주 후 그들의 포스터에 가장 덜 만족스러워했다. 포스터를 잠시 본 후에 선택한 사람들이 가장 만족했다. 또 다른 연구원은 가구 상점을 배경으로 한 연구로 실제 상황에서 같은 결과를 보여줬다. 가구 선택은 소비자가 하는 가장 인지적으로 힘든 선택 중 하나이다. 덜 의식적으로 검토한 후 가구를 선택했던 사람들은 매우 주의 깊게 검토한 후 샀던 사람들보다 더 만족했다.

> 실험에 따르면, 무엇을 선택할지에 대해 더 (A) 신중하게 생각했던 사람들은 자신들의 선택에 대해 덜 (B) 만족스러워한다.

(A) (B)
① 신중하게 …… 만족스러워
② 긍정적으로 …… 실망스러워
③ 비판적으로 …… 짜증나
④ 부정적으로 …… 실망스러워
⑤ 간단하게 …… 만족스러워

정답단추 우선 요약문을 읽으면 글에 언급된 실험을 통해 선택할 때 '어떻게' 생각했던 사람들이 그 선택에 '어떻게' 느꼈는지 찾아야 함을 알 수 있어. Timothy Wilson이 진행했던 포스터 선택 실험과 또 다른 연구원이 진행한 가구 선택 실험 모두 사람들이 선택할 때 더 깊게 생각할수록 후에 그 선택의 만족감이 떨어졌다고 했어. 따라서 답으로는 (A)에 carefully(신중하게), (B)에 satisfied(만족스러워)가 들어가는 ①이 적절해.

오답단서 ②, ③, ④ 모두 글의 내용과 관련이 없어서 오답이야. ⑤는 요약문에 넣어 보면 선택에 대해 더 간단하게 생각했던 사람들이 그 선택에 덜 만족스러워한다는 내용으로 글에 나온 연구 결과와 반대임을 알 수 있어. 따라서 ⑤도 답이 될 수 없어.

어휘확인 experiment 실험 survey (설문) 조사하다; 조사 consciously 의식하여, 의식적으로 examine 검토하다 cf. examination 검토; 시험 briefly 잠시; 간단하게 researcher 연구원 produce 보여주다; 생산하다 furniture 가구 selection 선택 cognitively 인지적으로 demanding 힘든 consumer 소비자 conscious 의식적인 purchase 구입; 구입하다 according to ~에 따르면
〈선택지 어휘〉 satisfy 만족시키다 positively 긍정적으로 disappoint 실망시키다 critically 비판적으로 annoy 짜증나게 하다 negatively 부정적으로

눈에 보이는 핵심 구문

Timothy Wilson(S) did(V_1) *an experiment* [in which he(S') gave(V') students a choice of five different art posters], // and then later surveyed(V_2) them ~.

··· in which ~ posters는 선행사 an experiment를 수식하는 관계사절이다. 관계대명사가 관계사절 내에서 전치사의 목적어로 쓰여 관계대명사 which 앞에 전치사 in이 위치했다.

유형 08 무관한 문장 찾기

I 정답 ②

해석 한눈에 보기 주제문 아시아인들과 여러 북미 원주민 문화는 침묵을 사회적 상호 작용의 중요하고 적절한 부분이라고 여긴다. ① 이러한 문화들에서 온 화자는 다른 화자에게 반응하기 전 약간의 침묵의 순간을 자주 가진다. (② 침묵은 분열과 분리를 유발하고, 관계에 심각한 문제를 일으킨다.) ③ 이러한 초기의 침묵은 화자에 대한 청자의 존중을 전달한다. 그것은 청자가 화자의 말을 들었고 충분히 그 말을 생각하고 있음을 나타낸다. ④ 침묵은 화자가 한 말을 알고, 그것에 대해 생각하고, 검토해 볼 시간으로 여겨진다. ⑤ 침묵을 귀하게 여기는 문화에서는 화자가 자신의 차례를 끝낸 후 너무 빨리 반응하는 것은 화자의 말과 생각에 충분한 주의와 생각을 기울이지 않았다는 것으로 해석된다.

정답단추 이 글은 사회적 상호 작용에서 중요하고 적절한 부분으로써의 침묵의 기능을 설명하고 있어. 그런데 ②는 침묵이 나쁜 결과를 낳는다는 내용으로 이 글의 전체적인 내용과 반대되는 내용이야.

오답단서 ①의 these cultures는 앞의 Asians and many Native American cultures를 대신하는 어구이며 앞 문장에 이어 침묵의 기능에 대해 추가 설명을 하고 있어. 그리고 ③, ④, ⑤도 침묵의 기능에 대한 추가 설명이야.

어휘확인 Asian 아시아인; 아시아의 Native American 북미 원주민 silence 침묵; 고요 appropriate 적절한 interaction 상호 작용 offer 내놓다; 제안하다 response 반응 division 분열; 분할 separation 분리 relationship 관계 initial 처음의, 초기의 convey 전달하다 listener 청자 respect 존경(심) indicate 나타내다 due 충분한; ~로 인한 prize 귀하게 여기다; 상 turn 차례; 돌다 interpret 해석하다 devote 기울이다 inadequate 불충분한 consideration 사려, 숙고; 고려사항

눈에 보이는 핵심 구문

~ it(S) indicates(V) // that the listener(S') has heard(V'₁) the speaker's words and (the listener)(S'₂) is giving(V'₂) them(= the speaker's words) due thought.

··· indicates의 목적어로 쓰인 that절에 두 개의 동사(has heard, is giving)가 and로 병렬 연결되어 있다. 대명사 them은 and 앞에 쓰인 the speaker's words를 대신한다.

II 정답 ④

해석 한눈에 보기 주제문 흰올빼미의 귀는 외부에서는 보이지 않지만 놀라운 청력을 가지고 있다. 흰올빼미의 얼굴 깃털은 소리를 귀로 인도하고 인간이 들을 수 없는 것을 듣는 능력을 준다. ① 양쪽 귀는 크기가 다르며, 하나가 다른 하나보다 더 높이 있다. ② 양쪽 귀의 다른 크기와 위치는 이 올빼미가 소리들을 구별하는데 도움이 된다. ③ 이 올빼미는 큰 사슴의 먼 발굽소리, 위에 있는 새의 날개의 펄럭임 그리고 아래에 있는 작은 동물의 땅 파는 소리를 동시에 들을 수 있다. (④ 실제로 그것은 어둠 속에서와 먼 거리에서도 잘 볼 수 있는 시력을 가진다.) ⑤ 어떤 소리가 이 올빼미의 흥미를 가장 끄는지를 선택한 후, 거대한 원형 안테나가 최상의 수신 상태를 포착하듯이 흰올빼미는 자신의 머리를 움직인다.

정답단추 흰올빼미의 청력에 관한 글이야. 그런데 ④는 흰올빼미의 청력이 아니라 어둠 속과 먼 거리에서도 볼 수 있다는 시력에 관한 내용이라서 이 글의 전체적인 내용과는 관련이 없어.

오답단서 ①, ②는 앞 문장에서 언급하고 있는 흰올빼미의 귀에 관한 보충 설명이야. ③은 흰올빼미가 들을 수 있는 소리를 구체적인 예를 들어 설명하고 있어. 마지막으로 ⑤는 흰올빼미가 소리를 들을 때의 모습을 묘사하고 있어.

어휘확인 snowy owl 흰[눈]올빼미 visible 보이는 incredible 놀라운; 믿을 수 없는 hearing 청력, 청각 feather 깃털 ability 능력 location 위치 distinguish 구별하다 distant (멀리) 떨어져 있는, 먼 hoofbeat 발굽소리 deer 사슴 flap 퍼덕거림 dig (구멍 등을) 파다 in fact 실제로; 실은 excellent 훌륭한 vision 시력; 시야 at a distance 멀리서 circular 원형의, 둥근 antenna 안테나; 더듬이 reception 수신 상태; 접수처

눈에 보이는 핵심 구문

After choosing which sound interests it most(= After the snowy owl chooses ~), / the snowy owl(S) moves(V) its head / like a large circular antenna / to pick up the best reception(부사적 용법(목적)).

··· 뜻을 명확히 하기 위해 접속사 After를 생략하지 않고 남겨 놓은 분사구문으로 After the snowy owl chooses ~ most로 바꿔 쓸 수 있다. to부정사구 to pick up ~ reception은 '~하기 위해서'라는 뜻의 목적을 나타내는 부사적 용법이다.

유형 09 글의 순서 배열

I 정답 ③

해석 한눈에 보기 어느 누구든 내릴 수 있는 가장 필수적인 결정 중 하나는 시간을 어떻게 투자하느냐이다. (B) 물론 시간을 어떻게 투자하는지는 우리가 단독으로 내릴 결정이 아니다. 인류의 구성원이기 때문에, 혹은 특정 문화와 사회에 속해 있기 때문에 많은 요인들이 우리가 해야 할 일들을 결정한다. (C) 그럼에도 불구하고, 개인이 선택할 수 있는 여지는 있으며 시간에 대한 통제권은 어느 정도 우리 손 안에 있다. 가장 억압적인 산업혁명 시대에조차 사람들은 시간에 대한 자유 의지를 포기하지 않았다. (A) 이 시대의 사람들은 공장에서 일주일에 80시간 이상 일했다. 하지만 술집에 가는 대신, 자신들의 얼마 안 되는 소중한 자유 시간을 독서나 정치 관여에 사용하는 일부의 사람들도 있었다.

정답단추 먼저, 주어진 글의 how we invest our time이 Of course로 시작하는 (B)에서 반복되고 있어서 주어진 글 다음에는 (B)가 와야 적절해. 그리고 시간 투자 결정에 여러 요소가 영향을 미친다는 (B)의 내용에 이어서 그럼에도 불구하고(Nevertheless) 우리가 통제권을 가진다는 내용의 (C)가 와야 해. 마지막으로 (A)의 this period는 (C)의 산업혁명을 대신하니까 (A)가 (C) 다음에 위치해. 따라서 올바른 순서는 ③ '(B) – (C) – (A)'임을 알 수 있어.

어휘확인 essential 필수적인 decision 결정 invest 투자하다 period 시대; 기간 precious 귀중한 get involved in ~에 관여하다 politics 정치 pub 술집 factor 요인, 인자 determine 결정하다 human race 인류 belong to ~에 속하다 certain 어느 정도의; 확실한 nevertheless 그럼에도 불구하고 room 여지; 방 personal 개인의 extent 정도 oppressive 억압적인 Industrial Revolution 산업혁명 free will 자유 의지 when it comes to ~에 대해서라면

눈에 보이는 핵심 구문

Many factors(S) determine(V) what we should do(O) // either because we(S'₁) are(V'₁) members of the human race, / or because we(S'₂) belong to(V'₂) a certain culture and society.

··· 두 개의 because가 이끄는 절이 상관접속사 「either A or B」로 병렬 연결되어 있다.

II 정답 ④

해석 한눈에 보기 고대 아테네에서 Plato의 추종자들이 어느 날 모여서 다음과 같은 질문을 자신에게 했다고 한다. "인간이란 무엇인가?" (C) 많은 생각을 한 후에 그들은 다음과 같은 답을 생각해냈다. "인간은 깃털 없는 두 발 동물이다." 모든 사람은 한 철학자가 살아 있는 깃털 없는 닭을 가지고 강당으로 난입할 때까지는 이 정의에 만족하는 것처럼 보였다. (A) 그는 그것을 손에 들고, "보시오! 내가 여러분들에게 인간을 보여주겠소."라고 외쳤다. 충격이 지나간 후에, 철학자들은 다시 시도했다. 그들은 인간이 넓은 발톱을 가진 깃털 없는 두 발 동물이라고 말했다. (B) 초기 철학의 역사에서 나오는 이 호기심을 끄는 이야기는 추상적이고 일반적인 정의를 내리려고 할 때 철학자들이 직면한 어려움의 종류들을 보여준다.

정답단추 내용 전개가 자연스럽게 연결되도록 순서를 정하면 돼. 고대 아테네에서 인간의 정의에 대한 질문을 던졌다는 주어진 글 다음에는 답을 생각해냈다는 (C)가 와야 해. 그리고 (C)의 그들이 닭을 든 철학자가 나타날 때까지는 만족했다는 내용이 (A)에서 이어지고 있지. 그리고 이 이야기(This story) 전체가 보여주는 점을 정리하고 있는 (B)가 마지막에 와야 적절해. 따라서 올바른 순서는 ④ '(C) – (A) – (B)'야.

어휘확인 ancient 고대의 Athens 아테네 follower 추종자 human being 인간 present 보여주다; 선물 stir 충격; 젓다 philosopher 철학자 featherless 깃털이 없는 biped 두 발 동물 broad (폭이) 넓은 nail 손톱 curious 호기심을 끄는, 기이한; 궁금한 philosophy 철학 face 직면하다; 얼굴 attempt 시도하다 abstract 추상적인 general 일반적인 definition 정의 a great deal of 많은, 다량의 thought 생각 come up with ~을 생각해 내다 content 만족하는; 내용물 burst into ~에 난입하다 lecture hall 강당

눈에 보이는 핵심 구문

This curious story(S) [from the history of early philosophy] / shows(V) *the kinds of difficulties* [(which[that]) philosophers(S') face(V')] // **when attempting to give abstract, general definitions**(= when they attempt ~).

··· 전치사구 from ~ philosophy가 This curious story를 수식해서 주어의 길이가 길어진 문장이다. when attempting to give ~ definitions는 의미를 명확하게 하려고 접속사를 생략하지 않은 분사구문이다. 절로 나타내면 when they attempt ~ definitions.로 쓸 수 있다.

I 정답 ③

해석 한눈에 보기 인생에서 여러분을 믿고 응원하는 사람들이 있다는 것은 좋은 일이다. 그들은 여러분이 성취하려고 노력하고 있는 것에 진심으로 관심을 가지며 여러분의 모든 목표와 노력을 지지한다. 우리는 각자 우리의 인생에서 자신의 능력을 확신하고 자신의 목표를 향해 앞으로 나아갈 수 있도록 우리를 격려해 주는 사람들이 필요하다. 하지만 여러분의 인생에서 일어나 여러분을 응원할 사람이 주변에 아무도 없을 때가 있을 것이다. 이런 일이 일어날 때, 우울해하지 마라. 주제문 대신에 여러분 자신의 치어리더가 되라. 어느 누구도 여러분의 장점과 소질을 여러분보다 더 잘 알지 못하고 그 어느 누구도 여러분에게 여러분보다 더 잘 동기를 부여할 수 없으므로, 동기를 부여하는 격려의 말을 여러분 자신에게 하라.

정답단추 주어진 문장이 But으로 시작하지만, 특별히 가리키는 내용이나 뚜렷한 지시어가 없으니 글의 흐름이 끊기는 곳을 찾아야 해. ③의 앞 문장에서 우리는 격려해 줄 사람이 필요하다고 했는데, ③ 다음 문장에서는 이럴 때 우울해하지 말라고 하는 걸로 보아 흐름이 끊기는 걸 알 수 있어. ③에 주어진 문장을 넣어서 다시 읽어보면 당신을 응원해 줄 사람이 없을 때가 ③ 다음 문장의 이런 일(this)이고 의미도 자연스럽게 이어짐을 알 수 있어. 따라서 ③이 주어진 문장이 들어가기에 가장 적절한 곳이야.

오답단서 ①, ②, ④, ⑤는 앞뒤 문장이 유기적으로 잘 연결되어 있어서 주어진 문장이 들어갈 수 없어.

어휘확인 cheer on ~을 응원하다 truly 진심으로 achieve 달성하다 support 지지하다 goal 목표; 골 encourage 격려하다 capability 능력 depressed 우울한 cheerleader 치어리더; 지지자 motivational 동기를 부여하는 cf. motivate 동기를 부여하다 pep talk 격려의 말 strength 장점; 힘

눈에 보이는 핵심 구문

Each of us(S) needs(V) *people* in our lives [who encourage us] // **so that** we(S′) can feel(V'_1) confident in our capabilities / and (can) move(V'_2) forward toward our goals.

⋯› 관계사절 who encourages us는 바로 앞의 our lives가 아닌 people을 수식한다. so that은 목적을 나타내는 접속사로 '~하도록, ~하기 위해서'라고 해석한다.

II 정답 ②

해석 한눈에 보기 상어에 대한 두려움이 풀장에서 수영하는 많은 사람들이 바닷물을 시도해보지 못하게 해왔다. 특히 작은 해변 지역에서의 일련의 상어 공격을 특징으로 하는 영화 'Jaws'는 많은 사람들이 바다를 피해야 한다고 설득시키는 생생한 장면을 제공했다. 하지만, 상어에 의해 공격을 받을 실제 가능성은 아주 낮다. 당신은 해변을 오가는 운전을 하는 동안 더 큰 위험을 무릅쓰게 된다. 국제 상어 공격 기록에 따르면 상어 공격의 적은 횟수는 이 커다란 물고기가 본래 사람을 먹지 않는다는 것을 보여준다. 대부분의 상어 공격은 단순히 잘못된 정체파악 때문이다. 2007년도에 인간에 대한 상어 공격이 전 세계적으로 71건 있었고 단 한 명의 사망자만 있었다고 보고되었는데, 이는 벌에 쏘이는 것과 뱀에 물리는 것에 의한 2007년도의 사망률보다 상당히 더 낮다.

정답단추 However로 시작하는 주어진 문장에 뚜렷한 단서가 없으니까 글의 흐름이 끊기는 곳을 찾아보자. ② 앞 문장은 영화 'Jaws'가 사람들에게 바다를 피하게 만들었다는 내용인데, ② 뒤 문장은 해변으로 차를 타고 오갈 때 더 위험하다는 내용으로 두 문장이 자연스럽게 이어지고 있지 않음을 알 수 있어. 그리고 ②에 주어진 문장을 넣어서 읽어보면 영화가 사람들에게 상어에 대한 공포감을 주었지만, 사실 상어가 공격하는 경우는 매우 적으며 오히려 운전이 더 위험하다는 식으로 세 문장이 자연스럽게 이어져. 따라서 ②가 답이야.

오답단서 ①은 뒷문장이 앞 문장에 이어 추가 설명하고 있고 ③, ④, ⑤도 앞뒤로 내용의 흐름이 끊기지 않아서 주어진 문장이 들어갈 수 없어.

어휘확인 actual 실제의 attack 공격하다; 공격 fear 공포, 두려움 keep A from v-ing A가 ~하지 못하게 하다 feature 특징으로 삼다; 특징 a series of 일련의 community 지역 사회; 주민 provide 주다 vivid 생생한 image 장면; 이미지 convince 설득하다; 확신시키다 risk 위험 according to ~에 따르면 file 기록; 문서 indicate 나타내다 feed on ~을 먹다 by nature 본래; 천성적으로 simply 그저 due to ~ 때문에 mistaken 잘못 알고 있는 identity 정체 파악; 신분 worldwide 전 세계적인 death 사망 significantly 상당히 rate -율, 비율; 속도 sting (곤충 따위의 침·가시에) 쏘인 상처; 쏘다 bite 물기; (이빨로) 물다

눈에 보이는 핵심 구문

In 2007, / there were(V_1) 71 reported shark attacks on humans(S_1) worldwide / and (there was)(V_2) *only one death*(S_2), // which is significantly lower / than ~.

⋯› there는 형식적인 주어로 「there is[are] ~」는 '~이 있다'로 해석한다. which가 이끄는 관계사절은 앞에 나온 선행사 only one death를 보충 설명하고 있다.

유형 11 장문 독해

I 정답 i) ④ ii) ④ iii) ④

해석 한눈에 보기 (A) Victoria라는 이름의 열네 살 소녀는 항상 노래하는 것을 좋아했다. 그녀는 자주 학교 뮤지컬을 지원했지만, 결코 주연 중 하나는 아니었다. 스포트라이트는 그녀의 마음을 끌지 못했으며 그녀는 코러스 단에 섞이는 것을 선호했다. 그때 (a) 그녀(Victoria)는 중대한 도전에 직면했다. (D) Victoria의 학교에서 해마다 열리는 교내 뮤지컬 공연이 몇 달 후에 열릴 것이었다. Victoria의 엄마는 그날 중요한 회의가 있었다. 그녀는 Victoria가 주연을 차지한다면 (d) 자신(엄마)이 회의를 빠지겠다고 약속했다. 그녀는 Victoria가 자신이 (e) 그녀(Victoria)를 믿고 있다는 것을 알길 원했다. 그녀는 또한 Victoria가 자신을 믿길 원했다. 엄마가 한 말은 Victoria를 한동안 깊은 생각에 잠기게 했다. (B) 그 다음에 Victoria는 시도해 보기로 했다. 'Into the Woods' 뮤지컬에는 많은 중요한 배역들이 있었다. 그녀는 요정 대모 배역에 지원했다. 놀랍게도 그녀는 그 배역을 따냈고, 곧 긴장되기 시작했다. 그녀는 소프라노로 노래해야 했는데, 이는 자기 음역보다 몇 음 높은 것이었다. 그리고 그 대본은 (b) 그녀(Victoria)가 한 시점에 무대로부터 6피트 위에 매달리도록 요구했다. (C) 하지만, Victoria는 결심했다. 그녀는 관객 모두가 온전히 (c) 자신(Victoria)에게 집중될 그 순간을 준비하기 위해 몇 달 동안 매일 연습했다. 중요한 그날, 두려움에도 불구하고, Victoria는 자신의 배역을 완벽히 연기했다. 그녀의 엄마가 관객 속에 자랑스러워하며 앉아 있었고, Victoria는 기쁨을 느꼈다.

정답단추 i) 주어진 글 (A)의 마지막에 나온 a serious challenge는 주연 역할을 기피하던 Victoria가 엄마가 공연을 보러 오게끔 하려면 뮤지컬에서 주연 역할을 해야 하는 상황을 가리키므로 (D)가 이어져야 해. 이런 상황에서 깊은 생각에 빠졌던(fall ~ while) Victoria가 주연을 한번 해 보기로 결심했다는 (B)가 그 다음에 와야 적절해. 그런데 Victoria가 맡게 된 역할은 자신의 음역대보다 높은 음의 노래를 해야 할 뿐 아니라 공중에 매달려야만 한다는 내용에 이어서 그래도 결단을 내리고 열심히 연습해서 완벽하게 연기를 했다는 (C)가 와야 해. 따라서 알맞은 순서는 ④ '(D) – (B) – (C)'야.

ii) 지문에서 she, her가 대신할 수 있는 대상은 Victoria와 엄마야. (a)는 첫 문장의 Victoria를 대신하는 she야. 요정 대모 역할에 관한 설명에서 무대에 매달려야 하는 건 Victoria니까 (b)도 Victoria를 가리킴을 알 수 있어. 관중이 모두 집중할 대상인 (c)도 첫 문장의 Victoria를 대신해. 그리고 Victoria가 주연을 맡으면 회의에 빠지기로 약속한 사람은 엄마이므로 (d)는 엄마를 가리켜. 그리고 엄마는 자신이 Victoria를 믿고 있음을 알기를 원했다는 내용에서 (e)는 Victoria야. 따라서 가리키는 대상이 다른 하나는 (d)야.

iii) Victoria는 몇 달 동안 매일 연습한 끝에 완벽한 공연을 했다고(Victoria played her role to perfection.) (C)에서 설명하고 있어. 그런데 ④에서는 무대에서 실수를 했다고 하고 있지? 따라서 글의 내용으로 적절하지 않은 것은 ④야.

오답단서 i) Victoria가 중대한 도전을 하게 되었다는 (A)에 이어서 그 도전을 해 보기로 했다는 (B)나 (C)가 올 것 같지만, 주연을 맡는 것에 관해 깊이 생각했다는 (D)의 위치가 어색해져. 따라서 ①, ②, ③은 답이 될 수 없지. 그리고 (C)는 Victoria가 공연을 완벽하게 마쳤다는 내용으로 Victoria가 맡게 된 배역에 대해서 설명하는 (B) 앞에 올 수 없어. 그래서 ⑤도 오답이야.
iii) ①은 (A)에서 Victoria는 주연을 맡기보다는 코러스 단에 섞이는 걸 좋아했다고 했으므로 적절해. 그리고 Victoria는 'Into the Woods' 뮤지컬에서 요정 대모 역할을 맡게 되었는데 이는 자신의 음역대 보다 몇 음 높았다는 내용이 (B)에서 나오니까 ②, ③도 적절한 내용이야. 마지막으로 주연을 맡으면 회의를 빼고 뮤지컬을 보러 오겠다는 엄마의 말에 Victoria는 깊은 고민을 했다고 (D)에서 설명했으니까 ⑤도 맞는 내용이야.

어휘확인 leading role 주연 spotlight 스포트라이트, 환한 조명 attract 마음을 끌다 prefer ~을 좋아하다 blend into ~와 뒤섞이다 chorus 합창단; 후렴 face 직면하다; 얼굴 give A a try A를 한번 해보다 offer 내놓다 a number of 많은, 다수의 role 배역; 역할 fairy 요정 godmother 대모 nerve 긴장; 신경 set in 시작되다 immediately 즉시 soprano 소프라노 several 몇몇의 note 음; 메모 range 범위 script 대본 call for ~을 요구하다; ~을 필요로 하다 feet 피트(길이의 단위) determine 결정하다 train 훈련하다 whole 전체의 audience 관중 focus on ~에 집중하다 entirely 전적으로 despite ~에도 불구하고 fear 두려움 to perfection 완벽히, 완전히 proudly 자랑스럽게 delighted 기뻐하는 annual 매년의 hold (행사 등을) 열다; 잡다 skip 빼먹다; 생략하다 land 차지하다, 획득하다; 땅 fall into ~에 빠지다 thought 생각 for a while 한동안; 잠시

눈에 보이는 핵심 구문

She(S) trained(V) every day for months / to prepare for *the moment*(부사적 용법(목적)) [when the whole audience(S′) would focus(V′) entirely on her].

⋯› to prepare로 시작하는 to부정사구는 여기서 목적을 나타내는 부사구로 '~하기 위해서'로 해석한다.

II 정답 i) ② ii) ①

해석 한눈에 보기 지난해 Roberta Vinci는 전미 오픈 테니스 선수권 대회에서 세계 1위 Serena Williams와 테니스 경기를 했다. 누구도 Vinci가 승리할 것이라고 생각하지 않았지만, 그녀는 승리했다. 경기 후 인터뷰에서 Vinci는 자기가 이기는 것이 가능하다고 여기지 않아서 승리에 대해 생각하지 않으려고 노력했다고 말했다. "마음속으로 저는 '공을 치고 달려. 생각하지 말고 그냥 달려'라고 말했고, 그 결과 승리했습니다." Vinci의 태도는 긍정을 너무 강조하는 오늘날의 우리 문화와 크게 대조된다. 만약 당신이 어떤 일이 불가능하다고 느낀다면, 당신은 충분히 긍정적으로 생각하고 있지 않다는 말을 들을 것이다. 그러나 만약 당신이 어떤 일이 불가능하거나 성공할 수 없다고 정말 믿는다면, 자신에게 그렇지 않다고 납득시키려고 노력하는 것은 불안을 증가시킬 수도 있고, 실제로도 전혀 도움이 되지 않는다. 주제문 그러므로 때때로 어려운 목표를 달성하는 최선의 방법은 그것이 가능하다는 생각을 그만하고, 그저 한 번에 한 단계씩 해 나가는 것이다. 목표에 지나치게 집중하는 것은 당신이 원하는 것을 성취할 수 없도록 만들 수 있다는 것을 기억하라. 목표를 잊어라. 단지 공을 치고 달려라.

i) ① 긍정적인 생각의 힘
② 생각하는 것을 멈추고 그 순간에 충실해라
③ 원래 계획을 제대로 유지해라
④ 신체적 활동이 불안을 낮춘다
⑤ 성공하고 싶은가? 실수로부터 배워라!

ii) ① 목표 ② 노력 ③ 명성
④ 운 ⑤ 기쁨

정답단추 i) 주어진 글은 Roberta Vinci가 세계 1위의 테니스 선수 Serena Williams와의 경기에서 승리한 이야기를 예로 들면서 이기는 것, 즉 긍정적인 생각에 집중하지 않고 경기에만 집중해서 승리를 거둘 수 있었음을 설명하고 있어. 그리고 두 번째 문단의 Therefore, sometimes ~ at a time.에서 어려운 목표를 이루려면 성공에 대한 생각보다는 목표를 이루기 위한 과정에 집중하라고 설명하고 있어. 따라서 이 내용을 가장 잘 나타내는 제목은 '생각하는 것을 멈추고 그 순간에 충실하라'는 내용의 ②야.
ii) 빈칸 문장은 '무엇'에 지나치게 집중하는 것은 원하는 것을 성취할 수 없게 만들 수 있다는 것을 기억하라는 내용이야. 이 문장 앞뒤에서 '무엇'의 단서를 찾을 수 있어. 앞에서는 목표 달성 가능성에 대한 생각은 그만하고 하나씩 하라는 내용이고, 뒤에서 '무엇'을 받고 있는 it을 잊고 단지 '공을 치고 달리라'고 하고 있지? 이를 종합하면 '무엇'은 빈칸 앞 문장의 목적(objective)임을 알 수 있어. 따라서 빈칸에 들어갈 말로 가장 적절한 것은 '목적'을 나타내는 단어인 ① 'goal'이야.

오답단서 i) ①은 이 글 전체에서 다루고 있는 소재 중 하나인 '긍정'을 포함한 선택지이지만, 이 글과는 반대되는 내용을 나타내는 제목이야. 그리고 ③, ⑤는 이 글의 내용과는 전혀 관련이 없어. ④는 본문에 언급된 anxiety를 사용했고, 테니스를 연상시키는 physical activity를 사용한 선택지이지만, 이 글 전체의 내용과는 무관해.

어휘확인 -ranked ~ 순위의 U.S. Open 전미 오픈 테니스[골프] 선수권 대회 hit 치다[때리다] attitude 태도 stand against ~에 반대하다 emphasize 강조하다 positivity 긍정; 확실함 positively 긍정적으로 succeed 성공하다 convince 확신시키다 otherwise 그렇지 않으면 increase 증가시키다 anxiety 불안 accomplish 성취하다 objective 목표 at a time 한 번에; 따로따로 focus on ~에 주력하다, ~에 초점을 맞추다 prevent A from v-ing A가 ~할 수 없도록 만들다 achieve 성취하다
〈선택지 어휘〉 positive 긍정적인 thinking 생각 on track 바르게, 제대로 진행되고 있는 physical 신체의 fame 명성

눈에 보이는 핵심 구문

However, / if you(S′) really believe(V′) / that something is impossible, [or] that you won't succeed, // then trying to convince yourself otherwise(S) / can increase(V₁) your anxiety, / [and] actually doesn't help(V₂) at all.

⋯› or는 believe의 목적어 역할을 하는 두 개의 that절을 병렬로 연결하고 있고, and는 두 개의 동사구를 병렬로 연결하고 있다. 주절의 주어는 trying to ~ otherwise로 otherwise(그렇지 않다고)는 that something is possible and that you will succeed를 나타낸다.

유형 12 심경, 분위기 파악

I 정답 ①

해석 한눈에 보기 일몰이 늦게 오고 있었다. 덥고 햇볕이 강한 날이었고 공기는 무겁고 고요했다. 나는 마을 광장 한가운데 있는 큰 분수대를 보았는데 거기에 물은 없었다. 광장은 무섭고 날카로운 표정으로 나를 응시하는 검은 고양이를 제외하고는 비어 있었다. 가게들은 문을 닫았고 주위에는 아무도 없었다. 어두워지자 나는 불안해지기 시작했다. 나는 건너편 카페로 가서 테이블에 앉아 가방을 옆자리에 두었다. 창가 테이블에 앉은 두 명의 거칠어 보이는 남자들을 제외하고는 카페는 비어 있었다. 그들은 위협적으로 나를 관찰하다가 갑자기 나를 향해 다가오기 시작했다. 나는 정말 도망치고 싶었다.

① 무서운 ② 기쁜 ③ 안도하는
④ 궁금한 ⑤ 무관심한

정답단추 'I'의 심경을 알려면 'I'가 처한 상황을 파악해야 해. 날은 어두워지는데 아무도 없는 마을 광장에 혼자 있던 'I'가 카페 테이블에 앉았는데, 거칠어 보이는 남자 두 명이 'I'를 지켜보다 갑자기 다가와서 정말 도망치고 싶었다고 하고 있어. 따라서 'I'의 심경으로 적절한 것은 ①이야.

어휘확인 late in ~에 늦은 fountain 분수 square 광장; 정사각형 except for ~을 제외하고는 stare at ~을 응시하다 sharp 날카로운 anxious 불안해하는 beside ~ 옆에 rough 거친 -looking ~으로 보이는 observe 관찰하다 threateningly 위협적으로 approach 다가오다 escape 달아나다
〈선택지 어휘〉 fearful 무서운 relieved 안도하는 curious 궁금한 indifferent 무관심한

눈에 보이는 핵심 구문

I walked over to a cafe / and sat down at a table, / **putting my bag on *the seat* [beside me]**.
(S: I, V_1: walked over, V_2: sat down, putting my = and I put my ~)

⋯→ 분사구문 putting ~ me는 and I put my ~의 부사절로 나타낼 수 있다.

II 정답 ②

해석 한눈에 보기 할아버지께서 말씀하셨다. "Viola, 한잔 안 할래?" Viola는 엄마를 흘긋 쳐다보고, "아니요, 안 돼요, Tate씨, 안 되겠어요."라고 말했다. 그는 그녀를 무시하고는 그녀의 손에 잔을 쥐어 주었고 그리고 또 한 잔을 SanJuanna의 손에 쥐어 주었다. 그들은 모두 일어서서 축하의 잔을 들어 올렸다. 우리는 웃으며 우유가 든 잔으로 그들을 따라 했다. 아버지께서 말씀하셨다. "우리의 건강을 위해, 우리의 지속적인 번영을 위해, 그리고, 이렇게 즐거운 날, 할아버지와 그의 과학적 업적을 위하여. 저는 당신이 시간을 보냈던 방식에 대해 의아해 했던 적이 있었음을 인정할 수밖에 없습니다. 하지만 당신은 그것이 모두 가치 있는 일이었음을 증명해 왔습니다. 오늘 밤 우리는 자랑스러운 가족입니다!" Harry는 '참으로 좋은 친구를 위하여'라는 노래의 후렴을 시작했고 그러고 나서 그들이 세 번의 건배를 하도록 이끌었다.

① 차분하고 평화로운 ② 즐겁고 신나는
③ 슬프고 비탄에 잠긴 ④ 위험하고 긴급한
⑤ 엄숙하고 성스러운

정답단추 이 글에서 Viola의 가족들이 할아버지의 과학적 업적을 축하하기 위해 모였으며, 아버지께서 건배사를 한 뒤 건배를 하고, 노래를 부르고 있는 상황임을 알 수 있어. in celebration, laughing, started up a chorus, giving three cheers 등의 어구로 즐겁고 신나는 분위기임을 알 수 있지. 따라서 이 글의 분위기로 적절한 것은 ②야.

어휘확인 glance at ~을 힐끗 보다 ignore 무시하다 in celebration ~을 축하하여 imitate 흉내 내다 continuing 지속적인, 계속적인 prosperity 번영 grand 아주 즐거운; 웅장한 occasion 축하; 때 scientific 과학의 accomplishment 업적 admit 인정하다 prove 증명하다 worthwhile ~할 가치가 있는 chorus 후렴 jolly 참으로, 아주; 행복한 fellow 친구 cheer 건배; 환호(성)

〈선택지 어휘〉 calm 차분한 festive 즐거운; 축제의 sorrowful 비탄에 잠긴, 슬픈 urgent 긴급한 solemn 엄숙한; 침통한 sacred 성스러운

눈에 보이는 핵심 구문

I must admit / that there were *times* [when I wondered about *the way* [(that[in which]) you spend your time]], // but you have proven it to be all worthwhile.
(S_1: I, V_1: must admit, V': were, S': times, S_2: you, V_2: have proven, O: it, C: to be all worthwhile)

⋯→ when이 이끄는 관계부사절에 the way를 수식하는 절이 포함되어 있다. you ~ worthwhile은 SVOC 구문으로 여기서는 'O가 C이다'로 해석한다.

유형 13 지칭 대상 파악

I 정답 ⑤

해석 한눈에 보기 나이 많은 어느 목수가 은퇴를 앞두고 있었다. 그는 자신의 사장에게 ① 자신(목수)의 가족과 함께 할 계획을 이야기했다. 그는 매주 받던 급여는 못 받겠지만 은퇴를 원했다. 사장은 훌륭한 직원이 그만 두는 것이 아쉬워서 개인적인 부탁으로 ② 그(목수)가 집을 한 채만 더 지어줄 수 있는지 물어보았다. 목수는 그러겠다고 대답했지만, ③ 그(목수)의 마음은 자신의 일에서 떠났다. 그는 형편없는 재료를 사용했고 그의 마지막 작업에 그다지 많은 시간이나 노력을 쏟지 않았다. 그것은 그가 평생 해 온 일을 마무리하는 방식으로는 바람직하지 않았다. ④ 그(목수)가 작업을 마무리 했을 때, 그의 사장은 집을 확인하러 왔다. 그 후 ⑤ 그(사장)는 현관 열쇠를 목수에게 건네며 "이 집은 당신에게 주는 선물입니다"라고 말했다.

정답단추 이 글에서는 목수와 사장, 두 명의 인물이 등장하고 있어. ①은 목수가 자신의 가족 이야기를 하는 것이므로 목수를 가리켜. ②는 사장이 집을 지어달라고 부탁한 사람이니까 목수를 가리키고, 자신의 일에서 마음이 뜬 사람인 ③도 목수를 지칭해. 그리고 ④의 작업을 마무리 한 사람은 목수이고, 목수에게 현관 열쇠를 준 사람인 ⑤는 사장을 가리켜. 따라서 가리키는 대상이 다른 하나는 ⑤야.

어휘확인 carpenter 목수 retire 은퇴하다 boss 사장; 상사 paycheck 급료 personal 개인적인 material 재료 unfortunate 적절하지 않은, 부적당한; 불행한 lifelong 평생 동안의 career 경력; 직업 check out 확인하다 hand 건네주다; 손 front-door 현관

눈에 보이는 핵심 구문

The boss was sorry **to see** his good worker go and asked ~.
(S: The boss, V_1: was, 부사적 용법(감정의 원인): to see, V_2: asked)

⋯→ to부정사구 to see ~ go는 감정의 원인을 나타내는 부사구이다. 지각동사인 see는 동사원형 또는 현재분사(v-ing)를 목적격 보어로 취할 수 있는데, 여기서는 동사원형이 쓰였다.

II 정답 ③

해석 한눈에 보기 Carol은 미국에 처음 왔다. 한 친구가 ① 그녀(Carol)를 점심 식사에 초대하기 위해 전화를 했다. 그녀는 오전 11시 30분에 34번가와 5번가의 모퉁이로 그녀를 태우러 가겠다고 제안했다. Carol은 도착했을 때 ② 그녀(Carol)는 자신의 머리 위에 표지판 하나를 발견했다. 그 것은 "서 있지 마시오."라고 적혀 있었다. Carol은 어떻게 해야 될지를 몰랐다. 그녀는 거리에서 왔다 갔다 하며 걷기 시작했다. 그녀는 그녀의 친구가 도착했을 때 서둘러 ③ 그녀(친구)의 차에 탔다. 그녀는 사람들이 그곳에 서 있으면 안 되기 때문에 그 모퉁이에서 만나기로 한 것은 좋지 않은 생각이었다고 흥분해서 말했다. ④ 그녀(Carol)의 친구는 "무슨 말 하는 거야? 당연히 거기 서 있어도 돼."라고 말했다. "아니야, 표지판에 '서 있지 마시오.' 라고 적혀 있어."라고 ⑤ 그녀(Carol)가 말했다. 그녀의 친구는 웃음을 터뜨렸다. "그것은 차를 거기에 주차할 수 없다는 뜻이야."

정답단추 이 글의 등장인물은 두 명으로 Carol과 그녀의 친구야. 먼저 친구가 식사에 초대한 사람은 Carol이므로 ①은 Carol을 가리켜. 그리고 ②는 시간 부사절의 주어와 같은 사람을 대명사로 받고 있으니까 Carol을 가리켜. ③은 Carol이 친구의 차에 탔으니까 친구를 의미해. 그리고 Carol의 친구가 Carol의 말에 대답하는 상황이니까 ④는 Carol을 가리키고, 표지판의 의미를 오해한 것은 Carol이니까 ⑤도 Carol을 의미해.

어휘확인 offer 제안하다 pick A up A를 (차에) 태우러 가다 avenue -가, 거리 notice ~을 알아차리다 back and forth 왔다갔다; 앞뒤로 get into (차에) 타다; ~에 들어가다 excitedly 흥분하여 allow 허가하다 burst into (갑자기) ~을 터뜨리다 laughter 웃음 park 주차하다; 공원

눈에 보이는 핵심 구문

She excitedly explained // that it was a bad idea / to meet at that corner because ~.
(S: She, V: explained, 가주어: it, V': was, 진주어(S'): to meet at that corner)

⋯→ that절에서 주어 자리에는 가주어 it이 쓰였고 to-v가 이끄는 명사구가 진주어로 쓰였다.

유형 14 세부 내용 파악

I 정답 ⑤

해석 한눈에 보기 나우루는 남서 태평양에 있는 섬나라이다. 솔로몬 제도의 북동쪽 약 800마일에 위치해 있으며, 가장 가까운 이웃은 동쪽으로 약 200마일 떨어진 바나바 섬이다. 나우루는 공식 수도는 없지만, 정부 건물들이 야렌에 위치해 있다. 약 10,000명의 인구를 가진 나우루는 남태평양에서 가장 작은 나라이고 면적으로는 세계에서 세 번째로 작은 나라이다. 국기에 있는 12개의 꼭짓점을 가진 별이 상징하듯이 나우루 원주민은 12개의 부족으로 이루어져 있으며 이들은 미크로네시아인, 폴리네시아인, 멜라네시아인이 혼합된 것으로 여겨진다. 그들의 모국어는 나우루어이지만, 영어가 행정 및 상업적인 목적으로 사용되기 때문에 널리 쓰인다.

정답단추 선택지와 글의 내용을 차례대로 비교해 보면서 읽다 보면 마지막 문장에서 나우루의 모국어는 나우루어지만, 영어도 널리 쓰인다고 했는데 ⑤에서는 다른 언어는 사용하지 않는다고 했어. 따라서 글의 내용과 일치하지 않는 것은 ⑤야.

오답단서 본문에서 나우루가 솔로몬 제도의 북동쪽 약 800마일에 위치해 있다고 했으니 ①은 일치하는 내용이야. 이 글에서 나우루는 수도는 없지만, 정부 건물들은 야렌에 있다고 했으니 ②도 맞는 내용이지. 그리고 나우루는 면적으로 따졌을 때 전 세계에서 세 번째로 작은 나라라는 내용도 글에 언급되어 있으므로 ③도 일치해. 마지막으로 나우루의 원주민은 12개의 부족으로 이루어져 있다는 ④의 내용도 글에서 확인할 수 있어.

어휘확인 southwestern 남서쪽의 Pacific Ocean 태평양 be located 위치하다 northeast 북동; 북동쪽의 mile 마일(거리 단위) official 공식적인 capital 수도 population 인구 area 면적; 지역 native 원주민의; 태어난 곳의 consist of ~으로 이루어지다 tribe 부족 mixture 혼합; 혼합물 native language 모국어 widely 널리 business 상업, 사업 purpose 목적

눈에 보이는 핵심 구문

Their native language is Nauruan, // [but] English is widely spoken / **as** it is used for ~.
(S1: Their native language, V1: is, S2: English, V2: is widely spoken, S': it, V': is used)

···› 두 개의 절이 but에 의해 병렬로 연결되어 있으며, 여기서 as는 이유를 나타내는 접속사로 쓰여 '~ 때문에'라고 해석한다.

II 정답 ⑤

해석 한눈에 보기 짧은 뿔도마뱀은 짧고 뭉뚝한 뿔들이 있는 작고 납작하며 둥그스름한 (체형을 가진) 도마뱀이다. 그것들은 북아메리카와 중앙아메리카의 사막과 반건조 기후 환경에서 발견된다. 날씨가 더울 때는 오전에 가장 활동적이고 오후에는 덜 활동적이다. 짧은 뿔도마뱀은 그들이 주변 환경에 섞일 수 있는 바위 근처의 부드럽고 모래가 많은 토양을 선호한다. 그것들의 색깔은 주변 환경에 따라 적갈색부터 누런 회색까지 다양한데, 그 이유는 색깔이 위장 기능을 제공하기 때문이다. 몸의 아랫면은 흰색 또는 밝은 회색이며, 반점이 없다. 위협을 받으면 그것들은 자신의 몸을 평소 크기의 두 배까지 부풀릴 수 있다. 그리고 만약 이것이 충분하지 않으면, 그들은 포식 동물을 교란시키기 위해 눈에서 피를 쏜다. 그 피는 3피트의 거리까지 날아갈 수 있다.

정답단추 선택지와 글의 내용을 차례로 비교했을 때, 글의 마지막 부분에 나오는 짧은 뿔도마뱀은 포식 동물을 교란시키기 위해 눈에서 피를 쏜다는 내용이 ⑤와 일치하지? 따라서 정답은 ⑤야.

오답단서 글에서 짧은 뿔도마뱀은 더운 날씨에서 오전에 가장 활동적이라고 했는데 ①에서는 오후라고 해서 일치하지 않아. 그리고 짧은 뿔도마뱀이 선호하는 토양은 ②에서 언급한 바닥에 붙어서 몸을 숨길 수 있는 딱딱한 토양이 아니라 바위 근처의 부드럽고 모래가 많아 주변 환경에 섞일 수 있는 토양이야. ③에서는 반점이 있다고 했는데 글에서는 반점이 없다고 하고 있어. 마지막으로 짧은 뿔도마뱀이 부풀릴 수 있는 몸의 크기는 두 배까지라고 했는데 ④에서는 세 배라고 해서 일치하지 않아.

어휘확인 horned 뿔이 있는 cf. horn 뿔 lizard 도마뱀 stubby 뭉툭한 semi-arid 반건조 기후의 Central America 중앙아메리카 prefer ~을 좋아하다 sandy 모래가 있는, 모래가 든 soil 토양, 흙 blend in with (주위 환경에) 섞여들다; 조화를 이루다 background 배경 vary 각기 다르다 depending on ~에 따라 surroundings 환경 since ~ 때문에; ~한 이후로 provide 제공하다 camouflage 위장 underside 아랫면 spot 반점, 점 threaten 위협하다 capable of ~을 할 수 있는 normal 평소의; 보통의 prove 드러나다; 증명하다 insufficient 불충분한 shoot 쏘다 confuse 교란시키다, 혼란시키다 predator 포식 동물, 포식자 distance 거리 up to ~까지 feet 피트(길이 단위)

눈에 보이는 핵심 구문

When (being) threatened, / they are capable of blowing their bodies up / to twice their normal size.
(= When they are threatened; S: they, V: are)

···› 분사구문 When threatened는 의미를 명확히 하려고 접속사를 생략하지 않은 형태이다. 부사절로 나타내면 When they are threatened이다. 부사절의 동사가 수동태여서 분사구문에서는 being이 생략되었다.

유형 15 실용 자료 파악

I 정답 ⑤

해석 한눈에 보기 **박물관에서의 밤**

여러분은 이집트 조각상과 함께 잠들거나 미라 옆에서 깨어나는 것을 상상해 보신 적이 있나요? '박물관에서의 밤'에 오세요! 여러분은 해진 후에 박물관을 탐험하면서 하룻밤을 보낼 수 있습니다!

시간과 장소

매월 세 번째 주말

(토요일 오후 6시 30분부터 일요일 오전 7시 30분까지)

입장료(가격)

8세부터 13세까지만(1인당 40달러)

포함사항

활동을 위한 자료, 야간 숙박, 아침 식사

(주의: 아침 식사 때까지 음식이 제공되지 않으므로 간식을 가져오세요.)

예약정보

- 박물관 웹사이트의 '박물관에서의 밤' 페이지를 통해 온라인으로 표를 예약하세요.
- 표를 예약하기 위해서는 박물관 웹사이트에서 회원으로 가입해야 합니다.
- 환불은 행사 2주전까지만 가능합니다.

정답단추 각 소제목과 선택지 내용을 비교해 보자. 본문의 예약정보에 해당하는 내용을 보면 환불이 행사 2주전까지 가능하다고 했는데 이는 ⑤의 내용과 일치해. 따라서 정답은 ⑤야.

오답단서 시간과 장소를 보면 매주 주말이 아니라 매월 세 번째 주말에만 행사가 진행된다고 했으니까 ①은 오답이야. ②는 8세 이상이면 가능하다고 했는데 안내문에서는 8세에서 13세까지라고 나이 제한을 하고 있어. 그리고 포함사항 내용을 보면 아침 식사까지 음식이 제공되지 않으니 간식을 가져오라고 했으니 이는 음식 반입이 가능하다는 뜻인데 ③에서는 음식 반입이 되지 않는다고 했으니 오답이야. 마지막으로 ④는 회원 가입이 필요 없다고 했는데 안내문의 예약정보를 보면 표 예약을 위해서는 회원 가입을 해야 한다고 했으니 일치하지 않아.

어휘확인 imagine 상상하다 Egyptian 이집트의 sculpture 조각품 mummy 미라 explore 탐험하다 admission 입장료 include 포함하다 material 자료; 재료 overnight 야간의; 밤사이에 accommodation 숙박; 숙소 provide 제공하다 booking 예약 cf. book 예약하다; 책 information 정보 sign up 가입하다 refund 환불 up to ~까지

눈에 보이는 핵심 구문

You can **spend a night exploring** the museum after dark!
(S: You, V: can spend)

···› 〈spend + 시간[돈] + v-ing〉는 '~하는데 시간[돈]을 보내다[쓰다]'라는 뜻의 구문이다.

유형 16 도표 자료 파악

I 정답 ④

해석 한눈에 보기 위 도표는 2014년의 세계 최상위 국제 관광 소비 국가를 보여준다. ① 중국은 총 1,650억 달러로 목록의 최상위에 있었다. ② 세계에서 두 번째로 돈을 많이 소비한 국가인 미국은 국제 관광에 러시아보다 두 배 더 많이 돈을 소비했다. ③ 독일은 미국보다 200억 달러 더 적게 돈을 소비했으며 3위를 차지했다. ④ 영국은 580억 달러를 소비했는데, 그것은 미국이 소비한 총액의 절반보다 더 적었다. ⑤ 다섯 개의 국가 중에서, 러시아는 국제 관광에 가장 적은 금액의 돈을 소비했다.

정답단추 세계 상위 국제 관광 소비 국가를 보여주는 도표의 내용을 각 문장의 내용과 비교해보면 도표에서 영국이 소비한 돈은 580억 달러로 미국이 소비한 1,120억 달러의 절반인 560억 달러보다 더 많아. 그런데 글에서 미국이 소비한 돈의 절반보다 더 적었다고 했으니까 도표의 내용과 일치하지 않음을 알 수 있어. 따라서 정답은 ④야.

오답단서 ①은 도표에서 확연히 드러나듯이 중국이 1,650억 달러로 다섯 국가 중 최상위 소비 국가임을 알 수 있어. 그리고 미국의 소비 금액인 1,120억 달러는 러시아가 소비한 500억 달러의 두 배, 즉 1,000억 달러보다 더 많으니까 ②도 도표와 일치하는 내용이야. 그리고 독일은 920억 달러를 소비했음을 알 수 있는데, 이는 미국이 소비한 1,120억 달러에 비해 200억 달러 적은 돈이니까 ③도 일치함을 알 수 있지. 마지막으로 ⑤는 러시아가 500억으로 다섯 국가 중 가장 적은 돈을 소비했음을 도표에서도 확인할 수 있어.

어휘확인 tourism 관광(업) spender 돈을 쓰는 사람 billion 10억 dollar 달러 total 총, 전체의 place 등위; 장소 amount 액수, 총액

눈에 보이는 핵심 구문

The United States of America (USA), / the world's second largest spender, / spent more than **twice as much** / **as** Russia on international tourism.
(S = The United States of America (USA) = the world's second largest spender, V = spent)

··· The ~ America (USA)와 the world's ~ spender는 동격 관계이다. 「배수사 + as + 원급 + as」는 '~보다 (몇) 배 …한'이라는 뜻의 구문이다.

유형 17 어법성 판단

I 정답 ③

해석 한눈에 보기 많은 고객들은 상품이 시장에서 구할 수 있다는 것을 알게 된 후에야 상품을 구매한다. 어떤 상품이 시장에 출시된 이후에도 한동안 광고가 되지 않았다고 가정해보자. 그렇다면 어떤 일이 일어날까? 고객들은 상품이 존재한다는 것을 알지 못해서, 그 제품이 그들에게 유용했을지라도 아마 사지 않을 것이다. 광고는 또한 사람들이 자신에게 최적의 상품을 찾을 수 있게 해준다. 사람들은 전체 범위의 상품들을 알게 되었을 때, 상품을 비교하고 구매할 수 있어서, 힘들게 번 돈으로 원하는 것을 얻는다. 그래서 광고는 일상생활에서 필수적인 것이 되었다.

정답단추 (A)가 있는 문장의 주어인 상품(a product)은 광고'하는' 것이 아니라 광고'되는' 것이니까 advertised가 적절해.
(B)는 대명사가 무엇을 대신하는지 파악해야 하는데, 문맥상 제품이 '고객들(customers)'에게 유용하더라도 구매하지 않는다는 내용이 되어야 하니까 them이 와야 해.
(C)는 앞에 선행사가 없고 뒤에는 불완전한 절이 왔으므로 선행사를 포함한 관계대명사 what이 적절해.

어휘확인 customer 고객, 손님 product 상품(= goods) aware ~을 알고 있는 available (사물이) 구할 수 있는 even if ~에도 불구하고 out (모두 이용할 수 있도록) 나와 있어; 밖으로 for a while 한동안; 잠시 advertise 광고하다 cf. advertising 광고 exist 존재하다 probably 아마 whole 전체의 range 범위; 다양성 compare 비교하다 purchase 구매 desire 바라다; 바람 hard-earned 힘들여 번 thus 그래서 necessity 필수적인 것, 필수품; 필요 daily life 일상생활

눈에 보이는 핵심 구문

Not knowing that the product exists, / customers would probably not buy it // even if the product **may have worked** for them.
(Not knowing that the product exists = Because customers don't know that ~, S = customers, V = would probably not buy)

··· 분사구문 Not knowing ~ exists는 Because customers don't know that the product exists로 바꿔 쓸 수 있다. may have p.p.는 '~했을지도 모른다'라는 뜻으로 과거의 불확실한 추측을 나타낸다.

II 정답 ④

해석 한눈에 보기 식량을 찾아다니는 것은 야생의 식량 자원을 탐색하는 수단이다. 이것은 오랫동안 사용되어 온 방법이며 수천 년 전으로 거슬러 올라가는 아마도 가장 오래된 식량 탐색 방법이다. 과거에는 사람들이 보통 숲, 강가, 동굴, 그리고 식량이 발견될 수 있는 거의 모든 곳에서 식량을 찾아다녔다. 찾아다니며 얻은 대부분의 식량들이 뿌리 작물, 잡초, 그리고 관목이었다. 요즘 식량을 찾아다니는 것이 또 다시 흔해지고 있다. 오늘날의 빠르게 진행되는 사회 속의 사람들은 필요에 의해서든 즐거움을 위해서든 이것에 참여하고 있다. 그 목적이 무엇이든 간에, 사람들은 이제 식량을 찾아다니는 것에 느리지만 확실하게 친숙해지고 있다. 점점 더 많은 사람들이 그것이 꽤 성취감을 주는 일이고 매우 유익한 것으로 생각한다.

정답단추 ④를 포함한 문장에서 in today's fast-paced society의 수식을 받는 People이 주어이고 문장에 다른 동사가 없으므로 ④가 이 문장의 동사자리임을 알 수 있어. 즉, 주어의 수와 문장의 시제에 맞춰서 engaging in은 engage in으로 고쳐야 해. 따라서 어법상 틀린 것은 ④야.

오답단서 ①은 앞의 선행사 a method를 수식하는 주격 관계대명사 자리니까 that은 옳아. ②를 포함한 문장에서 문맥상 음식이 '찾는' 곳이 아니라 '찾아지는' 곳이 자연스러우므로 수동형 be found는 적절해. 그리고 Most of the foods에서 the foods가 복수니까 ③의 were도 적절하지. 마지막으로 ⑤는 find의 목적어 it을 보충 설명하는 목적격 보어로 형용사가 적절하게 쓰였어.

어휘확인 forage 식량을 찾아다니다 means 수단 food resource 식량 자원 method 방법 possibly 아마 trace back to ~까지 거슬러 올라가다 commonly 보통 riverside 강가 cave 동굴 virtually 거의, 사실상 root (식물의) 뿌리 crop 작물 weed 잡초 shrub 관목 fast-paced 빨리 진행되는 engage in ~에 참여하다 necessity 필요(성) entertainment 즐거움; 오락 whatever 어떤 ~이든 purpose 목적 acquainted 알고 있는 fulfilling 성취감을 주는 beneficial 유익한

눈에 보이는 핵심 구문

In the past, / people commonly foraged for food / in forests, riversides, caves, and virtually *any place* [where food could possibly be found].
(S = people, V = foraged, S' = food, V' = could possibly be found)

··· 관계부사절 where ~ be found가 선행사 any place를 수식한다.

I 정답 ②

해석 한눈에 보기 느낌과 감정은 매일의 의사 결정에 매우 중요하다. 신경과학자인 Antonio Damasio는 감정 체계에 손상을 준 뇌 부상을 제외하고 모든 면에서 완벽하게 정상적인 사람들을 연구했다. 결과적으로, 그들은 세상 속에서 효과적으로 결정을 내리거나 기능을 (A) 할 수 없었다. 그들은 자신들이 어떻게 기능하고 있어야 했는지 정확하게 묘사할 수는 있었지만, 어디에 살고, 무엇을 먹고, 어떤 제품을 사서 사용할지는 결정할 수가 없었다. 이러한 결과는 의사 결정이 합리적이고 논리적인 사고의 핵심이라는 보편적 믿음을 (B) 반박한다. 그러나 최신 연구는 정서적 체계가 여러분이 좋고 나쁜 것 사이에서 빠른 선택을 하도록 돕고, 고려해야 할 것들의 수를 줄여주면서 여러분의 의사 결정에 중대한 (C) 도움을 준다는 것을 보여준다.

	(A)		(B)		(C)
①	할 수 있었다	……	반박한다	……	도움
②	할 수 없었다	……	반박한다	……	도움
③	할 수 없었다	……	반박한다	……	방해
④	할 수 없었다	……	지지한다	……	방해
⑤	할 수 있었다	……	지지한다	……	방해

정답단추 (A) 다음 문장에서 감정 체계에 손상이 있는 사람들이 설명은 할 수 있었지만 결정하지 못했다고 했으니까 그들이 효과적으로 결정을 내리거나 기능'할 수 없었다'는 내용이 되어야 자연스러워. 그래서 unable이 들어가야 해. 그리고 (B)를 포함한 앞 문장에서 논리적인 사고가 가능하더라도 의사 결정은 내리지 못했다는 연구 결과가 나왔으니까 의사 결정이 합리적이고 논리적 사고의 중심이라는 믿음을 '반박하고' 있어. 따라서 (B)는 contradicts가 적절해. (C)를 포함한 문장은 앞 내용을 반박하면서 정서적 체계가 빠른 선택에 도움이 되며, 경우의 수를 줄여준다고 했으니까 이는 의사 결정에 '도움'이 된다고 해야 적절해. 따라서 (C)에는 assistance가 들어가야 해.

어휘확인 emotion 감정 cf. emotional 감정의 crucial 중요한, 중대한 decision making 의사 결정 neuroscientist 신경과학자 perfectly 완벽하게 normal 정상적인 except for ~을 제외하고는 injury 부상 damage 손상을 주다; 손상 system 체계; 제도 decision 결정 function (제대로) 기능하다; 기능 effectively 효과적으로 describe 묘사하다 product 제품 finding 결과 contradict 반박하다 support 지지하다 common 보통의; 흔한 belief 믿음 heart 핵심; 마음 rational 합리적인 logical 논리적인 thought 사고, 생각 modern 최신의; 현대의 research 연구 affective 정서적인 provide 제공하다 critical 중대한; 비판적인 assistance 도움 interference 방해 rapid 빠른 selection 선택 consider 고려하다

눈에 보이는 핵심 구문

The neuroscientist Antonio Damasio(S) studied(V) / *people* [who were perfectly normal in every way / except for *brain injuries* [that damaged their emotional systems]].

⋯› 선행사 people을 수식하는 주격 관계대명사절 who ~ systems는 선행사 brain injuries를 수식하는 주격 관계대명사절 that ~ systems를 포함하고 있다.

II 정답 ④

해석 한눈에 보기 주제문 사람들이 똑같은 매일, 매주, 매달 그리고 계절 리듬을 공유할 때, 그들 간의 관계는 더욱 빠르게 형성되고 더욱 강한 상태를 유지한다. 그들은 서로를 더욱 깊이 신뢰하게 되고 ① 협력도 더 쉬워진다. 결국, 그들은 ② 자주 똑같은 일을 하고 똑같은 문제들을 함께 해결한다. 사실, 몇몇 조직들은 강한 유대를 유지하고 ③ 공유된 사고방식을 강화시키기 위해 정기적인 회의를 이용한다. 한 식품 회사의 최고 경영자는 그의 팀과 함께 매일 하는 간단한 회의에 대해 말한다. "빈번함이 만들어 내는 리듬은 관계가 ④ 약화되도록(→ 발전하도록) 하고 개인의 습관이 이해되게 하고 스트레스 요인들도 확인되게 한다. 이 모든 것은 팀의 구성원들이 자신의 역할 뿐만 아니라 그들이 어떻게 서로가 서로에게서 최상의 것을 얻어낼 수 있는지를 이해하도록 ⑤ 도와준다.

정답단추 이 글은 도입부에서 사람들이 같은 것을 공유할 때 관계 발전도 더 쉽고 결속력도 더 강하다고 말하고 있어. 그러므로 ④가 있는 최고 경영자의 말에서 빈번함이 만드는 리듬은 관계를 약화시키는 것이 아니라 발전시킨다는 내용이 와야 적절하지. 따라서 grow, develop 등이 들어가야 해.

오답단서 ①은 앞부분에서 신뢰가 더 깊어진다고 했으니까 협력(coordination)도 더 쉬워진다가 어울려. ②는 첫 문장에서 단서를 얻을 수 있는데, 똑같은 매일, 매주, 매달, 계절 리듬을 공유한다고 했으니까 똑같은 일을 자주(frequently) 한다는 의미가 되어야 해. ③도 바로 앞부분의 결속력이라는 단어를 통해 공유된(shared) 사고방식이 문맥상 옳다는 것을 알 수 있어. 마지막으로 ⑤는 사람들이 이렇게 같은 것을 자주 공유하면 자신뿐만 아니라 서로를 이해하도록 도와준다(helps)는 내용으로 글의 내용과 자연스럽게 이어져.

어휘확인 seasonal 계절적인 rhythm 리듬 connection 관계; 연결 form 형성되다; 종류 deeply 깊이 coordination 협력; 조화 after all 결국 frequently 자주 in fact 사실 several (몇)몇의 regular 정기적인 maintain 유지하다 bond 유대 reinforce 강화하다 mindset 사고방식 CEO 최고 경영자 frequency 빈번함; 빈도 generate 만들어내다 weaken 약화시키다 personal 개인의 stressor 스트레스 요인 identify 확인하다 role 역할

눈에 보이는 핵심 구문

All of this(S) helps(V) the members of the team(O) understand(C) / **not only** their roles / **but also** how they can get the best out of one another.

⋯› SVOC구문으로 목적격 보어 자리에 동사원형이 이끄는 동사구가 위치했다. 그리고 동사 understand의 목적어로 'A뿐만 아니라 B도'라는 뜻의 상관접속사 구문 「not only A but also B」가 쓰였다.

유형편

Chapter 1

특강 글의 핵심 내용 파악하기

Mini Test 1 ① 2 ② 3 (1) D (2) D (3) T 4 ① 5 ④ 6 ⑤ 7 ⓐ 8 ⓒ 9 ① 10 ② 11 ① 12 ①

Mini Test 해석

1 훌륭한 독자들은 정확한 이해를 이뤄 내기 위해 특정한 단계를 밟는다.

2 우리는 타인들이 신체적 매력 면에서 우리의 기준에 부합하지 않으면 그들의 성격에 대해 결코 알지 못할지도 모른다.

3 (1) 통계는 우리가 사람들에 대해 더 많이 알도록 도와줄 수 있다. (2) 우리는 또한 우리가 하는 일에 대해 결정을 내리는 데 도움이 되도록 통계를 사용할 수 있다. (3) 우리가 우리에게 도움이 되도록 통계를 사용할 수 있는 방법들이 많이 있다.

4 ① 주제문 대부분의 상황에서 사회적 증거는 매우 유용하다. ② 주차장이 가장 꽉 찬 식당은 대개 정말로 최고의 음식을 제공한다. ③ 당신은 남들이 하고 있는 것을 무시하기보다는 그것에 주의를 기울임으로써 인생에서 실수를 보다 더 적게 할 것이다. ④ 예를 들어, 고속도로를 운전할 때 당신 앞에 있는 모든 차들이 차선을 바꾸기 시작하면, 그 운전자들은 아마도 당신이 모르는 무언가를 알고 있을 것이다. ⑤ 만약 당신이 그 운전자들을 무시하면, 당신은 결국에 가서 무언가와 부딪치게 될지도 모른다.

5 ① 건강한 아이들은 TV나 컴퓨터를 끄고 야외로 놀러 나간다. ② 가능한 어느 곳이든지, 아이들은 자전거를 타거나 학교까지 걸어가야 한다. ③ 최근의 한 연구는 하루에 90분보다 적게 하는 운동은 아이를 큰 병에 걸리기 더 쉽게 만든다는 것을 발견했다. ④ 주제문 건강과 행복을 위해서 아이들은 매일 한 시간 반 이상의 적당한 운동을 해야 한다. ⑤ 적당한 운동은 빨리 걷기나 계단 오르기 또는 자전거 타기와 같은 그 모든 운동을 말한다.

6 ① 만약 당신이 근육을 키울 생각을 하고 있다면, 한계를 넘어 정말로 당신의 몸을 혹사시키고 싶은 유혹을 많이 느낄 수 있다. ② 많은 사람들은 운동이 고통스러워야 한다는 것에 동의하는 것 같다. ③ 하지만 이것이 정말로 이 문제의 진실일까? ④ 사실, 피로와 고통은 당신의 몸이 그것이 위험에 처해 있고 혹사되고 있다는 것을 말하는 방식이다. ⑤ 주제문 좋은 운동은 압박과 도전을 제공해야 하지만, 그것은 절대적으로 결코 고통스러워서는 안 된다.

7 주제문 많은 곤충들이 추운 겨울을 견디고 살아남지 못하지만, 어떤 곤충들은 봄까지 살아남을 수 있는 영리한 계획을 찾아내었다. 주 세부사항 예를 들어, 어떤 파리들은 겨울 동안 어느 따뜻한 집의 구석에서 지내기 때문에, 그것들이 밖으로 날아다니는 것을 보기가 쉽지 않다. 주 세부사항 어떤 꿀벌들은 좁은 공간에 함께 모여 그들의 날개를 빠르게 움직여 열을 냄으로써 따뜻함을 유지할 수 있다. 주 세부사항 어떤 모기들은 개구리처럼 겨울 추위 동안 잠을 잔다.

8 주 세부사항 아이들이 나이가 들어 십대가 되면, 그들은 종종 제멋대로 굴고 말썽에 휩싸인다. 부 세부사항 예를 들어, 아이들은 종종 늦게까지 밖에 있고 싶어 한다. 부 세부사항 그들은 자신의 친구들은 그렇게 하도록 허용된다고 말한다. 주제문 하지만 아이들이 제대로 키워지려면 부모는 지나치게 관대하지 않도록 주의해야 한다.

9 꼬마아이들은 공원에서 그네나 미끄럼틀을 타는 것을 즐긴다. 조금 더 큰 아이들은 공원의 운동장에서 리틀 야구 리그 경기나 다른 팀 스포츠를 할 수 있다. 십 대들은 잔디에서 축구하는 것을 좋아한다. 어른들은 산책을 할 수 있으며, 어르신들은 공원 벤치에 앉아서 새들에게 모이를 주는 것을 종종 즐긴다.

① 공원은 모두에게 있어 즐거운 장소이다.
② 공원은 도시 거주자들에게 정말로 중요하다.

10 어떤 아이들은 진지하고 책임감이 있다. 또 어떤 아이들은 대학 때나 그들의 첫 직장에서 경험을 쌓는 동안에 성숙한다. 또 어떤 사람들은 훨씬 더 긴 시간을 필요로 하고 어떤 사람들은 나이가 들어도 절대 진정으로 철이 들지 않는다.

① 인생의 어느 때에 성숙해지는 것은 중요하다.
② 사람들은 서로 다른 속도로 성숙해지는 것 같아 보인다.

11 블루스, 재즈, 클래식, 포크 음악을 즐기는 사람들은 창의적인 경향이 더 있는 것 같다. 반면에, 팝, 컨트리, 종교 음악을 좋아하는 사람들은 다른 사람을 신뢰하고 부지런한 경향이 있다. 록과 헤비메탈을 선호하는 사람들은 신체적으로 활동적이며 모험을 좋아하는 경향이 있다.

① 사람이 좋아하는 음악은 그 사람에 대해 실제로 상당히 많은 것을 말해줄지도 모른다.
② 음악은 우리의 기분에 영향을 미치고 심지어 우리가 세상을 인지하는 방식을 바꾸기도 한다.

12 수년 전 어느 일요일 저녁에, 우리는 오랫동안 매주 해오던 대로 뉴욕시에서 출발하여 프린스턴을 향해 차를 운전해 가고 있었다. 우리는 이상한 광경을 목격했는데, 불타고 있는 자동차 한 대가 도로변에 있었다. 우리가 그다음 일요일에 그 도로의 동일 지점에 다다랐을 때, 또 다른 자동차가 그곳에서 불타고 있었다. 하지만 이번에 우리는 우리가 첫 번째 경우에 그랬던 것보다 덜 놀랐다는 것을 발견했다. 이곳은 이제 '자동차가 불타는 장소'였던 것이다.

⬇

같은 종류의 사고의 (A)반복이 그것을 목격하는 놀라움을 (B)감소시켰다.

	(A)		(B)
①	반복	…	감소시켰다
②	반복	…	증가시켰다
③	예방	…	드러내었다
④	예방	…	감소시켰다
⑤	분석	…	증가시켰다

유형 01 주제

Check-Up 1 1 smartphones 2 However, smartphones ~ too much. 3 ② **001** ①
Check-Up 2 ③ **002** ④
Check-Up 3 ① **003** ③
실전적용독해 **004** ⑤ **005** ④ **006** ⑤

Check-Up 1

정답 1 smartphones 2 However, smartphones ~ too much. 3 ②

해석 [1-3] 많은 사람들은 스마트폰이 대단하다고 생각하는데, 스마트폰이 할 수 없는 것이 거의 없어서다. 그러나 우리가 스마트폰을 너무 많이 사용하면 중요한 신체적, 정서적 건강상의 문제를 유발한다. 보통의 스마트폰은 화장실에서 발견되는 박테리아 양의 최대 10배까지 가지고 있다! 3 ① 세계적인 스마트폰의 인기 ② 스마트폰에 의해 유발될 수 있는 건강상의 문제들

001 정답 ①

지문 All in One

전구의 발명 덕분에 / 19세기 후반의 / 우리는 이제 훨씬
1 Due to the invention of the electric light bulb / in the late 19th century, / we are now
S V

더 많은 빛에 노출되었다 / 밤에 / 우리가 노출되었던 것보다 / 초기 역사 동안 죽
exposed to much more light / at night // than we had been exposed to / throughout our early
V / 접속사 S' V'

이 다소 새로운 양식의 빛 노출은 / 거의 확실하다 / 우리의 수면 양식에
history. 2 This rather new pattern of light exposure / is almost certain / to have affected our
S V C

영향을 미쳤음이 / 빛에 대한 노출은 / 늦은 밤에 / 지연시키는 경향이 있다 / 생체시계의 주기를
patterns of sleep. 3 Exposure to light / in the late evening / tends to delay / the cycle of our
S V

그리고 우리에게 더 늦은 잠자는 시간을 선호하게 하는 / 빛에 대한 노출은 / 한밤중에
internal clock / and (to) lead us to prefer later sleep times. 4 Exposure to light / in the middle
S

더 예측할 수 없는 영향을 줄 수 있다 / 하지만 분명히 우리의 생체시계가 재설정되게 하기에 충분할
of the night / can have more unpredictable effects, / but can certainly be enough to cause our
V_1 V_2 C

수 있다 / 그리고 수면으로 돌아가는 것을 어렵게 만들지도 모른다
internal clock to be reset, / and may make it difficult to return to sleep.
V_3 가목적어 C 진목적어

① Effects of artificial light on our sleep rhythms
인공조명이 수면 리듬에 미치는 영향
② The importance of light to our physical health
신체 건강에 대한 빛의 중요성
③ Our ever-increasing exposure to light
우리의 계속 증가하는 빛에 대한 노출
④ The self-controlled working of our internal clock
우리의 생체시계의 자체 제어 작업
⑤ Sleep deprivation caused by overworking
과로로 인한 수면 부족

해석 한 눈에 보기 1 19세기 후반의 전구의 발명 덕분에, 우리는 이제 초기 역사 동안 죽 노출되었던 것보다 밤에 훨씬 더 많은 빛에 노출되었다. 주제문 2 이 다소 새로운 양식의 빛 노출은 우리의 수면 양식에 영향을 미쳤음이 거의 확실하다. 3 늦은 밤에 빛에 노출되면 생체시계의 주기가 지연되고 우리에게 더 늦은 잠자는 시간을 선호하게 하는 경향이 있다. 4 한밤중에 빛에 노출되면 더 예측할 수 없는 영향을 줄 수 있는데, 분명히 우리의 생체시계가 재설정되게 하기에 충분할 수 있고, 수면으로 돌아가는 것을 어렵게 만들지도 모른다.

정답단추 이 글의 글감은 전구의 light(빛)이고, This rather new pattern of light exposure is almost certain to have affected our patterns of sleep.에 글감에 대한 글쓴이의 견해가 담겨 있어. 이어지는 문장들은 수면 양식의 변화에 대한 보다 구체적인 내용, 즉 잠자는 시간이 늦어지고 수면이 어려워질 수 있다는 보충설명이야. 그러므로 이 글의 주제문은 This rather new pattern ~.이고 정답은 이를 가장 잘 반영한 ①이야.

오답단서 ②의 신체 건강에 대한 내용은 글에서 나오지 않으므로 답이 될 수 없어. 빛의 노출로 인한 수면 부족이 건강에 영향을 줄 수도 있지만, 너무 앞서간 추론이야. 또, 우리가 지금 훨씬 더 많은 빛에 노출되고 있는 것은 맞지만, 글감에 글쓴이의 견해를 더한 것이 주제문이 되므로, 글쓴이의 주장이 충분히 반영되지 않은 ③은 답이 될 수 없어. ④는 밤에 빛에 노출되면 생체시계가 재설정된다고 했으므로 오답이야. ⑤의 과로는 글에 나오지 않는 내용이야.

어휘확인

due to ~ 때문에, ~ 덕분에 **invention** 발명 **light bulb** 전구 **expose** 노출하다 **throughout** ~동안 죽, ~에 걸쳐 **rather** 다소 **exposure** 노출 **certain** 확실한, 분명한 **affect** 영향을 미치다 **tend to-v** ~하는 경향이 있다 **delay** 지연시키다 **cycle** 주기 **internal clock** 생체시계 **lead A to-v** A에게 ~하게 하다 **prefer** 선호하다 **unpredictable** 예측할 수 없는 **certainly** 분명히 **cause A to-v** A로 하여금 ~하게 하다 **reset** 재설정하다

〈선택지 어휘〉

artificial 인공의 **importance** 중요성 **physical** 신체의 **ever-increasing** 계속 증가하는 **self-controlled** 자체 제어되는 **deprivation** 부족 **overworking** 과로

지문 Flow

[원인]
전구의 발명으로 밤에도 빛에 노출됨

⬇

[결과 + 주제문]
새로운 양식의 빛 노출이 수면 양식에 영향을 미침

⬇

[보충설명1]
늦은 밤에 빛에 노출되면 생체시계 주기가 지연되어 잠자는 시간이 늦어짐

&

[보충설명2]
한밤중에 빛에 노출되면 생체시계가 재설정되고 수면을 어렵게 만들 수 있음

Check-Up 2

정답 ③

해석 ① 식물이나 동물 채집은 아이들에게 자연 세계에 대해 가르쳐 줄 수 있다. ② 우표 수집은 아이들에게 한 나라의 문화나 역사적 사건들을 보여준다. ③ 수집은 아이들에게 새로운 세상을 열어 줄 수 있다.

002 정답 ④

지문 All in One

1 People love / going to concerts. (사람들은 좋아합니다 / 콘서트에 가는 것을) 2 I do, too. (저도 그렇고요) 3 My observations / as a long-time concert-goer / led me to try to categorize / concert-goers into several types. (저의 관찰은 / 오랫동안 콘서트에 다닌 사람으로서 / 제가 분류하게 했습니다 / 콘서트 관객을 여러 가지 유형으로) 4 One of the types, "The Statue," / never wants to seem / like he's enjoying anything. (그 유형들 중 하나인 '동상' 형은 / 보이기를 원하지 않습니다 / 그가 무엇이든 즐기고 있는 것처럼) 5 He stands / with his arms folded firmly / and a blank stare towards the stage. (그는 서 있습니다 / 굳게 팔짱을 끼면서 / 그리고 무대 쪽을 멍하니 응시하며) 6 We can also see *people* [who have truly lost themselves in the music], // as they throw their hands in the air / like they just don't care / what anyone thinks. (우리는 또한 볼 수 있습니다 / 진정으로 음악에 몰두한 사람들을 / 허공으로 손을 흔들면서 / 그들이 그냥 신경 쓰지 않는 것처럼 / 누구든 생각하는 것에) 7 I would call / this group "The Fish-Out-Of-Water" type. (저는 부를 것입니다 / 이 그룹을 '물 밖의 물고기' 유형이라고) 8 The next type / is "The Girl-On-Shoulders." (다음 유형은 / '어깨 위의 소녀'입니다) 9 This person sits / on the shoulders of a guy / at the concert, // probably because they are too far back from the stage / or because they want a better view / or because they just want to get the attention of the performer. (이 사람은 앉아 있습니다 / 어떤 남자의 어깨 위에 / 콘서트에서 / 아마 그들이 무대에서 너무 멀리 떨어져 있기 때문에 / 또는 그들이 더 나은 시야를 원하기 때문에 / 또는 그들이 그저 공연자의 주목을 받고 싶기 때문에)

① Common purposes of concert-goers
콘서트 관객의 공통 목적

② Reasons people love concerts
사람들이 콘서트를 좋아하는 이유

③ The boom of the concert business
콘서트 사업의 호황

④ Different types of people at concerts
콘서트에서의 사람들의 여러 유형

⑤ How personality is reflected in choice of music
성격이 음악의 선택에 반영되는 방법

해석 한 눈에 보기 1 사람들은 콘서트에 가는 것을 좋아합니다. 2 저도 그렇고요. 주제문 3 오랫동안 콘서트에 다닌 사람으로서 저의 관찰은 제가 콘서트 관객을 여러 가지 유형으로 분류하게 했습니다. 4 그 유형들 중 하나인 '동상' 형은 그가 무엇이든 즐기고 있는 것처럼 보이기를 원하지 않습니다. 5 그는 굳게 팔짱을 끼고 무대 쪽을 멍하니 응시하며 서 있습니다. 6 우리는 또한 누가 어떻게 생각하든 그냥 신경 쓰지 않는 것처럼 허공으로 손을 흔들면서 진정으로 음악에 몰두한 사람들을 볼 수 있습니다. 7 저는 이 그룹을 '물 밖의 물고기' 유형이라고 부를 것입니다. 8 다음 유형은 '어깨 위의 소녀'입니다. 9 이 사람은 콘서트에서 어떤 남자의 어깨 위에 앉아 있는데, 아마 무대에서 너무 멀리 떨어져 있거나 더 나은 시야를 원하거나 그저 공연자의 주목을 받고 싶기 때문일 수 있습니다.

정답단추 주제문은 글 전체의 내용을 아우르므로 단락에서 가장 포괄적인 문장이 되어야 해. 또, 구체적이지 않으므로 나머지 보충설명을 통해 글이 말하고자 하는 바를 정확하게 파악할 수 있지. 이 글은 주제문에서 언급된 several types에 대한 구체적인 내용의 예시가 나열된 구조의 글이야. 즉, 콘서트 관객을 여러 유형으로 분류할 수 있다는 도입부에 이어서 '동상' 유형, '물 밖의 물고기' 유형, '어깨 위의 소녀' 유형에 대한 설명이 나열되고 있어. 그러므로, 글의 주제로 적절한 것은 ④야.

오답단서 ①, ②, ③은 모두 콘서트에 대한 내용이 나와서 헷갈리기 쉬워. 하지만 콘서트 관객의 공통 목적이나 콘서트를 좋아하는 이유, 콘서트 사업에 대한 내용은 글에 나오지 않으므로 오답이야. ⑤는 성격과 음악 선택에 대한 내용으로 글과는 전혀 상관없어.

어휘확인

observation 관찰 concert-goer 콘서트에 다니는 사람 lead A to-v A에게 ~하게 하다 categorize 분류하다 several 몇몇의 type 유형 statue 동상 fold (팔을) 끼다, 접다 firmly 단단히, 굳게 blank stare 멍한 눈으로 빤히 봄 lose oneself in ~에 몰두하다, ~에 넋을 잃다 care 신경 쓰다 guy 남자 view 시야 attention 주목, 관심 performer 공연자

〈선택지 어휘〉

common 공통의 purpose 목적 reason 이유 boom 붐, 호황 personality 성격 reflect 반영하다

지문 Flow

[주제문]
콘서트 관객은 몇 가지 유형으로 분류됨

↓

[예시1]
'동상' 유형 – 팔짱을 끼고 멍하니 무대를 응시함

&

[예시2]
'물 밖의 물고기' 유형 – 다른 사람 신경 쓰지 않고 음악에 몰두함

&

[예시3]
'어깨 위의 소녀' 유형 – 거리나 시야의 문제 또는 주목을 받고 싶어서 남자의 어깨 위에 앉아 있음

Check-Up 3

정답 ①

해석 (A) 돌고래들은 필요할 때 서로를 도와, 부상당한 돌고래들 아래쪽에서 헤엄을 치며 그것들이 숨을 쉴 수 있도록 해수면 위로 그것들을 떠받쳐 준다. (B) 쓰러진 코끼리들은 호흡하는 데 어려움을 겪는 경향이 있어서, 한 마리가 쓰러지면, 다른 코끼리들이 그 코끼리를 일으켜 세우려고 애쓴다. ① 부상당한 동물들을 돕는 동물들의 예 ② 더 강한 동물들로부터 도움을 구하는 동물들

003 정답 ③

지문 All in One

1 When you view an abstract painting, // don't search for recognizable images / from your world. (당신이 추상화를 볼 때 / 알아 볼 수 있는 이미지를 찾지 마라 / 당신의 세계에서) 2 Instead, / try to enter the artist's world / and (try to) feel / what the artist was (대신에 / 화가의 세계로 들어가라 / 그리고 느끼려고 해라 / 그 화가가 느끼고 있었던 것을)

어휘확인

view 보다 abstract painting 추상화 search 찾다, 살펴보다 recognizable 알아볼 수 있는 image 이미지 instead 대신에 artist 화가, 예술가 take a step back 한 걸음 물러서다 from a distance 멀리서

한 걸음 물러서라 / 그리고 그림을 보아라 / 멀리서 / 영향에 주목하라

feeling. 3 Take a step back / and view the painting / from a distance. 4 Note *the impact*

V₁ V₂ V

그것(그림)이 당신에게 미치는 / 자신에게 물어보라 / 무슨 감정을 / 색깔들과 모양들 그리고 선들이 나타내는지

[(which[that]) it has on you]. 5 Ask yourself / what emotions / the colors, shapes, and lines /

= the painting V IO DO 의문사 S'

더 가까이 가라 / 그리고 살펴봐라 / 붓놀림, 물감의 질감 그리고 세세한 것들의 배치를

suggest. 6 Move closer / and examine / [the brushstrokes, the texture of the paint, and the

V' V₁ V₂ O₂

봐라 / 어떻게 모든 부분들이 서로 관련되어 있는지 / 긴장을 늦춰라 / 그리고

arrangement of the details]. 7 See / how all the parts relate to each other. 8 Relax / and give

V 의문사 S' V' V₁ V₂

그림에게 시간을 주어라 / 당신이 더 오래 볼수록 / 그림은 더 의미 있어질 것이다

the painting time. 9 The longer you look, / the more meaningful the painting will become.

IO DO The+비교급 S₁ V₁ the+비교급 S₂ V₂

① 예술가의 심리 ② 추상화의 역사
③ 추상화 감상법 ④ 현대미술의 특징
⑤ 미술관 관람 예절

해석 한 눈에 보기 1 추상화를 볼 때는, 당신의 세계에서 알아볼 수 있는 이미지들을 찾으려 하지 마라. 2 대신에 그 화가의 세계로 들어가 그가 느끼고 있었던 것을 느끼려고 해보라. 3 한 걸음 뒤로 물러나 멀리서 그림을 보아라. 4 그것이 당신에게 미치는 영향에 주목하라. 5 색깔들과 모양들, 그리고 선들이 무슨 감정을 나타내는지 자문해 보라. 6 더 가까이 가서 붓놀림, 물감의 질감, 세세한 것들의 배치를 살펴보아라. 7 모든 부분들이 어떻게 서로 관련되어 있는지 보아라. 8 긴장을 늦추고 그림을 감상하는 시간을 가져라. 9 더 오래 볼수록, 그림이 더 의미 있어질 것이다.

정답단추 글에 주제문이 뚜렷하게 나타나 있지 않고 있어. 이럴 때는 공통적인 내용을 종합해야 하지. 추상화를 감상할 때 하지 말아야 할 것과 해야 할 것들을 명령문으로 나열한 게 보이지? 그러니까 이 글의 주제는 ③이야.

오답단서 ① '예술가의 심리', ④ '현대미술의 특징', ⑤ '미술관 관람 예절'은 글에 언급된 적이 없어. ② '추상화의 역사'는 추상화라는 것만 공통되는 부분일 뿐 역사에 관해서는 이야기한 적이 없으니 답이 될 수 없겠지?

note ~에 주목하다 impact 영향; 충격 emotion 감정 suggest 암시하다 examine 검토하다 brushstroke 붓놀림 texture 질감[감촉] paint 물감 arrangement 배치 detail 세부 사항 relate to ~와 관련되다 meaningful 의미 있는

지문 Flow

[보충설명1]
화가의 입장에서 추상화 보기

&

[보충설명2]
멀리서 추상화 살펴보기

&

[보충설명3]
가까이에서 추상화 살펴보기

&

[보충설명4]
시간을 들여 추상화 보기

⬇

[주제 도출]
추상화 감상법

실전적용독해

004 정답 ⑤

지문 All in One

무더운 여름날에는 / 식욕과 기력이 떨어진다 / 더위와 습도로

1 In the hottest days of summer, / appetites and energy are weakened / by heat and

S₁ S₂ V

인해 / 이것은 ~이다 / 아이스크림콘이나 아이스바가 ~처럼 보일 때

humidity. 2 This is // (the time) when it seems like an ice cream cone or a popsicle / is the

관계부사 접속사

완벽한 것처럼 / 그러나 동양 의학의 이론은 우리에게 말한다 / 찬 음식을 먹는 것은 답이 아니라고

perfect thing. 3 But a theory from oriental medicine tells us // that eating cold foods is not the

S V IO 접속사 DO

대신에 / 우리는 '더운' 음식을 먹어야 한다 / 더위를 이기기 위해 / 가장 인기 있는 여름 전통

answer. 4 Instead, / one should eat "hot" foods / to beat the heat. 5 The most popular

S V 부사적 용법(목적) S

음식은 / 한국에서 / 삼계탕이다 / 그것은 영계이다 / 쌀로 채워지고

traditional summer food / in Korea / is *samgyetang*. 6 It's *a young chicken* [stuffed with rice

V C S V C

국으로 끓여진 / 마늘 및 인삼과 함께 / 이 재료들은 강력한 열을 내주는 에너지를 가지고 있다

and boiled in soup / with garlic and ginseng]. 7 These ingredients have *powerful warming*

S V

신체의 기운을 북돋아 주고 / 정신을 자극해 주는 / 이런 종류의 '더운' 음식은

energy [that invigorates the body / and stimulates the mind]. 8 These kinds of "hot" foods /

관계대명사 S

잃어버리는 영양분을 대체해 주고 / 지나친 발한을 통해 / 우리를 건강하고

replace *the nutrients* [(which[that]) we lose / through excessive sweating,] // and keep us

V₁ 관계대명사 V₂ O

튼튼하게 느끼도록 유지해 준다

feeling healthy and strong.

C

① The ingredients of *samgyetang*
삼계탕의 재료
② Various healthy diets
다양한 건강 식단
③ Korean foods around the world
전 세계의 한국 음식
④ A recipe for better health
더 나은 건강을 위한 요리법
⑤ A hot meal to survive the heat
더위에서 살아남기 위한 더운 음식

어휘확인

appetite 식욕 weaken 약화시키다 humidity 습도 popsicle 아이스바 theory 이론 oriental medicine 동양 의학 answer 답, 대답 instead 대신에 beat 이기다, 물리치다 traditional 전통의 stuff A with B A를 B로 채우다 boil 끓이다 garlic 마늘 ginseng 인삼 ingredient 재료, 성분 invigorate 기운 나게 하다 stimulate 자극하다 replace 대체하다 nutrient 영양분 excessive 지나친 sweating 발한

〈선택지 어휘〉
various 다양한 survive 살아남다

지문 Flow

[도입]
여름에는 더위와 습도 때문에 식욕과 기력이 떨어져서 찬 음식을 찾게 됨

⬇

[주제문]
동양 의학에서는 더위를 이기려면 찬 음식 대신에 '더운' 음식을 먹어야 한다고 함

&

해석 한 눈에 보기 1 무더운 여름날에는, 식욕과 기력이 더위와 습도로 인해 떨어진다. 2 이때는 아이스크림콘이나 아이스바가 완벽한 것처럼 보이는 때이다. 주제문 3 그러나 동양 의학의 이론은 우리에게 찬 음식을 먹는 것은 답이 아니라고 한다. 4 대신에, 우리는 더위를 이기기 위해 '더운' 음식을 먹어야 한다. 5 한국에서 가장 인기 있는 여름 전통 음식은 삼계탕이다. 6 그것은 쌀로 채워지고 마늘 및 인삼과 함께 국으로 끓여진 영계이다. 7 이 재료들은 신체의 기운을 북돋아 주고 정신을 자극해 주는 강력한 열을 내주는 에너지를 가지고 있다. 8 이런 종류의 '더운' 음식은 우리가 지나친 발한을 통해 잃어버리는 영양분을 대체해 주고, 우리를 건강하고 튼튼하게 느끼도록 유지해 준다.

정답단추 이 글에서는 여름에는 식욕이 떨어져서 찬 음식을 찾는다는 내용의 처음 두 문장이 도입문이 되고, 이어지는 세 번째, 네 번째 문장이 나머지 글 전체의 내용을 포괄하는 주제문이야. 주제문의 '더운' 음식이 무엇인지는 이어지는 문장에서 삼계탕을 예로 들어 보충설명하고 있어. 따라서, 정답은 ⑤야.

오답단서 ①은 글의 세부적인 내용만을 다루고 있어. ②와 ④는 글이 다루고 있는 주제에 비해 범위가 너무 넓고, ③은 글에서 언급되고 있지 않기 때문에 적절하지 않아.

[보충설명 – 예시]
한국에서 가장 인기 있는 여름 음식은 삼계탕으로, 들어가는 재료들이 열을 내주는 에너지를 가지고 있음

⬇

[보충설명]
이러한 더운 음식은 발한으로 잃어버리는 영양분을 대체하여 건강을 유지시켜 줌

005 정답 ④

지문 All in One

사람들은 왜 되는가 / 스포츠팬이 / 스포츠팬들은 지원을 받는다 / 다른 팬과 이어짐으로써
1 Why are people / sports fans? 2 Sports fans receive support / by connecting with other fans
V S C S V

경기장에서 / 또는 일상생활에서 / 이 지원은 하게 한다 / 팬들로 하여금 위협에 대처하게
/ at a stadium / [or] in their day-to-day life. 3 This support allows / the fans to cope with
S V O C

그들의 정체성에 대한 / 경기 중 나쁜 결과와 같은 / 상대편의 팬들
threats / to their identity, / such as bad outcomes during a game, / opposing fans, / [and] poor

그리고 좋지 않은 팀 성적 / 단기적으로 / 어려운 생활환경뿐만 아니라
performance of the team / in the short-term, / [as well as] difficult life circumstances / in the

장기적으로 / 더욱이 / 가장 좋아하는 팀과의 애착이나 동일시는 / 이끌 가능성이
long-term. 4 Moreover, / attachment or identification with one's favorite team / is most likely
S V C

가장 크다 / 팬 층의 혜택으로 / 사회심리적인 혜택은 / 스포츠팬이 되는 것의
to lead / to the benefits of fandom. 5 The social-psychological benefits / of being a sports fan /
S

포함한다 / 더 낮은 수준의 외로움과 / 스트레스를 / 운동 경기 동안에
include / lower levels of loneliness / and stress / during sporting events, / a sense of
V

더 큰 지역사회와의 소속감을 / 그리고 더 나은 심리적 작용을
belonging to a larger community, / [and] better psychological functioning.

① The absence of sportsmanship in sports
스포츠에서의 스포츠맨 정신의 부재
② The importance of fans in sports events
스포츠 경기에서 팬의 중요성
③ The recent increasing popularity of sports
스포츠에 대한 최근의 인기 상승
④ The emotional gains from being a sports fan
스포츠팬이 되는 것에서 생기는 정서적 이득
⑤ What makes fans remain loyal to their team
팬들이 자신들의 팀에게 충심을 다하게 만드는 것

해석 한 눈에 보기 1 사람들은 왜 스포츠팬이 되는가? 2 스포츠팬들은 경기장이나 일상생활에서 다른 팬과 이어짐으로써 지원을 받는다. 3 이 지원은 팬들로 하여금 장기적으로 어려운 생활환경뿐만 아니라, 단기적으로 경기 중 나쁜 결과, 상대편의 팬들, 좋지 않은 팀 성적과 같은 그들의 정체성에 대한 위협에 대처하게 한다. 4 더욱이, 가장 좋아하는 팀과의 애착이나 동일시는 팬 층의 혜택으로 이끌 가능성이 가장 크다. 5 스포츠팬이 되는 것의 사회심리적인 혜택은 운동 경기 동안에 더 낮은 수준의 외로움과 스트레스, 더 큰 지역사회와의 소속감, 그리고 더 나은 심리적 작용을 포함한다.

정답단추 주제문이 뚜렷하게 나타나지 않아서 전체적인 내용을 보고 판단해야 해. 이 글은 사람들이 왜 스포츠팬이 되는가에 질문을 던지면서 스포츠팬이 되면 얻을 수 있는 여러 장점들에 대해서 나열하고 있어. 위협에 대처하고 애착과 동일시, 그리고 소속감을 가질 수 있다는 것과 더 나은 심리적 작용을 얻을 수 있다는 것을 모두 종합하면 글의 주제로 가장 적절한 것은 ④야.

오답단서 ①과 ③은 모두 스포츠에 대한 것이지만, 스포츠 정신이나 스포츠의 인기 상승에 대한 내용이 아니므로 답이 될 수 없어. 또한 ②와 ⑤는 스포츠팬에 대한 내용으로 오답으로 고르기 쉬워. 하지만, 팬의 중요성이나 팬들이 자신의 팀에 충심을 다하게 만드는 것에 대한 내용이라기보다 스포츠팬이 얻을 수 있는 혜택에 대한 내용이므로 오답이야.

어휘확인

fan 팬, 애호가 **connect with** ~와 연결하다, 이어지다 **stadium** 경기장 **day-to-day** 일상의 **cope with** ~에 대처하다 **threat** 위협 **identity** 정체성 **such as** ~와 같은 **outcome** 결과 **opposing** 상대편의 **performance** 성적, 성과 **in the short-term** 단기적으로(↔ **in the long-term** 장기적으로) **circumstances** 상황, 환경 **moreover** 더욱이, 또한 **attachment** 애착 **identification** 동일시, 일체화 **lead to** ~로 이끌다 **benefit** 이익; 혜택 **fandom** 팬 층, 팬인 것 **social-psychological** 사회심리적의 **include** 포함하다 **lower** 더 낮은 **level** 수준 **loneliness** 외로움 **sporting event** 운동 경기 **belong to** ~에 속하다 **community** 지역사회 **functioning** 기능, 작용

〈선택지 어휘〉

absence 부재 **sportsmanship** 스포츠맨 정신 **importance** 중요성 **recent** 최근의 **increasing** 증가하는 **popularity** 인기 **emotional** 감정적인 **gain** 이득 **loyal** 충실한, 성실한

지문 Flow

[질문]
사람들이 스포츠팬이 되는 이유는?

⬇

[대답]
• 자신들의 정체성에 대한 위협에 대처하게 됨
• 좋아하는 팀과의 애착과 동일시로 인한 혜택을 받음
• 외로움과 스트레스를 덜 느끼고, 소속감과 더 나은 심리적 작용을 얻음

⬇

[주제 도출]
스포츠팬이 되면 정서적인 면에서 여러 이익을 얻음

006 정답 ⑤

지문 All in One

우리가 타고나는 재능 / 그리고 우리가 우리 삶 내내
1 *The gifts* [(which[that]) we are born with] / [and] *those* [(which[that]) we work to develop
관계대명사 / = the gifts / 관계대명사

어휘확인

gift 재능; 선물 **develop** 계발하다 **throughout** ~동안 죽, 내내 **vary** 다양하다

계발하려고 애쓰는 것(재능)은 다양하다 형태와 기능에 있어서 어떤 것들에서는 우리가 매일 용도를 찾고
throughout our lives] / vary / in form and function. [2] Some we find use for every day, //
V S_1 V_1 O

반면에 다른 것들은 오직 가치가 있다 특정 상황에서 자주(여러 번)
while others are only of value / in specific circumstances. [3] Many times / we overlook
S_2 V_2 S V

우리는 기회를 간과한다 우리의 독특한 재능을 다른 사람들과 공유할 바로 비판에 대한 두려움이나 무력하게 만드는
opportunities [to share our unique gifts with others]. [4] It is fear of criticism or the paralyzing
(holds의 S 강조)

불확실성의 중압감이다 우리를 저지하는 것은 궁극적으로 우리는 의심한다 우리의 선천적인 재능들과
weight of uncertainty / that holds us back. [5] Ultimately, / we doubt / that our innate talents
강조구문 S_1 V_1 접속사 S'

숙련된 기술들이 진정으로 다른 사람들의 삶에 보탬이 될지 하지만 바로 세상 전체이다
and practiced skills / can truly add to others' lives, // but it is the world as a whole / that
V' 강조구문 (benefits의 S_2 강조)

이익을 보는 것은 우리가 기꺼이 우리의 재능들을 공유할 때 이것은 ~이다 당신의 영혼 속에 숨겨져 있는 모든 재능이
benefits / when we willingly share our gifts. [6] This is // because *every gift* [lying hidden in
V_2 S' V' S V 접속사 S'

가지고 있기 때문 필요를 채워줄 가능성을 다른 누군가의 삶 속에 당신의 타고난 능력은
your soul] has / *the potential* [to fill a need / in someone else's life]. [7] *Your natural ability* [to
V' S

상처를 달래주거나 동정심을 고무시키거나 조직하거나 혹은 고정관념을 벗어나 생각하는 요긴한 것이
soothe hurt, (to) inspire compassion, (to) organize, or (to) think outside the box] / can be a
V

될 수 있다 어려움에 처한 누군가에게
boon / to someone in need.

form 형태; 종류 function 기능 value 가치 specific 특정한 circumstances 상황, 환경 overlook 간과하다 opportunity 기회 share 공유하다 unique 독특한 fear 두려움 criticism 비판 paralyze 무력하게 만들다 weight 중압감, 부담; 무게 uncertainty 불확실성 hold A back A를 저지하다 ultimately 궁극적으로 doubt 의심하다 innate 선천적인, 타고난 talent 재능 practiced 숙련된 truly 진정으로 add to ~에 보태다 as a whole 전체로서 benefit 이득을 보다 willingly 기꺼이 hidden 숨겨진 soul 영혼 potential 가능성 fill 채우다 ability 능력 soothe 달래다 inspire 고무[격려]하다 compassion 동정심 organize 조직[준비]하다 think outside the box 고정관념에서 벗어나 생각하다 boon 요긴한 것 in need 어려움에 처한

〈선택지 어휘〉
pursue 추구하다 effective 효과적인 importance 중요성 necessity 필요성

① Benefits of pursuing one's gifts
자신의 재능을 추구하는 것의 이점
② The form and function of our gifts
우리의 재능들의 형태와 기능
③ Effective ways to use one's gifts
자신의 재능을 사용하기 위한 효과적인 방법들
④ The importance of developing our talents
우리의 재능을 계발하는 것의 중요성
⑤ The necessity of sharing one's gifts with others
자신의 재능을 다른 사람들과 공유하는 것의 필요성

해석 한 눈에 보기 [1] 우리가 타고나는 재능들과 우리가 일생을 통해 계발하려고 애쓰는 재능들은 형태와 기능에 있어 다양하다. [2] 어떤 것들에 대해서는 우리가 매일 용도를 찾게 되는 반면에, 다른 것들은 특정 상황에서만 가치가 있다. [3] 자주 우리는 우리의 독특한 재능을 다른 사람들과 공유하는 기회를 간과한다. [4] 우리를 저지하는 것은 바로 비판에 대한 두려움이나 무력하게 만드는 불확실성의 중압감이다. 주제문 [5] 궁극적으로 우리는 우리의 선천적인 재능들과 숙련된 기술들이 다른 사람들의 삶에 진정으로 보탬이 될 수 있을지 의심하지만, 우리가 기꺼이 우리의 재능들을 공유할 때 이익을 보는 것은 바로 세상 전체이다. [6] 이것은 당신의 영혼 속에 숨겨져 있는 모든 재능은 다른 누군가의 삶 속의 어떤 필요를 채워줄 가능성을 지니고 있기 때문이다. [7] 상처를 달래주거나, 동정심을 고무시키거나, 조직하거나, 혹은 고정관념을 벗어나 생각하는 당신의 타고난 능력은 어려움에 처한 누군가에게 요긴한 것이 될 수 있다.

정답단추 처음 두 문장에서 이 지문의 글감은 gifts(재능)라는 것을 알 수 있어. 이어서 글쓴이는 우리는 자주 재능을 다른 사람들과 공유하는 기회를 간과한다고 설명하며, 재능 공유가 세상 전체에 이득이 되므로 필요하다는 주제문이 나오고 있어. 이를 잘 반영한 선택지는 ⑤야.

오답단서 ①은 재능을 추구하는 것이라 했는데 글의 내용은 공유하는 것에 관한 거지? 그리고 이 글이 재능에 관한 글이긴 하지만 그 형태와 기능에 대한 글은 아니므로 ②는 답이 아니야. ③과 ④도 재능이라는 공통점 외에 글에 언급되지 않은 내용이라는 거 확실히 보이지?

지문 Flow

[도입]
• 재능은 다양하며 용도와 상황에 따른 가치가 있음
• 재능 공유의 기회가 있음에도 두려움이나 불확실성 때문에 하지 않음

⬇

[주제문]
재능 공유는 세상 전체에 이득이므로 필요함

⬇

[보충설명]
모든 재능은 어려움에 처한 다른 사람에게 도움이 될 가능성이 있음

유형 02 요지, 주장

Check-Up 1 ③ 007 ④
Check-Up 2 ① 008 ⑤
Check-Up 3 009 ⑤
Check-Up 4 010 ① 011 ④
실전적용독해 012 ④ 013 ⑤ 014 ⑤

Check-Up 1

정답 ③

해석 ① 사람들이 새로운 계획을 시작할 때 맞닥뜨리는 가장 큰 문제들 중 하나는 야심 찬 목표들 때문에 동기유발이 급격히 줄어든다는 것이다. ② 너무 많은 것을 너무 빨리하려고 시도하는 것은 전혀 아무것도 하지 않는 것보다 더 나쁘다. ③ 당신은 그 과정에서 작지만 구체적인 목표들을 세워야 한다.

007 정답 ④

지문 All in One

만약 당신이 누군가가 말하는 것을 들었다면 또는 스스로에게 말한 적이 있다면 ~와 같은 말을
1 If you've ever heard someone say, / or have said to yourself, / something like / "If I could
접속사 S' V'1 O' C' V'2 접속사 S'

'내가 정보를 기억할 수 있다면 내가 노래 가사를 기억하는 것처럼 나는 가장 똑똑한 사람이 될 텐데
remember information / like I remember song lyrics, / I'd be the smartest person / in the
V' 접속사 S'' V'' S V C

세상에서' 그 다음에 당신은 이미 경험했다 내가 주장하는 것을 음악이 우리에게 어떻게 영향을 미치는지에 대해
world," // then you have already experienced / what I claim / about how music influences us.
S V 관계대명사 간접의문문

그것은 왜인가 많은 학생들이 생각하는 것은 그들이 정보를 적절하게 배울 수 있다고 그것이 노래
2 Why is it // that many students feel / (that) they can adequately learn information / if it is in
V S 접속사 S' V' 접속사

가사의 형태이면 나는 생각한다 정보를 음악적으로 듣는 것이 듣는 사람에게 더 기억하기 쉬울 것이라고
lyrical form? 3 I believe // that hearing information musically / is catchier for the listener /
S V 접속사 S' V'1 C'1

그리고 학습을 덜 성가신 것으로 만들고 그리고 더 재미있는 활동으로
and makes learning less of a nuisance / and (makes learning) more of a fun activity. 4 By
V'2 O C'2 C'3

우리의 사고방식을 바꿈으로써 음악은 바꿀 수 있다 우리가 지식을 흡수하는 방법을 그리고 (우리가) 세상을
altering our mindset, / music can transform / how we absorb knowledge / and (how we)
S V 관계부사

바라보는 (방법을)
look at the world.

① 공부를 할 때는 익숙한 노래를 듣는 것이 좋다.
② 공부를 하면서 음악을 듣는 것은 좋지 않다.
③ 음악은 공부에서 오는 스트레스를 줄여줄 수 있다.
④ 우리는 음악을 지식 습득의 도구로 사용할 수 있다.
⑤ 사람에 따라 똑같은 음악을 다양하게 해석한다.

해석 한 눈에 보기 1 만약 당신이 "내가 노래 가사를 기억하는 것처럼 정보를 기억할 수 있다면, 나는 세상에서 가장 똑똑한 사람이 될 텐데."와 같은 말을 누군가가 하는 것을 듣거나 마음속으로 생각한 적이 있다면, 당신은 내가 음악이 우리에게 어떻게 영향을 미치는지에 대해 주장하는 것을 이미 경험한 것이다. 2 도대체 왜 많은 학생들은 정보가 노래 가사 형태이면 자신들이 그것을 적절하게 배울 수 있다고 생각하는 걸까? 주제문 3 나는 정보를 음악적으로 듣는 것이 듣는 사람에게 더 기억하기 쉬울 것이며, 학습을 덜 성가시고 더 재미있는 활동으로 만들 것이라고 생각한다. 4 우리의 사고방식을 바꿈으로써 음악은 우리가 지식을 흡수하고 세상을 바라보는 방법을 변화시킬 수 있다.

정답단추 글의 요지는 글쓴이의 주장이 담긴 주제문을 찾는 것이 가장 첫 번째 전략이야. 주제문은 주로 글의 앞이나 끝 부분에 있는 경우가 많은데, 이 글에서는 세 번째 문장인 I believe ~부터가 주제문이야. 음악이 정보 기억과 학습에 도움을 줄 수 있고 지식을 얻는 방법을 변화시킬 수 있다는 말을 통해 음악이 지식을 얻게 하는 도구임을 알 수 있어. 따라서 글의 요지로 가장 적절한 것은 ④야.

오답단서 ①, ②, ③은 공부와 음악의 상관관계에서 나올 법한 선택지이므로 답이 될 수 없어. ⑤의 같은 음악에 대한 다양한 해석은 글의 내용에서 다루지 않는 내용이야.

어휘확인

say to oneself 마음속으로 생각하다, 혼잣말하다 **information** 정보 **lyric** (노래의) 가사 **cf. lyrical** 노래 가사의; 서정적인 **claim** 주장하다 **influence** 영향을 미치다 **adequately** 적절히 **form** 형태 **musically** 음악적으로 **catchy** 기억하기 쉬운 **nuisance** 성가신 것 **alter** 바꾸다 **mindset** 사고방식 **transform** 변형시키다, 바꾸다 **absorb** 흡수하다 **knowledge** 지식

지문 Flow

[도입]
노래 가사는 기억이 잘 됨

⬇

[주제문]
• 정보를 음악적으로 들으면 더 기억하기 쉽고, 학습이 더 재미있어짐
• 음악은 지식을 흡수하고 세상을 바라보는 방법을 변화시킴

Check-Up 2

정답 ①

해석 ① 음악을 듣는 것은 자는 것보다 더 마음을 느긋하게 해줄 수 있다. ② 경찰은 그 사고로 세 명이 부상당했다고 말했다.

008 정답 ⑤

지문 All in One

(~라고) 가정해보자 어떤 사람이 도시에 싫증이 난다 즉, 스모그와 서두름에 그리고 그는
1 Suppose (that) / a person is tired of the city / — the smog and the hurry — // and he decides
V 접속사 S'1 V'1 C'1 S'2 V'2

떠나기로 결심한다 잠시 그는 자신의 차에 탄다 그리고 여행한다 자유와 휴식을 향해
to get away / for a while. 2 He gets into his car / and travels away / toward freedom and
S V1 V2

그러던 중에 그는 도로 한쪽으로 차를 댄다 시골 풍경의 조용한 아름다움을
relaxation. 3 Along the way, / he pulls over to the side of the road / to enjoy the quiet beauty
S V 부사적 용법(목적)

즐기기 위해 그가 무엇을 보는가 광고판들 한 광고판은 보여 준다 더러운 엔진
of a country scene. 4 What does he see? 5 Billboards! 6 One billboard shows / *giant dice*
S V S1 V1

오일을 떨어뜨리는 거대한 주사위를 또 다른 광고판은 보여 준다 거대한 접시 위에 떨어지는 거대한
[dripping dirty motor oil]; / another billboard displays / *huge slices of bread* [falling on
S2 V2

빵 한 조각을 아직도 또 다른 것이 파스텔 색깔의 화장실 휴지를 보여 준다 물건의 이름 철자를 적어 놓으면서
a giant plate]; / still another shows pastel toilet tissue, / spelling out the name of *the product*
S3 V3 분사구문

어휘확인

suppose 가정하다 **be tired of** ~에 싫증이 나다 **smog** 스모그 **get away** 떠나다 **for a while** 잠시 동안 **get into** ~에 타다 **freedom** 자유 **relaxation** 휴식 **pull over** 길 한쪽으로 차를 대다 **scene** 풍경 **billboard** 광고판 **dice** 주사위 **drip** 떨어뜨리다 **motor oil** 엔진 오일 **display** 전시하다, 보여 주다 **huge** 거대한 **pastel** 파스텔 색깔의 **spell out** 철자를 적다 **product** 상품 **numerous** 수많은 **replacement** 대체물 **seek** 찾다 **spoil** 망치다 **roadside** 길가

그가 구매해야 할 / 이 수많은 다른 광고판들은 / 보기 싫은 대체물이다

[(which) he should buy]. 7 These and numerous other billboards / are ugly replacements / for
관계대명사 / S / V / C

나무와 들판, 강, 호수, 사막, 언덕, 그리고 산들의 / 그가 찾고 있는

the trees and fields, rivers, lakes, deserts, hills, and *mountains* [(that) he is seeking].
관계대명사

이 보기 싫은 것들이 망친다 / 자연적인 길가의 아름다움에 대한 그의 즐거움을

8 These ugly things spoil / his enjoyment of natural roadside beauty.
S / V

① 도시를 이따금씩 떠나 있는 것은 재충전이 된다.
② 크고 눈에 띄는 옥외 광고판은 여행의 활력소이다.
③ 옥외 광고판을 통해 인기 있는 제품을 알 수 있다.
④ 옥외 광고판은 자연과 조화를 이루는 것이 좋다.
⑤ 옥외 광고판은 자연 풍경의 아름다움을 해친다.

해석 한 눈에 보기 1 어떤 사람이 도시, 즉, 스모그와 서두름에 싫증이 나서 잠시 떠나기로 결심한다고 가정해보자. 2 그는 자신의 차에 타고 자유와 휴식을 향해 여행한다. 3 그러던 중에, 그는 시골 풍경의 조용한 아름다움을 즐기기 위해 도로 한쪽으로 차를 댄다. 4 그가 무엇을 보는가? 5 광고판들! 6 한 광고판은 더러운 엔진 오일을 떨어뜨리는 거대한 주사위를 보여 준다. 또 다른 광고판은 거대한 접시 위에 떨어지는 거대한 빵 한 조각을 보여 준다. 아직도 또 다른 것이 그가 구매해야 할 물건의 이름 철자를 적어 놓으면서 파스텔 색깔의 화장실 휴지를 보여 준다. 7 이 수많은 다른 광고판들은 그가 찾고 있는 나무와 들판, 강, 호수, 사막, 언덕, 그리고 산들의 보기 싫은 대체물이다. 주제문 8 이 보기 싫은 것들이 자연적인 길가의 아름다움에 대한 그의 즐거움을 망친다.

정답단추 글쓴이의 주장, 즉 주관적인 견해를 담고 있는 주제문을 찾아 요지를 파악할 수 있어. 이 글은 자연 속에 존재하는 보기 싫은 광고판들로 인해 자연 풍경이 망쳐지고 있음을 안타까워하는 내용을 다루고 있는데, 그 내용이 마지막 한 문장에 주관적인 견해로 담겨 있어. 따라서 글의 요지로 가장 적절한 것은 ⑤야.

오답단서 ①은 글의 앞부분에 언급되지만 글 전체의 요지로 볼 수는 없어. ②, ③은 옥외 광고판의 장점을, ④는 좋은 옥외 광고판의 요건을 언급한 선택지로, 광고판이 자연을 망친다는 글의 내용과는 상반되므로 당연히 오답이야.

지문 Flow

[도입]
어떤 사람이 도시를 떠나 자유와 휴식을 위해 여행하기로 하는데, 시골 풍경의 아름다움 대신에 상품 광고판들을 보게 됨

⬇

[보충설명]
수많은 광고판이 자연 풍경의 보기 싫은 대체물이 되고 있음

⬇

[주제문]
자연 곳곳에 있는 광고판들이 자연 풍경의 아름다움을 망침

Check-Up 3

009 정답 ⑤

지문 All in One

작은 시골 학교들은 직면한다 / 폐쇄와 학생들을 보내는 것에 / 다른 더 큰 학교에

1 Small rural schools face / closure and sending students / to other larger schools.
S / V

시골 지역의 인구 감소는 / 폐쇄에 기여했을지도 모른다 / 일부 더 작은 학교의

2 Population decrease in rural areas / may have contributed to the closure / of some smaller
S / V

그러나 더 자주 / 그것은 틀린 판단일 뿐이다 / 보다 소수의 학교를

schools. 3 But more frequently, / it is just bad judgment / by *those* [who associate fewer
S V / C / 관계대명사

관리의 효율성과 연관시키는 사람들에 의한 / 크기가 늘어남에 따라 / 더 어렵다

schools with efficiency of management]. 4 As size increases, // it is more difficult / to
접속사 S′ V′ / 가주어 V / C

교육을 개인화하고 개별화하는 것은 / 또는 학생들의 성장 문제에 주의를 기울이는 것은

personalize and individualize education, / or to pay attention to problems in students'
진주어₁ / 진주어₂

이런 면에서 / 소수의 학생들에게 봉사하는 교사는 / 낭비가 아니다 / 대신에

growth. 5 In this respect, / *a teacher* [serving a few students] / is not a waste; // instead, / it is
S_1 / V_1 / C_1 / S_2 V_2

그것은 이점이다 / 학부모가 그러한 학교를 선택하도록 동기 부여할 수 있는 / 시골 지역 사회에서 학교 운영을

a benefit [that should motivate parents to choose such schools]. 6 Keeping schools running in
C_2 관계대명사 가능성, 추측: (아마) ~일 것이다 / S

유지하는 것이 / 효과적인 방법이다 / 성인 노동력을 끌어들이는 / 강력한 경제를 발전시키기 위해

rural communities / is *an effective way* [to attract adult workers / to develop strong
V / C / 부사적 용법(형용사 수식) / 부사적 용법(목적)

시골의 저개발 지역에

economies / in less-developed areas of the country].

① 학급의 크기를 줄여 교육의 질을 높여야 한다.
② 학교별 보조금을 규모에 따라 차등 지급해야 한다.
③ 시골 소학교들에 대한 보조금 지원을 늘려야 한다.
④ 학생별 특성에 맞게 커리큘럼을 다양화해야 한다.
⑤ 시골 소학교들을 폐쇄하는 대신 장점을 살려야 한다.

해석 한 눈에 보기 1 작은 시골 학교들은 폐쇄와 학생들을 다른 더 큰 학교에 보내는 상황에 직면한다. 2 시골 지역의 인구 감소는 일부 더 작은 학교의 폐쇄에 기여했을지도 모른다. 3 그러나, 그것은 보다 소수의 학교를 관리의 효율성과 연관시키는 사람들에 의한 틀린 판단일 뿐인 경우가 더 자주 있다. 4 크기가 늘어남에 따라, 교육을 개인화하고 개별화하거나 학생들의 성장 문제에 주의를 기울이는 것은 더 어렵다. 5 이런 면에서, 소수의 학생들에게 봉사하는 교사는 낭비가 아니다. 대신에, 그것은 학부모가 그러한 학교를 선택하도록 동기 부여할 수 있는 이점이다. 6 시골 지역 사회에서 학교 운영을 유지하는 것이 시골의 저개발 지역에 강력한 경제를 발전시키기 위해 성인 노동력을 끌어들이는 효과적인 방법이다.

정답단추 이 글에는 딱히 주제문으로 볼 수 있는 문장이 없어. 그러므로 요지를 찾으려면 각 문장에서 공통적으로

어휘확인

rural 시골의 **face** (상황에) 직면하다 **closure** 폐쇄 **population** 인구 **decrease** 감소 **contribute to** ~에 기여하다 **frequently** 자주 **judgment** 판단 **associate A with B** A를 B에 연관시키다 **efficiency** 효율성 **management** 관리 **increase** 증가하다 **personalize** 개인화하다 **individualize** 개별화하다 **pay attention to** ~에 주의를 기울이다 **growth** 성장 **in this respect** 이런 면에서, 이 점에서 **benefit** 이점 **motivate** 동기 부여하다 **run** 운영하다 **community** 지역 사회 **effective** 효과적인 **attract** 끌어들이다 **develop** 발전시키다 **economy** 경제 **less-developed** 저개발의

지문 Flow

[도입]
시골 인구 감소로 작은 학교를 폐쇄하고 학생들을 다른 큰 학교로 보냄

⬇

[비판]
관리의 효율성만 보는 잘못된 판단일 경우가 더 많음

⬇

[근거]
• 학교 규모가 커지면 교육의 개인화, 개별화, 학생 성장에 주의를 기울이기 어려움
• 시골 학교를 유지시키면 성인 노동력을 끌어들일 수 있어 지역 경제가 발전됨

다루는 내용을 살펴야 해. 이 글은 시골의 작은 학교는 소규모 수업의 효율성과 시골의 경제 발전이라는 측면에서 폐교시키지 말고 유지해야 한다는 내용이야. 따라서 글의 요지로 가장 적절한 것이 ⑤야.

오답단서 ①은 학교 크기가 작으면 폐교시킨다는 내용이 나오므로 오답이야. ②와 ③의 학교 보조금, ④의 커리큘럼 다양화는 글에서 언급되지 않으므로 정답이 될 수 없어.

[주장도출]
시골의 작은 학교를 폐쇄하지 말고 그것이 가지고 있는 장점을 살려야 함

Check-Up 4

010 정답 ①

지문 All in One

잉글랜드의 시인 Coleridge는 / 〈늙은 선원의 노래〉에 썼다 / 물

1 The English poet Coleridge / wrote in *The Rime of the Ancient Mariner*, / "water, / water

S = / V

사방에 물 / 하지만 마실 (물은) 한 방울도 없네 / 그것은 의미한다 / 사람이 있을 수 있다고 / 바다 한가운데에서

everywhere / but not *a drop* [to drink]." 2 It means // [that one can be / in the middle of the

S / V / = 앞의 인용문을 대신하는 대명사 It / S' / V'

그리고 여전히 갈증으로 죽을 (수 있다고) / 사우디아라비아 사람들은 비슷한 문제를 가지고 있다 / 모래는

ocean / and (one can) still die of thirst]. 3 The Saudi Arabians have a similar problem. 4 Sand

S / V / S

필수적이다 / 건축과 많은 다른 산업에 / 사우디아라비아는 / 둘러싸여 있다

is essential / for building and many other industries. 5 The Saudis / are surrounded / by

V / C / S_1 / V_1

모래로 가득 찬 사막으로 / 그러나 그것은 맞지 않는 모래 종류이다 / 건축과 산업에

deserts [(which are) full of sand], // but it's the wrong kind of sand / for building and

S_2 V_2

그래서 / 사우디아라비아는 강모래를 수입해야 한다 / 스코틀랜드로부터 / 이상하다

industry. 6 So / the Saudis have to import river sand / from Scotland. 7 It's strange // that a

S / V / 가주어 V / 진주어

사막 국가가 / 모래를 사야만 한다는 것이 / 유럽에서

desert nation / has to buy its sand / from Europe.

= a desert nation's

① All that glitters is not gold.
반짝이는 것이 다 금인 것은 아니다.

② Rome wasn't built in a day.
로마는 하루아침에 이루어지지 않았다.

③ Blood is thicker than water.
피는 물보다 진하다.

④ Kill two birds with one stone.
돌 하나로 두 마리의 새를 잡는다.

⑤ A bird in the hand is worth two in the bush.
손안에 있는 한 마리의 새가 숲속에 있는 두 마리의 가치가 있다.

해석 한 눈에 보기 1 잉글랜드의 시인 Coleridge는 〈늙은 선원의 노래〉에서 "사방이 물이지만 마실 물은 한 방울도 없네"라고 썼다. 2 이것은 사람이 바다 한가운데에 있어도 여전히 갈증으로 죽을 수 있다는 것을 의미한다. 3 사우디아라비아 사람들도 비슷한 문제를 겪고 있다. 4 모래는 건축 및 기타 많은 산업에 필수적이다. 5 사우디아라비아는 모래로 가득 찬 사막에 둘러싸여 있지만, 그것은 건축과 산업에 맞지 않는 종류의 모래이다. 6 그래서 사우디아라비아는 스코틀랜드에서 강모래를 수입해야 한다. 7 사막 국가가 유럽에서 모래를 사와야 한다는 것이 이상하다.

정답단추 이 글은 주제문이 뚜렷하지 않기 때문에 내용을 종합적으로 파악해서 그 내용이 시사하는 점에 집중해야 해. Coleridge의 시 구절과 사우디아라비아의 예를 통해 '겉보기에는 그럴듯하지만 실제로는 가치가 없을 수도 있다.'는 내용을 시사하고 있음을 알 수 있어. 따라서 이 글이 시사하는 바와 알맞은 속담은 ①이야.

오답단서 속담은 그 숨은 뜻까지 알고 있어야 해. ②는 '모든 일에는 노력이 필요하며 단기간에 되는 것이 아니다.'는 뜻이고, ③은 '혈연관계인 가족은 그 어떤 관계보다 가깝다.'는 뜻이야. ④는 일거양득, 즉, '동시에 두 가지 이득을 본다.'는 뜻으로 많이 접한 속담일 거야. 마지막으로 ⑤는 '내가 소유할 수 없는 것보다는 내 수중에 있는 것이 더 중요하다.'는 뜻이야.

어휘확인

English 잉글랜드의; 영어 **poet** 시인 **rime** (= rhyme) 노래; 운(음조가 비슷한 글자) **ancient** 늙은; 고대의 **mariner** 선원 **drop** 방울; 떨어뜨리다 **thirst** 갈증 **similar** 비슷한 **essential** 필수적인 **building** 건축; 건물 **industry** 산업 **be surrounded by** ~에 둘러싸이다 **full of** ~로 가득 찬 **kind** 종류; 친절한 **import** 수입하다 **river sand** 강모래 **nation** 국가

지문 Flow

[예시1]
Coleridge의 시 인용구

[예시2]
사막 국가인 사우디아라비아가 모래를 수입함

[시사점 도출]
겉보기에는 그럴듯해도 실제로는 가치가 없음

011 정답 ④

지문 All in One

한 보석상의 친구는 특별한 선물을 원했다 / 자신의 약혼녀를 위한 / 그래서 / 보석상은 500달러짜리

1 A jeweler's friend wanted a special present / for his fiancée. 2 So, / the jeweler picked out *a*

S / V / S / V

목걸이를 골랐다 / 자신이 기꺼이 ~할 / 친구가 250달러에 갖게 / 그런데 보석상이 250달러의

$500 necklace [that he was willing to / let his friend have for $250]. 3 But when the jeweler

관계대명사 / 접속사 / S'

가격을 불렀을 때 / 그의 친구의 얼굴은 어두운 표정이 되었다 / 그리고 물러나기 시작했다 / 거래에서부터

quoted the $250 price, // his friend's face fell, / and he began backing away / from the deal /

V' / S_1 / V_1 / S_2 / V_2

자신이 '정말 좋은' 어떤 것을 원했다는 이유로 / 보석상이 파악이 되자 / 일이 어떻게

because he wanted *something* ["really nice."] 4 When the jeweler realized / what had

접속사 / S' / V' / 접속사 / S' / V' / 간접의문문

어휘확인

jeweler 보석상 **fiancée** 약혼녀 **pick out** ~을 고르다 **necklace** 목걸이 **be willing to** 기꺼이 ~하다 **quote** 가격을 부르다 **fall** 어두운 표정이 되다 **back away from** ~에서 뒷걸음치다[물러나다] **deal** 거래 **realize** 깨닫다 **happen** 발생하다 **introduce** 소개하다 **regular** 정해진, 고정적인 **on the spot** 그 자리에서 **exchange** 교환하다 **drop** 깎다, 낮추다 **rather than** ~보다는 **offensive** 불쾌한 **overjoyed** 매우 기뻐하는

된 건지 / 그는 친구에게 전화를 걸어 / 그에게 요청했다 / 다시 와 달라고 / 이번에 / 보석상은

happened, // he called his friend / and asked him / to come back. 5 This time, / the jeweler

S V₁ V₂ O C S

새 목걸이를 소개했다 / 그것의 정가인 500달러에 / 그의 친구는 그것을 충분할 정도로 좋아했다 / 그것을 그

introduced the new piece / at its regular $500 price. 6 His friend liked it enough / to buy it

V S V 부사적 용법(부사 수식)

자리에서 구입하기에 / 하지만 돈이 거래되기 전에 / 보석상은 그에게 말했다

on the spot. 7 But before any money was exchanged, // the jeweler told him / that, as a

접속사 S′ V′ S V IO 접속사

결혼 선물로 자신이 가격을 깎아 주겠다고 / 250달러로 / 이번에는 / 250달러 세일 가격을 불쾌하게

wedding gift, he would drop the price / to $250. 8 This time, / rather than finding the $250

DO V′ O′

여기기보다는 / 친구는 아주 기뻐했다 / 그것을 가지게 되어

sales price offensive, // he was overjoyed / to have it.

C′ S V 부사적 용법(감정의 원인)

① 친한 사이라도 돈거래는 안 하는 것이 좋다.
② 상대방의 호의는 되도록 거절하지 말아야 한다.
③ 값비싼 물건은 그 값어치를 하게 마련이다.
④ 사람들은 가격으로 물건의 가치를 판단한다.
⑤ 선물은 가격보다 정성을 깃들이는 것이 좋다.

해석 한 눈에 보기 1 한 보석상의 친구가 자신의 약혼녀에게 줄 특별한 선물을 원했다. 2 그래서 보석상은 자신이 기꺼이 친구가 250달러에 갖게 할 500달러짜리 목걸이를 골랐다. 3 그런데 보석상이 250달러의 가격을 불렀을 때, 그의 친구가 실망을 하고는, 자신이 '정말 좋은' 어떤 것을 원했다는 이유로 거래를 안 하려고 했다. 4 보석상이 일이 어떻게 된 건지 파악이 되자, 그는 친구에게 전화를 걸어 그에게 다시 와 달라고 요청했다. 5 이번에, 보석상은 새 목걸이를 그것의 정가인 500달러에 소개했다. 6 그의 친구는 그것을 그 자리에서 구입할 정도로 그것을 좋아했다. 7 하지만 돈이 거래되기 전에, 보석상은 그에게 결혼 선물로 자신이 가격을 250달러로 깎아 주겠다고 말했다. 8 이번에는 250달러 세일 가격을 불쾌하게 여기기보다는 오히려 친구는 그것을 사게 되어 아주 기뻐했다.

정답단추 일화처럼 이야기체로 서술한 글에서는 주제문이 없는 경우가 많아. 이때는 글의 사건이나 상황을 종합하여 추론하고, 그 결과가 시사하는 점이 무엇인지를 생각해야 해. 이 글에서 보석상이 처음 제시한 가격에 따라 친구의 반응이 달라지는 것을 알 수 있지? 즉 물건의 가격이 가치 판단의 잣대가 된다는 것을 알 수 있어. 따라서 ④가 정답이야.

오답단서 ①과 ③은 글의 내용에서 언급된 친구와 목걸이의 가격과 같은 어구들을 활용하여 만든 오답이야. ②와 ⑤는 글에서 언급되지 않은 내용이야.

지문 Flow

[도입]
보석상의 친구가 약혼녀에게 줄 특별한 선물을 원함

[문제]
보석상이 500달러짜리 목걸이를 250달러에 팔려고 하자, 친구는 '정말 좋은' 물건을 사고 싶었다는 이유로 거절함

[해결]
보석상은 상황 파악 후에, 500달러 목걸이를 정가에 팔면서, 결혼 선물로 250달러로 깎아 주겠다고 말함

[결과]
친구가 기쁜 마음으로 목걸이를 삼

실전적용독해

012 정답 ④

지문 All in One

부모들은 종종 가진다 / 장래 직업적 성공에 높은 기대를 / 그들 자녀들의 / 그리고

1 Parents often have / high expectations of future career success / for their children, // and

S V

그들은 믿는다 / 학업의 성공이 / 그것과 가장 강력하게 관련되어 있다고 / 그러나 그러한 기대는

they believe // [that academic success / is most strongly linked to it]. 2 But those expectations

S V 접속사 S′ V′ 접속사 S

쓸모없는 것일 수 있다 / 만약 아이들이 기본적인 도구들을 갖고 있지 않다면 / 인생에서 성공하기 위한 / 정직함, 인내심,

/ can be useless // if children don't have *the basic tools* [to succeed in life]. 3 Values like

V C 접속사 S′ V′

책임감과 같은 가치관들은 / 필수적이다 / 사회의 효율적인 구성원이 되는 데

honesty, patience, and responsibility / are essential / to be an effective member of society.

S V 부사적 용법(목적)

그것들은 훨씬 더 중요하다 / 긴 안목으로 보면 / 성적표의 A학점들보다

4 Those are far more important / in the long run / than A's on student report cards. 5 Solid

S V S

학교 공부보다는 오히려 견고한 가치관들이 / 최상의 선물이다 / 부모가 줄 수 있는 / 그리고 가장

values rather than academic studies / are *the best gifts* [that parents can give] / and will

V₁ 관계대명사 S′ V′ V₂

큰 영향을 미칠 것이다 / 미래의 성공에

have the greatest effect / on future success.

① 성공을 위한 초석인 학업에 매진하라.
② 지나친 기대는 아이에게 부담을 준다.
③ 아이의 실수에 관대한 자세를 취하라.
④ 삶의 가치관 형성이 성적보다 중요하다.
⑤ 성공을 위해서는 인내의 시간이 필요하다.

해석 한 눈에 보기 1 부모는 종종 자녀의 장래 직업적 성공에 높은 기대를 걸고, 학업의 성공이 그것과 가장 강력하게 관련되어 있다고 믿는다. 주제문 2 그러나 그러한 기대는 만약 아이들이 인생에서 성공하기 위한 기본적인 도구들을 갖고 있지 않다면 쓸모없는 것일 수 있다. 3 정직함, 인내심, 책임감과 같은 가치관들은 사회의 효율적인 구성원이 되는 데 필수적이다. 4 그것들은 긴 안목으로 보면 성적표의 A학점들보다 훨씬 더 중요하다. 5 학교 공부보다는 오히려 견고한 가치관들이 부모가 줄 수 있는 최상의 선물이며 미래의 성공에 가장 큰 영향을 미칠 것이다.

정답단추 글의 요지는 글쓴이의 주장이야. 우선 주장을 나타내는 표현이 담긴 문장을 찾고 그 문장이 나머지 문장들

어휘확인

expectation 기대 career 직업 success 성공 academic 학업의 strongly 강하게, 강경히 link 관련되다 useless 쓸모 없는 basic 기본적인 tool 도구 succeed in ~에 성공하다 value 가치관 honesty 정직(성) patience 인내심 responsibility 책임감 essential 필수적인 effective 효과적인 in the long run 긴 안목으로 보면, 결국은 report card 성적표, 통지표 solid 견고한, 단단한 rather than ~보다는 have an effect on ~에 영향을 미치다

지문 Flow

[도입]
부모는 종종 학업의 성공이 장래 직업적 성공과 관련되어 있다고 믿음

[주제문]
학업의 성공보다 정직함, 인내심, 책임감과 같은 가치관이 더 필수적임

[보충설명1]
긴 안목으로 보면 성적표보다 훨씬 더 중요한 것들임

에 의해 뒷받침 되고 있는지를 파악하면 돼. 이 글에서 글쓴이는 자녀의 성공은 학업 성적과 가장 관련이 깊다고 생각하는 학부모들의 생각을 But으로 시작하는 문장으로 완곡하게 반박하며 '바람직한 가치관을 우선 갖추어야 한다'고 주장하고 있어. 따라서 ④가 가장 적절한 답이야.

오답단서 ①은 글의 내용과는 상반돼. ②와 ③의 내용은 글에서 다루고 있지 않아. 또한, ⑤의 내용은 세부적이므로 요지로는 적절하지 않아.

&

[보충설명2]
견고한 가치관이 최상의 선물이자 미래의 성공에 가장 큰 영향을 미침

013 정답 ⑤

지문 All in One

[1] Diversity is a wonderful thing // — diversity of culture, people, geography, history, and lifestyle all / makes the world a fascinating place. [2] Schools, / by their very nature, / are diverse organizations, // but in this period of rapid educational evolution / they are becoming more and more diverse / in terms of what is being taught, / how it is taught and assessed, / who is teaching, / and who is learning. [3] Our educational curriculum encourages diversity / and aims to be flexible; // that is a good thing / because students learn / in different ways. [4] Providing a diverse range of learning experiences / and allowing students to explore and inquire / make school learning programs today very different / from those of the past.

(다양성은 훌륭한 것이다 / 즉, 문화, 민족, 지리, 역사, 그리고 생활방식의 다양성 모두가 / 세상을 매혹적인 장소로 만든다 / 학교는 / 본질적으로 / 다양한 조직이다 / 하지만 이 급속한 교육 진화의 시기에 / 그것들은 / 점점 더 다양해지고 있다 / 가르치는 내용 면에서 / 가르치고 평가하는 방법 / 가르치는 사람 / 그리고 배우는 사람 / 우리의 교육과정은 다양성을 장려한다 / 그리고 융통성 있는 것을 목표로 한다 / 그것은 좋은 것이다 / 학생들이 배우기 때문에 / 여러 가지 방법으로 / 다양한 범위의 학습 경험을 제공하는 것 / 그리고 학생들이 탐구하고 질문할 수 있게 하는 것은 / 오늘날 학교 학습 프로그램들을 매우 다르게 만든다 / 과거의 그것들과)

(Diversity: S_1, is: V_1, a wonderful thing: C_1, diversity of ... all: S_2, makes: V_2, the world: O_2, a fascinating place: C_2; Schools: S_1, are: V_1, diverse organizations: C_1, they: S_2, are becoming: V_2, more and more diverse: C_2, what is being taught / how it is taught and assessed / who is teaching / who is learning: 간접의문문; Our educational curriculum: S, encourages: V_1, aims: V_2, that: S, is: V, a good thing: C, because: 접속사, students: S′, learn: V′; Providing ...: S_1, allowing students ...: S_2, make: V, school learning programs today: O, very different: C, those = school learning programs)

① 시대에 맞는 학교 교육이 필요하다.
② 다양성은 융통성 있게 가르쳐야 한다.
③ 교육과정 선택은 학생에 의해 이루어져야 한다.
④ 학교 커리큘럼은 상황에 따라 변화해야 한다.
⑤ 다양화되는 오늘날의 교육은 환영받을 만하다.

해석 한 눈에 보기 [1] 다양성은 훌륭한 것이다. 즉, 문화, 민족, 지리, 역사, 그리고 생활방식의 다양성 모두가 세상을 매혹적인 장소로 만든다. [2] 학교는 본질적으로 다양한 조직이지만, 이 급속한 교육 진화의 시기에 그것들은 가르치는 내용, 가르치고 평가하는 방법, 가르치는 사람, 그리고 배우는 사람의 측면에서 점점 더 다양해지고 있다. 주제문 [3] 우리의 교육 과정은 다양성을 장려하고 융통성 있는 것을 목표로 한다. 즉, 그것은 학생들이 여러 가지 방법으로 배우기 때문에 좋은 것이다. [4] 다양한 범위의 학습 경험을 제공하고 학생들이 탐구하고 질문할 수 있게 하는 것은 오늘날 학교 학습 프로그램들을 과거의 그것들과 매우 다르게 만든다.

정답단추 이 글은 도입 부분에서 '다양성'이라는 것에 대한 긍정적인 면을 서술한 뒤 구체적으로 학교에서도 여러 면에서 다양해지고 있는 점을 서술하고 있어. 그리고 이는 학생들로 하여금 여러 가지 방법으로 배우도록 하기 때문에 좋은 것이라고 주장하고 있지. 따라서 글의 요지로 가장 적절한 것은 ⑤야.

오답단서 ①은 글에 언급된 바가 없으므로 오답이야. ②는 다양성과 융통성이라는 단어만 보고 오답으로 고를 확률이 가장 높은 선택지야. 전혀 다른 내용인데, 첫 문장에 나오는 다양성이라는 말만 보고 답으로 고를 가능성이 있으므로 주의해야 해. ③과 ④는 교육과정의 선택과 변화에 대한 내용으로 교육의 다양성과는 거리가 먼 선택지야.

어휘확인

diversity 다양성 **geography** 지리 **fascinating** 매혹적인 **by one's very nature** 본질적으로 **diverse** 다양한 **organization** 조직 **period** 기간 **rapid** 빠른 **educational** 교육의 **evolution** 진화 **in terms of** ~ 면에서, ~에 관하여 **assess** 평가하다 **curriculum** 교육과정 **encourage** 장려하다 **aim** 목표로 하다 **flexible** 융통성 있는 **provide** 제공하다 **range** 범위 **explore** 탐구하다; 탐험하다 **inquire** 질문하다

지문 Flow

[도입]
다양성은 훌륭한 것인데, 학교도 여러 측면에서 점점 다양해지고 있음

[주제문]
다양성을 장려하는 교육 과정은 학생들이 여러 가지 방법으로 배울 수 있으므로 좋은 것임

[추가]
과거의 학습 프로그램들과는 매우 다른 것임

014 정답 ⑤

지문 All in One

[1] I edit a lot of job applications / to help my students. [2] Mostly / I shorten them. [3] I try not to change word choice / or do *something* [that would take away from the writer's original voice]. [4] It's a shame, // but I see many small but critical errors / — misspellings, grammatical errors / (including lack of capital letters), / and extremely casual writing / in formal

(나는 많은 취업 지원서를 교정본다 / 내 학생들을 돕기 위해 / 주로 / 나는 그것들을 짧게 한다 / 나는 단어 선택을 바꾸지 않으려고 한다 / 또는 글쓴이의 원래 목소리에서 벗어나는 어떤 것을 하지 않으려고 / 유감스럽게도 / 나는 작지만 중대한 많은 오류들을 본다 / 맞춤법 오류, 문법 오류 / 대문자 결여를 포함하는 / 그리고 극도로 격식이 없는 글을)

(I: S, edit: V, to help: 부사적 용법(목적); I: S, shorten: V; I: S, try: V, that: 관계대명사; It: S_1, 's: V_1, I: S_2, see: V_2)

어휘확인

edit (원고를) 손질하다, 교정보다 **job application** 취업 지원서 **mostly** 주로, 일반적으로 **shorten** 짧게 하다 **take away from** ~로부터 벗어나다 **original** 원래의 **critical** 중대한, 결정적인 **error** 오류 **misspelling** 오타 **grammatical** 문법적인 **including** 포함하여 **lack** 부족, 결여 **capital letter** 대문자 **extremely** 극히, 극도로 **casual** 격식이 없는 **formal** 공식적

공식적인 상황에서 / 이것은 멈춰야만 하는 것이다 / 당신이 직업을 구하기를 바란다면
circumstances. 5 This is *something* [which must stop] // if you ever hope to get a job / in the
S V C 관계대명사 접속사 S′ V′

현실 세계에서 / 신입사원 모집자들은 안다 / 총체적 부주의와 결합된 대문자의 결여가
real world. 6 Recruiters find / *the lack of capital letters* [combined with overall carelessness] /
S V O

매우 짜증난다는 것을 / 그리고 사실을 직시하자 / 그들이 고용한다는 / 나는 모든 사람이 진지하게 맹세
completely irritating. 7 And let's face it, / [they do the hiring]. 8 I want every person
C V = S V O

하기를 바란다 / 오류로 가득 찬 또 다른 이메일을 보내지 않기를 / 나는 지금 항의를
to solemnly swear / that they will never send another email full of errors. 9 I can hear the
C 접속사 S V

들을 수 있다 / 우리는 완벽할 수 없다 / 그렇지 않은가 / 잊지 마라 / 그것은 정확히 이러한 유형의 행동이다
protests now // — we cannot be perfect, / can we? 10 Don't forget! 11 It's precisely *this type of*
S V C 부가의문문 V S V C

돌아와서 당신을 이빨로 무는
behavior [that comes back and bites you].
관계대명사

① 구직용 자기소개서는 전문가의 검토를 받아야 한다.
② 구직 서류는 간단명료하게 작성하는 것이 좋다.
③ 서류 작성 시 용도에 맞는 문체를 선택해야 한다.
④ 지나친 완벽주의는 구직 활동에 좋지 않은 영향을 준다.
⑤ 구직 서류 작성 시 실수를 저지르지 않아야 한다.

해석 한 눈에 보기 1 나는 내 학생들을 돕기 위해 많은 취업 지원서를 교정본다. 2 주로 나는 그것들을 짧게 한다. 3 나는 단어 선택을 바꾸지 않으려고 하거나 글쓴이의 원래 목소리에서 벗어나는 것을 하지 않으려고 노력한다. 4 유감스럽게도 나는 맞춤법 오류, 문법 오류 (대문자 결여 포함) 같은 작지만 중대한 많은 오류들, 그리고 공식적인 상황에서 극도로 격식이 없는 글을 본다. **주제문** 5 현실 세계에서 직업을 구하기를 바란다면, 이것은 멈춰야만 하는 것이다. 6 신입사원 모집자들은 총체적 부주의와 결합된 대문자의 결여가 매우 짜증난다는 것을 안다. 7 그리고 그들이 고용한다는 사실을 직시하자. 8 나는 모든 사람이 오류로 가득 찬 또 다른 이메일을 보내지 않기를 진지하게 맹세하기를 바란다. 9 나는 지금 항의를 들을 수 있다. 우리는 완벽할 수 없다. 그렇지 않은가? 10 잊지 마라! 11 그것은 돌아와서 당신을 이빨로 무는 정확히 이러한 유형의 행동이다.

정답단추 글에서 글쓴이의 주장이 담긴 문장을 찾아 글쓴이가 무엇을 말하고 있는지 확인하는 게 중요해. 글쓴이의 주장은 '~해야 한다'의 의미를 가진 must, should 등으로 표현하는 경우가 많아. 이 글에서는 This is something which must stop ~ in the real world.가 주제문이지. 직업을 구하려면 이것을 하지 말라는 내용인데, 여기서 이것은 취업 지원서의 부주의한 오류를 말해. 즉, 취업 지원서를 쓸 때 실수를 하지 말라는 것이 핵심 내용이야. 따라서 글의 요지로 가장 적절한 것은 ⑤임을 알 수 있지?

오답단서 ①, ②, ③, ④ 모두 글의 내용에 유사 표현이 언급된 선택지들이야. 특히, ③은 공식적인 상황에서는 격식이 없는 글이 되지 않도록 해야 한다는 내용 때문에 답으로 고를 수 있는데, 특정한 세부 내용에 불과하므로, 핵심 내용을 담은 요지로 보기는 어려워.

인 circumstances 환경 recruiter 신인 모집자 combined with ~와 결합된 overall 전부의, 종합의 carelessness 부주의 completely 완전히, 매우 irritating 짜증나게 하는 do the hiring 고용하다 solemnly 진지하게 swear 맹세하다 protest 항의, 이의 precisely 정확히 behavior 행동 bite (이빨로) 물다

지문 Flow

[문제점]
• 취업 지원서의 많은 문법적 오류
• 극도로 격식 없는 글

[주제문]
직업을 구하려면 취업 지원서에 오류를 범하지 말아야 함

[보충설명]
고용자들이 부주의한 오류를 좋아하지 않으며, 이러한 실수가 취업을 방해함

유형 03 제목

Check-Up 1 ② **015** ③
Check-Up 2 **016** ②
Check-Up 3 **017** ⑤
실전적용독해 **018** ⑤ **019** ③ **020** ⑤

Check-Up 1

정답 ②
해석 광범위한 증거는 자연과의 접촉이 아이들의 교육, 개인적·사회적 기술, 그리고 건강과 행복을 향상시킨다는 것을 보여준다. ① 교육이 이루어지게 하는 방법 ② 자연은 아이들이 필요로 하는 것

015 정답 ③

지문 All in One

나는 생각한다 / 일부 과학기술이 기여하고 있다고 / 숙련 지연의 확산에 / 사실이다
1 I believe // some technology is contributing / to the spread of skill retardation. 2 The fact is
S V S′ V′ S V

우리가 총체적으로 더 나빠지고 있다는 것은 / 대부분의 일에서 / 수학, 글을 읽고 쓰는 능력, 지도 읽기 능력,
// that we're collectively getting worse / at most things / — math, literacy, being able to read
접속사 S′ V′ C′ C

실무 기술 / 그리고 심지어 우리의 기억 사용 / 특히 젊은 사람들은
maps, hands-on skills, / and even using our memory. 3 Young people in particular /
S_1

어휘확인

technology 과학기술 contribute 기여하다 spread 확산, 전파 retardation 지체, 지연, 방해 collectively 총체적으로 get worse 더 나빠지다, 악화되다 literacy 읽고 쓰는 능력 hands-on 직접 해보는, 실무에 참가하는 memory 기억 in particular 특히 prove 증명하다, 밝히다 skilled 숙련된

이미 밝혀지고 있다 / 이제껏 가장 숙련되지 않은 세대로 / 그리고 많은 기업들이 이를 인식한다

are already proving / to be the least skilled generation ever, // and a lot of companies recognize *this*, / which is why they're increasingly reluctant / to hire young graduates.

(V_1, S_2, V_2, 계속적 용법, 관계부사)

그것이 그들이 점점 더 꺼리는 이유이다 / 젊은 졸업생을 고용하기를

4 Even *my wife*, [who's a primary school teacher], / is often telling me / about the growing number of *kids* / she sees / [who lack basic skills and knowledge]. 5 This extends / to social skills, / too. 6 Young people are becoming less skilled / at basic human communication, handling conflicts, / and even dating or meeting people.

(S, 관계대명사, V, 삽입절, 관계대명사, S, V, S, V, C)

초등학교 교사인 나의 아내조차도 / 종종 내게 이야기한다 / 아이들의 수가 늘어나는 것에 대해서 / 그녀가 보기에 / 기본적인 기량과 지식이 부족한 / 이것은 확장된다 / 사회적 기술에 / 또한 / 젊은 사람들은 덜 숙련되고 있다 / 기본적인 인간의 의사소통, 갈등 대처에 / 그리고 심지어 데이트나 사람들과의 만남에도

① The Continual Advancement of Technology
과학기술의 지속적인 발전

② Where Technology Cannot Beat Humans
과학기술이 인간을 이길 수 없는 곳

③ Technology Is Making the Young Stupid
과학기술은 젊은 바보들을 만들고 있다

④ A New Generation of Technology Loving Kids
아이들을 사랑하는 신세대 과학기술

⑤ What Distinguishes Skilled and Unskilled People
숙련된 사람들과 숙련되지 않은 사람들을 구분하는 것

해석 한 눈에 보기 **주제문** 1 나는 일부 과학기술이 숙련 지연의 확산에 기여하고 있다고 생각한다. 2 우리가 수학, 글을 읽고 쓰는 능력, 지도 읽기 능력, 실무 기술, 그리고 심지어 우리의 기억 사용 같은 대부분의 일에서 총체적으로 더 나빠지고 있다는 것은 사실이다. 3 특히 젊은 사람들은 이미 이제껏 가장 숙련되지 않은 세대로 밝혀지고 있고, 많은 기업들이 이를 인식하는데, 그것이 그들이 젊은 졸업생을 고용하는 것을 점점 더 꺼리고 있는 이유이다. 4 초등학교 교사인 나의 아내조차도 종종 그녀가 보기에 기본적인 기량과 지식이 부족한 아이들의 수가 늘어나는 것에 대해 내게 이야기한다. 5 이것은 사회적 기술에도 확장된다. 6 젊은 사람들은 기본적인 인간의 의사소통, 갈등 대처, 그리고 심지어 데이트나 사람들과의 만남에도 덜 숙련되고 있다.

정답단추 글의 제목은 핵심 내용을 담고 있는 주제문을 찾아서 이를 제목으로 잘 표현한 선택지를 고르면 돼. 이 글에서는 I believe로 시작하는 첫 문장이 필자의 생각을 담고 있어. 일부 과학기술이 사람들을 덜 숙련되게 만든다는 내용이야. 일을 하는 데 기본적으로 필요한 기량이나 지식이 나빠지고 있고 특히 젊은 사람들이 숙련도가 떨어지고 있는데 초등학생들도 그런 아이들이 늘어나고 있다는 거야. 또한 젊은 사람들은 사회적 기술에서도 숙련도가 떨어진다는 보충설명내용이 이어지고 있어. 따라서 글의 주제문은 첫 문장이고 이를 제목으로 가장 적절히 표현한 것은 ③이야.

오답단서 ①, ②, ④는 모두 글에서 언급된 technology를 이용해서 만든 선택지야. 하지만 모두 글에서는 언급되지 않은 내용들이지. ⑤는 글에 과학기술이 숙련도를 떨어뜨린다는 내용은 나오지만, 숙련된 사람과 그렇지 않은 사람을 구분하는 것에 대한 내용은 나오지 않으므로 답이 될 수 없어.

generation 세대 recognize 인식하다 increasingly 점점 더 reluctant 꺼리는 hire 고용하다 graduate 졸업생 primary 초등의 lack 부족하다 knowledge 지식 extend 확장하다 communication 의사소통 handle 다루다 conflict 갈등

〈선택지 어휘〉

continual 지속적인 advancement 발전, 진보 stupid 어리석은 distinguish 구분하다 unskilled 숙련되지 않은

지문 Flow

[주제]
일부 과학기술로 인해 숙련 지연이 확산되고 있음

⬇

[보충설명1]
수학, 글을 읽고 쓰는 능력, 지도 읽기 능력, 실무 능력, 기억 사용 등에서 더 나빠지고 있음

⬇

[추가]
특히 젊은 사람들이 숙련도가 떨어지고, 기본 기량과 지식이 부족한 초등학생들도 늘어나고 있음

⬇

[보충설명 2]
젊은 사람들은 의사소통, 갈등 대처, 사람들과의 만남 등의 사회적 기술에서도 숙련도가 떨어짐

Check-Up 2

016 정답 ②

지문 All in One

1 BottleRocket is *a recycling service* [that supplies users / — mostly college students — / with *cardboard bins* [to fill with bottles]. 2 Users then request pickups / when their bins are full, // and when enough users are ready for pickup / in an area, / they collect the bins / and drop them off / at a recycling center. 3 Users can choose / how to be rewarded, / such as earning \$5 / per bin. 4 "I like the idea, // since college kids obviously have / *lots of cans and bottles* [to recycle], // but they are too lazy to go out and recycle themselves," / said *a student* [who uses BottleRocket's services]. 5 "The company is still expanding, // and may be able to recycle / electronics, such as old smartphones, and clothing / in the future," / the founder said.

(S, V, C, 관계대명사 / S_1, V_1, 접속사, S'_1, V'_1, C'_1 / 접속사, S'_2, V'_2, C'_2, = BottleRockets workers, V_3 / S, V, to부정사의 수동태 / S, V, 접속사(이유), S'_1, V'_1 / S'_2, V'_2, 'too ~ to ...': 너무 ~해서 …할 수 없다, V, S, 관계대명사 / S, V_1, V_2 / S, V)

BottleRocket은 재활용 서비스이다 / 사용자들에게 제공하는 / 대개 대학생들에게 / 판지 쓰레기통을 / 병으로 가득 채울 / 사용자들은 그런 다음 픽업을 요구한다 / 쓰레기통이 가득 찼을 때 / 그리고 충분한 사용자들이 픽업 준비가 되었을 때 / 한 지역에서 / 그들은 쓰레기통을 모은다 / 그리고 그것들을 가져다 놓는다 / 재활용 센터에 / 사용자들은 선택할 수 있다 / 보상받는 방법을 / 5달러 획득과 같이 / 쓰레기통 당 / 저는 그 생각이 맘에 들어요 / 대학생들이 분명히 가지고 있기 때문에 / 재활용할 수 있는 많은 캔과 병을 / 하지만 너무 게을러서 스스로 밖에 나가서 재활용할 수 없기 (때문에) / 한 학생이 말했다 / BottleRocket의 서비스를 사용하는 / 회사는 여전히 확장 중입니다 / 그리고 재활용할 수 있을 겁니다 / 오래된 스마트폰과 같은 전자제품과 의류를 / 장차 / 창립자는 말했다

① Recycling: A Principle of a Healthy Society
건강한 사회의 원칙인 재활용

② A New Recycling Service Appeals to Users
새로운 재활용 서비스가 사용자들의 관심을 끌다

어휘확인

recycling 재활용 supply A with B A에게 B를 제공하다 mostly 대개 cardboard 판지 bin 쓰레기통 fill with ~으로 가득 차다 request 요청하다, 요구하다 be ready for ~할 준비가 되다 area 지역 drop off 갖다 놓다 reward 보상하다 earning 획득; (일하며)벌기 obviously 분명히 recycle 재활용하다 expand 확장하다 electronics 전자제품 clothing 옷 founder 창립자, 설립자

〈선택지 어휘〉

principle 원칙 appeal 관심을 끌다 connect 연결하다 online 온라인으로

지문 Flow

[도입]
BottleRocket 재활용 서비스

⬇

③ Volunteers for a Better World
더 나은 세상을 위한 자원봉사자

④ College Students Turn to Starting their Own Businesses
대학생들이 자신의 사업을 시작하는 것으로 전환하다

⑤ A New Way of Being Connected with People Online
온라인으로 사람들과 연결되는 새로운 방법

해석 한 눈에 보기 1 BottleRocket은 사용자들, 대개 대학생들에게 병으로 가득 채울 판지 쓰레기통을 제공하는 재활용 서비스이다. 2 그러면 사용자들은 쓰레기통이 가득 찼을 때 픽업을 요청하고, 한 지역에서 충분한 사용자들이 픽업 준비가 되었을 때, 그들(BottleRocket)은 쓰레기통을 모아서 재활용 센터에 가져다 놓는다. 3 사용자들은 쓰레기통 당 5달러 획득과 같이 보상받는 방법을 선택할 수 있다. 4 "대학생들이 분명히 재활용할 수 있는 많은 캔과 병을 가지고 있지만, 너무 게을러서 스스로 밖에 나가서 재활용할 수 없기 때문에, 저는 그 생각이 맘에 들어요."라고 BottleRocket의 서비스를 사용하는 한 학생이 말했다. 5 "회사는 여전히 확장 중이며, 장차 오래된 스마트폰과 같은 전자제품과 의류를 재활용할 수 있을 겁니다."라고 창립자는 말했다.

정답단추 뚜렷한 주제문이 글에 나오지 않을 때는 글 전체의 내용을 종합해서 생각해봐. 재활용 서비스 BottleRocket에 대해 설명하는 글인데, 이것은 사용자들, 주로 대학생들에게 재활용 통을 제공하고 캔이나 병 같은 재활용 쓰레기를 모으면 픽업해 가는 서비스야. 한 대학생의 긍정적인 평가와 BottleRocket 회사의 확장 및 서비스 확대 계획을 통해 이 서비스가 사용자들에게 호응을 얻고 있음을 알 수 있어. 그러므로, 글의 제목으로 가장 적절한 것은 ②야.

오답단서 ①은 글에서 주로 다룬 Recycling이 나오기 때문에 오답으로 고를 가능성이 가장 높아. 하지만 너무 포괄적인 내용이라 제목으로 적절하지 않아. ③, ④, ⑤는 글에 언급된 내용이 아니므로 답이 될 수 없어.

[설명1]
서비스 내용: 대학생들에게 재활용 쓰레기통을 제공하고, 픽업해서 재활용 센터에 가져다주며 보상 제공

&

[설명2]
서비스 반응: 대학생들에게 적절한 서비스

&

[설명3]
서비스 회사 현황: 회사 확장 중이고 재활용 물품 확대 계획 중임

⬇

[주제 도출]
BottleRocket 재활용 서비스가 사용자들에게 호응을 얻고 있음

Check-Up 3

017 정답 ⑤

지문 All in One

음악은 우리를 둘러싼다 / 매일 / 우리에게 다가오면서 / 자동차 라디오, 엘리베이터 스피커, 노래하는

1 Music surrounds us / every day, / coming to us / from car radios, elevator speakers, the little

(Music: S, surrounds: V, coming to us: 분사구문(= as it comes ~))

아이들의 어린 목소리 / 그리고 셀 수 없을 정도로 많은 다른 출처로부터 / 그러나 / 음악은 가치가 있다

voices of singing children, / [and] countless other sources. 2 However, / music has value /

(music: S, has: V)

오락 이상의 / 증거가 있다 / 리듬과 소리가 우리의 감각에 영향을 미친다는

beyond entertainment. 3 There is evidence // that rhythm and sound have an effect on our

(is: V, evidence: S = that: 접속사, rhythm and sound: S'₁, have an effect on: V'₁)

그리고 결과적으로 / 근육 조절에 영향을 미친다는 / 연구들은 또한 시사한다 / 음악이 일부 신경 세포를

senses / [and], in turn, / influence muscle control. 4 Studies also suggest // that music can

(influence: V'₂, Studies: S, suggest: V, that: 접속사, music: S')

자극할 수 있다고 / 우리가 듣거나 느낄 때 / 리듬의 외부 원천을 / 음악과 같은

stimulate some neurons. 5 When we hear or feel / an outside source of rhythm / such as

(stimulate: V', When: 접속사, we: S', hear: V'₁, feel: V'₂)

우리의 몸은 자연스럽게 일치시키려고 노력한다 / 우리 자신의 리듬을 박자와

music, // our bodies naturally try to match / our own rhythms to the beat. 6 The beats per

(our bodies: S, try: V)

음악 한 곡의 분당 박자는 / 몸과 뇌를 자극한다 / 다양한 방식으로 / 예를 들어

minute of a piece of music / stimulate the body and brain / in various ways. 7 For example, /

(The beats per minute of a piece of music: S, stimulate: V)

분당 60박자는 / 좋다 / 자기 전에 / 그것이 되돌리는 데 도움이 되기 때문에 / 몸의 자연스러운

60 beats per minute / is good / before bed // because it helps to return / the body's natural

(60 beats per minute: S, is: V, good: C, because: 접속사, it: S', helps: V')

리듬을 평온한 상태로 / 분당 100박자는 / 가장 좋다 / 작업 등의 주의 집중에 도움을 주기에

rhythm to a calm state. 8 One hundred beats per minute / is best / to help with attention to a task, etc.

(One hundred beats per minute: S, is: V, best: C, to help: 부사적 용법(형용사 수식))

① The Importance of Music in Entertainment
오락에 있어서 음악의 중요성

② Music: A New Tool for Mental Growth
음악: 정신적 성장을 위한 새로운 도구

③ Does Music Really Make Us Feel Good?
음악은 정말 우리를 기분 좋게 하는가?

④ Is Music Entertainment or Art?
음악은 오락인가 아니면 예술인가?

⑤ How Music Affects Our Body and Brain
음악이 우리의 몸과 뇌에 영향을 미치는 방법

해석 한 눈에 보기 1 음악은 자동차 라디오, 엘리베이터 스피커, 노래하는 아이들의 어린 목소리, 그리고 셀 수 없을 정도로 많은 다른 출처로부터 우리에게 다가오면서 매일 우리를 둘러싼다. 주제문 2 그러나, 음악은 오락 이상의 가치가 있다. 3 리듬과 소리가 우리의 감각에 영향을 미치고, 결과적으로 근육 조절에 영향을 미친다는 증거가 있다. 4 연구들은 또한 음악이 일부 신경 세포를 자극할 수 있다고 시사한다. 5 우리가 음악과 같은 리듬의 외부 원천을 듣거나 느낄 때, 우리의 몸은 자연스럽게 우리 자신의 리듬을 박자와 일치시키려고 노력한다. 6 음악 한 곡의 분당 박자는 몸과 뇌를 다양한 방식으로 자극한다. 7 예를 들어, 분당 60박자는 몸의 자연스러운 리듬을 평온한 상태로 되돌리는 데 도움이 되기 때문에 자기 전에 좋다. 8 분당 100박자는 작업 등의 주의 집중에 도움을 주기에 가장 좋다.

어휘확인

surround 둘러싸다 **countless** 셀 수 없이 많은, 무수한 **source** (-s) 출처; 원천, 근원 **value** 가치 **beyond** ~을 넘어서 **entertainment** 오락 **evidence** 증거 **rhythm** 리듬 **have an effect on** ~에 영향을 미치다 **sense** 감각 **in turn** 결과적으로 **influence** 영향을 미치다 **muscle** 근육 **control** 조절 **suggest** 시사하다 **stimulate** 자극하다 **neuron** 뉴런, 신경 세포 **outside** 외부의 **such as** ~ 같은 **naturally** 자연스럽게 **match** 일치시키다 **beat** 박자 **per minute** 분당 **brain** 뇌 **various** 다양한 **return** 되돌리다 **natural** 자연스러운 **calm** 평온한, 침착한 **state** 상태 **attention** 주의 집중 **task** 작업, 임무 **etc.** (= et cetera) 등등

지문 Flow

[주제]
매일 우리 주변을 둘러싸는 음악이 오락 이상의 가치가 있음

⬇

[보충설명1]
• 리듬과 소리가 감각, 근육 조절에 영향을 미친다는 증거
• 음악이 신경 세포를 자극할 수 있다는 연구

&

[보충설명2]
음악을 듣거나 느낄 때 몸이 자연스럽게 박자를 탐

&

[보충설명3]
음악의 분당 박자는 몸과 뇌를 다양한 방식으로 자극함

정답단추 글의 핵심 내용을 담고 있는 주제문을 찾아서 이를 잘 반영한 제목을 골라야 해. However로 시작하는 두 번째 문장이 주제문으로 음악이 오락 이상의 가치가 있다고 하고 있어. 그 뒤에 보충설명으로 음악의 리듬과 소리에 몸이 반응하고, 뇌에도 다양한 방식으로 자극을 준다는 내용이 이어지고 있어. 이를 종합하여 가장 적절하게 표현한 제목은 ⑤야.
오답단서 ①은 음악이 오락 이상의 가치가 있다고 했으니 적절하지 않아. ②와 ④는 음악을 정신적 성장이나 예술 같은 측면에서 다루고 있지 않으므로 답이 될 수 없어. ③은 음악이 정말 우리의 기분을 좋게 하는지에 대해 언급하고 있지 않으니 오답이야.

[예시]
• 분당 60박자는 자기 전에 좋음
• 분당 100박자는 주의 집중에 좋음

실전적용독해

018 정답 ⑤

지문 All in One

1 The growth of the Internet (S) / has caused (V) *a revolution* / in the news media [that (관계대명사) is obvious in several ways]. 2 Younger people (S) / especially like (V) to reproduce / their own news, / choosing (분사구문) from the Internet's millions of blogs, UCC videos, and newspaper sites. (= as they choose from ~) 3 People (S_1) want (V_1) / their news (O) to be relevant to their personal interests (C), // and they (S_2) discard (V_2) everything else. 4 Another characteristic of today's news (S) / is (V) its focus on / analysis and opinion. 5 People (S) / want (V) to know more / than what's happening (간접의문문) / and where it's taking place (간접의문문). 6 That is, / they (S) want (V) to know // [what the events mean / to other people / and how the events will impact (간접의문문) them / in their own lives].

(인터넷의 성장은 / 혁명을 초래했다 / 뉴스 매체에 / 여러 가지 면에서 명백한 / 보다 젊은 사람들은 / 특히 재생산하는 것을 좋아한다 / 자기 자신들의 뉴스를 / 인터넷 상에 있는 수백만 개의 블로그, UCC 동영상, 신문 사이트에서 선별하여 / 사람들은 원한다 / 그들의 뉴스가 개인적인 관심사와 관련이 있기를 / 그리고 그 밖의 모든 것은 버린다 / 또 다른 오늘날의 뉴스의 특징은 / 초점을 둔다는 것이다 / 분석과 의견에 / 사람들은 / 더 많이 알기를 원한다 / 무슨 일이 일어나고 있는지보다 / 그리고 어디에서 일어나고 있는지 / 즉 / 그들은 / 알기를 원한다 / 사건이 무엇을 의미하며 / 다른 사람들에게 / 그것이 그들에게 어떻게 영향을 미칠 것인지 / 그들의 삶에서)

① The Power of the Media
매체의 힘
② What People Want These Days
사람들이 오늘날 원하는 것
③ The Role of Youth in the Media
매체에서 젊은이의 역할
④ The Decreasing Quality of News
뉴스의 떨어져 가는 품질
⑤ The Changing Character of News
변하고 있는 뉴스의 성격

해석 한 눈에 보기 주제문 1 인터넷의 성장은 뉴스 매체에 여러 가지 면에서 명백한 혁명을 초래했다. 2 보다 젊은 사람들은 특히 인터넷 상에 있는 수백만 개의 블로그, UCC 동영상, 신문 사이트에서 선별하여 자기 자신들의 뉴스를 재생산하는 것을 좋아한다. 3 사람들은 자신의 뉴스가 자신의 개인적인 관심사와 관련이 있기를 원하여, 그 밖의 모든 것을 버린다. 4 오늘날의 뉴스의 또 다른 특징은 그것이 분석과 의견에 초점을 둔다는 것이다. 5 사람들은 무슨 일이 일어나고 있고 어디에서 그것이 일어나고 있는지보다 더 많은 것을 알고 싶어 한다. 6 즉, 그들은 사건이 다른 사람들에게 무엇을 의미하며 그것이 그들의 삶에서 그들에게 어떻게 영향을 미칠 것인지를 알고 싶어 한다.
정답단추 제목은 글의 핵심 내용을 압축적으로 표현하기 때문에 핵심 내용을 찾아 함축하면 제목을 알아낼 수 있어. 이 글을 보면 '인터넷이 발달하여 뉴스를 재생산하고, 오늘날의 뉴스는 분석과 의견에 초점을 맞추고 있다'는 내용으로, 오늘날의 변화하고 있는 뉴스의 성격에 관한 것임을 알 수 있어. 그러므로 가장 적절한 제목은 ⑤야.
오답단서 ①, ③, ④는 글에 언급되지 않았어. 또한, ②는 제목이라 보기에는 세부적인 내용이라 제목으로 적절하지 않아.

어휘확인

growth 성장 **cause** 야기하다 **revolution** 혁명 **media** 매체, 미디어 **obvious** 명백한, 뻔한 **several** (몇)몇의 **especially** 특히 **reproduce** 재생산하다 **millions of** 수백만의 **UCC** (= User Created Content) 사용자 제작 콘텐츠 **be relevant to** ~와 관련되어 있다 **personal** 개인의 **interest** 관심, 흥미 **discard** 버리다 **characteristic** 특징 **focus** 초점, 중점 **analysis** 분석 **opinion** 의견 **take place** 일어나다, 개최되다 **that is (to say)** 즉, 다시 말하면 **mean** ~을 의미하다 **impact** 영향을 미치다

지문 Flow

[주제]
인터넷 성장은 뉴스 매체에 명백한 혁명을 초래함

[보충설명1]
젊은 사람들은 블로그, UCC 동영상, 신문 사이트를 선별하여 자신의 뉴스를 재생산하는 것을 좋아함

&

[보충설명2]
뉴스의 사실 보도보다 분석과 의견에 초점을 둠

[추가]
사람들은 사건이 다른 사람들에게 미치는 영향을 알고 싶어 함

019 정답 ③

지문 All in One

1 There are (V) around 45,000 surnames, or family names (S), / in England today. 2 But this (S) wasn't (V) always the case (C). 3 In fact, / in England's early history, / only the nobility (S) / had (V) two names.

(약 45,000개의 성(姓), 즉 가족 이름이 있다 / 오늘날 영국에는 / 그러나 이것이 항상 그러한 경우는 아니었다 / 사실 / 영국의 초기 역사에서는 / 오직 귀족만이 / 두 개의 이름을 가졌다)

어휘확인

around 약; 둘레에 **surname** 성(姓) (= family name, second name) **in fact** 사실은[실은] **nobility** 귀족 **common** 보통의; 흔한 **personal** 개인적인 **nickname** 애칭, 별명 **village** 마을 **country** 시골; 국가

보통 사람들은 사용했다 개인적인 이름 혹은 애칭만을 마을이나 시골에서는
4 Common people used / only a personal name or nickname. 5 In villages and in the country,
S V

성이 불필요했다 모든 사람이 알았기 때문에 'John'이나 'Mary'가 누구인지 그러나 1066년에
/ surnames were unnecessary // as everyone knew / who "John" or "Mary" was. 6 But in 1066,
S V C 접속사 S′ V′ 간접의문문 S″ V″

프랑스의 William이 영국을 정복했다 그리고 결정했다 모든 사람이 성을 가져야 한다고
/ William from France / conquered England // and ruled / that everyone should have a
S V_1 V_2 접속사 S′ V′

성이 있으면 더 쉬울 것이다 사람들을 기록하고 세금을 징수하기가
surname. 7 With surnames, / it would be easier / to keep records of people / and to collect
가주어 V C 진주어$_1$ 진주어$_2$

그 기록을 토대로 하여 이것은 의미했다 모든 사람이 선택해야 함을 아버지로부터
taxes / based on those records. 8 This meant // that everyone had to choose / *a second name*
분사구문(= which were based ~) S V 접속사 S′ V′

넘겨질 두 번째 이름을 그들의 아들과 딸들에게
[that would be passed on from fathers / to their sons and daughters].
주격 관계대명사

① The Value of the Surname
성의 가치
② Common Names in England
영국에서 흔한 이름들
③ The Origin of Family Names
성의 유래
④ The Great Conqueror, William
위대한 정복자 William
⑤ The Function of Family Names
성의 기능

해석 한 눈에 보기 1 오늘날 영국에는 약 45,000개의 성(姓), 즉 가족 이름이 있다. 2 그러나 이것이 항상 이랬던 것은 아니었다. 3 사실, 영국의 초기 역사에서는, 오직 귀족만이 두 개의 이름을 가졌다. 4 평민들은 개인적인 이름이나 애칭만을 사용했다. 5 마을이나 시골에서는, 모든 사람이 'John'이나 'Mary'가 누구인지 알고 있었기 때문에 성이 불필요했다. 6 그러나 1066년에 프랑스의 William이 영국을 정복했고 모든 사람이 성을 가져야 한다고 결정했다. 7 성이 있으면, 사람들에 대해 기록을 하고 그 기록을 토대로 하여 세금을 징수하기가 더 쉬울 것이다. 8 이것은 모든 사람이 아버지로부터 아들딸에게 넘겨질 두 번째 이름을 선택해야 함을 의미했다.

정답단추 이 글은 뚜렷한 주제문이 없어서 제목을 찾기 어려울 수 있어. 이럴 때는 글 전체 내용을 종합해서 생각하면 돼. 이 글의 전체 내용은 '귀족만 사용하던 성(姓)이 William에 의해서 평민들도 사용하게 되었다'니까 글의 제목으로 가장 적절한 것은 ③이야.

오답단서 ①은 '성(姓)'에 관련되긴 했지만 '가치'에 대해서는 언급한 적이 없어서 답이 될 수 없어. ②와 ④는 각각 글에서 언급한 '영국'과 'William'을 사용해 만든 오답이야. 그리고 ⑤는 글의 마지막 부분에 나온 세부 내용으로 제목으로는 적절하지 않아.

unnecessary 불필요한 conquer 정복하다 rule 결정을 내리다; 규칙 keep a record of ~을 기록하다 collect 징수하다 tax 세금 based on ~을 토대로 하여 pass on (to) (~에게) 넘겨주다
〈선택지 어휘〉
value 가치 origin 유래 conqueror 정복자 function 기능

지문 Flow

[도입]
오늘날 영국에 45,000개의 성이 있으나 항상 그러지는 않았음

[설명1]
과거: 귀족만이 성을 가졌고, 평민은 이름이나 애칭을 사용함

&

[설명2]
1066년: 프랑스의 영국 정복 이후, 세금 징수 편의를 위해 모든 사람이 성을 갖도록 규정함

[결과]
모든 사람이 아버지로부터 성을 물려받음

020 정답 ⑤

지문 All in One

나는 단체를 시작했다 위탁 양육 청소년들에게 적절한 옷을 제공하기 위한 지난 20016년 8월에
1 I started *an organization* [to provide decent clothing for foster care teens] / last August 2016.
S V

우리는 서비스를 제공한다 약 42명의 청소년들에게 매달 우리는 아니다 전형적인 자선 단체가 옷은
2 We serve / about 42 teens / every month. 3 We are not / a typical charity. 4 The clothes / are
S V S V C S V

중고이거나 닳아 해졌거나 더럽지 않다 우리는 새로운 속옷, 양말 그리고 기타 필수품을 제공한다
not used, worn-out, or dirty. 5 We provide new underwear, socks, and other essentials / to
C_1 C_2 C_3 S_1 V_1

가능한 한 많은 청소년들에게 그리고 모든 것은 신제품이다 나로서는 성공은 변화를 가져오고
as many teens as possible, // and everything / is brand-new. 6 As for me, / success is making
S_2 V_2 C S V_1

있다 그리고 다른 사람들을 돕고 있다 종종 잊혀진 우리는 동기를 부여
a difference // and (is) helping *others* [who have often been forgotten about]. 7 We have been
V_2 관계대명사 S V

할 수 있었다 지역 사회 구성원들에게 문제에 대한 인식을 가져옴으로써
able to motivate / our community members / by bringing awareness to this issue.

위탁 양육에 있는 청소년들은 품위 있는 쇼핑을 할 자격이 있다 새로운 의류와 액세서리를 고를
8 Teens in foster care / deserve to shop with dignity, / (to) choose new clothing and
S V

그리고 필요한 위생 필수품을 받을 청소년들은 우리 가게를 떠난다
accessories, / and (to) receive the necessary hygiene essentials. 9 Teens leave our shop / with
S V

자신감과 높아진 자존감으로
confidence and raised self-esteem.

① A New Trend in Shopping for Clothing
의류 쇼핑의 새로운 경향
② Clothing Items Favored by Stylish Teens
유행에 민감한 십대들이 좋아하는 의류 아이템
③ What Success Means to Most Teenagers
대부분의 십대들에게 성공이 의미하는 것
④ A Shop with More Fashion Choices for Teens
십대들을 위한 더 많은 패션 선택이 있는 가게

어휘확인

organization 단체 provide A for[to] B A를 B에게 제공하다 decent (상황에) 적절한 clothing 옷 foster care 위탁 양육 typical 전형적인 charity 자선 단체 used 중고의 worn-out 닳아 해진 underwear 속옷 essentials 필수품 brand-new 신제품의 success 성공 make a difference 변화를 가져오다 motivate 동기 부여하다 community 지역 사회 awareness 인식 issue 문제 deserve to-v ~할 가치가 있다 dignity 품위, 위엄 accessory 액세서리, 장신구 necessary 필요한 hygiene 위생 confidence 자신감 raised 높은 self-esteem 자존감
〈선택지 어휘〉
trend 경향 favor 호의를 보이다 stylish 유행을 따르는, 멋진 needy (경제적으로) 어려운

지문 Flow

[도입]
위탁 양육 청소년에게 옷을 제공하기 위해 단체를 시작함

⑤ An Organization for Helping Needy Teens
가난한 십대를 도와주는 단체

해석 한 눈에 보기 1 나는 지난 2016년 8월에 위탁 양육 청소년들에게 적절한 옷을 제공하기 위한 단체를 시작했다. 2 우리는 매달 약 42명의 청소년들에게 서비스를 제공한다. 3 우리는 전형적인 자선 단체가 아니다. 4 옷은 중고이거나 닳아 해졌거나 더럽지 않다. 5 우리는 가능한 한 많은 청소년들에게 새로운 속옷, 양말, 그리고 기타 필수품을 제공하며, 모든 것은 신제품이다. 6 나로서는, 성공은 변화를 가져오고 있고 종종 잊혀진 다른 사람들을 돕고 있다. 7 우리는 이 문제에 대한 인식을 가져옴으로써 지역 사회 구성원들에게 동기를 부여할 수 있었다. 8 위탁 양육에 있는 청소년들은 품위 있는 쇼핑을 하고, 새로운 의류와 액세서리를 고르고, 필요한 위생 필수품을 받을 자격이 있다. 9 청소년들은 자신감과 높아진 자존감으로 우리 가게를 떠난다.

정답단추 글의 제목은 글의 핵심 내용을 찾아 압축하면 돼. 이 글은 위탁 양육 청소년들에게 적절한 옷을 제공하는 단체의 활동 내용에 대해서 소개하고 있어. 즉 그 단체는 전형적인 자선 단체와는 달리 새 제품을 그 청소년들에게 제공함으로써 그들의 자신감과 자존감을 높여준다고 해. 따라서 글의 제목으로 가장 적절한 것은 ⑤야.

오답단서 ①, ②, ③, ④는 글에 나오는 어휘인 clothing, success, shop을 선택지에 넣어 그럴듯하게 만든 오답이야.

[설명]
단체의 활동 내용: 매달 약 42명의 청소년에게 새로운 속옷, 양말, 기타 필수품을 제공함

⬇

[결과]
위탁 양육 청소년들의 자신감과 자존감이 높아짐

유형 04 글의 목적 파악

Check-Up 1 1 ② 2 I hope you will someday be able to forgive me for ruining the last half an hour. **021** ④
Check-Up 2 3 ② 4 I cannot thank you enough for your help. 5 I would like to meet with you and Mr. Oliver sometime soon to see if we can resolve this situation. **022** ③
Mini Test 1 ① 2 ② 3 ① 4 ① 5 ②
실전적용독해 **023** ③ **024** ③ **025** ①

Check-Up 1

정답 1 ② 2 I hope you will someday be able to forgive me for ruining the last half an hour.
해석 1 ① 6월 1일부터 시작하여, 저희는 저희 단골 고객들에게 무료로 차량 점검을 제공해 드립니다. ② 이리하여 저희는 귀하의 차를 저희 정비소로 가져오시도록 귀하를 초대합니다. ③ 이 서비스는 6월 30일까지 월요일부터 금요일 오전 8시부터 오후 3시까지 계속될 것입니다.

021 정답 ④

지문 All in One

1 Dear Dorothy, (Dorothy에게)

2 I hope // (that) you're having a good morning. (나는 바라 / 네가 좋은 아침을 보내고 있기를) [I: S, hope: V, (that): 접속사, you: S′, 're having: V′] 3 Personally, / I feel terrible / about ruining your lovely lunch yesterday / by arguing with Celia / about Will Ladislaw. (개인적으로 / 나는 기분이 아주 안 좋아 / 어제 너의 즐거운 점심 식사를 망쳐버린 것에 대해 / Celia와 논쟁함으로써 / Will Ladislaw에 대해) [I: S, feel: V, terrible: C] 4 You certainly did *everything* [(that) you could (do) to save the situation], // and I apologize / for ignoring good taste and old friendships / in pursuing *a "discussion"* [that was completely inappropriate]. (너는 분명히 모든 것을 했어 / 상황을 수습하기 위해 네가 할 수 있는 / 그리고 나는 사과할게 / 좋은 맛과 오래된 우정을 무시한 것에 대해 / '토론'을 계속하느라 / 완전히 부적절한) [You: S_1, did: V_1, (that): 관계대명사, I: S_2, apologize: V_2, that: 관계대명사] 5 I talked to Celia / first thing this morning / and attempted to fix things with her, // but I feel a great deal worse / about what I did to you. (나는 Celia에게 이야기했어 / 오늘 아침에 맨 먼저 / 그리고 그녀와 함께 문제를 해결하려고 했어 / 하지만 나는 많은 잘못을 느꼈어 / 내가 너에게 한 것에 대해서는) [I: S_1, talked: V_1, attempted: V_2, I: S_2, feel: V_3, a great deal worse: C, what: 관계대명사] 6 The lunch was delicious, // and the first two hours were delightful. (점심은 맛있었어 / 그리고 처음 2시간은 즐거웠잖아) [The lunch: S_1, was: V_1, delicious: C_1, the first two hours: S_2, were: V_2, delightful: C_2] 7 I hope // (that) you will someday be able to forgive me / for ruining the last half an hour. (나는 바라 / 네가 언젠가 나를 용서할 수 있기를 / 마지막 30분을 망친 것에 대해) [I: S, hope: V, (that): 접속사, you: S′, will someday be able to forgive: V′]

8 Your friend, (너의 친구 Judy가)
Judy

① 친구들과의 모임 약속을 전달하려고
② 친구와 다툼이 있었던 것을 고백하려고

어휘확인

personally 개인적으로 **ruin** 망치다 **lovely** 즐거운; 사랑스러운 **argue with** ~와 논쟁하다 **certainly** 분명히 **save the situation** 상황을 수습하다 **apologize** 사과하다 **ignore** 무시하다 **pursue** (논쟁 등을) 계속하다 **discussion** 토론 **completely** 완전히 **inappropriate** 부적절한 **first thing** 맨 먼저 **attempt** 시도하다 **fix** (문제를) 해결하다 **a great deal** 많이 **delightful** 즐거운, 유쾌한 **forgive** 용서하다

지문 Flow

[소재]
Dorothy와 함께 한 점심 식사 때 일어난 일

⬇

[세부내용]
• 다른 친구(Celia)와 싸우느라 점심 식사를 망침
• 오늘 아침 Celia와 이야기 했으며 Dorothy에게 미안함을 느낌

⬇

[목적]
점심 식사의 마지막 30분을 망친 것에 대해 용서를 바라고 있음

③ 담장을 망가뜨린 것을 항의하려고　　④ 오찬 모임을 망친 것을 사과하려고
⑤ 모임에 늦게 도착하게 된 사정을 설명하려고

해석 한 눈에 보기 1 Dorothy에게 2 네가 좋은 아침을 보내고 있기를 바라. 3 개인적으로, 나는 어제 Will Ladislaw에 대해 Celia와 논쟁함으로써 너의 즐거운 점심 식사를 망쳐버린 것에 대해 기분이 아주 안 좋아. 4 너는 분명히 상황을 수습하기 위해 네가 할 수 있는 모든 것을 했고, 나는 완전히 부적절한 '토론'을 계속하느라 좋은 맛과 오래된 우정을 무시한 것에 대해 사과할게. 5 오늘 아침에 맨 먼저 Celia에게 이야기했고 그녀와 함께 문제를 해결하려고 했지만, 내가 너에게 한 것에 대해서는 많은 잘못을 느꼈어. 6 점심은 맛있었고, 처음 2시간은 즐거웠잖아. 7 나는 네가 언젠가 마지막 30분을 망친 것에 대해 나를 용서할 수 있기를 바라. 8 너의 친구, Judy가
정답단추　편지글은 앞부분에 인사말이 나와서 헷갈릴 수 있으니 주의해야 돼. 글의 끝부분에 목적이 나오는 경우가 많으므로, 글을 끝까지 읽으면서 글쓴이의 의도를 찾는 것이 중요해. 글쓴이는 자신이 개인적인 일 때문에 어제 Dorothy와의 점심 식사를 망쳐버린 것에 대해 기분이 안 좋다는 말로 시작하고 있어. 사과하려는 의도가 솔솔 풍기지? 이어서 바로 자신의 부적절한 행동에 대해 사과한다는 말이 나오고 자신을 용서해주길 바란다는 내용으로 마무리하고 있어. 따라서 글의 목적으로 가장 적절한 것은 ④야.
오답단서　①과 ⑤는 글쓴이와 Dorothy가 만난 상황을 친구들과의 모임이라는 말로 혼동을 주고 있는 선택지야. ②는 글쓴이가 Celia와 싸울 때 Dorothy가 그 자리에 있었으니까 답이 될 수 없고, ③은 글과 전혀 무관한 선택지야.

Check-Up 2

정답　3 ②　4 I cannot thank you enough for your help.
5 I would like to meet with you and Mr. Oliver sometime soon to see if we can resolve this situation.
해석　[3-5] 제가 레드우드 대학교의 빅 드림 장학금을 받게 되었습니다! 이것은 귀하께서 그 추천서를 써주셨기 때문에 가능했습니다. 귀하의 추천서가 장학금 위원회로 하여금 제게 기회를 주도록 설득했음에 틀림없습니다. 저는 귀하의 도움에 뭐라 감사의 말씀을 드려야 할지 모르겠습니다.

022　정답 ③

지문 All in One

1 Dear Ms. Dallas, (Dallas 씨께)

2 I very much enjoy working / for Stegner Publishing, // and you / in particular / have been most helpful / in introducing me to people / and (in) showing me around. (저는 일하는 것이 아주 즐겁습니다 / Stegner 출판사에서 / 그리고 당신은 / 특히 / 가장 도움이 되었습니다 / 저를 사람들에게 소개하는 데 / 그리고 저를 구경시켜 주는 데) [I: S_1, enjoy: V_1, you: S_2, have been: V_2, most helpful: C]
3 When I was interviewed for the job, // Mr. Oliver consistently used the term "production editor," / and the job duties [(that) he listed] / were those [generally associated with the position of production editor]. (제가 직업 때문에 인터뷰를 했을 때 / Oliver 씨는 지속적으로 '프로덕션 에디터'라는 말을 사용했습니다 / 그리고 그가 열거한 일 업무는 / 일반적으로 프로덕션 에디터의 직위와 관련된 것들이었습니다) [When: 접속사, I: S', was interviewed: V', Mr. Oliver: S, used: V, the job duties: S_2, (that): 관계대명사, were: V_2, those: C]
4 In my three weeks on the job, / however, / I have done nothing but copyediting. (3주 근무 동안 / 그러나 / 저는 원고 정리만 했습니다) [I: S, have done: V]
5 After speaking to you yesterday / and discovering / that this was not just a training stage but my permanent position, // I suspect / (that) there has been a misunderstanding. (어제 당신에게 말을 한 후에 / 그리고 알게 된 후에 / 이것이 단지 교육 단계가 아니라 저의 영구적인 일임을 알게 된 후에 / 저는 의심이 듭니다 / 오해가 있었다고) [that: 접속사, I: S, suspect: V, (that): 접속사, has been: V', a misunderstanding: S']
6 I would like to meet with you and Mr. Oliver / sometime soon / to see if we can resolve this situation. (저는 당신과 Oliver 씨와 만나고 싶습니다 / 언젠가 곧 / 우리가 이 상황을 해결할 수 있는지 보기 위해) [I: S, would like: V, to see: 부사적 용법(목적), if we can resolve this situation: 간접의문문]

7 Sincerely, (Adam Gillum 올림)
Adam Gillum

① 일을 그만둠을 통보하려고　　② 정식 직원 채용 여부에 대해 문의하려고
③ 담당 업무와 관련하여 만남을 제안하려고　　④ 직속상관이 누구인지 명확히 문의하려고
⑤ 출판사 전체 일의 흐름에 대해 문의하려고

어휘확인

publishing 출판사 **in particular** 특히 **helpful** 도움이 되는 **introduce** 소개하다 **show A around** A를 구경시켜 주다 **interview** 인터뷰하다 **consistently** 지속적으로 **term** 용어, 말 **duty** 임무 **list** 열거하다 **generally** 일반적으로 **associate with** ~와 관련이 있다 **position** 직위 **nothing but** 오직, 단지 **copyedit** 원고를 정리하다 **discover** 알다, 깨닫다 **training** 교육, 훈련 **permanent** 영구적인 **suspect** 의심하다 **misunderstanding** 오해 **resolve** 해결하다

지문 Flow

[소재]
Stegner 출판사에서 일하는 사람이 상사에게 보내는 편지글

[세부내용]
• 도움이 되어 준 것에 대한 감사함
• 취업 인터뷰에서 담당자가 말했던 업무와 자신이 3주 동안 해왔던 일이 연관이 없음
• 지금 하는 일이 자신의 고정 업무임을 알게 됨

[목적]
이 상황 해결을 위해 두 사람과 만나고 싶다고 제안함

해석 한 눈에 보기 1 Dallas 씨께 2 저는 Stegner 출판사에서 일하는 것이 아주 즐겁고, 특히 당신은 저를 사람들에게 소개하고 저를 구경시켜 주는 데 가장 도움이 되었습니다. 3 제가 직업 때문에 인터뷰를 했을 때, Oliver 씨는 지속적으로 '프로덕션 에디터'라는 말을 사용했으며, 그가 열거한 일 업무는 일반적으로 프로덕션 에디터의 직위와 관련된 것들이었습니다. 4 그러나, 3주 근무 동안, 저는 원고 정리만 했습니다. 5 어제 당신에게 말을 하고 이것이 단지 교육 단계가 아니라 저의 영구적인 일임을 알게 된 후에 저는 오해가 있었다는 의심이 듭니다. 6 저는 우리가 이 상황을 해결

할 수 있는지 보기 위해 언젠가 곧 당신과 Oliver 씨와 만나고 싶습니다. 7 Adam Gillum 올림

정답단추 글의 목적을 파악하려면 글을 쓴 의도가 가장 잘 드러나는 문장을 찾아야 하는데, 종종 but, however처럼 내용이 바뀌는 연결어 다음에 글쓴이의 의도가 드러나는 경우가 있어. 즉 글의 초반은 입사 초기에 도움이 되어 준 것에 대한 감사의 내용이지만 however 다음에는 자신이 면접 때 생각했던 업무와 지금 담당하는 업무가 다르다고 하면서, 뭔가 오해가 있음을 제기하고 이와 관련한 만남을 요청하고 있어. 따라서 글의 목적으로 가장 적절한 것은 ③이야.

오답단서 사직이나 채용에 대한 내용이 아니므로 ①과 ②는 답이 될 수 없어. ④는 두 사람의 상사 이름이 글에 나오므로 오답으로 고를 수 있지만, 직속상관을 묻는 내용은 나오지 않아. ⑤는 글쓴이가 출판사에 근무하는 것은 맞지만, 자신의 업무에 대해서만 언급하고 있으므로 오답임을 알 수 있어.

기출총정리

Mini Test 1 ① 2 ② 3 ① 4 ① 5 ②

Mini Test 해석 및 해설

1 **해석** 모든 나라의 13세 이상의 작가들은 동인도 출판사 단편 소설 공모전에 참가할 것이 장려되고 있습니다. 당신은 2017년 3월 1일까지 당신의 소설을 제출해야 합니다.

2 **해석** 여기에 암호를 해독해 주고 영향력 있는 경제 일간지에서 보일 수 있는 상당히 많은 예시들을 제공해 주는 초급자용 특강이 있다. ① 확인하려고 ② 광고하려고

3 **해석** 제 은행 명세서를 받았을 때, 저는 귀하가 제 카드에 두 번 청구했다는 것을 발견했습니다. 귀하께서 이 문제를 빨리 해결해 주실 수 있다면 감사하겠습니다.

4 **해석** 나는 학교 신문의 편집자가 되고 싶었지만, 담당 선생님이 다른 학생을 뽑았다. 나는 실망했지만, 계속해서 글을 썼고 그래서 지금 나는 어느 신문의 칼럼니스트이다. 그러니 절대 포기하지 마라! 당신은 훌륭하고 그것이 중요한 모든 것이다! ① 독려하려고 ② 문의하려고

5 **해석** 당신의 기부는 아주 많이 도움이 되어 왔지만, 여전히 기부의 필요성이 큽니다. 다 함께 우리는 삶을 변화시키고 있고 더 밝은 미래를 만들어 가고 있습니다만, 당신이 없다면, 그것은 가능하지 않을 것입니다.

실전적용독해

023 정답 ③

지문 All in One

1 Dear Mrs. Green,

2 We were so sorry / to learn that you have been hospitalized. 3 I have already stopped / your newspaper and mail delivery / for the time being. 4 Since I had a copy of your house key, // I went in to make sure / (that) all the faucets were off / and the windows (were) shut / (except for leaving one upstairs and one downstairs / open an inch / for air). 5 I've been going in / at night / and turning on a few lights // so it doesn't look empty. 6 I wasn't sure / (that) you were up to a phone call, // but I thought / you'd want to know / that the house is being looked after. 7 We are all hoping / and praying for your speedy recovery. 8 In the meantime, / if there is *anything* [(that) you'd like us to do], // please don't hesitate to call.

9 With best wishes,

Randy Lahey

① 병문안 가지 못함을 사과하려고
② 보안을 더 철저히 할 것을 당부하려고
③ 빈집 관리를 하고 있음을 알리려고
④ 집 관리 관련 세부 내용을 문의하려고
⑤ 전화 연락을 해달라고 요청하려고

어휘확인

hospitalize 입원하다 **mail delivery** 우편배달 **for the time being** 당분간, 잠시 동안 **make sure** 확인하다 **faucet** 수도꼭지 **shut** 닫다 **except for** ~을 제외하고 **downstairs** 아래층에 **turn on** (불을) 켜다 **be up to** ~을 감당할 수 있다, ~할 만큼 좋다 **look after** ~을 돌보다 **pray** 기도하다 **speedy** 빠른 **recovery** 회복 **in the meantime** 그동안 **hesitate** 주저하다

지문 Flow

[소재]
병원에 입원한 이웃에게 보내는 편지글

[세부내용]
- 신문과 우편배달을 중단함
- 수도꼭지와 창문을 점검함
- 비어 있는 것처럼 보이지 않게 밤에 몇몇 조명을 켜두었음

[목적]
빈집이 관리되고 있음을 그린 부인에게 알리고 있음

[맺음말]
다른 원하는 것이 있으면 전화하라고 함

해석 한 눈에 보기 1 Green 부인께 2 우리는 당신이 병원에 입원해 있다는 것을 알게 되어 유감입니다. 3 제가 이미 당신의 신문과 우편 배달을 당분간 중단시켰습니다. 4 제가 당신의 집 열쇠 복사본을 가지고 있었기 때문에, 저는 들어가서 모든 수도꼭지가 잠겨 있고 창문이 닫혀 있는지 확인했습니다. (통풍 때문에 위층에 하나와 아래층에 하나를 1인

치 열어 둔 채로 놔둔 것을 제외하고) 5 제가 밤에 들어가서 몇몇 조명을 켜고 있어서 집이 비어 있는 것처럼 보이지 않습니다. 6 당신이 전화 통화를 할 수 있는지 확실하지 않았습니다. 하지만 저는 당신이 집이 돌봐지고 있다는 것을 알고 싶을 거라고 생각했습니다. 7 우리는 모두 당신의 빠른 회복을 바라며 기도하고 있습니다. 8 그동안, 우리가 하기를 바라는 것이 있으면, 주저하지 말고 전화하십시오. 9 행복을 빌며, Randy Lahey올림

정답단추 글을 쓴 의도가 잘 드러난 문장을 찾으면 그게 답이야. 또한 연결어를 주의 깊게 봐야 하는데, 그 뒤에 진짜 목적이 나올 수도 있기 때문이지. 글쓴이는 병원에 입원한 Green 부인의 집에 들어가 부인 대신 집을 관리하고 있어. but I thought ~ 이후의 내용을 보면, Green 부인에게 그 사실을 알리려고 하는 것을 분명히 알 수 있어. 따라서 글의 목적으로 가장 적절한 것은 ③이야.

오답단서 ①은 앞부분의 내용에만 집중하면 답으로 고르기 쉬워. 하지만 글을 쓴 의도는 보통 뒤에 나오므로 끝까지 읽어야 해. ②는 집의 보안을 하는 사람은 글쓴이이므로 입장이 바뀐 선택지라고 볼 수 있어. ④는 집 관리 사항을 반대로 알려주고 있으므로 답이 아니야. ⑤는 마지막 문장 때문에 헷갈리기 쉬운데, 요구사항이 있으면 전화하라고 했으니 오답이야.

024 정답 ③

지문 All in One

1 We received // and read your manuscript / with surprise and delight. 2 It is the first time // (that) we have reviewed such a brilliant book / in the 67-year history / of this publishing house. 3 Every one of our editors was similarly impressed, // and we discussed your manuscript eagerly / for quite some time. 4 After several meetings / we agreed // that if we were to publish your book, / we could never match its standard. 5 *Any books* [that we publish / in the future] / will surely be nothing / in comparison to yours. 6 Therefore, / to our great regret, / we must return this astonishing work / to you // and beg your forgiveness / for our decision.

(저희는 받았고 / 그리고 귀하의 원고를 읽었습니다 / 놀라움과 기쁨으로 / 이것은 처음입니다 / 우리가 그렇게 훌륭한 책을 검토한 것은 / 67년 역사상 / 이 출판사의 / 저희 편집자 모두가 비슷하게 감명을 받았으며 / 저희는 귀하의 원고에 대해 열띠게 논의했습니다 / 한동안 / 여러 차례의 회의 후에 / 저희는 동의했습니다 / 만약 저희가 귀하의 책을 출판하려 한다면 / 저희는 절대 그 수준을 맞추지 못할 것이라는 데 / 저희가 출판하는 그 어떤 책도 / 미래에 / 분명히 아무것도 아닐 것입니다 / 귀하의 것과 비교해 볼 때 / 그러므로 / 정말 유감스럽게도 / 저희는 이 놀라운 작품을 돌려보내야 하며 / 귀하에게 / 그리고 귀하의 용서를 구해야 합니다 / 저희의 결정에 대해)

(S, V_1, V_2, 가주어 V, 접속사, 진주어, S_1, V_1, S_2, V_2, S V, 접속사 접속사, V', S', V', S, 관계대명사, V, C, S, V_1, V_2)

① 출판 일정을 의논하려고
② 원고 투고를 장려하려고
③ 책의 출판을 거절하려고
④ 원고 집필을 의뢰하려고
⑤ 훌륭한 원고를 칭찬하려고

해석 한 눈에 보기 1 저희는 귀하의 원고를 놀랍고 기쁜 마음으로 받아 읽어 보았습니다. 2 이 출판사의 67년 역사상 우리가 그렇게 훌륭한 책을 검토한 것은 처음입니다. 3 저희 편집자 모두가 비슷하게 감명을 받았으며, 저희는 귀하의 원고에 대해 한동안 열띠게 논의했습니다. 4 여러 차례의 회의 후에 저희는 만약 저희가 귀하의 책을 출판하려 한다면 저희는 절대 그 수준을 맞추지 못할 것이라는 데 동의했습니다. 5 저희가 앞으로 출판하는 그 어떤 책도 귀하의 것과 비교해 볼 때 분명히 아무것도 아닐 것입니다. 6 그러므로 정말 유감스럽게도 저희는 이 놀라운 작품을 귀하에게 돌려보내야 하며 저희의 결정에 대해 귀하의 용서를 구해야 합니다.

정답단추 이와 같은 편지글은 실제 목적이 나타나기 전에 의례적인 인사말이 등장해서 헷갈릴 수 있으니 글을 끝까지 읽고 글쓴이의 진짜 의도가 무엇인지 파악해야 해. 출판사에 들어온 원고에 대한 칭찬이 글 대부분을 차지하고 있지만, 이는 출판 거절을 위한 도입 설명이라 할 수 있어. 그리고 Therefore 이하의 마지막 문장에서 글의 실제 목적이 드러나고 있지. 너무나 훌륭한 원고임에도 작품을 돌려보내야 하며 용서를 구해야 한다는 내용으로 보아 이 글의 목적은 책의 출판을 거절하려는 것임을 알 수 있어. 따라서 정답은 ③이야.

오답단서 출판 일정과 원고 집필에 대한 내용은 언급되지 않았으므로 ①과 ④는 정답이 아니야. 또한, 이미 투고한 원고에 대한 편지니까 ②도 아니지. 마지막으로 도입부의 의례적인 인사말만 보고 ⑤를 선택할 수 있지만, 글의 실제 목적은 책의 출판을 거절하는 것이므로 답이 될 수 없어.

어휘확인

manuscript (책 등의) 원고 **delight** 기쁨 **brilliant** 훌륭한 **publishing house** 출판사 **similarly** 비슷하게 **impressed** 감명을 받은 **discuss** 논의하다 **eagerly** 열심히 **for some time** 한동안, 한참 **several** (몇)몇의 **publish** 출판하다 **match** (필요에) 맞추다 **standard** 수준[기준] **in comparison to** ~와 비교해 볼 때 **to one's regret** 유감스럽게도 **return** 돌려보내다 **astonishing** 정말 놀라운 **work** 작품; 일 **beg** 간청[애원]하다 **forgiveness** 용서 **decision** 결정

지문 Flow

[도입]
원고를 검토함

[세부내용]
편집자들이 원고에 대해 논의하였으나, 원고 수준을 출판사가 맞추지 못할 것임에 동의함

[목적]
원고를 출판하지 않기로 결정하고 원고를 돌려보내는 것에 대해 용서를 구함

025 정답 ①

지문 All in One

1 The Internet may be a writer's best resource, // but at my old age of 90, / computers are far too much trouble. 2 My stiff fingers cannot work / the mouse or the keyboard. 3 But I could

(인터넷은 작가의 가장 좋은 자원일지도 모릅니다 / 하지만 90세라는 나의 늙은 나이에 / 컴퓨터는 너무 큰 어려움입니다 / 내 굳은 손가락들은 사용할 수 없습니다 / 마우스 혹은 키보드를 / 그러나 나는 이)

(S_1, V_1, C_1, S_2, V_2, C_2, S, V, S, V)

어휘확인

resource 자원; 자료 **stiff** 굳은, 뻣뻣한 **work** (기계·장치 등을) 사용하다; 작품 **nor** (~이 아닌 것은) …도 그렇다 **sincere** 진심 어린 **gratitude** 감사 **expert** 전문가 **inspire** 고무하다 **in the first place** 애초에,

책을 쓸 수 없었을 것입니다 / 인터넷의 자료 없이는 / 몇몇 멋진 사람들의 도움 없이도 그랬을 것입니다

not have written this book / without the Internet's resources, // [nor] (접속사) without the help of some fantastic people. [4] My sincere gratitude (S) goes (V) / to Tanika Hasley, / the Internet expert, / and [to] *Deanne Warrick*, // [who (관계대명사(계속적 용법)) inspired me to write the book / in the first place]. [5] Also [to] my publisher, / Patricia Law, / for her encouragement and support. [6] And of course it (가주어) would be (V) a mistake (C) / not to mention my wonderful and supportive family (진주어). [7] I (S) couldn't have done (V) it / without you all.

나의 진심 어린 감사를 보냅니다 / Tanika Hasley에게 / 인터넷 전문가인 / 그리고 Deanne Warrick에게 / 나에게 그 책을 쓰도록 고무해 준 / 애초에 / 또한 제 출판업자에게도 / Patricia Law / 그녀의 격려와 지지에 대해 / 그리고 당연히 실수가 될 것입니다 / 나의 멋지고 힘을 주는 가족을 언급하지 않는 것은 / 나는 그것을 해낼 수 없었을 것입니다 / 여러분 모두가 없었다면

① to give thanks for help
도움에 감사를 표하려고

② to offer a job in publishing
출판계 일자리를 제안하려고

③ to praise the work of a poet
시인의 작품을 칭찬하려고

④ to request computer repairs
컴퓨터 수리를 요청하려고

⑤ to complain about a deadline
마감 일자에 대해 불평하려고

해석 한 눈에 보기 1 인터넷은 작가의 가장 좋은 자료일지도 모르지만, 90세라는 내 늙은 나이에, 컴퓨터는 너무나도 큰 어려움입니다. 2 내 굳은 손가락들은 마우스나 키보드를 사용하지 못합니다. 3 그러나 나는 인터넷 자료가 없었다면 이 책을 쓰지 못했을 것이며, 몇몇 멋진 사람들의 도움이 없었어도 못했을 것입니다. 4 내 진심 어린 감사를 인터넷 전문가인 Tanika Hasley에게 그리고 애초에 나에게 이 책을 쓰도록 고무해 준 Deanne Warrick에게 보냅니다. 5 또한, 제 출판업자 Patricia Law에게도 그녀의 격려와 지지에 대해 감사드립니다. 6 그리고 멋지고 힘을 주는 제 가족을 언급하지 않는 것은 당연히 실수가 될 것입니다. 7 나는 여러분 모두가 없었다면 이것을 해낼 수 없었을 것입니다.

정답단추 글의 목적을 파악하기 위해서는 글을 쓴 의도가 가장 잘 드러나는 문장을 찾아야 해. 그리고 종종 but, however 등의 내용을 전환하는 연결어 다음에 본론을 꺼낼 때가 있어서 글을 끝까지 읽어야 해. 이 글의 앞부분에서는 인터넷과 컴퓨터를 사용할 줄 몰라서 어려움을 겪었다고 하고 있어. 그러나 But I could not ~ people.부터 내용이 전환되면서 이러한 어려움을 극복하고 책을 쓸 수 있도록 도와준 사람들에게 감사를 표현하고 있지. 따라서 이 글의 목적은 감사를 표현하는 거니까 정답은 ①이야.

오답단서 ②의 publishing과 ③의 praise, work는 글에 언급된 표현을 활용한 오답으로 글의 전체적인 내용과는 거리가 멀어. ④와 ⑤의 내용은 글에서 언급되지 않았어.

먼저 **publisher** 출판업자; 출판사 **encouragement** 격려 **support** 지지, 지원 cf. **supportive** 힘을 주는
〈선택지 어휘〉
thanks 감사 **offer** 제안하다 **publishing** 출판 (사업) **request** 요청하다 **repair** 수리; 수리하다 **deadline** 마감 일자

지문 Flow

[문제점]
90세 작가로서 컴퓨터 사용이 어려움

[보충설명]
인터넷 자료와 다른 사람들의 도움이 없었다면 책을 쓰지 못했을 것임

[목적]
인터넷 전문가, 책을 쓰도록 해준 사람, 출판업자, 가족에게 감사를 전함

미니 모의고사 1

유형 01 | 유형 02 | 유형 03 | 유형 04

026 ④ 027 ② 028 ⑤ 029 ④ 030 ③ 031 ② 032 ④ 033 ① 034 ④
035 ④ 036 ① 037 ② 038 ① 039 ③ 040 ⑤ 041 ③ 042 ③ 043 ③

026 정답 ④

지문 All in One

[1] One of the earliest kinds of movie (S) / was (V) the "magic lantern" show (C). [2] A magic lantern show (S) / projected (V) painted images / from glass slides onto a screen. [3] The shows (S) were (V) popular (C) / in the 19th century. [4] Lantern men (S) traveled (V_1) widely // [and] attracted (V_2) big crowds / to their shows. [5] The glass slides (S_1) were (V_1) expensive (C), // [so] they (S_2) were replaced (V_2) / by film / when (접속사) photography (S'_1) was invented (V'_1). [6] But the pictures (S) still did not move (V). [7] Real movies (S) were finally made (V_1) // [and] (were) shown (V_2) / in France / in 1895 / by the Lumiere brothers. [8] They (S) invented (V) / *a machine* [which (관계대명사)

가장 초기의 영화 종류 중 하나는 / '환등기' 영화였다 / 환등기 영화는 / 색칠이 된 그림을 영사했다 / 유리 슬라이드에서 스크린으로 / 그 영화는 인기 있었다 / 19세기에 / 환등기 상영자는 널리 다녔다 / 그리고 많은 사람들을 끌어들였다 / 그들의 영화로 / 유리 슬라이드는 비쌌다 / 그래서 그들은 교체되었다 / 필름으로 / 사진 촬영술이 발명되었을 때 / 그러나 그 그림들은 여전히 움직이지 않았다 / 진짜 영화는 마침내 만들어졌다 / 그리고 상영되었다 / 프랑스에서 / 1895년에 / Lumiere 형제에 의해 / 그들은 발명했다

어휘확인
kind 종류; 친절한 **magic lantern** 환등기 **project** 영사하다 **image** 그림; 이미지 **slide** (환등기의) 슬라이드 **screen** 스크린, 화면 **century** 세기(世紀) **travel** 다니다 **widely** 널리 **attract** 끌어들이다 **crowd** 사람들, 군중 **replace** 대체하다 **photography** 사진 촬영술 **invent** 발명하다 **appear** ~인 것 같다
〈선택지 어휘〉
popularity 인기 **developmental** 발달의

많은 필름 이미지를 영사할 수 있는 기계를 / 매우 빠르게 / 그림이 움직이는 것 같도록 하기 위해

could project many filmed images / very quickly / to make a picture appear to move].

부사적 용법(목적) / make+목적어+동사원형(~가 …하게 하다)

① the popularity of movies 영화의 인기
② the inventor of movies 영화의 발명가
③ the difficulties of making movies 영화 제작의 어려움
④ the developmental process of movies 영화의 발달 과정
⑤ the relationship between photography and movies 사진과 영화의 관계

해석 한 눈에 보기 1 가장 초기의 영화 종류 중 하나는 '환등기(환등 장치를 이용하여 그림, 필름 등을 확대하여 스크린에 비추는 기계)' 영화였다. 2 환등기 영화는 색이 칠해진 그림을 유리 슬라이드에서 스크린 위로 영사시켰다. 3 이 영화는 19세기에 인기가 있었다. 4 환등기 상영자들은 널리 돌아다녔고 많은 사람들을 그들의 영화로 끌어들였다. 5 유리 슬라이드는 비싸서 사진 촬영술이 발명되자 그것들은 필름으로 대체되었다. 6 그러나 영상은 여전히 움직이지 않았다. 7 진짜 영화는 1895년에 Lumiere 형제에 의해 프랑스에서 마침내 만들어졌고 상영되었다. 8 그들은 그림이 움직이는 것 같게 하려고 많은 필름 이미지들을 매우 빠르게 영사할 수 있는 기계를 발명했다.

정답단추 주제문이 명백하지 않은 글이니까 전체 내용을 보고 정리해보자. 이 글은 '가장 초기의 영화 형태인 환등기 영화'에 관한 설명과 '그 후 필름이 사용되고 Lumiere 형제에 의해 진짜 움직이는 영화가 상영되었다'는 내용으로서 영화의 발달 과정을 시간순으로 설명하고 있어. 그러므로 이를 종합하면 ④가 주제임을 알 수 있어.

오답단서 ①, ②는 이 글의 세부 내용이니까 글 전체의 주제로는 적절하지 않아. ⑤는 글에 '사진 촬영술(photography)'이라는 단어가 나오긴 하지만 '사진과 영화의 관계'에 대해서는 언급하지 않았으니까 답이 될 수 없어.

지문 Flow

[도입]
가장 초기의 영화 중 하나였던 환등기 영화는 19세기에 인기를 끎

[과정1]
사진 촬영술의 발명 이후에 필름이 사용되었으나 영상은 움직이지 않음

[과정2]
프랑스의 Lumiere 형제는 필름 이미지를 빠르게 영사할 수 있는 기계를 발명하여 그림이 움직이는 듯한 진짜 영화를 상영함

[주제 도출]
영화의 발달 과정

027 정답 ②

지문 All in One

1 "One of the cleanest spots / in a public restroom / is usually the toilet seat. 2 A lot of people will wipe it / before using it, // and cleaners tend to clean it well," / says an expert. 3 "So / (there are) no worries // if you make contact. 4 The real threat lies beneath," // he says. 5 "The most dangerous spot / in restrooms / is always the floor." 6 According to research, / when the toilet flushes, // it sends *a spray of droplets* / into the air, / [which then settle onto any surfaces / within six feet of the flush]. 7 Those droplets can be carrying bacteria / from any number of diseases. 8 All that can be avoided / by closing the lid. 9 The only problem: / we forget to do it. 10 That means // the handle, the toilet paper dispenser, and even the little purse shelf / are hotspots / for bacteria to settle.

(가장 깨끗한 곳 중 하나는 / 공중 화장실에서 / 대개 변기입니다 / 많은 사람들이 닦을 것이다 / 그것을 사용하기 전에 / 그리고 청소부는 그것을 잘 청소하는 경향이 있습니다 / 어떤 전문가는 말한다 / 그러므로 / 걱정하지 마십시오 / 당신이 접촉하더라도 / 진정한 위협은 바로 아래에 있습니다 / 그가 말한다 / 가장 위험한 곳은 / 화장실에서 / 항상 바닥입니다 / 연구에 따르면 / 변기의 물이 내려질 때 / 작은 물방울이 뿌려지는데 / 공중으로 / 그 물방울은 그 다음에 어떤 표면에도 내려앉는다 / 변기물의 6피트 이내의 / 그러한 작은 물방울은 박테리아를 운반할 수 있다 / 많은 질병에서 오는 / 모두 피할 수 있다 / 뚜껑을 닫음으로써 / 유일한 문제 / 우리가 그렇게 하는 것을 잊는다 / 그것은 뜻한다 / 손잡이, 화장지 기계 및 작은 지갑 선반조차 / 핫스팟이다 / 박테리아가 내려앉을)

관계대명사(계속적 용법)

① How to best clean your bathroom 욕실을 가장 깨끗이 청소하는 방법
② What to remember in a restroom and why 화장실에서 기억해야 할 것과 그 이유
③ Disease-carrying bacteria living on toilet seats 변기에 사는 병을 옮기는 박테리아
④ Ways to prevent overuse of toilet paper 화장지의 남용을 막는 방법
⑤ Making toilets as comfortable as possible 변기를 가능한 한 편안하게 만들기

해석 한 눈에 보기 1 "공중 화장실에서 가장 깨끗한 곳 중 하나는 대개 변기입니다. 2 많은 사람들이 그것을 사용하기 전에 닦을 것이고, 청소부는 그것을 잘 청소하는 경향이 있습니다."라고 어떤 전문가는 말한다. 3 "그러므로 당신이 접촉하더라도 걱정하지 마십시오. 4 진정한 위협은 바로 아래에 있습니다."라고 그가 말한다. 5 "화장실에서 가장 위험한 곳은 항상 바닥입니다." 6 연구에 따르면, 변기의 물이 내려질 때, 작은 물방울이 공중으로 뿌려지는데, 그 물방울은 그 다음에 변기물의 6피트 이내의 어떤 표면에도 내려앉는다. 7 그러한 작은 물방울은 많은 질병에서 오는 박테리아를 운반할 수 있다. 주제문 8 그것 모두는 뚜껑을 닫음으로써 피할 수 있다. 9 유일한 문제는 우리가 그렇게 하는 것을 잊는다는 것이다. 10 그것은 손잡이, 화장지 기계 및 작은 지갑 선반조차 박테리아가 내려앉을 핫스팟이라는 뜻이다.

정답단추 주제는 글의 핵심 내용을 압축적으로 담고 있어야 하므로, 글에서 어떤 내용을 핵심적으로 다루고 있는지

어휘확인

spot 지점, 장소 **restroom** 화장실 **toilet seat** 변기 **wipe** 닦다 **tend to-v** ~하는 경향이 있다 **expert** 전문가 **make contact** 접촉하다 **threat** 위협 **beneath** (바로) 아래에 **according to** ~에 따르면 **research** 연구 **flush** (변기의) 물을 내리다; 변기 물내림 **spray** 물보라, 분무 **droplet** 작은 물방울 **settle** 내려앉다 **surface** 표면 **bacteria** 박테리아 **any number of** 많은, 얼마든지 **disease** 질병 **avoid** 피하다 **lid** 뚜껑 **handle** 손잡이 **dispenser** (손잡이, 단추 등을 눌러 안에 든 것을 바로 뽑아 쓸 수 있는) 기계[용기] **purse** 지갑 **shelf** 선반

<선택지 어휘>

prevent 막다 **overuse** 남용 **comfortable** 편안한 **as ~ as possible** 가능한 한 ~하게

지문 Flow

[도입]
화장실에서 가장 깨끗한 곳은 변기임

[대조]
화장실에서 가장 더러운 곳은 바닥임

[이유]
변기 물을 내릴 때 박테리아를 운반하는 작은 물방울이 6피트 거리까지 뿌려짐

[주장]
변기 뚜껑을 닫고 물을 내려야 함

를 파악해보자. 글에서는 화장실에서 가장 위험한 곳이 바닥이라고 말하고 있어. 그 이유가 변기 물을 내릴 때 물방울이 튀어서 바닥에 닿기 때문이라는 거야. 그래서 물을 내릴 때 잊지 말고 뚜껑을 닫고 내리라는 거지. 즉, 화장실에서 기억해야 하는 것과 그 이유에 대한 내용으로 구성되어 있음을 알 수 있어. 따라서 글의 주제로 가장 적절한 것은 ②야.
오답단서 ①의 욕실 청소 방법에 대해서는 글에 나오지 않으므로 오답이야. ③과 ④는 글에 나오는 내용을 선택지로 만들어서 답으로 고를 가능성이 있지만, 세부적인 내용이므로 답이 될 수 없어. ⑤의 편안한 변기에 대한 내용은 글에 전혀 나오지 않아.

028 정답 ⑤

지문 All in One

동네 학교 운동장에서 / 그곳에서는 당신이 편을 선택하는데 / 가능하다 / 단순히 경기하는 것이
1 On *the village school ground,* / [where you pick sides], // it is possible / to play simply / for
관계부사 / 가주어 V / C / 진주어

재미난 운동으로 / 하지만 / 위신이라는 문제가 생기자마자 / 전투적인 본능이 생겨난다
fun exercise. 2 But / as soon as the question of prestige arises, // the combative instincts are
S' / V' / S / V

경기해본 사람은 / 교내 축구 경기에서라도 / 이것을 안다
aroused. 3 *Anyone* [who has played / even in a school football match] / knows this. 4 At the
관계대명사 / S / V / 앞 문장 전체

국제적인 수준에서 / 스포츠는 솔직히 전쟁과 비슷하다 / 각 나라의 관중들은
international level, / sport frankly resembles warfare. 5 The spectators from each nation /
S / V / S

심각하게 믿는다 / 이러한 달리기, 뛰어오르기, 공차기 경쟁들이 / 국가적인 힘(국력)
seriously believe // that these contests of running, jumping, and kicking a ball / are tests of
V / 접속사 / S' / V' / C'

테스트라고 / 오늘날 행해지는 거의 모든 스포츠는 / 경쟁적이다 / 당신은 이기기 위해 경기를 한다
national power. 6 Nearly all sports practiced nowadays / are competitive. 7 You play to win, //
S / V / C / S_1 V_1 부사적 용법(목적)

그리고 경기는 의미가 거의 없다 / 당신이 최선을 다하지 않는 한 / 이기기 위해서
and the game has little meaning / unless you do your best / to win.
S_2 V_2 / 접속사 S' V' / 부사적 용법(목적)

① 스포츠의 재미는 경쟁을 한다는 데 있다.
② 스포츠는 경쟁보다 체력 증진이 목적이어야 한다.
③ 국제 경기를 전쟁으로 착각하면 안 된다.
④ 스포츠는 보는 것보다 참가하는 데 의의가 있다.
⑤ 요즘의 스포츠는 대부분 이기는 것을 목표로 한다.

해석 한 눈에 보기 1 동네의 학교 운동장에서는 당신이 편을 선택하는데, 단순히 재미난 운동 삼아 경기하는 것이 가능하다. 2 하지만 위신이라는 문제가 생겨나면 그 즉시, 전투 본능이 생겨난다. 3 교내 축구 경기에서라도 경기를 해본 사람이라면 누구나 이것을 안다. 4 국제적 수준에서, 스포츠는 솔직히 전쟁과 흡사하다. 5 각 나라의 관중들은 이러한 달리기, 뛰어오르기, 공차기 경쟁들이 국력 테스트라고 진지하게 믿는다. 주제문 6 오늘날 행해지는 거의 모든 스포츠는 경쟁적이다. 7 당신은 이기기 위해서 경기를 하기에, (경기에) 이기기 위해 최선을 다하지 않는 한 의미가 거의 없다.
정답단추 글의 요지는 글쓴이의 주장이니까 주장이 담긴 주제문을 찾고, 나머지 문장이 뒷받침하고 있는지 파악하면 돼. 소규모의 경기에서는 재미 삼아 경기하는 게 가능하지만, 위신 문제가 개입되면 전투 본능이 일어나고 특히 국제적인 규모의 경기에서는 경기가 마치 전쟁과 비슷하다고 하고 있지? 따라서 '오늘날 행해지는 거의 모든 스포츠는 경쟁적이다'라는 문장이 이 글의 주제문이야. 그러므로 글의 요지는 ⑤라고 볼 수 있어.
오답단서 ①, ②, ③, ④는 모두 지문에 나온 표현을 사용해서 그럴듯하게 만든 선택지이므로 답이 될 수 없어.

어휘확인

side 편[쪽] **simply** 단순히 **as soon as** ~하자마자 **prestige** 위신 **arise** (문제 등이) 생기다 **combative** 전투적인 **instinct** 본능 **arouse** (느낌·태도를) 불러일으키다 **frankly** 솔직히 **resemble** 비슷하다 **warfare** 전쟁 **spectator** 관중 **nation** 나라, 국가 **seriously** 진지하게 **nearly** 거의 **nowadays** 오늘날에는 **competitive** 경쟁적인 **unless** ~하지 않는 한 **do one's best** 최선을 다하다

지문 Flow

[도입]
운동 삼아 경기하는 것과 달리, 위신이 걸려 있는 경기에서는 전투 본능이 생겨남

⬇

[보충설명1]
국제적 수준의 스포츠는 전쟁과 흡사함

&

[보충설명2]
각 나라의 사람들은 스포츠를 국력 테스트라고 생각함

⬇

[주제 도출]
오늘날의 모든 스포츠는 경쟁적이므로, 이기지 않는 한 의미가 없음

029 정답 ④

지문 All in One

5월 19일에 / 나는 1,200달러짜리 텔레비전 한 대를 샀다 / 당신의 가게에서 / 가게를 돌아다닌 후에 / 며칠 동안
1 On May 19, / I bought a $1,200 TV / in your store // after shopping around / for several days.
S V / 접속사

당신의 판매원이 내게 말했다 / 내가 그것을 배달받을 수 있을 거라고 / 기차로 / 나의 집까지 / 단지 12
2 Your salesman told me // (that) I could have it delivered / by train / to my home, / for just
S / V / IO / 접속사

달러에 / 이것은 합리적인 제안인 것 같았다 / 그래서 나는 동의했다 / 그리고 요금을 지불했다 / 이틀 후에
$12. 3 This seemed like a reasonable offer, // so I agreed, / and paid the fee. 4 Two days later,
S_1 V_1 / S_2 V_2 / V_3

나는 전화를 받았다 / 기차역으로부터 / 80킬로미터 떨어진 / 내게 말하는 / 배달물이 도착했다고
/ I got *a call* / from the railway station, / 80 kilometers away, / [to tell me / (that) a delivery had
S V / 접속사

나를 위한 / 그런데 그들은 말했다 / 내가 24달러를 빚졌다고 / 수송을 위해 / 게다가 / 그들은 말했다
arrived / for me]. 5 But they said // that I owed $24 / for shipping. 6 Furthermore, / they said //
S V / 접속사 S' V' / S V

트럭이 내 텔레비전을 수송할 수 있다고 / 역에서 나의 집으로 / 추가 12달러에 / 당신은
(that) a truck could ship my TV / from the station to my home / for an additional $12. 7 You
접속사 S' V' / S

상상할 수 있다 / 내가 어떻게 느꼈을지 / 나는 기다리고 있을 것이다 / 당신의 답변을
can imagine // how I felt! 8 I will be waiting / for your reply.
V / 간접의문문 / S V

어휘확인

shop around (상품의 가격·품질 등을 비교하며) 가게를 돌아다니다 **several** (몇)몇의 **salesman** 판매원 **seem like** ~인 것 같다 **reasonable** 합리적인 **offer** 제안; 제안하다 **fee** 요금 **railway station** 기차역 **kilometer** 킬로미터(= km) **delivery** 배달물; 배달 **shipping** 수송 cf. **ship** 수송하다; 배 **furthermore** 더욱이 **additional** 추가의 **imagine** 상상하다 **reply** 답변; 대답하다

지문 Flow

[도입]
한 상점에서 텔레비전을 구입함

⬇

① 늑장 배달에 대해 항의하려고
② 직원의 친절에 대해 감사하려고
③ 물품 대금 지급 연기를 신청하려고
④ 배달 비용 추가에 대해 항의하려고
⑤ 물품 손상에 대한 배상을 청구하려고

해석 한 눈에 보기 1 5월 19일에, 저는 며칠 동안 가게를 돌아다닌 후에 귀하의 상점에서 1,200달러짜리 텔레비전 한 대를 샀습니다. 2 귀하의 판매원이 저에게 12달러만 내면 그것을 기차로 저의 집까지 배달받을 수 있을 것이라고 말했습니다. 3 이것은 합리적인 제안 같아서, 저는 동의했고, 요금을 지불했습니다. 4 이틀 후에, 저는 80킬로미터 떨어진 기차역으로부터 제게 배달물이 도착했다는 전화를 받았습니다. 5 그런데 그들은 제가 수송을 위해 24달러를 내야 한다고 말했습니다. 6 더욱이, 그들은 12달러를 추가로 내면 트럭이 제 텔레비전을 역에서부터 저의 집까지 배송해 줄 수 있을 것이라고 말했습니다. 7 귀하는 제가 어떤 기분이었을지 상상하실 수 있을 겁니다! 8 귀하의 답변을 기다리고 있겠습니다.

정답단추 글을 쓴 의도를 가장 잘 드러낸 문장을 찾아보자. 그리고 종종 연결어를 사용하여 글의 진짜 목적을 나타낼 때가 있으니까 끝까지 읽어봐야 해. 이 편지의 앞부분에서 TV를 사고 배송료 12달러를 지급했다고 했어. 그러나 But they said ~ for shipping.의 문장부터 추가 요금이 발생했다고 하고 있지? 그리고 마지막 문장을 통해 이 상황에 대한 답변을 요구하고 있음을 알 수 있어. 따라서 이 편지의 목적은 배달 추가 비용에 대해서 항의하고자 하는 것이므로 ④가 적절한 답이야.

오답단서 ①은 이 글의 소재인 배송을 포함한 내용이지만, 배송이 늦어졌다는 내용은 글에서 언급되지 않아서 정답이 될 수 없어. ②는 This seemed ~ the fee.까지만 보면 목적으로 생각할 수 있는 오답이야. 하지만 뒤이은 내용을 보면 추가 요금이 계속 발생하는 상황에 대해 불만을 이야기하고 있으니까 직원의 친절에 감사하기 위한 것이 아님을 알 수 있지. 그리고 물품 대금 지급과 손상을 포함한 ③과 ⑤는 이 글의 내용과는 무관해.

[전개]
집까지 배달을 약속 받고 요금을 지불함

[반전]
80킬로 떨어진 기차역에 배달물이 도착했고, 집까지 배송하려면 추가 수송비를 내야 한다고 알려줌

[목적]
그때 자신의 기분이 어땠을지 상상해보라고 함 — 화가 나서 항의하고 있음을 유추할 수 있음

030 정답 ③

지문 All in One

1 Many people believe // that they are unaffected / by advertising. 2 They may say // that they have complete freedom of choice / when (they are) shopping. 3 They may also say // that they use only their common sense and intelligence / when they choose / what to buy. 4 But advertising is a very powerful force / in modern society. 5 Companies spend billions / on advertising // as they compete fiercely / for our money. 6 Can you really believe // (that) they are throwing all that money away? 7 Advertisements are everywhere. 8 You can't escape them // no matter how hard you try. 9 *People* [who think // that ads have no influence / on their decisions / when (they are) shopping] / are just fooling themselves. 10 Just look at the brands / in your kitchen and bathroom.

(많은 사람이 믿는다 / 그들은 영향을 받지 않는다고 / 광고에 / 그들은 말할지도 모른다 / 그들이 완전한 선택의 자유를 가지고 있다고 / 쇼핑할 때 / 그들은 또한 말할지도 모른다 / 그들이 오직 그들의 상식과 지식만을 사용한다고 / 그들이 선택할 때 / 무엇을 살지 / 하지만 광고는 매우 강력한 힘이다 / 현대 사회에서 / 기업들은 수십억을 쓴다 / 광고에 / 그들이 치열하게 경쟁하기 때문에 / 우리의 돈을 위해 / 당신은 정말로 생각하는가 / 그들이 그 모든 돈을 버리고 있다고 / 광고는 어디에나 있다 / 당신은 그것에서 벗어날 수 없다 / 당신이 아무리 열심히 노력하더라도 / 생각하는 사람들은 / 광고가 아무런 영향을 미치지 않는다고 / 그들의 결정에 / 쇼핑할 때 / 스스로를 속이고 있다 / 상표를 보아라 / 당신의 주방과 욕실에 있는)

(S V 접속사 S′ V′ / S V 접속사 S′ V′ 접속사 S″ V″ / S V 접속사 S′ V′ 접속사 S″ V″ / S V C / S V 접속사 S′ V′ / S V 접속사 S′ V′ / S V / S V 양보 부사절(= however) S′ V′ / S 관계대명사 접속사 접속사 V / V)

① Overspending on Advertising
광고에의 과다 지출
② The Foolish Behaviors of Shoppers
구매자들의 어리석은 행동들
③ The Powerful Effects of Advertising
광고의 강력한 영향들
④ Freedom in Choosing Goods to Buy
구매할 물건을 고르는 자유
⑤ Escaping the Influence of Advertising
광고의 영향력에서 벗어나기

해석 한 눈에 보기 1 많은 사람이 자신은 광고에 영향을 받지 않는다고 믿는다. 2 그들은 자신들이 쇼핑할 때 완전한 선택의 자유를 갖고 있다고 말할지도 모른다. 3 그들은 또한 그들이 무엇을 사야 하는지 선택할 때 오직 자신들의 상식과 지식만을 사용한다고 말할지도 모른다. 주제문 4 하지만 광고는 현대 사회에서 매우 강력한 힘이다. 5 기업들은 우리의 돈을 두고 치열하게 경쟁하기 때문에 광고에 수십억을 쓴다. 6 당신은 정말로 그들이 그 모든 돈을 허비하고 있다고 생각하는가? 7 광고는 어디에나 있다. 8 당신은 당신이 아무리 열심히 노력하더라도 그것에게서 벗어날 수 없다. 9 쇼핑할 때 광고가 자신들의 결정에 아무런 영향을 미치지 않는다고 생각하는 사람들은 단지 자신을 속이고 있을 뿐이다. 10 한번 당신의 주방과 욕실에 있는 상표들을 보아라.

정답단추 글의 제목은 글의 핵심 내용을 찾아 압축하면 돼. 처음 세 문장의 '상품 구매 시 광고의 영향을 받지 않는다고 믿는 사람들이 많다'는 내용에 이어서 But으로 시작하는 네 번째 문장부터는 이에 대해 '광고는 어디에나 있고 심지어 광고의 영향을 안 받는다고 생각하는 사람도 집안을 둘러보면 광고 브랜드를 발견한다'는 내용으로 앞의 내용을 반박하며 글쓴이의 견해를 나타내고 있어. 따라서 이 글의 주제문이자 핵심 내용은 '광고는 현대 사회에서 매우 강력한 힘이다'라는 내용이며, 이를 가장 잘 반영한 제목은 ③이야.

오답단서 ①, ④, ⑤는 글에서 언급한 표현을 이용해 그럴듯하게 만든 선택지이고, ②는 이 글의 내용과 거리가 멀어.

어휘확인

unaffected 영향을 받지 않은 advertising 광고(= advertisement, ad); 광고업 complete 완전한 freedom 자유 common sense 상식 intelligence 지식 force 힘 modern 현대의 billion 10억 compete for ~을 위해 경쟁하다 fiercely 치열하게 throw away 버리다 escape 벗어나다 no matter how 어떻게 하든 have no influence on ~에 영향을 전혀 끼치지 못하다 decision 결정 fool 속이다 brand 상표

〈선택지 어휘〉

overspend (돈을) 너무 많이 지출하다 foolish 어리석은 behavior 행동 goods 물건, 상품 influence 영향력

지문 Flow

[통념]
많은 사람들은 자신이 광고에 영향을 받지 않으며, 쇼핑에 있어서 자신의 지식만을 사용한다고 생각함

[반박 + 주제]
현대사회에서 광고는 강력한 힘을 발휘함

[구체적 사실]
기업이 광고에 많은 돈을 쓰고 있으며, 우리는 주변의 광고에 쉽게 노출됨

[주장]
광고가 자신의 결정에 영향을 미치지 않는다고 생각하는 사람들은 자신을 속이는 것임

031 정답 ②

지문 All in One

당신이 50명을 위한 점심식사를 계획하든 / 혹은 500명을 위한 결혼식을 / Amberly Manor는 이상적인 장소
[1] Whether you are planning a lunch for 50 / or a wedding for 500, // Amberly Manor is the
접속사 S' V' / S V
입니다 / 당신에게 / Manor는 아주 유명합니다 / 5성급 서비스, 훌륭한 음식, 그리고
ideal place / for you. [2] The Manor is famed / for its five-star service, excellent food, and
C / S V
독특하고도 웅장한 디자인으로 / 저희 연회장은 단연 최고인데 / 시에서 / 쉽게 나뉘기 때문입니다
unique and magnificent design. [3] Our ballroom is the best / in the city, // as it is easily
S V C / 접속사 S'
분리된 공간들로 / 보다 더 작은 기능을 위해 / Manor의 고도로 숙련된 요리사,
divided / into separate rooms / for smaller functions. [4] The Manor's highly-trained chefs,
V' / S
웨이터와 매니저들은 보장합니다 / 당신의 당신의 모든 요구가 / 제공되도록 / 그 어떤 세세한 사항도
waiters, and managers ensure // that your every need / is provided for. [5] No detail will be
V / 접속사 S' V' / S_1
간과되지 않을 것이며 / 저희는 특별 요청도 환영합니다 / 그 어떤 종류의 / 저희는 당신과 함께 일하겠습니다
overlooked, // and we welcome special requests / of any nature. [6] We will work together
V_1 / S_2 V_2 / S V
당신의 완벽한 행사를 만들고 / 반드시 하도록 / 당신이 Amberly Manor를 나서는
with you / to create your perfect event // and (to) make sure / (that) you leave Amberly
부사적 용법(목적) / 부사적 용법(목적) / 접속사
좋은 기억을 가지고 / 평생 지속될
Manor / with *great memories* [to last a lifetime].

① Why Use a Dining Service?
왜 식사 서비스를 이용할까?

② Host Your Event at Our Place
당신의 행사를 저희 장소에서 주최하세요

③ An Invitation to Our Wedding Party
저희 결혼식 파티로의 초대

④ How to Make Valuable Memories
소중한 추억을 만드는 방법

⑤ How to Plan a Party Successfully
성공적으로 파티를 계획하는 방법

해석 한 눈에 보기 1 당신이 50명을 위한 점심식사를 계획하든 500명을 위한 결혼식을 계획하든, Amberly Manor는 당신에게 이상적인 장소입니다. 2 Amberly Manor는 5성급 서비스와 훌륭한 음식, 그리고 독특하고도 웅장한 디자인으로 아주 유명합니다. 3 저희 연회장은 시에서 단연 최고인데, 이는 보다 더 작은 기능을 위해 분리된 공간들로 쉽게 나뉘기 때문입니다. 4 Manor의 고도로 숙련된 요리사와 웨이터와 매니저들은 당신의 모든 요구가 제공되도록 보장합니다. 5 그 어떤 세세한 사항도 간과되지 않을 것이며, 저희는 그 어떤 종류의 특별 요청도 환영합니다. 6 저희는 당신의 완벽한 행사를 만들고 반드시 당신이 평생 지속될 좋은 기억을 가지고 Amberly Manor를 나서시도록 당신과 함께 일하겠습니다.

정답단추 고급스러운 시설과 훌륭한 서비스를 강조하며 Amberly Manor에서 행사를 주최해 보라는 광고문이야. 이를 가장 잘 압축한 제목은 ②임을 알 수 있어.

오답단서 ①, ③, ④, ⑤는 글에서 사용된 표현을 이용하여 오답을 유도하고 있어. 글에 나온 표현만 보고 섣불리 답을 고르면 안 돼.

어휘확인

ideal 이상적인 **famed** 아주 유명한 **star** (호텔·식당 등의 등급을 나타내는) 별 **excellent** 훌륭한 **unique** 독특한 **magnificent** 웅장한 **ballroom** 연회장 **divide into** ~으로 나누다 **separate** 분리된 **function** 기능 **highly-trained** 고도로 훈련된 **chef** 요리사 **waiter** 웨이터, 종업원 **manager** 매니저 **ensure** 보장하다 **provide** 제공하다 **detail** 세부 사항 **overlook** 간과하다 **request** 요청[신청] **nature** 종류[유형]; 자연 **make sure (that)** 반드시 ~하다 **memory** 기억; 추억 **last** 지속되다 **lifetime** 평생

〈선택지 어휘〉

dining 식사 **host** 주최하다 **invitation** 초대 **valuable** 소중한 **successfully** 성공적으로

지문 Flow

[도입]
식사나 결혼식을 위한 이상적인 장소인 Amberly Manor

⬇

[보충설명1]
5성급 서비스, 훌륭한 음식, 독특하고 웅장한 디자인으로 유명함

&

[보충설명2]
• 분리된 공간으로 나뉠 수 있는 연회장
• 숙련된 요리사, 웨이터, 매니저
• 특별한 요청 환영

⬇

[결론]
고객의 완벽한 행사와 평생 지속될 좋은 기억을 위해 노력하겠음

032 정답 ④

지문 All in One

식기세척기가 / 물을 내뿜고 있다 / 그 범람이 퍼져나가고 있다 / 부엌 바닥을 가로질러
[1] The dishwasher / is spouting water. [2] The flood is spreading / across the kitchen floor.
S V / S V
당신은 속으로 생각한다 / 만약 내가 손으로 설거지를 했다면 / 이런 일은 벌어지고 있지 않을 터라고
[3] You think to yourself, // "if I had washed the dishes by hand, / this wouldn't be happening."
S V / 접속사 S'_1 V'_1 / S'_2 V'_2
일이 잘못되면 / 우리는 비난할 데를 찾는다 / 그리고 종종 우리는 거울을 들여다본다
[4] When things go wrong, / we look to lay blame, // and often we look in the mirror.
접속사 S' V' C / S_1 V_1 / S_2 V_2
심리학자들은 발견한다 / 우리 중 많은 이들이 희생양이 되고 있다는 것을 / '모든 것은 내 잘못'이라는 접근법의
[5] Psychologists find // that many of us fall victim / to the "everything is my fault" approach /
S V / 접속사 S' V' C'
삶에 대한 / 우리가 종종 간과하는 두 가지는 ~이다 / 얼마나 적게 우리가 상황을 직접 통제하는가와
to life. [6] *Two things* [(which[that]) we often overlook] are / how little we directly control a
목적격 관계대명사 S / V / C_1
얼마나 적은 가치가 있는가를 / 우리의 시간을 보내는 것에 / 자신을 비난하며
situation // and how little value there is / in spending our time / blaming ourselves. [7] These
C_2 / S
이러한 생각들은 문제를 해결해 주지 않는다 / 비난은 과거에 관한 것이지만 / 행동 계획은 / 문제를 해결하기 위한
thoughts do not fix the problem. [8] Blame is about the past; // *a plan of action* [to fix a problem]
V / S_1 V_1 C_1 / S_2

어휘확인

dishwasher 식기 세척기 **spout** (액체를) 내뿜다, 분출하다 **flood** 범람, 홍수 **spread** 퍼지다 **across** 가로질러 **go wrong** 잘못되다 **look to-v** ~할 데를 찾다 **lay blame** 비난하다 **psychologist** 심리학자 **fall victim to** ~의 희생양이 되다 **fault** 잘못, 책임 **approach** 접근법 **overlook** 간과하다 **directly** 직접적으로 **situation** 상황 **value** 가치 **blame** 비난하다; 비난 **thought** (특정한) 생각 **fix** 해결하다; 고치다

지문 Flow

[가정]
식기세척기의 물이 부엌 바닥으로 넘치는 경우, 손으로 설거지를 했다면 그 일이 일어나지 않았을 것이라고 생각함

미래에 관한 것이다
/ is about the future.
V₂ C₂

① 과거를 돌아보는 것은 미래 설계에 중요하다.
② 일이 잘못되면 책임 소재부터 따져야 한다.
③ 자신이 한 일에 책임질 줄 아는 자세가 필요하다.
④ 문제 발생 시 자책하지 말고 해결을 해야 한다.
⑤ 인생을 가치 있게 살려면 현재를 열심히 살아야 한다.

해석 한 눈에 보기 1 식기세척기가 물을 내뿜고 있다. 2 그 범람이 부엌 바닥을 가로질러 퍼져나가고 있다. 3 당신은 속으로 '만약 내가 손으로 설거지를 했다면, 이런 일은 벌어지고 있지 않을 텐데.'라고 생각한다. 4 일이 잘못되면, 우리는 비난할 데를 찾다가, 종종 거울을 들여다본다(반성한다). 5 심리학자들은 우리 중 많은 이들이 삶에 대한 "모든 것은 내 잘못"이라는 접근법의 희생양이 되고 있다는 것을 발견한다. 주제문 6 우리가 종종 간과하는 두 가지는 얼마나 적게 우리가 상황을 직접 통제하는지와 우리가 우리 시간을 자신을 비난하며 보내는 것에 얼마나 적은 가치가 있는가이다. 7 이러한 생각들은 문제를 해결해 주지 않는다. 8 비난은 과거에 관한 것이지만, 문제를 해결하기 위한 행동 계획은 미래에 관한 것이다.

정답단추 글의 전반적인 내용을 살펴보자. 식기세척기의 예시와 심리학자들의 의견을 통해 많은 사람이 자신을 탓하는 태도를 보인다고 하고 있어. 하지만 이러한 태도는 우리가 상황을 거의 직접 통제하지 못하고, 자책하는 것은 가치가 거의 없다는 것을 간과하는 것이지. 그러므로 과거의 일을 비난하는 데 시간을 보내지 말고 앞으로 문제를 어떻게 해결할 것인지 행동 계획을 세우라는 것이 이 글의 요지야. 그래서 가장 적절한 답은 ④야.

오답단서 ①, ②, ③, ⑤는 모두 본문에서 언급된 표현으로 오답을 유도하고 있어. 그럴듯하게 보이지만 글의 요지와는 거리가 먼 내용이야.

&

[가정재진술]
일이 잘못됐을 때, 자신을 비난하고 반성하는 경향이 있음

⬇

[주제도출]
자신을 비난하는 데 시간을 보내는 것은 가치가 없고 문제를 해결해 주지 못하므로 문제를 해결하기 위한 행동 계획을 세워야 함

033 정답 ①

지문 All in One

1 Millions of tons of clothing (수백만 톤의 옷이, S) / are tossed (던져진다, V) / into garbage landfills (쓰레기 매립지로) / each year (매년). 2 They (S) rot (V₁) // and produce methane gas (V₂) (그것들은 썩어서 메탄가스를 만들어 낸다). 3 A major source of discarded clothes / in landfills (매립지의 버려진 옷들의 주된 원인은, S) / is (V) the "fast fashion" industry (C) ('패스트 패션' 산업이다). 4 "Fast fashion" (S) is (V) the modern trend (C) ('패스트 패션'은 현대의 추세이다) / towards low cost, low quality, and quickly changing fashion (저비용, 낮은 품질, 빠르게 변하는 패션을 향한). 5 We (S) don't care (V) (우리는 신경 쓰지 않는다) // if (접속사) the shoes (S'₁) are worn out (V'₁) soon (신발이 금방 닳는지) / or if (접속사) the clothes (S'₂) are poorly made (V'₂) (혹은 옷이 허술하게 만들어져 있는지에). 6 Instead (대신에), / we (S) just want (V) the latest "look." (우리는 그저 최신의 '겉모양'만을 원한다) 7 We (S₁) then discard (V₁) the clothes (우리는 그러고 나서 옷을 버리고) // and they (S₂) go (V₂) into a landfill (그러면 그것들은 매립지로 간다). 8 However (그러나), / consumers (S) must learn (V) (소비자들은 알아야 한다) // that (접속사) cheap and fast fashion (S') (싸고 빠른 패션은) / comes (V') at a very high cost (매우 높은 비용을 치러야 한다는 것을) / to the environment (환경에). 9 Buy (V₁) less (더 적게 사고) // and pay (V₂) more for *clothing* [that lasts] (관계대명사) (오래가는 옷에 더 많이 지불해라).

① The problem with fast fashion
패스트 패션의 문제점
② The size of the fashion industry
패션 산업의 크기
③ Problems with garbage landfills
쓰레기 매립지의 문제점
④ The high speed of change in fashion
패션의 빠른 변화 속도
⑤ Advantages of low-cost clothing
저비용 의류의 장점

해석 한 눈에 보기 1 매년 수백만 톤의 옷이 쓰레기 매립지로 던져진다. 2 그것들은 썩어서 메탄가스를 만들어 낸다. 3 매립지의 버려진 옷들의 주된 원인은 '패스트 패션' 산업이다. 4 '패스트 패션'은 저비용, 낮은 품질, 빠르게 변하는 패션을 향한 현대의 추세이다. 5 우리는 신발이 금방 닳는지 혹은 옷이 허술하게 만들어져 있는지에 신경 쓰지 않는다. 6 대신에 우리는 그저 최신의 '겉모양'만을 원한다. 7 우리는 그러고 나서 옷을 버리고 그러면 그것들은 매립지로 간다. 주제문 8 그러나 소비자들은 싸고 빠른 패션은 환경에 매우 높은 비용을 치러야 한다는 것을 알아야 한다. 9 더 적게 사고 오래가는 옷에 더 많이 지불해라.

정답단추 주제는 글의 핵심 내용을 담고 있는 것이어야 해. 이 글은 수많은 옷이 버려지고 이 옷들이 썩으면서 메탄가스를 방출하는 문제가 발생하고 있는데, 옷을 많이 버리는 주된 이유는 '패스트 패션' 산업이라고 말하고 있어. However로 시작하는 문장에도 있듯이 싸고 빠른 패션은 환경에 고비용을 발생시키는 문제를 가지고 있는 것이야. 그래서 글쓴이는 마지막 문장에서 '옷을 덜 사고 오래가는 옷에 돈을 많이 쓰라'고 '패스트 패션'에 따르지 말 것을 당부하고 있지. 그러므로 글의 주제로는 ①이 가장 적절해.

오답단서 ②, ③, ⑤의 fashion industry, garbage landfills, low-cost clothing은 글에서 사용된 어구로, 이를 이용하여 만든 선택지야. 또한, ④는 세부적인 내용이므로 글의 주제로는 적절하지 않아.

어휘확인

ton 톤(무게의 단위) **clothing** 의류 **toss** 던지다 **landfill** (쓰레기) 매립지 **rot** 썩다, 부패하다 **methane gas** 메탄가스 **major** 주요한, 중대한 **source** (문제의) 근원 **discard** 버리다 **industry** 산업 **modern** 현대의, 근대의 **trend** 추세, 경향 **cost** 비용, 값 **quality** 질 **wear out** 닳게[해지게] 하다 **poorly** 좋지 못하게 **instead** 대신에 **latest** 최신의 **consumer** 소비자 **at a (high) cost** (높은) 비용으로 **environment** 환경 **last** 오래가다, 지속되다

〈선택지 어휘〉
advantage 장점

지문 Flow

[문제제기]
매년 수많은 옷이 버려짐

⬇

[원인]
• 저비용, 낮은 품질, 유행을 따르는 '패스트 패션' 산업
• 최신의 '겉모양'만을 추구하는 사람들

⬇

[결론]
싸고 빠른 패션은 높은 환경 비용을 치러야 하므로, 더 적게 사고 오래가는 옷을 사야함.

034 정답 ④

지문 All in One

우리가 말을 할 때 / 항상 가능한 것은 아니다 / 정확하게 말하는 것이 / 우리가 말하고 싶은 것을
1 When we are speaking, // it's not always possible / to say exactly / what we want to say.
접속사 S′ V′ / 가주어 V / C / 진주어 / 관계대명사

광범위한 어휘를 소유한 화자는 거의 없고 / 심지어 그런 사람조차도 종종 부족하다 / 통제 수준이
2 Few speakers possess a wide vocabulary, // [and] even *those* [that do] often lack / *the level of*
S_1 V_1 / S_2 관계대명사 = possess V_2

완벽한 단어를 선택하는 데 필요한 / 발끈하여 / 그것은 ~이다
control [necessary to choose the perfect word] / in the heat of the moment. 3 That is // because
부사적 용법(형용사 수식) / S V

준비할 확실한 방법이 없기 때문에 / 다음에 무엇을 말할지 / 우리가 말을 하고 있을 때 / 말이 우리 머리에 불쑥
there is no *sure way* [to prepare / for what to say next / as we are speaking]. 4 Words pop into
V′ S′ / C / 접속사 S″ V″ / S V_1

나타나서(떠올라서) / 우리의 입 밖으로 나온다 / 부주의한 방식으로 / 글쓰기에서 / 그러나
our heads / [and] come out of our mouths / in a careless way. 5 In writing, / however, / we
V_2 / S

우리는 시간이 더 많다 / 쓸 / 우리가 말하고 싶은 것을 / 정확하게 / 훨씬 더 많은 편집은 / 가능하다
have more *time* [to write / what we want to say / correctly]. 6 Much more editing / is possible.
V / 관계대명사 / S V C

글을 쓰는 사람은 작업할 수도 있다 / 몇 시간씩 / 단 하나의 단락을 / 단지 그것을 '올바르게' 하기 위해
7 Writers can work / for hours / on a single paragraph / just to get it "right."
S V / 부사적 용법(목적)

① how to speak carefully
신중하게 말하는 방법

② factors to be considered in speech
연설에서 고려할 요소

③ why it's difficult to write
글쓰기가 어려운 이유

④ the difference between speaking and writing
말하기와 쓰기의 차이점

⑤ the necessity for accurate use of vocabulary
정확한 어휘 사용의 필요성

해석 한 눈에 보기 1 우리가 말을 할 때, 정확히 우리가 말하고 싶은 것을 말하는 것이 항상 가능한 것은 아니다. 2 광범위한 어휘를 소유하고 있는 화자는 거의 없으며, 그러한 화자조차도 종종 발끈하여 완벽한 단어를 선택하는 데 필요한 통제 수준이 부족하다. 3 그것은 우리가 말을 하고 있을 때는 다음에 무슨 말을 해야 하는지를 준비할 확실한 방법이 없기 때문이다. 4 말들이 머릿속으로 떠올라 되는대로 입 밖으로 나와 버린다. 5 그러나 글을 쓸 때는 우리가 말하고 싶은 것을 정확히 쓸 시간이 더 많이 있다. 6 훨씬 더 많은 편집이 가능하다. 7 글을 쓰는 사람은 하나의 단락을 단지 그것을 '올바르게' 하기 위해 몇 시간씩 작업할 수도 있다.

정답단추 주제문이 뚜렷하게 나타나지 않은 글이라서 전체적인 내용을 봐야 해. 이 글은 전반부에서 '말을 할 때는 아무리 어휘력이 풍부해도 원하는 말이 안 나올 때가 있다'라고 말하며 말하기의 어려움에 대해 언급하고 있어. 그러나 중반부 In writing, however, ~.부터는 글을 쓸 때는 충분한 시간이 있어 원하는 말을 정확히 표현할 수 있다며 글쓰기의 특징에 대해 얘기하고 있어. 따라서 이 글은 말하기와 쓰기의 차이점에 대한 내용으로 가장 적절한 주제는 ④야.

오답단서 ①은 이 글에서 말하기의 어려움에 대해 얘기하고 있긴 하지만, 신중하게 말하는 방법을 알려주진 않아서 답이 될 수 없어. ②는 이 글의 내용과는 거리가 있어. ③과 ⑤는 이 글에서 사용된 표현을 활용해서 만든 오답이라서 그럴 듯하게 보일 수 있지만, 둘 다 글에서 언급된 내용은 아니야.

어휘확인

exactly 정확히 **speaker** 화자(말하는 사람) **possess** 소유하다 **wide** 광범위한 **vocabulary** 어휘 **lack** ~이 부족하다 **in the heat of the moment** 발끈하여 **prepare** 준비하다 **pop** 불쑥 나타나다 **careless** 부주의한 **writing** 글쓰기 **correctly** 정확하게 **editing** 편집 **single** 단 하나의 **paragraph** 단락

〈선택지 어휘〉

necessity 필요성 **accurate** 정확한

지문 Flow

[도입]
말하고 싶은 것을 말하는 것이 항상 가능한 것은 아님

⬇

[보충설명]
말하는 중에는 다음에 할 말에 대한 준비를 할 수 없어서 머리에 떠오르는 대로 말하게 됨

⬇

[대조]
글을 쓸 때는 말하고 싶은 것을 정확히 쓸 수 있음

⬇

[보충설명]
편집이 가능하고, 수정을 위해 많은 시간 작업할 수 있음

035 정답 ④

지문 All in One

점점 더 많은 사람들이 고생하고 있다 / 어깨 통증으로 / 취해질 수 있는 몇 가지 조치가 있지만
1 More and more people are suffering / from shoulder pain. 2 There are *a few steps* [that can
S V / V_1 S_1 주격 관계대명사

아픈 어깨를 치료하기 위해 / 전문가들은 동의한다 / 최고의 전략이 예방이라는 것에
be taken] / to cure an aching shoulder, // but experts agree / that the best strategy is
부사적 용법(목적) / S_2 V_2 / 접속사 S′ V′

예방 전략의 한 가지 중요한 부분은 / 근육 힘(근력)과 유연성을 기르는 것이다
prevention. 3 One important part of the prevention strategy / is to build muscle strength and
C′ / S / V / C

그러나 훨씬 더 중요하다 / 올바른 가방을 선택하여 / 그것을 적절하게 들고 다니는 것이
flexibility. 4 But it's even more important / to select the right bag / [and] (to) carry it properly.
가주어 V 비교급 강조 C / 진주어₁ / 진주어₂

여행할 때는 / 가벼운 가방을 들고 다녀라 / 바퀴가 달린 / 만약 당신이 배낭이나 책가방을 들고 가야 한다면
5 When you travel, // carry light bags / with wheels. 6 If you must carry a backpack or book
접속사 S′ V′ / V / 접속사 S′ V′

학교에 / 당신은 똑바로 서야 한다 / 그리고 등 위쪽으로 가방을 메야 한다
bag / for school, // you should stand up straight / [and] keep the pack high on your back.
S V_1 / V_2

배낭을 메고 다니지 마라 / 그 어떤 무거운 가방도 / 한쪽 어깨로
7 Don't carry the pack, / [nor] any other heavy bags, / over one shoulder.
V / not A nor B(A도 아니고 B도 아니다)

어휘확인

suffer from ~으로 고생하다 **step** 조치 **cure** 치료하다 **aching** 아픈 **expert** 전문가 **strategy** 전략 **prevention** 예방 **muscle** 근육 **flexibility** 유연성 **select** 선택하다 **properly** 적절하게 **straight** 똑바로

〈선택지 어휘〉

pack (짐을) 싸다 **enemy** 적 **posture** 자세 **benefit** 이점, 혜택 **light** 가볍게; 빛; 밝은

지문 Flow

[주제]
어깨 통증에 대한 최고의 치료는 예방임

⬇

① What to Pack for Traveling
여행 갈 때 무엇을 싸야 하는가

② Stress: The Enemy of Health
스트레스는 건강의 적

③ Keeping Good Body Posture
좋은 신체 자세 유지하기

④ Prevention: The Best Cure for Shoulder Pain
예방이 어깨 통증의 최선의 치료법

⑤ The Benefits of Traveling Light
가볍게 여행하는 것의 이점들

해석 한 눈에 보기 1 점점 더 많은 사람들이 어깨 통증으로 고생하고 있다. 주제문 2 아픈 어깨를 치료하기 위해 취해질 수 있는 몇 가지 조치가 있지만, 전문가들은 최고의 전략이 예방이라는 것에 동의한다. 3 예방 전략의 한 가지 중요한 부분은 근력과 유연성을 기르는 것이다. 4 그러나 올바른 가방을 선택하여 그것을 적절하게 들고 다니는 것이 훨씬 더 중요하다. 5 여행할 때는, 바퀴가 달린 가벼운 가방을 들고 다녀라. 6 만약 당신이 배낭이나 책가방을 들고 학교에 가야 한다면, 똑바로 서서 등 위쪽으로 가방을 메야 한다. 7 배낭이나 그 어떤 무거운 가방도 한쪽 어깨에 메고 다니지 마라.

정답단추 글의 핵심 내용을 담고 있는 주제문을 찾고 이를 가장 잘 반영한 제목을 고르면 돼. 서두에서 어깨 통증을 겪는 사람이 많은데 가장 좋은 치료법은 예방이라는 내용에 이어서 가방을 올바르게 드는 방법이 구체적으로 언급되고 있어. 따라서 이 글의 제목은 핵심 내용을 적절하게 반영한 ④임을 쉽게 알 수 있지.

오답단서 ①과 ⑤는 travel을 이용하여 오답을 유도하고 있어. 또한, ②의 stress는 본문에 등장하지 않았고, ③은 본문의 핵심어인 '어깨 통증'으로 연상할 수 있는 것이지만 이 글의 내용과는 상관이 없어.

[예방전략]
• 근력과 유연성 기르기
• 올바른 가방을 적절하게 들고 다니기

⬇

[예시]
• 여행할 때는 바퀴 있는 가벼운 가방 사용하기
• 배낭은 등 위쪽으로 매기
• 한쪽 어깨로 가방 매지 않기

036 정답 ①

지문 All in One

1 With today's Internet and satellite technologies, / it is easy for military leaders / in far-away headquarters / to communicate with their armies. 2 Of course, / this wasn't always the case.
(오늘날의 인터넷과 위성 기술로 / 군대 지휘관들에게 쉽다 / 멀리 떨어진 본부에 있는 / 그들의 부대와 통신하는 것이 / 물론 / 이것은 항상 그러한 경우는 아니었다)
(it: 가주어, is: V, easy: C, for military leaders: to부정사의 의미상 주어, to communicate ~: 진주어; this: S, wasn't: V, the case: C)

3 Armies of the past / had to find other methods / of getting messages safely and quickly / through enemy lines.
(과거의 군대들은 / 다른 방법을 찾아야만 했다 / 메시지를 안전하고 빠르게 전달할 / 적의 경계선(전선)을 뚫고)
(Armies of the past: S, had to find: V)

4 One of those ways / was by pigeon. 5 This is // because pigeons have / *an amazing ability* [to find their homes] / at high speed / across great distances.
(그런 방법 중 하나가 / 비둘기에 의한 것이었다 / 이것은 ~이다 / 비둘기가 가지고 있기 때문(이다) / 그들의 집을 찾는 놀라운 능력을 / 빠른 속도로 / 먼 거리를 가로질러)
(One of those ways: S, was: V, by pigeon: C; This: S, is: V, because: 접속사, pigeons: S', have: V')

6 *The pigeons* [used for this sort of communication] / were usually kept in cages / at military camps.
(이런 종류의 통신에 사용된 비둘기들은 / 흔히 새장에서 키워졌다 / 군 야영지의)
(The pigeons: S, were ~ kept: V)

7 Then, / when the birds were released / with messages tied to their legs, // they would fly to *headquarters*, / [where the messages could be read].
(그러다가 / 그 새(비둘기)가 풀어지면 / 그들의 다리에 메시지가 묶인 채로 / 그들은 본부로 날아가곤 했는데 / 그곳에서 그 메시지가 읽힐 수 있었다)
(when: 접속사, the birds: S', were released: V', with messages tied to their legs: 분사구문 「with+명사+분사」: ~한 채로, they: S, would fly: V, where: 관계부사, the messages: S, could be read: V)

① Pigeons as Messengers
전령으로서의 비둘기

② Safe Handling of Wild Birds
야생 조류의 안전한 취급

③ Sending Messages in the Army
군대에서의 메시지 보내기

④ Pigeons' Instinct to Return Home
집으로 돌아가려는 비둘기의 본능

⑤ The Communication Forms of Today
오늘날의 통신 형태

해석 한 눈에 보기 1 오늘날의 인터넷과 위성 기술로, 멀리 떨어진 본부에 있는 군 지휘관들이 자신들의 부대들과 통신하기가 쉽다. 2 물론 이것이 항상 이랬던 것은 아니었다. 주제문 3 과거의 군대들은 적의 전선을 뚫고 안전하고 빠르게 메시지를 전달할 다른 방법들을 찾아야만 했다. 4 그러한 방법 중 하나가 비둘기에 의한 것이었다. 5 이것은 비둘기가 빠른 속도로 먼 거리를 가로질러 자신의 집을 찾아가는 놀라운 능력을 지니고 있기 때문이다. 6 이런 종류의 통신에 사용된 비둘기들은 흔히 군 야영지의 새장에서 키워졌다. 7 그러다가 비둘기가 그것들 다리에 메시지가 묶인 채로 풀어지면, 그것들은 본부로 날아가곤 했는데, 그곳에서 그 메시지가 읽힐 수 있었다.

정답단추 오늘날에는 인터넷과 위성 기술의 발달로 통신이 쉬워졌지만, 과거에는 통신 수단으로 비둘기를 사용하기도 했다는 내용이 나오지? 그리고 비둘기를 어떻게 통신에 이용했는지 자세한 설명이 이어지고 있어. 따라서 이를 가장 적절하게 반영한 제목은 ①이야.

오답단서 ②는 글에서 언급되지 않았고, ③, ④, ⑤는 세부적인 내용일 뿐이라서 답이 될 수 없어.

어휘확인

satellite (인공)위성 **technology** (과학) 기술 **military** 군대의; 군대 **headquarters** 본부, 사령부 **communicate** 통신하다 cf. **communication** 통신 **army** 부대, 군대 **method** 방법 **enemy** 적 **way** 방법; 길 **pigeon** 비둘기 **ability** 능력 **distance** 거리 **sort** 종류 **cage** 새장; 우리 **release** 풀어주다

〈선택지 어휘〉

messenger 전령, 전달자 **handling** 취급, 다루기 **instinct** 본능 **return** 돌아가다 **form** 형태

지문 Flow

[도입]
오늘날 인터넷과 위성 기술로 멀리 떨어진 본부와 부대 간의 통신이 쉬워짐

⬇

[비교 + 주제]
과거에는 비둘기가 메시지를 전달하는 수단으로 쓰임

⬇

[보충설명1]
비둘기가 빠른 속도로 자신의 집을 찾아가는 능력을 지녔음

&

[보충설명2]
통신용 비둘기가 메시지를 다리에 묶고 날아가 본부에 전달함

037 정답 ②

지문 All in One

사람의 눈처럼 / 물고기 눈은 갖고 있다 / 동공, 수정체 및 뇌로 연결되는 시신경을
1 Like the human eye, / a fish eye has / a pupil, a lens, and *optic nerves* [leading to the brain].
S V

그러나 대부분의 물고기는 / 눈이 위치해 있다 / 머리의 서로 반대되는 쪽에 / 그래서 그것들은 다른
2 But in most fish, / the eyes are placed / on opposite sides of the head, // so they can see
S_1 V_1 접속사 S_2 V_2

이미지를 볼 수 있다 / 각 눈으로 / 눈의 이러한 위치는 / 그들에게 매우 넓은 범위의 시야를 제공해 준다
different images / with each eye. 3 This location of their eyes / gives them a very wide field of
S V IO DO

최대 360도에 이르는 / 이것은 훨씬 더 넓다 / 사람의 시야 범위보다
vision / — up to 360 degrees. 4 This is much wider / than the human field of vision, // and
S_1 V_1 비교급 강조 C_1

그리고 특히 유용하다 / 물속에서 / 포식자들이 공격할 수 있는 / 어느 방향에서든
it's especially useful / under *the water*, [where predators can attack / from any direction / at
S_2 V_2 C_2 관계부사

언제든지 / 하지만 이것만이 유일하게 흥미로운 특징인 것은 아니다 / 그것들이 물속에서 살기 때문에 / 물고기는
any time]. 5 But this is not the only interesting feature. 6 Because they live in water, // fish
S V C 접속사 S′ V′ S_1

눈꺼풀이 없다 / 반면에 우리는 눈꺼풀이 필요하다 / 우리 눈을 촉촉하게 유지하기 위해
have no eyelids, // whereas we need them / to keep our eyes moist.
V_1 접속사 S_2 V_2 부사적 용법(목적)

① a fish's wide field of vision
물고기의 넓은 시야

② unique features of a fish's eyes
물고기 눈의 독특한 특징

③ similarities between fish eyes and human eyes
물고기 눈과 사람 눈의 유사점

④ the range of colors that a fish can see
물고기가 볼 수 있는 색깔 범위

⑤ advantages of a fish's wide field of view
물고기의 넓은 시야가 가지는 장점

해석 한 눈에 보기 1 사람의 눈처럼, 물고기의 눈도 동공, 수정체 및 뇌로 연결되는 시신경을 갖고 있다. 2 그러나 대부분의 물고기의 경우, 눈이 머리의 서로 반대되는 쪽에 위치해 있어서, 그것들은 각 눈으로 서로 다른 이미지를 볼 수 있다. 3 눈의 이러한 위치는 그것들에게 최대 360도에 이르는 매우 넓은 범위의 시야를 제공해 준다. 4 이것은 사람의 시야 범위보다 훨씬 더 넓으며, 포식자들이 언제든지 어느 방향에서든 공격할 수 있는 물속에서 특히 유용하다. 5 하지만 이것만이 유일하게 흥미로운 특징인 것은 아니다. 6 그것들이 물속에서 살기 때문에, 물고기는 눈꺼풀이 없는 반면에, 우리는 우리 눈을 촉촉하게 유지하기 위해 눈꺼풀이 필요하다.

정답단추 주제문이 없는 글일 때는 전체적인 글의 내용을 파악해 보자. 사람 눈과 물고기 눈은 비슷한 점도 있지만, 눈의 위치, 볼 수 있는 범위와 눈꺼풀의 유무에서 차이가 있다는 내용으로 물고기 눈의 특징에 대한 내용임을 알 수 있어. 이를 종합한 주제로는 ②가 가장 적절해.

오답단서 ①과 ⑤는 글의 주제가 되기에는 너무 세부적인 내용이야. 그리고 물고기 눈과 사람 눈의 유사점도 언급되지만, 차이점이 주된 내용이므로 ③은 정답이 될 수 없어. 또한, ④는 글에서 언급되지 않은 내용이야.

어휘확인

pupil 동공, 눈동자 **lens** (눈의) 수정체 **optic nerve** 시신경 **lead to** ~로 이어지다 **opposite** 정반대의 **image** 이미지 **location** 위치 **field** 범위; 들판 **vision** 시야, 시력 **up to** ~까지, 최대 ~ **degree** (각도·온도계 등의) 도 **especially** 특히 **useful** 유용한 **predator** 포식자 **attack** 공격하다 **feature** 특징 **eyelid** 눈꺼풀 **whereas** ~인 반면에 **moist** 촉촉한
〈선택지 어휘〉
similarity 유사점 **range** 범위

지문 Flow

[비교1]
물고기도 사람처럼 동공, 수정체, 시신경을 갖고 있음

⬇

[비교2]
물고기의 눈은 머리의 서로 반대되는 쪽에 위치해서 각 눈으로 다른 이미지를 볼 수 있으므로 사람보다 시야 범위가 넓음

⬇

[비교3]
물고기는 물속에 살아서 사람과 달리 눈꺼풀이 없음

038 정답 ①

지문 All in One

저는 차를 살 여유가 없는 가난한 대학생입니다 / 그래서 저는 아주 많이 의존합니다 / 제 자전거에
1 I am *a poor college student* [who can't afford a car], // so I rely heavily / on my bike. 2 As
S_1 V_1 C_1 관계대명사 S_2 V_2 접속사

제 고향의 대중교통이 / 공사로 고통 받고 있기 때문에 / 그리고 휘발유 가격이 계속 천문학적이
mass transit in my hometown / suffers from construction / and gas prices remain
S'_1 V'_1 S'_2 V'_2

기 (때문에) / 자전거 타기는 돌아다니기에 가장 좋은 방법일 것입니다 / 하지만 제가 가는 어디에나 / 자전거 타기가
astronomical, // biking should be *the best way* [to get around]. 3 But wherever I go, // biking is
C′ S V C 복합관계부사 S′ V′ S V

불필요하게 어렵습니다 / 자전거들은 인도에서 금지되어 있습니다 / 그런데도 자전거 전용 도로는 부족합니다
unnecessarily difficult. 4 Bikes are prohibited on sidewalks, // yet bike lanes are scarce. 5 I
C S_1 V_1 S_2 V_2 C S

저는 생각합니다 / 제가 제 목숨을 두고 있다고 / 부주의한 운전자들의 손에 / 제가 자전거를 탈 때마다
think // (that) I'm putting my life / in the hands of distracted drivers / every time I bike / in
V 접속사 S′ V′ 접속사 S″ V″

거리에서 / 포틀랜드는 앞으로 나아가 있습니다 / 그것은 거두고 있습니다 / 경제적 그리고 환경적 혜택을
the street. 6 Portland is moving forward. 7 It is reaping / the economic and environmental
S V S V

자전거 타기를 받아들이는 것의 / 저는 Jackson 시장님께 바랍니다 / 자전거 타기에 관한 그의 마음을 바꾸기를
benefits / of embracing cycling. 8 I expect Mayor Jackson / to change his mind about cycling /
S V O C_1

그리고 자전거 전용 도로를 만들기를 / 자전거 거치대를 설치하기를 / 그리고 주민들에게 촉구하기를 / 마력에서 페달력으로
and (to) create bike lanes, / (to) install bike racks, / and (to) urge residents / to switch from
C_2 C_3 C_4 부사적 용법(목적)

전환하도록
horsepower to pedal power.

어휘확인

college student 대학생 **afford** ~살 여유가 되다 **rely on** ~에 의존하다 **heavily** 아주 많이 **mass transit** 대중교통 **suffer from** ~로 고통 받다 **construction** 공사 **gas** 휘발유; 가스 **remain** 계속 ~이다 **astronomical** (양·가격 등이) 천문학적인, 어마어마한 **get around** 돌아다니다 **wherever** 어디에나 **unnecessarily** 불필요하게 **prohibit** 금지하다 **sidewalk** 인도 **yet** 그런데도; 아직 **bike lane** 자전거 전용 도로 **scarce** 부족한 **distracted** 부주의한; (정신이) 산만해진 **every time** ~할 때마다 **reap** (좋은 결과 등을) 거두다 **economic** 경제의 **environmental** 환경의 **benefit** 혜택, 이득 **embrace** 받아들이다; 껴안다 **expect** 바라다, 기대하다 **install** 설치하다 **bike rack** 자전거 거치대 **urge** 촉구하다 **resident** 주민 **switch** 전환하다; 스위치 **horsepower** 마력 **pedal** (자전거의) 페달

① 자전거 활성화 정책을 촉구하려고　　② 다른 도시의 모범 사례를 제시하려고
③ 자전거 시설의 교체를 건의하려고　　④ 운전자의 부주의를 상기시키려고
⑤ 자전거의 위험성을 지적하려고

해석 한 눈에 보기　1 저는 차를 살 여유가 없는 가난한 대학생이라서, 제 자전거에 많이 의존합니다. 2 제 고향의 대중교통이 공사 중이고 휘발유 가격이 계속 천문학적이기 때문에, 자전거를 타는 것이 돌아다니기에 가장 좋은 방법일 것입니다. 3 하지만 제가 어디를 가든지, 자전거를 타는 것이 불필요하게 어렵습니다. 4 자전거가 인도에서 금지되어 있는데도, 자전거 도로는 희박합니다. 5 저는 도로에서 자전거를 탈 때마다 제 목숨을 부주의한 운전자들의 손에 두고 있다는 생각이 듭니다. 6 포틀랜드는 앞으로 나아가고 있습니다. 7 이곳은 자전거를 받아들이는 것의 경제적 및 환경적 효과를 거두고 있습니다. 8 저는 Jackson 시장님께서 자전거 타기에 대한 생각을 바꿔서 자전거 도로를 만들고, 자전거 거치대를 설치하며, 주민들에게 마력(자동차)에서 페달력(자전거)으로 전환하도록 촉구하기를 바랍니다.
정답단추　글의 목적을 물을 때는 글을 끝까지 읽고 글쓴이의 의도가 잘 드러나는 문장을 찾아야 해. 글쓴이는 자전거를 이용하는 것이 본인에게 가장 좋은 방법인데 자전거 전용 도로가 거의 없어서 자전거 타기가 너무 힘들다고 하고 있어. 그리고 마지막 문장 I expect ~ pedal power.에서 글쓴이의 진짜 의도가 잘 드러나는데 자전거 도로와 거치대 만들기 및 자전거 활성화 정책을 Jackson 시장에게 청원하고 있어. 따라서 이 글의 목적은 ①이야.
오답단서　②는 다른 도시에 대해 말한 적이 없어서 답이 될 수 없어. ③은 자전거 전용 도로, 거치대와 같은 자전거 시설에 관해 건의를 한 건 맞지만, 교체에 대해서 언급하지는 않았기 때문에 오답이야. ④는 글의 일부분에서 언급된 것은 맞지만, 이 글 전체를 포함하는 목적은 아니야. 마지막으로 ⑤는 이 글의 궁극적인 목적과는 반대되는 내용이라서 답이 될 수 없어.

지문 Flow

[도입]
자전거를 이용하는 대학생

[문제제기]
자전거는 인도에서 금지되어 있는데, 자전거 도로가 희박하여 자전거 이용이 어려움

[주장]
자전거 도로를 만들고, 자전거 거치대를 설치하고, 주민들의 자전거 이용 촉구를 바람

039　정답 ③

지문 All in One

나는 1,000마일 떨어진 곳에 산다 / 나의 딸에게서 / 하지만 인터넷 덕분에 / 우리는
1 I live a thousand miles away / from my daughter. 2 But thanks to the Internet, / we have
S V　S V
함께 있어왔다 / 하루 종일 / 먼 거리에도 불구하고 / 나는 안다 / 모든 그녀의 삶과 / 그녀가 겪고 있는 것을
been together / all day. 3 Despite the distance, / I know / all about her life / and what she is
S V　관계대명사
그녀는 사랑니를 뺐다 / 오늘 아침에 / 우리가 대화를 할 수 없었더
going through. 4 She had her wisdom teeth pulled out / this morning. 5 If we had not been
S　have+목적어+과거분사(~이 …되게 하다)　접속사 S′ V′
라면 / 나는 매우 걱정했을 것이다 / 하지만 우리는 온라인상으로 / 채팅을 해왔다 / 그녀가 집에
able to talk, // I would have been so worried. 6 But we've been online, / chatting, // since she
가정법 과거완료　S V C　S V　접속사 S′
온 이후로 / 병원에서 / 나는 너무 기쁘다 / 내가 그녀와 이야기 할 수 있어서 / 이렇게 쉽게 / 그리고 비록 그녀가
got home / from the clinic. 7 I'm so glad // that I can talk to her / so easily. 8 And though she
V′　S V C　접속사 S′ V′　접속사 S′
아프고 피가 나고 있을지라도 / 그녀는 위로를 얻는다 / 나와 아주 가까이 있다고 느끼는 것으로부터
is in pain and (is) bleeding, // she gets comfort / from feeling so close to me. 9 How
V'_1　V'_2　S V　C
얼마나 멋진가 / 우리가 그렇게 쉽게 연락을 주고받을 수 있다는 게 / 우리가 사랑하는 사람들과
wonderful it is // that we can so easily keep in touch / with our loved ones!
S V　S′ V′

① 특히 몸이 아플 때 가족의 필요성을 느끼게 된다.
② 가족의 사랑은 무엇과도 바꿀 수 없이 소중하다.
③ 인터넷 덕분에 멀리 있는 가족과 연락이 용이하다.
④ 외국에 나가서야 비로소 가족의 소중함을 알게 된다.
⑤ 멀리 떨어진 가족과 연락하는 것을 게을리하면 안 된다.

해석 한 눈에 보기　1 나는 내 딸에게서 1,000마일 떨어진 곳에서 산다. 2 하지만 인터넷 덕분에, 우리는 하루 종일 함께 있어 왔다. 3 먼 거리에도 불구하고, 나는 그녀의 삶과 그녀가 겪고 있는 것을 모두 안다. 4 그녀는 오늘 아침에 사랑니를 뺐다. 5 우리가 대화를 할 수 없었더라면, 나는 무척 걱정했을 것이다. 6 그러나 우리는 그녀가 병원에서 집으로 돌아온 이후로 온라인상으로 채팅을 해 왔다. 7 나는 내가 그녀와 이렇게 쉽게 이야기할 수 있어서 너무 기쁘다. 8 그리고 비록 그녀가 아파하고 피가 나고 있을지라도, 그녀는 나와 아주 가까이 있다고 느끼는 것으로부터 위로를 얻는다. 주제문 9 우리가 사랑하는 사람들과 그렇게 쉽게 연락하고 지낼 수 있다는 것이 얼마나 멋진가!
정답단추　글쓴이의 개인적인 경험을 들어 주제를 설명하는 글이야. 즉, 인터넷을 이용하여 가족과 연락을 쉽게 할 수 있다는 것에 기쁘고 만족한다는 내용으로 마지막 문장이 주제문이라 할 수 있어. 따라서 글의 요지로는 ③이 가장 적절해.
오답단서　①, ②, ④는 모두 글에 언급된 내용을 사용해 그럴듯하게 만든 선택지야. ⑤는 '연락하는 것을 게을리 하면 안 된다'가 아니라 '요즘은 연락에 있어 거리가 문제 되지 않는다'는 것이 글의 요지라서 답이 될 수 없어.

어휘확인

mile 마일(거리 단위) **thanks to** ~ 덕분에 **all day** 하루 종일 **despite** ~에도 불구하고 **distance** 거리 **go through** 겪다 **wisdom tooth** 사랑니 **pull out** ~을 뽑다 **clinic** 병원 **though** 비록 ~일지라도 **in pain** 아픈 **bleed** 피를 흘리다 **comfort** 위로, 위안 **keep in touch with** ~와 연락을 주고받다

지문 Flow

[도입]
인터넷 덕분에 멀리 떨어져 사는 딸의 소식을 접할 수 있게 됨

[예시]
사랑니를 빼고 온 딸과 온라인으로 채팅함

[보충설명]
딸은 아파도 부모가 가까이 있다고 느끼는 것에서 위로를 얻음

[주제문]
사랑하는 사람들과 쉽게 연락하고 지낼 수 있다는 것은 좋은 것임

040 정답 ⑤

지문 All in One

'훌라'는 하와이의 전통적인 춤이다 / 특별한 노래와 음악에 맞춰진 / 흐르는 듯한 움직임과
1 *Hula* is *a traditional Hawaiian dance* [set to special chants and music [that combines
S V C 관계대명사

결합한 / 얼굴표정과 / '훌라'가 시작되었을 때 / 그것은 예배의 형태였다
flowing movement / with unique facial expressions]]. 2 When *hula* began, // it was a form of
접속사 S' V' S V C

Lot Kapúaiwa 왕자는 / '훌라'를 살아있게 유지했다 / 하와이에서 / 관심이 점점 더 줄어들었을 때에
worship. 3 Prince Lot Kapúaiwa / kept the *hula* alive / in Hawaii / at *a time* [when there was
S V O C 관계부사

그것에 대해 / 그 왕자는 그의 에너지와 강한 의지로 유명했다 / 그의
less and less interest / in it]. 4 The prince was noted for his energy and strong will. 5 One of
S V S

관심 중 하나가 / 하와이 문화를 홍보하고 보존하는 것이었다 / 특히 '훌라'를 / 그는
his interests / was to promote [and] (to) preserve Hawaiian culture, / especially the *hula*. 6 He
V C S

이것을 했다 / '훌라' 공연을 개최함으로써 / 그의 별장에서 / 많은 사람들에게 / '훌라'는 하와이인들의 세계관을
did this / by holding *hula* performances / at his cottage. 7 To many, / the *hula* represents the
V S V

나타낸다 / 감사하여 / 하와이 문화를 보존하려던 Lot 왕자의 노력에
Hawaiians' view of the world. 8 In appreciation of / *Prince Lot's efforts* [to preserve Hawaiian

'프린스 롯 훌라 축제'가 설립되었다 / 1978년에 / 해마다 / '훌라' 학교들이
culture], / the Prince Lot Hula Festival was established / in 1978. 9 Each year / *hula* schools
S V S

축제로 찾아온다 / 공연하기 위해 / 호놀룰루에서 / 이 축제는 또한 포함하고 있다 / 다른 하와이의 행사와
come to the festival / to perform / in Honolulu. 10 This festival also includes / other Hawaiian
V 부사적 용법(목적) S V

전시회를
activities and exhibits.

① Ways to perform the *hula*
'훌라'를 추는 방법들

② The diversity of Hawaiian culture
하와이 문화의 다양성

③ The uniqueness of Hawaiian dances
하와이 춤의 독특함

④ The importance of keeping traditions
전통을 지키는 것의 중요성

⑤ The origin of the Prince Lot Hula Festival
프린스 롯 훌라 축제의 기원

해석 한 눈에 보기 1 훌라는 흐르는 듯한 움직임과 얼굴 표정을 결합하여 특별한 노래와 음악에 맞춰진 하와이의 전통적인 춤이다. 2 '훌라'가 시작되었을 때, 그것은 예배의 형태였다. 3 Lot Kapúaiwa 왕자는 그것에의 관심이 점점 더 줄어드는 시점에 하와이에서 '훌라'를 살아있게 했다. 4 왕자는 그의 에너지와 강한 의지로 유명했다. 5 그의 관심 중 하나가 하와이 문화, 특히 '훌라'를 홍보하고 보존하는 것이었다. 6 그는 자신의 별장에서 '훌라' 공연들을 개최함으로써 그것을 했다. 7 많은 이들에게, '훌라'는 하와이인들의 세계관을 상징한다. 8 하와이 문화를 보존하려던 Lot 왕자의 노력에 감사하여, '프린스 롯 훌라 축제'가 1978년에 설립되었다. 9 해마다 '훌라' 학교들이 호놀룰루에서 공연하기 위해 이 축제에 찾아온다. 10 이 축제는 또한 다른 하와이 행사 및 전시회를 포함하고 있다.

정답단추 주제문이 뚜렷하게 드러나지 않는 글이므로 전체적인 내용을 봐야 해. 이 글은 하와이의 전통춤인 훌라를 지키기 위해 노력한 Lot 왕자와 그를 기념하기 위해 생긴 '프린스 롯 훌라 축제'의 유래에 관한 내용이야. 따라서 글의 주제는 ⑤가 가장 적절해.

오답단서 ①, ②, ③은 글에서 언급된 어구들을 사용해 만든 오답이야. Lot 왕자가 하와이의 전통을 지키려고 노력한 내용이 나와서 전통을 지키는 것의 중요성에 관한 글인 것 같지만, 글 전체 내용을 반영하지 않아서 ④는 답이 될 수 없어.

어휘확인

chant 노래; 구호 **combine** 결합하다 **flowing** 흐르는 듯한, 유려한 **movement** 움직임 **facial** 얼굴의 **expression** 표정 **form** 형태; 종류 **worship** 예배, 숭배 **alive** 살아 있는 **be noted for** ~로 유명하다 **will** 의지 **promote** 홍보하다 **preserve** 보존하다 **hold** 개최하다; 잡고 있다 **cottage** 별장, 작은 집 **represent** 나타내다 **view** –관(觀), 관점 **in appreciation of** ~에 감사하여 **establish** 설립하다 **perform** 공연하다 **include** 포함하다 **exhibit** 전시회

〈선택지 어휘〉

way 방법; 길 **diversity** 다양성 **uniqueness** 독특함 **importance** 중요성 **origin** 기원, 근원

지문 Flow

[도입]
전통 하와이 춤인 '훌라'는 특별한 노래와 음악에 맞춰 흐르는 듯한 움직임과 얼굴 표정을 결합시킴

⬇

[전개]
Lot Kapúaiwa 왕자가 하와이 문화, 특히 '훌라'를 홍보하고 보존시킴
→ 자신의 별장에서 '훌라' 공연을 개최함

&

[보충설명]
'훌라'는 하와이인의 세계관을 상징함

⬇

[결과]
1978년에 '훌라' 축제가 설립되었음

041 정답 ③

지문 All in One

과학과 과학기술의 세계에서 / 정확한 측정은 중요하다
1 In the worlds of science and technology, / precise measurement is critical / to success in
S V C

연구와 제품 개발의 성공에 / 비록 우리 대부분이 / 일상생활을 하는
research and product development. 2 Although most of us / in everyday life / don't perform
접속사 S' V'₁

실험을 하거나 첨단기술 제품을 설계하지 않을지라도 / 매우 많은 사람이 / 불필요한 정확성
experiments [or] design high-tech products, // a great many people / insist on using
V'₂ S V

사용을 고집한다 / 당신이 그들에게 시간을 물으면 / 그들은 '9시 59분'이라고 말할 것이다
unnecessary precision. 3 When you ask them for the time, // they'll say "9:59" / instead of
접속사 S' V' S V

'10시쯤' 대신에 / 그리고 그들은 당신에게 말할 것이다 / 그들이 자신들의 PC에 '15.1인치 화면'을 가지고 있다고
"about 10:00." 4 And they will tell you // (that) they have a "15.1-inch screen" on their PC /
S V IO 접속사 DO

어휘확인

technology 과학기술 **precise** 정확한 cf. **precision** 정확성 **measurement** 측정 **critical** 중대한; 비판적인 **success** 성공 **research** 연구 **product** 제품 **development** 개발 **although** 비록 ~일지라도 **perform** 행하다 **experiment** 실험 **high-tech** 첨단 기술의 **insist on** ~을 고집하다 **unnecessary** 불필요한 **precision** 정확성 **inch** 인치(길이 단위) **screen** 화면 **convince** 확신시키다 **variation** 차이 **crucial** 중대한, 결정적인 **scientific** 과학의 **investigation** 연구 **after all** 어쨌든; 결국에는 **sense** 느끼다

'15인치 화면' 대신에 / 이 사람들은 그들 스스로 확신해 왔다 / 작은 차이가 중요하다고

instead of a "15-inch screen." 5 These people have convinced themselves // that tiny variations
S V 접속사 S'

나는 이해한다 / 정확성이 중요하다는 것을 / 과학적 연구에서는 / 하지만 일상

are important. 6 I understand / that precision is crucial / in scientific investigations, // [but] it's
V' C' S_1 V_1 접속사 S' V' C' S_2 V_2

생활에서는 아니다 / 어쨌든 / 당신은 차이를 느끼지 못한다 / 9시 59분과 10시 사이의

not in everyday life. 7 After all, / you can't sense the difference / between 9:59 and 10:00.
S V

'근사치'는 대체로 충분하다

8 "Close" is usually good enough.
S V C

① 과학 실험에서는 정확한 측정이 중요하다. ② 현대 사회에서는 시간 개념이 정확해야 한다.
③ 일상생활에서는 정확성을 너무 따질 필요가 없다. ④ 전문용어와 일상용어는 구분해서 사용해야 한다.
⑤ 제품을 개발할 때는 항상 품질을 우선시해야 한다.

해석 한 눈에 보기 1 과학과 과학 기술의 세계에서, 정확한 측정은 연구와 제품 개발의 성공에 아주 중요하다. 2 비록 일상생활을 하는 우리 대부분이 실험을 하거나 첨단기술 제품을 설계하지 않을지라도, 매우 많은 사람이 불필요한 정확성 사용을 고집한다. 3 당신이 그들에게 시간을 물으면, 그들은 '10시쯤' 대신에 '9시 59분'이라고 말할 것이다. 4 그리고 그들은 당신에게 자신들의 PC에 '15인치 모니터' 대신에 '15.1인치 모니터'를 가지고 있다고 말할 것이다. 5 이런 사람들은 아주 작은 차이가 중요하다고 확신해 왔다. **주제문** 6 나는 정확성이 과학적 연구에서는 아주 중요하지만, 일상생활에서는 그렇지 않다고 생각한다. 7 어찌 되었건 간에, 당신은 9시 59분과 10시 사이의 차이를 느끼지 못한다. 8 '근사치'는 대체로 충분히 족하다.

정답단추 글의 요지는 전체적인 맥락을 먼저 살펴봐야 해. 첫 문장만 보고 섣불리 답을 고르면 안 되지. 이 글은 과학적 연구에서는 정확성이 절대적으로 중요하지만, 일상생활에서는 근사치로도 충분하다는 내용이야. 따라서 가장 적절한 글의 요지는 ③이야.

오답단서 ②, ⑤는 본문에 사용된 어구로 만든 오답이고, ④는 본문과 전혀 관계없는 내용이야. 그리고 첫 번째 문장만 읽고 ①을 답으로 선택하지 않도록 주의해야 해.

지문 Flow

[도입]
과학에서 정확한 측정은 연구와 제품 개발의 성공에 중요함

⬇

[비판]
많은 사람들이 일상생활에서도 불필요한 정확성 사용을 고집함

⬇

[예시]
'10시쯤' 대신에 '9시 59분'이라고 말하거나 '15인치 모니터' 대신에 '15.1인치 모니터'를 가지고 있다고 말함

⬇

[주제도출]
정확성이 과학적 연구에서는 중요하지만, 일상생활에서는 그렇지 않음

042 정답 ③

지문 All in One

날마다 / 뉴스 프로그램은 보도한다 / 여론 조사 결과를 / 비록 여론 조사가 주로

1 Day after day, / news programs report / the results of opinion polls. 2 Although the polls
S V 접속사 S'

정치적 장면과 관계가 있을지라도 / 그것은 때때로 다룬다 / 사회 및 경제적인 문제도

usually / have to do with the political scene, // they sometimes cover / social or economic
V' S V

많은 사람들이 듣는다 / 관심을 갖고 / 여론 조사 결과를 / 그들은 매료된다

issues. 3 Lots of people listen / with interest / to poll results. 4 They are fascinated // that the
S V S V 접속사

그 결과들이 보도되는 점에 / 아주 정확하게 / 그래서 그들은 믿는 경향이 있다

results are reported / with extraordinary precision. 5 And they tend to believe // that *the*
S' V' S V 접속사

결과들을 보도하는 권위자가 / 객관적이고 아는 것이 많다고 / 사실

authority figure [reporting the results] / is objective and knowledgeable. 6 In fact, / the reality
S' V' C' S

현실은 종종 많이 다르다 / 따라서 / 당신이 들을 때 / 여론 조사 결과를 / 당신은 그것을

is often much different. 7 So, / when you hear / the result of an opinion poll, // you should
V C 접속사 S' V' S V

곧이곧대로 믿어서는 안 된다 / 질문을 작성하는 사람들이 / 선입견이 있을 지도 모르고 / 혹은 표본

take it with a grain of salt. 8 *The people* [writing the questions] / might be biased, // [or] the
S_1 V_1

인구가 반영하지 않을지도 모른다 / 인구 전체를 / 더욱이

sample population might not reflect / the population as a whole. 9 Furthermore, / polls are
S_2 V_2 S

여론 조사는 흔히 사용된다 / 뉴스 단체들에 의해 / 단순히 필러로 / 시청자의 관심을 끌기 위한 어떤 것인

frequently used / by news organizations / simply as filler / — *something* [to grab the viewers'
V

질에 상관없이 / 이런 점들과 다른 잠재적인 문제점들이 / 여론 조사를 믿을

interest], / regardless of quality. 10 These and other potential problems / make polls
S V O

수 없게 만든다

unreliable.
C

① 여론 조사의 정확성을 높이자. ② 여론 조사를 공정하게 시행하자.
③ 여론 조사 결과를 과신하지 말자. ④ 여론 조사에 대한 사람들의 관심도를 높이자.
⑤ 여론 조사에 대한 사람들의 불신을 해소하자.

해석 한 눈에 보기 1 날마다, 뉴스 프로그램은 여론 조사 결과를 보도한다. 2 비록 여론 조사가 주로 정치적 장면과 관계가 있을지라도, 그것은 때로는 사회 및 경제적인 문제도 다룬다. 3 많은 사람이 관심을 갖고 여론 조사 결과를 듣는다. 4 그들은 그 결과들이 아주 정확하게 보도되는 점에 매료된다. 5 그래서 그들은 그 결과들을 보도하는 권위자

어휘확인

day after day 날마다 **report** 보도하다, 알리다 **result** 결과 **opinion poll** 여론 조사(= poll) **although** 비록 ~이긴 하지만 **have to do with** ~와 관계가 있다 **political** 정치와 관련된 **scene** 장면, 현장 **cover** 다루다 **social** 사회의 **economic** 경제의 **issue** 문제, 주제 **fascinated** 매료된 **extraordinary** 아주 대단한 **precision** 정확성 **tend to-v** ~하는 경향이 있다 **authority figure** 권위자 **objective** 객관적인 **knowledgeable** 아는 것이 많은 **in fact** 사실은 **reality** 현실 **take it with a grain of salt** 곧이곧대로 믿지 않다 **biased** 선입견이 있는 **sample** 표본 **population** 인구 **reflect** 반영하다 **as a whole** 전체로서 **furthermore** 더욱이 **frequently** 자주, 흔히 **organization** 단체, 기구 **simply** 단순히, 그저 **filler** (중요하지는 않으며 시간이나 공간을) 채우기 위한 것 **grab** (사로)잡다 **viewer** 시청자 **regardless of** ~에 상관없이 **quality** 질(質) **potential** 잠재적인 **unreliable** 믿을 수 없는

지문 Flow

[통념]
뉴스가 보도하는 여론 조사 결과에 많은 사람들이 관심을 가짐

⬇

[보충설명]
사람들은 결과를 보도하는 권위자가 객관적이고 아는 것이 많다고 믿음

⬇

가 객관적이고 아는 것이 많다고 믿는 경향이 있다. **주제문** 6 사실, 현실은 종종 많이 다르다. 7 따라서 당신이 여론 조사 결과를 들을 때, 그것을 있는 그대로 받아들여서는 안 된다. 8 질문을 작성하는 사람들이 선입견을 가졌을지도 모르고, 혹은 표본 인구가 인구 전체를 반영하지 않을지도 모른다. 9 더욱이, 여론 조사는 흔히 뉴스 단체들에 의해 질에 상관없이 시청자의 관심을 끌기 위한 어떤 것인 필러로 단순히 사용된다. 10 이런 점들과 기타 잠재적인 문제점들이 여론 조사를 믿을 수 없게 만든다.

정답단추　뉴스를 통해 접하는 여론 조사 결과가 맞는 것 같지만 현실은 다르다는 내용으로 여론 조사 결과를 곧이곧대로 믿어서는 안 된다는 필자의 주장이 나타나 있어. take it with a grain of salt의 의미를 모르더라도 바로 앞 문장의 '현실은 많이 다르다'는 문장을 통해 주제문 앞의 내용과 반대되는 내용일 것으로 추론할 수 있어. 또한, 마지막 문장을 통해서도 ③이 정답임을 알 수 있어.

오답단서　①, ②, ④, ⑤ 모두 '여론 조사'라는 핵심어와 본문에 사용된 어구들로 연상될 수 있는 것들이지만 본문의 내용과는 거리가 멀어.

[역접 + 주제문]
여론 조사 결과를 있는 그대로 받아들이지 말아야 함

↓

[이유]
- 질문 작성자의 선입견
- 표본 인구의 부정확성
- 관심 끌기용 필러로 사용
- 다른 잠재적 문제점들

043　정답 ③

지문 All in One

1 Today, / college students tend to identify college education / with preparing them for their jobs / and for contributing to their growth / in working as part of a team, / communicating effectively, / and applying knowledge. 2 A college education, / however, / has value / beyond delivering job skills. 3 College students enroll // because they want to develop / as whole people. 4 Whichever majors they choose, // they also participate in / athletics, leadership programs, student government, and service work. 5 Most of them also want / much more than a job / after school. 6 Whether they are studying / to become *therapists* [who heal injuries], / or *digital communications majors* [who improve online experiences], // students pursue a degree // because they want to live fulfilling, well-rounded lives / and make the world a better place. 7 Colleges and universities have / *the resources, the expertise,* and *the structures* in place / to provide a more satisfying and fulfilling full-course meal / of a college degree.

① 대학 교육의 목적은 시대의 요구에 따라야 한다.
② 대학은 직업 준비 프로그램의 다양화에 힘써야 한다.
③ 대학 교육의 가치는 직업 생활 준비 그 이상에 있다.
④ 대학 교육의 초점은 사회생활 준비에 맞춰져야 한다.
⑤ 전인 교육은 대학이 아니라 개인의 노력에 달려 있다.

해석 한 눈에 보기　1 오늘날, 대학생들은 대학 교육을 자신들의 직업을 준비하고 팀의 일원으로 일하고 효과적으로 의사소통하며 지식을 적용하는 데 있어 자신의 성장에 도움이 되는 것으로 인지하는 경향이 있다. **주제문** 2 하지만, 대학 교육은 직업 기술을 전달하는 것 이상의 가치가 있다. 3 대학생들은 전인적 인간으로 발전하기를 원하기 때문에 입학한다. 4 그들이 어떤 전공을 선택하던 간에, 그들은 또한 운동 경기, 리더십 프로그램, 학생 정부, 그리고 봉사 활동에 참여한다. 5 그들 중 대부분은 또한 학교를 졸업한 후에 일자리보다 훨씬 더 많은 것을 원한다. 6 그들이 부상을 치료하는 치료사 또는 온라인 경험을 향상시키는 디지털 커뮤니케이션 전공자가 되기 위해 공부를 하고 있든 간에, 학생들은 성취감을 주고 균형 잡힌 삶을 살고 세상을 더 나은 곳으로 만들고 싶기 때문에 학위를 딴다. 7 대학은 대학 학위에 대한 더 만족스럽고 성취감을 주는 풀코스 식사를 제공하기 위해 마련된 자원, 전문 기술, 그리고 조직 체계를 갖추고 있다.

정답단추　글의 서두에서 대학 교육이 직업 준비 과정으로만 여겨지는 경향이 있다고 하고 있어. 그러나 A college education, ~ skills.의 문장에서 대학 교육이 직업 준비 그 이상의 가치가 있다는 글쓴이의 견해가 드러나 있고, 그에 대한 보충설명이 이어지고 있지. 따라서 이 글의 요지로 적절한 것은 ③이야.

오답단서　①, ②, ④는 대학 교육이라는 같은 소재를 다룬 선택지들이지만, 핵심 내용과는 관련이 없어. 특히, ②와 ④는 대학 교육이 직업 준비를 위한 교육이라는 초반부 내용과 관련 있으므로 오답임을 알 수 있지. ⑤의 전인 교육은 글에 나오지 않는 내용이야.

어휘확인

tend to-v ~하는 경향이 있다 **identify** 인지하다 **education** 교육 **prepare** 준비하다 **contribute to** ~에 도움이 되다, ~에 기여하다 **growth** 성장 **communicate** 의사소통하다 **effectively** 효과적으로 **apply** 적용하다 **knowledge** 지식 **value** 가치 **beyond** ~은 넘어서, ~ 이상 **deliver** 전달하다 **enroll** 입학하다 **whichever** 어느 것이든지 **major** 전공; 주요한 **participate in** ~에 참여하다 **athletic** 운동 경기 **leadership** 지도(력) **government** 정부 **therapist** 치료사 **heal** 치료하다 **injury** 부상 **improve** 향상시키다 **online** 온라인의 **pursue** 추구하다, 수행하다 **degree** 학위 **fulfilling** 성취감을 주는 **well-rounded** 균형 잡힌 **university** 대학 **resource** 자원 **expertise** 전문 지식[기술] **in place** ~을 위한 준비가 되어 있는 **provide** 제공하다 **satisfying** 만족한

지문 Flow

[통념]
대학생들은 대학 교육을 직업을 준비하는 과정으로 생각함

↓

[역접 + 주제문]
대학 교육은 직업 기술 전달 이상의 가치가 있음

↓

[이유]
대학생들이 전인적인 인간이 되기를 원하기 때문

↓

[보충설명]
- 대학생들은 성취감을 주고 균형 잡힌 삶을 살며, 더 나은 세상을 만들고 싶어서 학위를 땀
- 대학은 이를 위한 자원, 기술, 조직 체계를 갖추고 있음

유형편

Chapter 2

유형 05 빈칸 추론

Check-Up 1 ② 044 ⑤
Check-Up 2 ② 045 ④
Check-Up 3 ① 046 ①
Check-Up 4 047 ④
Check-Up 5 1 ① 2 ① 048 ⑤
Mini Test 1 ① 2 ② 3 ②
실전적용독해 049 ③ 050 ⑤ 051 ① 052 ② 053 ③ 054 ④

Check-Up 1

정답 ②
해석 결론적으로 ______은[는] 당신이 당신 삶의 스트레스를 줄이는 데 도움을 줄 것이다.

044 정답 ⑤

지문 All in One

1 A strong memory(S) depends on(V) (강한 기억력은 달려 있다) / the health and vitality of your brain. (당신의 뇌의 건강과 활력에) 2 Whether(접속사) you(S′)'re(V′) *a student*(C′1) [studying for final exams], (당신이 기말 시험을 위해 공부하는 학생이든) / or *a working professional*(C′2) [interested in doing *all* [you can (do)] (또는 할 수 있는 모든 것을 하는 데 관심이 있는 전문직 종사자이든) / to stay mentally sharp](부사적 용법(목적)) (정신적으로 예리함을 유지하기 위해), // you(S) can improve(V) your memory and mental performance. (당신은 기억력과 정신적 수행력을 향상시킬 수 있다)

3 Indeed, (실제로) / the human brain(S) has(V) (인간의 뇌는 가지고 있다) / *an astonishing ability* [to adapt and change] (적응하고 변화할 수 있는 놀라운 능력을) / — even in old age. (심지어 노년기에도) 4 This ability(S) is known(V) (이 능력은 알려져 있다) / as neuro plasticity. (신경 가소성으로) 5 With the right stimulation, (적절한 자극으로) / your brain(S) can form(V1) new neural pathways, (뇌는 새로운 신경 연결 통로를 형성할 수 있다) / alter(V2) existing connections, (기존의 연결을 변경할) / and adapt and react(V3) (그리고 적응하고 반응할) / in ever-changing ways. (변화무쌍한 방식으로) 6 *This incredible ability* of the brain [to **reshape itself**](S) (스스로를 개조하는 뇌의 이 놀라운 능력은) / is(V) very important(C) (매우 중요하다) // when(접속사) it(S′) comes(V′) to learning and memory. (학습과 기억에 관한 한) 7 You(S) can take advantage of(V) the natural power of neuro plasticity (당신은 신경 가소성의 자연적 힘을 이용할 수 있다) / to increase your mental abilities,(부사적 용법(목적)) (당신의 정신 능력을 증진시키기 위해) / (to) enhance *your ability* [to learn new information](부사적 용법(목적)), (새로운 정보를 학습할 능력을 향상시키기 위해) / and (to) improve your memory.(부사적 용법(목적)) (기억력을 향상시키기 위해)

① store information
정보를 저장하다
② cut irrelevant connections
관련 없는 연결을 끊다
③ return to its original state
그것의 원래 상태로 되돌아가다
④ deceive itself
스스로를 속이다
⑤ reshape itself
스스로를 개조하다

어휘확인

depend on ~에 의존하다 vitality 활력 professional 전문직 종사자 mentally 정신적으로 cf. mental 정신적인 sharp 예리한, 날카로운 improve 개선하다, 향상시키다 memory 기억(력) performance 수행(력), 성과 indeed 정말로, 실로 astonishing 깜짝 놀랄 만한, 놀라운 ability 능력 adapt 적응하다 be known as ~로 알려지다 neuro plasticity 신경 가소성 stimulation 자극 form 형성하다 neural pathway 신경 연결 통로 alter 변경하다 existing 기존의 connection 연결 react 반응하다 ever-changing 변화무쌍한, 늘 변화하는 incredible 놀라운, 믿을 수 없는 reshape 개조하다, 모양을 고치다 take advantage of ~을 이용하다 natural 자연적인 increase 증진시키다 enhance 향상시키다
〈선택지 어휘〉
store 저장하다 irrelevant 관련 없는 original 원래의 state 상태 deceive 속이다

지문 Flow

[도입]
기억력은 뇌의 건강에 달려 있음

⬇

[주제문]
우리는 기억력과 정신적인 수행을 향상시킬 수 있음

⬇

해석 한 눈에 보기 1 강한 기억력은 당신의 뇌의 건강과 활력에 달려 있다. 주제문 2 당신이 기말 시험을 위해 공부하는 학생이든, 정신적으로 예리함을 유지하기 위해 할 수 있는 모든 것을 하는 데 관심이 있는 전문직 종사자이든, 당신은 기억력과 정신적인 수행을 향상시킬 수 있다. 단서 3 실제로, 인간의 뇌는 심지어 노년기에도 적응하고 변화할 수 있는 놀라운 능력을 가지고 있다. 4 이 능력은 신경 가소성으로 알려져 있다. 5 적절한 자극으로, 뇌는 새로운 신경 연결 통로를 형성하고, 기존의 연결을 변경하고, 변화무쌍한 방식으로 적응하고 반응할 수 있다. 6 학습과 기억에 관한 한, 스스로를 개조하는 뇌의 이 놀라운 능력은 매우 중요하다. 주제문 7 당신은 정신 능력을 증진시키고, 새로운 정보를 학습할 능력을 향상시키며, 기억력을 향상시키기 위해 신경 가소성의 자연적 힘을 이용할 수 있다.

정답단추 빈칸이 포함된 문장부터 읽으면, 빈칸은 뇌의 놀라운 능력을 서술한 부분임을 알 수 있어. 그리고, This라는 대명사가 있으므로 빈칸 문장 앞에 그 능력이 이미 서술되었다는 것도 파악할 수 있지. 따라서 뇌의 놀라운 능력이 '무엇'인지에 대해 빈칸 문장 앞부분에 중점을 두고 읽으면 돼. 〈단서〉 문장에 그러한 능력이 잘 드러나 있는데, 이를 다른 말로 표현하면 빈칸에 가장 적절한 것은 ⑤야.

오답단서 ①은 뇌의 기본적인 기능이지만, 본문에는 언급되지 않으므로 오답이야. ②는 새로운 신경 연결 통로를 형성하고 기존 연결을 변경한다는 내용은 나오지만, 연결을 끊는다는 내용은 없어서 답이 될 수 없지. 그리고 ③과 ④는 본문에 나오지 않는 내용이므로 답이 될 수 없어.

[보충설명]
이는 인간의 뇌가 적응하고 변화할 수 있는 능력, 즉 신경가소성을 가지고 있기 때문임

[주제반복]
정신 능력 증진, 학습 능력 향상, 기억력 향상을 위해 신경 가소성의 힘을 이용할 수 있음

Check-Up 2

정답 ②

해석 (A) 만약 당신이 바퀴벌레를 무서워한다면, 바퀴벌레 사진을 응시하기 시작하고 당신에게 바퀴벌레를 보여주는 영화를 보는 것은 좋은 생각이다. (B) 그런 다음에, 당신은 죽은 바퀴벌레들을 바닥에서 쓸어내 볼 수 있고, 그러면 결국에 가서는 실제로 그것들을 밟아버리거나 죽이기 전에 먼저 한두 마리의 기어 다니는 바퀴벌레를 바라볼 수 있을 것이다. → 당신이 만일 당신을 무섭게 만드는 것에 당신 자신을 점차적으로 덜 예민하게 만든다면 공포증을 효과적으로 극복할 수 있다. ① 당신의 무서운 경험을 당신의 친구들과 공유한다 ② 당신을 무섭게 만드는 것에 당신 자신을 점차적으로 덜 예민하게 만든다

045 정답 ④

지문 All in One

1 We are sometimes assigned group work / in the course of our lives. (우리는 때때로 우리의 공동 작업을 할당받는다 / 인생 행로에서) [We: S, are ... assigned: V]
2 Many people agree // that the biggest problem with group work / lies in / not always having the option of choosing your own group. (많은 사람들은 동의한다 / 공동 작업의 가장 큰 문제점이 / ~에 있다 / 항상 당신 자신의 그룹을 고르는 데 선택권이 없다는 것에) [Many people: S, agree: V, that: 접속사, the biggest problem with group work: S', lies in: V']
3 However, / if you do get this choice, // there are some important considerations [(which) you should take into account / to ensure (that) you get the most out of your group task]. (하지만 / 이 선택을 정말 하면 / 감안해야 할 몇 가지 중요한 고려 사항이 있다 / 당신은 공동 업무를 최대한으로 활용하는지 보증하기 위해서) [if: 접속사, you: S'₁, do: 강조, get: V'₁, are: V, some important considerations: S, (which): 관계대명사, to ensure: 부사적 용법(목적), (that): 접속사, you: S'₂, get: V'₂]
4 What makes group work worthwhile / is members' **diversity**. (공동 작업을 가치 있게 만드는 것은 / 구성원들의 다양성이다) [What makes group work worthwhile: S, is: V, members' diversity: C]
5 In order to ensure that your group task is rewarding, / it is important to choose *members* [that have *something* different from you [to bring to the project]]. (당신의 공동 업무가 반드시 보람 있도록 하기 위해 / 구성원을 선택하는 것이 중요하다 / 당신과 다른 점이 있는 / 프로젝트를 이끌) [In order to: 부사적 용법(목적), that: 접속사, your group task: S', is: V', it: 가주어, is: V, important: C, to choose members: 진주어, that: 관계대명사]
6 This can be done / in terms of gender, culture, [or] even *the amount of research* [or] *work experience* [(that) a member may have]. (이것은 행해질 수 있다 / 성별, 문화, 또는 심지어 구성원이 가지고 있을지도 모르는 연구나 업무 경험의 측면에서) [This: S, can be done: V, (that): 관계대명사]
7 Ensuring (that) your group has a number of different perspectives [and] ways of thinking / will add / to the wealth of *ideas* [created for your task]. (당신의 그룹이 많은 다른 시각과 사고방식을 가지고 있는지 보증하는 것이 / 더해질 것이다 / 당신의 업무를 위해 창조된 풍부한 아이디어에) [(that): 접속사, Ensuring ... ways of thinking: S, will add: V]

① loyalty 충성심
② cooperation 협력
③ trust 믿음
④ diversity 다양성
⑤ enthusiasm 열정

해석 한 눈에 보기 1 우리는 때때로 우리의 인생 행로에서 공동 작업을 할당받는다. 2 많은 사람들은 공동 작업의 가장 큰 문제점이 항상 당신 자신의 그룹을 고르는 데 선택권이 없다는 것에 있음에 동의한다. 3 하지만, 이 선택을 정말 한다면, 당신은 공동 업무를 최대한으로 활용하는지 보증하기 위해서 감안해야 할 몇 가지 중요한 고려 사항이 있다. 주제문 4 공동 작업을 가치 있게 만드는 것은 구성원들의 다양성이다. 단서 5 당신의 공동 업무가 반드시 보람 있도록 하기 위해, 프로젝트를 이끌 당신과 다른 점이 있는 구성원을 선택하는 것이 중요하다. 6 이것은 성별, 문화, 또는 심지어 구성원이 가지고 있을지도 모르는 연구나 업무 경험의 양 측면에서 행해질 수 있다. 단서 7 당신의 그룹이 많은 다양한 시각과 사고방식을 가지고 있는지 보증하는 것이 당신의 업무를 위해 창조된 풍부한 아이디어에 더해질 것이다.

정답단추 빈칸을 포함한 문장을 먼저 읽고, 무엇에 중점을 두어야 하는지 파악한 다음에 그 단서에 초점을 맞추어 글

어휘확인
assign 맡기다, 배정하다 option 선택권 consideration 고려 사항 take ~ into account ~을 감안하다, ~을 고려하다 ensure 보증하다, 보장하다 get the most out of ~을 최대한으로 활용하다 worthwhile 가치 있는 diversity 다양성 rewarding 보람 있는 in terms of ~의 측면에서 gender 성별, 성 amount 양 research 연구 a number of 많은 perspective 관점, 시각 the wealth of 풍부한
〈선택지 어휘〉
loyalty 충성심 cooperation 협력 enthusiasm 열정

지문 Flow

[도입]
공동 작업을 할 자신의 그룹을 고르는 선택권이 있다면 중요한 고려 사항이 있음

[주제문]
공동 작업 시 구성원들의 다양성이 중요함

[보충설명]
공동 작업을 이끌 당신과 다른 점(성별, 문화, 연구나 업무 경험 등의 측면)이 있는 구성원을 선택해야 함

을 읽으면 돼. 빈칸을 포함한 문장에서 공동 작업을 가치 있게 만드는 것이 구성원들의 '무엇'이라고 했어. '무엇'의 단서는 빈칸 문장 바로 다음 문장의 공동 업무를 위해 자신과 다른 점이 있는 구성원을 선택하는 것이 중요하다는 내용, 그리고 글의 마지막 문장의 그룹이 다양한 시각과 사고방식을 가질수록 업무 아이디어에 보탬이 된다는 내용에서 찾을 수 있지. 이를 통해 공동 작업을 가치 있게 만드는 것은 구성원들의 '다양성'으로 표현할 수 있어. 따라서 가장 적절한 것은 ④야.

오답단서 ①, ②, ③, ⑤는 모두 공동 작업으로 연상될 수 있는 단어들이야. 하지만 이 글은 구성원들을 다양하게 해야 한다는 내용이 주를 이루므로, 나머지 선택지들은 주제에서 벗어난 어휘들임을 알 수 있어.

Check-Up 3

정답 ①

해석 다시 말해, 협력하는 것은 더 나은 결과를 만들어 낸다. ← 연구에 의하면 거의 90%의 경우에 있어 협력하는 환경에 있는 사람들이 경쟁적인 환경에 있는 사람들을 능가한다고 한다. ① 협력하는 ② 독립적인

046 정답 ①

지문 All in One

길들여진 동물들은 ~이다 / 인간들과 함께 사는 것들 / 한 때 / 그들은 모두 야생
1 Domesticated animals are / *those* [that live with humans]. 2 At one point, / they were all
동물이었다 / 하지만 그것은 더 이상 사실이 아니다 / 수천 년에 걸쳐 / 길들여진 동물들은
wild animals, // but that is no longer the case. 3 Over thousands of years, / domestic animals
뚜렷한 변화를 겪어 왔다 / 더 작아지는 것과 같은 / 친척인 종의 야생 동물과 비교해서
have undergone distinct changes, / like becoming smaller / compared to wild animals of
그러나 / 가장 주목할 만한 변화는 ~이다 / 그들이 되어 왔다는 것
related species. 4 However, / the most remarkable transformation is // that they have come /
인간에게 의존하도록 / 생존을 위해 / 예를 들어 / 늑대들은 안다 / 서식처를 찾고 먹이를 사냥하는 방법을
to rely on humans / for survival. 5 For example, / wolves know / how to find shelter and
그리고 차이를 구분할 수 있다 / 적과 동지 사이의 / 개는 늑대와
hunt for food, // and can tell the difference / between enemies and friends. 6 The dog is
관계가 있다(친척이다) / 하지만 길들여진 것(개)의 생존 기술은 / 사라져 버렸다 / 그것은 기대한다
related to the wolf, // but the domesticated one's **survival skill** / has disappeared. 7 It expects
인간이 그것의 필요 모두를 제공해 줄 것을 / 그것은 좋은 삶을 살 수 없다 / 인간의 도움 없이는 / 많든
/ humans to provide all of its needs. 8 It can't live a good life / without human help. 9 To a
적든 어느 정도는(다소 정도의 차이는 있지만) 마찬가지이다 / 고양이와 농장 동물들에서도
greater or lesser degree, / the same is true / for cats and farm animals.

① survival skill
생존 능력
② hunting instinct
사냥 본능
③ physical strength
체력
④ ability to multiply
번식 능력
⑤ dependence on nature
자연에의 의존

해석 한 눈에 보기 1 길들여진 동물(가축)은 인간들과 함께 사는 것들이다. 2 한때 그것들은 모두 야생 동물이었지만, 더 이상은 그렇지 않다. 3 수천 년에 걸쳐, 가축은 친척뻘인 야생 동물과 비교해서 더 작아지는 것과 같은 뚜렷한 변화를 겪어 왔다. 주제문 4 그러나 가장 주목할 만한 변화는 그것들이 생존을 위해 인간에게 의존하게 되었다는 것이다. 5 예를 들어, 늑대는 서식처를 찾고 먹이를 사냥하는 방법을 알고 있고, 적과 동지 간의 차이를 구분할 수 있다. 6 개는 늑대와 친척 간이지만, 길들여진 개의 생존 능력은 사라져 버렸다. 7 그것은 인간이 그것의 필요 모두를 제공해 줄 것을 기대한다. 8 그것은 인간의 도움 없이는 좋은 삶을 살 수 없다. 9 다소 정도의 차이는 있지만, 고양이와 농장 동물들에서도 마찬가지이다.

정답단추 빈칸이 포함된 문장에서, 개는 늑대와 친척 간이지만 '무엇'이 사라졌다고 하고 있어. 빈칸 문장은 바로 앞 문장인 For example로 시작하는 예시 문장에 이어지는 것이므로, 주제문을 찾아서 빈칸을 알 수 있어. 여기서 주제문은 For example 바로 앞 문장인데, 길들여진 동물이 야생 동물과 비교해서 가장 큰 변화는 생존을 인간에게 의존하게 되었다는 내용이야. 야생 동물인 늑대는 서식지 탐색, 먹이 사냥, 적과 동지의 구분을 할 수 있는데, 길들여진 개는 생존을 인간에게 의존하다 보니 이러한 survival skill(생존 능력)이 사라져 버린 것이지. 따라서 정답은 ①이야.

오답단서 ②는 지문에 나온 hunt for food를 이용해 만든 오답이자 세부적인 내용이라 빈칸에 들어갈 말로는 적절하지 않아. 그리고 ③, ④, ⑤는 글의 내용과는 무관해서 답이 될 수 없어.

어휘확인

domesticated 길들여진(= domestic) **point** 때, 시점; 요점 **no longer** 더 이상 ~ 아닌 **case** 사실; 경우 **undergo** 겪다 **distinct** 뚜렷한 **compared to** ~와 비교해서 **related** 친척의; 관련된 **species** 종(생물 분류의 기초 단위) **remarkable** 주목할 만한 **transformation** 변화 **rely on** ~에 의존하다 **survival** 생존 **shelter** 서식처; 주거지 **tell the difference** 차이를 구분하다 **enemy** 적 **be related to** ~와 관계가 있다 **disappear** 사라지다 **expect** 기대하다 **provide** 제공하다 **to a degree** 어느 정도로 **true** 적용되는, 해당하는; 사실인

〈선택지 어휘〉

instinct 본능 **physical** 신체의 **ability** 능력 **multiply** 번식하다 **dependence** 의존

지문 Flow

[도입]
인간과 함께 사는 길들여진 동물은 한때 야생 동물이었지만 뚜렷한 변화를 겪음

⬇

[주제문]
가장 주목할 변화는 길들여진 동물이 생존을 위해 인간에게 의존하게 됨

⬇

[예시1]
늑대는 서식처를 찾고 먹이 사냥의 방법을 알지만, 친척 간인 개의 생존 능력은 인간이 필요한 것을 제공함으로써 사라짐

&

[예시2]
고양이와 농장 동물들도 이와 유사함

Check-Up 4

047 정답 ④

지문 All in One

[1] Some people miss out / on lots of fun, mind-expanding activities / because of the "always do your best" mentality. [2] You don't need to be / one of them. [3] Adjust your perception. [4] Realize / that it's okay / to be an (A) unexceptional pianist // if playing the piano makes you feel good. [5] And it's okay / to be an average golfer // if you like to play golf. [6] And it's okay / to be a mediocre artist // if you enjoy painting. [7] If there's *something* [(that) you enjoy], // just do it / and forget "their" standards. [8] If you like doing it, // concern with how well you do it / and with the evaluations of others / should be (B) irrelevant.

(문장 해석 주석: 어떤 사람들은 놓친다 / 많은 재미있고 생각을 확장하는(생각의 폭을 넓혀 주는) 활동들을 / '항상 최선을 다하라'는 사고방식 때문에 / 당신은 될 필요가 없다 / 그들 중 한 명이 / 당신의 인식을 조정해라 / 깨달아라 / 괜찮다는 것을 / 평범한 피아니스트가 되는 것도 / 만일 피아노를 연주하는 것이 당신을 기분 좋게 만든다면 / 그리고 괜찮다 / 보통의 골퍼가 되는 것도 / 만일 당신이 골프 치는 것을 좋아한다면 / 그리고 괜찮다 / 보통 밖에 안 되는 화가가 되는 것도 / 만일 당신이 그림 그리는 것을 즐긴다면 / 만약 당신이 즐기는 무언가가 있다면 / 그냥 그것을 하고 / '그들의' 기준을 잊어버려라 / 만일 당신이 그것을 하는 것을 좋아한다면 / 그것을 당신이 얼마나 잘하는지에 대한 걱정은 / 그리고 다른 사람들의 평가에 대한 (걱정은) / 상관없어야 한다)

(문장 성분 표시: S, V, 접속사, 가주어, C′, 진주어, S″, V″, O″, C″, S′, V′, 관계대명사, V_1, V_2, 간접의문문, C)

	(A)		(B)
①	exceptional 특출한	······	important 중요해야
②	exceptional 특출한	······	trivial 사소해야
③	excellent 뛰어난	······	unnecessary 불필요해야
④	unexceptional 평범한	······	irrelevant 상관없어야
⑤	unexceptional 평범한	······	essential 필수적이어야

해석 한 눈에 보기 1 어떤 사람들은 '항상 최선을 다하라'라는 사고방식 때문에 많은 재미있고 생각의 폭을 넓혀 주는 활동들을 놓친다. 주제문 2 당신은 그들 중 한 명이 될 필요가 없다. 3 당신의 인식을 조정해라. 4 만일 피아노 연주가 당신을 기분 좋게 만든다면 (A) 평범한 피아니스트가 되는 것도 괜찮다는 것을 깨달아라. 5 그리고 만일 당신이 골프 치는 것을 좋아한다면 보통의 골퍼가 되는 것도 괜찮다. 6 그리고 만일 당신이 그림 그리는 것을 즐긴다면 보통 밖에 안 되는 화가가 되는 것도 괜찮다. 주제문 7 만약 당신이 즐기는 무언가가 있다면, 그냥 그것을 하고 '그들의' 기준을 잊어버려라. 8 만일 당신이 그것을 하는 것을 좋아한다면, 당신이 그것을 얼마나 잘하는지와 다른 사람들의 평가에 대한 걱정은 (B) 상관없어야 한다.

정답단추 두 개의 빈칸이 있는 유형으로 각기 다른 세부사항에 하나씩 제시되고 있어. 우선 빈칸 (A) 뒤는 좋아한다면 평범한 골퍼와 그저 그런 화가가 되는 것도 괜찮다는 내용이야. 그래서 빈칸 (A)에는 '평범한(unexceptional)' 피아니스트가 되는 것도 괜찮다는 내용이 적절해. 또한, 빈칸 (B)의 앞에서는 다른 사람의 기준(항상 최선을 다하라)은 잊고 자신이 좋아하는 것을 그냥 하라는 내용이 나오고 있지? 그래서 (B)를 포함한 문장에서는 자신이 얼마나 잘하는지와 다른 사람의 평가는 '상관없는(irrelevant)' 것이라는 내용이 오는 것이 자연스러워. 따라서 가장 적절한 답은 ④라고 할 수 있어.

오답단서 ①, ②, ③의 빈칸 (A) 어휘 exceptional과 excellent는 모두 unexceptional(평범한)과 반대 의미를 지니고 있어. 또한, ①, ⑤의 빈칸 (B) 어휘인 important와 essential이 빈칸에 오게 되면 글 내용과는 정반대의 의미를 나타내기 때문에 적절하지 않아.

어휘확인

miss out ~을 놓치다 **expand** 확장하다 **because of** ~ 때문에 **do one's best** 최선을 다하다 **mentality** 사고방식 **adjust** 조정[조절]하다 **perception** 인식, 인지; 지각 **realize** 깨닫다 **unexceptional** 평범한 **average** 평균의, 보통의 **mediocre** 보통밖에 안 되는 **standard** 기준 **concern** 걱정, 우려 **well** 잘, 훌륭하게 **evaluation** 평가 **irrelevant** 상관없는, 무관한

〈선택지 어휘〉

exceptional 특출한 **trivial** 사소한 **unnecessary** 불필요한 **essential** 필수적인

지문 Flow

[도입]
'최선을 다하라'는 사고방식이 재미있고 생각의 폭을 넓혀 주는 활동을 놓치게 함

⬇

[주제문]
그러한 인식을 조정해야 함

⬇

[보충설명]
평범한 피아니스트, 보통의 골퍼, 그저 그런 화가가 되는 것도 좋아하는 일이라면 괜찮음

⬇

[주제 재진술]
당신이 즐기는 것을 그냥 하라. (그것을 얼마나 잘하느냐와 다른 사람들의 평가는 상관없다.)

Check-Up 5

정답 1 ① 2 ①

해석 [1-2] (A) 운동은 당신의 신체적, 정신적 건강 둘 다를 향상시키는 가장 쉬운 방법들 중 하나이다. (B) 약간의 규칙적인 운동은 당신을 하루 종일 보다 더 에너지가 넘치게 느끼도록 해주고, 밤에 더 잘 자게 해주고, 보다 더 예리한 기억력을 갖게 해주고, 당신 자신과 당신의 삶에 대해 보다 느긋하고 긍정적으로 느끼게 해 줄 수 있다.

048 정답 ⑤

지문 All in One

[1] Organisms of different species / can interact / in many ways. [2] They can compete, // or they can be *long-term partners* [helping each other survive]. [3] They can also form / one of the

(문장 해석 주석: 서로 다른 종의 생물체는 / 상호 작용할 수 있다 / 여러 방식으로 / 그들은 경쟁할 수 있다 / 혹은 서로 생존을 도와주는 그들은 장기적인 파트너가 될 수 있다 / 그들은 또한 형성할 수 있다)

(문장 성분 표시: S, V, S_1, V_1, S_2, V_2, C_2, S, V)

어휘확인

organism 생물체, 유기체 **species** 종(種) **interact** 상호 작용하다 **compete** 경쟁하다 **long-term** 장기적인 **survive** 생존하다 **form** 형성하다 **link** 고리 **food chain** 먹이사슬 **ecology** 생태계; 생태학 **a series of** 일련의 **nutrient** 영양소, 영양분 **flow** 흐르다

먹이 사슬의 고리들 중 하나를 / 즉 / 그들 중 하나가 / 다른 하나를 먹을 수 있다 / 생태계에서

links in a food chain. [4] (A) That is, / one of them / can eat the other. [5] In ecology, / a food chain is a series of *organisms* [that eat one another / so that energy and nutrients flow / from one to the next]. [6] (B) For example, / if you had a hamburger / for lunch, // you might be *part of a food chain* [that flows like this: grass → cow → human]. [7] What if you had lettuce / on your hamburger? [8] In that case, / you're also *part of a food chain* [that goes like this: lettuce → human].

먹이 사슬은 서로를 먹는 일련의 유기체들이다 / 에너지와 영양소가 흐르도록 / 하나에서 그 다음으로 / 예를 들어 / 당신이 햄버거를 먹었다면 / 점심으로 / 당신은 '풀 → 암소 → 인간', 이와 같이 흐르는 먹이 사슬의 일부가 될지도 모른다 / 당신이 양상추를 먹었다면 어떻게 될까 / 햄버거에 더해 / 그런 경우에 / 당신은 또한 먹이 사슬의 일부가 된다 / '양상추 → 인간', 이와 같이 진행되는

	(A)		(B)		(A)		(B)
①	However	……	In short	②	Fortunately	……	For example
③	However	……	Similarly	④	That is	……	On the other hand
⑤	That is	……	For example				

해석 한 눈에 보기 주제문 1 서로 다른 종의 생물체는 여러 방식으로 상호 작용할 수 있다. 2 그들은 경쟁할 수 있고, 혹은 서로 생존을 도와주는 장기적인 파트너가 될 수 있다. 3 그들은 또한 먹이 사슬의 고리들 중 하나를 형성할 수 있다. 4 (A) 즉, 그들 중 하나가 다른 하나를 먹을 수 있다. 5 생태계에서, 먹이 사슬은 에너지와 영양소가 하나에서 그 다음으로 흐르도록 서로를 먹는 일련의 유기체들이다. 6 (B) 예를 들어, 당신이 점심으로 햄버거를 먹었다면, 당신은 '풀→암소→인간', 이와 같이 흐르는 먹이 사슬의 일부가 될지도 모른다. 7 당신이 햄버거에 더해 양상추를 먹었다면 어떨게 될까? 8 그런 경우에, 당신은 또한 '양상추→인간', 이와 같이 진행되는 먹이 사슬의 일부가 된다.

정답단추 적절한 연결어를 찾기 위해서 빈칸 앞뒤 문장의 논리적 관계를 주의 깊게 살펴봐야 해. 빈칸 (A)의 앞에는 서로 다른 종의 생물체가 먹이 사슬을 형성할 수 있다는 내용이 나오고, 뒤에는 그것을 구체적으로 풀어 다시 설명하는 내용이 나와. 따라서 (A)에는 환언을 나타내는 연결어 That is가 적절해. 빈칸 (B)의 앞에는 생태계 먹이 사슬에서 에너지와 영양소의 이동에 대한 설명을 하고 있고, 뒤에는 그것의 예로 사람이 햄버거를 먹었을 때의 먹이 사슬에 대해 언급하고 있어. 따라서 (B)에는 예시를 나타내는 연결어 For example이 적절해. 이를 종합하면, 정답은 ⑤야.

lettuce 양상추, 상추

지문 Flow

[주제문]
서로 다른 종의 생물체는 여러 상호 작용을 함

⬇

[보충설명]
• 경쟁
• 생존을 돕는 파트너
• 먹이 사슬의 고리 형성: 에너지와 영양소가 흐르도록 하나가 다른 하나를 먹음

⬇

[예시1]
햄버거를 먹었다면, '풀→암소→인간'으로 흐르는 먹이 사슬의 일부가 됨

&

[예시2]
양상추를 먹었다면, '양상추→인간'으로 흐르는 먹이 사슬의 일부가 됨

기출총정리

Mini Test 1 ① 2 ② 3 ②

Mini Test 해석 및 해설

1 **해석** 실패는 능력의 부족 또는 동기유발의 부족 때문일지도 모른다. **반면에** 성공은 높은 수준의 능력과 함께 작용하는 높은 수준의 동기유발을 필요로 한다.
해설 빈칸 전후의 내용이 서로 대조를 이루고 있으므로 역접을 나타내는 연결어가 적절하다.

2 **해석** 누군가가 차를 타고 어딘가로 운전해 가는 시간 대부분에, 자동차 충돌과 같은 사고는 일어나지 않는다. 그러나 안전하기 위해서, 운전자와 탑승자는 항상 자신의 안전벨트를 매야 한다. **마찬가지로** 당신이 실험을 하든지 그냥 관찰만 하든지 간에, 당신은 실험실에서 항상 보호 장비를 착용하고 사용해야 한다.
해설 빈칸 앞은 안전을 위해 안전벨트를 매야 한다는 것이고, 빈칸 뒤는 실험실에서는 실험을 하든지 관찰만 하든지 간에 보호 장비를 착용해야 한다는 것으로, 서로 유사한 내용이 이어지고 있다.

3 **해석** 부모의 신체적 접촉이 그들의 사랑을 십 대에게 전달하는가? 답은 그렇기도 하고 아니기도 하다. 그 모든 것은 언제, 어디서, 어떻게 하느냐에 달려 있다. **예를 들어**, 포옹은 만일 그것이 십 대가 그의 친구들과 함께 있을 때 이루어진다면 당혹스러울지도 모른다. 그것은 십 대가 부모를 밀쳐내거나 "하지 마세요"라고 말하게 할지도 모른다.
해설 빈칸 뒤의 내용은 빈칸 앞의 질문에 대한 부정 답변의 구체적인 예이다.

실전적용독해

049 정답 ③

지문 All in One

당신이 카페에 가면 / 커피가 훌륭한 / 그리고 분위기와 직원이 친근하고 매력적인 / 당신은 다시 갈 것인가 / 대부분의 사람들에게 / 대답은 '그렇다'일 것이다 / 바로 이런 이유 때문이다 / 카페들이 거의 모든 곳에서 번성해온 것은 / 하지만

[1] If you were to go into *a café* [where the coffee is great, / and the atmosphere and staff are friendly and inviting], // would you go back? [2] For most people, / the answer would be yes. [3] It is precisely for this reason / that cafés have prospered almost everywhere. [4] However, /

어휘확인

atmosphere 분위기 **staff** 직원 **inviting** 매력적인, 마음을 끄는 **precisely** 바로, 정확하게 **prosper** 번성하다 **nowadays** 요즘에는 **provide** 제공하다 **lover** 애호가 **in peace** 편안히 **laptop** 노트북 컴퓨터 **paradox** 역설 **simultaneously** 동시에 **after all** 결국에는, 어쨌든 **surround** 둘러

카페 문화에서 가장 좋은 것은 / 요즘 / 당신이 사회적이 될 필요가 없다는 것이다 / 카페에서

the best thing about café culture / nowadays / is that you do not have to be social / in a café.

5 종종 / 카페는 공유된 공공의 공간을 제공한다 / 커피 애호가들이 편안히 그들의 음료를 즐기거나

Often, / cafés provide *shared public spaces* [where coffee lovers can enjoy their drink in

독서를 하거나 / 또는 노트북 컴퓨터를 가져와서 일을 할 수 있는 / 신경 쓰지 않고 / 다른

peace, / do some reading, / or bring their laptop and do some work / without caring / what

사람들이 그들을 어떻게 생각하는지 / ~가 있다 / 그러므로 / 역설이 / 혼자 있는 동안

others think of them]. 6 There is, / therefore, / a paradox / that while being alone, / you are

당신은 동시에 사회적이라는 / 어쨌든 / 당신은 사람들에 둘러싸인 카페에 있다

simultaneously being social. 7 After all, / you are in *a café* [surrounded with people], /

혼자라는 금기를 사회적으로 받아들일 수 있게 만들면서

making the taboo of being alone socially acceptable.

분사구문(= and this makes ~)

① accidentally 우연히 ② fortunately 운 좋게 ③ simultaneously 동시에

④ intentionally 고의적으로 ⑤ accordingly 그에 맞게

해석 한 눈에 보기 1 커피가 훌륭하고 분위기와 직원이 친근하고 매력적인 카페에 가면, 당신은 다시 갈 것인가? 2 대부분의 사람들에게, 대답은 '그렇다'일 것이다. 3 카페들이 거의 모든 곳에서 번성해온 것은 바로 이런 이유 때문이다. 4 하지만, 요즘 카페 문화에서 가장 좋은 것은 당신이 카페에서 사회적이 될 필요가 없다는 것이다. 5 종종, 카페는 커피 애호가들이 편안히 자신의 음료를 즐기거나, 독서를 하거나, 노트북 컴퓨터를 가져와서 다른 사람들이 그들을 어떻게 생각하는지 신경 쓰지 않고 일을 할 수 있는 공유된 공공의 공간을 제공한다. 주제문 6 그러므로 혼자 있으면서 당신은 동시에 사회적이라는 역설이 있다. 7 어쨌든, 당신은 사람들에 둘러싸인 카페에 있으면서, 혼자라는 금기를 사회적으로 받아들일 수 있게 만든다.

정답단추 빈칸이 있는 문장에 연결어 therefore가 있어. 따라서 빈칸이 있는 문장이 결론을 말하는 문장임을 알 수 있지. 우선 빈칸 문장의 앞뒤 글의 흐름을 살펴보자. 앞에서는 카페에서 사회적이 될 필요가 없다고 하면서, 카페에서 혼자 할 수 있는 일들에 대해 말하고 있어. 또한 뒤에서는 결정적으로 사람이 둘러싸인 카페에서 혼자 있는 것이 받아들여진다는 내용이 나오고 있어. 그러므로 빈칸이 있는 문장은 혼자 있으면서 '동시에' 사회적이 된다는 내용이 되어야 자연스러워. 따라서 빈칸에 들어갈 말로 가장 적절한 것은 ③이야.

오답단서 ①, ②, ④는 내용과는 어울리지 않는 부사들이야. ⑤는 앞의 내용에 대한 결과가 이어질 때 쓸 수 있는 부사이므로 역시 적절하지 않아.

싸다 **taboo** 금기 **acceptable** 받아들일 수 있는

〈선택지 어휘〉

accidentally 우연히 **fortunately** 운 좋게 **intentionally** 고의적으로 **accordingly** 그에 맞게

지문 Flow

[도입]
요즘 카페 문화에서는 사람들이 사회적이 될 필요가 없음

[보충 설명]
카페는 다른 사람들을 신경 쓰지 않고 일을 할 수 있는 공유된 공공의 공간을 제공함

[주제문]
카페는 혼자 있는 동시에 사회적, 즉 사람들에게 둘러 싸여 있는 역설적 공간임

050 정답 ⑤

지문 All in One

흰 코끼리는 극도로 희귀하다 / 그리고 신성하다고 오랫동안 여겨져 왔다

1 White elephants are extremely rare // and have long been regarded as divine / in South-

동남아시아에서 / 비록 그들이 종종 순백색으로 묘사될지라도 / 그들의 피부는 대체로 부드러운

East Asia. 2 Although they are often depicted as pure white, // their skin is usually *a soft*

불그스름한 갈색이다 / 연한 분홍색으로 변하는 / 젖었을 때 / 흰 코끼리를 유지하기 위해서

reddish-brown [that turns light pink / when (it is) wet]. 3 To keep a white elephant, / one

사람은 많은 돈을 써야만 한다 / 그것에게 특별한 음식을 먹이기 위해 / 그리고 접대하기 위해 / 그것에게 기도하러 오는 많은 순례자들을

must spend a lot of money / to feed it special food / and to serve / *the many pilgrims* [who

오래 전에 / 왕이 기쁨을 얻지 못하면(만족하지 않으면) / 궁정 관리에게

come to pray to it]. 4 Long ago, / if a king was not pleased / with a palace official, // he gave

그는 그 관리에게 흰 코끼리를 주었다 / 아무도 선물을 거절할 수 없었다 / 왕이 주는 / 하지만 코끼리는 쓸모가

the official a white elephant. 5 Nobody could refuse a gift / from the king. 6 But an elephant

없었다 / 관리에게 / 그리고 그것을 돌보는 비용은 / 재정적인 파산을 초래했다

was of no use / for the official // and the cost of caring for it / caused financial ruin. 7 This is

이것은 현대의 관용구인 '흰 코끼리'의 유래인데 / 이것은 쓸모없고 값비싼 짐을 의미한다

the origin of the modern idiom, "*white elephant*," // which means **a useless and expensive**

burden.

관계대명사 (계속적 용법)

① a useful and beautiful gift 유용하고 아름다운 선물 ② a symbol of one's wealth 사람의 부의 상징

③ a symbol of disliking someone 누군가를 싫어한다는 표시 ④ a very large object in a museum 박물관에 있는 매우 큰 물건

어휘확인

extremely 극도로 **rare** 희귀한 **regard A as B** A를 B로 여기다 **divine** 신성한 **South-East Asia** 동남아시아 **although** 비록 ~일지라도 **depict** 묘사하다 **reddish** 불그스름한 **pilgrim** 순례자 **pray** 기도하다 **please** 기쁘게 하다 **official** 관리[공무원] **refuse** 거절하다 **be of no use** 쓸모없다 **cost** 비용 **care for** ~을 돌보다 **financial** 재정의 **ruin** 파산 **origin** 유래, 기원, 근원 **modern** 현대의 **idiom** 관용구, 숙어 **useless** 쓸모없는 **burden** 짐

〈선택지 어휘〉

wealth 부(富), 재산 **dislike** 싫어하다 **object** 물건, 물체

지문 Flow

[도입]
동남아시아에서 신성하게 여겨지는 흰 코끼리는 기르는 데 많은 돈이 듦

[보충설명]
오래 전에, 왕이 궁정 관리에게 만족하지 않으면 선물로 흰 코끼리를 주었는데, 쓸모없는 흰 코끼리를 돌보다가 재정적 파산을 초래함

⑤ a useless and expensive burden
쓸모없고 값비싼 짐

해석 한 눈에 보기 1 흰 코끼리는 매우 희귀하여 동남아시아에서는 오랫동안 신성하다고 여겨졌다. 2 비록 그것들이 종종 순백색으로 묘사될지라도, 그것들의 피부는 대체로 젖으면 연한 분홍색으로 변하는 부드러운 불그스름한 갈색이다. 3 흰 코끼리를 기르기 위해서, 사람은 그것에게 특별한 음식을 먹이고 그것에게 기도하러 오는 많은 순례자를 접대하기 위해 많은 돈을 써야 한다. 4 오래 전에, 왕이 궁정 관리에게 만족하지 않으면, 그는 그 관리에게 흰 코끼리를 주었다. 5 아무도 왕이 주는 선물을 거절할 수 없었다. 6 하지만 코끼리는 관리에게 쓸모가 전혀 없었고 그것을 돌보는 비용은 재정적 파산을 초래했다. 7 이것은 오늘날의 관용어인 '흰 코끼리'의 유래인데, 이것은 쓸모없고 값비싼 짐을 의미한다.

정답단추 빈칸 추론 문제는 빈칸을 포함한 문장을 먼저 읽는 게 좋아. 이 글의 빈칸 문장을 보면 'white elephant'란 관용어가 '무엇'을 의미하는지 찾아야 함을 알 수 있어. 그다음으로 빈칸을 추론할 수 있는 단서를 찾아 압축하면 돼. 이 글의 빈칸 문장 앞 내용은 '왕이 맘에 안 드는 관리에게 흰 코끼리를 선물로 줄 수 있는데, 이는 거부할 수 없을 뿐 아니라 기르는 데는 엄청난 돈이 들어 결국 파산하게 된다'고 하고 있어. 이를 통해 'white elephant'는 '쓸모없고 비싸기만 한 짐'임을 알 수 있어. 따라서 빈칸에 들어갈 말로 ⑤가 가장 적절해.

오답단서 ①, ②, ④는 이 글의 내용과 무관한 어구라서 답이 될 수 없어. ③은 '왕이 만족하지 않는 관리에게 흰 코끼리를 준다'는 내용에서 유추할 수 있지만, 이는 세부 내용이라서 정답이 될 수 없어.

[결과]
'흰 코끼리'는 오늘날 관용어로서 쓸모없고 값비싼 짐을 의미함

051 정답 ①

지문 All in One

만약 시간 부족에 대한 걱정이 / 시간이 매우 귀중하다는 생각에서 생겨난다면
1 If worries about lack of time / stem from the sense [that time is highly valuable], // then *one*
접속사 S′ V′ 접속사 S′ V′

이런 압박감을 줄이기 위해 우리가 할 수 있는 최선의 것 중 하나는 / 우리의 시간을 거저 주는 것일지도
of the best things [(that) we can do to reduce this sense of pressure] / may be to give our time
관계대명사 S V

모른다 / 사실 / 새로운 연구는 시사한다 / 다른 사람들을 돕기 위한 시간을 거저 주는 것은 / 실제로 시간적
away. 2 Indeed, / new research suggests // that giving *time* away [to help others] / can actually
S V 접속사 S′ V

압박감을 완화시켜 줄 수 있다고 / 어떤 회사들은 그들의 직원들에게 제공하는데
alleviate feelings of time pressure. 3 Some companies provide their employees / with
S V

다른 사람들을 도울 그들의 시간을 내는 기회를 / 이것은 어쩌면 시간 스트레스와 피로감을 줄여 줄지도
opportunities [to volunteer their time to help others], / potentially reducing feelings of time
분사구문(= and they potentially reduce ~)

모를 / 그리고 구글은 직원들에게 장려한다 / 그들 시간의 20%를 쓰도록
stress and burnout. 4 And Google has encouraged employees / to use 20 percent of their
S V

그들 자신의 개인적인 프로젝트에 / 비록 이 프로젝트 중 몇몇은 이익을 가져왔을지라도
time / on their own personal projects. 5 Although some of these projects have resulted in
접속사 S′ V′

이 자유 시간을 제공하는 가장 큰 이득은 / 직원들의 생각을 줄이는 데에 있을지도 모른다
profit, // the greatest benefit of giving this free time / might lie in reducing employees' sense /
S V

그들의 시간이 부족하다는
[that **their time is scarce.**]
접속사 S′ V′ C′

① their time is scarce
그들의 시간이 부족하다

② they are so stressed
그들이 너무 스트레스를 받고 있다

③ they have to help others
그들이 다른 사람들을 도와야 한다

④ they are wasting their time
그들이 그들의 시간을 낭비하고 있다

⑤ they are not given free time
그들에게 자유 시간이 주어지지 않는다

해석 한 눈에 보기 주제문 1 만약 시간 부족에 대한 걱정이 시간이 매우 귀중하다는 생각에서 생겨난다면, 이런 압박감을 줄이기 위해 우리가 할 수 있는 최선의 것 중 하나는 우리의 시간을 거저 주는 것일지도 모른다. 2 사실 새로운 연구에 따르면 다른 사람들을 돕기 위해 시간을 거저 주는 것은 실제로 시간적 압박감을 완화시켜 줄 수 있다고 한다. 3 어떤 회사들은 그들의 직원들에게 시간을 내서 다른 사람들을 도울 기회를 제공하는데, 이것은 어쩌면 시간 스트레스와 피로감을 줄여줄지도 모른다. 4 그리고 구글은 직원들에게 그들 시간의 20%를 그들 자신의 개인적인 프로젝트에 쓰도록 장려한다. 5 비록 이 프로젝트 중 몇몇은 이익을 가져왔을지라도, 이 자유 시간을 제공하는 가장 큰 이득은 그들의 시간이 부족하다는 직원들의 생각을 줄이는 데에 있을지도 모른다.

정답단추 빈칸을 포함한 문장을 먼저 읽어 보자. 직원들의 '어떤' 생각을 줄이는 것이 가장 큰 이득이 있는지를 찾아야 해. 앞선 직원들에게 개인의 프로젝트에 시간의 20%를 투자하고 장려한 구글의 예시를 통해 직원들에게 시간 압박감을 줄여주고자 함을 알 수 있어. 따라서 '시간이 부족하다'는 직원들의 생각을 줄여준다는 내용이 와야 문맥이 자연스러워. 그러므로 정답은 ①이야.

오답단서 ②, ③은 글에서 언급된 어구를 사용한 선택지이만, 글 전체 내용과는 무관해서 답이 될 수 없어. 또한, ④는 시간에 대한 내용이지만, 글의 내용과는 반대되고 있으므로 오답이야. ⑤ 역시 그들에게 다른 사람들을 도울 자유 시간이 주어졌으므로, 사실과는 다른 내용이야.

어휘확인

lack 부족, 결핍 **stem from** ~에서 생겨나다 **sense** 생각, 의식 **highly** 매우, 대단히 **valuable** 귀중한, 소중한 **pressure** 압박감, 압력 **give away** 기부하다[선물로 주다] **indeed** 사실, 실(제)로 **research** 연구 **suggest** 시사[암시]하다 **alleviate** 완화하다 **provide** 제공하다, 주다 **employee** 직원, 고용인 **opportunity** 기회 **volunteer** 자진하여 하다, 지원하다 **potentially** 어쩌면, 가능성이 있게 **burnout** 극도의 피로(감) **encourage** 장려[권장]하다 **personal** 개인적인 **although** 비록, 그러나 **result in** (결과적으로) ~을 낳다[야기하다] **profit** 이익, 수익 **benefit** 이득, 혜택 **lie** (생각·특질·문제 등이)있다, 발견되다; 눕다 **scarce** 부족한, 드문

〈선택지 어휘〉

stressed 스트레스를 받는[느끼는]

지문 Flow

[주제문]
시간이 부족하다는 압박감을 줄이는 방법은 우리의 시간을 거저 주는 것임

[보충설명]
- 연구에 따르면 실제로 시간적 압박감을 완화시켜 줌
- 어떤 회사에서는 다른 사람들을 도울 시간을 제공하여 스트레스와 피로감을 줄여줌
- 구글은 시간의 20%를 개인 프로젝트에 쓰도록 직원들에게 장려하는데, 이는 시간이 부족하다는 직원들의 생각을 줄여 줌

052 정답 ②

지문 All in One

형용사에 대한 훌륭한 점은 / 당신이 반의어를 암기할 필요가 없다는 것이다
1 The great thing about adjectives / is that you don't need to memorize the antonyms. 2 *All*
S / V 접속사 / C / S

당신이 필요한 것은 / 부정 불변화사(예를 들어 not)이다 / 형용사에 적용할 수 있는
[(that) you need] / is *a negative particle* (e.g. not) [that you can apply to an adjective / in
관계대명사 / V / C / 관계대명사

대화에서 / 예를 들어 / 당신은 '저 남자는 살찌지 않았다'라고 말할 수 있다 / '저 남자는 비쩍 말랐다' 대신에
conversation]. 3 (A) For example, / you can say "That man is not fat" / instead of "That man is
S V

두 말이 정확히 똑같지는 않더라도 / 당신은 반의어를 알게 될 것이다 / 시간이
skinny," // though the two do not sound exactly alike. 4 You'll pick up the antonyms / over
접속사 S' V' C' / S V

지나면서 / 당신이 배움에 따라 / 점점 더 많은 단어들을 / 마찬가지로 / 당신은 암기할 필요가 없다
time // as you learn / more and more words. 5 (B) Likewise, / you don't need to memorize /
접속사 S' V' / S V

수천 개의 명사를 / 만약 당신이 모른다면 / '세탁기'라는 단어를 / 예를 들어
thousands of nouns. 6 If you don't know / the word for "washing machine" / for example, //
접속사 S' V'

당신은 말할 수 있다 / '내 옷을 세탁하는 물건'이라고 / 'thing'은 알고 있기에 매우 유용한 단어이다
you could say / "*the thing* [(which) I wash my clothes in]." 7 "Thing" is *a very handy word* [to
S V / 관계대명사 / S V C

스스로를 무장시켜라 / 충분한 기본 언어로 / 그러면 당신은 더 이상 애쓸 필요가 없을 것이다
know]. 8 Arm yourself / with enough basic language // and you'll no longer need to struggle
V_1 「명령문, and ~」: …해라, 그러면 할 것이다 / S_2 V_2

가장 적절한 단어를 찾으려고 / 당신이 말하고 싶은 것에 대한
/ to find the best word / for what you want to say.
부사적 용법(목적) / 관계대명사

	(A)		(B)
①	However	……	Likewise
②	For example	……	Likewise
③	That is	……	However
④	In other words	……	On the other hand
⑤	Indeed	……	On the other hand

해석 한 눈에 보기 1 형용사에 대한 훌륭한 점은 당신이 반의어를 암기할 필요가 없다는 것이다. 2 당신이 필요한 것은 대화에서 형용사에 적용할 수 있는 부정 불변화사(예를 들어 not)이다. 3 (A) 예를 들어, 두 말이 정확히 똑같지는 않더라도, '저 남자는 비쩍 말랐다' 대신에 '저 남자는 살찌지 않았다'라고 말할 수 있다. 4 점점 더 많은 단어들을 배움에 따라, 당신은 시간이 지나면서 반의어를 알게 될 것이다. 5 (B) 마찬가지로, 당신은 수천 개의 명사를 암기할 필요가 없다. 6 예를 들어, '세탁기'라는 단어를 모른다면, '내 옷을 세탁하는 물건'이라고 말할 수 있다. 7 'thing'은 알고 있기에 매우 유용한 단어이다. **주제문** 8 충분한 기본 언어로 스스로를 무장시켜라, 그러면 당신은 말하고 싶은 것에 대한 가장 적절한 단어를 찾으려 더 이상 애쓸 필요가 없을 것이다.

정답단추 빈칸 앞뒤 문장의 관계를 파악하면 적절한 연결어를 찾을 수 있어. 빈칸 (A) 앞에는 형용사의 반의어를 암기하는 대신에 부정어 not을 이용할 수 있다는 내용이 나오고, 뒤에는 그것에 대해 문장을 예로 들어 말하고 있어. 따라서 빈칸 (A)에는 예시를 나타내는 연결어 For example이 적절해. 빈칸 (B) 앞에는 형용사를 많이 알게 되면 반의어도 덩달아 많이 알게 된다는 내용이 나오고, 빈칸 뒤에서도 기본 언어를 사용해서 명사를 설명하면 되므로 수많은 명사를 암기할 필요가 없다는 내용이야. 따라서 빈칸 (B)에는 유사 내용을 추가해서 설명하는 연결어 Likewise가 적절해. 이를 종합하면 정답은 ②야.

어휘확인

adjective 형용사 **memorize** 암기하다 **antonym** 반의어 **negative** 부정적인 **particle** 불변화사 (관사, 전치사, 접속사 등 어형 변화가 없는 것) **e.g.** 예를 들면 **apply** 적용하다 **conversation** 대화 **instead of ~** 대신에 **skinny** 비쩍 마른 **exactly** 정확히 **pick up** (정보를) 알게 되다 **over time** 시간이 지나면서 **noun** 명사 **washing machine** 세탁기 **handy** 유용한, 편리한 **arm** 무장하다 **basic** 기본의 **struggle** 애쓰다, 노력하다

지문 Flow

[사실1]
형용사의 장점은 반의어를 외울 필요가 없고, not 같은 불변화사를 적용하면 됨
• 예시: 말랐다 ≒ 살찌지 않았다

⬇

[사실2]
명사는 암기할 필요가 없음
• 예시: 세탁기 = 내 옷을 세탁하는 물건

⬇

[주제문]
기본 언어를 알면, 가장 적절한 단어를 찾으려고 애쓰지 않아도 됨

053 정답 ③

지문 All in One

셰르파 사람들은 / 대략 15만 명이 있는데 / 주로 산악 지역에서 산다
1 *The Sherpa people*, / [of whom there are approximately 150,000], // mainly live in the
S / 전치사+관계대명사 / V

네팔 동쪽의 / 타고난 등산가들인 / 그들은 더 높은 고도에 산다
mountainous regions / of eastern Nepal. 2 Natural born mountaineers, / they live at higher
= S V

다른 어떤 사람들보다 / 유럽인들과의 접촉에 앞서 / 그들은 야크를 모는 목동이자
altitudes / than any other humans. 3 Prior to contact with Europeans, / they were yak herders
S V C

상인이었다 / 히말라야 산맥에서 / 그러나 / 서양 탐험가들의 도래는
and traders / in the Himalayas. 4 (A) However, / the arrival of western explorers / changed
S V

셰르파의 생활 방식을 영원히 바꿨다 / 초기 영국 원정에서 / 셰르파는 대단한 칭찬을 받았다
the Sherpa lifestyle forever. 5 On early British expeditions, / the Sherpas earned high praise /
S V

그들의 산악 기술에 대해 / 그들은 헌신적이었고, 정직했고, 진심 어렸고 강인했다
for their mountain skills. 6 They were dedicated, honest, sincere, and strong. 7 (B) As a
S V C

어휘확인

Sherpa 셰르파(히말라야에 사는 부족, 등반가들을 위한 안내나 짐 운반 등의 일을 자주 함) **approximately** 대략, 거의 **mainly** 주로 **mountainous** 산악의 **region** 지역, 지방 **eastern** 동쪽에 위치한 **natural born** 타고난 **mountaineer** 등산가 **altitude** (해발) 고도 **prior to A** A에 앞서 **yak herders** 야크(티베트산 들소)를 모는 목동 **trader** 상인 **Himalayas** 히말라야 산맥 **arrival** 도래 **western** 서양의 **explorer** 탐험가 **lifestyle** 생활 방식 **British** 영국의 **expedition** 원정 **earn** 받다[얻다] **dedicated** 헌신적인 **sincere** 진심 어린 **essential** 필수적인 **standard of living** 생활수준 **basis** 기초 **economy** 경제

결과적으로 그들은 모든 히말라야 원정에서 필수적인 부분이 되었다 가이드와 파트너로서의 그들의
result, / they became an essential part of all Himalayan expeditions. 8 Their work as guides
S V C S

일은 산악 원정에서 그들의 생활수준을 향상시켰다 그리고 그들 경제의
and partners / on mountain expeditions / improved their standard of living // and became
V_1 V_2

기초가 되었다 히말라야 원정은 이제 ~이다 셰르파 문화의 가장 중요한 부분
the basis of their economy. 9 Himalayan expeditions are now / the most important part of
C_2 S V C

Sherpa culture.

	(A)		(B)
①	In fact	……	Instead
②	That is	……	However
③	However	……	As a result
④	Otherwise	……	For example
⑤	For example	……	Therefore

해석 한 눈에 보기 1 셰르파 사람들은 대략 15만 명이 있는데, 주로 네팔 동쪽의 산악 지역에 산다. 2 타고난 등산가인 그들은 다른 어떤 사람들보다 더 높은 고도에 산다. 3 유럽인들과의 접촉에 앞서, 그들은 히말라야 산맥의 야크를 모는 목동이자 상인이었다. 4 (A) 그러나 서양 탐험가들의 도래는 셰르파의 생활양식을 영원히 바꿨다. 5 초기 영국 원정에서, 셰르파는 그들의 산악 기술에 대해 대단한 칭찬을 받았다. 6 그들은 헌신적이었고, 정직했고, 진심 어렸고, 강인했다. 7 (B) 결과적으로, 그들은 모든 히말라야 원정에서 필수적인 일부분이 되었다. 8 산악 원정에서 가이드와 파트너로서의 그들의 일은 그들의 생활수준을 향상시켰고 그들 경제의 기초가 되었다. 9 히말라야 원정은 이제 셰르파 문화의 가장 중요한 부분이다.

정답단추 연결어는 문장과 문장을 긴밀하게 이어주는 역할을 하니까 빈칸 앞뒤 문장의 관계를 살펴보면 돼. 빈칸 (A)의 앞은 셰르파가 유럽인과 접촉하기 전의 삶에 대한 내용이고 뒤는 서양인의 도래로 바뀐 삶에 대해 언급하고 있어. 즉, 앞뒤 내용이 역접 관계이므로 (A)에는 In fact, However 등이 적절해. 빈칸 (B)의 앞뒤는 셰르파족의 산악 기술과 훌륭함에 대해 언급한 다음 그들이 히말라야 원정의 필수 요소가 되었고 생활수준을 향상시켰다는 내용으로 서로 인과 관계임을 알 수 있지. 따라서 (B)에는 As a result, Therefore 등이 올 수 있어. 이를 종합하면 정답은 ③이야.

지문 Flow

[도입]
네팔 산악 지역에 사는 타고난 등산가, 셰르파 사람들

⬇

[보충설명]
히말라야 산맥의 야크를 모는 목동이자 상인이었음

⬇

[역접]
서양 탐험가들의 등장으로 셰르파의 산악 기술이 인정받음

⬇

[결과]
셰르파는 히말라야 산악 원정의 가이드와 파트너로서 일하게 되었고, 셰르파 문화의 가장 중요한 부분이 됨

054 정답 ④

지문 All in One

우리가 세상에서 보는 것은 현실의 객관적인 관점이 아니라 우리의 성향에 기반을 둔 현실의 관점(이다)
1 What we see in the world // is not an objective view of reality / but *a view of reality* [based
관계대명사 S V C_1 C_2

어떤 이들은 주장해왔다 성공적인 의사소통의 비결이
on our predispositions]. 2 Some have argued // that the key to successful communication / in
S V 접속사 S′

관계에서의 이 과정을 이용하는 것이라고 사물을 보는 사람을 찾아냄으로써
a relationship / is taking advantage of this process / by finding *someone* [who looks at things
V′ O′ 관계대명사

당신이 하는(보는) 것과 같은 방식으로 다시 말해 세계를 보는 사람을 찾아라
/ *the same way* [(as) you do]]. 3 (A) In other words, / find *someone* [who sees the world / *the*
V_1 관계대명사

당신이 하는(보는) 것과 같은 방식으로 그러면 당신은 찾을 것이다 관계를 보는 누군가를
same way [(as) you do]], // and you will find / *someone* [who will see a relationship / *the*
「명령문, and ~」 S_2 V_2 관계대명사

당신이 하는(보는) 것과 같은 방식으로 그 이론 뒤의 논리에도 불구하고 사실은
same way [(as) you do]]. 4 Despite the logic behind the theory, / in reality, / relationship
전치사 S

관계 성공은 달려 있지 않다 사물을 보는 것에 같은 방식으로 대신에 다른 사람의 관점에
success does not depend / on seeing things / the same way. 5 (B) Instead, / respect of the
V S

대한 존중이 훨씬 더 중요하다 그것에 대한 끊임없는 동의보다
other person's view / is far more important / than constant agreement with it.
V 비교급 강조 C

	(A)		(B)
①	As a result	……	On the other hand
②	In addition	……	Likewise
③	However	……	For example
④	In other words	……	Instead
⑤	Therefore	……	Moreover

해석 한 눈에 보기 1 우리가 세상에서 보는 것은 현실에 대한 객관적인 관점이 아니라 우리의 성향에 기반을 둔 현실에 대한 관점이다. 2 어떤 이들은 관계에서의 성공적인 의사소통의 비결이 당신이 보는 것과 같은 방식으로 사물을 보는 사람을 찾아냄으로써 이 과정을 이용하는 것이라고 주장해 왔다. 3 (A) 다시 말해, 당신이 보는 것과 같은 방식으로 세상을 보는 누군가를 찾아내면 당신은 당신이 보는 것과 같은 방식으로 관계를 보는 누군가를 찾게 될 것이다. 주제문 4 이 이론 뒤의 논리에도 불구하고, 사실, 관계의 성공은 사물을 같은 방식으로 보는 것에 달려 있지 않다. 5 (B) 대신에, 다른 사람의 관점에 대한 존중이 그것에 대한 끊임없는 동의보다 훨씬 더 중요하다.

정답단추 빈칸 (A) 뒤는 당신과 같은 관점으로 세상을 보는 사람을 찾으라는 내용이야. 이는 앞의 문장을 비슷한 말

어휘확인

objective 객관적인 view 관점; 견해 reality 현실 based on ~에 기반을 두다 predisposition 성향, 경향 argue 주장하다 key 비결; 열쇠 successful 성공적인 cf. success 성공 relationship 관계 take advantage of ~을 이용하다 despite ~에도 불구하고 logic 논리 theory 이론 in reality 사실은 depend on ~에 달려 있다 respect 존중, 존경 far 훨씬; 멀리 constant 끊임없는 agreement 동의

지문 Flow

[도입]
우리가 세상에서 보는 것은 우리의 성향에 기반을 둔 현실에 대한 관점이며, 관계의 성공 비결은 자신과 같은 방식으로 사물을 보는 사람을 찾아내는 것임

⬇

[재진술]
자신과 같은 방식으로 세상을 보는 사람을 찾아내면, 관계도 같은 방식으로 보는 사람을 찾게 되는 것임

⬇

[주제문]
사실, 관계의 성공은 사물을 같은 방식으로 보는 것과는 다름

⬇

로 한 번 더 설명하고 있어. 그래서 (A)에는 연결어 In other words가 적절해. 빈칸 (B) 앞에서는 사물을 보는 같은 관점이 관계 성공의 비결인 것은 아니라고 언급하고, 빈칸을 포함한 문장에서는 상대방의 관점을 존중하는 것이 더 중요하다며 앞의 내용을 반박하고 대안을 제시하고 있어. 따라서 (B)에는 Instead가 오는 것이 자연스러워. 이를 종합하면 정답은 ④임을 알 수 있어.

[보충설명]
다른 사람의 관점에 대한 존중이 동의보다 더 중요함

유형 06 함의 추론

Check-Up 1 ① **055** ②
실전적용독해 **056** ③ **057** ④ **058** ②

Check-Up 1

정답 ①

055

정답 ②

지문 All in One

사람들의 감정 상태는 완전히 바꾸어 놓을 수 있다 / 자신들의 생각, 결정, 그리고 상호작용을
1 People's emotional states can completely alter / their thinking, decisions, and interactions.
S V O

당신의 친구 Snooky가 ~에 설득될 수 있을지도 모른다 / 당신이 하는 주장에
2 Your friend Snooky may be convinced / by *an argument* [(which[that]) you are making] /
S_1 V_1 관계대명사

만약 그녀가 그날 마침 불안하다면 / 그러나 영향을 받지 않을 수도 있다 / 그녀가 마침 여유 있다면
if she happens to be anxious that day, // but unaffected / if she happens to be relaxed. 3 Under
접속사 S′ V′ C′ V_2 접속사 S′ V′ C′

여러 가지의 감정 상태에서 / 사람들은 처리할 준비가 되어 있다 / 특정한 자극을
different emotional states, / people are prepared to attend / to particular cues. 4 This principle
S V S

이러한 원리는 명심할 만큼 중요하다 / 이 원리는 설명한다 / 예를 들어 / 왜 공포 캠페인이 무의미할 수 있는지
is *important* to keep in mind. 5 It explains, / for example, / why fear campaigns can be useless
V C 부사적 용법 S V S′ V′ C'_1

특정한 시간과 장소에서는 / 그러나 다른 경우에는 효과적일 수 있는지를 / 따라서 만약 당신이 다른 사람들에게
/ in a certain time and place, / yet effective in another. 6 Thus if you attempt to give advice
C'_2 접속사 S′ V′ O′

효과적으로 조언하려고 시도한다면 / 계속해서 승리하는 선수 / 방금 끔찍한 진단을 받은 환자
effectively to others // — to *a player* [who keeps winning], *a patient* [who has just received an
관계대명사 관계대명사

또는 친구와 한창 싸움 중인 고객 / 당신은 먼저 Snooky를
awful diagnosis], or a client in the midst of fighting with friends — // you need to pull a
S V

끄집어낼 필요가 있다
Snooky first.

① reveal yourself to them immediately
그들에게 즉시 자신을 드러내다

② figure out what their feelings are now
그들의 감정이 지금 어떠한지 파악하다

③ obtain their personal information quickly
그들의 개인 정보를 빠르게 얻다

④ consider what Snooky has done for them
Snooky가 그들을 위해 무엇을 했는지 고려하다

⑤ think about them not emotionally but reasonably
감정적으로가 아니라 이성적으로 그들에 대해 생각하다

해석 한 눈에 보기 1 사람들의 감정 상태는 자신들의 생각, 결정, 그리고 상호작용을 완전히 바꾸어 놓을 수 있다. 단서 2 당신의 친구 Snooky가 만약 그날 마침 불안하다면, 그녀는 당신이 하는 주장에 설득될 수 있을지도 모르지만, 만약 그녀가 마침 여유 있다면 영향을 받지 않을 수도 있다. 3 여러 가지의 감정 상태에서, 사람들은 특정한 자극을 처리할 준비가 되어 있다. 4 이러한 원리는 명심할 만큼 중요하다. 5 예를 들어, 이 원리는 왜 공포 캠페인이 특정한 시간과 장소에서는 무의미할 수 있지만, 다른 경우에는 효과적일 수 있는지를 설명한다. 주제문 6 따라서 만약 당신이 계속해서 승리하는 선수, 방금 끔찍한 진단을 받은 환자, 또는 친구와 한창 싸움 중인 고객과 같은 사람들에게 효과적으로 조언하려고 시도한다면, 당신은 먼저 Snooky를 끄집어낼 필요가 있다.

정답단추 밑줄 친 어구에 등장하는 Snooky의 함축적 의미를 우선 파악해야 해. 초반의 예시에서 가상의 친구 Snooky가 등장하는데, 불안한 상태이면 상대방의 주장에 설득될 수 있고, 여유로움을 느끼면 상대방의 주장에 영향을 받지 않는다고 했어. 이를 근거로 밑줄 포함 문장에서 조언을 시도하기 위해 'Snooky를 끄집어내야' 한다고 주장하므로 밑줄 친 어구의 의미는 '그들의 감정이 지금 어떠한지 파악하다'야. 따라서 정답은 ②야.

오답단서 Snooky가 어떤 감정 상태인지에 따라 다른 사람과의 상호작용이 달라진다고 했을 뿐, Snooky가 사람들을

어휘확인
emotional 감정적인 **state** 상태 **completely** 완전히 **alter** 바꾸다 **interaction** 상호작용 **convince** 설득하다 **happen to** 마침[우연히] ~하다 **anxious** 불안한 **unaffected** 영향을 받지 않는 **attend to** ~을 처리하다 **cue** (행동) 자극; 단서, 신호 **keep in mind** 명심하다 **attempt to** ~하려고 시도하다 **diagnosis** 진단 **in the midst of** ~하는 중에
〈선택지 어휘〉
reveal 드러내다 **figure out** 파악하다, 알아내다 **obtain** 얻다 **reasonably** 이성적으로

지문 Flow

[도입]
사람의 감정 상태는 생각, 결정, 상호작용을 완전히 바꾸어 놓을 수 있음

[예시1]
당신의 친구(Snooky)가 불안하다면 당신의 주장에 설득되지만, 친구가 여유가 있다면 그렇지 않음

[예시2]
공포 캠페인이 특정한 시간과 장소에서는 무의미할 수 있지만, 다른 경우에는 효과적일 수 있음

[주제문]
당신이 누군가에게 효과적으로 조언하려고 한다면, 그들의 감정을 파악할 필요가 있음

위해서 무엇을 했는지 고려하라는 내용은 없으므로 ④는 오답이야. 또한 '감정 상태(emotional states)'가 결정에 영향을 미친다는 내용이지만 사람들을 감정적이 아니라 이성적으로 생각하라는 내용의 글은 아니므로 ⑤도 오답이 돼.

실전적용독해

056 정답 ③

지문 All in One

[1] A rewarding part of dog ownership (개의 주인인 것의 보람 있는 부분은, S) / is (V) successfully training your dog (당신의 개를 성공적으로 훈련시키는 것이다, C(동명사구)). [2] Training (훈련은, S) is (V_1) an *excellent way* [to bond with your dog] (당신의 개와 유대감을 형성하는 아주 좋은 방법이다) / and (그리고) will help (V_2) you (O) (당신을 도와줄 것이다) / build a good relationship with it (그것과 좋은 관계를 맺는 것을, C).

[3] Teaching your dog to sit (당신의 개에게 앉는 것을 가르치는 것은, S(동명사구)) / is (V) *a great step* (C) [to start with your training] (훈련을 시작하는 아주 좋은 단계이다, 형용사적 용법). [4] If (접속사) you're (S′) to have (V′) your dog (O′) sit (C′) (만약 당신의 개가 앉게 하려면) / as (접속사) you (S″) wish (V″) (당신이 원하는 대로), // you (S) need to hold (V) a tasty treat (당신은 맛있는 간식을 들고 있을 필요가 있다), / with him in a standing position (개를 서 있게 한 채로).

[5] Keeping the treat near your dog's nose (개의 코 근처에 간식을 두고서, 분사구문(= As you keep ~)), / move (V) your hand (O) (손을 움직여라) / in an arc (둥근 활 모양으로) / over his head (개의 머리 위로).

[6] As (접속사) the dog (S′) raises (V′) his head (개가 고개를 들면서) / to follow the treat (간식을 따라가려고, 부사적 용법(목적)), // his bottom (S) will go (V) on the floor (개의 엉덩이가 바닥에 놓일 것이다). [7] The instant he sits (개가 앉자마자), // praise him and give him the treat (개를 칭찬하면서 간식을 주어라). [8] Practice this a number of times (이것을 여러 번 연습하라) / in short (짧지만) but regular sessions (주기적인 기간으로). [9] You (S) can now add (V) the cue word 'sit' (당신은 이제 '앉아'라는 지시어를 덧붙일 수 있다) // as (접속사) he (S′) goes (V′) to sit (개가 앉으려 할 때). [10] Training your dog this way for a few days (당신의 개를 며칠 동안 이 방식으로 훈련시키는 것은, S(동명사구)) / should allow (V) your efforts (O) to bear fruit (C(to부정사)) (당신의 노력이 결실을 보게 할 것이다).

① take a pleasant walk with your dog
당신의 개와 기분 좋은 산책을 할

② become best friends with your dog
당신의 개와 가장 친한 친구가 될

③ make your dog sit whenever you want
당신이 원할 때 언제든지 당신의 개가 앉도록 할

④ train your dog effectively outdoors
당신의 개를 효과적으로 야외에서 훈련시킬

⑤ order your dog not to move his position
당신의 개가 움직이지 않도록 지시할

어휘확인

rewarding 보람 있는 **ownership** 소유 **bond** 유대감을 형성하다; 유대 **treat** 간식; 만족[기쁨]을 주는 것 **arc** 둥근[활] 모양 **bottom** 엉덩이; 맨 아랫부분 **the instant** ~하자마자 **praise** 칭찬하다 **session** 기간, 시간; 활동 **bear fruit** 결실을 보다, 열매를 맺다

지문 Flow

[도입]
개의 주인의 보람은 개를 성공적으로 훈련시키는 것임

⬇

[주제]
개에게 앉는 것을 가르치는 것은 훈련을 시작하는 아주 좋은 단계

⬇

[보충설명]
간식을 활용한 훈련으로 '앉아'라는 지시어를 훈련시킬 수 있음

⬇

[결론]
이러한 방식으로 며칠간 훈련시킨다면 원하는 것을 얻을 수 있음

해석 한 눈에 보기 1 개의 주인인 것의 보람 있는 부분은 당신의 개를 성공적으로 훈련시키는 것이다. 2 훈련은 당신의 개와 유대감을 형성하는 아주 좋은 방법이고 당신이 개와 좋은 관계를 맺는 것을 도와줄 것이다. 주제문 3 당신의 개에게 앉는 것을 가르치는 것은 훈련을 시작하는 아주 좋은 단계이다. 4 만약 당신이 원하는 대로 당신의 개가 앉게 하려면, 당신은 개를 서 있게 한 채로 맛있는 간식을 들고 있을 필요가 있다. 5 개의 코 근처에 간식을 두고서, 개의 머리 위로 손을 둥근 활 모양으로 움직여라. 6 개가 간식을 따라가려고 고개를 들면서, 개의 엉덩이가 바닥에 놓일 것이다. 7 개가 앉자마자, 개를 칭찬하면서 간식을 주어라. 8 이것을 짧지만 주기적인 기간으로 여러 번 연습하라. 9 당신은 이제 개가 앉으려 할 때 '앉아'라는 지시어를 덧붙일 수 있다. 10 당신의 개를 며칠 동안 이 방식으로 훈련시키는 것은 당신의 노력이 결실을 보게 할 것이다.

정답단추 개에게 앉는 것을 가르치는 훈련에 대해 방법 위주로 구체적으로 설명하고 있어. 훈련 방법이 서술된 후, 밑줄 친 어구를 포함한 마지막 문장에서 이러한 방식으로 훈련시킨다면 노력이 '결실을 보게' 된다고 했지. 즉 밑줄 친 어구는 '당신이 원할 때 언제든지 당신의 개가 앉도록 하는 것'이란 의미이고 정답은 ③이야.

오답단서 ②는 글 초반에 언급된 '개와 좋은 관계를 맺는 것을 도와준다'라는 내용에 근거하여 만든 오답이야. 글의 내용이 개의 훈련 중 '개를 앉게 하기'에 한정되었으므로 ④와 ⑤는 정답이 될 수 없어.

057 정답 ④

지문 All in One

[1] *A wise woman* (S) [who was hiking in the mountains] (관계대명사) (산에서 등산하고 있던 한 현명한 여성이) / found (V) a precious stone (O) in a stream (개울에서 귀중한 돌을 발견했다).

[2] The next day (다음날) / she (S_1) met (V_1) *another hiker* (O_1) [who was hungry] (관계대명사) (그녀는 배가 고픈 다른 등산객을 만났다), // and the wise woman (S_2) opened (V_2) her (O_2) (그리고 그 현명한 여성은 가방을 열었다)

어휘확인

stream 개울, 시내 **hesitation** 주저, 망설임 **comfort** 편안함 **security** (미래를 위한) 보장, 안정; 보안 **instantly** 즉시 **enable** ~을 할 수 있게 하다

〈선택지 어휘〉

priceless 귀중한, 소중한

자신의 음식을 나누어 주기 위해 귀중한 돌을 보고 배고픈 등산객은 여성에게 물었다
bag / to share her food. 3 Seeing the precious stone, / the hungry hiker asked the woman /
분사구문(= As soon as he(= the hungry hiker) saw ~) S V IO

자신이 그것을 가질 수 있는지 그녀는 그 돌을 그에게 주었다 주저하지 않고 그 남자는 떠났다 자신의 행운에 기뻐하면서
if he could have it. 4 She gave it to him / without hesitation. 5 The man left, / pleased with his
DO S V O S V 분사구문(= while he was pleased)

그는 알았다 그 돌이 충분히 가치가 있다는 것을 자신에게 평생 동안 편안함과 안정을 주기에
good fortune. 6 He knew // the stone was worth enough / to give him comfort and security for
S V S' V' C'

하지만 며칠 후 그는 그 돌을 돌려주기 위해 돌아왔다 그 현명한 여성에게 그는
a lifetime. 7 But a few days later / he came back to return the stone / to the wise woman. 8 He
S V 부사적 용법(목적)

말했다 "저는 이 돌이 얼마나 가치가 있는지 알아요 그러나 저는 이것을 돌려줄게요 희망하면서 당신이 저에게
said: // "I know how valuable the stone is, // but I give it back / in the hope / that you can give
S_1 V_1 O_1 접속사 S_2 V_2 S' V'

값을 따질 수 없는 것을 줄 수 있을 것이라고 당신 내면의 것을 저에게 주세요 저에게 이 돌을 즉시
me something beyond price. 9 Give me what you have within you / [that instantly enabled
IO' DO' V IO DO 관계대명사 V'

줄 수 있게 해주었던 처음에
you to give me the stone / in the first place]."
O' OC'

① the same luck that she has
그녀가 가진 것과 똑같은 행운

② a more precious stone hidden in her bag
그녀의 가방에 숨겨진 더 귀중한 돌

③ all the money and jewelry she has collected so far
그녀가 지금까지 모은 모든 돈과 보석

④ the warm heart willing to give up her priceless things
그녀의 귀중한 것을 기꺼이 포기하려는 따뜻한 마음

⑤ the courage that makes her hike alone in the mountain
그녀가 혼자 산을 등산하게 한 용기

지문 Flow

[발단]
등산하던 현명한 여성이 귀중한 돌을 발견함

[전개]
여성이 만난 등산객이 그 돌을 달라고 하자, 여성은 주저 없이 줌

[절정]
며칠 후 등산객이 그 돌을 돌려주며 값을 따질 수 없는 것을 받길 원함

[결말]
'더 귀중한 것'은 '현명한 여성이 귀중한 돌을 즉시 줄 수 있었던 내면'이었음

해석 한 눈에 보기 1 산에서 등산하고 있던 한 현명한 여성이 개울에서 귀중한 돌을 발견했다. 2 다음날 그녀는 배가 고픈 다른 등산객을 만났고, 그 현명한 여성은 자신의 음식을 나누어 주기 위해 가방을 열었다. 3 귀중한 돌을 보고 배고픈 등산객은 여성에게 자신이 그 귀중한 돌을 가질 수 있는지 물었다. 4 그녀는 주저하지 않고 그 돌을 그에게 주었다. 5 자신의 행운에 기뻐하면서 그 남자는 떠났다. 6 그는 그 돌이 자신에게 평생 동안 편안함과 안정을 주기에 충분히 가치가 있다는 것을 알았다. 7 하지만 며칠 후 그는 그 돌을 그 현명한 여성에게 돌려주기 위해 돌아왔다. 8 그는 "저는 이 돌이 얼마나 가치가 있는지 알지만, 저는 당신이 저에게 값을 따질 수 없는 것을 줄 수 있을 것이라고 희망하면서 이 것을 돌려줄게요. 단서 9 처음에 저에게 이 돌을 즉시 줄 수 있게 해주었던 당신 내면의 것을 저에게 주세요."라고 말했다.

정답단추 밑줄 어구가 포함된 문장에서 등산객은 귀중한 돌을 여성에게 돌려주며 '값을 따질 수 없는 (매우 귀중한) 것'을 받고 싶다고 했어. 이어지는 문장에서 그가 여성이 처음에 귀중한 돌을 즉시 줄 수 있게 한 내면에 있는 것을 달라고 한 것으로 보아, 정답은 ④ '그녀의 귀중한 것을 기꺼이 포기하려는 따뜻한 마음'이야.

오답단서 ①은 현명한 여성이 귀중한 돌을 발견하고, 등산객 또한 여성으로부터 그 귀중한 돌을 건네받은 행운이 있었다는 내용과 good luck 어휘를 이용해 만든 오답이야. ②와 ③은 밑줄 표현과 관련될 만한 귀중한 것들을 제시하지만 글의 주제와 연결되지 않은 무관한 오답이야.

058 정답 ②

지문 All in One

(라고) 말하는 몇몇 사람들이 있다 나는 나만의 사람이다 (~은) 상관없다 다른 사람들이
1 There are *some people* [who say], // "I'm my own person. // It doesn't matter / what others
V S S V C 가주어 V 진주어

생각하는 것 하지만 그들은 실망한다 다른 사람들이 그들을 정중하게 대하지 않으면 그들의 시간을
think." 2 Yet they feel disappointed // when others don't treat them politely, fail to respect
S V C 접속사 S' V'_1 O'_1 V'_2 O'_2

존중하지 않으면 또는 그들의 정보를 무시하면 이와 같은 사람들은 불평한다 그들이 얻지 못하면
their time, [or] ignore their information. 3 These same people complain // when they don't get
V'_3 S V 접속사 S' V'

자신이 원하는 직업이나 기대하는 급여를 그들은 이해하지 못한다 왜 최고의
/ *the job* [they want] [or] *the salary* [they expect]. 4 They don't understand / why the best
O'_1 O'_2 S V S'

직원들이 자신들을 위해 일하는 것을 싫어하는지 다른 사람들의 동기는 그들에게 수수께끼로 남아 있다
employees hate to work for them. 5 Other people's motivations remain a mystery to them.
V' O' S V C

다른 사람들로부터 지지와 승인을 얻는 것은 항상 운에 맡기는 상황인 것처럼 보인다
6 Gaining support and acceptance from others / always seems like a hit-or-miss situation //
S(동명사구) V

그들이 노력을 주도할 때 똑같은 함정에 빠지기 전에 이것을 생각하라
when they're leading the effort. 7 Before falling into that same trap, // consider this: // other
접속사 S' V' O' V O

다른 사람들의 인식이 그들의 현실을 만든다는 점을 당신 자신의 사실, 의도, 동기가 그들의 현실을 만들지 않는다
people's perceptions create their reality. 8 Your own facts, intentions, and motives do not
S V O S V

사람들은 알 수 없다 당신이 어떻게 생각하는지와 무엇을 의도하는지 항상 인지하라
(create their reality). 9 People can't see / how you think [and] what you intend. 10 Always be
O S V O_1 O_2 V

당신의 행동이 다른 사람들에게 어떻게 보이는지를
aware / of how your actions look to other people.
C S' V'

어휘확인

politely 정중하게, 예의 바르게 **motivation** 동기(=motive) **acceptance** 승인, 동의 **trap** 함정, 덫 **perception** 인식; 지각, 자각 **be aware of** ~을 인지하다[알다]
〈선택지 어휘〉
recognize 인정하다; 알아보다
accomplishment 성과, 업적

지문 Flow

[예시]
• 다른 사람들의 생각을 상관하지 않는 사람들은 자신이 존중받지 못하면 실망하고 불평함
• 원하는 직업, 급여를 받지 못하거나 최고의 직원이 같이 일하기 싫어하는 것을 이해하지 못함
• 노력할 때 타인의 지지와 승인을 운에 맡김

① getting angry at your poor results
당신의 부진한 결과에 화를 내기

② thinking about not others but yourself
다른 사람들이 아닌 당신 자신에 대해 생각하기

③ looking at the bright side of your reality
당신 현실의 밝은 면을 바라보기

④ spending too much time on team projects
팀 프로젝트에 너무 많은 시간을 소비하기

⑤ giving up recognizing others' accomplishments
다른 사람들의 성과를 인정하기를 그만두기

해석 한 눈에 보기 1 "나는 나만의 사람이다. 다른 사람들이 생각하는 것은 상관없다."라고 말하는 몇몇 사람들이 있다. 2 하지만 그들은 다른 사람들이 그들을 정중하게 대하지 않거나 그들의 시간을 존중하지 않으면, 또는 그들의 정보를 무시하면 실망한다. 3 이와 같은 사람들은 자신이 원하는 직업을 얻지 못하거나 그들이 기대하는 급여를 받지 못하면 불평한다. 4 그들은 왜 최고의 직원들이 자신들을 위해 일하는 것을 싫어하는지 이해하지 못한다. 5 다른 사람들의 동기는 그들에게 수수께끼로 남아 있다. 6 그들이 노력을 주도할 때 다른 사람들로부터 지지와 승인을 얻는 것은 항상 운에 맡기는 상황인 것처럼 보인다. 주제문 7 똑같은 함정에 빠지기 전에, 다른 사람들의 인식이 그들의 현실을 만든다는 점을 생각하라. 8 당신 자신의 사실, 의도, 동기가 그들의 현실을 만들지 않는다. 9 사람들은 당신이 어떻게 생각하는지 그리고 무엇을 의도하는지 알 수 없다. 주제문 10 당신의 행동이 다른 사람들에게 어떻게 보이는지를 항상 인지하라.

정답단추 다른 사람들이 생각하는 것은 상관하지 않고 자신의 생각만 집중하는 사람들은 타인의 행동이 기대와 다를 때 실망하고 이해하지 못한다고 하며 다양한 예시가 언급되고 있어. 밑줄 친 어구에서 이러한 현상을 '똑같은 함정에 빠지는 것'으로 표현하며, 이를 피하기 위해서 타인의 인식이 현실임을 인식하라고 주장하지. 따라서 밑줄 친 어구의 의미는 '다른 사람들이 아닌 당신 자신에 대해 생각하는 것'이므로 정답은 ②야.

오답단서 ①은 글의 초반에 언급된, 기대에 못 미치는 부정적 대우를 받는다는 내용을 이용해서 만든 오답이야. 또한 ③은 주제문에 등장한 reality(현실)를 활용한 오답으로, 밝은 면만 보라는 것은 글의 주제와 거리가 멀어.

[주제문]
(착각하는) 함정에 빠지기 전에 다른 사람들의 인식이 현실을 만든다는 점을 생각해야 함

⬇

[보충설명]
당신은 사람들의 현실을 만들지 않으며, 사람들은 당신의 생각과 의도를 알 수 없음

⬇

[주제 재진술]
당신의 행동이 다른 사람에게 어떻게 보이는지 항상 인지해야 함

유형 07 요약문 완성

Check-Up 1 ○ **059** ④
Check-Up 2 ① **060** ⑤
Check-Up 3 ② **061** ⑤
실전적용독해 **062** ④ **063** ④

Check-Up 1

정답 ○
해석 **059** 지문의 요약문 참조

059 정답 ④

지문 All in One

1 Good decision-making(S) is(V) a *skill*(C) [that(관계대명사) comes easily to some people, / not so easily to others].
(훌륭한 의사 결정은 기술이다 / 어떤 사람들에게는 쉽게 오는 / 다른 사람들에게는 그렇게 쉽게 오지 않는)

2 Choices(S) are(V) confusing(C). (선택은 혼란스럽다) 3 Choices(S) can make(V) you(O) anxious(C). (선택은 당신을 불안하게 만들 수 있다) 4 They(S) can cost(V) you(IO) peace of mind(DO), // even after(접속사) you(S′)'ve made(V′) the decision. (그것들은 당신에게 마음의 평화를 잃게 할 수 있다 / 심지어 당신이 결정을 내린 후에도)

5 In order to be a good decision-maker(부사적 용법(목적)), / you(S) should first learn(V) to accept / that(접속사) you(S′) can't have(V′) it all. (훌륭한 의사 결정자가 되기 위해서 / 당신은 먼저 받아들이는 것을 배워야 한다 / 모든 것을 한꺼번에 가질 수는 없다는)

6 Decisions(S) force(V) us(O) to close / the door on other possibilities, / small ones [and] big ones(C). (사실을 결정은 우리로 하여금 닫도록 강요한다 / 다른 가능성들에 대한 문을 / 작은 가능성들과 큰 가능성들)

7 You(S) can't order(V) every delicious dish / on the menu. (당신은 모든 맛있는 음식을 주문할 수는 없다 / 메뉴에서)

8 And there will be(V) *paths*(S_1) [not taken], / *careers*(S_2) [not chosen], / *experiences*(S_3) [not encountered]. (그리고 가지 않은 길들이 있을 것이다 / 선택되지 않은 직업들이 / 마주치지 않은 경험들이)

9 Also, / more thinking(S) is not(V) always better thinking(C). (또한 / 더 많은 생각이 항상 더 나은 생각이 되는 것은 아니다)

10 It's(가주어 V) often good(C) / to think through your decisions(진주어). (종종 좋다 / 결정을 통해 생각하는 것이)

11 But don't overdo(V) it(= thinking). (그러나 그것을 지나치게 하지 마라)

12 Many good decisions(S) can be made(V) / based as much on intuition(분사구문) / as on precise assessment of endless data. (많은 좋은 결정을 내릴 수 있다 / 많은 직관에 근거해서 / 끝없는 데이터의 정확한 평가만큼)

⬇

어휘확인

decision-making 의사 결정 **cf. decision-maker** 의사 결정자 **confusing** 혼란스러운 **anxious** 불안해하는 **cost** 희생시키다, 잃게 하다 **make a decision** 결정하다 **force A to B** A가 B하도록 강요하다 **possibility** 가능성 **career** 직업; 경력 **encounter** 마주치다 **overdo** 지나치게 하다 **intuition** 직관 **precise** 정확한 **assessment** 평가 **endless** 끝없는 **willingly** 기꺼이 **option** 선택사항 **lead to** ~로 이어지다

지문 Flow

[도입]
훌륭한 의사 결정은 어떤 이들에게는 쉽지 않고 불안하게 함

⬇

[주장1]
훌륭한 의사 결정자가 되기 위해서는 모든 것을 한꺼번에 가질 수는 없다는 것을 인정해야 함

13 선택을 하는 것은 의미한다 / 기꺼이 다른 선택사항을 잃는 것을 / 그리고 그것에 쓰는 더 많은 시간이

Making a choice means / willingly (A) losing other options, // and more time [spent on it] / does not always (B) lead to a good one.

항상 좋은 선택으로 이어지는 것은 아니다 (one = choice)

(A)		(B)	(A)		(B)
① taking	……	change	② taking	……	lead to
③ taking	……	follow	④ losing	……	lead to
⑤ losing	……	change			

해석 한 눈에 보기 1 훌륭한 의사 결정은 어떤 사람들에게는 쉽게 오고, 다른 사람들에게는 그렇게 쉽게 오지 않는 기술이다. 2 선택은 혼란스럽다. 3 선택은 당신을 불안하게 만들 수 있다. 4 심지어 당신이 결정을 내린 후에도, 그것들은 당신에게 마음의 평화를 잃게 할 수 있다. 5 훌륭한 의사 결정자가 되기 위해서, 당신은 먼저 모든 것을 한꺼번에 가질 수는 없다는 사실을 받아들이는 것을 배워야 한다. 6 결정은 우리로 하여금 다른 가능성들, 작은 가능성들과 큰 가능성들에 대한 문을 닫도록 강요한다. 7 당신은 메뉴에서 모든 맛있는 음식을 주문할 수는 없다. 8 그리고 가지 않은 길들, 선택되지 않은 직업들, 마주치지 않은 경험들이 있을 것이다. 9 또한, 더 많은 생각이 항상 더 나은 생각이 되는 것은 아니다. 10 결정을 통해 생각하는 것이 종종 좋다. 11 그러나 그것을 지나치게 하지 마라. 12 끝없는 데이터의 정확한 평가만큼 많은 직관에 근거해서 많은 좋은 결정을 내릴 수 있다.

13 선택을 하는 것은 기꺼이 다른 선택사항을 (A) 잃는 것을 의미하고, 그것(선택을 하는 것)에 더 많은 시간을 쓰는 것이 항상 좋은 선택으로 (B) 이어지는 것은 아니다.

정답단추 요약문에서 알 수 있듯이 선택을 하는 것이 다른 선택을 '어떻게 하는' 것이며, 선택하는 데 더 많은 시간을 들이는 것이 항상 좋은 선택을 '어떻게 하는' 것은 아닌지를 찾으면서 글을 읽어야 해. 의사 결정에 있어서 선택은 불안을 주는데, 그 이유는 모든 것을 한꺼번에 가질 수 없기 때문이라는 거야. 또한 많이 생각한다고 좋은 결정을 내리는 건 아니라고 했어. 따라서 빈칸 (A)에 들어갈 말은 losing, 빈칸 (B)에 들어갈 말은 lead to가 가장 적절해. 이를 종합하면 답은 ④야.

오답단서 어떤 선택을 하면 다른 선택을 못한다고 했는데 ①, ②, ③의 (A)는 글의 내용과 반대라서 답이 될 수 없어.

[보충설명]
결정은 다른 가능성을 잃는 것임

[주장2]
더 많이 생각한다고 좋은 결정을 하는 것이 아님

[보충설명]
직관에 근거해서도 많은 좋은 결정을 내릴 수 있음

Check-Up 2

정답 smell(s), ①

해석 바닐라 냄새는 사람들이 긴장을 풀도록 돕는다. 계피와 사과 냄새는 많은 사람들에게 그들의 고향을 생각나게 한다. → 냄새는 당신이 느끼는 방식을 바꿔 놓을 수 있다. ① 냄새 ② 맛

060 정답 ⑤

지문 All in One

1 As a driver, / you will encounter / both green and red lights. (운전자로서 / 당신은 마주칠 것이다 / 녹색불과 빨간불 둘 다를) 2 Most of us don't give this a second thought, // because the greens and reds average out over time / and we're all in the same boat. (우리들 대부분은 이것을 한 번 더 곰곰이 생각하지 않는다(재고하지 않는다) // 녹색불과 빨간불은 시간이 지나면서 결국 평균이 되고 / 우리는 모두 같은 상황에 놓이기 때문이다) 3 In other words, / most of us don't take it personally. (다시 말해 / 우리들 대부분은 그것을 개인적으로 받아들이지 않는다) 4 But there are / *unfortunate souls* [who have fallen / into the trap of perceiving every red light] / as a personal insult or sign of their lack of control. (하지만 ~ 있다 / 빠져버린 불행한 영혼들이 / 모든 빨간불을 인지하는 덫에 / 개인적인 모욕이나 그들의 통제 부족에 대한 표시로) 5 They respond by driving recklessly, / stepping on the accelerator pedal / to speed through the intersection // before the yellow light turns red. (그들은 무모하게 운전함으로써 반응한다 / 가속 장치 페달을 밟으면서 / 교차로를 관통해 질주하기 위해 // 노란불이 빨간불로 바뀌기 전에) 6 This is *a silly way* [to drive] / and *no way* [to navigate your life]. (이것은 어리석은 운전 방법이다 / 그리고 당신의 인생 방향을 찾아가는 방식이 아니다) 7 Red lights are not barriers / to your progress; // they are *your cue* [to relax, breathe, step back from responsibility, and think]. (빨간불은 장애물이 아니다 / 당신의 진전에 대한 // 그들은 당신이 긴장을 풀고, 숨을 쉬며, 책임감에서 한 발 물러서서, 생각하라는 신호이다)

8 *Many of the things* [troubled individuals view as (A) *obstacles*, / such as red lights], / are in fact *opportunities* [giving them *a chance* [to (B) refresh themselves]]. (불안해하는 개인들이 장애물로 보는 것들 중 많은 것들이 / 빨간불 같이 / 사실 그들 자신을 다시 생기롭게 할 가능성을 제공하는 기회들이다)

어휘확인

encounter 마주치다 give A a thought A를 곰곰이 생각하다 average out 결국 평균이 (~이) 되다 in the same boat 같은 상황에 있는 in other words 다시 말해 personally 개인적으로 cf. personal 개인적인 unfortunate 불행한 soul 영혼 fall into ~에 빠지다 trap 덫 perceive 인지하다 insult 모욕 lack 부족 recklessly 무모하게 accelerator 가속 장치 pedal (자전거·자동차 등의) 페달 speed 빨리 가다; 속도 intersection 교차로 silly 어리석은 navigate 길을 찾다 barrier 장애물 progress 진전 cue 신호 relax 긴장을 풀다 step back ~에서 물러나다 responsibility 책임감 troubled 불안해하는 individual 개인 obstacle 장애물 in fact 사실은 opportunity 기회 refresh 생기를 되찾게 하다

〈선택지 어휘〉

convenience 편리함 evaluate 평가하다

지문 Flow

[도입]
운전자로서 녹색불과 빨간불을 둘 다 만나게 됨

	(A)		(B)
①	conveniences	……	evaluate
②	conveniences	……	save
③	obstacles	……	protect
④	obstacles	……	express
⑤	obstacles	……	refresh

해석 한 눈에 보기 1 운전자로서 당신은 녹색불과 빨간불 둘 다를 만나게 될 것이다. 2 우리들 대부분은 이것을 재고하지 않는데, 녹색불과 빨간불이 시간이 지나면서 결국 평균이 되고 우리가 모두 같은 상황에 놓이기 때문이다. 3 다시 말해 우리 대부분은 그것을 개인적으로 받아들이지 않는다. 4 하지만 모든 빨간불을 개인적인 모욕이나 자신들의 통제력 부족에 대한 표시로 인식하는 덫에 빠진 불행한 영혼들이 있다. 5 그들은 노란불이 빨간불로 바뀌기 전에 교차로를 관통해 질주하기 위해 가속 페달을 마구 밟으면서 무모하게 운전함으로써 반응한다. 6 이것은 어리석은 운전 방법이고 당신의 인생 방향을 찾아가는 방식이 아니다. 주제문 7 빨간불은 당신의 전진에 대한 장애물이 아니라, 그것은 당신이 긴장을 풀고, 숨을 쉬며, 책임감에서 한발 물러서서, 생각하라는 신호이다.

8 불안해하는 개인들이 빨간불 같이 (A) 장애물로 보는 것 중 많은 것이 사실은 그들 자신을 (B) 다시 생기롭게 할 가능성을 제공하는 기회들이다.

정답단추 요약문을 먼저 읽고, 불안해하는 사람들이 빨간불을 '무엇'으로 보는지와 그것이 사실은 우리에게 '무엇을 할' 기회를 주는지 찾으며 읽는 게 좋아. 이 글은 도로의 빨간불이 반복적으로 등장하고 있는데, 이를 '편리함'이라기보다는 '장애물'로 생각하는 사람들이 있다고 했어. 그런데 마지막 문장에서 빨간불은 사실 장애물이 아닌 스스로 되돌아볼 수 있게 해 주는 신호라고 했지. 따라서 주제문이라 볼 수 있는 마지막 문장과 요약문을 비교하면 barriers는 obstacles로, cue to relax, breathe는 refresh로 바꿔 쓸 수 있음을 알 수 있어. 이를 종합하면 답은 ⑤야.

> [문제]
> 빨간불에 무모한 운전으로 반응하는 사람들이 있음
>
> ⬇
>
> [보충설명]
> 이는 어리석은 운전 방법으로, 인생 방향을 찾아가는 방식이 아님
>
> ⬇
>
> [주제문]
> 빨간불은 전진에 대한 장애물이 아니라, 긴장을 풀고 숨을 쉬며 책임감에서 물러나서 생각하라는 신호임

Check-Up 3

정답 ②

해석 인간과 돌고래는 둘 다 그들 시간의 대부분을 그들 자신의 종의 다른 대상들 주변에서 보낸다. → 인간처럼, 돌고래도 사회적인 동물이다. ① 지적인 ② 사회적인

061 정답 ⑤

지문 All in One

1 The words "travel" and "vacation" / are often used interchangeably, // but careful examination indicates some differences / between the two. 2 Vacation implies an escape / from your everyday life / — from your work and duties — // while travel may offer / *the opportunity* [to become totally lost in a different culture]. 3 Two types of journeys occur / during travel. 4 The outer journey describes / the physical experience of travel: / where you went, / what you saw, / and what you did. 5 The inner journey is characterized / by your interpretation of the experience. 6 It describes / what you learned, / and how it changed your perspective on life.

('여행'과 '휴가'라는 단어는 / 종종 바꿔서 사용된다 / 하지만 세심한 검토는 몇몇 차이점을 나타낸다 / 이 둘 사이의 / 휴가는 탈출하는 것을 의미한다 / 일상생활에서 / 즉 직장과 업무에서 / 반면에 여행은 제공할 수도 있다 / 다른 문화에 완전히 빠져 있는 기회를 / 두 가지 종류의 여정이 생긴다 / 여행하는 동안 / 외부 여정은 묘사한다 / 여행의 신체적 경험을 / 당신이 간 곳 / 당신이 본 것 / 그리고 당신이 한 것 / 내부 여정은 특징지어진다 / 그 경험에 대한 당신의 해석으로 / 그것은 설명한다 / 당신이 배운 것 / 그리고 그것이 인생에 대한 당신의 관점을 바꾼 방법)

⬇

7 Unlike the mere escape from (A) routine of vacation, / travel involves / both a real physical journey and an important (B) personal one.

(휴가가 일상에서 단순히 탈출한다는 것과는 달리 / 여행은 포함한다 / 실제의 신체적 여정과 중요한 개인적 여정을 둘 다)

	(A)		(B)
①	place	……	psychological
②	place	……	mental
③	routine	……	social
④	routine	……	geographical
⑤	routine	……	personal

해석 한 눈에 보기 주제문 1 '여행'과 '휴가'라는 단어는 종종 바꿔서 사용되지만, 세심한 검토는 이 둘 사이의 몇몇 차이점을 나타낸다. 2 휴가는 일상생활에서, 즉 직장과 업무에서 탈출하는 것을 의미하는 반면에, 여행은 다른 문화에 완전히 빠져 있는 기회를 제공할 수도 있다. 3 여행하는 동안 두 가지 종류의 여정이 생긴다. 4 외부 여정은 당신이 간 곳, 당신이 본 것, 그리고 당신이 한 것 같은 여행의 신체적 경험을 묘사한다. 5 내부 여정은 그 경험에 대한 당신의 해석으

어휘확인

interchangeably 바꿔서, 교환하여 **examination** 검토, 조사 **indicate** 나타내다 **imply** 의미하다, 함축하다 **escape** 탈출; 탈출하다 **duty** 업무, 임무; 의무 **offer** 제공하다 **opportunity** 기회 **totally** 완전히, 전적으로 **journey** 여정, 여행 **occur** 생기다, 발생하다 **outer** 외부의(↔ inner 내부의) **describe** 묘사하다, 설명하다 **physical** 신체적인 **characterize** 특징짓다 **interpretation** 해석 **perspective** 시각, 관점 **unlike** ~와는 달리 **mere** 단순한 **routine** 일상 **personal** 개인적인

〈선택지 어휘〉

psychological 심리적인 **mental** 정신적인 **geographical** 지리적인

지문 Flow

> [주제문]
> 여행과 휴가 사이에는 차이점이 있음
>
> ⬇
>
> [보충설명]
> 휴가는 일상생활에서 벗어나는 것인 반면에, 여행은 다른 문화에서만 경험할 수 있는 기회를 제공함
>
> ⬇
>
> [보충설명에 대한 보충설명]
> 여행하는 동안, 신체적 경험과 관련된 외부 여정과 그 경험에 대한 해석과 관련된 내부 여정을 경험하게 됨

로 특징지어진다. 6 그것은 당신이 배운 것, 그리고 그것이 인생에 대한 당신의 관점을 바꾼 방법을 설명한다.

> 7 휴가가 (A) 일상에서 단순히 탈출한다는 것과는 달리, 여행은 실제의 신체적 여정과 중요한 (B) 개인적 여정을 둘 다 포함한다.

정답단추 이 글은 요약문을 통해 '무엇'으로부터 탈출하는 휴가와는 달리, 여행은 신체적 여정과 중요한 '어떤' 여정 둘 다를 포함한다고 하면서 휴가와 여행의 차이를 구별하는 내용임을 알 수 있어. 두 번째 문장을 보면 휴가는 일상생활(everyday life)에서 탈출하는 것이라고 말하고 있어. 따라서 (A)에 들어갈 말은 everyday life와 같은 뜻을 가진 routine이야. 다섯 번째 문장과 여섯 번째 문장을 살펴보면, 여행하는 동안 생기는 두 가지 여정 중 내부 여정은 그 경험에 대한 당신의 해석이고 당신이 배운 것, 그리고 그것이 인생에 대한 시각을 바꾼 방법을 설명한다고 나와 있어. 이 내용을 다른 말로 압축해서 표현하면 (B)에는 personal이 가장 적절해. 이를 종합하면 답은 ⑤야.

오답단서 ①과 ②는 휴가를 단순히 장소에서의 탈출로 보고 있기 때문에 답이 될 수 없어. ③과 ④는 내부 여정을 사회적이고 지리적인 여정으로 볼 수 없으므로 오답이야.

실전적용독해

062 정답 ④

지문 All in One

1 What you do before sleep / influences the quality of your sleep. (수면 전에 당신이 하는 것이 / 당신의 수면의 질에 영향을 준다) [What you do before sleep: 관계대명사, S; influences: V]

2 Researchers have identified / *a variety of practices* and *habits* [that can help us maximize *the hours* [we spend sleeping]]. (연구원들은 발견했다 / 우리가 잠자는 데 보내는 시간을 최대화하도록 도움을 줄 수 있는 다양한 습관과 버릇들을) [Researchers: S; have identified: V; that: 관계대명사]

3 Invest a little time // before you get into your bed. (약간의 시간을 투자하라 // 당신이 침대에 들어가기 전에) [Invest: V; before: 접속사; you: S′; get: V′]

4 Then / you will wake up refreshed / the next day. (그러면 / 상쾌한 기분으로 잠이 깰 것이다 / 다음날에) [you: S; will wake up: V]

5 Ease the change / from wake time to sleep time / with a period of relaxing activities / an hour or so / before bed. (변화를 덜어 주어라 / 깨어 있는 시간에서 잠을 자는 시간까지 / 마음을 느긋하게 하는 활동들로 / 한 시간 가량 / 취침 전에) [Ease: V]

6 Take a bath / (the rise, then fall in body temperature promotes drowsiness), / read a book, / watch television, / or practice relaxation exercises. (목욕을 하라 / (체온의 상승, 그 다음에 하락이 졸음을 촉진한다) / 책을 읽어라 / 텔레비전을 봐라 / 또는 휴식 운동을 연습하라) [Take: V_1; read: V_2; watch: V_3; practice: V_4]

7 Avoid stressful, stimulating activities / — doing work, discussing emotional issues. (스트레스가 많고 자극적인 활동들을 피하라 / 일하기, 감정적인 문제 토론하기 같은) [Avoid: V]

8 They can cause the body to release / *a stress hormone* [which is associated with increasing alertness]. (그것들은 신체가 방출하게 할 수 있다 / 증가하는 각성도와 연관 있는 스트레스 호르몬을) [They: S; can cause: V; the body: O; to release: C; which: 관계대명사]

⬇

> 9 *The activities* [(which) you choose] / before bedtime / (A) affect the quality of your sleep, // so choose (B) light ones / to wake up feeling refreshed. (당신이 선택하는 활동들은 / 취침 시간 전에 / 당신의 수면의 질에 영향을 미친다 // 그러므로 가벼운 활동들을 선택하라 / 상쾌한 기분을 느끼면서 잠이 깨도록) [(which): 관계대명사; you: S; affect: V_1; choose: V_2; to wake up: 부사적 용법(목적)]

	(A)		(B)
①	describe	……	favorite
②	describe	……	learning
③	affect	……	additional
④	affect	……	light
⑤	affect	……	flexible

해석 한 눈에 보기 주제문 1 당신이 수면 전에 하는 것이 당신의 수면의 질에 영향을 준다. 2 연구원들은 우리가 잠자는 데 보내는 시간을 최대화하도록 도움을 줄 수 있는 다양한 습관과 버릇들을 발견했다. 3 당신이 침대에 들어가기 전에 약간의 시간을 투자하라. 4 그러면 다음날에 상쾌한 기분으로 잠이 깰 것이다. 5 취침 전에 한 시간 가량 마음을 느긋하게 하는 활동들로 깨어 있는 시간에서 잠을 자는 시간까지 변화를 덜어 주어라. 6 목욕을 하고 (체온의 상승, 그 다음에 하락이 졸음을 촉진한다), 책을 읽거나, 텔레비전을 보거나, 휴식 운동을 연습하라. 7 일하기, 감정적인 문제 토론하기 같은 스트레스가 많고 자극적인 활동들을 피하라. 8 그것들은 신체가 증가하는 각성도와 연관 있는 스트레스 호르몬을 방출하게 할 수 있다.

> 9 취침 시간 전에 당신이 선택하는 활동들은 당신의 수면의 질에 (A) 영향을 미친다. 그러므로 상쾌한 기분을 느끼면서 잠이 깨도록 (B) 가벼운 활동들을 선택하라.

어휘확인

influence 영향을 미치다 **quality** 질(質) **researcher** 연구원 **identify** 발견하다, 찾다 **a variety of** 다양한 **maximize** 최대화하다 **invest** 투자하다 **refreshed** 기분이 상쾌한 **ease** 덜어 주다 **relaxing** 마음을 느긋하게 해주는 **take a bath** 목욕하다 **rise** 상승 (↔ **fall** 하락) **temperature** 온도 **promote** 촉진하다 **drowsiness** 졸음 **relaxation** 휴식 **stressful** 스트레스가 많은 **stimulating** 자극적인 **emotional** 감정적인 **issue** 문제 **release** 방출하다 **hormone** 호르몬 **be associated with** ~와 연관[관련]되다 **increasing** 증가하는 **alertness** 각성도, 빈틈없음 **affect** 영향을 미치다

〈선택지 어휘〉

describe 묘사하다 **additional** 추가의 **flexible** 유연한; 신축성 있는

지문 Flow

[주제문]
자기 전의 행동이 수면의 질에 영향을 줌

⬇

[보충설명1]
취침 전 한 시간 정도 느긋한 활동(목욕, 독서, TV 시청, 휴식 운동 연습 등)을 함으로써 잠자는 행동과의 차이를 없앰

⬇

[보충설명2]
각성을 증가시키는 호르몬을 방출하는 스트레스가 많고 자극적인 활동(일하기, 감정적인 문제 토론하기 등)은 피함

정답단추 글을 읽기 전에 요약문을 먼저 읽는 게 좋아. 이 글에서는 첫 문장이 요약문의 내용을 추론할 수 있는 직접적인 단서인데, 취침 전 활동이 수면의 질에 영향을 준다고 했어. 또한 글의 중반부에 스트레스가 많고 자극적인 활동이 아닌 목욕, 독서, TV 시청, 휴식 운동 같은 느긋하게 할 수 있는 활동을 하라고 했어. 편하게 할 수 있는 활동들이니까 가볍게 할 수 있는 활동들로 볼 수 있겠지? 따라서 빈칸 (A)에 들어갈 말은 affect, 빈칸 (B)에 들어갈 말은 light가 가장 적절해. 이를 종합하면 답은 ④야.

오답단서 ①, ③, ⑤는 가장 좋아하는 활동, 추가 활동, 유연한 활동이 본문에 언급되지 않았으므로 오답이야. ②는 학습 활동을 스트레스가 많고 자극적인 활동으로 볼 수 있으니까 답이 될 수 없어.

063 정답 ④

지문 All in One

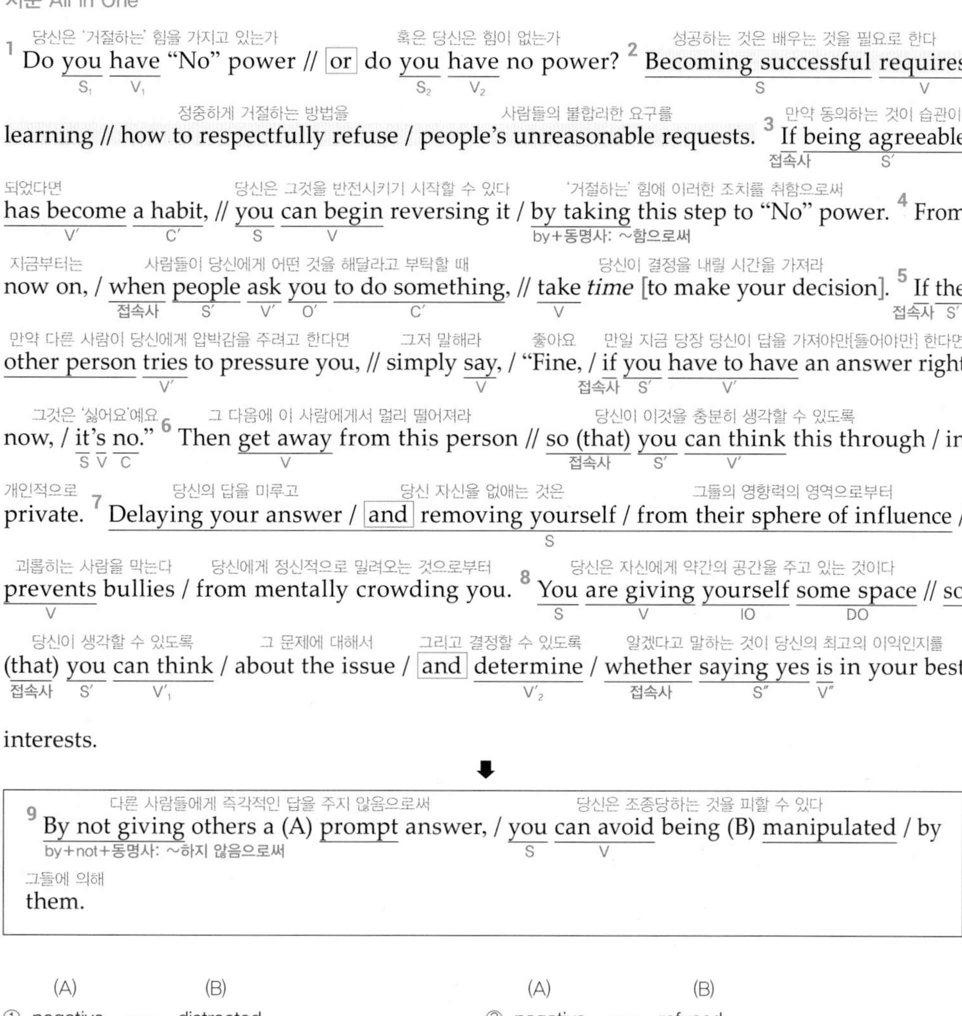

1 Do you have "No" power // or do you have no power? 2 Becoming successful requires learning // how to respectfully refuse / people's unreasonable requests. 3 If being agreeable has become a habit, // you can begin reversing it / by taking this step to "No" power. 4 From now on, / when people ask you to do something, // take *time* [to make your decision]. 5 If the other person tries to pressure you, // simply say, / "Fine, / if you have to have an answer right now, / it's no." 6 Then get away from this person // so (that) you can think this through / in private. 7 Delaying your answer / and removing yourself / from their sphere of influence / prevents bullies / from mentally crowding you. 8 You are giving yourself some space // so (that) you can think / about the issue / and determine / whether saying yes is in your best interests.

9 By not giving others a (A) prompt answer, / you can avoid being (B) manipulated / by them.

	(A)		(B)
①	negative	......	distracted
②	negative	......	refused
③	prompt	......	detected
④	prompt	......	manipulated
⑤	prompt	......	hindered

어휘확인

successful 성공한 require 필요로 하다 respectfully 정중하게 refuse 거절하다 unreasonable 불합리한 request 요구 agreeable 동의하는 reverse 반전시키다 take (a) step 조치를 취하다 from now on 지금부터는 decision 결정 pressure 압박감을 주다 simply 그저, 간단히 then 그 다음에 get away from ~에서 멀리 떨어지다 think through 충분히 생각하다 in private 개인적으로 delay 미루다 sphere 영역 influence 영향력 prevent 막다 bully (약자를) 괴롭히는 사람 mentally 정신적으로 crowd (생각이 마음속에) 밀려오다 issue 문제 whether ~인지 (아닌지) interest 이익; 흥미 prompt 즉각적인 manipulate 조종하다

〈선택지 어휘〉

negative 부정적인 distract 산만하게 하다 detect 발견하다 hinder 방해하다

지문 Flow

[주제문]
부당한 요구를 정중하게 거절하는 방법을 배우는 것이 필요함

⬇

[방법1]
사람들에게 부탁을 받으면 결정을 내릴 시간을 가져야 함

&

[방법2]
그 사람들에게서 떨어져 혼자 충분히 생각해야 함

⬇

[결과]
답을 미루고 그들의 영향력에서 벗어남으로써 당신의 정신적인 압박감을 막아주며, 자신에게 이익이 되는 결정을 하게 해줌

해석 한 눈에 보기 1 당신은 '거절하는' 힘을 지니고 있는가 아니면 당신은 아무런 힘이 없는가? 주제문 2 성공하는 것은 사람들의 부당한 요구를 정중하게 거절하는 방법을 배우는 것을 필요로 한다. 3 만일 동의하는 것이 습관이 되었다면, 당신은 '거절하는' 힘에 이러한 조치를 취함으로써 그것을 반전시키기 시작할 수 있다. 4 지금부터 사람들이 당신에게 어떤 것을 해달라고 부탁하면, 결정을 내릴 시간을 가져라. 5 만일 상대방이 당신에게 압박감을 주려고 한다면, 그저 "좋아요. 만일 당신이 지금 당장 답을 들어야만 한다면, 그것은 '싫어요'예요."라고 말해라. 6 그 다음에 당신이 이것을 혼자서 충분히 생각할 수 있도록 이 사람에게서 멀리 떨어져라. 7 답을 미루고 당신 자신을 그들의 영향력의 영역에서 없애는 것은 괴롭히는 사람이 당신에게 정신적으로 밀려오는 것을 막아준다. 8 당신이 그 문제에 대해 생각해 보고 알겠다고 말하는 것이 당신에게 최고의 이익인지를 결정할 수 있도록 당신은 자신에게 약간의 공간을 주고 있는 것이다.

9 다른 사람들에게 (A) 즉각적인 답을 제공하지 않음으로써, 당신은 그들에게 (B) 조종당하는 것을 피할 수 있다.

정답단추 글 전체를 한 문장으로 압축한 요약문을 먼저 읽어 보자. 이 글의 핵심인 다른 사람들에게 '어떠한' 답을 하지 않음으로써, '어떻게 되는' 것을 피할 수 있는지에 대해 찾아야 한다는 걸 알 수 있어. 이 글은 부당한 부탁에 대해 습관적으로 수락하지 말고 시간을 갖고 결정하라는 것과, 혼자서 충분히 생각할 수 있도록 타인의 영향력에서 벗어나라는 내용이야. 따라서 답으로는 (A)에 prompt, (B)에는 manipulated가 들어가는 ④가 적절해.

오답단서 ①, ②는 글의 내용을 제대로 반영하지 않은 negative(부정적인) 때문에 답이 아님을 쉽게 알 수 있어. ③도 detected(발각되는)가 글의 내용과 관련이 없어서 오답이야. ⑤는 hindered(방해받는)의 뜻과 글에서 정신적으로 밀려오는 것을 막아 준다는 내용만 보면 그럴듯하게 보이지만, 자세히 보면 yes라고 말하도록 방해받는 것을 피한다는 게 아니라 조종당하는 것을 피한다는 내용이 되어야 자연스러우므로 답이 될 수 없어.

미니 모의고사 2 유형 05 | 유형 06 | 유형 07

064 ⑤ 065 ⑤ 066 ② 067 ④ 068 ③ 069 ② 070 ② 071 ④ 072 ①
073 ④ 074 ④ 075 ⑤ 076 ② 077 ④ 078 ④ 079 ③ 080 ① 081 ⑤

064 정답 ⑤

지문 All in One

동물원은 길고 다양한 역사를 가지고 있다 / 5,000년 이상 거슬러 올라가는 / 이국적인 동물 수집으로
1 Zoos(S) have(V) *a long* and *varied history* [dating back over 5,000 years / to the exotic animal collections / of Egyptian pharaohs]. (이집트 파라오들의)

그것들의 인기에도 불구하고 / 최근 수십 년 동안
2 Despite their popularity, / in recent decades, / conflict(S) has emerged(V) / over the traditional zoo. (갈등이 생겨왔다 / 전통적인 동물원에 대한)

어떤 사람들은 믿는다 / 동물원이 일반 대중들을 장려한다고
3 Some people(S) believe(V) // (that)(접속사) zoos(S′) encourage(V′) the general public(O′) / to appreciate and (to) respect the animal world(C′). (동물 세계를 인정하고 존중하도록)

게다가 / 그들은 말한다
4 (A) Moreover, / they(S) say(V) // (that)(접속사) zoos(S′) can protect(V′₁) animals / against diseases and natural enemies, / and (can) be(V′₂) a shelter / for threatened animals. (동물원이 동물을 보호할 수 있고 / 질병과 자연의 적(천적)에게서 / 피난처가 될 수 있다고 / 위협받고 있는 동물들의)

이와는 반대로 / 또 어떤 사람들은 주장한다 / 동물을 가두는 것은 잔인하다고
5 (B) In contrast, / others(S) claim(V) // that(접속사) it(가주어) is(V′) cruel(C′) to keep animals / in zoos(진주어). (동물원에)

이 사람들은 주장한다 / 작고 인위적인 우리는 유발한다고
6 These people(S) argue(V) // that(접속사) the small, unnatural houses(S′) cause(V′) / unnecessary stress and suffering. (불필요한 스트레스와 고통을)

그들은 말한다 / 동물원이 만들어줘야 한다고 / 자연 서식지
7 They(S) say(V) // (that)(접속사) zoos(S′) must create(V′) / *environments* [which(관계대명사) look like the natural homes / of the animals]. (같아 보이는 환경을 / 동물의)

	(A)		(B)
①	Moreover	……	For example
②	However	……	Moreover
③	Therefore	……	For example
④	For instance	……	In contrast
⑤	Moreover	……	In contrast

해석 한 눈에 보기 1 동물원은 이집트 파라오들의 이국적인 동물 수집으로 5,000년 이상 거슬러 올라가는 길고 다양한 역사를 지니고 있다. 2 그것의 인기에도 불구하고, 최근 수십 년 동안, 전통적 동물원에 대한 갈등이 대두되어 왔다. 3 어떤 사람들은 동물원이 일반 대중들에게 동물 세계를 인정하고 존중하도록 장려한다고 믿는다. 4 (A) 게다가, 그들은 동물원이 질병과 천적에게서 동물을 보호할 수 있고, 위협받고 있는 동물들의 피난처가 될 수 있다고 말한다. 5 (B) 이와는 반대로, 또 어떤 사람들은 동물을 동물원에 가두는 것은 잔인하다고 주장한다. 6 이 사람들은 작고 인위적인 우리가 불필요한 스트레스와 고통을 유발한다고 주장한다. 7 그들은 동물원이 동물의 자연 서식지 같아 보이는 환경을 만들어줘야 한다고 말한다.

정답단추 연결사 문제는 앞뒤 문장의 문맥을 주의 깊게 살펴봐야 해. 빈칸 (A)의 앞뒤 모두 동물원을 찬성하는 입장의 주장이니까 첨가를 나타내는 Moreover(게다가)가 적절해. 그리고 빈칸 (B)의 앞뒤는 각각 동물원에 찬성하는 사람과 반대하는 사람의 의견이 이어지고 있으니까 대조를 나타내는 In contrast(이와 반대로)를 써야 해. 따라서 가장 적절한 답은 ⑤야.

어휘확인

varied 다양한 date back (to) ~까지 거슬러 올라가다 exotic 이국적인 Egyptian 이집트의 pharaoh 파라오(고대 이집트의 왕) despite ~에도 불구하고 popularity 인기 recent 최근의 decade 10년 conflict 갈등, 충돌 emerge 생겨나다 encourage 장려하다 general public 일반 대중 appreciate 인정하다 respect 존중하다 moreover 게다가 natural 자연의 (↔ unnatural 인위적인) enemy 적 shelter 피난처 threaten 위협하다 in contrast 이와는 반대로 claim 주장하다 cruel 잔인한 argue 주장하다 house (가축 등의) 우리 cause 유발하다 unnecessary 불필요한 suffering 고통 home 서식지

지문 Flow

[문제 제기]
길고 다양한 역사를 지닌 동물원이 최근에 갈등을 겪음

⬇

[옹호 주장]
- 사람들이 동물 세계를 인정하고 존중하도록 장려함
- 천적 보호와 피난처 제공

⬍

[반대 주장]
- 동물을 동물원에 가두는 것은 잔인함
- 스트레스와 고통 유발
- 자연 서식지와 유사한 환경을 만들어줘야 함

065 정답 ⑤

지문 All in One

크거나 유용한 데이터 파일들이 / 진정으로 복잡할 필요는 없다
1 Large or useful data files(S) / need not be(V) genuinely complex(C).

과학에서 / 우리는 추구한다 / 이런 식으로 '자연스러운' 설명을 / 왜냐하면 그것들이 더 믿을 수 있는 경향이 있기 때문이다
2 In science, / we(S) seek(V) / *explanations* [that(관계대명사) are "natural" in this way] // because(접속사) they(S′) tend(V′) to be more reliable / and to connect to other useful ideas. (그리고 다른 유용한 아이디어들과 관련되는)

우리는 혐오한다 / 긴 목록의 예외와 특별한 경우를
3 We(S) abhor(V) / long lists of exceptions and special cases.

어휘확인

data 데이터, 자료 file (컴퓨터에서 정보를 모아 놓은) 파일 genuinely 진정으로 complex 복잡한 seek 추구하다; 찾다 explanation 설명 natural 자연스러운 way 방식, 방법 tend to-v ~하는 경향이 있다 reliable 믿을 수 있는 connect 관련짓다 abhor 혐오하다 exception 예외 consider 생각하다 goal 목표; 골

4 Consider, / for example, / the goal of theoretical physics. 5 In theoretical physics, / we try to summarize / the results of a great number of observations [and] experiments / in terms of a few powerful laws. 6 We try, / in other words, / to produce / *the shortest possible program* [that outputs the world]. 7 In that precise sense, / it's a quest / for **simplicity**.

(생각해 봐라 / 예를 들어 / 이론 물리학의 목표를 / 이론 물리학에서 / 우리는 요약하려고 노력한다 / 아주 많은 양의 관찰과 실험의 결과를 / 몇몇 강력한 법칙 면에서 / 우리는 노력한다 / 다시 말해서 / 제작하려고 / 세상을 출력해 내는 가능한 가장 짧은 프로그램을 / 관계대명사 / 그러한 엄밀한 의미에서 / 그것은 추구이다 / 단순함의)

① truth 진실
② laws 법칙
③ precision 정확성
④ complexity 복잡성
⑤ simplicity 단순함

해석 한 눈에 보기 1 크거나 유용한 데이터 파일들이 진정으로 복잡할 필요는 없다. 2 과학에서 우리는 이런 식으로 '자연스러운' 설명을 추구하는데 그것들이 더 믿을 수 있고 다른 유용한 아이디어들과 관련되는 경향이 있기 때문이다. 3 우리는 긴 목록의 예외와 특별한 경우를 혐오한다. 4 예를 들어 이론 물리학의 목표를 생각해 보라. 5 이론 물리학에서, 우리는 아주 많은 양의 관찰과 실험의 결과를 몇몇 강력한 법칙 면에서 요약하려고 노력한다. 주제문 6 다시 말해 우리는 세상을 출력해 내는 가능한 한 가장 짧은 프로그램을 만들어 내기 위해 노력한다. 7 그러한 엄밀한 의미에서 그것은 단순함의 추구이다.

정답단추 빈칸이 포함된 마지막 문장을 먼저 읽어보자. 앞에서 말하는 내용이 '무엇'을 추구하는 것인지 파악하는 데 중점을 두면 되는 것을 알 수 있지? 글의 앞 내용을 읽으면 우리는 과학에서 간단한 설명을 더 신뢰하고, 예외나 특별한 경우를 혐오하며, 많은 관찰과 실험을 몇몇 법칙으로 요약하려 한다는 세부적인 내용을 알 수 있어. 그리고 주제문은 in other words가 포함된 문장으로, 세상을 표현하는 가장 짧은 프로그램을 만들어내려고 한다고 하고 있어. 이는 곧 단순함을 추구한다는 뜻이니까 빈칸에는 ⑤가 적절해.

오답단서 ①, ③은 각각 이 글의 내용과 무관해서 답이 될 수 없어. ②는 글의 다섯 번째 문장 a few powerful laws에 나온 어구를 활용한 오답이야. ④는 글의 내용과 반대되는 말이야.

theoretical 이론의, 이론적인 **physics** 물리학 **summarize** 요약하다 **observation** 관찰 **experiment** 실험 **in terms of** ~ 면에서 **a few** 몇몇, 조금 **law** 법칙; 법 **in other words** 다시 말해서 **produce** 제작하다 **output** 출력해 내다 **precise** 엄밀한 **sense** 의미; 감각 **a quest for** ~을 추구함 **simplicity** 단순함, 간단함

〈선택지 어휘〉

truth 진실 **precision** 정확성 **complexity** 복잡성

지문 Flow

[도입]
크거나 유용한 데이터 파일이 복잡할 필요는 없음

⬇

[보충설명]
우리는 긴 목록의 예외와 특별한 경우를 혐오함

⬇

[예시]
이론 물리학에서, 많은 관찰과 실험의 결과를 법칙으로 요약하려고 함

⬇

[주제문]
세상을 출력해 내는 가장 짧은 프로그램을 만들려고 노력함 → 단순함의 추구

066 정답 ②

지문 All in One

1 Science-fiction TV series / [and] movies like *Star Wars* / may be entertaining, // [but] they **violate key laws of physics**. 2 Spaceships on these shows all travel faster / than the speed of light, // [but] it's physically impossible / to do that. 3 Similarly, / the acceleration of such spaceships / would be [so] extreme / [as to] break apart nearly any vessel, / making the impossible journeys unsurvivable / even in theory. 4 Also, / *the way* [in which the stars pass / by the windows of the spaceships] / is unnatural. 5 If the spaceships were really traveling / at the speed of light, // the stars would appear / as *a bright light show*, [spreading out in a rainbow of colors]. 6 But, / in those movies, / they appear small [and] still, // just like they do to us / down here on earth.

(공상과학 TV 시리즈와 / 〈스타워즈〉와 같은 영화는 / 재미있을지는 모르지만 / 그러나 그것들은 / 물리학의 중요한 법칙을 위반한다 / 이러한 프로그램들의 우주선은 모두 더 빠르게 움직이지만 / 빛의 속도보다 / 그러나 물리적으로 불가능하다 / 그렇게 하는 것은 / 유사하게 / 그러한 우주선의 가속화는 / 극심할[매우 심할] 것이다 / 거의 모든 우주선을 산산이 부술 정도로 / 불가능한 여행을 생존할 수 없게 만든다 / 이론적으로도 / 또한 / 별들이 지나가는 방식도 / 우주선의 창문 옆으로 / 부자연스럽다 / 만약 우주선이 정말로 움직인다면 / 빛의 속도로 / 별들은 나타날 것이다 / 환한 광선 쇼로 / 무지갯빛으로 퍼져나가는 / 하지만 / 그런 영화들에서 / 그것들은 작고 정지한 것 같다 / 꼭 그것들이 우리에게 그러는 것처럼 / 아래의 여기 지구에서)

① are also realistic 또한 현실적이다
② violate key laws of physics 물리학의 중요한 법칙을 위반한다
③ are old-fashioned and boring 구식이고 지루하다
④ can be dangerous to children 아이들에게 위험할 수 있다
⑤ are difficult for us to understand 우리가 이해하기에 어렵다

어휘확인

science-fiction 공상과학 **series** (라디오·텔레비전 등의) 시리즈 **entertaining** 재미있는 **violate** 위반하다 **key** 중요한 **law** 법칙; 법 **physics** 물리학 **cf. physically** 물리적으로 **spaceship** 우주선 **similarly** 유사하게 **acceleration** 가속화 **extreme** 극심한, 극도의 **apart** 산산이 **nearly** 거의 **vessel** (대형) 선박 **journey** 여행, 여정 **unsurvivable** 생존할 수 없는 **theory** 이론 **pass by** ~ 옆을 지나다 **unnatural** 부자연스러운 **appear** 나타나다, ~인 것 같다 **spread out** 퍼져나가다 **still** 정지한

〈선택지 어휘〉

realistic 현실적인 **old-fashioned** 구식의

지문 Flow

[주제문]
공상과학 TV 시리즈와 영화는 물리학의 법칙에 위배됨

⬇

[근거1]
우주선이 빛의 속도보다 빠르게 움직이는 것은 물리적으로 불가능함
→ 우주선의 가속화는 우주선을 산산이 부숴버려 생존할 수 없음

&

해석 한 눈에 보기 주제문 1 공상과학 TV 시리즈와 〈스타워즈〉 같은 영화는 재미있을지는 모르지만, 그것들은 물리학의 중요한 법칙을 위반한다. 2 이러한 프로그램에 등장하는 우주선은 모두가 빛의 속도보다 더 빠르게 움직이지만, 그렇게 하는 것은 물리적으로 불가능하다. 3 유사하게, 그러한 우주선의 가속화는 거의 모든 우주선을 산산이 부숴 버릴 정도로 매우 심할 것인데 이것은 불가능한 여행을 이론적으로도 생존할 수 없게 만든다. 4 또한, 별들이 우주선의 창문 옆으로 지나가는 방식도 부자연스럽다. 5 만약 우주선이 정말로 빛의 속도로 움직인다면, 별들은 무지갯빛으로 퍼져나가는 환한 광선 쇼처럼 보일 것이다. 6 하지만 그런 영화들에서 그것들은 꼭 아래의 여기 지구에서 우리에게 그러는 것처럼 작고 정지한 것 같아 보인다.

정답단추 빈칸을 포함하고 있는 문장은 공상과학 TV 시리즈와 〈스타워즈〉 같은 영화는 재미있을지는 모르지만 그것들은 '무엇하다'고 나와 있어. '무엇하다'에 중점을 두고 나머지 내용을 읽어야 해. 빈칸 다음을 보면 영화에 나오는 우주선의 속도나 우주선에서 바라본 별의 움직임이 물리적으로 불가능하다는 구체적인 설명이 나오고 있어. 따라서 빈칸에는 ②가 적절하고, 빈칸이 포함된 문장이 모든 글의 내용을 아우르는 주제문이라는 것도 알 수 있어.

오답단서 ①은 글의 내용에 반대되는 내용이야. 또한, ③, ④, ⑤는 글의 내용과는 무관하여 정답이 될 수 없어.

[근거2]
우주선 창문에 지나가는 별의 부자연스러운 이동 방식
→ 퍼져나가는 광선 쇼처럼 보이지 않고 정지된 것처럼 보임

067 정답 ④

지문 All in One

시간이 측정되는 수학 시험에 대해 언급한 연구 결과가 / 게시되었다 / 블로그에 / 시간이 측정되는
1 *A research finding* [related to timed math testing] / was posted / on a blog: / "Timed math
S / V / S

수학 시험은 학생들을 실망시킬 수 있다 / 수학 불안과 그 과목에 대한 장기적인 두려움으로 이끌면서
tests can discourage students, / leading to math anxiety [and] a long-term fear of the subject."
V / 분사구문(= and lead to ~)

그 짧은 진술은 논쟁을 시작하게 했다 / 시간이 측정되는 시험의 장점에 대한 / 그 논쟁은 청중을 나눴다
2 The brief statement started a debate / on the merits of timed testing. 3 The debate divided
S / V / S / V

절반으로 / 한쪽은 주장했다 / 시간이 측정되는 시험이 가치가 있다고 / 실제 마감 시간이 있기
the audience / in half. 4 One side argued // that timed testing was valuable // because there are
S / V / 접속사 / S′ / V′ / C′ / 접속사 / V″

때문에 / 삶과 직업에 있어 / 그리고 그것들을 놓치는 것에 대한 실제 결과(가 있기 때문에) / 다른 사람들은 생각했다
real deadlines / in life [and] careers / — [and] real consequences to missing them. 5 Others felt
S''_1 / S''_2 / S / V

시간이 측정되는 시험이 일종의 두려움을 일으켜서 / 아이들에게 / 학생들의 사고력에 해를 끼친다
// that timed testing causes a kind of fear / in children, / damaging students' ability to think /
접속사 / S′ / V′ / 분사구문(= and this damages ~ and hurts ~)

그리고 더 심오한 학습을 해친다고 / 그러한 의견 차이에도 불구하고 / 많은 교사들은 생각한다 / 시간이 측정되는
[and] hurting deeper learning. 6 Despite the disagreement, / many teachers felt / that timed
S / V / 접속사 / S′

시험들이 중요한 단계라고 / 수학적인 능숙함으로 가는 길의 / 그것들이 속도를 향상시키기 때문에
tests are an important step / on the road to mathematical fluency, // as they improve speed /
V′ / C′ / 접속사 / S″ / V''_1

그리고 복잡한 문제 해결을 위한 기초를 마련하기 (때문에) / 많은 교사들에게 / 학생들을 실제 상황에
[and] lay a foundation for complex problem solving. 7 To many teachers, / not preparing
V''_2 / S

대비시키지 않는 것은 / 시간이 측정되는 시험으로 / '아이들을 실패하게 하는 것'처럼 느껴졌다
students for real-life situations / with timed testing / felt like "setting the kids up for failure."
V

⬇

> 수학 불안에 대한 모든 염려에도 불구하고 / 대다수의 교사는 동의한다
> 8 Despite all the (A) concerns about math anxiety, / the majority of teachers agree / on
> S / V
>
> 시간이 측정되는 수학 시험의 필요성에
> the (B) necessity of timed math testing.

	(A)		(B)
①	criticisms	……	defects
②	merits	……	benefits
③	merits	……	uselessness
④	concerns	……	necessity
⑤	concerns	……	weaknesses

해석 한 눈에 보기 1 시간이 측정되는 수학 시험에 대해 언급한 연구 결과가 블로그에 게시되었다. "시간이 측정되는 수학 시험은 학생들을 실망시켜서, 수학 불안과 그 과목에 대한 장기적인 두려움으로 이끌 수 있다." 2 그 짧은 진술은 시간이 측정되는 시험의 장점에 대한 논쟁을 시작하게 했다. 3 그 논쟁은 청중을 절반으로 나눴다. 4 한쪽은 삶과 직업에 있어 실제 마감 시간이 있고, 그것들을 놓치는 것에 대한 실제 결과가 있기 때문에, 시간이 측정되는 시험이 가치가 있다고 주장했다. 5 다른 사람들은 시간이 측정되는 시험이 아이들에게 일종의 두려움을 일으켜서, 학생들의 사고력에 해를 끼치고, 더 심오한 학습을 해친다고 생각했다. 6 그러한 의견 차이에도 불구하고, 많은 교사들은 시간이 측정되는 시험들이 속도를 향상시키고 복잡한 문제 해결을 위한 기초를 마련하기 때문에, 수학적인 능숙함으로 가는 길의 중요한 단계라고 생각한다. 7 많은 교사들에게, 시간이 측정되는 시험으로 학생들을 실제 상황에 대비시키지 않는 것은 '아이들을 실패하게 하는 것'처럼 느껴졌다.

> 8 수학 불안에 대한 모든 (A) 염려에도 불구하고, 대다수의 교사는 시간이 측정되는 수학 시험의 (B) 필요성에 동의한다.

어휘확인

research finding 연구 결과 **relate to** ~에 대해 언급하다 **time** 시간을 측정하다 **post** (웹사이트에) 게시하다, 올리다 **discourage** 실망시키다 **anxiety** 불안 **long-term** 장기적인 **fear** 두려움, 공포 **brief** 짧은 **statement** 진술 **debate** 논쟁 **merit** 장점 **divide** 나누다 **audience** 청중 **in half** 절반으로 **argue** 주장하다; 다투다 **valuable** 가치 있는 **deadline** 마감 시간, 기한 **career** 직업, 경력 **consequence** 결과 **damage** 해를 끼치다, 손상을 주다 **ability** 능력 **despite** ~에도 불구하고 **disagreement** 의견 차이 **mathematical** 수학적인 **fluency** 능숙함 **improve** 향상시키다, 개선하다 **foundation** 기초 **complex** 복잡한 **real-life** 실제의 **situation** 상황 **failure** 실패 **concern** 염려, 걱정 **majority** 다수 **necessity** 필요(성)

〈선택지 어휘〉

criticisms 비판 **defect** 단점, 결점 **benefit** 이득 **uselessness** 무용성, 쓸모없음 **weakness** 약점

지문 Flow

[소재]
시간을 측정하는 수학 시험

⬇

[옹호 주장1]
삶과 직업에도 마감 시간이 있으므로 가치가 있음

⬇

[반대 주장]
두려움을 일으켜서 학생들의 사고력에 해를 끼침

⬇

[옹호 주장2]
많은 교사들은 시간을 측정하는 시험이 수학을 능숙하게 하는 중요한 단계라고 생각해서, 그것으로 실제 상황에 대비시킴

정답단추 글 전체를 한 문장으로 압축한 요약문을 먼저 읽고, 빈칸에 들어갈 말의 단서를 글을 읽으면서 찾아보자. 이 글은 시간을 측정하는 수학 시험에 대한 내용이야. 이것에 대한 의견이 둘로 나뉘는데, 한쪽은 삶과 직업처럼 마감 시간이 있는 시험도 그 나름의 가치가 있다고 했고, 다른 한쪽은 그런 시험이 아이들에게 불안과 두려움을 주기 때문에 사고력 학습에 해를 끼친다고 했어. 그럼에도 교사들은 시간을 측정하는 시험이 수학을 능숙하게 하는 데 중요한 단계로 여긴다고 했어. 따라서 빈칸 (A)에 들어갈 말로는 concerns가, 빈칸 (B)에 들어갈 말로는 necessity가 가장 적절해. 이를 종합하면 답은 ④야.

오답단서 ①의 (B) defects와 ⑤의 (B) weaknesses는 수학 교사들이 시간을 측정하는 시험을 중요시한다고 했으므로, 단점, 약점이 답이 될 수는 없어. ②와 ③의 (A) merits는 수학 불안이 장점이 될 수 없으므로 오답이야.

068 정답 ③

지문 All in One

어렵다 / 삶을 상상하는 것은 / 돈과 빚에 대한 걱정에서 자유로운 / 돈을 쓰는 것은
1 It's hard / to imagine *a life* [free from the worries of money and debt]. 2 Spending money /
가주어 V C / 진주어 / S

늘어나는 빚 없이 / 제로섬 게임과 같다 / 그러니까 / 만일 당신이 더 많이 쓰고 싶다면
without increasing debt / is like a zero-sum game. 3 So, / if you want to spend more / on
V C / 접속사 S′ V′

교육에 / 당신은 덜 써야 한다 / 여흥에 / 마찬가지로 / 만일 당신이 경력을 원한다면
education, // you have to spend less / on entertainment. 4 (A) Likewise, / if you want a career,
S V / 접속사 S′ V′

당신은 가족과의 시간을 희생해야 한다 / 만일 당신이 보다 많은 가정생활을 원한다면 / 당신은 희생을 해야 한다
// you have to sacrifice family time. 5 If you want more family life, // you have to make
S V / 접속사 S′ V′ / S V

일에서 / 하지만 / 시간은 돈과 같지 않은데 / 그것은 사라진다 / 당신이
sacrifices / at work. 6 (B) However, / time is not like *money*, // which disappears / as you
S V C / 관계대명사(계속적 용법) / 접속사

쓰는 만큼 / 당신이 시간을 쓰는 방식은 / 효율성의 척도이다 / 양이 아니라
spend it. 7 *The way* [you spend your time] / is a measure of efficiency, / not quantity. 8 When
= money / S V C / 접속사

당신이 시간을 보다 잘 사용할 때 / 당신은 더 많은 것을 할 수 있고 / 일과 가족 측면 둘 다의 균형을 유지할 수 있다
you use your time better, // you can do more / and balance both the work and family sides
S′ V′ / S V_1 / V_2

당신 인생의
/ of your life.

	(A)		(B)
①	In fact	……	Similarly
②	Instead	……	Furthermore
③	Likewise	……	However
④	Likewise	……	In other words
⑤	Instead	……	Otherwise

해석 한 눈에 보기 1 돈과 빚에 대한 걱정에서 자유로운 삶을 상상하는 것은 어렵다. 2 늘어나는 빚 없이 돈을 쓰는 것은 제로섬 게임과 같다. 3 그러니까 만일 당신이 교육에 더 많이 쓰고 싶다면, 당신은 여흥에 덜 써야 한다. 4 (A) 마찬가지로, 만일 당신이 경력을 원한다면, 당신은 가족과의 시간을 희생해야 한다. 5 만일 당신이 보다 많은 가정생활을 원한다면, 당신은 일에서 희생을 감수해야 한다. 6 (B) 하지만 시간은 돈과 같지 않은데, 그것(돈)은 쓰는 만큼 없어진다. 주제문 7 당신이 시간을 쓰는 방식은 양이 아니라 효율성의 척도이다. 8 당신이 시간을 보다 잘 사용할 때, 당신은 더 많은 것을 할 수 있고 당신 인생의 일과 가족 측면 둘 다의 균형을 맞출 수 있다.

정답단추 연결어를 포함한 빈칸 문장의 앞뒤 글의 흐름을 살펴보자. 빈칸 (A)의 앞뒤는 돈을 어느 한쪽에 더 쓰려면 다른 한쪽에서는 아껴야 한다는 비슷한 내용이 이어지니까 (A)에서는 유사성을 나타내는 Likewise가 와야 해. 그리고 빈칸 (B)의 앞은 돈을 어느 한쪽에 쓰는 만큼 다른 쪽에서는 희생을 해야 한다는 내용이지만, 뒤에서는 시간은 쓴다고 없어지는 것이 아니라 효율적으로 사용할수록 더 많은 일을 할 수 있다고 반대되는 내용이 나오고 있지. 그래서 대조를 나타내는 However가 적절해. 따라서 올바른 답은 ③이야.

어휘확인

imagine 상상하다 debt 빚, 부채 increase 늘다 zero-sum game 제로섬 게임(승자의 득점과 패자의 실점을 합치면 0이 되는 게임) education 교육 entertainment 여흥, 오락 likewise 마찬가지로 career (특정한 일을 하면서 보내는) 경력 sacrifice 희생하다; 희생 disappear 사라지다 way 방식 measure 척도, 기준 efficiency 효율(성) quantity 양(量)

지문 Flow

[설명1]
늘어나는 빚 없이 돈을 쓰는 것은 제로섬 게임과 같음

&

[설명2]
• 교육에 더 많이 쓰려면 여흥을 줄여야 함
• 경력을 원하면 가족과의 시간을 희생해야 함
• 더 많은 가정생활을 원하면 일에서 희생을 감수해야 함

⬇

[주제문]
하지만, 시간은 쓰는 만큼 없어지는 돈과 같지 않고, 양이 아니라 효율성의 척도로 시간을 써야 함

⬇

[보충설명]
시간을 효율적으로 사용하면 더 많은 것을 할 수 있고, 일과 가족 둘 다에 균형을 맞출 수 있음

069 정답 ②

지문 All in One

마음속에 떠올리기는 기술이다 / 목표를 달성하기 위해서 대부분의 사람들이 사용하는 / 그리고 그들은 일반적으로
1 Visualization is *a skill* [that most people use to accomplish their goals], and they usually
S_1 V_1 C_1 / 관계대명사 / 부사적 용법(목적) / S_2

시각에 의지한다 / 마음속에서 이미지를 만들어내기 위해 / 하지만, 다른 네 개의 감각들이 있다
turn to the sense of sight / to create images in their minds. 2 However, there are *four other*
V_2 / 부사적 용법(목적)

마음속에 떠올리는 데 강력한 도구인 / 더 강력하게 스스로 마음속에 떠올리기 위해서
senses [that are powerful visualizing tools]. 3 To visualize yourself more powerfully, /
관계대명사 / 부사적 용법(목적)

당신의 이미지를 보충하라 / 청각, 후각, 촉각, 그리고 미각으로 / 당신은
supplement your images / with the senses of hearing, smell, touch, and taste. 4 You can

어휘확인

visualization 마음속에 떠올리기, 시각화 cf. visualize 마음속에 떠올리다, 상상하다 accomplish 달성하다, 성취하다 turn to ~에 의지하다 supplement 보충하다 driver 골프채, 드라이버 dew-covered 이슬로 덮인 downplay 간과하다, 무시하다 adopt 채택하다; 입양하다 become equipped with ~을 갖추다 cf. equip (장비를) 갖추다
<선택지 어휘>
doubt 의심하다

마음속에 떠올리기의 효과를 극적으로 높일 수 있다 / 최대한 많은 수의 감각을 이용함으로써

dramatically increase the impact of visualization / by using the maximum number of senses. [5] If you're working / to improve your golf game, // you can visualize yourself better / with various senses / such as hearing (that) your driver hit the ball straight / or touching the dew-covered grass. [6] It will help achieve your goal more effectively. [7] The importance of visualization / cannot be downplayed. [8] Adopt the technique // and you will become equipped with powerful forces in your life.

(당신이 노력하고 있다면 / 당신의 골프 경기를 향상시키기 위해 / 당신은 마음속에 스스로 더 잘 떠올릴 수 있다 / 다양한 감각으로 / 당신의 골프채가 공을 정통으로 치는 소리를 듣는 것과 같은 / 또는 이슬로 덮인 잔디를 만지는 것과 같은 / 이것은 당신의 목표를 더 효과적으로 달성하는 것을 도울 것이다 / 마음속에 떠올리기의 중요성은 / 간과되어서는 안 된다 / 이 기술을 채택하라 / 그러면 당신은 삶에서 강력한 힘을 갖추게 될 것이다)

(If 접속사, you S', 're working V', to improve 부사적 용법(목적), you S, can visualize V, hearing 동명사, (that) 접속사, your driver S', hit V', or, touching 동명사, Adopt the technique V_1 「명령문, and ~」, you S_2, will become V_2)

① Doubt the power of visualization
마음속에 떠올리기의 힘을 의심하라

② Use as many senses as possible
가능한 한 많은 감각을 이용하라

③ Work hard to accomplish your goal
당신의 목표를 이루기 위해 열심히 일하라

④ Visualize yourself with your friends
친구들과 함께 있는 자신을 마음속으로 그려라

⑤ Focus on what you have in mind now
지금 당신의 마음에 있는 것에 집중하라

해석 한 눈에 보기 [1] 마음속에 떠올리기는 목표를 달성하기 위해서 대부분의 사람들이 사용하는 기술이고, 그들은 일반적으로 마음속에서 이미지를 만들어내기 위해 시각에 의지한다. [2] 하지만, 마음속에 떠올리는 데 강력한 도구인 다른 네 개의 감각들이 있다. 주제문 [3] 더 강력하게 스스로 마음속에 떠올리기 위해서, 당신의 이미지를 청각, 후각, 촉각, 그리고 미각으로 보충하라. [4] 당신은 최대한 많은 수의 감각을 이용함으로써 마음속에 떠올리기의 효과를 극적으로 높일 수 있다. [5] 당신이 당신의 골프 경기를 향상시키기 위해 노력하고 있다면, 당신의 골프채가 공을 정통으로 치는 소리를 듣는 것 또는 이슬로 덮인 잔디를 만지는 것과 같은 다양한 감각으로 마음속에 스스로 더 잘 떠올릴 수 있다. [6] 이것은 당신의 목표를 더 효과적으로 달성하는 것을 도울 것이다. [7] 마음속에 떠올리기의 중요성은 간과되어서는 안 된다. 주제문 [8] 이 기술을 채택하라, 그러면 당신은 삶에서 강력한 힘을 갖추게 될 것이다.

정답단추 목표를 달성하기 위해 마음속에 떠올리기를 할 때 일반적으로 시각에 의지하지만, 시각, 청각, 후각, 촉각 등 최대한 많은 감각을 동원하는 것이 훨씬 더 효과적이라는 내용이야. 마지막에 주제를 다시 한번 언급하는 문장에서 '이 기술을 채택하라'는 어구의 의미는 '가능한 한 많은 감각을 이용하라'이므로 정답은 ②야.

오답단서 글의 핵심어인 '마음속에 떠올리기(visualization)'가 포함되었지만, 그것을 의심하는 것과는 관련이 없는 내용이므로 ①은 오답이야. ③도 역시 visualize가 등장하지만 친구와 자신을 마음속에 그리라는 내용이 글에 언급되지 않았으므로 정답이 될 수 없어.

지문 Flow

[통념]
대부분의 사람들은 목표 달성을 위해 마음속에서 이미지를 만들어내는 것을 시각에 의지함

⬇

[주제문]
마음속에 떠올리는 데 다른 네 개의 감각인 청각, 후각, 촉각, 미각으로 보충하라

⬇

[보충 설명]
최대한 많은 수의 감각을 이용함으로써 마음속에 떠올리기의 효과를 극적으로 높일 수 있음

⬇

[예시]
골프 경기에서 골프공 치는 소리 등 보다 다양한 감각으로 떠올리면 목표 달성에 효과적임

⬇

[주제문 재진술]
다양한 감각으로 마음속에 떠올리기를 하면 강력한 힘을 갖춤

070 정답 ②

지문 All in One

[1] How and when / do secrets, and the revelation of secrets, / give rise to shame and embarrassment? [2] Sometimes / the causes of shame / are open secrets. [3] Open secrets are *things* [that everyone knows / but still pretends to be secret]. [4] And so / one has to live / with the publicity of this open secret. [5] Shame is *the feeling* [that often accompanies the public revelation of *a secret* [that is considered morally wrong / in some way]]. [6] But / one only feels shame / about *actions* [that **one accepts as faults**]. [7] Someone may exclaim: / "Shame on you for using that language!" [8] But / if we do not feel / that our language was inappropriate or blameworthy, // then we need not feel shame. [9] In other words, / one feels shame // when (one is) judged by other people / for *a fault* [that one agrees is a fault].

(어떻게 그리고 언제 / 비밀과 비밀에 대한 폭로가 ~ 하는가 / 수치심과 당혹감을 생기게 / 때때로 / 수치심의 원인은 / 공개 비밀이다 / 공개 비밀은 모든 사람이 아는 것이다 / 하지만 여전히 비밀인 척하는 / 그래서 / 사람은 살아야 한다 / 이 공개 비밀이 널리 알려진 채 / 수치심은 감정이다 / 비밀에 대한 공개적인 폭로에 종종 동반되는 / 도덕적으로 잘못이라 여겨지는 / 어떤 면에서 / 그러나 / 사람은 단지 수치심을 느낀다 / 그가 잘못으로 인정하는 행동에 대해서 / 누군가 외칠지도 모른다 / 저 언어를 사용하는 것을 부끄러워하세요 / 하지만 / 우리가 느끼지 않으면 / 언어가 부적절하거나 비난 받을 만하다고 / 그 다음에 우리는 부끄러움을 느낄 필요가 없다 / 다시 말해서 / 사람은 수치심을 느낀다 / 다른 사람들에 의해 판단될 때 / 그가 동의하기에 잘못인 잘못으로)

(secrets ... of secrets S, give rise to V, the causes of shame S, are V, open secrets C, Open secrets S, are V, things C, that 관계대명사, one S, has to live V, Shame S, is V, the feeling C, that 관계대명사, that 관계대명사, one S, feels V, that 관계대명사, Someone S, may exclaim V, "Shame on you V', if 접속사, we S', do not feel V', that 접속사, our language S", was V", inappropriate $C"_1$, blameworthy $C"_2$, we S, need not feel V, one S, feels V, when 접속사, (one S', is) judged V', that 관계대명사, one agrees 삽입절)

① are against social rules
사회적 규칙에 위배되는

② one accepts as faults
그가 잘못으로 인정하는

어휘확인

revelation 폭로, 누설 **give rise to** ~이 생기게 하다 **shame** 수치심 **embarrassment** 당혹, 당황 **pretend** ~인 체하다 **publicity** 널리 알려짐, 공표 **accompany** 동반하다 **consider** ~로 여기다 **morally** 도덕적으로 **fault** 잘못 **exclaim** 외치다 **language** 언어 **inappropriate** 부적절한 **blameworthy** 비난 받을 만한 **in other words** 다시 말해서 **judge** 판단하다

〈선택지 어휘〉
blame 비난하다 **hide** 숨다 **threat** 위협 **safety** 안전

지문 Flow

[도입]
비밀과 폭로가 수치와 당혹감을 생기게 하는 때와 방법은 무엇인가

⬇

[설명]
수치심은 도덕적으로 잘못이라고 생각하는 비밀이 공개적으로 폭로될 때 동반되는 감정임

⬇

③ are blamed by others
다른 사람들에 의해 비난 받는

④ one cannot hide well
그가 잘 숨을 수 없는

⑤ are threats to one's safety
사람의 안전에 위협이 되는

[역접]
사람은 자신이 잘못이라고 생각하는 비밀에만 수치심을 느낌

[주제문]
자신이 잘못이라고 생각하는 것을 다른 사람들이 잘못이라고 할 때 수치심을 느낌

해석 한 눈에 보기 1 어떻게 그리고 언제 비밀과 비밀에 대한 폭로가 수치심과 당혹감을 생기게 하는가? 2 때때로 수치심의 원인은 공개 비밀이다. 3 공개 비밀은 모든 사람이 알고 있지만 여전히 비밀인 척하는 것이다. 4 그래서 사람은 이 공개 비밀이 널리 알려진 채 살아야 한다. 5 수치심은 어떤 면에서 도덕적으로 잘못이라 여겨지는 비밀에 대한 공개적인 폭로에 종종 동반되는 감정이다. 6 그러나 사람은 그가 잘못으로 인정하는 행동에 대해서만 수치심을 느낀다. 7 누군가 "저 언어를 사용하는 것을 부끄러워하세요!"라고 외칠지도 모른다. 8 하지만 우리의 언어가 부적절하거나 비난 받을 만하다고 느끼지 않으면, 그 다음에 우리는 부끄러움을 느낄 필요가 없다. 주제문 9 다시 말해서, 사람은 그가 동의하기에 잘못인 잘못으로 다른 사람들에 의해 판단될 때 수치심을 느낀다.

정답단추 빈칸에 있는 문장에 연결어 But이 있으므로, 당연히 앞의 내용과는 반대되는 내용이 되어야겠지? 앞뒤 문맥을 확인하면서 사람이 '무슨' 행동에 수치심을 느끼는지 찾아보자. 먼저 빈칸 앞에서 수치심은 도덕적으로 잘못이라 여겨지는 비밀에 대한 공개적인 폭로에서 생긴다고 했어. 하지만 빈칸 뒤에서는 자신이 쓰는 말이 부적절하거나 비난 받을 만하다고 생각하지 않으면 수치심을 느낄 필요가 없다는 내용이 예로 나와. 즉, 이것은 자기가 잘못으로 인정하는 행동에 수치심을 느낀다는 말이야. 따라서 빈칸에 들어갈 말로 가장 적절한 것은 ②야.

오답단서 ①, ③은 도덕적으로 잘못이라 여겨지면서 자신도 인정하는 잘못에만 수치심을 느낀다는 글의 내용과 어긋나므로 오답이야. ④는 드러나는 잘못이 아니라 인정하는 잘못에 초점을 두고 있으므로 답이 될 수 없어. ⑤는 글에서 다루지 않았으므로 적절하지 않아.

071 정답 ④

지문 All in One

1 "A rolling stone gathers no moss" is a well-known saying / in both America and Japan. ('구르는 돌은 이끼가 끼지 않는다'는 잘 알려진 속담이다 / 미국과 일본 두 곳에서)

2 For Americans, / a rolling stone means // *someone* [who is free-spirited and always moving]. (미국인들에게 / 구르는 돌은 의미한다 / 자유분방하고 항상 움직이는(활동적인) 사람을) 3 That kind of person / is usually considered cool // because they aren't tied down / by *the constraints* [that hold most of us back]. (그런 유형의 사람은 / 대개 멋지다고 여겨진다 / 그들은 얽매어 있지(묶여 있지) 않기 때문이다 / 우리 대부분을 저지하는 제약들에) 4 Moss represents the bad things / about staying in one place and getting old. (이끼는 나쁜 것들을 대표한다 / 한 곳에 머무르다 늙어가는 것에 대한) 5 The Japanese, / on the other hand, / see a rolling stone / as *a person* [who fails to keep a steady job], / *someone* [who avoids responsibilities and has no cares]. (일본인들은 / 반면에 / 구르는 돌을 본다 / 고정적인 직장을 유지하는 데 실패하는 사람으로 / (즉) 책임을 회피하고 걱정이 없는 사람으로) 6 As for moss, / it represents / *the kind of wisdom* or *wealth* [that grows only in peace and stillness] // and would never be found / on a rolling stone. (이끼에 대해서 말하자면 / 그것은 나타낸다 / 오직 평화와 고요 속에서만 자라는 종류의 지혜나 부를 / 그리고 절대로 발견되지 않을 것이다 / 구르는 돌에서는)

(1: S = "A rolling stone gathers no moss", V = is, C = a well-known saying / 2: S = a rolling stone, V = means, who: 관계대명사 / 3: S = That kind of person, V = is usually considered, C = cool, because: 접속사, S' = they, V' = aren't tied down, that: 관계대명사 / 4: S = Moss, V = represents / 5: S = The Japanese, V = see, who: 관계대명사 / 6: S = it, V_1 = represents, that: 관계대명사, V_2 = would never be found)

⬇

> 7 America and Japan share the same proverb, // but it has different (A) meanings / because of each culture's (B) viewpoint / on rolling stones and moss. (미국과 일본은 동일한 속담을 공유한다 / 하지만 그것은 다른 의미를 가진다 / 각 문화의 관점 때문에 / 구르는 돌과 이끼에 대한)
>
> (S_1 = America and Japan, V_1 = share, S_2 = it, V_2 = has)

	(A)		(B)
①	uses	……	experience with
②	forms	……	thoughts about
③	origins	……	focus on
④	meanings	……	viewpoint on
⑤	purposes	……	attitude about

어휘확인

moss 이끼 well-known 잘 알려진 saying 속담(= proverb) American 미국인 free-spirited 자유분방한 consider 여기다 cool 멋진; 시원한 tie down ~을 얽매다 constraint 제약 hold back ~을 저지하다 represent 대표하다; 나타내다 steady 고정적인; 꾸준한 responsibility 책임 as for ~에 대해서 말하자면 wealth 부(富) stillness 고요, 정적 viewpoint 관점
〈선택지 어휘〉
form 형태; 종류 thought 생각 origin 유래 purpose 목적 attitude 태도[자세]

지문 Flow

[도입]
'구르는 돌에는 이끼가 끼지 않는다'는 속담

⬇

[비교1]
미국인들에게 구르는 돌은 자유분방하며 활동적인 사람을 의미하고, 이끼는 한 곳에 머무르다 늙어가는 나쁜 것을 의미함

&

[비교2]
일본인들에게 구르는 돌은 고정적인 직장을 유지하지 못하고 책임을 회피하는 사람으로 여겨지고, 이끼는 지혜나 부의 축적을 의미함

해석 한 눈에 보기 1 '구르는 돌에는 이끼가 끼지 않는다'는 미국과 일본 두 곳에서 잘 알려진 속담이다. 2 미국인들에게, 구르는 돌은 자유분방하며 항상 활동적인 사람을 의미한다. 3 그런 유형의 사람은 대체로 멋지다고 여겨지는데 그들은 우리 대부분을 저지하는 제약들에 묶여 있지 않기 때문이다. 4 이끼는 한곳에 머무르다 늙어가는 것에 대한 나쁜 것을 대표한다. 5 반면에 일본인들은 구르는 돌을 고정적인 직장을 유지하지 못하는 사람, 즉 책임을 회피하고 걱정이 없는 사람으로 여긴다. 6 이끼에 대해 말하자면, 그것은 오직 평화와 고요 속에서만 자라는 종류의 지혜나 부를 의미하여 구르는 돌에서는 절대 발견되지 않을 것이다.

> 7 미국과 일본은 같은 속담을 공유하지만, 그것은 서로 다른 (A) 의미를 지니는데 구르는 돌과 이끼에 대한 각 문화의 (B) 관점 때문이다.

정답단추 먼저 요약문을 읽고 미국과 일본에는 공통된 속담이 있지만, 구르는 돌과 이끼에 대한 '무엇'이 달라서 속담의 '무엇'도 다르다는 내용을 파악한 다음, 나머지 글에서 '무엇'을 찾는 데 집중해야 해. 글 중간의 on the other hand를 기준으로 앞부분에는 구르는 돌을 긍정적으로 보고 이끼는 부정적으로 보는 미국인의 생각이, 뒷부분에는 이와 반대되는 일본인의 생각이 나와 있어. 따라서 이를 요약해 나타내면 두 나라에서 공통적인 속담이 구르는 돌과 이끼에 대한 다른 '관점(viewpoint)' 때문에 속담의 '의미(meanings)'도 달라진다는 내용이 적절해. 이를 종합하면 정답은 ④야.

072 정답 ①

지문 All in One

1 An egg cream is / *a refreshing cold drink* [that originated in New York City soda shops / about a hundred years ago]. 2 It's made of milk, flavored syrup, and soda water. 3 It contains neither eggs nor cream, // but it's called an egg cream nevertheless. 4 That's just the way it is. 5 Likewise, / people are not always predictable, // instruction manuals are sometimes unclear, // and fast food may or may not be served fast. 6 It's important to recognize and accept // that things won't always make sense. 7 That's really okay // because both the logical and the nonsensical are threads / in *the same rich tapestry* [that we call life].

8 We need to (A) accept the fact // [that the world does not always operate (B) rationally].

	(A)		(B)
①	accept	……	rationally
②	reject	……	legally
③	accept	……	sensitively
④	dispute	……	legally
⑤	reject	……	rationally

해석 한 눈에 보기 1 에그 크림은 약 100년 전에 뉴욕 시의 탄산음료 가게에서 생겨난 상쾌하게 해주는 찬 음료이다. 2 그것은 우유, 향이 나는 시럽, 소다수로 만들어진다. 3 그것은 달걀도 크림도 함유하고 있지 않지만, 그럼에도 불구하고 에그 크림이라고 불린다. 4 그것은 그냥 그렇게 되었다. 5 마찬가지로, 사람들이 항상 예측 가능한 것은 아니며, 사용 설명서가 때때로 불명확하고, 패스트푸드가 빨리 나오기도 하고 아니기도 하다. 주제문 6 상황이 항상 이해가 되는 것은 아니라는 것을 인식하고 받아들이는 것이 중요하다. 7 그것은 정말로 괜찮은데 논리적인 것과 터무니없는 것 둘 다 우리가 인생이라고 부르는 하나의 풍성한 태피스트리 안의 실들이기 때문이다.

8 우리는 세상이 항상 (B) 이성적으로 돌아가는 것은 아니라는 사실을 (A) 받아들일 필요가 있다.

정답단추 먼저 요약문 내용을 파악하고, 글 전체를 읽는 게 좋아. 세상이 항상 '어떠한 방법으로' 돌아가는 것은 아니라는 사실을 우리가 '무엇해야' 하는지에 대해 찾으면 되겠지? 이 글은 에그 크림, 사람, 사용 설명서, 패스트푸드를 예로 들면서 결국 상황은 예측 불가능하고 비논리적일 수 있으므로 이를 인정하는 게 중요하다는 내용이야. 다시 말해 세상은 항상 '이성적으로(rationally)' 돌아가는 것이 아니므로 '받아들일(accept)' 필요가 있다는 거야. 따라서 정답은 ① 이야.

어휘확인

refreshing 상쾌하게 하는 **originate in** ~에서 생겨나다 **soda** 탄산음료, 소다 **flavored** 향[맛]이 나는 **syrup** 시럽 **contain** ~이 함유되어 있다 **neither A nor B** A도 B도 아니다 **nevertheless** 그럼에도 불구하고 **likewise** 마찬가지로 **predictable** 예측 가능한 **instruction manual** 사용 설명서 **unclear** 분명하지 않은 **recognize** 인식하다 **thing** 상황; 물건 **make sense** 이해가 되다 **logical** 논리적인 **nonsensical** 터무니없는 **thread** 실 **rich** 풍성한; 부유한 **tapestry** 태피스트리(여러 가지 색실로 그림을 짜 넣은 직물) **operate** 운용되다(돌아가다) **rationally** 이성적으로
〈선택지 어휘〉
reject 거부하다 **legally** 합법적으로 **sensitively** 민감하게 **dispute** 반박하다

지문 Flow

[도입]
에그 크림은 달걀과 크림이 들어가지 않았지만 그냥 그렇게 불림

[추가]
사람들이 항상 예측 가능한 것은 아님

[예시]
• 불명확한 사용 설명서
• 빨리 나오기도 하고 아니기도 한 패스트푸드

[주제문]
상황이 항상 이해가 되는 것은 아니라는 것을 받아들여야 함

073 정답 ④

지문 All in One

1 It is vital // that young people **control** and **direct / their own learning**. 2 More specifically, / they must have *the right* [to decide] // if, when, how much, and by whom they want to be taught. 3 Furthermore, / they must be allowed / to decide // whether they want to go to

어휘확인

vital 매우 중요한 **direct** 관리하다, 감독하다 **learning** 학습 **specifically** 구체적으로 **right** 권리 **furthermore** 더 나아가 **allow** 허용하다 **whether ~ or not** ~인지 아닌지 **university** 대학 **attend** 다니다 **determine** 결정하다 **freedom** 자유 **advanced** 선진의 **education** 교육 **thought** (특정한) 생각 **guarantee** 보장하다 **success** 성공

그리고 얼마나 오랫동안 (그러고 싶은지를) 정말로 대학에 다니는 사람들에게는 최고다
university [or not], / [and] for how long. 4 For *those* [who do attend university], / it's best // that
관계대명사 가주어 V C
그들이 허용되는 것이 그들 자신의 수업 과정을 결정하도록 이것은 보호되는 자유다
they are allowed / to determine their own course of study. 5 This is *a freedom* [that is
진주어 S V C 관계대명사
모든 선진 사회에서 자기 자신의 교육을 선택할 수 있는 자유는
protected / in all advanced societies]. 6 *Freedom* [to choose one's own education] / is an
S V
중요한 일부분이다 생각의 자유의 그러므로 그것은 우리가 보호해야 하는 권리이다
important part / of freedom of thought. 7 Therefore, / it is *a right* [that we must protect] / in
C S V C 관계대명사
미래의 성공을 보장하기 위해 우리 사회의
order to guarantee the future success / of our society.
부사적 용법(목적)

① obtain a high level of education
높은 수준의 교육을 받는

② think whatever they want to think
생각하고 싶은 것은 무엇이든 생각하는

③ learn to be strong through hardship
역경을 통해 강해지는 법을 배우는

④ control and direct their own learning
그들 자신의 학습을 통제하고 관리하는

⑤ lead an independent life from their parents
그들의 부모로부터 독립적인 인생을 이끌어가는

해석 한 눈에 보기 주제문 1 젊은이들이 그들 자신의 학습을 통제하고 관리하는 것은 매우 중요하다. 2 더 구체적으로, 그들은 그들이 언제, 얼마나 많이, 그리고 누구에 의해 교육을 받고 싶은지를 결정할 권리를 가져야 한다. 3 더 나아가, 그들은 대학에 가고 싶은지 아닌지 그리고 얼마나 오랫동안 그러고 싶은지를 결정하도록 허용되어야 한다. 4 정말로 대학에 다니는 사람들에게는, 그들이 그들 자신의 수업 과정을 결정하도록 허용되는 것이 가장 좋다. 5 이것은 모든 선진 사회에서 보호되는 자유다. 6 자기 자신의 교육을 선택할 수 있는 자유는 생각의 자유의 중요한 일부분이다. 7 그러므로 그것은 우리가 우리 사회의 성공적인 미래를 보장하기 위해 보호해야 하는 권리이다.

정답단추 빈칸이 포함된 문장은 젊은이들에게 '무엇'이 매우 중요하다는 내용이야. 나머지 글을 읽고 '무엇'을 찾으면 돼. More specifically로 시작하는 두 번째 문장부터 앞 문장 내용을 뒷받침하는 부연 설명이 이어지고 있지? 이를 요약하면 '언제, 얼마나, 누구에 의해 교육받을지 젊은이들이 스스로 교육을 결정하고 관리하는 것이 필요하다'는 내용이야. 이를 정리해보면 빈칸에 들어갈 가장 적절한 답은 ④이고, 더불어 빈칸이 포함된 문장이 주제문이라는 것도 알 수 있어.

오답단서 이 글은 학습에 대한 주제를 다루고 있는 데 반해 ②, ③, ⑤는 그 주제와는 전혀 상관없는 내용이라서 정답이 될 수 없어. ①은 글에 사용된 어휘인 '교육'을 활용하여 오답을 유도하고 있지만, 마찬가지로 주제와는 무관한 내용이므로 정답으로 적절하지 않아.

〈선택지 어휘〉
obtain 받다, 얻다 **high level** 높은 수준 **whatever** ~하는 것은 무엇이든지 **hardship** 역경, 고난 **independent** 독립적인

지문 Flow

[주제문]
젊은이들이 자신의 학습을 통제하고 관리하는 것의 중요성

⬇

[보충설명1]
자신의 교육과 관련한 모든 것을 결정할 권리를 가져야 함

&

[보충설명2]
자신의 교육을 선택할 수 있는 자유는 생각의 자유의 중요한 일부분임

⬇

[결론]
그것은 우리 사회의 성공적인 미래를 보장하기 위해 보호해야 할 권리임

074 정답 ④

지문 All in One

누구도 놀라지 않는다 여름의 햇볕이 내리쬐는 따뜻함이 사람들을 행복하게 만든다는 것에
1 No one is surprised / that the sunny warmth of summer / makes people happy, // [but] the
S_1 V_1 접속사 S' V' O' C'
그러나 날씨의 영향은 거기서 멈추지 않는다 비 오는 날씨는 우리를 자기 성찰적이고 사색적으로
influence of weather doesn't stop there. 2 Rainy weather makes us introspective [and]
S_2 V_2 S V O C
만드는데 그것은 결과적으로 우리의 기억력을 강화시킨다 한 연구에서 사람들은 더 정확하게
thoughtful, / which in turn (A) enhances our memory. 3 In one study, / people more
관계대명사(계속적 용법) S
기억했다 상점의 특징을 비 오는 날에 훨씬 더 놀라운 것은 관계이다
accurately remembered / the features of a store / on rainy days. 4 More surprising still is the
V C V
날씨 변화와 우울증 그리고 다양한 종류의 사고들 사이의
relationship / [between] changes in weather / [and] depression, [and] various kinds of
주어가 길어 「보어+동사+주어」로 도치된 형태 S
이 연관성은 따뜻함과 사람의 친절함 사이의 비유 이상이다
accidents. 5 The association / [between] warmth [and] human kindness / is more than a
S_1 V_1 C_1
최근의 연구들은 보여줘 왔다 사람들이 낯선 사람들을 더 호감 있게 생각한다는 것을
metaphor; // recent studies have shown / that people find strangers more (B) likeable / when
S_2 V_2 접속사 S' V' O' C' 접속사
뜨거운 커피 한 잔을 들고 있을 때 따뜻함과 친절함의 비유는 확장된다 사회적 고립
(they're) holding a cup of hot coffee. 6 The warmth-kindness metaphor extends / to social
S″ V″ S_1 V_1
으로 사람들은 문자 그대로 더 차갑게 느낀다 그들이 사회적으로 고립되어 있을 때
exclusion: // people literally feel colder / when they've been socially isolated.
S_2 V_2 C 접속사 S' V'

	(A)		(B)
①	worsens	……	familiar
②	worsens	……	likeable
③	resets	……	familiar
④	enhances	……	likeable
⑤	enhances	……	threatening

어휘확인
surprised 놀라는 **influence** 영향 **introspective** 자기 성찰적인 **thoughtful** 사색적인, 생각에 잠긴 **in turn** 결과적으로 **enhance** 강화[향상]시키다 **memory** 기억력 **study** 연구; 공부 **accurately** 정확하게 **feature** 특징 **still** (비교급을 강조하여) 훨씬 **relationship** 관계 **depression** 우울증 **various** 다양한 **accident** 사고 **association** 연관성 **kindness** 친절(함) **metaphor** 비유, 은유 **recent** 최근의 **likeable** 호감이 가는 **extend** 확장하다 **exclusion** 고립; 제외 **literally** 문자 그대로 **isolate** 고립시키다, 격리하다

〈선택지 어휘〉
worsen 악화시키다 **familiar** 친근한 **reset** 다시 설정하다 **threatening** 위협적인, 협박하는

지문 Flow

[주제문]
날씨는 사람들에게 영향을 미침

⬇

[보충설명1]
비 오는 날씨는 기억력을 강화시킴

&

해석 한 눈에 보기 주제문 1 누구도 햇볕이 내리쬐는 여름의 따뜻함이 사람들을 행복하게 만든다는 것에 놀라지 않지만, 날씨의 영향은 거기서 멈추지 않는다. 2 비 오는 날씨는 우리를 자기 성찰적이고 사색적으로 만드는데, 그것은 결과적으로 우리의 기억력을 (A) 강화시킨다. 3 한 연구에서 사람들은 비 오는 날에 상점의 특징을 더 정확하게 기억했다. 4 훨씬 더 놀라운 것은 날씨 변화와 우울증 그리고 다양한 종류의 사고들 사이의 관계이다. 5 따뜻함과 사람의 친절함 사이의 연관성은 비유 이상으로, 최근의 연구들은 사람들이 뜨거운 커피 한 잔을 들고 있을 때 낯선 사람들을 더 (B) 호감 있게 생각한다는 것을 보여줘 왔다. 6 따뜻함과 친절함의 비유는 사회적 고립으로 확장되는데, 사람들은 그들이 사회적으로 고립되어 있을 때 문자 그대로 더 차갑게 느낀다.

정답단추 빈칸을 추론할 수 있는 단서는 빈칸을 포함한 문장의 주변에 있을 가능성이 높아. 우선 빈칸을 포함한 문장을 읽어보자. 빈칸 (A)가 포함된 문장은 비 오는 날은 우리를 생각에 잠기게 하여 우리의 기억력을 '무엇'한다고 했어. 다음 문장에서 연구에 따르면 사람들이 비 오는 날에 매장의 특징을 더욱 더 정확하게 기억했다고 했으니까 (A)에는 '강화시킨다(enhances)'가 오는 것이 적절해. 또한, 빈칸 (B)의 단서도 빈칸을 포함한 문장의 다음 문장에 제시되어 있어. 이 문장에서 따뜻함과 친절함의 관계는 사람들이 사회적으로 고립될 때 실제로 더 춥게 느끼는 것으로 확장된다고 하고 있지? 그러니까 뜨거운 커피를 들고 있을 때는 낯선 사람을 '호감 있게(likeable)' 생각한다는 내용이 되어야 자연스러워. 따라서 가장 적절한 답은 ④야.

오답단서 빈칸 (A)에는 기억력을 강화시킨다는 내용이 와야 하니까 ①, ②, ③의 빈칸 (A) 어휘인 worsen(악화시키다)과 reset(다시 설정하다)은 올 수 없어. 또한, 빈칸 (B)에서도 ①, ③, ⑤의 familiar(친근한)와 threatening(위협적인)은 문맥상 정답이 될 수 없어.

[보충설명2]
날씨 변화와 우울증 그리고 다양한 사고들 사이에 관계가 있음

&

[보충설명3]
따뜻함과 친절함 사이에도 연관이 있음

⬇

[예시1]
따뜻한 커피를 들고 있는 낯선 사람들을 더 호감 있게 생각함

&

[예시2]
사람들은 사회적으로 고립되어 있을 때 더 차갑게 느낌

075 정답 ⑤

지문 All in One

1 One of the reasons [(why[that]) the violin is difficult to learn to play] is // that its fingerboard contains no *visual aids* [to help the beginner acquire competence / in fingering]. 2 Unlike the guitar, / (A) for instance, / the violin has no frets, / that is, / no *small metal bars* or *bumps* [to guide the fingers]. 3 Therefore, / the beginner must learn exact positions / and literally feel his or her way, / unaided, / from position to position / up the fingerboard of the instrument. 4 Until the learner develops skill, // many notes are painfully out of tune. 5 Even when skill increases, // the player may still sound poor / unless he or she has a good ear. 6 (B) Thus, / not only does the beginner suffer, / he or she can also torture / *those* [listening], // as many a patient parent or sacrificial sibling / can tell you.

(바이올린 연주를 배우기 어려운 이유들 중의 하나는 / 지판에 시각 보조물이 없다는 것이다 / 초보자가 능숙함을 얻는 데 도움이 되는 / 운지법에 있어 / 기타와 달리 / 예를 들어 / 바이올린은 프렛이 없다 / 즉 / 작은 금속 막대나 돌기가 없다 / 손가락을 이끌기 위한 / 따라서 / 초보자는 정확한 위치를 배워야 한다 / 그리고 문자 그대로 더듬어 나가야 한다 / 도움이 없이 / 위치에서 위치로 / 악기의 지판을 따라 / 학습자가 기술을 연마할 때까지 / 고통스럽게도 많은 음들이 맞지 않는다 / 기술이 늘어났을 때조차도 / 연주자는 여전히 안 좋게 들릴지도 모른다 / 그들이 좋은 음감을 가지고 있지 않으면 / 따라서 / 초보자는 고통을 당할 뿐만 아니라 / 그들은 고문할 수도 있다 / 듣고 있는 사람들을 / 많은 인내심이 강한 부모나 희생적인 형제자매가 ~하는 것처럼 / 당신에게 말할 수 있다)

	(A)		(B)		(A)		(B)
①	instead	……	Thus	②	as a result	……	Moreover
③	as a result	……	Likewise	④	for instance	……	Likewise
⑤	for instance	……	Thus				

해석 한 눈에 보기 1 바이올린 연주를 배우기 어려운 이유들 중의 하나는 지판에 초보자가 운지법에 있어 능숙함을 얻는 데 도움이 되는 시각 보조물이 없다는 것이다. 2 (A) 예를 들어, 기타와 달리, 바이올린은 프렛이 없다. 즉, 손가락을 이끌기 위한 작은 금속 막대나 돌기가 없다. 3 따라서, 초보자는 정확한 위치를 배우고 문자 그대로 악기의 지판을 따라 위치에서 위치로 도움이 없이 더듬어 나가야 한다. 4 학습자가 기술을 연마할 때까지, 고통스럽게도 많은 음들이 맞지 않는다. 5 기술이 늘어났을 때조차도, 연주자가 좋은 음감을 가지고 있지 않으면 여전히 안 좋게 들릴지도 모른다. 6 (B) 따라서, 초보자는 고통을 당할 뿐만 아니라, 많은 인내심이 강한 부모나 희생적인 형제자매가 당신에게 말할 수 있는 것처럼, 그들은 듣고 있는 사람들을 고문할 수도 있다.

정답단추 연결어는 두 문장을 이어주는 역할을 하므로, 빈칸 앞뒤 문장의 문맥을 잘 살펴보도록 해. 빈칸 (A) 앞에는 바이올린은 운지할 때 도움을 주는 시각 보조물이 없어서 배우기 어렵다는 내용이 나오는데, 뒤에서 그 예로 바이올린에 프렛이 없음을 말하고 있어. 따라서 (A)에는 예시를 나타내는 연결어 for instance가 적절해. 빈칸 (B) 앞에는 초보자들이 바이올린을 잘 연주하게 되기 전까지는 음이 맞지 않으며, 연주자의 음감이 좋지 않아도 음이 맞지 않는다는 내용이 나오고, 뒤에는 그것으로 인해 본인 포함 듣는 가족들도 고통을 받는다고 나와 있어. 따라서 (B)에는 결과를 나타내는 연결어 Thus가 적절해. 이를 종합하면 답은 ⑤야.

어휘확인

fingerboard 지판(指板)(기타나 바이올린에서 손가락으로 현을 누르는 곳) **contain** 포함하다 **visual** 시각적인 **aid** 보조물, 보조도구 **beginner** 초보자 **acquire** 얻다, 습득하다 **competence** 능숙함 **fingering** 운지법(악기를 연주할 때 손가락을 쓰는 방법) **unlike** ~와 달리 **fret** 프렛(현악기의 지판을 구분하는 작은 돌기) **metal** 금속의 **bar** 막대기 **bump** 돌기 **guide** 이끌다, 안내하다 **therefore** 따라서, 그러므로 **exact** 정확한 **position** 위치 **literally** 문자 그대로 **feel one's way** 더듬어 나가다 **unaided** 도움이 없는 **instrument** 악기 **develop** 발전시키다 **painfully** 고통스럽게 **out of tune** 음이 맞지 않는 **increase** 증가하다 **unless** 만약 ~이 아니면, ~이 아닌 한 **good ear** 좋은 음감 **suffer** 고통 받다 **torture** 고문하다 **patient** 인내심 있는 **sacrificial** 희생적인 **sibling** 형제자매

지문 Flow

[도입]
시각 보조물이 없어서 바이올린 연주는 배우기 어려움

⬇

[예시]
기타와 달리 바이올린은 프렛이 없어서, 감으로 정확한 위치를 잡아야 함

⬇

[문제점]
• 연주 기술을 연마할 때까지 음이 맞지 않음
• 연주자의 음감이 좋지 않으면 음이 맞지 않음

⬇

[결과]
자신이 고통을 받고, 부모 형제를 고문하게 됨

076 정답 ②

지문 All in One

[1] It has long been known // that dolphins are among the smartest creatures / on Earth, / possessing sophisticated communication skills [and] the capacity for true learning. [2] But their uniqueness among species / doesn't end there. [3] Dolphins are social creatures // [and] can establish strong social bonds. [4] They will stay with injured [or] ill individuals, / even helping them to breathe / by bringing them to the surface / if (it is) needed. [5] This tendency does not appear / **to be limited to their own species**. [6] The dolphin Moko in New Zealand / has been observed guiding a female whale together with her calf / out of *shallow water* [where they had been stranded several times]. [7] They have also been seen protecting swimmers from sharks / by moving in circles / around the swimmers / [or] swimming toward sharks / to make them go away.

(오랫동안 알려져 왔다 / 돌고래가 가장 똑똑한 생명체 중 하나로 / 지구에서 / 정교한 의사소통 기술과 진정한 학습을 위한 능력을 소유하고 있어서 / 하지만 / 종들 중에서 그것들의 독특함은 / 거기서 끝나지 않는다 / 돌고래는 사회적 동물이다 / 그리고 강한 사회적 유대감을 형성할 수 있다 / 그것들은 다쳤거나 병든 개체와 함께 머무를 것이다 / 심지어 그것들이 숨을 쉬도록 돕는다 / 그것들을 수면으로 데리고 감으로써 / 만약 필요하다면 / 이러한 경향은 ~인 것 같지 않다 / 그것들 자신의 종에 국한되어 있는 / 뉴질랜드의 돌고래 Moko는 / 새끼와 함께 있는 한 암컷 고래를 안내하는 것이 관찰되어져 왔다 / 그것들이 여러 번 오도 가도 못하고 있던 얕은 물에서 빠져나오게 / 그것들은 또한 상어로부터 수영객들을 보호하는 것도 보여져 왔다(목격되어 왔다) / 원을 그리며 움직임으로써 / 수영객들 주변을 / 또는 상어들을 향해 헤엄쳐 감으로써 / 그것들이 가버리게 만들기 위해)

(문법 표시: S, V, 접속사, S′, V′, C′, 분사구문(= as they possess ~), V₁, C, V₂, 분사구문(= as they help them ~), 관계부사, 부사적 용법(목적))

① to be an inborn characteristic
타고난 특징인

② to be limited to their own species
그것들 자신의 종에 국한되어 있는

③ in emergency circumstances
응급 상황에 있는

④ in moving individually
각각 따로 이동하는

⑤ to last throughout their whole lives
그들의 전 생애 동안 지속되는

해석 한 눈에 보기 1 돌고래는 정교한 의사소통 기술과 진정한 학습 능력을 소유하고 있어서 지구에서 가장 똑똑한 생명체 중 하나로 오랫동안 알려져 왔다. 2 하지만 종들 중에서의 그것들의 독특함은 거기서 끝나지 않는다. **주제문** 3 돌고래는 사회적 동물이며 강력한 사회적 유대감을 형성할 수 있다. 4 그것들은 다쳤거나 병든 개체들과 함께 있어 줄 것인데, 심지어 필요하면 그것들을 해수면으로 데리고 감으로써 그것들이 숨을 쉬도록 돕기까지 한다. 5 이러한 경향은 그것들 자신의 종에 국한되어 있는 것 같지 않다. 6 뉴질랜드의 돌고래 Moko는 한 암컷 고래를 새끼와 함께 그것들이 여러 번 오도 가도 못하고 있던 얕은 물에서 빠져나오게 안내하는 것이 관찰되어져 왔다. 7 그것들은 또한 수영객들 주변을 원을 그리며 움직이거나 상어들을 가버리게 하려고 그것들을 향해 헤엄쳐 감으로써 상어들로부터 수영객들을 보호하는 것도 목격되어 왔다.

정답단추 빈칸이 포함된 문장을 먼저 읽으면 돌고래의 이런 경향이 '무엇'인 것 같지 않은지에 대해 찾아야 함을 알 수 있어. '이런 경향(This tendency)'은 빈칸 문장 앞 내용인 사회적 동물인 돌고래가 유대감이 매우 강해 다치거나 병든 돌고래들을 지키고 돕는다는 걸 의미해. 그리고 빈칸 문장 뒤에서는 돌고래 Moko를 예로 들면서 같은 돌고래뿐만 아니라 다른 종인 고래나 사람들까지도 돕는다는 내용이지? 따라서 빈칸 문장은 돌고래의 이러한 경향이 자신의 종에만 국한되지 않는다는 내용이 와야 자연스러우니까 가장 적절한 답은 ②야.

오답단서 ①은 지문에서 언급한 돌고래의 '독특함(uniqueness)'을 '특징(characteristic)'으로 나타냈지만, '타고난(inborn)'은 글에서 언급되지 않기 때문에 오답이야. ③은 지문에서 예로 들고 있는 '다쳤거나 병들고, 얕은 물에서 빠져나오지 못하는 상황'이 응급 상황이긴 하지만, 빈칸에 넣었을 때 글 전체의 내용을 포함하지 않아서 답이 될 수 없어. ④, ⑤는 글의 내용과는 무관한 말이라서 오답이야.

어휘확인

creature 생명체; 동물 possess 소유하다 sophisticated 정교한 capacity 능력; 용량 true 진정한 learning 학습 uniqueness 독특함 species 종(種) establish 형성하다; 설립하다 bond 유대감 injured 다친 individual 개체; 개인 tendency 경향 appear ~인 것 같다 observe 관찰하다 female 암컷의; 여성인 calf (고래·소 등의) 새끼 shallow 얕은 strand 오도 가도 못 하게 하다 go away (떠나) 가다

〈선택지 어휘〉

inborn 타고난 characteristic 특징 emergency 응급; 비상 circumstance 상황 individually 각각 따로 last 지속되다; 마지막 throughout ~ 동안 죽 whole 전부의

지문 Flow

[통념]
돌고래는 지구상에서 가장 똑똑한 생명체 중 하나로, 의사소통 기술과 학습 능력을 소유하고 있음

⬇

[주제]
돌고래는 사회적 동물이며 사회적 유대감을 형성함

⬇

[예시]
• 다쳤거나 병든 개체들과 함께 있어주거나 도움을 줌
• 암컷 고래와 새끼들을 얕은 물에서 빠져나오게 하려고 안내함
• 상어로부터 수영객들을 보호함

077 정답 ④

지문 All in One

[1] *Father Jim Scott*, / [who has been an academic administrator / for most of his career], / believes / [it] is his habit / of directing his focus outward / instead of inward / [that] has consistently landed him / in leadership roles. [2] He tells a story / about *a young man* [who

(Jim Scott 신부님은 / 학업 관리자(학장)인 / 그의 경력 대부분이 / 믿는다 / 자신의 습관이라고 / 그의 (관심) 초점을 바깥쪽으로 향하는 / 안쪽 대신에 / 그 자신이 지속해서 차지해온 것은 / 지도자의 역할을 / 그는 이야기를 말한다 / 조언을 구하러 왔던 한 젊은이에 관한)

(문법 표시: S, 관계대명사(계속적 용법), V, 강조구문, S′, V′, S, V, 관계대명사)

어휘확인

Father (가톨릭교 등의) 신부 academic 학업의 administrator 관리자 career (특정한 일을 하면서 보내는) 경력 direct ~로 향하다 outward 바깥쪽으로 향하는(↔ inward 안쪽으로 향하는) instead of ~ 대신에 consistently 지속적으로 land (직장·일자리 등을) 차지하다 leadership 지도자[직]

사회생활을 시작하기 전에 / Jim 신부님은 대답했다
came to ask for advice / before embarking on his career]. [3] Father Jim responded, // "My
접속사 / S / V / S

자네에게 해줄 나의 충고는 / 아주 간단하네 / 자네가 누구를 만나든지 / 자네가 그들을 어디에서 만나든지
advice to you / is very simple. [4] No matter whom you meet, / no matter where you meet
V / C / = who(m)ever / S'_1 / V'_1 / = wherever / S'_2 / V'_2

언제나 생각해라 / 그들이 훨씬 더 낫다고 / 자네보다 / 내가 둘러볼 때
them, // always presume / that they're much better / than you are. [5] When I look around, //
V / 접속사 / S' / V' / C' / S'' / V'' / 접속사 / S' / V'

내가 사람들이 겪는 것을 보게 되는 가장 치명적인 취약점은 / 그들이 그들 자신을
the most devastating Achilles' heel [that I see people suffering from] is / that they take
S / 관계대명사 / V / 접속사 / S' / V'

너무 진지하게 여기는 것이라네 / 매우 중요한 반면에 / 다른 사람들을 진지하게 여기는 것은 / 자네 자신을
themselves too seriously. [6] While it's very important / to take others seriously, // don't take
O' / 가주어 V' / C' / 진주어 / V

그만큼 진지하게 여기지 말게 / 이러한 끊임없는 관심이다 / 다른 사람들의 '실체'에 대한
yourself that seriously." [7] It is this constant attention / to the "realness" of others / that
강조구문 / S

이상적인 지도자를 만드는 것은
makes for an ideal leader.
V

⬇

지도력의 비결은 / 진실한 겸손과 / 진정한 관심과 존중이다 [8] The keys to leadership / are genuine (A) modesty / and real interest in and (B) respect S / V / C 다른 사람들에 대한 / for others.

	(A)		(B)		(A)		(B)
①	confidence	……	curiosity about	②	confidence	……	guidance for
③	modesty	……	protection of	④	modesty	……	respect for
⑤	modesty	……	openness toward				

해석 한 눈에 보기 **주제문** 1 Jim Scott 신부님은 그의 경력 대부분을 학장으로 지내 온 분으로, 자신을 계속해서 지도자 자리에 있게 해온 것은 바로 관심의 초점을 안쪽으로가 아니라 바깥쪽으로 향하게 하는 자신의 습관이라고 믿는다. 2 그는 사회생활을 시작하기 전에 조언을 구하러 왔던 한 젊은이에 관한 이야기를 한다. 3 Jim 신부님은 "내가 자네에게 해줄 충고는 아주 간단하네. 4 자네가 누구를 만나든지, 자네가 그들을 어디에서 만나든지, 언제나 그들이 자네보다 훨씬 더 낫다고 생각하게. 5 내가 (주변을) 둘러볼 때, 내가 사람들이 겪는 것을 보게 되는 가장 치명적인 취약점은 그들이 그들 자신을 너무 진지하게 여기는 것이라네. 6 다른 사람들을 진지하게 여기는 것은 매우 중요하지만, 자네 자신을 그렇게 진지하게 여기지 말게."라고 대답했다. **주제문** 7 이상적인 지도자를 만드는 것은 다른 사람들의 '실체'에 대한 이러한 끊임없는 관심이다.

8 지도력의 비결은 진정한 (A) 겸손과 다른 사람들에 대한 진정한 관심과 (B) 존중이다.

정답단추 요약문은 글 전체를 한 문장으로 압축하고, 글의 핵심 내용만을 담고 있어. 따라서 본문을 읽기 전에 요약문을 먼저 읽어보면 일부 추론할 수 있을 거야. 요약문을 먼저 보면 다른 사람들에 대한 진실한 '무엇'이 지도력의 비결인지에 대해 찾아야 한다는 것을 알 수 있지? 이 글을 읽어보면 오랜 경력 동안 신부님을 지도자의 자리에 머물게 만든 힘은 자신을 낮추고 타인을 높이는 태도였다는 내용이야. 그래서 요약문의 빈칸 (A)에는 modesty(겸손)가, 빈칸 (B)에는 respect for(~에 대한 존중)가 와야 해. 따라서 가장 적절한 답은 ④야.

role 역할 ask for advice 조언[충고]을 구하다 embark on ~을 시작하다 no matter whom 누구를 ~하더라도 no matter where 어디서 ~하더라도 presume ~라고 생각하다 devastating 치명적인 Achilles' heel 취약점, 아킬레스건 seriously 진지하게 that 그만큼 constant 끊임없는 attention 관심; 주의 realness 실체; 진실 ideal 이상적인 key 비결, 핵심 genuine 진실한 modesty 겸손 respect 존중

〈선택지 어휘〉
confidence 자신감 curiosity 호기심 guidance 안내, 지도 protection 보호 openness 솔직함

지문 Flow

[주제문]
Jim Scott 신부님을 계속 지도자 자리에 있게 해준 것은 관심의 초점을 바깥쪽으로 향하게 하는 습관임

⬇

[일화 소개]
사회생활을 시작하기 전에 조언을 구하러 온 젊은이 이야기
→ 다른 사람들을 자신보다 더 낫다고 생각하고, 자신보다 그들을 진지하게 여기라는 조언을 해줌

⬇

[주제 재진술]
이상적인 지도자를 만드는 것은 다른 사람들에 대해 끊임없는 관심을 주는 것임

078 정답 ④

지문 All in One

스포츠 경기에서 / 코치는 주의해야 한다 / 청소년의 참가가 과업이 되지 않도록
[1] In a sports game, / coaches should be cautious / that youth participation does not become
S / V / C / 접속사 / S' / V'

아이들에게 / 경기의 결과가 / 더 중요해서는 안 된다
work / for children. [2] The outcome of the game / should not be more important / than the
C / S / V / C

스포츠와 다른 교훈을 배우는 과정보다 / 하지만 오늘날 아이들의 스포츠 환경에서
process of learning sport and other lessons. [3] In today's youth sport setting, however, / young

어린 선수들은 더 걱정할지도 모른다 / 누가 승리할지에 대해 / 즐거운 시간을 보내고 스포츠를 즐기는 대신
athletes may be worrying more / about who will win / instead of enjoying themselves and
간접의문문

경기 후에 / 많은 코치들이 날카로운 매로 변하는 경향이 있다 / 그래서 아이들은
the sport. [4] Following a game, / many coaches tend to turn into a sharp hawk. [5] So *children*
S

실수를 했거나 자신이 잘하지 못했다고 생각한 / 그들과 대화하기를 꺼리는데
[who made mistakes or thought (that) they didn't perform well] / are reluctant to talk with
관계대명사 V'_1 / V'_2 / 접속사 / S'' / V'' / V

이는 어린 선수들이 알고 있기 때문이다 / 비난받게 되어 있을 것을 / 자신들이 한 일에 대해
them, // since the young players know / (that) they're supposed to be criticized / for what they
접속사 / S' / V' / 접속사 / S'' / V'' / 관계대명사

어휘확인

cautious 주의하는, 신중한 participation 참가, 참여 outcome 결과 setting (어떤 일이 일어나는) 환경, 장소 athlete 운동선수 hawk ((조류)) 매 reluctant 꺼리는, 주저하는 criticize 비난하다 cf. criticism 비난, 비판 burnout 극도의 피로 reinforcement 강화 regardless of ~에 상관없이

〈선택지 어휘〉
analyze 분석하다 be eager to ~에 열심이다 fault 결점, 잘못

지문 Flow

[주제문]
스포츠 경기에서 코치는 청소년의 참가가 아이들에게 과업이 되지 않도록 주의해야 함

⬇

did. 6 But criticism can create high levels of stress, / leading to burnout. 7 Positive reinforcement should be provided, / regardless of the outcome. 8 It has a greater effect / on children's learning in sports / than criticism.

(하지만 비난은 높은 수준의 스트레스를 만들 수 있고 / 극도의 피로를 이끌어낸다 / 분사구문(= and it leads to burnout) / 긍정적인 강화가 제공되어야 한다 / (경기) 결과에 상관없이 / 그것은 더 많은 영향을 끼친다 / 스포츠에서 아이들의 학습에 / 비난보다)

① analyze the game through technology
기술로 경기를 분석하다

② focus on searching for the best player
최고의 선수를 찾는 것에 집중하다

③ have children practice harder than before
아이들이 전보다 더 열심히 훈련하도록 하다

④ be eager to find fault with young players
어린 선수들의 결점을 열심히 찾는다

⑤ be forced to develop new skills for children
아이들을 위한 새로운 기술을 개발하도록 강요받다

해석 한 눈에 보기 주제문 1 스포츠 경기에서 코치는 청소년의 참가가 아이들에게 과업이 되지 않도록 주의해야 한다. 2 경기의 결과가 스포츠와 다른 교훈을 배우는 과정보다 더 중요해서는 안 된다. 3 하지만 오늘날 아이들의 스포츠 환경에서, 어린 선수들은 즐거운 시간을 보내고 스포츠를 즐기는 것보다는 누가 승리할지에 대해 더 걱정할지도 모른다. 4 경기 후에, 많은 코치들이 날카로운 매로 변하는 경향이 있다. 5 그래서 실수를 했거나 자신이 잘하지 못했다고 생각한 아이들은 그들과 대화하기를 꺼리는데, 이는 어린 선수들이 자신들이 한 일에 대해 비난받게 되어 있을 것을 알고 있기 때문이다. 6 하지만 비난은 높은 수준의 스트레스를 만들 수 있고 극도의 피로를 이끌어낸다. 주제문 7 경기 결과에 상관없이 긍정적인 강화가 제공되어야 한다. 8 그것은 스포츠에서 아이들의 학습에 비난보다 더 많은 영향을 끼친다.

정답단추 스포츠 경기가 아이들에게 과업이 되지 않아야 한다는 첫 문장 주제문에 이어서, 오늘날 아이들은 스포츠를 하면서 즐거운 시간을 보내는 것보다는 승리에 대해 걱정을 한다고 했어. 실수했거나 잘하지 못했다고 생각한 어린 선수들은 코치들이 자신들의 실수나 플레이에 대해서 비난할 것을 알고 있다고 했으므로 경기 후의 코치를 가리키는 밑줄 친 어구의 의미는 ④ '어린 선수들의 결점을 열심히 찾는다'가 적절해.

오답단서 경기가 끝난 후에 경기 분석을 철저하게 하는 것은 글의 전체적인 내용과는 관련이 없으므로 ①은 오답이야. ③과 ⑤는 어린이들이 경기를 즐기기보다는 경기에서 승리하는 것에 대해 더 걱정을 한다는 점에 착안해서 만든 오답이야.

[보충설명]
스포츠 경기의 결과가 스포츠와 다른 교훈을 배우는 과정보다 더 중요해서는 안 됨

[역접]
오늘날 아이들은 스포츠를 즐기는 것보다는 누가 승리할지를 걱정함

[보충설명]
아이들은 실수를 하거나 잘하지 못하면 코치에게 비난받고 스트레스를 받음

[주제문 재진술]
스포츠 경기 결과에 상관없이 긍정적인 강화가 제공되어야 함

079 정답 ③

지문 All in One

1 As parents, / we all get a lot of well-meaning advice / on how to raise our children. 2 Usually / it centers on *the techniques of child control* [that have been used by others with success]. 3 But / **someone else's child is not your child**. 4 One parent may offer / *the time-honored advice* [to spank your child on his behind]. 5 That will make him listen! 6 Maybe. 7 Then again, / you may have the type of *child* [who does not respond to physical punishment]. 8 There are such children. 9 If that is the case, // you may as well go out / and spank your car tire. 10 Understanding what makes your child different from other children / should be *the first step* / toward understanding his developmental needs, / on which you can start to build a sound relationship / with your child.

(부모로서 / 우리 모두는 많은 선의의 조언을 얻는다 / 자녀를 양육하는 방법에 대한 / 대개 / 그것은 아동 통제 기술에 중심을 둔다 / 다른 사람들에 의해 성공적으로 사용되었던 / 관계대명사 / 그러나 / 다른 누군가의 자녀는 당신의 자녀가 아니다 / 어떤 부모는 제공할지도 모른다 / 전통적인 조언을 / 자녀의 엉덩이를 때리는 / 그것이 그가 말을 듣게 해줄 거야 / 아마도 / 그렇지 않고 / 당신은 체벌에 반응하지 않는 유형의 자녀가 있을지도 모른다 / 관계대명사 / 그런 아이들이 있다 / 그렇다면 / 접속사 / 당신은 밖에 나가는 게 좋다 / 그리고 / 자동차 타이어를 때리는 게 / 무엇이 당신의 자녀를 다른 아이들과 다르게 만드는지 아는 것이 / 간접의문문 / 첫 단계가 되어야 하며 / 그의 발달상의 필요를 이해하는 / 그것에서 당신은 건전한 관계를 쌓기 시작할 수 있다 / 전치사+관계대명사 / 자녀와)

① it's important to apply them step by step
단계적으로 그것들을 적용하는 것이 중요하다

② using a little violence sometimes works
약간의 폭력을 사용하는 것은 때때로 효과가 있다

③ someone else's child is not your child
다른 누군가의 자녀는 당신의 자녀가 아니다

④ it usually hurts more than cures the relationship
그것은 대개 관계를 치료하는 것 이상으로 아프게 한다

⑤ techniques not based on a sound theory promise failure
건전한 이론에 근거하지 않은 기술들은 실패를 약속한다

해석 한 눈에 보기 1 부모로서, 우리 모두는 자녀를 양육하는 방법에 대한 많은 선의의 조언을 얻는다. 2 대개 그것은 다른 사람들에 의해 성공적으로 사용되었던 아동 통제 기술에 중심을 둔다. 3 그러나 다른 누군가의 자녀는 당신의 자녀가 아니다. 4 어떤 부모는 자녀의 엉덩이를 때리는 전통적인 조언을 제공할지도 모른다. 5 그것이 그가 말을 듣게

어휘확인

well-meaning 선의의 **center on** ~에 초점을 두다 **technique** 기술 **success** 성공 **offer** 제공하다 **time-honored** 전통 있는, 유서 깊은 **spank** 엉덩이를 때리다 **behind** 엉덩이 **then again** 그렇지 않고, 반대로 **respond** 반응하다 **physical** 신체적인 **punishment** 벌 **developmental** 발달상의 **sound** 건전한 **relationship** 관계

〈선택지 어휘〉
apply 적용하다 **step by step** 단계적으로, 점차로 **violence** 폭력 **work** 효과가 있다 **based on** ~에 근거[기반]를 둔, ~에 기초한 **theory** 이론 **promise** 약속하다 **failure** 실패

지문 Flow

[소재]
자녀 양육에 대한 조언

[부정적 의견]
조언은 다른 사람들에 의해 성공적으로 사용된 통제 기술에 중심을 두고 있지만, 다른 사람들의 자녀는 자신의 자녀가 아님

[예시]
체벌을 조언 받았지만, 자신의 자녀가 벌에 반응하지 않을 수 있음

해줄 거야! **6** 아마도. **7** 그렇지 않고, 당신은 체벌에 반응하지 않는 유형의 자녀가 있을지도 모른다. **8** 그런 아이들이 있다. **9** 그렇다면, 당신은 밖에 나가서 자동차 타이어를 때리는 게 좋다. 주제문 **10** 무엇이 당신의 자녀를 다른 아이들과 다르게 만드는지 아는 것이 그의 발달상의 필요를 이해하는 첫 단계가 되어야 하며, 그것에서 당신은 자녀와 건전한 관계를 쌓기 시작할 수 있다.

정답단추 앞뒤 글의 문맥을 살펴서, 빈칸에 들어갈 문장의 단서를 찾아보자. 우선 빈칸 앞에 대조를 나타내는 연결어 But이 있으므로, 앞의 내용과 상반된 내용이 들어감을 알 수 있어. 빈칸 앞에는 자녀 양육 방법에 대한 조언이 그동안 성공적으로 사용되었던 아동 통제 기술에 중심을 두고 있다는 내용이 나와. 빈칸 뒤에서는 체벌을 하는 전통적인 조언에 대한 내용을 다시 다루면서, 이것에 반응하지 않는 아이가 있을 수 있다고 했어. 이를 통해서 빈칸에는 모든 자녀에게 같은 양육 방법을 적용할 수 없다는 의미로, 다른 사람의 자녀는 당신의 자녀가 아니라는 내용이 들어가야 문맥이 자연스러워져. 따라서 빈칸에 들어갈 말로 가장 적절한 것은 ③이야.

오답단서 ①과 ②는 통제 기술 사용에 동의하는 내용이므로 답으로 적절하지 않아. ④, ⑤는 글의 마지막 문장에 나오는 a sound relationship을 이용한 오답으로, 글의 내용과는 관련이 없어.

[주제문]
자신의 자녀가 다른 아이들과 다른 점을 이해함으로써 자녀와 건전한 관계를 쌓을 수 있음

080 정답 ①

지문 All in One

당신은 생각하는가 / 실험에서 사람들을 관찰하는 것이 / 행동을 방해할 수 있다고
1 Do you think // observing people in an experiment / can interfere with *the behavior* [that is
S′ V′
연구되고 있는 / 가정해 보자 / 직원들이 성격 검사를 치르라고 요청받는다고
being studied]? **2** Suppose // employees are asked to take a personality test / as part of
V S′ V′
직업 만족도에 대한 연구의 일환으로 / 직원들은 / 그들의 답변이 상사에 의해 확인될 것이라는 걸 아는
research on job satisfaction. **3** *The employees* [knowing that their answers will be checked
S
그들의 검사 응답을 일부러 왜곡할 수도 있는데 / 그들이 개인적 성향을
by their boss] / may deliberately distort their test responses // because they do not want to
V 접속사 S′ V′ O′
드러내길 원하지 않기 때문이다 / 또 다른 예시로 / 연구를 생각해 보자
reveal personal tendencies. **4** For another example, / consider *research* [to investigate the
V O
제트 엔진 소음이 미치는 영향을 조사하는 / 항공사 정비사들의 능률에 / 만약 그 정비사들이 알고 있다면
effects of jet engine noise / on the efficiency of airline mechanics]. **5** If the mechanics are
접속사 S′ V′
자신들이 심리학 연구의 일부라는 것을 / 그들은 일부러 더 빠르게 또는
aware / that they are part of a psychological research study, // they may deliberately work
C′ 접속사 S″ V″ C″ S V
더 느리게 일할지도 모른다 / 그들이 일반적인 근무일에 일했던 것보다 / 그들이 관찰되지 않았던
faster or slower / than they would on *a normal workday* [when they were not being
접속사 S′ V′ 관계부사 S″ V″
따라서, (~이) 추론된다 / 당신의 단순한 행위가 변화를 줄 수 있다 / 사람들이 행동하는 방식에
observed]. **6** It is inferred, therefore, / that your simple act can vary / how people behave.
가주어 진주어

① keeping an eye on people
사람들을 계속 지켜보는 것
② making an effort to change
변화하려고 노력하는 것
③ distorting opinions deliberately
일부러 의견을 왜곡하는 것
④ sticking to the original attitude
원래의 태도를 고수하는 것
⑤ getting rid of personal tendencies
개인적 성향을 없애는 것

해석 한 눈에 보기 **1** 당신은 실험에서 사람들을 관찰하는 것이 연구되고 있는 행동을 방해할 수 있다고 생각하는가? **2** 직원들이 직업 만족도에 대한 연구의 일환으로 성격 검사를 치르라고 요청받는다고 가정해 보자. **3** 그들의 답변이 상사에 의해 확인될 것이라는 걸 아는 직원들은 그들의 검사 응답을 일부러 왜곡할 수도 있는데 이는 그들이 개인적 성향을 드러내길 원하지 않기 때문이다. **4** 또 다른 예시로, 항공사 정비사들의 능률에 제트 엔진 소음이 미치는 영향을 조사하는 연구를 생각해 보자. **5** 만약 그 정비사들이 자신들이 심리학 연구의 일부라는 것을 알고 있다면, 그들은 자신들이 관찰되지 않았던 일반적인 근무일보다 일부러 더 빠르게 또는 더 느리게 일할지도 모른다. 주제문 **6** 따라서, 당신의 단순한 행위가 사람들이 행동하는 방식에 변화를 줄 수 있다는 것이 추론된다.

정답단추 실험에서 사람들을 관찰하는 것이 연구되는 행동을 방해할 수 있다는 요지의 글이야. 실험 대상자는 자신의 답변이 확인될 것이라는 걸 안다면 응답을 일부러 왜곡할 수도 있으며, 예시에서 정비사들은 자신들이 연구의 일부라는 것을 안다면 일부러 근무 속도를 다르게 할지도 모른다고 했어. 마지막에 오는 주제문에서 '밑줄 친 어구(당신의 단순한 행위)가 사람들의 행동에 변화를 준다'라고 했으므로 밑줄 친 어구 의미로 적절한 것은 ① '사람들을 계속 지켜보는 것'이야.

오답단서 ③은 설문조사에 응한 직원들이 자신들의 대답을 왜곡한다는 내용을 활용하여 만든 선택지로, 밑줄 친 부분은 관찰자의 행동을 의미하기 때문에 오답이야.

어휘확인

observe 관찰하다 **experiment** 실험 **interfere with** ~을 방해하다 **personality test** 성격 검사 **satisfaction** 만족(도) **deliberately** 일부러, 의도적으로 **distort** 왜곡하다 **tendency** 성향 **investigate** 조사하다, 수사하다 **efficiency** 능률, 효율 **airline** 항공사 **mechanic** 정비사, 정비공 **normal** 일반적인, 정상적인 **infer** 추론하다

〈선택지 어휘〉

keep an eye on ~을 계속 지켜보다, ~을 감시하다 **stick to** ~을 고수하다; ~을 지키다 **get rid of** ~을 제거하다, ~을 없애다

지문 Flow

[질문]
실험에서 사람들을 관찰하는 것이 연구를 방해할 수 있는가?

⬇

[예시1]
상사가 성격 검사 답변을 확인할 수 있다는 것을 아는 직원들은 답변을 왜곡할 수 있음

⬇

[예시2]
제트 엔진 소음이 정비사의 능률에 미치는 영향을 조사하는 연구가 사실 심리학 연구라는 것을 알면 정비사들은 일의 속도를 평소와 달리 함

⬇

[주제문]
단순한 행위(관찰하는 행위)가 사람들의 행동 방식에 변화를 줄 수 있음

081 정답 ⑤

지문 All in One

[1] In order to lead, / one must first learn to follow. [2] *The first step* [to become a leader] / is to become a sincere follower / first. [3] The crown of a leader attracts many individuals // as it seems to represent / power and control over others. [4] These are only the cheap thoughts / of *a person* [who seeks to establish control over others], / however. [5] Remember, / (that) these are *the people* [who are weak]. [6] True leaders know / the value of responsibilities and duties. [7] A true leader never controls, / but instead supports; // never overpowers, / but instead gives power; // never demands obedience / except from himself. [8] Strong men find *a way* [to control their minds], // because the most difficult and rewarding battle / is the battle with yourself; // and leaders are already winners / in their own noticeable way.

⬇

[9] True leadership comes from the power of controlling (A) oneself, / and from the (B) awareness / that the leader is *the one* [who has to follow].

(A)		(B)	(A)		(B)
① others	······	superstition	② others	······	belief
③ others	······	recognition	④ oneself	······	suspicion
⑤ oneself	······	awareness			

해석 한 눈에 보기 1 이끌기 위해서, 사람은 따라야 한다는 것을 먼저 배워야 한다. 2 지도자가 되는 첫 번째 단계는 먼저 진실한 추종자가 되는 것이다. 3 지도자의 왕관은 권력과 다른 사람들에 대한 지배를 나타내는 것으로 보이기 때문에, 많은 사람들을 끌어들인다. 4 그러나, 이것들은 다른 사람들에 대한 지배를 확립하려고 노력하는 사람의 저급한 생각일 뿐이다. 5 기억하라, 이들은 약한 사람들이다. 주제문 6 진정한 지도자들은 책임과 의무의 가치를 알고 있다. 7 진정한 지도자는 결코 통제하지 않고, 대신에 지지한다. 절대 힘으로 제압하려 하지 않고, 대신에 권력을 부여한다. 자신을 제외하고는 결코 순종을 요구하지 않는다. 8 강한 사람들은 가장 어렵고 보람 있는 전투가 그들 자신과의 싸움이기 때문에, 자신들의 마음을 통제할 방법을 찾는다. 그리고 지도자들은 자신만의 눈에 띄는 방법으로 이미 승자들이다.

9 진정한 지도력은 (A) 자기 자신을 통제하는 힘과, 지도자는 따라야 하는 사람이라는 (B) 의식에서 온다.

정답단추 먼저 요약문 내용을 파악하고, 전체 글을 읽는 게 빈칸 어휘를 찾는 데 도움이 돼. 요약문은 진정한 지도력이 어디에서 나오는지를 말하고 있는데, 글의 처음 두 문장에서 지도자는 따라야 하는 사람이며, 진실한 추종자가 되는 것이 지도자가 되는 첫 번째 단계라고 했어. 또한 타인을 지배하려는 약한 사람들과 달리, 강한 사람들인 진정한 지도자들은 자신의 마음을 통제할 방법을 찾는다고 했어. 따라서 빈칸 (A)에 들어갈 말로 oneself, 빈칸 (B)에 들어갈 말로 awareness가 가장 적절해. 이를 종합하면 답은 ⑤야.

오답단서 ①, ②, ③의 other를 빈칸에 넣으면, 진정한 지도자는 자신을 제외한 다른 사람들은 통제하지 않는다는 글의 내용과 반대의 내용임을 알 수 있어. 그리고 suspicion은 글의 내용과 무관해. 따라서 ④도 오답이야.

어휘확인

sincere 진실한, 진정한 **crown** 왕관 **attract** 끌어들이다 **individual** 사람, 개인 **represent** 나타내다 **thought** 생각, 사고 **seek to** ~하려고 노력하다 **establish** 확립하다, 설립하다 **responsibility** 책임 **duty** 임무 **instead** 대신에 **support** 지지하다 **overpower** 제압하다 **demand** 요구하다 **obedience** 순종; 복종 **except** ~을 제외하고 **rewarding** 보람 있는 **battle** 전투, 싸움 **noticeable** 눈에 띄는, 주목할 만한 **leadership** 지도력 **awareness** 의식

〈선택지 어휘〉

superstition 미신 **belief** 믿음 **recognition** 인식 **suspicion** 의심

지문 Flow

[도입]
지도자가 되는 첫 단계는 진실한 추종자가 되는 것임

⬇

[대조]
권력이나 타인에 대한 지배를 위해 지도자가 되려는 사람은 약한 사람들임

⬇

[주제문]
진정한 지도자들은 책임과 의무의 가치를 알고 있음

⬇

[보충설명]
• 통제하는 대신 지지하고, 힘으로 제압하는 대신 권력을 부여하고, 순종을 요구하지 않음
• 자신의 마음을 통제할 방법을 찾음

유형편

Chapter 3

유형 08 무관한 문장 찾기

Check-Up 1 ② 082 ③
Check-Up 2 (A) ○ (B) × 083 ③
Mini Test 1 ② 2 ②
실전적용독해 084 ④ 085 ③ 086 ③

Check-Up 1

정답 ②

082 정답 ③

지문 All in One

음악 교육과정의 중요한 요소는 / 종종 음악 공연에 참석하는 것이다
1 An important element of a music course / is, often, attending a musical performance
S / V / C_1

콘서트나 오페라와 같은 / 그리고 그 다음에 보고서를 쓰는 것(이다) / 콘서트에 가기 전에
/ — such as a concert or an opera — / and then writing a report. 2 Before you go to a concert,
C_2 / 접속사 S′ V′

당신은 콘서트 예절을 재확인해야 한다 / 가능하다면 / 콘서트홀에 도착하라
// you need to review concert etiquette. 3 ① If (it is) possible, // arrive at the concert hall / at
S V / 접속사 S'_1 V'_1 C′ / V

최소한 공연 15분 전에 / 당신이 휴식을 취하면서 프로그램 노트를 읽을 수 있도록
least fifteen minutes before the performance, / so that you can relax and read the program
접속사 S'_2 V'_2 V'_3

또한 명심하라 / 많은 콘서트홀에서 / 늦게 온 사람들은 자리를 잡는 것이 허용되지 않는
notes. 4 ② Bear in mind, too, // that at many concert halls, / latecomers aren't allowed to take
V / 접속사 / S′ V′

다는 것을 / 음악이 잠시 끊길 때까지 / 당신이 늦었을 때 / 하지만 / 당신은
their seats / until some break in the music occurs. 5 (③ When you're late, // however, / you can
접속사 S″ V″ / 접속사 S′ V′ C′ / S

여전히 환불을 요청할 수 있다 / 당신이 도착하기만 하면 / 콘서트가 완전히 끝나기 전에
still ask for a refund / as long as you arrive / before the concert is completely finished.)
V / 접속사 S'_2 V'_2 / 접속사 S″ V″

공연 중에 / 절대적인 침묵은 연주자가 집중하는 데 도움을 준다
6 ④ During the performance, / absolute silence helps the performers to concentrate // and
S V_1 O_1 C

그리고 음악적 경험의 감정적 강렬함을 증가시킨다 / 연주자는 산만해질 수 있다
increases the emotional intensity of the musical experience. 7 ⑤ Performers can be distracted
V_2 O_2 / S V

잡담, 기침, 콧노래, 또는 가끔의 잡음으로 / 이는 또한 다른 청중들을 혼란스럽게 하고
/ by *talking, coughing, humming,* or *occasional noises* / — which will also distract // and
관계대명사 V'_1

짜증나게 할 것이다
annoy other audience members.
V'_2

해석 한 눈에 보기 1 음악 교육과정의 중요한 요소는 종종 콘서트나 오페라와 같은 음악 공연에 참석한 다음에 보고서를 쓰는 것이다. 주제문 2 콘서트에 가기 전에, 당신은 콘서트 예절을 재확인해야 한다. 3 ① 가능하다면, 휴식을 취하면서 프로그램 노트를 읽을 수 있도록 최소한 공연 15분 전에 콘서트홀에 도착하라. 4 ② 많은 콘서트홀에서, 늦게 온 사람들은 음악이 잠시 끊길 때까지 자리를 잡는 것이 허용되지 않음을 또한 명심하라. 5 (③ 하지만, 당신이 늦었을 때, 콘서트가 완전히 끝나기 전에 도착하기만 하면 여전히 환불을 요청할 수 있다.) 6 ④ 공연 중에, 절대적인 침묵은 연주자가 집중하는 데 도움을 주며 음악적 경험의 감정적 강렬함을 증가시킨다. 7 ⑤ 연주자는 잡담, 기침, 콧노래, 또는 가끔의 잡음으로 산만해질 수 있으며, 이는 또한 다른 청중들을 혼란스럽게 하고 짜증나게 할 것이다.

정답단추 무관한 문장을 고르는 문제는 보통 선택지 번호가 없는 문장이 주제문인 경우가 많아. 이 글에서는 두 번째 문장이 주제문인데, 이 문장을 통해 콘서트 예절에 대한 세부사항이 뒤에 이어질 것을 짐작할 수 있어. 그런데 ③은 공연에 늦게 도착해도 공연이 끝나지만 않았으면 환불이 가능하다는 내용이어서 글의 주제인 '콘서트 예절'과는 무관해.

어휘확인

element 요소 **attend** 참석하다 **etiquette** 예절, 에티켓 **relax** 휴식을 취하다 **bear in mind** ~을 명심하다 **latecomer** 늦게 오는 사람 **allow** 허용하다, 허락하다 **refund** 환불(금) **as long as** ~하는 한 **completely** 완전히 **absolute** 절대적인; 완전한 **silence** 침묵, 고요 **concentrate** 집중하다 **increase** 증가시키다 **emotional** 감정의, 정서의 **intensity** 강렬함 **distract** (정신을) 산만하게 하다 **humming** 콧노래 (부르기) **occasional** 가끔의 **annoy** 짜증나게 하다 **audience** 청중

지문 Flow

[주제문]
콘서트에 가기 전에 예절 재확인해야 함

⬇

[보충설명1]
• 공연 15분 전 도착
• 늦게 도착 시 휴게 시간에만 착석 가능

⬇

[무관한 문장]
늦게 도착 시 공연이 끝나기 전이라면 환불 요청 가능

⬇

[보충설명2]
• 공연 중 침묵 → 잡담, 기침, 콧노래, 잡음 등은 공연자와 청중 모두를 방해함

오답단서 ①, ②, ④는 모두 콘서트 예절에 대한 세부적인 사항이므로 연결이 자연스러워. ⑤는 마지막 세부사항에 대한 추가적인 설명을 하고 있어.

Check-Up 2

정답 (A) ○ (B) ×

해석 햇볕에의 지나친 노출은 건강에 안 좋다. (A) 수년에 걸친 너무 많은 햇볕에의 반복적이고 장기적인 노출은 피부에 손상을 유발할 수 있다. (B) 햇볕 노출의 영향은 의사와 미디어에 의해 크게 과장되어 왔다.

083 정답 ③

지문 All in One

1 News that many of us are consuming twice the recommended amount of salt / is serious cause for concern. 2 ① An expert says // (that) the biggest problem / is that people are failing to realize / just how much salt they are adding to their food, / either while cooking or at the table. 3 ② People are also consuming hidden salt / in some of our most common foods, / including breads, processed meats, soups, sauces, and salty snacks. 4 (③ They tend to consume / about the same amount of salt / no matter where they live, // and this amount hasn't changed much / in decades.) 5 ④ *The easiest and most effective way* [to reduce salt intake] / is to boost the amount of *fresh foods* [we consume] / and cut back on processed food. 6 ⑤ Recent changes to food labelling / have been helpful, // but easily accessible information / on recommended daily salt intake / is still badly needed.

어휘확인

consume 소비하다 recommend 권장하다 amount 양 concern 우려, 걱정, 염려 expert 전문가 fail to-v ~하지 못하다 add 첨가하다 at the table 식사 중 hidden 숨겨진 common 흔한 including ~을 포함하여 processed 가공한 decade 10년 effective 효과적인 intake 섭취(량) boost 증가시키다 cut back on ~을 줄이다 recent 최근의 label 라벨을 붙이다 accessible 접근 가능한 badly 너무, 몹시

지문 Flow

[소재]
사람들의 소금 과다 섭취는 우려의 원인임

[문제]
사람들이 얼마나 많은 소금을 섭취하는지 깨닫지 못함

[예시]
빵, 가공육, 수프, 소스, 간식 등에 숨겨진 소금 섭취

[무관한 문장]
사람들은 어디에 살든지 같은 양의 소금을 섭취함

[해결]
• 신선한 음식을 섭취하고 가공 식품을 줄여야 함
• 일일 섭취 소금 권장량을 쉽게 알 수 있는 정보가 필요함

해석 한 눈에 보기 1 우리들 중 많은 사람들이 소금 권장량의 두 배를 소비한다는 뉴스는 심각한 우려의 원인이다. 2 ① 전문가가 말하길, 가장 큰 문제는 사람들이 요리 중에나 또는 식사 중에 얼마나 많은 소금을 자신들의 음식에 첨가하는지 깨닫지 못하고 있다는 것이다. 3 ② 사람들은 또한 빵, 가공육, 수프, 소스, 그리고 짭짤한 간식 등을 포함하여 우리의 가장 흔한 음식의 일부에 숨겨진 소금을 소비하고 있다. 4 (③ 그들이 어디에 살든지 거의 같은 양의 소금을 소비하는 경향이 있으며, 이 양은 수십 년 간 별로 변하지 않았다.) 5 ④ 소금 섭취를 줄이는 가장 쉽고 효과적인 방법은 우리가 소비하는 신선한 음식의 양을 늘리고 가공 식품을 줄이는 것이다. 6 ⑤ 식품 라벨 대한 최근의 변화가 도움이 되었지만, 일일 권장 소금 섭취량에 대해 쉽게 접근할 수 있는 정보가 여전히 너무 필요하다.

정답단추 글 안의 모든 문장은 단 한가지의 주제를 적절하게 뒷받침해야 해. 이 글은 사람들이 소금 섭취를 과다하게 하는 것에 대한 우려와 문제점, 그리고 이를 해결하기 위해 소금 섭취를 줄이는 방법들이 설명되고 있어. 모든 문장들이 공통되게 말하고 있는 '소금의 과다 섭취'가 주제라고 할 수 있어. 그런데 ③은 사는 곳에 상관없이 같은 양의 소금을 섭취한다는 내용으로 '소금의 섭취'라는 핵심어가 포함되긴 하지만 주제와는 관련이 없는 문장이야.

오답단서 ①, ②는 사람들이 실제 섭취하는 소금의 양을 깨닫지 못하며, 흔한 음식에 숨겨진 소금도 섭취한다는 내용이 자연스럽게 이어지고 있어. ④, ⑤는 소금 섭취를 줄이기 위해 할 수 있는 방법을 알려주고 있으므로 관련이 있는 문장들이야.

기출총정리

기출총정리 해석

1 **주제문:** 당신이 공부를 하거나 강의실에 앉아 있을 때 의자에서 얼마나 자주 자세를 바꾸는지 생각해 보라. **흐름과 유관한 문장:** 불편함을 인식하고 반응하는 우리의 능력은 몸에 대한 신체적 손상을 예방하는 데 아주 중요하다. **흐름과 무관한 문장:** 교실에서의 움직임이나 소음은 학생들이 공부에 집중하는 것을 방해할지도 모른다.

2 **주제문:** 북아메리카의 캐나다 산갈가마귀들은 그들의 놀라운 기억력을 이용하여 생존한다. **흐름과 유관한 문장:** 그것은 매년 최대 5천 개의 조그만 장소에 적어도 3만 개의 견과를 숨기지만, 그것은 그것이 숨긴 장소의 약 75%의 위치를 기억할 수 있다. **흐름과 무관한 문장:** 그 새는 소나무의 솔방울을 비틀어 열고 견과를 빼내기 위해 그것의 강력한 부리를 사용한다.

3 **주제문:** 당신이 위험에 처해 있고 두려움을 느낄 때, 당신의 몸은 자동으로 당신의 혈액 속에 아드레날린이라고 불리는 화학 물질을 만들어낸다. **흐름과**

유관한 문장: 그러나 당신이 굉장히 두려울 때, 당신의 몸은 너무 많은 아드레날린을 만들어낼 수 있는데, 이것은 당신의 근육들을 당신이 전혀 움직이지 못할 정도로 단단해지게 한다. **흐름과 무관한 문장:** 그것이 당신이 근육을 강화하기 위해 운동을 하는 이유이다.

4 **주제문:** 당신의 무릎은 날마다 아주 많은 스트레스를 받으므로 당신은 그것을 잘 돌볼 필요가 있다. **흐름과 유관한 문장:** 무릎의 힘을 늘리기 위해, 당신은 주변 근육들을 강화시켜야 하는데, 이것들이 지지 체계 역할을 해서이다. **흐름과 무관한 문장:** 다음번에 당신이 산책을 하거나 조깅을 하러 나갈 때는, 당신의 심장과 폐가 당신을 위해서 얼마나 열심히 일하고 있는지 기억하라.

Mini Test 1 ② 2 ②

Mini Test 해석 및 해설

1 **해석** 당신이 음식을 한 입 베어서 씹기 시작할 때, 그것은 더 작아지고, 더 부드러워지고 삼키기가 더 쉬워진다. ① 음식이 입에서 떨어지지 못하도록 당신의 입술이 닫히고 당신의 치아는 음식을 더 작은 조각들로 부순다. ② 위에서 소화된 음식에서 나오는 영양분들은 곧장 혈액으로 흡수될 수 있다. ③ 당신의 음식이 이리저리 움직일 때, 그것은 침에 뒤덮이게 되는데, 이것은 음식의 어떤 성분들을 보다 작은 조각들로 분해시키는 데 도움을 준다.
해설 음식의 소화 과정 중 입에서 일어나는 소화 작용에 대한 설명이다. ②는 '음식'이라는 부분은 관련되지만 위에서의 소화 작용에 대한 내용이므로 흐름과 무관하다.

2 **해석** 한 스코틀랜드 회사가 '전자 탐지기 개'라고 불리는 새로운 보안 장치를 개발했다. ① 이 장치는 레이저를 사용하여 대기 중에 있는 가스 상태의 폭발 물질을 식별한다. ② 많은 개들이 승객들의 짐에서 폭발 물질의 냄새를 맡고 탐지하도록 훈련받는다. ③ 이 기계는 현재 공항에서 사용되는 금속탐지기와 비슷하게 생겼다.
해설 한 회사가 고안한 새로운 보안 장치를 주제로 하고 있다. ①, ③은 이 장치에 대한 기능과 생김새에 대한 내용이라서 주제와 연관되지만, ②는 폭발물 탐지견과 관련되는 내용이므로 흐름과 무관하다.

실전적용독해

084 정답 ④

지문 All in One

[1] Health-conscious people (건강에 특별한 관심이 있는 사람들은, S) / generally prefer (일반적으로 녹차를 선호한다, V) green tea / to black tea (홍차보다, ~보다), // possibly because (아마 녹차가 겪기 때문일 것이다, 접속사) green tea (S′) has undergone (V′) / less processing (적은 공정을). [2] But recent studies (하지만 최근의 연구들은 발견했다, S) have found (V) // that (접속사) black tea (S′) is (V′) just as good (C′) for you / as its green cousin (홍차가 당신에게 똑같이 좋다는 것을 / 그것의 녹색 사촌만큼). [3] ① The studies (S) show (V) (그 연구는 보여준다) // that (접속사) black tea (S′) can prevent (V′) many illnesses and diseases (홍차가 많은 질환과 질병을 예방할 수 있다는 것을) / just like (접속사) green tea (S″) can (prevent ~ diseases) (V″) (녹차가 할 수 있는 것처럼). [4] ② For example (예를 들어), / drinking black tea (홍차를 마시는 것은, S) / can lower (V) the risk of stroke (뇌졸중의 위험을 낮출 수 있다), / a serious concern (심각한 걱정거리인) / for anyone over forty (40세 이상의 누구에게든지). [5] ③ It (그것은, S) can (V) reduce (줄일 수 있다) / the risk of heart disease, too (심장병의 위험도). [6] (④ However (그러나), / an estimated 17 million people (1,700만 명으로 추정되는 사람들이, S) / die (V) of strokes and heart attacks (뇌졸중과 심장마비로 사망한다) / every year (매년).) [7] ⑤ Furthermore (더욱이), / drinking just one cup a day (하루에 단 한잔만 마셔도, S) / significantly improves (V) the function of the blood vessels (혈관 기능을 크게 향상시킨다).

해석 한 눈에 보기 [1] 건강에 특별한 관심이 있는 사람들은 일반적으로 홍차보다 녹차를 선호하는데, 아마도 녹차가 더 적은 공정을 거치기 때문일 것이다. 주제문 [2] 하지만 최근의 연구들은 홍차가 그것의 녹색 사촌만큼 똑같이 당신에게 좋다는 것을 발견했다. [3] ① 그 연구들은 홍차가 꼭 녹차가 그럴 수 있는 것처럼 많은 질환과 질병을 예방할 수 있다는 것을 보여준다. [4] ② 예를 들어, 홍차를 마시는 것은 40세 이상의 누구에게든지 심각한 걱정거리인 뇌졸중의 위험을 낮출 수 있다. [5] ③ 그것은 또한 심장병의 위험도 줄일 수 있다. [6] (④ 그러나 1,700만 명으로 추정되는 사람들이 매년 뇌졸중과 심장마비로 사망한다.) [7] ⑤ 더욱이 하루에 단 한 잔만 마셔도 혈관 기능을 크게 향상시킨다.

정답단추 무관한 문장을 고르는 문제에서는 선택지 번호가 없는 문장이 대개 주제문이거나 도입 내용이야. 이 글에서는 첫 두 문장이 각각 도입문과 주제문이지. 이 두 문장을 통해 홍차의 건강 관련 효능을 연구한 결과가 이어질 것임을 짐작할 수 있어. 그런데 ④는 한 해에 뇌졸중과 심장마비로 죽는 사람들의 숫자에 대한 설명이어서 글의 주제인 '홍차의 효능'과는 무관해.

오답단서 ①은 홍차가 질병 예방에 효과가 있다는 내용이고 ②, ③은 이를 뒷받침하는 예시 문장이야. ⑤는 혈관 기능 개선이라는 또 다른 홍차의 효능을 언급한 문장이라서 주제와 관련이 있는 문장이지.

어휘확인

health-conscious 건강에 특별한 관심이 있는 **generally** 일반적으로 **prefer** ~을 선호하다 **green tea** 녹차 **black tea** 홍차 **possibly** 아마 **undergo** 겪다 **processing** 공정(工程); 처리 **recent** 최근의 **study** 연구; 공부 **cousin** 사촌 **prevent** 예방하다 **lower** ~을 낮추다 **risk** 위험 **stroke** 뇌졸중 **concern** 걱정 **heart disease** 심장병 **estimated** 추정되는 **heart attack** 심장마비 **furthermore** 더욱이 **significantly** 크게 **function** 기능 **blood vessel** 혈관

지문 Flow

[통념]
건강을 챙기는 사람들은 홍차보다 녹차를 더 선호함

⬇

[주제문]
홍차가 녹차만큼 건강에 좋음

⬇

[보충설명1]
홍차가 녹차만큼 질병 예방 효과가 있음 – 뇌졸중, 심장병 등의 위험을 줄임

⬇

[무관한 문장]
매년 뇌졸중과 심장마비로 1,700만 명이 사망함

⬇

[보충설명2]
하루에 한 잔의 홍차는 혈관 기능을 크게 향상시킴

085 정답 ③

지문 All in One

투표는 중요하다 / 정치 제도의 건전함과 정치 제도에 참여하는 사람들 둘 다에게

1 Voting matters / both to the health of the political system and to *the people* [who

S V 관계대명사

그것은 시민으로서 당신의 목소리를 듣게 하는 방법이다 / 그리고 당신이 지역 사회에 대해

participate in it]. 2 It's *a way* [to make your voice heard as a citizen / and to show you care

S V C

관심이 있음을 보여 주는 / 당신이 그것에 대해 생각하면 / 그렇게 / 놀랍지 않다

about your community]. 3 ① When you think about it / like that, // it's not surprising / that

접속사 S' V' 가주어 V C 진주어

투표자들이 지역 사회에 관심이 많은 경향이 있다는 것이 / 여러 면에서 / 정치 이외에 / 통계에 따르면

voters tend to be community-minded / in many ways / besides just politics. 4 ② According to

투표자들은 알려져 있다 / 자원 봉사를 더 많이 하는 것으로 / 투표자들은 몇 가지 그룹으로

statistics, / voters are known / to be more engaged in volunteering. 5 (③ Voters are classified

S V S V

분류된다 / 참여하는 이유에 따라 / 그들은 또한 더 정보통이다

into several groups / according to *their reasons* [to participate].) 6 ④ They are also more

S V C

지역의 일에 대해서 / 특히 / 그들은 자신들의 지역 사회에 더 관심이 많다

informed / about local affairs. 7 ⑤ Especially, / they are more concerned about their

S V_1 C

그리고 그들 주변 세상에 영향을 미치게 할 능력에 대한 더 큰 감을 가지고 있다

communities / and have *a greater sense of their ability* [to impact the world around them].

V_2

해석 한 눈에 보기 **주제문** 1 투표는 정치 제도의 건전함과 정치 제도에 참여하는 사람들 둘 다에게 중요하다. 2 그것은 시민으로서 당신의 목소리를 듣게 하고, 당신이 지역 사회에 대한 관심이 있음을 보여 주는 방법이다. 3 ① 당신이 그것에 대해 그렇게 생각하면, 투표자들이 정치 이외에 여러 면에서 지역 사회에 관심이 많은 경향이 있다는 것이 놀랍지 않다. 4 ② 통계에 따르면, 투표자들은 자원 봉사를 더 많이 하는 것으로 알려져 있다. 5 (③ 투표자들은 참여하는 이유에 따라 몇 가지 그룹으로 분류된다.) 6 ④ 그들은 또한 지역의 일에 대해서 더 정보통이다. 7 ⑤ 특히, 그들은 자신들의 지역 사회에 더 관심이 많고, 그들 주변 세상에 영향을 미치게 할 자신들의 능력을 더 크게 느낀다.

정답단추 첫 두 문장에서 투표가 정치와 정치인 모두에게 중요하며, 시민이 지역 사회에 대한 관심을 보여 주는 방법이라고 했어. 이어지는 문장들은 투표자들의 경향, 특히 지역 사회에 관심이 많은 경향이 있다는 내용과 모두 연결되는데, ③은 투표자들이 투표 참여 이유에 따라 분류된다는 내용이므로 무관한 문장이야.

오답단서 ①, ②, ④, ⑤는 모두 투표자들이 지역 사회에 관심이 많다는 내용으로 주제를 뒷받침하는 문장들이야.

어휘확인

voting 투표 political 정치적인 cf. politics 정치, 정치학 participate in ~에 참여하다, ~에 참가하다 citizen 시민 community 지역 사회 voter 투표자, 유권자 community-minded 지역 사회에 관심이 많은 according to ~에 따르면 statistics 통계, 통계학 be engaged in ~에 종사하다 classify 분류하다 informed 정보통의, 소식에 밝은 local 지역의 affair 일, 사건 concerned 관심 있는 ability 능력 impact 영향을 주다

지문 Flow

[주제문]
투표는 정치의 건전함과 정치에 참여하는 사람들 모두에게 중요하며, 시민의 목소리와 지역 사회에 대한 관심을 보여 주는 방법임

⬇

[보충설명1]
투표자들은 지역 사회에 관심이 많음
• 자원 봉사를 더 많이 함

⬇

[무관한 문장]
참여 이유에 따라 투표하는 사람들이 분류됨

⬇

[보충설명 추가]
• 투표자들은 지역의 일에 더 정보통임

⬇

[보충설명2]
자신들이 사는 지역 사회에 더 관심이 많고 자신들의 능력을 더 크게 느낌

086 정답 ③

지문 All in One

우리 대부분은 카페인을 섭취한다 / 날마다 / 하지만 우리는 정말로 얼마나 많이 알고 있는가 / 그것의 영향에

1 Most of us consume caffeine / every day, // but how much do we really know / about its

S_1 V_1 S_2 V_2

대해 / 우리 몸에 미치는 / 쓴맛을 가진 이 천연 물질은 / 중추신경계를 자극하여

effect / on our body? 2 ① *This natural substance* [with a bitter taste] / stimulates the central

S V

당신이 더 초롱초롱하게 느끼게 만든다 / 보통의 복용량에서 / 그것은 실제로 건강상 이점을

nervous system, / making you feel more alert. 3 ② In moderate doses, / it can actually offer

분사구문(= and it makes ~) S V

제공하여 / 기억력, 집중력, 정신 건강을 증진시키는 데 도움을 줄 수 있다

health benefits, / helping to boost memory, concentration, and mental health. 4 (③ If

분사구문(= and it can help ~) 접속사

만일 누군가가 마신다면 / 카페인을 제거한 커피 5잔을 / 카페인 복용량은 / 도달할 수 있을 것이다

someone drinks / five cups of decaffeinated coffee, // the dose of caffeine / could reach / the

S' V' S V

카페인이 있는 커피 1잔의 수준에 / 그리고 특히 카페인은 연관이 있다

level of a cup of caffeinated coffee.) 5 ④ And caffeine in particular has been associated / with

S V

가능성 있는 감소와 / 알츠하이머병과 특정 암에 걸릴 위험에 있어

a possible decrease / in the risk of getting Alzheimer's disease and certain cancers. 6 ⑤ But

하지만 카페인 남용은 / 유발할 수 있다 / 불안감, 초조, 급격한 심장박동 수를

caffeine overuse / can cause / anxiety, restlessness, and a rapid heart rate.

S V

어휘확인

consume 섭취하다 caffeine 카페인 natural 천연의 substance 물질 bitter (맛이) 쓴 stimulate 자극하다 central nervous system 중추신경계 alert 정신이 초롱초롱한 moderate 보통의 dose (약의) 복용량 offer 제공하다 benefit 이점 boost 증진시키다; 신장시키다 memory 기억력 decaffeinated 카페인을 제거한 (↔ caffeinated) in particular 특히 associate 연관 짓다 decrease 감소 risk 위험 Alzheimer's disease 알츠하이머병, 치매 certain 특정한 cancer 암 overuse 남용(하다) anxiety 불안감 restlessness 초조 rapid 급격한 heart rate 심장박동 수

지문 Flow

[주제문]
카페인이 우리 몸에 미치는 영향을 알고 있는가

해석 한 눈에 보기 **주제문** [1] 우리 대부분은 날마다 카페인을 섭취하지만, 우리는 우리 몸에 미치는 카페인의 영향에 대해 정말로 얼마나 많이 알고 있는가? [2] ① 쓴맛을 가진 이 천연 물질은 중추신경계를 자극하여, 당신이 더 초롱초롱하게 느끼게 해준다. [3] ② 적당히 복용하면, 그것은 실제로 건강상의 이점들을 제공하여, 기억력, 집중력, 정신 건강을 증진시키는 데 도움을 줄 수 있다. [4] (③ 만일 누군가가 카페인을 제거한 커피 5잔을 마신다면, 카페인 복용량은 카페인이 있는 커피 1잔 수준에 달할 수 있을 것이다.) [5] ④ 그리고 특히 카페인은 알츠하이머병과 특정 암에 걸릴 위험을 감소시켜 줄 수 있다는 것과 연관이 있다. [6] ⑤ 하지만 카페인 남용은 불안감, 초조, 급격한 심장박동 수를 유발할 수 있다.

정답단추 첫 문장에서 짐작해볼 수 있듯이, 카페인이 우리 몸에 미치는 영향을 나열하고 있는 글이야. 그런데 ③은 카페인이 없는 커피 5잔은 카페인이 있는 커피 1잔과 같다는 내용으로 카페인이 인체에 미치는 영향과는 무관한 내용이야. 즉, 카페인이라는 주제와는 관련 있지만, 글의 전체 흐름과는 관계가 없어.

오답단서 ①, ②, ④는 카페인이 우리 몸에 미치는 긍정적인 영향이고, ⑤는 카페인을 남용했을 때 우리 몸에 미치는 부정적인 영향으로 이 네 문장은 모두 '카페인이 우리 몸에 미치는 영향'이라는 주제의 세부 내용이야.

[장점1]
카페인은 중추신경계를 자극하여 정신을 차리게 해주고, 기억력, 집중력, 정신 건강을 증진시킴

[무관한 문장]
카페인을 제거한 커피 5잔은 카페인 커피 1잔과 카페인 복용량이 같음

[장점2]
치매와 특정 암에 걸릴 위험을 감소시킴

[단점]
남용 시 불안감, 초조, 급격한 심장박동 수를 유발함

유형 09 글의 순서 배열

Check-Up 1 1 (A) Leonardo da Vinci (B) the Renaissance 2 ① **087** ④

Check-Up 2 3 Don't[don't] let the water tap run, turn it off firmly 4 ① **088** ②

실전적용독해 **089** ② **090** ③

Check-Up 1

정답 1 (A) Leonardo da Vinci (B) the Renaissance 2 ①

해석 [1-2] Leonardo da Vinci는 르네상스기라고 불리는 시대에 살았다. 그는 화가 훨씬 그 이상이었기 때문에 그 시대의 위대한 예술가가 되었다. 예를 들어, 그는 과학자이자, 발명가이자, 건축가이자, 음악가이자, 수학자였다.

087 정답 ④

지문 All in One

당신은 졸린 기분이 드는가 / 낮에 / 그렇다면 / 당신은 확실한가 / 그것이 정말 졸음이라는 것이 / 단지 피곤한 것보다는

[1] Do you feel sleepy / during the day? [2] If so, // are you sure / (that) it's really sleepiness / rather than just being tired?

그것들은 서로 다른 것들이다 / 그리고 중요하다 / 하나를 다른 것과 구별하는 것이

(C) [3] They are different things, // and it's important / to distinguish one from the other.

우리가 졸린 기분일 때 / 의식적인 싸움이다 / 깨어 있는 채로 있는 것은

[4] When we feel sleepy, // it is a conscious struggle / to remain awake.

반면에 / 우리가 피곤할 때 / 우리는 피로감을 느낄지도 모른다 / 하지만 여전히 비교적 정신을 차린 채 있을(지도 모른다) / 좋은 생각이다 / 밤 시간 동안 모든 잠을 자려고 노력하는 것은 / 그러므로 가볍게 졸린 기분이라면 / 낮에 / 최선을 다하라 / 그것과 싸우기 위해

(A) [5] On the other hand, / when we are tired, // we may feel fatigued / but still remain relatively alert. [6] It is a good idea / to try to save all your sleep for night time, // so if you feel mildly sleepy / during the day, / do your best / to fight it.

예를 들어 / 점심시간에 운동하는 것은 / 좋은 생각일 수 있다 / 대낮에 나가는 것은 / 또한 매우 중요하다 / 자연적인 빛이 우리가 정신을 차리고 있는 데 도움을 주기 때문에 / 커피와 에너지 음료는 또한 줄 수 있다 / 우리에게 '힘'을 / 낮은 에너지의 시간 동안

(B) [7] For example, / exercising at lunchtime / can be a good idea. [8] Getting out in the daylight / is also very important // because natural light helps (to) keep us alert. [9] Coffee and energy drinks can also give / us a "boost" / during times of low energy.

어휘확인

sleepiness 졸음, 졸림 **distinguish A from B** A와 B를 구별하다 **conscious** 의식하는, 자각하는 **struggle** 싸움, 투쟁 **remain** 계속[여전히] ~이다 **awake** 깨어 있는 **on the other hand** 반면에 **fatigued** 피로한 **relatively** 비교적 **alert** 정신이 초롱초롱한, 기민한 **mildly** 가볍게, 약간 **lunchtime** 점심시간 **in the daylight** 대낮에 **boost** (신장시키는) 힘, 격려

지문 Flow

[도입]
(C) 졸음과 피곤함은 서로 다른 것임

[보충설명]
(A) 졸릴 때는 억지로 깨어 있어야 하지만, 피곤할 때는 억지로 깨어 있는 것은 아님

[주장]
밤에 잠을 잘 수 있도록 낮에는 졸음과 싸워라

① (A) - (C) - (B)　② (B) - (A) - (C)　③ (B) - (C) - (A)
④ (C) - (A) - (B)　⑤ (C) - (B) - (A)

해석 한 눈에 보기 1 낮에 졸린 기분이 드는가? 2 그렇다면, 단지 피곤한 것보다는 정말 졸음이 확실한가? (C) 3 그것들은 서로 다른 것들이며, 하나를 다른 것과 구별하는 것이 중요하다. 4 우리가 졸린 기분일 때, 깨어 있는 채로 있는 것은 의식적인 싸움이다. (A) 5 반면에, 우리가 피곤할 때, 우리는 피로감을 느끼지만, 여전히 비교적 정신을 차린 채 있을지도 모른다. 6 밤 시간 동안 모든 잠을 자려고 노력하는 것은 좋은 생각이므로, 낮에 가볍게 졸린 기분이라면 최선을 다해 그것과 싸워라. (B) 7 예를 들어, 점심시간에 운동하는 것은 좋은 생각일 수 있다. 8 자연적인 빛이 우리가 정신을 차리고 있는 데 도움을 주기 때문에 대낮에 나가는 것은 또한 매우 중요하다. 9 커피와 에너지 음료는 또한 낮은 에너지의 시간 동안 우리에게 '힘'을 줄 수 있다.

정답단추 글의 흐름이나 순서를 알려주는 연결어, 대명사 등을 잘 살펴보고 이를 근거로 글을 배열하면 돼. 주어진 문장은 졸린 기분과 피곤함에 대해 말하고 있어. (C)의 They가 이 둘을 가리키고 있고, 그 둘을 구별하는 것이 중요하다고 하므로 바로 뒤에 이어지는 것이 적절해. (A)는 대조를 나타내는 On the other hand로 시작하면서, 피곤할 때 정신은 깨어 있는 상태임을 말하고 있는데, (C)의 마지막에서 졸릴 때 깨어 있는 채로 있는 것은 의식적인 싸움이라고 했으므로 (C)의 뒤에 (A)가 오는 것이 자연스러워. (B)는 (A)에서 말하는 낮에 졸린 것을 참기 위해 할 수 있는 일의 예를 들고 있으므로, 마지막에 오는 것이 적절해. 따라서 글의 순서로 가장 적절한 것은 ④ '(C) – (A) – (B)'야.

[예시 방법]
(B) • 점심시간에 운동하기
• 대낮에 햇빛 쐬기
• 커피와 에너지 음료 마시기

Check-Up 2

정답 3 Don't[don't] let the water tap run, turn it off firmly 4 ①

해석 [3-4] (A) 지구는 오직 우리가 마시고 사용할 만큼의 많은 물을 가지고 있다. 수도꼭지를 불필요하게 틀어놓지 말고 그것을 단단히 잠가라. (B) 당신이 수도꼭지를 틀어놓지 않고 반드시 그것을 단단히 잠그면, 당신은 물을 절약하도록 돕고 있는 것이다.

088 정답 ②

지문 All in One

1 Archimedes(S) was(V) a famous ancient Greek scientist(C). [Archimedes는 유명한 고대 그리스인 과학자였다] 2 A legend(S) says(V) [한 전설은 말한다] // that(접속사) he(S′) was(V′) the first(C′) [그가 첫 번째(최초)라고] / to use the sun's rays [태양 광선을 이용한] / to start a fire. [불을 피우기 위해 — 부사적 용법(목적)]

(B) 3 He(S) did(V) it [그는 그것을 했다] / to defend his country [그의 나라를 지키려고 — 부사적 용법(목적)] / against Rome. [로마에 대항해서] 4 Rome(S_1) had come(V_1) by sea [로마는 바다로 왔다] / to invade, [침략하러 — 부사적 용법(목적)] // and Roman ships(S_2) [그리고 로마의 배들은] / were about to attack(V_2) Syracuse, [시라쿠사를 막 공격하려고 했다] / Archimedes' home city. [Archimedes의 고향 도시인] (Syracuse = Archimedes' home city)

(A) 5 Knowing that something had to be done, [무언가 행해져야 한다는 것을 알았던 — 분사구문(= Because he knew ~)] / he(S) hatched(V) a plan. [그는 계획을 만들었다] 6 Archimedes(S) took out(V_1) a mirror [Archimedes는 거울을 꺼냈다] // and held it up(V_2) [그리고 그것을 들어올렸다] / to the sun. [태양을 향해] 7 He(S) knew(V) [그는 알았다] // (that)(접속사) the rays of the sun(S′) [태양의 광선이] / would reflect(V′) off the glass [유리에 반사될 것이라고] / onto the Roman ships. [로마의 배들 위로]

(C) 8 After a while, [얼마 후] / *the intense heat* [of *the sun's rays* [reflected by Archimedes' mirror]](S) [Archimedes의 거울에 의해 반사된 태양 광선의 강렬한 열기는] / caused(V) a ship(O) [배에 야기했다] / to catch fire(C). [불이 붙게] 9 The whole fleet(S_1) was burned(V_1), [전체 함대가 불탔다] // and Syracuse(S_2) was saved(V_2). [그리고 시라쿠사는 구해졌다]

① (A) - (C) - (B)　② (B) - (A) - (C)　③ (B) - (C) - (A)
④ (C) - (A) - (B)　⑤ (C) - (B) - (A)

해석 한 눈에 보기 1 Archimedes는 유명한 고대 그리스의 과학자였다. 2 한 전설에 따르면 그는 태양 광선을 이용해 불을 피운 최초의 사람이었다. (B) 3 그는 로마에 대항하여 자신의 나라를 지키려고 그렇게 했다. 4 로마가 바다를 이용해 침략해 왔고, 로마의 배들이 Archimedes의 고향 도시인 시라쿠사를 막 공격하려고 했다. (A) 5 뭔가 행해져야 한다는 것을 알았던 그는 하나의 계획을 세웠다. 6 Archimedes는 거울 하나를 꺼내 그것을 태양을 향해 높이 들었다. 7 그는 태양 광선이 유리에서 로마 배들 위로 반사될 것을 알았다. (C) 8 얼마 후, Archimedes의 거울에 반사된 태양 광선의 강렬한 열기는 배에 불이 붙게 했다. 9 전체 함대가 불에 탔고, 시라쿠사는 구해졌다.

정답단추 이 문제는 시간 전개상의 인과관계 등을 고려하면 돼. 주어진 문장은 Archimedes가 최초로 태양 광선을 이용해 불을 지폈다는 내용이니까 그가 고향을 지키려고 태양 광선을 사용했다는 내용인 (B)가 뒤이어 나오는 것이 자연스러워. (B)를 뒷받침하는 태양 광선을 사용한 구체적인 방법에 관한 내용인 (A), 그리고 얼마 후(After a while)에 로마 함대가 함락되고 시라쿠사가 구해졌다는 (C)로 이어지는 것이 적절해. 따라서 알맞은 글의 순서는 '(B) – (A) – (C)'야.

어휘확인
ancient 고대의 **Greek** 그리스인 **legend** 전설 **ray** 광선 **defend** 지키다, 방어하다 **Rome** 로마 **invade** 침략하다 **be about to-v** 막 ~하려는 참이다 **attack** 공격하다 **hatch** (비밀리에 계획 등을) 만들어내다 **mirror** 거울 **reflect** 반사하다 **intense** 강렬한 **catch fire** 불붙다 **whole** 전체의 **fleet** 함대

지문 Flow

[인물소개]
고대 그리스의 과학자 Archimedes는 태양으로 불을 피운 최초의 사람

[사실1]
(B) 로마의 배가 Archimedes의 나라를 공격하려고 함

&

[사실2]
(A) 거울로 태양 광선을 로마 배들에게 반사시킴

[결과]
(C) 로마 배에 불이 붙어, 전체 함대가 불에 탐

089 정답 ②

지문 All in One

HIV는 면역 체계를 공격하는 바이러스이다 / 면역 체계는 우리 몸의 자연적인 방어이다

1 HIV is *a virus* [that attacks *the immune system*], / which is our body's natural defence /

S V 관계대명사 C 관계대명사(계속적 용법)

질병에 대한 / 그 바이러스는 파괴한다 / 한 유형의 백혈구를 / 면역 체계의

against illness. 2 The virus destroys / *a type of white blood cell* / in the immune system /

S V_1

보조 T 림프구라고 불리는 / 그리고 그 자신의 복제물을 만든다 / 이 세포 안에 / 보조 T 림프구는

[called a T-helper cell], // and makes copies of itself / inside these cells. 3 T-helper cells are

V_2 S

또한 불린다 / CD4 세포로

also referred to / as CD4 cells.

V

HIV가 더 많은 CD4 세포를 파괴하면서 / 그리고 그 자신의 복제물을 더 많이 만들(면서)

(B) 4 As HIV destroys more CD4 cells / and makes more copies of itself, // it gradually breaks

접속사 S' V'_1 V'_2 S V

그것은 점차 사람의 면역 체계를 파괴한다

down a person's immune system.

이것은 의미한다 / HIV 감염자가 / 치료를 받고 있지 않은

(A) 5 This means // (that) *someone* [living with HIV], / who is not receiving treatment, / will

S V 접속사 S' 관계대명사 V'

점점 더 어렵다는 것을 알게 될 것이다 / 감염과 질병을 물리치기가

find it harder and harder / to fight off infections and diseases.

가목적어 C' 진목적어

10년 혹은 15년 후에 / HIV를 치료를 받지 않은 채 둔다면 / 면역 체계는 너무 심하게 손상될지도 모른다

(C) 6 After 10 or 15 years, / if HIV is left untreated, // the immune system may be so severely

S'_1 V'_1 S V

그것은 더 이상 스스로 전혀 방어할 수 없을 수 있다

damaged / (that) it can no longer defend itself at all.

S_2 V_2 so+형용사/부사+(that): 매우 ~하여 …하다

① (A) - (C) - (B) ② (B) - (A) - (C) ③ (B) - (C) - (A)
④ (C) - (A) - (B) ⑤ (C) - (B) - (A)

해석 한 눈에 보기 1 HIV는 면역 체계를 공격하는 바이러스인데, 면역 체계는 질병에 대한 우리 몸의 자연적인 방어이다. 2 그 바이러스는 보조 T 림프구라고 불리는 면역 체계의 한 유형의 백혈구를 파괴하고, 이 세포 안에 그 자신의 복제물을 만든다. 3 보조 T 림프구는 또한 CD4 세포로 불린다. (B) 4 HIV가 더 많은 CD4 세포를 파괴하고 그 자신의 복제물을 더 많이 만들면서 그것은 점차 사람의 면역 체계를 파괴한다. (A) 5 이것은 치료를 받고 있지 않은 HIV 감염자가 감염과 질병을 물리치기가 점점 더 어렵다는 것을 알게 될 것임을 의미한다. (C) 6 10 또는 15년 후, HIV를 치료받지 않은 채 놔두면, 면역 체계가 너무 심하게 손상되어 더 이상 스스로 전혀 방어할 수 없을 지도 모른다.

정답단추 주어진 문장은 HIV 바이러스에 대한 설명이야. 즉, 면역을 담당하는 보조 T 림프구(CD4 세포)를 파괴하고, 거기에 자신의 복제물을 만든다는 것이지. (B)는 그 영향으로 사람의 면역 체계가 파괴된다고 말하고 있으니까 그 다음 순서로 적절해. 그 다음에 치료를 받고 있지 않은 HIV 감염자에게 일어나는 상황에 대해 말하고 있는 (A)가 이어지고, 치료받지 않은 채로 내버려두면 그 결과로 면역 체계가 완전히 기능을 할 수 없다는 내용의 (C)가 이어지는 것이 시간적으로 자연스러운 흐름이야. 따라서 글의 순서로 가장 적절한 것은 ② '(B) – (A) – (C)'야.

어휘확인

HIV 에이즈 바이러스(= **human immunodeficiency virus**) **virus** 바이러스 **the immune system** 면역 체계 **defence** 방어 cf. **defend** 방어하다 **destroy** 파괴하다 **white blood cell** 백혈구 **T-helper cell** 보조 T 림프구 **refer to A as B** A를 B로 부르다 **CD4** 보조 T 림프구 등의 표면에 있는 항원 **cell** 세포 **gradually** 점차 **break down** 파괴하다 **treatment** 치료 **fight off** ~와 싸워 물리치다 **infection** 감염 **untreated** 치료를 받지 않는 **severely** 심하게 **damaged** 손상[손해]을 입은

지문 Flow

[소재]
HIV 바이러스

[설명]
면역 체계의 백혈구인 보조 T 림프구(CD4 세포)를 파괴하고, 그 안에 자신의 복제물을 만듦

[결과]
(B) HIV바이러스가 CD4 세포를 많이 파괴하고 복제물을 많이 생성하면, 서서히 면역 체계를 파괴함

[진행과정1]
(A) 치료 받고 있지 않은 HIV 감염자는 감염과 질병을 물리치기 점점 어려워짐

&

[진행과정2]
(C) 치료 받지 않으면 면역 체계의 손상으로 스스로 방어할 수 없게 됨

090 정답 ③

지문 All in One

우리는 개인이다 / 우리 자신의 판단에 책임이 있는 / 그리고 우리 자신의 자유 의지를 소유하고 있는

1 We are *individuals*, / [responsible for our own judgments / and in possession of our own

S_1 V_1 C_1

그럼에도 불구하고 / 우리는 보다 큰 어떤 것의 일부분이다

free will], // but nonetheless / we are part of something larger.

S_2 V_2 C_2

어떤 사람들은 그것을 집단 무의식이라고 부를지도 모른다 / 다른 사람들은 그것을 '정신' 또는 '삶의 힘(생명력)'이라고 부를지도 모른다

(B) 2 Some may call it the collective unconscious. 3 Others may label it "spirit" or "life

S V O C S V O C

그러나 당신이 선택한 말이 무엇이든지 간에 / 당신은 자신감을 얻는다 / 아는 것으로부터

force." 4 But whatever your word of choice (may be), // you gain confidence / from knowing

복합관계부사(무엇이든지 간에) S'_1 V'_1 S V

우리가 고립되어 있지 않음을 / 서로에게서

/ that we are not isolated / from one another.

접속사 S'_2 V'_2

어휘확인

individual 개인 **responsible for** ~에 책임이 있는 **judgment** 판단, 판단력 **possession** 소유; 재산 **free will** 자유 의지 **nonetheless** 그럼에도 불구하고 **collective** 집단적인 **unconscious** 무의식 **label** (…을) ~로 부르다 **spirit** 정신 **force** 힘 **whatever** 무엇이든지 간에 **gain** 얻다 **confidence** 자신감 **isolate** 고립시키다 **furthermore** 더욱이 **connectedness** 유대감, 소속의식 **imply** 내포하다 **certain** 어떤 **responsibility** 책임감, 책임 **harm** 해를 끼치다 **exploit** 착취하다 **awareness** 인식,

더욱이 / 이런 유대감은 / 어떤 책임감을 내포한다

(C) [5] Furthermore, / this feeling of connectedness / implies certain responsibilities. [6] If we

S / V / 접속사 S'_1

만일 우리가 모두 더 큰 그림의 일부분이라면 / 우리는 다른 사람들에게 해를 끼쳐서는 안 된다 / 우리 자신에게 해를 끼치는

are all part of a larger picture, // then we must not harm others / because we will be

V'_2 / C' / S / V / 접속사 S'_2 V'_2

셈이 되기 때문에 / 우리는 착취해서는 안 된다 / 우리는 우리 자신을 착취하는 셈이 되기 때문에

harming ourselves. [7] We must not exploit // because we will be exploiting ourselves.

S / V / 접속사 S' / V'

이러한 책임에 대한 당신의 인식은 / 당신의 가치 체계를 창출한다 / 이것의 정확한 세부사항은

(A) [8] Your awareness of these responsibilities / creates your value system. [9] The exact details

S / V / S_1

달려 있을 것이다 / 당신의 양육과 당신의 문화에 / 그러나 당신의 신념이 강하다면

of this / will depend / on your upbringing and your culture, // but if your belief is

V_1 / 접속사 S' V'

그것은 당신과 당신의 가까운 친구들을 지탱해 줄 것이다 / 인생의 어려움에 직면할 때

strong, / it will sustain you and your close friends / in the face of life's challenges.

C' S_2 V_2

① (A) - (C) - (B) ② (B) - (A) - (C) ③ (B) - (C) - (A)
④ (C) - (A) - (B) ⑤ (C) - (B) - (A)

해석 한 눈에 보기 1 우리는 개인들로, 우리 자신의 판단에 책임이 있으며 우리 자신의 자유 의지를 소유하고 있지만, 그럼에도 불구하고 우리는 보다 큰 어떤 것의 일부분이다. (B) 2 어떤 사람들은 그것을 집단 무의식이라고 부르지도 모른다. 3 다른 사람들은 그것을 '정신' 또는 '생명력'이라고 부르지도 모른다. 4 그러나 당신이 선택한 말이 무엇이든지 간에, 당신은 우리가 서로에게서 고립되어 있지 않음을 아는 것으로부터 자신감을 얻는다. (C) 5 더욱이 이런 유대감은 어떤 책임감을 내포한다. 6 만일 우리가 모두 더 큰 그림의 일부분이라면, 우리는 우리 자신에게 해를 끼치는 셈이 되기 때문에 다른 사람들에게 해를 끼쳐서는 안 된다. 7 우리는 우리 자신을 착취하는 셈이 되기 때문에 착취해서는 안 된다. (A) 8 이러한 책임에 대한 당신의 인식은 당신의 가치 체계를 창출한다. 9 이것의 정확한 세부사항은 당신의 양육과 당신의 문화에 달려 있지만, 당신의 신념이 강하다면, 그것은 인생의 어려움에 직면할 때 당신과 당신의 가까운 친구들을 지탱해 줄 것이다.

정답단추 이 글의 지시어 표현을 살펴보면 글의 순서를 알 수 있어. 우선 주어진 문장에서 '우리는 보다 큰 어떤 것의 일부분이다'의 something larger를 (B)에서 it으로 받고 있어. 그리고 그것(it)이 '집단 무의식, 정신, 생명력일 수 있는데 그것이 무엇이든 우리가 고립되어 있지 않다'는 내용으로 자연스럽게 이어지지. 그다음으로 Furthermore로 시작해 '이런 유대감(this feeling of connectedness)'에 대해서 부연 설명하는 (C)가 오는 것이 적절해. 마지막으로 (A)의 these responsibilities는 (C)의 certain responsibilities를 가리키는 표현으로, (A)에서 이에 대해 보충 설명하고 있어. 이러한 지시어의 흐름을 따라가면 글의 올바른 순서는 ③ '(B) – (C) – (A)'임을 알 수 있어.

인지 **create** 창출[창조]하다 **value** 가치 **system** 체계 **exact** 정확한 **detail** 세부사항 **depend on** ~에 달려 있다 **upbringing** 양육 **belief** 신념, 확신 **sustain** 지탱하다 **close** (사이가) 가까운 **in the face of** ~에 직면하여 **challenge** 어려움, 시련

지문 Flow

[도입]
우리는 개인들이지만, 보다 큰 어떤 것의 일부분임

⬇

[보충설명1]
(B) 우리가 서로 고립되어 있지 않다는 것에 자신감을 얻음

&

[보충설명2]
(C) 이러한 유대감은 책임감을 내포하여, 자신처럼 전체의 일부인 다른 사람에게도 해를 끼쳐서는 안 됨

⬇

[결론]
(A) 책임에 대한 인식은 가치 체계를 창출하고, 인생의 어려움에 직면할 때 당신과 친구들을 지탱해 줌

유형 10 문장 삽입

Check-Up 1 ①, ②, ③ **091** ③
Check-Up 2 2 Ⓐ 3 ② **092** ②
실전적용독해 **093** ④ **094** ④ **095** ④

Check-Up 1

정답 ①, ②, ③

091 정답 ③

지문 All in One

나는 사람들에게 '행운'을 빌어준다 / 하지만 나는 단지 제한된 믿음을 가지고 있다 / 운에 있어서 / 대신에 / 나는 생각한다

[1] I wish people "Good Luck!", // but I only have a limited belief / in luck. [2] Instead, / I believe

S_1 V_1 IO DO / S_2 V_2 / S V

우리가 우리 자신의 행운을 만든다고 / 두 사람이 제공받을 수 있다 / 같은 자원을 가지고 같은 상황을

// (that) we make our own luck. (①) [3] Two people could be given / the same situation with

접속사 S' V' / S / V_1

그리고 완전히 다른 결과를 만들어 낼 (수 있다) / 몇몇은 그것을 '운이 좋은' 것으로

the same resources // and create completely different outcomes. (②) [4] Some might regard it

V_2 / S V_1

여길지도 모른다 / 또는 운을 변명으로 사용할지도 (모른다) / '나는 단지 운이 나빠.'라고 말하면서 / 또는 '그녀는 나보다 더 운이 좋아.'

as "lucky" // or use luck as an excuse, / saying "I'm just unlucky," / or "She's luckier than

V_2 / 분사구문(= as they say ~)

나는 생각하지 않는다 / 그것이 운이라고 / 하지만 / 오히려 그것은 태도이다 / 어떻게 당신이 세상을

me." [5] (③ I don't believe // (that) it's luck, / however.) [6] Rather it's attitude: / how you choose

S V / 접속사 S' V' C' / S V C

어휘확인

limited 제한된 **belief** 믿음, 신념 **situation** 상황 **resource** 자원, 재원 **completely** 완전히 **outcome** 결과 **regard A as B** A를 B로 여기다[간주하다] **rather** 오히려 **attitude** 태도 **interact** 상호 작용하다 **within** ~ 이내에 **be up to** ~에 달려 있다 **provide** 제공하다, 주다 **approach** 접근하다 **be in charge** 책임지고 있다 **opportunity** 기회 **embrace** 껴안다, 포옹하다 **with joy** 기쁨으로

바라보기를 선택하는지 / 그리고 그 안에서 상호 작용하기를 / 당신의 태도와 당신이 세상을 보는 법은

to look at the world / and (to) interact within it. (④) 7 Your attitude and how you view the world / is everything in life, // and it's up to you. (⑤) 8 As every moment of every day / provides you with choices / about how to approach life, // you are in charge, / and you can either complain and run away / or greet opportunity and embrace it / with joy.

삶의 전부이다 / 그리고 그것은 당신에게 달려 있다 / 매일 매 순간이 ~하기 때문에 / 당신에게 선택권을 제공하기 / 삶에 접근하는 방법에 관한 / 당신은 책임지고 있다 / 그리고 당신은 불평하고 도망갈 수 있거나 / 또는 기회를 맞이하고 기회를 잡을 (수 있다) / 기쁨으로

해석 한 눈에 보기 1 나는 사람들에게 '행운'을 빌어주지만, 나는 단지 운에 있어서 제한된 믿음을 가지고 있다. 주제문 2 대신에, 나는 우리가 우리 자신의 행운을 만든다고 생각한다. 3 두 사람이 같은 자원을 가지고 같은 상황을 제공받아서 완전히 다른 결과를 만들어 낼 수 있다. 4 몇몇은 그것을 '운이 좋은' 것으로 여기거나, "나는 단지 운이 나빠." 또는 "그녀는 나보다 더 운이 좋아."라고 말하면서 운을 변명으로 사용할지도 모른다. 5 하지만, 나는 그것이 운이라고 생각하지 않는다. 6 오히려 그것은 태도이다. 즉, 어떻게 당신이 세상을 바라보고 그 안에서 상호 작용하기를 선택하는지. 7 당신의 태도와 당신이 세상을 보는 법은 삶의 전부이고, 그것은 당신에게 달려 있다. 8 매일 매 순간이 당신에게 삶을 접근하는 방법에 관한 선택권을 제공하기 때문에, 당신은 책임지고 있으며, 불평하고 도망가거나 또는 기쁨으로 기회를 맞이하고 기회를 붙잡을 수 있다.

정답단추 문장의 위치를 찾는 문제는 글의 흐름을 알려주는 연결어나 지시어, 대명사 등을 활용해서 앞뒤 문장의 관계를 파악하면 돼. 주어진 문장을 보면 however가 있으므로 앞뒤가 서로 역접 관계일 것임을 알 수 있지. 주어진 문장은 필자가 자신은 그것을 운이라고 생각하지 않는다는 의견을 말하는 것으로, 앞에는 그것을 운으로 생각한다는 내용이 언급되어야 함을 알 수 있어. 따라서 주어진 문장이 들어가기에 가장 적절한 곳은 ③이야.

오답단서 ①, ②의 앞과 뒤는 스스로 행운을 만들 수 있으며, 같은 상황에서도 다른 결과를 만들어 낼 수 있다는 내용과 함께 몇몇 사람들은 그것을 운이라고 생각한다는 내용이 자연스럽게 이어지고 있어. ④, ⑤의 앞과 뒤는 필자가 운이라고 생각하지 않는 이유를 설명하는 문장들이 유기적으로 연결되어 있어.

지문 Flow

[주제문]
행운은 스스로 만드는 것

[보충설명]
같은 상황에서도 다른 결과를 만들어 낼 수 있음

[주장]
운이 좋거나 나쁘다고 생각할지 모르지만, 그것은 운 때문이 아님

[추가]
세상을 바라보고 그 안에서 상호 작용하는 방법을 선택하는 태도에 결과가 달려 있음

[결론]
매순간 삶에 대한 선택을 하기 때문에, 책임은 자신에게 있고 운도 스스로 선택하는 것임

Check-Up 2

정답 1 Ⓐ 2 ②

해석 [1-2] 중력이 있는 물체는 사물을 자기 쪽으로 끌어당긴다. 물체가 클수록 중력이 세다. 예를 들어, 목성은 너무 커서 다른 모든 행성들이 그 안에 들어가도 맞다. 이와 같이, 목성은 다른 모든 행성들보다 더 강한 중력을 갖고 있다.

해설 1 Ⓐ 뒤에 있는 예시는 앞 내용과 맞지 않으므로 이 부분에서 글의 흐름이 끊긴다. 2 Ⓐ 뒤의 예시의 내용이 목성은 다른 모든 행성들이 그 안에 들어갈 수 있을 만큼 크기가 커서 가장 중력이 세다는 것이므로, Ⓐ 자리에는 '물체가 클수록 중력이 세다'는 말이 들어가야 글의 흐름이 논리적이다.

092 정답 ②

지문 All in One

1 A lot of people are under the impression / that to be fluent in another language / means / that you speak it / as well as (your native language), / or almost as well as, your native language. (①) 2 However, / I have my own definition of fluency / in a language. 3 (② That is, / we are fluent enough // if we're able to use the target language / to learn more of the target language.) 4 For example, / if you don't know the word for *tail* / in your target language / but you know how to describe / *the long body part behind a dog or cat,* // then you've demonstrated a high level of fluency. (③) 5 That's it. 6 Does it seem tough? (④) 7 Try it with some basic words / in your target language / to find out if you are fluent or not. (⑤) 8 You'll quickly see / what fluency is all about.

많은 사람들은 생각하고 있다 / 다른 언어에 유창하다는 것은 / 의미한다 / 당신이 그것을 말하는 것을 / (모국어)만큼 잘 / 또는 거의 모국어만큼 잘 / 하지만 / 나는 유창함에 대한 나만의 정의를 가지고 있다 / 언어에 있어서 / 즉 / 우리는 충분히 유창하다 / 우리가 목표 언어를 사용할 수 있다면 / 목표 언어에 대해 더 많이 배우기 위해 / 예를 들어 / 만약 당신이 '꼬리'라는 단어를 모른다면 / 목표 언어에서 / 하지만 당신이 설명하는 법을 알고 있다면 / '개나 고양이 뒤에 길이가 긴 몸 부분'을 / 그러면 당신은 높은 수준의 유창함을 증명했다 / 그게 전부다 / 그것이 힘들어 보이는가 / 몇 가지 기본 단어로 그것을 해 봐라 / 목표 언어의 / 당신이 유창한지 아닌지 알아보기 위해 / 당신은 빨리 알게 될 것이다 / 유창함이 무엇인지

해석 한 눈에 보기 1 많은 사람들은 다른 언어에 유창하다는 것은 당신이 그것을 모국어만큼 잘 또는 거의 모국어만큼 잘 말하는 것을 의미한다고 생각하고 있다. 2 하지만, 나는 언어에 있어서 유창함에 대한 나만의 정의를 가지고 있다. 주제문 3 즉, 우리가 목표 언어에 대해 더 많이 배우기 위해 목표 언어를 사용할 수 있다면, 우리는 충분히 유창하다.

어휘확인

be under the impression that ~하다고 생각하고 있다 **fluent** 유창한 **cf. fluency** 유창함 **native** 모국의, 태어난 곳의 **definition** 정의 **describe** 설명하다, 묘사하다 **demonstrate** 증명하다

지문 Flow

[소재]
언어의 유창성

[통념]
다른 언어를 모국어만큼 잘 해야 유창하다고 함

[주장]
목표 언어를 사용하여 더 많은 목표 언어를 배울 수 있다면, 유창한 것임

[예시]
'꼬리'라는 단어 대신 '개나 고양이 뒤에 길이가 긴 몸 부분'이라는 말로 설명함

4 예를 들어, 만약 당신이 목표 언어에서 '꼬리'라는 단어를 모르지만, '개나 고양이 뒤에 길이가 긴 몸 부분'을 설명하는 법을 알고 있다면, 당신은 높은 수준의 유창함을 증명했다. 5 그게 전부다. 6 그것이 힘들어 보이는가? 7 당신이 유창한지 아닌지 알아보기 위해 목표 언어의 몇 가지 기본 단어로 그것을 해 봐라. 8 당신은 유창함이 무엇인지 빨리 알게 될 것이다.

정답단추 주어진 문장은 That is라는 연결어와 함께 목표 언어에 유창하다는 것이 어떤 것인지 설명해주고 있어. That is는 앞의 내용을 구체적으로 설명할 때 쓰는 연결어로, 이에 대해 언급한 문장 뒤에 들어가야 자연스럽다는 것을 알 수 있어. ②의 앞에서 필자는 언어의 유창함에 대한 자신만의 정의가 있다고 했는데, ②의 뒤에서 그 정의를 설명하는 내용이 나오지 않고 바로 예시가 이어지고 있으므로 흐름이 끊겨 있지. 따라서 주어진 문장이 들어가기에 가장 적절한 곳은 ②야.

오답단서 ①의 앞에는 다른 사람들이 생각하는 언어의 유창성이 나오고, 뒤에는 필자가 생각하는 언어의 유창성이 나와서 연결이 자연스러워. ③, ④, ⑤의 앞과 뒤는 목표 언어의 기본 단어로도 유창함을 증명할 수 있다는 내용이 유기적으로 연결되어 있어.

[결론]
목표 언어의 기본 단어만으로도 유창함을 증명할 수 있음

실전적용독해

093 정답 ④

지문 All in One

커다란 눈과 조용하고 주의 깊은 행동으로 인해 / 올빼미는 숲 속의 가장 훌륭한 사냥꾼들 중 하나이다

1 With their huge eyes [and] quiet, watchful behavior, / owls(S) are(V) among the greatest hunters of the forest(C). (①)

2 During the daytime(낮 동안), / when(접속사) they(S′) are not hunting(V′)(그들이 사냥을 하고 있지 않을 때), // they(S) keep(V) their eyes(O) half-shut(C)(그것들은 눈을 반쯤 감고 있다). (②)

3 But when(접속사) the sun(S′) goes down(V′)(그러나 해가 지면), // they(S) can see(V) far(비교급 강조) better(그것들은 훨씬 더 잘 볼 수 있다) / than almost any other animal(거의 다른 어떤 동물보다도). (③)

4 They(S) open(V₁) their eyes(O) wide(C)(그것들은 눈을 크게 뜬다) / to let in(부사적 용법(목적))(들어오게 하기 위해) / [as] much light [as] possible(가능한 한 많은 빛을) // [and](그래서) become(V₂) skillful hunters(C)(능숙한 사냥꾼이 된다).

5 (④ However(하지만), / they(S) cannot move(V) their eyes(그것들은 눈을 움직이질 못한다) // as(접속사) mammals(S′) do(V′).(포유동물이 하는 것처럼))

6 Instead(대신에), / they(S) rely on(V) turning their heads(그것들은 고개를 돌리는 것에 의존한다) / almost 180 degrees(거의 180도로) / to find(부사적 용법(목적)) their prey(그것들의 먹이를 찾기 위해). (⑤)

7 As soon as(접속사) they(S′) find(V′) it(먹이를 발견하자마자), // they(S) swiftly catch(V) it(그것들은 재빨리 그것을 포획한다) / with a swoop of their silent wings(조용한 날갯짓 일격으로).

해석 한 눈에 보기 주제문 1 커다란 눈과 조용하고 주의 깊은 행동으로 인해, 올빼미는 숲 속의 가장 훌륭한 사냥꾼들 중 하나이다. 2 낮 동안, 그들이 사냥을 하고 있지 않을 때, 그것들은 눈을 반쯤 감고 있다. 3 그러나 해가 지면, 그것들은 거의 다른 어떤 동물보다도 훨씬 더 잘 볼 수 있다. 4 그것들은 가능한 한 많은 빛을 들어오게 하려고 눈을 크게 떠서 능숙한 사냥꾼이 된다. 5 하지만 그것들은 포유동물이 하는 것처럼 눈을 움직이질 못한다. 6 대신에, 그것들은 먹이를 찾기 위해 고개를 거의 180도로 돌리는 것에 의존한다. 7 먹이를 발견하자마자, 그것들은 조용한 날갯짓 일격으로 그것을 재빨리 포획한다.

정답단추 글의 흐름을 알려주는 지시어와 연결어를 활용해 보자. 주어진 문장에 나온 연결어 however를 이용해 문장의 위치를 파악하고 지시어 they가 가리키는 내용을 찾아야 해. 우선 첫 문장을 통해 이 글은 올빼미의 사냥법에 관한 내용임을 알 수 있어. 따라서 they는 올빼미를 의미하고 있음을 추론할 수 있지. 또한, 올빼미는 밤이 되면 눈을 크게 뜨고 사냥을 한다는 내용이 전개되다가, Instead로 시작되는 문장에서 글의 흐름이 끊어져. 그럴 경우 Instead가 포함된 문장 앞에 주어진 문장을 넣어 보고 글의 흐름이 자연스러운지를 파악해 보면 되는데, 글의 흐름이 매끄럽게 연결되므로 주어진 문장은 ④에 위치하는 것이 가장 적절해.

오답단서 ①, ②, ③, ⑤의 앞뒤 문장은 유기적으로 잘 연결되어 있어서 주어진 문장을 삽입하면 글의 연결이 어색해져.

어휘확인

huge 큰, 거대한 **quiet** 조용한(= silent) **watchful** 주의 깊은 **behavior** 행동 **owl** 올빼미 **hunter** 사냥꾼 **daytime** 낮 **shut** (눈이) 감긴 **go down** (해·달이) 지다 **let in** ~을 들어오게 하다 **skillful** 능숙한 **mammal** 포유동물 **rely on** ~에 의존하다 **degree** (각도·온도 등의) 도 **prey** 먹이 **as soon as** ~하자마자 **swiftly** 빨리, 신속히 **swoop** 일격; 급습

지문 Flow

[주제문]
숲 속의 가장 훌륭한 사냥꾼 중 하나인 올빼미

[보충설명1]
낮에는 눈을 반쯤 감고 있지만, 밤에는 눈을 크게 떠 훨씬 더 잘 볼 수 있음

&

[보충설명2]
눈을 움직이지 못하는 대신에 고개를 180도로 돌림

&

[보충설명3]
먹이를 발견하면 조용한 일격으로 재빨리 포획함

094 정답 ④

지문 All in One

1 Every person(S) is born(V)(모든 사람은 태어난다) / with *a particular potential*(특정한 잠재력을 가지고) [which(관계대명사) is unique to him](그 자신에게 유일한). (①)

2 People(S₁) are(V₁) of different types(C₁)(사람들은 유형이 다르다) // [and] not all of them(S₂) are(V₂) brilliant students(C₂).(그리고 그들 모두가 훌륭한 학생들은 아니다) (②)

3 Therefore(그러므로), / how to prepare for exams(S)(시험을 준비하는 방법은) / is(V) a big question(C)(큰 문제이다). (③)

4 First of all(우선), / before starting with their studies(분사구문(= before students start ~))(공부를 시작하기 전에), /

어휘확인

be born 태어나다 **particular** 특정한 **potential** 잠재력 **unique to** ~에 유일한 **type** 유형 **brilliant** 훌륭한 **prepare for** ~을 준비하다 **first of all** 우선 **design** 계획하다, 고안하다 **timetable** 시간표(= schedule) **describe** 설명하다 **material** 자료 **cover** 다루다, 포함하다

students should design / *their own timetable* [which describes *all the material* [that has to be covered] / and tells them / how much needs to be studied / each day]. 5 (④ A schedule like this / should be made / for *each subject* [that focuses on different priorities].) 6 Tough subjects and *the ones* [in which a student is weak] / should be given more hours, // and easier ones should be given / less hours with sufficient intervals / between each subject. (⑤) 7 It's very important / that these breaks (should) be included / in the timetable itself.

필요를 나타내는 형용사 뒤의 that절이 '~해야 한다'를 의미할 때: that+S+(should)+동사원형

해석 한 눈에 보기 1 모든 사람은 그 자신에게 유일한 특정한 잠재력을 가지고 태어난다. 2 사람들은 유형이 다르고 그들 모두가 훌륭한 학생들은 아니다. 3 그러므로, 시험을 준비하는 방법은 큰 문제이다. 4 우선, 공부를 시작하기 전에 학생들은 다루어져야 하는 모든 자료를 설명하고 매일 얼마나 공부해야 하는지 그들에게 알려주는 그들 자신의 시간표를 계획해야 한다. 5 이와 같은 시간표는 서로 다른 우선순위에 초점을 맞춘 각 과목별로 만들어져야 한다. 6 어려운 과목들과 학생이 약한 과목들은 더 많은 시간을 할애해야 하고, 더 쉬운 과목들은 각 과목 간에 충분한 간격을 두고 더 적은 시간을 할애해야 한다. 7 이러한 휴식 시간을 시간표 자체에 포함시키는 것이 매우 중요하다.

정답단추 주어진 문장에 지시어가 있으면 글에서 어떤 내용을 가리키는지 찾아보도록 해. 지시어와 연결어는 문장의 위치를 찾을 수 있는 핵심 힌트거든. 주어진 문장의 A schedule like this로 보아, 앞에는 시간표에 대한 내용이 나와야 하는데, ④의 앞부분에서 시간표에 대해 다루고 있어. 그러므로 this는 앞의 시간표를 설명하는 부분을 가리킨다고 볼 수 있지. 또한 주어진 문장에서 우선순위에 따라 과목별로 시간표가 만들어져야 한다고 했는데, ④의 뒤에서 어렵고 약한 과목들과 쉬운 과목들 간의 공부 시간의 할애에 대한 내용이 나오고 있어. 따라서 주어진 문장이 들어갈 위치로 가장 적절한 곳은 ④야.

오답단서 ①, ②, ③은 사람마다 유형이 달라서 시험을 준비하는 방법이 문제가 되는데, 우선 공부 시작 전에 자신만의 시간표를 만들어야 한다는 내용이 유기적으로 연결되고 있어. ⑤는 쉬운 과목을 공부할 때 충분한 간격을 두고 더 적은 시간을 할애해야 한다고 하면서, 휴식 시간이 시간표에 포함되는 것이 중요하다고 이어서 말하고 있어.

focus on ~에 초점을 맞추다 priority 우선순위 tough 어려운, 힘든 sufficient 충분한 interval 간격 break 휴식 (시간) include 포함하다

지문 Flow

[도입] 사람마다 유형이 다르고 모두 훌륭한 학생들이 아니므로 시험 준비 방법이 큰 문제가 됨

[주장] 공부하기 전에 무엇을 얼마나 공부해야 하는지 적은 시간표를 만들어야 함

[보충설명] 각 과목에 우선순위를 두어 시간표를 만들어야 함

&

[보충설명] 어렵고 약한 과목에는 시간을 더 할애하고, 쉬운 과목은 시간을 덜 할애함

095 정답 ④

지문 All in One

1 The substitution of more abundant materials / for scarce minerals / is an important goal / of manufacturing. (①) 2 The search for substitutes / is driven in part by economics: // *one effective way* [to cut production costs] / is to substitute an inexpensive or abundant material / for an expensive or scarce one. (②) 3 As a result, / plastics, ceramic composites, and glass fibers / have been substituted for scarcer materials / in many industries. (③) 4 Earlier in the 20th century, / tin was a critical metal / for the can-making industry; // since then, / plastic, glass, and aluminum / have been substituted for tin. 5 (④ Although substitution can extend / our mineral supplies, // it is not a cure-all / for resource shortages.) 6 There are *certain minerals* [for which no known substitutes exist / on Earth]. (⑤) 7 For example, / *no substance* [having the unique properties of platinum] / has yet been found.

전치사+관계대명사(= (which) no known substitutes exist for)

해석 한 눈에 보기 주제문 1 희박한 광물질을 보다 풍부한 물질로 대체하는 것은 제조업의 중요한 목표이다. 2 대체물의 탐색은 부분적으로 경제학에 의해 추진되는데, 생산비를 줄이는 효과적인 한 가지 방법은 비싸고 희박한 물질을 값싸고 풍부한 물질로 대체하는 것이다. 3 그 결과, 플라스틱, 세라믹 조성물, 유리 섬유가 많은 산업 분야에서 보다 희귀한 물질들을 대체해 왔다. 4 일찍이 20세기에, 주석은 깡통 제조 산업 분야에 아주 중요한 금속이었는데, 그때 이후로

어휘확인

substitution 대체 cf. substitute 대체물; 대체하다 abundant 풍부한 material 물질, 재료, 원료 scarce 희박한, 드문 mineral 광물(질) manufacturing 제조업 drive 추진시키다 in part 부분적으로 economics 경제학 effective 효과적인 cut 줄이다, 삭감하다 inexpensive 값싼 ceramic composite 세라믹 조성물(합성물) fiber 섬유 industry 산업 century 세기(世紀) tin 주석 critical 아주 중요한 metal 금속 aluminum 알루미늄 extend 확장하다 supply 비축[공급](량) cure-all 만병통치약 shortage 부족, 결핍 certain 어떤 substance 물질 unique 고유한 property 성질, 특성 platinum 백금

지문 Flow

[주제문] 희박한 광물질을 풍부한 물질로 대체하는 것이 제조업의 중요한 목표

[보충설명] 생산비를 줄이는 효과적인 방법으로 대체물을 탐색함

플라스틱, 유리, 알루미늄이 주석을 대체해왔다. 5 비록 대체가 광물질의 비축량을 확장시킬 수 있을지라도, 그것이 자원 부족에 대한 만병통치약은 아니다. 6 지구상에는 알려진 대체물질이 존재하지 않는 광물질이 있다. 7 예를 들어, 백금의 고유한 성질을 갖고 있는 물질은 아직 발견되지 않았다.

정답단추 주어진 문장에 뚜렷한 단서가 없어. 이럴 때는 먼저 글의 흐름이 끊기는 곳을 찾아야 해. ④의 앞에서는 대체물의 구체적인 예시들이 이어지다가, 뒤에서 갑자기 어떤 광물질은 알려진 대체물질이 지구상에 없다는 내용이 나오면서 글의 흐름이 끊어짐을 알 수 있어. 이 문장은 주어진 문장을 뒷받침할 수 있는 내용이니까 ④가 주어진 문장이 들어가기에 가장 적절한 곳이라 할 수 있어.

오답단서 ①, ②, ③, ⑤는 앞뒤로 글의 흐름이 끊기는 부분 없이 매끄럽게 연결되어 있어. 그래서 주어진 문장이 들어가기에는 적절하지 않아.

[예시]
깡통 제조에 중요한 금속이었던 주석을 플라스틱, 유리, 알루미늄이 대체함

⬇

[반론 + 주어진 문장]
대체물이 자원 부족에 대한 만병통치약은 아님

⬇

[예시]
대체물질이 없는 백금 같은 광물질이 있음

미니 모의고사 3 유형 08 | 유형 09 | 유형 10

096 ② 097 ③ 098 ② 099 ② 100 ③ 101 ② 102 ② 103 ④ 104 ③
105 ④ 106 ④ 107 ④ 108 ③ 109 ② 110 ④ 111 ③ 112 ③ 113 ④

096 정답 ②

지문 All in One

1 One of *the benefits* [(which[that]) you get from travel] / is that you can experience history / in *the places* [(which) you visit]. 2 You can read about history / in a book, // but you can feel it / when you see it / in person. 3 Many places offer / more than meets the eye. 4 ① For example, / Breckenridge, Colorado, is known for its ski resort, // but this former Victorian mining town / has done a great job / of preserving Victorian homes. 5 (② Many of them have been modernized / by *the young housewives* [who desire them].) 6 ③ Boston is an exciting party town, // but you can also evoke the American Revolution / by walking the Freedom Trail. 7 ④ A walk through the Coliseum in Rome / will transport you / back to the days of the Roman Empire. 8 ⑤ It may be impressive / in pictures, // but it's overwhelming / when you see it in real life.

(1 여행에서 얻는 이점들 중 하나는 (S) / 관계대명사 / 역사를 경험할 수 있다는 것이다 (V, 접속사, C) / 당신이 방문한 곳에서 (관계대명사) 2 당신은 역사에 대해 읽을 수 있다 (S_1, V_1) / 책에서 / 하지만 당신은 그것을 느낄 수 있다 (S_2, V_2) / 당신이 그것을 볼 때 (접속사, S′, V′) / 직접 3 많은 곳들은 제공한다 (S, V) / 눈으로 만나는 것 이상을 4 예를 들어 / 콜로라도 주의 브레킨리지는 스키 리조트로 유명하다 (S_1, V_1) / 하지만 이 옛날 빅토리아 시대의 탄광 마을은 (S_2) / 훌륭한 일을 했다 (V_2) / 빅토리아 시대의 주택을 보존하는 5 그것들 중 많은 것들이 현대화되었다 (S, V) / 젊은 주부들에 의해 / 그것들을 바라는 (관계대명사) 6 보스턴은 신나는 파티 마을이다 (S_1, V_1, C) / 하지만 당신은 또한 미국 독립 혁명을 불러일으킬 수도 있다 (S_2, V_2) / 프리덤 트레일을 걸음으로써 7 로마의 콜로세움을 따라 걷다 보면 (S) / 당신은 가 있을 것이다 (V) / 로마 제국의 시대로 8 그것은 인상적일지 모른다 (S_1, V_1, C_1) / 사진에서 / 하지만 그것은 압도적이다 (S_2, V_2, C_2) / 실제로 당신이 그것을 보면 (접속사, S′, V′))

해석 한 눈에 보기 주제문 1 여행에서 얻는 이점들 중 하나는 당신이 방문한 곳에서 역사를 경험할 수 있다는 것이다. 2 책에서 역사에 대해 읽을 수 있지만, 직접 볼 때 그것을 느낄 수 있다. 3 많은 곳들은 눈으로 만나는 것 이상을 제공한다. 4 ① 예를 들어, 콜로라도 주의 브레킨리지는 스키 리조트로 유명하지만, 이 옛날 빅토리아 시대의 탄광 마을은 빅토리아 시대의 주택을 보존하는 훌륭한 일을 했다. 5 (② 그것들 중 많은 것들이 그것들을 바라는 젊은 주부들에 의해 현대화되었다.) 6 ③ 보스턴은 신나는 파티 마을이지만, 당신은 또한 프리덤 트레일을 걸음으로써 미국 독립 혁명을 불러일으킬 수도 있다. 7 ④ 로마의 콜로세움을 따라 걷다 보면 당신은 로마 제국의 시대로 가 있을 것이다. 8 ⑤ 그것은 사진에서 인상적일지 모르지만, 실제로 그것을 보면 압도적이다.

정답단추 무관한 문장을 고르는 문제에서는 글의 앞부분이 주제문인 경우가 많아서, 주제를 파악한 후에 그것을 뒷받침하지 않는 문장을 고르면 답을 찾기 쉬워. 이 글은 첫 문장이 주제문인데, 여행지에 가면 그곳의 역사적인 경험을 할 수 있다고 했어. 그 뒤에 그에 대한 몇 가지 예들이 이어지고 있지. 그런데 ②는 그 예들 중 하나인 콜로라도 주 브레킨리지에 있는 빅토리아 시대의 주택을 젊은 주부들이 현대화시켰다는 내용으로, 여행지에서 역사적 경험을 할 수

어휘확인

benefit 이익, 혜택 in person 직접 offer 제공하다 be known for ~으로 유명하다 resort 리조트, 휴양지 former 옛날의, 이전의 mining 탄광, 채광 preserve 보존하다 modernize 현대화하다 housewife 주부 desire 바라다 evoke 불러일으키다 revolution (정치적인) 혁명 transport 이동시키다 empire 제국 overwhelming 압도적인

지문 Flow

[주제문]
여행의 이점으로 방문지의 역사를 경험할 수 있음

⬇

[보충설명]
책에서보다 직접 그것을 보는 것이 더 좋음

⬇

[예시1]
빅토리아 시대의 주택을 보존한 브레킨리지의 탄광 마을

⬇

[무관한 문장]
많은 주택들이 젊은 주부들에 의해 현대화됨

⬇

[예시2]
• 미국 독립 혁명을 생각나게 하는 보스턴의 프리덤 트레일
• 로마 제국을 경험할 수 있는 콜로세움

있다는 글의 주제와는 관련이 없어.

오답단서 ①, ③, ④는 여행지에서 역사 경험을 할 수 있는 예들이므로 글의 내용을 뒷받침하는 문장들이야. ⑤는 사진보다 실제로 유적지를 봤을 때 감동이 더 크다는 말이므로 주제와 관련이 있어.

097 정답 ③

지문 All in One

오스트레일리아는 유일한 섬이다 / 또한 대륙이기도 한 / 그러나 이것이 유일하게 흥미로운 사실인

1 Australia is *the only island* [that is also a continent], // [but] that's far from the only

S₁ V₁ C₁ 관계대명사 S₂ V₂ C₂

것은 전혀 아니다 / 그것에 관해 / 그것은 약 77배 더 크다 / 남한보다

interesting fact / about it. (①) 2 It is around 77 times bigger / than South Korea, // [but] has

S₁ V₁ C V₂

그러나 고작 2천만 명을 갖고 있다 / 반면에 남한은 그 수의 두 배 이상을 갖고 있다

only 20 million people, / [whereas] South Korea has more than twice that number. (②) 3 Not

접속사 S′ V′

놀랄 것 없이 / 오스트레일리아는 인구 밀도가 가장 낮은 대륙이다 / 지구에서 / 남극 대륙을

surprisingly, / Australia is the least densely populated continent / on Earth / excluding

S V C

제외하고 / 하지만 흥미로운 사실은 ~이다 / 적은 인구에도 불구하고 / 오스트레일리아가

Antarctica. 4 (③ But an interesting fact is // that, despite its low population, / Australia is

S V C S′ V′

민족적으로 다양하다는 것 / 예를 들어 / 대부분의 오스트레일리아 사람들은 / 영국인 조상을 가지고 있다

ethnically diverse.) 5 For example, most Australian people / have British ancestry, / which is a

C′ S V 계속적 용법

이것은 식민지화의 결과이다 / 18세기 후반과 19세기 동안에 있었던 / 다른 오스트레일리아인들은

result of colonization / during the late 18th and 19th centuries. (④) 6 Other Australians

S

오스트레일리아 원주민들과 사람들을 포함한다 / 약 120개의 서로 다른 나라에서 온

include the Aborigines [and] people / from around 120 different countries. (⑤) 7 In

V

특히 / 1970년대 이후로 / 아주 많은 수의 이주자들이 / 이주해 왔다 / 아시아에서

particular, / since the 1970s, / a great number of migrants / have come / from Asia.

S V

해석 한 눈에 보기 1 오스트레일리아는 또한 대륙이기도 한 유일한 섬인데, 이것이 그것에 관해 유일하게 흥미로운 사실인 것은 전혀 아니다. 2 그것은 남한보다 약 77배 더 크지만, 고작 2천만 명을 갖고 있는 반면에, 남한은 그 수의 두 배 이상을 갖고 있다. 3 놀라운 일은 아니지만, 오스트레일리아는 지구에서 남극 대륙을 제외하고 인구 밀도가 가장 낮은 대륙이다. 4 하지만 적은 인구에도 불구하고, 오스트레일리아가 민족적으로 다양하다는 것은 흥미로운 사실이다. 5 예를 들어, 대부분의 오스트레일리아 사람들은 영국인 조상을 가지고 있는데, 이것은 18세기 후반과 19세기 동안에 있었던 식민지화의 결과이다. 6 다른 오스트레일리아인들은 오스트레일리아 원주민들과 약 120개의 서로 다른 나라에서 온 사람들을 포함한다. 7 특히, 1970년대 이후로, 아주 많은 수의 이주자들이 아시아에서 이주해 왔다.

정답단추 먼저 주어진 문장은 '오스트레일리아는 적은 인구에도 불구하고 민족적으로 다양하다'는 내용이야. ③의 앞부분은 오스트레일리아의 낮은 인구 밀도에 대해 언급하고 있지? 또한, 뒷부분의 For example로 시작하는 문장은 다양한 민족 구성에 관한 예시를 들고 있어. 따라서 주어진 문장의 가장 적절한 위치는 ③임을 알 수 있어.

오답단서 ①, ②, ④, ⑤는 앞뒤 문장이 자연스럽게 이어지고 있어서 주어진 문장이 들어가기에는 적절하지 않아. 특히, ②의 앞, 뒤 문장이 인구에 관한 내용이긴 하지만, '다양한 민족 구성'과 관련된 내용은 나오지 않아서 주어진 문장의 위치로는 적절하지 않아.

어휘확인

continent 대륙 **far from** 전혀 ~이 아닌 **times** ~배(倍)가 되는 **whereas** 반면에, 반면 **not surprisingly** 놀랄 것 없이 **densely** 밀집하여 **populate** 살다, 거주하다 cf. **population** 인구 **excluding** ~을 제외하고 **Antarctica** 남극 대륙 **despite** ~에도 불구하고 **ethnically** 민족적으로 **diverse** 다양한 **ancestry** 조상, 선조 **colonization** 식민지화 **include** 포함하다 **Aborigine** 오스트레일리아 원주민 **in particular** 특히 **migrant** 이주자

지문 Flow

[소개]
오스트레일리아는 대륙이기도 한 유일한 섬

⬇

[사실1]
남한보다 77배 크지만, 인구는 절반 정도임

&

[사실2]
적은 인구에도 불구하고 민족적으로 다양함

⬇

[예시]
- 과거 식민지화의 결과로 인한 영국인 조상
- 오스트레일리아의 원주민
- 이주해 온 약 120여 개국의 사람들

098 정답 ②

지문 All in One

유사는 혼합된 모래 지역이다 / 너무 많은 물과 / 영화에서

1 Quicksand is an area of *sand* [that has been mixed / with too much water]. 2 In movies, / it

S V C 관계대명사 S

그것은 액체처럼 반응을 보인다 / 그리고 사람들을 아래로 빨아들인다 / 그리고 그들을 죽인다

behaves like a liquid / [and] sucks people down / [and] kills them.

V₁ V₂ V₃

그러나 유사에 대한 진실은 ~이다 / 그것이 정말로 위험하지는 않다는 것 / 당신은 그저 필요하다

(B) 3 But the truth about quicksand is // that it isn't really dangerous. 4 You just need / to keep

S V 접속사 C S V

당신의 정신을 차리는 것이 / 만약 당신이 뜻하지 않게 유사에 발을 디딘다면 / 그리고 가라앉기 시작한(다면) / 당황하지

your wits about you. 5 If you accidentally step in quicksand / [and] begin to sink, // don't

접속사 S′ V′₁ V′₂ V

마라

panic.

침착해라 / 가능한 한 거의 움직이지 말고 / 당신의 양팔을 펴고 / 뒤로 젖혀라

(A) 6 Stay calm. 7 Move [as] little [as] possible, / spread your arms, / [and] lean back // just as if

V C V₁ V₂ V₃ 가정법

마치 당신이 뜨려고 하는 것처럼 / 등을 대고 / 수영장에서 / 이것은 당신의 몸 표면적을 증가시

you were trying to float / on your back / in a swimming pool. 8 This will increase your

S′ V′ S V₁

어휘확인

quicksand 유사(流沙) **area** 지역 **behave** 반응을 보이다 **liquid** 액체 **suck** 빨아들이다 **truth** 진실 **keep A's wits about A** 정신을 차리다 **accidentally** 뜻하지 않게 **sink** 가라앉다 **panic** 당황하다 **calm** 침착한 **lean** (몸을) 젖히다 **float** (물에) 뜨다 **increase** 증가시키다 **surface area** 표면적 **gently** 부드럽게 **mess** 엉망진창인 상태 **afterward** 나중에 **otherwise** 그 외에는 **harm** 해, 피해

지문 Flow

[도입]
유사는 물과 혼합된 모래 지역으로, 영화에서는 사람들을 아래로 빨아들여 죽임

킬 것이다 그리고 당신이 가라앉는 것을 멈추게 한다

body's surface area // and make you stop sinking.

(C) [9] When you have stopped, // you can gently swim / using only your arms / to get out of the quicksand. [10] Of course you'll be a complete mess / afterward, // but otherwise no harm / will have been done.

① (A) - (C) - (B) ② (B) - (A) - (C) ③ (B) - (C) - (A)
④ (C) - (A) - (B) ⑤ (C) - (B) - (A)

[반박]
(B) 유사는 위험하지 않으며, 발이 빠지려고 해도 당황하지 않기

[보충설명1]
(A) 침착하고, 거의 움직이지 말고, 양팔을 펴고, 몸을 뒤로 젖히기

&

[보충설명2]
(C) 양팔로 수영해서 유사에서 빠져나오기

해석 한 눈에 보기 1 유사(流沙)는 너무 많은 물과 혼합된 모래 지역이다. 2 영화에서, 그것은 액체처럼 작용하여 사람들을 아래로 빨아들여 그들을 죽인다. (B) 3 그러나 유사에 대한 진실은 그것이 정말로 위험하지는 않다는 것이다. 4 당신은 그저 정신만 차리면 된다. 5 만일 당신이 어쩌다 유사에 발을 디뎌 가라앉기 시작한다면, 당황하지 마라. (A) 6 침착해라. 7 가능한 한 거의 움직이지 말고, 양팔을 펴고, 마치 꼭 당신이 수영장에서 등을 대고 뜨려고 할 때처럼 뒤로 젖혀라. 8 이것은 당신 몸의 표면적을 넓혀서 당신이 가라앉는 것을 멈추게 한다. (C) 9 당신이 멈추었을 때, 당신은 양팔만을 이용하여 부드럽게 수영해서 유사에서 빠져나올 수 있다. 10 물론 당신은 나중에 완전히 엉망진창이 되어 있을 것이지만, 그 외에는 어떤 해도 입지 않았을 것이다.

정답단추 주어진 글은 유사의 정의와, 영화에서 이것이 매우 위험하게 그려진다는 내용이야. (B)는 But으로 시작하면서 실제로는 유사가 위험하지 않다고 앞 내용을 반박하는 내용으로 주어진 글 뒤에 오는 것이 자연스러워. 그리고 당황하지 말라는 (B)의 마지막 문장 다음에 침착함을 유지하라는 명령문과 몸이 가라앉는 것을 막기 위한 대처 방법을 포함하고 있는 (A)가 이어서 와야 해. 마지막으로 가라앉는 게 멈추면 양팔만을 이용해 헤엄쳐서 빠져나오라는 내용의 (C)가 오는 것이 적절해. 따라서 이 글의 알맞은 순서는 ② '(B) – (A) – (C)'야.

099 정답 ②

지문 All in One

[1] People love to sit in hot tubs / to relieve tense muscles, // but hot baths are not recommended / for everyone. [2] In fact, / for some people, / a hot bath can be a very dangerous thing. [3] ① As hot water increases the heart rate, // a hot tub can be dangerous / for people / with high blood pressure. [4] (② Therefore, / you should get some exercise / every day / to reduce blood pressure / in a healthy way.) [5] ③ Body temperature also increases / in hot water, // which can lead / to loss of essential body fluids. [6] ④ Furthermore, / when body temperature rises, // blood sugar burns faster. [7] ⑤ This can be very risky / for *people* [who have diabetes].

해석 한 눈에 보기 1 주제문 사람들은 긴장한 근육을 완화하기 위해 뜨거운 욕조에 앉아 있기를 아주 좋아하지만, 뜨거운 목욕이 모든 사람에게 추천되지는 않는다. 2 사실, 어떤 사람들에게, 뜨거운 목욕은 매우 위험한 것일 수 있다. 3 ① 뜨거운 물은 심장박동 수를 증가시키기 때문에, 뜨거운 욕조는 고혈압이 있는 사람들에게 위험할 수 있다. 4 (② 그러므로 당신은 건강한 방법으로 혈압을 낮추려면 매일 약간의 운동을 해야 한다.) 5 ③ 체온 또한 뜨거운 물 속에서 높아지는데, 이것은 필수적인 체액의 손실을 초래할 수 있다. 6 ④ 더욱이 체온이 올라가면, 혈당이 더 빨리 연소한다. 7 ⑤ 이것은 당뇨병이 있는 사람에게 매우 위험할 수 있다.

정답단추 이 글에서는 선택지가 없는 첫 두 문장이 각각 주제문과 보충설명문이야. 이 두 문장을 읽고 나면 뜨거운 목욕이 좋지 않은 사람들의 예시가 뒤이어 나올 것을 예상할 수 있어. ②는 앞 문장의 blood pressure가 반복되어 자연스러운 것 같지? 하지만, 혈압을 줄이려면 날마다 운동을 하라는 내용으로 이 글의 핵심인 뜨거운 목욕과는 무관해. 따라서 ②가 전체 흐름과 관계없는 문장이야.

오답단서 ①은 심장박동 수를 증가시켜 고혈압 환자에게 위험하다는 내용이므로 자연스럽게 이어지고 있어. 그리고 ③, ④, ⑤도 뜨거운 목욕이 필수 체액의 손실을 주고, 혈당이 빨리 연소하여 당뇨 환자에게 위험하다는 내용으로 글의 흐름에서 벗어나지 않아.

어휘확인

tub 욕조 **relieve** 완화하다 **tense** 긴장한 **in fact** 사실 **increase** 증가시키다; 증가하다 **heart rate** 심장박동 수 **blood pressure** 혈압 **body temperature** 체온 **lead to** ~로 이어지다 **loss** 손실 **essential** 필수적인 **fluid** 액체 **furthermore** 더욱이 **rise** 오르다 **blood sugar** 혈당 **risky** 위험한 **diabetes** 당뇨병

지문 Flow

[주제문]
뜨거운 목욕이 모든 사람에게 좋지는 않음

[보충설명1]
뜨거운 물은 심장박동 수를 증가시켜, 고혈압 환자에게 위험함

[무관한 문장]
혈압을 낮추기 위해 매일 운동을 해야 함

[보충설명2]
체온도 높아져 체액의 손실을 초래함

&

[보충설명3]
체온 상승은 혈당을 더 빨리 연소시켜, 당뇨병 환자에게 위험함

100 정답 ③

지문 All in One

모든 아기는 다르다 / 그리고 언어 기술을 계발할 것이다 / 자기 자신의 속도로
[1] Every baby is different / and will develop language skills / at its own rate. (①) [2] While
S V_1 C V_2 접속사

몇몇이 말하고 있는 반면에 / 완전한 문장으로 / 18개월까지 / 그 나이의 다른 몇몇은 / 준비가 전혀 되어 있지 않다
some are speaking / in full sentences / by 18 months, // others of that age / are nowhere near
S′ V′ S V

마법의 방법은 없다 / 일찍 말하는 아이의 능력을 보장할
ready. (②) [3] There is no *magic method* [that will guarantee *a child's ability* [to talk early]].
V 관계대명사 S

그럼에도 불구하고 / 부모와 다른 돌보는 사람이 할 수 있는 것이 있다 / 아기들이 자신의 필요를 말로
[4] (③ Still, / there are *things* [that parents and other caregivers can do] / in order to encourage
V 관계대명사 S 부사적 용법(목적)

나타내도록 격려하기 위해 / 아기들과 이야기하는 것이 중요하다 / 가급적 '유아어'를 사용하지
babies to put their needs into words.) [5] Talking to babies is important, / preferably without
S V C

않고 / 아기들은 말하는 것을 배운다 / 다른 사람들의 말을 듣는 것에서 / 그러므로 말에 신중한 어른들은
using "baby talk." (④) [6] Babies learn to talk / from listening to others, // so *adults* [who are
S_1 V_1 S_2 관계대명사

자녀들을 도와줄 것이다 / 효과적으로 의사소통도 하도록
careful with their speech] / will help their children / to communicate effectively, too. (⑤) [7] It
V_2 O C 가주어

특히 도움이 된다 / 이야기하는 것이 / 친절한 구어체 방식으로 / 당신이 보는 것들을
is especially helpful / to talk / in a friendly, conversational manner / — pointing out *things*
V C 진주어

가리키는 것 / 그리고 활동들을 설명하는 것 / 당신이 하루를 보내면서
[that you see] / and describing activities / as you go about your day.
관계대명사

해석 한 눈에 보기 1 주제문 모든 아기는 다르고 자기 자신의 속도로 언어 기술을 계발할 것이다. 2 몇몇은 18개월까지 완전한 문장으로 말하는 반면에, 그 나이의 다른 몇몇은 준비가 전혀 되어 있지 않다. 3 일찍 말하는 아이의 능력을 보장할 마법의 방법은 없다. 4 그럼에도 불구하고, 아기들이 자신의 필요를 말로 나타내도록 격려하기 위해 부모와 다른 돌보는 사람이 할 수 있는 것이 있다. 5 가급적 '유아어'를 사용하지 않고, 아기들과 이야기하는 것이 중요하다. 6 아기들은 다른 사람들의 말을 듣는 것에서 말하는 것을 배우므로, 말에 신중한 어른들은 자녀들이 효과적으로 의사소통도 하도록 도와줄 것이다. 7 당신이 하루를 보내면서 당신이 보는 것들을 가리키고 활동들을 설명하는 것 같이 친절한 구어체 방식으로 이야기하는 것이 특히 도움이 된다.

정답단추 글의 흐름의 단서가 되는 연결어를 활용해 보자. 주어진 문장에 역접을 나타내는 연결어 Still이 있어. 이것으로 주어진 문장의 내용과 반대되는 내용이 나온 다음에 들어간다는 것을 짐작할 수 있지. 주어진 문장은 아기들이 필요한 것을 말로 할 수 있도록 부모나 돌보는 사람이 할 수 있는 일이 있다는 내용이야. 그런데 ③ 앞에 아이가 일찍 말하게 할 수 있는 비법은 없다고 했으므로, 주어진 문장이 그 뒤에 이어지는 것이 자연스러워. 또한 ③ 뒤에는 그것의 자세한 방법에 대해 언급하고 있지. 따라서 주어진 문장이 들어가기에 가장 적절한 곳은 ③이야.

오답단서 ①, ②의 앞과 뒤는 아기들의 언어 발달 속도가 달라서 문장으로 말하는 시기도 다르다는 내용과, 일찍 말하게 하는 방법이 따로 있는 것은 아니라는 내용이 연결되고 있어서 흐름이 어색하지 않아. ④, ⑤는 아기들은 어른들의 말을 배우므로, 유아어를 사용하지 않고 말을 가려서 의사소통하는 것이 도움이 된다는 내용이 유기적으로 연결되어 있으므로 자연스러워.

어휘확인

develop 계발하다 rate 속도 nowhere near ~에 도저히 미치지 못하는 method 방법 guarantee 보장하다 still 그럼에도 불구하고 caregiver 돌보는 사람 encourage 격려하다 put A into words A를 말로 나타내다 preferably 가급적, 오히려 effectively 효과적으로 conversational 구어의, 일상 대화에서 쓰이는 describe 설명하다, 묘사하다

지문 Flow

[주제문]
모든 아기는 다르고, 각자의 속도로 언어 기술을 계발함

↓

[보충설명]
아기마다 완전한 문장을 말하는 시기가 다르고, 일찍 말하게 할 방법은 없음

↓

[역접]
아기가 요구사항을 말로 나타내도록 부모나 돌보는 사람이 격려할 방법이 있음

↓

[보충설명]
유아어를 사용하지 않고 아기와 이야기하는 것이 좋음

↓

[추가]
친절한 구어체 방식으로 이야기하는 것이 도움이 됨

101 정답 ②

지문 All in One

허리케인 바람은 도달하지 못할지도 모른다 / 동일한 속도에 / 토네이도 바람과 / 하지만
[1] Hurricane winds may not reach / the same speeds / as the winds in tornados, // but
S_1 V_1

허리케인은 훨씬 더 큰 피해를 초래한다
hurricanes cause far more damage.
S_2 V_2 비교급 강조

토네이도는 좁다 / 맨 아랫부분이 / 그래서 보통 오직 좁은 지역에만 미친다 / 폭[직경]이 1km도
(A) [2] A tornado is narrow / at its base // and usually only covers a small area / of less than a
S V_1 C V_2

안 되는 / 이와 비교해서 / 허리케인은 (폭이) ~이다 / 폭이 최대 1,500km까지
kilometer across. [3] In comparison, / a hurricane can measure / up to 1,500 kilometers
S V

맨 아랫부분의
wide / at its base.

또 하나의 이유는 ~이다 / 토네이도는 한 시간 동안 지속된다는 것 / 기껏해야 / 더욱이
(C) [4] Another reason is // that a tornado lasts an hour / at the most. [5] Furthermore, / the
S V 접속사 C S_1

평균적인 토네이도는 형성된다 / 상대적으로 사람들이 적게 사는 지역에서 / 미국 중서부의
average tornado forms / in the relatively unpopulated areas / of the Midwestern United
V_1

어휘확인

hurricane 허리케인 reach ~에 도달하다 tornado 토네이도 cause ~을 초래하다 damage 피해, 손상 narrow 좁은 base 맨 아랫부분 cover (범위가) …에 미치다 area 지역 in comparison 이와 비교해서 measure (길이·양 등이) ~이다 up to 최대 ~, ~까지 last 지속되다; 계속되다 at (the) most 기껏해야 furthermore 더욱이 average 평균의 form 형성되다 relatively 상대적으로 unpopulated 사람이 살지 않는 Midwestern 중서부의 travel 이동하다 typically 일반적으로 coastal 해안의 destroy 파괴하다

그리고 그것은 보통 그다지 멀리 이동하지 않는다
States, // and it usually doesn't travel very far.
S₂ V₂

반면에 허리케인은 여러 날 동안 계속되고 수천 킬로미터를 이동할 수 있다
(B) [6] On the other hand, / hurricanes can last for many days // and travel thousands of kilometers / over the sea. [7] Also, / when they reach land, // it is typically near *a large coastal city* [where there are *many buildings* [to destroy]].

바다 너머로 / 또한 / 그것이 육지에 도달할 때 / 그것은 일반적으로 커다란 해안 도시에 인접해 있다 / 파괴할 많은 건물들이 있는
(S, V₁, V₂, 접속사, S', V', S V, 관계부사)

① (A) - (B) - (C) ② (A) - (C) - (B) ③ (B) - (C) - (A)
④ (C) - (A) - (B) ⑤ (C) - (B) - (A)

해석 한 눈에 보기 주제문 1 허리케인 바람은 토네이도 바람과 같은 속도에 도달하지 못할지는 몰라도, 훨씬 더 큰 피해를 초래한다. (A) 2 토네이도는 맨 아랫부분이 좁아서 보통 폭이 1km도 안 되는 좁은 지역에만 영향을 미친다. 3 이와 비교해서, 허리케인은 맨 아랫부분의 폭이 최대 1,500km에 도달할 수 있다. (C) 4 또 하나의 이유는 토네이도는 기껏해야 한 시간 동안 지속된다는 것이다. 5 더욱이, 토네이도는 평균적으로 상대적으로 사람들이 적게 사는 미국 중서부의 지역에서 형성되고 그것은 보통 그다지 멀리 이동하지 않는다. (B) 6 반면에, 허리케인은 여러 날 동안 계속되고 바다 너머로 수천 킬로미터를 이동할 수 있다. 7 또한, 그것이 육지에 도달할 때, 그것은 일반적으로 파괴할 많은 건물들이 있는 커다란 해안 도시에 인접해 있다.

정답단추 주어진 글은 허리케인이 토네이도보다 바람 속도는 느리지만, 훨씬 더 큰 피해를 입힌다는 내용이야. (A)는 주어진 글의 내용에 대한 이유를 보충 설명하고 있으니까 그다음으로 오는 것이 자연스러워. 또한, Another reason으로 시작해서 두 번째 이유를 언급하는 (C)가 다음 순서로 적절해. 그리고 (B)의 연결어 On the other hand를 통해 토네이도를 설명하던 앞선 문단의 내용이 전환되면서 허리케인을 설명하는 것으로 보아 마지막 순서임을 알 수 있어. 따라서 이 글의 가장 올바른 순서는 ② '(A) – (C) – (B)'야.

지문 Flow

[주제문]
허리케인은 토네이도보다 더 큰 피해를 유발함

⬇

[보충설명1]
(A) 토네이도는 좁은 지역에 영향을 미치지만, 허리케인은 넓은 지역에 영향을 미침

&

[보충설명2]
(C) 토네이도는 1시간 동안 지속되고, 사람이 적은 지역에 형성되며, 멀리 이동하지 않음

&

[보충설명3]
(B) 허리케인은 여러 날 동안 계속되고, 멀리 이동하며, 커다란 해안 도시에 인접함

102 정답 ②

지문 All in One

[1] The water cycle is // how Earth's water recycles itself. [2] Whether (it's) flowing in a river, / melting from a glacier, / or washing ashore on a sandy beach, // Earth's water is constantly in motion. [3] The water cycle describes // exactly how it is recycled. [4] First, / the sun evaporates water / from Earth's surface. (①) [5] This water vapor / rises to the sky // and forms clouds. [6] (② When the clouds get too heavy, // the water is released.) [7] Then it returns to Earth / in the form of rain or snow. (③) [8] This can sink / into the ground // and get filtered / by sand and rock. (④) [9] It also runs off the surface of Earth / into rivers, lakes, and oceans. (⑤) [10] There, / the sun evaporates the water, // and the whole cycle begins again.

물의 순환은 ~이다 / 지구의 물이 스스로 재순환시키는 방식 / 강으로 흐르든 / 빙하로부터 녹든 / 혹은 모래로 뒤덮인 바닷가(모래사장)의 해안으로 밀려오든 / 지구의 물은 끊임없이 움직이고 있다 / 물의 순환은 묘사한다 / 정확히 어떻게 그것이 재순환되는지를 / 먼저 / 태양이 / 물을 증발시킨다 / 지구의 표면(지표면)으로부터 / 이 수증기는 / 하늘로 올라간다 / 그리고 / 구름을 형성한다 / 구름이 너무 무거워질 때 / 물이 방출된다 / 그러면 그것은 지구로 돌아온다 / 비나 눈의 형태로 / 이것은 스며들 수 있다 / 땅속으로 / 그리고 / 여과된다 / 모래나 돌에 의해 / 그것은 또한 지구의 표면에서 흘러나와 / 강, 호수, 바다로 (간다) / 거기에서 / 태양은 물을 증발시킨다 / 그리고 전체 순환(과정)이 다시 시작된다

(S, V, C, S', V'₁, V'₂, V'₃, 간접의문문, V₁, V₂, 접속사, C', S₁, S₂)

해석 한 눈에 보기 주제문 1 물의 순환은 지구의 물이 스스로를 재순환시키는 방식이다. 2 강으로 흐르든, 빙하에서 녹든, 모래사장의 해변으로 밀려오든 간에, 지구의 물은 끊임없이 움직이고 있다. 3 물의 순환은 정확히 어떻게 그것이 재순환되는지를 묘사한다. 4 먼저, 태양이 지표면으로부터 물을 증발시킨다. 5 이 수증기는 하늘로 올라가 구름을 형성한다. 6 구름이 너무 무거워지면, 물이 방출된다. 7 그러면 그것은 비나 눈의 형태로 지구로 돌아온다. 8 이것은 땅속으로 스며들어 모래와 돌에 의해 여과될 수 있다. 9 그것은 또한 지표면에서 흘러나와 강, 호수, 바다로 간다. 10 거기에서 태양은 수분을 증발시키고, 전체 순환(과정)이 다시 시작된다.

정답단추 첫 문장을 통해 지구의 물의 순환 과정이 글의 주제임을 알 수 있어. 주어진 문장이 구름이 너무 무거워지면 물이 방출된다는 내용이니까, 앞에 구름이 형성된다는 내용이 있고 뒤에 비나 눈의 형태로 지구로 돌아온다는 내용이 있는 ②의 위치가 주어진 문장이 들어가기에 가장 적절해. ②의 앞 문장에 있는 clouds를 주어진 문장에서 the clouds로 받았고, 주어진 문장의 the water를 다음 문장에서 it으로 받은 것에 주목하면 돼.

오답단서 ①, ④, ⑤는 각각 앞, 뒤 문장이 물의 순환 과정을 차례로 설명해 주고 있어서 주어진 문장이 들어갈 곳으로 적절하지 않아. ③은 주어진 문장의 the clouds가 ③의 앞, 뒤 문장에서 언급되지 않아서 답이 될 수 없어.

어휘확인

cycle 순환 recycle 재순환시키다; 재활용하다 whether ~이든 flow 흐르다 glacier 빙하 wash (물이) 밀려오다 ashore 해안으로 sandy 모래로 뒤덮인 constantly 끊임없이 in motion 움직이고 있는 describe 묘사하다 exactly 정확히 evaporate (물 등을) 증발시키다 surface 표면 water vapor 수증기 rise 오르다 form 형성시키다; 형태 release 방출하다 return 돌아오다 sink into 스며들다 filter 여과하다 run off ~에서 흘러나오다 whole 전체의

지문 Flow

[주제문]
물의 순환은 지구의 물이 스스로를 재순환시키는 방식

⬇

[보충설명]
태양이 물을 증발시킴
→ 올라간 수증기가 구름을 형성함
→ 구름이 무거워지면 비나 눈이 내림
→ 땅속으로 스며들어 다시 강, 호수, 바다로 감

⬇

[결론]
계속 반복하여 순환 과정이 이루어짐

103 정답 ④

지문 All in One

많은 용도가 있다 / 단단하고 투명한 물질에는 / 우리가 유리라고 알고 있는

1 There are many uses / for *the solid, see-through substance* [that we know as glass], // and without it, / the world around us / would be a very different place. 2 ① *Glass* [made into windows] / allows us to see the outdoors / from indoors, // and brings natural light / into buildings. 3 ② *The very thin glass* [used in electric light bulbs] / lets rays of light pass through. 4 ③ *Bottles, jars, vases, and containers* [made of clear or colored glass] / let us view their contents. 5 (④ Also, / glass bottles should be separated by color / to be recycled.) 6 ⑤ *Glass* [used to make eyeglasses] / helps people with poor eyesight / to see the world normally.

(there are = V₁, many uses = S₁, that = 관계대명사, without it = but for, the world around us = S₂, would be = V₂, a very different place = C; Glass = S, allows = V₁, us = O, to see the outdoors = C, brings = V₂; The very thin glass = S, lets = V, rays of light = O, pass through = C; Bottles… = S, let = V, us = O, view = C; glass bottles = S, should be separated = V, to be recycled = 부사적 용법(목적); Glass = S, helps = V, people with poor eyesight = O, to see the world = C)

(그것이 없다면 / 우리를 둘러싼 세상은 / 매우 다른 곳이 될 것이다 / 창문으로 만들어지는 유리는 / 우리가 실외를 보게 해주고 / 실내에서 / 자연 빛(자연광)을 가져온다 / 건물 안으로 / 전기 전구에 사용되는 매우 얇은 유리는 / 빛의 광선이 통과해 지나가도록 둔다 / 투명하거나 색을 입힌 유리로 만든 병과 단지, 꽃병, 그리고 그릇은 / 우리가 그 내용물을 보게 해준다 / 또한 / 유리병은 색깔별로 분리되어야 한다 / 재활용되기 위해서 / 안경을 만드는 데 사용되는 유리는 / 안 좋은 시력을 가진 사람들을 돕는다 / 세상을 정상적으로 볼 수 있도록)

해석 한 눈에 보기 **주제문** 1 우리가 유리라고 알고 있는 단단하고 투명한 물질에는 많은 용도가 있으며, 그것이 없다면 우리를 둘러싼 세상은 매우 다른 곳이 될 것이다. 2 ① 창문으로 만들어지는 유리는 우리가 실내에서 실외를 보게 해주고, 자연광을 건물 안으로 가져온다. 3 ② 전구에 사용되는 매우 얇은 유리는 빛의 광선이 통과해 지나가도록 둔다. 4 ③ 투명하거나 색을 입힌 유리로 만든 병과 단지, 꽃병, 그리고 그릇은 우리가 그 내용물을 보게 해준다. 5 (④ 또한, 유리병은 재활용되기 위해서 색깔별로 분리되어야 한다.) 6 ⑤ 안경을 만드는 데 사용되는 유리는 안 좋은 시력을 가진 사람들이 세상을 정상적으로 볼 수 있도록 돕는다.

정답단추 글의 첫 문장이 주제문이면, 이어서 주제문을 뒷받침하는 내용이 나올 것을 예상할 수 있어. 따라서 주제문을 뒷받침하지 않는 문장을 고르면 정답을 쉽게 찾을 수 있어. ④는 '유리병의 재활용'에 관한 내용이므로 글의 흐름과 무관해.

오답단서 ①, ②, ③, ⑤ 모두 주제문을 뒷받침하는 '유리의 용도'에 대한 예시를 나열하고 있으므로 정답이 될 수 없어.

어휘확인

use 용도 **solid** 단단한 **see-through** 투명한 **substance** 물질 **allow** ~하게 해주다, 가능하게 하다 **outdoor** 실외(↔ **indoor** 실내) **electric** 전기의 **light bulb** (백열) 전구 **ray** 광선 **pass through** ~을 통과하다 **jar** (잼·꿀 등을 담아두는) 단지 **vase** 꽃병 **container** 그릇 **clear** 투명한 **content** (보통 **pl.**) 내용물 **separate** 분리하다 **recycle** 재활용하다 **eyeglasses** 안경 **poor** 안 좋은 **eyesight** 시력 **normally** 정상적으로

지문 Flow

[주제문]
유리는 많은 용도로 사용됨

⬇

[예시1, 2]
• 창문이나 전구를 만드는 유리는 빛을 통과시킴
• 유리로 만든 병이나 그릇은 내용물을 보여줌

⬇

[무관한 문장]
유리병은 재활용되기 위해 색깔별로 분리되어야 함

⬇

[예시3]
안경용 유리는 시력이 나쁜 사람에게 도움을 줌

104 정답 ③

지문 All in One

1 Up until the early 19th century, / wristwatches were considered "uncool."
(19세기 초까지 / 손목시계는 '멋지지 않은' 것으로 여겨졌다; wristwatches = S, were considered = V, "uncool" = C)

(B) 2 In the Western world, / pocket watches were a masculine status symbol, // while wristwatches were considered feminine and impractical.
(서양 세계에서는 / 회중시계가 남성적인 지위의 상징이었다 / 반면에 / 손목시계는 여성적이고 비실용적으로 여겨졌다; pocket watches = S, were = V, a masculine status symbol = C, while = 접속사(대조), wristwatches = S′, were considered = V′, feminine and impractical = C′)

(C) 3 That attitude began to change // as soldiers discovered / (that) wristwatches were far more practical / on the battlefield / than a pocket watch, / though changes were small / until World War I.
(그런 태도는 변하기 시작했다 / 군인들이 발견했을 때 / 손목시계가 훨씬 더 실용적이라는 것을 / 전쟁터에서 / 주머니 시계(회중시계)보다 / 비록 변화가 작았을지라도 / 제1차 세계 대전까지는; That attitude = S, began = V, as = 접속사, soldiers = S′₁, discovered = V′₁, (that) = 접속사, wristwatches = S″, were = V″, far = 비교급 강조, more practical = C″, though = 접속사, changes = S′₂, were = V′₂, small = C′)

(A) 4 Millions of soldiers were given a wristwatch / at that time, / something more accessible / than a pocket watch // while they were in uniform. 5 *These "trench watches"* [(which [that]) the soldiers carried / during battle] / gave watches / in general / a masculine reputation.
(수백만 명의 병사들에게 손목시계가 주어졌다 / 그때 / 이용이 더 쉬운 것인 / 주머니 시계(회중시계)보다 / 그들이 군복을 입고 있는 동안에는 / 군인들이 소지했던 이 '군인용 시계'는 / 전투 중에 / 시계에 가져다주었다 / 일반적으로 / 남성적인 평판을; Millions of soldiers = S, were given = V, a wristwatch = something more accessible, while = 접속사, they = S′, were = V′, in uniform = C′, These "trench watches" = S, which [that] = 관계대명사, gave = V, watches = IO, a masculine reputation = DO)

어휘확인

up until ~까지 **century** 세기(世紀) **wristwatch** 손목시계 **consider** ~로 여기다 **uncool** 멋지지 않은 **Western** 서양의 **pocket watch** 회중시계 **masculine** 남성적인(↔ **feminine** 여성적인) **status** 지위 **impractical** 비실용적인(↔ **practical** 실용적인) **attitude** 태도 **soldier** 군인 **discover** 발견하다 **battlefield** 전쟁터 **though** 비록 ~일지라도 **accessible** 이용이 쉬운 **trench** 군인용; 참호 **in general** 일반적으로 **reputation** 평판

지문 Flow

[도입]
19세기 초까지 손목시계는 멋지지 않은 것으로 여겨짐

⬇

[보충설명1]
(B) 회중시계는 남성적 지위의 상징인 반면에, 손목시계는 여성적이고 비실용적으로 여겨짐

&

① (A) - (B) - (C)　　② (B) - (A) - (C)　　③ (B) - (C) - (A)
④ (C) - (A) - (B)　　⑤ (C) - (B) - (A)

해석 한 눈에 보기 1 19세기 초까지, 손목시계는 '멋지지 않은' 것으로 여겨졌다. (B) 2 서양 세계에서는, 회중시계(몸에 지닐 수 있게 만든 작은 시계)가 남성적 지위의 상징인 반면에, 손목시계는 여성적이고 비실용적으로 여겨졌다. (C) 3 그러한 태도는 군인들이 손목시계가 회중시계보다 전쟁터에서 훨씬 더 실용적이라는 것을 발견하면서, 비록 변화가 제1차 세계 대전까지는 작았을지라도 변하기 시작했다. (A) 4 그때 수백만 명의 병사들에게 그들이 군복을 입고 있는 동안에는 회중시계보다 이용이 더 쉬운 것인 손목시계를 줬다. 5 군인들이 전투 중에 소지했던 이 '군인용 시계'는 시계에 일반적으로 남성적인 평판을 가져다주었다.
정답단추 과거에는 손목시계를 멋지지 않다고 여겼다는 내용의 주어진 글 뒤에는 그에 대한 자세한 설명, 즉 손목시계가 여성적이고 비실용적인 것으로 간주되었다는 내용의 (B)가 오는 것이 자연스러워. (C)의 그러한 태도(That attitude)는 (B)의 내용을 가리키므로 이어서 (C)가 와야 해. 마지막으로는 손목시계를 대하는 태도가 언제 어떻게 바뀌었는지 구체적으로 설명하고 있는 (A)로 이어지는 게 적절해. 따라서 글의 적절한 순서는 ③ '(B) – (C) – (A)'야.

[보충설명2]
(C) 군인들이 손목시계가 더 실용적임을 발견하면서 변화가 생김

[결과]
(A) 군인들에게 손목시계를 주었고, '군인용 시계'가 남성적인 평판을 가져다 줌

105 정답 ④

지문 All in One

1 Nowadays (요즘에는), / more and more mothers with young children (어린아이를 둔 점점 더 많은 엄마들이)(S) / work (V) outside the home (집 바깥에서 일을 한다). 2 This (S) represents (V₁) a huge shift (이것은 거대한 변화를 나타낸다) / in the distribution of the workforce (노동력 분포에 있어서) // and has (V₂) a real impact (그리고 실질적인 영향을 미친다) / on the lives of many women and families (많은 여성과 가족의 삶에). 3 ① Our country (S) has been (V₁) slow (C) (우리나라는 느려 왔다) / to acknowledge this (이것을 인정하는 데)(부사적 용법(형용사 수식)), // and has done (V₂) little (그리고 거의 아무것도 하지 않아 왔다) / to improve working mothers' lives (일하는 엄마들의 삶을 개선하는 데에)(부사적 용법(목적)). 4 ② The biggest problem (S) is (V) (가장 큰 문제는 ~이다) / the lack of affordable childcare facilities (C) (적당한 비용의 탁아 시설의 부족). 5 ③ Day-care centers (S₁) are (V₁) few (C₁) (주간 보호 시설(탁아소)은 거의 없고), / their fees (S₂) are (V₂) high (C₂) (보육비는 비싸고), // and many mothers (S₃) don't have (V₃) *relatives* (많은 엄마들은 친척이 없다) [to take care of children (아이들을 돌봐줄)]. 6 (④ On the other hand (반면에), / it (가주어) is (V) true (C) (그것은 사실이다) // that fathers do more (아빠들이 더 많은 것을 한다는 것)(진주어) / to help with childcare (육아를 돕기 위해)(부사적 용법(목적)).) 7 ⑤ Childcare in this country (S) (이 나라의 보육은) / is (V) far from satisfactory (C) (만족과는 거리가 멀다(전혀 만족스럽지 않다)) / for working mothers (일하는 엄마들에게).

해석 한 눈에 보기 1 요즘에는 어린아이를 둔 점점 더 많은 엄마들이 집 바깥에서 일한다. 2 이것은 노동력 분포에서 거대한 변화를 나타내며 많은 여성과 가족의 삶에 실질적인 영향을 미친다. 주제문 3 ① 우리나라는 이것을 인정하는 데 느려 왔고, 그래서 일하는 엄마들의 삶을 개선하는 데에 거의 아무것도 하지 않아 왔다. 4 ② 가장 큰 문제는 적당한 비용의 탁아 시설의 부족이다. 5 ③ 탁아소는 거의 없고, 보육비는 비싸고, 많은 엄마들은 아이들을 돌봐줄 친척이 없다. 6 (④ 반면에, 아빠들이 육아를 돕기 위해 더 많은 것을 한다는 것은 사실이다.) 주제문 7 ⑤ 이 나라의 보육은 일하는 엄마들에게 전혀 만족스럽지 않다.
정답단추 단락 내의 모든 문장은 하나의 주제를 적절하게 뒷받침해야 해. 이 글의 주제는 '우리나라에 일하는 엄마들은 많아지는데 그들의 삶은 전혀 만족스럽지 않다'는 것이야. 이와 관련된 세부 내용이 서술되어야 하는데 ④는 '아빠들이 육아를 돕고 있다'는 내용으로 주제와는 동떨어져 있음을 알 수 있어.
오답단서 ⑤는 이 내용을 담고 있는 주제문이자 결론이라 할 수 있어. ①, ②, ③은 '일하는 엄마들을 위한 지원과 보육시설이 부족하다'는 내용으로 주제문을 뒷받침하고 있어.

어휘확인
nowadays 요즘에는 represent 나타내다 huge 거대한 shift (방향의) 변화 distribution 분포; 분배 workforce 노동력, 노동인구 impact 영향 acknowledge (사실을) 인정하다 improve 개선하다; 개선되다 lack 부족 affordable (가격이) 적당한 childcare 탁아, 육아 facility 시설 day-care center 주간 보호 시설 fee 요금 relative 친척 take care of ~을 돌보다 far from 전혀 ~이 아닌 satisfactory 만족스러운

지문 Flow

[도입]
일하는 엄마들이 늘어나서 여성과 가족의 삶에 영향을 미침

[주제문]
우리나라는 일하는 엄마의 삶을 개선하지 못했음

[보충설명]
적당한 비용의 탁아 시설 부족함

[무관한 문장]
아빠들이 육아를 돕기 위해 많은 것을 함

[주제문 반복]
우리나라의 보육이 일하는 엄마들에게 만족스럽지 않음

106 정답 ④

지문 All in One

1 We (S) often try (V) (우리는 종종 노력한다) / to avoid following (따라가는 것을 피하려고) / in a parent's footsteps (부모님의 발자취를). (①) 2 But (하지만), / actually (실제로), / it's (가주어 V) a great idea (C) (훌륭한 생각이다) / to study the example of your ancestors (당신 조상의 예를 연구하는 것은)(진주어), // as revealed in the stories (이야기 속에 드러나 있듯이)(분사구문(= as it is revealed ~)) / of how they spent their lives (그들이 어떻게 그들의 삶을 보냈는지에 대한)(간접의문문). (②) 3 You (S) may find (V) (당신은 발견할지도 모른다) / clues to what to do (O) (무엇을 해야 하는지에 대한 단서가) / based on shared talents or interests (공유된 재능과 관심에 기반을 두고)(독립 분사구문).

어휘확인
follow in A's footsteps A의 발자취를 따라가다 ancestor 조상 reveal 드러내다 clue 단서 based on ~에 기반[기초]을 둔 compelling 강력한 medical school 의과대학 firefighter 소방관 run 이어지다 despise 경멸하다 all day 온종일 think twice 재고하다 business school 경영 대학원 wear out 지치다 construction 건설

있을지도 모른다 / 강력한 이유가 / 그렇게 많은 의과 대학 학생들이 ~을 가지고 있는
(③) 4 There may be / *a compelling reason* [why so many medical school students have / *a*
(V, S, 관계부사)

의사인 부모(아버지 혹은 어머니)를 / 혹은 농부나 소방관이 몇몇 가정에 이어지는 / 하지만 당신은
parent [who's a doctor]] / or [why farmers or firefighters run in some families]. 5 (④ But you
(관계대명사, 관계부사, S)

발견할지도 모른다 / 그만큼 강력한 신호를 / 무엇을 하지 말아야 하는지에 대해 / 만약 당신의 어머니가 경멸하셨다면
may find / *signs* [that are just as strong / about what *not* to do].) 6 If your mother despised /
(V, 관계대명사, 접속사, S′, V′)

온종일 사무실에 앉아 있는 것을 / 당신은 재고할지도 모른다 / 경영 대학원에 대해
sitting in an office all day, // you might think twice / about business school. (⑤) 7 On the
(S, V)

반면에 / 당신의 삼촌이 일찍 지치셨다면 / 건설 노동자로 / 사무직이 그렇게 나빠 보이지
other hand, / if your uncle wore out early / as a construction worker, // a desk job might not
(접속사, S′, V′, S)

않을지도 모른다
look too bad.
(V)

desk job 사무직

지문 Flow

[주제문]
조상의 예를 연구하는 것은 훌륭한 생각임

⬇

[보충설명1]
공유된 재능으로 자신이 무엇을 해야 하는지에 대한 단서를 찾을 수 있음
•의대생의 부모가 의사
•대대로 이어져 오는 농부, 소방관 집안

&

[보충설명2]
자신이 무엇을 하지 말아야 하는지에 대한 신호를 발견할지도 모름

⬇

[예시]
부모나 친척의 직업과 반대되는 직업을 선택할 수 있음

해석 한 눈에 보기 1 우리는 종종 부모의 발자취를 따르는 것을 피하려고 노력한다. 주제문 2 하지만 실제로, 당신 조상의 예를 연구하는 것은, 그들이 어떻게 그들의 삶을 보냈는지에 대한 이야기 속에 드러나 있듯이, 훌륭한 생각이다. 3 당신은 공유된 재능과 관심에 기반을 둬서 당신이 무엇을 해야 하는지에 대한 단서를 찾을 수 있을지도 모른다. 4 그렇게 많은 의과 대학 학생들이 의사인 부모를 갖고 있거나 혹은 농부나 소방관이 몇몇 가정에 (대대로) 이어져 오는 강력한 이유가 있을지도 모른다. 5 하지만 당신은 무엇을 하지 말아야 하는지에 대해 꼭 그만큼 강력한 신호를 발견할지도 모른다. 6 만일 당신의 어머니가 온종일 사무실에 앉아 있는 것을 경멸하셨다면, 당신은 경영 대학원에 대해 재고할지도 모른다. 7 반면에, 당신의 삼촌이 건설 노동자로 일찍 지치셨다면, 사무직이 그다지 나빠 보이지 않을지도 모른다.

정답단추 But으로 시작하는 주어진 문장은 하지 말아야 하는 것에 대한 신호를 찾을지도 모른다는 내용이야. ④의 앞부분에서는 조상의 사례를 통해 무엇을 해야 하는지에 대한 실마리를 찾을 수 있다고 언급하고 있어. 그에 반해 뒷부분은 조상의 사례를 통해 하지 말아야 할 것을 알게 된다는 것의 예시를 나열하고 있어서 내용의 전환이 있음을 알 수 있지. 따라서 주어진 문장이 들어가기에 가장 적절한 곳은 ④야.

오답단서 ①, ②, ③의 앞, 뒤 문장은 조상의 사례를 연구했을 때, 도움이 되는 점에 관해 언급하고 있어서 유기적으로 연결되어 있어. 그리고 ⑤는 앞뒤로 하지 말아야 할 것에 관한 두 가지 예시를 제시하고 있어서 주어진 문장이 들어갈 자리로는 적절하지 않아.

107 정답 ④

지문 All in One

공장에서 만들어진 유독가스와 / 자동차에서 나오는 매연은 / 대기 오염을 유발한다
1 *Toxic gases* [produced by factories] / and *fumes* [from motor vehicles] / cause *air pollution*,
(S, V)

끔찍한 결과를 가져오는
/ which has terrible consequences.
(계속적 용법)

그것은 폐 손상과 피부 문제를 유발할 뿐만 아니라 / 사람에게 / 또한 건물도
(C) 2 Not only does it cause lung damage and skin problems / in humans, // but it also
(S_1, V_1, S_2)

손상시킨다 / 이것은 ~이다 / 산성비가 결과이기 때문 / 수분과 혼합된 유독한 대기 오염의
damages buildings. 3 This is // because acid rain is the result / of toxic air pollution mixed
(V_2, S, V, S′, V′, C′)

구름 속의
with moisture / in clouds.

이 부식성의 액체는 충분히 강하다 / 거의 그 어떤 표면도 부식시킬 만큼 / 시간이 흐르면서 / 그것은
(A) 4 This corrosive liquid is strong enough / to erode almost any surface / over time. 5 It eats
(S, V, C, 부사적 용법(형용사 수식), S, V)

갉아먹는다 / 돌, 대리석 및 기타 건축 자재들을
away / at stone, marble, and other building materials.

그 결과 / 그것은 엄청난 손상을 초래해 왔다 / 고대 대리석 건물들에 / 인도에서는
(B) 6 As a result, / it has caused great damage / to ancient marble buildings. 7 In India, / for
(S, V)

예를 들어 / 그 유명한 타지마할의 흰 대리석 표면이 / 파괴되고 있다 / 슬프게도
example, / the white marble surface of the famed Taj Mahal / is being destroyed. 8 Sadly, /
(S, V)

행해 질 수 있는 것이 거의 없다 / 이러한 파괴를 막기 위해 / 이 문제의 근원이 제거되지 않으면
there is *little* [that can be done] / to prevent this destruction // unless the source of the
(V, S, 관계대명사, 부사적 용법(목적), 조건 접속사, S′)

problem is removed.
(V′)

① (A) - (C) - (B)　② (B) - (A) - (C)　③ (B) - (C) - (A)
④ (C) - (A) - (B)　⑤ (C) - (B) - (A)

어휘확인

toxic 유독성의 fume (불쾌한) 연기, 가스 motor vehicle 자동차 cause ~을 유발하다 pollution 오염, 공해 consequence 결과 lung 폐 damage 손상, 피해; 손상을 주다 acid rain 산성비 moisture 수분 corrosive 부식성의 liquid 액체 erode 부식시키다 surface 표면 eat away ~을 갉아먹다 marble 대리석 material 자재, 재료 ancient 고대의 famed 유명한 destroy 파괴하다 sadly 슬프게도 prevent 막다, 예방하다 destruction 파괴 unless ~하지 않는 한 source 근원

지문 Flow

[주제문]
유독가스와 매연은 대기 오염을 유발하여 끔찍한 결과를 낳음

⬇

[보충설명]
(C) 사람의 폐 손상과 피부 문제 유발, 건물 손상 야기

⬇

[이유]
(A) 산성비로 인한 유독한 대기 오염과 건축 자재들의 부식

⬇

해석 한 눈에 보기 주제문 1 공장에서 만들어진 유독가스와 자동차에서 나오는 매연은 대기 오염을 유발하는데, 이것은 끔찍한 결과를 낳는다. (C) 2 그것은 사람에게 폐 손상과 피부 문제를 유발할 뿐만 아니라 건물도 손상시킨다. 3 이것은 산성비가 구름 속의 수분과 혼합된 유독한 대기 오염의 결과이기 때문이다. (A) 4 이 부식성의 액체는 시간이 흐르면서 거의 그 어떤 표면도 부식시킬 만큼 충분히 강하다. 5 그것은 돌, 대리석 및 기타 건축 자재들을 갉아먹는다. (B) 6 그 결과, 그것은 고대 대리석 건물들에 엄청난 손상을 초래해 왔다. 7 예를 들어 인도에서는, 그 유명한 타지마할의 흰 대리석 표면이 파괴되고 있다. 8 슬프게도, 이 문제의 근원이 제거되지 않으면 이러한 파괴를 막기 위해 취해질 수 있는 것이 거의 없다.

정답단추 주어진 문장은 대기 오염이 끔찍한 결과를 가져온다는 내용이야. 이어서 이 끔찍한 결과가 폐 손상, 피부 문제, 건물 손상이며 산성비가 이러한 손상을 초래하는 이유라는 것을 언급하고 있는 (C)가 오는 게 자연스러워. (A)의 This corrosive liquid는 '산성비'를 의미하는 것이니 이어서 (A)가 와야겠지? 또한, (A)는 (C)에 이어서 산성비가 건물에 어떻게 해를 입히는지를 구체적으로 설명하고 있기도 하므로 글의 흐름이 자연스럽게 이어지지. 그리고 (A)에 대한 실제 예를 든 (B)가 뒤이어 오는 것이 자연스러우니까, 가장 적절한 글의 순서는 ④ '(C) – (A) – (B)'라 할 수 있어.

[결과]
(B) 인도의 타지마할 같은 고대 대리석 건물의 손상을 초래함

108 정답 ③

지문 All in One

1 When you, the leader, delegate responsibility / to others, // not only the organization but also you / benefit. 2 ① In the process, / you develop leadership skills and abilities / in your people // and enhance their initiative, creativity, and competence. 3 ② You build their confidence and self-esteem // and let them flex their own leadership muscles. 4 (③ The key to leadership is / not to focus on making other people follow, / but (to focus) on making yourself *the kind of person* / [(who[that]) they want to follow].) 5 ④ When people at every level feel / (that) they are trusted / and (are) empowered to act, // the entire organization is able / to move decisively / and (to) respond quickly / to changing situations. 6 ⑤ As a result, / your image may be enhanced: // instead of being judged / on your individual performance, / you are judged / by the magnified effectiveness of *the team or organization* [(which[that]) you lead].

(리더인 당신이 책임을 위임할 때 / 다른 사람들에게 / 조직뿐만 아니라 당신도 / 혜택을 본다 / 그 과정에서 / 당신은 리더십 기술과 능력을 발달시킨다 / 당신 사람(조직원)들의 / 그리고 그들의 진취력, 창조성, 역량을 향상시킨다 / 당신은 그들의 자신감과 자긍심을 기르고 / 그리고 그들이 그들 자신의 리더십 근육을 풀게 한다 / 리더십의 핵심은 ~이다 / 다른 사람들이 따르도록 만드는 데 집중하는 것이 아니라 / 당신 자신을 그런 종류의 사람으로 만드는 데 (집중하는 것이다) / 그들이 따르고 싶은 / 모든 수준에 있는 사람들이 느낄 때 / 자신이 신뢰받고 있고 / 행동할 수 있는 권한을 부여받았다고 / 그 전체 조직은 ~할 수 있다 / 단호히 움직이고 / 빠르게 대응을 하고 / 변화하는 상황에 / 결과적으로 / 당신의 이미지가 향상될지도 모르는데 / 판단되는 대신에 / 당신의 개인적인 능력에 대해 / 당신은 판단된다 / 팀이나 조직의 확대된 효율성에 의해 / 당신이 이끄는)

해석 한 눈에 보기 주제문 1 리더인 당신이 다른 사람들에게 책임을 위임할 때, 조직뿐만 아니라 당신도 혜택을 본다. 2 ① 그 과정에서, 당신은 당신 조직원들의 리더십 기술과 능력을 발달시키고 그들의 진취력, 창조성, 역량을 향상시킨다. 3 ② 당신은 그들의 자신감과 자긍심을 기르고 그들이 그들 자신의 리더십 근육을 풀게 한다. 4 (③ 리더십의 핵심은 다른 사람들이 따르도록 만드는 데 집중하는 것이 아니라 당신 자신을 그들이 따르고 싶은 종류의 사람으로 만드는 데 집중하는 것이다.) 5 ④ 모든 수준에 있는 사람들이 자신이 신뢰받고 있고 행동할 수 있는 권한을 부여받았다고 느낄 때, 그 조직 전체는 변화하는 상황에 단호히 움직이고 빠르게 대응할 수 있다. 6 ⑤ 결과적으로 당신의 이미지가 향상될지도 모르는데, 당신의 개인적인 능력에 관해 판단되지 않고, 당신은 당신이 이끄는 팀이나 조직의 확대된 효율성에 의해 판단된다.

정답단추 첫 문장이 주제문으로 리더가 조직원들에게 리더의 책임을 위임함으로써 리더와 조직 모두 혜택을 본다는 내용이야. 그러니 나머지 문장들은 이 주제를 뒷받침하는 문장들이 와야 해. 그러나 ③은 앞 문장의 leadership이 반복되어 얼핏 이어진 내용으로 보이기 쉽지만 리더십의 정의에 해당하는 말로 글의 주제와는 무관하다고 볼 수 있어.

오답단서 ①은 주제문의 '다른 사람들에게 책임을 위임할 때'를 그 과정(the process)으로 받아 부연 설명을 이어나가고 있어. ② 역시 ①과 연결되는 내용이야. ④, ⑤는 주제문 내용의 긍정적인 결과를 나타내고 있으므로 글의 흐름상 자연스러워.

어휘확인

delegate (권한·책임 등을) 위임하다 **responsibility** 책임 **not only A but (also) B** A뿐만 아니라 B도 **organization** 조직 **benefit** 혜택[득]을 보다 **develop** 발달하다 **leadership** 리더십, 지도력 **ability** 능력 **enhance** (가치·지위 등을) 향상시키다 **initiative** 진취력 **creativity** 창조성 **competence** 역량, 능력 **confidence** 자신감 **self-esteem** 자긍심 **flex** (준비 운동으로) 몸을 풀다 **key** 핵심, 비결 **focus on ~**에 집중하다 **empower** 권한을 주다 **entire** 전체[전부]의 **decisively** 단호히 **situation** 상황 **individual** 개인적인 **performance** 능력, 성과 **magnify** 확대하다 **effectiveness** 효율성

지문 Flow

[주제문]
리더가 다른 사람들에게 책임을 위임할 때, 조직뿐만 아니라 리더도 혜택을 봄

⬇

[보충설명1]
조직원들의 리더십 기술과 능력을 발달시키고, 자신감과 자긍심을 기르게 함

⬇

[무관한 문장]
리더십의 핵심은 조직원이 따르게 만드는 것이 아니라, 그들이 따르고 싶은 사람이 되는 것임

⬇

[보충설명2]
자신이 신뢰받고 있고 권한을 부여받았다고 느낄 때 조직은 변화하는 상황에 빠르게 대응할 수 있음

&

[보충설명3]
리더는 개인적 능력으로 판단되기보다는 조직의 효율성에 의해 판단됨

109 정답 ②

지문 All in One

쓰레기 투기는 엄청난 문제이다 / 도시들의 / 하지만 몇몇 훌륭한 해결책들이 고안되어 왔다

[1] Waste dumping is an enormous problem / for cities, // but some brilliant solutions have been devised.

S1 V1 C S2 V2

버려진 차량 문제를 들어 보자 / 한 예로 / 오래된 차량들은 처리하기 어렵기 때문에

(B) [2] Take the issue of abandoned vehicles / as an example. [3] Because old vehicles are difficult

V 접속사 S' V' C'

많은 사람들은 그냥 떠나버린다 / 그것들에게서 / 뉴욕 하나만으로도

to dispose of, // many people simply walk away / from them. [4] In New York alone, /

부사적 용법(형용사 수식) S V

약 4만 대의 자동차들이 남겨진다 / 길거리에 / 매년

around 40,000 cars are left / on the streets / every year.

S V

이것들 대부분은 결국 처하게 된다(가게 된다) / 고물 처리장에 / 다른 망가진 자동차들과 낡은 기기들과 함께

(A) [5] Most of these eventually end up / in junkyards / alongside other wrecked cars and old appliances.

S V

그곳에서 / 그것들은 납작하게 만들어진다 / 그들이 보내지기 전에 / 철강 공장으로 / 재활용을 위해

[6] There, / they are flattened // before they are sent / to a steel mill / for recycling.

S V 접속사 S' V'

납작하게 만드는 과정 후에 / 남은 금속 조각은 콘크리트와 혼합된다 / 그리고 벽돌로 만들어진다

(C) [7] After the flattening process, / extra scrap metal is mixed with concrete // and (is) made into bricks.

S V1 V2

이것들은 매우 인기 있다 / 건축 산업에서 / 그것들의 뛰어난 내구성 때문에

[8] These are very popular / in the building industry / because of their great strength.

S V C

① (A) - (C) - (B) ② (B) - (A) - (C) ③ (B) - (C) - (A)
④ (C) - (A) - (B) ⑤ (C) - (B) - (A)

해석 한 눈에 보기 주제문 1 쓰레기 투기는 도시들의 엄청난 문제이지만, 몇몇 훌륭한 해결책들이 고안되어 왔다. (B) 2 버려진 차량 문제를 예로 들어 보자. 3 오래된 차량은 처리하기가 어려워서 많은 사람은 그것들을 외면하고 그냥 떠나버린다. 4 뉴욕에서만, 매년 약 4만 대의 자동차들이 길거리에 남겨진다. (A) 5 이것들 대부분은 다른 망가진 자동차들과 낡은 기기들과 더불어 결국 고물 처리장으로 가게 된다. 6 그곳에서 그것들은 재활용을 위해 철강 공장으로 보내지기 전에 납작하게 만들어진다. (C) 7 납작하게 만드는 과정 후에, 남은 금속 조각은 콘크리트와 혼합되어 벽돌로 만들어진다. 8 이것들은 뛰어난 내구성 때문에 건축 산업에서 매우 인기 있다.

정답단추 글의 흐름이나 순서를 알려주는 표현에 유의하면서 글을 배열해야 해. 주어진 문장은 쓰레기 투기 문제에 대한 몇 가지 해결책이 고안되어 왔다는 내용이야. (B)를 보면 쓰레기 투기 문제 중 하나인 버려진 차량에 대한 예를 들고 있으므로 주어진 글 다음으로 오는 것이 자연스러워. 그리고 버려진 차량들을 these로 받아 고물 처리장으로 보내진 후 재활용을 위해 납작하게 만든다고 설명하는 (A)가 뒤이어 와야 해. 마지막으로는 이 압착 과정을 the flattening process로 대신하고 압착 후 남은 금속 조각을 콘크리트와 섞어서 재활용한다는 내용의 (C)가 오는 게 자연스러워. 따라서 글의 알맞은 순서는 ② '(B) – (A) – (C)'야.

어휘확인

waste 쓰레기; 낭비하다 **dumping** 투기[폐기] **enormous** 엄청난, 막대한 **brilliant** 훌륭한 **solution** 해결책 **devise** 고안하다 **take** (예로) 들어 보다; 가지고 가다 **issue** 문제; 주제 **abandoned** 버려진 **vehicle** 차량 **dispose of** ~을 처리하다 **simply** 그냥 **walk away (from)** (힘든 상황·관계를 외면하고) 떠나다 **alone** ~ 하나만으로도; 혼자 **leave** 남기다; 떠나다 **eventually** 결국 **end up** 결국 (어떤 상황에) 처하게 되다 **junkyard** 고물 처리장 **alongside** ~와 함께; ~옆에 **wrecked** 망가진 **appliance** (가정용) 기기 **flatten** 납작하게 만들다 **steel mill** 철강 공장 **recycling** 재활용 **extra** 남은; 추가의 **scrap** 조각 **metal** 금속 **concrete** 콘크리트 **brick** 벽돌 **industry** 산업 **strength** 내구성; 힘

지문 Flow

[주제문]
쓰레기 투기는 도시의 큰 문제지만 해결책들이 고안됨

⬇

[해결책]
버려진 차량: 고물 처리장에서 납작하게 만들어서 재활용을 위해 철강 공장으로 보내고, 남은 금속 조각은 건축 자재로 씀

110 정답 ④

지문 All in One

전반적인 건강과 체력은 / 좀처럼 얻어지지 않는다 / 특정 팀 스포츠를 함으로써는

[1] All-around health and fitness / is seldom achieved / through practicing specific team

S V

농구와 축구 같은 / 그리고 몇몇 대체 운동들이 건강과

sports, / such as basketball and football. (①) [2] And while some alternative sports do

접속사(대조) S' V'

체력을 증진시키는 반면에 / 사이클링, 수영, 조깅, 그리고 힘(근력) 운동 같은

promote health and fitness, / such as cycling, swimming, jogging, and strength training, //

미국 문화는 저항해왔다(거부해왔다) / 이런 활동들을 인식하는 것을 / 아이들을 위한 진정한 운동으로

American culture has resisted / recognizing these activities / as true sports for children. (②)

S V

이것은 유감스럽다 / 부모들은 그들의 아이들을 격려해야 한다 / 이런 활동에 참여하도록

[3] This is unfortunate. (③) [4] Parents should encourage their children / to participate in these activities.

S V C S V O C

이전의 세대들은 가질 필요가 없었다 / 건강과 체력 키우는 활동에

[5] (④ Previous generations did not have to give / health and fitness building

S V IO

어휘확인

all-around 전반적인 **fitness** 체력, 건강 **seldom** 좀처럼 ~않는 **achieve** 얻다 **specific** 특정한 **alternative** 대체의 **promote** 증진시키다 **resist** 저항하다 **recognize** 인식하다 **unfortunate** 유감스러운 **encourage** 격려하다 **participate** 참여하다 **previous** 이전의 **generation** 세대 **give A (some) thought** A에 관해 (곰곰이) 생각하다 **daily life** 일상생활 **work** 직장; 일하다 **grocery** 식료품 **chore** (정기적으로 하는) 일 **manually** 손으로 **rather than** ~보다는 **diet** 식단 **complex** 복합적인; 복잡한 **carbohydrate** 탄수화물 **make an effort** 노력하다 **conscious** 의식적인

activities / much thought — // they were part / of their daily lives.) [6] There was no choice but / to walk to work or school, / carry groceries, / work in the fields, / do chores manually / rather than by machine, / and eat diets high in complex carbohydrates. (⑤) [7] All this has changed, / however, // and most of us / now have to make a conscious effort / to get *the exercise* [(which[that]) our bodies need].

해석 한 눈에 보기 1 전반적인 건강과 체력은 농구 및 축구 같은 특정 팀 스포츠를 함으로써는 좀처럼 얻어지지 않는다. 2 그리고 사이클링, 수영, 조깅, 근력 운동 같은 몇몇 대체 운동들이 정말로 건강과 체력을 증진시키는 반면에, 미국 문화는 이런 활동들을 아이들을 위한 진정한 운동으로 인식하기를 거부해 왔다. 3 이것은 안타까운 일이다. 주제문 4 부모들은 그들의 자녀들이 이러한 활동에 참여하도록 격려해야 한다. 5 이전의 세대들은 건강과 체력을 키우는 활동들에 많은 생각을 들일 필요가 없었는데, 그것들은 그들의 일상생활의 일부분이었기 때문이다. 6 직장이나 학교로 걸어가고, 식료품을 들고 가고, 들판에서 일하고, 집안일을 기계보다는 오히려 손으로 하고, 복합 탄수화물이 높은 식단을 먹는 것 외에 선택의 여지가 없었다. 7 그러나 이 모든 것이 변했고 우리 대부분은 이제 우리 몸이 필요로 하는 운동을 얻기 위해 의식적인 노력을 해야 한다.

정답단추 주어진 문장은 전 세대는 체력 활동이 일상생활의 일부분이라 주의를 기울이지 않았다는 내용이야. 그리고 이 글의 주제문은 아이들이 운동하도록 장려해야 한다는 ④의 앞 문장이야. 그런데 ④ 다음 문장에서 일상생활의 예시를 나열하면서 선택권이 없었다며 내용 전환이 되고 있어서 주제문의 내용과 자연스럽게 이어지지 않음을 알 수 있어. 따라서 주어진 문장의 적절한 위치는 ④야.

오답단서 ①, ②, ③의 앞뒤 문장은 모두 여러 운동이 미국에서 등한시됐지만, 자녀들이 운동하도록 장려해야 한다는 내용이 자연스럽게 이어지고 있어서 주어진 문장이 들어갈 수 없어. ⑤ 다음 문장의 주어 This는 앞 문장 내용 전체를 대신하고 있어. 따라서 ⑤도 주어진 문장이 들어가기에 적절하지 않아.

지문 Flow

[사실]
팀 스포츠보다 사이클링, 수영, 조깅 같은 운동이 건강과 체력을 증진시킴

[주제]
부모들은 자녀들이 건강과 체력을 증진시키는 운동에 참여하도록 격려해야 함

[보충설명]
예전에는 건강과 체력을 키우는 활동이 일상생활의 일부분이었지만, 이제는 운동을 위해 의식적인 노력을 해야 함

111 정답 ③

지문 All in One

[1] It's been said // that we only use 10 percent / of our brain. [2] ① Keeping the brain strong and sharp / isn't a goal / just for seniors; // it's *something* [(that) we should strive for / throughout our lives]. [3] ② Exercise your brain regularly and thoroughly, // and you can virtually guarantee / that cognitive function will remain / in top form / into your seventies, eighties, and beyond. [4] (③ It also provides *the opportunity* [to learn / about the underlying causes of cognitive loss / in aging individuals].) [5] ④ Numerous studies have shown // that *people* [who lead lives / with little mental stimulation] / experience greater cognitive loss / as they age. [6] ⑤ Their memory fades // and they have trouble performing *simple mental tasks* [that come easily / to *those* [who "exercise" their brain often]].

해석 한 눈에 보기 1 우리는 오직 우리 뇌의 10%만 사용한다는 말이 전해져 왔다. 주제문 2 ① 뇌를 강하고 날카롭게 유지하는 것은 단지 노인들만을 위한 목표가 아니라, 우리의 인생 내내 얻으려고 노력해야 하는 어떤 것이다. 3 ② 당신의 뇌를 규칙적이고 철저하게 운동시켜라, 그러면 당신은 인지 기능이 당신의 70대, 80대, 그리고 그 이후에도 최고의 형태로 남아 있게 될 것을 사실상 보장한다. 4 (③ 그것은 또한 늙어가는 개인들의 인지적인 손실의 근본적인 원인에 대해 배울 기회를 제공한다.) 5 ④ 많은 연구는 정신적인 자극이 거의 없는 삶을 사는 사람들이 나이가 들어가면서 더 큰 인지적인 손실을 경험한다는 것을 보여줘 왔다. 6 ⑤ 그들의 기억력이 희미해지고 그들은 뇌를 자주 '운동시키는' 사람들에게는 쉽게 다가오는 단순한 정신적 일을 수행하는 데 어려움을 겪는다.

정답단추 이 글은 뇌도 운동을 시켜 줘야 나이가 들어서도 인지 기능이 떨어지지 않는다는 내용으로 ①이 주제문이야. ③은 cognitive loss를 이용해 앞 문장에 나온 cognitive function과 자연스럽게 이어지는 것처럼 보이지만, 노인의 인지 기능 손실 원인을 배울 기회를 제공한다는 내용은 글의 주제와 무관할 뿐 아니라 뒤이어 나오는 내용과 연결되지

어휘확인

percent 퍼센트 sharp 날카로운 senior 노인, 고령자 strive for ~을 얻으려고 노력하다 throughout 내내 regularly 규칙적으로 thoroughly 철저히 virtually 사실상 guarantee 보장하다 cognitive 인지의 function 기능 remain 남다 form 형태 beyond 그 이후에 provide 제공하다 opportunity 기회 underlying 근본적인 loss 손실 age 늙다, 나이가 들다 individual 개인 numerous 많은 lead (특정한 유형의 삶을) 살다 mental 정신적인 stimulation 자극 memory 기억력 fade 희미해지다 perform 수행하다

지문 Flow

[주제문]
뇌를 강하고 날카롭게 유지하기 위해 평생 노력해야 함

[보충설명]
뇌를 규칙적이고 철저하게 운동시키면, 나이가 들어도 최상의 형태로 남게 됨

[무관한 문장]
노인들의 인지적 손실의 근본 원인에 대해 배울 기회를 제공함

않아. 따라서 ③이 전체 흐름과 관계없는 문장이야.

오답단서 ②, ④, ⑤는 모두 주제문인 ①을 뒷받침하는 문장으로 자연스럽게 이어지고 있어서 정답이 될 수 없어.

[보충설명]
정신적 자극이 없는 삶을 살아온 사람이 기억력이 희미해지고, 정신적 일을 수행하는 데 어려움을 겪는 더 큰 인지적 손실을 경험함

112 정답 ③

지문 All in One

당신은 한번이라도 멈춰서 생각해본 적이 있는가 / 우리가 먹는 음식이 단지 연료라고 / 우리의 신체가
1 Do you ever stop to think // that *the food* [(which[that]) we eat] is merely *fuel* [to keep our
S V 접속사 S′ 관계대명사 V′ C′

건강하게 기능하도록 해주는 / 많은 면에서 / 그것은 전혀 다르지 않다 / 휘발유를 구입하는 것과
body functioning healthily]? 2 In many ways, / it's no different / from purchasing gasoline /
S V C

우리의 자동차를 운행하기 위해 / 안타깝게도 / 우리의 미뢰는 즐거움 측정기가 되어 왔다
to run our automobiles. (①) 3 Unfortunately, / our taste buds have become a pleasure gauge
부사적 용법(목적) S V C

품질 측정기라기보다는 / 우리는 더 이상 찾지 않는다 / 건강한(몸에 좋은) 맛을
/ rather than a quality gauge. (②) 4 We no longer look for / *the taste* [that is healthy].
S V 관계대명사

대신에 / 우리는 초점을 맞춘다 / 음식이 얼마나 기분 좋게 해주는가에 / 우리의 미각을 / 음식과 음료수는
5 (③ Instead, / we focus on // how pleasing the food is / to our palate.) 6 Food and drinks have
S V 간접의문문 S V_1

즐거움의 대상이 되었고 / 더 이상 여겨지지 않는다 / 그저 필요한 연료의 원천으로
become things of pleasure // and are no longer viewed / just as a source of needed fuel. (④)
C V_2

그러나 건강하지 않은(몸에 좋지 않은) 먹을 음식을 선택하는 것은 / 하루 종일 / 엄청 건강에 해로운 행동이다
7 But choosing *unhealthy foods* [to eat] / throughout the day / is an extraordinarily unhealthy
S V C

잘못된 것은 아무것도 없다 / 식사를 즐기는 것에는 / 그러나 당신은 명심해야 한다
behavior. (⑤) 8 There is nothing wrong / with enjoying a meal, // but you should keep in
V_1 S_1 S_2 V_2

당신 몸이 무엇을 정말로 필요로 하는지 / 동시에
mind / what your body really needs / at the same time.
간접의문문

해석 한 눈에 보기 1 당신은 한번이라도 잠깐 멈춰 서서 우리가 먹는 음식이 단지 우리의 신체가 건강하게 기능하도록 해주는 연료일 뿐이라고 생각해 본 적이 있는가? 2 많은 면에서, 그것은 우리의 자동차를 운행하기 위해 휘발유를 구입하는 것과 전혀 다르지 않다. 3 안타깝게도, 우리의 미뢰는 품질 측정기라기보다는 오히려 즐거움 측정기가 되어 왔다. 4 우리는 더 이상 몸에 좋은 맛을 찾지 않는다. 5 대신에 우리는 음식이 우리의 미각을 얼마나 기분 좋게 해주는가에 초점을 맞춘다. 6 음식과 음료수는 즐거움의 대상이 되었고 더 이상 그저 필요한 연료의 원천으로 여겨지지 않는다. 7 그러나 몸에 좋지 않은 먹을 음식을 하루 종일 선택하는 것은 엄청 건강에 해로운 행동이다. 8 식사를 즐기는 것에는 잘못된 것이 전혀 없으나, 당신은 동시에 당신 몸이 무엇을 정말로 필요로 하는지를 명심해야 한다.

정답단추 주어진 문장은 음식이 미각을 기분 좋게 해주는 정도에 더 초점을 맞춘다는 내용이고, 맨 앞의 Instead를 단서로 앞선 문장에는 대조되는 내용이어야 함을 알 수 있어. ③의 앞의 문장은 우리는 더는 건강한 음식을 찾지 않는다는 내용으로 주어진 문장과 대조되고 있어. 따라서 주어진 문장이 들어가기에 가장 적절한 곳은 ③이야.

오답단서 ①, ②의 앞뒤는 우리가 자동차에 연료를 넣듯이 건강을 위해 음식을 먹지만, 맛이 있는 것에만 집중한다는 내용으로 자연스럽게 이어지고 있어. 또한, ④, ⑤의 앞뒤에서는 음식을 즐거움의 대상으로만 인식하는 것은 나쁘며, 건강한 음식의 필요성을 명심해야 한다는 내용으로 글의 흐름이 유기적으로 연결되고 있지. 따라서 ①, ②, ④, ⑤는 주어진 문장이 들어갈 곳으로 적절하지 않아.

어휘확인

ever 한번이라도 **merely** 단지, 그저 **fuel** 연료 **function** 기능하다 **healthily** 건강하게 **cf. healthy** 건강한(↔ **unhealthy** 건강하지 않은) **purchase** 구입하다 **run** 운행하다 **automobile** 자동차 **unfortunately** 안타깝게도, 불행하게도 **taste bud** (혀의) 미뢰 **gauge** 측정기 **rather than** ~보다는 **quality** 질(質) **no longer** 더 이상 ~ 아닌 **focus on** ~에 초점을 맞추다 **pleasing** 기분 좋은 **palate** 미각, 구미 **thing** 대상 **pleasure** 즐거움 **view** ~라고 여기다 **source** 원천, 근원 **throughout** ~ 동안 죽 **extraordinarily** 엄청나게 **behavior** 행동 **keep in mind** 명심하다 **at the same time** 동시에

지문 Flow

[도입]
음식은 신체가 건강하게 기능하도록 해주는 연료

⬇

[역접]
미뢰는 즐거움을 위한 측정기였고, 더 이상 몸에 좋은 맛을 찾지 않음

⬇

[보충설명]
음식이 미각을 기분 좋게 해주는 것에 초점을 맞춤

⬇

[결론]
식사를 즐기는 것은 좋지만, 몸이 정말로 필요로 하는 음식을 선택해야 함

113 정답 ④

지문 All in One

사람들은 항상 찾아왔다 / 식품을 보존하는 방법을 / 훈제하기, 염장하기,
1 People have always looked / for *ways* [to preserve food]. 2 Preservation methods like
S V S

피클로 만들기(절이기), 말리기와 같은 보존 방법들은 / 사용되어 왔다 / 수천 년 동안
smoking, salting, pickling, and drying / have been used / for thousands of years.
V

그러나 발견된 이후로 / 차가운 온도가 ~을 늘인다는 것이 / 신선한 식품의 수명을
(B) 3 But since it was discovered / that cold temperatures lengthen / the life of fresh foods, //
접속사 S′ V′ 접속사 S″ V″

사람들은 노력해왔다 / 더 나은 기술을 찾기 위해 / 냉장 보관의 / 이런 기술들의 가장
people have worked / to find better techniques / of cold preservation. 4 The earliest of
S V 부사적 용법(목적) S

이른 것은 / 자연이 제공해야 했던 것에 의존했다
these techniques / relied on what nature had to offer.
V 관계대명사

고대 로마인들은 얼음과 눈을 모았다 / 식품 저장을 위해 / 이것은 상당히 좋은 효과가
(C) 5 The ancient Romans collected ice and snow / for food preservation. 6 This worked fairly
S V S_1 V_1

어휘확인

way 방법; 길 **preserve** 보존하다 **cf. preservation** 보존 **method** 방법 **like** (예를 들어) ~와 같은 **smoke** 훈제하다 **salt** 염장하다(소금에 절여 저장하다) **pickle** 피클을 만들다 **since** ~이후[부터] **discover** 발견하다 **lengthen** 늘이다 **life** 수명 **work** 노력하다; 효과가 있다 **technique** 기술, 기법 **rely on** ~에 의존하다 **offer** 제공하다 **ancient** 고대의 **fairly** 상당히 **remain** 남다 **common** 흔한 **practice** 관습 **for some time** 꽤 오랫동안 **far from** 전혀 ~이 아닌 **convenient** 편리한 **invent** 발명하다 **wood** 나무, 목재 **shelf** 선반 **improvement** 진보, 향상

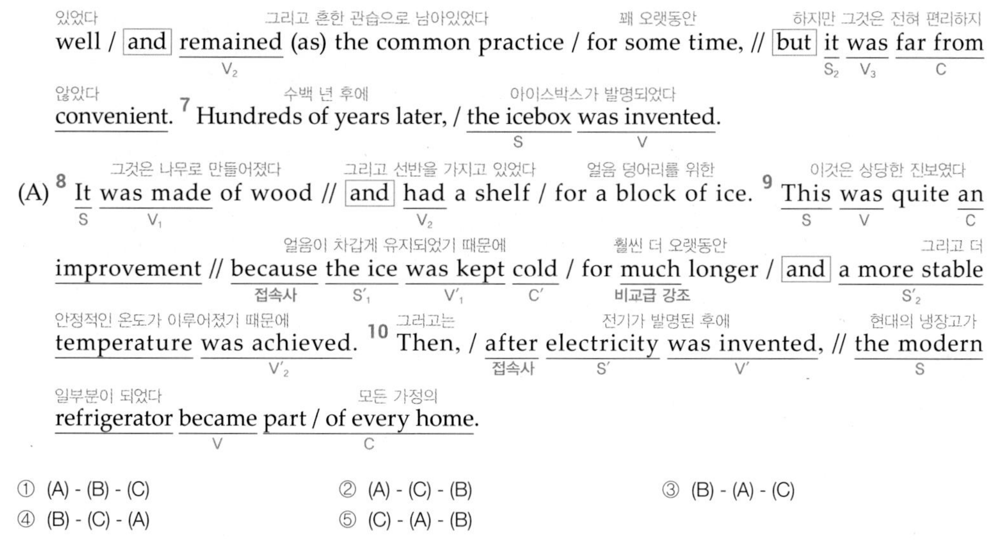

① (A) - (B) - (C)　　② (A) - (C) - (B)　　③ (B) - (A) - (C)
④ (B) - (C) - (A)　　⑤ (C) - (A) - (B)

stable 안정적인 **achieve** 이루다 **then** 그러고는 **electricity** 전기 **modern** 현대의 **refrigerator** 냉장고

지문 Flow

[도입]
음식을 보존하는 다양한 방법으로 훈제, 염장, 절이기, 말리기 등이 사용됨

⬇

[주제문]
(B) 찬 온도가 식품의 수명을 연장하기 때문에, 더 나은 냉장 보관 기술을 찾기 위해 노력함

⬇

[예시1]
(C) 고대 로마인들은 얼음과 눈을 사용하였고, 수백 년 후에 아이스박스가 발명됨

&

[예시2]
(A) 아이스박스는 나무로 만들어지고 얼음 선반이 있었고, 전기 발명 후에는 냉장고를 사용함

해석 한 눈에 보기 1 사람들은 항상 식품을 보존하는 방법을 찾아 왔다. 2 훈제하기, 염장하기, 절이기, 말리기와 같은 보존 방법들이 수천 년 동안 사용되어 왔다. (B) 주제문 3 그러나 차가운 온도가 신선한 식품의 수명을 연장한다는 것이 발견된 이후로, 사람들은 더 나은 냉장 보관 기술을 찾아내기 위해 노력해 왔다. 4 이러한 기술의 가장 이른 것은 자연이 제공해야 하는 것에 의존했다. (C) 5 고대 로마인들은 식품 저장을 위해 얼음과 눈을 모았다. 6 이것은 상당히 좋은 효과가 있었고 꽤 오랫동안 흔한 관습으로 남아 있었지만, 그것은 전혀 편리하지 않았다. 7 수백 년 후에, 아이스박스가 발명되었다. (A) 8 그것은 나무로 만들어졌고 얼음 덩어리를 위한 선반이 있었다. 9 이것은 얼음이 훨씬 더 오랫동안 차갑게 유지되었고 더욱 더 안정적인 온도가 이루어졌기 때문에 상당한 진보였다. 10 그러고는 전기가 발명된 후에, 현대식 냉장고가 모든 가정의 일부분이 되었다.

정답단추 주어진 글은 훈제, 염장, 절임, 건조와 같은 식품 저장법이 사용됐다는 내용으로, 이어서 But으로 시작해 '차가운 온도의 장점을 발견한 후 냉장 보존 기술을 찾으려 노력했지만, 자연에 의지했다'는 내용의 (B)가 오는 것이 적절해. 그다음으로는 냉장 보존 기술의 구체적인 예를 들고 있는 (C)가 와야 해. 마지막으로 (C)의 the icebox를 It으로 받아 아이스박스에 대한 자세한 설명과 오늘날의 냉장고에 관해 설명하는 (A)가 이어지는 것이 자연스러워. 따라서 글의 알맞은 순서는 ④ '(B) – (C) – (A)'야.

유형편

Chapter 4

유형 11 장문 독해

Check-Up 1 1 (D) 2 (A) 3 (C) 4 (B)
Check-Up 2 **114** ③ **115** ③ **116** ③
Check-Up 3 **117** ③ **118** ④
실전적용독해 **119** ④ **120** ⑤ **121** ③ **122** ⑤ **123** ⑤ **124** ④ **125** ④

Check-Up 1

정답 1 (D) 2 (A) 3 (C) 4 (B)

Check-Up 2

114 정답 ③ **115** 정답 ③ **116** 정답 ③

지문 All in One

Roy는 9살짜리 소년이었다 / 여느 소년들과 같은 / 희망과 호기심으로 가득한 / 그러나 당신은
(A) [1] Roy was a nine-year-old boy / like any other, / full of hope and curiosity. [2] But you'd
S V C S V
그가 돌아다니는 것을 결코 보지 못했을 것이다 / 다른 아이들과 / 그것은 ~였다 / Roy가 아픈 아이였기 때문
never find him running around / with the other children. [3] That was // because Roy was a
O C S V 접속사 C
백혈병이라고 부르는 치명적인 질병을 앓고 있는 / 병이 나아지고 있긴 했지만
sick child, / ill with *the deadly disease* [called leukemia]. [4] Though the disease had been
접속사 S′ V′
그 병이 다시 악화될 가능성이 항상 있었다 / 언제든지
getting better, // there was always *the chance* of it getting worse again / at any moment.
C′ V S =
그러나 그 어린 아이는 한 번도 불평하거나 울지 않았다 / 운명으로 그(Roy)에게 주어진 잔인한 패에
[5] But the little one did not once complain or weep / over *the cruel hand* [given to (a) him by
S V_1 V_2
그는 단지 그가 가장 좋아하는 창문에 앉아서 / 놀고 있는 아이들을 보았다 / 그의 침묵은
fate]. [6] He merely sat at his favorite window, / watching the children at play. [7] His silence was
S V 분사구문(= as he watched ~) S V
가슴 아팠다 / 그의 부모인 Mathew와 Susan에게 / Susan은 그의 차분한 받아들임을 더 참기 힘들다고 느꼈다
heart-breaking / to his parents, Mathew and Susan. [8] Susan found his calm acceptance more
C = S V O C
unbearable.

얘야 / TV를 보는 게 어때니 / 또는 게임을 하는 게 (어떠니) / 그녀가 말할 것이다
(C) [9] "Darling, / why don't you watch television / or play computer games?" / she would say;
S V_1 V_2 S_1 V_1
그리고 대답은 ~일 것이다 / 아니요 엄마 관심 없어요. / 때때로 / Mathew가
// and the answer would be, / "No, Mummy, not interested." [10] Sometimes / Mathew would
S_2 V_2 C_2 S V_1
그(Roy)와 함께 앉았을 것이다 그리고 그를 알게 되려고 노력했을 (것이다) / 그(Roy)를 웃게 하는 것을 알아내려고
sit with (d) him / and try to get to know him, / to find out what would make (e) him laugh.
V_2 관계대명사
Roy가 약간 미소 지을지라도 / 그의 부모를 행복하게 하기 위해 / 그는 결코 웃지 않았다 / 또한
[11] Though Roy would smile a little / to make his parents happy, // he never laughed, / nor
접속사 S′ V′ 부사적 용법(목적) S_1 V_1 부정어
어떤 것을 요구하지도 않았다
did he ask for anything.
조동사 S_2 V_2
어느 날 / Susan이 앉아 있었을 때 / 그녀의 아들이 아이들의 저녁 놀이를 즐기고 있는 것을 보면서 / 그녀는
(B) [12] One day, / as Susan sat / watching her son enjoy the evening play of the children, // she
접속사 S′ V′ 분사구문(= as she was watching ~) S

어휘확인

curiosity 호기심 **deadly** 치명적인 **leukemia** 백혈병 **get better** 좋아지다 (↔ **get worse** 악화되다) **weep** 울다, 눈물을 흘리다 **cruel** 잔인한, 잔혹한 **hand** (카드 놀이에서 손에 쥐게 된) 패 **fate** 운명 **merely** 단지 **silence** 침묵, 고요 **heart-breaking** 가슴이 아픈 **calm** 차분한, 침착한 **acceptance** 받아들임 **unbearable** 참을 수 없는 **suddenly** 갑자기 cf. **sudden** 갑작스러운 **thrill** 전율 **rush** 달리다, 돌진하다 **unusual** 특이한, 드문 **surprisingly** 놀랍게도 **extremely** 극도로, 극히 **happiness** 행복 **overjoyed** 매우 기뻐하는 **lap** 무릎 **be filled with** ~로 가득 차다 **joy** 기쁨 **hold ~ in one's arm** 끌어안다

지문 Flow

[발단]
9살짜리 소년 Roy가 백혈병을 앓고 있음

⬇

[전개]
Roy는 한 번도 자신의 병에 대해 불평하지 않고 창문에 앉아 놀고 있는 아이들을 봄

⬇

[위기]
Roy의 부모는 웃지 않는 Roy를 웃게 하려고 애씀

⬇

갑자기 그(Roy)가 큰 소리로 웃는 것을 보았다 / 갑작스런 기쁨의 전율을 느끼며 / Susan은 달려갔다

suddenly saw (b) him laugh loudly. 13 With a sudden thrill of joy, / Susan rushed / to see the

V O C / S V 부사적 용법(목적)

Roy의 특별한 흥분의 원인을 보기 위해 / 어린 소년이 / 거의 2살인 / Roy에게 그(어린 소년)의 코를

cause of Roy's unusual excitement. 14 A little boy, / hardly 2 years old, / was pushing (c) his

S / V

밀어 올리고 있었다 / 놀랍게도 / Roy 또한 우스운 몸짓을 하고 있었다 / 작은 녀석에게

nose up at Roy. 15 Surprisingly, / Roy was also making funny gestures / at *the little guy*, [who

S V / 계속적 용법

그는 Roy의 모든 행동을 베낀 / 이것은 잠시 동안 계속되었고 / Susan을 매우 행복하게 했다

copied every action of Roy's]. 16 This went on for some time, / making Susan extremely

S V / 분사구문

Roy가 마침내 웃고 있었다는 행복

happy / — happy that Roy was finally laughing!

=

그날 밤 / 그녀는 그녀의 작은 행복을 Mathew와 함께 나누었다 / 그 또한 매우 기뻤다

(D) 17 That night, / she shared her tiny piece of happiness with *Mathew*, [who was also

S V / 관계대명사(계속적 용법)

그는 Roy를 무릎에 앉히고 노래를 불렀다 / 내 작은 Roy는 작은 소년을 보았고

overjoyed]. 18 He took Roy onto his lap and sang, // "My little Roy saw a tiny boy / and was

S V_1 V_2 / S V_1 V_2

기쁨으로 가득했지 / 그들의 얼굴은 기쁨으로 빛나고 있었다 / 그들이 아들을 끌어안았을 때

filled with joy." 19 Their faces were shining with joy // as they held their son in their arms.

S V / 접속사 S' V'

[절정]
Roy가 2살짜리 소년과 우스운 몸짓을 하면서 큰 소리로 웃음

[결말]
Roy의 부모가 Roy가 웃은 것에 대해 기쁘고 행복해 함

114 ① (B) - (C) - (D) ② (B) - (D) - (C) ③ (C) - (B) - (D)
④ (C) - (D) - (B) ⑤ (D) - (C) - (B)

115 ① (a) ② (b) ③ (c) ④ (d) ⑤ (e)

116 ① Roy는 백혈병으로 병이 호전되고 있었다. ② Roy는 아픈 것에 대해 전혀 불평하지 않았다.
③ 부모는 Roy가 고요히 지내는 것에 안심했다. ④ Roy는 꼬마를 만나 즐거운 시간을 보냈다.
⑤ Roy는 TV와 컴퓨터 게임에 흥미가 없었다.

해석 한 눈에 보기 (A) 1 Roy는 희망과 호기심으로 가득한 여느 소년들과 같은 9살짜리 소년이었다. 2 그러나 당신은 그가 다른 아이들과 돌아다니는 것을 결코 보지 못했을 것이다. 3 그것은 Roy가 아픈 아이였고, 백혈병이라고 부르는 치명적인 질병을 앓고 있기 때문이었다. 4 병이 나아지고 있긴 했지만, 언제든지 그 병이 다시 악화될 가능성이 항상 있었다. 5 그러나 그 어린 아이는 운명으로 (a) 그(Roy)에게 주어진 잔인한 패에 한 번도 불평하거나 울지 않았다. 6 그는 단지 그가 가장 좋아하는 창문에 앉아서 놀고 있는 아이들을 보았다. 7 그의 침묵은 그의 부모인 Mathew와 Susan에게 가슴 아팠다. 8 Susan은 그의 차분한 받아들임을 더 참기 힘들다고 느꼈다. (C) 9 "얘야, TV를 보거나 컴퓨터 게임을 하는 게 어떠니?"라고 그녀가 말하면, 대답은 "아니요, 엄마, 관심 없어요."일 것이다. 10 때때로 Mathew가 (d) 그(Roy)와 함께 앉아서 그를 알게 되려고, (e) 그(Roy)를 웃게 하는 것을 알아내려고 노력했을 것이다. 11 Roy가 그의 부모를 행복하게 하기 위해 약간 미소 지을지라도, 그는 결코 웃지도 어떤 것을 요구하지도 않았다. (B) 12 어느 날, Susan이 자신의 아들이 아이들의 저녁 놀이를 즐기고 있는 것을 보면서 앉아 있었을 때, 그녀는 갑자기 (b) 그(Roy)가 큰 소리로 웃는 것을 보았다. 13 갑작스러운 기쁨의 전율을 느끼며, Susan은 Roy의 특별한 흥분의 원인을 보기 위해 달려갔다. 14 거의 2살인 어린 소년이 Roy에게 (c) 그(어린 소년)의 코를 밀어 올리고 있었다. 15 놀랍게도, Roy 또한 작은 녀석에게 우스운 몸짓을 하고 있었고, 그는 Roy의 모든 행동을 베꼈다. 16 이것은 잠시 동안 계속되었고, Susan은 매우 행복했다. Roy가 마침내 웃고 있었다는 행복! (D) 17 그날 밤, 그녀는 그녀의 작은 행복을 Mathew와 함께 나누었고, 그 또한 매우 기뻤다. 18 그는 Roy를 무릎에 앉히고 노래를 불렀다. "내 작은 Roy는 작은 소년을 보았고 기쁨으로 가득했지." 19 그들의 얼굴은 아들을 끌어안았을 때 기쁨으로 빛나고 있었다.

정답단추

114 각 단락의 내용이 자연스럽게 이어지는지를 파악하려면, 사건의 전개에 따른 등장인물의 행동과 심경 변화, 연결어, 지칭어 등을 살펴봐야 해. (A)에는 백혈병에 걸린 Roy가 자신의 병을 받아들이면서 친구들이 노는 모습을 침묵으로 바라본다는 내용이 나와. 그 다음에 그 모습을 안타까워하는 엄마가 Roy에게 TV 보기, 컴퓨터 게임하기 같은 일을 제안하는 (C)로 이어지는 게 자연스러워. (C)에서는 Roy가 웃지는 않는다는 내용이 나오는데, (B)에서 Roy가 꼬마를 만나 웃는다는 내용이 나오므로 (B)가 그 뒤에 이어져야 함을 알 수 있어. 그리고 마지막으로 웃음을 찾은 Roy를 보고 부모가 기뻐하는 내용이 와야 글의 흐름상 적절해. 따라서 글의 순서로 가장 적절한 것은 ③ '(C) – (B) – (D)'야.

115 대명사가 가리키는 대상을 찾을 때는 대명사의 앞뒤를 살펴서 명사를 파악한 후에, 대명사 자리에 그 명사를 대입해서 자연스러운지 확인하는 것이 좋아. 이 글에서 he로 받을 수 있는 사람은 Roy, Roy의 아버지, 2살짜리 꼬마야. 자신의 병에 대해 불평하거나 울지 않는다는 (a)는 앞에서 계속 언급한 Roy임을 알 수 있어. (b)는 Susan이 자신의 아들을 보고 있었다고 했으므로 Roy를 가리켜. 그리고 (c)는 Roy에게 코를 들어 보인 사람 즉, 2살짜리 꼬마를 대신하고 있지. 그리고 (d)는 Mathew가 함께 앉은 사람이므로 Roy임을 알 수 있고, (e)도 (d)에 이어지는 내용이니까 Roy를 의미해. 따라서 가리키는 대상이 다른 하나는 ③의 (c)야.

116 각 선택지를 먼저 읽은 후에, 순서대로 본문의 내용과 대조해 보자. (A)의 후반부에서 Roy의 부모는 Roy가 아무 말도 않고 창가에서 친구들이 노는 것을 보는 것이 가슴 아프다고 했고, Roy가 소리 내어 웃지 않아서 그를 웃게 하려고 노력했다고 했으므로, 글의 내용으로 적절하지 않은 것은 ③이야.

오답단서

116 ①은 (A)에서 Roy의 병이 나아지고 있다고 했으므로 적절한 설명이야. ②도 (A)에서 Roy가 자신의 운명의 장난 같은 자신의 병에 대해 불평하지 않았다고 했으므로 글의 내용과 일치해. ④는 (B)에서 Roy가 꼬마를 만나 그가 하는 행동을 보고 크게 웃었고, 서로 우스운 몸짓을 하며 놀았다는 글의 내용으로 알 수 있어. ⑤는 (C)에서 엄마가 TV를 보거나 컴퓨터 게임을 하라는 말에 Roy가 관심 없다고 답하니까 글의 내용과 일치해.

Check-Up 3

117 정답 ③ 118 정답 ④

지문 All in One

디지털 발자국은 ~에 관한 온라인 포트폴리오다 우리가 누구인지 우리가 무엇을 하는지 그리고 연계에 의해
1 Digital footprints are online portfolios of / who we are, / what we do, / and by association,
S V C 간접의문문 간접의문문

우리가 무엇을 알고 있는지 그것은 삶의 보증된 부산물이다 인터넷에 연결된 세상 속에서 그래서 만약
/ what we know. 2 They are a guaranteed by-product of life / in a connected world. 3 So if you
간접의문문 S V C 접속사 S'

당신이 인터넷에 접속하면 또는 소셜 미디어를 사용하면 당신은 디지털 발자국을 만든다 당신이 웹사이트에 접속할 때마다
ever get online / or use social media, // you create a digital footprint. 4 Every time you get on
V'_1 V'_2 S V 접속사 S' V'_1

링크를 클릭하거나 사진을 올리거나 상태를 업데이트할 (때마다) 그것은 추적된다 사람들은 인터넷
a website, / click on a link, / post a picture, / or update a status, // it is tracked. 5 People can
V'_2 V'_3 V'_4 S V S V_1

에 접속할 수 있다 어떤 검색 엔진으로 구글 같은 혹은 어떤 소셜 미디어 사이트로 그리고 당신에
go online / to any search engine, / such as Google, / or (to) any social media site // and learn
V_2

대해 배울 수 있다 당신이 비공개라고 생각하는 모든 것은 그렇지 않다 하지만 당신이 왜 신경 써야 하는가?
about you. 6 *Everything* [that you think is **private**] / isn't. 7 But why should you care? 8 Does it
S 관계대명사 삽입절 V S V S

정말로 중요한가 누군가가 이것들을 모두 찾아볼 수 있다는 것이 사실 이것은 당신의 삶에 영향을 미칠 수 있다
really matter // that someone can look up all of this stuff? 9 Actually, / this can affect your life
V 접속사 S' V' S V

중대한 방법으로 그것은 당신이 직업을 얻지 못하게 야기할 수 있다 혹은 심지어 당신이 원하는 대학에 가지 못하게
/ in major ways. 10 It can cause you not to get a job, / or even not to get into *the college* [that
S V O C_1 C_2 관계대명사

2009년도의 한 설문 조사는 발견했다 275명의 미국 채용 담당자 중 70%가 말했다는 것을 그들이 지원자를
you want]. 11 A 2009 survey found // that 70% of 275 U.S. recruiters said / (that) they have
S V 접속사 S' V' 접속사 S'' V''

거부해왔다고 그들이 온라인으로 찾은 정보를 토대로 하여
rejected candidates / based on *information* [(which[that]) they found online] / [that conflicted
관계대명사 관계대명사

회사 기준에 모순되는 당신은 가지고 있을 수 있다 당신이 해온 모든 사회 활동을 보여주는
with company standards]. 12 You could have / *an extremely impressive resume* [showing *all*
S_1 V_1

대단히 인상적인 이력서를 하지만 만일 당신의 디지털 발자국이 보여준다면
of the community work [(that) you have done]], // but if your digital footprint shows / a
관계대명사 접속사 S' V'

당신 성격의 다른 면을 당신은 절대로 당신의 꿈을 이루지 못할지도 모른다 부디
different side of your personality, / you may never achieve your dream. 13 Hopefully, / you
S_2 V_2 S

당신이 당신의 디지털 발자국을 알고 있기를 바란다 그리고 그것이 당신에게 어떻게 영향을 미칠 수 있는지를
will be aware of your digital footprint / and how it can affect you.
V C 간접의문문

117
① Do Not Look Up Others' Digital Footprints
다른 사람들의 디지털 발자국을 찾지 마라
② Searching Online Portfolios: An Invasion of Privacy
온라인 포트폴리오를 찾는 것: 사생활 침해
③ Be Cautious about What You Post Online
인터넷에 게시하는 것을 조심해라
④ Advantages and Disadvantages of Digital Footprints
디지털 발자국의 장점과 단점
⑤ Spam Mailers: Digital Footprint Trackers
스팸 메일을 보내는 사람들: 디지털 발자국 추적자들

118
① necessary
필요하다고
② improper
부적절하다고
③ appropriate
적절하다고
④ private
비공개라고
⑤ satisfactory
만족스럽다고

해석 한 눈에 보기 1 디지털 발자국은 우리가 누구이고, 우리가 무엇을 하며, 그리고 연계하여 우리가 무엇을 알고 있는지에 관한 온라인 포트폴리오이다. 2 그것은 네트워크 세상 속의 삶의 보증된 부산물이다. 3 따라서 만일 당신이 온라인에 접속하거나 소셜 미디어를 이용하면, 당신은 디지털 발자국을 만든다. 4 당신이 웹사이트에 접속하거나, 링크를 클릭하거나, 사진을 올리거나, 상태를 업데이트할 때마다, 그것은 추적된다. 5 사람들은 구글 같은 그 어떤 검색 엔진이나 그 어떤 소셜 미디어에 온라인으로 접속해서 당신에 대해 알아낼 수 있다. 6 당신이 비공개라고 생각하는 모든 것이 그렇지 않다. 7 그런데 당신은 왜 신경 써야 하는가? 8 누군가가 이 모든 것을 찾아볼 수 있다는 것이 정말로 중요한가? 9 사실 이것은 당신의 인생에 중대한 방식으로 영향을 미칠 수 있다. 10 그것은 당신이 직업을 구하지 못하게 혹은 심지어 당신이 원하는 대학에 들어가지 못하게 할 수 있다. 11 2009년도의 한 설문 조사는 미국 채용 담당자 275명 중 70%가 그들이 회사 기준과 모순되는 온라인상에서 발견한 정보를 토대로 하여 지원자를 거부해 왔다고 말했다는 것을 발견했다. 12 당신은 자신이 해온 모든 사회 활동을 보여 주는 대단히 인상적인 이력서를 갖고 있을 수 있지만, 만일 당신의 디지털 발자국이 당신 성격의 이면을 보여 준다면, 당신은 결코 꿈을 이루지 못할지도 모른다. 13 부디 당신이 당신의 디지털 발자국과 그것이 당신에게 어떻게 영향을 미칠 수 있는지를 알고 있기를 바란다.

어휘확인

online 온라인의 **portfolio** 포트폴리오[작품집] **association** 연계; 협회 **guaranteed** 보증된 **by-product** 부산물 **connected** 인터넷에 연결된; 연속된 **get online** 인터넷에 접속하다(= go online) **social media** 소셜 미디어, 사회 매체 **every time** ~할 때마다 **website** 웹사이트(= site) **click** (마우스를) 클릭하다 **link** ((컴퓨터)) 링크; 관계 **post** (웹사이트에 정보·사진 등을) 올리다 **update** 업데이트하다(가장 최근의 정보를 알려주다); 갱신하다 **status** 상태; 지위 **track** 추적하다 cf. **tracker** 추적자 **search engine** 검색 엔진 **private** 비공개의[사적인] **matter** 중요하다; 문제 **look up** (컴퓨터 등에서 정보를) 찾아보다 **stuff** 것들, 물건 **affect** 영향을 미치다 **major** 중대한 **way** 방법; 길 **survey** 설문 조사 **recruiter** 채용 담당자 **reject** 거부하다 **candidate** 지원자 **based on** ~을 토대로 하여 **information** 정보 **conflict with** ~와 모순되다 **standard** 기준 **extremely** 대단히, 극히 **resume** 이력서 **community** 사회; 주민 **personality** 성격 **achieve** 이루다, 성취하다 **hopefully** 부디 **be aware of** ~을 알다

〈선택지 어휘〉
invasion 침해; 침략 **cautious** 조심스러운 **advantage** 장점(↔ **disadvantage** 단점) **spam mailer** 스팸 메일을 보내는 사람들 cf. **spam** 스팸 메일 (통신이나 인터넷을 통해 무차별적으로 대량 살포되는 광고성 전자 메일) **improper** 부적절한 **appropriate** 적절한 **satisfactory** 만족스러운

지문 Flow

[도입]
디지털 발자국은 네트워크 세상 속의 삶의 부산물

⬇

[보충설명]
온라인 접속, 소셜 미디어 이용, 웹사이트 접속, 링크 클릭, 사진 업로드 등으로 만들어진 디지털 발자국은 추적 가능함

⬇

[문제 제기]
디지털 발자국이 공개적이라는 것에 대해 왜 신경 써야 하는가?

⬇

[주장]
디지털 발자국은 인생에 중대한 영향을 미칠 수 있음

⬇

정답단추

117 제목을 고르는 문제는 글의 시사점을 압축적으로 표현한 것을 찾으면 돼. 이 글의 전반부에서는 우리가 인터넷에서 활동한 흔적인 디지털 발자국에 관해 설명하고 있어. 글의 중반부 A 2009 survey found ~.에서 디지털 발자국에 대한 설문 조사 내용을 토대로 디지털 발자국은 취직이나 대학 입학 등 인생에 큰 영향을 미칠 수 있으므로 주의할 것을 당부하고 있어. 따라서 글의 내용을 가장 잘 압축한 제목은 인터넷에 게시하는 것을 주의하라는 내용의 ③이야.

118 빈칸 문제는 빈칸을 포함한 문장을 먼저 읽고 무엇에 중점을 두어야 하는지 파악한 다음 나머지를 읽는 게 좋아. 빈칸이 포함된 문장은 당신이 '무엇'이라고 생각하는 모든 것이 그렇지 않다는 내용이지? 이 문장 앞에서 '무엇'의 단서를 찾을 수 있어. 그 내용을 보면 웹사이트 접속하기, 링크 클릭하기, 사진 올리기, 상태 업데이트하기 등의 디지털 발자국이 검색 엔진이나 소셜 미디어를 통해 쉽게 추적할 수 있고 결국 당신에 대해 알 수 있다고 하고 있어. 이를 다르게 말하면 우리가 개인적으로 한 것들, 즉 비공개라고 생각하는 것이 사실은 그렇지 않음을 의미해. 따라서 빈칸에 들어갈 말로 가장 적절한 것은 ④ 'private'이야.

오답단서

117 ①, ④, ⑤는 글의 소재인 디지털 발자국을 활용해 만든 제목이야. 하지만, 디지털 발자국의 영향을 주의하라는 글의 주제와는 관련이 없어서 답이 될 수 없어. ②도 글에 언급된 내용이지만, 온라인상의 흔적을 찾는 것이 사생활 침해라는 것을 강조하는 게 아니라 그 흔적으로 사생활이 침해될 수 있으므로 조심하라는 내용이므로 제목으로 옳지 않아.

[보충설명]
취업이나 진학에 중대한 영향을 미칠 수 있음

실전적용독해

119 정답 ④ **120** 정답 ⑤ **121** 정답 ③

지문 All in One

(A) [1] I've watched Kevin / with admiration // as he has strived / to meet *goals* [(which) others might think impossible]. [2] At nineteen, / he decided to try his hand / at competitive powerlifting. [3] This wasn't a natural choice / for a former cyclist, // but (a) he was determined / to break the national record / for dead lifts.

(나는 Kevin을 지켜봐 왔다 / 감탄과 함께 / 그가 노력했을 때 / 다른 사람들은 불가능하다고 생각할지도 모르는 목표를 달성하려고 / 19세에 / 그는 시도해보기로 결정했다 / 경쟁적인 역도를 / 이것은 자연스러운 선택은 아니었지만 / 전 사이클 선수에게 / 그러나 그(Kevin)는 결심했다(마음먹었다) / 국가 기록을 깨겠다고 / 데드리프트의)

(S: I, V: 've watched; 접속사: as, S′: he, V′: has strived; 부사적 용법(목적): to meet; 관계대명사: (which); S: he, V: decided; S_1: This, V_1: wasn't, C: a natural choice; but; S_2: he, V_2: was determined)

(D) [4] Kevin identified the best trainer / in northern California // and drove two hours each way, / several times a week, / to learn from (e) him. [5] Kevin read *everything* [(that) he could / about the sport], // carefully crafted *a diet* [to build more muscle], // and spent hours training / at the gym.

(Kevin은 최고의 트레이너를 찾아냈고 / 캘리포니아 북부에 있는 / 갈 때마다 2시간씩 운전을 했다 / 일주일에 몇 번씩 / 그(트레이너)에게서 배우기 위해 / Kevin은 그가 읽을 수 있는 모든 것을 읽었고 / 그 스포츠에 관해 / 더 많은 근육을 키워 줄 식단을 세심하게 공들여 만들었으며 / 몇 시간씩 훈련을 하며 보냈다 / 체육관에서)

(S: Kevin, V_1: identified, V_2: drove; 부사적 용법(목적): to learn; S: Kevin, V_1: read; 관계대명사: (that); V_2: crafted; V_3: spent)

(B) [6] After several years of weight training, / he entered a competition / to see how (b) he stacked up against others. [7] We arose at 5:00 a.m. // and drove three hours to Fresno / for a formal meet. [8] The gym was filled / with *weight lifters* [who'd been competing / for years]. [9] I was worried // (that) (c) he would be disappointed / with his performance.

(수년간의 근력 단련 후에 / 그는 대회에 참가했다 / 그(Kevin)가 다른 선수들과 얼마나 견줄만한지 알아보기 위해 / 우리는 새벽 5시에 일어나서 / 프레즈노로 3시간을 운전해 갔다 / 공식 경기를 위해 / 체육관은 가득 차 있었다 / 시합에 참가해왔던 역도 선수들로 / 수년간 / 나는 걱정스러웠다 / 그(Kevin)가 실망할까 봐 / 자신의 성적에)

(S: he, V: entered; 부사적 용법(목적): to see; 간접의문문: how (b) he stacked up against others; S: We, V_1: arose, V_2: drove; S: The gym, V: was filled; 관계대명사: who; S: I, V: was, C: worried; 접속사: (that), S′: he, V′: would be, C′: disappointed)

(C) [10] But Kevin blew away / both the federation's state and national records / by lifting 590 pounds — // this was 50 pounds more / than the previous record holder. [11] Was he lucky? [12] Of course / he was lucky. [13] All the cards lined up / for him / that day. [14] But (d) he would never have succeeded // unless he had put tremendous effort / behind his goals.

(그러나 Kevin은 수월하게 이겼다 / 연맹의 주 기록과 전국 기록 둘 다를 / 590파운드를 들어 올림으로써 / 이것은 50파운드가 더 많았다 / 이전의 기록 보유자보다 / 그가 운이 좋았던 걸까? / 물론 / 그는 운이 좋았다 / 모든 카드가 (모든 게) 척척 맞아떨어졌다 / 그에게 / 그날 / 그러나 그(Kevin)는 결코 성공하지 못했을 것이다 / 만일 그가 엄청난 노력을 들이지 않았다면 / 그의 목표 뒤에서)

(S: Kevin, V: blew away; S: this, V: was, C: 50 pounds more; V: Was, S: he, C: lucky; S: he, V: was, C: lucky; S: All the cards, V: lined up; S: he, V: would never have succeeded; 접속사: unless, S′: he, V′: had put)

어휘확인

admiration 감탄 **strive to-v** ~을 얻으려고 노력하다 **meet** 충족시키다; 경기[대회] **goal** 목표; 골문 **try one's hand at** ~을 시도해 보다 **competitive** 경쟁을 하는 cf. **competition** 대회; 경쟁 **compete** (시합 등에) 참가하다; 경쟁하다 **powerlifting** 역도 **natural** 자연스러운 **former** 예전의 (= previous) **cyclist** 사이클리스트, 자전거 타는 사람 **be determined to-v** ~하기로 결심하다 **break a record** 기록을 깨다 **dead lift** (기계를 쓰지 않고) 바로 들어올리기 **identify** 찾다; 확인하다 **trainer** 트레이너 **several** (몇)몇의 **craft** 공들여 만들다 **build muscle** 근육을 키우다 **gym** 체육관 **weight training** 근력 단련, 웨이트 트레이닝 **enter** (대회 등에) 참가하다; 들어가다 **see** 알다, 이해하다; 보다 **stack up (against)** (~와) 견줄 만하다 **arise** (잠자리에서) 일어나다; 생기다 **formal** 공식적인; 격식을 차린 **be filled with** ~로 가득 차다 **weight lifter** 역도 선수 **for years** 수년간 **disappointed** 실망한 **blow away** ~을 수월하게 이기다 **federation** 연맹[연합] **state** (미국 등에서) 주(州) **pound** 파운드(무게 단위) **previous** 이전의 **holder** 보유자[소유자] **succeed** 성공하다 **unless** ~하지 않는 한 **put effort** 노력을 들이다 **tremendous** 엄청난

지문 Flow

[발단]
전 사이클 선수였던 Kevin은 19세에 역도를 시작하면서 데드리프트 국가 기록을 깨기로 마음먹음

119 ① (B) - (D) - (C) ② (C) - (B) - (D) ③ (C) - (D) - (B)
④ (D) - (B) - (C) ⑤ (D) - (C) - (B)

120 ① (a) ② (b) ③ (c) ④ (d) ⑤ (e)

121 ① 19살에 역도 선수가 되려고 결심했다. ② 한때 사이클 선수였다.
③ 훈련 없이 경기에 참가했다. ④ 신기록으로 우승했다.
⑤ 역도에 관한 책을 읽었다.

[전개]
최고의 트레이너를 찾아 배웠고, 관련 지식에 대해 읽었고, 근육을 위한 식단에 신경을 썼고, 많은 시간 훈련을 했음

[위기]
수년 후에 대회에 참가함

[절정]
이전 기록을 모두 깨는 기록으로 우승함

[결말]
운도 좋았지만, Kevin의 엄청난 노력이 그를 성공하게 함

해석 한 눈에 보기 (A) **1** 나는 Kevin이 다른 사람들은 불가능하다고 여길지도 모르는 목표를 달성하려고 노력했을 때 감탄하면서 지켜봐 왔다. **2** 19세에 그는 경쟁적인 역도를 해보기로 했다. **3** 이것은 전 사이클 선수에게 자연스러운 선택은 아니었지만, (a) 그(Kevin)는 데드리프트의 국가 기록을 깨겠다고 마음먹었다. (D) **4** Kevin은 캘리포니아 북부에 있는 최고의 트레이너를 찾아냈고 (e) 그(트레이너)에게서 배우기 위해 일주일에 몇 번씩 갈 때마다 2시간씩 운전을 했다. **5** Kevin은 그가 그 스포츠에 관해 읽을 수 있는 모든 것을 읽었고, 더 많은 근육을 만들어 줄 식단을 세심하게 짰으며, 체육관에서 몇 시간씩 훈련하며 보냈다. (B) **6** 수년간의 근력 훈련 후에, 그는 (b) 그(Kevin)가 다른 선수들과 얼마나 견줄만한지 알아보기 위해 대회에 참가했다. **7** 우리는 새벽 5시에 일어나서 공식 경기를 위해 프레즈노로 3시간을 운전해 갔다. **8** 체육관은 수년간 경기에 참가해왔던 역도 선수들로 가득 차 있었다. **9** 나는 (c) 그(Kevin)가 자신의 성적에 실망할까 봐 걱정스러웠다. (C) **10** 그러나 Kevin은 590파운드를 들어 올림으로써 연맹의 주 기록과 전국 기록 둘 다를 날려버렸는데, 이것은 이전의 기록 보유자보다 50파운드가 더 많았다. **11** 그가 운이 좋았던 걸까? **12** 물론 그는 운이 좋았다. **13** 그날 모든 게 그에게 착착 맞아떨어졌다. **14** 그러나 만일 그가 그의 목표 뒤에서 엄청난 노력을 하지 않았다면 (d) 그(Kevin)는 결코 성공하지 못했을 것이다.

정답단추

119 시간 순서에 따라 내용이 전개되고 있어서 내용상 흐름이 자연스러운지를 잘 살펴봐야 해. 이 글은 전 사이클 선수였던 한 역도 선수가 신기록을 세우기까지의 과정을 묘사하고 있어. (A)는 전 사이클 선수였던 Kevin이 역도 선수가 되기로 했다는 내용이야. 따라서 이를 이루기 위해 트레이너를 찾고, 식단을 짜고, 체육관에서 훈련했다는 내용의 (D)가 다음으로 오는 게 적절해. 이 과정이 (B)의 After several years of weight training으로 계속 이어지고 있어. 그러면서 경기에 참가하는 Kevin이 실망할까 봐 걱정된다는 말로 끝나고 있지. 그다음에 그러한 우려와는 달리 국가 신기록을 세우면서 우승을 했고 Kevin의 엄청난 노력이 있었다는 내용의 (C)가 뒤이어 와야 자연스러워. 그러므로 올바른 글의 순서는 ④ '(D) – (B) – (C)'임을 알 수 있어.

120 제시된 대명사를 앞뒤 문장에 나온 등장인물을 대입해보면서 무엇을 지칭하는지 확인하면서 읽어야 해. 우선 (a)는 바로 앞에 나온 전 사이클 선수를 가리키고 있지? 그리고 앞선 문장에서 Kevin에 대한 설명이 이어지고 있으므로 전 사이클 선수가 곧 Kevin이라는 것을 알 수 있어. (b)는 Kevin이 훈련 과정을 끝내고 경기에 참가한다는 내용으로 Kevin을 대신하고 있어. 또한, (c), (d)는 글쓴이가 경기에 참가한 Kevin을 걱정하고, 칭찬하는 내용으로 모두 Kevin을 가리키고 있어. 마지막으로 (e)의 바로 앞에서 Kevin이 캘리포니아 북부에 있는 최고의 트레이너를 찾았단 내용으로 새로운 등장인물인 트레이너를 받고 있음을 알 수 있어. 따라서 가리키는 대상이 다른 것은 ⑤야.

121 꼼꼼하게 각 선택지의 내용을 지문의 내용과 대조해 보자. 확인한 내용은 선택지 옆에 따로 표시해두어도 좋아. Kevin은 수년간의 훈련 끝에 다른 선수들과 견줄 만한지 알아보기 위해 대회에 참가한 것으로 훈련 없이 경기에 참가했다는 ③의 설명은 지문의 내용과 일치하지 않아. 따라서 ③이 답이야.

오답단서

121 ①은 (A)에서 Kevin은 19살 때 역도에 도전하기로 했다는 내용을 찾을 수 있어. 또한, 뒤이은 설명에서 Kevin이 전 사이클 선수였다고 했으니까 ②도 일치하는 설명이야. 그다음 ④는 (C)에서 연맹의 주 기록과 전국 기록을 둘 다 깨버렸다고 했으니 신기록을 세워 우승했다는 설명은 적절하다는 걸 알 수 있지. ⑤는 (D)의 마지막 문장에서 그가 그 스포츠에 관해 읽을 수 있는 것은 모두 읽었다는 내용으로 확인할 수 있어.

122 정답 ⑤ 123 정답 ⑤

지문 All in One

(인생은 힘들 수 있다 / 돌아다니는 것 / 항상 / 그리고 느끼지 않는 것 / 실제로 당신이 정말 원하는 어떤 것도 끝낸 것처럼)

1 Life(S) can be(V) hard(C) / — running around / all the time / [and] never feeling / like you actually get *anything* [(that)(관계대명사) you really want] done.

(습관이 도움을 줄 수 있다) **2** Habits(S) can help(V).

(그것들은 나를 도와주었다 / 더 조직화되게 / 그리고 나의 하루에서 더 많은 시간을 찾게) **3** They(S)'ve helped(V) me(O) / to get more organized(C_1) / [and] find(C_2) more time in my day.

(습관은 당신 삶의 일부가 된 것들이다 / 심지어 당신이 그것들에 대해 생각조차 하지 않고 / 어떤 뇌 공간도 차지하지 않기 때문에 / 당신에게 더 많은 시간을 주는 경향이 있다 / 당신이 심지어 그것을 깨닫지 않고도)

4 Habits(S_1) are(V_1) *things*(C) [that(관계대명사) become part of your life / without you even thinking about them], // [and] because(접속사) they(S′) don't take up(V′) any brain space, / they(S_2) tend(V_2) to give you more time / without you even realizing it.

(당신이 이를 닦을 때 / 매일 / 당신은 그것을 결코 하지 않은 것에 대해 생각하는가 / 아니면 그것을 그냥 하는가)

5 When(접속사) you(S′) brush(V′) your teeth / each day, // do you(S_1) think(V_1) about not doing it at all, / [or] do you(S_2) just do(V_2) it?

(결국 / 우리 모두는 이를 닦는다 / 매일 아침과 저녁에 / 그것은 몇 분이 소요된다)

6 After all, / we all(S) brush(V) our teeth / every morning [and] evening // — it(S) takes(V_1) a few minutes /

어휘확인

run around 돌아다니다 **all the time** 항상 **actually** 실제로, 사실은 **habit** 습관 **get organized** 조직화되다 **take up** 차지하다 **tend to-v** ~하는 경향이 있다 **realize** 깨닫다 **brush one's teeth** 이를 닦다 **avoid** 피하다 **positive** 긍정적인 **nature** 천성 **smoothly** 순조롭게, 평탄하게

〈선택지 어휘〉

create 창조하다 **be full of** ~으로 가득 차다 **unexpected** 예기치 않은 **difficulty** 어려움 **remove** 없애다, 제거하다 **helper** 도우미 **meaningless** 의미 없는 **practical** 유용한, 실용적인

그러고 나서 끝난다 / 우리는 그것을 피할 길을 찾지 못한다 / 우리는 그것이 해야 할 필요가 있음을 알기 때문에

and then is done. [7] We don't find *a way* [to avoid it], // as we know (that) it needs to be done,

그리고 몇 시에 그리고 하루 중 언제 그것을 해야 하는지 알기 (때문에) / 그것은 하기에 아주 단순해져서

/ and we know what time and when in our day we should do it. [8] It has become so **simple**

우리는 그것을 그냥 한다 / 그것은 습관이 되었다 / 만약 우리가 만들 수 있다면 / 많은 긍정적인 것들을

to do / that we just do it. [9] It's become a habit. [10] If we can make / lots of positive things / in

우리 인생에서 / 이와 같은 습관으로 / 그 결과 그것들을 제2의 천성이 되게 한다면 / 그 다음에 우리는 스스로를 도울 수 있다

our life / a habit like this, / so that they become second nature, // then we can help ourselves,

그리고 우리의 삶은 더 원활하게 돌아갈 것이다 / 매일 매일

/ and our lives will run more smoothly / each and every day.

122 ① Habits Create Who We Are
습관은 우리가 누구인지 창조한다
② Life Is Full of the Unexpected
인생은 예기치 못한 것으로 가득 차 있다
③ Tips to Get Organized in Your Study
공부에서 조직화되는 비결
④ The Difficulty of Removing Bad Habits
나쁜 습관을 없애는 것의 어려움
⑤ Habit: A Helper in Managing Our Life
습관: 우리의 인생을 관리하는 도우미

123 ① hard 어려워 ② meaningless 의미 없어 ③ special 특별해 ④ practical 유용해 ⑤ simple 단순해

지문 Flow

[주제문]
습관이 인생에 도움을 줄 수 있음

[보충설명]
습관은 삶을 조직화시켜 많은 시간을 찾게 해줌

[예시]
매일 이를 닦을 때 생각하지 않고 습관처럼 단순하게 행동함

[주제 재진술]
긍정적인 것들을 습관으로 만들어서 제2의 천성이 되게 하면, 삶이 순조로워질 것임

해석 한 눈에 보기 1 인생은 힘들 수 있는데, 그것은 항상 돌아다니는 것이며 실제로 당신이 정말 원하는 어떤 것도 끝낸 것처럼 느끼지 않는 것이다. 주제문 2 습관이 도움을 줄 수 있다. 3 그것들은 나를 더 조직화시키고 나의 하루에서 더 많은 시간을 찾게 도와주었다. 4 습관은 심지어 당신이 그것들에 대해 생각조차 하지 않고 당신 삶의 일부가 되는 것들이며, 어떤 뇌 공간도 차지하지 않기 때문에 당신이 심지어 그것을 깨닫지 않고도 당신에게 더 많은 시간을 주는 경향이 있다. 5 매일 이를 닦을 때, 당신은 그것을 결코 하지 않은 것에 대해 생각하는가, 아니면 그것을 그냥 하는가? 6 결국, 우리 모두는 매일 아침과 저녁에 이를 닦고, 그것은 몇 분이 소요되고 나서 끝난다. 7 우리는 그것이 해야 할 필요가 있음을 알고, 몇 시에 그리고 하루 중 언제 그것을 해야 하는지 알기 때문에 그것을 피할 길을 찾지 못한다. 8 그것은 하기에 아주 단순해져서 우리는 그것을 그냥 한다. 9 그것은 습관이 되었다. 주제문 10 만약 우리가 인생에서 많은 긍정적인 것들을 이와 같은 습관으로 만들어서 그 결과 제2의 천성이 되게 할 수 있다면, 그 다음에 우리는 스스로를 도울 수 있고 우리의 삶은 매일 매일 더 순조롭게 돌아갈 것이다.

정답단추

122 글의 제목 문제는 핵심 내용을 가장 잘 압축한 것을 제목으로 고르면 돼. 이 글은 습관이 인생에 도움을 줄 수 있다는 내용으로 시작하고 있어. 습관은 모르는 사이에 삶의 일부가 되니까, 인생에서 긍정적인 것들을 습관으로 만들면 인생에 도움이 될 수 있고, 순조로운 삶을 살 수 있다는 것이 핵심 내용이야. 따라서 글의 제목으로 가장 적절한 것은 ⑤야.

123 빈칸 문제는 빈칸을 포함한 문장을 먼저 읽고 무엇에 중점을 두어야 하는지 파악한 후에 나머지 내용을 읽는 것이 좋아. 빈칸을 포함한 문장은 그것은 하기에 아주 '무엇'해서 우리가 그냥 그것을 한다는 내용이야. 여기서 그것은 이를 닦는 것이지. 이를 닦는 것은 특별한 생각 없이 아침저녁으로 하는 일이고, 불과 몇 분 안에 끝나는 일이야. 또한 언제 해야 하는지도 이미 알고 있는 것이지. 즉, 아주 단순하게 할 수 있는 일이라는 말이야. 따라서 빈칸에 들어갈 말로 가장 적절한 것은 ⑤ 'simple'이야.

오답단서

122 ①은 '습관'이라는 단어가 나오지만, 습관이 우리의 인생에 도움을 줄 수 있다는 내용과는 동떨어지므로 답이 될 수 없어. ②, ③은 지문에서 다루지 않은 내용이므로 오답이야. ④는 좋은 습관을 만들면 인생에 도움이 된다는 내용은 있지만, 나쁜 습관에 대한 내용은 언급되지 않으므로 제목으로 적절하지 않아.

124 정답 ④ 125 정답 ④

지문 All in One

우리 중 많은 사람들이 자랐다 / 들으면서 / 우리가 우리 자신의 운명을 통제한다는 것을

[1] Many of us have grown up / being told / that we are in control of our own fate / — that we

우리가 궁극적인 통제를 한다는 것을 / 성공하는지 아닌지에 대해 / 일부 사람들은 여전히 이 개념을 지지할지도

have ultimate control / over whether we succeed or not. [2] While some may still hold onto

모르지만 / 그것은 종종 우울증과 실패감의 근원이 된다 / 우리가 인생에서 성공하지 못할 때

this notion, // it is often the root of depression and sense of failure / when we don't succeed

어떤 나라가 부자가 되기 위해서는 / 훌륭한 경제 및 정부 체제와 확립된 사회 기반 시설이 필요하다

in life. [3] In order for a country to be rich, / you need a good system of economics and

다른 요소들 중에서 / 하지만 / '부유한'

government, and an established infrastructure, / among other factors. [4] However, / being a

어휘확인

fate 운명 ultimate 궁극적인, 최후의 succeed 성공하다 notion 개념, 관념 root 근원, 뿌리 depression 우울증 economics 경제 government 정부 established 확립된 infrastructure 사회 기반 시설 factor 요인, 인자 citizen 시민 focus on ~에 주력하다, ~에 초점을 맞추다 money-related 돈에 관련된 tend to-v ~하는 경향이 있다 rate 비율 situation 상황, 처지 successful 성공적인 cf. success 성공 unprepared 준비가 되지 않은 personal 개인의 business 사업

나라가 된다는 것은 / 의미하지 않는다 / 그 나라의 시민들이 행복하다는 것을 / 사람들이 돈과 관련된 목표에 집중하는 사회는
"rich" country / doesn't mean // that its citizens are happy. 5 *Societies* [where the people focus on money-related goals] / tend to have high rates of depression. 6 What can be said / about this situation?

높은 비율의 우울증을 겪는 경향이 있다 / 무엇을 말할 수 있겠는가 / 이러한 상황에 대해

7 All of the successful [and] "rich" countries in the world / have *a culture* [focused on success], // [and] that leaves people **unprepared** / for personal [or] business failure. 8 Constant innovation is often a top priority / in such a social atmosphere. 9 Engineers [and] those in technical fields drive innovation, // [and] it is often these workers / that suffer from a great sense of failure / from being unable to advance. 10 Remember, / failure is natural / [and] to be expected. 11 Life is not just about succeeding. 12 You still have to go on // if you're met with difficulties / on your journey.

세계의 성공적이고 '부유한' 모든 국가들은 / 성공에 중점을 둔 문화를 가지고 있다 / 그리고 그것은 사람들을 준비가 되지 않은 상태로 둔다 / 개인적 또는 사업적 실패에 / 끊임없는 혁신은 종종 최우선 순위이다 / 그러한 사회적 분위기에서 / 엔지니어와 기술 분야의 사람들은 혁신을 추진시킨다 / 그리고 흔히 바로 이러한 노동자들이다 (강조구문) / 큰 실패감으로 고통 받는 사람은 / 진보할 수 없는 것으로부터 / 기억하라 / 실패는 자연스럽다는 것을 / 그리고 예상될 수 있음을 / 인생은 단지 성공하는 것에 관한 것이 아니다 / 당신은 여전히 계속해야 한다 / 당신이 어려움을 만나면 / 여정에서

constant 끊임없는 innovation 혁신, 쇄신 priority 우선 사항 atmosphere 분위기 technical (과학) 기술의, 기술적인 drive 추진시키다 suffer from ~으로 고통 받다 advance 진보하다, 전진하다 expect 예상하다 journey 여정, 여행

〈선택지 어휘〉
financially 재정적으로, 금융적으로 create 만들어 내다, 창조하다 obsession 집착, 강박 상태 modern 현대의, 근대의 pressure 압력, 압박 shortcut 지름길 unnoticed 눈에 띄지 않는 eager 열망하는 respected 높이 평가되는 ignorant 무지한, 무식한

지문 Flow

[주제문]
성공 여부가 자신에게 달려 있다는 말을 들으면서 자라면 성공하지 못했을 때 우울증과 실패감의 근원이 됨

↓

[보충설명]
부유한 나라가 곧 그 나라의 시민들이 행복한 것은 아님

↓

[보충설명 재진술]
부유한 나라들은 성공에 중점을 둔 문화를 가지고 있어서, 혁신이 최우선 순위인 분위기에서 사람들이 실패감으로 고통 받음

↓

[첨언]
실패는 자연스러운 것임

124 ① What Makes a Country Financially Successful
무엇이 국가를 재정적으로 성공하게 하는가
② Successful Nations Create Successful People
성공한 국가는 성공적인 국민들을 만든다
③ The Obsession of Modern Man with Success
성공한 현대인들의 집착
④ Cultural Pressure to Succeed Brings People Down
성공하기 위한 문화적 압력은 사람들을 패배시킨다
⑤ Innovation as a Shortcut to Economic Success
경제적 성공의 지름길로서의 혁신

125 ① unnoticed 눈에 띄지 않는
② eager 열망하는
③ respected 평판이 좋은
④ unprepared 준비가 안 된
⑤ ignorant 무지한

해석 한 눈에 보기 **주제문** 1 우리 중 많은 사람들이 우리가 우리 자신의 운명을 통제한다는, 즉, 우리가 성공하는지 아닌지에 대해 궁극적인 통제를 한다는 말을 들으면서 자랐다. 2 일부 사람들은 여전히 이 개념을 지지할지도 모르지만, 우리가 인생에서 성공하지 못할 때 그것은 종종 우울증과 실패감의 근원이 된다. 3 어떤 나라가 부자가 되기 위해서는, 다른 요소들 중에서 훌륭한 경제 및 정부 체제와 확립된 사회 기반 시설이 필요하다. 4 하지만, '부유한' 나라가 된다는 것은 그 나라의 시민들이 행복하다는 것을 의미하지 않는다. 5 사람들이 돈과 관련된 목표에 집중하는 사회는 높은 비율의 우울증을 겪는 경향이 있다. 6 이러한 상황에 대해 무엇을 말할 수 있겠는가? 7 세계의 성공적이고 '부유한' 모든 국가들은 성공에 중점을 둔 문화를 가지고 있으며, 그것은 사람들을 개인적 또는 사업적 실패에 준비가 되지 않은 상태로 둔다. 8 끊임없는 혁신은 종종 그러한 사회적 분위기에서 최우선 순위이다. 9 엔지니어와 기술 분야의 사람들은 혁신을 추진시키며, 진보할 수 없는 것으로부터 큰 실패감으로 고통 받는 사람은 흔히 바로 이러한 노동자들이다. 10 실패는 자연스럽고 예상될 수 있음을 기억하라. 11 인생은 단지 성공하는 것에 관한 것이 아니다. 12 당신은 여정에서 어려움을 만나면 여전히 계속해야 한다.

정답단추

124 글의 제목은 글의 핵심 내용을 담고 있는 주제문을 찾아서 이를 가장 잘 반영한 것을 고르면 돼. 글의 초반부에서 우리는 성공 여부가 우리 자신에게 달려 있다는 말을 들으면서 자라서 성공하지 못했을 때 우울증과 실패감을 겪는다고 했어. 뒤이어서 보충설명이 이를 더 구체적으로 뒷받침하고 있어. 두 번째 단락도 유사한 내용이 이어지고 있는데, 문화 자체가 성공에 중점을 둔 나라들은 사람들이 실패했을 때 고통을 준다는 것이야. 이 두 단락은 모두 성공을 중시하는 문화가 사람들을 부정적인 감정으로 이끈다는 것이므로 글의 제목으로 가장 적절한 것은 ④야.

125 빈칸 추론 문제는 빈칸을 포함한 문장을 먼저 읽는 게 좋아. 빈칸 문장을 보면 부유한 국가는 성공에 중점을 둔 문화를 가지고 있어서 사람들을 실패에 '무엇'한 상태로 둔다고 하고 있어. 뒤이은 문장에서 이러한 사회 분위기는 혁신을 추진시키고, 진보할 수 없음으로부터 사람들은 큰 실패감으로 고통을 받는다고 했어. 즉, 사람들이 실패에 준비되지 않은 것이지. 그러므로 빈칸에 들어갈 말로 가장 적절한 것은 ④야.

오답단서

124 ①, ②, ③, ⑤는 모두 성공을 키워드로 만든 선택지들이야. ①, ②는 부유한 국가들이 가지는 성공 문화에 대한 내용이 나오긴 하지만, 부분적인 내용이므로 답이 될 수 없어. ③은 글에 나오지 않는 내용으로 만든 선택지야. ⑤도 글의 후반부에 혁신에 대한 내용이 나오긴 하지만, 성공이 중점인 문화에서 혁신이 최우선 순위가 된다는 내용이므로 제목으로 적절하지 않아.

125 ①은 내용상 어색해서 답이 될 수 없어. ②, ③은 실패와는 연관성이 적은 선택지들이니까 적절하지 않아. ⑤는 오답으로 고를 수 있는 가능성이 가장 높은데, 성공에 중점을 두는 분위기 때문에 실패에 준비가 안 되어 있다는 말이지, 실패에 무지한 것은 아니라서 답이 될 수 없어.

유형 12 심경, 분위기 파악

Check-Up 1 1 ② 126 ④
Check-Up 2 3 ② 127 ⑤
Mini Test 1 ② 2 ① 3 ② 4 ①
실전적용독해 128 ② 129 ④ 130 ①

Check-Up 1

정답 1 ②
해석 나는 모든 것이 엉망이 되어 있는 것을 발견했다. 싱크대 위의 창문이 깨져 있었고, 수백 개의 유리 조각들이 우리 부엌 바닥을 엉망진창으로 만들어 놓았다. 내 다리가 너무 심하게 떨리고 있어서 나는 거의 가만히 서 있을 수가 없었다.

126 정답 ④

지문 All in One

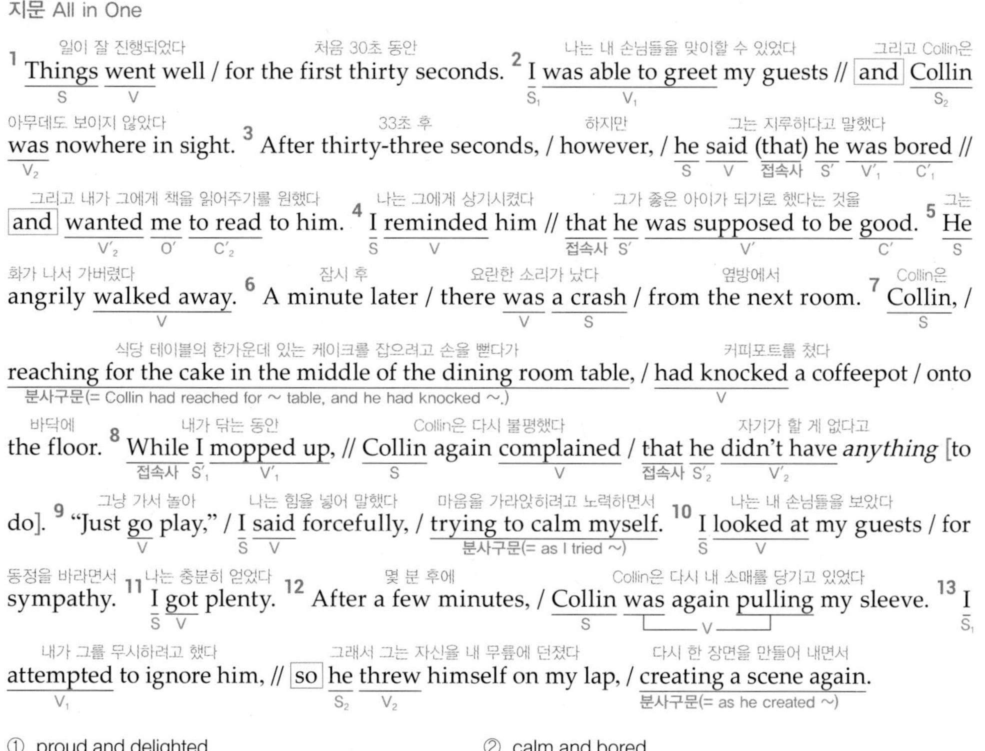
1 Things went well / for the first thirty seconds. 2 I was able to greet my guests // and Collin was nowhere in sight. 3 After thirty-three seconds, / however, / he said (that) he was bored // and wanted me to read to him. 4 I reminded him // that he was supposed to be good. 5 He angrily walked away. 6 A minute later / there was a crash / from the next room. 7 Collin, / reaching for the cake in the middle of the dining room table, / had knocked a coffeepot / onto the floor. 8 While I mopped up, // Collin again complained / that he didn't have *anything* [to do]. 9 "Just go play," / I said forcefully, / trying to calm myself. 10 I looked at my guests / for sympathy. 11 I got plenty. 12 After a few minutes, / Collin was again pulling my sleeve. 13 I attempted to ignore him, // so he threw himself on my lap, / creating a scene again.

① proud and delighted
자랑스럽고 기쁜
② calm and bored
평온하고 지루한
③ disappointed and nervous
실망스럽고 초조한
④ embarrassed and annoyed
당황스럽고 짜증이 난
⑤ expectant and hopeful
기대하고 희망에 찬

해석 한 눈에 보기 1 일이 처음 30초 동안 잘 진행되었다. 2 나는 내 손님들을 맞이할 수 있었고 Collin은 아무데도 보이지 않았다. 3 그러나 33초 후, 그는 지루하다고 말했고, 내가 그에게 책을 읽어주기를 원했다. 4 나는 그가 좋은 아이가 되기로 했다는 것을 그에게 상기시켰다. 5 그는 화가 나서 가버렸다. 6 잠시 후 옆방에서 요란한 소리가 났다. 7 Collin은 식당 테이블의 한가운데 있는 케이크를 잡으려고 손을 뻗다가 커피포트를 쳐서 바닥에 쓰러뜨렸다. 8 내가 닦는 동안, Collin은 자기가 할 게 없다고 다시 불평했다. 9 "그냥 가서 놀아."라고 단호하게 말하면서 나는 마음을 가라앉히려고 노력했다. 10 나는 동정을 바라면서 내 손님들을 보았다. 11 나는 충분히 얻었다. 12 몇 분 후에, Collin은 다시 내 소매를 당기고 있었다. 13 내가 그를 무시하려고 했으므로, 그는 자신을 내 무릎에 던져서 다시 한 장면을 만들어냈다.

정답단추 필자의 심경을 묻는 문제니까, 필자가 처한 상황을 파악하는 것이 우선이야. 필자가 집에 손님을 초대한 상황에서, 필자의 아들이 보채고 말썽을 피우며 필자를 귀찮게 하고 있어. forcefully, trying to calm myself, ignore 등의 어구에서 필자의 심경을 유추할 수 있지. 따라서 'I'의 심경으로 가장 적절한 것은 ④야.

어휘확인
greet 맞이하다 **guest** 손님 **in sight** 보이는 곳에, 시야 안에 **bored** 지루한 **remind** ~에게 생각나게 하다 **be supposed to** ~하기로 되어 있다 **angrily** 화내어, 성나서 **crash** 요란한 소리, 충돌 **reach for** ~을 잡으려고 손을 뻗다 **knock** 치다[부딪치다] **coffeepot** 커피포트 **mop up** (물을) 닦아내다, 훔치다 **forcefully** 힘을 넣고, 격렬하게 **calm oneself** 마음을 가라앉히다 **sympathy** 동정, 연민 **plenty** 충분히, 많이 **sleeve** 소매 **attempt** 시도하다 **ignore** 무시하다 **scene** 장면
〈선택지 어휘〉
delighted 아주 기뻐하는 **disappointed** 실망한 **embarrassed** 당황스러운 **annoyed** 짜증이 난 **expectant** 기대하는 **hopeful** 희망에 찬

지문 Flow

[발단]
집에 손님이 옴

[전개]
Collin이 지루하다고 책을 읽어 달라고 했는데, 들어주지 않음

[위기]
옆방에서 요란한 소리가 났고 Collin이 커피포트를 바닥에 쓰러뜨림

[절정]
다시 불평을 하는 Collin에게 가서 놀라고 하면서 마음을 가라앉히려고 노력함

[결말]
몇 분 후, Collin이 다시 옆에 와서 내 무릎에 몸을 던짐

Check-Up 2

정답 3 ②
해석 커다란 굉음 / 화염 / 두 번 더 폭발 / 이미 바다 속으로 가라앉은

127 정답 ⑤

지문 All in One

1 Linda leaned over / to admire *the bouquet of peach-colored roses* [(which) she had just bought]. 2 It was a smell (that) she remembered / from her childhood. 3 Her mind wandered fancifully / from the flowers to *the wonderful smell of fresh bread* [coming from the bakery next door]. 4 Standing to the side of the entrance / was an amateur juggler. 5 With his wildly colored costume, / he attracted / *an audience of children* [who giggled / each time he made a mistake]. 6 She walked a bit closer, / careful not to disturb the gathered children. 7 She watched a few minutes, // and found herself giggling too. 8 He finished his performance / with a bow / toward Linda. 9 She took a deep bow in return // and handed him a rose.

① lonely 외로운
② sympathetic 동정적인
③ depressing 우울한
④ mysterious 불가사의한
⑤ pleasant 즐거운

해석 한 눈에 보기 1 Linda는 몸을 구부려 자신이 방금 산 복숭아 빛깔의 장미꽃 다발에 감탄했다. 2 그것은 자신의 어린 시절부터 기억하는 바로 그 냄새였다. 3 그녀의 마음이 상상에 빠져 꽃에서부터 옆집 제과점에서 나는 갓 구운 빵의 좋은 냄새로 흘러갔다. 4 입구 옆에는 한 아마추어 저글러가 서 있었다. 5 그는 아주 화려한 복장을 하고 자신이 실수할 때마다 킥킥거리며 웃는 아이들 관중의 마음을 사로잡았다. 6 그녀는 모여 있는 아이들을 방해하지 않으려고 조심하면서 조금 더 가까이 걸어갔다. 7 그녀는 몇 분간 쳐다보았고, 자신 역시 킥킥거리며 웃고 있는 것을 발견했다. 8 그는 Linda에게 고개 숙여 인사하면서 공연을 마쳤다. 9 그녀는 답례로 고개를 깊이 숙여 인사했고, 그에게 장미 한 송이를 건넸다.

정답단추 분위기를 묻는 문제인 만큼 전체적인 맥락에서 글의 분위기를 파악해야 해. 따라서 글의 사건이나 등장인물 묘사에 쓰인 형용사나 부사 등의 수식어구에 주목하여 글을 읽어보자. admire, rose, wandered fancifully, fresh bread, giggled 등의 어휘를 통해 즐겁고 평화로운 분위기를 느낄 수 있지. 따라서 가장 적절한 답은 ⑤라고 할 수 있어.

어휘확인

lean over ~로 몸을 구부리다 **admire** 감탄하다; 존경하다 **bouquet** 꽃다발 **peach-colored** 복숭아 색의 **rose** 장미(꽃) **childhood** 어린 시절 **wander** (마음·생각이) 다른 데로 팔리다 **fancifully** 상상 속에나 나올 것 같이; 비현실적으로 **entrance** (출)입구 **amateur** 아마추어 **juggler** 저글러(물건을 이리저리 던지며 묘기 부리는 사람) **wildly** 아주, 극도로 **colored** 색깔이 있는 **attract** 유혹하다, 마음을 끌다 **audience** 관중[관객] **giggle** 킥킥거리며 웃다 **make a mistake** 실수를 하다 **a bit** 조금, 약간 **disturb** 방해하다 **bow** (고개 숙여 하는) 인사 cf. **take a bow** 인사를 하다 **in return** 답례로 **hand** 건네주다

〈선택지 어휘〉
sympathetic 동정적인 **depressing** 우울한 **pleasant** 즐거운

지문 Flow

[발단]
Linda는 장미꽃 다발을 구입함

[전개]
꽃향기를 맡으면서 마음이 상상에 빠짐

[절정]
빵집 입구 옆에서 공연하는 저글러를 아이들과 함께 구경하면서 아이들에 동화됨

[결말]
공연이 끝난 후, 저글러와 인사를 나누었고 그에게 장미 한 송이를 줌

기출총정리

Mini Test 1 ② 2 ① 3 ② 4 ①

Mini Test 해석 및 해설

1 **해석** 나는 처음으로 살아있는 고래를 보고 있었다. 나는 각 고래의 몸 전체를 볼 수는 없었고, 그것들이 물을 내뿜기 위해 수면 위로 올라올 때 그것들의 등만을 볼 수 있었다. 그러나 그것은 나를 아주 흥분하게 만들기에 충분했다. 나는 야생에서 그렇게 큰 동물을 본 적이 없었다. 말만으로는 이 최초의 광경이 어떻게 나에게 영향을 미쳤는지 묘사할 수 없다. ① 무관심한 ② 매료된

2 **해석** 그런 후에 그는 아주 많은 갖가지 명령어를 입력했다. 그것은 전혀 소용이 없었다. 그는 짜증이 나서 침착하게 있을 수가 없었다. 어떤 이유인지 그는 거듭되는 오류 메시지를 받고 있었다. 그는 그것들이 무엇을 의미하는지를 이해할 수 없었다. 그는 짜증이 나서 머리를 흔들었다. ① 짜증 난 ② 안도하는

3 **해석** 마침내 더 이상의 경고 없이 그 동물이 시야에 나타났다. 그는 자신의 맥박이 목구멍에서 요동치는 것을 느꼈다. 그의 생각들이 서로 필사적인 경주를 하고 있는 것 같았다. ① 활기찬 ② 긴박한

4 **해석** 갇힌 광부들을 구해 내기 위해 애쓰던 세 명의 구조대원들 또한 광산의 한쪽 벽이 폭발하여 그들을 묻어 버리면서 사망했다. 그들은 광부들의 어떤 징후도 보거나 듣지 못하여, 여섯 명 모두가 실종되었고 어쩌면 죽은 것으로 여겨졌다. 모든 구조 노력은 결국 포기되었다. ① 비극적이고 낙심시키는 ② 무섭고 불가사의한

128 정답 ②

지문 All in One

경찰관들은 그들의 순찰차에서 나왔다 / 그리고 주차장을 건넜다 / 걸어서 / 그들은
1 The officers exited their patrol car // [and] crossed the parking lot / on foot. 2 They
S_1 V_1 V_2 S

아파트로 다가갔다 / 조심스럽게 / Tennant는 속삭였다 / 그의 후배 파트너인 Roscoe에게
approached the apartment / with caution. 3 Tennant whispered / to his junior partner,
V S V =

출입구 반대편으로 가라 / 그리고 문을 열어봐라 / 그 어린 경찰관은 조용하고
Roscoe, // "Get to the other side of the doorway / [and] try the door." 4 The younger officer
V_1 V_2 S

빠르게 움직였다 / 그가 하라고 훈련받았던 대로 / 그는 부드럽게 손잡이를 돌렸다
moved quietly [and] quickly, // as he had been trained to do. 5 He gently turned the doorknob.
V 접속사 S′ V′ S V

그것은 잠겨 있지 않았다 / 지금이야 / Tennant가 소리쳤다 / 그들은 함께 아파트로 뛰어들었다
6 It wasn't locked. 7 "Now!" // shouted Tennant. 8 Together they burst into the apartment. 9 A
S V V S S V S

몇 초가 지났다 / 그들이 방을 훑어보는 동안 / 그때 / 큰 소리가 났다 / 아파트의 뒤쪽에서
few seconds passed // as they scanned the room. 10 Then, / a loud noise came / from the back
V 접속사 S′ V′ S_1 V_1

그리고 Roscoe는 재빨리 달려갔다 / 소리를 향해서 / Tennant가 소리쳤다 / 안돼
of the apartment, // [and] Roscoe ran quickly / toward the sound. 11 Tennant shouted / "No!"
S_2 V_2 S_1 V_1

하지만 몇 초 후 / 그 어린 경찰관은 쓰러져 있었다 / 바닥에 / 심한 총상으로 피를 흘리며
// [but] seconds later, / the young officer was lying / on the floor, / bleeding from a serious
S_2 V_2 분사구문(= as he bled from ~)

그의 어깨에
bullet wound / to his shoulder.

① festive and noisy 축제 같고 시끄러운
② tense and urgent 긴장되고 긴박한
③ hopeful and lively 희망차고 활기찬
④ strange and confusing 이상하고 혼란스러운
⑤ happy and harmonious 행복하고 조화로운

해석 한 눈에 보기 1 경찰관들이 그들의 순찰차에서 나와 주차장을 걸어서 건넜다. 2 그들은 조심스럽게 아파트로 다가갔다. 3 Tennant는 그의 후배 파트너인 Roscoe에게 "출입구 반대편으로 가서 문을 열어봐."라고 속삭였다. 4 그 어린 경찰관은 그가 훈련받았던 대로 조용하고 재빠르게 움직였다. 5 그는 부드럽게 손잡이를 돌렸다. 6 그것은 잠겨 있지 않았다. 7 "지금이야!"라고 Tennant가 소리쳤다. 8 그들은 함께 아파트로 뛰어들었다. 9 그들이 방을 훑어보는 동안 몇 초가 지났다. 10 그때 큰 소리가 아파트 뒤쪽에서 났고, 그래서 Roscoe는 재빨리 소리가 나는 쪽으로 달려갔다. 11 Tennant가 "안 돼!"라고 소리쳤지만, 몇 초 후 그 어린 경찰관은 바닥에 쓰러져 있었고, 심한 총상으로 어깨에 피를 흘리고 있었다.

정답단추 글의 분위기를 묻는 문제는 전체적인 맥락을 파악하는 것이 중요하니까 글의 상황을 상상하며 읽는 게 좋아. 또한 형용사나 부사 등의 수식어구를 주목해서 볼 필요가 있어. 이 글은 두 명의 경찰관이 아파트에 잠입했다가 한 명이 총에 맞아서 상처를 입는 장면을 묘사하고 있어. with caution, quietly and quickly, bleeding from a serious bullet wound 등의 표현에서 긴장되고 긴박한 상황임을 느낄 수 있지. 따라서 정답은 ②야.

어휘확인

officer (직함을 나타내어) 경찰관; 장교 **exit** 나가다; 출구 **patrol car** 순찰차 **parking lot** 주차장 **on foot** 걸어서 **approach** 다가가다 **with caution** 조심스럽게 **whisper** 속삭이다 **junior** 후배, 부하 **doorway** 출입구 **quietly** 조용히 **doorknob** 손잡이 **lock** 잠그다 **burst into** ~로 갑자기 뛰어들다 **scan** 훑어보다 **then** 그때 **bleed** 피를 흘리다 **bullet wound** 총상(총에 맞은 상처)

〈선택지 어휘〉

festive 축제 같은, 축하하는 **tense** 긴장한 **urgent** 긴박한 **hopeful** 희망에 찬 **lively** 활기찬 **confusing** 혼란스러운 **harmonious** 조화로운

지문 Flow

[발단] 경찰관들이 아파트로 다가감

↓

[전개] 후배 파트너를 출입구 반대편으로 가서 문을 열게 함

↓

[위기] 그들은 아파트로 뛰어들어 방을 훑어봄

↓

[절정] 아파트 뒤쪽에서 큰 소리가 났고, 후배 경찰관이 그쪽으로 달려감

↓

[결말] 후배 경찰관이 총상으로 바닥에 쓰러짐

129 정답 ④

지문 All in One

어떤 여성이 내 자리에 앉았다 / 교회에서 / 얼마 전에 / 그것은 그렇게 중요하지 않았다 / 정말 / 그녀는
1 A lady took my seat / in church / a while back. 2 It's not that important / really. 3 She is a
S V S V C S V

매우 좋은 숙녀분이다 / 그리고 좋은 친구이기도 (하다) / 어떤 사람이라도 편해야 한다 / 어디에나
very nice lady, / [and] a good friend, too. 4 Any person should be comfortable / sitting
C_1 C_2 S_1 V_1 C_1

앉아 있으면서 / 그러므로 그것이 큰 문제는 아니다 / 나는 확신한다 / 그녀가 내 자리에 앉을 의도가 아니었다고 / 나는 내 자리를
anywhere, // [so] it's no big deal. 5 I'm sure / (that) she didn't intend to take my seat. 6 I love
S_2 V_2 C_2 S V C 접속사 S′ V′ S V

아주 좋아한다 / 그러나 / 나는 결코 요란을 피우지 않을 것이다 / 자리에 대해 / 그녀는 아마도 개인적인 것을 의도하지 않았
my seat. 7 But / I would never raise a fuss / about a seat. 8 She probably didn't intend
S V S V

을 것이다 / 내 자리에 앉음으로써 / 사실 / 약 3개월 전이었다
anything personal / by taking my seat. 9 Actually, / it was about three months ago // when
S V 접속사

그녀가 내 자리에 앉았던 때 / 나는 정말 모른다 / 왜 그녀가 그 자리를 차지했는지 / 나는 그녀에게 결코 아무 짓도 하지 않았기 때문에
she took my seat. 10 I really don't know / why she took it, // since I've never done anything to
S′ V′ S V 간접의문문 = my seat 접속사 S′ V′

어휘확인

a while back 얼마 전에 **a big deal** 큰 사건, 큰 거래 **intend** 의도하다, 작정하다 **raise a fuss** 요란을 피우다, 호들갑을 떨다 **probably** 아마 **insensitive** 무신경한, 둔감한 **parking** 주차

〈선택지 어휘〉

pleasant 즐거운 **regretful** 후회하는

지문 Flow

[발단] 어떤 여성이 교회에서 내 자리에 앉음

↓

나는 결코 그녀의 자리에 앉지 않았다 / 그러나 보아라 / 이것은 위대한 사회적 불공평이 시작되는 방식이다

her. 11 I've never taken her seat. 12 But see! 13 This is *the way* [great social injustices begin]: /

무신경한 사람들이 교회에서 다른 사람들의 자리를 차지하는 것 / 사람들은 단지 앉을 것이다 / 그들이 마음에

insensitive people taking other people's seats in church. 14 People will just sit / *anywhere*

드는 어디에나 / 그리고 그들이 그 다음에 할 일은 / 내 주차 자리도 차지하는 것이다

[they please]. 15 And *the next thing* [(that) they'll do] / is (to) take my parking place, too.

S 관계대명사 V C

① pleasant 즐거운
② regretful 후회하는
③ excited 흥분된
④ upset 화가 난
⑤ lonely 외로운

[전개]
사람은 어디에나 편히 앉을 수 있어야 하고, 그녀도 다른 의도 없이 그 자리에 앉았다고 생각해서 그냥 둠

⬇

[위기]
3개월째 계속 그 여성이 내 자리에 앉음

⬇

[결과]
사회적 불공평이 시작됨

⬇

[추측]
사람들은 마음에 드는 어디에나 앉을 것이고, 내 주차 자리도 차지할 것임

해석 한 눈에 보기 1 어떤 여성이 얼마 전에 교회에서 내 자리에 앉았다. 2 그것은 정말 그렇게 중요하지 않았다. 3 그녀는 매우 좋은 숙녀분이고, 좋은 친구이기도 하다. 4 어떤 사람이라도 어디에나 앉아 있으면서 편해야 하므로, 그것이 큰 문제는 아니다. 5 나는 그녀가 내 자리에 앉을 의도가 아니었다고 확신한다. 6 나는 내 자리를 아주 좋아한다. 7 그러나 나는 결코 자리에 대해 요란을 피우지 않을 것이다. 8 그녀는 아마도 내 자리에 앉음으로써 개인적인 것을 의도하지 않았을 것이다. 9 사실, 그녀가 내 자리에 앉았던 때는 약 3개월 전이었다. 10 나는 그녀에게 결코 아무 짓도 하지 않았기 때문에, 왜 그녀가 그 자리를 차지했는지 정말 모른다. 11 나는 결코 그녀의 자리에 앉지 않았다. 12 그러나 보아라! 13 이것은 위대한 사회적 불공평이 시작되는 방식이다. 무신경한 사람들이 교회에서 다른 사람들의 자리를 차지하는 것. 14 사람들은 단지 그들이 마음에 드는 어디에나 앉을 것이다. 15 그리고 그들이 그 다음에 할 일은 내 주차 자리도 차지하는 것이다.

정답단추 글에 심경을 알 수 있는 어휘가 나오지 않는 경우, 필자의 심경을 알기 위해서 자신을 글의 주인공으로 가정하고 상상해보는 것도 좋은 방법이야. 필자는 교회에서 3개월째 자신의 자리에 앉은 여성에 대해 말하고 있어. 사람들은 어디에나 앉을 수 있고, 여자도 어떤 의도 없이 그 자리에 앉았을 테니 그는 비켜 달라는 말을 하지 않았어. 하지만 그는 그런 상황을 불공평하다고 생각하고 있어. 의도를 가지지 않고 무신경한 사람들이 다른 사람에게 피해를 줌으로써 자신이 피해를 보고 있다는 것이지. 이런 상황에서 필자는 화가 났을 거야. 따라서 필자의 심경으로 가장 적절한 것은 ④야.

130 정답 ①

지문 All in One

어느 금요일 오후 / 나는 가는 길이었다 / 로스앤젤레스에서 팜스프링스로 / 내가 멈춰

1 One Friday afternoon, / I was on my way / from Los Angeles to Palm Springs. 2 As I came

S V 접속사 S'1 V'1

서면서 / 긴 자동차 줄 뒤에 / 나는 백미러를 흘깃 보고 발견했다

to a stop / behind a long line of cars, // I glanced in my rear-view mirror to discover / that the

S V 부사적 용법(결과) 접속사

내 뒤의 차가 멈추지 않고 있다는 것을 / 사실 / 그것은 나를 향해 오고 있었다 / 엄청난 속도로

car behind me was not stopping. 3 In fact, / it was coming toward me / with tremendous

S'2 V'2 S V

나는 깨달았다 / 그 운전자가 주의를 기울이지 않고 있다는 것을 / 그리고 내가 세게 부딪히리라는 것을

speed. 4 I realized // that the driver was not paying attention / and that I was going to be hit

S V 접속사 S'1 V'1 접속사 S'2 V'2

나는 내 눈을 감았다 / 숨을 쉬었다 / 그리고 내 손들을 떨어뜨렸다 / 내 옆으로 / 그때 나는

hard. 5 I closed my eyes, / took a breath, / and dropped my hands / to my sides. 6 Then I was

S V1 V2 V3 S V

부딪혔다 / 막대한 힘으로 / 움직임과 소음이 멈췄을 때 / 나는 내 눈을 떴다

hit / with enormous force. 7 When the movement and noise stopped, // I opened my eyes.

접속사 S' V' S V

내 차는 압축되었다 / 아코디언처럼 / 하지만 나는 괜찮았다 / 경찰은 내게 말했다 / 내가

8 My car was compacted / like an accordion, // but I was fine. 9 The police told me / (that) I

S1 V1 S2 V2 C S1 V1 IO 접속사

운이 좋았다고 / 내가 긴장을 풀고 있어서 / 근육의 긴장은 가능성을 증가시키기 때문이다 / 중상의

was lucky / (that) I had relaxed, // for muscle tension increases the likelihood / of severe

DO 접속사 = because S2 V2

injury.

① frightened → relieved
겁먹은 안도하는

② excited → disappointed
신이 난 실망한

③ ashamed → proud
부끄러운 자랑스러운

④ comfortable → anxious
편안한 불안한

⑤ curious → annoyed
궁금한 짜증 난

해석 한 눈에 보기 1 어느 금요일 오후에 나는 로스앤젤레스에서 팜스프링스로 가는 길이었다. 2 긴 자동차 행렬 뒤에 멈춰 서면서, 나는 백미러를 흘깃 보았다가 내 뒤의 차가 멈추지 않고 있다는 것을 발견했다. 3 사실 그것은 엄청난 속도로 나를 향해 오고 있었다. 4 나는 그 운전자가 주의를 기울이지 않고 있다는 것, 그리고 내가 세게 부딪히리라는 것을 깨달았다. 5 나는 눈을 감았고, 심호흡했고, 양손을 양옆으로 내렸다. 6 그때 나는 막대한 힘에 부딪혔다. 7 그 움

어휘확인

on one's way to ~로 가는 길[도중]에 **come to a stop** 멈춰 서다 **glance** 흘깃 보다 **rear-view mirror** (자동차의) 백미러 **discover** 발견하다 **in fact** 사실 **tremendous** 엄청난 **realize** 깨닫다 **pay attention (to)** (~에) 주의를 기울이다 **hit** 부딪치다; 때리다 **take a breath** 숨을 쉬다 **then** 그때 **enormous** 막대한 **force** 힘 **movement** 움직임 **compact** 압축하다; 다지다 **accordion** 아코디언 **relax** (근육 등의) 긴장을 풀다; 휴식을 취하다 **tension** 긴장 **increase** 증가시키다 **likelihood** 가능성 **severe injury** 중상(아주 심한 부상)

〈선택지 어휘〉

frightened 겁먹은 **relieved** 안도하는 **disappointed** 실망한 **anxious** 불안한 **curious** 궁금한 **annoyed** 짜증이 난

지문 Flow

[발단]
어느 금요일 오후, 로스앤젤레스에서 팜스프링스로 차로 이동함

⬇

[전개]
긴 자동차 행렬 뒤에 멈춰 서면서 백미러를 통해 뒤에 오는 차를 봄

⬇

[위기]
뒤에 오는 차가 엄청난 속도로 달려와서 세게 부딪힘

직임과 소음이 멈췄을 때, 나는 눈을 떴다. 8 내 차가 아코디언처럼 찌그러져 있었지만, 나는 괜찮았다. 9 경찰은 내게 내가 긴장을 풀고 있어서 운이 좋았다고 말했는데, 근육의 긴장은 중상의 가능성을 증가시키기 때문이다.
정답단추 필자의 심경 변화를 묻는 유형이니까 등장인물이 처한 상황을 파악하는 게 중요해. 또한, 사건의 흐름 묘사에 쓰인 어구도 주의 깊게 살펴보자. 필자는 운전 중 뒤차가 멈추지 않아서 세게 부딪힐 것을 알았으니 처음에는 겁을 먹었을 거야. 사고 후에 차는 완전히 찌그러졌지만, 필자는 크게 다치지 않았다고 했으니 안도했겠지? 따라서 필자의 심경 변화로 적절한 것은 ①이야.

[절정]
차가 아코디언처럼 찌그러짐

[결말]
근육에 긴장을 풀고 있어서 다행히 다치지 않음

미니 모의고사 4 유형 11 | 유형 12

131 ④ 132 ② 133 ② 134 ⑤ 135 ④ 136 ⑤ 137 ③ 138 ④ 139 ③
140 ④ 141 ⑤ 142 ④ 143 ④ 144 ① 145 ⑤ 146 ① 147 ③ 148 ⑤

131 정답 ④

지문 All in One

1 When George got to Belle's house, // there had already been a visitor there / before him. 2 Ed Handby had come to the door / and was calling Belle / out of the house. 3 George had wanted / to ask this woman / to come away with him / and to be his wife, // but when he saw her standing / by the door / with Ed, // he lost his self-assurance // and his face turned red. 4 "You stay away from that kid," // he yelled, / and then, / not knowing what else to say, / turned to go away. 5 "If I see you together again, // I won't be able to control myself," // he added. 6 George had come to express his love, / not to threaten, // and now was angry with himself / for losing his temper / in front of everyone.

(주석: George가 Belle의 집에 도착했을 때 / 이미 그곳에 방문한 사람이 있었다 / 그 이전에 / Ed Handby가 문 앞에 왔다 / 그리고 Belle을 불러내고 있었다 / 집 밖으로 / George는 원했다 / 이 여성에게 요청하기를 / 자신과 함께 떠나 달라고 / 그리고 그의 아내가 되어 달라고 / 하지만 그가 그녀가 서 있는 것을 보았을 때 / 문 옆에 / Ed와 함께 / 그는 자신감을 잃었다 / 그리고 그의 얼굴은 달아올랐다 / 당신은 그 애와 떨어져 있어 / 그가 소리쳤다 / 그리고 그 다음에 / 다른 무슨 말을 해야 할지 몰라서 / 돌아서 갔다 / 만약 내가 너희를 다시 함께 본다면 / 나는 자제할 수 없을 거야 / 그가 덧붙였다 / George는 그의 사랑을 표현하기 위해 왔다 / 협박하려고가 아니라 / 그런데 이제 스스로 화가 났다 / 화를 냈기 때문에 / 모두 앞에서)

(문법: When 접속사, George S′, got V′; had already been V, a visitor S; Ed Handby S, had come V_1, was calling V_2; George S_1, had wanted V_1; when 접속사, he S′, saw V′, her O′, standing C′; he S_2, lost V_2; his face S_3, turned V_3, red C; You S, stay away V; he S, yelled V_1; not knowing what else to say 분사구문(= because he didn't know ~); turned V_2; If 접속사, I S′, see V′; I S, won't be able to control V; he S, added V; George S, had come V_1, to express 부사적 용법(목적), to threaten 부사적 용법(목적); was V_2, angry C)

① satisfied 만족스러운 ② frightened 겁먹은 ③ pleased 기쁜
④ jealous 질투하는 ⑤ hopeful 희망에 찬

해석 한 눈에 보기 1 George가 Belle의 집에 도착했을 때, 이미 그 이전에 그곳에 방문한 사람이 있었다. 2 Ed Handby가 문 앞에 와서 Belle을 집 밖으로 불러내고 있었다. 3 George는 이 여성에게 자신과 함께 떠나서 아내가 되어 달라고 요청하고 싶었지만, 그녀가 Ed와 함께 문 옆에 서 있는 것을 보았을 때, 그는 자신감을 잃었고 얼굴은 달아올랐다. 4 "당신은 그 애와 떨어져 있어."라고 그가 소리쳤고, 그 다음에 다른 무슨 말을 해야 할지 몰라서, 돌아서 갔다. 5 "만약 내가 너희를 다시 함께 본다면, 나는 자제할 수 없을 거야."라고 그가 덧붙였다. 6 George는 협박하려고가 아니라 그의 사랑을 표현하기 위해 왔는데, 이제 모두 앞에서 화를 냈기 때문에 스스로 화가 났다.
정답단추 등장인물의 심경을 묻는 문제이므로 그 사람이 처한 상황을 파악하는 게 중요해. George가 Belle에게 청혼을 하러 갔는데, Belle과 Ed가 함께 있는 것을 보았으니 아마도 질투가 났을 거야. George가 한 말을 통해 George의 질투 어린 심경을 엿볼 수 있지. 따라서 George의 심경으로 가장 적절한 것은 ④야.

어휘확인
visitor 방문객 **self-assurance** 자신(감) **yell** 소리 지르다 **threaten** 협박하다, 위협하다 **lose one's temper** 화를 내다

지문 Flow

[발단]
George가 Belle의 집에 도착했을 때, 이미 Ed가 와서 Belle을 불러내고 있었음

[전개]
George는 Belle에게 청혼하러 왔지만, 다른 사람과 있는 것을 보고 자신감을 잃음

[위기]
George가 Belle에게 Ed와 만나지 말라고 소리침

[절정]
또한 George는 둘이 함께 있는 것을 보면 참지 않겠다고 함

[결말]
George는 질투 때문에 화를 내버린 자신에게 화가 남

132 정답 ②

지문 All in One

[1] Warren was a middle-aged professor. [2] But the college faced a budget shortfall, // and took the step of eliminating / a number of its departments, / including Warren's. [3] For him, / everything seemed to have been destroyed. [4] Instead of giving up, / however, / Warren realized // how much the world had to offer. [5] He chose / to focus on *the opportunity* [set / before him]. [6] Never before had he had / *the chance* [to start again], / [to decide / what he wanted to do / and where he wanted to do it]. [7] He wound up taking a year off / from the world / to live in a rural town. [8] And how did he feel / at the end of the year? [9] "I've never been better."

(Warren은 중년의 교수였다 / 그런데 대학이 예산 부족에 직면했다 / 그리고 / 없애는 조치를 취했다 / 그것의 많은 학과를 / Warren의 것을 포함하여 (= college's) / 그에게 / 모든 것이 파괴된 것처럼 보였다 / 포기하는 대신에 / 그러나 / Warren은 / 깨달았다 / 세상이 제공할 수 있는 것(기회)이 얼마나 많은지를 (간접의문문) / 그는 선택했다 / 놓여 있는 기회에 초점을 맞추는 것을 / 그의 앞에 / 그는 전에는 절대로 가졌던 적이 없었다 (부정어, 조동사 S V) / 다시 시작할 기회를 / 결정할 (기회를) / 그가 무엇을 하길 원했는지 (간접의문문) / 그리고 어디에서 그가 그것을 하길 원했는지 (간접의문문) / 그는 1년의 휴가를 얻게 되었다 / 세상으로부터 / 시골 마을에서 살았다 (부사적 용법(결과)) / 그리고 그가 어떻게 느꼈을까 / 그해의 마지막에 / 저는 더 좋은 적이 없었어요)

① relaxed → frightened
여유 있는 무서운
② discouraged → satisfied
낙심한 만족한
③ proud → ashamed
자랑스러운 부끄러운
④ comfortable → anxious
편안한 불안한
⑤ curious → annoyed
궁금한 짜증 난

해석 한 눈에 보기 1 Warren은 중년의 교수였다. 2 그런데 대학이 예산 부족에 직면하여, Warren 교수의 학과를 포함한 많은 학과를 없애는 조치를 취했다. 3 그에게 있어 모든 것이 파괴된 것처럼 보였다. 4 그러나 포기하는 대신 Warren은 세상이 제공할 수 있는 것(기회)이 얼마나 많은지를 깨달았다. 5 그는 자신 앞에 놓여 있는 기회에 초점을 맞추는 쪽을 선택했다. 6 이전에 그는 한 번도 다시 시작할, 즉 그가 무엇을 하고 싶고 그것을 어디에서 하고 싶은지를 결정할 기회를 가져본 적이 없었다. 7 그는 세상으로부터 1년간 휴가를 얻게 되어서 시골마을에서 살았다. 8 그리고 그가 그해의 마지막에 어떻게 느꼈을까? 9 "저는 이보다 더 좋은 적이 없었어요."

정답단추 심경의 변화를 묻는 문제니까 우선 등장인물이 처한 상황을 파악하면서 심경을 묘사하는 표현들에 유의해야 해. 이 글은 Warren 교수가 대학에서 실직하게 되어 절망을 느꼈지만, 포기하지 않고 그것을 기회로 삼아 자신이 그동안 하지 못했던 것을 하면서 만족을 느끼게 되었다는 내용이야. For him, everything ~ destroyed.와 마지막 문장 I've never been better.가 Warren 교수의 심경 변화를 추론할 수 있는 결정적 단서라고 할 수 있어. 따라서 Warren 교수의 심경 변화로는 ②가 적절해.

어휘확인

middle-aged 중년의 **professor** 교수 **face** 직면하다; 얼굴 **budget** 예산 **shortfall** 부족 **take a step** 조치를 취하다 **eliminate** 없애다 **a number of** 많은, 다수의 **department** 학과 **include** 포함하다 **destroy** 파괴하다 **realize** 깨닫다 **have A to offer** A를 제공할 수 있다 **focus on** ~에 초점을 맞추다 **opportunity** 기회 **wind up v-ing** (어떤 장소·상황에) 처하게 되다 **take off** 휴가를 얻다, 쉬다 **rural** 시골의
〈선택지 어휘〉
relaxed 여유 있는 **frightened** 무서운 **discouraged** 낙심한 **satisfied** 만족한 **anxious** 불안한 **curious** 궁금한 **annoyed** 짜증 난

지문 Flow

[발단]
예산 부족으로 Warren 교수의 학과가 없어짐

[전개]
그는 포기하지 않고 세상이 제공하는 기회에 초점을 맞추는 것을 선택함

[절정]
그는 1년 휴가를 얻게 되어서 시골마을에서 삶

[결말]
그는 만족감을 느낌

133 정답 ② 134 정답 ⑤ 135 정답 ④

지문 All in One

(A) [1] One day / a young mother left her daughter Bonnie / with their next-door neighbor // while (a) she went to work. [2] Later in the day, / as Bonnie was playing on the neighbor's front lawn, // a car came flying around the corner, / out of control. [3] It flew up onto the lawn // and hit the little girl, / knocking her into the street. [4] By the time the police and the ambulance arrived, // she had stopped breathing.

(어느 날 / 한 젊은 엄마가 자신의 딸 Bonnie를 맡겼다 / 옆집 이웃에게 / 자신(엄마)이 일하러 가 있는 동안에 (접속사 S' V') / 그날 나중에 / Bonnie가 이웃집 앞마당 잔디에서 놀고 있을 때 / 차 한 대가 모퉁이를 돌아 날아 왔다 / 중심을 잃고 / 그것은 잔디 위로 날아 올라왔고 / 그리고 / 그 어린 소녀를 치어 / 도로로 나동그라지게 했다 (분사구문(= and it knocked ~)) / 경찰과 구급차가 도착했을 때쯤에 / 그 아이는 숨을 멈췄다)

(C) [5] One of the nurses at the hospital / called the mother // and shared this terrible news / as gently as possible. [6] Although the hospital offered / to send *someone* [to drive the

(병원의 간호사들 중 한 명이 / 소녀의 엄마에게 전화했고 / 이 끔찍한 소식을 말했다 / 가능한 한 조심스럽게 / 병원이 제안했지만 / 엄마를 태워줄 사람을 보내겠다고)

어휘확인

leave with ~에게 맡기다 **next-door** 옆집의 **front** 앞쪽 **lawn** 잔디(밭) **out of control** 중심을 잃은, 통제불능의 **onto** ~(위)로 **hit** (사람·물건·차 등이) ~에 부딪히다, 충돌하다 **knock** (때리거나 타격을 가해) ~한 상태가 되게 만들다; 노크하다 **by the time** ~할 때쯤에 **ambulance** 구급차 **although** (비록) ~이긴 하지만 **offer** 제안하다 **drive** 태워다 주다 **insist on** ~을 고집하다 **emotionless** 감정이 없는 **lifelessly** 죽은 것처럼 **table** 수술대; 테이블 **completely** 완전히 **break down** 허물어지다[감정을 주체하지 못하다] **injury** 부상 **remain** 계속 ~이다 **staff** (전체) 직원 **emergency room** 응급실 **pay phone** 공중전화 **relative** 친척 **policeman** 경찰관 **first** 최초의 인물; 첫째 **scene** 현장 **walk**

mother in], // (c) she insisted on making the long drive herself. [7] Finally the mother walked into the hospital, / (being) emotionless // until she saw her little girl lying lifelessly on the table. [8] She completely broke down.

(B) [9] The doctors sat down with her // and explained her daughter's injuries / and what they had done / to try to save her life. [10] This didn't help the mother. [11] The nurse sat down with (b) her // and explained how they had done everything possible / to save her little girl. [12] The mother remained upset — so hurt // that the staff thought / (that) they might have to treat this poor mother. [13] Then the mother walked through the emergency room / to the pay phone, / to call her relatives.

(D) [14] Seeing (d) her, / *the policeman* [who had been sitting there / for almost four hours] / stood up. [15] He had been *the first* [to arrive on the scene], / the *one* [who had held little Bonnie in his arms]. [16] He walked up to this mother // and told her what had happened, / adding, / "I just want you to know / (that) she was not alone." [17] The mother was so grateful / to hear // that in her daughter's last moments / on this earth, / (e) she was held and (was) loved. [18] The mother finally felt consoled, / knowing (that) her daughter had felt love / at the end of life, // even if it was from a stranger.

133 ① (B) - (D) - (C) ② (C) - (B) - (D) ③ (C) - (D) - (B) ④ (D) - (B) - (C) ⑤ (D) - (C) - (B)

134 ① (a) ② (b) ③ (c) ④ (d) ⑤ (e)

135 ① Bonnie는 이웃집에서 놀다가 차 사고를 당했다. ② 간호사가 사고 소식을 엄마에게 알렸다. ③ 엄마는 직접 운전해서 병원으로 왔다. ④ 간호사의 말이 엄마에게 위안을 주었다. ⑤ 경찰관은 사고를 당한 Bonnie를 안아 주었다.

해석 한 눈에 보기 (A) 1 어느 날 한 젊은 엄마가 (a) 자신(엄마)이 일하러 가 있는 동안에 자신의 딸 Bonnie를 옆집 이웃에게 맡겼다. 2 그날 나중에, Bonnie가 이웃집 앞마당 잔디에서 놀고 있을 때, 차 한 대가 느닷없이 모퉁이를 돌아 중심을 잃고 달려왔다. 3 그것은 붕 날아올라 잔디 위를 덮쳤고 그 어린 소녀를 치어, 도로로 나동그라지게 했다. 4 경찰과 구급차가 도착했을 무렵, 그 아이는 숨을 멈춘 상태였다. (C) 5 병원에 있던 간호사 중 한 명이 이 끔찍한 소식을 소녀의 엄마에게 가능한 한 조심스럽게 전했다. 6 병원이 사람을 보내 엄마를 차로 데려오겠다고 제안했지만, (c) 그녀(엄마)는 그 장거리 운전을 스스로 하겠다고 고집했다. 7 마침내 엄마가 병원으로 걸어 들어왔는데, 자신의 어린 딸이 죽은 것처럼 수술대 위에 누워 있는 것을 볼 때까지 감정을 억누르고 있었다. 8 그녀가 감정을 주체하지 못하고 완전히 허물어졌다. (B) 9 의사들이 그녀와 함께 앉았고 딸의 부상과 딸의 목숨을 살려 보려고 무엇을 했는지를 설명했다. 10 이것은 엄마에게 도움이 되지 않았다. 11 간호사가 (b) 그녀(엄마)와 함께 앉아 그녀의 어린 딸을 구하기 위해 그들이 가능한 모든 것을 어떻게 했는지를 설명했다. 12 엄마는 고통스러운 채로 계속 있었는데, 너무 아파해서 의료진들은 이 불쌍한 엄마를 치료해야 할지도 모른다고 생각했다. 13 그 때 엄마는 응급실을 지나 공중전화로 걸어갔는데 친척들에게 전화하기 위해서였다. (D) 14 (d) 그녀(엄마)를 보자, 그곳에서 거의 4시간 동안 앉아 있었던 경찰관이 일어섰다. 15 그는 현장에 처음으로 도착한 사람이었고, 자신의 양팔로 어린 Bonnie를 안았던 사람이었다. 16 그는 이 엄마에게로 걸어가 그녀에게 무슨 일이 일어났는지를 말해 주면서 "저는 다만 어머니가 따님이 혼자가 아니었다는 것을 아셨으면 해요."라고 덧붙였다. 17 엄마는 자신의 딸의 이 세상에서의 마지막 순간에 (e) 그녀(Bonnie)가 안겨져 있었고 사랑받고 있었다는 말을 듣고 너무나 고마웠다. 18 엄마는 마침내 위안을 느꼈는데, 자신의 딸이 비록 낯선 사람으로부터였지만 생의 마지막에 사랑을 느꼈다는 것을 알게 되었기 때문이다.

up (to) (~ 쪽으로) 걸어가다 **grateful** 고마워하는 **earth** 세상; 지구 **console** 위안을 주다, 위로하다 **even if** (비록) ~일지라도

지문 Flow

[발단]
한 젊은 엄마가 자신의 딸 Bonnie를 이웃에게 맡김

[전개]
자동차가 앞마당에서 놀고 있던 Bonnie를 치어 숨지게 함

[위기]
간호사가 엄마에게 소식을 전했고 병원으로 달려온 엄마는 감정을 주체하지 못함

[절정]
의사와 간호사가 딸을 살리기 위해 한 일을 말하지만, 엄마는 계속 고통스러워함

[결말]
엄마는 딸을 현장에서 데려온 경찰관의 이야기를 듣고 자신의 딸이 생의 마지막 순간에 사랑을 느꼈음을 알게 되어서 비로소 위안을 받음

정답단추

133 글의 순서는 각 문단을 읽고 내용상 자연스럽게 이어지는지를 파악해야 해. 이를 위해서는 사건의 전개에 따른 등장인물의 심경 변화와 동작 그리고 연결어, 지칭어 등을 유심히 살펴보는 게 좋아. 먼저 (A)는 이웃집에 맡겨진 Bonnie가 자동차 사고를 당해서 죽었다는 내용이야. 그다음으로는 그 소식을 듣고 병원으로 달려온 엄마가 고통스러워한다는 내용의 (C)가 오는 것이 자연스러워. 그리고 소녀의 엄마를 의사들과 간호사가 위로하지만, 소용이 없다는 (B)가 오고, 마지막으로 현장에 처음 도착해 딸을 안아 주었던 경찰이 엄마를 위로하자 마침내 엄마가 위안을 받는다는 내용의 (D)가 와야 글이 유기적으로 잘 연결될 수 있어. 따라서 이 글의 적절한 순서는 ② '(C) – (B) – (D)'야.

134 각각의 대명사가 가리키는 대상을 찾을 때는 밑줄 친 대명사의 앞뒤를 자세히 살펴볼 필요가 있어. 우선 (a)는 딸을 맡기고 일을 간 엄마를 가리키고 있어. 또한, (b), (c), (d)는 병원에서 교통사고로 죽은 딸아이를 마주하는 엄마의 심경 변화를 다루고 있는 상황에서 나오고 있으므로 모두 엄마를 지칭해. 그러나 (e)는 문맥상 바로 앞 문장에서 언급된 경찰의 팔에 안겨 죽은 딸(Bonnie)을 가리키고 있어. 그래서 지칭 대상이 다른 하나는 (e)야.

135 지문과 선택지의 내용이 일치하는지 판단하기 위해서는 반드시 지문에서 근거를 찾아 확인하는 것이 좋아. (B) 단락에서 간호사의 거듭된 위로와 설명에도 엄마는 계속 고통스러워했다고 하고 있지? 그리고 경찰관이 딸아이가 마지막에 혼자가 아니었다고 하자 비로소 엄마는 위안을 받았다고 했으니까, 간호사의 말이 엄마에게 위안을 주었다는 것은 글의 내용과 일치하지 않아. 따라서 정답은 ④야.

오답단서

135 (A)에서 Bonnie가 이웃집 앞마당 잔디에서 놀다가 차 사고를 당했다고 했으니 ①은 지문과 일치하는 내용이야. 또한, ②, ③은 (C)의 간호사가 엄마에게 전화해서 소식을 전했고, 그녀 스스로 운전을 하여 병원에 왔다는 내용을 통해 확인할 수 있지. 마지막으로 ⑤의 경찰관이 사고를 당한 Bonnie를 안아주었다는 내용은 (D)에서 찾을 수 있어.

136 정답 ⑤ 137 정답 ③

지문 All in One

(모든 사람은 결정을 내린다 / 항상 / 그 중 일부는 크다 / 그 중 일부는 작다)
1 Everybody makes decisions / all the time — // some of them (are) big, / some of them (are) small.

(우리는 만족감을 얻는다 / 결정의 결과에서 뿐만이 아니라 / 우리가 가정을 생각하는 데 보내는 시간의 양에서도)
2 We gain satisfaction / not just from the outcome of the decision / but also from *the amount of time* [(that) we spend considering *what-ifs*].

(가정은 일어날 수 있는 모든 가능한 것들이다 / 당신의 행동의 결과로서 / 그리고 한계가 없다 / 그것들에는)
3 What-ifs are *all the possible things* [that might happen / as a result of your actions], // and there is no limit / to them.

(그러나 생각하는데 시간을 보내는 것은 / 모든 다른 상상이 가능한 시나리오에 대해 / 가치를 약화시킬 수 있다 / 당신이 내린 결정의)
4 But spending time thinking / about every other imaginable scenario / can **weaken** the value / of *a decision* [(which) you have made].

(가정은 우리를 돕지 않는다 / 가능한 최고의 결과를 만들도록 / 우리가 이미 내린 결정에 대해)
5 What-ifs do not help us / create the best possible outcome / for *the decisions* [(which) we have already made].

(영화감독 Blake Edwards의 첫 번째 경험은 / 영화 업계에서 / 그를 만들었다 / 그 스스로를 의심하도록)
6 Film director Blake Edwards' first experience / in the movie business / made him / doubt himself.

(가정을 생각하는데 많은 시간을 보냈기 때문에 / 저는 계속해서 제 결정을 바꿨습니다 / 잠재적인 투자자들을 기쁘게 하려고 노력하기 위해)
"7 Spending a great deal of time imagining what-ifs, / I continuously changed my decisions / to try to please the potential investors.

(그랬더니 그들은 결정했습니다 / 돈을 투자하지 않기로 / 제 프로젝트에)
8 Then they decided / not to invest money / in my project.

(그것이 ~였습니다 / 앉았을 때 / 그리고 생각했을 (때) / 제가 바꿨던 모든 것에 관해 / 그들을 기쁘게 하려고)
9 That was // when I sat down / and thought / about *everything* [(that) I had changed / to please them]."

(그는 결국 결정했다 / 만약 그가 정말로 영화를 만들 것이라면 / 그것은 그의 영화가 되어야 한다는 것을 / 그들의 것이 아닌)
10 He eventually decided // that if he was really going to make the movie, / it had to be his movie, / not theirs (= their movie).

(나중에 / 그가 말했다 / 그의 영화는 활기를 띄었다고 / 오직 '내가 가정에 대해 생각하는 것을 멈추었을' 때만)
11 Later, / he said // (that) his movie came alive / only when "I stopped thinking about what-ifs."

(문법 표시: 1 Everybody S_1, makes V_1, some of them S_2, (are) V_2, big C_1, some of them S_3, (are) V_3, small C_2 / 2 We S, gain V / 2 (that) 관계대명사 / 3 What-ifs S, are V, all the possible things C, that 관계대명사, is V, no limit S / 4 spending ~ scenario S, can weaken V / 4 (which) 관계대명사 / 5 What-ifs S, do not help V, us O, create C, (which) 관계대명사 / 6 Film director Blake Edwards' first experience S, made V, him O, doubt C / 7 Spending a great deal 분사구문, I S, changed V, to try 부사적 용법(목적) / 8 they S, decided V / 9 That S, was V, when 관계부사, I S′, sat V'_1, thought V'_2, (that) 관계대명사, to please 부사적 용법(목적) / 10 He S, decided V, that 접속사, if 접속사, he S″, was ~ going to make V″, it S′, had to be V′ / 11 he S, said V, (that) 접속사, his movie S′, came V′, alive C′, when 접속사, I S″, stopped V″)

136 ① The Importance of Saving Time
시간을 아끼는 것의 중요성
② Living Today in Dangerous Situations
위험한 상황 속에서 오늘을 살아가는 것
③ Considering Potential Investors in Projects
프로젝트의 잠재적 투자자 고려하기
④ The Necessity of Supporting the Movie Industry
영화 산업 후원의 필요성
⑤ The Uselessness of Thinking about Other Possibilities
다른 가능성들에 대해 생각하는 것의 무용성

어휘확인

make a decision 결정을 내리다 **cf. decision** 결정 **all the time** 항상; 내내 **satisfaction** 만족(감) **not just[only] A but also B** A뿐만 아니라 B도 **outcome** 결과 **amount** 양; 총액 **consider** 생각하다; 고려하다 **what-if** 가정 **as a result of** ~의 결과로서 **imaginable** 상상이 가능한 **cf. imagine** 상상하다 **scenario** (미래에 가능한 일을 묘사한) 시나리오 **weaken** 약화시키다 **value** 가치 **film director** 영화감독 **business** 업계, 사업 **doubt** 의심하다 **a great deal of** 많은 **continuously** 계속해서 **please** 기쁘게 하다 **potential** 잠재적인 **investor** 투자자 **cf. invest** 투자하다 **eventually** 결국 **come alive** 활기를 띠다

〈선택지 어휘〉

importance 중요성 **save** 아끼다; 구하다 **situation** 상황 **necessity** 필요(성) **support** 후원하다; 지지하다 **industry** 산업 **uselessness** 무용성, 쓸모없음 **possibility** 가능성 **replace** 대신하다 **indicate** 나타내다 **calculate** 계산하다

지문 Flow

[도입]
모든 사람은 결정을 내리지만, 그에 따른 가정도 할 수 있음

⬇

[주제]
다른 시나리오에 대한 생각(가정)으로 시간을 보내는 것은 자신의 결정에 대한 가치를 약화시킴

⬇

[보충설명]
가정은 결정에 대한 최고의 결과물을 만드는 데 도움이 되지 않음

⬇

137 ① replace 대신할 ② indicate 나타낼 ③ weaken 약화시킬
④ calculate 계산할 ⑤ imagine 상상할

[예시]
투자자를 기쁘게 하려고 자신의 결정을 계속 바꿨던 영화감독이 결국 투자를 받지 못했고, 결국 그는 자신의 영화를 만들기 위해 가정에 대한 생각을 멈춤

해석 한 눈에 보기 1 모든 사람은 항상 결정을 내리는데, 그중 일부는 크고, 그중 일부는 작다. 2 우리는 결정의 결과에서 뿐만이 아니라 우리가 '가정'하면서 보내는 시간의 양에서도 만족감을 얻는다. 3 가정은 당신 행동의 결과로 일어날 수 있는 모든 가능한 것들이며, 그것에는 한계가 없다. 주제문 4 그러나 모든 다른 상상할 수 있는 시나리오에 대해 생각하면서 시간을 보내는 것은 당신이 내린 결정의 가치를 약화시킬 수 있다. 5 가정은 우리가 이미 내린 결정에 대한 가능한 최고의 결과물을 만드는 데 도움이 되지 않는다. 6 영화 업계에서 영화감독 Blake Edwards의 첫 번째 경험은 그를 스스로에 대해 의심하게 하였다. "7 가정을 생각하는데 많은 시간을 보냈기 때문에, 저는 잠재 투자자들을 기쁘게 하려고 노력하기 위해 제 결정을 계속해서 바꿨습니다. 8 그랬더니 그들은 제 프로젝트에 돈을 투자하지 않기로 했습니다. 9 그때가 제가 자리에 앉아서 그들을 기쁘게 하려고 제가 바꿨던 모든 것에 대해 생각해 본 때였습니다." 10 그는 결국 만일 그가 정말로 영화를 만들 것이라면, 그것은 그들의 것이 아니라 그의 영화가 되어야 한다고 결정을 내렸다. 11 나중에, 그는 자신의 영화는 오직 '내가 가정에 대해 생각하는 것을 멈추었을' 때만 활기를 띠었다고 말했다.

정답단추

136 글의 제목은 전체적인 내용을 압축해서 나타낸다는 거 기억하지? 이 글은 앞부분에서 가정을 생각하는 데 많은 시간을 보내는 것은 오히려 결정의 가치를 약화한다고 언급하고 있어. 그리고 Film director ~ himself.부터는 영화감독인 Blake Edwards의 경험을 예로 들어 주제를 뒷받침하고 있지. 따라서 이를 종합한 제목으로는 ⑤가 적절해.

137 빈칸 문제는 빈칸이 포함된 문장을 먼저 읽고 나머지 글을 통해 빈칸에 들어갈 말을 찾아야 해. 빈칸 문장은 가정을 생각하면서 시간을 보내는 것이 이미 내린 결정에 '어떤' 영향을 미친다는 내용이야. 바로 다음 문장에서 가정을 자꾸 생각하면 우리가 이미 내린 결정에 대해 도움이 되지 않는다고 했고, 뒤이어 영화감독 Blake Edwards의 예시가 이어지며 이를 뒷받침하고 있어. 즉, 가정을 생각하는 것은 이미 내린 결정의 가치를 '약화시킬 수 있다'는 것이므로 빈칸에는 ③이 들어가야 적절해.

오답단서

136 ①은 글에서 자주 언급된 Time을 사용해 만든 제목이지만, 이 글이 시간을 아끼는 중요성에 관한 내용은 아니야. ②는 이 글의 내용과는 전혀 관련이 없어. ③은 글에서 언급된 potential investor와 project가 포함된 제목으로 Blake Edwards의 예시를 보면 답이 될 수 있을 것 같지만, 전체적인 글 내용을 포괄하지는 않아. 마지막으로 ④도 movie business를 movie industry로 다르게 표현한 제목이지만 전체적인 글의 내용과는 관련이 없어.

138 정답 ④

지문 All in One

1 With 30 seconds remaining, / the Huskers(S) will attempt(V) a field goal. 2 After a hard-fought game by both teams, / the Huskers(S) are(V) behind by just one point. 3 The ball(S) is(V) on the 35-yard line. 4 Jeff's mind(S_1) is racing(V_1), // his heart(S_2) is pounding(V_2), // and his palms(S_3) are sweating(V_3). 5 He(S) takes(V_1) a deep breath, / says(V_2) a prayer, / "God bless this kick," / and waits(V_3) for the snap. 6 All(S) goes(V) well; // he(S_1) kicks(V_1) the ball / and watches(V_2) in what(관계대명사) seems like slow motion / as(접속사) the ball(S') sails(V') beautifully between the goal posts. 7 The fans(S) give(V) each other(IO) hugs(DO) and high-fives // as if(가정법 과거) they(S') were(V') on the field themselves. 8 His teammates and TV crews(S) bombard(V) the boy.

(30초가 남아 있는 상태에서 / Huskers팀은 필드골을 시도할 것이다 / 양 팀이 격전을 벌인 뒤에 / Huskers팀은 단 1점을 뒤지고 있다 / 공은 35야드 선상에 있다 / Jeff의 머리는 바쁘게 돌아가고 있고 / 그의 가슴은 쿵쾅거리고 있으며 / 그의 손바닥에는 땀이 나고 있다 / 그는 심호흡하고 / 기도를 하며 / 신이여 이 킥을 축복해 주소서 / 스냅을 기다린다 / 모든 것이 잘되어 가서 / 그는 공을 차고 / 느린 동작과 같은 모습으로 본다 / 마치 / 공이 골대 사이로 아름답게 나아갈 때 / 팬들은 서로를 안고 하이파이브를 한다 / 그들 스스로가 경기장에 있는 것처럼 / 그의 팀 동료들과 TV (중계)팀이 소년을 향해 쏟아 붓는다(우르르 달려든다))

① scary and mysterious 무섭고 불가사의한
② sad and miserable 슬프고 불행한
③ relieved and comforted 안심하고 위안 받은
④ tense and festive 긴장되고 즐거운
⑤ quiet and peaceful 조용하고 평화로운

어휘확인

remain 남아 있다 **attempt** 시도하다 **field goal** 필드골(필드에서 킥하여 얻은 골) **after** ~ 뒤에[후에] **hard-fought** 격전을 벌이는 **behind by** ~만큼 뒤진 **yard** 야드(길이의 단위) **mind** 머리; 마음 **race** (뇌·심장 기능 등이) 바쁘게 돌아가다; 경주하다 **pound** (가슴이) 쿵쾅거리다; 쿵쿵 뛰다 **take a breath** 숨을 쉬다 **say a prayer** 기도를 하다 **God** 신 **bless** (신의) 축복을 빌다 **snap** 스냅(공을 다리 사이로 패스하는 것) **go well** 잘되어 가다 **slow motion** 느린 동작 **sail** (미끄러지듯이) 나아가다; 항해하다 **beautifully** 아름답게 **goal post** 골대 **give ~ a hug** ~을 안다 **high-fives** 하이파이브 **as if** 마치 ~인 것처럼 **teammate** 팀 동료 **crew** 팀, 조 **bombard** 쏟아 붓다[퍼붓다]

〈선택지 어휘〉

miserable 불행한, 비참한 **relieve** 안도하게 하다 **comfort** 위안[위로]하다 **tense** 긴장한 **festive** 즐거운, 축하하는

지문 Flow

[발단]
30초가 남은 상황에서 1점을 뒤진 Huskers팀이 필드골을 시도함

⬇

[절정]
Jeff가 심호흡하고 기도하는 마음으로 스냅을 기다린 후 공을 참

해석 한 눈에 보기 1 30초가 남아 있는 상태에서 Huskers팀이 필드골을 시도할 것이다. 2 양 팀이 격전을 벌인 끝에 Huskers팀이 단 1점을 뒤지고 있다. 3 공은 35야드 선상에 있다. 4 Jeff의 머리는 바쁘게 돌아가고 있고, 그의 가슴은 쿵쾅거리고 있으며, 손바닥에는 땀이 나고 있다. 5 그는 심호흡하고, '신이여, 이 킥을 축복해 주소서'라고 기도하며, 스냅을 기다린다. 6 모든 것이 잘되어 가서, 그는 공을 차고 공이 골대 사이로 아름답게 날아갈 때 느린 동작 같은 모습으로 본다. 7 팬들은 마치 그들 스스로가 경기장에 있는 것처럼 서로 부둥켜안고 하이파이브를 한다. 8 그의 팀 동료들과 TV 중계팀이 소년에게 우르르 달려든다.

정답단추 전체적인 맥락에서 글의 분위기를 파악해야 해. 글을 읽으면서 글의 상황을 머릿속에 상상해봐. 그리고 형용사, 부사 등의 수식어구를 주목해서 보도록 하자. 이 글을 쭉 읽어 보면 Jeff가 속한 팀이 1점을 뒤진 상태였는데 필드골을 성공시켜 환호하는 내용인 걸 알 수 있어. 또한, Jeff's mind ~ sweating.에서 긴장된 분위기를 느낄 수 있지. 더

나아가 give each other hugs and high-fives, bombard the boy 등과 같은 표현으로 즐거운 분위기가 잘 묘사되어 있어. 따라서 가장 적절한 답은 ④야.

[결말]
공이 골대 사이로 날아가자 팬들은 부둥켜안고, 팀 동료들과 TV 중계팀은 Jeff에게 달려감

139 정답 ③

지문 All in One

1 My train was quickly approaching a crossing // when suddenly a yellow school bus appeared ahead! 2 This was *a situation* [(which) I had mentally prepared for] // but [(which I had) never believed / would really happen]. 3 I slammed on the emergency brake, // shut my eyes, // prayed, // and waited / for the terrible crash. 4 There was *nothing else* [(that) I could do]. 5 When the train finally stopped, // I opened my eyes / and saw the bus / in front of the train. 6 My prayers had been answered! 7 If it had been any closer, // it would have been a disaster. 8 I got down / from the train. 9 The driver also got out of the bus // and ran / to give me a great big hug! 10 Oh, / we were both in tears!

(내 기차가 빠르게 건널목에 다가가고 있었다 / 갑자기 노란색 학교 버스 한 대가 앞에 나타났을 때 / 이것은 내가 마음속으로 대비했던 상황이었다 / 하지만 절대 믿지 않았던 (상황이었다) / 실제로 일어날 것이라고는 / 나는 비상 브레이크를 급히 밟았다 / 내 눈을 감았다 / 기도했다 / 그리고 기다렸다 / 끔찍한 충돌을 / 그 밖에 내가 할 수 있는 것은 아무것도 없었다 / 기차가 마침내 멈춰 섰을 때 / 나는 내 눈을 떴다 / 그리고 버스를 보았다 / 기차 앞에 있는 / 내 기도들이 응답되었다 / 만약 그것이 조금만 더 가까웠더라면 / 그것은 참사였을 것이다 / 나는 내렸다 / 기차로부터 / 그 운전자 또한 버스에서 내렸다 / 그리고 달려왔다 / 나에게 아주 커다란 포옹을 하려고 / 오 / 우리는 둘 다 눈물을 흘리고 있었다)

(S, V, S′, V′, 접속사, 관계대명사, C, V_1, V_2, V_3, V_4, 가정법 과거완료, 부사적 용법(목적))

① gloomy → excited (우울한 → 신나는)
② confident → disappointed (자신감 있는 → 실망한)
③ desperate → relieved (절박한 → 안도한)
④ hopeful → discouraged (희망에 찬 → 낙심한)
⑤ joyful → sorrowful (즐거운 → 슬픈)

해석 한 눈에 보기 1 내 기차가 빠르게 건널목에 다가가고 있는데 바로 그때 갑자기 노란색 학교 버스 한 대가 앞에 나타났다! 2 이것은 내가 마음속으로는 대비했었지만 실제로 일어날 것이라고는 한 번도 생각해 보지 않은 상황이었다. 3 나는 비상 브레이크를 쾅 밟았고, 눈을 감았고, 기도했고, 끔찍한 충돌을 기다렸다. 4 내가 할 수 있는 것은 그밖에 아무것도 없었다. 5 기차가 마침내 멈춰 섰을 때, 나는 눈을 떴고 버스가 기차 앞에 있는 것을 보았다. 6 내 기도가 응답되었던 것이다! 7 그것이 조금만 더 가까웠었더라면, 그것은 참사였을 것이다. 8 나는 기차에서 내렸다. 9 버스 기사도 차 밖으로 나와 내게 아주 커다란 포옹을 하려고 달려왔다! 10 오, 우리는 둘 다 눈물을 흘리고 있었다!

정답단추 필자의 심경 변화를 알기 위해서는 이 글의 주인공이 되어 상황을 상상해보는 게 좋아. 필자가 기차를 운전하던 중이었는데 갑자기 학교 버스가 나타나 급하게 브레이크를 밟고 눈을 감고 기도하며 충돌을 기다리는 심정은 절박함 그 자체였을 거야. 그리고 기차가 멈춘 후 충돌이 일어나지 않은 것을 보고는 버스 운전기사와 함께 포옹하며 안도감을 느꼈어. 따라서 필자의 심경은 절박함에서 안도감으로 변했으니까 정답은 ③이야.

어휘확인

approach 다가가다 **crossing** 건널목 **appear** 나타나다 **situation** 상황 **mentally** 마음속으로 **prepare for** ~을 대비하다; ~을 준비하다 **slam on** (브레이크 등을) 급히 밟다 **emergency brake** 비상 브레이크 **shut** (눈을) 감다; (문을) 닫다 **pray** 기도하다 cf. **prayer** 기도 **disaster** 참사 **get down from** ~으로부터 내리다(= get out of) **give ~ a hug** ~을 포옹하다 **in tears** 눈물을 흘리며

〈선택지 어휘〉

gloomy 우울한 **disappointed** 실망한 **desperate** 절박한 **relieved** 안도한 **hopeful** 희망에 찬 **discouraged** 낙심한 **joyful** 즐거운 **sorrowful** 슬픈

지문 Flow

[발단]
기차가 건널목에 다가가던 중, 노란색 학교 버스를 발견함

[위기]
비상 브레이크를 밟고, 눈을 감고 기도함

[절정]
기차가 멈췄을 때, 버스가 기차 앞에 있는 것을 확인함

[결말]
참사를 면했고, 기사들은 눈물을 흘리며 기뻐함

140 정답 ④

지문 All in One

1 Being a parent of a child / with special needs / produces a lot of conflicting emotions. 2 I recall, / for instance, / *a school concert* [in which my son was asked to be the flag-bearer / during several songs]. 3 His face shone with pride / as he tried to hold up the pole, // and at first, / my husband and I shared / his emotions. 4 We felt a warmth / from knowing / that he had a meaningful role / in the concert / and that he was enjoying / a sense of accomplishment. 5 Then, / like a bolt of lightning, / I was struck / by the moving mouths of

(자녀의 부모가 되는 것은 / 특수 교육이 필요한 / 많은 상반되는 감정을 만들어 낸다 / 나는 기억난다 / 예를 들어 / 내 아들이 기수가 되어 달라는 요청을 받았던 학교 콘서트를 / 몇몇 곡 동안 / 그의 얼굴은 자부심으로 빛났다 / 그가 깃대를 들어 올리려고 했을 때 / 처음에는 / 남편과 내가 공유했다 / 그의 감정을 / 우리는 따뜻함을 느꼈다 / 아는 것에서 / 그가 의미 있는 역할을 했다는 것을 / 콘서트에서 / 그가 즐기고 있었다는 것을 / 성취감을 / 그런 다음 / 번개처럼 / 나는 감전되었다 / 다른 모든 5학년 학생들의 움직이는)

(S, V, 전치사+관계대명사, S_1, V_1, 접속사, S′, V′, S_2, V_2, S'_1, V'_1, S'_2, V'_2)

어휘확인

special needs 특수 교육; 특수 요구 **produce** 만들어 내다 **conflicting** 상반되는, 서로 싸우는 **emotion** 감정 **recall** 기억해 내다, 상기하다 **for instance** 예를 들어 **flag-bearer** 기수(旗手) **during** ~ 동안 **several** 몇몇의 **shine** 빛나다(-shone-shone) **pride** 자부심 **hold up** 들어 올리다 **pole** 깃대 **at first** 처음에 **warmth** 따뜻함 **meaningful** 의미 있는 **role** 역할 **sense** -감, 느낌; 감각 **accomplishment** 성취 **a bolt of lightning** 번개 **be struck by** ~에 감전되다; ~에 끌리다 **read music** 악보를 읽다 **remind A of B** A에게 B를 생각나게 하다 **limitation** 한계 **sink** 가라앉다(-sank-sunk) **difference** 차이 **peer** 또래,

입에 의해 / 그들은 모든 노래를 불렀고 / 모든 악보를 읽었다
all the other fifth-graders. 6 They sang all the songs // [and] read all the music. 7 (Being)
S V₁ V₂ 분사구문

내 아들의 한계가 생각나서 / 나는 더 이상 미소를 지을 수 없었다 / 내 마음은 가라앉았다
Reminded of my son's limitations, / I was no longer able to smile. 8 My heart sank // as I
(= Because[since] I was reminded ~) S V S V 접속사 S'

그의 차이점에 대해 생각하면서 / 그리고 그가 서 있는 것을 보면서 / 또래들과 떨어져
thought about his differences / [and] saw him standing / apart from his peers.
V'₁ V'₂ O' C'

① pleased → annoyed (기쁜 → 화가 난)
② sad → pleased (슬픈 → 기쁜)
③ bored → excited (지루한 → 신이 난)
④ proud → sad (자랑스러운 → 슬픈)
⑤ indifferent → interested (무관심한 → 흥미 있는)

해석 한 눈에 보기 1 특수 교육이 필요한 자녀의 부모가 되는 것은 많은 상반되는 감정을 만들어 낸다. 2 예를 들어, 나는 아들이 학교 콘서트를 위해 몇몇 곡 동안 기수(旗手)가 되어 달라는 요청을 받았던 것을 기억한다. 3 그가 깃대를 들어 올리려고 했을 때 그의 얼굴은 자부심으로 빛났고, 처음에는 남편과 내가 그의 감정을 공유했다. 4 우리는 그가 콘서트에서 의미 있는 역할을 했고 성취감을 즐기고 있었다는 것을 아는 것에서 따뜻함을 느꼈다. 5 그런 다음, 번개처럼 나는 다른 모든 5학년 학생들의 움직이는 입에 감전되었다. 6 그들은 모든 노래를 불렀고 모든 악보를 읽었다. 7 내 아들의 한계가 생각나서, 나는 더 이상 미소를 지을 수 없었다. 8 그의 차이점에 대해 생각하고 그가 또래들과 떨어져서 있는 것을 보면서 내 마음은 가라앉았다.

정답단추 심경의 변화를 묻고 있으니까 먼저 등장인물이 처한 상황을 파악하면서 심경을 묘사하는 표현들을 찾아보자. 이 글은 아들이 학교 콘서트에서 기수로 활약했을 때는 그 모습이 자랑스러웠지만, 또래 친구들이 노래를 부를 때는 함께 노래하지 못하는 아들을 보고 안타까워서 슬퍼하는 감정을 엿볼 수 있어. 글의 전반부인 His face shone ~ his emotions.에서 자랑스러워하는 감정을 알 수 있고, 글의 후반부인 Reminded of my son's limitations, ~ from his peers.에서 슬픈 감정을 알 수 있어. 따라서 필자의 심경 변화로 가장 적절한 것은 ④야.

동료

지문 Flow

[주장]
특수 아동의 부모는 자녀에 대해 상반된 감정을 느낌

[예시]
• 학교 콘서트에서 기수로 서 있었던 아들에게 자부심을 느낌
• 또래들이 노래하는 동안 노래를 하는 대신에 기수로 서 있었던 아들에게 안타까움을 느낌

141 정답 ⑤ 142 정답 ④ 143 정답 ④

지문 All in One

나는 체스판을 응시했다 / 믿지 않으며 / 나는 토너먼트 경기를 지게 생겼다
(A) 1 I stared at the chessboard / in disbelief. 2 I was going to lose a tournament game / to *a*
S V S V

두 살 더 어린 선수에게 / 나보다 / 내 상대 / Max는 / 내 킹을 체크 메이트할 수
player [who was two years younger / than I was]. 3 My opponent, / Max, / could put my king
관계대명사 S = V

있을 것이다 / 단 세 수만으로 / 나는 오직 바랐다 / 그(Max)가 그 기회를 보지 못하기를
in mate / in only three moves. 4 I only hoped // that (a) he didn't see the opportunity. 5 (There
S V 접속사 S' V'

그런 행운은 없었다
was) No such luck.
V S

그(Max)는 자신의 비숍을 움직여 자리에 두면서 / 경기를 마지막으로 유발시켰다(몰고 갔다) / 나는 슬프게 바라보
(D) 6 (e) He moved his bishop into position, / setting up the end of the game. 7 I looked sadly
S V 분사구문(= and he set up ~) S V

았다 / 서 계시던 엄마를 / 방의 한쪽에 / 그녀는 알았다 / 경기가 끝난 것을
over / at *my mom* [who was standing / at the side of the room]. 8 She knew / (that) the game
관계대명사 S V₁ 접속사 S'

그러나 미소 지었다 그리고 엄지손가락을 치켜세우는 몸짓을 해주었다 / 어쨌거나 / 다시 체스판으로 돌아와 / 나는
was over // [but] smiled / [and] gave a thumbs-up sign / anyway. 9 Back at the chessboard, / I
V' C' V₂ V₃ S

마지막으로 의미 없는 몇 수를 더 두었다 / 경기를 공식적으로 만들기(마치기) 위해 / 그리고 체스판으로 부터 나와 걸어갔다
made a few last meaningless moves / to make the game official // [and] walked away from the
V₁ 부사적 용법(목적) V₂

내가 할 수 있는 한 빨리 / 곧장 엄마에게로
board / [as] fast [as] I could — / straight to my mom.

모두가 Bobby Fischer가 될 수 있는 것은 아니야 Greg / 엄마가 말씀하셨다 / 엄마는 알고 계셨다
(C) 10 "Not everybody can be Bobby Fischer, Greg," // my mom said. 11 She knew // how I
S V C S V S V 간접의문문

내가 얼마나 Bobby Fischer처럼 되고 싶어 했는지 / 신비롭고 훌륭했던 체스 챔피언인
always wanted to be like Bobby Fischer, / the mysterious [and] brilliant chess champion.
=

Fischer는 미국 체스 챔피언이었다 / 그가 겨우 14살이었을 때 / 나는 깨달았다
12 Fischer was the U.S. Chess Champion // when he was only fourteen years old. 13 I realized
S V C 접속사 S' V' C' S V

내가 그(Bobby Fischer)처럼 되지 못하리라는 것을 / 눈물이 눈에서 솟아오르기 시작했다 / 그리고 나는
// (that) I was not going to be like (d) him. 14 Tears started to well up in my eyes, // [and] I
접속사 S' V' C' S₁ V₁ S₂

메스꺼움이 느껴지기 시작했다 / 우리가 준비가 되어가고 있을 때 / 경기장을 떠날 / 나는 Max가
started feeling sick. 15 As we were getting ready / to leave the competition room, // I saw Max
V₂ 접속사 S' V' S V O

어휘확인

stare at ~을 응시하다 chessboard 체스판 in disbelief 믿지 않는 tournament 토너먼트 opponent (게임·대회 등의) 상대 king ((체스)) 킹 mate(= checkmate) ((체스)) 체크 메이트(킹이 붙잡히게 된 상황, 완전히 패배한 상황) move ((체스)) 수, 두기; 두다, 옮기다 opportunity 기회 bishop ((체스)) 비숍(체스의 말 중 하나) position 자리, 위치 set up 유발시키다 look over ~을 살펴보다 sadly 슬프게 sign 몸짓; 징후 anyway 어쨌든 meaningless 의미 없는 official 공식적인 straight 곧장 brilliant 훌륭한 chess 체스 champion 챔피언, 선수권 대회 우승자 realize 깨닫다 well up 솟아 오르다 feel sick 메스꺼움을 느끼다, 구역질이 나다 get ready 준비를 하다 approach 다가오다[가다] catch up 따라잡다 way 방법 knight ((체스)) 나이트; 기사 attack 공격하다 extend (신체 일부분을) 내밀다 for a second 잠깐 동안, 잠시 react 반응하다 look up at ~을 쳐다보다 then 그때 proudly 자랑스럽게 shake hands 악수하다 stomach 속, 위, 배

지문 Flow

[발단]
나는 두 살 어린 선수인 Max와 체스 경기를 함

[전개]
Max가 비숍을 움직여 경기를 마지막으로 몰고 갔고, 나는 의미 없는 몇 수 후에 경기를 마치고 엄마에게 감

내게 다가오고 있는 것을 보았다
approaching me.
C

(B) 16 "You played a great game," // Max said / as (b) he caught up to me. "17 I especially liked / the way [you used your knights to attack]. 18 I think // you could have had me," // he said / as he extended his hand toward me. 19 For a second, / I didn't know / how to react. 20 I looked up at my mom, // and she just smiled. 21 Then I turned to Max // and proudly shook (c) his hand. "22 Thanks a lot, Max. 23 It was a great game," // I said. 24 Already the sick feeling in my stomach / was gone. 25 "Maybe someday / you can be the next Bobby Fischer!"

(대단한 경기를 하셨어요 / Max가 말했다 / 그(Max)가 나를 따라잡았을 때 / 특히 좋았어요 / 나이트를 사용해서 공격하는 방법이 / 저는 생각해요 / 저를 지게 할 수도 있었다고 / 그는 말했다 / 내게 손을 내밀면서 / 잠깐 동안 / 나는 몰랐다 / 어떻게 반응해야 하는지 / 나는 엄마를 쳐다보았고 / 어머니는 그저 미소 지으셨다 / 그때 나는 Max에게 돌아서서 / 자랑스럽게 그(Max)와 악수했다 / 정말 고마워 Max / 멋진 경기였어 / 나는 말했다 / 이미 속이 메스꺼웠던 느낌은 / 사라졌다 / 어쩌면 언젠가 / 네가 다음(차세대) Bobby Fischer가 될 수 있을 거야)

[위기]
14살에 전미 체스 챔피언이 된 Bobby Fischer처럼 되고 싶었지만 그러지 못한 나를 엄마가 위로함

[절정]
경기장을 떠나려 할 때, 나에게 Max가 다가와 칭찬하는 말을 함

[결말]
나는 Max와 악수하며, 그에게 감사와 칭찬을 전함

141 ① (B) - (D) - (C) ② (C) - (B) - (D) ③ (C) - (D) - (B)
④ (D) - (B) - (C) ⑤ (D) - (C) - (B)

142 ① (a) ② (b) ③ (c) ④ (d) ⑤ (e)

143 ① 체스 경기에서 Max에게 졌다. ② Fischer 같은 챔피언이 되고 싶었다.
③ 실망감에 눈물을 흘렸다. ④ Max를 찾아가 우승을 축하했다.
⑤ 경기가 끝난 후 곧장 어머니에게 달려갔다.

해석 한 눈에 보기 (A) 1 나는 믿지 않으며 눈으로 체스판을 응시했다. 2 나는 토너먼트 경기를 나보다 두 살 더 어린 선수에게 지게 생겼다. 3 내 상대 선수인 Max는 단 세 수만 더 두면 내 킹을 붙잡을 수 있을 것이다. 4 나는 (a) 그(Max)가 그 기회를 보지 못하기만을 바랐다. 5 그런 행운은 없었다. (D) 6 (e) 그(Max)는 자신의 비숍을 움직여 자리에 두면서 경기를 마지막으로 몰고 갔다. 7 나는 방의 한쪽에 서 계시던 엄마를 슬프게 바라봤다. 8 엄마는 경기가 끝난 것을 알고 계셨지만 어쨌거나 미소 지으시며 엄지손가락을 치켜세워 주셨다. 9 다시 체스판으로 돌아와, 나는 마지막으로 의미 없는 몇 수를 더 두어 경기를 공식적으로 마치고 가능한 한 빨리 체스판으로부터 멀리 빠져나와 곧장 엄마에게로 갔다. (C) 10 "모두가 Bobby Fischer가 될 수 있는 것은 아니야, Greg."라고 엄마가 말씀하셨다. 11 엄마는 내가 얼마나 그 신비로울 정도로 훌륭했던 체스 챔피언인 Bobby Fischer처럼 되고 싶어 했는지 알고 계셨다. 12 Fischer는 자신이 겨우 14살이었을 때 전미 체스 챔피언이 되었다. 13 나는 내가 (d) 그(Bobby Fischer)처럼 되지 못하리라는 것을 깨달았다. 14 눈물이 눈에서 솟아오르기 시작했고, 메스꺼움이 느껴지기 시작했다. 15 우리가 경기장을 떠날 준비를 하고 있을 때, 나는 Max가 내게 다가오고 있는 것을 보았다. (B) 16 "대단한 경기를 하셨어요."라고 Max가 (b) 자신(Max)이 나를 따라잡았을 때 말했다. 17 "특히 나이트를 써서 공격하는 방법이 좋았어요. 18 저를 이길 수도 있었다고 생각해요." 그는 내게 손을 내밀면서 말했다. 19 잠깐 동안, 나는 어떻게 반응해야 하는지 몰랐다. 20 나는 엄마를 쳐다보았고, 어머니는 그저 미소 지으셨다. 21 그때 나는 Max에게 돌아서서 자랑스럽게 (c) 그(Max)의 손을 잡고 악수했다. 22 "정말 고마워, Max. 23 멋진 경기였어."라고 나는 말했다. 24 이미 속이 메스꺼웠던 느낌은 사라져 버렸다. 25 "어쩌면 언젠가 네가 차세대 Bobby Fischer가 될 수 있을 거야!"

정답단추

141 글의 전개가 자연스럽게 연결되어야 하니까 대명사나 한정사 등의 쓰임을 유의하여 보자. 또한, 각 단락의 뒷부분에 언급된 내용이 다음 단락의 앞부분에서 계속 이어지는 경우가 있다는 점도 명심해. 이 글은 체스 경기에서 어린 상대 선수 Max에게 진 뒤에 어머니와 상대 선수에게서 위로를 받았던 경험을 다루고 있어. 우선 (A)는 경기 중 자신이 지게 될 것을 알았다는 내용이야. 그리고 결과적으로 경기에 지고 나서 엄마에게 바로 달려갔다는 내용의 (D)가 오는 것이 자연스러워. 그다음 엄마에게서 위로를 받았지만, 패배감이 들었는데 Max가 다가왔다는 내용의 (C)가 이어진 뒤, 그에게서 격려를 받자 상대에게 진정으로 축하할 수 있게 되었다는 내용의 (B)가 오는 것이 자연스러워. 따라서 적절한 답은 ⑤ '(D) – (C) – (B)'야.

142 지문에서 등장한 he, his, him으로 받을 수 있는 대상은 Max와 Bobby Fischer야. 각각의 대명사가 나오면 앞뒤 문장을 확인해서 그 대상을 찾아야 해. ①은 바로 앞 문장에서 언급한 Max를 대신하고 있어. 또한, ②, ③은 Max와 서로 격려와 칭찬을 나누는 상황에서 나오고 있어 모두 Max를 지칭하고 있음을 알 수 있어. 그러나 ④는 앞 문장의 Bobby Fischer를 대신하고 있어. 마지막으로 ⑤는 Max와의 경기 내용이 나와 있으므로 Max를 가리키고 있는 거야. 따라서 가리키는 대상이 다른 하나는 ④야.

143 가장 먼저 선택지와 본문의 내용이 일치하는 것을 고르는 문제인지 불일치하는 것을 고르는 문제인지 지시문을 반드시 확인해야 해. 그리고 선택지를 먼저 읽고 순서대로 본문과 대조하면 돼. Max가 먼저 다가와 훌륭한 경기였다고 자신을 위로해 주었다고 했으므로 Max를 찾아가 우승을 축하해주었다는 ④는 본문의 내용과 일치하지 않아. 따라서 ④가 정답이야.

오답단서

143 ①은 (A)에서 자신보다 두 살 어린 Max에게 체스 경기를 졌다는 내용과 일치해. ②, ③은 (C)를 보면 자신은 Fischer와 같은 체스 챔피언이 되고 싶었고, 그처럼 될 수 없음을 느끼자 눈물이 솟구쳤다는 문장을 통해 확인할 수 있어. ⑤는 (D)의 마지막 문장으로 알 수 있어.

지문 All in One

당신은 상상하는 것조차도 두려워하는가 / 커다란 일이 일어날 수 있다고 / 당신의 인생에서
1 Are you afraid even to imagine / (that) great things could happen / in your life // because
V S C 접속사 S′ V′ 접속사

당신이 실망감에 직면할 수 없기 때문에 / 희망이 산산조각이 나는 것을 보는 것의 / 많은 사람들이 그런 식으로 느낀다
you can't face the disappointment / of seeing hopes go to pieces? 2 A lot of people feel that
S″ V″ S V

그러나 두려워할 필요가 없다 / 최악의 상황조차도 / 인생은 쉽지 않을지도 모른다
way. 3 But there's *no need* [to be afraid / of even the worst situation]. 4 Life may not be easy, //
V S S_1 V_1 C_1

하지만 당신은 항상 그것을 더 좋게 만들 수 있다 / 특히 만약 당신이 기억한다면 / 삶이 당신에게 레몬을 주었을 때
but you can always make it better, / especially if you remember, / when life gives you
S_2 V_2 O C_2 접속사 S′ V′ 접속사 S″ V″ IO″

레모네이드를 만들라는 (말을) / 여기에 좋은 예가 있다 / 거친 권투 세계에서의
lemons — / make lemonade. 5 Here's a good example, / from the tough world of boxing.
DO″ V_3 V S

Gene Tunney는 재능 있는 헤비급 권투선수였다 / KO 파워를 가진 / 양손에
6 Gene Tunney was a talented heavyweight boxer, / with knockout power / in both hands.
S V C

불행하게도 / 그는 너무 많은 뼈를 부러뜨렸다 / 그의 양손의 / 너무 여러 번 / (그래서) ~ 보였다
7 Unfortunately, / he broke so many bones / in his hands / so many times // that it looked /
S V 접속사 S′ V′

그의 경력이 끝났던 것처럼 / 많은 권투선수는 포기했을 것이다 / 만약 그들이 Tunney의 처지였더라면
like his career was over. 8 Many fighters would have given up // if they had been in Tunney's
접속사 S″ V″ C″ S V 가정법 과거완료 접속사 S′ V′

그러나 Tunney는 그만두지 않았다 / 그는 그저 바꿨다 / 운동에 대한 그의 전체적인 접근법을
shoes. 9 But Tunney didn't quit. 10 He simply changed / his entire approach to his sport.
S V S V

그는 그의 스타일을 바꿨다 / 크게 휘두르는 공격적인 선수의 그것에서
11 He altered his style, / from that of a big-swinging aggressive fighter / to that of a master
S V = style = style

계획, 사고, 전략의 고수의 그것으로 / Tunney의 새로운 과학적인 스타일은 효과가 좋았다 / 그리고 그는
of planning, thinking, and strategy. 12 Tunney's new scientific style worked well, // and he
S_1 V_1 S_2

헤비급 권투 세계 챔피언이 되었다 / 1926년에 / Tunney처럼 / 당신은 적응
became the heavyweight boxing champion of the world / in 1926. 13 Like Tunney, / you can
V_2 C_2 S V

할 수 있다 / 인생이 던져주는 것에 / 당신에게 / 당신은 포기할 필요가 없다 / 일이 잘 풀리지 않을 때
adjust / to what life throws / at you. 14 You don't need to give up // when things don't work
관계대명사 S V 접속사 S′ V′

당신이 바라는 식으로
out / the way you hope.
= how

144 ① Keep Fighting: Failure Is Not the End
계속 싸워라: 실패는 끝이 아니다
② Face Your Fears Head On to Find Yourself
자기 자신을 찾기 위해 두려움에 정면으로 직면해라
③ Gene Tunney: Legend of Heavyweight Boxing
Gene Tunney: 헤비급 권투의 전설
④ Who Can Avoid the Troubles of Life?
누가 인생의 어려움을 피할 수 있는가?
⑤ Better to Fail Than Never to Try
아예 시도하지 않는 것보다는 실패하는 것이 더 낫다

145 ① 재능 있는 헤비급 권투선수였다.
② 양손 펀치력이 매우 강했다.
③ 손뼈가 부러지는 부상을 여러 번 입었다.
④ 힘든 상황에서도 포기하지 않았다.
⑤ 부상 후 전략에 능한 코치가 되었다.

어휘확인

imagine 상상하다 **face** 직면하다; 얼굴 **disappointment** 실망(감) **go to pieces** 산산조각이 나다; 절망하다 **way** 방식 **situation** 상황 **lemonade** 레모네이드 **boxing** 권투, 복싱 **cf. boxer** 권투선수 (= **fighter**) **talented** 재능이 있는 **heavyweight** ((권투)) 헤비급 **knockout** ((권투)) 케이오(**KO**), 녹아웃 **unfortunately** 불행하게도 **career** 경력; 직업 **be in one's shoes** ~의 처지가 되다 **quit** 그만두다 **simply** 그저, 그냥 **entire** 전체의 **approach** 접근법 **alter** 바꾸다 **swinging** 휘두르는; 흔들리는 **aggressive** 공격적인 **master** 고수, 달인; 주인 **planning** 계획 **thinking** 사고[생각] **strategy** 전략 **scientific** 과학적인 **work** 효과가 있다; 일하다 **champion** 챔피언 **adjust** 적응하다 **work out** (일이) 잘 풀리다

〈선택지 어휘〉

fear 두려움 **head on** 정면으로 **legend** 전설

지문 Flow

[주제문]
최악의 상황에서도 두려워할 필요가 없음

⬇

[보충설명]
인생은 쉽지 않지만, 최악의 상황도 더 좋게 만들 수 있음

⬇

[예시]
양손에 KO 파워를 지닌 권투선수 Gene Tunney는 양손의 뼈가 여러 번 부러져서 경력이 끝날 위기에 처했지만, 포기하지 않고 자신의 스타일을 바꿔 세계 챔피언이 됨

⬇

[주제문 재진술]
주어진 상황에 적응하고, 일이 바라는 대로 풀리지 않을 때도 포기하지 말아야 함

해석 한 눈에 보기 1 당신은 희망이 산산조각 나는 것을 보는 것의 실망감에 직면할 수 없어서 당신의 인생에서 커다란 일이 일어날 수 있다고 상상하는 것조차도 두려워하는가? 2 많은 사람이 그런 식으로 느낀다. 주제문 3 그러나 최악의 상황조차도 두려워할 필요가 전혀 없다. 4 인생이 쉽지 않을지도 모르지만, 당신은 언제나 그것을 더 좋게 만들 수가 있는데, 특히 인생이 당신에게 레몬을 주면, 레모네이드를 만들라는 말을 기억한다면 말이다. 5 여기에 거친 권투 세계에서의 좋은 예가 있다. 6 Gene Tunney는 양손에 KO 파워를 지닌 재능 있는 헤비급 권투선수였다. 7 불행히도, 그는 양손의 너무 많은 뼈를 너무나도 여러 번 부러뜨려서 그의 경력은 끝나는 것처럼 보였다. 8 많은 권투선수는 만일 그들이 Tunney의 처지였더라면 포기했을 것이다. 9 그러나 Tunney는 그만두지 않았다. 10 그는 그저 자신의 운동에 대한 전체적인 접근법을 바꿨을 뿐이다. 11 그는 자신의 스타일을 크게 휘두르는 공격적인 선수의 그것에서 계획, 사고, 전략 고수의 그것으로 바꿨다. 12 Tunney의 새로운 과학적 스타일은 효과가 좋았고, 그는 1926년에 헤비급 권투 세계 챔피언이 되었다. 주제문 13 Tunney처럼 당신도 인생이 당신에게 던져주는 것에 적응할 수 있다. 14 당신은 일이 당신이 바라는 식으로 풀리지 않을 때 포기할 필요가 없다.

정답단추

144 글의 제목으로는 전체 내용을 가장 잘 압축해서 나타내는 걸 고르면 돼. 이 글은 최악의 상황을 두려워할 필요가 없다고 하면서 권투선수 Gene Tunney를 예로 들고 있어. Tunney는 수많은 부상을 입고도 좌절하지 않고 스타일을 바꿔 결국 헤비급 권투 세계 챔피언이 되었지. 또한 마지막 두 문장, Like Tunney, ~ you hope.에서 포기하지 말고 계속 싸울 것을 강조하고 있어. 따라서 글의 내용을 잘 나타낸 제목은 ①이야.

145 글의 내용과 불일치하는 것을 고르는 문제야. 글의 중후반부에서 Gene Tunney는 부상 후 권투 스타일을 바꿔 헤비급 권투 세계 챔피언이 되었다고 했지? 그런데 ⑤에서는 부상 후 전략에 능한 코치가 되었다고 했으니 일치하지 않음을 알 수 있어. 따라서 답은 ⑤야.

오답단서

144 최악의 상황을 두려워하지 말라고 언급했지만, 자신을 찾기 위한 것이라는 내용은 나오지 않아서 ②는 답이 될 수 없어. ③은 Gene Tunney를 활용한 제목이지만, 이 글에서 Gene Tunney는 예시로 제시된 것으로 글 전체 내용을 포함하는 제목이 될 수는 없어. 또한, 이 글은 인생의 어려움에도 포기하지 말고 계속 맞서 싸우라는 내용이니까 아무도 인생의 어려움을 피할 수 없다는 ④는 지문의 내용과 거리가 멀어. 마지막으로 ⑤는 포기하지 말고 계속 맞서라는 글의 내용과 일치하지 않으므로 적절하지 않아.

145 ①은 글에서 언급된 a talented heavyweight boxer의 내용이야. ②는 with knockout power in both hands로 확인할 수 있어. 손뼈가 많이 부러졌다는 내용은 Unfortunately, he ~ over.를 통해 알 수 있으니까 ③도 일치해. 마지막으로 ④는 많은 부상에도 불구하고 Tunney는 권투를 하는 스타일을 바꿔서 세계 챔피언이 되었다는 걸로 보아 글의 내용과 일치함을 알 수 있어.

146 정답 ① 147 정답 ③ 148 정답 ⑤

지문 All in One

맑은 날이었다 / 나는 먼지와 흙으로 덮여 있었다 / 내가 땅 위를 뒹굴어서
(A) [1] It was a sunny day. [2] I was covered with dust [and] dirt // as I rolled on the ground, /
S V C / S V / 접속사 S' V'

놀면서 / 그저 또 다른 평범한 하루였다 / 내 2학년의 / 내 선생님인 Robertson
playing. [3] (It was) Just another ordinary day / in my second grade class. [4] My teacher, Mrs.
분사구문 / S V C / S =

부인은 멀리서 내 엄마에게 손을 흔들었다 / 그리고 그 다음에 가까이 걸어왔다 / Bit 부인, 우리 잠깐 이야기할 수 있을
Robertson, waved at my mom from afar / [and] then walked closer. [5] “Mrs. Bit, can we talk for
V_1 / V_2 / 조동사 S V

까요 / 그녀(Robertson 선생님)는 말했다 웃으면서 / 나의 엄마가 방 안으로 걸어 들어갔다 / 그리고 나는 밖에서 기다렸다
a second?” // (a) she said, / smiling. [6] My mom walked into a room, // [and] I waited outside, /
S V 분사구문 / S_1 V_1 / S_2 V_2

좋은 소식일 거라고 짐작하면서 / 잠시 후 / 나의 엄마가 방에서 나왔다
assuming that it would be great news. [7] After a while, / my mom came out of the room //
분사구문 / S V_1

그리고 나를 바라보았다 / 나는 즉시 느꼈다 / 뭔가 잘못되었다는 것을
[and] looked at me. [8] I felt immediately // that something was wrong.
V_2 / S V / 접속사 S' V' C'

집으로 오는 길에 / 나는 엄마에게 그녀(Robertson 선생님)가 뭐라고 말했는지 물었다 / 네 성적이 떨어지고 있대 / 그녀는
(B) [9] On our way home, / I asked her what (b) she had said to her. “[10] You're failing. [11] She
S V IO 간접의문문 DO / S V / S

말했어 / 네가 그녀의 반에서 성적이 떨어지고 있는 유일한 학생이라고 / 그녀는 말했어 / 그녀는 네가 3학년으로 올라가지
said // that you're *the only one* [failing in her class]. [12] She said // (that) she's pretty sure that
V 접속사 S' V' C' / S_1 V_1 / 접속사 S' V' C' 접속사

못할 것을 꽤 확신한다고 / 미안하다 / 나의 엄마는 슬프게 말했다
you're not going to make it into third grade, / I'm sorry,” / my mom said sadly. [13] *Those*
S'' V'' / S_2 V_2 / S V / S

그녀가 입 밖에 낸 그 말은 / 내 어린 시절의 모든 부분을 망쳤다 / 나는 겨우 10살이었다 / 그때
words [she uttered] / ruined every piece of my childhood. [14] I was only ten years old / then.
V / S V C

떨어지는 성적과 나와 다른 학생들에 대한 그녀(Robertson 선생님)의 비교는 / 나를 느끼게 했다
(D) [15] The failing grades [and] (e) her comparison of me with other students / made me feel /
S / V O C

내가 아무것도 아닌 것처럼 / 아무도 나를 믿지 않았고 / 심지어 나 자신도 믿지 않았다 / 그 후 곧
like I was nothing. [16] No one believed in me, / not even myself. [17] Shortly afterwards / I
접속사 S' V' C' / S V / S

나는 다른 학교로 전학을 갔다 / 거기서 나는 새로운 선생님을 만났다 / 그녀는 내가 전에 가졌던 선생님과는 거리가
transferred to *another school*, / [where I met a new teacher]. [18] She was far from *the one* [I'd
V / 관계부사(계속적 용법) / S V

멀었다 / 그녀는 한 번 내 옆에 앉았다 / 그리고 우리는 이야기했다 / 나는 그룹 활동을 계획 중이야
had before]. [19] She sat beside me one time, // [and] we talked. [20] “I am planning a group
S_1 V_1 / S_2 V_2 / S V_1

그래서 네가 그룹 리더가 될 수 있는지 궁금하구나 / 그녀는 말했다 / 기분 좋게
activity / [and] wondering if you could be a group leader,” // she said, / cheerfully.
V_2 접속사 S' V' C' / S V

나는 망설였다 / 처음에 / 그러나 그녀(새로운 선생님)는 모든 것을 했다 / 나를 설득하기 위해 / 그리고 그것은 효과가 있었다
(C) [21] I hesitated / at first. [22] But / (c) she did everything / to convince me, // [and] it worked.
S V / S_1 V_1 / 부사적 용법(목적) / S_2 V_2

나는 그룹을 성공적으로 이끌었다 / 그 순간부터 / 나는 다시 미소 짓는 것을 배웠다 / 때때로
[23] I successfully led the group. [24] From that moment, / I learned to smile again. [25] From time
S V / S V

나는 이전 선생님에게서 들었던 것으로 고통 받아야 했다 / 하지만
to time, / I had to suffer from what I'd heard from my previous teacher, / though. [26] Some of
S V 관계대명사 / S

내 행복의 일부는 영원히 사라졌다 / 그녀(Robertson 선생님)의 모진 말 때문에 / 그 날 / 나는 대개는
my happiness was forever lost / because of (d) her sharp words / that day. [27] Though I mostly
V C / 접속사 S'

어휘확인

be covered with ~로 덮여 있다 **dust** 먼지 **dirt** 더러움, 먼지 **wave** 손을 흔들다 **from afar** 멀리서 **for a second** 잠시, 잠깐 **assume** 추측하다, 추정하다 **after a while** 잠시 후에 **immediately** 즉시 **utter** 입 밖에 내다, 발언하다 **ruin** 망치다 **childhood** 어린 시절 **comparison** 비교 **shortly** 곧 **afterwards** 나중에, 그 뒤에 **transfer** 이동하다, 전학 가다 **wonder** 궁금하다, 궁금해하다 **cheerfully** 기분 좋게 **hesitate** 망설이다 **convince** 납득시키다, 확신시키다 **work** 효과가 있다 **successfully** 성공적으로 **from time to time** 때때로 **suffer** 시달리다, 고통 받다 **previous** 이전의 **happiness** 행복 **sharp** 날카로운, 모진 **mostly** 대개는

지문 Flow

[발단]
엄마가 학교에 방문하여 선생님을 만남

⬇

[전개]
성적이 떨어지고 있고, 3학년으로 올라가지 못할 거라는 말을 들음

⬇

[위기]
떨어지는 성적과, 다른 학생들과 자신을 비교하는 선생님 때문에 자신감이 상실됨

⬇

[절정]
전학을 가서 새로운 선생님을 만나, 그룹 리더 임무를 성공적으로 마친 뒤, 자신감이 생김

⬇

[결말]
다시 자신을 믿게 되었지만, 말의 진정한 힘을 배우게 됨

자신을 다시 믿었지만 / 나는 말의 진정한 힘을 배웠다

believed in myself again, // I had learned the true power of speech.

V′ / S V

146 ① (B) - (D) - (C) ② (C) - (B) - (D) ③ (C) - (D) - (B)
④ (D) - (B) - (C) ⑤ (D) - (C) - (B)

147 ① (a) ② (b) ③ (c) ④ (d) ⑤ (e)

148
① Robertson 선생님이 엄마에게 할 말을 미리 알고 있었다.
② Robertson 선생님은 내 성적이 곧 좋아질 거라고 격려했다.
③ 글쓴이는 성적이 뒤처진다고 해서 속상해하지는 않았다.
④ 글쓴이는 리더를 맡겠다고 선생님께 자원했다.
⑤ 글쓴이는 단체 활동을 성공적으로 이끌었다.

해석 한 눈에 보기 (A) **1** 맑은 날이었다. **2** 나는 놀면서 땅 위를 뒹굴어서 먼지와 흙으로 덮여 있었다. **3** 그저 내 2학년의 또 다른 평범한 하루였다. **4** 내 선생님인 Robertson 부인은 멀리서 내 엄마에게 손을 흔들었고 그 다음에 가까이 걸어갔다. **5** "Bit 부인, 우리 잠깐 이야기를 나눌 수 있을까요?" (a) 그녀(Robertson 선생님)는 웃으면서 말했다. **6** 나의 엄마가 방 안으로 걸어 들어갔고, 나는 좋은 소식일 거라고 짐작하며 밖에서 기다렸다. **7** 잠시 후, 나의 엄마가 방에서 나와 나를 바라보았다. **8** 나는 즉시 뭔가 잘못되었다는 것을 느꼈다. (B) **9** 집으로 오는 길에, 나는 엄마에게 (b) 그녀(Robertson 선생님)가 엄마에게 뭐라고 말했는지 물었다. "**10** 네 성적이 떨어지고 있대. **11** 그녀는 네가 그녀의 반에서 성적이 떨어지고 있는 유일한 학생이라고 말했어. **12** 그녀는 네가 3학년으로 올라가지 못할 거라고 꽤 확신하며 말하더구나. 미안하다." 나의 엄마는 슬프게 말했다. **13** 그녀가 입 밖에 낸 그 말은 내 어린 시절의 모든 부분을 망쳤다. **14** 나는 그때 겨우 10살이었다. (D) **15** 떨어지는 성적과 나와 다른 학생들에 대한 (e) 그녀(Robertson 선생님)의 비교는 나를 아무것도 아닌 것처럼 느끼게 했다. **16** 아무도 나를 믿지 않았고, 심지어 나 자신도 믿지 않았다. **17** 그 후 곧 나는 다른 학교로 전학을 갔고, 거기서 새로운 선생님을 만났다. **18** 그녀는 내가 전에 만났던 선생님과는 거리가 멀었다. **19** 그녀는 한 번 내 옆에 앉았고, 우리는 이야기했다. **20** "나는 그룹 활동을 계획 중이고 네가 그룹 리더가 될 수 있는지 궁금하구나." 그녀는 기분 좋게 말했다. (C) **21** 나는 처음에 망설였다. **22** 그러나 (c) 그녀(새로운 선생님)는 나를 설득하기 위해 모든 것을 했고, 그것은 효과가 있었다. **23** 나는 그룹을 성공적으로 이끌었다. **24** 그 순간부터, 나는 다시 미소 짓는 것을 배웠다. **25** 하지만 때때로, 나는 이전 선생님에게서 들었던 것으로 고통 받아야 했다. **26** 그 날 (d) 그녀(Robertson 선생님)의 모진 말 때문에 내 행복의 일부는 영원히 사라졌다. **27** 나는 대개는 내 자신을 다시 믿었지만, 나는 말의 진정한 힘을 배웠다.

정답단추

146 이 글은 시간 순서에 따라 전개되고 있어서, 내용이 자연스럽게 이어지는지 살펴봐야 해. 각 단락에서 순서를 나타내는 단서를 찾아보자. (A)는 엄마가 학교에 방문해서 선생님을 만나는 상황이야. (B)의 On our way home에서 집으로 돌아오는 상황임을 알 수 있으므로, 그 뒤에 이어지는 것이 자연스러워. 또한 엄마는 선생님이 말한 것을 알려주고 (D)에서 필자가 그로 인해 자신감을 잃은 상황이 나와. 그 후, 전학을 가게 된 필자가 새로운 선생님을 만나고, (C)에서 필자가 선생님의 제안으로 그룹 리더가 되어 그룹을 성공적으로 이끌면서 자신감을 찾았다는 내용으로 글이 마무리 돼. 따라서 글의 순서로 가장 적절한 것은 ①이야.

147 이 글은 등장인물이 많아. 특히 she, her로 가리킬 수 있는 인물이 필자의 엄마, 과거의 선생님(Robertson 선생님), 새로운 선생님이지. 따라서 구분이 헷갈릴 수 있으니 앞뒤 문맥을 살피면서 확인해야 해. (a), (b)는 필자의 엄마가 학교에 방문해서 만난 Robertson 선생님을 가리키고, (e)도 필자를 다른 학생들과 비교한 그 선생님을 가리켜. 그런데 (c)는 그 이후에 전학 가서 만난 새로운 선생님을 가리키므로 Robertson 선생님과 다른 사람이지. (d)는 필자에게 모진 말을 한 선생님으로 Robertson 선생님을 가리켜. 따라서 정답은 ③이야.

148 글의 순서대로 선택지가 제시된다는 사실은 알고 있지? 그러니까 읽으면서 해당 내용이 나오는 곳을 찾아 확인하는 것이 효율적이야. (C)에서 필자는 선생님의 설득으로 그룹의 리더를 맡아 그룹을 성공적으로 이끌었다는 내용이 나와. 따라서 글의 내용으로 적절한 것은 ⑤야.

오답단서

148 필자는 엄마를 기다리며 좋은 소식일 것으로 추정했으므로 ①은 정답이 아니야. 또한, Robertson 선생님은 필자가 진급하지 못할 것이라 확신했으므로 ②도 일치하지 않아. ③ 역시 필자는 떨어지는 성적으로 자신감이 사라졌다고 했으므로 오답이야. 마지막으로 ④는 새로운 선생님이 먼저 리더를 해보라고 제안했으니까 일치하지 않는 내용이야.

유형편

Chapter 5

유형 13 지칭 대상 파악

Check-Up 1 1 they: ② their: ① 2 **149** 해석 참조 **149** ③ **150** ④
Mini Test **1** (A) ① (B) ② (C) ① **2** (A) ① (B) ① (C) ②
실전적용독해 **151** ⑤ **152** ③ **153** ④

Check-Up 1

정답 1 they: ② their: ① 2 **149** 해석 참조
해석 1 ① 도마뱀은 발바닥에 50만 개의 아주 작은 ② 털이 있는데, 그것(털)이 그것들의(도마뱀들의) 놀라운 오르기 기술의 비결이다.

149 정답 ③

지문 All in One

[1] Two men were walking / through a desert. (두 남자가 걷고 있었다 / 사막을 가로질러; Two men: S, were walking: V) [2] At some point / they had an argument, // and one of them slapped ① the other in the face. (어떤 시점에서 / 그들은 논쟁을 벌였다 / 그리고 / 그들 중 한 명이 다른 사람(얼굴 맞은 사람)의 얼굴을 찰싹 때렸다; they: S_1, had: V_1, one of them: S_2, slapped: V_2) [3] The man was hurt, // and he wrote in the sand: / "TODAY MY BEST FRIEND SLAPPED ME IN THE FACE." (그 남자는 기분이 상했다 / 그리고 그는 모래에 썼다 / 오늘 나의 가장 친한 친구는 내 얼굴을 찰싹 때렸다; The man: S_1, was hurt: V_1, he: S_2, wrote: V_2, MY BEST FRIEND: S, SLAPPED: V) [4] Then they started walking again, // until they found *an oasis*, / where they decided to take a bath. (그런 다음 그들은 다시 걷기 시작했다 / 오아시스를 발견할 때까지 / 거기서 그들은 목욕하기로 결정했다; they: S, started: V, until: 접속사, they: S′, found: V′, where: 관계부사(계속적 용법)) [5] There / ② *the one* [who had been slapped] / got stuck in some mud // and started to drown. (거기서 / 얼굴을 맞았던 사람이 / 진흙에 빠져 꼼짝 못하게 되었다 / 그리고 익사하기 시작했다; the one: S, who: 관계대명사, got: V_1, stuck: C, started: V_2) [6] Luckily, / ③ his friend saved him. (운 좋게도 / 그의 친구(때린 사람)가 그를 구해주었다; his friend: S, saved: V) [7] This time / ④ the man wrote on a stone: / "TODAY MY BEST FRIEND SAVED MY LIFE." (이번에 / 그 남자(얼굴 맞은 사람)는 돌에 썼다 / 오늘 내 가장 친한 친구는 내 생명을 구했다; the man: S, wrote: V, MY BEST FRIEND: S, SAVED: V) [8] Out of curiosity, / his friend asked him, // "After I hurt you, / you wrote in the sand, / and now you write on a stone / — why?" (호기심에서 / 그의 친구가 그에게 물었다 / 내가 당신의 기분을 상하게 한 후에 / 당신은 모래 위에 썼습니다 / 그리고 지금은 당신이 돌 위에 썼네요 / 왜죠; his friend: S, asked: V, After: 접속사, I: S′, hurt: V′, you: S_1, wrote: V_1, you: S_2, write: V_2) [9] ⑤ He replied, // "When someone hurts us, / we should write it down in *sand*, / where winds of forgiveness can erase it away. (그(얼굴 맞은 사람)는 대답했다 / 누군가가 우리의 기분을 상하게 하면 / 우리는 모래에 그것을 써야 합니다 / 그곳에서 용서의 바람이 그것을 지워 없애 줍니다; He: S, replied: V, When: 접속사, someone: S′, hurts: V′, we: S, should write: V, where: 관계부사(계속적 용법)) [10] But, / when someone does something good for us, // we must write it in *stone*, / where no wind can ever erase it." (그러나 / 누군가가 우리를 위해 좋은 일을 할 때는 / 우리는 돌에 그것을 써야 합니다 / 그곳에는 바람이 없어서 그것을 지울 수 없습니다; when: 접속사, someone: S′, does: V′, we: S, must write: V, where: 관계부사(계속적 용법))

해석 한 눈에 보기 **1** 두 남자가 사막을 가로질러 걷고 있었다. **2** 어떤 시점에서 그들은 논쟁을 벌였고, 그들 중 한 명이 ① 다른 사람(얼굴 맞은 사람)의 얼굴을 찰싹 때렸다. **3** 그 남자는 기분이 상했고, 그는 모래에 썼다. "오늘 나의 가장 친한 친구는 내 얼굴을 찰싹 때렸다." **4** 그런 다음 오아시스를 발견할 때까지 다시 걷기 시작했고, 그들은 거기서 목욕을 하기로 결정했다. **5** 거기서 얼굴을 맞았던 ② 사람은 진흙에 빠져 꼼짝 못하게 되었고 익사하기 시작했다. **6** 운 좋게도, ③ 그의 친구(때린 사람)가 그를 구해주었다. **7** 이번에 ④ 그 남자(얼굴 맞은 사람)는 돌에 썼다. "오늘 내 가장 친한 친구는 내 생명을 구했다." **8** 호기심에서 그의 친구가 그에게 물었다. "내가 당신의 기분을 상하게 한 후에, 당신은 모래 위에 썼는데, 지금은 돌 위에 썼네요. 왜죠?" **9** ⑤ 그(얼굴 맞은 사람)는 대답했다. "누군가가 우리의 기분을 상하게 하면, 모래에 그것을 써야 하는데, 그곳에서 용서의 바람이 그것을 지워 없애줍니다. **10** 그러나, 누군가가 우리를 위해 좋은 일을 할 때는, 돌에 그것을 써야 하는데, 그곳에는 바람이 없어서 그것을 지울 수 없습니다."

정답단추 이 글에는 사막을 걷고 있는 두 남자가 나와. 따라서 밑줄 친 부분이 둘 중 누구인지 구분하면서 읽으면 돼.

어휘확인

argument 논쟁, 언쟁 **slap A in the face** A의 얼굴을 찰싹 때리다 **oasis** 오아시스 **take a bath** 목욕하다 **get stuck** 꼼짝 못하게 되다 **drown** 익사하다 **curiosity** 호기심 **reply** 대답하다 **forgiveness** 용서 **erase** 지우다

지문 Flow

[발단]
두 남자가 사막을 걸음

[전개]
두 사람은 언쟁을 했고, 한 사람이 다른 사람의 얼굴을 때리자 맞은 사람은 기분이 상해 모래에 글을 씀

[위기]
얼굴을 맞았던 사람이 진흙에 빠져 익사할 위기에 처함

[절정]
그의 친구가 그를 구해주자, 이번에는 돌에 글을 씀

[결말]
모래와 돌에 각각 글을 쓴 이유를 묻자, 모래에 쓴 글은 지워지지만, 돌에 쓴 글은 지워지지 않는다고 함

글의 초반부에서 두 사람 중 한 사람은 얼굴을 맞았고, 다른 한 사람은 얼굴을 때렸어. 그것을 토대로 ①, ②는 얼굴을 맞은 사람임을 알 수 있고, ④, ⑤도 그를 가리키는 말이야. ③은 얼굴을 맞은 사람의 친구이므로 때린 사람이겠지? 따라서 정답은 ③이야.

150 정답 ④

지문 All in One

1 When Father was seventy // he had cancer, / and he was forced to stay in bed / for half a year / while his condition gradually got worse. 2 Because of ① his age, / surgery was not considered, // and death became just a matter of time. 3 Toward the end, / for almost a month, / we expected each day to be ② his last. 4 My sisters, brother, and I / took turns in caring for him / in his last hours. 5 The last time I visited Father // the doctor told me / (that) ③ he would probably hold out / for four or five more days, / so I returned that night to my place / to change my clothes. 6 But / when I got there / the next morning, // ④ he was announcing / that he had just drawn his last breath. 7 ⑤ He was said to be alert / to the very end, / giving detailed instructions / about whom to notify of his death.

(아버지가 70세였을 때 / 그는 암에 걸리셨다 / 그리고 그는 침대에 누워 있어야 했다 / 반년 동안 / 그의 상태가 서서히 악화되는 동안에 / 그(아버지)의 나이 때문에 / 수술은 고려되지 않았다 / 그리고 죽음은 단지 시간문제가 되었다 / 끝 무렵에 / 거의 한 달 동안 / 우리는 매일이 그(아버지)의 마지막 날이 되리라고 예상했다 / 나의 자매들, 형제, 그리고 나는 / 교대로 그를 돌보는 일을 했다 / 그의 마지막 시간에 / 내가 아버지를 마지막으로 방문했을 때 / 의사는 내게 말했다 / 그(아버지)가 아마 더 버티실 거라고 / 4~5일 간 / 그래서 나는 그날 밤 집에 돌아갔다 / 옷을 갈아입으러 / 그러나 / 내가 거기에 도착했을 때 / 다음 날 아침에 / 그(의사)는 알리고 있었다 / 그가 방금 마지막 숨을 쉬었다고 / 그(아버지)는 정신을 차리고 있었다고 말해진다 / 끝까지 / 세부적인 지시를 하면서 / 그의 죽음을 알려야 할 사람에 대해)

(1 When: 접속사, Father: S'_1, was: V'_1, seventy: C'_1, he: S_1, had: V_1, he: S_2, was forced: V_2, while: 접속사, his condition: S'_2, got: V'_2, worse: C'_2 / 2 surgery: S_1, was not considered: V_1, death: S_2, became: V_2, a matter of time: C_2 / 3 we: S, expected: V, each day: O, to be his last: C / 4 My sisters, brother, and I: S, took: V / 5 The last time: 접속사, I: S′, visited: V′, the doctor: S_1, told: V_1, me: IO, (that): 접속사, (that) ~ days: DO, I: S_2, returned: V_2, to change my clothes: 부사적 용법(목적) / 6 when: 접속사, I: S'_1, got: V'_1, he: S, was announcing: V, that: 접속사, he: S'_2, had just drawn: V'_2 / 7 He: S, was said: V, to be alert: C, giving ~: 분사구문(= and he gave ~))

해석 한 눈에 보기 1 아버지는 70세에 암에 걸리셨고, 상태가 서서히 악화되는 동안에 아버지는 반년 동안 침대에 누워 있어야 했다. 2 ① 그(아버지)의 나이 때문에, 수술은 고려되지 않았고, 죽음은 단지 시간문제가 되었다. 3 끝 무렵에, 거의 한 달 동안, 우리는 매일이 ② 그(아버지)의 마지막 날이 되리라고 예상했다. 4 내 자매들, 형제, 그리고 나는 교대로 그의 마지막 시간에 그를 돌보는 일을 했다. 5 내가 아버지를 마지막 방문했을 때, 의사는 내게 ③ 그(아버지)가 아마 4~5일 간 더 버티실 거라고 말해서, 나는 그날 밤 옷을 갈아입으러 집에 돌아갔다. 6 그러나 다음 날 아침에 내가 거기에 도착했을 때, ④ 그(의사)는 그가 방금 마지막 숨을 쉬었다고 알리고 있었다. 7 ⑤ 그(아버지)는 그의 죽음을 알려야 할 사람에 대해 세부적인 지시를 하면서, 끝까지 정신을 차리고 있었다고 말해진다.

정답단추 이 글에는 세 명의 인물이 등장해. 필자, 필자의 아버지, 의사. 그 중 he로 지칭할 수 있는 사람은 필자의 아버지와 의사야. 대명사가 가리키는 대상을 찾기 위해서는 앞뒤에 나오는 명사를 자세히 살펴봐야 해. ①, ②, ③은 병원에 있는 필자의 아버지를 가리키는 것이고, ⑤도 아버지의 임종 직전을 설명하고 있으니 아버지를 가리켜. 그런데 ④는 아버지가 마지막 숨을 쉬었다고 알리는 사람이니까 의사로 볼 수 있지. 따라서 정답은 ④야.

어휘확인

cancer 암 **be forced to-v** ~하도록 강요받다 **gradually** 서서히 **get worse** 악화되다 **surgery** 수술 **consider** 고려하다 **death** 죽음 **expect** 예상하다, 기대하다 **take turns** 교대로 하다 **care for** ~을 돌보다 **hold out** 버티다, 견디다 **draw one's breath** 숨을 쉬다, 살아 있다 **alert** 정신을 바짝 차린 **detailed** 상세한 **instruction** 지시 **notify** 알리다, 통지하다

지문 Flow

[발단] 아버지가 암에 걸려서 반년 동안 침대에 누워 계심

⬇

[전개] 형제자매들과 교대로 아버지를 돌봄

⬇

[위기] 자신이 마지막으로 방문했을 때, 4~5일 더 버티실 거라는 의사의 말을 듣고 옷을 갈아입으러 밤에 집으로 감

⬇

[결말] 다음 날 아침 아버지에게 갔을 때, 방금 전에 돌아가심

기출총정리

Mini Test 1 (A) ① (B) ② (C) ① 2 (A) ① (B) ① (C) ②

Mini Test 해석 및 해설

1 해석 용은 파충류의 피부, 코끼리의 몸통, 말의 머리, 도마뱀의 꼬리를 갖고 있다. (A) 그것들(용들)은 많은 마법의 힘을 가지고 있다고 알려져 있다. (B) 그것들(마법의 힘) 중 하나는 불을 뿜어내는 것이다. 어떤 이야기에서 용들은 착하고 현명한 반면에, 또 어떤 이야기에서 (C) 그것들(용들)은 사악한 괴물이다. ① 용들 ② 마법의 힘 ③ 어떤 이야기들

2 해석 몇 년 전에 (A) 그들(모건과 산즈)이 우림 깊은 곳에 캠프를 설치하고 있는 동안, 모건과 산즈는 한 무리의 침팬지가 멀리서 시끄럽게 소리를 내고 있는 것을 들었다. (B) 그들(모건과 산즈)은 침팬지들이 나무 사이를 급하게 움직이고 있다고 생각했다. 그 침팬지들은 더 시끄럽게 소리 지르고 있었고, (C) 그것들(침팬지들)은 곧바로 캠프를 향해 오고 있는 것 같았다. ① 모건과 산즈 ② 침팬지들 ③ 나무들

151 정답 ⑤

지문 All in One

비서로 일하는 / 국제공항에서 / 내 여동생은 사무실을 두고 있다

[1] Working as a secretary / at an international airport, / my sister had an office / next to *the*

분사구문(= When she was working ~) S V

보안 요원들이 임시로 용의자들을 유치해 두는 방 옆에 / 어느 날 / 한 보안 요원이 한 남자(전화 수리공)를

room [where security temporarily holds suspects]. [2] One day / a security officer was

관계부사 S V

심문하고 있었는데 / 바로 그때 그가 갑자기 호출되었다 / 다른 비상사태로

questioning ① a man // when he was suddenly called away / on another emergency. [3] To the

접속사 S' V'

내 여동생과 그녀의 동료들의 공포에도 / 그(전화 수리공)는 혼자 남겨졌다 / 잠기지 않은 방에

horror of my sister and her colleagues, / ② he was left alone / in the unlocked room. [4] After a

S V

몇 분 후에 / 그 문이 열렸다 / 그리고 그(전화 수리공)가 걸어 나오기 시작했다 / 용기를 내서

few minutes, / the door opened // and ③ he began to walk out. [5] Gathering her courage, /

S_1 V_1 S_2 V_2 분사구문(= After she gathered ~)

비서 중 한 명이 소리쳤다 / 그곳으로 다시 돌아가세요 / 나오지 마세요 / 지시를 받을 때까지

one of the secretaries yelled, // "Get back in there, / and don't you come out / until you're

S V V_1 V_2 접속사 S' V'

그(전화 수리공)는 안쪽으로 뛰어 들어갔다 / 그리고 문을 큰소리로 닫았다 / 보안 요원이 돌아왔을 때

told!" [6] ④ He ran inside // and shut the door loudly. [7] When the security guard returned, //

S V_1 V_2 접속사 S' V'

그 여자들은 전했다 / 무슨 일이 있었는지를 / 한마디 말도 없이 / 그(보안 요원)는 그 방으로 걸어 들어갔다

the women reported / what had happened. [8] Without a word, / ⑤ he walked into the room //

S V 간접의문문 S V_1

그리고 겁에 질린 전화 수리공 한 명을 풀어주었다

and released one frightened telephone repairman.

V_2

해석 한 눈에 보기 [1] 국제공항에서 비서로 일하는, 내 여동생은 보안 요원들이 임시로 용의자들을 유치해 두는 방 옆에 있는 사무실을 썼다. [2] 어느 날 한 보안 요원이 ① 한 남자(전화 수리공)를 심문하고 있었는데 바로 그때 그가 다른 급한 일로 갑자기 호출되었다. [3] 내 여동생과 그녀의 동료들이 무섭게도, ② 그(전화 수리공)는 잠기지 않은 방에 혼자 남겨졌다. [4] 몇 분 후에, 그 문이 열렸고 ③ 그(전화 수리공)가 걸어 나오기 시작했다. [5] 용기를 내서, 비서 중 한 명이 "그곳으로 다시 돌아가서, 지시를 받을 때까지 나오지 마세요!"라고 소리쳤다. [6] ④ 그(전화 수리공)는 안쪽으로 뛰어 들어가서 문을 큰소리로 닫았다. [7] 보안 요원이 돌아왔을 때, 그 여자들은 무슨 일이 있었는지를 설명했다. [8] 한마디 말도 없이 ⑤ 그(보안 요원)는 그 방으로 걸어 들어가서 겁에 질린 전화 수리공 한 명을 풀어주었다.

정답단추 각각의 대명사가 가리키는 대상을 정확히 찾기 위해서는 대명사가 주로 앞뒤에 언급된 명사를 대신해서 쓰이는 경우가 많다는 걸 명심하고 지문을 살펴보자. 이 지문에서는 a man, he가 될 수 있는 대상은 두 명의 남자 등장인물인 보안 요원과 전화 수리공이야. 글의 앞부분에서 보안 요원이 한 남자(전화 수리공)를 데리고 와 심문을 하다가 잠시 자리를 비우게 되지. 그 후 상황 전개는 전화 수리공, 여동생과 여동생 동료들 사이에서 일어나고 있어. 다시 말해, ①~④는 앞에 언급된 전화 수리공을 계속 가리키고 있음을 알 수 있어. 그리고 다시 보안 요원이 돌아왔다는 문장 뒤에 ⑤는 앞 문장의 되돌아온 보안 요원을 지칭하고 있어. 따라서 정답은 ⑤야.

어휘확인

secretary 비서 **airport** 공항 **have** (특정한 위치에) 두고 있다[두다] **security** 보안 요원(= security officer, security guard) **temporarily** 임시로 **hold** (사람을) 유치하다 **suspect** 용의자 **question** 심문하다 **call away** ~을 호출하다, ~을 불러내다 **emergency** 비상(사태) **horror** 공포(감) **colleague** 동료 **leave alone** 혼자 있게 해주다 **unlocked** 잠겨 있지 않은 **after** ~ 후에[뒤에] **open** (문을) 열다 **gather courage** 용기를 내다 **get back** 돌아오다[가다] **shut** (문 등을) 닫다 **return** 돌아오다 **release** 풀어 주다 **frightened** 겁에 질린 **repairman** 수리공

지문 Flow

[발단]
여동생은 국제공항에서 임시로 용의자를 유치하는 방 옆에 있는 사무실에서 비서로 근무함

⬇

[전개]
보안 요원이 한 남자를 심문하던 중 호출되어서, 그 남자 홀로 방에 남겨짐

⬇

[위기]
그 남자가 방에서 나오려 하자 비서 중 한 명이 소리쳤고 그 남자는 다시 들어감

⬇

[결말]
보안 요원이 돌아오자, 그 여자들이 있었던 일을 설명했고, 방에 들어가 겁에 질린 전화 수리공을 풀어줌

152 정답 ③

지문 All in One

많은 아테네인들은 느꼈다 / Socrates가 위험했다는 것을 / 그리고 의도적으로 정부에 저항하고 있었다는 것을

[1] Many Athenians felt // that Socrates was dangerous / and was deliberately going against

S V 접속사 S' V'_1 C' V'_2

기원전 399년에 / Socrates가 70세였을 때 / 그들 중 한 명인 / Meletus가

the government. [2] In 399 BC, / when Socrates was 70 years old, // one of them, / Meletus, /

접속사 S' V' C' S =

그(Socrates)를 법정에 데려갔다(세웠다) / Meletus는 주장했다 / Socrates가 아테네의 신들을 등한시하고 있었다는 것을

took ① him to court. [3] Meletus claimed // that Socrates was neglecting the Athenian gods, /

V S V 접속사 S' V'_1

그리고 새로운 신들을 소개하고 있었다는 것을 / 그(Socrates) 자신의 / Socrates는 아테네의 젊은이들을 가르치고 있었다

and (was) introducing new gods / of ② his own. [4] Socrates was teaching the young men of

V'_2 S V O

나쁘게 행동하라고 / 그(Meletus)에 따르면 / 그들을 조장하고 있었다 / 정부에 등을 돌리도록

Athens / to behave badly, / according to ③ him, / encouraging them / to turn against the

C 분사구문(= and he was encouraging ~)

사실이든 아니든 / 이것들은 매우 심각한 주장이었다 / 아마도

authorities. [5] (Whether they were) True or not, / these were very serious claims. [6] Perhaps

접속사 S' V' C' S V C

어휘확인

Athenian 아테네인(사람); 아테네의 cf. **Athens** 아테네 **deliberately** 의도적으로 **go against** ~에 저항하다 **BC** 기원전 **claim** 주장하다; 주장 **neglect** 등한시하다; 방치하다 **god** 신 **young man** 젊은이, 청년 **behave** 행동하다 **badly** 나쁘게 **according to** ~에 따르면 **encourage** 조장하다(↔ **discourage** 막다, ~을 못하게 말리다) **turn against** ~에게 등을 돌리다 **authorities** 정부 **true** 사실인 **perhaps** 아마도 **state religion** 국교(국가에서 법으로 정해 온 국민이 믿도록 하는 종교) **evidence** 증거 **demonstrate** 입증하다 **flaw** 결함 **democracy** 민주주의 **match** 들어맞다; 성냥 **certainly** 확실하게 **charge** 고발; 요금

Socrates는 정말로 그(Socrates)의 학생들을 막았을지도 모른다 / 국교를 따르는 것으로부터 / 그리고 약간의

Socrates really did discourage ④ his students / from following the state religion, // and there is some evidence / that he enjoyed demonstrating the flaws / in Athenian democracy. [7] That would have matched well / with ⑤ his character. [8] What is certainly true is // that many Athenians believed the charges.

증거가 있다 / 그가 결함을 입증하는 것을 즐겼다는 / 아테네 민주주의의 / 그것은 잘 들어맞았을 것이다 / 그(Socrates)의 성격과 / 확실하게 사실인 것은 ~이다 / 많은 아테네인들이 그 고발을 믿었다는 것

해석 한 눈에 보기 1 많은 아테네인은 Socrates가 위험하고 의도적으로 정부에 저항하고 있다고 느꼈다. 2 기원전 399년, Socrates가 70세였을 때, 그들 중 한 명인 Meletus는 ① 그(Socrates)를 법정에 세웠다. 3 Meletus는 Socrates가 아테네 신들을 등한시하고 있었고, ② 그(Socrates) 자신의 새로운 신들을 소개하고 있다고 주장했다. 4 ③ 그(Meletus)에 따르면 Socrates는 아테네의 젊은이들에게 나쁘게 행동하라고 가르치면서, 그들에게 정부에 등을 돌리도록 조장하고 있었다는 것이다. 5 사실이든 아니든, 이런 것들은 매우 심각한 주장이었다. 6 아마도 Socrates가 정말로 ④ 그(Socrates)의 제자들에게 나라의 종교를 따르지 말라고 했을지도 모르며, 그가 아테네 민주주의의 결함을 입증하기를 즐겼다는 약간의 증거가 있다. 7 그것은 ⑤ 그(Socrates)의 성격과 잘 들어맞았을 것이다. 8 확실하게 사실인 것은 많은 아테네인이 그 고발을 믿었다는 것이다.

정답단추 밑줄 친 대명사가 가리키는 대상을 찾는 문제에서는 앞뒤 문장을 유심히 살펴봐야 해. 이 글에서는 Socrates와 Meletus라는 두 명의 인물이 등장하고 있어. 먼저 Meletus가 법정에 데려간 사람은 앞에 나온 Socrates이니까 ①은 Socrates를 의미해. 그리고 ②는 같은 문장의 주어로 쓰인 Socrates를 대신하고 있지. ③은 Socrates가 젊은이들이 정부에 등을 돌리도록 조장하고 있었다고 주장하는 사람이니까 Meletus를 가리켜. ④는 같은 문장의 주어인 Socrates를 가리키고, ⑤도 앞의 Socrates에 관한 설명이니까 Socrates를 가리키는 것을 알 수 있어. 따라서 가리키는 대상이 다른 하나는 ③이야.

지문 Flow

[발단]
많은 아테네인들은 Socrates가 정부에 저항한다고 생각했음

[전개1]
Meletus는 Socrates를 법정에 세웠고, 젊은이들에게 정부에 등을 돌리도록 조장한다고 주장했음

&

[전개2]
Socrates가 제자들에게 나라의 종교를 따르지 말라고 했을지도 모르며, 아테네 민주주의의 결함을 입증하기를 즐겼다는 증거가 있음

[결과]
많은 아테네인은 그 고발을 믿었음

153 정답 ④

지문 All in One

[1] When I begin to write // I always find / (that) there is *one character* [who refuses to come alive]. [2] There is nothing psychologically false / about ① him, // but it takes great effort / to find words for him. [3] *All the technical skill* / [(that) I have acquired / through the years] / has to be employed / in making ② him appear alive to my readers. [4] Sometimes / I get a sour satisfaction // when a famous reviewer praises / ③ him as the best-written character / in the story. [5] I'm left wondering / how ④ he could somehow be unable to see / the complete awkwardness of this character. [6] This character lies heavily on my mind // whenever I start to work / like an ill-digested meal on the stomach, / robbing me of the pleasure of creation / in *any scene* [where ⑤ he is present].

해석 한 눈에 보기 1 글쓰기를 시작할 때, 나는 살아 움직이기를 거부하는 한 인물이 있다는 것을 발견한다. 2 ① 그(한 인물)에 대해 심리적으로 잘못된 것은 없지만, 그에게 쓸 단어들을 찾는 것은 많은 노력을 필요로 한다. 3 수년간 내가 습득한 모든 기교는 ② 그(한 인물)가 내 독자들에게 생생하게 보이도록 하는 데 사용되어야 한다. 4 때때로 유명한 평론가가 ③ 그(한 인물)를 이야기에서 가장 잘 쓰인 인물이라고 칭찬할 때 나는 불쾌한 만족감을 얻는다. 5 나는 왜 그런지 모르겠지만 어떻게 ④ 그(평론가)가 이 인물의 완전한 어색함을 볼 수 없는지 궁금하다. 6 이 인물은 위에서 잘 소화되지 않는 음식과 같이, 내가 일하기 시작할 때마다 마음속에 크게 자리 잡고 있으며, ⑤ 그(한 인물)가 존재하는 모든 장면에서 나로부터 창작의 즐거움을 빼앗아 간다.

정답단추 밑줄 친 him[he]가 가리키는 대상이 누구인지 앞뒤 문장의 명사를 잘 살피면서 파악해 보자. 우선 ①은 앞 문장의 one character를 가리키는 말이야. ②, ③, ⑤도 필자의 글 속에 존재하는 인물을 가리키는 말이고. 그런데 ④는 필자의 인물을 칭찬한 평론가를 가리키고 있지. 따라서 정답은 ④야.

어휘확인

refuse 거부하다, 거절하다 **psychologically** 심리(학)적으로 **false** 잘못된, 틀린 **technical** 기술적인 **acquire** 습득하다 **employ** 사용하다, 쓰다 **appear** (~처럼) 보이다, ~인 것 같다 **satisfaction** 만족(감) **reviewer** 평론가, 비평가 **somehow** 왜 그런지 (모르겠지만) **awkwardness** 어색함 **heavily** 크게, 심하게 **ill-digested** 제대로 소화되지 않은 **stomach** 위, 복부 **rob A of B** A에게 B를 빼앗다 **creation** 창작, 창조 **scene** 장면 **present** 존재하는

지문 Flow

[도입]
글에서 살리기 힘든 인물이 있음

[보충설명]
- 그 인물을 위한 단어 찾기에 많은 노력이 필요함
- 독자들에게 그 인물이 생생하게 보이도록 자신의 모든 기교를 사용해야 함

[추가]
평론가가 그 인물에 대해 칭찬하면 불쾌한 만족감을 얻음

[결론]
잘 소화되지 않는 음식처럼 이 인물은 마음속에 크게 자리 잡고 있으며, 그가 나오는 장면에서는 창작의 즐거움이 사라짐

유형 14 세부 내용 파악

Check-Up 1 1 ○ 2 ○ 3 × **154** ④
Check-Up 2 **155** ③
Check-Up 3 **156** ③
실전적용독해 **157** ⑤ **158** ⑤ **159** ⑤

Check-Up 1

정답 1 ○ 2 ○ 3 ×
해석 1 부채파초는 인도양의 동아프리카 해안에서 좀 떨어져 나와 있는 마다가스카르 섬이 원산지인 식물의 한 종(種)이다. 2 그것은 위쪽 끝에 녹색 잎들이 달린 기다란 줄기들이 기둥으로부터 거대한 손부채처럼 뻗어 있기 때문에 '부채파초'라는 이름이 붙여졌다. 3 그것은 햇빛이 가득한 곳에서 가장 잘 번성하고 자라므로, 특히 실내에서 키워질 때 많은 빛을 필요로 한다.

154 정답 ④

지문 All in One

대만은 방문하기 쉬운 나라이다 / 개별적으로 여행하는 사람이 / 그리고 이 기차 여행은
1 Taiwan is *an easy country* [to visit / as an independent traveler], // and this train tour gives
S1 V1 C1 S2 V2
훌륭히 소개한다 / 그 나라가 제공해야 하는 최선의 것에 대해 / 종일 탐험을 시작으로
a fine introduction / to *the best* [(that) the country has to offer]. 2 Beginning with a full-day
관계대명사
수도인 타이베이의 / 이 9박 10일의 여행은 / 최대한 활용한다
exploration / of the capital city of Taipei, / this 9 nights and 10 days tour / takes full
= S V
그 나라의 훌륭한 철도망을 / 핑시로의 여정에서
advantage of / the country's excellent railway network. 3 On *your journey to Pingxi* [to
그 나라의 독특한 등불 축제를 경험하는 / 대만의 일 년 중 가장 큰 행사인
experience the city's spectacular Lantern Festival / — the biggest event of Taiwan's calendar
=
여러분은 멈출 것이다 / 수많은 관심 포인트에서 / 가장 좋은 부분은 포함한다
year —] / you will make stops / at numerous points of interest. 4 Highlights include / a stop
S V S V
네이완에서 정차를 / 전통적인 하카 음식을 먹기 위해 / 그리고 타이난에서 정차를 / 과거의 역사적 수도였던
in Neiwan / for traditional Hakka cuisine / and one in Tainan, / the historic former capital.
= a stop =
여러분은 또한 볼 것이다 / 잊을 수 없는 일출을 / 아리산 산악 철도에서
5 You'll also view / an unforgettable sunrise / from *the Alishan Mountain Railway*, / which
S V 관계대명사
그 철도는 원래 통나무를 수송하기 위해 건설되었다 / 숲에서 / 하지만 이제는 수천 명의 관광객을 태우고 있다
was originally built to transport logs / from the forest / but now carries thousands of tourists
매년
/ each year.

① Taipei 관광을 포함한다.
② 9박 10일 일정의 코스이다.
③ Pingxi에서 열리는 등불 축제에 간다.
④ Hakka와 Tainan 전통 요리를 맛본다.
⑤ 해돋이 관광을 포함한다.

해석 한 눈에 보기 1 대만은 개별적으로 여행하는 사람이 방문하기 쉬운 나라이고, 이 기차 여행은 그 나라가 제공해야 하는 최선의 것에 대해 훌륭히 소개한다. 2 수도인 타이베이의 종일 탐험을 시작으로, 이 9박 10일의 여행은 그 나라의 훌륭한 철도망을 최대한 활용한다. 3 대만의 일 년 중 가장 큰 행사인 핑시의 독특한 등불 축제를 경험하는 핑시로의 여정에서, 여러분은 수많은 관심 포인트에서 멈출 것이다. 4 가장 좋은 것은 전통적인 하카 음식을 먹기 위해 네이완에서 정차하고, 과거의 역사적 수도였던 타이난에서 정차한다는 것이다. 5 여러분은 또한 아리산 산악 철도에서 잊을 수 없는 일출을 볼 것인데, 그 철도는 원래 숲에서 통나무를 수송하기 위해 건설되었지만 이제는 매년 수천 명의 관광객을 태우고 있다.

정답단추 먼저 본문의 내용과 일치하는 것을 찾아야 하는지 불일치하는 것을 찾아야 하는지를 확인하도록 해. 이 문제는 일치하지 않는 것을 찾는 문제이니까, 본문을 읽으면서 선택지와의 일치 여부를 순서대로 확인하면 돼. 또한 선택지를 먼저 읽는 것은 문제를 푸는 시간을 절약할 수 있지. 이 글은 대만의 기차 여행에 대한 내용이야. 글의 후반부에서 기차는 하카(Hakka) 음식을 먹기 위해 네이완에서 정차하고, 과거의 역사적 수도였던 타이난에서 정차한다고 했어. 이것을 보면 Hakka는 지명 이름이 아니고, 타이난에서 전통 요리를 먹는다는 내용은 없다는 걸 알 수 있지. 따라서 ④가 글의 내용과 일치하지 않아.

오답단서 ①은 타이베이 관광으로 여행이 시작된다고 했으니 일치해. ②는 this 9 nights and 10 days tour라는 표현에서 일치함을 알 수 있어. ③은 핑시에서 등불 축제를 경험할 수 있다고 했으니 일치해. ⑤는 잊을 수 없는 일출을 보게 될 거라는 마지막 문장을 통해 일치함을 알 수 있어.

어휘확인

independent 독자적인, 독립적인 **traveler** 여행객 **give an introduction** 소개하다 **full-day** 하루 종일의 **exploration** 탐험, 탐사 **capital** 수도 **take an advantage of** ~을 이용하다 **railway** 철도 **network** (그물처럼 얽혀 있는 도로 등의) 망 **experience** 경험하다 **spectacular** 독특한 **lantern** 등, 랜턴 **calendar year** 역년 (1월 1일부터 12월 31일까지의 기간) **numerous** 수많은 **highlight** 가장 좋은 부분, 하이라이트 **include** 포함하다 **traditional** 전통적인 **cuisine** 음식; 요리(법) **historic** 역사적으로 유명한 **former** 전의, 이전의 **view** 보다 **unforgettable** 잊을 수 없는 **sunrise** 일출 **originally** 원래 **transport** 수송하다 **log** 통나무

지문 Flow

[소개]
대만의 기차 여행

⬇

[세부사항1]
9박 10일의 일정으로, 수도인 타이베이 관광으로 시작함

&

[세부사항2]
• 핑시 – 등불 축제 관람
• 네이완 – 하카 음식 경험
• 타이난 – 과거 수도 방문

&

[세부사항3]
아리산 산악 철도에서 일출 관람

Check-Up 2

155 정답 ③

지문 All in One

[1] 미국 바닷가재는 몸집이 큰 바닷가재이다 / 그리고 상업적인 목적이 된 바다 생물
The American lobster is a large-bodied lobster, / and a commercially targeted sea species.

[2] 그것은 무게에 달한다 / 적어도 45파운드(20kg)의 / [3] 게와 다른 바닷가재와 마찬가지로
It reaches weights / of at least 45 pounds (20 kg). Along with crabs and other lobsters, / the

미국 바닷가재는 10개의 다리가 있다 / 그리고 단단한 껍질로 덮여 있다 / 그것을 다른 동물로부터
American lobster has ten legs, // and it is covered with *a hard shell* [that provides it with

보호해주는 / 미국 바닷가재의 앞 다리는 변형된다
some protection / from other animals]. [4] The American lobster's front legs are modified / into

매우 큰 집게발로 / 두 개의 집게발은 서로 약간 다르다 / 하나는 더 강하면서
very large claws. [5] The two claws are slightly different from each other, / with one being

파쇄용으로 사용 / 반면에 다른 하나는 더 날카롭다 / 절단용으로 사용 / 낮에는
stronger / (used for crushing) / while the other is sharper / (used for cutting). [6] During the

미국 바닷가재가 숨어 있을 만한 장소에 있다 / 바위가 많은 바다 해안을 따라 / 저녁 시간과
day, / American lobsters remain in hiding places / along rocky ocean shores. [7] During the

밤에 / 각 개체들은 훨씬 더 활동적이다 / 그리고 해변을 따라서 다양한 음식을
evening hours and at night, / individuals are much more active // and search along the shore

찾는다 / 썩어 가는 유기물과 일부 조류를 포함한
for a variety of foods, / including rotting organic matter, and some algae.

(S: The American lobster, V: is, C_1: a large-bodied lobster, C_2: a commercially targeted sea species / S: It, V: reaches / S_1: the American lobster, V_1: has, S_2: it, V_2: is covered with, that: 관계대명사 / S: The American lobster's front legs, V: are modified / S: The two claws, V: are, C: different, with+목적어+분사 / while: 접속사 / S: American lobsters, V: remain / S: individuals, V_1: are, much: 비교급 강조, V_2: search)

① 상업적인 목적으로 이용된다. ② 적어도 20kg의 무게에 달한다.
③ 두 개의 똑같은 집게발을 가지고 있다. ④ 낮에는 암초에 몸을 숨긴 채로 있다.
⑤ 저녁과 밤 시간에 먹이를 찾아 활동한다.

해석 한 눈에 보기 1 미국 바닷가재는 몸집이 큰 바닷가재이고, 상업적인 목적이 된 바다 생물이다. 2 그것은 적어도 45파운드(20kg)의 무게에 달한다. 3 게와 다른 바닷가재와 마찬가지로, 미국 바닷가재는 10개의 다리가 있으며, 다른 동물로부터 보호해주는 단단한 껍질로 덮여 있다. 4 미국 바닷가재의 앞 다리는 매우 큰 집게발로 변형된다. 5 두 개의 집게발은 서로 약간 다른데, 하나는 더 강하고 (파쇄용으로 사용), 반면에 다른 하나는 더 날카롭다 (절단용으로 사용). 6 낮에는 미국 바닷가재가 바위가 많은 바다 해안을 따라 숨어 있을 만한 장소에 있다. 7 저녁 시간과 밤에, 각 개체들은 훨씬 더 활동적이고, 해변을 따라서 썩어 가는 유기물과 일부 조류를 포함한 다양한 음식을 찾는다.

정답단추 불일치하는 것을 찾는 것임을 명심하고, 선택지와 내용이 일치하는지 비교하며 읽어보자. 오답 선택지는 본문의 내용과 반대되는 표현을 사용한 경우가 많은데, 글의 중반부에 미국 바닷가재의 두 집게발이 서로 다르다고 했어. 하나는 더 강해서 부수는 용도로 쓰고, 다른 하나는 더 날카로워서 자르는 용도로 쓴다고 했지. 그런데 ③에서는 두 개의 똑같은 집게발을 가지고 있다고 했으니 글의 내용과 일치하지 않는 것은 ③이야.

오답단서 ①은 첫 문장에, ②는 두 번째 문장에 그 내용이 나와. ④, ⑤는 미국 바닷가재가 낮에는 바위가 많은 해안을 따라 숨어 있고, 밤에 먹이 활동을 한다고 했으므로 일치하는 내용이야.

어휘확인

lobster 바닷가재 **large-bodied** 몸집이 큰 **commercially** 상업적으로 **targeted** 목표가 된 **species** 종 **reach** ~에 이르다 **at least** 적어도, 최소한 **crab** 게 **shell** 껍질, 껍데기 **provide A with B** A에게 B를 제공하다 **protection** 보호 **modify** 변형하다 **claw** (게의) 집게발 **slightly** 약간, 조금 **crush** 으깨다, 분쇄하다 **remain** 머무르다, 체재하다 **shore** 해안 **individual** 개체; 개인 **a variety of** 다양한 **including** ~을 포함하여 **rot** 썩다 **organic matter** 유기물 **algae** 해조류, 해초

지문 Flow

[소재]
미국 바닷가재

↓

[특징1]
몸집이 커서 상업적인 목적으로 이용됨

&

[특징2]
• 10개의 다리와 단단한 껍질로 덮여 있음
• 두 개의 서로 다른 집게발을 가지고 있음 (하나는 파쇄용, 다른 하나는 절단용)

&

[특징3]
낮에는 바위가 많은 해안가에 숨어 있다가, 밤에 나와서 먹이 활동을 함

Check-Up 3

156 정답 ③

지문 All in One

[1] Wangari Maathai는 ~였다 / 국제적으로 유명한 케냐의 과학자
Wangari Maathai was / an internationally renowned Kenyan scientist. [2] Having earned

미국의 두 대학에서 학위를 받은 후 / 그녀는 케냐로 돌아왔다 / 그리고 박사 학위를 취득했다
degrees from two U.S. colleges, / she returned to Kenya / and earned her PhD / from the

나이로비 대학교에서 / 그리고 그 다음에 교수로 일했다 / 수의학과에서
University of Nairobi, / and then worked as a professor / in their department of veterinary

1976년에 / Maathai는 나무 심기 프로그램을 홍보하기 시작했다 / 숲을 보호하고
medicine. [3] In 1976, / Maathai began promoting a tree-planting program / to save forests

케냐 여성들에게 장작을 제공하기 위해 / 곧 그린벨트 운동으로 알려졌고
and (to) provide firewood for Kenyan women. [4] Soon known as the Green Belt Movement, /

그 프로그램은 수백만 그루의 나무를 심게 했다 / 1997년에 / 그녀는 대통령직과 의원직 출마에 실패했다
the program led to the planting of millions of trees. [5] In 1997, / she ran unsuccessfully for

(S: Wangari Maathai, V: was, C: an internationally renowned Kenyan scientist / Having earned: 분사구문(= after she had earned ~) / S: she, V_1: returned, V_2: earned, V_3: worked / S: Maathai, V: began, to save: 부사적 용법(목적), (to) provide: 부사적 용법(목적) / Soon known as ~: 분사구문 / S: the program, V: led / S_1: she, V_1: ran)

어휘확인

internationally 국제적으로 **renowned** 유명한 **Kenyan** 케냐의 **earn** 받다, 얻다 **degree** 학위; 각도 **return** 돌아오다 **PhD** 박사 (학위) (= Doctor of Philosophy) **professor** 교수 **department** 학과, 부서 **veterinary medicine** 수의학 **promote** 홍보하다 **provide** 제공하다 **firewood** 장작 **movement** (조직적인) 운동 **run for** ~에 출마하다 **unsuccessfully** 실패하여, 불운하게 **president** 대통령 **seat** (의회·위원회 등의) 의석[자리] **parliament** 의회, 국회 **elect** 선출하다 **appoint** 임명하다, 지명하다 **ministry** 장관의 직무; (정부의 각) 부처 **natural resource** 천연 자원 **wildlife** 야생

하지만 2002년 12월에 / 그녀는 국회의원으로 선출되었다 / 그리고 2003년에 / 그녀는 환경, 천연 자원 및 야생동물부 장관에 임명되었다

president and for a seat in Parliament, // but in December of 2002 / she (S_2) was elected (V_2) to Parliament, / and in 2003 / she (S_3) was appointed (V_3) to the Ministry of Environment, Natural Resources and Wildlife. [6] She (S) won (V) the Nobel Peace Prize / in 2004, / with the Nobel committee praising (with+목적어+현재분사) / "her contribution to environmentally-friendly development, democracy, and peace." [7] She (S) was (V) *the first African woman* [to win a Nobel Prize] (C).

그녀는 노벨 평화상을 수상했다 / 2004년에 / 노벨위원회가 칭찬하면서 / '환경 친화적인 개발, 민주주의, 그리고 평화에 대한 그녀의 공헌'을 / 그녀는 최초의 아프리카 여성이었다 / 노벨상을 수상한

① 미국에서 대학교수로 재직했다.
② 아프리카에서 수의사로 일했다.
③ 그린벨트 운동으로 알려진 사회운동을 전개했다.
④ 공직에 야망이 있었으나 뜻을 이루지 못했다.
⑤ 노벨상을 수상한 최초의 여성이다.

해석 한 눈에 보기 [1] Wangari Maathai는 국제적으로 유명한 케냐의 과학자였다. [2] 미국의 두 대학에서 학위를 받은 후, 그녀는 케냐로 돌아와 나이로비 대학교에서 박사 학위를 취득했고, 그 다음에 수의학과에서 교수로 일했다. [3] 1976년에 Maathai는 숲을 보호하고 케냐 여성들에게 장작을 제공하기 위해 나무 심기 프로그램을 홍보하기 시작했다. [4] 곧 그린벨트 운동으로 알려졌고, 그 프로그램은 수백만 그루의 나무를 심게 했다. [5] 1997년에, 그녀는 대통령과 의원직 출마에 실패했지만, 2002년 12월에 그녀는 국회의원으로 선출되었으며, 2003년에 그녀는 환경, 천연 자원 및 야생동물부 장관에 임명되었다. [6] 노벨위원회가 '환경 친화적인 개발, 민주주의, 그리고 평화에 대한 그녀의 공헌'을 칭찬하면서, 그녀는 2004년에 노벨 평화상을 수상했다. [7] 그녀는 노벨상을 수상한 최초의 아프리카 여성이었다.

정답단추 먼저 일치 혹은 불일치 중 어느 것을 고르는 건지 확인한 후, 선택지를 읽고, 해당 내용이 나오는 곳을 글에서 찾는 게 효율적이야. Wangari Maathai는 나무 심기 프로그램을 홍보했는데, 그것이 그린벨트 운동으로 알려져, 수백만 그루의 나무를 심게 했다고 했으므로, ③이 글의 내용과 일치해.

오답단서 ①, ②는 케냐의 나이로비 대학교의 수의학과 교수로 일했다고 했으므로 내용과 일치하지 않아. ④는 처음에는 대통령과 의원직 출마에 실패했지만, 나중에 국회의원으로 선출되었고, 환경, 천연 자원 및 야생동물부 장관에 임명되었다고 했으므로 일치하지 않는 내용이야. ⑤는 노벨상을 탄 최초의 아프리카 여성이므로 내용과 일치하지 않아.

동물 **committee** 위원회 **praise** 칭찬하다 **contribution** 기여 **development** 개발, 발달 **democracy** 민주주의

지문 Flow

[인물 소개]
2004년 노벨 평화상을 수상한 과학자 Wangari Maathai

[세부사항1]
미국에서 학위를 받은 후, 케냐로 돌아와 박사 학위를 받고, 수의학과 교수로 일함

&

[세부사항2]
나무 심기 프로그램을 홍보하여 그린벨트 운동으로 확산시킴

&

[세부사항3]
국회의원과 환경, 천연 자원 및 야생동물부 장관에 임명되어 공직 생활을 함

[맺음말]
환경 친화적인 개발, 민주주의, 그리고 평화에 대한 공헌으로 노벨상을 수상한 최초의 아프리카 여성이 됨

실전적용독해

157 정답 ⑤

지문 All in One

[1] Hummingbirds (S) are (V) *very small birds* [which (관계대명사) are native / to the Americas and the western hemisphere] (C). [2] They (S) were given (V) / the name "hummingbird" / because of *the easily recognizable humming sound* [(which[that]) (관계대명사) their wings make / when (접속사) they (S') fly (V')]. [3] The bee hummingbird (S) is (V) the world's smallest bird (C). [4] It (S) is (V_1) only five centimeters long (C) // and weighs (V_2) about *1.8 grams*, / which (관계대명사(계속적 용법)) is about the same weight / as a penny. [5] Most hummingbirds (S) migrate (V_1) north / in the early spring // and return (V_2) south / in the early fall. [6] They (S) have (V) a lifespan of nine to twelve years. [7] Hummingbirds (S) are (V) very curious (C_1) / and aggressive (C_2) with each other. [8] One of the best-known facts about hummingbirds (S) is (V) // that (접속사) they can fly backwards (C). [9] No other bird in the world (S) / can do (V) this.

벌새는 ~가 원산지인 아주 작은 새다 / 미대륙과 서반구 / 그것들에게는 주어졌다 / '벌새'라는 이름이 / 쉽게 알 수 있는 윙윙거리는 소리 때문에 / 그것들의 날개가 내는 / 그것들이 날 때 / 꿀벌벌새는 세계에서 가장 작은 새다 / 그것은 길이가 겨우 5cm밖에 안 되고 / 무게가 약 1.8g인데 / 이것은 거의 같은 무게이다 / 1페니와 / 대부분의 벌새는 북쪽으로 이동한다 / 이른 봄에 / 그리고 남쪽으로 돌아온다 / 이른 가을에 / 그것들은 9~12년의 수명을 가진다 / 벌새는 매우 호기심이 강하고 / 서로에게 공격적이다 / 벌새에 대해 가장 잘 알려진 사실들 중 하나는 ~이다 / 그것들이 뒤로 날 수 있다는 것 / 전 세계의 그 어떤 다른 새도 / 이것을 하지 못한다

① 가장 작은 것은 크기가 동전만 하다.
② 초봄부터 초가을까지는 남쪽에 산다.
③ 다 자라려면 9~12년이 걸린다.
④ 온순한 성격으로 떼 지어 다닌다.
⑤ 유일하게 뒤로 날 수 있는 새다.

어휘확인

hummingbird ((조류)) 벌새 **native** 원산(지)의 **Americas** 미대륙 전체 **western** 서쪽에 위치한 **hemisphere** (지구의) 반구 **recognizable** 쉽게 알 수 있는 **humming** 윙윙거리는 **centimeter** 센티미터(= cm) **gram** 그램(= g, gm) **penny** 페니(영국의 동전 단위) **migrate** 이동하다 **north** 북쪽으로 **return** 돌아오다 **south** 남쪽으로 **lifespan** 수명 **curious** 호기심이 강한 **aggressive** 공격적인 **best-known** 가장 잘 알려진 **backwards** 뒤로

지문 Flow

[도입]
벌새는 날개가 내는 윙윙거리는 소리 때문에 '벌새'라는 이름이 주어짐

[세부사항1]
크기가 아주 작으며, 이른 봄에 북쪽으로 이동하고 이른 가을에 남쪽으로 돌아옴

&

해석 한 눈에 보기 1 벌새는 미대륙과 서반구가 원산지인 아주 작은 새다. 2 그것들이 날 때 그것들의 날개가 내는 쉽게 알 수 있는 윙윙거리는 소리 때문에 그것들에게는 '벌새'라는 이름이 주어졌다. 3 꿀벌 벌새는 세계에서 가장 작은 새다. 4 그것은 길이가 겨우 5cm밖에 안 되고 무게가 약 1.8g인데, 이것은 1페니와 거의 같은 무게이다. 5 대부분의 벌새는 이른 봄에 북쪽으로 이동하고 이른 가을에 남쪽으로 돌아온다. 6 그것들은 9~12년의 수명을 가진다. 7 벌새는 매우 호기심이 강하고 서로에게 공격적이다. 8 벌새에 대해 가장 잘 알려진 사실 중 하나는 그것들이 뒤로 날 수 있다는 것이다. 9 전 세계의 그 어떤 다른 새도 이렇게 하지 못한다.

정답단추 선택지를 먼저 읽고, 순서대로 본문과 대조하며 정답을 골라야 해. 비교하면서 글을 읽어가다 보면 마지막 두 문장에 벌새는 뒤로 날 수 있으나 다른 새들은 그러지 못한다는 내용이 있지? 따라서 ⑤가 글의 내용과 일치하는 정답이야.

오답단서 선택지와 글의 내용을 순서대로 비교하며 살펴보자. 지문에서는 벌새의 크기가 아니라 무게를 동전과 비유하고 있으므로 ①의 내용은 맞지 않아. ②에서는 초봄부터 초가을까지 남쪽에 산다고 하였지만 지문에 따르면 남쪽이 아닌 북쪽에 산다고 했으므로 일치하지 않아. 또한, ③에서 평균 수명이 9~12년이므로 다 자라는 데 9~12년이 걸린다는 설명은 옳지 않고, 마지막으로 본문에서 벌새의 성향은 공격적이라고 하고 있으므로 ④의 설명도 옳지 않아.

[세부사항2]
9~12년의 수명을 가지며, 호기심이 강하고 공격적임

&

[세부사항3]
뒤로 날 수 있는 것이 다른 새들과 다름

158 정답 ⑤

지문 All in One

1 The story of the voyageurs (S: 보이저 이야기는) / is (V) *a colorful feature of Canadian history* (C: 캐나다 역사의 다채로운 하나의 특징이다) [that (관계대명사) is celebrated to this day] (오늘날까지 기념되고 있는). 2 Voyageur (S₁) means (V₁) "traveler" / in French (보이저는 '여행자'를 의미하며 / 프랑스어로), // [and] many of the voyageurs (S₂) were (V₂) of French descent (보이저 중 많은 이들이 프랑스 혈통이었다). 3 They (S) were (V) *men* [who (관계대명사) made their living / in the 18th century / transporting goods to distant parts of Canada / by canoe] (C) (그들은 생계를 꾸리던 사람들이었다 / 18세기에 / 상품들을 캐나다의 먼 지역들로 수송하며 / 카누로). 4 Among *the goods* [(which[that]) (관계대명사) they transported] (그들이 수송하던 상품들 중에서), / the vast majority (S) were (V) *furs* (C) [that (관계대명사) would be sold / in the larger cities, / such as Montreal] (엄청난 다수는 팔릴 모피였다 / 보다 더 큰 도시들에서 / 몬트리올같이). 5 Voyageurs (S) had to be (V) strong [and] courageous (보이저는 강하고 용감해야 했는데), // since (접속사) they (S′) canoed (V′) / through vast wilderness (그들이 카누로 갔기 때문이다 / 방대한 황무지를). 6 They (S) were (V) also cheerful, optimistic, [and] fun-loving men (C) / with a sense of humor (그들은 또한 쾌활하고 낙천적이고 즐겁게 생활하는 사람들이었다 / 유머 감각이 있는). 7 But eventually the railroad (S₁) replaced (V₁) the canoe (하지만 결국 철도가 카누를 대체하였고) / as *the most efficient* [and] *inexpensive way* [to transport goods] (가장 효율적이고 저렴한 방법으로서 / 상품을 수송하는), // [and] voyageurs (S₂) soon disappeared (V₂) (그래서 보이저는 곧 사라졌다).

① 대부분은 프랑스인의 후손들이다.
② 카누를 타고 캐나다에서 무역을 했다.
③ 거친 환경에서 생활하는 강인한 사람들이었다.
④ 성격이 활기차고 긍정적인 사람들이었다.
⑤ 카누가 철도를 대체하면서 호황을 누렸다.

해석 한 눈에 보기 1 보이저 이야기는 오늘날까지 기념되고 있는 캐나다 역사의 다채로운 하나의 특징이다. 2 보이저는 프랑스어로 '여행자'를 의미하며, 보이저 중 많은 이들이 프랑스 혈통이었다. 3 그들은 18세기에 상품들을 카누로 캐나다의 먼 지역들로 수송하며 생계를 꾸리던 사람들이었다. 4 그들이 수송하던 상품 중에서, 엄청난 다수는 몬트리올같이 보다 더 큰 도시들에서 팔릴 모피였다. 5 보이저는 강하고 용감해야 했는데, 방대한 황무지를 카누로 갔기 때문이다. 6 그들은 또한 쾌활하고, 낙천적이고, 즐겁게 생활하는 사람들이었으며 유머 감각이 있었다. 7 하지만 결국 철도가 상품을 수송하는 가장 효율적이고 저렴한 방법으로서 카누를 대체하였고, 그래서 보이저는 곧 사라졌다.

정답단추 지시문을 읽고 일치 혹은 불일치 중 어느 것을 고르는 건지 파악한 뒤 선택지를 읽고, 순서대로 본문과 대조하며 정답을 찾으면 돼. 마지막 문장에서 철도가 카누를 대체하면서 보이저는 사라졌다는 내용을 확인할 수 있지? 그러나 ⑤에서는 그 반대로 카누가 철도를 대체하면서 호황을 누렸다고 했으므로 글의 내용과 일치하지 않아. 따라서 ⑤가 정답이야.

오답단서 순서대로 선택지와 글의 내용을 살펴보자. ①은 두 번째 문장에서 대부분 프랑스 혈통이었다는 내용을 찾을 수 있어. ②도 그다음 문장에서 바로 찾을 수 있지. 또한, 보이저는 방대한 황무지를 카누로 갔기 때문에 강하고 용감해야 한다는 문장에서 ③의 내용을 확인할 수 있어. 마지막으로 보이저는 쾌활하고 낙천적이라는 설명(they were also ~ humor.)을 통해 ④의 설명도 일치함을 알 수 있어.

어휘확인

voyageur 보이저(캐나다의 뱃사공) **colorful** 다채로운 **feature** 특징, 특성 **Canadian** 캐나다의 **traveler** 여행자 **descent** 혈통, 가문 **make one's living** 생계를 꾸리다 **century** 세기, 100년 **transport** 수송하다; 수송 **goods** 상품, 제품 **distant** 먼, 떨어져 있는 **canoe** 카누; 카누로 가다 **vast** 엄청난[방대한] **majority** 다수 **courageous** 용감한 **wilderness** 황무지, 황야 **cheerful** 쾌활한 **optimistic** 낙천[낙관]적인 **fun-loving** 재미를 추구하는 **sense** 감각 **humor** 유머, 익살 **eventually** 결국, 종내 **railroad** 철도 **replace** 대체하다 **efficient** 효율적인 **inexpensive** 저렴한, 비싸지 않은 **disappear** 사라지다

지문 Flow

[도입]
보이저는 오늘날까지 기념되고 있는 캐나다 역사의 다채로운 하나의 특징임

⬇

[세부사항1]
프랑스어로 '여행자'를 의미하고, 대부분이 프랑스 혈통으로 카누로 상품을 수송하며 생계를 꾸리던 사람들이었음

&

[세부사항2]
강하고 용감하며, 쾌활하고, 낙천적이고, 유머 감각이 있고, 즐겁게 생활하는 사람들이었음

&

[세부사항3]
철도가 카누를 대체하면서 보이저는 곧 사라졌음

159 정답 ⑤

지문 All in One

1 George Eyser (S) was born (V₁) / in Germany / in 1870 (George Eyser는 태어났다 / 독일에서 / 1870년에) // [and] emigrated (V₂) to the St. Louis area / at age (그리고 세인트루이스 지역으로 이민을 갔다 / 14살 때)

어휘확인

emigrate 이민을 가다 **area** 지역 **adolescence** 청소년기 **hit** ~와 부딪치다;

언제가 청소년기 시절에 / 그는 그의 왼쪽 다리를 잃었다 / 열차에 의해 치인 후에

fourteen. [2] Sometime during his adolescence, / he lost his left leg / after being hit by a train.

S V 분사구문(= after he was hit ~)

그는 갖추게 되었다 / 나무로 된 다리를 / 그가 달리고 뛰는 것을 가능하게 했다 / 만일 당신이

[3] He was outfitted / with a wooden leg, / which allowed him to run [and] jump. [4] If you were

S V 관계대명사(계속적 용법) 접속사 S′ V′

독일인이라면 / 체조는 중요 부분이었다 / 세인트루이스 지역 사회 경험의 / 그리고

German, / gymnastics was part and parcel / of the St. Louis community experience, // [and]

C′ S_1 V_1 C_1

Eyser의 왼쪽 다리 결핍은 / 이것을 바꾸지 않았다 / 전혀 / 체조 선수로서의 Eyser의 경험은 / 성과를

Eyser's lack of a left leg / did not change this / at all. [5] Eyser's experience as a gymnast / paid

S_2 V_2 S V

올렸다 / 비록 1904년 올림픽의 참가자들이 / 아마추어 선수로 평가되었지만 / Eyser는

off. [6] Even though the competitors in the 1904 Olympics / were ranked as amateurs, // Eyser

접속사 S′ V′ S

압도했다 / 그는 금메달을 땄다 / 평행봉, 도마, 그리고 밧줄 타기에서

dominated. [7] He took gold medals / on the parallel bars, vault, [and] in the rope climb.

V S V

① 14세에 St. Louis로 이민 왔다.
② 열차 사고로 한쪽 다리를 잃었다.
③ 나무로 된 의족에 의지한 채 운동했다.
④ 체조가 인기 있던 지역에서 성장했다.
⑤ 쟁쟁한 프로 선수들을 이기고 금메달을 땄다.

해석 한 눈에 보기 [1] George Eyser는 1870년에 독일에서 태어났고 14살 때 세인트루이스 지역으로 이민을 갔다. [2] 언젠가 청소년기 시절에, 그는 열차에 치인 후 왼쪽 다리를 잃었다. [3] 그는 나무로 된 다리를 갖추게 되었는데, 이것은 그가 달리고 점프하는 것을 가능하게 했다. [4] 만일 당신이 독일인이라면, 체조는 세인트루이스 지역 사회 경험의 중요한 부분이었는데, Eyser의 왼쪽 다리 결핍은 이것을 전혀 바꾸지 않았다. [5] 체조 선수로서의 Eyser의 경험은 성과를 올렸다. [6] 비록 1904년 올림픽 참가자들이 아마추어들로 평가되었지만, Eyser는 이들을 압도했다. [7] 그는 평행봉, 도마, 밧줄 타기에서 금메달을 땄다.

정답단추 먼저 지시문을 읽고 일치 혹은 불일치 중 어느 것을 고르는 건지 파악해야 해. 그리고 선택지를 먼저 읽은 후에 해당 내용이 나오는 곳을 글에서 찾아 읽는 게 효율적이야. 마지막 문장에서 1904년 올림픽 참가자들은 아마추어 선수들이라고 했는데 ⑤는 '프로 선수들'이라고 표현했지? 따라서 ⑤가 글의 내용과 일치하지 않아.

오답단서 ①은 첫 번째 문장으로 확인할 수 있어. ②는 지문에서 Eyser가 열차에 치여서 왼쪽 다리를 잃었다고 했으니까 일치하는 내용이지. 그리고 나무로 된 다리 덕에 달리고 점프할 수 있다고 했으니까 ③도 글의 내용과 일치해. 마지막으로 ④는 세인트루이스 지역에서 체조가 중요한 부분(part and parcel)이라고 언급하고 있어서 일치함을 알 수 있어.

때리다 **outfit** (복장·장비를) 갖추어 주다 **allow** 가능하게 하다; 허락하다 **gymnastics** 체조, 체육 **part and parcel** 중요 부분, 요점 **community** 지역 사회 **lack** 결핍 **gymnast** 체조 선수 **pay off** 성과를 올리다 **even though** 비록 ~일지라도 **competitor** (시합) 참가자; 경쟁자 **rank** (등급·등위·순서를) 평가하다 **amateur** 아마추어 선수 **dominate** (경기에서) 압도하다; 지배하다 **parallel bars** 평행봉 **vault** ((체조)) 도마 **rope climb** 밧줄 타기

지문 Flow

[인물 소개]
George Eyser는 1870년에 독일에서 태어남

⬇

[사건]
열차 사고로 왼쪽 다리를 잃었지만, 나무로 된 다리를 갖추어 달리고 점프하게 됨

⬇

[화제 전환]
체조는 세인트루이스 지역사회 경험의 중요한 부분이었고, 체조 선수로서 Eyser는 성과를 올림

⬇

[결과]
1904년 올림픽에 출전하여 평행봉, 도마, 밧줄 타기에서 금메달을 땀

유형 15 실용 자료 파악

Check-Up 1 1 Ⓐ 2 Ⓑ 3 Ⓒ 4 Ⓓ **160** ④
Check-Up 2 **161** ⑤
실전적용독해 **162** ② **163** ④

Check-Up 1

정답 1 Ⓐ 2 Ⓑ 3 Ⓒ 4 Ⓓ

해석

활동
나무 위의 집, 정글 다리, 이야기 들려주기, 보트 여행, 동물 집짓기, 미끄러운 비탈길 내려가기, 습지 걷기

시간
- 4월 초부터 10월 말까지
- 오전 10시부터 오후 5시까지

입장료
6세 미만 …… 무료
6–14세 …… 10달러
15–65세 …… 13달러
65세 초과 …… 7.5달러
- 단체 요금: 1인당 7달러 (12명 이상의 단체)

음식물 및 음료
개인 음식을 가져올 수 있습니다.
레스토랑과 두 개의 다과 판매점이 있습니다.

160 정답 ④

지문 All in One

직위 / 임시 보조 교사
1 **Job Title:** Temporary Assistant Teacher

위치 / 헨라이코, 버지니아 주, 미국
2 **Location:** Henrico, VA, US

기관명 / HCPS(헨라이코 카운티 공립학교)
3 **Organization Name:** HCPS(Henrico County Public Schools)

필수 직무
4 **Essential Duties**

학생들을 위한 교수 활동 계획하기
5 – Plan instructional activities for students

학생들의 발달에 대한 성적 평가 및 유지하기
6 – Assess [and] maintain records of students' progress

다양한 교수 전략 활용하기 / 학생들의 성공을 장려하기 위해
7 – Utilize a variety of instructional strategies / in order to promote student success
(in order to promote: 부사적 용법(목적))

최소 자격
8 **Minimum Qualifications**

학사 학위가 필요합니다
9 Bachelor's Degree (is) required.
(Bachelor's Degree: S / (is) required: V)

추가 정보
10 **Additional Information**

하루 당 83.84달러
11 $83.84/per day

이 공석은 열려 있습니다 / 채워질 때까지
12 This vacancy is open / until (it is) filled.
(This vacancy: S / is: V / open: C / until: 접속사 / it: S' / is filled: V')

이 자리에 대한 구체적인[상세한] 질문은 / HCPS에 연락하십시오 / 804-795-7030로
13 FOR SPECIFIC QUESTIONS ABOUT THIS POSITION / PLEASE CONTACT HCPS / at 804-795-7030.
(CONTACT: V)

지원 방법
14 **How To Apply**

이 직책을 고려한다면 / 증빙 서류와 대학 성적 증명서를 아래로 우편으로 보내주십시오
15 To be considered for this position, / please mail written references and college transcripts to:
(To be considered: 부사적 용법(조건) / mail: V)

헨라이코 카운티 공립학교 / 인적 자원부 / 사서함 23120
16 Henrico County Public Schools / Department of Human Resources / P.O. Box 23120 /
나인 마일가 3820 / 헨라이코, 버지니아 우편번호 23223-0420
3820 Nine Mile Road / Henrico, VA 23223-0420

① 임시 보조 교사를 구하는 것이다.
② 업무에는 학생 성적 평가가 포함된다.
③ 학사 학위 이상인 자가 지원 가능하다.
④ 마감일 없이 상시 지원 가능하다.
⑤ 제출 서류는 우편으로 우송해야 한다.

해석 한 눈에 보기 1 **직위:** 임시 보조 교사 2 **위치:** 헨라이코, 버지니아 주, 미국 3 **기관명:** HCPS(헨라이코 카운티 공립학교) 4 **필수 직무** 5 – 학생들을 위한 교수 활동 계획하기 6 – 학생들의 발달에 대한 성적 평가 및 유지하기 7 – 학생들의 성공을 장려하기 위해 다양한 교수 전략 활용하기 8 **최소 자격** 9 학사 학위가 필요합니다. 10 **추가 정보** 11 하루 당 83.84달러 12 이 공석은 채워질 때까지 열려 있습니다. 13 이 자리에 대한 구체적인 질문은 HCPS에 804-795-7030로 연락하십시오. 14 **지원 방법** 15 이 직책을 고려한다면, 증빙 서류와 대학 성적 증명서를 아래로 우편으로 보내주십시오. 16 헨라이코 카운티 공립학교, 인적 자원부, 버지니아주, 헨라이코, 나인 마일가 3820, 사서함 23120, 우편번호 23223-0420

정답단추 선택지를 읽고, 해당하는 부분의 소제목을 찾아 일치 여부를 확인하도록 해. 이 안내문은 임시 보조 교사를 구하는 구인 광고야. This vacancy is open until filled.로 보아, 교사를 구할 때까지 이 광고가 유효한 거야. 그러니까 그 후에는 지원할 수 없는 것이지. 따라서 글의 내용과 일치하지 않는 것은 ④야.

오답단서 ①은 Job Title에서 확인할 수 있어. ②는 필수 직무의 두 번째 항목에 해당하는 내용이야. ③은 최소 자격으로 학사 학위가 필요하다고 했으므로 일치하는 내용이야. ⑤는 How to Apply에 나오는 내용으로서 일치해.

어휘확인

temporary 임시의, 일시적인 **assistant** 보조원, 조수 **location** 위치, 장소 **VA** ((우편)) 버지니아(= **Virginia**) **county** 카운티, 군(郡) **essential** 필수적인 **duty** 의무, 임무 **instructional** 교육용의 **assess** 평가하다 **maintain** 유지하다 **progress** 발달, 진보 **utilize** 활용하다 **a variety of** 다양한 **strategy** 전략 **promote** 장려하다, 촉진하다 **qualification** 자격, 자격증 **bachelor's degree** 학사 학위 **require** 필요하다, 요구하다 **additional** 추가의 **vacancy** 공석, 결원 **specific** 구체적인 **position** 자리, 위치 **apply** 지원하다, 신청하다 **consider** 고려하다 **references** 증빙 서류 **transcript** (학교의) 성적증명서 **department** 부서 **human resources** 인적 자원; (회사의) 인사부 **P.O. Box** 사서함(= **post-office box**)

지문 Flow

[소재]
임시 보조 교사 구인 광고

[세부사항1]
필수 직무: 교수 활동 계획, 성적 평가 및 유지, 다양한 교수 전략 활용

&

[세부사항2]
• 최소 자격: 학사 학위
• 급료: 하루 당 83.84달러
• 충원 시까지 공고 유효함

&

[세부사항3]
지원 방법: 증빙 서류와 대학 성적 증명서 우편 송부

Check-Up 2

161 정답 ⑤

지문 All in One

곤충들의 세상입니다
1 **It's a Bug's World**

'곤충들의 세상입니다'가 바꿀 것입니다 / 쇼츠타운 마을 회관을 이번 4월에 정글로
2 It's a Bug's World is turning / Shortstown Village Hall into a jungle this April!
(It's a Bug's World: S / is turning: V)

시간 / 2017년 4월 22일 10:00~13:00
3 When: 22 April 2017 10:00 ~ 13:00

어휘확인

informal 비공식의 **exhibition** 전시회 **opportunity** 기회 **face to face** 직면한, 서로 얼굴을 맞대고 **a wide variety of** 매우 다양한 **exotic** 이국적인 **insect** 곤충 **despite** ~에도 불구하고 **reputation** 명성, 평판 **available** 이용할 수 있는 **keeper** (동

장소 쇼츠타운 마을 회관, 쇼츠타운, 베드퍼드
4 Where: Shortstown Village Hall, Shortstown, Bedford

이 무료의 비공식적인 교육 전시회는 직접 만날 흥미로운 기회입니다
5 This FREE informal, educational exhibition is *an exciting opportunity* [to meet face to face / with a wide variety of exotic insects / and (to) see for yourselves that, / despite their reputation, / they're not scary at all].
(S: This FREE informal, educational exhibition / V: is / C: an exciting opportunity / 매우 다양한 종류의 이국적인 곤충을 / 그리고 ~라는 것을 스스로 알게 될 / that: 접속사 / 그들의 명성에도 불구하고 / 전혀 무서운 것이 아니라는 것을 / S′: they / V′: 're / C′: not scary)

사육사와 함께 할 수 있는 동물 다루기 경험
6 • *Animal handling experiences* [available with their keepers]

판매용 품목 동물 장비 및 동물 주제의 기타 관련 상품과 같은
7 • Items for sale, / such as animal equipment and other related, animal-themed goods

영감을 받게 하는 정보 및 상호적인 활동
8 • *Information and interactive activities* [to get you inspired]

공인되고 경력이 있는 사육사가 당신의 질문에 답변해 드릴 겁니다
9 • Qualified and experienced keepers / will answer your questions.
(S: Qualified and experienced keepers / V: will answer)

마을 회관에서 주차는 제한됩니다 그리고 지역 주민들은 행사에 걸어오실 것을 요청드립니다
10 Parking is restricted at the Village Hall, // and it is requested that local residents walk to the event.
(S₁: Parking / V₁: is restricted / 가주어: it / V₂: is requested / 접속사: that / 진주어: local residents walk to the event)

① 3시간 동안 단 1회 진행되는 행사이다.
② 참가비는 무료이다.
③ 동물을 직접 만져 볼 수 있다.
④ 전문 사육사에게 사육 관련 내용을 질의할 수 있다.
⑤ 주차장이 따로 없어 주차는 불가능하다.

해석 한 눈에 보기 1 **곤충들의 세상입니다** 2 '곤충들의 세상입니다'가 쇼츠타운 마을 회관을 이번 4월에 정글로 바꿀 것입니다! 3 시간: 2017년 4월 22일 10:00~13:00 4 장소: 쇼츠타운 마을 회관, 쇼츠타운, 베드퍼드 5 이 무료의 비공식적인 교육 전시회는 매우 다양한 종류의 이국적인 곤충을 직접 만나고, 그들의 명성에도 불구하고, 전혀 무서운 것이 아니라는 것을 스스로 알게 될 흥미로운 기회입니다. 6 •사육사와 함께 할 수 있는 동물 다루기 경험 7 •동물 장비 및 동물 주제의 기타 관련 상품과 같은 판매용 품목 8 •영감을 받게 하는 정보 및 상호적인 활동 9 •공인되고 경력이 있는 사육사가 당신의 질문에 답변해 드릴 겁니다. 10 마을 회관에서 주차는 제한되며, 지역 주민들은 행사에 걸어오실 것을 요청드립니다.

정답단추 이 글은 It's a Bug's World라는 이름의 행사를 홍보하는 안내문으로, 일치하지 않는 것을 고르는 문제야. 글 안의 단서와 선택지의 순서가 일치하므로, 차례로 글에서 단서를 찾으면 돼. 글의 마지막 문장에서 마을 회관에 제한적이나마 주차를 할 수 있다는 내용이 나오므로 ⑤는 글의 내용과 일치하지 않아.

오답단서 ①은 10시에서 1시까지 진행된다고 했으므로 일치하는 내용이야. ②는 This FREE informal, educational exhibition에서 무료 행사라고 했으므로 내용과 일치함을 알 수 있어. ③, ④는 행사에서 할 수 있는 활동에 대한 선택지로 모두 글에서 언급된 내용이야.

물의) 사육사 **equipment** 장비 **related** 관련된 **interactive** 상호적인 **inspire** 영감을 주다 **parking** 주차 **restrict** 제한하다, 한정하다 **request** 요청하다 **resident** 주민

지문 Flow

[소재]
It's a Bug's World라는 행사 홍보

⬇

[세부사항1]
•시간: 2017년 4월 22일 10:00~13:00
•장소: 쇼츠타운 마을 회관

&

[세부사항2]
무료의 비공식적인 교육 전시회에서 다양한 곤충을 경험할 수 있음
•행사 내용: 동물 다루기 체험, 동물 장비와 동물 주제 기타 관련 상품 판매, 정보와 상호적인 활동, 질의응답

&

[세부사항3]
주차는 마을 회관에서 제한적으로 이용 가능

실전적용독해

162 정답 ②

지문 All in One

크리스틴 스쿨 IB 국제 학교
1 **Kristin School IB World School**

사립 남녀 공학의 통학 학교 유치원에서 13학년을 위한 4—18세
2 A private, co-educational day school / for grades K—13 / (ages 4—18).

우리의 임무
3 Our mission:

우리 학생들에게 우수한 다방면의 교육을 제공하기 그리고 그들을 책임 있는 세계 시민이 되도록 준비시키기
4 To provide our students with a superior all-round education / and to prepare them to be *responsible world citizens* [who think creatively, reason critically, communicate effectively, and learn enthusiastically / throughout life].
(to be: 부사적 용법(목적) / who: 관계대명사 / 창조적으로 생각하고, 비판적으로 추론하고, 효과적으로 의사소통하고, 열정적으로 배우는 / 평생)

오클랜드의 노스 쇼어의 올버니에 위치함 오클랜드 시내에서 30분
5 (It is) Located in Albany on Auckland's North Shore / (30 minutes from downtown Auckland / and 50 minutes from Auckland International Airport)
(S: It / V: is / 그리고 오클랜드 국제공항에서 50분)

교사진과 학생의 비율 1:10
6 Ratio of teaching staff to students: 1:10

유학생의 비율 3%
7 Percentage of international students: 3%

어휘확인

private 사립의 **co-educational** 남녀 공학의 **day school** 통학 학교(기숙학교와 대조적으로 학생들이 집에서 다니는 사립학교) **mission** 임무 **provide** 제공하다 **superior** 우수한 **all-round** 다방면의, 전반적인 **education** 교육 **responsible** 책임 있는 **citizen** 시민 **creatively** 창조적으로 **reason** 추론하다, 논하다 **critically** 비판[비평]적으로; 혹평하여 **effectively** 효과적으로 **enthusiastically** 열정적으로 **throughout life** 평생, 일생 동안 **locate** 위치하다 **ratio** 비율 **staff** 직원 **percentage** 비율; 퍼센트 **academic year** 학년(도)

지문 Flow

[소재]
크리스틴 스쿨 IB 국제 학교 홍보

⬇

8 학사 일정
Academic Year:

9 1월 하순—12월 첫째 주
Late January — first week of December

10 각 2—3주간의 방학/휴일 4월, 7월, 그리고 9월에
Study breaks/holidays of 2 — 3 weeks each / in April, July, and September.

① 공립학교로서 남녀 공학이다. ② Auckland 시내에서 30분 거리이다.
③ 한 반 평균 인원이 10명이다. ④ 학사 일정은 1월 초에서 12월 초이다.
⑤ 1년에 총 2~3주의 단기방학이 있다.

해석 한 눈에 보기 1 **크리스틴 스쿨 IB 국제 학교** 2 유치원에서 13학년(4—18세)을 위한 사립 남녀 공학의 통학 학교 3 우리의 임무: 4 우리 학생들에게 우수한 다방면의 교육을 제공하고 평생 그들이 창조적으로 생각하고, 비판적으로 추론하고, 효과적으로 의사소통하고, 열정적으로 배우는 책임 있는 세계 시민이 되도록 준비시키는 것 5 오클랜드의 노스 쇼어의 올버니에 위치함 (오클랜드 시내에서 30분 그리고 오클랜드 국제공항에서 50분) 6 교사진과 학생의 비율: 1:10 7 유학생의 비율: 3% 8 학사 일정: 9 1월 하순—12월 첫째 주 10 4월, 7월, 그리고 9월에 각 2—3주간의 방학/휴일

정답단추 국제 학교를 소개하는 안내문의 모든 내용을 읽을 필요는 없어. 선택지를 읽고, 해당하는 부분을 찾아 빠르게 일치 여부를 확인하도록 해. 글의 중반부에 학교의 위치를 설명하면서, 오클랜드 시내에서 30분 그리고 오클랜드 국제공항에서 50분 거리라고 했어. 따라서 글의 내용과 일치하는 것은 ②야.

오답단서 ①은 첫 번째 문장에서 사립 남녀 공학 학교라고 했으므로 일치하지 않아. ③은 교사와 학생의 비율이 1:10이라는 것이지, 한 반 평균 인원수에 대한 내용이 아니므로 오답이야. ④는 Late January로 보아, 1월 하순부터 학사 일정이 시작되므로 일치하지 않는 내용이야. ⑤는 4월, 7월, 9월에 각 2—3주간의 방학이 있다고 했으므로 내용과 일치하지 않아.

[세부사항1]
사립 남녀 공학 학교 (유치원—13학년)

&

[세부사항2]
• 임무: 우수한 다방면의 교육 제공, 책임 있는 세계 시민 양성

&

[세부사항3]
• 위치: 오클랜드의 노스 쇼어의 올버니(오클랜드 시내에서 30분, 오클랜드 국제공항에서 50분 거리)

&

[세부사항4]
• 교사와 학생 비율: 1:10
• 유학생 비율: 3%
• 학사 일정: 1월 하순—12월 첫째 주
• 방학: 4월, 7월, 9월에 2—3주

163 정답 ④

지문 All in One

1 나를 멀리 데려가 주세요
Take Me Away (V)

2 역사 내내 / 작가들은 가상의 세계를 창조해왔습니다
Throughout history, / writers (S) have created (V) imaginary worlds. 3 이제 우리를 멀리 데려갈 당신의 차례입니다 Now it('s) (가주어 V) your turn to take us away / (진주어) 상상의 나라로 to a land of make-believe.

4 여기에 방법이 있습니다(방법 안내)
Here's how (V S)

5 가상의 세계를 만드세요 / 뚜렷한 특징들과 랜드마크들이 있는
Create (V) an imaginary world / with distinct features and landmarks. 6 그러고 나서 이 가상의 장소를 배경으로 설정된 단편 소설 혹은 시를 쓰세요 Then write (V) *a short story* [or] *a poem* [set in this imaginary place]. 7 당신은 삽화를 포함할 수 있습니다 / 당신의 가상 세계에 대한 You (S) can include (V) an illustration / of your imaginary world. 8 4명의 우승자가 저희의 초대(객원) 심사위원에 의해 선정될 것입니다 Four winners (S) will be selected (V) by our guest judge. 9 우승 출품작들은 실릴 것입니다 / 〈라이트 나우〉의 4월호에 Winning entries (S) will be published (V) / in the April issue of *Write Now*.

10 알아둘 규칙
***Rules* [to Know]**

11 대회는 참여할 수 있습니다 / 5—12학년 학생들이
• The contest (S) is (V) open (C) / to students in grades 5 — 12.

12 시는 400단어를 초과해서는 안 됩니다 / 소설은 더 길어서는 안 됩니다 / 800단어보다
• Poems (S_1) should not exceed (V_1) 400 words, // [and] stories (S_2) should be (V_2) no longer / than 800 words (C_2).

13 모든 출품작들은 우체국 소인이 찍혀 있어야 합니다 / 2017년 12월 20일까지
• All entries (S) must be postmarked (V) / by Dec. 20, 2017.

14 대회 출품작을 우편으로 여기로 보내 주십시오 / 〈라이트 나우〉 잡지 '나를 멀리 데려가 주세요' 코네티컷주 스탬퍼드시 사서함 1200, 스탬퍼드 1번가 200번지 우편번호 069-0024
• Mail (V) contest entries to: / *Write Now* Magazine "Take Me Away" 200 First Stamford Place, P.O. Box 1200 Stamford, CT 069-0024

① 판타지 장르의 글쓰기 대회 안내문이다. ② 선정된 글은 4월호 잡지에 실린다.
③ 4학년은 제출할 수 없다. ④ 모든 글은 400~800단어여야 한다.
⑤ 우편 발송을 해야 한다.

어휘확인

take A away (to B) A를 (B로) 멀리 데리고 가다 **throughout** 내내 **imaginary** 가상의 **turn** 차례; 돌다 **make-believe** 상상, 환상 **distinct** 뚜렷한 **feature** 특징 **landmark** 랜드마크(멀리서 보고 위치 파악에 도움이 되는 대형 건물 같은 것) **then** 그러고 나서; 그때 **short story** 단편 소설 **set** (연극·소설·영화의) 배경을 설정하다 **include** 포함하다 **illustration** 삽화 **winner** 우승자 **select** 선정하다 **guest** 초대받은 사람, 손님 **judge** 심사위원; 판사 **entry** 출품작; 입장 **publish** 싣다; 출판하다 **issue** (잡지·신문 같은 정기 간행물의) 호; 주제 **open to A** A가 참여할 수 있는 **grade** 학년; 품질 **exceed** 초과하다 **postmark** 우편물의 소인을 찍다 **mail** 우편으로 보내다; 우편물 **P.O. Box** 사서함(= **post-office box**) **CT** ((우편)) 코네티컷(= **Connecticut**)

지문 Flow

[도입]
글쓰기 대회 안내문

⬇

[세부사항1]
대회 출품 방법: 가상의 세계 만들어서 그 장소를 배경으로 단편소설이나 시 쓰기(삽화 포함 가능)

&

[세부사항2]
작품 선정: 심사위원이 4인의 우승자를 선정하여 〈라이트 나우〉 4월호에 개재함

⬇

해석 한 눈에 보기 1 **나를 멀리 데려가 주세요** 2 역사 내내, 작가들은 가상의 세계를 창조해 왔습니다. 3 이제는 당신이 우리를 멀리 상상의 나라로 데려갈 차례입니다. 4 **방법 안내** 5 뚜렷한 특징들과 랜드마크들이 있는 가상의 세계를 만드세요. 6 그러고 나서 이 가상의 장소를 배경으로 하는 단편소설이나 시를 쓰세요. 7 당신은 당신의 가상 세계에 대한 삽화를 포함할 수 있습니다. 8 4인의 우승자가 저희의 객원 심사위원에 의해 선정될 것입니다. 9 우승 작품은 〈라이트 나우〉 4월호에 실릴 것입니다. 10 **알아둘 규칙** 11 •대회는 5－12학년 학생들이 참여할 수 있습니다. 12 •시는 400단어를 초과해서는 안 되고, 소설은 800단어를 넘어서는 안 됩니다. 13 •모든 출품작에는 2017년 12월 20일까지 우체국 소인이 찍혀 있어야 합니다. 14 •대회 출품작을 우편으로 이곳으로 보내 주십시오: 〈라이트 나우〉 잡지 '나를 멀리 데려가 주세요' 코네티컷주, 스탬퍼드시 사서함 1200, 스탬퍼드 1번가 200번지 우편번호 069-0024

정답단추 실용문은 소제목으로 내용이 구분되어 있을 때가 많아서 선택지를 읽고 그에 해당하는 소제목의 내용을 확인하는 게 효율적이야. 이 실용문은 잡지사에서 실시하는 소설과 시 공모 안내문이야. ④에서 모든 글이 400~800단어여야 한다고 설명하고 있지? 그런데 지문의 소제목 중 '알아둘 규칙'의 내용을 보면 시는 400단어 미만, 소설은 800단어 미만이어야 한다고 하고 있어. 따라서 ④는 안내문의 내용과 일치하지 않아.

오답단서 ①, ②는 '방법 안내'라는 소제목 내용에서 확인할 수 있어. 먼저 안내문에서 가상의 세계를 배경으로 한 글쓰기를 하라고 했으니까 ①의 판타지 장르의 글쓰기 대회라는 설명과 일치해. 그리고 ②는 우승 작품이 〈라이트 나우〉의 4월호에 실릴 예정이라고 했으니까 옳은 설명이지. ③, ⑤는 소제목 '알아둘 규칙' 내용에서 찾을 수 있는데 첫 번째, 세 번째 규칙과 각각 일치하는 내용이야. 첫 번째 규칙에서 5~12학년 학생이 대상이라고 했으니 4학년은 제출할 수 없다는 ③의 설명과 일치해. 그리고 세 번째 규칙에서 모든 작품에는 우체국 소인이 찍혀 있어야 한다고 했으니까 우편 발송을 해야 한다는 ⑤의 내용도 안내문과 일치함을 알 수 있어.

[추가사항]
출품 시 알아둘 4가지 규칙에 대해 설명함(참여 대상, 작품의 제한 단어 수, 제출 기한, 우편 제출)

유형 16 도표 자료 파악

Check-Up 1 1 ○ 2 × **164** ③
Mini Test 1 ○ 2 ○ 3 × 4 ○ 5 × 6 × 7 ○ 8 × 9 the strongest 10 five times 11 steadily
12 had reached their peak 13 × 14 ○ 15 ○
실전적용독해 **165** ⑤ **166** ④

Check-Up 1

정답 1 ○ 2 ×
해석 1 1891년과 1901년 사이에 미국으로의 이민자 수는 급격히 증가했다. 2 1910년 이후 캐나다로의 이민자 수는 미국의 수치를 초과했다.

164 정답 ③

지문 All in One

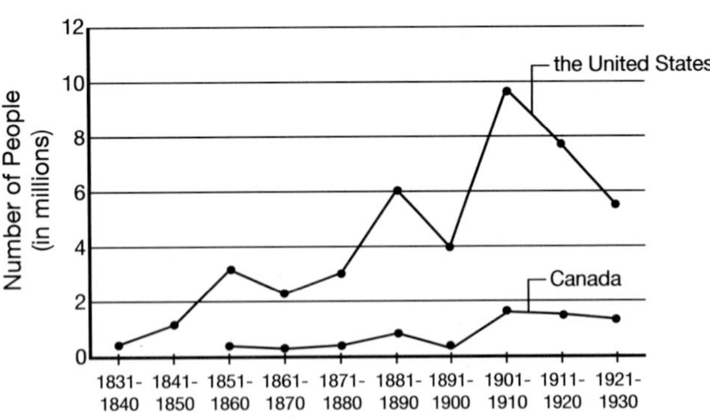

[1] The chart above(S, 위 도표는) shows(V, 보여 준다) / the immigration trends of the United States and Canada(미국과 캐나다의 이민 경향을) / during the years 1831 – 1930(1831–1930년 동안). [2] ① The number of immigrants to the U.S.(S, 미국으로의 이민자 수는) / reached(V) its peak(최고치에 이르렀다) / during the period from 1901 – 1910(1901–1910년 기간 동안에), / which was the same with Canada(이는 캐나다와 동일했다; which: 관계대명사(계속적 용법)). [3] ② After 1910(1910년 이후), / the number(S) of immigrants to the U.S.(미국으로의 이민자 수가) / began(V) to drop(떨어지기 시작했다), / falling to less than 6 million(6백만 명 미만으로 떨어졌다; 분사구문(= and it fell to ~)) / in the 1921 – 1930 period(1921–1930년 기간에). [4] ③ The number of immigrants to Canada(S_1, 캐나다로의 이민자 수는) / was(V_1) comparatively smaller(C_1, 비교적 더 적었다) / than that of(미국의 이민자; that = the number of immigrants)

어휘확인
chart 도표, 차트 **immigration** 이민 **trend** 경향, 추세 **immigrant** 이민자 **peak** 최고치, 절정 **period** 기간, 시기 **comparatively** 비교적 **continue** 계속되다 **increase** 증가하다 **decline** 감소하다 **go beyond** ~을 넘어서다, ~을 초과하다

지문 Flow

[소재]
1831－1930년 동안 미국과 캐나다의 이민 경향을 보여 주는 도표

⬇

[진술1]
1901－1910년에 미국과 캐나다의 이민자 수가 최고치임 (미국이 5배 많음)

&

[진술2]
1910년 이후, 미국 이민자 수가 떨어짐 → 1921－1930년에 6백만 명 미만으로 떨어짐

&

수보다 / 모든 기간에서 / 그러나 그것은 계속 증가했다 / 1910년까지 / 그때 감소하기 시작했다
the U.S. / in all periods, // but it continued to increase / until *1910*, / when it started to decline. 5 ④ The number of immigrants to the U.S. / when it reached its peak / was more than five times bigger / than that to Canada in its peak. 6 ⑤ Canada never saw its number of immigrants go beyond 2 million / during the given periods.

(S₂ it, V₂ continued; when: 관계부사(계속적 용법); 미국으로의 이민자 수는 (S) / 최고치에 이르렀을 때 (삽입절) / was (V) / 5배 이상 더 많았다 (C); 최고치에 있는 캐나다로의 이민자 수보다, that = the number of immigrants; 캐나다는 (S) 이민자의 수가 2백만 명을 넘어서는 것을 (O) 결코 보지 못했다 (V), go beyond 2 million (C); 주어진 기간 동안)

[진술3]
캐나다 이민자 수가 1910년까지 증가하다가 감소함 (→ 1891—1900년에 한 번 아래로 꺾임)

&

[진술4]
캐나다 이민자 수는 2백만 명을 넘지 못함

해석 한 눈에 보기 1 위 도표는 1831—1930년 동안 미국과 캐나다의 이민 경향을 보여 준다. 2 ① 미국으로의 이민자 수는 1901—1910년 기간에 최고치에 이르렀는데, 이는 캐나다와 동일했다. 3 ② 1910년 이후, 미국으로의 이민자 수가 떨어지기 시작했고, 1921—1930년 기간에 6백만 명 미만으로 떨어졌다. 4 ③ 캐나다로의 이민자 수는 모든 기간에서 미국의 이민자 수보다 비교적 더 적었지만, 그것은 1910년까지 계속 증가했는데, 그때 감소하기 시작했다. 5 ④ 미국으로의 이민자 수는 최고치에 이르렀을 때, 최고치에 있는 캐나다로의 이민자 수보다 5배 이상 더 많았다. 6 ⑤ 캐나다는 주어진 기간 동안 이민자의 수가 2백만 명을 넘어서는 것을 결코 보지 못했다.

정답단추 도표의 제목과 도입 부분의 내용을 보고 무엇에 관한 도표인지 먼저 알아야 해. 그 다음에 글을 읽으면서 각 문장들이 도표의 내용과 일치하는지 확인하면 돼. 도표의 제목을 보면, 1831—1930년 동안 미국과 캐나다의 이민자 수를 비교한 도표임을 알 수 있어. 도표를 보면, 캐나다로의 이민자 수는 모든 기간에서 미국의 이민자 수보다 적었고, 계속 증가하다가 1891—1900년에 한번 아래로 꺾였어. 따라서 1910년까지 계속 증가했고, 그 이후로 감소했다는 ③은 도표와 일치하지 않아.

오답단서 ①은 도표에서 미국과 캐나다로의 이민자 수가 최고치인 때가 1901—1910년이므로 일치하는 설명이야. ②는 미국으로의 이민자 수가 1910년 이후에 떨어지기 시작해서 1921—1930년에 6백만 명 미만이 되었으므로 일치해. ④는 미국으로의 이민자 수가 최고치였을 때 천만 명 정도였고, 캐나다는 2백만 명에 좀 못 미쳤으므로, 5배 이상 많았다는 설명은 옳아. ⑤는 도표에서 캐나다로의 이민자수가 2백만 명을 넘지 못하므로 일치하는 설명이야.

기출총정리

Mini Test 1 ○ 2 ○ 3 × 4 ○ 5 × 6 × 7 ○ 8 × 9 the strongest 10 five times 11 steadily 12 had reached their peak 13 × 14 ○ 15 ○

Mini Test 해석 및 해설

1 **해석** 위의 5개 국가 중, 태국이 두 해에 가장 많은 고무 생산국이었다.
2 **해석** 태국에 의해 생산된 고무의 양은 두 해에 그 어떤 다른 나라의 그것보다 더 많았다.
3 **해석** 인도네시아는 2010년에만 두 번째로 많은 고무 생산국이었다.
4 **해석** 말레이시아는 2004년과 2010년 둘 다에서 인도보다 더 많은 고무를 생산했다.
5 **해석** 2010년에 인도와 베트남은 둘 다 2004년으로부터 약간의 감소를 보였다.
6 **해석** 말레이시아의 그것이 2010년에 그랬던 것처럼, 인도의 생산도 약간 감소했다.
7 **해석** 베트남은 2004년과 2010년 둘 다에서 5개 국가 중 가장 적은 고무의 양을 생산했다.
8 **해석** 2004년에 인도네시아에 의해 생산된 고무의 양은 같은 해에 베트남의 그것보다 약 3배 더 많았다.
9 **해석** 2007년에 이 세 지역에서의 하이브리드 자동차 판매량은 미국에서 가장 강세였다.
10 **해석** 2009년에 아시아에서의 하이브리드 자동차 판매량은 그것이 2007년에 그랬던 것보다 5배 더 많았다.
11 **해석** 미국에서의 하이브리드 자동차 판매량은 꾸준히 줄어든 반면에 아시아와 유럽의 그것은 계속 증가했다.
12 **해석** 2010년에 아시아에서의 하이브리드 자동차 판매량은 절정에 다다랐는데, 판매량에서 미국과 유럽 둘 다를 능가했다.
13 **해석** 2011년의 모든 매체의 광고 수입은 2002년도에 비해 증가했다.
14 **해석** 텔레비전 광고 수입은 2002년과 2011년 사이의 기간 내내 매년 최고를 차지했다.
15 **해석** 2002년에 인터넷 광고 수입은 그 어떤 다른 매체의 것보다 더 적었지만, 2011년에 그것은 라디오와 신문 광고 수입을 능가했다.

165 정답 ⑤

지문 All in One

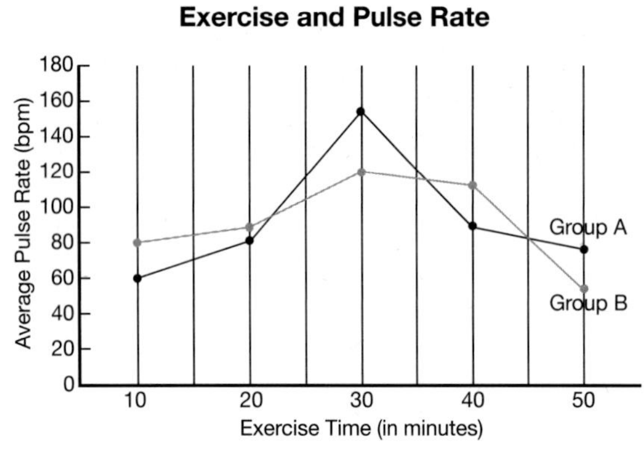

[1] This graph compares the effects of exercise / on the average heart rates / of a group of office workers / and another group of former college athletes. [2] ① The heart rate of both groups / was highest at 30 minutes of exercise. [3] ② The rate of Group A / was lower at 10 minutes / than at 50 minutes. [4] ③ Between 40 and 50 minutes, / the pulse rate of Group B / decreased more dramatically / compared with Group A. [5] ④ During the last five minutes of exercise, / the rate of Group B / was lower / than that of Group A. [6] ⑤ As a result, / it can be said // that there is more variation / in the pulse rate of former athletes / than that of office workers.

(이 그래프는 운동의 영향을 비교한다 / 평균 심장박동 수에 있어 / 사무직 근로자 한 집단의 / 그리고 대학 운동선수 출신인 다른 그룹의 / 두 그룹의 심장박동 수는 / 운동 30분쯤에 가장 높았다 / A 집단의 심장박동 수는 / 10분쯤에 더 낮았다 / 50분쯤보다 / 40분과 50분 사이에 / B 집단의 맥박 수는 / 더 급격하게 감소했다 / A 집단과 비교하여 / 마지막 5분의 운동 동안 / B 집단의 맥박 수는 / 더 낮았다 / A 집단의 것보다 / 그 결과 / ~라고 말해질 수 있다 / 더 많은 변화가 있다고 / 운동선수 출신들의 맥박 수에 / 사무직 근로자의 것보다)

(S: This graph, The heart rate of both groups, The rate of Group A, the pulse rate of Group B, the rate of Group B, it; V: compares, was, decreased, can be said; C: highest, lower; that = the rate; that 접속사; V′: is; S′: more variation; that = the pulse rate)

해석 한 눈에 보기 1 이 그래프는 운동이 사무직 근로자 한 집단과 대학 운동선수 출신 한 집단의 평균 심장박동 수에 미치는 영향을 비교한다. 2 ① 두 집단의 심장박동 수는 운동 30분쯤에 가장 높았다. 3 ② A 집단 심장박동 수는 50분쯤보다 10분쯤에 더 낮았다. 4 ③ 40분과 50분 사이에, B 집단의 맥박 수는 A 집단과 비교하여 훨씬 더 급격하게 감소했다. 5 ④ 마지막 5분 동안, B 집단의 맥박 수는 A 집단의 그것보다 더 낮았다. 6 ⑤ 그 결과 사무직 근로자의 맥박 수보다 운동선수 출신들의 맥박 수에 더 많은 변화가 있다고 할 수 있다.

정답단추 도표와 지문 내용이 일치하는지 하나씩 확인하면 돼. 도표를 보면 사무직 근로자로 구성된 A 집단의 맥박 수는 60~160이지만, 운동선수 출신의 B 집단은 50~120임을 알 수 있어. 즉, 변화 정도가 더 큰 것은 A 집단이지? 따라서 운동선수 출신 집단의 맥박 수에 더 많은 변화가 있다고 한 ⑤는 잘못된 설명이야.

오답단서 ①은 두 집단 모두 30분에 평균 심장박동 수가 가장 높은 것을 확인할 수 있으므로 글의 내용과 일치해. 10분에 A 집단의 평균 맥박 수는 60이고, 이는 50분의 평균 맥박 수인 80보다 더 낮아서 ②도 일치해. 그리고 40분과 50분 사이에 A 집단보다 B 집단의 수치가 더 많이 감소했으므로 ③의 더 급격히 감소했다(decreased more dramatically)는 표현은 적절해. 마지막으로 45분과 50분 사이에 B 집단의 맥박 수가 A 집단보다 더 낮은 것을 확인할 수 있으므로 ④도 글의 내용과 일치함을 알 수 있어.

어휘확인

pulse rate 맥박 수, 심장박동 수(= **heart rate**) **average** 평균의 **office worker** 사무직 근로자 **former** 이전의 **athlete** 운동선수 **compare** 비교하다 **decrease** 감소하다 **dramatically** 급격하게; 극적으로 **compared with** ~와 비교하여 **variation** 변화

지문 Flow

[소재]
운동이 사무직 근로자(A 집단)와 운동선수 출신(B 집단)의 평균 심장박동 수에 미치는 영향을 비교하는 그래프

[진술1]
두 집단의 심장박동 수는 운동 30분쯤에 가장 높음

&

[진술2]
A 집단의 심장박동 수는 50분쯤보다 10분쯤에 더 낮음

&

[진술3]
B 집단의 심장박동 수는 40—50분쯤에 A 집단보다 더 급격하게 감소하여, 마지막 5분 동안 A 집단보다 더 낮아짐

&

[진술4]
사무직 근로자보다 운동선수 출신의 심장박동 수에 변화가 더 많음

지문 All in One

Children Involved in Selected Leisure
Activities, Victoria, by Age

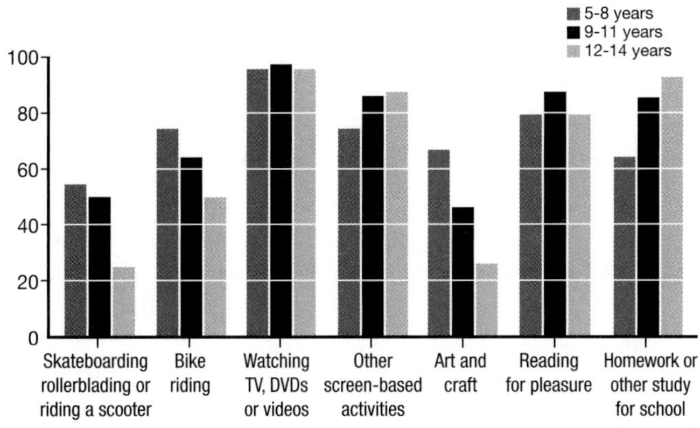

위 그래프는 보여준다 / 5－14세 아이들이 선호하는 여가 활동을
1 The above graph shows / the preferred leisure activities of the children aged 5 — 14 / in
S V

빅토리아 주의 / 데이터를 통해 ~은 분명하다 / 조용한 활동들이 / TV, DVD, 비디오 시청, 숙제 및 기타 학교
Victoria. 2 ① It is clear from the data // that quiet activities / such as watching TV, DVDs, or
가주어 V C 접속사 S′

공부와 같은 / 요즘은 더 인기가 있다는 것은 / 활동적인
videos, and homework [or] other study for school / are more popular nowadays / than active
V′ C′

활동들보다 / 스케이트보드 타기, 롤러블레이드 타기, 스쿠터 타기와 같은 / 즐거움을 위해 하는 독서는
ones / such as skateboarding, rollerblading, [or] riding a scooter. 3 ② Reading for pleasure
= activities 진주어 S

비교적 인기가 있었지만 / 모든 연령대에서 / 9－11세 연령대에서 가장 그랬다
was relatively popular / among all age groups, // [but] most so for those 9 — 11 years old. 4 ③
V C

여가 활동은 / 연령대별로 가장 차이가 컸던 / 예술과 공작 활동이었는데
The leisure activities / with the greatest differences between age groups / were *art* [and] craft
S V C

여기에서의 참여율은 보다 더 높았다 / 5－8세 연령대에서
activities, // where the participation rates were higher / in the 5 — 8 year age group. 5 ④
관계부사(계속적 용법)

숙제와 기타 학교 공부는 / 더 낮은 참여율을 보였다 / 12－14세 연령대에서
Homework [and] other study for school / had lower participation rates / in the 12 — 14 year
S V

스케이트보드 타기는 가장 인기가 적은 활동이었다 / 7개 중에서
age group. 6 ⑤ Skateboarding was the least popular activity / among the seven / for the
S V C

가장 어린 연령대에게
youngest age group.

해석 한 눈에 보기 1 위 그래프는 빅토리아 주의 5－14세 아이들이 선호하는 여가 활동을 보여준다. 2 ① 데이터를 통해 요즘은 TV, DVD, 비디오 시청, 숙제 및 기타 학교 공부와 같은 조용한 활동들이 스케이트보드 타기, 롤러블레이드 타기, 스쿠터 타기와 같은 활동적인 활동들보다 더 인기가 있다는 것은 분명하다. 3 ② 즐거움을 위해 하는 독서는 비교적 모든 연령대에서 인기가 있었지만, 9－11세 연령대에서 가장 그랬다. 4 ③ 연령대별로 가장 차이가 컸던 여가 활동은 예술과 공작 활동이었는데, 여기에서의 참여율은 5－8세 연령대에서 보다 더 높았다. 5 ④ 숙제와 기타 학교 공부는 12－14세 연령대에서 더 낮은 참여율을 보였다. 6 ⑤ 스케이트보드 타기는 가장 어린 연령대에 7개 중에서 가장 인기 없는 활동이었다.

정답단추 도표의 제목과 도입 부분을 활용해 무엇에 관한 도표인지를 우선 파악하자. 그리고 지문을 읽으면서 각 문장의 설명이 도표의 내용과 일치하는지 확인해보자. 이 도표는 빅토리아 주의 5－14세 아이들이 선호하는 여가 활동을 보여주고 있어. 도표를 보면 숙제와 기타 학교 공부 활동에서 가장 높은 참여율을 보이는 연령대는 12－14세라는 것을 확인할 수 있어. 그러므로 12－14세 연령대에서 더 낮은 참여율을 가졌다는 ④의 설명은 도표의 내용과 일치하지 않으므로 정답은 ④야.

오답단서 ①은 도표를 보면 조용한 활동(TV, DVD, 비디오 시청, 숙제와 기타 학교 공부)이 활동적인 활동(스케이트보드 타기, 롤러블레이드 타기, 스쿠터 타기)보다 모든 연령대에서 참여율이 높다는 것을 통해 더 인기가 많다는 것을 알 수 있어. 다음으로 도표에서 독서는 거의 모든 연령대에서 참여율이 높지만 9~11세 연령대에서 가장 그러하므로 ②는 옳은 설명이야. 그리고 연령대별로 가장 차이가 큰 것은 예술과 공작 활동이고, 5~8세 연령대에서 가장 참여율이 높다는 걸 도표에서 알 수 있으니 ③도 일치해. 마지막으로 도표에서 총 7개의 활동에서 가장 어린 연령대인 5~8세의 참여율을 가리키는 막대를 보면 막대가 가장 낮은 활동이 스케이트 타기이므로 ⑤의 설명은 적절해.

어휘확인
leisure 여가 skateboarding 스케이트보드 타기 rollerblading 롤러블레이드 타기 scooter 스쿠터(소형 오토바이) based 기반을 둔 reading 독서 prefer 선호하다 aged ~세[살]의 data 데이터[자료] nowadays 요즘에는 relatively 비교적 age group 연령대 participation 참여, 참가 rate －율, 비율

지문 Flow

[소재]
빅토리아 주의 5－14세 아동이 선호하는 여가 활동을 보여주는 그래프

⬇

[진술]
조용한 활동이 활동적인 활동보다 더 인기가 있음

⬇

[보충설명]
• 독서: 모든 연령대에서 인기 있음, 9－11세에서 가장 인기 있음
• 예술과 공작: 연령대별로 가장 차이가 큼, 5－8세의 참여율이 높음
• 숙제와 기타 학교 공부: 12－14세의 참여율이 낮음(→ 높음)
• 스케이트보드 타기: 어린 연령대에서 가장 인기 없음

미니 모의고사 5 유형 13 | 유형 14 | 유형 15 | 유형 16

167 ④ 168 ③ 169 ③ 170 ④ 171 ⑤ 172 ⑤ 173 ⑤ 174 ③ 175 ③
176 ② 177 ④ 178 ③ 179 ③ 180 ③ 181 ④ 182 ② 183 ⑤

167 정답 ④

지문 All in One

Robert Baden-Powell은 육군 중장이었다 / 영국 육군의 / 작가
1 Robert Baden-Powell was a lieutenant-general / in the British Army, / a writer, / and a
S V C_1 C_2

그리고 주요한 설립자 / 보이 스카우트 조직의 / 1899년에 / 전쟁 중에 / 그(Baden-Powell)는
primary founder / of the Boy Scout Movement. 2 In 1899, / during a war, / ① he commanded a
C_3 S V

한 영국 부대를 지휘했다 / 마페킹이라는 마을에서 / 남아프리카의 / 마페킹은 적에 의해 둘러싸였다
British military unit / in the town of Mafeking, / South Africa. 3 Mafeking was surrounded
S_1 V_1

그리고 그(Baden-Powell)는 부족했다 / 그것을 방어할 군대가 / 상황은 절망적이었다
by the enemy, // and ② he lacked / *the troops* [to defend it]. 4 The situation was desperate, //
S_2 V_2 S_1 V_1 C

그리고 그(Baden-Powell)는 도움이 필요했다 / 한 장교가 제안했다 / 그들이 고용하자고 / 그들을 도울 현지
and ③ he needed help. 5 An officer suggested // that they (should) employ / *local boys* [to
S_2 V_2 S V 접속사 S′ V′

소년들을 / 그(장교)는 소년들에게 주었다(시켰다) / 군대식 훈련을 / 그룹별로 / 그리고 그들을 일하게 했다
assist them]. 6 ④ He gave the boys / military-style training / in groups // and got them to
S V_1 IO DO V_2 O C

감시원과 전령으로서 / Baden-Powell은 깊은 인상을 받았다 / 그 광경에
work / as watchers and messengers. 7 Baden-Powell was impressed / at the sight. 8 When
S V 접속사

그(Baden-Powell)가 영국으로 돌아왔을 때 / 그는 훈련 캠프를 조직했다 / 소년들을 위해 / 그리고 그것이 시작이었다
⑤ he returned to England, / he organized training camps / for boys, // and that was the
S′ V′ S_1 V_1 S_2 V_2 C

국제 스카우트 조직의
beginning / of the international Scout Movement.

해석 한 눈에 보기 1 Robert Baden-Powell은 영국 육군의 중장이고, 작가이고, 보이스카우트 연맹의 주요 설립자였다. 2 1899년, 전쟁 중에, ① 그(Baden-Powell)는 남아프리카의 마페킹이라는 마을에서 한 영국 부대를 지휘했다. 3 마페킹은 적에게 둘러싸여 있었는데, ② 그(Baden-Powell)는 마을을 방어할 군대가 부족했다. 4 상황이 절망적이어서 ③ 그(Baden-Powell)는 도움이 필요했다. 5 한 장교가 그들이 그들을 도울 현지 소년들을 고용하자고 제안했다. 6 ④ 그(장교)는 그룹별로 소년들에게 군대식 훈련을 시켰고 그들을 감시원과 전령으로 일하게 했다. 7 Baden-Powell은 그 광경에 깊은 인상을 받았다. 8 ⑤ 그(Baden-Powell)가 영국으로 돌아왔을 때, 그는 소년들을 대상으로 훈련 캠프를 조직했고, 그것이 국제 스카우트 연맹의 시작이었다.

정답단추 이 글에서는 Robert Baden-Powell과 장교, 두 사람이 등장하므로 글을 읽으면서 둘 중 누구를 의미하는지 구분하며 읽으면 돼. ①, ②, ③은 군대를 지휘하며 병력이 모자라 도움이 필요했던 사람으로 모두 Baden-Powell을 가리키고, ④는 소년들을 군사력에 동원하자고 제안하고 훈련을 시킨 사람인 장교를 의미해. 마지막으로 깊은 인상을 받은 Baden-Powell이 영국에 돌아와 스카우트를 조직했으므로 ⑤는 Baden-Powell을 대신하는 것을 알 수 있어. 따라서 가리키는 대상이 다른 것은 ④야.

어휘확인

lieutenant-general 육군 중장 **British** 영국의 **army** 육군; 군대 **primary** 주요한 **founder** 설립자 **Boy Scout** 보이 스카우트 cf. **scout** 스카우트 **movement** (사회적) 운동 조직 **war** 전쟁 **command** (군대에서) 지휘하다 **military** 군대의, 군사의 **unit** 부대; 단위 **surround** 둘러싸다 **enemy** 적 **lack** ~이 부족하다 **troop** 군대 **defend** 방어하다 **situation** 상황 **desperate** 절망적인 **suggest** 제안하다 **employ** 고용하다 **local** 현지의 **assist** 돕다 **watcher** 감시원 **messenger** 전령; 전달자 **impress** 깊은 인상을 주다 **sight** 광경; 시력 **return** 돌아오다 **organize** 조직하다 **beginning** 시작

지문 Flow

[인물소개]
Robert Baden-Powell
• 영국 육군의 중장
• 작가
• 보이스카우트 연맹의 주요 설립자

⬇

[일화]
1899년에 남아프리카 마페킹에서 영국 부대를 지휘하던 중, 적에 대항할 군대가 부족하자, 한 장교가 현지 소년들에게 군대식 훈련을 시켜 감시원과 전령으로 일하게 함

⬇

[결과]
Baden-Powell은 그것을 본떠 영국으로 돌아와서 소년들을 대상으로 훈련 캠프를 조직함 → 국제 스카우트 연맹의 시작

168 정답 ③

지문 All in One

Poon Lim은 세계적으로 유명해진 중국의 선원이었다 / 놀라운 생존 경험 후에
1 Poon Lim was *a Chinese sailor* [who became world-famous / after an amazing survival
S V C 관계대명사

그는 일하고 있었다 / 영국의 무역선에서 / 제2차 세계 대전 중에 / 그 배는
experience]. 2 He was working / on a British merchant ship / during World War II. 3 The ship
S V S

가는 도중이었다 / 케이프타운에서 수리남으로 / 그 배가 독일의 잠수함에 의해 폭격 당했을 때
was on its way / from Cape Town to Suriname. 4 When the ship was bombed by German
V 접속사 S'_1 V'_1

Poon Lim은 뛰었다(뛰어내렸다) / 그것이 불타서 가라앉자 / 그는 바다에 있었다 / 2시간 동안
submarines, // Poon Lim jumped / as it burned and sank. 5 He was in the sea / for two hours
S V 접속사 S'_2 V'_2 V'_3 S V

구명보트가 떠내려 왔을 때 / 그는 올라탔다 / 그리고 물, 음식, 손전등을 발견했다
// when a lifeboat floated by. 6 He climbed in // and found water, food, and a flashlight.
접속사 S′ V′ S V_1 V_2

어휘확인

world-famous 세계적으로 유명한 **survival** 생존 cf. **survive** 생존하다 **British** 영국의 **merchant ship** 무역선 **World War II** 제2차 세계 대전 **on one's way to** ~로 가는 도중에 **bomb** 폭격하다; 폭탄 **submarine** 잠수함 **lifeboat** 구명보트, 구명정 **flashlight** 손전등 **supply** 비축량; 공급 **run low** 다 떨어져 가다 **rely on** ~에 의존하다 **fishing** 낚시 **seabird** 바닷새 **rainwater** 빗물 **amazingly** 놀랍게도 **eventually** 결국 **rescue** 구조하다 **coast** 해안 **return** 돌아오다

비축량이 다 떨어져 갈 때 / 그는 낚시와 바닷새를 잡는 것에 의존했다 / 먹기 위해 / 그리고

[7] When supplies ran low, // he relied on fishing [and] catching seabirds / to eat / [and]

접속사 S' V' C' / S V / 부사적 용법(목적)

빗물을 모으는 것에 (의존했다) / 마시기 위해 / 놀랍게도 / 그는 133일 동안 생존했다 / 바다 위에서

gathering rainwater / to drink. [8] Amazingly, / he survived for 133 days / on the ocean / in

부사적 용법(목적) / S V

그 구명보트에서 / 결국 그는 구조되었다 / 브라질 해안 근처에서 / 그리고 영국에 돌아왔다

that lifeboat. [9] Eventually he was rescued / near the coast of Brazil // [and] returned to

S V_1 / V_2

위대한 영웅으로

England / as a great hero.

① 2차 대전 때 군인으로 참전했다.
② 배가 뒤집혀 바다에 표류했다.
③ 구명보트에서 물과 음식을 발견했다.
④ 바다에서 5달 넘게 생존했다.
⑤ 브라질 어선에 의해 구조되었다.

해석 한 눈에 보기 [1] Poon Lim은 놀라운 생존 경험 후에 세계적으로 유명해진 중국의 선원이었다. [2] 그는 제2차 세계 대전 중에 영국의 무역선에서 일하고 있었다. [3] 그 배는 케이프타운에서 수리남으로 가는 도중이었다. [4] 그 배가 독일 잠수함의 폭격을 받았을 때, Poon Lim은 배가 불타서 가라앉자 바다로 뛰어내렸다. [5] 그가 2시간 동안 바다에 있었는데 그때 구명보트 하나가 떠 내려왔다. [6] 그는 올라탔고 물, 음식, 손전등을 발견했다. [7] 비축량이 다 떨어져 갈 때, 그는 먹기 위해 낚시와 바닷새 잡는 것에 그리고 마시기 위해 빗물을 모으는 것에 의존했다. [8] 놀랍게도 그는 바다 위에서 그 구명보트를 타고 133일 동안 생존했다. [9] 결국 그는 브라질 해안 근처에서 구조되었고 위대한 영웅으로 영국에 돌아왔다.

정답단추 선택지와 본문의 내용이 일치하는 것을 고르는 문제야. 본문과 선택지의 내용을 차례대로 비교하면서 답을 찾으면 돼. 다섯 번째, 여섯 번째 문장에서 Poon Lim이 바다에 표류하고 있다가 떠내려 온 보트에서 음식과 물을 발견했다고 했으니까 ③은 지문의 내용과 일치함을 알 수 있어.

오답단서 Poon Lim은 영국 무역선에서 일했다고 했으므로 ①은 일치하지 않아. ②는 배가 뒤집힌 것이 아니고 폭격에 맞아 불타고 가라앉아서 표류하게 되었다는 내용이라 답이 될 수 없어. 그리고 Poon Lim이 바다에서 지낸 기간은 133일, 즉 4달 반 정도이지? 그런데 ④에서 5달 넘게 지냈다고 했으니 본문의 내용과 일치하지 않아. 마지막으로 ⑤는 본문에서 구조된 장소로 브라질 해안 근처라고 언급했지만, 어느 나라 배에 의해 구조되었는지는 나오지 않아서 답이 될 수 없어.

지문 Flow

[인물소개]
생존 경험 후에 유명해진 중국의 선원 Poon Lim

[사건]
그가 제2차 세계 대전 중에 영국의 무역선에서 일하던 중, 독일 잠수함의 폭격을 받아 배가 가라앉음

[전개]
그는 바다에 뛰어들었고, 떠내려 온 구명보트에 올라타 133일 동안 생존함

[결과]
브라질 해안에서 구조되어 영국으로 돌아옴

169 정답 ③

지문 All in One

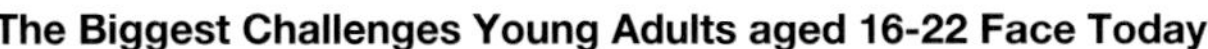

The Biggest Challenges Young Adults aged 16-22 Face Today

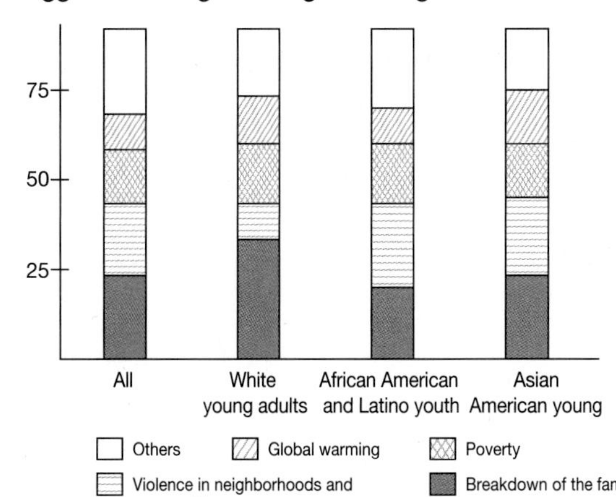

위 그래프는 보여 준다 / 16—22세의 젊은 성인들이 무엇을 / 그들의 삶에 강한 영향을 주는 주요한

[1] The above graph shows / what young adults [aged 16 — 22] feel / are *the primary issues*

S V / 간접의문문

문제라고 생각하는지 / 응답자의 24퍼센트는 / 생각한다

[impacting their lives]. [2] ① Twenty-four percent of the respondents / consider / the

S_1 V_1 O

가족의 붕괴가 오늘날 그들의 세대가 직면한 가장 긴급한 문제라고

breakdown of the family to be *the most pressing issue* [facing their generation today], // [but]

C

하지만 몇 가지 중요한 차이가 / 인종 및 민족 집단 간의 / 정말로 존재한다 / 백인 젊은

several significant differences / among racial and ethnic groups / do exist. [3] ② White young

S_2 / 강조 V_2 / S

성인들은 가족 붕괴를 1위로 선정했다 / 빈곤 및 지구 온난화가 뒤따랐다

adults named family breakdown as number one, / followed by poverty and global warming.

V

아프리카계 미국인과 라틴계 젊은이들은 / 하지만 / 믿었다 / 자신들의 지역 사회 내의

[4] ③ African American and Latino youth, / however, / believed // (that) violence in their

S / V / 접속사 / S'

어휘확인

global warming 지구 온난화 **poverty** 가난, 빈곤 **violence** 폭력, 폭행 **neighborhood** 이웃 **community** 지역 사회 **breakdown** 붕괴, 몰락 **primary** 주요한, 주된 **issue** 문제, 쟁점 **impact** 강한 영향을 주다 **respondent** 응답자 **consider** 생각하다, 간주하다 **pressing** 긴급한 **generation** 세대 **significant** 중요한 **racial** 인종 간의 **ethnic** 민족의 **exist** 존재하다 **name A as B** A를 B로 선정하다 **meanwhile** 한편, 그 사이에 **equally** 똑같이 **overall** 전반적으로 **insecure** 불안한 **related to** ~와 관련 있는 **relationship** 관계 **community** 지역 사회 **safety** 안전

지문 Flow

[소재]
16—22세의 젊은이들의 삶에 영향을 주는 문제가 무엇인지 보여 주는 그래프

[진술]
응답자의 24퍼센트가 가족의 붕괴를 가장 긴급한 문제로 생각하지만, 인종과 민족 간의 차이가 존재함

폭력이 그들의 세대가 직면한 가장 긴급한 문제라고 / 빈곤 및 지구 온난화가
communities was *the most pressing issue* [facing their generation], / followed by poverty

뒤따랐다 / 아시아계 미국인 젊은 성인들은 / 한편 / 가족 붕괴를 1위 문제
and global warming. [5] ④ Asian American young adults, / meanwhile, / named family

로 선정했다 / 하지만 그들은 생각했다 / 이웃 폭력이 거의 똑같이 중요하다고
breakdown as the number-one issue, // but they felt / (that) neighborhood violence was

전반적으로 / 미국 젊은 성인들은 불안을 느끼지만
almost equally important. [6] ⑤ Overall, / though American young adults feel insecure /

빈곤과 지구 온난화와 관련하여 / 그들은 더 불안을 느낀다 / 자신들의 가족 관계와 지역
related to poverty and global warming, // they feel more insecure / about their family

사회 안전에 대해
relationships and community safety.

[예시]
- 백인: 가족 붕괴 〉 빈곤 〉 지구 온난화 〉 이웃과 지역 사회의 폭력
- 아프리카 & 라틴계: 이웃과 지역 사회의 폭력 〉 가족 붕괴 〉 빈곤 〉 지구 온난화
- 아시아계: 가족 붕괴 = 이웃과 지역 사회의 폭력 〉 빈곤 = 지구 온난화

[결론]
미국 젊은이들은 가족 관계와 사회 안전에 대해 더 불안을 느낌

해석 한 눈에 보기 1 위 그래프는 16—22세의 젊은 성인들이 무엇을 그들의 삶에 강한 영향을 주는 주요한 문제라고 생각하는지 보여 준다. 2 ① 응답자의 24퍼센트는 가족의 붕괴가 오늘날 그들의 세대가 직면한 가장 긴급한 문제라고 생각하지만, 인종 및 민족 집단 간의 몇 가지 중요한 차이가 정말로 존재한다. 3 ② 백인 젊은 성인들은 가족 붕괴를 1위로 선정했고, 빈곤 및 지구 온난화가 뒤따랐다. 4 ③ 하지만, 아프리카계 미국인과 라틴계 젊은이들은 자신들의 지역 사회 내의 폭력이 그들의 세대가 직면한 가장 긴급한 문제라고 믿었고, 빈곤 및 지구 온난화가 뒤따랐다. 5 ④ 한편, 아시아계 미국인 젊은 성인들은 가족 붕괴를 1위 문제로 선정했지만, 그들은 이웃 폭력이 거의 똑같이 중요하다고 생각했다. 6 ⑤ 전반적으로, 미국 젊은 성인들은 빈곤과 지구 온난화와 관련하여 불안을 느끼지만, 자신들의 가족 관계와 지역 사회 안전에 대해 더 불안을 느낀다.

정답단추 이 그래프는 16—22세의 젊은 성인들이 오늘날 직면한 가장 긴급한 문제가 무엇인지 보여 주고 있어. 그래프에 나타난 정보를 파악하고, 지문 내용과 하나씩 비교하도록 해. 그래프를 보면, 아프리카계 미국인과 라틴계 젊은이들은 이웃과 지역 사회의 폭력이 1위였고, 그 다음이 가족 붕괴와 빈곤임을 알 수 있어. 따라서 지역 사회의 폭력 다음에 빈곤과 지구 온난화가 뒤따랐다는 ③의 설명은 도표와 일치하지 않아.

오답단서 ①은 전체 그래프에서 전체 응답자 중 25퍼센트가 살짝 못 미치게 가족의 붕괴를 문제라고 생각하고 있음을 알 수 있고, 인종과 집단 간의 차이를 다른 그래프들로 보여 주고 있으므로 일치하는 설명이야. ②는 백인 젊은이들의 그래프가 가족 붕괴, 빈곤, 지구 온난화의 순서이므로 일치하는 설명이야. ④는 아시아계 미국인 젊은이들의 그래프에서 가족 붕괴와 이웃과 지역 사회 내의 폭력의 비율이 거의 같으므로 일치하는 설명이야. ⑤는 전체 그래프를 보면, 긴급한 문제로 생각하는 비율이 가족 붕괴, 이웃과 지역 사회 내의 폭력, 빈곤, 지구 온난화의 순서야. 따라서 앞의 두 항목에 더 불안을 느끼므로 일치하는 설명이야.

170 정답 ④

지문 All in One

지능, 헌신, 그리고 전략적 사고에 대한 가장 존경받는 테스트 중 하나로서
1 As one of the most-respected tests of intelligence, dedication, and strategic thinking, / it is

놀랄 일이 아니다 / 많은 나라가 주장해 온 것은 / 자신들이 체스의 탄생지라는 칭호를 받을 만하다고
no surprise // that many countries have claimed / that they deserve the title of the birthplace

그러나 이제 일반적으로 동의되고 있다 / 그 게임이 기원을 가지고 있다는 데 / 인도에 / 그것(체스)이
of chess. [2] But it is now generally agreed / that the game had its origins / in India, // since ① it

인도 문학에 언급되어 있기 때문이다 / 기원전 500년으로 거슬러 올라가는 / 1500년 후에
is mentioned in Indian literature / dating from 500 BC. [3] One thousand five hundred years

그것(체스)은 스페인에 등장했다 / 그곳에서부터 / 그것(체스)은 빠르게 퍼졌다 / 유럽의 나머지 지역에
later, / ② it appeared in Spain. [4] From there, / ③ it quickly spread / over the rest of Europe.

1924년에 / 국제체스연맹이 설립되면서 / 파리에 / 그것(국제체스연맹)은
[5] In 1924, / when the International Chess Federation was established / in Paris, // ④ it played a

큰 역할을 했다 / 체스 게임의 인기를 퍼뜨리는 데 / 전 세계로 / 오늘날
large part / in spreading the popularity of the game of chess / all over the world. [6] Today, /

그것(체스)은 세계에서 가장 인기 있는 게임들 중 하나이다
⑤ it is one of the world's most popular games.

해석 한 눈에 보기 1 지능, 헌신, 전략적 사고에 대한 가장 존경받는 테스트 중 하나로서, 많은 나라가 자신들이 체스의 탄생지라는 칭호를 받을 만하다고 주장해 온 것은 놀랄 일이 아니다. 2 그러나 이제 그 게임이 인도에 그 기원을 두고 있다는 데 일반적으로 의견이 모여지고 있는데, ① 그것(체스)이 기원전 500년으로 거슬러 올라가는 인도 문학에 언급되어 있기 때문이다. 3 1500년 후에 ② 그것(체스)은 스페인에 등장했다. 4 그곳에서부터 ③ 그것(체스)은 유럽의 나머지 지역에 급속도로 퍼졌다. 5 1924년에 국제체스연맹이 파리에 설립되면서 ④ 그것(국제체스연맹)은 체스 게임의 인기를 전 세계로 퍼뜨리는 데 보다 더 큰 역할을 했다. 6 오늘날 ⑤ 그것(체스)은 세계에서 가장 인기 있는 게임들 중 하나이다.

어휘확인

respected 존경을 받는 **intelligence** 지능 **dedication** 헌신 **strategic** 전략적인 **thinking** 사고[생각] **claim** 주장하다 **deserve** ~을 받을 만하다 **title** 칭호; 제목 **birthplace** 탄생지[발생지], 출생지 **generally** 일반적으로 **origin** 기원, 근원 **since** ~ 때문에 **Indian** 인도의; 인도인 **literature** 문학 **date from** ~부터 시작되다 **BC** 기원전 **appear** 나타나다, 생기다 **federation** 연맹[연합] **establish** 설립하다 **play a[one's] part** 역할을 하다 **popularity** 인기 *cf.* **popular** 인기 있는

지문 Flow

[소재]
지능, 헌신, 전략적 사고에 대한 테스트로서의 체스 게임

[보충설명]
- 인도에 그 기원을 두는 것이 일반적인 의견인데, 기원전 500년의 인도 문학에 언급되어 있기 때문임
- 1500년 후, 스페인에 등장하고 유럽 전역으로 퍼짐
- 1924년에 파리에 국제체스연맹이 설립된 후, 전 세계적으로 인기를 끎

정답단추 대명사는 주로 앞뒤에 언급된 명사를 대신하는 경우가 많아. 그러니까 가리키는 대상을 정확히 찾기 위해서는 대명사의 앞뒤를 자세히 살펴봐야 해. 글의 앞부분은 체스의 유래에 대한 설명으로 ①, ②, ③은 모두 첫 문장에 언급된 체스를 가리키고 있어. ④는 같은 문장 앞부분에서 언급된 국제체스연맹을 대신하고 있어. 마지막 문장의 ⑤는 세계적으로 가장 인기 있는 게임 중 하나라고 했으므로 체스를 말하고 있는 거야. 따라서 it이 가리키는 대상이 다른 것은 ④야. 그리고 it에 해당 단어를 넣어 읽어 보면서 글의 흐름이 자연스러운지 확인하는 것을 잊지 마.

171 정답 ⑤

지문 All in One

1 Mistletoe grows on the branches or trunk of a tree // and sends out *roots* [that enter the tree and steal its food]. 2 But / it is also capable of growing on its own / — using photosynthesis. 3 Some people have thought // that mistletoe had mystical powers, // and down through the centuries / it became associated with many myths and customs. 4 In the Middle Ages, / branches of mistletoe were hung from ceilings / to defend against evil spirits. 5 In Europe, / they were placed over house and barn doors / to prevent the entrance of witches. 6 Kissing under the mistletoe / was first associated with a Greek festival / and later with early marriage practices. 7 At Christmas time, / *a young lady* [standing under a ball of mistletoe] / could not refuse to be kissed. 8 Such a kiss could mean / deep romance or lasting friendship and goodwill.

(겨우살이는 나무의 가지나 줄기에서 자란다 / 그리고 나무에 들어가서 그것의 양분을 훔치는 뿌리를 내린다 / 그러나 / 그것은 또한 혼자서 성장할 수 있다 / 광합성을 이용하여 / 어떤 사람들은 생각했다 / 겨우살이가 신령스러운 힘을 가졌다고 / 그리고 수세기 동안 내려오면서 / 그것은 많은 신화 및 풍습과 연관되게 되었다 / 중세 시대에 / 겨우살이의 가지들은 천장에 매달려 있었다 / 악령을 방어하기 위해 / 유럽에서는 / 그것을 집과 헛간 문 위에 두었다 / 마녀들의 출입을 막기 위해 / 겨우살이 아래에서 키스하는 것은 / 처음에는 그리스 축제와 관련이 있었다 / 그리고 나중에는 이른 결혼 풍습과 관련이 있었다 / 크리스마스 때 / 겨우살이 뭉치 아래에 서 있는 젊은 여자는 / 키스 받는 것을 거부할 수 없었다 / 그러한 키스는 의미할 수 있었다 / 깊은 로맨스 또는 지속적인 우정과 호의를)

(S: Mistletoe, V₁: grows, V₂: sends, 관계대명사: that / S: it, V: is, C: capable / S₁: Some people, V₁: have thought, 접속사: that, S': mistletoe, V': had / S₂: it, V₂: became, C: associated / S: branches of mistletoe, V: were hung, 부사적 용법(목적): to defend / S: they, V: were placed, 부사적 용법(목적): to prevent / S: Kissing under the mistletoe, V: was, C: associated / S: a young lady [standing under a ball of mistletoe], V: could not refuse / S: Such a kiss, V: could mean)

① 뿌리를 나무속에 박아 자라기도 한다.
② 광합성을 통해 스스로 자랄 수도 있다.
③ 많은 민간 풍습들과 연관이 있다.
④ 나쁜 기운을 쫓는 데 쓰이기도 했다.
⑤ 덩굴에 키스하는 크리스마스 풍습이 있다.

해석 한 눈에 보기 1 겨우살이는 나무의 가지나 줄기에서 자라며, 나무에 들어가서 그것의 양분을 훔치는 뿌리를 내린다. 2 그러나 그것은 또한 광합성을 이용하여 혼자서 성장할 수 있다. 3 어떤 사람들은 겨우살이가 신령스러운 힘을 가졌다고 생각했고, 수세기 동안 내려오면서 그것은 많은 신화 및 풍습과 연관되게 되었다. 4 중세 시대에, 겨우살이의 가지들은 악령을 방어하기 위해 천장에 매달려 있었다. 5 유럽에서는, 마녀들의 출입을 막기 위해 그것을 집과 헛간 문 위에 두었다. 6 겨우살이 아래에서 키스하는 것은 처음에는 그리스 축제와 관련이 있었고 나중에는 이른 결혼 풍습과 관련이 있었다. 7 크리스마스 때, 겨우살이 뭉치 아래에 서 있는 젊은 여자는 키스 받기를 거부할 수 없었다. 8 그러한 키스는 깊은 로맨스 또는 지속적인 우정과 호의를 의미할 수 있었다.

정답단추 먼저 지시문에서 내용과 불일치하는 것을 고르는 문제임을 확인하고, 본문을 읽으면서 선택지와의 일치 여부를 순서대로 확인해봐. 글의 후반부에 크리스마스에 겨우살이 뭉치 아래에 서 있는 젊은 여자는 키스를 거부할 수 없다는 내용이 나오므로 덩굴에 키스한다는 내용이 아니야. 따라서 글의 내용과 일치하지 않는 것은 ⑤야.

오답단서 ①은 첫 문장에서 확인할 수 있어. ②는 두 번째 문장에 그 내용이 나오는데, 광합성으로 혼자서 자랄 수 있다고 했어. ③은 수세기 동안 겨우살이가 많은 신화와 풍습과 연관이 있다고 했으므로 내용과 일치해. ④는 중세 시대에는 악령을 쫓기 위해서, 유럽에서는 마녀의 출입을 막기 위해서 사용되었다고 했으므로 내용과 일치함을 알 수 있어.

어휘확인

mistletoe 겨우살이(줄기를 크리스마스 장식에 쓰는 덩굴식물) trunk (나무의) 몸통, 줄기 steal 훔치다 capable 할 수 있는 photosynthesis 광합성 mystical 신령스러운 century 세기 associated 관련된 myth 신화 custom 풍습, 관습 ceiling 천장 defend 방어하다 barn 헛간 prevent 막다, 예방하다 entrance 입장, 등장; 입구 witch 마녀 marriage 결혼 (생활) refuse 거부[거절]하다 romance 로맨스, 연애 goodwill 호의, 친선

지문 Flow

[소재]
겨우살이

[특징]
- 나무의 가지나 줄기에서 자라고, 나무에 뿌리를 내려 양분을 얻음
- 광합성으로 자생 가능함
- 신령스러운 힘을 가졌다고 여겨졌고, 많은 신화 및 풍습과 연관됨

[예시]
- 중세: 악령을 쫓기 위해 천장에 매달아 놓음
- 유럽: 마녀의 출입을 막기 위해 집과 헛간 문 위에 둠
- 겨우살이 아래에서 키스하는 풍습
  - 그리스 축제와 관련 있음
  - 이른 결혼 풍습과 관련됨
  - 크리스마스에 겨우살이 아래에 있는 여자에게 키스할 수 있음

172 정답 ⑤

지문 All in One

1 Modern Library's collection of eight thousand items / includes general histories of art and exhibition catalogues. 2 All materials must be used or viewed / in the library. 3 We offer wireless access, color scanners, and onsite access / to the library's resources.

(현대 도서관의 8천 개 품목의 소장품은 / 예술의 일반적인 역사와 전시 카탈로그들을 포함하고 있습니다 / 모든 자료는 사용되거나 열람되어야 합니다 / 도서관 내에서 / 저희는 무선 열람, 컬러 스캐너, 현장 열람을 제공합니다 / 도서관 자료에 대한)

(S: Modern Library's collection of eight thousand items, V: includes / S: All materials, V₁: must be used, V₂: viewed / S: We, V: offer)

어휘확인

modern 현대의 include 포함하다 general 일반적인 catalogue 카탈로그, 목록 material 자료; 직물 view 열람하다, 보다 offer 제공하다 wireless 무선의 access 접근 scanner 스캐너 onsite 현장의 resource 자료; 자원 hour(s) (영업 등을 하는) 시간 national holiday 국가 공휴

4 시간
Hours

5 매일 오전 10시 — 오후 5시
Daily 10:00 a.m. — 5:00 p.m.

6 국가 공휴일에는 휴관 / 금요일에는 오후 3시에 도서관이 폐관됨 / 연휴가 낀 주말 전
((We're) Closed on national holidays; // the library closes at 3:00 p.m. on Fridays / before holiday weekends.)

7 이야기 시간(스토리타임)
Storytime

8 스토리타임은 특별 프로그램입니다 / 3~7세 아이들을 위해 제공되는
• Storytime is *a special program* [offered for children ages three through seven].

9 그것은 월요일부터 금요일까지는 오후 3시부터 오후 3시 30분에 열립니다 / 그리고 일요일에는 오후 2시에
• It is held Monday — Friday from 3:00 p.m. — 3:30 p.m. / and Sundays at 2:00 p.m.

10 공간이 제한되어 있습니다 / 먼저 오면 / 먼저 응대합니다(선착순입니다)
• Space is limited. 11 First come, // first served.

① 자료들을 외부로 가지고 나갈 수 있다.
② 유선으로만 온라인 자료에 접근이 가능하다.
③ 연휴가 낀 주말이 시작되기 전 금요일에는 열지 않는다.
④ 3세 아동은 Storytime에 참가할 수 없다.
⑤ Storytime 참가는 선착순이다.

해석 한 눈에 보기 1 현대 도서관의 8천 개 품목의 소장품은 예술의 일반적인 역사와 전시 카탈로그들을 포함하고 있습니다. 2 모든 자료는 도서관 내에서 사용되거나 열람되어야 합니다. 3 저희는 도서관 자료에 대한 무선 열람, 컬러 스캐너, 현장 열람을 제공합니다. 4 **시간** 5 매일 오전 10시 – 오후 5시 6 (국가 공휴일에는 휴관, 연휴가 낀 주말 전 금요일에는 오후 3시에 도서관이 폐관됨) 7 **스토리타임** 8 •스토리타임은 3~7세 아이들을 위해 제공되는 특별 프로그램입니다. 9 •그것은 월요일부터 금요일까지는 오후 3시부터 오후 3시 30분에, 그리고 일요일에는 오후 2시에 열립니다. 10 •공간이 제한되어 있습니다. 11 선착순입니다.

정답단추 도서관 안내문의 모든 문장을 샅샅이 읽을 필요는 없어. 선택지를 읽고 해당하는 소제목을 찾아 빠르게 훑으며 확인하자. 또한, 주로 선택지 순서와 지문 단서의 순서가 일치하는 경우가 많아서 순서대로 보면 돼. 마지막 문장에 스토리타임은 선착순으로 참가할 수 있다고 나와 있지? 따라서 안내문과 선택지 내용이 일치하는 건 ⑤야.

오답단서 자료들은 도서관 내에서만 사용하거나 열람할 수 있다고 했으니까 외부로 나갈 수 없어. 따라서 ①은 안내문의 내용과 일치하지 않아. 또한, ②는 안내문에서 도서관 자료는 무선으로도 접근할 수 있다고 했으니까 오답이야. ③은 안내문에서 연휴가 낀 주말이 되기 전 금요일은 오후 3시까지 개관한다고 했으니 답이 될 수 없어. 마지막으로 스토리타임은 3~7세 아이를 위한 프로그램이니까 3세 아동이 참가할 수 없다는 ④도 옳지 않아.

일 **first come, first served** 선착순

지문 Flow

[소재]
현대 도서관의 안내문

[세부사항]
• 모든 자료는 도서관 내에서 사용되거나 열람되어야 함(무선 열람, 컬러 스캐너, 현장 열람 제공)
• 이용 시간
• 3~7세 아동을 위한 특별 프로그램인 스토리타임

173 정답 ⑤

지문 All in One

1 명상은 ~이다 / 자기 유도 형태의 마인드컨트롤 / 행해져 온 / 수천 년 동안
Meditation is / *a self-induced form of mind control* [that has been practiced] / for thousands of years.

2 그것(명상)은 인기를 얻기 시작했다 / 서양에서 / 1960년대에 / 특히 비틀스가 인도로 여행을 간 후에
① It started to gain popularity / in the West / in the 1960s, // especially after The Beatles traveled to India / to study and practice it.
그것을 공부하고 행하기 위해 (부사적 용법 (목적))

3 기본적으로 / 그것(명상)은 조용히 앉아있는 것을 포함한다 / 대개 바닥에 / 당신의 눈이 감긴 채로 / 그리고 단 하나의 이미지나 소리에 집중하는 것(을 포함한다) / 당신의 마음을 맑게 하기 위해
Basically, / ② it involves sitting quietly, / usually on the floor / with your eyes closed, / and focusing on a single image or sound / in order to clear your mind.
(with+명사+분사; 부사적 용법 (목적))

4 잘 알려져 있다 / 그것(명상)의 규칙적인 수행이 / 혈압을 낮출 수 있다는 것 / 행복감을 증가시킬 수 있다는 것 / 그리고 정신적 각성[주의력]을 신장시킬 수 있다는 것은
It's well known // that regular practice of ③ it / can lower blood pressure, / increase feelings of wellbeing, / and boost mental alertness.
(가주어, 접속사, 진주어)

5 그것(명상)을 포함해 온 사람들은 / 그들의 일상의 규칙적인 일과로 / 주장한다 / 스트레스가 상당히 줄어들었다고
People [who have incorporated ④ it / into their daily routines] / claim // that stress is significantly reduced.
(관계대명사, 접속사)

6 그것(스트레스)이 너무 적게 남아서 / 그것은 쉽게 처리될 수 있다 / 당신을 편안하고 건강한 상태로 만들어 준다
So little of ⑤ it remains // that it can easily be dealt with, / which leaves you relaxed and healthy.
(「so ~ that ...」 구문, 접속사, 관계대명사(계속적 용법))

해석 한 눈에 보기 1 명상은 수천 년 동안 행해져 온 자기 유도 형태의 마인드컨트롤이다. 2 ① 그것(명상)은 1960년대에, 특히 비틀스가 그것을 공부하고 수행하기 위해 인도로 여행을 간 후에, 서양에서 인기를 얻기 시작했다. 3 기본적으로 ② 그것(명상)은 대개 눈을 감고 바닥에 조용히 앉아 있는 것과 마음을 비우기 위해 하나의 이미지나 소리에 집중하는 것을 포함한다. 4 ③ 그것(명상)의 규칙적인 수행은 혈압을 낮추고, 행복감을 증가시키고, 정신적 각성[주의력]을

어휘확인

meditation 명상 **self-induced** 자기 유도의 **form** 형태; 종류 **mind control** 마인드컨트롤, 마음 조절 **practice** 행하다; 수행 **popularity** 인기 **the West** 서양; 서부 지방 **basically** 기본적으로 **involve** 포함하다 **quietly** 조용히 **focus on** ~에 집중하다 **single** 단 하나의 **image** 이미지, 심상 **in order to-v** ~하기 위해 **well known** 잘 알려진 **regular** 규칙적인 **lower** 낮추다 **blood pressure** 혈압 **increase** 증가시키다 **wellbeing** 행복 **boost** 신장시키다 **alertness** 각성(도), 민첩(성) **incorporate** (일부로) 포함하다 **routine** 규칙적인 일과 **claim** 주장하다 **significantly** 상당히 **remain** 남아 있다 **deal with** ~을 처리하다 **leave** (어떤 상태 등에) 있게 만들다 **relaxed** 편안한

지문 Flow

[소재]
수천 년 동안 행해져 온 자기 유도 형태의 마인드컨트롤인 명상

신장시킬 수 있다는 것은 잘 알려져 있다. 5 ④ 그것(명상)을 일상의 규칙적인 일과에 포함해 온 사람들은 스트레스가 상당히 줄어들었다고 주장한다. 6 ⑤ 그것(스트레스)이 너무 적게 남아서 그것은 쉽게 처리될 수 있는데, 이것은 당신을 편안하고 건강한 상태로 만들어 준다.

정답단추 대명사 it[It]이 가리키는 대상을 앞뒤 문장에서 찾으며 읽어야 해. ①은 앞 문장에 나온 Meditation(명상)을 대신하고 있어. 그리고 뒤이어 명상에 대한 구체적인 설명이 이어지고 있으므로 ②, ③, ④도 모두 명상을 가리켜. 그런데 ⑤는 앞 문장에서 언급한 명상을 통해 줄어드는 stress(스트레스)를 가리키고 있어. 따라서 it[It]이 가리키는 대상이 다른 것은 ⑤야. 대상을 찾은 다음에는 밑줄 친 대명사에 넣어 읽어보고 문맥이 자연스러운지 확인하자.

[보충설명]
- Beatles가 명상을 공부하고 수행하기 위해 인도로 간 후에 서양에서 인기를 끎
- 눈을 감고 바닥에 조용히 앉아 있거나, 마음을 비우기 위해 하나의 이미지나 소리에 집중함

⬇

[결과]
명상의 규칙적인 수행은 혈압 저하, 행복감 증가, 정신적 각성[주의력] 신장과 스트레스 감소 효과가 있음

174 정답 ③

지문 All in One

1 (Having been) Dedicated as a UNESCO World Heritage Site / in 1994, / the Nazca Lines of South America are / among *the most fascinating historical objects* [found anywhere in the world]. 2 These gigantic lines were discovered / in the 1930s / by airplane pilots. 3 (Having been) Drawn in Peru's Nazca Desert more than 3,000 years ago, / they depict / such things as birds, monkeys, and abstract designs. 4 Mysteriously, / it is impossible to see the pictures // if one is standing on the ground. 5 One can only see them from the sky. 6 It's hard to imagine // how primitive people achieved / such gigantic, detailed designs. 7 Various theories have been proposed / about *the methods* [used to make the Nazca Lines], // but there is *no exact evidence* [to explain / the reason why (they were made) and how they were made].

(유네스코 세계문화유산 보호지역으로 헌정되어서 / 1994년에 / 남미의 나스카 라인은 ~ 있다 / 세계 어디에서나 발견된 가장 매력적인 역사적인 물체들(유산들) 중에 / 이 거대한 라인들은 발견되었다 / 1930년대에 / 비행기 조종사들에 의해 / 페루의 나스카 사막에 3천 년보다도 더 오래전에 그려졌는데 / 그것들은 묘사한다 / 새, 원숭이, 추상적인 디자인과 같은 것들을 / 신비롭게도 / 그 그림들을 보는 것은 불가능하다 / 만일 우리가 땅에 서 있다면 / 우리는 그것들을 오직 하늘에서만 볼 수 있다 / 상상하는 것은 어렵다 / 어떻게 원시 시대 사람들이 이뤄냈는지 / 그렇게 거대하고 정교한 디자인을 / 다양한 이론들이 제시되었지만 / 나스카 라인을 만드는 데 사용된 방법들에 대해 / 그러나 ~을 설명해줄 정확한 증거는 없다 / 그것들이 만들어진 이유와 방법을)

(완료형 수동태 분사구문 / S / V / S / V / 완료형 수동태 분사구문 / S / V / 가주어 V / C / 진주어 / 접속사 S' / V' / S / V / 가주어 V / C / 진주어 / 간접의문문 / S / V / 부사적 용법(목적) / V / S / 관계부사 / 관계부사(= the way))

① 1930년대에 비행기 조종사들이 발견했다.
② 동물과 기하학적 문양이 그려져 있다.
③ 지상에서는 그림의 일부만 볼 수 있다.
④ 거대할 뿐 아니라 정밀하게 그려졌다.
⑤ 만들어진 방법과 동기는 정확하지 않다.

해석 한 눈에 보기 1 1994년에 유네스코 세계문화유산 보호지역으로 헌정되어서, 남미의 나스카 라인은 세계 그 어느 곳에서 발견된 가장 매력적인 역사적 유산 중 하나이다. 2 이 거대한 라인은 1930년대에 비행기 조종사들에 의해 발견되었다. 3 페루의 나스카 사막에 3천 년보다도 더 오래전에 그려졌는데, 그것은 새, 원숭이, 추상적인 디자인과 같은 것들을 묘사한다. 4 신비롭게도 만일 우리가 땅에 서 있다면 그 그림들을 보는 것은 불가능하다. 5 우리는 그것들을 오직 하늘에서만 볼 수 있다. 6 원시 시대 사람들이 어떻게 그렇게 거대하고 정교한 디자인을 이뤄냈는지 상상하는 것은 어렵다. 7 나스카 라인을 만드는 데 사용된 방법들에 대해 다양한 이론들이 제기되었지만, 그것들이 만들어진 이유와 방법을 설명해 줄 정확한 증거는 없다.

정답단추 문제를 풀기 전 선택지와 본문의 내용이 일치하는 것을 찾아야 하는지 불일치하는 것을 찾아야 하는지를 반드시 확인해야 해. 일치하지 않는 것을 고르는 문제라는 걸 명심하고, 본문을 읽으면서 선택지와의 일치 여부를 순서대로 확인해보자. Mysteriously로 시작하는 부분을 보면 나스카 라인은 지상에서는 그림을 볼 수 없고 하늘에서만 볼 수 있다고 했으니까 ③이 본문의 내용과 일치하지 않는 설명이야.

오답단서 선택지와 글의 내용을 비교하면서 살펴보자. 우선 지문에서 이 거대한 라인은 1930년대에 비행기 조종사들이 발견했다고 하였으므로 ①은 옳은 내용이야. 또한, 새, 원숭이(동물)와 추상적(기하학적)인 문양이 그려져 있으므로 ②도 일치해. 또한, 나스카 라인은 상상하기 어려울 만큼 거대하고 정교한 디자인을 가지고 있다고 하고 있어 ④의 내용도 일치해. 마지막으로 ⑤는 지문의 마지막 문장에서 확인할 수 있어.

어휘확인
dedicate 헌정하다 **UNESCO** 유네스코(국제연합교육과학문화기구) **World Heritage Site** 세계문화유산 **fascinating** 매력적인 **historical** 역사적인 **object** 물체; 물건 **anywhere** 어디(에)나 **gigantic** 거대한 **discover** 발견하다 **depict** 묘사하다 **abstract** 추상적인 **mysteriously** 신비롭게 **imagine** 상상하다 **primitive** 원시 시대의 **achieve** 이루다; 성취하다 **detailed** 정교한, 상세한 **various** 다양한 **theory** 이론 **propose** 제시하다 **method** 방법 **exact** 정확한 **evidence** 증거

지문 Flow

[소재]
유네스코 세계문화유산 보호지역으로 헌정된 페루의 나스카 라인

⬇

[세부사항1]
1930년대에 비행기 조종사들이 나스카 사막에서 발견함

&

[세부사항2]
새, 원숭이, 추상적인 디자인을 묘사하고 있으며, 하늘에서만 볼 수 있음

&

[세부사항3]
나스카 라인이 만들어진 이유와 방법을 설명할 정확한 증거가 없음

지문 All in One

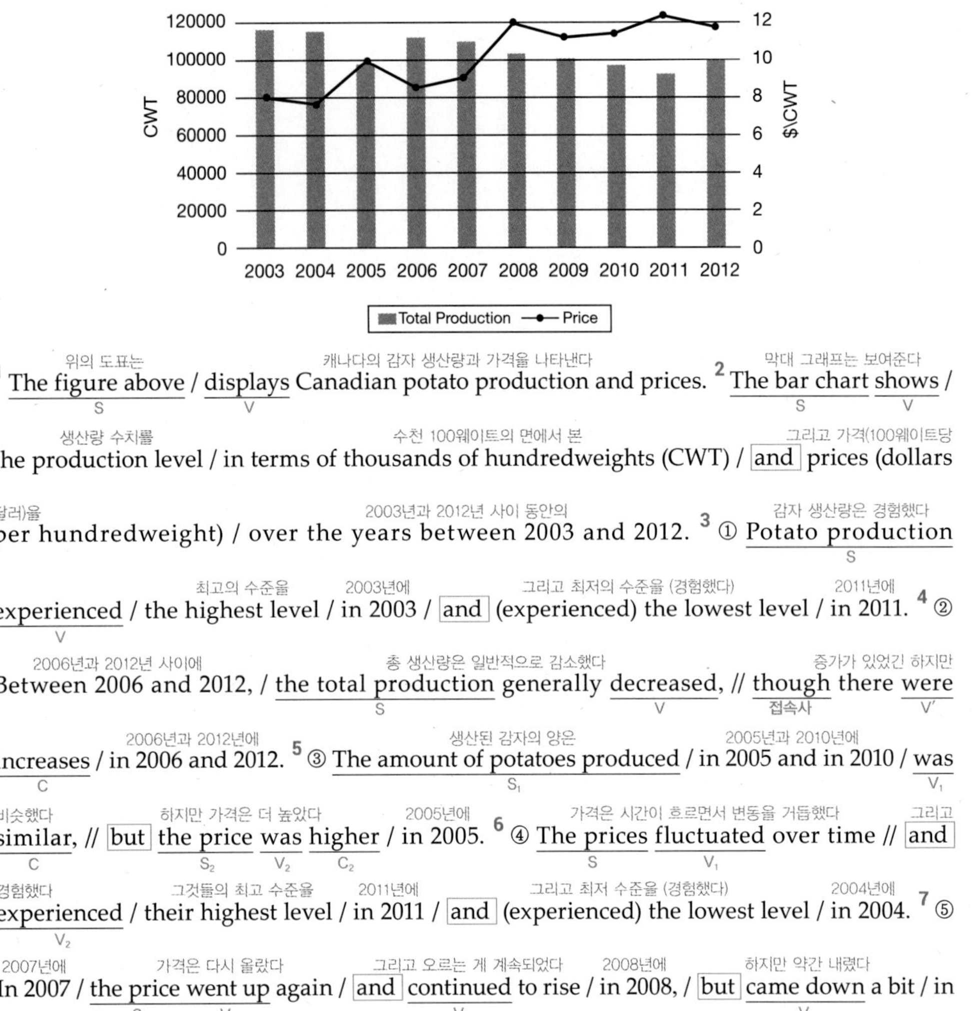

1 The figure above / displays Canadian potato production and prices. 2 The bar chart shows / the production level / in terms of thousands of hundredweights (CWT) / and prices (dollars per hundredweight) / over the years between 2003 and 2012. 3 ① Potato production experienced / the highest level / in 2003 / and (experienced) the lowest level / in 2011. 4 ② Between 2006 and 2012, / the total production generally decreased, // though there were increases / in 2006 and 2012. 5 ③ The amount of potatoes produced / in 2005 and in 2010 / was similar, // but the price was higher / in 2005. 6 ④ The prices fluctuated over time // and experienced / their highest level / in 2011 / and (experienced) the lowest level / in 2004. 7 ⑤ In 2007 / the price went up again / and continued to rise / in 2008, / but came down a bit / in 2009.

해석 한 눈에 보기 1 위의 도표는 캐나다의 감자 생산량과 가격을 나타낸다. 2 막대 그래프는 2003년과 2012년 사이 기간의 수천 100웨이트의 면에서 본 생산량 수치와 가격(100웨이트당 달러)을 보여준다. 3 ① 감자 생산량은 2003년에 최고의 수준을 그리고 2011년에 최저의 수준을 경험했다. 4 ② 2006년과 2012년 사이에, 총 생산량은 2006년과 2012년에 증가가 있었지만, 일반적으로 감소했다. 5 ③ 2005년과 2010년에 생산된 감자의 양은 비슷했지만, 가격은 2005년에 더 높았다. 6 ④ 가격은 시간이 흐르면서 변동을 거듭했는데, 2011년에 최고 수준을 그리고 2004년에 최저 수준을 경험했다. 7 ⑤ 2007년에 가격은 다시 올랐고 2011년에도 계속 올랐지만 2009년에는 약간 내렸다.

정답단추 도표 자료 파악 문제는 도표의 제목과 첫 문장에 소개되는 도표의 성격을 통해 도표를 파악한 다음, 글을 읽으면서 도표와 꼼꼼히 비교해야 하는 거 기억하지? 이 도표에서 막대 그래프는 감자 생산량을, 꺾은선 그래프는 가격임을 혼동하지 않도록 유의해야 해. 꺾은선 그래프를 보면 2005년에 비해 2010년의 감자 가격이 더 높았음을 알 수 있어. 그런데 지문에서는 2005년의 가격이 더 높았다고 하고 있어 도표의 내용과 일치하지 않는 것은 ③이야.

오답단서 감자 생산량이 2011년에 최저 수준, 2003년에 최고 수준이라는 ①의 내용은 막대 그래프의 수치와 일치해. 생산량을 나타내는 막대 그래프에서 2006년과 2012년 사이의 총 생산량은 2006년과 2012년만 증가했을 뿐 나머지는 모두 감소했기 때문에 ②의 내용과 일치해. 그리고 가격을 나타내는 꺾은선 그래프를 보면 시간의 흐름에 따라 변동을 거듭했고, 2011년에 최고점을, 그리고 2004년에 최저점을 기록했다는 ④의 내용과 일치함을 알 수 있어. 마지막으로 2007년부터 2008년까지 가격이 오르다가 2009년에 약간 감소한 것을 꺾은선 그래프에서 확인할 수 있으니까 ⑤도 맞는 내용이야.

어휘확인

Canadian 캐나다의 **production** 생산량; 생산 **figure** 도표; 수치 **display** 나타내다; 전시하다 **bar chart** 막대 그래프 **in terms of** ~ 면에서 **dollar** 달러 **per** ~당 **total** 총, 전체의 **generally** 일반적으로 **decrease** 감소하다; 감소(↔ **increase** 증가하다; 증가) **though** 비록 ~할지라도 **amount** 양; 총액 **similar** 비슷한 **fluctuate** 변동을 거듭하다 **go up** (가격·기온 등이) 오르다 **continue** 계속되다 **rise** 오르다 **come down** (가격·기온·비율 등이) 내리다 **a bit** 약간

지문 Flow

[소재]
2003년~2012년의 캐나다의 감자 생산량과 가격을 나타내는 그래프

[진술1]
생산량: 2003년에 최고, 2011년에 최저
2006~2012년에 생산량 증가함 (2006년, 2012년 제외)

&

[틀린 진술]
2005년과 2010년의 생산량은 비슷했지만, 가격은 2005년에 더 높음(→ 2010년의 가격이 더 높음)

&

[진술2]
가격: 2011년에 최고, 2004년에 최저
2007년부터 계속 오르다가 2009년에 약간 내림

176 정답 ②

지문 All in One

그린빌 교향악단
1 **GREENVILLE SYMPHONY ORCHESTRA**

David S. Pollitt, 음악 감독
2 David S. Pollitt, Music Director

명곡 시리즈
3 MASTERWORKS SERIES

10월 19일 토요일 오후 8시 / 그리고 10월 20일 일요일 오후 3시 / 평화 센터
4 Saturday, October 19, 8:00 p.m. / and Sunday, October 20, 3:00 p.m., / The Peace Center

Mozart
5 MOZART

진혼곡 D 단조
6 The Requiem in D minor

Mendelssohn
7 MENDELSSOHN

바이올린 협주곡 E 단조
8 Violin Concerto in E Minor

Robert McDuffie의 바이올린 협연
9 ROBERT McDUFFIE, *Violin*

중간 휴식 시간
10 *Intermission*

Tchaikovsky
11 TCHAIKOVSKY

교향곡 4번 F 단조
12 Symphony No. 4 in F Minor

늦게 오시는 분들은 입장하지 못할 겁니다 / 공연 도중에
13 Latecomers will not be admitted / during the performance.
S V

① 토요일 2회, 일요일 1회 공연이다.
② 모두 세 작곡가의 곡들이 연주된다.
③ Robert McDuffie가 오케스트라를 총 감독한다.
④ 중간 휴식시간 없이 공연이 계속된다.
⑤ 공연 시작 후 10분까지는 입장이 가능하다.

해석 한 눈에 보기 **1 그린빌 교향악단** 2 David S. Pollitt, 음악 감독 3 명곡 시리즈 4 10월 19일 토요일 오후 8시와 10월 20일 일요일 오후 3시, 평화 센터 5 Mozart 6 진혼곡 D 단조 7 Mendelssohn 8 바이올린 협주곡 E 단조 9 Robert McDuffie의 바이올린 협연 10 중간 휴식 시간 11 Tchaikovsky 12 교향곡 4번 F 단조 13 늦게 오시는 분들은 공연 도중에 입장하지 못할 겁니다.

정답단추 이 글은 그린빌 교향악단 공연 팸플릿인데, 소제목으로 잘 구분되어 있어서, 선택지와 소제목을 잘 활용하면 일치하는 선택지를 쉽게 찾을 수 있어. 소제목에서 음악가의 이름을 보면, 이 콘서트에 Mozart, Mendelssohn, Tchaikovsky의 음악이 연주됨을 알 수 있어. 따라서 글의 내용과 일치하는 것은 ②야.

오답단서 ①은 토요일 오후 8시, 일요일 오후 3시 공연이므로, 토요일에도 1회 공연임을 알 수 있어. ③은 Robert McDuffie가 Mendelssohn의 곡에서 바이올린 협연을 하므로 일치하지 않는 내용이야. ④는 Intermission에서 일치하지 않는 내용임을 알 수 있어. ⑤는 마지막 문장에서 공연 도중에 입장할 수 없다고 했으므로 일치하지 않는 내용이야.

어휘확인

symphony orchestra 교향악단 **director** 감독 **masterwork** 명작 **requiem** 진혼곡(죽은 사람의 영혼을 위로하기 위한 미사 음악), 레퀴엠 **minor** ((음악)) 단조 **intermission** 중간 휴식 시간 **latecomer** 늦게 오는 사람 **admit** (입장을) 허락하다 **performance** 공연

지문 Flow

[소재]
그린빌 교향악단 공연 팸플릿

[세부사항1]
• 일시: 10월 19일 토요일 오후 8시 / 10월 20일 일요일 오후 3시
• 장소: 평화 센터

&

[세부사항2]
Mozart, Mendelssohn, Tchaikovsky의 음악 연주

&

[세부사항3]
늦게 오는 사람은 공연 도중에 입장 불가능

177 정답 ④

지문 All in One

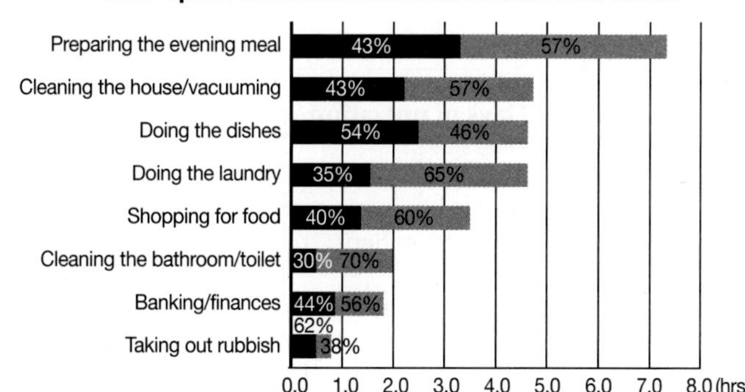

	Taking out rubbish	Banking/finances	Cleaning the bathroom/toilet	Shopping for food	Doing the laundry	Doing the dishes	Cleaning the house/vacuuming	Preparing the evening meal
■ Man(hrs)	0.5	0.8	0.6	1.4	1.6	2.5	2.1	3.2
■ Woman(hrs)	0.3	1.0	1.4	2.1	3.0	2.1	2.8	4.2

어휘확인

vacuum 진공청소기로 청소하다 **do the dishes** 설거지를 하다 **do (the) laundry** 빨래하다 **toilet** 화장실 **banking** 은행업무 **finances** 재정; 돈 **rubbish** 쓰레기 **average** 평균의 **partner** 배우자; 파트너 **a range of** 다양한 **routine** 일상의 **household** 가정 **although** (비록) ~이긴 하지만 **tend to-v** ~하는 경향이 있다 **extent** 정도 **participation** 참여, 참가 **vary** (상황에 따라) 다르다 **according to** ~에 따라 **percentage** 비율, 퍼센트 **share** 몫; 나누다 **time-consuming** (많은) 시간이 걸리는

[1] The above graph shows / *the average time* [spent by men and their partners / in a range of routine household tasks] / in Australia. [2] ① Although women tend to do most of the housework, // the extent of men's participation varies / according to task. [3] ② *The only tasks* [where men report / that they do more / than their partners] / are doing the dishes / and taking out the rubbish. [4] ③ For all other tasks, / men's partners spend more time / each week, / with women spending much more time / than men / (in) doing the laundry, / cleaning the bathroom and toilet, / and food shopping. [5] ④ The biggest difference in the percentage share / for men and women / is shown / in cleaning the house and vacuuming. [6] ⑤ The graph also shows // that preparing the evening meal / was the most time-consuming task / and taking out the rubbish / was the least.

(위 그래프는 보여준다 / 남자와 그들의 배우자들에 의해 소비된 평균적인 시간을 / 다양한 일상적인 가정(집안)일에 / 호주에서 / 비록 여자들이 집안일의 대부분을 하는 경향이 있지만 / 남자들의 참여 정도는 다르다 / 일에 따라 / 남자들이 보고하는 유일한 일들은 / 그들이 더 많이 한다고 / 그들의 배우자들보다 / 설거지하기이다 / 그리고 쓰레기 버리기(이다) / 다른 모든 일에 대해서 / 남자들의 배우자들이 더 많은 시간을 보낸다 / 매주 / 여자들은 훨씬 더 많은 시간을 보낸다 / 남자들보다 / 빨래하기 / 욕실과 화장실 청소하기 / 그리고 음식 장보기에 / 몫의 비율에서 가장 큰 차이는 / 남자와 여자의 / 보인다 / 집 청소하기와 진공청소기로 청소하는 것에서 / 그 그래프는 또한 보여준다 / 저녁 식사를 준비하는 것이 / 가장 많은 시간이 걸리는 일이라는 것을 / 그리고 쓰레기를 버리는 것이 / 가장 적은 (시간이 걸리는 일이라는) 것을)

(S: The above graph, V: shows / 접속사: Although, S′: women, V′: tend / S: the extent of men's participation, V: varies / S: The only tasks, 관계부사: where, 접속사: that, S′: they, V′: do, V: are, C_1: doing the dishes, C_2: taking out the rubbish / S: men's partners, V: spend / with+명사+분사 / S: The biggest difference in the percentage share, V: is shown / S: The graph, V: shows, 접속사: that, S'_1: preparing the evening meal, V'_1: was, C'_1: the most time-consuming task, S'_2: taking out the rubbish, V'_2: was, C'_2: the least)

해석 한 눈에 보기 [1] 위 그래프는 호주의 남자와 그들의 배우자들이 다양한 일상적인 집안일에 소비하는 평균 시간을 보여준다. [2] ① 비록 여자들이 대부분의 집안일을 하는 경향이 있지만, 남자들의 참여 정도는 일에 따라 다르다. [3] ② 남자들이 자신들이 그들의 배우자보다 더 많이 한다고 보고하는 유일한 일들은 설거지하기와 쓰레기 버리기이다. [4] ③ 다른 모든 일에 대해서, 남자의 배우자들이 매주 더 많은 시간을 보내는데, 여자들은 빨래하기, 욕실과 화장실 청소하기, 음식 장보기에 남자들보다 훨씬 더 많은 시간을 쓴다. [5] ④ 남자와 여자에 대한 몫의 비율에서 가장 큰 차이는 집 청소하기와 청소기 돌리기에서 보인다. [6] ⑤ 그 그래프는 또한 저녁 식사를 준비하는 것이 가장 시간이 오래 걸리는 일이고 쓰레기를 버리는 것이 시간이 가장 적게 걸리는 일이었음을 보여준다.

정답단추 이 그래프와 표는 호주의 부부가 일상적인 집안일에 쓰는 시간과 비율을 보여주고 있어. 두 자료에 나타난 정보를 파악하고, 지문 내용과 꼼꼼히 비교하는 게 좋아. ④에서 언급한 cleaning the house and vacuuming은 남자와 여자에 대한 몫의 비율이 각각 43%와 57%로 그 차이는 14%에 불과해. 그리고 가장 차이가 큰 것은 남녀 몫의 비율이 각각 30%와 70%로 차이가 40%인 cleaning the bathroom and toilet이야. 따라서 ④가 도표의 내용과 일치하지 않아.

오답단서 그래프에서 남자의 집안일 참여 비율을 보면 집안일의 종류에 따라 달라지는 것을 확인할 수 있으므로 ①의 내용은 일치해. ②도 그래프를 보면 남자가 쓰레기 버리기와 설거지하기를 더 많이 하고 나머지 일은 여자가 더 많이 한다는 것을 알 수 있으니까 옳아. 그리고 비율 차이가 가장 많이 나는 집안일은 욕실과 화장실 청소하기(40%), 빨래하기(30%), 음식 장보기(20%)로 ③도 맞는 설명이야. 마지막으로 도표를 보면 저녁 준비가 3.2시간과 4.2시간으로 가장 오래 걸리는 집안일이고, 쓰레기 버리기가 0.5시간과 0.3시간으로 가장 적게 걸리는 집안일이야. 따라서 ⑤의 내용도 일치한다는 것을 알 수 있어.

지문 Flow

[소재]
호주의 부부가 다양한 집안일에 소비하는 평균 시간을 보여주는 그래프

[진술1]
남자는 설거지와 쓰레기 버리기를 더 많이 함

&

[진술2]
여자는 빨래, 욕실과 화장실 청소, 음식 장보기에 많은 시간을 씀

&

[틀린 진술]
남녀 몫의 비율이 가장 큰 것은 집 청소하기와 청소기 돌리기임(→ 욕실과 화장실 청소임)

&

[진술3]
저녁 식사 준비가 시간이 가장 오래 걸리고, 쓰레기 버리기가 시간이 가장 적게 걸림

178 정답 ③

지문 All in One

[1] **A380 Flight Schedule** (A380 비행 일정표)

노선(출발 — 도착) Route(from — to)	항공기 번호 Flight number	출발 Departure	도착 Arrival	운항일 Days of operation
뉴욕(JFK) — 서울(인천) New York (JFK) — Seoul (Incheon)	K082	14:00	17:20+1	화요일, 목요일, 토요일 Tue, Thu, Sat (9월 1일부터 매일 운항) (Daily from Sept. 1)
서울(인천) — 뉴욕(JFK) Seoul (Incheon) — New York (JFK)	K081	11:00	11:55	화요일, 토요일 Tue, Sat (9월 1일부터 매일 운항) (Daily from Sept. 1)
로스앤젤레스 — 서울(인천) Los Angeles — Seoul (Incheon)	K018	12:30	17:30+1	화요일, 목요일, 토요일 Tue, Thu, Sat (10월 20일부터 매일 운항) (Daily from Oct. 20)

어휘확인

flight 비행; 항공기(= **aircraft**) **route** 노선, 경로 **departure** 출발 **arrival** 도착 **operation** 운항, 운용 **subject** ~될 수 있는 **notice** 예고, 알림 **indicate** 나타내다 **gate** (공항의) 탑승구 **prior to** ~전에, ~에 앞서 **passenger** 승객 **allow** 허용[허락]하다 **check** (비행기 등을 탈 때 수하물을) 부치다 **baggage** 수하물 **carry-on** (기내) 휴대용 가방 **per** ~당

지문 Flow

[소재]
A380 비행 일정표

서울(인천) — 로스앤젤레스 Seoul (Incheon) — Los Angeles	K017	15:00	09:50	화요일, 토요일 Tue, Sat (10월 20일부터 매일 운항) (Daily from Oct. 20)

2 비행 일정과 항공기 종류는 / 변경될 수 있습니다 / 예고 없이
• Flight schedules and aircraft types / are subject to change / without notice.
(S: Flight schedules and aircraft types, V: are, C: subject)

3 '+1'은 하루 뒤에 도착함을 나타냅니다
• '+1' indicates arrival after one day.
(S: '+1', V: indicates)

4 출발 탑승구는 닫힙니다 / 예정된 출발의 20분 전에
• Departure gates close / 20 minutes prior to scheduled departure.
(S: Departure gates, V: close)

5 승객들은 허용됩니다 / 체크인한(기내에 부치는) 수하물 2개와 기내 휴대용 수하물 하나가 / 1인당
• Passengers are allowed / two pieces of checked baggage plus one carry-on / per person.
(S: Passengers, V: are allowed)

[보충설명 1]
서울과 뉴욕, 서울과 로스앤젤레스의 왕복 비행 일정표

&

[보충설명 2]
• 비행 일정과 항공기 종류는 예고 없이 변경 가능함
• 출발 탑승구는 출발 20분 전에 닫힘
• 1인당 가방 2개와 기내 수하물 1개가 허용됨

① 10월 20일부터는 모두 매일 운항한다.
② K082는 일주일에 3일 운항 중이다.
③ K018은 서울에 오후 6시 30분에 도착한다.
④ 비행기 기종은 사전 안내 없이 변경될 수 있다.
⑤ 이륙 20분 전까지는 탑승을 완료해야 한다.

해석 한 눈에 보기 1 **A380 비행 일정표** 2 비행 일정과 항공기 종류는 예고 없이 변경될 수 있습니다. 3 '+1'은 하루 뒤에 도착함을 나타냅니다. 4 출발 탑승구는 예정된 출발의 20분 전에 닫힙니다. 5 승객들은 1인당 체크인한 가방 2개와 기내 휴대 수하물 하나가 허용됩니다.

정답단추 우선 무엇에 관한 도표인지 파악하자. 위 도표는 A380의 비행 노선, 비행 일정, 참고 사항을 보여주고 있지? 선택지와 일정표의 숫자와 세부 정보, 하단의 참고 사항에 나오는 세부 사항을 꼼꼼히 확인해야 해. 일정표 아래의 참고 사항에 나와 있듯이 도착시각인 17:30+1에서 '+1'은 다음 날을 나타내는 표시이므로 도착시각은 오후 6시 30분이 아닌 5시 30분이야. 따라서 표의 내용과 일치하지 않는 것은 ③이야.

오답단서 운항일을 보면 K082, K081이 9월 1일부터, K018, K017이 10월 20일부터 매일 운항한다고 했으므로 10월 20일부터는 모두 매일 운행한다는 ①의 내용은 일정표와 일치해. 또한, K082의 운항일을 보면 화요일, 목요일, 토요일을 운항하고 있으니까 ②에서 일주일에 3일 운항 중이라는 설명은 옳아. ④와 ⑤는 일정표 아래의 세부 사항에서 쉽게 찾을 수 있어. 비행 일정과 항공기 종류는 예고 없이 변경될 수 있다고 하였고, 출발 탑승구는 출발의 20분 전에 닫힌다고 나와 있으므로 ④와 ⑤의 내용과 일치해.

179 정답 ③

지문 All in One

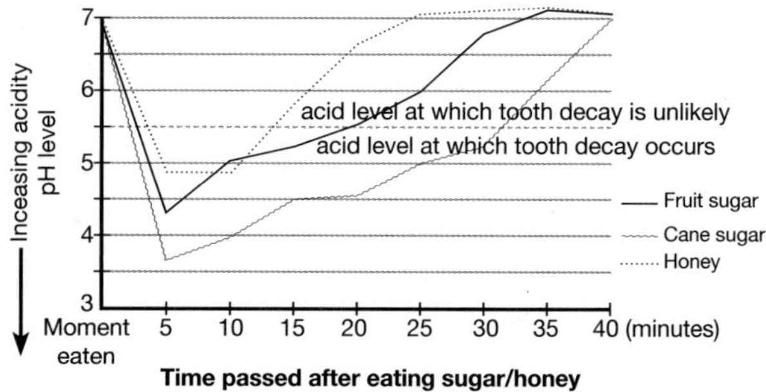

1 위 그래프는 보여준다 / 입안의 산 수치를 / 단 음식을 먹은 후에 / 과당, 사탕수수로 만든 설탕, 그리고 꿀을 비교함으로써
The above graph shows / the level of acid in the mouth / after eating sweet foods / by comparing fruit sugar, cane sugar, [and] honey.
(S: The above graph, V: shows)

2 단 음식은 pH를 내려가게 한다 / 잠깐 // 그리고 더 오래 pH 수치가 5.5 아래일수록 / 충치가 발생할 기회는 더 커진다
Sweet foods cause pH to drop / for a while, // [and] the longer pH levels remain below 5.5, / the greater the opportunity for tooth decay to occur (is).
(S: Sweet foods, V: cause, O: pH, C: to drop / C_1: the longer, S_1: pH levels, V_1: remain, C_2: the greater, S_2: the opportunity, V_2: (is))

3 꿀은 가장 덜 위험한 물질인 것처럼 보인다 // 왜냐하면 입안의 산이 pH 5.5 이상으로 돌아오기 때문이다 / 15분 이내로
① Honey seems to be the least risky substance // because mouth acid returns to above pH 5.5 / in under fifteen minutes.
(S: Honey, V: seems, 접속사: because, S': mouth acid, V': returns)

4 그리고 과당은 약 20분 정도 걸린다 / pH 5.5 이상으로 돌아가는 데
② And fruit sugar takes about 20 minutes for it / to go back to above pH 5.5.
(S: fruit sugar, V: takes, to go back: 부사적 용법 (목적))

5 그에 반해서 / 사탕수수로 만든 설탕을 먹은 후에 / pH 수치는 pH 5.5 이상으로
③ In contrast, / after eating cane sugar, / pH levels do not rise
(S: pH levels, V: do not rise)

어휘확인
acid ((화학)) 산 **cf. acidity** 산성 **level** 수치, 수준 **consumption** 소비 **pH** ((화학)) 피에이치, 페하(용액의 수소 이온 농도 지수) **tooth decay** 충치 **unlikely** 있을 것 같지 않은 **occur** 발생하다 **fruit sugar** 과당 **cane sugar** 사탕수수로 만든 설탕 **compare** 비교하다 **for a while** 잠깐, 잠시 **remain** 계속 ~이다 **opportunity** 기회 **risky** 위험한 **substance** 물질 **in contrast** 그에 반해서 **rise** 올라가다 **risk** 위험 **implication** 시사하는 바, 암시 **appear** ~인 것 같다 **preferable to** ~보다 더 나은

지문 Flow

[소재]
단 음식을 먹은 후의 입안의 산 수치를 보여주는 그래프

⬇

[진술]
단 음식은 pH를 내려가게 하는데, pH 수치가 5.5 아래에 오래 있을수록 충치가 발생함

⬇

올라가지 않는다 적어도 35분이 경과할 때까지 과당, 사탕수수로 만든 설탕, 그리고 꿀을
above pH 5.5 // until at least 35 minutes have passed. [6] ④ By comparing fruit sugar, cane
접속사 S′ V′

비교함으로써 우리는 발견한다 사탕수수로 만든 설탕이 초래한다는 것을 셋 중 가장 큰 위험을
sugar, and honey, / we find // that cane sugar produces / the greatest risk of the three. [7] ⑤
S V 접속사 S′ V′

시사하는 바는 그렇다면 ~이다 꿀이나 과당이 더 나은 것 같다는 것 사탕수수로 만든 설탕보다
The implications, / then, / are // that honey or fruit sugar appear preferable / to cane sugar.
S V 접속사 C

[예시]
pH 5.5 이상으로 돌아오는 데 걸리는 시간 • 꿀: 15분 이내 • 과당: 약 20분 • 설탕: 35분 이상(→ 30분 정도)

⬇

[결론]
설탕이 충치에 가장 큰 위험을 초래함

해석 한 눈에 보기 1 위 그래프는 과당, 사탕수수로 만든 설탕, 꿀을 비교함으로써 단 음식을 먹은 후의 입안의 산 수치를 보여준다. 2 단 음식은 pH를 잠깐 내려가게 하는데, pH 수치가 5.5 아래에 더 오래 있을수록, 충치가 발생할 기회는 더 커진다. 3 ① 꿀은 15분 이내에 입 안의 산이 pH 5.5 이상으로 돌아오기 때문에 가장 덜 위험한 물질처럼 보인다. 4 ② 그리고 과당은 pH 5.5 이상으로 되돌아오는 데 약 20분이 걸린다. 5 ③ 그에 반해서, 사탕수수로 만든 설탕을 먹은 후에는, pH 수치가 최소 35분이 지나갈 때까지도 pH 5.5 이상으로 올라가지 않는다. 6 ④ 과당, 사탕수수로 만든 설탕, 꿀을 비교함으로써, 우리는 설탕이 셋 중에서 가장 큰 위험을 초래한다는 것을 발견한다. 7 ⑤ 그렇다면 시사하는 바는 꿀이나 과당이 설탕보다 더 나은 것 같다는 것이다.

정답단추 이 그래프는 과당, 설탕, 꿀을 먹었을 때 시간의 흐름에 따른 입안의 산성도 변화를 보여주고 있어. 그래프를 보면 설탕을 섭취한 후 입안의 pH 수치가 5.5로 돌아오기까지 30분이 조금 넘게 걸렸음을 확인할 수 있어. 그런데 ③에서는 최소 35분까지 pH 5.5 이상으로 올라가지 않는다고 했으니 그래프와 일치하지 않아.

오답단서 그래프에서 pH 5.5 이상으로 돌아오는 데 가장 짧은 시간이 걸린 것은 꿀이니까 ①은 일치해. 과당이 pH 5.5 이상이 되는 건 약 20분부터니까 ②의 내용도 그래프와 일치한다는 것을 알 수 있어. 과당, 설탕, 꿀 중에 입안의 pH 수치가 5.5까지 돌아오는 시간이 가장 긴 것은 설탕이지? 이것은 이가 썩을 기회가 더 많다는 걸 의미하니까 설탕이 가장 위험하다는 ④의 내용은 옳아. 마지막으로 이 그래프를 통해 알 수 있는 건 설탕보다는 꿀과 과당이 더 낫다는 점이니까 ⑤의 내용과도 일치해.

180 정답 ③

지문 All in One

1 닥터 툼스
Dr. TUMS

2 효능
Uses

3 ~의 완화를 위한 것입니다
for the relief of

4 산성 소화불량과 속 쓰림
• acid indigestion and sour stomach

5 과식에 따른 두통을 동반한 배탈
• upset stomach with headache from overeating

6 맛
Flavors

7 씹어 먹는 닥터 툼스 알약은 4가지 맛으로 나옵니다 체리, 레몬, 딸기, 그리고 귤
Dr. TUMS chewable tablets come in 4 flavors: / cherry, lemon, strawberry, and tangerine.
S V

8 복용법
Directions

9 완전히 용해시키세요 4온스의 물에 알약 2정을 섭취 전에
Fully dissolve / 2 tablets in 4 ounces of water / before taking.
V 분사구문(= before you take them)

10 어른과 12세 이상의 아이는 4시간마다 2알을 복용하세요
Adults and children over 12 years and over: // take 2 tablets every 4 hours.
S V

11 8알을 초과하지 마세요 24시간 내에
Do not exceed 8 tablets / in 24 hours.
V

12 60세 이상의 어른은 4시간마다 2알을 복용하세요
Adults 60 years old and over: // take 2 tablets every 4 hours.
S V

13 4알을 초과하지 마세요 24시간 내에
Do not exceed 4 tablets / in 24 hours.
V

14 유효 성분
Active Ingredients

15 1,000 밀리그램의 탄산칼슘 씹어 먹는 알약 1정당
1,000 milligrams of Calcium Carbonate / per chewable tablet.

16 경고
Warnings

17 사용하지 마세요 만일 당신이 알레르기가 있다면 아스피린이나 기타 어떤 진통제에
Do not use // if you are allergic / to aspirin or any other pain reliever.
V 접속사 S′ V′ C′

① 소화 불량이나 복통에 먹는 약이다.
② 다양한 맛으로 출시되고 있다.
③ 60세 이상 성인은 하루에 8알을 넘게 먹으면 안 된다.

어휘확인

use 효능, 용도 **relief** 완화; 안도 **acid** ((화학)) 산성의 **indigestion** 소화불량 **sour stomach** 속 쓰림, 위산과다 **upset stomach** 배탈 **overeating** 과식 **flavor** 맛 **chewable** 씹을 수 있는 **tablet** 정제(둥글넓적한 모양의 약제) **come** (상품·물품 등이) 나오다 **tangerine** 귤 **direction** 복용법, 지시 **fully** 완전히 **dissolve** 용해시키다, 녹이다 **ounce** 온스(무게 단위) **take** (약을) 복용하다[먹다] **exceed** 초과하다 **ingredient** 성분, 재료 **milligram** 밀리그램(= mg) **Calcium Carbonate** 탄산칼슘 **per** ~당 **be allergic to** ~에 알레르기가 있다 **aspirin** 아스피린 **pain reliever** 진통제

지문 Flow

[소재]
약 닥터 툼스

⬇

[세부사항1]
• 효능: 소화불량, 속 쓰림, 과식에 따른 두통을 동반한 배탈 • 맛: 4가지(체리, 레몬, 딸기, 귤) • 복용법: 4온스 물에 알약 2정을 용해시킴

&

[세부사항2]
대상에 따른 복용 수량 안내 • 4시간마다 2알 복용 • 하루 8알 초과하지 말 것 • 60세 이상은 하루 4알 초과하지 말 것

&

④ 성인은 1회 섭취 시 2,000밀리그램의 탄산칼슘을 섭취한다.
⑤ 다른 진통제에 알레르기 증상이 있으면 복용해선 안 된다.

해석 한 눈에 보기 1 **닥터 툼스** 2 **효능** 3 다음 증상을 완화해 줍니다. 4 산성 소화불량과 속 쓰림 5 과식에 따른 두통을 동반한 배탈 6 **맛** 7 씹어 먹는 닥터 툼스 알약은 체리, 레몬, 딸기, 귤의 4가지 맛으로 나옵니다. 8 **복용법** 9 섭취 전에 4온스의 물에 알약 2정을 완전히 용해시키세요. 10 **어른과 12세 이상의 아이는** 4시간마다 2알을 복용하세요. 11 24시간 내에 8알을 초과하지 마세요. 12 **60세 이상의 어른은** 4시간마다 2알을 복용하세요. 13 24시간 내에 4알을 초과하지 마세요. 14 **유효 성분** 15 씹어 먹는 알약 1정당 1,000mg의 탄산칼슘 16 **경고** 17 만일 당신이 아스피린이나 기타 어떤 진통제에 알레르기가 있다면 사용하지 마세요.
정답단추 모든 문장을 읽을 필요 없이 선택지와 소제목을 활용하자. 이 글은 약 복용법 안내문으로 내용이 소제목으로 잘 구분되어 있어서 선택지를 먼저 읽고 해당 내용을 빠르게 찾아 확인하면 돼. ③의 60세 이상 성인은 하루에 8알을 넘게 먹으면 안 된다는 내용을 지문에서 찾아보면, 8알이 아닌 4알임을 알 수 있어. 그리고 8알을 초과하지 말라고 한 대상은 성인 및 12세 이상의 아이들에게 해당하는 내용이야. 따라서 안내문과 일치하지 않는 정답은 ③이야.
오답단서 ①, ②는 효능(uses)과 맛(flavors)의 소제목 아래의 내용에서 쉽게 찾을 수 있어. 또한, ④는 간단한 계산이 필요한 경우로, 성인은 1회 섭취 시 2정을 복용해야 하는데 1정당 1,000mg의 탄산칼슘이 들어 있으므로 1회 섭취 시 2,000mg의 탄산칼슘을 섭취해야 함을 알 수 있어. 마지막으로 ⑤는 경고(warning) 아래 내용에 나와 있어.

[세부사항3]
- 유효 성분: 1정당 1,000mg의 탄산칼슘
- 경고: 아스피린이나 기타 어떤 진통제에 알레르기가 있다면 복용 금지

181 정답 ④

지문 All in One

1 George Burns was born in New York / on January 20, 1896. 2 He was *a comedian* [best known / for his long-running radio [and] television show / with his wife Gracie Allen]. 3 When they first teamed up onstage / to perform a comedy act / in the 1930s, // he had the experience / [and] she was new / to the business. 4 George took the lead // [and] had Gracie feed him the straight lines / while he told all the jokes. 5 The act was a disaster. 6 The next night / George took the straight lines // [and] gave Gracie all the laugh lines. 7 The rest is show business history. 8 First onstage, / then on radio, / [and] then on TV, / the real-life [and] stage couple / played their roles perfectly. 9 For George Burns, / standing out of the spotlight / in the act // while his wife was the center of the show / was simply a recognition of ability. "10 Gracie had / *a talent* [(which[that]) the audience loved]. 11 I had / *a talent* [(which[that]) the audience didn't (love)]. 12 I knew / how to write it, // [and] she knew / how to say it."

① 뉴욕 태생의 방송 코미디언이었다.
② 1930년대에 Gracie와 팀을 이루었다.
③ 무대에서는 부인이 더 조명을 받았다.
④ 부인보다 웃기는 데 재능이 많았다.
⑤ 쇼의 대본을 쓰는 재능이 있었다.

해석 한 눈에 보기 1 George Burns는 1896년 1월 20일에 뉴욕에서 태어났다. 2 그는 아내인 Gracie Allen과 함께 하는 그의 장수 라디오와 텔레비전 쇼로 가장 잘 알려진 코미디언이었다. 3 그들이 1930년대에 코미디 공연을 하기 위해 처음으로 무대에서 한 팀이 되었을 때, 그는 경험이 있었고 그녀는 그 분야가 처음이었다. 4 George가 주도권을 잡고 자신이 내내 우스갯소리를 하는 동안에 Gracie가 그에게 (우스갯소리를 유도하는) 진지한 대사를 던지게 했다. 5 그 공연은 완전한 실패였다. 6 다음 날 밤에는 George가 진솔한 대사를 맡고 Gracie에게 모든 우스개 대사를 줬다. 7 그 뒤는 쇼비즈니스 역사이다. 8 처음에는 무대에서, 다음에는 라디오에서, 그리고 그다음은 TV에서, 실생활에서도 무대에서도 부부인 이 커플은 그들의 역할을 완벽히 했다. 9 George Burns에게, 그의 아내가 쇼의 중심에 있는 동안에 공연의 스포트라이트에서 벗어나 있는 것은 단순히 능력의 인정이었다. "10 Gracie는 관객이 사랑하는 재능을 가지고 있었어요. 11 저는 관객이 사랑하지 않은 재능을 가지고 있었고요. 12 나는 쓰는 법을 알고 있었고, 그녀는 말하는 법을 알고 있었지요."
정답단추 지시문에서 불일치하는 것을 찾으라고 한 것을 명심하고 선택지와 비교하면서 글을 읽어보자. George Burns가 주도적으로 웃기는 역할을 했던 첫 번째 공연은 대실패였지만, 아내가 그 역을 대신하고부터는 성공했다고 하고 있어. 다시 말해, George보다 Gracie가 웃기는 재능이 더 많았음을 알 수 있어. 따라서 ④는 지문과 일치하지 않아.

어휘확인

comedian 코미디언 **best known** 가장 잘 알려진 **long-running** 오래 계속되어 온 **wife** 아내 **team up** 한 팀이 되다 **onstage** 무대 위에서 **perform** 공연하다 **act** (여러 파트로 구성된 쇼의 한) 파트, 공연; 행동 **new (to)** 처음 시작한 **business** 일; 사업 **take the lead** 주도권을 잡다 **feed A straight lines** A에게 (우스갯소리를 유도하는) 진지한 대사를 주다 **disaster** 완전한 실패(작); 재난 **show business** 쇼비즈니스, 연예 공연업 **real-life** 실생활의 **couple** 부부; 두 사람 **play a role** 역할을 하다 **perfectly** 완벽하게 **spotlight** 스포트라이트, 환한 조명 **simply** 단순히 **recognition** 인정 **ability** 능력 **audience** 관객

지문 Flow

[소재]
코미디언 George Burns

[보충설명]
- 1896년 1월 20일 뉴욕 출생
- 아내(Gracie Allen)와 함께 하는 라디오와 TV 쇼로 잘 알려짐

[일화]
아내 Gracie와 처음 같이 공연을 했을 때, 그가 주도적으로 웃기는 역할을 했던 첫 공연은 실패했지만, 두 사람의 역할을 바꾸어 공연한 이후로는 성공함

[이유]
남편은 쓰는 재능이 있었고, 아내는 말하는 재능이 있었음

오답단서 George Burns가 뉴욕 출신 코미디언이라는 사실은 첫 번째와 두 번째 문장에 나와 있으므로 ①은 일치해. ②의 내용도 아내인 Gracie와 무대에서 공연하려고 한 팀이 된 건 1930년대라고 했으니까 글의 내용과 일치해. ③은 For George Burns, ~ ability.에서 찾을 수 있어. 그리고 ⑤는 글의 마지막 부분에서 George의 말인 I knew how to write it, ~.에서 대본을 쓰는 재능이 있었다는 걸 확인할 수 있어.

182 정답 ②

지문 All in One

쿨 피트니스
1 **Cool Fitness**

저희는 완벽하게 선정된 것을 제공합니다 / 유산소 운동 장비, 종합 헬스 기구, 그리고 체력 단련 수업의
2 We provide a complete selection / of cardio equipment, weight machines, and fitness classes.
S V

저희는 또한 편안한 시설을 제공합니다 / 저희 회원들에게 / 그들이 운동 프로그램을 막 시작하는 것이든 / 상급 수준에 있든 간에
3 We also provide a comfortable facility / for our members, // whether they are just starting an exercise program / or are at an advanced level.
S V 접속사 S′ V′₁ V′₂

혜택
4 **• Benefits**

모든 신입 회원에게는 개인 훈련 시간이 주어집니다 / 저희 트레이너 중 한 명과 함께
5 All new members are given a personal training session / with one of our trainers.
S V

이 과정들은 회원들에게 무료입니다
6 These sessions are free to members.
S V C

저희는 항상 이용 가능합니다 / 설명을 제공하는 데 있어 / 저희 모든 장비의 정확한 사용에 대한
7 We are always available / to provide instruction / in the correct use of all of our equipment.
S V C 부사적 용법(목적)

활동
8 **• Activities**

회원들은 정기적으로 참여할 기회를 가집니다 / 체육관에서 후원되는 자선 및 사회 행사 둘 다에 / 운동을 넘어서는 공동체 의식을 키우는
9 Members regularly have *the opportunity* [to participate / in *both charity and social events* [sponsored by the gym]] — building *a sense of community* [that goes beyond exercise].
S V 분사구문(= and these events build ~) 관계대명사

(이용) 시간
10 **• Hours**

11 월요일 — 목요일 Monday — Thursday	오전 6:00 — 오후 10:00 6:00 AM — 10:00 PM
12 금요일 Friday	오전 7:00 — 오후 9:00 7:00 AM — 9:00 PM
13 토요일 — 일요일 Saturday — Sunday	오전 8:00 — 오후 10:00 8:00 AM — 7:00 PM

① 운동을 처음 시작하는 사람들도 가입할 수 있다.
② 할인된 가격에 개인 훈련을 받을 수 있다.
③ 언제든지 기구 사용에 대한 지도를 받을 수 있다.
④ 원하면 사회봉사 활동에 참여할 수 있다.
⑤ 주말은 금요일보다 이용시간이 3시간 더 짧다.

해석 한 눈에 보기 **1 쿨 피트니스** 2 저희는 유산소 운동 장비, 종합 헬스기구, 체력 단련 교실의 완벽히 엄선된 프로그램을 제공합니다. 3 저희는 또한 저희 회원들에게 그들이 운동 프로그램을 막 시작하는 것이든 상급 수준에 있든 간에 편안한 시설을 제공합니다. **4 •혜택** 5 모든 신입 회원에게는 저희 트레이너 중 한 명과 함께하는 개인 훈련 과정이 제공됩니다. 6 이 과정은 회원들에게 무료입니다. 7 저희는 저희 모든 장비의 정확한 사용에 대한 교육을 제공하는 데 있어 항상 이용 가능합니다. **8 •활동** 9 회원들은 정기적으로 체육관에서 후원하는 자선 및 사회 행사 둘 다에 참여할 기회를 가지고, 운동을 넘어서는 공동체 의식을 키우게 됩니다. **10 •시간** 11 월요일—목요일 오전 6:00—오후 10:00 12 금요일 오전 7:00—오후 9:00 13 토요일—일요일 오전 8:00—오후 7:00

정답단추 선택지의 정오를 판단할 수 있는 지문 내의 단서는 주로 선택지의 순서와 일치해. 따라서 선택지의 차례대로 불일치 여부를 판별해 나가면 돼. 혜택(Benefits)에서 These sessions are ~.의 문장을 통해 회원이 되면 개인 훈련을 무료로 받을 수 있다고 하고 있으므로 ②가 안내문과 일치하지 않아.

오답단서 안내문의 도입부에서 운동을 막 시작하는 사람들도 가입할 수 있다고 하고 있으므로 ①의 내용은 일치해. ③과 ④의 내용도 각각 혜택(Benefits)과 활동(Activities)의 소제목 아래 내용에서 쉽게 찾을 수 있어. ⑤의 이용 시간은 간단한 계산이 필요한데, 금요일은 오전 7시부터 오후 9시로 총 14시간이며 주말은 오전 8시부터 오후 7시까지로 총 11시간이니까 주말이 금요일보다 이용 시간이 3시간 짧다는 설명은 옳다는 것을 알 수 있어.

어휘확인

fitness 피트니스; 체력 단련 **provide** 제공하다 **selection** 선정된 것들 **cardio** 유산소 운동, 심장 (강화 운동) **equipment** 장비 **weight machine** 종합 헬스 기구 **facility** 시설[기관] **whether** ~이든 아니든 **advanced** 상급[고급]의 **benefit** 혜택 **personal** 개인의 **session** 시간[기간] **trainer** 트레이너, 훈련[교육]시키는 사람 **available** 이용할 수 있는 **instruction** 설명 **regularly** 정기적으로 **opportunity** 기회 **participate** 참여하다 **charity** 자선 **sponsor** 후원하다 **gym** 체육관 **sense** 의식; 감각 **community** 공동체 **go beyond** ~을 넘어서다

지문 Flow

[소재]
쿨 피트니스 회원 모집

⬇

[세부사항1]
• 엄선된 프로그램 제공
• 수준에 맞는 시설 제공

&

[세부사항2]
• 신입 회원에게 무료로 트레이너와 함께 하는 개인 훈련 제공
• 전 회원에게 체육관 후원 행사에 참여 기회 제공

&

[세부사항3]
이용 시간 안내

183 정답 ⑤

지문 All in One

1 동물 보호 협회
The Animal Care Society

2 예! Yes! 3 저는 동물 보호 협회의 회원이 되고 싶습니다 I want to become a member of The Animal Care Society / 그리고 싸움에 합류하고 (싶습니다) and join the fight / 동물 학대를 끝내기 위해서 to end animal cruelty // 그것이 일어나는 곳이라면 어디에서든지 wherever it occurs. 4 1년에 겨우 25달러의 비용이 듭니다 It costs just $25 a year / 협회의 회원이 되기 위해서는 to be a member of the Society.

(I: S, want: V_1, join: V_2, to end: 부사적 용법(목적), wherever: 복합관계부사, It: S, costs: V, to be: 부사적 용법(목적))

5 가입에 대한 감사의 표시로서 **As a thank you for joining,** / 당신은 받을 것입니다 **you'll receive:** (you: S, 'll receive: V)

6 1년 구독권 • A one-year subscription / 협회 격월지 〈마이 애니멀스〉 to our bimonthly magazine, *My Animals*

7 주간 소식지 • A weekly newsletter / 동물에 대한 간단한 조치를 취하는 것에 대한 about taking simple actions for animals

8 조사 보고서 • Investigative reports / 동물 보호 분야로부터의 from the animal protection field

9 당신은 또한 받습니다 **You'll also get:** (You: S, 'll get: V)

10 초대 • Invitations / 협회에서 주최되는 행사와 특별 강연으로의 to *the events* and *special lectures* [held by the Society]

11 개인별 안부 카드 • A personalized greeting card / 특별 메시지와 함께 with a special message

12 질문이 있으신가요? (Do you) Have a question / 동물 보호 협회 회원 자격에 대해 about your ACS membership? (you: S, Have: V)

13 저희에게 편지를 보내 주시거나, animalcare@society.org로 이메일을 보내 주시거나, 102-242-1200으로 전화해 주세요.
Write to us, / email *animalcare@society.org*, / or call 102-242-1200. (Write: V_1, email: V_2, call: V_3)

① 일 년에 25달러를 내면 회원이 될 수 있다. ② 일 년 동안 잡지를 무료로 구독할 수 있다.
③ 동물을 위한 조치에 관한 주간 뉴스레터를 받는다. ④ 동물 보호에 관한 조사 보고서를 받는다.
⑤ 정부 주관 행사에 초대받는다.

해석 한 눈에 보기 1 **동물 보호 협회** 2 예! 3 저는 동물 보호 협회의 회원이 되어서 동물 학대가 일어나는 곳이라면 어디에서든지 그것을 끝내기 위한 싸움에 합류하고 싶습니다. 4 협회의 회원이 되기 위해서는 1년에 겨우 25달러의 비용이 듭니다. 5 **가입에 대한 감사의 표시로 당신은 다음의 혜택을 받게 됩니다.** 6 •협회 격월지 〈마이 애니멀스〉의 1년 구독권 7 •동물에 대한 간단한 조치를 취하는 것에 대한 주간 소식지 8 •동물 보호 분야로부터의 조사 보고서 9 **이와 함께 다음의 혜택도 받게 됩니다.** 10 •협회에서 주최되는 행사와 특별 강연으로의 초대 11 •특별 메시지가 담긴 개인별 안부 카드 12 동물 보호 협회 회원 자격에 대해 질문이 있으신가요? 13 저희에게 편지를 보내 주시거나, animalcare@society.org로 이메일을 보내 주시거나, 102-242-1200으로 전화해 주세요.

정답단추 이 글은 동물 보호 협회의 회원이 되는 방법과 혜택을 소개하는 안내문이야. 또한, 지문 내의 단서의 위치와 선택지의 순서가 일치해서 차례대로 지문에서 단서를 찾아 나가면 돼. 두 번째 소제목 You'll also get에서 협회(Society) 주관 행사에 초대받는다고 했으므로 정부 주관 행사에 초대받는다는 내용의 ⑤는 안내문의 내용과 일치하지 않아. 따라서 ⑤가 정답이야.

오답단서 동물 보호 협회의 회원이 되기 위해서 25달러의 비용이 든다고 했으므로 ①은 옳은 설명이야. 또한, ②, ③, ④는 모두 첫 번째 소제목인 As a thank ~ receive의 내용에서 차례대로 찾을 수 있어.

어휘확인

society 협회; 사회 **cruelty** 학대 **wherever** ~하는 곳은 어디든지 **occur** 일어나다, 발생하다 **cost** (비용이) ~들다 **subscription** 구독 **bimonthly** 격월의, 2개월 마다의 **newsletter** 소식지 **take action** 조치를 취하다 **investigative** 조사의 **protection** 보호 **invitation** 초대 **lecture** 강연, 강의 **personalized** 개인화된 **greeting** 안부의 말; 인사 **membership** 회원 자격 **email** ~로 이메일을 보내다

지문 Flow

[소재]
동물 보호 협회 회원 가입 안내문

⬇

[세부사항1]
1년에 25달러의 비용이 듦

&

[세부사항2]
혜택:
•협회지 1년 구독권, 주간 소식지, 조사 보고서
•행사와 강연 초대, 개인별 안부 카드

&

[세부사항3]
회원 자격에 대한 문의 사항 안내

유형편

Chapter 6

유형 17 어법성 판단

Check-Up 1 184 ③

Check-Up 2 185 ④

실전적용독해 186 ③ 187 ③ 188 ⑤ 189 ③ 190 ⑤ 191 ⑤

Check-Up 1

184 정답 ③

지문 All in One

대부분의 성인은 필요로 한다 / 7~8시간의 수면을 / 하룻밤에 / 일부 사람들이 필요로 할지라도

1 Most adults need / seven to eight hours of sleep / per night, // although some people need /
(S V 접속사 S' V')

더 많거나 더 적은 수면 시간을 / 적당히 휴식을 취하기 위해 / 충분한 수면을 취하지 않는 것 / 또는 좋지 않은

more or less sleep time / to be (A) adequately rested. 2 Not getting enough sleep / or poor
(부사적 용법(목적), S)

수면의 질은 / 심각한 결과를 초래한다 / 만약 당신이 충분한 수면을 취하고 있다(면) / 하지만 여전히 항상

quality of sleep / (B) has serious consequences. 3 If you're getting enough sleep / but still feel
(V 접속사 S' V'_1 V'_2)

졸린 느낌이 들면 / 당신은 수면 장애를 가지고 있을 수 있다 / 수면 장애는 방해한다 / 사람의 능력을

sleepy all the time, // you could have a sleep disorder. 4 Sleep disorders disrupt / *a person's*
(C' S V S V)

잠이 들거나 자고 있는 상태를 유지하려는 / 수면 의사들이 묻는 첫 번째 질문은

ability [to fall asleep or stay asleep]. 5 *The first question* [(that) sleep doctors (C) ask / when
(S 관계대명사)

새 환자들이 자신의 수면 클리닉을 방문할 때 / '충분한 수면을 취하고 계십니까?'이다 / 그것은 중요한

new patients visit their sleep clinic] / is "Are you getting enough sleep?" 6 That's a big
(V C S V C)

질문이다 / 왜냐하면 의사들이 생각하기 때문에 / 많은 환자들이 (충분한 수면을 취하지) 않는다고

question // because doctors think / (that) a lot of patients are not (getting enough sleep).
(접속사 S' V' 접속사 S'' V'')

그들은 잠이 부족하다 / 부분적으로 또는 때때로 또는 항상

7 They're lacking sleep, / either partially or occasionally or all the time.
(S V)

	(A)		(B)		(C)
①	adequate	······	has	······	ask
②	adequate	······	have	······	are asked
③	adequately	······	has	······	ask
④	adequately	······	has	······	are asked
⑤	adequately	······	have	······	ask

해석 한 눈에 보기 주제문 1 일부 사람들이 적당히 휴식을 취하기 위해 더 많거나 더 적은 수면 시간을 필요로 할지라도, 대부분의 성인은 하룻밤에 7~8시간의 수면을 필요로 한다. 2 충분한 수면을 취하지 않거나 수면의 질이 좋지 않으면 심각한 결과를 초래한다. 3 만약 충분한 수면을 취하고 있지만 여전히 항상 졸린 느낌이 들면, 수면 장애를 가지고 있을 수 있다. 4 수면 장애는 잠이 들거나 자고 있는 상태를 유지하는 사람의 능력을 방해한다. 5 수면 의사들이 새 환자들이 자신의 수면 클리닉을 방문할 때 묻는 첫 번째 질문은 '충분한 수면을 취하고 계십니까?'이다. 6 의사들은 많은 환자들이 그렇지 않다고 생각하기 때문에 그것은 중요한 질문이다. 7 그들은 부분적으로 또는 때때로 또는 항상 잠이 부족하다.

정답단추 먼저 네모 안의 문법 사항을 파악하는 것이 문제를 빨리 푸는 요령이야. (A)에는 to부정사의 부사적 용법으로 쓰인 동사를 수식하는 부사 adequately가 들어가야 해. (B)에는 「A or B」가 주어로 쓰일 때, B에 수를 일치시켜야 하는데, B가 poor quality of sleep이므로 has가 옳아. (C)에는 수면 의사가 질문을 받는 것이 아니라 질문을 '하는' 것이므로 능동의 의미를 갖는 ask가 적절해.

어휘확인

adult 성인 **per night** 하룻밤에 **adequately** 적당히 **rest** 쉬다, 휴식하다 **quality** 질 **serious** 심각한 **consequence** 결과 **sleepy** 졸린 **disorder** 장애 **disrupt** 방해하다 **ability** 능력 **fall asleep** 잠이 들다 **patient** 환자 **sleep clinic** 수면 클리닉 **lack** 부족하다 **partially** 부분적으로 **occasionally** 때때로 **all the time** 항상

지문 Flow

[주제문]
성인은 하룻밤에 7~8시간 수면을 필요로 함

⬇

[보충설명]
충분한 수면을 취하지 않거나 수면의 질이 좋지 않으면 심각한 결과를 초래함

⬇

[보충설명]
충분한 수면에도 졸리면 수면 장애의 가능성 있음

⬇

[보충설명]
수면 클리닉을 방문하는 많은 환자들은 충분한 수면을 취하고 있지 않음

Check-Up 2

185 정답 ④

지문 All in One

당신은 외롭거나 고립되어 있다고 느끼는가 / 사람들 사이에서 / 즐기는 것을 배워라 / 당신 자신의 교제를
1 Do you feel lonely [or] isolated / among people? 2 Learn to enjoy / your own company! 3 It
S V C₁ C₂ V S

기분이 이상할지도 모른다 / 처음에는 / 당신이 둘러싸이는 것에 익숙하다면 / 다른 사람들에 의해 / 그러나
might feel weird / at first // if you're used to ① being surrounded / by other people. 4 But, /
V C 접속사 S' V'

혼자서 시간을 보내는 것은 / 실제로 자유롭게 하는 것일 수 있다 / 혼자 있는 것의 자유는 / 자신의 생각들과
spending time alone / can be really ② liberating. 5 The freedom [to be alone / with your
S V C S

함께 / 좋은 방법이 될 수 있다 / 긴장을 푸는 / 편안함을 느끼도록 해봐라 / 단지 자신뿐인 것에
thoughts] / can be a great way [to relax]. 6 Try [and] feel ③ comfortable / with just yourself /
V C V₁ V₂ C

교제를 위해서 / 일반적으로 / 우리가 사람들에 대해 생각할 때 / 우리가 주변에 있고 싶은
for company. 7 Generally / when we think of people [(who(m)[that]) we want to be around], //
접속사 S' V' 관계대명사

그들은 사람들이다 / 다른 사람들에게 매력적인 자신감을 가진
they are people [who have a confidence [④ what(→ which[that]) is attractive to others]].
S V C 관계대명사

혼자가 되는 것을 배우는 것은 / 그리고 당신 자신의 교제를 좋아하는 것은 / 한 걸음이다 / 이런 종류의 자신감
8 Learning to be on your own / [and] (to) ⑤ like your own company / is a step / towards this
S V C

을 향한
kind of confidence.

해석 한 눈에 보기 1 당신은 외롭거나 사람들 사이에서 고립되어 있다고 느끼는가? 주제문 2 당신 자신의 교제를 즐기는 것을 배워라! 3 다른 사람들에 의해 둘러싸이는 것에 익숙하다면, 처음에는 기분이 이상할지도 모른다. 4 그러나, 혼자서 시간을 보내는 것은 실제로 자유롭게 하는 것일 수 있다. 5 자신의 생각들과 함께 혼자 있는 것의 자유는 긴장을 푸는 좋은 방법이 될 수 있다. 6 교제를 위해서 단지 자신뿐인 것에 편안함을 느끼도록 해봐라. 7 일반적으로 우리가 주변에 있고 싶은 사람들에 대해 생각할 때, 그들은 다른 사람들에게 매력적인 자신감을 가진 사람들이다. 8 혼자가 되는 것을 배우는 것과 당신 자신의 교제를 좋아하는 것을 배우는 것은 이런 종류의 자신감을 향한 한 걸음이다.

정답단추 전체를 다 읽지 않아도 선택지가 포함된 문장을 읽고 밑줄 친 부분의 문법을 파악하면 시간을 절약할 수 있어. ④는 what 이하가 a confidence를 수식하는 관계사절이 되어야 하는데, 앞에 선행사가 있으므로 선행사를 포함하는 관계대명사 what은 쓸 수 없어. 따라서 관계대명사 which나 that을 쓰는 것이 옳아.

오답단서 ①은 be used to v-ing는 '~하는 것에 익숙하다'라는 의미이므로 어법상으로나 내용상으로나 쓰임이 옳아. ②는 be의 보어로 쓰인 동명사이므로 liberating은 어법상 쓰임이 적절해. ③은 feel이 형용사를 보어로 취하는 동사이므로 comfortable은 어법상 옳아. ⑤는 Learning의 목적어로 to부정사인 to be와 to like가 병렬 연결된 문장이므로 어법상 적절해. to like에서 to는 생략된 것이지.

어휘확인

lonely 외로운 isolated 고립된 company 교제, 사귐 weird 이상한 be used to v-ing ~하는 데 익숙하다 surround 둘러싸다 spend (시간을) 보내다 alone 혼자서 liberate 자유롭게 하다, 해방하다 freedom 자유 thought 생각, 사고 relax 긴장을 풀다 comfortable 편한 generally 일반적으로 confidence 자신감 attractive 매력적인 be on one's own 혼자서 towards ~을 향하여

지문 Flow

[주제문]
외롭거나 고립되어 있다고 느낄 때 자신과의 교제를 즐겨라.

⬇

[보충설명1]
자유로워지는 것이고, 긴장을 완화시키는 좋은 방법임

&

[보충설명2]
교제를 위해서도 필요함

실전적용독해

186 정답 ③

지문 All in One

당신의 심장을 관리하는 것에 관한 한 / 당신이 보는 것은 중요할지도 모른다
1 When it comes to taking care of your heart, // what you watch may be [as] important / [as]
접속사 S' V' 관계대명사 S V C

당신이 먹거나 하는 것만큼 / 메릴랜드 대학에서의 한 연구는 / 발견했다 / 코미디를 보는 것이 당신의 심장에
what you eat or do. 2 A study at the University of Maryland / found // that watching comedy
관계대명사 S V 접속사 S'

좋다는 것을 / 운동만큼 / 그 연구는 40명의 성인을 참여시켰다
is [as] good for your heart / (A) [as] exercise. 3 The study involved 40 adults, // (B) [whose
V' C' S V 관계대명사(계속적 용법)

그들의 심장은 관찰되었다(측정되었다) / 그들이 슬픈 영화를 보았을 때 / 그리고 웃긴 영화를 / 웃긴
hearts were monitored / as they watched a sad movie / [and] a funny movie]. 4 The funny
접속사 S' V' S

영화는 피의 흐름을 증가시켰다 / 반면에 슬픈 영화는 그것을 감소시켰다 / 그 연구원들은 주장했다
movie increased blood flow // [while] the sad movie decreased it. 5 The researchers claimed //
V 접속사(대조) S' V' S V

슬픈 영화를 보는 것은 비슷한 영향을 미친다고 / 수학 문제를 푸는 것처럼 / 반면에 웃긴 영화를 보는
that watching sad movies has a similar effect / as doing math problems, / [while] the effect of
접속사 S'₁ V'₁ 접속사(대조) S'₂

것의 영향은 / 에어로빅 운동과 같다고 / 그러니 / 만약 당신이 무언가 좋은 일을 하고 싶다면
watching funny movies / (C) is like aerobic exercise. 6 So, / if you want to do something good
V'₂ C' 접속사 S' V'

어휘확인

when it comes to ~에 관한 한 university 대학 involve 참여시키다; 포함하다 monitor 관찰하다; 측정하다 increase 증가시키다(↔ decrease 감소시키다) flow 흐름 while 반면에; ~하는 동안 researcher 연구원 claim 주장하다 similar 비슷한 do a problem 문제를 풀다 aerobic 에어로빅 make a point of 반드시 ~하다

지문 Flow

[주제문]
심장 관리에 있어서 먹는 것만큼 보는 것도 중요함

⬇

당신의 심장에 반드시 코미디를 봐라
/ for your heart, // make a point of watching comedy.
V

	(A)		(B)		(C)
①	as	……	who	……	is
②	as	……	whose	……	are
③	as	……	whose	……	is
④	than	……	whose	……	are
⑤	than	……	who	……	is

해석 한 눈에 보기 주제문 1 당신의 심장을 관리하는 것에 관한 한, 당신이 보는 것은 당신이 먹거나 하는 것만큼이나 중요할지도 모른다. 2 메릴랜드 대학의 한 연구는 코미디를 보는 것이 운동만큼 당신의 심장에 좋다는 것을 발견했다. 3 이 연구는 40명의 성인을 참여시켰는데, 그들의 심장이 그들이 슬픈 영화와 웃긴 영화를 볼 때 측정되었다. 4 웃긴 영화는 피의 흐름(혈류)을 증가시키는 반면에 슬픈 영화는 그것을 감소시켰다. 5 연구원들은 슬픈 영화를 보는 것이 수학 문제를 푸는 것과 비슷한 영향을 미치는 반면에, 웃긴 영화를 보는 것의 영향은 에어로빅 운동과 같다고 주장했다. 6 그러니 만일 당신이 당신의 심장에 뭔가 좋은 일을 하고 싶다면, 반드시 코미디를 봐라.

정답단추 (A)의 앞을 보면 is as good for your heart가 있지? 여기에서 연상할 수 있는 표현은 'A는 B만큼 좋다'라는 뜻의 「A as good as B」야. as 사이에 형용사나 부사의 원급을 사용하여 두 대상을 비교하지. than은 「A+형용사나 부사의 비교급+than B」처럼 비교급과 함께 쓰여. 따라서 (A)에는 as가 와야 해. (B)는 선행사 40 adults를 대신 받으며 뒤의 명사 hearts를 수식하는 소유격 관계대명사가 필요한 자리야. 따라서 whose가 적절해. 또한 whose hearts ~ movie는 선행사 40 adults를 부연 설명하고 있어. (C)는 while절의 동사 자리로 단수 주어 the effect가 of ~ movies의 수식을 받고 있어. 따라서 수일치의 원칙으로 단수동사 is를 써야 해.

[보충설명]
한 연구에서 코미디가 운동만큼 심장이 좋음을 발견함

⬇

[주장 재진술]
심장을 좋게 하려면 코미디를 봐라.

187 정답 ③

지문 All in One

인생은 짧다는 이야기의 교훈은 이것이다 당신에게 주어진 모든 날을 이용하라
1 The moral of the story [that life is short] / is this: // take advantage of *every day* [(that) you
S = V C V 관계대명사

이 말은 의도적이다 많은 우리의 연장자들이 제안했다는 점에서
are (A) given]. 2 This phrasing is intentional, // in that many of our elders suggested / that
S V C 접속사 S′ V′ 접속사

하루하루는 선물로 받아들여지고 그리고 그런 식으로 대해져야 한다고 라틴어 격언 하나가 흔히
each day (should) (B) be taken as a gift / and (be) treated that way. 3 A Latin aphorism has
S″ V″1 V″2 S V

사용되어 왔다 '카르페 디엠' 영화 〈죽은 시인의 사회〉에 의해 유명해진
come into common usage: / "carpe diem." 4 (Having been) Made famous by the movie *Dead*
분사구문

그것은 보통 '오늘을 즐겨라'로 번역된다 원래 라틴어의 의미는
Poets Society, / it is usually translated as "seize the day." 5 The meaning of the original Latin,
S V S

그러나 그날을 '수확하는 것'에 더 가깝다 하루하루는 가지고 있다 수확되지 않은 풍부함을
/ however, / is closer to "harvesting" the day. 6 Each day has / an unharvested abundance / of
V C S V

많은 젊은 사람들이 놓치는 기쁨과 즐거움과 아름다움의 아주 흔한 사람의 실패는
pleasure, enjoyment, and beauty [that many younger people miss]. 7 A very common human
관계대명사 S

인생의 기쁨을 이용하지 못하는 것이다 그리고 살아 있다는 바로 그 즐거움에 주목하지 (못하는 것
failing / is not taking advantage of life's pleasures / and (C) attending to the very joy of
V C_1 C_2

이다)
being alive.

	(A)		(B)		(C)
①	giving	……	be	……	attendance
②	giving	……	was	……	attendance
③	given	……	be	……	attending
④	given	……	was	……	attending
⑤	given	……	be	……	attendance

해석 한 눈에 보기 주제문 1 인생은 짧다는 이야기의 교훈은 당신에게 주어진 모든 날을 이용하라는 것이다. 2 이 말은 많은 우리의 연장자들이 하루하루는 선물로 받아들여지고 그런 식으로 대해져야 한다고 제안했다는 점에서 의도적이다. 3 라틴어 격언 하나가 흔히 사용되어 왔는데 그것은 '카르페 디엠'이다. 4 영화 〈죽은 시인의 사회〉에 의해 유명해진 그것은 보통 '오늘을 즐겨라'로 번역된다. 5 그러나 원래 라틴어의 의미는 그날을 '수확하는 것'에 더 가깝다. 6 하루하루는 많은 젊은이들이 놓치는 수확되지 않은 수많은 기쁨과 즐거움과 아름다움을 지니고 있다. 7 아주 흔한 사람의 실패는 인생의 기쁨을 이용하지 못하고 살아 있다는 바로 그 즐거움에 대해 주목하지 못하는 것이다.

정답단추 (A)가 있는 문장에서 you 이하는 선행사 every day를 수식하는 관계대명사절인데 모든 날은 당신이 '주는' 것이 아니고 당신에게 '주어지는' 것이므로 given이 적절해. SVOO 구조로 쓰인 「give+A(사람)+B(사물)」에서 간접목적어 A를 주어로 쓴 수동태 〈A is given B〉인데, B가 관계대명사절의 수식을 받는 선행사로 앞에 쓰여서 생략된 형태야. (B)는

어휘확인

moral 교훈; 도덕 **take advantage of** ~을 이용하다 **phrasing** 말, 표현 **intentional** 의도적인 **in that** ~라는 점에서 **elder** 연장자 **suggest** 제안하다 **take** 받아들이다; 가지고 가다 **Latin** 라틴어 **aphorism** 격언 **come into usage[use]** 쓰이게 되다 **common** 흔한 **translate** 번역하다 **seize the chance** 오늘을 즐기다; 기회를 잡다 **cf. seize** 붙잡다 **original** 원래의 **close** (다른 무엇과) 가까운 **harvest** 수확하다 **unharvested** 수확되지 않은 **abundance** 풍부 **enjoyment** 즐거움 **attend** 주의를 기울이다, 주목하다 **joy** (큰) 즐거움 **alive** 살아 있는
〈선택지 어휘〉
attendance 출석, 참석

지문 Flow

[주제문]
인생은 짧다는 교훈은 자신에게 주어진 모든 날을 이용하라는 것

⬇

[보충설명]
이 말은 연장자들이 의도적으로 제안한 것임

⬇

[보충설명]
라틴어 격언 'carpe diem'의 원래 의미는 그날을 '수확하는 것'

⬇

[주장 재진술]
기쁨과 즐거움이 있는 하루하루를 놓치지 말고, 인생의 기쁨과 살아 있다는 즐거움에 주목해야 함

동사 형태만 보고 섣불리 판단해서는 안 돼. '명령, 요구, 제안, 필요' 등을 나타내는 동사나 형용사 뒤에 that절이 당위성(~해야 하다)을 나타내면 that절에는 조동사 should를 써야 해. 그러나 이 should는 생략 가능해서 동사원형만이 남게 되는 경우도 있지. 많은 연장자들이 하루하루를 선물로 여겨야 한다고 제안했다(suggest)는 내용으로 당위성을 나타내고 있으므로 be를 쓰는 것이 적절해. (C)를 포함한 문장은 is의 주격 보어인 동명사구 taking ~ pleasures와 함께 접속사 and에 의해 not에 공통으로 연결되는 병렬구조를 이루고 있어. 따라서 taking ~ pleasures와 똑같은 동명사구가 위치해야 하는 자리이므로 attending이 어법상 옳아.

188 정답 ⑤

지문 All in One

Jean-Paul Sartre의 〈상상계〉는 / 상세한 글이다 / 상상력의 본질에 관한 / 그것은 결과물이다 / 10년이 넘는 연구의 / Sartre가 많은 발상들을 연구하고 발달시키는 동안

1 Jean-Paul Sartre's *The Imaginary* (S) / is (V) a detailed essay (C) / about the nature of imagination. 2 It (S) is (V) the result (C) / of *more than a decade's work*, // over the course of (A) which (관계대명사) Sartre researched and developed many ideas.

이것들은 포함한다 / 예를 들어 / 철학의 본질 / 그리고 / 그것의 관계 / 심리학과의

3 These (S) include (V), / for example, / the nature of philosophy / and its relation / to psychology.

상상력에 대한 그의 이론은 발전된다 / 그리고 부분적으로 옹호된다 / 논의와 응용을 통해 / 이 분야들의 / 그의 생각에 대한

4 His theory of imagination (S) is developed (V_1) // and (B) (is) defended (V_2) partly / through discussions and applications / of these areas / of his thought.

그것 자체로 흥미로울 뿐만 아니라 / 그 연구는 토대를 제공한다 / Sartre의 많은 후기 작품의 / 인간 조건에 대한

5 As well as being interesting on its own, / the work (S) provides (V) foundations / for much of Sartre's later work / on the human condition.

자유와 그릇된 신념에 관한 그의 이론들은 / 예를 들어 / 그리고 / 문학의 본질에 관한 / 차분하게 활용한다 / 강조된 생각들과 주제들을 / 이 책에서

6 His theories of freedom and bad faith, / for example, / and of the nature of literature, (S) / quietly (C) draw (V) / on thoughts and themes emphasized / in this book.

	(A)		(B)		(C)
①	what	……	defends	……	draw
②	what	……	defended	……	draws
③	which	……	defends	……	draw
④	which	……	defended	……	draws
⑤	which	……	defended	……	draw

해석 한 눈에 보기 1 Jean-Paul Sartre의 〈상상계〉는 상상력의 본질에 대한 상세한 글이다. 2 그것은 10년이 넘는 연구의 결과물로, 그 동안 Sartre는 많은 발상을 연구하고 발달시켰다. 3 예를 들어 이것들은 철학의 본질과 그것의 심리학과의 관계를 포함한다. 4 상상력에 대한 그의 이론은 그의 이런 분야의 생각에 대한 논의와 응용을 통해 부분적으로 발전되고 옹호된다. 5 그 자체로 흥미로울 뿐만이 아니라, 그 연구는 인간의 조건에 대한 Sartre의 많은 후기 작품의 토대를 제공한다. 6 예를 들어, 자유와 그릇된 신념, 그리고 문학의 본질에 관한 그의 이론들은 이 책에서 강조된 생각들과 주제들을 차분하게 활용한다.

정답단추 (A)는 선행사 more than a decade's work를 부연 설명하는 관계사절의 일부이므로 관계대명사 which가 적절해. 관계대명사 what은 선행사를 포함하므로 여기서는 적절하지 않아. (B)에는 주어인 His theory of imagination이 무엇을 옹호하는 것이 아니라 옹호되는 것이니까 수동태를 만들어 주는 과거분사 defended가 적절해. 앞에 쓰인 is developed와 병렬구조로서 앞에 is가 생략된 형태야. (C)에는 주어가 복수 형태인 His theories이므로 복수동사 draw가 와야 해. of freedom and bad faith와 of the nature of literature는 His theories를 수식하는 구라는 걸 유의하자.

어휘확인

detailed 상세한 **essay** 글; 에세이 **nature** 본질; 자연 **imagination** 상상력 **decade** 10년 **work** 연구; 작품; 일하다 **over the course of** ~ 동안 **research** 연구하다 **develop** 발달시키다 **include** 포함하다 **philosophy** 철학 **relation** 관계 **psychology** 심리학 **theory** 이론 **defend** 옹호하다 **partly** 부분적으로 **discussion** 논의 **application** 응용 **area** 분야; 지역 **thought** 생각 **as well as** ~뿐만 아니라 **provide** 제공하다 **foundation** 토대[기초] **condition** 조건; 상태 **freedom** 자유 **faith** 신념, 믿음 **literature** 문학 **quietly** 차분하게 **draw on** ~을 활용하다 **theme** 주제 **emphasize** 강조하다

지문 Flow

[도입]
Sartre의 〈상상계〉는 상상력의 본질에 대한 글로, 많은 발상을 연구하고 발달시킴

⬇

[보충설명]
Sartre는 자신의 발상을 철학 및 심리학과 연관시켰고, 상상력에 대한 그의 이론은 논의와 응용을 통해 발전됨

⬇

[보충설명]
이 책은 인간의 조건에 대한 Sartre의 후기 작품의 토대를 제공함

⬇

[예시]
자유와 그릇된 신념, 문학의 본질에 대한 이론들은 이 책의 생각과 주제를 활용함

189 정답 ③

지문 All in One

조용하고, 어둡고, 시원한 환경은 / 숙면을 촉진하는 데 도움을 줄 수 있다 / 왜 박쥐가 동굴을 선택한다고 생각하는가 / 주간 수면을 위해

1 A quiet, dark, and cool environment (S) / can help (V) promote sound sleep. 2 Why (의문사) do you think (삽입절) bats (S) choose (V) caves / for their daytime sleep?

그러한 환경을 이루기 위해 / 외부 소음의 음량을 낮춰라 / 귀마개 또는 '백색소음' 기기로 / 두꺼운 커튼, 암막 커튼, 또는

3 ① To achieve such an environment, / lower (V) the volume of outside noise / with earplugs or a "white noise" appliance. 4 Use (V) heavy curtains,

어휘확인

promote 촉진하다 **sound sleep** 숙면 **bat** 박쥐 **cave** 동굴 **daytime** 주간; 주간의 **achieve** 이루다, 성취하다 **lower** 낮추다 **earplug** 귀마개 **white noise** 백색소음, 잡음 **appliance** (가정용) 기기 **curtain** 커튼 (= **shade**) **blackout** 암막; 정전 **cue** 단서, 신호 **comfortably** 편안하게 **ventilate** 환기하다 **equip** 장비를 갖추다 **mattress** (침

blackout shades, or an eye mask / to block light, *a powerful cue* [② that tells the brain that it's time to wake up]. 5 Keep the temperature comfortably cool / — between 60 and 75°F — / and the room well ③ ventilate(→ ventilated). 6 And make sure // (that) your bedroom is equipped with a comfortable mattress and pillows. 7 Also, / if a pet regularly wakes you / during the night, // you may want to consider / ④ keeping it out of your bedroom. 8 Keeping computers, TVs, and work materials out of the room / ⑤ strengthens the mental association / between your bedroom and sleep.

해석 한 눈에 보기 주제문 1 조용하고, 어둡고, 시원한 환경은 숙면을 촉진하는 데 도움을 줄 수 있다. 2 왜 박쥐가 주간 수면을 위해 동굴을 선택한다고 생각하는가? 3 그러한 환경을 이루기 위해, 귀마개 또는 '백색소음' 기기로 외부 소음의 음량을 낮춰라. 4 깨어날 때라는 것을 뇌에 알리는 강력한 단서인 빛을 가리기 위해 두꺼운 커튼, 암막 커튼, 또는 눈가리개를 사용하라. 5 온도를 화씨 60~75도 사이로 편안히 서늘하게 유지하고, 방을 환기가 잘 되게 하라. 6 그리고 침실에 편안한 매트리스와 베개가 구비되어 있는지 확인하라. 7 또한, 애완동물이 밤에 규칙적으로 당신을 깨우면, 당신의 침실 밖에 그것을 두는 것을 고려하고 싶어 할지도 모른다. 8 컴퓨터, TV, 그리고 업무 자료를 방 밖에 두는 것은 침실과 잠 사이의 정신적 연관성을 강화한다.

정답단추 선택지가 포함된 문장을 먼저 읽고 어법을 파악한 후, 문제를 풀면 시간을 절약할 수 있어. ③이 있는 문장에서 and 뒤에 나오는 the room은 앞의 동사 Keep에 이어지는 목적어야. 따라서 뒤에 이어지는 목적격 보어는 형용사의 형태가 되어야 하는데, the room과 well ventilate의 관계가 수동이므로 과거분사형인 well ventilated가 적절해. 그래서 어법상 틀린 것은 ③이야.

오답단서 ①은 '~하기 위해서'라는 뜻의 목적을 나타내는 to부정사의 부사적 용법으로 쓰임이 적절해. ②는 선행사 a powerful cue를 수식하는 관계사절을 이끄는 주격 관계대명사이므로 어법상 옳아. ④는 consider의 목적어로 동명사 keeping이 쓰였으므로 적절한 표현이야. ⑤는 주어가 Keeping computers ~ the room으로 단수 취급하는 동명사구니까 동사도 단수형으로 올바르게 쓰였어.

대의) 매트리스 **pillow** 베개 **wake** 깨우다; 깨다 **consider** 고려하다 **material** 자료; 재료 **strengthen** 강화하다 **association** 연관성

지문 Flow

[주제문]
조용하고, 어둡고, 시원한 환경은 숙면에 도움을 줄 수 있음

⬇

[방법]
- 귀마개나 '백색소음' 기기로 외부 소음의 음량 낮추기
- 두꺼운 커튼, 암막 커튼, 눈가리개 사용하기
- 서늘한 온도 유지와 환기가 잘 되게 하기
- 편안한 매트리스와 베개 구비하기
- 밤에 애완동물과 따로 자기
- 컴퓨터, TV, 업무 자료를 방 밖에 두면, 침실과 잠의 연관성이 강화됨

190 정답 ⑤

지문 All in One

1 If you walk into any classroom today, // you will quickly notice / that it is quite different / from those of the past. 2 For one thing, / computers in the classroom are as common // as blackboards once were (common). 3 And this is true / at all levels of education. 4 Many universities require / all students ① to have a powerful personal computer and high-speed Internet access. 5 The situation / at primary and secondary schools / ② is changing swiftly, / too. 6 Now, / children ③ are used to computer-based learning systems. 7 At kindergartens, / you are likely to see / *three- and four-year-olds* [④ using computers]. 8 One company sells *a computer* / for children as young / as two / [that gives instructions and ⑤ ask(→ asks) questions / in a friendly voice].

해석 한 눈에 보기 1 만일 당신이 오늘날의 그 어떤 교실에 들어가더라도, 당신은 그것이 예전의 그것들과 상당히 다르다는 것을 금방 알아차릴 것이다. 2 첫째로, 교실 안의 컴퓨터들이 칠판이 한때 그랬던 것만큼 흔하다. 3 그리고 이것은 모든 수준의 교육 현장에 적용된다. 4 많은 대학은 모든 학생이 성능 좋은 개인용 컴퓨터와 고속 인터넷 접속을 갖고 있을 것을 요구한다. 5 초등학교와 중등학교에서의 상황도 빠르게 변하고 있다. 6 이제 아이들은 컴퓨터 기반 학습 체제에 익숙하다. 7 유치원에서, 당신은 서너 살 아이들이 컴퓨터를 사용하고 있는 것을 볼 가능성이 있다. 8 한 기업은 두 살만큼 어린아이들을 위한 친절한 목소리로 지시하고 질문을 하는 컴퓨터를 판다.

어휘확인

notice 알아차리다 **for one thing** 우선 첫째로 **common** 흔한 **true** 적용되는; 사실인 **education** 교육 **university** 대학 **require** 요구하다 **powerful** 성능 좋은; 강력한 **personal** 개인의 **high-speed** 고속의 **access** 접속; 접근 **situation** 상황 **primary school** 초등학교 **secondary school** 중등학교 **swiftly** 빠르게 **be used to A** A에 익숙하다 **computer-based learning** 컴퓨터 기반 학습 **system** 체제; 시스템 **kindergarten** 유치원 **be likely to-v** ~할 것 같다 **instruction** 지시; 설명

지문 Flow

[소재]
예전과는 다른 교실 모습

⬇

[보충설명]
컴퓨터가 흔하고, 모든 수준의 교육 현장에 적용됨

⬇

[예시1]
초등, 중등, 대학의 학생들은 컴퓨터 기반 교육 체제에 익숙함

정답단추 ⑤를 포함한 문장에서 that 이하는 앞에 멀리 떨어져 있는 선행사 a computer를 수식하는 주격 관계대명사 절이야. 즉, 선행사가 단수라서 여기에 이어지는 동사로 gives가 왔지. ask는 gives와 병렬구조를 이루고 있으니까 asks로 고쳐야 해. 따라서 어법상 틀린 것은 ⑤야.

오답단서 ①은 「require A to-v」가 쓰인 것으로 'A가 ~할 것을 요구하다'란 뜻이야. 따라서 to have는 어법상 옳아. ②가 있는 문장의 주어는 The situation으로 단수니까 단수동사 is가 적절해. at ~ schools는 주어를 수식하는 형용사 기능의 전명구일 뿐이니까 헷갈리지 않도록 주의해야 해. ③의 「be used to A」는 'A에 익숙하다'라는 의미로 쓰여. 글의 내용을 보아도 아이들이 컴퓨터 기반 교육 체제에 익숙하다는 내용이 자연스러우므로 are used to는 어법상 옳은 표현이야. 참고로 「be used to-v」와 같이 to 뒤에 동사원형이 오면 '~하는 데 쓰이다'란 뜻으로 의미가 전혀 달라져. 마지막으로 ④의 「see+목적어+목적격 보어」에서 목적격 보어로 동사원형이나 분사가 올 수 있는데, 현재분사가 왔을 때는 동작의 진행을 강조하는 것이므로 using은 어법상 문제가 없어.

&

[예시2]
유치원생도 컴퓨터 사용을 하고, 유아를 위한 컴퓨터도 판매되고 있음

191 정답 ⑤

지문 All in One

[1] Thanks to research (연구 덕분에) / by medical professionals and sports scientists, (의료 전문가들과 스포츠 과학자들에 의한) / we(S) know(V) (우리는 알고 있다) // that(접속사) fitness(S′) (체력 단련이) makes(V′₁) us(O′₁) healthier(C′) (우리를 보다 더 건강하게 만들어 주고) / [and] ① improves(V′₂) the quality of our lives(O′₂). (그리고 우리의 삶의 질을 높여 준다는 것을) [2] But what level of fitness should(조동사) we(S₁) aim(V₁) for, (하지만 우리는 어떤 수준의 체력 단련을 목표로 해야 하는가) // [and] how much time and effort should(조동사) we(S₂) devote(V₂) (그리고 우리는 얼마나 많은 시간과 노력을 쏟아야 하는가) / to our personal workout routines? (우리 개인의 운동 일과에) [3] We all(S) need(V) to be ② fit enough(형용사+enough+to부정사) (우리 모두는 충분히 건강할 필요가 있다) / to do ordinary work (일상적인 일을 할 만큼) / [and] (to) maintain minimum health levels. (최소한의 건강 수준을 유지할 만큼) [4] But not all(부분부정) people(S) do(V) the same kind of work. (그러나 모든 사람들이 똑같은 종류의 일을 하는 것은 아니다) [5] Nor(부정어) ③ do(조동사) they(S) do(V) the same workout, (그들은 또한 똑같은 운동을 하는 것도 아닌데) // because(접속사) they(S′) need(V′) different levels of physical strength. (그들은 서로 다른 수준의 신체적인 힘을 필요로 하기 때문이다) [6] Professional athletes(S) need(V) ④ much(비교급 강조) more exercise ((프로) 운동선수는 훨씬 더 많은 운동이 필요하다) // than(접속사) teachers or office workers(S′) do(V′) (교사나 사무직 근로자가 (운동)하는 것보다) / to perform their jobs successfully(부사적 용법(목적)). (그들의 직업을 성공적으로 수행하기 위해) [7] Thus, (이와 같이) / *a fitness program* [⑤ was designed(→ designed) / for your needs](S) (고안된 체력 단련 프로그램은 / 당신의 요구에 맞게) / will be(V) enough(C) (충분할 것이다) / to keep you fit(부사적 용법(목적)) (당신을 건강하게 유지시켜 주기에) / for life. (평생)

해석 한 눈에 보기 [1] 의료 전문가들과 스포츠 과학자들에 의한 연구 덕분에, 우리는 체력 단련이 우리를 더욱 더 건강하게 만들어 주고 우리의 삶의 질을 높여 준다는 것을 알고 있다. [2] 하지만 우리는 어떤 수준의 체력 단련을 목표로 해야 하며, 우리는 우리 개인의 운동 일과에 얼마나 많은 시간과 노력을 쏟아야 하는가? [3] 우리 모두는 일상적인 일을 하고 최소한의 건강 수준을 유지할 만큼 충분히 건강할 필요가 있다. [4] 그러나 모든 사람이 똑같은 종류의 일을 하는 것은 아니다. [5] 그들은 또한 똑같은 운동을 하는 것도 아닌데, 그들은 서로 다른 수준의 신체적 힘이 필요하기 때문이다. [6] 프로 운동선수는 그들의 직업을 성공적으로 수행하기 위해 교사나 사무직 근로자가 하는 것보다 훨씬 더 많은 운동이 필요하다. 주제문 [7] 이와 같이 당신의 요구에 맞게 고안된 체력 단련 프로그램은 당신을 평생 건강하게 유지해 주기에 충분할 것이다.

정답단추 전체 내용을 다 읽지 않고 선택지가 포함된 문장을 읽고 밑줄 친 부분에서 묻고 있는 문법사항을 파악하면 시간을 절약할 수 있어. ⑤가 있는 문장 전체의 주어는 a fitness program이고 동사는 will be이므로 was designed는 주어를 수식하는 과거분사 designed가 되어야 옳아. 따라서 어법상 틀린 것은 ⑤야.

오답단서 ①은 주절의 주어 we와 동사 know의 목적어인 that절의 주어 fitness 중 어느 주어에 속하는 동사인지 봐야 해. 내용을 보면 that절의 단수동사 makes와 병렬구조에 있다는 것을 알 수 있어. 따라서 improves가 어법상 옳아. ②는 「형용사/부사+enough to-v」 구문으로 '~할 만큼 충분히 …한[하게]'의 의미로 쓰여. 따라서 fit enough는 「형용사+enough」에 해당하므로 알맞은 표현이야. ③이 있는 문장의 Nor ~ workout의 「nor+조동사+S+V」 구문은 '~도 … 아니다'라는 의미로 쓰여. 그리고 조동사의 형태는 nor가 쓰인 부분의 동사 형태에 맞춰야 해. 여기서는 they do라고 쓰인 거로 봐서 동사가 일반동사임을 알 수 있으니 조동사 do가 오는 것이 옳아. ④의 much는 비교급으로 사용된 more(더 많은)를 수식하는 부사로 '훨씬'이라는 의미이므로 어법상 문제가 없어. 참고로 이와 같은 비교급 강조 수식 부사로는 still, a lot, far, even 등이 있어.

어휘확인

thanks to ~ 덕분에 **research** 연구 **medical** 의료[의학]의 **professional** 전문가, 전문직 종사자; 전문적인 **fitness** 체력 단련 **quality** 질 **aim for** ~을 목표로 하다 **devote** 쏟다, 바치다 **personal** 개인의 **workout** 운동 **routine** 일과, 일상 **fit** 건강한 **maintain** 유지하다 **minimum** 최소한의 **physical** 신체의 **athlete** 운동선수 **office worker** 사무직 근로자 **perform** 수행하다 **successfully** 성공적으로 **thus** 이와 같이 **need** 요구; 필요 **keep fit** 건강을 유지하다 **for life** 평생

지문 Flow

[도입]
체력 단련은 건강하게 만들고 삶의 질을 높여줌

⬇

[문제제기]
어떤 수준으로 얼마나 체력 단련을 해야 하는지 의문을 가짐

⬇

[보충설명]
모든 사람은 다른 수준의 신체적 힘이 필요하므로, 똑같은 운동을 할 수는 없음

⬇

[예시]
프로 운동선수는 사무직 근로자보다 더 많은 운동이 필요함

⬇

[결론]
자신의 필요에 맞게 고안된 체력 단련 프로그램으로 건강을 유지해야 함

Check-Up 1 192 ④ 193 ②
Check-Up 2 × 194 ②
실전적용독해 195 ④ 196 ⑤ 197 ③ 198 ② 199 ④

Check-Up 1

192 정답 ④

지문 All in One

1 Countless studies show // that *a life* [that's full of friends and fun] / comes with benefits to the brain. 2 Humans are highly social animals. 3 We're not meant to survive, / let alone succeed, / in (A) isolation. 4 Relationships stimulate our brains // — in fact, / interacting with others / may be the best kind of brain exercise. 5 Moreover, / laughter is especially good for your brain. 6 You probably have heard / that laughter is the best medicine, // and that holds true for the brain / as well as the body. 7 Unlike *other emotional responses*, / [which are (B) limited to specific areas of the brain], / laughter engages multiple regions / across the whole brain. 8 Furthermore, / listening to jokes and making your own / (C) activates *areas of the brain* [vital to learning and creativity]. 9 As psychologist Daniel Goleman notes / in his book *Emotional Intelligence*, // "Laughter seems to help people / think more broadly and associate more freely."

	(A)		(B)		(C)
①	association 유대	......	limited 제한적인	......	activates 활성화시킨다
②	association 유대	......	unlimited 제한 없는	......	activates 활성화시킨다
③	isolation 고립	......	limited 제한적인	......	paralyzes 마비시킨다
④	isolation 고립	......	limited 제한적인	......	activates 활성화시킨다
⑤	isolation 고립	......	unlimited 제한 없는	......	paralyzes 마비시킨다

해석 한 눈에 보기 주제문 1 무수한 연구들은 친구들과 재미로 가득 찬 삶이 뇌에 이익을 가져온다는 것을 보여 준다. 2 인간은 고도의 사회적 동물이다. 3 우리는 (A) 고립 속에서 성공하기는커녕 생존하지 못할 것이다. 4 관계는 우리의 두뇌를 자극한다. 실제로, 다른 사람들과 상호 작용하는 것이 최상의 두뇌 운동일 수 있다. 5 게다가, 웃음은 특히 당신의 두뇌에 좋다. 6 당신은 아마도 웃음이 최고의 약이라는 것을 들었을 것이고, 그것은 신체뿐만 아니라 두뇌에도 사실이다. 7 뇌의 특정 부위에 (B) 제한적인 다른 정서적 반응과는 달리, 웃음은 뇌 전체에 걸쳐 다수의 영역을 관여한다. 8 더욱이, 농담을 듣고 자신의 것으로 만드는 것은 학습과 창의력에 중요한 두뇌 영역을 (C) 활성화시킨다. 9 심리학자 Daniel Goleman이 자신의 저서 〈감성 지능〉에 적어 놓은 것처럼 "웃음은 사람들이 더 널리 생각하고 더 자유롭게 연관 짓는 것을 돕는 것 같다."

정답단추 네모 안에 맞는 적절한 단어를 묻고 있지만, 글의 내용을 정확히 이해해야 문제를 풀 수 있어. 네모가 있는 문장의 앞뒤 내용을 읽고 자연스럽게 이어지는 어휘를 고르면 돼. 우선, 인간은 사회적 동물이라는 내용 다음에 (A)인 '이곳'에서 성공은커녕 생존도 못한다고 했어. 관계가 뇌를 자극한다는 내용으로 보아, 고립 상태에서 생존을 못한다는 내용이 자연스러워. 따라서 isolation이 적절해. association은 '유대'라는 상반된 뜻의 어휘야. (B)가 있는 문장에서 웃음은 다른 정서적 반응과 달리, 전 뇌에 걸쳐 다수 영역에 관여한다고 했으므로, 다른 정서적 반응은 뇌에서 제한적임을 알 수 있어. 따라서 limited가 적절하고, unlimited는 반의어로 '무제한의'이라는 뜻이야. (C)에는 농담을 듣고 자기 것으로 만드는 것은 학습과 창의력에 중요한 두뇌 영역을 활성화시킨다는 내용이 문맥상 자연스러우니까 activates가 적절해. paralyze는 '마비시키다'라는 뜻으로 문맥상 어울리지 않아.

어휘확인

countless 무수한, 셀 수 없이 많은 **benefit** 이익, 이득 **be meant to-v** v할 예정이다; v하지 않으면 안 되다 **survive** 생존하다, 살아남다 **let alone** ~커녕, ~은 고사하고 **succeed** 성공하다 **isolation** 고립, 분리 **relationship** 관계 **stimulate** 자극하다 **interact** 상호 작용하다 **moreover** 게다가, 더욱이 **laughter** 웃음 **hold true** 사실이다 **emotional** 정서의, 감정의 **response** 반응, 대답 **specific** 특정한; 구체적인 **engage** 관계하다, 종사하다 **multiple** 다수의, 다양한 **region** 영역; 지방, 지역 **furthermore** 더욱이 **activate** 활성화시키다 **vital** 중요한, 필수적인 **creativity** 창의력; 창조력 **psychologist** 심리학자 **intelligence** 지능 **broadly** 널리 **associate** 연관 짓다
〈선택지 어휘〉
association 유대; 협회 **unlimited** 제한 없는, 무제한의 **paralyze** 마비시키다

지문 Flow

[주제문]
친구들과 재미있는 삶이 뇌에 이익을 줌

⬇

[보충설명1]
인간은 사회적 동물이고 사람들과 상호 작용하는 것이 최상의 두뇌 운동임

&

[보충설명2]
웃음이 두뇌에 좋음 → 웃음은 전 뇌에 걸쳐 다수 영역에 관여함

⬇

[추가]
농담을 듣고 자신의 것으로 만드는 것은 학습과 창의력에 중요한 두뇌 영역을 활성화시킴

193 정답 ②

지문 All in One

우리 중 많은 사람들이 얼마나 기진맥진하는지를 고려하면 8시간의 일과 후에 인상적이다
[1] Considering how exhausted many of us are / after an eight-hour workday, // it is impressive
독립 분사구문 가주어 V C

Winston Churchill이 하루에 16시간씩 일했다는 것은 심지어 70대가 되어서도 그가 어떻게 그것을 했을까
/ that Winston Churchill worked 16 hours a day, / even into his seventies. [2] How did he do it?
진주어 S V

매일 아침 11까지 그는 침대에서 일했다 심지어 중요한 회의도 열었다
[3] Every morning until 11 o'clock, / he worked in bed, / even (A) holding important
S V 분사구문(= and he even held ~)

그의 침실에서 점심 식사 후에 그는 한 시간 동안 잠을 잤다 그리고 저녁에는 그는
conferences / in his bedroom. [4] After lunch, / he slept for an hour, // and in the evening / he
S_1 V_1 S_2

두 시간을 더 잤다 저녁 식사 전에 그것은 피로의 치료가 아니었다 그는 그것을 치료할 필요가
slept for two more hours / before supper. [5] It wasn't a cure for tiredness. [6] He didn't need to
V_2 S V C S V

없었다 대신에 그는 그것을 예방했다 그의 잦은 낮잠 덕분에 그는 일할 수 있었다
cure it. [7] Instead, / he (B) prevented it. [8] Thanks to his frequent naps, / he was able to work /
= tiredness S V S V

활기찬 태도와 많은 에너지를 갖고 자정을 지나 오래도록까지
with a (C) lively attitude and plenty of energy, / until long past midnight.

	(A)		(B)		(C)
①	holding 열었다	……	prevented 예방했다	……	live 살아 있는
②	holding 열었다	……	prevented 예방했다	……	lively 활기찬
③	holding 열었다	……	predicted 예측했다	……	lively 활기찬
④	handing 건넸다	……	predicted 예측했다	……	lively 활기찬
⑤	handing 건넸다	……	prevented 예방했다	……	live 살아 있는

해석 한 눈에 보기 [1] 우리 중 많은 사람들이 8시간의 일과 후에 얼마나 기진맥진하는지를 고려하면, Winston Churchill이 심지어 70대가 되어서도 하루에 16시간씩 일했다는 것은 인상적이다. [2] 그가 그것을 어떻게 했을까? [3] 매일 아침 11시까지, 그는 침대에서 일했는데, 심지어 그의 침실에서 중요한 회의도 (A) 열었다. [4] 점심 식사 후에, 그는 한 시간 동안 잠을 잤고, 저녁에는 저녁 식사 전에 두 시간을 더 잤다. [5] 그것은 피로의 치료가 아니었다. [6] 그는 그것을 치료할 필요가 없었다. [7] 대신에 그는 그것을 (B) 예방했다. [8] 그의 잦은 낮잠 덕분에, 그는 자정을 지나 오래도록까지 (C) 활기찬 태도와 많은 에너지를 갖고 일할 수 있었다.

정답단추 문장 앞뒤의 문맥을 살펴 자연스럽게 이어지는 어휘를 골라야 해. (A)의 hold는 '(회의 등을) 열다, 개최하다'란 뜻으로 뒤에 나오는 목적어 important conferences와 함께 쓰여 문맥상 '회의를 열다'란 의미가 자연스러우므로 holding이 적절해. hand는 '건네다'라는 뜻이야. (B)는 피로의 치료를 위해 낮잠을 자는 것이 아니라 낮잠을 자서 피로를 '예방했다'라는 문맥이 자연스러우니 prevented가 들어가야 해. predict는 '예측하다'라는 의미야. (C)의 경우 낮잠 덕분에 '활기찬' 태도로 일할 수 있었다는 문맥이 자연스러우므로 lively가 적절해. 흔히 부사형 접미사로 사용되는 -ly로 끝나기 때문에 lively를 부사로 생각하기 쉽지만 형용사라는 점에 유의하자. 형용사 live는 '살아 있는; 생방송의'라는 의미야.

어휘확인

considering ~을 고려[감안]하면 **exhausted** 기진맥진한 **workday** 일과, 근무 (시간) **impressive** 인상적인, 인상 깊은 **hold** (회의 등을) 열다, 개최하다 **conference** 회의 **supper** 저녁 식사 **cure** 치료; 치료하다 **tiredness** 피로 **prevent** 예방하다, 막다 **thanks to** ~ 덕분에 **frequent** 잦은, 빈번한 **nap** 낮잠 **lively** 활기찬 **attitude** 태도 **plenty of** 많은
〈선택지 어휘〉
live 살아 있는; 살다 **predict** 예측하다 **hand** 건네주다; 손

지문 Flow

[도입]
Winston Churchill은 70대에도 하루 16시간 일함

⬇

[보충설명]
- 오전 11시까지 침대에서 일함
- 점심 식사 후에 한 시간 낮잠을 잠
- 저녁 식사 전에 두 시간 더 잠으로써 피로를 예방함

⬇

[결론]
잦은 휴식(낮잠) 덕분에 늦게까지 활기차게 일할 수 있었음

Check-Up 2

정답 ×
해석 다른 사람의 언어로 의사소통하려고 노력하는 것은 그 사람에 대한 당신의 무례를 보여준다.

194 정답 ②

지문 All in One

다음 상황을 생각해 보라 당신이 딱 한 번 사용할 봉지는 상점에서 구매한 물건을 가져
[1] Consider the following situation: // *a bag* [that you will use just once / to carry a purchase
V S 관계대명사 부사적 용법(목적)

오기 위해 집으로 지구를 손상시킬 수 있다 다가올 수백 년 동안
from a store / to your home] / can ① harm the earth / for hundreds of years to come.
V

어떤 좋은 일도 일어나지 않는다 비닐봉지를 받아들이는 것에서 구매 물건들과 함께 만일 당신이 고려
[2] Nothing good can come / from accepting plastic bags / with purchases, // unless you
S V 접속사 S'

하지 않는다면 말이다 그것이 당신에게 제공하는 불편함(→ 편리함)을 비록 당신이
consider / the ② inconvenience(→ convenience) [(which[that]) it affords you]. [3] Even if you
V' 관계대명사 접속사 S'

상점으로 걸어가거나 자전거를 타고 가는 노력을 할지라도 줄이기 위해 당신이 그렇지 않으면 운전을 함으로써 끼칠지도 모르는
make an effort to walk or cycle to a shop / to reduce / *the environmental harm* [you might
V' 부사적 용법(목적)

어휘확인

consider 생각하다; 고려하다 **situation** 상황, 처지 **purchase** 구매한 것 **harm** 손상시키다; 해, 피해 **come** 오다; (어떤 일이) 일어나다 **unless** ~하지 않는 한 **inconvenience** 불편(함) **afford** 제공하다 **even if** ~일지라도 **make an effort** 노력하다 **environmental** 환경의 **otherwise** (만약) 그렇지 않으면 **a bunch of** ~ 한 묶음[다발, 송이] **counter** 반박하다 **remain** (없어지지 않고) 남다 **fossil fuel** 화석 연료 **carbon** 탄소 **release** 방출하다; 풀어 주다 **manufacture** 제조하다

환경적 해를 / 비닐봉지 한 꾸러미는 / 그런 노력을 반박할 수 있다(거스를 수 있다) / 이것은

otherwise do by driving], // a bunch of plastic bags / can ③ counter the efforts. [4] This is

~ 때문이다 / 비록 당신이 봉지를 재사용하고 재활용할지라도 / 사실은 남아 있기 / 그것들이 화석 연료로

because // even if you reuse and recycle the bags, / the fact ④ remains / that they are made

만들어졌다는 / 불가능하다 / 방출된 모든 탄소를 제거하는 것은

from fossil fuels. [5] It is impossible / to remove *all the carbon* [that was ⑤ released / while

비닐을 제조하면서

manufacturing the plastic].

해석 한 눈에 보기 1 다음 상황을 곰곰이 생각해 보라: 당신이 상점에서 구매한 물건을 집으로 가져오기 위해 딱 한 번 사용할 봉지는 앞으로 수백 년 동안 지구를 ① 손상시킬 수 있다. **주제문** **2** 구매 물건들과 함께 비닐봉지를 받아들이는 것에서 그 어떤 좋은 일도 생기지 않는데, 만일 당신이 그것이 당신에게 제공하는 ② 불편함(→ 편리함)을 고려하지 않는다면 말이다. **3** 비록 당신이 상점으로 걸어가거나 자전거를 타고 가는 노력을 하지 않고 운전을 함으로써 당신이 끼칠지도 모르는 환경적 해를 줄이더라도 비닐봉지 한 꾸러미는 그런 노력을 ③ 거스를 수 있다. **4** 이것은 비록 당신이 봉지를 재사용하고 재활용할지라도 그것이 화석 연료로 만들어졌다는 사실은 ④ 남아 있기 때문이다. **5** 비닐을 제조하면서 ⑤ 방출된 모든 탄소를 제거하는 것은 불가능하다.

정답단추 우선 글의 전체적인 이해가 중요해. 앞뒤 문맥을 세밀히 살펴보고 밑줄 친 단어가 해당 문장 내의 문맥에서 자연스러운지 확인해야 해. 이 글은 도입부에서 비닐봉지가 지구를 훼손한다는 걸 생각해 보라고 시작하고 있어서 비닐봉지 사용을 자제하라는 내용의 글임을 알 수 있어. 그러므로 ②를 포함한 문장은 비닐봉지가 편리하지만, 그 외에는 좋은 점이 전혀 없다는 내용이 되어야 자연스러워. 따라서 inconvenience의 반의어인 convenience가 들어가야 해.

오답단서 ①의 바로 다음 문장에서 비닐봉지를 받아들이는 것에서 그 어떤 좋은 일도 생기지 않는다고 했으니 비닐봉지 사용을 자제하라는 내용임을 알 수 있어. 따라서 비닐봉지의 사용이 앞으로 수백 년 동안 지구를 손상시킨다(harm)가 어울려. ③은 even if를 통해서 환경적 해를 줄이기 위한 다양한 노력과 반대되는 결과가 나와야 함을 알 수 있어. 즉, 다양한 노력에도 불구하고 비닐봉지 한 꾸러미는 그 노력을 거스를 수 있다(counter)는 의미가 되어야 해. ④의 경우 바로 앞부분에서 even if로 시작되어 당신이 비닐봉지를 재사용하고 재활용한다는 가정이 나오고 있어. 뒷문장과의 흐름으로 보면 그럼에도 비닐봉지들이 화석 연료로 만들어진 사실은 여전하다는 의미의 remain이 와야 해. ⑤가 있는 문장에서 비닐 제조 과정에서 발생한 모든 탄소를 제거하는 것은 불가능하다고 하고 있지? 따라서 이 제조 과정 속에서 방출된 탄소이므로 released가 문맥상 옳아.

지문 Flow

[도입]
비닐봉지가 수백 년 동안 지구를 손상시킬 수 있음

[주장]
편리함을 빼고는 비닐봉지를 쓰는 것에는 장점이 없음

[보충설명]
환경적 해를 줄이기 위해 다른 노력을 할지라도, 비닐봉지 사용은 그런 노력을 무효로 만듦

[보충설명]
비닐봉지는 화석 연료로 만들어졌으며, 비닐 제조 시 방출된 탄소는 제거 불가능하기 때문

실전적용독해

195 정답 ④

지문 All in One

십대 초반과 십대들은 노력하고 있다 / 세상을 이해하고 자기 자신을 발견하려고

[1] Pre-teens and teenagers are trying / to understand the world [and] find their own selves, //

그래서 이것은 그들에게 매우 힘든 시기일 수 있다 / 부모는 도울 수 있다 / 적극적으로 청소년의 불안정한

[so] this can be a very hard time for them. [2] Parents can help / by actively attempting to

자신감을 강화하려고 시도함으로써 / 자녀들에게 웃고 / 말하는 동안 눈을

strengthen a teen's (A) unstable self-confidence. [3] Smiling at their children, / holding eye

마주 치며 / 어려운 시기나 과업 중에 그들을 격려하고 / 잘된 일에 대해

contact while speaking, / encouraging them during a difficult time or task, / praising them

그들을 칭찬하고 / 의견을 묻고, / 그들의 관심사에 관심을 갖는 것은

for a job well done, / asking for their opinion, / [and] taking an interest in their interests / are

부모가 자녀의 자신감을 발전시키는 것을 도울 수 있는 모든 방법이다 / 부모는 또한 알고 있어야 한다

all ways [that parents can help (B) foster their child's self-confidence]. [4] Parents should also

자신들의 의견과 약속이 십대들에게 큰 의미가 있음을

be aware // that their opinions [and] promises mean a great deal to their teens. (C)[5] Careless

부주의한 발언과 약속은 쉬운 방법이다 / 십대의 자부심을 망치는 / 그리고 어떠한 희생을 치르더라도

remarks [and] promises are *easy ways* [to ruin a teen's self-esteem], // [and] should be avoided

피해야 한다

at all costs.

	(A)		(B)		(C)
①	stable 안정된	……	foster 발전시키는	……	Careful 주의 깊은
②	stable 안정된	……	undermine 약화시키는	……	Careless 부주의한
③	stable 안정된	……	undermine 약화시키는	……	Careful 주의 깊은
④	unstable 불안정한	……	foster 발전시키는	……	Careless 부주의한

어휘확인

pre-teen 십대 초반 청소년 **teenager** 십대 **actively** 적극적으로, 활발히 **attempt** 시도하다 **strengthen** 강화하다 **unstable** 불안정한 **self-confidence** 자신(감), 자기 과잉 **hold eye contact** 눈을 마주치다 **encourage** 격려하다 **foster** 발전시키다, 조성하다 **aware** 알고 있는 **mean a great deal** 깊은 뜻이 있다 **careless** 부주의한, 조심성 없는 **remark** 발언, 말, 언급 **ruin** 망치다 **self-esteem** 자부심 **at all costs** 어떤 희생을 치르더라도

〈선택지 어휘〉

stable 안정된 **undermine** 약화시키다

지문 Flow

[도입]
십대는 세상을 이해하고 자신을 발견하는 시기

[주제문]
부모는 자녀의 불안정한 자신감을 강화시키는 데 도움을 줄 수 있음

⑤ unstable …… undermine …… Careful
불안정한 약화시키는 주의 깊은

해석 한 눈에 보기 1 십대 초반과 십대들은 세상을 이해하고 자기 자신을 발견하려고 노력하고 있어서, 이것은 그들에게 매우 힘든 시기일 수 있다. 주제문 2 부모는 청소년의 (A) 불안정한 자신감을 강화하려고 적극적으로 시도함으로써 도울 수 있다. 3 자녀들에게 웃고, 말하는 동안 눈을 마주 치며, 어려운 시기나 과업 중에 그들을 격려하고, 잘된 일에 대해 그들을 칭찬하고, 의견을 묻고, 그들의 관심사에 관심을 갖는 것은 부모가 자녀의 자신감을 (B) 발전시키는 것을 도울 수 있는 모든 방법이다. 4 부모는 또한 자신들의 의견과 약속이 십대들에게 큰 의미가 있음을 알고 있어야 한다. 5 (C) 부주의한 발언과 약속은 십대의 자부심을 망치는 쉬운 방법이며, 어떠한 희생을 치르더라도 피해야 한다.

정답단추 우선 글의 전체적인 내용 이해가 중요하고, 그 다음에 네모 안 어휘를 포함한 문장의 앞뒤 문맥이 자연스러운지 확인해서 적절한 어휘를 골라야 해. 이 글은 십대들이 자신감을 키우는 데 부모에게 도움을 받을 수 있다는 내용이야. (A)는 앞에서 청소년기는 힘든 시기일 수 있다고 하였으므로, unstable이 적절해. stable은 반의어로 '안정된'이라는 뜻이야. (B)가 있는 문장에서 부모가 자녀들에게 웃고, 말하면서 눈을 마주치고, 격려하고, 칭찬하는 등의 행동은 도움을 주는 방법이므로, 자신감을 발전시키는, 즉 foster가 적절해. undermine은 반대의 뜻으로 '약화시키다'라는 뜻이야. (C)다음 내용을 보면 부모의 의견과 약속이 십대들에게 큰 의미가 있다고 했으므로, '부주의한' 발언과 약속을 하면 자부심을 망치기 쉽다는 내용이 와야 해. 따라서 Careless가 적절해. Careful은 '주의 깊은'이라는 의미로 반대의 뜻이야.

[보충설명1]
자녀들에게 웃기, 말하면서 눈을 마주치기, 격려하기, 칭찬하기, 의견 묻기, 자녀의 관심사에 관심 갖기

&

[보충설명2]
부주의한 발언과 약속 피하기

196 정답 ⑤

지문 All in One

1 When (we're) faced with many responsibilities, // it is almost always helpful / to make a schedule. 2 However, / it is important for each individual / to choose *the type of schedule* [that (A) fits his or her circumstances best]. 3 Some students work better / with a detailed schedule, // whereas others work better / with a brief list of *things* [to do]. 4 Circumstances also (B) influence / the type of *schedule* [(which[that]) a student should make]. 5 There are on-campus students, / commuting students, / employed students, / and night-class students, // and each has different scheduling requirements. 6 Every student should tailor / the principles of schedule building / to his or her personal circumstances, // rather than (C) adopt / *some ideal model* [which fits hardly anybody].

(많은 책무들에 직면했을 때 / 거의 항상 도움이 된다 / 일정을 세우는 것은 / 하지만 / 각 개인에게 중요하다 / 일정 유형을 선택하는 것은 / 그 혹은 그녀의 상황에 가장 잘 맞는 / 몇몇 학생들은 (공부를) 더 잘 한다 / 상세한 일정으로 / 다른 학생들이 더 잘하는 반면에 / 할 일의 간단한 목록으로 / 상황은 또한 영향을 미친다 / 일정 유형에 / 학생이 세워야 하는 / 교내에 있는 학생들이 있다 / 통학하는 학생들 / 고용된 학생들 / 그리고 야간 수업 학생들 / 그리고 각각은 서로 다른 일정 세우기 요건을 가진다 / 모든 학생은 맞춰야 한다 / 일정 세우는 원칙을 / 그 혹은 그녀의 개인적인 상황에 / 채택하기보다는 / 누구에게도 거의 맞지 않는 어떤 이상적인 모델을)

(When: 접속사, we're: S′, faced: V′, it: 가주어, is: V, helpful: C, to make a schedule: 진주어; it: 가주어, is: V, important: C, for each individual: 의미상 주어, to choose ~: 진주어, that: 관계대명사; Some students: S_1, work: V_1, whereas: 접속사, others: S′, work: V′; Circumstances: S, influence: V, which[that]: 관계대명사; There are: V_1, students: S_1, and, each: S_2, has: V_2; Every student: S, should tailor: V_1, adopt: V_2, which: 관계대명사)

	(A)		(B)		(C)
①	fills 채우는	……	include 포함한다	……	adapt 적응하기
②	fills 채우는	……	influence 영향을 미친다	……	adopt 채택하기
③	fits 맞는	……	include 포함한다	……	adapt 적응하기
④	fits 맞는	……	influence 영향을 미친다	……	adapt 적응하기
⑤	fits 맞는	……	influence 영향을 미친다	……	adopt 채택하기

해석 한 눈에 보기 1 많은 책무에 직면했을 때, 일정을 세우는 것은 거의 항상 도움이 된다. 주제문 2 하지만 각 개인이 자신의 상황에 가장 (A) 맞는 유형의 일정을 선택하는 것이 중요하다. 3 어떤 학생들은 상세한 일정으로 공부를 더 잘하지만, 다른 학생들은 할 일의 간단한 목록으로 공부를 더 잘한다. 4 상황 또한 학생이 세워야 하는 일정의 유형에 (B) 영향을 미친다. 5 교내에 있는 학생들, 통학하는 학생들, 고용된 학생들, 야간 수업을 받는 학생들이 있는데, 각각은 서로 다른 일정 세우기 요건들을 갖고 있다. 주제문 6 모든 학생은 누구에게도 거의 맞지 않는 어떤 이상적인 모델을 (C) 채택하기보다는 일정을 세우는 원칙을 자신의 개인적 상황에 맞춰야 한다.

정답단추 어휘 추론 문제에서는 해당 문장의 내용에서 문맥상 자연스러운 어휘를 선택해야 해. (A)에는 일정을 세울 때는 개인의 상황에 '맞는' 유형을 선택하는 것이 중요하다는 내용이 되어야 자연스러우므로 fits가 들어가야 해. fill은 '채우다'란 뜻이야. (B)는 뒤에서 교내에 있는지, 통학하는지, 고용되었는지 등의 상황에 따라 일정의 유형이 서로 달라진다는 내용이 나오고 있으니까 상황이 일정 유형에 '영향을 미친다'는 influence가 적절해. include는 '포함하다'란 뜻이야. 마지막으로 (C)가 있는 문장은 아무에게도 안 맞는 이상적인 계획표를 '채택하기'보다는 개인의 상황에 맞는 일정을 세워야 한다는 내용이 자연스러우니까 adopt가 들어가야 해. adapt는 '적응하다'라는 뜻이야.

어휘확인

face 직면하다; 얼굴 **responsibility** 책무, 책임 **individual** 개인; 개인의 **fit** 들어맞다; 맞다 **circumstance** 상황 **detailed** 상세한 **whereas** ~인 반면에 **brief** 간단한; 짧은 **influence** 영향을 미치다 **on-campus** 교내의 **commuting** 통학하는; 통근 **employed** 고용된 **requirement** 요건 **tailor** (특정한 목적에) 맞추다; 재단사 **principle** 원칙 **personal** 개인적인 **rather than** ~보다는 **adopt** 채택하다; 입양하다 **ideal** 이상적인 **hardly** 거의 ~ 아니다

〈선택지 어휘〉

fill 채우다 **include** 포함하다 **adapt** 적응하다

지문 Flow

[도입]
책무가 많을 때 일정을 세우는 것이 도움이 됨

⬇

[주제문]
자신의 상황에 맞는 일정을 선택하는 것이 중요함

⬇

[보충설명]
• 상세한 일정 vs. 할 일의 간단한 목록
• 학생의 상황도 세워야 하는 일정의 유형에 영향을 미침

⬇

[주제 재진술]
일정을 세울 때 자신의 개인적인 상황에 맞춰야 함

197 정답 ③

지문 All in One

[1] It is important / not to overlook the health of our hearing. [2] By reducing *the noises* [(which) we hear] / to under ninety decibels / or by taking simple precautions / such as wearing ear plugs / when (we're) working around loud equipment, // we can (A) prevent damage to our hearing. [3] The drawbacks of hearing loss / certainly (B) outweigh the inconveniences of prevention. [4] The sense of hearing is important for survival // and should be taken care of / just as we take care of our lives. [5] More and more advances are being (C) developed every year / to improve hearing problems, // but they are expensive / and do not always cure the problem. [6] Prevention is the only one-hundred-percent cure / for hearing impairments.

(이것은 중요하다 / 우리의 청력 건강을 간과하지 않는 것은 / 우리가 듣는 소음을 줄임으로써 / 90데시벨 미만으로 / 혹은 단순한 예방책을 취함으로써 / 귀마개를 착용하는 것과 같은 / 시끄러운 장비 주변에서 일할 때 / 우리는 청력에 대한 손상을 예방할 수 있다 / 청력 손실의 문제점은 / 분명히 예방의 불편함보다 더 크다 / 청각은 생존을 위해 중요하며 / 돌보아져야 한다 / 꼭 우리가 우리의 인생을 돌보는 것처럼 / 해마다 점점 더 많은 진보가 이루어지고 있지만 / 청력 문제를 개선하기 위해 / 그러나 그것들은 비싸고 / 항상 그 문제를 치료해 주는 것은 아니다 / 예방이 유일한 100%의 치료법이다 / 청력 장애의)

(가주어 V, C, 진주어, 관계대명사, 접속사 S' V', S V, S, V, S V₁ C V₂, 접속사 S' V', S₁ V₁, 부사적 용법(목적), S₂ V₂ C, 부분부정, V₃, S V C)

	(A)		(B)		(C)
①	prevent 예방할	……	lessen ~을 줄인다	……	determined 결정되고
②	prevent 예방할	……	outweigh ~보다 더 크다	……	determined 결정되고
③	prevent 예방할	……	outweigh ~보다 더 크다	……	developed 이루어지고
④	protect 보호할	……	lessen ~을 줄인다	……	developed 이루어지고
⑤	protect 보호할	……	outweigh ~보다 더 크다	……	developed 이루어지고

해석 한 눈에 보기 [1] 우리의 청력 건강을 간과하지 않는 것은 중요하다. [2] 우리가 듣는 소음을 90데시벨 미만으로 줄임으로써 혹은 시끄러운 장비 주변에서 일할 때 귀마개를 착용하는 것과 같은 단순한 예방책을 취함으로써, 우리는 청력에 대한 손상을 (A) 예방할 수 있다. [3] 청력 손실의 문제점은 분명히 예방의 불편함(B)보다 더 크다. [4] 청각은 생존을 위해 중요하며 꼭 우리가 우리의 인생을 돌보는 것처럼 돌보아져야 한다. [5] 청력 문제를 개선하기 위해 해마다 점점 더 많은 진보가 (C) 이루어지고 있지만, 그것들은 비싸고 항상 그 문제를 치료해 주는 것은 아니다. [6] 예방이 청력 장애의 유일한 100%의 치료법이다.

정답단추 (A)가 포함된 문장을 보면 소음을 90dB 미만으로 줄이거나 귀마개를 끼는 등의 예방책을 통해서 우리는 청력 손상을 '예방할' 수 있다는 내용이므로 prevent가 들어가야 해. protect는 '보호하다'라는 의미야. (B)는 다음 문장에서 청각은 생존에 필요한 것이라 인생을 돌보는 것처럼 신경 써야 한다고 했으므로 청력 손실의 문제점이 청력 예방의 불편함'보다 더 크다'는 것을 알 수 있어. 따라서 outweigh가 들어가야 해. lessen은 '줄이다'라는 뜻이니까 답이 될 수 없어. (C)의 경우 청력 문제를 개선하기 위해 해마다 점점 더 많은 진보가 '이루어지고' 있으나 그것은 비싸고 문제가 항상 해결되는 것이 아니라는 내용이 되어야 자연스러우므로 developed가 와야 해. determine은 '결정하다'라는 뜻이야.

어휘확인

overlook 간과하다 hearing 청력, 청각 decibel 데시벨(음의 세기를 나타내는 단위) take (조치·방법 등을) 취하다 precaution 예방책 ear plug (소음방지용) 귀마개 equipment 장비, 용품 prevent 예방하다 cf. prevention 예방 damage 손상 drawback 문제점, 결점 loss 손실 certainly 분명히 outweigh ~보다 더 크다 inconvenience 불편, 애로 sense 감각 survival 생존 advance 진보, 발전 develop (기술 등이) 개발되다 impairment (신체적·정신적) 장애

〈선택지 어휘〉

lessen 줄이다

지문 Flow

[주제문]
청력 건강을 간과하지 않는 것이 중요함

⬇

[보충설명]
- 청력 손상의 예방책
  - 소음을 90dB 미만으로 줄임
  - 시끄러운 장비 주변에서 일할 때 귀마개 착용
- 청력 손실의 문제점이 예방의 불편함보다 큼
- 청력 문제 개선법은 비싸고 항상 치료되는 것이 아님

⬇

[결론]
청력 장애는 예방이 유일한 치료법임

198 정답 ②

지문 All in One

[1] Most kids and teens are emotional / at times, // so it can be ① hard for parents to distinguish between normal behavior and cause for concern. [2] Short-term (less than two weeks) sadness / is usually not thought to be alarming. [3] However, / when feelings of sadness or hopelessness last, // a larger problem may ② disappear(→ exist). [4] *Kids* [who were once good students / but now don't ③ care about their academic responsibilities] / may be depressed. [5] *Any child* [who talks about running away from home] / should be evaluated by

(대부분의 어린이와 청소년은 감정적이다 / 때때로 / 그래서 부모가 정상적인 행동과 걱정의 이유를 구별하는 것이 어려울 수 있다 / 단기(2주 미만) 슬픔은 / 보통 걱정스럽게 생각되지 않는다 / 하지만 / 슬픔이나 절망감이 계속될 때 / 더 큰 문제가 사라질(→ 나타날)지도 모른다 / 한때 좋은 학생이었던 아이들은 / 하지만 지금은 학업 책임에 대해 신경 쓰지 않는 / 우울할지도 모른다 / 집에서 도망가는 것에 대해 이야기하는 어떤 아이라도 / 전문 상담자에 의해 평가되어야 한다)

(S V C, 가주어 V C 의미상 주어, 진주어, S, V, 접속사 S', V' S V, S 관계대명사 V'₁, V'₂, V, C, S 관계대명사, V)

어휘확인

emotional 감정의, 정서의 at times 때때로 distinguish 구별하다 behavior 행동 concern 걱정, 우려 sadness 슬픔 alarming 걱정스러운, 두려운 hopelessness 절망, 가망 없음 disappear 사라지다 responsibility 책임, 책무 depressed 우울한 cf. depression 우울증 evaluate 평가하다 professional 전문적인, 직업의 counselor 상담사 count on 의지하다, ~을 믿다 seriously 심각하게 assistance 도움, 지원 ignore 무시하다 symptom 증상 tragic 비극적인, 비극의 consequence (발생한 일의) 결과

그 아이들은 도움을 청하고 있다 / 그리고 그들의 주변 사람들에게 의지하고 있다

a professional counselor. [6] Those kids are calling out for help // and are counting on *those* around them / [to take them ④ seriously]. [7] It is far better / to seek assistance than to ⑤ ignore the symptoms of *depression*, / [which can have tragic consequences].

자신들을 심각하게 받아들이는 / 훨씬 더 낫다 / 우울증의 증상을 무시하기보다는 도움을 청하는 것이 / 그것은 비극적인 결과를 가져올 수 있다

(S / V_1 / V_2 / 가주어 V 강조 C / 진주어 / 관계대명사(계속적 용법))

해석 한 눈에 보기 1 대부분의 어린이와 청소년은 때때로 감정적이어서, 부모가 정상적인 행동과 걱정의 이유를 구별하는 것이 ① 어려울 수 있다. 2 단기(2주 미만) 슬픔은 보통 걱정스럽게 생각되지 않는다. 3 하지만, 슬픔이나 절망감이 계속될 때, 더 큰 문제가 ② 사라질(→ 나타날)지도 모른다. 4 한때 좋은 학생이었지만 지금은 학업 책임에 대해 ③ 신경 쓰지 않는 아이들은 우울할지도 모른다. 5 집에서 도망가는 것에 대해 이야기하는 어떤 아이라도 전문 상담자에 의해 평가되어야 한다. 6 그 아이들은 도움을 청하고 있으며, 자신들을 ④ 심각하게 받아들이는 그들의 주변 사람들에게 의지하고 있다. 7 우울증의 증상을 ⑤ 무시하기보다는 도움을 청하는 것이 훨씬 더 나은데, 그것(우울증)은 비극적인 결과를 가져올 수 있다.

정답단추 밑줄 친 어휘가 있는 문장의 앞뒤 내용을 파악하고, 해당 어휘가 문맥에 적절한지 살펴봐. 두 번째 문장에서 단기 슬픔은 걱정스럽지 않다고 했는데 그다음 문장이 이와 역접으로 연결되었으므로 슬픔이나 절망이 장기화되면 아마도 더 큰 문제가 생길 거야. 따라서 ②는 disappear가 아니라 exist나 occur, happen 등을 써야 자연스러운 흐름이 돼.

오답단서 ①은 어린이와 청소년은 감정적이라고 했으므로 정상적인 행동과 걱정의 이유를 구별하기 '어렵다'고 해야 문맥이 자연스러워. ③이 있는 문장은 한때 좋은 학생들이 but 뒤에서 지금은 학업에 신경을 쓰지 않는 아이들이 되어서 우울증을 겪을 수 있다는 내용이므로 care about은 문맥상 쓰임이 적절해. ④를 포함한 문장은 우울증을 겪는 아이들이 주변 사람들에게 도움을 요청하는데, 그 사람들은 그 아이들의 상태를 심각하게 받아들여야 해. 따라서 seriously는 문맥상 자연스러워. ⑤가 있는 마지막 문장은 우울증을 무시하는 것보다, 도움을 요청하는 것이 좋은 결과를 가져온다는 흐름이므로, ignore는 적절한 어휘야.

지문 Flow

[도입]
대부분의 어린이와 청소년은 감정적이어서 정상적인 행동과 걱정의 이유를 구별하기 어려움

[보충설명]
• 단기 슬픔은 걱정스럽지 않지만, 슬픔이나 절망감이 장기화되면 큰 문제가 나타날지도 모름
• 학업에 신경 쓰지 않는 아이들 또는 가출하고 싶다고 말하는 아이들은 우울함

[의견]
우울증의 결과는 비극적일 수 있으므로 무시하는 것보다 도움을 청하는 것이 나음

199 정답 ④

지문 All in One

[1] Through their shared secrets, / *the time* [(that) they spend alone], / and *the knowledge* [(which[that]) they gain], / siblings learn to ① cooperate / and (to) get along together. [2] With their learning and knowledge, / siblings also build a personal history. [3] That is not to say // that brothers and sisters have ② identical histories. [4] Each child in a family / experiences life differently, / relates differently to parents, / and creates a different and ③ unique environment / for the other. [5] Yet there is a family ethos, / as well as *a pool of memory* [that transcends individual experiences / and forms a ④ different (→ common) past / for siblings]. [6] The pull of memory and the rewards of sibling companionship / ⑤ draw adult brothers and sisters / to each other / in spite of their differences.

그들의 공유된 비밀을 통해 / 그들이 혼자 보내는 시간 / 그리고 그들이 얻는 지식(을 통해) / 형제자매들은 협력하는 것을 배운다 / 그리고 사이좋게 지내는 것을 / 그들의 배움과 지식으로 / 형제자매들은 또한 개인적인 이력을 쌓는다 / 그것은 말하는 것은 아니다 / 형제들과 자매들이 똑같은 이력을 가진다고 / 한 가정의 각각의 아이는 / 삶을 다르게 경험한다 / 부모와 다르게 관계가 있다(관계를 맺는다) / 그리고 다르고 독특한 환경을 만들어낸다 / 상대방에게 / 그런데 가족 기풍이 있다 / 개인의 경험을 초월한 기억의 웅덩이뿐만 아니라 / 그리고 다른(→ 공통의) 과거를 형성하는 / 형제자매에게 / 기억을 끌어당기는 힘과 형제자매 우애의 보상은 / 어른 형제들과 자매들을 끌어당긴다 / 서로에게로 / 그들의 차이에도 불구하고

(관계대명사 / 관계대명사 / S V / S V / S V C / 접속사 S' V' / S V_1 / V_2 / V_3 / V S / 관계대명사 / V'_1 / V'_2 / S V)

해석 한 눈에 보기 1 그들의 공유된 비밀과 그들이 혼자 보내는 시간과 그들이 얻는 지식을 통해, 형제자매들은 ① 협력하며 사이좋게 지내는 법을 배운다. 2 그들의 배움과 지식으로, 형제자매들은 또한 개인적 이력을 쌓아가기도 한다. 3 그것은 형제자매들이 ② 똑같은 이력을 가진다고 말하는 것이 아니다. 4 한 가정의 각각의 아이는 삶을 서로 다르게 경험하고, 부모와 서로 다르게 관계를 맺으며, 상대방에게 다르고 ③ 독특한 환경을 만들어 낸다. 5 그런데 개인적 경험을 초월하여 형제자매들에게 ④ 다른(→ 공통의) 과거를 형성해 주는 기억 덩어리뿐만이 아니라 가풍도 있다. 6 기억을 끌어당기는 힘과 형제자매 간 우애의 보상은 그들의 차이에도 불구하고 어른이 된 형제자매들을 서로에게로 ⑤ 끌어당긴다.

정답단추 글을 전체적으로 이해한 다음 밑줄 친 어휘가 적절한지 앞뒤 문맥을 통해 판단해야 해. Each child ~ for the other.에서 형제자매들은 삶을 다르게 경험하기 때문에 각자 다른 이력을 만들어 나간다고 했어. 뒤이어 이런 각기 다른 개인적인 경험을 초월한 기억과 가풍이 있어 어른이 된 형제자매들을 서로에게로 끌어당긴다고 설명하고 있어. 따라서 기억과 가풍은 형제자매들에게 '다른(different)' 과거가 아니라 '공통의(common)' 과거를 만들어 준다고 해야 적절하므로 낱말의 쓰임이 적절하지 않은 것은 ④야.

오답단서 ①은 형제자매들이 함께 잘 지내는 법을 배운다고 했으니까 cooperate(협력하며)는 자연스러워. ②와 ③은

어휘확인

knowledge 지식 **sibling** 형제자매 **cooperate** 협력하다 **get along** 사이좋게 지내다 **learning** 배움, 학습 **personal** 개인적인 **history** 이력; 역사 **identical** 똑같은 **relate to** ~와 관계가 있다; ~와 관련되다 **ethos** 기풍, 정신 **as well as** ~뿐만 아니라 **memory** 기억 **transcend** 초월하다 **individual** 개인의 **form** 형성시키다; 종류 **pull** 끌어당기는 힘; 당기다 **reward** 보상 **companionship** 우애, 우정 **draw** 끌어 당기다; 그리다 **in spite of** ~에도 불구하고

지문 Flow

[도입]
형제자매는 협력하며 함께 잘 지내는 동시에, 자신들의 배움과 지식으로 개인적 이력을 쌓음

[보충설명]
서로 삶을 다르게 경험하고, 부모와 다른 관계를 맺음

[반박]
개인적 경험을 초월한 공통의 과거를 형성하는 기억이나 가풍이 있음

[결론]
기억의 힘과 형제자매 간의 우애는 그들의 차이에도 불구하고 서로를 끌어당김

앞뒤 문장의 설명을 보면 문맥상 자연스럽다는 것을 알 수 있어. 형제자매들은 개인적인 이력을 쌓는다고 했는데 이는 똑같은 이력을 가지는 게 아니라 다른 삶의 경험, 부모와 서로 다른 관계 등 각자 독특한 환경을 만들어 낸다는 의미니까 각각 identical과 unique가 와야 해. 마지막으로 기억의 흡인력과 우애의 보상이 있기에 서로 다른 형제자매가 어른이 되어서도 서로 끌어당긴다는 내용에서 draw의 쓰임은 자연스러우니까 ⑤도 적절하게 쓰였어.

미니 모의고사 6 유형 17 | 유형 18

200 ① 201 ⑤ 202 ④ 203 ③ 204 ② 205 ② 206 ④ 207 ③ 208 ①
209 ② 210 ③ 211 ① 212 ③ 213 ⑤ 214 ③ 215 ④ 216 ①

200 정답 ①

지문 All in One

1 Exploration(S: 탐험은) was(V) a driving force(C: 원동력이었다) / behind the success of human civilizations(인간 문명의 성공 뒤의) / and(그리고) our mastery of the environment(환경에 대한 우리의 지배). 2 In fact(사실), / cultures(S: 문화는) / such as the Vikings(바이킹과 같은) / defined(V) themselves(주로 그들 자신을 정의했다) primarily / in terms of exploration(탐험의 관점에서). 3 Nowadays(요즘에는), / however(하지만), / there are(V) few areas(S) of our planet(우리의 행성(지구)의 지역은 거의 없다) / [that(관계대명사) (A) remain untouched and unexplored](본래 그대로이거나 탐험되지 않은 채로 남아 있는). 4 Especially since the beginning of the great Age of Exploration(특히 대항해 시대의 시작 이후로) / in the early 15th century(15세기 초의), / explorers and scientists(S) have been (B) uncovering(V) the secrets(탐험가들과 과학자들은 비밀을 알아 내오고 있다) / of remote mountains(외진 산), / deep forests(깊은 숲), / huge oceans(거대한 바다), / and(그리고) the freezing polar regions(꽁꽁 얼 정도로 추운 극지방의). 5 Curiosity and ambition(호기심과 야망은) / led(V) adventurers(O)(모험가들을 이끌었다) / to go into the unknown(C_1: 미지의 세계로 가도록) / and to put themselves(C_2: 그리고 그들 자신을 처하도록) / in extreme danger(극도로 위험한 상황에). 6 Because of *those* [(C) who(관계대명사) went before us](우리보다 앞서간 사람들 때문에), / there are not(V) so many *mysteries*(S) [left to discover / on Earth](발견하도록 남겨진 수수께끼가 그다지 많지 않다 / 지구에는).

	(A)		(B)		(C)
①	remain	……	uncovering	……	who
②	remain	……	uncovered	……	which
③	remains	……	uncovering	……	who
④	remains	……	uncovered	……	which
⑤	remain	……	uncovered	……	who

해석 한 눈에 보기 1 탐험은 인간 문명의 성공과 환경에 대한 우리의 지배 뒤의 원동력이었다. 2 사실, 바이킹 같은 문화는 주로 탐험의 관점에서 그들 자신을 정의했다. 3 하지만 요즘에는 본래 그대로이거나 탐험되지 않은 채로 남아 있는 지구상의 지역은 거의 없다. 4 특히 15세기 초의 대항해 시대의 시작 이후로, 탐험가들과 과학자들은 외진 산, 깊은 숲, 거대한 바다, 꽁꽁 얼게 할 정도로 추운 극지방의 비밀을 밝혀 오고 있다. 5 호기심과 야망은 모험가들을 미지의 세계로 향하게 하고 그들 자신을 매우 위험한 상황에 처하게 했다. 6 우리보다 앞서간 사람들 덕분에, 지구상에는 발견해야 할 수수께끼가 그다지 많이 남아 있지 않다.

정답단추 (A)의 remain은 관계사절 내의 동사이므로 선행사에 수를 일치시켜야 해. of our planet의 수식을 받는 areas가 선행사이므로 복수동사 remain이 와야 해. (B)는 능동과 수동을 구분하는 문제로, 문맥상 탐험들과 과학자들이 비밀을 '알아내는' 것이므로 능동형인 uncovering을 쓰는 것이 옳아. (C)의 경우 선행사 those는 앞 문장의 adventurers를 가리키고 있으므로 사람 선행사를 대신 받는 관계대명사 who가 적절해.

어휘확인

exploration 탐험 **driving force** 원동력, 추진력 **success** 성공 **civilization** 문명 **mastery** 지배, 장악 **in fact** 사실(은) **Viking** 바이킹(스칸디나비아의 한 부족) **define** 정의하다 **primarily** 주로 **in terms of** ~ 면에서 **nowadays** 요즘에는 **area** 지역 **planet** 행성 **remain** 남다; 계속 ~ 이다 **untouched** 본래 그대로의 **unexplored** 탐험되지 않은 **since** ~이후[부터] **beginning** 시작 **the Age of Exploration** 대항해 시대 **century** 세기 **explorer** 탐험가 **uncover** 알아내다 **remote** 외진 **huge** 거대한 **freezing** 꽁꽁 얼게 추운 **polar** 극지의 **region** 지역, 지방 **curiosity** 호기심 **ambition** 야망 **adventurer** 모험가 **the unknown** 미지의 세계[것(들)] **put** (어떤 상태에) 처하게 하다 **extreme** 극도의 **discover** 발견하다

지문 Flow

[도입]
탐험은 인간 문명의 성공과 환경에 대한 지배의 원동력

↓

[주제문]
지구상에서 탐험되지 않는 지역이 거의 없음

↓

[보충설명]
15세기 초 대항해 시대 이후로, 여러 외진 곳의 비밀이 밝혀짐

↓

[주제 재진술]
위험을 무릅쓴 모험가들 덕분에 지구상에 발견할 수수께끼가 많이 남아 있지 않음

201 정답 ⑤

지문 All in One

소설 읽기를 즐기는 많은 사람들은 / 또한 즐긴다 / 그 소설을 토대로 한 영화를 보는 것을
1 Many [① who enjoy reading novels] / also enjoy / watching *movies* [that are based on those
S 관계대명사 V 관계대명사

소설이 소생되는 것을 보는 것은 / 대형 화면에 / ~일 수 있다 / 혹자는 말할지도 모른다 / 새로운
novels]. 2 Seeing a story ② come to life / on the big screen / can be, // one might say, // a novel
S V 삽입절 C

경험 / 그러나 만일 당신이 책을 읽으면 / 영화를 본 후에 / 불가능할 것이다
experience. 3 But if you read the book / after seeing the movie, // it will be impossible / not ③
접속사 S′ V′ 가주어 V C 진주어

그 영화의 배우들과 배경을 보지 않는다는 것은 / 당신의 마음의 눈으로 / 그것은 애석한 일이다 / 독서하는 것의 즐거움
to see the movie's actors and settings / in your mind's eye. 4 That's a shame // because part of
S V C 접속사 S′

중 일부분은 (~이기) 때문이다 / '당신'이 상상하게 되는 것 / 등장인물들과 배경의 세부 사항을
the fun of reading is / ④ that *you* get to imagine / the details of the characters and settings.
V′ 접속사 S″ V″ C′

만일 그 일의 많은 것이 이미 이루어졌다면 / 당신을 위해 / 당신의 독서 경험은
5 If much of that work already has been done / for you, // your reading experience / will be
접속사 S′ V′ S V

덜 활기차고 덜 즐거울 것이다 / 소설의 길이에 상관없이
less ⑤ actively(→ active) and less enjoyable. 6 Regardless of a novel's length, / *the movie*
C_1 C_2 S

그것을 토대로 하는 영화 대본은 될 것이다 / 90~120쪽 사이로 / 1쪽이 / 촬영 1분당
script [that is based on it] will be / between 90 and 120 pages / — one page / for each minute
관계대명사 = novel V C

of shooting.

해석 한 눈에 보기 1 소설 읽기를 즐기는 많은 사람은 그 소설을 토대로 하는 영화를 보는 것 또한 즐긴다. 2 혹자는 소설이 대형 화면에 소생되는 것을 보는 것은 새로운 경험일 수 있다고 말할지도 모른다. 3 그러나 만일 당신이 영화를 본 후에 책을 읽으면, 당신의 마음의 눈으로 그 영화의 배우들과 배경을 보지 않는다는 것은 불가능할 것이다. 4 독서하는 것의 즐거움 중 일부분은 '당신'이 등장인물들과 배경의 세부적인 것을 상상하게 되는 것이기 때문에 그것은 애석한 일이다. 5 만일 그 일의 많은 것이 이미 당신을 위해 이루어졌다면, 당신의 독서 경험은 덜 활기차고 덜 즐거울 것이다. 6 소설의 길이에 상관없이, 그것을 토대로 하는 영화 대본은 90~120쪽 사이로 촬영 1분당 1쪽이 될 것이다.

정답단추 밑줄 친 부분에서 묻고 있는 문법사항을 정확히 파악하여 확인해보자. ⑤는 will be의 주격 보어 자리이므로 부사 actively가 아닌 형용사 active가 되어야 해. 주격 보어로는 명사와 형용사만 가능해. 부사는 동사를 수식하는 어구로 보어 자리에는 올 수가 없어. 또한, 뒤의 enjoyable과 병렬구조를 이뤄야 한다는 것도 놓치지 말자.

오답단서 ①에는 선행사 many가 사람을 가리키므로 사람 선행사를 취하는 관계대명사 who가 올바르게 쓰였어. 지각동사 see는 목적격 보어로 동사원형이나 현재분사를 취하니까 ②의 come은 적절하게 쓰였어. ③이 포함된 문장에서 to see ~ eye는 앞에 있는 가주어 it을 대신하는 진주어로 쓰인 to부정사이므로 어법상 적절해. ④의 that은 명사절을 이끄는 접속사로서 because절에서 주어는 part ~ reading, 동사는 is, that ~ settings는 is의 보어 역할을 하고 있으므로 어법상 옳은 표현이야.

어휘확인

novel 소설 **be based on** ~을 토대로 하다 **come to life** 소생하다, 활기를 띠다 **screen** 화면, 스크린 **setting** (연극·소설 등의) 배경 **shame** 애석한 일, 아쉬운 일 **get to-v** ~하게 되다 **imagine** 상상하다 **detail** 세부 사항 **actively** 활발히, 활동적으로 **enjoyable** 즐거운 **regardless of** ~에 상관없이 **length** 길이 **script** 대본, 원고 **page** 쪽, 페이지 **shooting** (영화) 촬영

지문 Flow

[도입]
소설을 토대로 한 영화를 보는 것은 새로운 경험임

⬇

[주제문]
영화를 보고 책을 읽으면, 독서를 통해 얻게 되는 상상의 즐거움을 빼앗기게 됨

⬇

[보충설명]
독서 경험이 덜 활기차게 덜 즐겁게 됨

⬇

[추가]
소설의 길이에 상관없이 90~120쪽으로 영화 대본이 만들어짐

202 정답 ④

지문 All in One

우리의 연장자들 중 가장 현명한 분은 알고 있다 / 생기든 일은 무엇이든 받아들일 줄을 / 어려움들에 적응하며
1 The wisest of our elders knows / to accept whatever may come, / adapting to difficulties /
S V 복합관계사 분사구문

그것들이 발생할 때 / 절대 잃어버리지 않으면서 / 사는 것에 내재된 즐거움을 / 문제점들에도
when they arise // while never (A) losing / the sense of joy inherent to living / in spite of
접속사 분사구문

불구하고 / 나는 이런 인생관을 부르고 싶다 / '그럼에도 불구하고 행복해'라고 / 이것은 대조된다
problems. 2 I like to call this outlook / "happy in spite of." 3 This (B) contrasts / with *the*
S V S V

다수에 의해 소유되는 관점과 / 그것을 나는 부르겠다 '그렇게 되기만 하면 행복해'라고 / 일반적으로
viewpoint [held by the majority], // [which I'd call / "happy if only."] 4 In general, / the
관계대명사(계속적 용법)

젊은이들의 인생관은 말한다 / '내가 ~하기만 하면 나는 행복할 텐데' / 그 진술은 완성될 수 있다
outlook of the young says: // "I would be happy if only I..." 5 The statement can be completed
S V S V C 접속사 S′ S V

수많은 방법으로 / 내가 살이 빠지면 / 짝을 찾으면 / 건강해지면 / 부자가 되면 / 등등이
/ in any numbers of ways: // if I lose weight, / find a mate, / get healthy, / get rich, / and on
접속사 S′ V'_1 V'_2 V'_3 V'_4

있다 / 연구원들은 믿는다 / 그러한 '그렇게 되기만 하면 행복해' 태도는 / 그저
and on. 6 Researchers believe // that such a "happy if only" attitude / will do nothing but
S V 접속사 S′ V'_1

실망으로 이어질 뿐이다
lead to (C) disappointment.
V'_2

어휘확인

elder 연장자 **whatever** ~하는 것은 무엇이든 **adapt to** ~에 적응하다 **arise** 발생하다 **sense** ~ 느낌[감] **joy** 즐거움 **inherent** 내재된, 고유한 **in spite of** ~에도 불구하고 **outlook** 인생관 **contrast with** ~와 대조를 이루다 **viewpoint** 관점[시각] **majority** 다수 **in general** 일반적으로, 보통 **statement** 진술 **numbers of** 수많은, 다수의 **lose weight** 살이 빠지다 **mate** 짝, 배우자 **on and on** 기타 등등; 계속해서 **researcher** 연구원 **attitude** 태도 **do nothing but** ~하기만 하다, ~만 할 뿐이다 **lead to** ~로 이어지다 **disappointment** 실망

〈선택지 어휘〉

contentment 만족 **comply** 순응하다, 준수하다

	(A)		(B)		(C)
①	getting 가지지	……	contrasts 대조되는데	……	contentment 만족
②	losing 잃어버리지	……	contrasts 대조되는데	……	contentment 만족
③	getting 가지지	……	complies 응하는데[따르는데]	……	contentment 만족
④	losing 잃어버리지	……	contrasts 대조되는데	……	disappointment 실망
⑤	getting 가지지	……	complies 응하는데[따르는데]	……	disappointment 실망

해석 한 눈에 보기 **1** 우리의 연장자 중 가장 현명한 분은 무슨 일이 생길지라도, 문제점들에도 불구하고 사는 것에 내재된 즐거움을 절대 (A) 잃어버리지 않으면서 어려움이 생길 때 그것들에 적응하며 받아들일 줄을 안다. **2** 나는 이런 인생관을 "그럼에도 불구하고 행복해"라고 부르고 싶다. **3** 이것은 다수에 의해 소유되는 관점과 (B) 대조되는데, 그것을 나는 "그렇게 되기만 하면 행복해"라고 부르겠다. **4** 일반적으로 젊은이들의 인생관은 "내가 ~하기만 하면 나는 행복할 텐데"라고 말한다. **5** 그 진술은 수많은 방법으로 완성될 수 있는데, 내가 살이 빠지면, 짝을 찾으면, 건강해지면, 부자가 되면 등등이 있다. **6** 연구원들은 그러한 "그렇게 되기만 하면 행복해" 태도는 오직 (C) 실망만을 초래할 것이라고 믿는다.

정답단추 네모 안 어휘를 포함한 문장 앞뒤의 문맥이 자연스럽게 이어지는 어휘를 골라야 해. (A)가 있는 문장 다음을 보면 어려움에 적응하고 받아들이는 인생관을 '그럼에도 불구하고 행복해'라고 표현한다고 했으니 내재된 기쁨을 '잃어버리지' 않는다는 내용이 적절해. 따라서 (A)에는 losing이 들어가야 해. 그리고 이어지는 내용에서 '그렇게 되기만 하면 행복해' 태도와는 '대조되는' 태도니까 (B)에 들어갈 말은 contrast가 적절해. comply는 '응하다, 따르다'라는 뜻이야. 마지막으로 젊은이들의 '그렇게 되기만 하면 행복해' 인생관은 결국 '실망'에 이르게만 할 것이라는 내용이 자연스러우므로 (C)에는 disappointment가 들어가야 해. contentment는 '만족'이라는 뜻이야.

지문 Flow

[진술]
현명한 연장자는 문제점이 있어도 삶의 즐거움을 잃지 않고, 어려움에 적응함

⬇

[보충설명]
'그럼에도 불구하고 행복해'라는 인생관

⬇

[대조]
젊은이들은 '~하면 행복할 텐데'라는 조건이 있는 행복을 말함

⬇

[보충설명]
'그렇게 되기만 하면 행복해'는 실망을 초래하는 인생관

203 정답 ③

지문 All in One

[1] Many fruits and vegetables(S, 많은 과일과 채소는) experience(V, 경험한다) / rapid ① losses(급격한 손실을) / in their nutritional value(그들의 영양가의) / when(접속사) (they(S') are) stored(V') in a refrigerator(냉장고에 저장될 때) / for several days(며칠 동안). [2] This(S) occurs(V) partly(이것은 부분적으로 발생한다) // because(접속사) the produce(S') has already spent(V') a few days(그 농산물이 이미 며칠을 보냈기 때문에) / in transport [and] on store shelves(운송 과정과 상점 진열대에서) / ② before(접속사) you(S") buy(V") it(당신이 그것을 사기 전에). [3] Try(V) the two following options(다음의 두 가지 선택 사항을 시도해 보라). [4] One(하나는), / look for(V) locally grown fresh produce(현지에서 재배된 신선한 농산물을 찾아라) // — it(S) has usually traveled(V_1) ③ longer(→ shorter) distances(그것은 대체로 더 먼(→ 더 짧은) 거리를 이동해 왔고) / [and] thus still has(V_2) most of its nutritional value(이리하여 영양소 대부분을 여전히 갖고 있다). [5] The second option(S) is(V) to use frozen produce(C)(두 번째 선택 사항은 냉동 농산물을 이용하는 것이다). [6] While(접속사) frozen fruits and vegetables(S') may seem(V') / to ④ lack the flavor and appeal of fresh produce(냉동 과일과 채소가 신선한 농산물의 맛과 매력이 부족한 것 같아 보일지도 모르겠지만), // they(S_1) are treated(V_1) immediately with flash freezing(그것들은 순간 냉동으로 즉시 처리되는데) / after being picked(수확된 후, 분사구문(= after they are picked)), / [and] this(S_2) can ⑤ slow down(V_2)(이것은 속도를 늦출 수 있다) / the loss of vitamins and nutrients(비타민과 영양분의 손실의).

해석 한 눈에 보기 **1** 많은 과일과 채소는 냉장고에 며칠 동안 저장될 때 영양소의 급격한 ① 손실을 경험한다. **2** 이것은 그 농산물이 당신이 그것을 사기 ② 전에 이미 며칠을 운송 과정과 상점 진열대에서 보냈기 때문에 부분적으로 발생한다. **3** 다음의 두 가지 선택 사항을 시도해 보라. **4** 하나는, 현지에서 재배된 신선한 농산물을 찾아라. 그것은 대체로 ③ 더 먼(→ 더 짧은) 거리를 이동해 왔고 이리하여 영양소 대부분을 여전히 갖고 있다. **5** 두 번째 선택 사항은 냉동 농산물을 이용하는 것이다. **6** 냉동 과일과 채소가 신선한 농산물의 맛과 매력이 ④ 부족한 것 같아 보일지도 모르겠지만, 그것들은 수확된 후 순간 냉동으로 즉시 처리되는데, 이것은 비타민과 영양분의 손실의 ⑤ 속도를 늦출 수 있다.

정답단추 문장에 쓰인 단어의 쓰임이 적절한지를 알기 위해서는 지문의 전반적인 내용을 정확히 이해해야 해. 이 글은 과일과 채소를 냉장고에 오래 보관하면 영양소 손실이 있으므로 현지에서 재배된 농산물을 먹으면 운송 거리가 '더 짧아져' 영양소의 손실 속도를 늦출 수 있다는 내용이야. 즉, ③의 longer는 shorter로 바꾸어야 적절해.

오답단서 과일과 채소를 냉장고에 오래 보관하면 영양소가 '손실'되므로 ①의 losses는 맞는 표현이야. 또한, 운송되고 진열되는 것은 소비자가 사기 '전'이므로 ②의 before도 옳아. 두 번째 선택 사항은 냉동 농산물에 관한 내용으로 냉동 농산물은 신선한 농산물의 맛과 매력이 '부족한(lack)' 것처럼 보이지만 냉동은 영양소 손실을 '늦추어 준다(slow down)'고 하고 있어. 따라서 문맥상 ④, ⑤의 쓰임은 자연스러워.

어휘확인

rapid 급격한, 빠른 **loss** 손실, 분실 **nutritional value** 영양가 **store** 저장하다; 상점 **refrigerator** 냉장고 **several** (몇)몇의 **occur** 발생하다 **partly** 부분적으로 **produce** 농산물[농작물] **transport** 운송, 수송 **shelf** 진열대, 선반 **option** 선택 사항 **look for** 찾다, 구하다 **locally** 현지[지역]에서 **grown** 재배된; 성장한 **distance** 거리 **thus** 이렇게 하여 **frozen** (식품이) 냉동된 **lack** 부족하다 **flavor** 맛, 풍미 **appeal** 매력 **treat** 처리하다 **immediately** 즉시, 즉각 **flash freezing** 순간 냉동, 급속 냉동 **pick** 수확하다; 고르다 **slow down** (속도·진행을) 늦추다 **vitamin** 비타민 **nutrient** 영양분, 영양소

지문 Flow

[문제제기]
채소와 과일이 냉장고에 오래 보관되면 영양소가 손실됨

⬇

[해결책]
• 현지의 농산물 찾기
• 냉동 농산물 이용하기

⬇

[보충설명]
더 짧은 거리 이동과 수확 후 즉시 냉동으로 인해 영양분 손실의 속도를 늦춤

204 정답 ②

지문 All in One

만일 당신이 아는 것이 많게 들리기 원한다면 / 당신은 차이를 배워야 한다

1 If you want to sound knowledgeable, // you must learn the difference / [between] visual

접속사 S′ V′ / S V

시각 효과와 특수 효과 간의 / 특수 효과는 만들어진다 / 세트장에서 / 폭풍우처럼 보이게 만드는 데

effects [and] special effects. 2 *Special effects* are created / on the set. 3 *The wind, lightning,*

S V S

사용되는 바람과 번개와 비 기계는 / 특수 효과 팀의 도구이다

[and] rain machines [that are used to (A) simulate a storm] / are tools of the special effects

관계대명사 V C

'시각 효과'는 만들어진다 / 세트장 밖에서 / 그리고 그 다음에 더해진다 / 촬영 후 편집 작업 시에

team. 4 *Visual effects* are created / off the set // [and] then (are) added / in post-production.

V_1 V_2

시각 효과 종사자들은 얘기하면서 많은 시간을 보낸다 / 블루 스크린에 대해 / 영화사가 슈퍼맨이 날아가는

5 Visual effects people spend a lot of time talking / about blue screens. 6 When the studio (B)

S V 접속사 S′

것을 보여주고 싶을 때 / 그들은 배우를 들어 올릴 것이다 / 말 그대로 파란색인 스크린 앞에

wants to show Superman flying, // they'll lift the actor / in front of *a screen* [that is literally

V′ S V_1 관계대명사

그리고 그 다음 그들이 찍는 것을 겹쳐 놓을 것이다 / 다른 배경에서 / 기상

blue], / [and] then superimpose [what they shoot] / against another background. 7 Weather

V_2 관계대명사 S

캐스터들은 같은 기술을 사용한다 / 당신에게 보여주고자 / 기상도를 가로질러 이동하는 구름 모양을

reporters use the same technique / to show you / *the cloud patterns* [(C) moving across the

V 부사적 용법(목적)

그것은 예술적 감성을 결합하는 기술이다 / 훌륭한 기술적 전문

weather map]. 8 It's *a technique* [that combines artistic sensibilities / with great technical

S V C 관계대명사

지식 및 혁신과

expertise [and] innovation].

	(A)		(B)		(C)
①	simulate	……	wants	……	moved
②	simulate	……	wants	……	moving
③	simulate	……	will want	……	moving
④	simulating	……	wants	……	moved
⑤	simulating	……	will want	……	moving

해석 한 눈에 보기 1 만일 당신이 아는 것이 많게 들리기 원한다면, 당신은 시각 효과와 특수 효과 간의 차이를 알아두어야 한다. 2 '특수 효과'는 세트장에서 만들어진다. 3 폭풍우처럼 보이게 만드는 데 사용되는 바람과 번개와 비 기계는 특수 효과 팀의 도구이다. 4 '시각 효과'는 세트장 밖에서 만들어진 다음에 촬영 후 편집 작업 시 더해진다. 5 시각 효과 담당자들은 많은 시간을 블루 스크린에 관해 얘기하면서 보낸다. 6 영화사가 슈퍼맨이 날아가는 것을 보여주고 싶을 때, 그들은 말 그대로 파란색인 스크린 앞에서 배우를 들어 올린 다음 그들이 다른 배경에서 찍는 것을 겹쳐놓을 것이다. 7 기상 캐스터들은 이와 같은 기술을 사용하여 당신에게 기상도를 가로질러 이동하는 구름 모양을 보여준다. 8 그것은 예술적 감성을 훌륭한 기술적 전문 지식 및 혁신과 결합하는 기술이다.

정답단추 (A)의 「be used to-v」는 '~하는 데 사용되다'라는 의미로 쓰여. 비슷한 형태의 「be used to v-ing」는 '~하는 데 익숙하다'라는 의미야. 이 문장은 폭풍우처럼 보이게 만드는 데 바람, 번개, 비 기계가 사용된다는 것이므로 simulate가 오는 것이 적절해. (B)의 시간이나 조건 등을 나타내는 부사절은 미래를 현재시제로 대신하기 때문에 wants가 와야 해. (C)는 바로 앞의 수식 받는 명사구 the cloud patterns와 분사의 관계가 능동이므로 현재분사형인 moving을 써야 해.

어휘확인

sound ~처럼 들리다; 소리 knowledgeable 아는 것이 많은 visual effect 시각 효과 special effect 특수 효과 set (연극·영화의) 세트[무대 장치] wind 바람 lightning 번개 simulate ~처럼 보이게 만들어지다 tool 도구 post-production 필름 촬영 후의 편집 people (특정 직종 분야의) 종사자들; 사람들 blue screen 블루 스크린(푸른 배경으로 찍은 장면을 다른 장면에 겹치는 특수 효과) studio 영화사; 스튜디오 screen (영화의) 스크린, 화면 literally 말 그대로 then 그 다음에 superimpose 겹쳐놓다, 덧붙이다 shoot (영화를) 찍다[촬영하다] background 배경 weather reporter 기상캐스터 technique 기술, 기법 cf. technical 기술적인 weather map 기상도, 일기도 combine 결합하다 artistic 예술의 sensibility 감성[감수성] expertise 전문 지식[기술] innovation 혁신

지문 Flow

[도입]
특수 효과와 시각 효과의 차이

⬇

[보충설명1]
특수 효과는 세트장에서 만들어지고, 시각 효과는 세트장 밖에서 만들어진 후에 편집 작업에서 더해짐

&

[보충설명2]
시각 효과에서 블루 스크린 이용이 보편적임

⬇

[예시]
•배우 촬영분과 배경 사진을 겹침
•기상캐스터와 기상도를 겹침

⬇

[결론]
예술과 기술 혁신의 결합

205 정답 ②

지문 All in One

시간대를 통과하여 여행하는 사람들은 / 또는 야간 근무를 하는 / 일반적으로 두 가지 증상이

1 *Individuals* [who travel across time zones / [or] work the night shift] / typically have two

S 관계대명사 V'_1 V'_2 V

있다 / 하나는 불면증이다 / 그들이 잠을 자려고 할 때 / 익숙하지 않은 시간에

symptoms. 2 One is insomnia / when they are trying to sleep / at unfamiliar times, // [and]

S_1 V_1 C_1 접속사 S'_1 V'_1

그리고 다른 하나는 과도한 졸림이다 / 내부 시계가 깨어 있어야 한다고 말하는 시간 동안

the other is excessive sleepiness / during *the time* [when their internal clock says that they

S_2 V_2 C_2 관계부사

모든 야간 근무 근로자들의 절반은 규칙적으로 보고한다 / 깜빡 졸고 잠이 든다고

should be (A) awake]. 3 Half of all night shift workers regularly report / (B) nodding off [and]

S V

직장에서 일할 때 / 이것은 보여져야 한다 / 중요한 관심사로

falling asleep // when they are at work. 4 This should be seen / as an important concern /

접속사 S′ V′ S V

어휘확인

individual 개인 time zone 시간대 night shift 야간 근무 typically 일반적으로, 보통 symptom 증상 insomnia 불면증 unfamiliar 익숙지 않은 excessive 과도한 sleepiness 졸림 internal 내부의 shift worker 교대 근무 근로자 regularly 규칙[정기]적으로 nod off 깜빡 졸다 concern 관심사; 우려, 걱정 given that ~ ~을 고려하면 airline 항공사 controller 관제사 physician 내과 의사, 의사 safety 안전(함) employ 고용하다 profession 전문직, 직업 peak 최고조, 절정 function 기능하다, 작용

개인과 사회 둘 다에 / ~을 고려하면 / 항공기 조종사, 항공 교통 관제사,
both for individuals and society, / given that / airline pilots, air traffic controllers,
접속사 S′
내과 의사, 간호사, 경찰 및 기타 공공 안전 근로자가 / 모두 전문직에 고용되는 것을
physicians, nurses, police, and other public safety workers / are all employed in *professions*
V′
야간 근무 동안 최대로 기능하는 것이 중대할지도 모르는
[in which peak functioning during a night shift may be (C) critical].
전치사+관계대명사

	(A)		(B)		(C)
①	awake 깨어 있어	……	nodding off 깜빡 졸고	……	optional 선택적일
②	awake 깨어 있어	……	nodding off 깜빡 졸고	……	critical 중대할
③	asleep 자고 있어	……	nodding off 깜빡 졸고	……	critical 중대할
④	asleep 자고 있어	……	setting off 시작하고	……	critical 중대할
⑤	asleep 자고 있어	……	setting off 시작하고	……	optional 선택적일

해석 한 눈에 보기 주제문 1 시간대를 통과하여 여행하거나 야간 근무를 하는 사람들은 일반적으로 두 가지 증상이 있다. 2 하나는 익숙하지 않은 시간에 잠을 자려고 할 때 나타나는 불면증이고, 다른 하나는 내부 시계가 (A) 깨어 있어야 한다고 말하는 시간 동안의 과도한 졸림이다. 3 모든 야간 근무 근로자들의 절반은 직장에서 일할 때 (B)깜빡 졸고 잠이 든다고 규칙적으로 보고한다. 4 이것은 항공기 조종사, 항공 교통 관제사, 내과 의사, 간호사, 경찰 및 기타 공공 안전 근로자가 모두 야간 근무 동안 최대로 기능하는 것이 (C) 중대할지도 모르는 전문직에 고용되는 것을 고려하면, 개인과 사회 둘 다에 중요한 관심사로 보여져야 한다.

정답단추 글의 전체 내용을 이해한 뒤 적절한 어휘를 골라 앞뒤 문맥과 자연스럽게 이어지는지 확인해 보자. 이 글은 야간 근무를 하는 사람들이 불면증과 졸림이라는 두 가지 증상의 수면 장애를 겪는다는 내용이야. (A)는 두 가지 증상 중 졸림 증상에 대한 내용으로, 내부 생체 시계가 졸릴 때 깨어 있으라는 신호를 보내므로, awake가 적절해. asleep은 반의어로 '자고 있는'이라는 뜻이야. (B)는 야간 근무자들의 절반이 직장에서 깜박 존다고 하는 것이 문맥상 자연스러우므로, '졸다'라는 뜻의 nod를 사용한 nodding off가 적절해. set off는 '시작하다, 개시하다'라는 뜻이야. (C)는 전문직 종사자들은 야간 근무에도 최상의 기능으로 업무를 보는 것이 중요한 상황이므로, critical이 적절해. optional은 '선택적인'이라는 뜻이야.

하다 **critical** 중대한, 중요한
〈선택지 어휘〉
optional 선택적인 **set off** 시작하다, 개시하다; 출발하다

지문 Flow

[주제]
시간대 여행이나 야간 근무를 하는 사람에게 나타나는 증상

[보충설명1]
불면증: 익숙한 시간에 잠을 자지 않아서

&

[보충설명2]
과도한 졸림: 생체 시계가 깨어 있어야 한다고 해서

[결론]
전문직 종사자는 야간 근무 시에도 충실히 업무를 해야 하므로, 조는 것이 문제가 될 수 있음

206 정답 ④

지문 All in One

1 We are ① constantly brainwashed to believe // that more wealth will make us happier. 2 We
(우리는 믿도록 끊임없이 세뇌된다 / 더 많은 부가 우리를 더 행복하게 해줄 것이라고 / 우리는; S V / 접속사 S′ V′ / S)
certainly need ② sufficient money / in the current economic system // and, as the comedian
(분명히 충분한 돈이 필요하다 / 현재의 경제 체제에서 / 그리고 희극 배우; V / 접속사 S′)
Woody Allen observed, / "Money is better than poverty." 3 It is, / however, / ③ sensible / to
(Woody Allen이 말한 것처럼 / '돈은 가난보다 낫다' / ~이다 그러나 현명하다; V′ / S V C / 가주어 V C)
take a step back occasionally. 4 As the economist Adam Smith pointed out, / if we want to
(가끔은 한 걸음 물러서는 게 / 경제학자 Adam Smith가 지적한 것처럼 / 만약 우리가 빠져나; 진주어 / 접속사 S'_1 V'_1 / 접속사 S'_2 V'_2)
escape / from the trap of anxiety and ④ independence(→ dependence) on money, // we must
(오고 싶다면 / 불안의 덫과 돈에 대한 독립(→ 의존)으로부터 / 우리는; S V_1)
look at *ways* [to spend less] / rather than find *ways* [to make more money]. 5 We can never
(덜 쓰는 방법을 살펴야 한다 / 더 많은 돈을 버는 방법을 찾기보다는 / 우리는 절대; 접속사 V_2 / S V)
earn enough / to satisfy our ever-increasing needs. 6 Only through ⑤ frugality can we learn
(충분히 벌 수가 없다 / 계속 증가하는 우리의 욕구를 충족시켜 줄 만큼 / 오직 검소함을 통해서만이 우리는 배울 수 있다; enough+to부정사 / 부사구 조동사 S V)
// how satisfying it is to be free from concern.
(근심으로부터 자유로운 것이 얼마나 만족스러운지; 간접의문문 가주어 진주어)

해석 한 눈에 보기 1 우리는 더 많은 부(富)가 우리를 더 행복하게 해줄 것이라고 믿도록 ① 끊임없이 세뇌된다. 2 우리는 현 경제 체제에서 분명히 ② 충분한 돈이 필요하며, 희극 배우 Woody Allen이 말한 것처럼 "돈은 가난보다 낫다." 3 그러나 가끔은 한 걸음 물러서는 게 ③ 현명하다. 주제문 4 경제학자 Adam Smith가 지적한 것처럼, 만약 우리가 불안의 덫과 돈에 대한 ④ 독립(→ 의존)에서 빠져나오고 싶다면, 우리는 더 많은 돈을 버는 방법을 찾기보다는 덜 쓰는 방법을 살펴야 한다. 5 우리는 결코 계속 증가하는 우리의 욕구를 충족시켜 줄 만큼 충분히 벌 수 없다. 6 오직 ⑤ 검소함을 통해서만이 우리는 근심이 없는 것이 얼마나 만족스러운지 배울 수 있다.

정답단추 밑줄 친 어휘가 앞뒤 문맥과 자연스럽게 이어지는지 살펴보자. ④의 뒤부분에서 돈을 더 많이 버는 방법을 찾기보다는 적게 쓰는 방법을 찾아야 한다고 하고 있어. 따라서 앞의 the trap of anxiety와 대등한 의미가 되어야 하고, 문맥상 돈에 대한 '독립'이 아닌 '의존'에서의 탈출이 되어야 하니까 ④는 independence가 아닌 dependence가 되어야 해. 따라서 쓰임이 적절하지 않은 것은 ④야.

오답단서 ①의 '끊임없이(constantly)' 세뇌된다는 내용과 ②의 '충분한(sufficient)' 돈 모두 문맥상 적절하게 사용되었어. ③은 부의 중요성에 관해 설명한 앞 내용에 이어 however로 시작하여 그러나 가끔은 한 걸음 물러나는 것이 '현명

어휘확인
constantly 끊임없이 **brainwash** 세뇌시키다 **wealth** 부, (많은) 재산 **certainly** 분명히 **sufficient** 충분한 **current** 현재의 **economic** 경제의 **system** 체제, 제도 **comedian** 희극 배우, 코미디언 **observe** (의견을) 말하다; 관찰하다 **poverty** 가난, 빈곤 **sensible** 현명한; 분별 있는 **take a step back** 한 걸음 물러서다 **occasionally** 가끔 **economist** 경제학자 **point out** 지적하다 **escape** 빠져 나오다[벗어나다] **trap** 덫 **anxiety** 불안, 염려 **independence** 독립(↔ **dependence** 의존) **way** 방법; 길 **rather than** ~보다는 **make money** 돈을 벌다 **earn** (돈을) 벌다 **satisfy** 충족시키다, 만족시키다 **ever-increasing** 계속 증가하는 **need** 욕구; 필요 **frugality** 검소 **concern** 근심, 우려

지문 Flow

[도입]
우리는 부가 행복의 척도라고 믿도록 세뇌됨

[주장]
돈에 대한 의존에서 빠져나오고 싶으면, 돈을 더 버는 방법보다 돈을 덜 쓰는 방법을 찾아야 함

하다'는 내용으로 이어지므로 sensible의 쓰임은 자연스러워. 마지막으로 ⑤를 포함한 문장은 앞의 돈을 적게 쓰는 방법을 찾아야 한다는 내용에 이어 마지막 결론을 내는 문장이지? 따라서 '검소함'을 통해서만이 우리는 얼마나 만족스러운지 배울 수 있다는 내용은 글의 흐름과 일치하니까 frugality는 적절해.

[이유]
욕구를 충족할 만큼 돈을 벌 수 없으므로, 검소함으로 만족감을 배워야 함

207 정답 ③

지문 All in One

[1] Television is such a universal part / of our lives // that we seldom give it a second thought. [2] However, / if aliens came to Earth / from outer space / and watched TV for a day, // they would be convinced / that all humans are either very successful and attractive, / or (are) about to die / by violence. [3] Television (A) affects us more / than we know. [4] We worry // that *the horrifying things* [that we see / on television] / will happen / to us. [5] And we feel (B) frustrated // because *the success* [that everyone seems to possess / on television] / hasn't yet come / to us. [6] (C) Separate the illusion / from [what you know is real]. [7] Let reality be your judge.

	(A)		(B)		(C)
①	affects 영향을 미친다	……	frustrated 좌절감을	……	Suspect 의심해라
②	effects 초래한다	……	frustrated 좌절감을	……	Suspect 의심해라
③	affects 영향을 미친다	……	frustrated 좌절감을	……	Separate 구분해라
④	effects 초래한다	……	exhausted 기진맥진함을	……	Separate 구분해라
⑤	affects 영향을 미친다	……	exhausted 기진맥진함을	……	Suspect 의심해라

해석 한 눈에 보기 1 텔레비전은 우리 삶의 너무나 보편적인 부분이라서 우리는 좀처럼 그것에 대해 깊이 생각하지 않는다. 2 하지만 만약 외계인이 외계에서 지구로 와서 하루 동안 TV를 본다면, 그들은 모든 인간이 굉장히 성공해서 매력적이거나, 폭력에 의해 죽음이 임박해 있다고 확신할 것이다. 3 텔레비전은 우리가 아는 것보다 더 많이 우리에게 (A) 영향을 미친다. 4 우리는 우리가 텔레비전에서 보는 무서운 일들이 우리에게 일어날까 봐 걱정한다. 5 그리고 우리는 (B) 좌절감을 느끼는데 텔레비전에서 모든 사람이 소유하고 있는 것으로 보이는 성공이 아직 우리에게 오지 않았기 때문이다. 6 당신이 알기에 현실인 것과 환상을 (C) 구분해라. 7 현실이 당신의 판사이도록 하라.

정답단추 우선 글의 전반적인 흐름을 아는 것이 중요해. 그리고 해당 문장 앞뒤 문맥을 살펴 가장 자연스럽게 연결되는 어휘를 골라야 해. (A)의 뒤에서 우리가 텔레비전을 보며 걱정과 좌절감을 느끼게 된다고 했으므로 텔레비전이 우리에게 '영향을 미친다'는 내용이 와야 해. 따라서 (A)에는 affects가 적절해. effect는 '(결과를) 초래하다'라는 뜻이야. (B)를 포함한 문장에서 텔레비전에서 모든 사람이 소유하고 있는 것으로 보이는 성공이 우리에게는 멀게 느껴진다고 하고 있어. 이에 대해서 '좌절감을' 느낀다고 해야 자연스러우므로 frustrated가 적절해. exhausted는 '기진맥진한'이라는 뜻이야. 마지막으로 (C)는 환상과 현실을 '구분하라'는 표현이 의미상 자연스러우니까 Separate가 들어가야 해. 또한, separate A from B의 어구를 통해서도 정답의 단서를 얻을 수 있어. 이처럼 하나의 어구와 같이 쓰이는 표현을 알아두면 문제 푸는 시간을 절약할 수 있어. suspect는 '(~일 것으로) 의심하다'라는 뜻이야.

어휘확인

universal 보편적인 seldom 좀처럼 ~ 않는 give a thought ~을 생각하다 alien 외계인 outer space 우주 공간 convince 확신시키다 successful 성공한 cf. success 성공 attractive 매력적인 be about to-v 막 ~하려는 참이다 die 죽다 violence 폭력 affect ~에 영향을 미치다[주다] horrifying 무서운, 소름 끼치는 frustrated 좌절한, 실망한 possess 소유하다 separate 구분하다 illusion 환상 reality 현실

〈선택지 어휘〉

suspect 의심하다 effect (결과를) 초래하다, 가져 오다 exhausted 기진맥진한

지문 Flow

[도입]
텔레비전은 우리 삶의 보편적인 부분이라서 우리가 이를 깊이 생각하지 않음

⬇

[보충설명]
텔레비전에 나오는 것은 성공한 사람들과 폭력적인 내용뿐임

⬇

[문제 제기]
텔레비전은 우리에게 많은 영향을 미침 (걱정, 좌절감)

⬇

[주장]
현실과 환상을 구분하라

208 정답 ①

지문 All in One

[1] Various forms of writing have existed / for thousands of years, // and nowadays, / being able to read and write / is an essential skill. [2] However, / there was *a time* [(A) when writing was very hard to do], // because pens did not exist. [3] *Bird feathers*, / [called quills], / were used to (B) write / until the invention of the pen / in the 18th century. [4] The new pen had *a*

어휘확인

various 다양한 form 형태, 종류 writing 글; 쓰기 exist 존재하다 nowadays 요즘에는 essential 필수적인 time (특정한 일이 일어나는) 때 feather 깃털, (새의)털 quill 깃펜 invention 발명 cf. invent 발명하다 century 세기 metal 금속 point (사물의 뾰족한) 끝 nib 펜촉 repeatedly 반복적으로 dip (액체에) 살짝 담그다 ink 잉크 fountain pen 만년필 refillable 다시 채울 수 있는, 리필이 가능한 supply 공급(통)

끝을 가지고 있었는데 펜촉이라고 불리는 그것은 반복적으로 잉크에 담가졌다 글을 쓰는 동안
metal point, / [called a nib], // [which was repeatedly dipped in ink / while writing]. [5] The
관계대명사 S

만년필은 발명되었다 19세기에 그것은 다시 채울 수 있는 잉크 공급통과 강철 펜촉을 가지고
fountain pen was invented / in the 19th century. [6] It had a refillable ink supply and a steel
V S V

있었다 글을 쓰는 사람들이 글쓰기를 멈춰야 했던 시절은 가버렸다 몇 글자마다 그리고 펜을 잉크에
nib. [7] Gone were *the days* [when writers had to stop writing / every few words / and (C) dip
C V S 관계부사 V'_1 V'_2

담가야 했던
their pens in ink].

	(A)		(B)		(C)
①	when	……	write	……	dip
②	when	……	writing	……	dip
③	when	……	write	……	dipping
④	which	……	writing	……	dip
⑤	which	……	write	……	dipping

해석 한 눈에 보기 1 다양한 형태의 글은 수천 년간 존재해 왔고, 오늘날 읽고 쓸 수 있는 것은 필수적인 기술이다. 2 하지만 쓰는 것이 매우 어려운 때가 있었는데, 펜이 존재하지 않았기 때문이다. 3 깃펜(quill)이라고 불리는 새의 깃털이 18세기에 펜이 발명될 때까지 글을 쓰는 데 사용되었다. 4 새로운 펜은 펜촉(nib)이라고 불리는 금속(의 뾰족한) 끝을 가지고 있었는데, 그것은 글을 쓰는 동안 반복적으로 잉크에 담가졌다. 5 만년필은 19세기에 발명되었다. 6 그것은 다시 채울 수 있는 잉크 공급통과 강철 펜촉이 달려 있었다. 7 글을 쓰는 사람들이 몇 글자마다 글쓰기를 멈추고 펜을 잉크에 담가야 했던 시절은 가버렸다.

정답단추 (A) 이후의 절이 「S+V+C」를 갖춘 완전한 문장이며 선행사가 a time이므로 때를 나타내는 관계부사 when이 와야 적절해. 관계부사는 「전치사+관계대명사」로 바꿔 쓸 수도 있으니까 when을 at which로 바꿔 쓸 수도 있어. (B)의 「be used to-v」는 '~하는 데 사용되다'라는 의미로 사용되지만, 「be used to v-ing」는 '~하는 데 익숙하다'라는 뜻으로 쓰여. 형태가 비슷하여 헷갈릴 수 있으니 주의하자. 이 글에서는 문맥상 글을 '쓰는 데 사용되었다'는 의미가 되어야 자연스러우니까 write가 와야 해. (C)는 병렬구조를 묻는 질문이야. when 이하의 관계부사절이 the days를 수식하고 있어. 관계부사절 내의 주어는 writers이고 동사는 had to stop이야. 그리고 had to에 dip 이하가 접속사 and로 병렬로 연결된 구조여야 글의 내용이 자연스러우므로 dip이 적절해.

steel 강철 **days** (특정한 때나 역사적인) 시절[시대], 시기

지문 Flow

[도입]
읽고 쓰는 것은 필수적인 기술이지만, 과거에는 펜이 없어서 쓰는 것이 어려웠음

⬇

[18세기]
깃펜 이후에 펜촉이 있는 새로운 펜이 발명됨

⬇

[19세기]
만년필이 발명됨

⬇

[추가]
펜을 잉크에 담그며 글쓰기를 했던 시절은 사라짐

209 정답 ②

지문 All in One

1830년에 처음 세워진 도심지에 이탈리아의 비아 포르탈바 18번지의
[1] (Having been) First ① established in 1830 / in the town center / at Via Port'Alba 18, Italy, /
분사구문(= Antica Pizzeria Port'Alba was first established ~)

안티카 피체리아 포르탈바는 널리 알려져 있다 세계 최초의 피자 전문점으로 이 식당은 대체했다
Antica Pizzeria Port'Alba is widely believed / to be the world's first pizzeria. [2] The restaurant
S V S

피자를 만들던 행상들을 그리고 그것을 거리로 가져오던
replaced / *street vendors* [who would make pizza / and (would) bring it onto the street, /
V 관계대명사 V'_1 V'_2 = pizza

따뜻하게 하여 작은 양철 난로에 그것은 곧 잘 알려진 만남의 장소가 되었다
keeping it ② warmly(→ warm) / in small tin stoves]. [3] It soon became a well-known meeting
분사구문 S V C

그 거리에 살고 있는 남성들에게 대부분의 단골손님은 돈이 거의 없었다 그래서 만들어진 피자는
place / for men living on the street. [4] Most patrons had little money, // so *the pizzas* [made] /
S_1 V_1 S_2

대체로 단순했다 지불 시스템이 개발되었다 고객들에게 지불하는 것을 허용하는
③ were usually simple. [5] *A payment system* was developed / [that allowed customers to pay
V_2 C S V 관계대명사

최대 8일 까지 식사 후 그래서 생긴 이 지역의 농담 하나는 ~이었다 포르탈바의 피자는
/ up to eight days / after their meal]. [6] A resulting local joke was // that a pizza from Port'Alba
S V 접속사 가정법 과거 S'

그 사람의 마지막 공짜 식사가 될지도 모른다는 것 만일 어떤 사람이 죽으면 돈을 지불하기 전에 어떤 단골손님은 시를 창작했다
/ might be someone's last free meal / if they ④ died / before they paid. [7] Some patrons created
V' C' 접속사 S'' V'' S V

피자를 기리기 위해
poetry / ⑤ to honor the pizzas.
부사적 용법(목적)

해석 한 눈에 보기 1 1830년에 이탈리아의 비아 포르탈바 18번지의 도심에 처음 세워진, 안티카 피체리아 포르탈바(포르탈바의 오래된 피자 전문점)는 세계 최초의 피자 전문점으로 널리 알려져 있다. 2 이 식당은 피자를 만들어 그것을 거리로 가져와 작은 양철 난로에 따뜻하게 했던 거리의 행상인들을 대체했다. 3 그것은 곧 그 거리에 사는 남성들에게 잘 알려진 만남의 장소가 되었다. 4 대부분의 단골손님은 돈이 거의 없어서, 만들어진 피자는 대체로 단순했다. 5 고객들에게 식사 후 최대 8일 까지 지불하는 것을 허용하는 지불 시스템이 개발되었다. 6 그래서 생긴 이 지역의 농담 하나가 포르탈바의 피자는 만일 어떤 사람이 돈을 지불하기 전에 죽으면 그 사람의 마지막 공짜 식사가 될지도 모른다는 것이었다. 7 어떤 단골손님들은 피자를 기리기 위해 시를 창작했다.

어휘확인

establish 세우다, 설립하다 **town center** 도심지, 번화가 **pizzeria** 피자 전문점 **widely** 널리 **replace** 대체하다 **vendor** 행상인, 노점상 **tin** 양철 **stove** 난로, 스토브 **well-known** 잘 알려진, 유명한 **meeting place** 만남의 장소, 집회소 **patron** 단골손님, 고객(= **customer**) **payment** 지불 **develop** 개발하다 **allow** 허용하다 **up to** ~까지 **local** (특정) 지역의 **die** 죽다 **poetry** 시 **honor** 기리다, 찬미하다

지문 Flow

[도입]
1830년 이탈리아에 세워진 세계 최초의 피자 전문점, 안티카 피체리아 포르탈바

⬇

[보충설명1]
거리에서 피자를 팔던 행상인들을 대체했고, 만남의 장소가 됨

&

[보충설명2]
고객들이 식사 후 최대 8일 후에 지불하는 시스템을 적용함

&

정답단추 어법 유형은 다른 유형과는 달리 선택지가 포함된 문장만을 읽고 문제를 풀 수 있는 경우가 많아. 시간을 좀 더 절약하기 위해서는 밑줄 친 부분에서 묻고 있는 문법사항을 정확히 파악하는 것이 중요해. ②를 포함한 문장에 쓰인 구문은 「keep+목적어+목적격 보어(형용사)」로 '~을 …하게 유지하다'라는 의미야. 목적격 보어는 흔히 우리말로 부사처럼 해석하지만 보어로는 명사와 형용사만 가능해. 따라서 warmly가 아닌 warm이 되어야 하므로 어법상 틀린 것은 ②야.
오답단서 ①의 First established ~ Italy는 앞에 Having been이 생략된 분사구문으로, 주절의 주어인 Antica Pizzeria Port'Alba의 부연 설명이야. 주어가 설립하는 것이 아니라 '설립되는' 것이 맞으므로 수동형인 established는 어법상 옳아. ③은 앞의 the pizzas를 주어로 하므로 were가 와야 해. 앞의 made는 the pizzas를 뒤에서 수식하는 과거분사야. ④가 있는 문장은 「If+주어+동사의 과거형 ~, 주어+조동사의 과거형+동사원형」 형태의 가정법 과거 구문으로 현재나 미래에 있을 법하지 않은 내용을 가정 혹은 상상할 때 사용하며 '만일 ~라면 …일 것이다'라는 뜻이야. 이를 바탕으로 보면 if절의 과거형 동사 died는 어법상 적절해. ⑤의 to honor 이하는 술부인 created poetry의 목적을 나타내는 부사 기능의 to부정사구로 사용되어서 문맥 및 어법상 자연스러워.

[보충설명3]
공짜 피자로 인식되어서, 우스갯소리가 만들어지거나 피자를 기리는 시가 창작됨

210 정답 ③

지문 All in One

만일 당신이 운전을 한다면 (~이) 현명하다 당신의 차에 대해 조금 더 많이 배워 두는 것 단순히 그것을 주차하는 법보다
1 If you drive, // it's wise / to learn a bit more about your car / than simply how to park it. 2 In
접속사 S′ V′ 가주어V C 진주어

사실 많은 기초적인 정비와 많은 긴급 수리는 실제로 상당히 단순하다
fact, / a lot of basic maintenance [and] many emergency repairs / are actually quite simple.
S V C

예를 들어 (~은) 어렵지 않다 바람 빠진 타이어를 교체하는 방법을 배워두는 것 당신의 사용 설명서가
3 For example, / it's not hard / to learn how to change a flat tire. 4 Your instruction manual /
가주어 V C 진주어 S

자동차 안에 있는 당신에게 말해 줄 것이다 정확히 어떻게 해야 하는지를 명심하라 당신이 적절한 도구를 갖추어 두는 것을
in your car / will tell you / exactly what to do. 5 Make sure // (that) you have the (A) *proper*
V IO DO V 접속사 S′ V′

렌치 같은 나사들을 풀 수 있는 매우 중요하다 나사를 푸는 것은
tool, / such as a wrench, / [to loosen the nuts]. 6 It is very important / to loosen the nuts /
가주어V C 진주어

잭을 사용하기 전에 자동차를 땅에서 들어올리기 위해 펑크 난 타이어가 땅에서 떨어지면
before using the jack / to (B) raise the car off the ground. 7 When the flat tire is off the
부사적 용법(목적) 접속사 S′ V′

나사들을 완전히 제거해라 그리고 그것을 대체하라 예비 타이어로 당신은
ground, // remove the nuts completely / [and] replace it / with your spare tire. 8 You must
V_1 V_2 S V

이 타이어를 단단히 부착시켜야 한다.
attach this tire (C) tightly.

	(A)		(B)		(C)
①	proper 적절한	……	rise 오르기	……	tightly 단단히
②	proper 적절한	……	raise 들어올리기	……	strictly 엄격하게
③	proper 적절한	……	raise 들어올리기	……	tightly 단단히
④	prompt 즉각적인	……	rise 오르기	……	strictly 엄격하게
⑤	prompt 즉각적인	……	raise 들어올리기	……	tightly 단단히

해석 한 눈에 보기 주제문 1 만일 당신이 운전을 한다면, 단순히 주차하는 법보다 당신의 차에 대해 조금 더 많이 배워두는 것이 현명하다. 2 사실 많은 기초적 정비와 많은 긴급 수리는 실제로 상당히 단순하다. 3 예를 들어, 펑크 난 타이어를 교체하는 방법을 배워 두는 것은 어렵지 않다. 4 당신의 자동차 안에 있는 사용 설명서가 정확히 어떻게 해야 하는지 당신에게 말해 줄 것이다. 5 나사들을 풀 수 있는 렌치 같은 (A) 적절한 도구를 갖추어 두는 것을 명심하라. 6 자동차를 땅에서 (B) 들어올리기 위해 잭을 사용하기 전에 나사를 푸는 것은 매우 중요하다. 7 펑크 난 타이어가 땅에서 떨어지면, 나사들을 완전히 제거하고 그것을 예비 타이어로 대체해라. 8 당신은 이 타이어를 (C) 단단히 부착시켜야 한다.
정답단추 (A)는 나사들을 풀 수 있는 렌치 같은 '적절한' 도구를 준비하라는 말이 문맥상 자연스러우므로 proper가 적절해. prompt는 '즉각적인'이라는 뜻이야. (B)의 rise는 '오르다'라는 뜻의 자동사로 목적어를 취할 수 없고, raise는 '들어올리다'라는 뜻의 타동사로 목적어를 취할 수 있어. 여기서는 the car라는 목적어를 취할 수 있는 타동사가 필요하니까 raise가 들어가야 해. 마지막으로 (C)에서는 타이어를 '엄격하게(strictly)' 부착시킨다는 말보다는 '단단히' 부착시킨다는 의미가 자연스러우니까 tightly가 와야 해.

어휘확인

a bit 조금 **simply** 단순히, 그저 **park** 주차하다 **in fact** 사실 **basic** 기초[기본]적인 **maintenance** 정비; 유지 **emergency** 긴급, 비상 **repair** 수리, 보수 **flat tire** 바람 빠진 타이어 **instruction manual** 사용 설명서 **exactly** 정확히 **make sure** ~을 명심하다, ~을 확실히 하다 **proper** 적절한 **tool** 도구, 연장 **wrench** 렌치[스패너] **loosen** 풀다 **nut** 나사, 너트 **jack** 잭(자동차 타이어를 갈 때처럼 무거운 것을 들어올릴 때 쓰는 기구) **completely** 완전히 **replace** 대체[대신]하다 **spare** 예비용의; (자동차 타이어) 스페어 **tire** (차바퀴의) 타이어 **attach** 부착하다, 붙이다 **tightly** 단단히
<선택지 어휘>
rise 오르다 **strictly** 엄격히 **prompt** 즉각적인, 신속한

지문 Flow

[주제문]
차에 관련된 것, 즉 기초 정비와 긴급 수리 등을 배워 두는 것이 현명함

[예시]
펑크 난 타이어 교체는 사용 설명서대로 하면 됨

[보충설명1]
자동차를 들어올리기 위해 잭을 사용하기 전에 나사를 풀어줌

&

[보충설명2]
펑크 난 타이어가 땅에서 떨어지면, 나사를 완전히 빼고 예비 타이어로 교체함

211 정답 ①

지문 All in One

(~라고들) 한다 8시간의 수면보다 더 적게 자는 것은 수행 능력에 심각하게 영향을 미칠 수 있다고
1 It's said // that getting fewer than eight hours of sleep / can seriously impact performance.
가주어 V S′ V′ 진주어

어휘확인

seriously 심각하게 **impact** 영향을 주다 **recent** 최근의 **research** 연구(= **study**)

그러나 최근의 연구는 이러한 주장을 전적으로 지지하지 않는다 연구들은 발견해 왔다
[2] However, / recent research does not entirely (A) support this claim. [3] Studies have found //
S V S V
만일 8시간씩 자는 사람이 제한되면 6시간 미만의 수면으로 일주일 동안 그들의
that if eight-hour sleepers are restricted / to less than six hours of sleep / for a week, / their
접속사 접속사 S″ V″ S′
수행 능력이 떨어진다는 것을 하지만 이러한 연구들 대부분은 참여시켜왔다 젊은 8시간 수면자들을
performance drops. [4] However, / most of these studies have involved / young, eight-hour
V′ S V
추가적인 연구는 보여줘 왔다 더 어리고 더 많이 자는 사람들이 더 민감하다는 것을
sleepers. [5] Further research has shown // that younger and longer sleepers are more (B)
S V 접속사 S′ V′ C′
수면 손실의 영향에 나이가 더 든 사람들을 참여시키는 몇 안 되는 연구 중 하나는 발견했다
sensitive / to the effects of sleep loss. [6] One of *the few studies* [involving older people] / found
S V
수면 손실 후의 그들의 수행 능력이 크게 변하지 않았다는 것을 그들은 대표하기 때문에
// that their performance after sleep loss / was not significantly altered. [7] Since they represent
접속사 S′ V′ 접속사 S′ V′
수면이 부족한 인구의 큰 집단을 이러한 발견은 나타낸다
/ a large group of the sleep-deprived population, // these findings indicate / that our
S V 접속사 S″
실생활에서의 수면 손실에 대한 우리의 이해가 결코 완전하지 않다는 것을
understanding of real-world sleep loss / is far from (C) complete.
V″

	(A)		(B)		(C)
①	support 지지하는	……	sensitive 민감하다는	……	complete 완전하지
②	support 지지하는	……	sensory 감각적이라는	……	incomplete 불완전하지
③	support 지지하는	……	sensitive 민감하다는	……	incomplete 불완전하지
④	deny 부정하는	……	sensory 감각적이라는	……	complete 완전하지
⑤	deny 부정하는	……	sensitive 민감하다는	……	complete 완전하지

해석 한 눈에 보기 1 8시간의 수면보다 더 적게 자는 것은 수행 능력에 심각하게 영향을 미칠 수 있다고들 한다. 2 그러나 최근의 연구는 이러한 주장을 전적으로 (A) 지지하는 것은 아니다. 3 연구들은 만일 8시간씩 자는 사람이 일주일 동안 6시간 미만의 수면으로 제한되면 그들의 수행 능력이 떨어진다는 것을 발견해 왔다. 4 하지만 이러한 연구들 대부분은 젊은 8시간 수면자들을 참여시켜 왔다. 5 추가적인 연구는 더 어리고 더 많이 자는 사람들이 수면 손실의 영향에 더 (B) 민감하다는 것을 보여줘 왔다. 6 나이가 더 든 사람들을 참여시키는 몇 안 되는 연구 중 하나는 수면 손실 후의 그들의 수행 능력이 크게 변하지 않았다는 것을 발견했다. 7 그들은 수면이 부족한 인구의 큰 집단을 대표하기 때문에, 이러한 발견은 실생활에서의 수면 손실에 대한 우리의 이해가 결코 (C) 완전하지 않다는 것을 나타낸다.

정답단추 해당 문장의 앞뒤 문맥을 보고 어휘의 쓰임이 자연스러운지 파악해야 해. (A)의 문장은 However로 시작해 앞선 문장의 전적으로 '지지하는' 것은 아니라는 내용이 이어져야 자연스러우므로 support가 적절해. deny는 '부정하다'라는 뜻이야. (B)에서는 젊은이들이 수면 손실의 영향을 더 많이 받는다는 내용으로 그 영향에 '민감하다'고 하는 것이 문맥상 적절하므로 sensitive가 와야 해. sensory는 '감각적인'이라는 뜻이야. (C)를 보면 이 글에서 수면 손실의 영향이 나이에 따라 차이가 있다는 내용으로 단순히 수면 손실이 악영향을 끼칠 것이라는 우리의 이해는 '완전하지' 않다고 볼 수 있지? 따라서 complete가 들어가야 해. incomplete는 complete의 반의어로 '불완전한'이라는 뜻이야.

entirely 전적으로 **support** 지지하다 **claim** 주장 **sleeper** 잠을 자는 사람 **restrict** 제한하다 **involve** 참여시키다; 수반하다 **further** 추가의, 더 이상의 **sensitive** 민감한 **loss** 손실 **significantly** 크게, 상당히 **alter** 변하다 **represent** 대표하다 **sleep-deprived** 수면이 부족한 **population** 인구 **indicate** 나타내다 **understanding** 이해 **real-world** 실생활의, 현실 세계의 **far from** 결코[전혀] ~이 아닌 **complete** 완전한

〈선택지 어휘〉
sensory 감각적인, 감각의 **incomplete** 불완전한, 미완성의 **deny** 부정[부인]하다

지문 Flow

[통념]
8시간 미만의 수면이 수행 능력에 나쁜 영향을 줌

⬇

[연구1]
8시간 자는 사람들을 대상으로 6시간 미만의 수면 제한을 했을 때 수행 능력이 저하됨

&

[연구2]
• 어리고 더 많이 자는 사람들이 수면 손실의 영향에 더 민감함
• 나이가 많은 사람들은 수면 손실 후에 수행 능력에 크게 변화가 없음

⬇

[결과]
수면 손실에 대한 우리의 이해가 완전하지 않음

212 정답 ③

지문 All in One

우리의 어머니들은 우리를 위해 너무나 많은 일을 해주셔서 우리의 인생 내내 당연할 뿐이다 우리가
[1] Our mothers do [so] much for us / throughout our lives // [that] it is only natural / (that) we
S V 접속사 S′ V′ C′ 접속사 S″
그분들에게 고마워하고 싶어 해야 한다는 것은 미국에서는 어머니의 날이 기념된다 5월의 둘째 주 일요일에
should want to thank them. [2] In America, / Mothers' Day is celebrated / on the second
V″ S V
우리의 어머니들에게 공식적으로 감사를 표하는 날이다 그리고 그들을 알게 해드리는 우리의
Sunday of May. [3] It is *a day* [to acknowledge our mothers], / [and] [(to) let them (A) know / our
S V C
사랑과 존경을 그분들에 대한 학교에 있는 아이들은 장려된다 특별한 카드와 선물을 만들도록
love and respect / for them]. [4] Children at school are encouraged / to make special cards and
S V
상점들은 어머니의 날 카드들로 가득 차 있다 웃긴 메시지가 담긴 것들에서부터 감동적인 시가 담긴 것들까지
gifts. [5] Stores fill with Mothers' Day cards, / [from] those with funny messages [to] those with
S V = cards = cards
많은 가정은 그들의 어머니에게 대접한다 특별한 여행과 레스토랑 음식을
(B) touching poems. [6] Many families treat their mothers / to special outings and restaurant
S V
어머니의 날은 분명히 중요하다 하지만 우리는 또한 잊지 말아야 한다 가장 중요한
meals. [7] Mothers' Day is clearly important. [8] But we also should not forget // (C) what the
S V C S V 간접의문문
선물이 무엇인지 그것은 우리의 사랑을 보여주는 것이다 매일
greatest gift is. [9] That is showing our love / every day.
S V C

어휘확인

throughout 내내 **natural** 당연한, 정상적인 **Mothers' day** 어머니의 날 **acknowledge** (공식적으로) 감사를 표하다 **respect** 존경 **encourage** 장려[권장]하다 **touching** 감동적인 **treat** 대접하다; 다루다 **outing** 여행 **clearly** 분명히 **great** 중요한; 큰

지문 Flow

[도입]
어머니에게 감사의 마음을 갖는 것은 당연한 일임

⬇

[예시]
미국에서 5월 둘째 주 일요일은 어머니의 날

⬇

	(A)		(B)		(C)
①	know	……	touched	……	what
②	to know	……	touched	……	that
③	know	……	touching	……	what
④	to know	……	touching	……	what
⑤	to know	……	touching	……	that

[보충설명]
감사와 사랑, 존경을 표하는 날이며, 특별한 카드와 선물을 마련하거나 특별한 여행이나 음식을 대접함

⬇

[주장]
잊지 말아야 할 가장 중요한 선물은 우리의 사랑을 매일 보여주는 것임

해석 한 눈에 보기 1 우리의 어머니들은 우리의 인생 내내 우리를 위해 너무나 많은 일을 해주셔서 우리가 그분들에게 고마워하고 싶어 해야 한다는 것은 당연할 뿐이다. 2 미국에서는 5월의 둘째 주 일요일에 어머니의 날이 기념된다. 3 이날은 우리의 어머니들에게 공식적으로 감사를 표하고, 그분들에 대한 우리의 사랑과 존경을 알게 해드리는 날이다. 4 학교에 있는 아이들은 특별한 카드와 선물을 만들도록 장려된다. 5 상점들은 웃긴 메시지가 담긴 것들에서부터 감동적인 시가 담긴 것들까지 어머니의 날 카드들로 가득 차 있다. 6 많은 가정은 그들의 어머니에게 특별한 여행과 레스토랑 음식을 대접한다. 7 어머니의 날은 분명히 중요하다. 8 하지만 우리는 또한 가장 중요한 선물이 무엇인지 잊지 말아야 한다. 9 그것은 우리의 사랑을 매일 보여주는 것이다.

정답단추 (A)의 앞 사역동사 let은 「let+목적어+목적격 보어(동사원형)」의 5형식 문장을 취하고, '~가 …하게 하다'라는 의미를 가지고 있어. 목적격 보어 자리에는 반드시 동사원형이 와야 해서 know가 오는 것이 적절해. (B)에서는 적절한 동사의 형태를 선택해야 하는데 감정을 나타내는 동사가 명사를 수식할 경우에 주체에 따라 형태가 달라져. 주체가 사람이면 수동의 과거분사(p.p.)를, 사물이면 능동의 현재분사(v-ing)를 써. 이 글에서 touch는 '감동시키다'의 뜻을 가진 감정 동사로 시는 '감동을 주는' 것이므로 능동 현재분사인 touching이 와야 해. (C) 뒤의 절이 〈S+V〉이고 동사 is가 불완전자동사로 보어가 있어야 하는 불완전한 절이야. 그래서 보어 역할을 하는 동시에 동사 forget의 목적어 역할을 하는 간접의문문을 이끄는 의문사 what이 와야 적절해. 접속사 that은 완전한 절만을 뒤에 동반할 수 있어서 이 자리에는 올 수 없어.

213 정답 ⑤

지문 All in One

1 The new year has always served / as a time of reflection, celebration, and starting over. 2 But not every culture has chosen / to celebrate the occasion / at the same time of the year / or in the same way. 3 For example, / in ancient Babylonia, / more than 4,000 years ago, / the beginning of a new year was always celebrated / ① around the end of March. 4 This is a *natural time* [to celebrate / the coming of a new year], // as it is the beginning of *spring* [when new crops ② are planted]. 5 ③ Like us, / the Babylonians made New Year's resolutions. 6 Of course, / they didn't resolve / to lose weight or (to) quit ④ smoking. 7 *The most common resolution* [made by the Babylonians] / ⑤ were(→ was) to return / *farming tools* [(which[that]) they had borrowed].

(끊어 읽기 해석: 새해는 언제나 역할을 해왔다 / 반성과 축하와 새로운 시작의 시간으로서 / 하지만 모든 문화가 정해온 것은 아니다 / 그때를 기념할 것을 / 일 년 중 같은 때에 / 혹은 같은 방식으로 / 예를 들어 / 고대 바빌로니아에서 / 4천 년도 훨씬 전에 / 새해의 시작은 항상 기념되었다 / 3월 말쯤에 / 이것은 기념하기에 자연스러운 시기이다 / 새해의 도래를 / 새로운 농작물이 심어지는 봄의 시작이기 때문이다 / 우리처럼 / 바빌로니아인들은 새해 결심들을 했다 / 물론 / 그들은 결심하지는 않았다 / 살을 빼거나 담배를 끊겠다는 / 바빌로니아인들에 의해 이루어진 가장 흔한 결심은 / 돌려주는 것이었다 / 그들이 빌렸던 농기구를)

(문장 구조: 1 The new year(S) has always served(V) / 2 not every: 부분부정, culture(S) has chosen(V) / 3 the beginning of a new year(S) was always celebrated(V) / 4 This(S) is(V) a natural time(C), as: 접속사, it(S') is(V') the beginning of spring(C'), when: 관계부사 / 5 the Babylonians(S) made(V) / 6 they(S) didn't resolve(V) / 7 The most common resolution(S) were(→ was)(V) farming tools(C), (which[that]): 관계대명사)

해석 한 눈에 보기 1 새해는 언제나 반성과 축하, 새로운 시작의 시간 역할을 해왔다. 주제문 2 하지만 모든 문화가 그 때를 일 년 중 같은 때에 혹은 같은 방식으로 기념하기로 정해온 것은 아니다. 3 예를 들어, 고대 바빌로니아에서, 4천 년도 훨씬 전에, 새해의 시작은 항상 3월 말쯤에 기념되었다. 4 이때는 새해의 도래를 기념하기에 자연스러운 시기인데, 이때가 새로운 농작물이 심어지는 봄의 시작이기 때문이다. 5 우리처럼, 바빌로니아인들은 새해 결심들을 했다. 6 물론 그들은 살을 빼거나 담배를 끊겠다는 결심을 하지는 않았다. 7 바빌로니아인들이 했던 가장 흔한 결심은 그들이 빌렸던 농기구를 돌려주는 것이었다.

정답단추 ⑤의 were는 문장의 동사로 주어의 수와 일치하는지 확인해야 해. 이 문장에서 주어는 단수인 The most common resolution으로 과거분사구인 made by the Babylonians의 수식을 받아 길어졌어. the Babylonians가 were 바로 앞에 있지만, 주어로 혼동하지 않도록 주의하자. 따라서 동사로는 were가 아닌 단수동사 was가 와야 하니까 어법상 틀린 것은 ⑤야.

오답단서 ①의 around는 이 글에서는 전치사로 '~쯤에, ~경에'라는 뜻이고, 문맥상 '3월 말쯤에'라는 의미로 자연스러워. ②를 보면 농작물은 사람에 의해 '심어지는' 것이므로 수동태인 are planted가 와야 해. ③의 Like는 동사가 아닌 전치사로 us와 함께 '우리처럼'으로 자연스럽게 사용되었으므로 옳은 형태야. 마지막으로 ④ 앞에 있는 동사 quit은 동명사만을 목적어로 취하여 '~하는 것을 그만두다[끊다]'라는 의미로 쓰여. 따라서 quit smoking은 '담배 피우는 것을 끊는다'는 것으로 어법상 적절해.

어휘확인

new year 새해, 신년 **serve as** ~의 역할을 하다 **reflection** 반성; 상[모습] **celebration** 축하 cf. **celebrate** 축하하다, 기념하다 **start over** 다시 시작하다 **occasion** (어떤 일이 일어나는 특정한) 때 **way** 방식; 길 **ancient** 고대의 **Babylonia** 바빌로니아(메소포타미아 남부의 고대 왕국) cf. **Babylonian** 바빌로니아인 **beginning** 시작 **natural** 자연스러운 **coming** 도래, 시작 **crop** 농작물 **make a resolution** 결심하다 (= **resolve**) **lose weight** 살을 빼다 **quit** 그만두다 **smoking** 담배 피우기, 흡연 **common** 흔한 **return** 돌려주다 **farming tool** 농기구

지문 Flow

[도입]
새해는 새로운 시작의 시간 역할을 함

⬇

[주제문]
모든 문화에서 같은 때에 혹은 같은 방식으로 기념되는 것은 아님

⬇

[보충설명1]
고대 바빌로니아에서는 새해 시작을 3월 말쯤에 기념함

⬇

[보충설명2]
바빌로니아인들의 흔한 새해 결심은 빌렸던 농기구를 돌려주는 것

214 정답 ③

지문 All in One

1 It seems / that the feeling of affection is universal / among peoples / all over the world, // but different cultures have / *their own ways* [to express it]. 2 It's common / in the West / ① to greet friends and family / by kissing. 3 Kissing became an accepted part of greeting / thanks to the French. 4 They ended their dances / with a kiss / between partners. 5 This custom soon spread / ② throughout Europe, // and is still a widely recognized expression / of friendliness. 6 On the other hand, / ③ another(→ other) cultures have different greetings. 7 For example, / some tribal South Americans show // ④ how happy they are / to see loved ones / by weeping loudly. 8 The crying is a way / of ⑤ communicating love / for them.

해석 한 눈에 보기 주제문 1 애정의 감정은 전 세계 사람들에게 보편적인 것으로 보이지만, 각기 다른 문화들은 그것을 표현하는 그들 자신의 방식을 갖고 있다. 2 서양에서는 친구와 가족을 키스함으로써 맞이하는 것이 흔하다. 3 키스하는 것은 프랑스인들 덕분에 용인된 인사의 일부분이 되었다. 4 그들은 춤을 파트너 간의 키스로 끝냈다. 5 이 관습은 곧 유럽 도처로 퍼졌고, 여전히 널리 인정되는 다정함의 표현이다. 6 반면에, 다른 문화들은 다른 인사법을 갖고 있다. 7 예를 들어, 몇몇 남아메리카 부족민들은 그들이 사랑하는 사람을 보게 되어 얼마나 기쁜지를 큰소리로 울으로써 보여준다. 8 우는 것은 그들에게 있어 사랑을 전달하는 한 가지 방법이다.

정답단추 밑줄이 포함된 문장을 읽고 어법을 파악하여 정답을 고르면 시간을 절약할 수 있어. ③의 another는 단수명사와 함께 쓰이는데, 뒤에는 복수명사인 cultures가 왔어. 따라서 어법상 틀린 것은 ③이야. another 대신 복수명사와 함께 쓰이는 other는 올 수 있어.

오답단서 ①이 있는 문장은 「It is+형용사+to-v」 구문이 쓰인 것으로 '~하는 것이 …하다'라는 의미야. It은 가주어이고, 뒤에 나오는 to greet 이하의 to부정사구가 진주어야. ②의 throughout은 '곳곳에'라는 의미의 전치사로 문맥상 유럽 '곳곳으로' 퍼졌다는 말은 자연스러워. ④는 show의 목적어로 간접의문문이 사용된 경우야. 간접의문문은 「의문사(+형용사/부사)+S+V」의 어순을 취하니까 적절하게 사용되었다는 걸 알 수 있어. 마지막으로 ⑤는 of와 같은 전치사 뒤에는 명사 종류가 와야 하고, 뒤의 명사 love를 목적어로 취해야 해. 따라서 동사와 명사의 성격을 모두 갖춘 동명사 communicating은 적절하게 쓰였어.

어휘확인

affection 애정, 애착 **universal** 보편적인 **common** 흔한 **greeting** 인사 **thanks to ~** 덕분에 **custom** 관습 **throughout** 곳곳에, 도처에 **widely** 널리 **recognized** 인정된, 알려진 **friendliness** 다정함, 호의 **tribal** 부족의 **weep** 울다, 눈물을 흘리다 **way** 방법; 길

지문 Flow

[주제문]
문화마다 애정 표현의 방식이 다름

⬇

[예시1]
서양에서는 키스로 애정 표현을 함

&

[예시2]
남아메리카 부족민은 큰소리로 울으로써 애정 표현을 함

215 정답 ④

지문 All in One

1 Whether we would like to be (affected) or not, // it is an undeniable fact / that all of us are affected by our emotions. 2 And when it comes to emotions, / in most cases, // a moderate level of emotional involvement / intensifies communication / and makes it more personal. 3 However, / too much emotional involvement / can be an ① obstacle to communication. 4 For example, / too much anger / can create *an environment* [where ② reasonable discussion is impossible]. 5 Likewise, / prejudice / (automatically rejecting certain people or ideas), / stereotyping / (placing individuals into categories), / and boredom all ③ hinder effective communication. 6 Such emotions tend to create / *a blocked mind* [that is closed / to new ideas], / ④ accepting(→ rejecting/ignoring) *ideas* [that don't agree / with one's world view].

어휘확인

whether ~이든 아니든 **undeniable** 부인할 수 없는 **affect** 영향을 미치다 **emotion** 감정; 정서 cf. **emotional** 감정의 **when it comes to** ~에 관한 한 **moderate** 적절한, 적당한 **involvement** 개입 **intensify** 강화하다 **personal** 개인적인 **obstacle** 장애, 장애물 **anger** 분노, 화 **reasonable** 합리적인, 타당한 **discussion** 논의, 상의 **likewise** 마찬가지로 **prejudice** 편견 **automatically** 자동적으로 **reject** 거부하다 **certain** 특정한; 어떤 **stereotyping** 유형화, 고정 관념 **place** (특정한 상황에) 두다; 장소 **individual** 개인 **category** 범주, 카테고리 **boredom** 지루함 **hinder** 방해하다 **effective** 효과적인 **tend to-v** ~하는 경향이 있다 **blocked** 막힌 **world view** 세계관 **develop** 성장시키다 **open** 개방된; 열려 있는 **free from** ~가 없는; ~을 면한 **bias** 편견 **lifelong** 평생의 **awareness** 인식, 의식

감정적 편견이 없는 개방적인 사고방식을 기르는 것은 / 시작되는 평생의 과정이다

7 ⑤ Developing *an open mind* [that is free from emotional bias] / is *a lifelong process* [that begins / with awareness of the problem].

(S: Developing an open mind / 관계대명사: that / V: is / C: a lifelong process / 관계대명사: that / 문제에 대한 인식과 함께)

해석 한 눈에 보기 1 우리가 그러고 싶든 아니든 간에, 우리가 모두 우리의 감정에 영향을 받는다는 것은 부인할 수 없는 사실이다. 2 그리고 감정에 관한 한, 대부분의 경우에, 적절한 수준의 감정적 개입은 의사소통을 강화하고 그것을 더 개인적으로 만든다. 3 그러나 너무나 큰 감정적 개입은 의사소통에 ① 장애가 될 수 있다. 4 예를 들어, 너무나 많은 분노는 ② 합리적인 논의가 불가능한 환경을 만들 수 있다. 5 마찬가지로, 편견(자동으로 특정 사람들이나 생각을 거부하는 것), 유형화(개인들을 범주로 나누는 것), 지루함 모두는 효과적인 의사소통을 ③ 방해한다. 6 그런 감정은 새로운 생각들에 닫혀서 막힌 사고방식을 만들어 내는 경향이 있어, 자신의 세계관과 일치하지 않는 생각들을 ④ 받아들인다(→ 거부한다/무시한다). 7 감정적 편견이 없는 개방적인 사고방식을 ⑤ 기르는 것은 문제에 대한 인식과 함께 시작되는 평생의 과정이다.

정답단추 밑줄 친 어휘가 속한 문장 앞뒤 내용을 파악하고 해당 어휘의 쓰임이 적절한지 살펴보자. ④의 앞 문장을 보면 편견, 유형화, 지루함은 효과적인 의사소통을 방해한다고 하고 있어. 그리고 이러한 감정들은 새로운 생각에 닫혀 있는 사고방식을 만들어 내고, 자신의 세계관과 일치하지 않는 생각들을 거부하거나(rejecting) 무시한다고(ignoring) 해야 자연스러워. 따라서 '받아들인다'는 뜻의 accepting은 문맥상 적절하지 않으므로 정답은 ④야.

오답단서 ①을 포함한 문장은 적당한 수준의 감정적 개입은 의사소통을 강화하고 더 개인적으로 만든다는 앞 문장에 뒤이어 However 연결어로 시작하고 있지. 따라서 너무나 큰 감정적 개입은 의사소통에 장애(obstacle)가 된다는 내용이 되어야 해. ②는 앞 문장에 대한 예시로 너무 큰 분노는 합리적인(reasonable) 논의가 불가능하다는 내용이 자연스러워. 또한, ③의 hinder를 포함한 문장은 Likewise를 사용하여 앞과 비슷한 문맥을 이어가고 있으니까 편견, 유형화와 지루함은 효과적인 의사소통을 마찬가지로 '방해한다'는 내용이 알맞아. 마지막 문장으로는 개방적인 사고방식을 '길러야 한다'는 결론이 와야 자연스러우므로 ⑤의 Developing이 적절하게 쓰였음을 알 수 있어.

지문 Flow

[도입]
우리는 감정에 영향을 받으며, 적절한 감정 개입은 의사소통을 강화시킴

⬇

[반론]
큰 감정 개입은 의사소통의 장애가 됨

⬇

[예시]
• 분노는 합리적 논의를 불가능하게 함
• 편견, 유형화, 지루함이 효과적인 의사소통을 방해함

⬇

[결과]
막힌 사고방식을 만들어 자신의 세계관과 맞지 않는 생각을 거부함

⬇

[결론]
감정적 편견이 없는 개방적 사고방식을 길러야 함

216 정답 ①

지문 All in One

1 There are *many illnesses and health problems* [that we must watch out for / as we age], // and among them, / a stroke is one of the most terrifying / for a variety of reasons. 2 For one thing, / most victims have no warning / that they will suffer a fatal stroke. 3 One out of three incidences of stroke / results in (A) sudden death. 4 Only the lucky few / get any warning signs. 5 Not even (B) sensible eating and weight control / can protect everyone / from a stroke. 6 *The best way* [to (C) prevent a stroke] / is to see your doctor / for regular checkups. 7 This is especially important // if there is a history of stroke / in your family.

(조심해야 하는 많은 질병과 건강 문제들이 있다 / 우리가 나이 들어감에 따라 / 그리고 그것들 중에 / 뇌졸중은 가장 무서운 것들 중 하나이다 / 다양한 이유로 / 우선 첫째로 / 대부분의 희생자들은 경고를 가지지 않는다 / 그들이 치명적인 뇌졸중에 고통 받을 것이라는 / 뇌졸중 발생 3건 중 하나는 / 갑작스러운 사망을 낳는다 / 불과 운이 좋은 몇 명만이 / 그 어떤 경고 신호를 받는다 / 심지어 분별 있는 식사와 체중 조절조차도 / 모든 사람을 보호하지는 못한다 / 뇌졸중으로부터 / 뇌졸중을 예방하는 가장 좋은 방법은 / 당신의 의사를 만나보는 것이다 / 정기 검진을 위해 / 이것은 특히 중요하다 / 뇌졸중 이력이 있다면 / 당신 집안에)

	(A)		(B)		(C)
①	sudden 갑작스러운	……	sensible 분별 있는	……	prevent 예방하는
②	sudden 갑작스러운	……	sensitive 민감한	……	prevent 예방하는
③	sudden 갑작스러운	……	sensible 분별 있는	……	preserve 유지하는
④	predicted 예상된	……	sensible 분별 있는	……	prevent 예방하는
⑤	predicted 예상된	……	sensitive 민감한	……	preserve 유지하는

해석 한 눈에 보기 1 우리가 나이 들어감에 따라 조심해야 하는 많은 질병과 건강 문제들이 있는데, 그것 중에 뇌졸중은 다양한 이유로 가장 무서운 것 중 하나이다. 2 첫째로 대부분의 희생자는 그들이 치명적인 뇌졸중으로 고통 받을 것이라는 경고를 전혀 받지 않는다. 3 뇌졸중 발생 3건 중 하나는 (A) 갑작스러운 사망을 낳는다. 4 불과 운이 좋은 몇 명만이 그 어떤 경고 신호를 받는다. 5 심지어 (B) 분별 있는 식사와 체중 조절조차도 모든 사람을 뇌졸중으로부터 보호하지는 못한다. 6 뇌졸중을 (C) 예방하는 가장 좋은 방법은 정기 검진을 위해 당신의 의사를 만나보는 것이다. 7 이것은 당신 집안에 뇌졸중 이력이 있다면 특히 중요하다.

정답단추 (A)는 바로 앞 문장에서 뇌졸중 환자 대부분이 아무런 사전 경고를 받지 않는다고 했으므로 '갑작스러운' 사망으로 이어진다는 문맥이 자연스러워. 따라서 sudden이 들어가야 해. predicted는 '예상된'이라는 뜻이야. (B)는 바로 뒤에 이어지는 식사와 체중 조절(eating and weight control)을 수식하는 자리니까 문맥상 '분별 있는'이라는 뜻의 sensible이 적절해. sensitive는 '민감한'이라는 뜻이야. (C)는 뇌졸중을 '예방하는' 가장 좋은 방법이라는 내용이 자연스러우니까 prevent가 와야 해. preserve는 '유지하는'이라는 뜻이야.

어휘확인

illness 질병[병] **watch out for** ~에 대해 조심하다[주의하다] **stroke** 뇌졸중 **terrifying** 무서운, 겁나게 하는 **a variety of** 다양한, 여러 가지의 **for one thing** 우선 첫째로 **victim** 희생자, 피해자 **suffer** (질병 등에) 고통 받다, 시달리다 **fatal** 치명적인 **incidence** 발생 **result in** ~을 낳다 **sudden** 갑작스러운 **death** 사망 **sensible** 분별 있는, 합리적인 **weight control** 체중 조절 **prevent** 예방하다 **regular checkup** 정기 검진 **history** (개인·가정의) 이력[내력]

〈선택지 어휘〉

sensitive 민감한 **preserve** 유지하다, 보존하다 **predicted** 예상된

지문 Flow

[도입]
많은 질병들 중에 가장 무서운 것 중 하나인 뇌졸중의 위험성

⬇

[보충설명1]
희생자들이 뇌졸중의 경고를 전혀 받지 못함 → 갑작스러운 사망

&

[보충설명2]
식사와 체중 조절로도 보호받지 못함

⬇

[결론]
정기 검진을 통해 예방하는 것이 가장 좋은 방법임

실전편

독해 모의고사 1회

217 ② 218 ④ 219 ③ 220 ⑤ 221 ② 222 ③ 223 ① 224 ④ 225 ⑤
226 ④ 227 ① 228 ③ 229 ④ 230 ③ 231 ⑤ 232 ② 233 ② 234 ④

217 정답 ②

지문 All in One

생물은 문제가 없다 / 세계의 많은 부분이 해마다 꽁꽁 언다 / 그리고 생물은
1 Life doesn't have a problem. 2 Much of the world freezes solid every year, // and life carries
S V O S_1 V_1 S_2 V_2

계속 나아가거나 땅속에서 기다린다 / 그것의 뿌리, 굴, 씨앗 안에서 / 따뜻해질 때까지
on or waits underground, / in its roots, burrows and seeds, / until things warm up. 3 The
V_3 접속사 S′ V′ S

똑같은 일이 일어난다 / 극심한 가뭄이 있는 곳들에서 / 어떤 씨앗들은 수십 년을 기다릴 수 있다
same happens in places / with extreme droughts. 4 Some seeds can wait for decades / in very
V S V

아주 메마른 땅에서 / 비가 오면 / 그것들은 활성화된다 / 그리고 싹이 나고 꽃을 피우기 시작한다
dry ground. 5 When rain comes, // they are activated / and begin to sprout and blossom / as
접속사 S′ V′ S V_1 V_2 O_2

평상시처럼 / 너무나 많은 종류의 생명체가 있어서 / 너무나 많은 다양한 환경에 잘 적응된
usual. 6 There are so many types of *living things* [well-adapted to so many different
V S

그 어떤 유형의 부정적인 변화들이 일어난다고 할지라도 / 어떤 종은
circumstances] // that, no matter what sort of adverse changes come about, / some will find
접속사 = whatever(양보) S′ V'_1

그것들이 적합하다고 생각한다 / 그리고 번성하고 진화할 것이다 / 산불, 허리케인, 가뭄, 또는 지진을
them suitable / and will thrive and evolve. 7 Forest fires, hurricanes, droughts, or
O'_1 OC'_1 V'_2 V'_3

생물은 그것들 모두에 침착하게 대처한다
earthquakes: // life takes them all in stride.

① to be harmed a lot by natural disasters
자연재해에 의해 많이 해를 입다
② to continue with the cycle despite trials
시련에도 불구하고 자신의 순환을 계속하다
③ to depend seriously on various circumstances
다양한 환경에 심각하게 의존하다
④ to be much more precious than any other thing
다른 어떤 것보다 훨씬 더 소중하다
⑤ to cause a negative natural phenomenon by chance
우연히 부정적인 자연 현상을 야기하다

해석 한 눈에 보기 1 생물은 문제가 없다. 2 세계의 많은 부분이 해마다 꽁꽁 얼고, 생물은 계속 나아가거나 따뜻해질 때까지 땅속에 있는 뿌리, 굴, 씨앗 안에서 기다린다. 3 극심한 가뭄이 있는 곳들에서 똑같은 일이 일어난다. 4 어떤 씨앗들은 아주 메마른 땅에서 수십 년을 기다릴 수 있다. 5 비가 오면, 그것들은 활성화되어 평상시처럼 싹이 나고 꽃을 피우기 시작한다. 주제문 6 너무나 많은 다양한 환경에 잘 적응하는 너무나 많은 종류의 생명체가 있어서 그 어떤 유형의 부정적인 변화들이 일어난다고 할지라도, 어떤 종은 그것들이 적합하다고 생각해서 번성하고 진화할 것이다. 7 산불, 허리케인, 가뭄, 또는 지진. 생물은 그것들 모두에 침착하게 대처한다.

정답단추 메마른 땅에서 수십 년간 기다린 씨앗도 비가 오면 다시 꽃을 피우는 것처럼, 그 어떤 부정적인 변화가 생겨도 생명은 그 변화에 적응해서 번성한다고 했어. 즉 생물은 시련에도 불구하고 자신의 순환을 계속한다는 것이 주제이므로 정답은 ②야.

오답단서 ①, ⑤는 밑줄 친 부분 바로 앞에 산불, 허리케인 등 자연재해와 관련된 구체적인 어휘가 언급되었다는 점을 착안해서 만든 오답이야. 또한 글에서 생명이 '다양한 환경에 적응한다'고 했지만 그것에 의존한다는 내용이 아니므로 ③은 오답이야.

어휘확인

freeze 얼다 **solid** 단단한; 고체의 **carry on** 계속 나아가다, 견디다 **root** 뿌리 **burrow** 굴, 구멍 **extreme** 극심한 **drought** 가뭄 **decade** 10년 **activate** 활성화하다 **sprout** 싹이 나다 **blossom** 꽃을 피우다 **adapt to** ~에 적응하다 **circumstance** 환경, 상황 **adverse** 부정적인 **come about** 일어나다, 생기다 **suitable** 적합한 **thrive** 번성하다, 번창하다 **evolve** 진화하다 **take A in stride** A에 침착하게 대처하다

〈선택지 어휘〉

natural disaster 자연재해 **cycle** 순환, 사이클 **despite** ~에도 불구하고 **trials** 시련 **phenomenon** 현상 **by chance** 우연히

지문 Flow

[예시1]
세계가 꽁꽁 얼어도, 생물은 땅속에서 따뜻해질 때까지 기다림

&

[예시2]
가뭄에서 어떤 씨앗들은 수십 년을 기다리며, 비가 오면 싹트고 꽃을 피움

⬇

[주제문]
생물은 다양한 환경에서 어떤 부정적 변화에도 번성하고 진화할 것임

⬇

[주제문 재진술]
생물은 부정적 변화(산불, 허리케인, 가뭄, 지진)에 침착하게 대처함

218 정답 ④

지문 All in One

1 Confucius reportedly said, / "*Short pencil better / than long memory.*" 2 Taking notes / is a proven memory technique. 3 However, / standard note taking / usually involves writing down ideas / in a more or less word-for-word fashion. 4 This is actually more repetition / than involvement. 5 We are repeating in a written form / what we heard [or] saw. 6 Although we can listen at / up to 800 words per minute, // *the speaker* [(who(m)) we are listening to] / can only speak / about 135 words per minute / [and] we can only write / about 40 words per minute! 7 Trying to take notes word-for-word / will cause us to miss / a great deal of incoming material. 8 Additionally, / the process of trying to remember / what was previously said / [and] (to) write it down / while listening to new material / causes inaccuracies / [and] actually interferes with thinking.

(전하는 바에 따르면 공자는 ~라고 말했다 / 더 좋은 짧은 연필 / 긴 기억력보다 / 필기하기는 / 증명된 기억 기술이다 / 하지만 / 일반적인 필기는 / 대체로 생각들을 적는 것을 수반한다 / 거의 말 그대로 쓰는 방식으로 / 이것은 사실상 더 많은 반복이다 / 참여보다는 / 우리는 글 형태로 반복하고 있다 / 우리가 듣거나 본 것을 / 비록 / 우리가 들을 수 있을지라도 / 분당 최대 800단어를 / 우리가 귀를 기울이는 화자는 / 오직 말할 수 있다 / 분당 약 135단어를 / 그리고 우리는 오직 쓸 수 있다 / 분당 약 40단어를 / 글자 그대로 필기하려고 애쓰는 것은 / 우리로 하여금 놓치게 할 것이다 / 들어오는 다량의 자료를 / 게다가 / 기억하려고 노력하는 과정은 / 앞서 말해진 것을 / 그리고 받아 적으려는 (과정은) / 새로운 자료를 듣는 동안에 / 부정확함을 유발한다 / 그리고 / 사실상 사고를 방해한다)

(1 Confucius: S, said: V / 2 Taking notes: S, is: V, a proven memory technique: C / 3 standard note taking: S, involves: V / 4 This: S, is: V, more repetition: C / 5 We: S, are repeating: V, what: 관계대명사 / 6 Although: 접속사, we: S′, can listen: V′, the speaker: S_1, who(m): 관계대명사, can only speak: V_1, we: S_2, can only write: V_2 / 7 Trying to take notes word-for-word: S, will cause: V, us: O, to miss: C / 8 the process of trying to remember ~ new material: S, what: 관계대명사, (to) write it down: = what was previously said, causes: V_1, interferes: V_2)

① how to take notes effectively
효과적으로 필기하는 방법

② various ways to improve memory
기억력을 증진하는 다양한 방법들

③ the positive effects of writing on memory
쓰기가 기억력에 미치는 긍정적인 영향

④ the problems with copying when taking notes
필기할 때 그대로 받아 적는 것의 문제점

⑤ the process of forming and storing memories
기억을 형성하고 저장하는 과정

해석 한 눈에 보기 **1** 전하는 바에 따르면 공자는 "긴 기억력보다 더 좋은 짧은 연필"이라고 말했다고 한다. **2** 필기하기는 증명된 기억 기술이다. **3** 하지만 일반적인 필기는 대체로 생각들을 거의 말 그대로 쓰는 방식으로 받아 적는 것을 수반한다. **4** 이것은 사실상 참여보다는 오히려 반복이다. **5** 우리는 우리가 듣거나 본 것을 글 형태로 반복하고 있는 것이다. **6** 비록 우리가 분당 최대 800단어를 들을 수 있을지라도, 우리가 귀를 기울이고 있는 화자는 오직 분당 약 135단어를 말할 수 있을 뿐이며 우리는 오직 분당 약 40단어를 쓸 수 있을 뿐이다! **7** 글자 그대로 필기하려고 애쓰는 것은 들어오는 많은 정보를 우리로 하여금 놓치게 할 것이다. **8** 게다가 새로운 정보를 듣는 동안에 앞서 말해진 것을 기억하여 그것을 받아 적으려고 노력하는 과정은 부정확함을 유발하고 사실상 사고를 방해한다.

정답단추 서두에서 필기하기는 증명된 기억 기술이라고 언급하며 필기하기의 긍정적인 면을 보여주고 있어. 그러나 이어지는 문장들은 모두 필기하기의 문제점들을 제기하고 있으므로 이 글의 주제로 가장 적절한 것은 ④야.

오답단서 필기하기에 관한 글이지만 필기하는 것을 부정적으로 보고 있고, 또 효과적으로 필기하는 방법에 대해서는 언급하지 않았으므로 ①은 적절하지 않아. ②, ③, ⑤ 역시 글에 등장한 일부 어구들을 이용하여 만든 것이나 글의 주제와는 연관이 없어.

어휘확인

Confucius 공자 **reportedly** 전하는 바에 따르면 **memory** 기억력, 기억 **take notes** 필기하다 **proven** 증명된 **technique** 기술 **standard** 일반적인 **involve** 수반[포함]하다; 참여시키다 cf. **involvement** 참여, 개입 **more or less** 거의, 다소 **word-for-word** 정확히 말한[글자] 그대로 **fashion** 방식; 유행 **repetition** 반복 **although** 비록 ~일지라도 **up to** 최대 ~, ~까지 **per** ~당[마다] **a great deal of** 다량의, 많은 **incoming** 들어오는, 도착하는 **material** 자료; 재료 **additionally** 게다가 **previously** 앞서, 사전에 **inaccuracy** 부정확함 **interfere with** ~을 방해하다

〈선택지 어휘〉
effectively 효과적으로 **various** 다양한 **positive** 긍정적인 **form** 형성하다 **store** 저장하다

지문 Flow

[도입]
필기하는 것이 기억에 좋음

⬇

[보충설명1]
생각을 그대로 적는 일반적인 필기는 참여보다는 반복의 행위임

⬇

[보충설명2]
글자 그대로 필기하려는 것은 많은 정보를 놓치게 함

⬇

[주장]
받아 적으려고 노력하는 것은 부정확함을 유발하고 사고를 방해함

⬇

[주제도출]
듣는 그대로 적는 필기는 문제점들이 있음

219 정답 ③

지문 All in One

1 Based solely on external appearances, / it is easy to think // that the current generation of youth / is revolutionary — / somehow fundamentally different / from *anything* [that came before]. 2 (A) Despite *the unique way* [(that) they dress [and] speak], / however, / today's teenagers are not different / from any other generation's. 3 Our grandparents also adopted strange new behaviors // [and] used slang / to show their independence / from adults / when

(단지 외적인 모습만을 토대로 하면 / ~라고 생각하기 쉽다 / 현재의 젊은 세대가 / 혁명적이며 / 왠지 근본적으로 다르다 / 전에 있었던 그 어떤 것과 / 그들이 입고 말하는 독특한 방식에도 불구하고 / 그러나 / 오늘날의 십대들은 다르지 않다 / 그 어떤 다른 세대의 십대들과 / 우리의 조부모님들도 또한 이상하고 새로운 행동을 채택했다 / 그리고 속어를 사용했다 / 그들의 독립을 보여주려고 / 어른으로부터의)

(1 Based solely on external appearances: 분사구문(= If you base your opinion solely on ~), it: 가주어, is: V, easy: C, to think: 진주어, that: 접속사, to think ~: 부사적 용법(형용사 수식), the current generation of youth: S′, is: V′, revolutionary: C'_1, that: 관계대명사 / 2 that: = in which, today's teenagers: S, are: V, different: C / 3 Our grandparents: S, adopted: V_1, used: V_2, to show: 부사적 용법(목적), when: 접속사)

어휘확인

based on ~을 토대로 하여 **solely** 단지, 오로지 **external** 외면적인, 외부의 **appearance** 모습 **current** 현재의 **generation** 세대 **youth** 젊음, 어린 시절 **revolutionary** 혁명적인 **somehow** 왠지; 어떻게든 **fundamentally** 근본적으로 **despite** ~에도 불구하고 **adopt** 채택하다 **behavior** 행동 **slang** 속어 **independence** 독립(성) **show off** ~을 과시[자랑]하다 **membership** (단체의) 일원임; 회원 자격 **peer** 또래 **form** 형성하다(= shape) **bond** 유대(감), 결속(감) **identity** 정체성

그들이 십 대였을 때 / 십 대들이 속어를 사용할 때 / 그들은 사실 그들이 일원임을 과시하고 있는 것이다

they were teenagers. 4 When teenagers use slang, // they are actually (B) showing off their

S′ V′ C′ 접속사 S′ V′ S V

그들의 특별한 또래 집단의 / 그들은 강한 유대감을 형성하고 있다 / 그들의 또래와

membership / in their special group of peers. 5 They are forming strong bonds / with their

S V_1

그리고 그들의 정체성을 형성하고 있다 / 동일한 언어를 말함으로써

peers / and (are) shaping their identities / by (C) speaking the same language.

V_2

	(A)		(B)		(C)
①	Despite	……	shown	……	speak
②	Although	……	showing	……	speak
③	Despite	……	showing	……	speaking
④	Although	……	showing	……	speaking
⑤	Although	……	shown	……	speak

해석 한 눈에 보기 1 단지 외적인 모습만을 토대로 하면, 현재의 젊은이들 세대가 혁명적이며 전에 있었던 그 어떤 것과도 왠지 근본적으로 다르다고 생각하기 쉽다. 주제문 2 그러나 그들이 입고 말하는 독특한 방식에도 불구하고, 오늘날의 십 대들은 그 어떤 다른 세대의 십 대들과 다르지 않다. 3 우리의 조부모님들 또한 이상하고 새로운 행동을 채택했고, 그들이 십 대였을 때 어른으로부터의 그들의 독립을 보여주려고 속어를 사용했다. 4 십 대들이 속어를 사용할 때, 그들은 사실상 그들이 그들의 특별한 또래 집단의 일원임을 과시하고 있는 것이다. 5 그들은 동일한 언어를 말함으로써 그들 또래와의 강한 유대감을 형성하고 있고 그들의 정체성을 갖추고 있다.

정답단추 (A)의 despite와 although의 의미는 '~에도 불구하고'로 비슷하지만 despite는 전치사이고 although는 접속사야. 접속사는 주어와 동사를 갖춘 절을 이끌어야 하는데, 여기서는 뒤에 (that) they dress and speak에 의해 수식을 받는 명사구 the unique way가 왔으니 구를 이끄는 전치사 Despite가 적절해. (B)에는 과거분사 shown과 현재분사 showing이 있네. 이럴 땐 주어와의 관계를 따져 능동인지 수동인지를 구분해야 해. 주어 they는 teenagers를 가리키며, 십 대들이 자신들이 또래의 일원임을 '과시한다'는 문맥이 자연스러우므로 능동의 현재분사 showing이 적절해. (C)는 전치사 by의 목적어 자리이므로 명사 종류가 와야 하고 동시에 뒤의 the same language를 목적어로 취할 수 있는 것이 필요하므로 동사와 명사의 역할을 동시에 하는 동명사 speaking이 적절해.

지문 Flow

[도입]
외적인 모습만으로 판단하면 현재 젊은 세대가 혁명적이고 근본적으로 이전과는 다름

⬇

[주제문]
오늘날의 십 대들은 다른 세대의 십 대들과 다르지 않음

⬇

[보충설명1]
조부모님도 십 대였을 때 이상한 행동을 하거나 속어를 사용했음

&

[보충설명2]
십 대의 속어 사용은 특별한 또래 집단의 일원임을 과시하고, 강한 유대감을 형성하는 것임

220 정답 ⑤

지문 All in One

맨해튼 중심가는 / 당신이 농업을 연상할 장소가 결코 아니다

1 Downtown Manhattan / is hardly *a place* [(which[that]) you would associate with ①

S V 관계대명사 C

그러나 / 당신은 볼지도 모른다 / 토마토 씨앗을 심고 있는 한 무리의 농부를

agriculture]. 2 However, / you may see / *a group of farmers* [planting tomato seeds] / in the

S V

뉴욕시의 한가운데에서 / 가까운 미래에 / 새로운 개념의 농법이 / 수직 농법이라고

middle of New York City / in the near future. 3 *A new concept of farming*, [called vertical

S

불리는 / 수행되고 있다 / 고층건물에서 / 유리 벽과 태양 전지판을 갖춘 / 각 층은

farming], / is being carried out / in skyscrapers / with glass walls and solar panels. 4 Each

V S

가지고 있다 / 농작물이 생산될 수 있는 대형 모종 밭을 / 강력하게 통제된 환경에서

floor has / *large planting beds* [where crops can be produced / in a heavily ② controlled

V 관계부사

그러한 실내의 식품 생산은 필요로 하지 않는다 / 곤충과 해충의 성장을 억제해 주는

environment]. 5 Such ③ indoor food production does not require / *any insecticides* [to control

S_1 V_1

그 어떤 살충제도 / 따라서 / 소비자는 혜택을 받을 수 있다 / 유기농 식품으로부터

the growth of insects and pests], // and thus, / consumers can benefit / from ④ organic

S_2 V_2

게다가 / 모든 종류의 농작물이 재배될 때 / 도시 환경에서 / 화물 및

foods. 6 In addition, / as crops of all kinds will be grown / in an urban setting, // cargo and

접속사 S′ V′ S

선적 서비스가 / 필요할(→ 불필요할) 것이다 / 이는 ~을 의미한다 / 온실가스 배출이 없을 것이

shipping services will be ⑤ necessary(→ unnecessary), / [which means / that there will be no

V C 관계대명사(계속적 용법) 접속사

라는 것

greenhouse gas emissions].

해석 한 눈에 보기 1 맨해튼 중심가는 당신이 ① 농업을 연상할 장소가 결코 아니다. 주제문 2 그러나 당신은 가까운 미래에 뉴욕시의 한가운데에서 한 무리의 농부들이 토마토 씨앗을 심고 있는 것을 보게 될지도 모른다. 3 수직 농법이라고 불리는 새로운 개념의 농법이 유리 벽과 태양 전지판을 갖춘 고층건물에서 수행되고 있다. 4 각 층은 농작물이 강력하게 ② 통제된 환경에서 생산될 수 있는 대형 모종 밭을 갖추고 있다. 5 그러한 ③ 실내의 식품 생산은 곤충과 해충의 성장을 억제해 주는 그 어떤 살충제도 필요로 하지 않으며, 따라서 소비자는 ④ 유기농 식품으로부터 혜택을 얻을 수 있다. 6 게다가 모든 종류의 농작물이 도시 환경에서 재배될 때, 화물 및 선적 서비스가 ⑤ 필요할(→ 불필요할) 것인데, 이는 온실가스 배출이 전혀 없을 것임을 의미한다.

정답단추 적절한 낱말의 쓰임을 묻는 문제에서는 글의 전체적인 이해가 중요해. 도심 고층건물에서 농작물을 재배하

어휘확인

downtown 중심가 **hardly** 결코[전혀] ~아니다 **associate with** ~을 연상하다 **agriculture** 농업 **plant** (나무·씨앗 등을) 심다; 식물 **concept** 개념 **vertical** 수직의, 세로의 **carry out** ~을 수행하다 **skyscraper** 고층건물 **solar panel** 태양 전지판 **planting bed** 모종 밭 **crop** (농)작물 **heavily** 몹시, 심하게 **controlled** 통제된 **indoor** 실내의 **production** 생산 **require** 필요로 하다 **insecticide** 살충제 **growth** 성장 **insect** 곤충 **pest** 해충 **benefit** 혜택을 받다 **organic** 유기농의 **in addition** 게다가 **urban** 도시의 **setting** 환경 **cargo** 화물 **shipping** 선적 **greenhouse gas** 온실가스 **emission** (빛·열·가스 등의) 배출

지문 Flow

[주제문]
곧 도시 한 가운데에서 농업을 하게 될 수 있음

⬇

[보충설명1]
새로운 개념의 수직 농법:
유리 벽과 태양 전지판을 갖춘 고층건물에서 수행됨

⬇

[보충설명2]
각 층은 농작물이 통제된 환경에서 생산될 수 있는 대형 모종 밭을 갖춤

는 수직 농법에 대한 글로, 그 농법에 대한 소개와 장점이 나열된 글이야. 그러므로 마지막 문장은 도시에서 기른 농작물은 도시에서 소비되므로 화물 및 선적 서비스가 '불필요하게' 되어 운송으로 인한 온실가스 배출이 없을 것이라는 내용이 되어야 자연스럽지. 따라서 ⑤는 necessary의 반의어인 unnecessary가 되어야 해.

오답단서 맨해튼 중심가에서 ①을 연상하기 힘들다고 하고 있는데, 바로 다음 문장에 한 무리의 농부들이 뉴욕시에서 토마토 씨앗을 심는 모습을 볼 수도 있을 것이라고 말하고 있어. 농부들이 씨앗을 심는 건 농업(agriculture)을 의미하지. 글에서 소개하는 수직 농법이 유리 벽과 태양 전지판을 갖춘 고층건물에서 수행된다는 점으로 미루어봤을 때, 통제된(controlled) 환경에서 농작물이 생산된다는 점을 추측할 수 있지. 마찬가지로 수직 농법은 실내의(indoor) 식품 생산이니, ②와 ③에선 올바른 단어가 쓰였어. 수직 농법에서는 그 어떤 살충제도 필요하지 않다고 했으니, 수직 농법으로 재배되는 농작물은 유기농(organic) 식품임을 알 수 있어. 따라서 ④도 그 쓰임이 적절해.

[장점]
- 살충제가 필요 없어서 유기농 식품을 얻을 수 있음
- 화물 및 선적 서비스가 불필요해서 온실가스 배출이 없음

221 정답 ②

지문 All in One

어메이징 하트랜드 달리기 대회
1 ***Amazing Heartland Race***

당신은 당신의 마을을 얼마나 잘 아시나요 / 그것은 무엇으로 유명한가요 / 커피를 마시기에 가장 좋은 곳은 어디인가요
2 How well do you know your town? 3 What is it famous for? 4 Where's *the best place* [to grab a coffee]?
(you: S, know: V / is: V, it: S / 's: V, the best place: S)

가장 맛있는 음식은 어떤가요 / 당신의 이웃에서
5 What about the best food / in your neighborhood?

와서 발견하세요 / 아니 재발견하세요 / 당신의 마을을 / 달리면서 / 어메이징 하트랜드 달리기 대회는
6 Come discover, / or rediscover, / your town // as you run! 7 The Amazing Heartland Race / will
(V_1 V_2 V_3 접속사 S′ V′ / S V)

당신이 보도록 해줄 것 입니다 / 당신이 전에 결코 본 적이 없는 고향 마을의 일면을 / 마을의 주요 지형지물을
have you seeing / *a side of your hometown* [that you've never seen before], // as you run past the
(O C / 관계대명사 / 접속사 S′ V′)

지나쳐 달리면서 / 당신이 살며 놀고 있는
landmarks / in *the town* [that you live and play in]!
(관계대명사)

5명의 구성원으로 된 팀을 구성하고 / 지금 등록하세요
8 Form a team of 5 members / and register now!
(V_1 V_2)

등록은 2017년 4월 30일에 마감합니다
9 Registration closes on 30 April 2017.
(V)

달리기 대회 세부사항
10 ***Race Details***

날짜: 2017년 6월 3일 (토요일)
11 Date: 3 June 2017 (Saturday)

시간: 오전 9시 ~ 오후 5시
12 Time: 9:00 a.m. to 5:00 p.m.

이 5개 마을 중 어떤 곳을 달립니다 / 베독 / 쥬링 / 퀸스타운 / 토아 파요 / 이순
13 Race in any of these 5 towns / - Bedok / Juring / Queenstown / Toa Payoh / Yishun

더 많은 정보를 위해서는 / www.hdb.gov.sg/heartlandbeat를 방문하세요
14 For more information, / visit www.hdb.gov.sg/heartlandbeat.
(V)

① 고향 마을을 더 잘 알 수 있는 기회를 제공한다.
② 전체 다섯 팀으로 구성된다.
③ 등록 마감은 2017년 4월 30일이다.
④ 여덟 시간 동안 진행된다.
⑤ 다섯 마을 중 한 곳에서 달리게 된다.

해석 한 눈에 보기 1 **어메이징 하트랜드 달리기 대회** 2 당신은 당신의 마을을 얼마나 잘 아시나요? 3 그것은 무엇으로 유명한가요? 4 커피를 마시기에 가장 좋은 곳은 어디인가요? 5 당신의 동네에서 가장 맛있는 음식은 어떤가요? 6 오셔서 달리면서 당신의 마을을 발견, 아니 재발견하세요. 7 어메이징 하트랜드 달리기 대회는 당신이 살며 놀고 있는 마을의 주요 지형지물을 지나쳐 달리면서 당신이 전에 결코 본 적이 없는 고향 마을의 일면을 보게 해줄 겁니다! 8 5명의 구성원으로 된 팀을 구성하고 지금 등록하세요! 9 등록은 2017년 4월 30일에 마감합니다. 10 **달리기 대회 세부사항** 11 날짜: 2017년 6월 3일 (토요일) 12 시간: 오전 9시 ~ 오후 5시 13 이 5개 마을 (베독 / 쥬링 / 퀸스타운 / 토아 파요 / 이순) 중 어떤 곳을 달립니다. 14 더 많은 정보를 위해서는, www.hdb.gov.sg/heartlandbeat를 방문하세요.

정답단추 다섯 마을 중 한 곳을 골라 달리면서 마을을 재발견해 보라는 달리기 행사 홍보 내용이야. 전체가 다섯 팀이라는 것이 아니라, 5명으로 구성된 팀을 등록하라고 했으므로 ②는 일치하지 않는 설명이야.

오답단서 선택지의 순서대로 지문에서 단서를 찾아보자. 마을의 주요 지형지물을 지나쳐 달리면서 동네를 재발견할 기회라고 했으니, ①은 지문과 일치해. 등록 마감은 2017년 4월 30일이고, 시간은 오전 9시부터 오후 5시까지, 즉 여덟 시간이라고 지문에 명시되어 있으니 ③, ④도 일치하는 설명이야. 또한, 2017년 6월 3일은 달리기 행사의 날짜이지, 등록 마감일은 아니야. 마지막으로 다섯 개의 마을 중 한 곳에서 달리게 된다며 마을 이름을 나열해 놓은 부분에서 ⑤도 지문과 일치하는 설명임을 알 수 있어.

어휘확인

grab 급히[잠깐] ~을 먹다 **neighborhood** 이웃; 지역 **discover** 발견하다 **rediscover** 재발견하다 **past** (위치상으로) ~을 지나서 **landmark** 주요 지형지물, 랜드마크 **form** 구성하다, 형성하다 **register** 등록하다 **cf. registration** 등록, 신고 **detail** 세부 사항 **information** 정보

지문 Flow

[소재]
어메이징 하트랜드 달리기 대회 안내문

[보충설명]
마을을 달리면서 자신의 고향의 새로운 일면을 재발견할 수 있는 기회임

[세부사항1]
- 5명이 한 팀으로 등록함
- 2017년 4월 30일 등록 마감

&

[세부사항2]
- 대회 날짜: 2017년 6월 3일 토요일
- 시간: 오전 9시—오후 5시
- 달리는 장소: 5개 마을 중 하나

222 정답 ③

지문 All in One

세쿼이아 국립공원은 위치해 있다 / 시에라 네바다 산맥 남쪽에 / 캘리포니아 동부 지역에 있는
1 Sequoia National Park is located / in the southern Sierra Nevada, / in the eastern part of
S V

그것은 국립공원으로 공표되었다 / 1890년에 / 미국에서 세 번째로 / 그것의 동쪽 경계선
California. 2 It was declared a National Park / in 1890, / the third in the USA. 3 On its eastern
S V 부사구

에는 / 가장 높은 산이 있다 / 알래스카를 제외하고 / 미국에서 / 휘트니 산이 / 세쿼이아
border / is the highest mountain / outside of Alaska / in the USA, / Mt. Whitney. 4 Sequoia
V S =

국립공원은 고향이다 / 유명한 자이언트 세쿼이아 나무들의 / 제너럴 셔먼 나무를 포함하는
National Park is the home / of the famed Giant Sequoia trees, / including the General
S V C

약 2,200년 된 / 제너럴 셔먼 나무는 또한 가장 큰 나무이다
Sherman tree. 5 Approximately 2,200 years old, / the General Sherman is also the largest tree
S V C

지구에서 / 가장 큰 열 그루의 나무 중 다섯 그루가 있다 / 세계에서 / 세쿼이아 국립공원에
/ on Earth. 6 There are five out of the ten largest trees / in the world / in Sequoia National
V S

수천 명의 관광객들이 온다 / 나무들을 보러 / 그리고 그것들의 장엄한 아름다움에 감탄한다
Park. 7 Thousands of sightseers come / to see them // and marvel at their majestic beauty /
S V_1 부사적 용법(목적) V_2

매년
every year.

① 캘리포니아 주 남부에 있다.
② 미국에서 최초로 설립된 국립공원이다.
③ Giant Sequoia 나무의 원산지이다.
④ 세계에서 가장 오래된 나무가 있다.
⑤ 현재는 사람들의 접근이 차단되었다.

해석 한 눈에 보기 **1** 세쿼이아 국립공원은 캘리포니아 동부 지역에 있는 시에라 네바다 산맥 남쪽에 위치해 있다. **2** 그것은 1890년에 미국에서 세 번째로 국립공원으로 공표되었다. **3** 그것의 동쪽 경계선에는 알래스카를 제외하고 미국에서 가장 높은 산인 휘트니 산이 있다. **4** 세쿼이아 국립공원은 제너럴 셔먼 나무를 포함하는 유명한 자이언트 세쿼이아 나무들의 고향이다. **5** 약 2,200년 된, 제너럴 셔먼 나무는 또한 지구에서 가장 큰 나무이기도 하다. **6** 세계에서 가장 큰 열 그루의 나무 가운데 다섯 그루가 세쿼이아 국립공원에 있다. **7** 수천 명의 관광객들이 매년 이 나무들을 보러 와서 그것들의 장엄한 아름다움에 감탄한다.

정답단추 글과 선택지의 내용이 일치하는지 꼼꼼하게 비교하며 읽어 내려가야 해. 네 번째 문장에서 세쿼이아 국립공원이 자이언트 세쿼이아 나무들의 고향(the home of the famed Giant Sequoia trees)이라고 했으므로 ③이 글의 내용과 일치해.

오답단서 ①은 첫 번째 문장에서 확인할 수 있어. 세쿼이아 국립공원은 캘리포니아 주 남부가 아니라 동부 지역에 있지. 미국에서 세 번째로 공표된 국립공원이라는 것을 두 번째 문장에서 확인할 수 있으니 ②도 일치하지 않아. 세계에서 가장 오래된 것이 아니라 가장 큰 나무가 있다고 했고, 마지막 문장에서 매년 많은 관광객들이 방문한다고 했으므로 ④와 ⑤도 글의 내용과 일치하지 않아.

어휘확인

be located in ~에 위치해 있다 **southern** 남쪽의 **eastern** 동쪽의 **declare** 공표[선언]하다 **border** 경계(선), 국경(선) **outside of** ~이외에; ~의 바깥쪽에 **home** 고향; 집 **famed** 유명한 **including** ~을 포함하여 **approximately** 대략, 거의 **sightseer** 관광객 **marvel at** ~에 감탄하다[경이로워하다] **majestic** 장엄한

지문 Flow

[지형 소개]
세쿼이아 국립공원은 캘리포니아 동부의 네바다 산맥 남쪽에 위치함

⬇

[세부사항1]
• 미국에서 세 번째로 국립공원으로 공표됨
• 알래스카를 제외하고 미국에서 가장 높은 산인 휘트니 산이 있음

&

[세부사항2]
• 자이언트 세쿼이아 나무의 고향
• 약 2,200년 된, 세계에서 가장 큰 나무인 제너럴 셔먼 나무가 있음

&

[세부사항3]
매년 수천 명의 관광객들이 보러 옴

223 정답 ①

지문 All in One

4번가는 호텔에서 멀지 않았다 / 그리고 쇼핑 중심지의 심장부에 있었다
1 Fourth Street was not far from the hotel // and was at the heart of the central shopping area
S V_1 C V_2

빙엄턴 중심가의 / 아침에 / 비가 많이 내렸다 / Kelly는 궁금해했다
/ in downtown Binghamton. 2 In the morning, / it rained a lot. 3 Kelly wondered // whether
S V S V 접속사

그녀가 붐비는 쇼핑 지역을 방문해야 하는지 어떤지 / 그러나 그녀가 나왔을 때쯤에는
she should visit the crowded shopping area. 4 But by the time she had emerged / from the
S′ V′ 접속사 S′ V′

호텔에서 / 구름이 끼었던 하늘이 마침내 맑아지고 있었고 / 해가 비치기 시작하고 있었다 / 공기는
hotel, // cloudy skies were finally clearing / and the sun was beginning to shine. 5 The air
S_1 V_1 S_2 V_2 S

맑았다 / 그리고 은은한 냄새로 유혹적이었다 / 꽃들과 약간 젖은 나뭇잎들의
was clear / and (was) inviting with the delicate scent / of flowers and slightly wet tree leaves.
V_1 C V_2

햇빛이 악센트를 제공하여 / 사람들의 대화에 / 오후의 산책을 숨이 멎을 듯이
6 The sun provided an accent / to the conversation of people, / making the afternoon walk
S V 분사구문(= and it made ~)

매력적이게 만들었다 / 그녀가 걸어가면서 / 그녀는 무수한 상점들을 지났다 / 다양한
breathtakingly attractive. 7 As she walked, // she passed countless stores, / various
접속사 S′ V′ S V

식당들과 / 몇몇 가옥들을
restaurants, / and some houses.

어휘확인

heart 심장[중심]부; 심장 **area** 지역 **downtown** 중심가 **whether** ~인지 어떤지 **crowded** (사람들이) 붐비는 **emerge** 나오다, 모습을 드러내다 **clear** (날씨가) 맑아지다; 맑은 **inviting** 유혹적인 **delicate** (색깔·냄새 등이) 은은한 **scent** 냄새, 향기 **slightly** 약간, 조금 **provide** 제공하다 **accent** 악센트, 강세 **conversation** 대화 **breathtakingly** 숨이 멎을 듯이 **attractive** 매력적인 **countless** 무수한 **various** 다양한

〈선택지 어휘〉

lively 활기찬 **urgent** 급박한, 시급한 **calm** 조용한; 침착한 **amusing** 재미있는 **thrilling** 긴장감 있는

① fresh and lively
신선하고 활기찬
② busy and urgent
분주하고 급박한
③ calm and lonely
조용하고 외로운
④ funny and amusing
웃기고 재미있는
⑤ exciting and thrilling
신이 나고 긴장감 있는

해석 한 눈에 보기 **1** 4번가는 호텔에서 멀지 않았고 빙엄턴 중심가의 쇼핑 중심지의 심장부에 있었다. **2** 아침에 비가 많이 내렸다. **3** Kelly는 자신이 붐비는 쇼핑 지역을 방문해야 하는지 어떤지 궁금해했다. **4** 그러나 그녀가 호텔에서 나왔을 때쯤에는, 구름이 끼었던 하늘이 마침내 개고 있었고 해가 비치기 시작하고 있었다. **5** 공기는 꽃들과 약간 젖은 나뭇잎들의 은은한 냄새로 맑고 유혹적이었다. **6** 햇빛이 사람들의 대화에 악센트를 제공하여, 오후의 산책을 숨이 멎을 듯이 매력적이게 만들었다. **7** 그녀는 걸어가면서, 무수한 상점들과 다양한 식당들과 몇몇 가옥들을 지나쳐 갔다.
정답단추 글의 분위기를 머릿속에 상상하며 읽어 보자. 오전에 비가 와서 관광을 해야 하나 하던 차에 마침내 비가 그치고 날씨가 맑아져 기분 좋게 산책을 즐기고 있는 모습이 그려지지? 지문에 등장한 형용사, 부사 등의 수식어구에 주목해서 글을 읽는 것도 도움이 돼. shine, clear and inviting with the delicate scent of flowers, breathtakingly attractive 등의 표현에서 신선하고 활기찬 분위기를 파악할 수 있어.

지문 Flow

[상황1]
아침에 비가 내려서 Kelly가 쇼핑 지역 방문에 대해 걱정함

&

[상황2]
오후에 하늘이 개고 해가 비침

⬇

[결말]
맑은 공기와 매력적인 햇빛이 오후의 산책을 즐겁게 했고, Kelly는 쇼핑 지역을 방문함

224 정답 ④

지문 All in One

1 A study has found // that people [who have **similar diets**] / **are likely to have similar personalities**. **2** For example, / vegetarians are usually artistic // and don't really like competitive sports or jobs. **3** They tend to be thoughtful and caring, / especially with animals, // and they tend to embrace / open-mindedness, different cultures, and new ideas. **4** On the other hand, / meat-eaters tend to be more active / than vegetarians. **5** They enjoy competitive sports, / prefer careers in business, / have a lot of ambition, // and like to get things done quickly. **6** They also tend to be more rigid / in their thinking // and more likely to embrace traditional viewpoints. **7** Of course, / these stereotypes are not absolute truths, / but simply common observations.

(한 연구는 밝혀냈다 / 접속사 / 비슷한 식사를 하는 사람들은 / 관계대명사 / 비슷한 성격을 가지기 쉽다 / 예를 들어 / 채식주의자들은 대체로 예술적이다 / 그리고 경쟁적인 운동이나 직업을 그다지 좋아하지 않는다 / 그들은 사려 깊고 배려하는 경향이 있다 / 특히 동물에게 / 그리고 그들은 수용하는 경향이 있다 / 열린 마음, 다른 문화와 새로운 아이디어를 / 반면에 / 고기를 먹는 사람들은 더 활동적인 경향이 있다 / 채식주의자들보다 / 그들은 경쟁적인 운동을 즐긴다 / 업무 경력을 선호한다 / 많은 야망을 가지고 있다 / 그리고 일이 빨리 처리되는 것을 좋아한다 / 그들은 또한 보다 더 엄격하고 / 그들의 사고에 있어전통적인 관점을 더 잘 받아들이는 경향이 있다 / 물론 / 이러한 고정관념은 절대적인 사실은 아니다 / 단지 일반적인 관찰일 뿐)

① firm beliefs are not willing to change
굳은 믿음(을 가진 사람들)은 변하려 하지 않는다
② different viewpoints tend to have different appetites
다른 견해(를 가진 사람들)는 다른 식욕을 가지는 경향이 있다
③ a balanced diet tend to stay in shape
균형 잡힌 식사(를 하는 사람들)는 건강을 유지하고 있는 경향이 있다
④ similar diets are likely to have similar personalities
비슷한 식사(를 하는 사람들)는 비슷한 성격을 가지기 쉽다
⑤ eating problems are able to overcome them
식이 장애(가 있는 사람들)는 그것을 극복할 수 있다

해석 한 눈에 보기 주제문 **1** 한 연구가 비슷한 식사를 하는 사람들은 비슷한 성격을 가지기 쉽다는 것을 밝혀냈다. **2** 예를 들어, 채식주의자들은 대체로 예술적이고 경쟁적인 운동이나 직업을 그다지 좋아하지 않는다. **3** 그들은 사려 깊고 배려하는 경향이 있는데, 특히 동물에게 그러하고, 그들은 열린 마음과 다른 문화와 새로운 아이디어를 수용하는 경향이 있다. **4** 반면에, 고기를 먹는 사람들은 채식주의자들보다 더 활동적인 경향이 있다. **5** 그들은 경쟁적인 운동을 즐기며, 업무 경력을 선호하고, 많은 야망을 갖고 있고, 일이 빨리 처리되는 것을 좋아한다. **6** 그들은 또한 그들의 사고에 있어 보다 더 엄격하고 전통적인 견해를 더 잘 받아들이는 경향이 있다. **7** 물론 이러한 고정관념은 절대적인 사실이 아니라 단지 일반적인 관찰일 뿐이다.
정답단추 빈칸을 포함한 문장을 보면 빈칸에는 연구에서 밝혀진 결과가 나온다는 것을 알 수 있어. 뒤이어 채식주의자의 성격과 고기를 먹는 사람의 성격이 나열되고 있지. 이를 다른 말로 표현하면 비슷한 식습관을 가진 사람들은 비슷한 성격을 가진다고 할 수 있어. 따라서 빈칸에 들어갈 말로 가장 적절한 것은 ④야.
오답단서 ①은 지문에 사용된 어구를 활용해 만든 오답이야. 또한, 두 부류의 비슷한 식습관을 가진 사람들을 비교한 것이지, 다른 견해를 가진 사람들을 비교하고 있지는 않으니 ②도 정답이 될 수 없어. ③은 본문의 내용과는 전혀 관련이 없어. ⑤ 역시 식이 장애에 대해 본문에서 언급한 적이 없으므로 빈칸에 적절하지 않아.

어휘확인

similar 비슷한 **be likely to-v** ~하기 쉽다 **personality** 성격 **vegetarian** 채식주의자 **artistic** 예술적인 **competitive** 경쟁적인 **tend to-v** ~하는 경향이 있다 **thoughtful** 사려 깊은 **caring** 배려하는 **embrace** 받아들이다; 안다, 포옹하다 **open-mindedness** 열린 마음 **meat-eater** 고기 먹는 사람 **prefer** 선호하다 **career** 경력; 직업 **business** (직장의) 일, 업무 **ambition** 야망 **rigid** 엄격한 **thinking** 사고, 생각 **viewpoint** 관점, 시각 **stereotype** 고정관념 **absolute** 절대적인 **truth** 사실 **simply** 단지, 그저 **common** 일반적인, 보통의 **observation** 관찰; 의견
〈선택지 어휘〉
firm 굳은, 견고한 **belief** 믿음, 신념 **be not willing to-v** ~하려 하지 않다 **appetite** 식욕 **balanced** 균형 잡힌 **stay in shape** 건강을 유지하다 **overcome** 극복하다

지문 Flow

[주제문]
비슷한 음식을 먹는 사람들은 비슷한 성격을 가지기 쉬움

⬇

[예시1]
• 채식주의자
– 예술적이고, 경쟁적이지 않으며, 사려 깊고 배려함
– 열린 마음으로 다른 문화와 새로운 아이디어를 수용함

&

[예시2]
• 육식주의자
– 활동적이고, 경쟁적이며, 야망이 많고, 신속한 일 처리를 좋아함
– 사고가 더 경직적이고 전통적인 견해를 더 잘 수용함

225 정답 ⑤

지문 All in One

만약 당신이 당신 자신에 대한 개인 정보를 내어 주는 것에 저항한다면 다른 사람들에게 당신은 자신에게 부여
[1] If you resist giving away personal information about yourself / to others, // you might be
접속사 S′ V′ S V

하고 있는 것일지도 모른다 너무 많은 중요성을 만약 당신이 자세히 살펴본다면 당신이 드러낼지도 모르는 것을 당신은
giving yourself / too much importance. [2] If you look closely / at what you might reveal, // you
접속사 S'_1 V'_1 관계대명사 S

아마도 발견할 것이다 어떤 것도 사실상 커다란 비밀이 아니라는 것을 즐거운 친밀한 관계는
will probably find / that nothing is actually a great secret. [3] Enjoyable close relationships /
V 접속사 S'_2 V'_2 C′ S

갖기 불가능하다 만약 당신이 준비가 되어 있지 않으면 당신 자신에 대한 것들을 드러낼
are impossible to have // unless you are prepared / to reveal things about yourself. [4] Of
V C 부사적 용법(형용사 수식) 접속사 S′ V′

물론 어떤 생각이나 감정들은 발설되지 않은 채로 있는 것이 가장 좋다 특히 사무실에서나 혹은 완전히 낯선 사람
course, / some thoughts and feelings / are best left unspoken, / especially in the office or
S V

들과 함께 있을 때 그러나 개인적인 어떤 것도 공유하기를 거부하는 것은 거의
with complete strangers. [5] However, / **refusing to share anything personal** / is almost a
S V C

당신이 외로울 것이라는 보장이다 평생 동안 따라서 다음번에 누구가가 관심을 보일 때
guarantee that you will be lonely / all your life]. [6] Thus, / the next time someone shows an
= 접속사 S′ V′

당신의 배경이나 개인적인 감정이나 혹은 견해에 대해 당신은 모험을 해야 한다
interest / in your background, personal feelings, or opinions, // you should take a risk; /
S V

즉 당신 자신에 대한 독특한 어떤 것을 드러내고 기분이 좋아지는 보상을 즐겨라
reveal something unique about yourself, / and enjoy the reward of feeling good.
V_1 V_2

① distrusting people's motives
다른 사람의 동기를 불신하는 것

② revealing other people's secrets
다른 사람들의 비밀을 폭로하는 것

③ being interested in a close relationship
친밀한 관계에 관심을 갖는 것

④ avoiding getting along with strangers
낯선 사람들과 잘 지내기를 피하는 것

⑤ refusing to share anything personal
개인적인 어떤 것도 공유하기를 거부하는 것

해석 한 눈에 보기 **1** 만약 당신이 다른 사람들에게 자신에 대한 개인적인 정보를 내어주는 것에 저항한다면, 당신은 자신에게 너무 많은 중요성을 부여하고 있는 것일지도 모른다. **2** 만약 당신이 드러낼지도 모르는 것을 당신이 자세히 살펴본다면, 당신은 아마도 어떤 것도 사실상 커다란 비밀이 아니라는 것을 발견할 것이다. **3** 즐거운 친밀한 관계는 만약 당신이 자신에 대한 것들을 드러낼 준비가 되어 있지 않으면 갖기 불가능하다. **4** 물론, 어떤 생각이나 감정은 발설되지 않은 채로 있는 것이 가장 좋은데, 특히 사무실에서나 혹은 완전히 낯선 사람들과 함께 있을 때 그렇다. **5** 그러나 개인적인 어떤 것도 공유하기를 거부하는 것은 거의 당신이 평생 외로울 것이라는 보장이다. 주제문 **6** 따라서, 다음번에 누군가가 당신의 배경이나, 개인적인 감정이나, 혹은 견해에 관심을 보일 때, 당신은 모험을 해야 한다. 즉, 자신에 대한 독특한 어떤 것을 드러내고, 기분이 좋아지는 보상을 즐겨라.

정답단추 빈칸에 들어갈 '무엇'이 사람을 평생 외롭게 만들 것인지를 찾아야 해. 세 번째 문장에서 즐거운 친밀한 관계는 자신을 드러낼 준비가 되어 있지 않으면 불가능하다고 말하고 있어. 또한 빈칸을 포함한 문장 뒤에서 자신에 대한 개인적인 어떤 것을 공유하는 모험을 해야 한다고 하고 있지? 따라서 '개인적인 어떤 것도 공유하기를 거부하는 것'이 외롭게 만든다는 것을 알 수 있어. 따라서 빈칸에는 ⑤가 적절해.

오답단서 자신에 대해 드러내면 다른 사람들과 친밀한 관계를 맺을 수 있다는 이 글의 주제를 잘 생각해보자. ①의 다른 사람의 동기에 대한 불신이 어떠한 영향을 미칠 것이라는 언급은 전혀 없었어. 다른 사람에게 자신에 대한 개인적인 정보를 내어주지 않는 것이 다른 사람의 동기에 대한 불신 때문이라고 넘겨짚으면 안 돼. ②, ④는 지문에서 사용된 어구를 활용해 만든 선택지야. ③은 본문의 내용과는 관련이 없지.

어휘확인

resist 저항하다 **give away** 내어[거저] 주다 **personal** 개인적인, 개인의 **information** 정보 **importance** 중요성 **closely** 자세히 **reveal** 드러내다, 폭로하다 **probably** 아마 **enjoyable** 즐거운 **relationship** 관계 **unless** 만약 ~이 아니면 **thought** 생각 **unspoken** 말로 하지[입 밖에 내지] 않은 **refuse** 거부[거절]하다 **guarantee** 보장(하는 것) **thus** 따라서 **background** 배경 **take a risk** 모험하다 **reward** 보상

〈선택지 어휘〉

distrust 불신하다 **motive** 동기, 이유 **get along with** ~와 잘 지내다

지문 Flow

[도입]
자신의 개인적 정보를 주기를 거부하는 것은 자신에게 너무 많은 중요성을 부여하는 것이며 사실상 큰 비밀이 아님

⬇

[보충설명1]
친밀한 관계를 원한다면 자신에 대한 것을 드러내야 함

&

[보충설명2]
개인의 것을 공유하지 않으면 평생 외로울 것임

⬇

[주제문]
누군가 당신의 개인적인 것에 관심을 보일 때, 자신을 드러내어 기분이 좋아지는 보상을 받아야 함

226 정답 ④

지문 All in One

신체적이든 아니든 간에 벌은 단순히 아이들에게 가르친다 규칙을 어기면
[1] Whether physical or not, // punishment simply teaches children / that if they break rules /
접속사 S V IO 접속사 접속사 S″ V″

부정적 결과를 겪을 것이라고 벌이 아이들에게 반드시 가르쳐주는 것은 아니다
they will suffer negative consequences. [2] Punishment does not necessarily teach children /
S′ V′ S V IO

왜 규칙이 있는지 왜 규칙이 중요한지 또는 어떻게 그들이 규칙을 가장 잘 따를 수 있는지
why the rules are in place, / why the rules are important, / or how they can best follow the
DO_1(간접의문문) DO_2(간접의문문) DO_3(간접의문문)

벌은 또한 가르치지 않는다 아이들이 책임을 지도록 또는 고려하도록
rules. [3] Punishment also does not teach / children to be responsible / or to take into account
S V O C_1 C_2

어휘확인

physical 신체적인 **punishment** 벌, 처벌 **simply** 단순히 **suffer** 겪다, 고통 받다 **negative** 부정적인 **consequence** 결과 **necessarily** 반드시 **in place** 가동 중인; 제자리에 **responsible** 책임 있는 **take into account** ~을 고려하다 **thought** 생각, 사고 **discipline** 훈육, 규율 **on the other hand** 반면에 **appropriate** 적절한 **behavior** 행동 **means** 수단 **better oneself** 더 잘 살다, 출세하다

다른 사람들의 생각, 필요, 또는 경험을 　　　　　　　　　　　　　　　　　훈육은 　　　　　　　반면에 　　　　　　　항상

/ the thoughts, needs, or experiences of others. [4] Discipline, / on the other hand, / always

S

교훈을 담고 있다 　　　　　　　아이들이 아는 데 도움을 주는 　　　　　　　적절한 행동이 무엇인지를 　　　　　　　그리고

carries *a lesson* [which helps children to understand / what appropriate behaviors are / and

V 　　　　　　관계대명사 　　　　　　　　　　　　　　간접의문문

왜 그것들이 허용되었는지를 　　　　　　　우리 사회에서 　　　　　자녀를 훈육하는 것은 　　　　　실제로 자녀들에게

why they have become accepted / in our society]. [5] Disciplining children / is really a means

간접의문문 　　　　　　　　　　S 　　　　V 　　　C

가르치는 수단이다 　　　　　　　　더 잘 사는 방법을

of teaching children / how to **better** themselves.

① spoil 망치는 　② define 정의하는 　③ punish 처벌하는

④ better 더 잘 사는 　⑤ free 풀어 주는

해석 한 눈에 보기 1 신체적이든 아니든 간에, 벌은 단순히 아이들에게 규칙을 어기면 부정적 결과를 겪을 것이라고 가르친다. 2 벌은 왜 규칙이 있는지, 왜 규칙이 중요한지, 또는 어떻게 그들이 규칙을 잘 따를 수 있는지를 반드시 아이들에게 가르쳐주는 것은 아니다. 3 벌은 또한 아이들이 책임을 지거나 다른 사람들의 생각, 필요, 또는 경험에 대해 고려하도록 가르치지 않는다. 4 반면에, 훈육은 항상 아이들이 적절한 행동이 무엇인지 그리고 왜 그것들이 우리 사회에서 허용되었는지를 아는 데 도움을 주는 교훈을 담고 있다. 주제문 5 자녀를 훈육하는 것은 실제로 자녀들에게 더 잘 사는 방법을 가르치는 수단이다.

정답단추 빈칸 추론 문제는 빈칸을 포함한 문장을 먼저 읽는 게 좋아. 빈칸이 있는 문장을 보면 자녀를 훈육하는 것이 자녀들에게 '무엇'하는 방법을 가르치는 수단이라는 내용이지. 바로 앞 내용을 살펴보면, 벌과 달리 훈육은 아이들에게 적절한 행동이 무엇인지, 왜 그렇게 하는지 알려주는 교훈을 담고 있다고 했으니까, 훈육은 자녀들에게 '더 잘 사는 방법'을 가르치는 수단이 된다고 볼 수 있어. 따라서 빈칸에 들어갈 말로 가장 적절한 것은 ④야.

〈선택지 어휘〉

define 정의하다 punish 처벌하다

지문 Flow

[도입]
벌은 규칙을 어기면 좋지 않은 결과를 겪는다는 것을 가르침

⬇

[보충설명]
• 벌은 규칙의 존재나 중요성의 이유를 설명하지 않음
• 벌은 아이들이 책임을 지거나 다른 사람들을 배려하도록 하지 않음

⬇

[비교]
훈육은 사회에서 허용되는 적절한 행동이 무엇인지 알려주는 교훈을 담고 있음

⬇

[주제도출]
자녀 훈육은 자녀들에게 더 잘 사는 방법을 가르치는 수단임

227 정답 ①

지문 All in One

나쁜 기억을 지워버리는 알약 　　　　　　　이것은 영화에서 나오는 어떤 것처럼 들린다 　　　　　　그러나

[1] *A pill* [to erase bad memories]? [2] This sounds like something out of a movie, // but it may

S_1 V_1 S_2 V_2

현실에 더 가까울지도 모른다 　당신이 생각하는 것보다 　이 약은 　　'프로프라놀롤'이라는 이름의 　　고통스러운 기억을 치유할

be closer to reality / than you think. [3] *The drug*, / [named "Propranolol,"] / has *the potential*

C_2 S V

수 있는 잠재력을 갖고 있다 　　　　　　이 약은 연결을 끊는다 　　　　　　그 기억과 그에 관련된 감정 간의

[to heal painful memories]. [4] The drug breaks the link / between the memory and its

S V

환자가 정신적 충격을 받은 사건에 대해 생각하고 있는 동안에 　　　　　그러면 　　　고통이

related emotions // while the patient is thinking about the traumatic event. [5] Then, / the pain

접속사 S' V' S

사라진다 　　　하지만 　　이 약을 비판하는 사람들은 주장한다 　　　　우리의 기억이 우리를 인간으로 만든다고

disappears. [6] (A) However, / critics of the drug insist // that our memories make us human, /

V S V 접속사 S'_1 V'_1 O'_1 C'_1

그리고 고통스러운 사건들이 우리를 도와준다고 　　　우리가 더 나은 사람이 되도록 　　　또한 　　그들은 염려한다

and that painful events help us / to become better people. [7] (B) Also, / they are concerned //

접속사 S'_2 V'_2 O'_2 C'_2 S V C

이 약이 무분별하게 사용되어 　　　　　일상적인 사건들에서 생기는 평범한 감정을 지우게 될까 봐

that the drug will be used carelessly, / to erase *the normal feelings* [that come from everyday

접속사 S' V' 부사적 용법(결과) 관계대명사

사소한 말다툼과 당혹스러운 상황과 같은

events / like minor arguments and embarrassing situations].

	(A)		(B)
①	However	……	Also
②	Similarly	……	Otherwise
③	Moreover	……	Instead
④	For example	……	Therefore
⑤	On the other hand	……	Nevertheless

해석 한 눈에 보기 1 나쁜 기억을 지워버리는 알약? 2 이것은 영화에서 나오는 어떤 것처럼 들리지만, 그것은 당신이 생각하는 것보다 현실에 더 가까울지도 모른다. 3 '프로프라놀롤'이라는 이름의 이 약은 고통스러운 기억을 치유할 수 있는 잠재력이 있다. 4 이 약은 환자가 정신적 충격을 받은 사건에 대해 생각하고 있는 동안에 그 기억과 그에 관련된 감정 간의 연결고리를 끊는다. 5 그러면 고통이 사라진다. 6 (A) 하지만 이 약을 비판하는 사람들은 우리의 기억이 우리를 인간으로 만들며, 고통스러운 사건들이 우리를 더 나은 사람이 되도록 도와준다고 주장한다. 7 (B) 또한, 그들은 이 약이 무분별하게 사용되어 사소한 말다툼과 당혹스러운 상황과 같은 일상적인 사건들에서 생기는 평범한 감정을 지우게 될까 봐 염려한다.

정답단추 (A)의 앞뒤에는 각각 고통스러운 기억을 지우는 약의 효과와 이를 비판하는 사람들의 주장이 나오므로 상반된 내용을 연결하는 접속사가 들어가야 해. 따라서 (A)에는 '대조'를 나타내는 연결어 However가 적절해. (B)에는 이 약을 비판하는 사람들의 또 다른 주장이 이어지므로 '첨가'를 나타내는 Also가 들어가야 자연스러워.

어휘확인

erase 지우다, 없애다 memory 기억 out of ~에서, reality 현실 drug 약, 의약품 potential 잠재력, 가능성 heal 치료하다, 고치다 painful 고통스러운 link 연결, 관련 related 관련된 emotion 감정 patient 환자 traumatic 정신적 충격이 큰 then 그러면; 그 때 disappear 사라지다 critic 비판하는 사람, 비평가 insist 주장하다 concerned 염려[걱정]하는 carelessly 무분별하게, 경솔하게 normal 평범한 minor 사소한 argument 말다툼 embarrassing 당혹스러운, 난처한 situation 상황

지문 Flow

[도입]
나쁜 기억을 지워버리는 약, 프로프라놀롤

⬇

[보충설명]
환자가 정신적 충격을 받은 사건에 대해 생각하는 동안, 그 기억과 관련된 감정 간의 연결고리를 끊어서 고통을 사라지게 함

⬇

[반박]
• 고통스러운 기억이 더 나은 인간이 되도록 도와줌
• 약의 무분별한 사용으로 일상적인 사건에서 생기는 감정까지 지워질 수 있음

228 정답 ③

지문 All in One

1 Studies in American society show / (that) white teachers have lower expectations / that their black students will graduate and go to college, // and that lower expectations for black and Latino students / are one possible explanation / for observed achievement gaps. 2 ① Meanwhile, / black students receive suspensions / at nearly four times the rate / for white students. 3 ② As solutions, / many school systems have banned suspensions / for subjective categories / such as disobedience, // and (have) begun to rethink teacher training. 4 (③ As a result, / the costs for the new teacher training program / have doubled.) 5 ④ At the same time, / school districts have made a push / to hire more teachers of color, / motivated by *findings* / [showing that students of color do better in school / if they have a teacher of the same race]. 6 ⑤ As one expert said, // "Focus should be made / on fostering a culture of equity / and ensuring that all kids have access to high-quality teaching."

해석 한 눈에 보기 1 미국 사회의 연구에 의하면 백인 교사들은 자신들의 흑인 학생들이 졸업하고 대학에 진학한다는 기대가 더 낮았고, 흑인과 라틴계 학생들에 대한 그 더 낮은 기대는 관찰된 성취도 차이에 대한 하나의 가능성 있는 설명이다. 2 ① 한편, 흑인 학생들은 백인 학생들에 비해 거의 4배 비율로 정학을 받는다. 3 ② 해결책으로, 많은 학교 제도는 불복종(반항)과 같은 주관적 범주에 대한 정학을 금지하고, 교사 연수를 다시 생각하기 시작했다. 4 (③ 그 결과, 새로운 교사 연수 프로그램 비용이 두 배가 되었다.) 5 ④ 동시에, 학군들은 같은 인종의 선생님을 가지면 유색 인종의 학생들이 학교에서 더 잘한다는 것을 보여 주는 연구 결과에 의해 동기 부여되어서 더 많은 유색 인종의 선생님을 고용하도록 밀고 나갔다. 주제문 6 ⑤ 한 전문가가 말했듯이, "형평성 문화를 조성하고 모든 아이들이 양질의 가르침에 접근하도록 보장하는 것에 초점이 맞춰져야 한다."

정답단추 글 안의 모든 문장은 하나의 주제를 적절하게 뒷받침해야 해. 이 글은 학교에서 인종적인 이유로 불평등이 일어날 수 있다는 문제를 다루고 있어. 도입 부분은 백인 교사들이 유색 인종의 학생들에 대한 기대치가 낮으며, 그것이 학생들의 성취도에 차이를 준다는 내용으로 시작하고, 그것에 대한 해결책으로 주관적인 정학을 금지하고, 교사 연수를 다시 재고하고, 유색 인종의 교사를 고용하는 것 등을 말하고 있지. 그런데 ③은 교사 연수 비용이 두 배가 되었다는 내용이어서 글의 주제인 '학교 교육의 형평성'과는 무관해.

오답단서 ①은 문제점에 대한 내용이고, ②와 ④는 문제점에 대한 해결책이므로 자연스럽게 연결돼. ⑤는 글의 주제문에 해당하는 문장이야.

어휘확인

lower 더 낮은 **expectation** 기대, 예상 **graduate** 졸업하다 **possible** 가능한 **explanation** 설명 **observe** 관찰하다 **achievement** 성취, 업적 **gap** 차이 **meanwhile** 한편, 그 동안에 **suspension** 정학 **solution** 해결책 **ban** 금하다 **subjective** 주관적인 **category** 범주 **disobedience** 불복종, 반항 **rethink** 다시 생각하다 **cost** 비용 **double** 두 배가 되다 **at the same time** 동시에 **district** 지구, 지역 **make a push** 밀고 나가다 **hire** 고용하다 **motivate** 동기를 부여하다 **finding** (연구) 결과 **race** 인종 **expert** 전문가 **foster** 조성하다, 발전시키다 **equity** 형평(성), 공평 **ensure** 보장하다 **have access to** ~로 접근하다 **high-quality** 양질의

지문 Flow

[문제점]
- 백인 교사들의 흑인과 라틴계 학생들에 대한 낮은 기대치가 성취도의 차이를 가져옴
- 흑인 학생들이 백인 학생들보다 정학을 4배나 더 받음

↓

[해결책1]
- 주관적 이유로 정학 금지
- 교사 연수

↓

[무관한 문장]
교사 연수 프로그램 비용이 두 배가 됨

↓

[해결책2]
- 유색 인종 교사 고용

↓

[주제도출]
형평성 문화를 조성하고 학생들에게 양질을 교육을 보장해야 함

229 정답 ④

지문 All in One

1 It should come as no surprise // that the fastest way to transport food / is by aircraft. (①) 2 Also, / it is *the most expensive way* [to move food]. (②) 3 So between nearby countries, / food is usually transported / over land / by truck or train. (③) 4 Ships are usually used to transfer it / between very distant countries // because they are able to carry such large volumes. 5 (④ However, / there are *times* [when aircraft are useful / in getting food / to

어휘확인

come as no surprise 놀라운 일이 아니다 **transport** 수송하다 **aircraft** 항공기 **nearby** 가까운 **transfer** 수송하다 **distant** 먼, (멀리) 떨어져 있는 **suppose** 가정하다; 추측하다 **earthquake** 지진 **starve** 굶어 죽다

지문 Flow

[소재]
음식물 수송의 가장 빠른 방법은 항공기

↓

사람들에게 가정해 보자 홍수나 지진이 났다고 그리고 사람들이 다다를 수 없었다고
people].) 6 Suppose // (that) there was a flood [or] an earthquake / [and] people could not be
V 접속사 V′₁ S′₁ S′₂ V′₂
기차나 트럭으로 만약 음식물이 수송되지 못하면 항공기에 의해
reached / by train [or] truck. (⑤) 7 If food could not be transported / by aircraft, // those
접속사 S′ V′ S
그 사람들은 굶어 죽을지도 모른다
people might starve.
V

해석 한 눈에 보기 1 음식물을 수송하는 가장 빠른 방법은 항공기에 의한 것이라는 것은 전혀 놀라운 일이 아닐 것이다. 2 또한 그것은 음식물을 운반하는 가장 비싼 방법이기도 하다. 3 그래서 가까운 나라들 간에는, 음식물이 일반적으로 트럭이나 기차에 의해 육로를 거쳐 수송된다. 4 배는 일반적으로 아주 많은 양을 운반할 수 있기 때문에 매우 먼 나라들 간의 그것을 수송하는 데 쓰인다. 5 하지만 항공기가 사람들에게 음식물을 전달하는 데 유용한 때가 있다. 6 홍수나 지진이 났는데 사람들이 기차나 트럭으로 다다를 수 없었다고 가정해 보라. 7 만일 음식물이 항공기에 의해 수송되지 못하면, 그 사람들은 굶어 죽을지도 모른다.

정답단추 첫 문장을 읽고 음식물과 항공 수송에 관한 글임을 짐작할 수 있지? 전반부는 항공 수송이 빠르지만 비용이 많이 들어 주로 육로와 배로 음식을 나른다는 내용인 반면, Suppose 이하의 두 문장은 항공기로 음식을 수송해야 하는 경우를 설명하고 있어. 내용이 상반되므로 ④에는 However가 들어가는 게 적절해.

오답단서 ①, ②, ③, ⑤는 앞뒤로 글의 흐름이 끊기는 부분 없이 매끄럽게 연결되어 있어. 그래서 주어진 문장이 들어가기에는 적절하지 않아.

[비판]
항공기가 비싸서, 가까운 나라 간에는 육로를 이용하고, 먼 나라 간에는 배를 이용함

⬇

[대조]
홍수나 지진이 났을 때, 음식물을 빠르게 전달하는 데는 항공기가 유용함

230 정답 ③

지문 All in One

다른 사람들을 용인한다는 것은 〈미국 문화유산 사전〉에 따르면 의미한다 인정하고
1 To tolerate others, / according to *The American Heritage Dictionary*, / means, / to recognize
S V
존중하는 것을 그들과 그들의 믿음이나 관습을 반드시 그들에게 동의하거나 그들을 동정하지 않고도
[and] respect / them [and] their beliefs [or] practices, / without necessarily agreeing [or]
반면에 이 단어는 다른 사람들을 참는 것을 의미할 수 있다
sympathizing with them. 2 On the other hand, / the word can mean to put up with others, //
S V
당신이 그들을 경멸할지라도 어떤 힘이 ~하기 때문에 사회적 규범과 같은 당신이 그렇게 할
though you may despise them, / because some force, / such as social norms, / requires that
접속사 S′₁ V′₁ 접속사 S′₂ V′₂ 접속사
것을 요구하기 나에게는 ~으로 보인다 사람들이 종종 사용하는 척하는 것 그 단어의 첫 번째 의미를
you do so. 3 It seems to me / that people often pretend to use / the first meaning of the word
S″ V″ S V 접속사 S′ V′
그들이 실제로 두 번째 의미를 염두에 두었을 때 그런 경우에 사람들은
// when they really have in mind the second meaning. 4 In such cases, / people are
접속사 S″ V″ S₁ V₁
위선적이다 그들이 그 단어를 사용할 때 그리고 나는 그들을 존경하지 않는다 그들은 다른 사람들을
hypocritical / when they use the word, // [and] I do not admire them. 5 They pretend to
C 접속사 S′ V′ S₂ V₂ S₁ V₁
존중하는 체 한다 그러나 실제로 그들은 단지 그들을 참고 있는 것이다 그것은 그들이 말하고 있는
respect others, // [but] in reality / they are merely putting up with them. 6 It is as though they
S₂ V₂ S V 접속사 S′
것과 같다 점잖게 굴어라 그러면 나는 호의적일 것이다 당신이 있는 것을 허용할 정도로 충분히 또는
are saying: / Behave yourself, / [and] I will be gracious / enough to permit you to exist. 7 Or, /
V′ V₁ S₂ V₂ 형용사+enough+to부정사
당신이 나의 우월함을 받아들이면 나는 당신을 용인할 것이다
if you will accept my superiority, / I will tolerate you.
접속사 S′ V′ S V

⬇

그것의 공식적인 의미와는 달리 불평등의 의미는 종종 암시된다
8 Contrary to its official meaning, / a sense of (A) unequalness is often implied / by *the*
S V
'용인하다'라는 단어로 그것을 내가 인정할 수 없다는 것을 알게 된다
word "tolerate," / [which I find (B) unacceptable].
관계대명사(계속적 용법)

	(A)		(B)
①	modesty	……	admirable
②	modesty	……	unacceptable
③	unequalness	……	unacceptable
④	unequalness	……	admirable
⑤	balance	……	understandable

해석 한 눈에 보기 1 〈미국 문화유산 사전〉에 따르면, 다른 사람들을 용인한다는 것은 반드시 그들에게 동의하거나 그들을 동정하지 않고도, 그들과 그들의 믿음이나 관습을 인정하고 존중하는 것을 의미한다. 2 반면에, 이 단어는 사회적 규범과 같은 어떤 힘이 당신이 그렇게 할 것을 요구하기 때문에, 당신이 그들을 경멸할지라도, 다른 사람들을 참는 것을 의미할 수 있다. 3 나에게는 사람들이 실제로 두 번째 의미를 염두에 두었을 때, 종종 그 단어의 첫 번째 의미를

어휘확인

tolerate 용인하다, 참다 **according to** ~에 따르면 **heritage** 유산 **recognize** 인정하다 **respect** 존중하다 **belief** 믿음 **practice** 관습, 관행 **necessarily** 반드시, 필연적으로 **sympathize** 동정하다 **on the other hand** 반면에 **put up with** ~을 참다 **despise** 경멸하다 **force** 힘 **norm** 규범 **require** 요구하다 **pretend** ~인 체하다 **have in mind** 염두에 두다 **hypocritical** 위선적인 **admire** 존경하다, 칭찬하다 **in reality** 실제로는 **merely** 단지 **behave oneself** 점잖게 굴다 **gracious** 호의적인, 친절한 **permit** 허용하다, 허락하다 **exist** 존재하다 **superiority** 우월성 **contrary to** ~와 반대로 **official** 공식적인 **unequalness** 불평등 **imply** 암시하다, 함축하다 **unacceptable** 인정할 수 없는, 받아들일 수 없는

〈선택지 어휘〉
modesty 겸손 **admirable** 존경스러운 **understandable** 이해할 수 있는

지문 Flow

[소재]
다른 사람들을 용인하는 것의 의미

⬇

[보충설명]
• 의미1: 동의나 동정 없이, 타인과 그들의 믿음이나 관습을 인정하고 존중하는 것
• 의미2: 사회 규범 때문에, 타인을 경멸할지라도 참는 것

⬇

[비판]
두 번째 의미를 감추고 첫 번째 의미를 사용하는 척 하는 사람들은 위선적임

⬇

사용하는 척하는 것으로 보인다. **4** 그런 경우에, 사람들은 그 단어를 사용할 때 위선적이며, 나는 그들을 존경하지 않는다. **5** 그들은 다른 사람들을 존중하는 체 하지만, 실제로 그들은 단지 그들을 참고 있는 것이다. **6** 그것은 그들이 이렇게 말하고 있는 것과 같다. "점잖게 굴어라, 그러면 내가 당신이 있는 것을 허용할 정도로 충분히 호의적일 것이다." **7** 또는, 당신이 나의 우월함을 받아들이면, 나는 당신을 용인할 것이다.

[보충설명]
다른 사람들을 존중하는 척 하지만, 단지 참고 있는 것일 뿐임

8 그것의 공식적인 의미와는 달리, '용인하다'라는 단어는 (A) 불평등의 의미를 종종 암시하는데, 나는 그것을 (B) 인정할 수 없다는 것을 안다.

정답단추 글을 읽기 전에 요약문을 보면 글의 내용을 어느 정도 추론할 수 있는데, 이 글은 '용인하는 것'에 대한 사람들의 이면성을 다룬 내용이야. tolerate는 원래 다른 사람들을 인정하고 존중하는 것을 말하지만, 사실상 그것의 이면에는 다른 사람들을 참는다는 의미를 포함하고 있어. 필자는 말로는 용인한다고 하면서 실제로는 다른 사람들을 참고 있는 사람들을 위선적이라고 생각하고 있어. 또한 그들은 다른 사람들에게 자신의 우월함을 인정하면 그들을 용인할 거라는 식으로 생각하고 있는 것 같다고 했어. 우월함을 인정하면 참아주겠다는 의미에서 둘 사이의 관계는 불평등한 거야. 그런 의미에서 필자는 그 단어를 인정할 수 없다는 것이지. 따라서 빈칸 (A)에 들어갈 말로는 unequalness, 빈칸 (B)에 들어갈 말로는 unacceptable이 가장 적절해. 이를 종합하면 답은 ③이야.
오답단서 ①, ②는 겸손이 남을 존중하며 자신을 낮추는 행동이므로, '용인하다'의 이면적 의미인 참는 것과는 어울리지 않아. ④는 필자가 그 단어를 존경스럽게 생각하지 않으므로 오답이야. ⑤는 둘 다 본문의 내용과 어울리지 않는 선택지로 답이 될 수 없어.

231 정답 ⑤

지문 All in One

1 Before(접속사) you(S') start(V') a writing project, // it's(가주어 V) good(C) / to have a brainstorming session(진주어) / to get creative writing ideas.(부사적 용법(목적))
(당신이 쓰기 과제를 시작하기 전에 / ~이 좋다 / 브레인스토밍 시간을 갖는 것이 / 창의적인 쓰기 아이디어를 얻기 위해)

2 Sit,(V_1) think,(V_2) and write(V_3) down / every single idea [that(관계대명사) comes into your head].
(앉아서, 생각하고, 그리고 적어두어라 / 머릿속에 떠오르는 생각 하나하나를 모두)

(C) 3 When(접속사) you(S') are(V') ready(C') / to start writing, // just let(V_1) your ideas(O) flow,(C) / and don't worry(V_2) too much / about correct spelling or grammar.
(당신이 준비가 되었을 때 / 쓰기를 시작할 / 그저 생각이 흘러가게 두어라 / 그리고 너무 많이 걱정하지 마라 / 정확한 철자나 문법에 대해)

4 This(S) is not(V) the time(C) [to be a perfectionist(형용사적 용법)].
(지금은 ~할 때가 아니다 / 완벽주의자가 될)

(B) 5 After(접속사) you've(S') finished(V') the initial rough copy, // review(V) it carefully.
(당신이 처음의 대략적인 원고를 완성한 후에는 / 그것을 주의 깊게 검토해라)

6 Take(V) some extra time at this stage / to be really thorough.(부사적 용법(목적))
(이 단계에서 약간의 추가 시간을 가져라 / 정말로 철저해지기 위해)

7 Think(V_1) of better words and clearer sentences, // and fix(V_2) all obvious mistakes.
(더 나은 단어와 더 명백한 문장을 생각해 내라 / 그리고 모든 명백한 실수를 고쳐라)

(A) 8 Your final copy(S) should be(V) double-spaced.
(당신의 최종 원고는 한 행씩 띄어져 있어야 한다)

9 Then, / give(V) it(IO) one last check(DO) / before printing.
(그리고 나서 / 마지막으로 한 번 더 확인해라 / 인쇄하기 전에)

10 Make(V) sure(C) // (that)(접속사) your name and the title of your essay(S') / are written(V') clearly / on the first page.
(확실히 해라 / 당신의 이름과 당신 리포트의 제목이 / 명확히 적혀 있는지 / 첫 페이지에)

① (A) - (B) - (C) ② (B) - (A) - (C) ③ (B) - (C) - (A)
④ (C) - (A) - (B) ⑤ (C) - (B) - (A)

해석 한 눈에 보기 **1** 당신이 쓰기 과제를 시작하기 전에, 창의적인 쓰기 아이디어를 얻기 위해 브레인스토밍 시간을 갖는 것이 좋다. **2** 앉아서, 생각하고, 그리고 머릿속에 떠오르는 생각 하나하나를 모두 적어두어라. (C) **3** 당신이 쓰기 시작할 준비가 되었을 때는, 그저 당신의 생각들이 흘러가게 두고, 정확한 철자나 문법에 대해 너무 많이 걱정하지 마라. **4** 지금은 완벽주의자가 될 시간이 아니다. (B) **5** 당신이 처음의 대략적인 원고를 완성한 후에는, 그것을 주의 깊게 검토해라. **6** 이 단계에서 정말로 철저해지기 위해 약간의 추가 시간을 가져라. **7** 더 나은 단어와 더 명확한 문장을 생각해 내고 모든 명백한 실수를 고쳐라. (A) **8** 당신의 최종 원고는 한 행씩 띄어져 있어야 한다. **9** 그리고 나서 인쇄하기 전에 그것을 마지막으로 한 번 더 확인해라. **10** 당신의 이름과 당신 리포트의 제목이 첫 페이지에 명확히 적혀 있는지 확실히 해라.
정답단추 주어진 문장은 쓰기 과제를 시작하기 전 아이디어를 얻는 방법을 설명하고 있어. (A)는 최종 원고를 확인할 때에 관한 내용인 것을 final copy에서 파악할 수 있어. (B)는 최초의 초고를 완성한 후, 즉 완성된 초안을 검토할 때의 내용이니까 글을 쓰기 시작한 다음 단계에 대한 설명이겠지? (C)에서 '당신이 쓰기 시작할 준비가 되었을 때'라고 했으니, 주어진 문장 다음에 와야 한다는 걸 알 수 있어. 이를 종합해서 쓰기 과제를 작성하는 방법을 순서대로 바르게 연결하면 글의 순서는 ⑤의 '(C) – (B) – (A)'가 돼.

어휘확인
brainstorming 브레인스토밍(자유롭게 아이디어를 끌어내는 방식) **session** 시간[기간] **single** 하나하나의; 단 하나의 **come into A's head** A의 머릿속에 떠오르다 **flow** 흐르다 **spelling** 철자(법) **grammar** 문법 **perfectionist** 완벽주의자 **initial** 처음의 **rough** 대략적인; 거친 **copy** 원고; 복사(본) **extra** 추가의 **thorough** 철저한, 완전한 **obvious** 명백한 **double-spaced** 한 행씩 띄어서 쓴 **then** 그러고 나서 **make sure (that)** 확실히[반드시] ~하다 **essay** 리포트, 과제물 **clearly** 명확히, 또렷하게

지문 Flow

[도입]
글쓰기 전에 창의적인 쓰기 아이디어를 얻기 위해 브레인스토밍을 하는 것이 좋음

⬇

[보충설명1]
생각들이 흘러가게 두고, 철자나 문법에 대해 걱정하지 말아야 함

&

[보충설명2]
대략적인 원고 완성 후에 주의 깊게 검토하여 실수를 고쳐야 함

&

[보충설명3]
인쇄 전에 다시 확인하고 이름과 제목도 다시 확인해야 함

지문 All in One

한 남자가 퇴근해서 집에 왔다 늦게 기진맥진하여 평소대로 그의 어린 아들이 아직도
1 (A) 1 A man came home from work, / late [and] exhausted / — as usual. 2 His little boy was
S V S V

깨어있었다 침대에 앉은 채로 그 자신이 자러 가기 전에 그 남자는 앉았다 그의 아들
still awake, / sitting up in bed. 3 Before going to sleep himself, / the man sat down / next to
C 분사구문 분사구문(= Before he went ~) S V

옆에 잘 자라는 인사를 하려고 그가 항상 하던 대로 아빠 아빠는 한 시간에 얼마나 많은 돈을 버세요
his son / to say goodnight // as he always did. 4 "Daddy, how much money do you make an
부사적 용법(목적) 접속사 S′ V′ S V

그(아들)가 물었다 네 아빠는 한 시간에 20달러를 번다 남자가 대답했다 그리고 한숨을 쉬었다
hour?" // (a) he asked. 5 "Your Daddy makes $20 an hour," // the man replied, / then sighed.
S V S V S V_1 V_2

이제 자거라
6 "Now go to sleep."
V 부사적 용법(목적)

그러나 어린 아들은 누우려 하지 않았다 그는 매우 꼿꼿이 앉아서 침대 가장자리 가까이에
(C) 7 But the little boy wouldn't lie down. 8 He sat up very straight / near the edge of the bed,
S V S V_1

자신의 아버지를 쳐다보았다 그리고 정중하게 질문을 했다 아빠 제가 10달러를 빌릴 수 있을까요
/ looked at his father, // [and] politely asked a question. 9 "Daddy, may I borrow $10?" 10 The
V_2 V_3 S V S

남자는 짜증 나 보였다 너는 단지 알고 싶었니 내가 얼마나 많은 돈을 버는지 그래서
man looked annoyed. "11 Did you only want to know / how much money I make // so that
V C S V 간접의문문 접속사

네가 돈을 좀 뜯을 수 있게 나에게서 너는 이미 충분한 장난감과 잡동사니를 갖고 있잖니 어린 아들은
you can squeeze some / out of me? 12 You already have enough toys [and] junk!" 13 The little
S′ V′ S V S

자신(아들)의 고개를 가로저으며 말했다 안녕히 주무세요, 아빠
boy shook (c) his head [and] said, // "Goodnight, Daddy."
V_1 V_2

남자는 일어나서 밖으로 걸어 나와 침실 문을 닫았다 그날은 또 하나의 긴 하루였다
(B) 14 The man got up, / walked out, // [and] closed the bedroom door. 15 It had been another
S V_1 V_2 V_3 S_1 V_1 C_1

그리고 그가 고대하고 있던 유일한 것은 자는 것이었다 그러나 그때
long day // [and] *the only thing* [(that) he was looking forward to] / was sleep. 16 But then (b)
관계대명사 S_2 V_2 C_2

그(아빠)는 생각했다 어쩌면 그의 아들이 정말로 필요로 하는 어떤 일이 있을지도 모른다고 그 10달러를 그는
he thought // maybe there was *something* [(that) his boy really needed / that $10 for]. 17 He
S V V S′ 관계대명사 S

침실 문을 다시 열었다 미안하다 아가야 오늘은 긴 하루였는데 내가 내 스트레스를
opened the bedroom door again. 18 "I'm sorry, baby. 19 It's been a long day, // [and] I took my
V S V C S_1 V_1 C S_2 V_2

너에게 풀었구나 여기 그 10달러가 있다 오 고마워요 아빠 어린 아들은 기뻤다
stress out on you. 20 Here's that $10." 21 "Oh, thank you, Daddy!" 22 The little boy was
V S V S V

delighted.
C

그러더니 그(아들)는 매트리스 밑으로 손을 뻗었다 그리고 봉투 하나를 꺼냈다 달러 지폐로
(D) 23 Then, / (d) he reached under his mattress // [and] pulled out *an envelope* [full of dollar
S V_1 V_2

가득 찬 너는 왜 10달러를 요구했니 너는 이미 부자잖아 아빠가 말했다 또다시 그는
bills]. 24 "Why did you ask for $10? 25 You're rich already!" / said the father. 26 Again he was
S V S V C V S S V

약간 짜증이 났다 그 모든 것이 행동이었다고 생각하니 장난감 살 돈을 얻기 위한 저는 아직
slightly annoyed, / thinking that it had all been an act / to get money for toys. 27 "I didn't
C 분사구문(= because he thought ~) 부사적 용법(목적) S_1 V_1

충분히 갖고 있지 않았어요 아빠 그런데 지금은 그래요 그(아들)가 말했다 제가 이제 20 달러를 갖고 있어요 제가 한 시간을 살
have enough yet, Daddy, / [but] now I do," // (e) he said. "28 I have $20 now. 29 Can I buy an
S_2 V_2 S V S V S V

수 있을까요 아빠의 시간에서
hour / of your time?"

232 ① (B) - (C) - (D) ② (C) - (B) - (D) ③ (C) - (D) - (B) ④ (D) - (B) - (C) ⑤ (D) - (C) - (B)

233 ① (a) ② (b) ③ (c) ④ (d) ⑤ (e)

234 ① 아들은 장난감을 사기 위해 20달러가 필요했다.
② 아버지는 아들에게 돈의 소중함을 가르쳐 주었다.
③ 아들은 아버지의 스트레스를 덜어 주고 싶었다.
④ 아들은 아버지와 함께 시간을 보내고 싶었다.
⑤ 아버지는 용돈을 달라는 아들의 부탁을 흔쾌히 들어주었다.

어휘확인

exhausted 기진맥진한, 녹초가 된 **as usual** 평소대로, 늘 그렇듯이 **reply** 대답하다 **sigh** 한숨 쉬다[쉬며 말하다] **lie down** 눕다 **edge** 가장자리, 끝 **politely** 정중하게, 공손하게 **annoyed** 짜증 난 **squeeze** 짜내다 **junk** 잡동사니, 폐물 **shake A's head** A의 고개를 가로젓다 **look forward to** ~을 고대[기대]하다 **take A out on B** A를 B에게 풀다[B에게 화풀이를 하다] **delighted** 기쁜 **reach** (손·팔을) 뻗다[내밀다]; ~에 닿다 **mattress** 매트리스 **pull out** ~을 꺼내다 **full of** ~로 가득 찬 **slightly** 약간, 조금

지문 Flow

[발단]
녹초가 되어 퇴근한 아빠를 기다리던 어린 아들이 아빠에게 시간 당 받는 수당을 물어봄

[전개]
아들이 아빠에게 10달러를 빌리려고 하지만, 아빠는 거절함

[절정]
아빠는 아들에게 미안한 마음이 들어 다시 10달러를 주기로 함

[결말]
아들은 가지고 있던 10달러와 빌린 10달러를 합해 아빠의 한 시간을 사려고 함

해석 한 눈에 보기 (A) **1** 한 남자가 평소대로 늦게 기진맥진하여 퇴근해서 집에 왔다. **2** 그의 어린 아들이 아직도 깨어서 침대에 앉아 있었다. **3** 자신이 자러 가기 전에, 그 남자는 자신이 항상 하던 대로 잘 자라는 인사를 하려고 그의 아들 옆에 앉았다. **4** "아빠, 아빠는 한 시간에 얼마나 많은 돈을 버세요?"라고 (a) 그(아들)가 물었다. **5** "네 아빠는 한 시간에 20달러를 번단다."라고 남자가 대답하고, 이어서 한숨을 쉬면서 말했다. **6** "이제 자거라." (C) **7** 그러나 어린 아들은 누우려 하지 않았다. **8** 그는 침대 가장자리 가까이에 매우 꼿꼿이 앉아서, 자신의 아버지를 쳐다보며, 정중하게 질문을 했다. **9** "아빠, 제가 10달러를 빌릴 수 있을까요?" **10** 남자는 짜증 나 보였다. **11** "너는 단지 내게서 돈을 좀 뜯어가려고 내가 얼마나 많은 돈을 버는지 알고 싶었던 거니? **12** 너는 이미 충분한 장난감과 잡동사니를 갖고 있잖니!" **13** 어린 아들은 (c) 자신(아들)의 고개를 가로저으며 말했다. "안녕히 주무세요, 아빠." (B) **14** 남자는 일어나서, 밖으로 걸어 나와, 침실 문을 닫았다. **15** 그날은 또 하나의 긴 하루였고 그가 고대하고 있던 유일한 것은 자는 것이었다. **16** 그런데 그때 (b) 그(아빠)는 어쩌면 그의 아들이 그 10달러를 정말로 필요로 하는 어떤 일이 있을지도 모른다고 생각했다. **17** 그는 침실 문을 다시 열었다. **18** "미안하다, 아가야. **19** 오늘은 긴 하루였는데 내가 내 스트레스를 너에게 풀었구나. **20** 여기 그 10달러가 있다." **21** "오, 고마워요, 아빠!" **22** 어린 아들은 기뻤다. (D) **23** 그러더니 (d) 그(아들)는 매트리스 밑으로 손을 뻗어 달러 지폐로 가득 찬 봉투 하나를 꺼냈다. **24** "너는 왜 10달러를 요구했니? **25** 너는 이미 부자잖아!"라고 아빠가 말했다. **26** 또 다시 그는 그 모든 것이 장난감 살 돈을 얻기 위한 행동이었다고 생각하니 약간 짜증이 났다. **27** "저는 아직 충분히 갖고 있지 않았어요, 아빠, 그런데 지금은 그래요." (e) 그(아들)가 말했다. **28** "제가 이제 20달러를 갖고 있어요. **29** 제가 아빠 시간에서 한 시간을 살 수 있을까요?"

정답단추

232 각 문단을 읽고 글의 순서를 드러내는 단서를 찾아보자. 먼저 (A)는 한 남자가 늦게 녹초가 되어 퇴근해서 집에 돌아왔는데 잠을 자지 않고 있던 아들이 아빠에게 시간당 얼마를 받고 일하느냐고 물어서 그것에 대답해 주고 얼른 자라고 말하는 내용이야. (C)는 But으로 시작해서 아들이 누우려 하지 않고 10달러를 빌려달라고 하고 아빠는 그런 아들에게 짜증을 낸다는 내용이니 (A) 뒤에 이어지는 것이 적절하겠지? 짜증을 내고 아들 방을 나온 아버지는 미안한 마음에 다시 들어가 아들에게 10달러를 준다는 내용의 (B)는 (C) 뒤에 이어서 오면 돼. (D)는 아들은 자신이 모아두었던 돈과 방금 받은 10달러를 합쳐 20달러를 주면서 아버지의 한 시간을 사려는 내용이야. 따라서 (A)에 이어질 가장 적절한 순서는 ② '(C) – (B) – (D)'야.

233 이 글의 등장인물은 아들과 아빠 두 사람이니, 제시된 대명사가 누구를 가리키는지 하나하나 확인해 보자. 먼저 (a)는 아빠에게 한 시간에 얼마나 많은 돈을 버냐고 물었으니, 아들을 가리키겠지. (b)는 아들이 10달러가 정말로 필요할 거라고 생각하는 사람이니 아빠를 가리켜. (c)는 자신의 고개를 저으며 아빠에게 '안녕히 주무세요.'라고 말하고 있으니 아들이야. 10달러를 받은 아들이 매트리스 밑에 있는 봉투를 꺼내는 것이니 (d)도 아들이고, 아빠에게 10달러를 왜 달라고 했는지 설명하는 부분의 (e)가 가리키는 것도 아들이야. 따라서 가리키는 대상이 다른 하나는 (b)야.

234 아들은 20달러로 매일 녹초가 되어 집에 돌아오는 아버지의 시간을 사고 싶어 시간당 얼마를 받고 일하는지, 또 10달러를 빌려줄 수 있는지 물었던 거야. 이는 아버지와 함께 시간을 보내고 싶은 아들의 심경을 나타내므로 ④가 지문과 일치하는 내용이야.

오답단서

234 아들이 20달러가 필요했던 건 아버지와 함께 시간을 보내고 싶은 마음에 아버지의 한 시간을 사고 싶어서였으니 ①은 옳지 않아. 지문에서 아버지가 아들에게 돈의 소중함을 가르쳐 주거나 아들이 아버지의 스트레스를 덜어 주고 싶어 한 부분은 찾을 수 없으므로 ②, ③도 내용과 일치하지 않아. 또한, 돈을 빌려달라는 아들의 요구를 아버지가 흔쾌히 들어주지는 않았어. 따라서 ⑤도 정답이 될 수 없어.

실전편

독해 모의고사 2회

235 ③	236 ⑤	237 ⑤	238 ②	239 ④	240 ④	241 ⑤	242 ⑤	243 ⑤
244 ④	245 ②	246 ④	247 ④	248 ④	249 ②	250 ②	251 ④	252 ②

235 정답 ③

지문 All in One

다른 사람들의 견해에 대한 개방성이 / 당신에게 당신의 지적 독립성을 잃게 할 수 있는가
1 Could openness to other people's viewpoints / cause you to lose your intellectual
조동사 S V O C

그렇다 / 하지만 단지 당신이 그들의 견해를 무조건 수용할 때만 / 당신이
independence? 2 Yes, / but only if you accept their views unconditionally. 3 As long as you
접속사 S'

그 견해들을 점검하는 한 / 그것들을 받아들이기 전에 / 당신은 두려워할 것이 없을 것이다 / Carol Tavris의 예를 들어보자
test their ideas / before accepting them, // you will have nothing to fear. 4 Take the example of
V' 분사구문(= before you accept ~) S V

심리학자이자 Yale 대학교의 교수인 / 그녀는 자신의 연구를 시작했다
Carol Tavris, / (a psychologist and a professor at Yale University). 5 She began her work / by
=

널리 퍼진 믿음을 고려하면서 / 화를 솔직하게 표현하는 것이 / 우리가 화를 덜 느끼게 한다는
considering the widespread belief / that expressing anger openly / make us feel less angry.
= S' V' O' C'

하지만 그녀는 거기서 멈추지 않았다 / 그녀는 또한 고려했다 / 반대가 되는 견해와 관련된 연구 결과들의 정확성을
6 But she didn't stop there. 7 She also considered / opposing views and the correctness of

그녀의 결론은 / 화를 표현하는 것이 / 화를 강화하고 심지어 심화시킨다는
related findings. 8 Her conclusion / that expressing anger / tends to reinforce and even (to)
S = S' V'

개방성의 결과였다 / 모든 견해에 대한 / 또한 모든 것을 면밀히 조사하는 그녀의 능력의
intensify it / was the result of openness / to all viewpoints / plus *her ability* [to scrutinize
= anger V C 형용사적 용법

everything].

① discussing the matter with other experts
다른 전문가들과 문제를 논의하는 것

② blindly researching favorable opinions
찬성하는 의견을 맹목적으로 조사하는 것

③ considering others' views in a critical way
다른 사람들의 견해를 비판적으로 수용하는 것

④ expressing openly that she could be wrong
그녀가 틀릴 수 있다는 것을 솔직하게 표현하는 것

⑤ making changes to the current environment
현재 상황에 변화를 만드는 것

해석 한 눈에 보기 1 다른 사람들의 견해에 대한 개방성이 당신의 지적 독립성을 잃게 할 수 있는가? 2 그렇다. 하지만 단지 당신이 그들의 견해를 무조건 수용할 때만 그렇다. 주제문 3 다른 사람들의 견해를 받아들이기 전에 당신이 그 견해들을 점검하는 한, 당신은 두려워할 것이 없을 것이다. 4 심리학자이자 Yale 대학교의 교수인 Carol Tavris의 예를 들어보자. 5 그녀는 화를 솔직하게 표현하는 것이 우리가 화를 덜 느끼게 한다는 널리 퍼진 믿음을 고려하면서 자신의 연구를 시작했다. 6 하지만 그녀는 거기서 멈추지 않았다. 7 그녀는 또한 반대가 되는 견해와 관련된 연구 결과들의 정확성을 고려했다. 8 화를 표현하는 것이 화를 강화하고 심지어 심화시킨다는 그녀의 결론은 모든 견해에 대한 개방성뿐만 아니라 모든 것을 면밀하게 조사하는 능력의 결과였다.

정답단추 다른 사람의 견해에 대한 개방성(견해를 받아들이는 것)은 지적 독립성을 잃어버리게 하지만 그것은 무조건적으로 수용할 때만 그렇고, 견해를 받아들이기 전에 점검한다면 그것은 바람직하다는 주제야. 이어지는 예시의 심리학자는 '분노 표출'에 관해 널리 퍼진 믿음(화를 표출하라)과 반대가 되는 견해도 받아들였지만 정확성을 고려해 결론으로 냈어. 따라서 밑줄 친 어구 '모든 것을 면밀하게 조사하는 능력'이란 다른 사람들의 견해를 비판적으로 수용하는 것이므로 정답은 ③이야.

오답단서 찬성하는 의견만을 맹목적으로 조사한 것은 Carol Tavris의 연구 내용과 거리가 멀어 ②는 오답이야.

어휘확인

openness 개방성, 마음이 열려 있음 **viewpoint** 견해, 관점 **intellectual** 지적인, 지능의 **unconditionally** 무조건 **psychologist** 심리학자 **widespread** 널리 퍼진, 광범위한 **openly** 솔직하게, 공공연하게 **opposing** 반대의, 대립되는 **related** 관련된 **reinforce** 강화하다 **intensify** 심화시키다 **scrutinize** 면밀히 조사하다

〈선택지 어휘〉

blindly 맹목적으로, 무턱대고; 보지 않고 **favorable** 찬성하는; 호의적인 **critical** 비판적인

지문 Flow

[도입]
다른 사람의 견해에 대한 개방성은 지적 독립성을 침해할 수 있음

⬇

[주제문]
다른 사람의 의견을 받아들이기 전에 그 견해들을 점검해야 함

⬇

[예시]
- Carol Tavris는 화를 솔직하게 표현하는 것이 화를 덜 느끼게 한다는 널리 퍼진 믿음과, 반대가 되는 견해와 관련된 연구 결과들도 고려함
- 널리 퍼진 믿음에 대한 추가적인 노력의 결과로 화를 표현하는 것이 심지어 화를 심화시킨다는 결론을 내림

236 정답 ⑤

지문 All in One

만약 당신이 당신의 아이들에게 부탁한다면 / 부엌을 청소해 달라고 / 그들이 반드시 알게 해라 / 그것이 당신에게
[1] If you ask your children / to clean the kitchen, // make sure (that) they know / what that
접속사 S'_1 V'_1 O′ C′ V C 접속사 S'_2 V'_2 관계대명사

의미하는 것을 / 많은 부모들은 화를 낸다 / 그들의 아이들이 집안일을 엉망으로 할 때
means to you. [2] Many parents get upset / when their children do a terrible job with chores, //
S V C 접속사 S'_1 V'_1

그들이 시간을 전혀 가져본 적이 없음에도 불구하고 / 훈련을 위한 / 훈련받는 시간을 가지는 것은 / 또한 의미하지
even though they have never taken time / for training. [3] Taking time for training / also does
접속사 S'_2 V'_2 S V

않는다 / 아이들이 일을 할 것임을 / 당신이 좋아할 만큼 잘 / 항상은 평생의 과정이다
not mean // (that) children will do things / as well as you would like. [4] Improvement is a
접속사 S'_1 V'_1 S'_2 V'_2 S V C

그리고 / 기억해라 / 당신이 그들이 하기를 바라는 것이 / 최우선
lifelong process. [5] And, / remember, / *the things* [(which[that]) you want them to do] / may
V S′ 관계대명사 V′

순위가 아닐지도 모른다는 것을 / 그들에게 / 그들이 어른이 될 때까지 / 비록 청결과 예의범절이
not be a high priority / for them // until they become adults. [6] Even though cleanliness and
C′ 접속사 S″ V″ C″ 접속사 S′

최우선 순위가 아닐지라도 / 아이들에게 / 그들은 여전히 이런 자질들을 배워야 할 필요가 있다
manners / may not be a high priority / for children, // they still need to learn these qualities.
V′ C′ S V

어른들은 / 그러나 / 기억할 필요가 있다 / 아이들은 아이들이라는 것을
[7] Adults, / however, / need to remember // that kids are kids.
S V 접속사 S′ V′ C′

① 부모는 자녀에게 솔선수범해야 한다.
② 가정교육을 위한 시간을 따로 마련해야 한다.
③ 아이들의 요구를 모두 들어줘서는 안 된다.
④ 자녀의 잘못된 행동에 일일이 화를 내서는 안 된다.
⑤ 가정교육 시 아이들에 대한 이해가 선행되어야 한다.

해석 한 눈에 보기 **1** 만약 당신이 당신의 아이들에게 부엌을 청소해 달라고 부탁한다면, 그것이 당신에게 의미하는 것을 그들이 반드시 알게 해라. **2** 많은 부모들은 비록 그들의 아이들이 훈련받는 시간을 전혀 가져본 적이 없음에도 불구하고 그들이 집안일을 엉망으로 할 때 화를 낸다. **3** 훈련받는 시간을 가지는 것 또한 아이들이 당신이 좋아할 만큼 일을 잘할 것임을 의미하지는 않는다. **4** 향상은 평생의 과정이다. **5** 그리고 당신이 그들이 하기를 바라는 것들이 그들이 어른이 될 때까지 그들에게 최우선 순위가 아닐지도 모른다는 것을 기억하라. **6** 비록 청결과 예의범절이 아이들에게 최우선 순위가 아닐지라도, 그들은 여전히 이런 자질들을 배워야 할 필요가 있다. **7** 그러나 어른들은 아이들은 아이들이라는 것을 기억할 필요가 있다.

정답단추 이 글은 아이들에게 가정교육을 할 때 주의해야 할 어른들의 태도에 관한 내용이야. 아이들에게 집안일이나 예법을 가르칠 때는 충분한 훈련이 필요하고, 또 훈련한다고 해서 바로 잘하지는 않을 것이라는 점, 집안일이 아이들의 주요 관심사가 아니라는 점, 아이들은 아이들일 뿐이라는 것을 기억하라는 내용을 종합해 보면 가정교육에 있어서는 아이들을 이해하는 것이 먼저 필요하다는 것이 이 글의 요지라는 것을 알 수 있어. 따라서 정답은 ⑤야.

오답단서 ①과 ③의 내용은 글에서 다루고 있지 않아. 가정교육을 할 때 주의해야 할 점을 다루지만 시간을 따로 마련해야 한다는 ②의 내용은 본문에 언급되지 않아. ④는 글에서 부모들이 화를 내는 것이 바람직하지 않다고는 하지만 세부적인 내용이므로 글의 요지로 적절하지 않아.

어휘확인

make sure 반드시 ~하다, ~하도록 확실히 하다 **chores** 집안일 **improvement** 향상 **lifelong** 평생의, 일생의 **high priority** 최우선 순위 **cleanliness** 청결 **manners** 예의범절 **quality** (사람의) 자질

지문 Flow

[도입]
아이들에게 부엌 청소(집안일)를 부탁할 때, 그것이 어떤 일인지 알게 해야 함

⬇

[보충설명1]
아이들은 집안일을 훈련받지 않았고, 훈련받았어도 잘하지 못함

&

[보충설명2]
집안일, 청결, 예의범절이 아이들의 최우선 순위가 아니지만, 가르쳐야 함

⬇

[주장]
아이들은 아이들일 뿐임을 기억해야 함

237 정답 ⑤

지문 All in One

수족관은 인기가 있다 / 전 세계적으로 / 그리고 아주 다양한 물고기들이 / 가정용으로
[1] Aquariums are popular / around the world, // and a wide variety of fish / are kept
S_1 V_1 C S_2 V_2

키워지고 있다 / 그것들 중에 / 키싱구라미가 인기가 있다 / 그것(키싱구라미)의 기이한 습성 때문에
domestically. [2] Among them, / the kissing gourami is popular / because of ① its unusual
S V C

다른 물고기, 식물, 그리고 다양한 물체들에 키스를 하는 / 그것(키싱구라미)은 수출되고 있다 / 일본, 유럽, 북미
habit / of kissing other fish, plants, and various objects. [3] ② It is exported / to Japan, Europe,
= S V

및 전 세계 기타 지역으로 / 대량으로 / 그것(키싱구라미)은 빠른 속도로 자라서
North America, and other parts of the world / in great numbers. [4] ③ It matures quickly, //
S V_1

급격히 너무 커진다 / 작은 수조에 비해 / 그것(키싱구라미)이 먹는 것을 좋아하기 때문에
and rapidly gets too big / for a small fish tank. [5] Since ④ it likes to eat / *the slimy seaweed*
V_2 C 접속사 S′ V′

자라는 끈적끈적한 해초를 / 당신의 수족관 내부에서 / 당신은 유리를 그다지 자주 청소할 필요가 없다
[which grows / on the inside of your aquarium], // you don't need to clean the glass very
관계대명사 S V

그것은 매우 유용하다 / 해초를 먹는 물고기로 / 그것(해초)의 증식을 억제하도록 도와주므로
often. [6] It is very useful / as a seaweed eater, // helping to control ⑤ its growth.
S V C 분사구문(= because it helps ~)

어휘확인

aquarium 수족관 **a variety of** 다양한 **domestically** 가정적으로; 국내에서 **unusual** 기이한, 특이한 **habit** 습성; 버릇 **various** 다양한 **object** 물체 **export** 수출하다 **in great numbers** 대량으로, 다수로 **mature** 성숙하다 **rapidly** 급격히, 빨리 **fish tank** 수조, 어류 탱크 **slimy** 점액성의, 끈적끈적한 **seaweed** 해초 **growth** 증식; 성장

지문 Flow

[도입]
가정용으로 다양한 물고기들이 수족관에서 키워지는데 키싱구라미가 인기 있음

⬇

해석 한 눈에 보기 1 수족관은 전 세계적으로 인기가 있고, 아주 다양한 물고기들이 가정용으로 키워지고 있다. 2 그것들 중에 키싱구라미가 인기가 있는데 다른 물고기, 식물, 그리고 다양한 물체들에 키스를 하는 ① 그것(키싱구라미)의 기이한 습성 때문이다. 3 ② 그것(키싱구라미)은 일본, 유럽, 북미 및 전 세계 기타 지역으로 대량으로 수출되고 있다. 4 ③ 그것(키싱구라미)은 빠른 속도로 자라서, 작은 수조에 비해 급격히 너무 커진다. 5 ④ 그것(키싱구라미)은 당신의 수족관 내부에서 자라는 미끌미끌한 해초를 먹는 것을 좋아하기 때문에, 당신은 유리를 그다지 자주 청소할 필요가 없다. 6 그것은 해초를 먹는 물고기로 아주 유용하여, ⑤ 그것(해초)의 증식을 억제하도록 도와준다.

정답단추 ①, ②, ③, ④는 다른 물고기나 식물, 물체 등에 키스하는 습관이 있고, 전 세계로 수출되며, 성장 속도가 빠르고, 수족관 안쪽의 해초를 먹는 것을 좋아하는 키싱구라미를 가리켜. 그런데 마지막 문장은 키싱구라미가 해초를 먹어서 해초의 증식을 억제한다는 내용으로 ⑤는 해초(seaweed)를 가리키고 있어. 따라서 ⑤가 정답이야.

[보충설명]
- 다른 물고기나 식물, 물체 등과 키스를 하는 그것의 기이한 습성이 있음
- 전 세계에 대량 수출됨
- 성장 속도가 빠름
- 해초를 먹어서, 잦은 수족관 청소가 불필요하고 해초 증식을 억제함

238 정답 ②

지문 All in One

1 South Korean weather researchers(S: 한국의 기상 연구원들은) expect(V: 예상한다) / this year's yellow dust season(O: 올해의 황사 철이) to be milder(C: 더 약할 것으로) / than those(= yellow dust seasons) of recent years(최근 몇 년의 황사 철보다). 2 Still(그럼에도), / the dust(S: 황사는) caused(V: ~하게 했다) / the Korea Meteorological Administration(O: 한국 기상청으로 하여금) to give warnings(C: 경고를 하도록) / in Seoul [and] several other (A) surrounding cities(서울과 몇몇 다른 주변 도시들에) / on Sunday(일요일에). 3 High levels of *the yellow dust particles*(S: 높은 수준의 황사 입자는), / which(관계대명사(계속적 용법)) can cause breathing illness(호흡기 질환을 일으킬 수 있는), / remained(V: 대기 중에 머물렀다) in the air / through Monday afternoon(월요일 오후까지). 4 Accordingly(따라서), / KMA officials(S: 한국 기상청 직원들은) recommend(V: 권고한다) // that(접속사) all outdoor activities(S'₁: 모든 야외 활동을 취소할 것을) (B) be canceled(V'₁) / during yellow dust warnings(황사 경고 동안에), / [and] that(접속사) the young, old, [and] weak(S'₂: 그리고 어린이, 노약자들은 실내에 머물 것을) stay(V'₂) indoors. 5 The dust(S) typically comes(V) from the Chinese [and] Mongolian deserts(황사는 전형적으로 중국과 몽골의 사막에서 와서), / potentially (C) bringing(분사구문: 잠재적으로 가져온다) / along with it(= the dust: 그것과 함께) / bacteria [and] industrial wastes(박테리아와 산업 폐기물을).

	(A)		(B)		(C)
①	surrounding	……	are	……	bringing
②	surrounding	……	be	……	bringing
③	surrounding	……	be	……	bring
④	surrounded	……	are	……	bring
⑤	surrounded	……	be	……	bring

해석 한 눈에 보기 1 한국의 기상 연구원들은 올해의 황사 철이 최근 몇 년의 황사 철보다 더 약할 것으로 예상한다. 2 그럼에도, 황사는 한국 기상청으로 하여금 일요일에 서울과 몇몇 다른 주변 도시들에 경고를 하게 했다. 3 호흡기 질환을 일으킬 수 있는 높은 수준의 황사 입자는 월요일 오후까지 대기 중에 머물렀다. 4 따라서, 한국 기상청 직원들은 황사 경고 동안에 모든 야외 활동을 취소하고, 어린이, 노약자들은 실내에 머물 것을 권고한다. 5 황사는 전형적으로 중국과 몽골의 사막에서 와서, 잠재적으로 그것과 함께 박테리아와 산업 폐기물을 가져온다.

정답단추 어법 문제는 선택지가 포함된 문장만을 읽고 문제를 풀 수 있는 경우가 많아. (A)는 '둘러싸고 있는' 도시들(cities)로 능동의 현재분사 surrounding이 되어야 해. (B)의 주절 동사 recommend가 권고를 나타내므로, that절의 동사는 당위성을 나타내기 위해 〈should+동사원형〉 또는 동사원형으로 써야 해. 조동사 should가 생략된 것으로 be가 들어가야 해. (C)는 앞 문장의 결과를 나타내는 분사구문이 적절해. 따라서 현재분사형의 bringing이 들어가고, it brings로 바꿔 쓸 수도 있어. 참고로 동사원형 bring은 주어 The dust와 수가 일치하지 않으므로 정답이 될 수 없어.

어휘확인

researcher 연구원 **expect** 예상하다, 기대하다 **yellow dust** 황사 **mild** 약한[순한] **recent** 최근의 **the Korea Meteorological Administration** 한국 기상청 **several** 몇몇의 **surrounding** 주위의, 둘레의 **particle** 입자 **breathing** 호흡 **illness** 질병, 병 **remain** 남아 있다 **accordingly** 따라서 **official** 직원, 공무원 **recommend** 권고하다, 추천하다 **cancel** 취소하다 **indoors** 실내에서 **typically** 전형적으로 **potentially** 잠재적으로 **bacteria** 박테리아 **industrial** 산업의

지문 Flow

[도입]
기상 연구원들이 올해 황사 철이 최근 몇 년의 황사 철보다 더 약할 것이라고 예상함

⬇

[대조]
한국 기상청에서 서울과 주변 도시에 황사 경고를 했고, 높은 수준의 황사가 대기 중에 머물렀음

⬇

[보충설명1]
야외 활동을 취소하고, 어린이와 노약자는 실내에 있을 것을 권고함

&

[보충설명2]
황사는 중국과 몽골 사막에서 오는데, 박테리아와 산업 폐기물을 동반함

239 정답 ④

지문 All in One

1 "Stress(S) causes(V) illness!"(스트레스는 질병을 유발한다) 2 If(접속사) you(S') want(V') to stay physically [and] mentally healthy(육체적으로나 정신적으로 건강을 유지하고 싶으면), // avoid(V) stressful events(스트레스가 많은 사건을 피해라). 3 This(S) is(V) *a memorable message*(C: 이것은 기억에 남는 메시지이다) / [(which[that])(관계대명사) the majority of research [and] studies on stress(스트레스에 관한 대다수의 연구가) / have delivered to us(우리에게 전달한)]. 4 But(그러나) / such simple advice(S: 그렇게 단순한 조언은) / is(V) just (A) impossible to(C: 따르기가 불가능하다)

어휘확인

physically 육체적으로 (↔ **mentally** 정신적으로) **stressful** 스트레스가 많은 **memorable** 기억할 만한 **majority** 대다수 **research** 연구, 조사 **moreover** 게다가, 더욱이 **prescription** 처방전 **opportunity** 기회 **notion** 개념, 관념 **ignore** 무시하다 **assume** 가정하다 **passive** 수동적인, 소극적인 **initiative** 진취성, 결단력 **creativity**

스트레스가 많은 사건이 위험하더라도 / 많은 것들은 / 사랑하는 사람의 죽음처럼

follow. [5] Even if stressful events are dangerous, // many / — like the death of a loved one — /
부사적 용법(형용사 수식) 접속사 S′ V′ C′ S

피할 수가 없다 / 게다가 / 스트레스가 많은 사건을 모두 피하라는 경고는

are impossible to avoid. [6] Moreover, / *any warning* [to avoid all stressful events] / is a
V C 부사적 용법(형용사 수식) S V

처방이다 / 문제점뿐만 아니라 기회에서 멀어지는 / 모든 스트레스가 당신을

prescription / for staying away from opportunities as well as trouble. [7] The notion that all
C S

아프게 한다는 개념은 / 또한 / 우리가 사람들에 대해 알고 있는 것의 대부분을 무시한다 / 우리는 가정한다

stress makes you sick / also (B) ignores a lot of what we know about people. [8] It assumes /
V 관계대명사 S V

우리 모두가 약하고 수동적이라고 / 어려움에 직면할 때 / 그러나 / 인간의 힘, 진취성과 독창성은

(that) we're all weak and passive / in the face of difficulty. [9] But / what about human
접속사 S′ V′ C′1 C′2

어떠한가 / 많은 사람들은 스트레스 시기를 극복한다 / 더 많은 육체적,

strength, initiative, and creativity? [10] Many come through periods of stress / with (C) more
S V

정신적 힘으로 / 이전에 그들이 가졌던 것보다

physical and mental strength / than they had before.
접속사 S′ V′

	(A)		(B)		(C)
①	possible 가능	……	ignores 무시한다	……	more 더
②	possible 가능	……	reflects 반영한다	……	less 덜
③	impossible 불가능	……	ignores 무시한다	……	less 덜
④	impossible 불가능	……	ignores 무시한다	……	more 더
⑤	impossible 불가능	……	reflects 반영한다	……	more 더

해석 한 눈에 보기 **1** "스트레스는 질병을 유발한다!" **2** 육체적으로나 정신적으로 건강을 유지하고 싶으면, 스트레스가 많은 사건을 피해라. **3** 이것은 스트레스에 관한 대다수의 연구가 우리에게 전달한 기억에 남는 메시지이다. **4** 그러나 그렇게 단순한 조언은 따르기가 (A) 불가능하다. **5** 스트레스가 많은 사건이 위험하더라도, 사랑하는 사람의 죽음처럼 많은 것들은 피할 수가 없다. **6** 게다가, 스트레스가 많은 사건을 모두 피하라는 경고는 문제점뿐만 아니라 기회에서 멀어지는 처방이다. **7** 모든 스트레스가 당신을 아프게 한다는 개념은 또한 우리가 사람들에 대해 알고 있는 것의 대부분을 (B) 무시한다. **8** 우리는 어려움에 직면할 때 우리 모두가 약하고 수동적이라고 가정한다. **9** 그러나 인간의 힘, 진취성과 독창성은 어떠한가? **10** 많은 사람들은 이전에 그들이 가졌던 것보다 (C) 더 많은 육체적, 정신적 힘으로 스트레스 시기를 극복한다.

정답단추 네모 안 어휘를 포함한 문장의 앞뒤 문맥을 잘 살펴보고, 자연스럽게 이어지는 어휘를 골라보자. 이 글은 스트레스와 관련된 오해에 대한 글이야. 보통 스트레스를 피하는 게 좋다고만 알고 있는데, 사실 스트레스를 극복하는 인간의 측면도 있다는 내용이야. (A)의 앞 advice는 스트레스를 피하라는 조언을 가리켜. 그러나 이 문장이 앞 문장과 역접 관계이고, 뒤이은 내용에서 스트레스를 피할 수 없다고 하고 있으므로 impossible이 적절해. (B)는 스트레스를 피해야 한다는 조언에 대한 비판에 해당되므로, 스트레스가 병이 된다는 개념 때문에 우리가 알고 있는 사람들의 진취적이고, 독창적인 부분이 무시되고 있다는 내용이 되어야 해. 따라서 ignores가 적절해. reflect는 '반영하다'라는 뜻이야. (C) 역시 사람들이 육체적, 정신적 힘으로 스트레스를 극복한다는 내용이 되어야 하므로, more가 문맥상 더 자연스러워. 힘이 많아야 스트레스를 극복할 수 있잖아. 따라서 ④가 답이야.

독창력, 창조성 **come through** (몹시 앓다가) 극복하다 **period** 시기, 기간 **physical** 육체적인 (↔ **mental** 정신적인)

지문 Flow

[도입]
스트레스는 질병을 유발하므로 피하라는 연구가 대다수임

[주제문]
그런 조언은 단순해서 따르기가 불가능함

[보충설명]
• 스트레스를 피할 수 없는 경우가 있음
• 스트레스가 문제점뿐만 아니라 기회가 되기도 함
• 스트레스가 병이 된다는 개념으로 인간의 능동적 측면이 무시됨

[결론]
사람들은 약하지만, 인간의 힘, 진취성, 독창성으로 스트레스를 극복함

240 정답 ④

지문 All in One

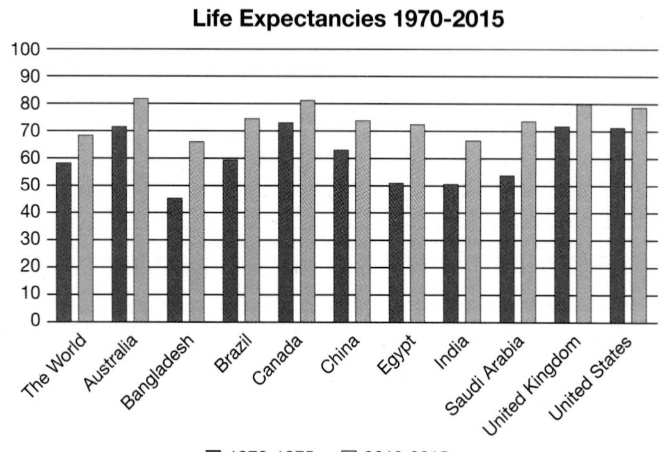

어휘확인

life expectancy 기대 수명 **demonstrate** (증거를 들어가며) 보여 주다, 증명하다 **worldwide** 전 세계적인 **average** 평균의 **survey** 조사 **remain** 남아 있다 **recent** 최근의 **increase** 증가; 증가하다 **in contrast** 그에 반해서 **comparatively** 비교적 **original** 원래의

지문 Flow

[소재]
1970－1975년과 2010－2015년 기간 사이의 기대 수명의 변화를 보여 주는 그래프

위 그래프는 보여 준다 / 기대 수명의 변화를 / 1970—1975년과 2010—2015년의

1 The graph above demonstrates / the change in life expectancy / between the periods 1970 —

S V

기간 사이의 / 4개국이 전 세계 평균 기대 수명 아래에 있었던 반면에

1975 and 2010 — 2015. 2 ① While four countries were below the worldwide average life

접속사 S′ V′

1970—1975년 조사에서 / 단지 2개국이 평균 이하로 남아 있었다

expectancy / in the 1970 — 1975 survey, // only two countries remained below the average / in

S V

더 최근의 조사에서 / 호주, 캐나다, 그리고 영국은 가장 높은 기대 수명을 기록한 3개국이었다

the more recent survey. 3 ② Australia, Canada, [and] the United Kingdom were *the three*

S V C

두 조사에서 / 사람들이 평균

countries [that recorded the highest life expectancy / in both surveys]. 4 ③ Among *the four*

관계대명사

75년 이상 산 4개국 중에서 / 가장 최근의 조사에서

countries [whose people lived more than 75 years on average / in the more recent survey], /

관계대명사

미국이 가장 낮은 평균 연령을 기록했다 / 가장 큰 증가를 보였다

the United States recorded the lowest average age. 5 ④ The biggest increases were seen / in

S V S V

방글라데시, 이집트, 그리고 사우디아라비아에서 / 그 나라들 모두 평균 50세 미만을 기록했다

Bangladesh, Egypt, and Saudi Arabia, / all of which recorded an average of less than 50 / in

관계대명사(계속적 용법)

더 이전 조사에서 / 그에 반해서 / 더 높은 숫자를 기록했던 국가들은

the earlier survey. 6 ⑤ In contrast, / *countries* [that had recorded higher numbers] / made

S 관계대명사 V

비교적 더 적은 증가를 했다 / 지난 40년 동안 / 원래 숫자가 더 낮았던 국가들보다

comparatively smaller increases / during the last forty years / than those with lower original

= countries

numbers.

[보충설명1]
이전 조사에서는 4개국이 세계 평균 기대 수명 이하였고, 최근 조사에서는 2개국이었음

&

[보충설명2]
호주, 캐나다, 영국이 상위 3개국이며, 기대 수명이 75세 이상인 국가로 미국이 포함됨

&

[보충설명3]
방글라데시, 이집트, 사우디아라비아가 증가 폭이 컸는데, 이전 조사에서는 모두 평균 50세 미만이었음(→ 방글라데시만 50세 미만이었음)

⬇

[결과]
기대 수명이 높은 나라가 낮은 나라보다 증가 폭이 적음

해석 한 눈에 보기 1 위 그래프는 1970—1975년과 2010—2015년 기간 사이의 기대 수명의 변화를 보여 준다. 2 ① 1970—1975년 조사에서는 4개국이 전 세계 평균 기대 수명 아래에 있었던 반면에, 더 최근의 조사에서는 단지 2개국이 평균 이하로 남아 있었다. 3 ② 호주, 캐나다, 그리고 영국은 두 조사에서 가장 높은 기대 수명을 기록한 3개국이었다. 4 ③ 가장 최근의 조사에서, 사람들이 평균 75년 이상 산 4개국 중에서, 미국이 가장 낮은 평균 연령을 기록했다. 5 ④ 방글라데시, 이집트, 그리고 사우디아라비아에서 가장 큰 증가를 보였는데, 그 나라들 모두 더 이전 조사에서는 평균 50세 미만을 기록했다. 6 ⑤ 그에 반해서, 더 높은 숫자를 기록했던 국가들은 원래 숫자가 더 낮았던 국가들보다 지난 40년 동안 비교적 더 적은 증가를 했다.

정답단추 우선 무엇에 관한 그래프인지 파악하자. 위 그래프는 1970년부터 2015년까지 각 나라들의 기대 수명의 변화를 보여 주고 있어. 선택지의 설명이 그래프와 일치하는지 꼼꼼히 확인하도록 해. 그래프를 보면, 방글라데시, 이집트, 사우디아라비아에서 기대 수명이 가장 크게 증가했는데, 그 나라들 중 이전 조사에서는 평균 50세 미만을 기록한 나라는 방글라데시뿐이야. 따라서 ④가 그래프의 내용과 일치하지 않는 설명이야.

오답단서 ①은 그래프에서 이전 조사에서는 방글라데시, 이집트, 인도, 사우디아라비아 4개국이 전 세계 평균 기대 수명의 평균 이하였고, 최근 조사에서는 방글라데시, 인도 2개국이 평균 이하였으므로 일치해. ②는 두 조사에서 모두 호주, 캐나다, 영국이 높은 기대 수명을 가진 3개국이므로 일치하는 설명이야. ③은 그래프에서 호주, 캐나다, 영국, 미국 중 미국의 기대 수명이 가장 낮다는 걸 확인할 수 있어. ⑤는 기대 수명이 높은 나라들이 낮은 나라들보다 증가 폭은 적으므로 일치하는 설명이야.

241 정답 ⑤

지문 All in One

1830년 12월 10일에 태어난 / 매사추세츠 주 애머스트에서 / Emily Dickinson은 학교를 그만 두었다

1 Born on December 10, 1830 / in Amherst, Massachusetts, / Emily Dickinson left school / as a

분사구문(= Emily Dickinson was born ~, and she ~) S V

십 대에 / 결국 외로운 삶을 살았다 / 다른 사람들과 떨어져 / 그곳에서 그녀는

teenager, / eventually living a lonely life / away from the company of others. 2 There, / she

분사구문(= ~, and eventually lived ~.) S

몰래 몇 묶음의 시집을 창작했다 / 그리고 수백 통의 편지를 썼다 / 그녀의 여동생 Lavinia의 발견

secretly created bundles of poetry / [and] wrote hundreds of letters. 3 Due to a discovery by

V_1 V_2

덕분에 / Dickinson의 놀라운 작품은 출판되었다 / 그녀의 사후에 / 그리고 그녀는

her sister Lavinia, / Dickinson's remarkable work was published / after her death, // [and] she

S_1 V_1 S_2

이제 간주된다 / 미국 문학에서 가장 중요한 인물 중 한 명으로

is now considered / (as) one of the most important figures of American literature. 4 Though

V_2 접속사

Dickinson이 학교를 떠난 정확한 이유는 / 알려지지 않고 있지만 / ~라고들 한다

the precise reasons for Dickinson's departure from school / are unknown, // it is said / that

S′ V′ C′ 가주어 V 진주어

그녀의 연약한 감정 상태가 / 역할을 했을지도 모른다 / 그녀를 학교에서 끌어내려는 그녀의 아버지의 결정에

her weak emotional state / may have played a role / in *her father's decision* [to pull her from

어휘확인

eventually 결국 **secretly** 몰래 **bundle** 묶음, 꾸러미 **poetry** 시집, 시 **due to** ~ 덕분에, ~ 때문에 **discovery** 발견 **remarkable** 놀라운, 놀랄 만한 **publish** 출판하다 **death** 죽음 **consider** (~을 …으로) 간주하다[여기다]; 고려하다 **figure** 인물 **literature** 문학 **precise** 정확한 **departure** 떠남, 출발 **unknown** 알려지지 않은 **emotional** 감정의, 정서의 **play a role** 역할을 하다 **decision** 결정 **chief** 주된 **caregiver** 간병인, 돌보는 사람 **pass away** 죽다, 사망하다 **homestead** 농가, 농장 **respective** 각자의, 각각의

Emily와 그녀의 여동생 Lavinia는 주된 간병인으로 지냈다 　병든 어머니를 돌보는
school]. [5] Emily [and] her sister Lavinia served as chief caregivers / for their sick mother //
S 　V

그녀가 세상을 떠날 때까지 　1882년에 　Emily도 그녀의 여동생도 결혼하지 않았다 　그리고 그들은
until she passed away / in 1882. [6] [Neither] Emily [nor] her sister ever married, // [and] they
접속사 S′ V′ 　S_1 　V_1 　S_2

함께 살았다 　농가에서 　그들 각자가 죽을 때까지
lived together / at the homestead / until their respective deaths.
V_2

① 십 대 시절에 학교를 그만두었다.　② 한 농장에서 은둔의 삶을 살았다.
③ 작품이 여동생에 의해 발견되었다.　④ 사후에 작품이 출간되었다.
⑤ 병든 어머니를 돌보다가 사망하였다.

해석 한 눈에 보기 **1** 1830년 12월 10일, 매사추세츠 주 애머스트에서 태어난 Emily Dickinson은 십 대에 학교를 그만 두었고, 결국 다른 사람들과 떨어져 외로운 삶을 살았다. **2** 그곳에서, 그녀는 몰래 몇 묶음의 시집을 창작하고 수백 통의 편지를 썼다. **3** 그녀의 여동생 Lavinia의 발견 덕분에, Dickinson의 놀라운 작품은 그녀의 사후에 출판되었으며, 그녀는 이제 미국 문학에서 가장 중요한 인물 중 한 명으로 간주된다. **4** Dickinson이 학교를 떠난 정확한 이유는 알려지지 않고 있지만, 그녀의 연약한 감정 상태가 그녀를 학교에서 끌어내려는 그녀의 아버지의 결정에 역할을 했을지도 모른다고들 한다. **5** Emily와 그녀의 여동생 Lavinia는 1882년에 그녀가 세상을 떠날 때까지 병든 어머니를 돌보는 주된 간병인으로 지냈다. **6** Emily도 그녀의 여동생도 결혼하지 않았고, 그들은 그들 각자가 죽을 때까지 농가에서 함께 살았다.

정답단추 선택지와 본문의 내용이 일치하지 않는 것을 고르는 문제야. 본문과 선택지의 내용을 순서대로 비교하면서 답을 찾으면 돼. 글의 후반부에서 Emily Dickinson은 여동생과 함께 병든 어머니가 세상을 떠날 때까지 간병을 했다고 했으므로, ⑤는 글의 내용과 일치하지 않아.

오답단서 ①은 첫 번째 문장을 통해 일치함을 알 수 있어. ②는 첫 번째 문장에서 은둔 생활을 했다고 했고, 마지막 문장에서 죽을 때까지 농가에서 살았다고 했으므로 일치하는 내용이야. ③, ④는 여동생의 발견으로 Emily Dickinson의 작품들이 사후에 출간되었다고 했으므로 내용과 일치해.

지문 Flow

[인물 소개]
Emily Dickinson은 1830년 12월 10일, 매사추세츠 주 애머스트에서 태어남

⬇

[세부사항1]
십 대에 학교를 그만두고 은둔 생활을 하면서, 수많은 작품을 씀

⬇

[추가]
여동생 Lavinia가 그녀의 사후에 작품을 발견하여 출간하였고, 지금은 미국 문학의 중요한 인물로 간주됨

⬇

[세부사항2]
병든 어머니를 돌아가실 때까지 여동생과 함께 돌봄

&

[세부사항3]
결혼하지 않고 죽을 때까지 농가에서 여동생과 함께 지냄

242 　정답 ⑤

지문 All in One

나는 끝없이 나의 길을 간다 　텅 빈 해변을 따라 　나는 알고 있다 　파도가 부딪히고 있다는 것을
[1] I make my way endlessly / along an empty beach. [2] I am aware / that waves are crashing /
S V 　S_1 V_1 C_1 접속사 S'_1 V'_1

저 멀리 어딘가에서 　그러나 그 소리가 불확실하고 희미하여 　마치 내가 실제로 그곳에 있지 않은 것 같다
somewhere in the distance, // [but] their sound is unclear and faint, / as if I'm not really there.
S_2 V_2 C_2 접속사 S'_2 V'_2

저 멀리에 빛줄기 하나가 있다 　그러나 ~인 것 같다 　내가 걸으면 걸을수록 　그것이 내게서 더 멀어지는 것
[3] There's a light in the distance, // [but] it seems / the more I walk, / the further away it gets
V_1 S_1 　S_2 V_2 　「the+비교급 ~, the+비교급 …」

나는 마침내 포기한다 　나는 알기 때문에 　내가 절대 그곳에 도달하지 못할 것임을 　해는 거의 진다
from me. [4] I finally give up, // since I know / (that) I'll never reach it. [5] The sun is almost gone,
S V 접속사 S′ V′ 접속사 S″ V″ 　S V

검붉은 바닷속으로 사라져 가면서 　낮은 구름들이 타고 있다 　해가 낮게 저물면서 　그것들
/ disappearing into a dark red sea. [6] Low clouds are glowing // as the sun sinks low. [7] Behind
분사구문(= as it disappears ~) 　S V 접속사 S′ V′

뒤로 　섬의 검은 그림자가 　나타난다 　그것의 산들이 　하늘의 검은색 거인들 같다
them / the dark shadow of an island / appears. [8] Its mountains / seem like black giants in the
= clouds 　S V 　S V

갑자기 모든 것이 녹아들어 간다 　완전한 어둠 속으로 　이제는 나에게 길을 보여줄 달조차 없다
sky. [9] Suddenly everything melts / into total darkness. [10] There is not even *a moon* [to show
S V 　V S

me the way] now.

① calm and gentle 조용하고 부드러운　② joyful and festive 즐겁고 흥겨운　③ noisy and crowded 시끄럽고 혼잡한
④ thrilling and exciting 스릴 있고 흥미로운　⑤ hopeless and gloomy 절망적이고 우울한

해석 한 눈에 보기 **1** 나는 텅 빈 해변을 따라 끝없이 길을 간다. **2** 나는 파도가 저 멀리 어딘가에서 부딪히고 있다는 것을 알고 있지만, 그 소리가 불확실하고 희미하여 마치 내가 실제로 그곳에 있지 않은 것 같다. **3** 저 멀리에 빛줄기 하나가 있지만, 내가 걸으면 걸을수록 그것이 내게서 더 멀어지는 것 같다. **4** 나는 마침내 포기하는데, 내가 절대 그곳에 도달하지 못할 것을 알기 때문이다. **5** 해는 거의 저서, 검붉은 바닷속으로 사라져 가고 있다. **6** 낮은 구름이 해가 낮게 저무는 가운데 붉게 타고 있다. **7** 그것들 뒤로 어느 섬의 검은 그림자가 나타난다. **8** 그것의 산들이 하늘의 검은색 거인들 같다. **9** 갑자기 모든 것이 완전한 어둠 속으로 녹아들어 간다. **10** 이제는 나에게 길을 보여줄 달조차 없다.

정답단추 글의 상황을 머릿속에 그림을 그리듯 상상하며 읽어 보자. 텅 빈 해변, 멀어지는 빛, 태양이 지고 난 후의 어둠 등을 표현한 어구가 보이지? 또, give up, never reach, dark red sea 등을 통해서도 이 글의 전체적인 분위기는 절망적이고 우울하다는 것을 알 수 있어. 따라서 이 글의 분위기로 가장 적절한 것은 ⑤야.

어휘확인

make A's way 길을 가다 **endlessly** 끝없이, 영원히 **aware (that)** (~을) 알고 있는 **crash** 부딪히다; 충돌하다 **somewhere** 어딘가에[에서] **in the distance** 멀리서 **unclear** 불확실한 **faint** 희미한 **disappear** 사라지다 **glow** (불 등이) 타다, 빛나다 **sink** 가라앉다 **appear** 나타나다 **melt into** ~ 속으로 녹아들다[사라져 버리다] **total** 완전한; 전체의 **darkness** 어둠
〈선택지 어휘〉
calm 조용한; 침착한 **gentle** 부드러운, 온화한 **joyful** 즐거운, 기쁜 **festive** 흥겨운 **crowded** 혼잡한, 복잡한 **thrilling** 스릴 있는 **hopeless** 절망적인 **gloomy** 우울한

지문 Flow

[발단]
파도 소리가 멀리서 들리는 텅 빈 해변을 따라 걸어감

⬇

[전개]
멀리 있는 빛줄기가 걸을수록 더 멀어짐 → 더 가기를 포기함

⬇

[절정]
해가 바닷속으로 저물고, 섬의 검은 그림자가 나타남

⬇

[결말]
갑자기 완전한 어둠이 와서 길을 보여줄 달조차 없음

243 정답 ⑤

지문 All in One

드문 일이다 / 최첨단 기술이 / 손을 뻗는 것은 / 그리고 우리를 만지는 것은
1 It is a rare thing / for cutting-edge technology / to reach out / and touch us / on an
가주어 V_1 C_1 for+목적격(의미상 주어) 진주어

감정적 수준으로 / 그러나 그것이 그렇게 할 때 / 그 결과는 뛰어나고 예상 밖일 수 있다
emotional level, // but when it does, / the result can be brilliant and unexpected. 2 For
접속사 S′ V′ S_2 V_2 C_2

예를 들어 / 미국과 영국의 연구원들은 / 사람의 얼굴 표정을 이용하는 소프트웨어를 개발해 냈다
example, / researchers in America and England / have developed *software* [that uses
S V 관계대명사

미술 작품을 만들어 내기 위해 / 사람들은 그림을 본다
people's facial expressions] / to generate a work of art. 3 People view a painting / on a
부사적 용법(목적) S V

컴퓨터 모니터에 있는 / 그 동안 웹캠은 그들의 얼굴을 기록한다 / 컴퓨터는 개인의 감정을 인식할 수 있다
computer screen // while a webcam records their faces. 4 The computer can recognize an
접속사 S′ V′ S V

눈과 입의 움직임을 분석함으로써 / 보는 사람의 표정이 변할 때마다
individual's emotions / by analyzing eye and mouth movements. 5 Each time the viewer's
접속사 S′

컴퓨터는 색깔과 붓놀림을 바꾼다 / 그 사람의 기분에 맞도록
expression changes, // the computer changes colors and brushstrokes / to match the person's
V′ S V 부사적 용법(목적)

컴퓨터는 이 모든 것을 한다 / 실시간으로 / 이것은 ~을 의미한다 / 보는 사람의 감정이
mood. 6 The computer does all of this / in real time, // which means / that **the viewer's**
S V 관계대명사(계속적 용법) 접속사

미술 작품을 변화시킨다는 것을
emotions / change the artwork.

① facial expressions change quickly
얼굴 표정이 빠르게 바뀐다

② using high-tech software is easy
첨단 기술 소프트웨어를 사용하는 것이 쉽다

③ its artwork is better than human artwork
그것의 예술 작품이 사람의 예술 작품보다 더 낫다

④ the best colors are selected automatically
가장 좋은 색깔이 자동으로 선택된다

⑤ the viewer's emotions change the artwork
보는 사람의 감정이 미술 작품을 변화시킨다

해석 한 눈에 보기 주제문 1 최첨단 기술이 손을 뻗어 감정적 수준으로 우리를 만지는 것은 드문 일이지만, 그것이 그렇게 할 때 그 결과는 뛰어나고 예상 밖일 수 있다. 2 예를 들어, 미국과 영국의 연구원들은 사람 얼굴의 표정을 이용하여 미술 작품을 만들어 내는 소프트웨어를 개발해 냈다. 3 사람들이 컴퓨터 모니터에 있는 그림을 보고 있는 동안 웹캠이 그들의 얼굴을 기록한다. 4 컴퓨터는 눈과 입의 움직임을 분석함으로써 개인의 감정을 인식할 수 있다. 5 보는 사람의 표정이 바뀔 때마다, 컴퓨터는 그 사람의 기분에 맞도록 색깔과 붓놀림을 바꾼다. 6 컴퓨터는 이 모든 것을 실시간으로 하는데, 이것은 보는 사람의 감정이 미술 작품을 변화시킨다는 것을 의미한다.

정답단추 빈칸을 포함하는 문장을 먼저 읽고, 이 컴퓨터가 하는 작업이 '무엇'을 의미하는지 찾아보자. 도입부에서 최첨단 기술이 우리의 감정 수준까지 도달한다고 말하고 있고, 이어서 이를 보충 설명하는 예시로 컴퓨터가 사람의 표정을 읽어 미술 작품을 만드는 소프트웨어가 개발됐다는 내용과 그 작동 원리에 대해 말하고 있어. 즉 감정에 따라 표정이 바뀌고 그에 따라 그림이 달라진다는 내용이므로 빈칸에 들어갈 말은 ⑤가 적절해.

오답단서 이 글에선 빈칸 문장의 바로 앞 문장이 주요 단서가 돼. 속도와 관계없이 표정이 바뀌기만 하면 컴퓨터가 실시간으로 그것을 그려내는 것이니 ①의 표정이 빠르게 바뀌는 것과도 상관이 없어. 또한, ②, ③, ④는 글의 내용과 거리가 멀어.

어휘확인

rare 드문, 보기 힘든 **cutting-edge** 최첨단의, 칼날의 **emotional** 감정적인 **brilliant** 뛰어난 **unexpected** 예상 밖의 **researcher** 연구원 **develop** 개발하다; 발달시키다 **software** 소프트웨어 **facial** 얼굴의 **expression** 표정, 표현 **generate** 만들어 내다, 생성하다 **work of art** 미술품, 예술품 (= artwork) **webcam** 웹캠(컴퓨터에 연결할 수 있는 비디오카메라) **recognize** 인식하다 **individual** 개인의 **emotion** 감정, 정서 **analyze** 분석하다 **movement** 움직임 **brushstroke** 붓놀림 **match** 맞추다, 어울리다 **mood** 기분, 분위기 **real time** 실시간(의)

〈선택지 어휘〉
high-tech 첨단 기술의 **select** 선택하다 **automatically** 자동적으로

지문 Flow

[주제문]
최첨단 기술이 우리의 감정 수준에 도달함

⬇

[보충설명1]
미국과 영국의 연구원들이 사람의 표정으로 미술 작품을 만드는 소프트웨어를 개발함

&

[보충설명2]
사람들이 모니터의 그림을 보는 동안, 웹캠이 얼굴을 기록하여 감정을 인식하고, 기분에 맞게 색깔과 붓놀림을 바꿈

⬇

[결론]
보는 사람의 감정이 미술 작품을 변화시킴

244 정답 ④

지문 All in One

사회적 동물로서 / 우리 삶의 많은 부분은 / 추측함을 중심으로 돌아간다 / 다른 사람들이
1 As social animals, / a large portion of our lives / revolves around guessing // what others
S V 관계대명사

생각하거나 느낄지도 모르는 것을 / 그리고 우리는 여러 가지 요령들을 개발해 왔다 / 이것을 위한 / 예를 들어
may be thinking or feeling. 2 And we've developed several tricks / for this. 3 For example, /
S V

많은 사람들이 믿는다 / 우리의 눈이 진실을 드러낸다고 / 우리가 어떻게 느끼고 있는지에 대해 / 우리가 누군가
many people believe / that our eyes reveal the truth / about how we are feeling: // when we
S V 접속사 S′ V′ 간접의문문 접속사 S'_1

를 정말로 좋아할 때 / 우리는 생각한다 / 그 사람이 아마 알 수도 있을 것이라고 / 우리가 그렇다는 것을
really like someone, / we think / that the person can probably tell / that we do / just by
V'_1 S V 접속사 S'_2 V'_2 접속사 S″ V″

오직 우리 눈을 들여다봄으로써 / 그런데 / 과학자들은 그것을 증명해 왔다 / 그들은 발견해 왔다 / 우리의 동공이 크기를
looking into our eyes. 4 Now, / scientists have proven it. 5 They've found // that our pupils
S V S V 접속사 S′

어휘확인

portion 부분 **revolve around** ~을 중심으로[위주로] 돌아가다 **guess** 추측[짐작]하다 **develop** 개발하다; 발달시키다 **several** 여러 가지의; 몇몇의 **trick** 요령; 속임수 **reveal** 드러내다, 밝히다 **truth** 진실 **probably** 아마 **tell** 알다, 판단하다; 말하다 **look into** ~을 들여다보다 **prove** 증명하다 **pupil** 동공, 눈동자 **depending on** ~에 따라

〈선택지 어휘〉
fingerprint 지문 **expand** 확장[확대]되다 **let in** ~을 들어오게 하다

바꾼다는 것을 우리의 감정에 따라 동공은 작고 검은 원이다 우리 눈의 가운데에

change size / depending on our feelings. 6 Pupils are the little black circles / in the middle

V′ S V C

있는 그것은 더 커진다 당신이 좋아하는 누군가나 어떤 것을 볼 때

of our eyes. 7 They get bigger / when you look at *someone* [or] *something* [(that) you like] //

S V C_1 접속사 S'_1 V'_1 관계대명사

그리고 더 작아진다 당신이 좋아하지 않는 것을 볼 때

[and] smaller / when you look at *things* [(which[that]) you don't like].

C_2 접속사 S'_2 V'_2 관계대명사

① are unique like fingerprints
지문처럼 독특하다

② move when we are telling lies
우리가 거짓말을 할 때 움직인다

③ get smaller when we are angry
우리가 화가 났을 때 더 작아진다

④ change size depending on our feelings
우리의 감정에 따라 크기를 바꾼다

⑤ expand to let in more light when it's dark
날이 어두울 때 더 많은 빛을 들이려고 확장된다

해석 한 눈에 보기 주제문 **1** 사회적 동물로서, 우리 삶의 많은 부분은 다른 사람들이 생각하거나 느낄지도 모르는 것을 추측하는 것을 중심으로 돌아간다. **2** 그리고 우리는 이것을 위한 여러 가지 요령들을 개발해 왔다. **3** 예를 들어, 많은 사람은 우리의 눈이 우리가 어떻게 느끼고 있는지에 대한 진실을 드러낸다고 믿는데, 그래서 우리가 누군가를 정말로 좋아할 때, 우리는 그 사람이 어쩌면 우리가 그렇다는 것을 오직 우리 눈을 들여다봄으로써 알 수도 있을 것으로 생각한다. **4** 그런데 과학자들이 그것을 증명해 왔다. **5** 그들은 우리의 동공이 우리의 감정에 따라 크기를 바꾼다는 것을 발견해 왔다. **6** 동공은 우리 눈의 가운데에 있는 작고 검은 원이다. **7** 그것은 당신이 좋아하는 누군가나 어떤 것을 볼 때 더 커지고 당신이 좋아하지 않는 것을 볼 때 더 작아진다.

정답단추 빈칸이 포함된 문장을 읽고 과학자들이 동공에 대해 알아낸 사실이 '무엇'인지 찾으며 글을 읽어 보자. 마지막 문장에서 우리가 좋아하는 대상을 볼 때 동공의 크기가 커지고, 좋아하지 않는 것을 볼 때 동공의 크기가 작아진다는 내용이 언급되었으므로 빈칸에는 감정에 따라 크기가 바뀐다는 내용의 ④가 적절해.

오답단서 ①, ⑤는 본문의 내용과는 전혀 관련이 없어. 세 번째 문장에서 많은 사람은 우리의 눈이 진실을 드러낸다고 믿는다고 했지만, 이걸 보고 우리가 거짓말할 때 움직인다는 내용의 ②가 들어가야 한다고 섣불리 추측해선 안 돼. 동공은 좋아하지 않는 것을 볼 때 더 작아진다고 했으므로 ③은 지문의 내용과 일치하지 않아.

지문 Flow

[주제문]
우리는 사회적 동물로서, 다른 사람의 생각과 감정을 추측하고 요령을 개발함

⬇

[보충설명]
우리의 눈에 감정에 대한 진실이 드러나므로, 눈을 보고 그것을 알 수 있음

⬇

[추가]
과학자들이 동공이 감정에 따라 크기를 바꾼다는 것을 발견함

⬇

[결론]
좋아하는 것을 볼 때는 동공이 커지고, 좋아하지 않는 것을 볼 때는 동공이 작아짐

245 정답 ②

지문 All in One

대부분의 사람들은 겪는다 어느 정도의 불안을 시험을 준비할 때 이것은

1 Most people suffer / some degree of anxiety // when (they're) preparing for a test. 2 This can

S V 접속사 S′ V′ S V

어느 것이든 될 수 있다 가벼운 긴장감에서부터 완전한 공황 발작에 이르기까지 당신의 불안 수준이 무엇이든 간에

be anything / [from] a mild nervous feeling [to] a full panic attack. 3 Whatever your level of

C 복합관계사 S′

그것을 줄이는 것을 배우는 것은 매우 중요하다 시험을 위해 효과적으로 공부하기 위해

anxiety (is), // learning to reduce it / is very important / to study effectively for a test. 4 Leave

V′ S V C 부사적 용법(목적) V

자신에게 남겨 두어라 공부할 많은 시간을 시험 전날 밤까지 기다리는 것은 공부를

yourself / **plenty of time for studying**. 5 Waiting until the night before a test / to start

IO DO S 부사적 용법(목적)

시작하려고 당신의 불안감을 증가시킬 것 같다 당신은 시간이 부족하고 성급해지고

studying / is likely to increase your anxiety. 6 You will be short of time, rushed,

V S V_1 V_2

당황하게 될 것이고 육체적으로 피곤할 것이다 질문을 할 시간이 없어서 또는 필요한 정보를 찾아 볼

overwhelmed, [and] physically tired, / with no *time* [to ask questions / [or] look up necessary

V_3 V_4

(시간이 없어서) 기다리는 대신에 마지막 순간까지 공부를 시작하라 시험 일정이 잡히자마자

information]. 7 Instead of waiting / until the last minute, / start studying // as soon as a test is

V 접속사 S′ V′

준비하는 며칠로 인해 당신은 더 여유 있게 느낄 것이다

scheduled. 8 With *several days* [to prepare], / you'll feel more relaxed.

S V C

① time to make plans
계획을 세울 시간

② plenty of time for studying
공부할 많은 시간

③ enough energy to start the work
일을 시작할 충분한 에너지

④ a few places to study most efficiently
가장 효율적으로 공부할 몇몇 장소들

⑤ freedom to pursue your own study schedule
자신의 학습 일정을 추구할 자유

해석 한 눈에 보기 **1** 대부분의 사람들은 시험을 준비할 때 어느 정도의 불안을 겪는다. **2** 이것은 가벼운 긴장감에서부터 완전한 공황 발작에 이르기까지 어느 것이든 될 수 있다. 주제문 **3** 당신의 불안 수준이 무엇이든 간에, 그것을 줄이는 것을 배우는 것은 시험을 위해 효과적으로 공부하기 위해 매우 중요하다. **4** 공부할 많은 시간을 자신에게 남겨 두어라. **5** 공부를 시작하려고 시험 전날 밤까지 기다리는 것은 당신의 불안감을 증가시킬 것 같다. **6** 당신은 질문을 하거나 필요한 정보를 찾아 볼 시간이 없어서, 시간이 부족하고, 성급해지고, 당황하게 될 것이고, 육체적으로 피곤할 것

어휘확인

suffer (고통 등을) 겪다, 받다 **anxiety** 불안 **mild** 가벼운, 순한 **panic attack** 공황 발작 **reduce** 줄이다, 감소시키다 **effectively** 효과적으로 **plenty of** 많은 **be likely to** ~할 것 같다 **increase** 증가시키다 **be short of** ~이 부족하다 **rush** 서두르다 **overwhelm** 당황하게 하다, 압도하다 **look up** 찾아 보다 **necessary** 필요한 **instead of ~** 대신에 **schedule** 일정을 잡다 **several** 몇몇의 **relaxed** 여유 있는, 느긋한

〈선택지 어휘〉

efficiently 효율적으로 **freedom** 자유 **pursue** 추구하다

지문 Flow

[도입]
대부분의 사람은 시험 준비 시 불안을 겪음

⬇

[주제문]
불안 해소는 효과적인 시험공부에 중요하며, 공부할 시간을 많이 남겨 두어야 함

⬇

[보충설명]
시험에 임박해서 공부를 하면 불안감이 증가하므로, 시험 일정이 잡히면 바로 공부를 시작해야 함

이다. **7** 마지막 순간까지 기다리는 대신에, 시험 일정이 잡히자마자 공부를 시작하라. **8** 준비하는 며칠로 인해, 당신은 더 여유 있게 느낄 것이다.

정답단추 빈칸을 추론할 수 있는 단서는 빈칸을 포함한 문장의 주변에 있을 가능성이 높아. 우선 빈칸을 포함한 문장을 살펴보자. 빈칸이 있는 문장을 보면, 스스로에게 남겨 두어야 하는 것이 '무엇'인지 찾아야 돼. 그 단서는 뒤에 나와. 시험 전날 밤에 공부를 시작하는 것은 불안감을 증가시키고, 시간이 부족해서 성급하고 당황할 것이므로, 시험 일정이 나오자마자 공부를 하라는 거지. 따라서 빈칸에 들어갈 말로 가장 적절한 것은 ②야.

오답단서 ①의 계획을 세울 시간이 아니라 공부할 시간이 필요한 거야. ④는 불안 해소가 효과적인 공부에 좋다는 내용은 나오는데, 공부 장소는 언급되지는 않았어. 에너지와 자유에 대해서 언급하지 않으므로 ③과 ⑤는 내용과 무관해.

246 정답 ④

지문 All in One

많은 연구원들과 정치가들은 / 불행한 실수를 한다 / 나라들 사이를
[1] Many researchers [and] politicians / make the unfortunate mistake / of distinguishing
S / V

구분하는 / '서양'이나 '동양'으로 / 비록 특정한 문화적 특징들이 공유되긴 하지만
between countries / as "Western" [or] "Eastern." [2] Although certain cultural characteristics
접속사 / S'

'서양' (나라들) 사이에서 / 그리고 동양 나라들 사이에서 / 그 같은 나라들도 다르다
are shared / among "Western" / [and] among "Eastern" countries, // the same countries differ
V' / S / V

많은 중요한 분야(면)에서 / 예를 들어 / 유럽 자체 내의 종교적 차이는
/ in many important areas. [3] (A) For example, / religious differences within Europe itself /
S

아마도 의미한다 / 남유럽이 더 유사하다는 것을 / 남미 구교 국가들 중 많은 수와
probably mean // that Southern Europe is more similar / to much of Catholic South America /
V / 접속사 / S' / V' / C'

북유럽보다 / Samuel Huntington은 / 잘 알려진 정치학자인 / 주장했다
than to Northern Europe. [4] Samuel Huntington, / a well-known political scientist, / argued /
S = / V

말하는 것이 더 낫다고 / '서양'과 '나머지'라고 / 여기서 그 구별은
that it is better to speak / of *the "West"* [and] *the "Rest,"* // where the distinction is based on
접속사 가주어 V' C' / 진주어 / 관계부사(계속적 용법)

경제 활동과 부를 토대로 한다 / 그러나 / 급격한 경제 발달로
economic activity [and] wealth. [5] (B) However, / with the rapid economic development / of

비서양 국가들 중 일부의 / 이것은 또한 점차 부적절해질 것이다
some of the non-West nations, / this too will become increasingly irrelevant.
S / V / C

	(A)		(B)		(A)		(B)
①	In addition	……	However	②	In addition	……	Instead
③	In addition	……	Therefore	④	For example	……	However
⑤	For example	……	Therefore				

해석 한 눈에 보기 주제문 **1** 많은 연구원과 정치가들이 나라들 사이를 '서양'이나 '동양'으로 구분하는 불행한 실수를 저지른다. **2** 비록 특정한 문화적 특징들이 '서양' 나라들 사이에서 그리고 '동양' 나라들 사이에서 공유될지라도, 그 나라들도 많은 중요한 면에서 다르다. **3** (A) 예를 들어, 유럽 자체 내의 종교적 차이는 아마도 남유럽이 북유럽보다 남미 구교 국가 중 많은 수와 더 유사하다는 것을 의미한다. **4** 잘 알려진 정치학자인 Samuel Huntington은 '서양'과 '나머지'라고 말하는 것이 더 낫다고 주장했는데, 여기서 그 구분은 경제 활동과 부를 토대로 한다. **5** (B) 그러나, 비서양 국가 중 일부의 급격한 경제 발달로, 이것 또한 점차 부적절해질 것이다.

정답단추 빈칸 앞뒤 문장의 관계를 파악하면 적절한 연결어를 찾을 수 있어. (A)의 앞 문장은 같은 서양 또는 동양 국가로 분류된 나라 중에서도 차이가 있다는 내용이야. (A) 뒤에서는 이에 대한 구체적인 예로 유럽 내의 종교적 차이를 들고 있으므로 For example이 들어가야 자연스러워. 그리고 (B) 앞에서는 Samuel Huntington이 언급한 서양과 나머지의 구분 기준이 경제 활동과 부라고 했는데, (B) 뒤를 보면 이것 역시 부적절해질 것이라는 상반된 내용이 나왔으니까 However가 적절해. 따라서 이를 종합하면 정답으로 알맞은 것은 ④야.

어휘확인

researcher 연구원 politician 정치가 make a mistake 실수를 하다 unfortunate 불행한 distinguish 구분하다 cf. distinction 구분 Western 서양의 Eastern 동양의 although 비록 ~이긴 하지만 certain 특정한 cultural 문화의 characteristic 특징 differ 다르다 area 분야; 지역 religious 종교의 within ~ 이내에[안에] probably 아마도 Southern 남쪽의 similar 유사한 Catholic 구교의 well-known 잘 알려진 political scientist 정치학자 argue 주장하다 be based on ~을 토대로 하다 economic 경제의 wealth 부(富), 재산 rapid 급격한; 빠른 development 발달 nation 국가 increasingly 점점 더 irrelevant 부적절한; 무관한

지문 Flow

[주제문]
나라들을 '서양'과 '동양'으로 구분하는 실수를 저지름

⬇

[보충설명]
문화적 특징들이 서양과 동양 나라들 간에 공유될지라도, 많은 면에서 다름

⬇

[예시]
유럽 국가들의 종교적 차이

⬇

[추가]
경제 활동과 부를 토대로, '서양'과 '나머지'로 구분하자는 주장이 있음

⬇

[반론]
비서양 국가들의 경제 발달로 그러한 구분도 부적절함

247 정답 ④

지문 All in One

행성은 별(항성) 궤도를 도는 거대한 둥근 물체이다 / 그들은 주로 기체로 만들어졌을지도 모른다
[1] A planet is *a massive round object* [which orbits a star]. [2] They may be primarily made of
S / V / C / 관계대명사 / S / V

목성처럼 / 혹은 고체로 / 지구 혹은 화성처럼 / 어떤 것들은 고리나 위성을 가지고 있다 / 반면에
gas, / like Jupiter, / [or] solid, / like Earth [or] Mars. [3] [Some] have rings [or] moons // while
S / V / 접속사

어떤 것들은 그렇지 않다 / 고대 그리스인들은 지도를 그린 최초의 사람들이었다 / 그리고 이 물체들 이름을
[others] do not (have ~ moons). [4] The ancient Greeks were *the first* [to map / [and] name these
S' / V' / S / V / C

어휘확인

planet 행성 massive 거대한 object 물체 orbit 궤도를 돌다; 궤도 star 별, 항성 primarily 주로 gas 기체, 가스 Jupiter 목성 solid 고체 moon 위성 ancient 고대의 Greek 그리스인 map 지도를 그리다 name 이름을 지어주다 wanderer 방랑자 cf. wander 돌아다니다 randomly 무작위로 from place to place 이곳저곳

지어준　　　　　　그들은 그것들을 행성이라고 불렀다　　　　　　　그것은 '방랑자'를 의미한다　　　　　　　　방랑자들은 무작위로

objects]. 5 ① They called them "planets," // which means "wanderers." 6 ② Wanderers travel

S　V　　　관계대명사(계속적 용법)　　　S　V_1

돌아다닌다　　　이곳저곳을　　　　　그리고 영구적인 집이 없다　　　　　그리스인들은 믿었다

randomly / from place to place // and have no permanent home. 7 ③ The Greeks believed //

V_2　　　S　V

그 행성들이 자유롭게 돌아다닌다고　　　하늘에서　　　　8개의 대행성들이 있다　　　　그리고 3개의

that the planets wandered freely / in the sky. 8 (④ There are eight major planets / and three

접속사　S′　V′　　　　V_1　S_1

소행성들이　　　　우리 태양계에　　　　그리고 이 행성들은 태양의 궤도를 돈다　　　　그러나

minor planets / in our solar system, // and these planets orbit the sun.) 9 ⑤ However, /

S_2　V_2

현대의 과학은 증명해 왔다　　　행성들이 고정된 궤도를 갖고 있다는 것을　　　그리고 그들의 이동이 매우 정확히 예측될

modern science has proved // that the planets have fixed orbits, / and their movement can be

S　V　접속사　S'_1　V'_1　S'_2　V'_2

수 있다는 것을

predicted very accurately.

해석 한 눈에 보기 1 행성은 별(항성)의 궤도를 도는 거대하고 둥근 물체이다. 2 그것들은 목성처럼 주로 기체로 혹은 지구나 화성처럼 고체로 만들어졌을지도 모른다. 3 어떤 것들은 고리나 위성을 가지지만 어떤 것들은 그렇지 않다. 4 고대 그리스인들이 이 물체들의 지도를 그리고 이름을 지은 최초의 사람들이었다. 5 ① 그들은 그것들을 '행성'이라고 불렀는데, 그것은 '방랑자'를 의미한다. 6 ② 방랑자는 무작위로 이곳저곳을 돌아다니며 영구적인 보금자리가 없다. 7 ③ 그리스인들은 행성이 하늘을 자유롭게 돌아다닌다고 믿었다. 8 (④ 우리 태양계에는 8개의 대행성과 3개의 소행성이 있으며, 이 행성들은 태양의 궤도를 돈다.) 9 ⑤ 그러나 현대 과학은 행성이 고정된 궤도를 갖고 있고, 그들의 이동이 매우 정확히 예측될 수 있다는 것을 증명해 왔다.

정답단추 글을 읽으면서 흐름에서 벗어나는 문장을 찾으면 돼. 이 글은 행성에 관한 글로 행성에 관심을 가졌던 고대 그리스인들의 이야기가 이어지고 있어. 그런데 ④는 태양계를 구성하는 여러 행성에 대한 설명으로 전체 내용과 무관할 뿐 아니라 그리스인들이 행성이 자유롭게 돌아다닌다고 믿었다는 앞 문장에 자연스럽게 이어지지 않아. 따라서 글의 흐름과 관계없는 문장은 ④야.

오답단서 ①, ②, ③은 그리스인들이 행성을 이리저리 떠도는 방랑자로 여겼다는 내용으로 자연스럽게 이어지고 있어. 마지막으로 ⑤도 그리스인들의 생각과 달리 행성은 일정 궤도를 주기적으로 돌고 있다는 내용으로 ③과 자연스럽게 이어져.

permanent 영구적인 **freely** 자유롭게 **major planet** 대행성(↔ **minor planet** 소행성) **solar system** 태양계 **modern** 현대의 **prove** 증명하다 **fixed** 고정된 **movement** 이동 **predict** 예측하다 **accurately** 정확히

지문 Flow

[도입]
행성은 별의 궤도를 도는 거대한 둥근 물체로, 기체 또는 고체로 만들어졌고, 고리나 위성을 가짐

⬇

[보충설명]
• 그리스인들이 최초로 행성의 지도를 그리고 이름을 지었음
• 그리스인들은 행성이 하늘을 자유롭게 돌아다닌다고 믿음

⬇

[무관한 문장]
태양계에 대행성 8개와 소행성 3개가 있으며, 태양의 궤도를 돔

⬇

[반론]
행성은 고정된 궤도가 있고, 이동이 예측 가능함

248 정답 ④

지문 All in One

거북은 가장 오래된 생물 중 하나이다　　　지구상에서　　　　육지 거북은 토터스라고 불린다

1 Turtles are among the oldest creatures / on Earth. (①) 2 Land turtles are called tortoises, //

S　V　　　S_1　V_1

그리고 그것들의 몸은 만들어져 있다　　　모든 것을 아주 느리게 하도록　　　Aesop의 유명한 이야기에도 불구하고

and their bodies are made / to do everything very slowly. (②) 3 Despite Aesop's famous

S_2　V_2

육지 거북은 달리기 경주를 절대 이기지 못할 것이다　　　토끼와 겨루는　　　그것의 무겁고 단단한

story, / the tortoise will never win a running race / against a rabbit. (③) 4 Its heavy and

S　V　S

등딱지는　　그것의 몸통을 너무 뻣뻣하게 만든다　　달리기에는　　그러나 단단한 등딱지를 가진 이 파충류는

hard shell / makes its body too stiff / for running. 5 (④ But these hard-shelled reptiles / don't

V　O　C　S　V

빨리 달릴 필요가 없다　생존하기 위해　　육지 거북은 숨을 수 있다　　자신의 등딱지 안으로　　그들이 적에 의해

need to run fast / to survive.) 6 Tortoises can hide / inside their shells // when they are

부사적 용법(목적)　S　V　접속사　S′　V′

공격받았을 때　　　또한　　대부분의 육지 거북은 야채뿐인 음식만을 먹기 때문에　　　그들은 달릴

attacked by enemies. (⑤) 7 Also, / since most tortoises eat only vegetarian food, // they don't

접속사　S′　V′　S　V_1

필요가 없다　　그리고 동물을 잡을　　그들의 저녁거리를 위해

need to run / and catch animals / for their dinner.

V_2

해석 한 눈에 보기 1 거북은 지구상에서 가장 오래된 생물 중 하나이다. 2 육지 거북은 '토터스'라고 불리는데, 그것들의 몸은 모든 것을 아주 느리게 하도록 만들어져 있다. 3 Aesop의 유명한 이야기에도 불구하고, 육지 거북은 토끼와 겨루는 달리기 경주를 절대 이기지 못할 것이다. 4 그것의 무겁고 단단한 등딱지는 그것의 몸통을 달리기에는 너무 뻣뻣하게 만든다. 5 그러나 단단한 등딱지를 가진 이 파충류는 생존하기 위해 빨리 달릴 필요가 없다. 6 육지 거북은 그들이 적에 의해 공격받았을 때 자신의 등딱지 안으로 숨을 수 있다. 7 또한, 대부분의 육지 거북은 채식만을 하므로, 그들은 그들의 저녁거리를 위해 달려가서 동물을 잡을 필요가 없다.

정답단추 주어진 문장이 필요한 부분은 주로 글의 흐름이 끊기는 부분으로 갑자기 글의 흐름이 바뀌어 논리적으로 어색한 부분을 찾으면 돼. ④의 앞은 육지 거북이 매우 느려서 뛰지 못한다는 내용인데, 뒤는 육지 거북이 빨리 뛰지 않아도 된다고 하여 내용이 상반되고 있어. 따라서 내용을 전환하는 But으로 시작하여 육지 거북이 생존하기 위해 뛸 필요가 없다는 내용의 주어진 문장이 ④에 들어가면 자연스러워. 이를 넣어 다시 읽어보고, 자연스럽게 이어지는지 확인하는 것을 잊지 마.

어휘확인

turtle (모든 종류의) 거북; 바다 거북 **creature** 생물 **tortoise** 육지 거북 **despite** ~에도 불구하고 **shell** 등딱지, 껍데기 cf. **hard-shelled** 단단한 등딱지[껍질]의 **stiff** 뻣뻣한 **reptile** 파충류 **survive** 생존하다 **hide** 숨다 **attack** 공격하다 **enemy** 적 **vegetarian** 야채뿐인; 채식주의자

지문 Flow

[도입]
가장 오래된 생물 중 하나인 거북은 태생적으로 느림

⬇

[이유]
무겁고 단단한 등딱지가 달릴 수 없게 만듦

⬇

[대조]
거북은 생존을 위해 빨리 달릴 필요가 없음

⬇

[이유]
• 적에게 공격받았을 때 등딱지 안으로 숨을 수 있음
• 채식을 하므로 먹이를 얻기 위해 달려가 동물을 잡을 필요 없음

249 정답 ②

지문 All in One

어떤 사람들은 그들의 방과 일터를 유지한다 / 아주 청결한 상태로 / 그들에게

[1] Some people keep their rooms [and] workspaces / in a spotless condition. [2] For them, /
S V

모든 것은 적절한 장소를 가지고 있다 / 그리고 그들은 편히 쉬는 것이 불가능하다는 것을 발견한다 / 모든 것이 정확히 알맞은 곳에

everything has a proper place, // [and] they find it impossible to relax / unless everything is
S_1 V_1 S_2 V_2 가목적어 C 진목적어 접속사 S' V'

있지 않는 한 / 다른 사람들은 방과 책상을 갖고 있다 / 완전한 혼돈 상태로 / 그들은

exactly where it belongs. [3] Others have rooms [and] desks / in a state of complete chaos. [4] They
관계부사 S V S

좀처럼 재고하지 않는다 / 어떤 것이 어디에 두어져 있어야 하는지를 / 하지만 이 사람들이 어떤 것을

rarely give a second thought / to where anything should be stored. [5] But when these people
V 간접의문문 접속사 S'

필요로 할 때 / 그들은 종종 그것을 바로 찾을 수 있다 / 무질서가 항상 무정돈과 동등한 것은 아니다

need something, // they can often find it straight away. [6] Disorder does not always equal
V' S V S V

그것은 중요하지 않다 / 만약 다른 사람들이 생각한다면 / 당신의 방이 재난 지역처럼 보인다고

disorganization. [7] It doesn't matter // if other people think / (that) your room looks like a
S V 접속사 S' V' 접속사 S'' V''

만약 당신이 모든 것을 찾을 수 있다면 / 당신이 그것을 필요로 할 때 / 만약 당신이 물건들을 유지할 수 있다면

disaster area. [8] If you can find everything / when you need it, / if you can keep things / in
접속사 S'_1 V'_1 접속사 S'' V'' 접속사 S'_2 V'_2

꽤 좋은 상태로 / 그리고 만약 당신이 편하게 느낀다면 / 당신의 공간에서 / 그러면 당신은 정리 정돈되었다(된 사람이다)

fairly good condition, / [and] if you feel comfortable / in your space, // then you are organized!
접속사 S'_3 V'_3 C' S V

⬇

> 정리 정돈은 공간이 어떻게 보이는지에 관한 것이 아니다 / 그러나 그것이 어떻게 기능하는지에 (관한 것이다)
>
> [9] Organization is [not] about how a space (A) looks, // [but] how it (B) functions.
> S V 간접의문문 간접의문문

	(A)		(B)
①	looks	……	changes
②	looks	……	functions
③	looks	……	is cleaned
④	works	……	functions
⑤	works	……	changes

해석 한 눈에 보기 1 어떤 사람들은 자신의 방과 일터를 아주 청결한 상태로 유지한다. 2 그들에게는, 모든 것이 적절한 장소를 갖고 있어서, 그들은 모든 것이 그것이 알맞은 곳에 정확히 있지 않으면 편히 쉬는 것이 불가능하다고 생각한다. 3 또 어떤 사람들은 방과 책상을 완전한 혼돈 상태로 갖고 있다. 4 그들은 좀처럼 어떤 것이 어디에 두어져 있어야 하는지를 재고하지 않는다. 5 하지만 이 사람들이 어떤 것을 필요로 할 때, 그들은 종종 그것을 바로 찾을 수 있다. 6 무질서가 항상 무정돈과 동등한 것은 아니다. 7 다른 사람들이 당신의 방이 재난 지역 같아 보인다고 생각할지라도 그것은 중요하지 않다. 주제문 8 만약 당신에게 그것이 필요할 때 모든 것을 찾을 수 있다면, 만약 당신이 물건들을 꽤 좋은 상태로 보관할 수 있다면, 그리고 만약 당신이 당신의 공간에서 편안하게 느낀다면, 그러면 당신은 정리 정돈된 사람이다.

> 9 정리 정돈은 공간이 어떻게 (A) 보이는지에 관한 것이 아니라 그것이 어떻게 (B) 기능하는지에 관한 것이다.

정답단추 요약문을 먼저 읽고 (A), (B)에 들어갈 말을 찾아야 해. 요약문은 정리 정돈의 정의를 내리고 있으니까 글에서 정리 정돈에 대해서 무엇이라고 설명하는지를 살펴보자. 이 글은 방을 깨끗이 하는 사람도 있고 지저분하게 하는 사람도 있는데, 지저분해 보여도 물건을 찾는 데 문제가 되지 않는다면 정리 정돈이 된 사람이라는 내용이야. 이를 가장 잘 반영하면 요약문의 (A)에는 looks(보이는)가, (B)에는 functions(기능하는)가 들어가서 정리 정돈은 보이는 게 다가 아니라 그 기능에 달려있다는 내용이 되어야 적절해. 따라서 정답은 ②야.

오답단서 (A)의 works와 (B)의 changes는 글의 내용과 관련이 없어. 그리고 (B)의 is cleaned는 글의 처음에 언급된 in a spotless condition과 비슷한 표현이지만, 이 글에서는 정리 정돈이 깨끗한 정도에 기준을 두는 게 아니라 기능에 기준을 둔다고 했으니까 적절하지 않아. 종합하면 ①, ③, ④, ⑤는 답이 될 수 없어.

어휘확인

workspace 일터; (사무실 내의) 업무 공간 **spotless** 아주 청결한, 티끌 하나 없는 **condition** 상태 **proper** 적절한 **relax** 편히 쉬다 **unless** ~하지 않는 한 **exactly** 정확히 **belong** 알맞은 위치에 있다 **state** 상태 **chaos** 혼돈 **rarely** 좀처럼 ~하지 않는 **second thought** 재고, 다시 생각함 **store** 두다, 보관하다; 가게 **straight away** 바로, 즉시 **disorder** 무질서 **equal** ~와 같다; ~에 필적하다 **disorganization** 무정돈 (↔ **organization** 정리 정돈; 조직 **cf. organize** 정리하다) **matter** 중요하다; 문제 **disaster** 재난 **area** 지역 **fairly** 꽤 **function** 기능하다

〈선택지 어휘〉

work 작용하다; 일하다

지문 Flow

[도입]
방과 일터를 청결하게 유지하는 사람들은 모든 것을 적절한 장소에 둠

⬇

[대조]
방과 책상을 어질러진 상태로 두는 사람들이 있는데, 그들도 필요한 물건을 바로 찾을 수 있음

⬇

[주장]
무질서가 무정돈과 동등한 것은 아님

⬇

[주제도출]
필요할 때 그 물건을 찾을 수 있고, 그것을 잘 보관할 수 있고, 그 공간에서 편안함을 느낀다면, 정리 정돈된 사람임

250 정답 ②

지문 All in One

별들은 주로 수소와 헬륨으로 이루어져 있다 / 가장 가벼운 두 가지 원소인 / 우주에서

[1] Stars consist mainly of hydrogen [and] helium, / the two lightest elements / in the universe.
S V =

하지만 / 지구는 대부분 더 무거운 원소로 이루어져 있다 / 산소, 규소, 알루미늄 같이

(A) [2] However, / Earth is made up mostly of heavier elements, / such as oxygen, silicon, [and]
S V

이 원소들이 어디에서 생겨났는지에 대한 대답은 / 다소 놀랍다

aluminum. [3] The answer to where these elements came from / is somewhat surprising.
S 간접의문문 V C

어휘확인

star 별 **consist of** ~으로 이루어져 있다 (= **be made up of**) **mainly** 주로 **hydrogen** 수소 **helium** 헬륨 **element** 원소; 요소 **universe** 우주 **mostly** 대부분 **oxygen** 산소 **silicon** 규소, 실리콘 **aluminum** 알루미늄 **come from** ~에서 생겨나다 **somewhat** 다소, 약간 **billion** 10억 **back then** 그 당시에 **alive** 살아 있는

이것들 모두는 별들에 의해 만들어졌다 수십 억 년 전에
4 All of them were made by the stars / billions of years ago.

그 당시에 별들이 살아 있었을 때 막대한 압력과 열이 가벼운 원소들을
(C) 5 Back then, / when the stars were alive, // enormous pressure and heat / fused their light
융합해서 만들어 냈다 더 무거운 원소들을 점점 더 많은 별들이 변해가면서
elements to produce / heavier elements. 6 As more and more of the stars were turned /
무거운 원소들로 별들은 서서히 에너지가 없어졌고 불안정해졌다 그때
into heavy elements, // the stars slowly ran out of energy / and became unstable. 7 Then,
별들이 폭발했다 그것들이 죽으면서
/ the stars exploded // as they died.
그러한 폭발은 무거운 원소들을 융합했다 훨씬 더 무거운 원소들로 그리고 그것들을 날려버렸다
(B) 8 Those explosions fused the heavy elements / into even heavier ones // and threw them /
광대한 거리들을 가로질러 그 원소들이 새로운 태양계들을 만들어 냈다 우리의 것을 포함하여
across vast distances. 9 Those elements created new solar systems, / including ours.

(부사적 용법(결과); ones = elements; ours = our solar system)

① (A) - (B) - (C) ② (A) - (C) - (B) ③ (B) - (A) - (C)
④ (B) - (C) - (A) ⑤ (C) - (B) - (A)

해석 한 눈에 보기 1 별들은 주로 우주에서 가장 가벼운 두 가지 원소인 수소와 헬륨으로 이루어져 있다. (A) 2 하지만 지구는 대부분 산소, 규소, 알루미늄 같이 더 무거운 원소로 이루어져 있다. 3 이 원소들이 어디에서 생겨났는지에 대한 대답은 다소 놀랍다. 4 이것들 모두는 수십 억 년 전에 별들에 의해 만들어졌다. (C) 5 별들이 살아 있던 그 당시에, 엄청난 압력과 열이 그것들의 가벼운 원소들을 융합하여 더 무거운 원소들을 만들어 냈다. 6 점점 더 많은 별이 무거운 원소들로 변해가면서, 별들은 서서히 에너지가 없어졌고 불안정해졌다. 7 그러다 별들이 죽으면서 폭발했다. (B) 8 그러한 폭발은 무거운 원소들을 융합하여 훨씬 더 무거운 원소들로 만들었고 광대한 거리를 가로질러 그것들을 날려버렸다. 9 그 원소들이 우리의 것을 포함하여 새로운 태양계들을 만들어 냈다.

정답단추 글의 흐름이나 순서를 알려주는 연결어, 대명사, 한정어 등의 쓰임을 주의 깊게 살펴보고 이를 근거로 글을 배열해보자. 우선 연결어 however로 시작하는 (A)를 보면 이와 반대로 지구는 더 무거운 원소들로 이루어졌다는 내용으로 주어진 문장과 자연스럽게 이어지고 있어. 그다음으로 (A)의 끝에 나오는 billions of years ago를 (C)의 Back then으로 받고 있어. 마지막으로 이 폭발로 생긴 더 무거운 원소들이 태양계를 만들었다는 내용의 (B)가 (C)에 이어서 오는 것이 적절해. 따라서 가장 알맞은 순서는 ②야.

enormous 막대한, 거대한 pressure 압력; 압박 fuse 융합시키다 run out of ~이 없어지다 unstable 불안정한 explode 폭발하다 cf. explosion 폭발 vast 광대한, 방대한 distance 거리 solar system 태양계 include 포함하다

지문 Flow

[도입]
별은 수소와 헬륨 등의 가벼운 원소로 이루어짐

[대조]
지구는 산소, 규소, 알루미늄 같은 무거운 원소로 이루어졌는데, 이것도 수십 억 년 전에 별에 의해 만들어짐

[보충설명]
별이 압력과 열로 가벼운 원소를 융합하여 더 무거운 원소를 만들어 냈고, 서서히 에너지가 없어져 결국 폭발함

[결과]
폭발로 인해 더 무거운 원소가 만들어졌고, 그 원소들이 새로운 태양계를 만들어 냄

251 정답 ④ 252 정답 ②

지문 All in One

알약 하나를 하루에 세 번 드세요 3일 동안 그러면 당신은 괜찮아지실 겁니다 라고 의사가 말했다
1 "Take one pill three times a day / for three days / and you'll be fine," // said the doctor.
환자는 했다 의사가 말한 것을 그리고 나아짐을 느끼기 시작했다 그러나 그 알약은
2 The patient did / what the doctor said, // and started to feel better. 3 However, / the pills
약 성분을 전혀 함유하지 않았다 그렇다면 환자는 왜 나아졌다고 느꼈을까 필시 그것은 '플라세보(위약)
contained no medicine. 4 Then, / why did the patient feel better? 5 Most likely, / it was due to
효과' 때문이었을 것이다 임상 실험에서 어떤 사람들에게는 위약이 주어진다 진짜 약 대신에
the "placebo effect." 6 In clinical tests, / some people are given placebos / instead of real
위약은 약인 것 같아 보인다 하지만 아니다 과학자들은 아주 잘 알고 있다
medicine. 7 A placebo appears to be medicine // but (it) is not. 8 Scientists know very well /
정신력에 달린 문제의 중요성을 약에 관한 한 수천 개의 실험과
the importance of mind over matter // when it comes to medicine. 9 Thousands of trials and
연구가 보여줘 왔다 환자의 50%에서 75% 사이가 좋아진다는 것을 위약으로 치료
studies have shown // that between 50 and 75 percent of patients improve / when (they are)
받을 때 이것은 모든 문제에 적용된다 사소한 알레르기와 화상에서부터
treated with placebos. 10 This is true for all problems, / from minor allergies and burns /
우울증과 암까지 한 가지 질문 어떤 종류의 위약이 가장 효과가 있을까? 알약의
to depression and cancer. 11 One question: // what type of placebo works best? 12 The size
크기와 색깔은 중요한 것 같지 않다 하지만 치료법의 종류는 그렇다 주사는
and color of a pill / does not seem to matter, // but the type of treatment does. 13 Injections,
예를 들어 더 커다란 플라세보 효과를 만든다 알약이 그러는 것보다 그러나 가장 큰 영향은 오는 것
/ for example, / produce greater placebo effects // than pills do. 14 But the biggest impact

(관계대명사; 접속사)

어휘확인

take (약을) 먹다; 가지고 가다 patient 환자 contain ~이 함유되어 있다 most likely 필시 due to ~ 때문에 placebo effect 플라세보 효과(위약 투여에 의한 심리 효과로 실제로 병이 호전되는 일) cf. placebo 플라세보, 위약(환자에게 심리적 효과를 얻도록 하려고 주는 가짜 약) clinical 임상의 appear ~인 것 같다 importance 중요성 mind over matter 정신력에 달린 문제 cf. matter 문제; 중요하다 when it comes to ~에 관한 한 trial 실험; 재판 treat 치료하다; 다루다 cf. treatment 치료(법) true 적용되는; 사실인 minor 사소한, 작은 allergy 알레르기 burn 화상; 불에 타다 depression 우울증 cancer 암 work 효과가 있다; 일하다 injection 주사 impact 영향 behavior 행동 display 보이다; 전시하다 confidence 자신감 be responsible for ~의 원인이다; ~에 책임이 있다

〈선택지 어휘〉
drug 약 harmless 해가 없는 alternative 대안 unscientific 비과학적인 myth 통념; 신화 take control of ~을 지배하다 physical 신체의 appearance 외모 background 환경, 배경 university 대학 education 교육

같다 / 의사의 행동으로부터 / 더 많은 관심을 보여주는 의사들이 / 그들의

appears to come / from **the doctor's behavior.** 15 *Doctors* [who show greater interest / in their

V / 관계대명사 V'1 / S

환자에게 / 그리고 더 많은 자신감을 보이는 / 그들의 일에 / 더 많고 더 강한 플라세보 효과의 원인이다

patients, / and display greater confidence / in their work,] / are responsible for more and stronger placebo effects.

V'2 / V / C

251 ① Good Doctors Are Better Than Good Drugs
좋은 의사는 좋은 약보다 더 낫다
② Placebos: A Harmless Alternative to Traditional Medicine
위약: 전통 의학의 해롭지 않은 대안
③ The Placebo Effect: An Unscientific Myth
플라세보 효과: 비과학적인 통념
④ Placebos: What They Are and When They Work Best
위약: 무엇이며 언제 효과가 가장 좋은가
⑤ Mind Over Matter: Take Control of Your Health
정신력으로 당신의 건강을 지배하라

252 ① the patient's age 환자의 나이 ② the doctor's behavior 의사의 행동 ③ physical appearance 신체적 외모
④ family background 가정 환경 ⑤ university education 대학 교육

지문 Flow

[도입]
아무 성분이 없는 약을 복용한 환자는 나아짐을 느낌 → 플라세보(위약) 효과

⬇

[보충설명]
모든 질병을 망라하고 위약 처방을 받은 환자들의 50—75%가 치료에 효과가 있었음

⬇

[추가]
가장 효과가 좋은 위약은 알약의 크기와 색깔보다 치료법(주사)과 의사의 행동에서 영향을 받음

⬇

[보충설명]
환자에게 더 관심을 보이고, 자신의 일에 더 많은 자신감을 보이는 의사들이 플라세보 효과에 가장 큰 영향을 줌

해석 한 눈에 보기 1 "한 알씩, 하루에 세 번, 3일 동안 드세요. 그러면 괜찮아지실 겁니다."라고 의사가 말했다. 2 환자는 의사가 말한 것을 했고 나아짐을 느끼기 시작했다. 3 그러나 그 알약은 약 성분을 전혀 함유하지 않았다. 4 그렇다면 환자는 왜 나아졌다고 느꼈을까? 5 필시 그것은 '플라세보(위약) 효과' 때문이었을 것이다. 6 임상 실험에서, 어떤 사람들은 진짜 약 대신에 위약을 받는다. 7 위약은 약인 것 같아 보이지만 아니다. 8 과학자들은 약에 관한 한 정신력의 중요성을 아주 잘 알고 있다. 9 수천 개의 실험과 연구가 위약으로 치료받을 때 환자의 50—75% 사이가 좋아진다는 것을 보여줘 왔다. 10 이것은 사소한 알레르기와 화상에서부터 우울증과 암까지 모든 문제에 적용된다. 11 한 가지 질문을 해 보자. 어떤 종류의 위약이 가장 효과가 좋을까? 12 알약의 크기와 색깔은 중요한 것 같지 않지만, 치료법의 종류는 그래 보인다. 13 예를 들어, 주사는 알약이 그러는 것보다 더 커다란 플라세보 효과를 낸다. 14 그러나 가장 큰 영향은 의사의 행동에서 나오는 것 같다. 15 환자에게 더 많은 관심을 보이고 자신의 일에 더 많은 자신감을 보이는 의사들이 더 많고 더 강한 플라세보 효과의 주된 원인이다.

정답단추

251 글의 핵심 내용을 가장 잘 압축한 제목을 찾으면 돼. 이 글은 약처럼 보이지만 약 성분이 없는 위약과 이에 대한 실험 그리고 위약의 효과가 가장 좋을 때를 설명하고 있어. 따라서 이 글의 제목으로 적절한 것은 ④야.

252 빈칸을 포함한 문장을 먼저 읽고 앞뒤 문맥을 살펴보면 알약보다는 주사가 더 큰 플라세보를 효과를 내지만 가장 큰 효과를 내는 것이 '무엇'이라고 설명하고 있어. 그리고 바로 다음 문장에서 플라세보 효과에 가장 크게 영향을 주는 요인으로 의사가 환자에게 관심을 더 가지고 자기 일에 자신감을 더 보이는 것이라고 설명하고 있지. 즉, 의사의 행동이 플라세보 효과에 가장 큰 영향을 준다는 것이므로 빈칸에 들어갈 말은 ②야.

오답단서

251 ①은 글에서 언급된 의사와 약을 사용한 제목이긴 하지만 글의 내용과는 거리가 멀어. ②도 이 글의 소재인 위약을 포함하지만 전통 의학에 관한 내용은 글에 나오지 않았어. 그리고 이 글이 플라세보 효과에 관해 설명하고 있지만, 이것을 비과학적인 통념이라고 하지는 않아서 ③도 오답이지. 마지막으로 ⑤는 Scientists know ~ to medicine.의 내용과 이어지지만, 글 전체 내용을 포함하는 제목이 아니라서 답이 될 수 없어.

실전편

독해 모의고사 3회

253 ④ 254 ⑤ 255 ② 256 ③ 257 ② 258 ⑤ 259 ④ 260 ③ 261 ②
262 ③ 263 ④ 264 ④ 265 ③ 266 ④ 267 ③ 268 ④ 269 ⑤ 270 ②

253 정답 ④

지문 All in One

배우는 가장 귀중한 교훈 중 하나는 / 사업에서 / '평생 가치'의 개념이다
1 One of *the most valuable lessons* [to learn / in business] / is the concept of "lifetime value."
S V C

이것은 ~이다 / 고객이 당신에게 가치 있는 것 / 평균 기간 동안 / 그 혹은 그녀가 충실한 상태로
2 This is // what a customer is worth to you / over the average period / of *time* [that he or she
S V 관계대명사 관계부사

있는 시간의 / 당신에게 / 그것은 엄청나게 도움이 되는 개념이다 / 분명히 / 다른 고객들은 다른 가치를
stays loyal / to you]. 3 It is a tremendously helpful concept. 4 Obviously, / different customers
S V C S_1

가지고 있다 / 하지만 당신은 여전히 타당한 추측을 할 수 있다 / 가정해보자
have different values, // but you can still make a reasonable guess. 5 Let's assume // (that)
V_1 S_2 V_2 V O C 접속사

당신이 점심을 사먹는 고객을 가지고 있다고 / 당신에게서 / 한 주에 3일을 / 평균적으로 그는 하루
you have *a customer* [who buys his lunch / from you / three days a week]. 6 On average he
S' V' 관계대명사 S

에 8파운드를 쓴다 / 이것은 일주일에 24파운드이다 / 우리는 그에게 휴가 6주를 허용할 것이다 / 그래서 그것은
spends *£8 a day*, / [which is £24 a week]. 7 We'll allow him six weeks of vacation, // so that's
V 관계대명사(계속적 용법) S_1 V_1 접속사 S_2 V_2

1년에 1,104파운드이다 / 우리가 가정한다면 / 그가 당신과 머무른다고 / 4년 동안 / 그러면 이것은 동일하다
£1,104 a year. 8 If we assume / that he stays with you / for four years, // then this equates / to
C 접속사 S' V' 접속사 S" V" S V

총 4,416파운드의 가치와 / 이것은 당신에게 매우 다른 견해를 준다 / 당신이 그를 어떻게 대해야 하는지에 대해
a total value of £4,416. 9 This gives you a very different view / on how you should treat him /
S V IO DO 간접의문문

매일
on a daily basis.

① 고객에 따른 맞춤 서비스를 개발해야 한다.
② 고객의 다양한 요구를 수용하는 것은 어렵다.
③ 단골 고객을 대상으로 한 할인 정책은 효과가 좋다.
④ 고객과의 관계를 장기적으로 유지하는 것이 중요하다.
⑤ 질 높은 서비스는 단골 고객을 만드는 지름길이다.

해석 한 눈에 보기 주제문 **1** 사업에서 배우는 가장 귀중한 교훈 중 하나는 '평생 가치'의 개념이다. **2** 이것은 고객이 당신에게 충실한 상태로 있는 평균 기간 동안 당신에게 가치 있는 정도이다. **3** 그것은 엄청나게 도움이 되는 개념이다. **4** 분명히 서로 다른 고객은 서로 다른 가치를 가지고 있지만, 당신은 여전히 타당한 추측을 할 수 있다. **5** 당신이 한 주에 3일을 당신에게서 점심을 사 먹는 고객을 갖고 있다고 가정해 보자. **6** 평균적으로 그는 하루에 8파운드를 쓰는데, 이것은 일주일에 24파운드이다. **7** 우리는 그에게 6주의 휴가를 허용할 것이라, 그것은 1년에 1,104파운드이다. **8** 만약 그가 당신과 4년간 머무른다고 가정하면, 이것은 총 4,416파운드의 가치와 같다. **9** 이것은 당신에게 당신이 그를 매일 어떻게 대해야 하는지에 대한 아주 다른 견해를 제공한다.

정답단추 글의 시사점을 알기 위해서는 글 전체 내용 파악이 선행되어야 해. 이 글은 앞의 두 문장에서 고객이 충실한 기간에 생기는 가치인 '평생 가치'가 사업에 중요하다고 설명하고 있어. 이것을 하루에 8파운드의 점심을 사 먹는 고객의 예시를 들어 설명하고 있어. 더 나아가 이 고객이 6주의 휴가 기간에 가게에 오지 않더라도 1년이면 1,104파운드이고 4년이 되면 4,416파운드의 가치가 있음을 구체적으로 보여주고 있어. 이를 종합하면 장기 고객은 사업에 엄청난 이윤을 가져다주므로 고객과의 관계를 장기적으로 유지하는 것이 중요하다는 점을 시사하고 있음을 알 수 있어. 따라서 정답은 ④야.

오답단서 ①, ②는 이 글에서 자주 언급된 '고객'을 포함한 선택지이지만, 글에서 언급되지 않은 내용을 담고 있어. 그리고 이 글이 '단골손님'에 관한 내용이긴 하지만, 이를 대상으로 한 할인 정책이나 질 높은 서비스에 대해서는 다루고 있지 않아서 ③, ⑤도 답이 될 수 없어.

어휘확인

valuable 귀중한 **cf. value** 가치 **lesson** 교훈; 수업 **business** 사업 **concept** 개념 **lifetime** 평생 **customer** 고객 **worth** ~의 가치가 있는 **average** 평균의 **period** 기간 **loyal** 충실한 **tremendously** 엄청나게 **obviously** 분명히 **reasonable** 타당한 **guess** 추측 **assume** 가정하다; 추정하다 **on average** 평균적으로 **allow** 허용하다 **equate** 동일시하다 **total** 총, 전체의 **on a daily basis** 매일

지문 Flow

[주제문]
사업에서 중요한 '평생 가치'의 개념

[보충설명]
고객이 당신에게 충실한 상태로 있는 기간 동안 당신에게 생기는 가치

[예시]
일주일에 3일, 하루에 8파운드의 점심을 사먹는 고객은 1년에 1,104파운드의 가치가 있고, 해가 갈수록 가치가 늘어남

[결론]
장기 고객은 사업에 큰 이윤을 가져오므로, 관계를 장기적으로 유지해야 함

254 정답 ⑤

지문 All in One

[1] Are you swimming / against the tide? [2] Do you feel *the need* [to escape from rules and tradition], / [to live life / according to your own ideas and desires]? [3] No problem! [4] We provide / you with *everything* [(that) you need] / to design your environment / in line with your own personal style. [5] Live life / to your own design! [6] There is no limit to *your freedom* [to determine your individual wall design]. [7] Whether you choose a pattern of shapes for the wallpaper / in your child's room / or decorate a modern kitchen / with romantic flowery wallpaper — // anything goes! [8] Remember: / exceptional wallpaper does not necessarily mean / great expense; / reasonably priced wall coverings can be used / to create a unique and attractive wall. [9] And for those with deeper pockets, / our hand-made Luxury Wallpapers / with beautiful bead detail / will fit the bill.

① 좋은 가족 휴양지를 소개하려고
② 디자인 프로그램을 안내하려고
③ 저렴한 인테리어 방법을 알려주려고
④ 벽지 고르는 방법을 설명하려고
⑤ 다양한 벽지를 갖춘 상점을 광고하려고

해석 한 눈에 보기 **1** 당신은 유행에 거스르고 있습니까? **2** 당신은 규칙과 전통에서 벗어나 당신 자신의 생각과 욕구에 따라 삶을 살아야 할 필요를 느끼십니까? **3** 문제 없습니다! **4** 저희는 당신 자신의 개인 스타일에 따라 당신의 환경을 설계하도록 당신이 필요한 모든 것을 제공합니다. **5** 당신 자신만의 디자인으로 삶을 살아보세요! **6** 개별 벽 디자인을 결정할 자유에는 제한이 없습니다. **7** 자녀 방에 있는 벽지에 들어갈 모양의 무늬를 고르시든지 낭만적인 꽃무늬 벽지로 현대적인 부엌을 꾸미시든지, 어떤 것이든 하세요! **8** 기억하세요. 탁월한 벽지가 반드시 큰 비용을 의미하지는 않습니다. 합리적으로 값이 매겨진 벽지가 독특하고 매력적인 벽을 만드는 데 사용될 수 있습니다. **9** 그리고 주머니 사정이 좋은 분들에게는 아름다운 구슬 세부 장식이 달린 저희 수제 '고급 벽지'가 만족시킬 것입니다.

정답단추 글의 목적을 파악하기 위해서는 글을 쓴 의도가 가장 잘 드러나는 문장을 찾아야 해. 글의 앞부분에서 이미 자신만의 디자인으로 주변을 설계할 수 있도록 모든 것을 제공한다는 내용이 나와. 즉, 디자인과 관련된 물건을 파는 곳의 광고임을 짐작할 수 있어. 이어서 벽지를 자유롭게 고를 수 있다는 내용이 나오고, 비싼 벽지가 꼭 좋은 건 아니라는 내용도 나와. 마지막 부분에 결정적으로 돈이 많으면 수제 '고급 벽지'를 살 수 있다는 내용으로 마무리되고 있지. 따라서 글의 목적으로 가장 적절한 것은 ⑤야.

오답단서 ①은 본문과 전혀 상관없는 내용이니 답은 당연히 아니야. ②와 ③은 디자인과 인테리어라는 단어로 혼동을 주기 위한 선택지일 뿐 글의 내용과는 상관없는 선택지야. ④는 오답으로 고를 가능성이 가장 큰데, 벽지에 대한 내용이 많이 나오긴 해도 벽지를 고르는 방법은 나와 있지 않으니까 오답이야.

어휘확인

swim against the tide 유행에 거스르다, 시류에 역행하다 **escape from** ~에서 달아나다 **tradition** 전통 **according to** ~에 따라서 **desire** 욕구 **provide A with B** A에게 B를 제공하다 **environment** 환경 **in line with** ~에 따라, ~와 함께 **personal** 개인의 **limit** 제한; 한계 **freedom** 자유 **determine** 결정하다 **individual** 개개의 **wallpaper** 벽지 **decorate** 꾸미다 **romantic** 낭만적인 **flowery** 꽃무늬의 **exceptional** 탁월한, 특출난 **necessarily** 반드시 **expense** 비용 **reasonably** 합리적으로 **priced** 정가가 붙은 **unique** 독특한 **attractive** 매력적인 **deep pocket** 부, 재력 **luxury** 고급의 **bead** 구슬 **detail** 세부 장식 **fit the bill** 만족시키다, 꼭 알맞다

지문 Flow

[목적]
자신만의 스타일로 자신의 환경을 설계하도록 필요한 모든 것을 제공하는 상점을 광고함

⬇

[세부사항1]
개별 벽 디자인 결정에 제한이 없음

&

[세부사항2]
비싸지 않은 좋은 벽지로 독특하고 매력적인 벽을 만들 수 있음

⬇

[추가]
돈이 많은 사람들을 위한 수제 벽지도 구비하고 있음

255 정답 ②

지문 All in One

[1] A long time ago, / Johann encountered his friend Hans in the forest / and said, "Hans, I got *that horse* [(which[that]) I wanted] at a good price. I'm really lucky." [2] In a second, however, / Johann realized (that) he had made a big mistake; // he shouldn't have talked / about his good luck out loud. [3] Johann immediately ran to the nearest tree / and started knocking on it. [4] He believed // that the gods lived in trees, / and if they heard about any human happiness,

어휘확인

encounter 만나다 **in a second** 곧, 금세 **out loud** 소리 내어 **knock on** ~을 치다[때리다] **drive away** ~을 떠나게 만들다 **suffer** ~을 겪다; 고통받다 **reversal** 뒤바뀜, 전환 **literally** 말[문자] 그대로 **knock on wood** 행운을 빌다 **phrase** 문구, 어구 **fulfill** 이행하다
〈선택지 어휘〉
inner 내면의

그들이 문제를 일으킬 것이라고 (믿었다) / they would cause problems. [5] Johann은 Johann, [(사람들의) 말을 듣는 숲에서 자신이 한 일을 인식한 aware of what he had done in the listening forest], 나무를 쳤다 knocked on the wood / 신을 몰아내기 위해 to drive the gods away / 행운이 뒤바뀌는 일을 겪지 않기를 희망하면서 in the hope that his good fortune would suffer no reversal. [6] 더 이상 관습이 아니었을 때조차도 Even when it was no longer a custom / 말 그대로 '나무를 치는' 것이 to literally "knock on wood," // 이 문구는 오늘날까지 남아있었고 the phrase has remained to this day / 똑같은 목적을 이행한다 to fulfill the same purpose.

(S'₂ they, V'₂ would cause, S Johann, 관계대명사 what, V knocked, 부사적 용법(목적) to drive, the hope = that절, S' his good fortune, V' would suffer, 가주어 it, V was, C a custom, 진주어 to literally "knock on wood," 부사적 용법(결과) to fulfill)

① helping friends in danger
위험에 처한 친구들을 돕는 것

② keeping good luck as it is
현 상황의 행운을 유지하는 것

③ remembering your mistake
당신의 실수를 기억하는 것

④ believing trees to be their god
나무를 그들의 신이라고 믿는 것

⑤ understanding your inner voice
당신 내면의 목소리를 이해하는 것

해석 한 눈에 보기 1 오래전에 Johann은 숲에서 친구 Hans를 만나서 "Hans, 난 내가 원했던 그 말을 좋은 가격에 구입했어. 나는 정말로 운이 좋아."라고 말했다. 2 하지만, 곧 Johann은 자신이 큰 실수를 저질렀다는 것을 깨달았다. 그는 자신의 행운에 대해서 소리 내어 말하지 않았어야 했다. 3 Johann은 즉시 가장 가까이에 있는 나무로 뛰어가서 나무를 두드리기 시작했다. 4 그는 신들이 나무에 살고 있으며, 만약 신들이 인간의 행복에 대해 들었다면, 그들이 문제를 일으킬 것이라고 믿었다. 5 (사람들의) 말을 듣는 숲에서 자신이 한 일을 인식한 Johann은 자신의 행운이 뒤바뀌는 일을 겪지 않기를 희망하면서 신을 몰아내기 위해 나무를 쳤다. 주제문 6 말 그대로 '나무를 치는' 것이 더 이상 관습이 아니었을 때조차도 이 문구는 남아서 오늘날까지 똑같은 목적을 이행한다.

정답단추 영어 표현 knock on wood(행운을 빌어)의 유래를 설명하는 글이야. 숲에서 행운을 말하면 나무에 살고 있는 신이 듣고 문제를 일으킬 것이라고 믿었던 Johann은 행운이 뒤바뀌지 않기를 희망하여 신을 몰아내기 위해 나무를 쳤다고 했어. 밑줄 포함 문장은 '똑같은 목적'을 이행하기 위해 '나무를 친다'는 문구가 남았다는 의미이므로, 밑줄 친 어구가 의미하는 정답은 ②야.

오답단서 위험에 처한 친구를 돕는 것과 관련된 내용은 없으므로 ①은 정답이 될 수 없어. ③은 주인공 Johann이 실수했다는 내용과 관련하여, ④는 '신들이 나무에 살고 있다'라는 내용과 관련해서 만든 오답이야.

지문 Flow

[발단]
Johann이 친구 Hans를 만나 자신의 행운에 대해서 말함

[전개]
Johann은 신들이 인간의 행복에 대해 듣는다면 그들이 문제를 일으킬 것이라고 믿어, 실수를 저지른 것을 깨달음

[절정]
자신의 행운이 뒤바뀌는 일을 겪지 않기를 희망하면서 신을 몰아내기 위해 나무를 침

[결말(주제문)]
knock on wood(나무를 치다)라는 문구는 오늘날까지 남아서 사용됨

256 정답 ③

지문 All in One

[1] 아주 맥 빠지는 일이다 It's very frustrating / 물건을 잃어버리거나 잘못 두는 것 to lose or (to) misplace things / 혹은 늦게 오는 사람을 기다리는 것은 or (A) to wait for *someone* [who is late]. [2] 또한 나쁘다 It's also bad // 당신이 목표를 달성하지 못할 때 when you fail to achieve a goal / 계획 부족으로 through *lack* [of planning]. [3] 이와 같은 때에는 At times like these, / 느껴질 수 있다 it can feel // 당신의 삶이 자신의 통제 하에 있지 않은 것처럼 like your life is not under your control. [4] 그러나 But / 더 나쁜 것은 ~이다 what's worse is // 이런 모든 일들이 대개 유발된다는 것 that all these things are usually (B) caused / 엉망과 무질서에 의해 by mess and disorder. [5] 우울증, 불안, 분노, 낮은 자존감 그리고 황폐해진 인간관계 Depression, anxiety, anger, low self-esteem, and ruined relationships / 또한 생겨날 수 있다 can also result. [6] 엉망과 무질서는 ~이다 Mess and disorder are / 눈에 띄지 않고 자라는 두 가지 형태의 암이다 *two forms of cancer* [that grow unnoticed / 그것들이 다루기 힘들어질 때까지 until they become unmanageable]. [7] 그러니 정리를 잘해라 So get organized! [8] 그것은 만든다 It makes / 당신이 자신을 통제하도록 you (C) control yourself // 그리고 자유롭게 해준다 and frees / 당신이 정말로 즐기는 일을 하도록 you to do *the things* [you really enjoy].

(가주어 It, V 's, C frustrating, 진주어 to lose ~ late; 가주어 It, V 's, 접속사 when, S' you, V' fail, 진주어 through lack of planning; S it, V can feel, 접속사 like, S' your life, V' is; S what's worse, V is, 접속사 that, S' all these things, V' are caused; S Depression ~ relationships, V can result; S Mess and disorder, V are; 관계대명사 that, 접속사 until, S' they, V' become, C' unmanageable; V get, C organized; S It, V₁ makes, O₁ you, C₁ control yourself, V₂ frees, O₂ you, C₂ to do the things)

	(A)		(B)		(C)
①	waiting	……	caused	……	control
②	waiting	……	causing	……	to control
③	to wait	……	caused	……	control
④	to wait	……	caused	……	to control
⑤	to wait	……	causing	……	control

해석 한 눈에 보기 1 물건을 잃어버리거나 잘못 두는 것 혹은 늦게 오는 사람을 기다리는 것은 아주 맥 빠지는 일이다. 2 계획 부족으로 인해 목표를 달성하지 못하는 것 또한 나쁘다. 3 이와 같을 때에는, 당신의 삶이 자신의 통제 하에 있지 않은 것처럼 느껴질 수 있다. 4 그러나 더 나쁜 것은 이 모든 일이 대체로 엉망과 무질서에 의해 유발된다는 것이다. 5 우울증, 불안, 분노, 낮은 자존감, 황폐해진 인간관계도 생겨날 수 있다. 6 엉망과 무질서는 그것들이 다루기 힘들

어휘확인

frustrating 맥 빠지게 하는; 불만스러운 **misplace** 잘못 두다; 제자리에 두지 않다 **achieve** 달성하다 **goal** 목표; 득점 **lack** 부족; ~이 없다 **planning** 계획 **under one's control** ~의 통제 하에 있는 **worse** 더 나쁜 **mess** 엉망 **disorder** 무질서; 엉망 **depression** 우울증 **anxiety** 불안 **anger** 분노 **self-esteem** 자존감; 자부심 **ruined** 황폐해진, 폐허가 된 **relationship** 관계 **form** 형태; 종류 **cancer** 암 **unnoticed** 눈에 띄지 않는 **unmanageable** 다루기 힘든 **get organized** 정리하다

지문 Flow

[도입]
물건 분실, 늦게 오는 사람 기다리기, 계획 부족으로 목표 달성에 실패하는 것은 좋지 않음

[보충설명]
스스로 삶을 통제하지 못하는 것 같음

[원인]
모든 것은 엉망과 무질서에 의해 생겨남

어질 때까지 눈에 띄지 않고 자라는 두 가지 형태의 암이다. 주제문 7 그러니 정리를 잘하라! 8 그것은 당신이 자신을 통제하게 해주고 당신이 정말로 즐기는 일을 하도록 당신을 자유롭게 해준다.

정답단추 (A)를 포함한 문장에서 진주어 자리에 등위접속사 or가 위치해서 to부정사구를 병렬로 연결해주고 있어. 따라서 (A)에는 to wait가 적절해. (B)는 능동·수동을 구분하는 문제로 문맥상 이 모든 일이 엉망과 무질서 때문에 '유발된다'라는 의미가 되어야 하니까 수동인 caused가 와야 해. (C)가 있는 문장은 SVOC 구문으로 동사 makes는 사역동사로 〈make+O+C(동사원형, 분사)〉 형태로 쓰여. 따라서 목적격 보어 자리에는 to부정사가 아닌 동사원형인 control이 와야 해.

[보충설명]
엉망과 무질서는 우울증, 불안 등 여러 가지 좋지 않은 결과를 낳는 암과 같은 존재임

⬇

[주제]
정리 잘하기

257 정답 ②

지문 All in One

1 Language can strengthen social relationships / as well as convey facts. 2 Conversations between parents and children, / or "small talk" between acquaintances, / may not provide a lot of new information // but are ① vital for forming bonds / between individuals. 3 Familiar legends and stories / ② weaken(→ strengthen) a community's sense of history and values.

(언어는 사회적 관계를 강화할 수 있다 / 사실을 전달할 뿐만 아니라 / 부모와 자녀 간의 대화나 / 지인들 간의 '잡담'은 / 많은 새로운 정보를 제공하지 않을지도 모른다 / 그러나 유대감이 형성되는 데 필수적이다 / 개인들 간의 / 익숙한 전설과 이야기는 / 공동체의 역사의식과 가치들을 약화시킨다(→ 강화시킨다))

(S: Language, V₁: can strengthen, V₂: convey, S: Conversations, V₁: may not provide, V₂: are, C: vital for forming bonds, S: Familiar legends and stories, V: weaken)

4 Language can also highlight social distinctions. 5 People speak ③ differently / to friends, / to *those* [(who are) younger or older than themselves], / and to employers. 6 In some societies, / rulers and elders are addressed / with *special titles* [that show ④ respect]. 7 People may also use / *words or dialects* [that are considered "prestigious"] / to make themselves appear ⑤ more cultured or important.

(언어는 또한 사회적 차이를 강조할 수 있다 / 사람들은 다르게 얘기한다 / 친구들에게 / 그들보다 어리거나 나이가 많은 사람들에게 / 그리고 고용주에게 / 몇몇 사회에서는 / 통치자와 연장자가 칭해진다 / 존경을 드러내는 특별한 칭호로 / 사람들은 또한 사용할지도 모른다 / '일류'라고 여겨지는 말이나 통용어를 / 자신을 더 교양 있고 중요하게 보이게 하려고)

(S: Language, V: can also highlight, S: People, V: speak, who: 관계대명사, S: rulers and elders, V: are addressed, that: 관계대명사, S: People, V: may also use, that: 관계대명사, to make: 부사적 용법(목적))

해석 한 눈에 보기 1 언어는 사실을 전달할 뿐만 아니라 사회적 관계를 강화할 수 있다. 2 부모와 자녀 간의 대화나 지인들 간의 '잡담'은 많은 새로운 정보를 제공하지 않을지는 몰라도 개인들 간의 유대감을 형성하는 데 ① 필수적이다. 3 익숙한 전설과 이야기는 공동체의 역사의식과 가치관을 ② 약화시킨다(→ 강화시킨다). 4 언어는 또한 사회적 차이를 강조할 수 있다. 5 사람들은 친구들에게, 자기보다 어리거나 나이가 많은 사람들에게, 고용주에게 ③ 다르게 얘기한다. 6 몇몇 사회에서는, 통치자와 연장자가 ④ 존경을 드러내는 특별한 칭호로 칭해진다. 7 사람들은 또한 자신을 ⑤ 더 교양 있고 중요하게 보이게 하려고 '일류'라고 여겨지는 말이나 통용어를 사용할지도 모른다.

정답단추 글의 전체 내용을 파악해야만 밑줄 친 어휘의 쓰임이 적절한지 판단할 수 있어. 이 글의 내용을 보면 언어의 여러 기능을 설명하고 있지? 그러므로 언어가 단순 사실 전달뿐 아니라 유대감 형성, 공동체 의식 강화, 사회적 차이 강조 등의 기능을 한다고 해야 글이 일관적으로 흘러가게 돼. 즉, 공동체 의식을 약화시킨다는 부분의 weaken을 반의어 strengthen으로 바꿔야 해. 따라서 낱말의 쓰임이 적절하지 않은 것은 ②야.

오답단서 ①의 앞 문장에서 언어는 사회적 관계를 강화할 수 있다고 하고 있어. 그러므로 잡담은 개인들 간의 유대감을 형성하는 데 '필수적(vital)'이라는 내용이 와야 해. 또한, ③은 사람들은 친구들에게, 자기보다 어리거나 나이가 많은 사람들에게, 고용주에게 '다르게(differently)' 얘기한다고 해야 자연스러워. ④에서는 특별한 칭호로 칭해지는 대상이 통치자와 연장자이므로 '존경(respect)'을 드러낸다는 내용이 적절해. 마지막으로 ⑤의 일류라고 여겨지는 말이나 통용어를 사용하는 이유가 자신을 '더(more)' 교양 있고 중요한 사람으로 보이기 위함이라는 내용이 이어져야 자연스러우므로 어휘의 쓰임이 적절해.

어휘확인

strengthen 강화하다 **relationship** 관계 **as well as** ~뿐만 아니라 **convey** 전달하다 **conversation** 대화; 회화 **small talk** 잡담, 수다 **acquaintance** 지인, 아는 사람 **provide** 제공하다 **vital** 필수적인 **form** 형성되다 **bond** 유대 **individual** 개인 **familiar** 익숙한, 친숙한 **legend** 전설 **weaken** 약화시키다(↔ **strengthen** 강화시키다) **community** 공동체, 사회 **sense** 의식; 감각 **value** 가치 **highlight** 강조하다 **distinction** 차이[대조] **employer** 고용주 **ruler** 통치자, 지배자 **elder** 연장자 **address** 호칭을 쓰다; 주소 **respect** 존경 **dialect** (어떤 사회·계급·직업의) 통용어, 은어; 방언 **consider** (~을 …로) 여기다[생각하다] **prestigious** 일류의 **appear** ~처럼 보이다, ~인 것 같다 **cultured** 교양 있는

지문 Flow

[도입]
언어는 사실을 전달하고 사회적 관계를 강화시킴

⬇

[보충설명]
• 대화나 '잡담'은 개인 간의 유대감을 형성함
• 전설과 이야기는 공동체 역사의식과 가치관 강화

⬇

[추가진술]
언어는 사회적 차이도 강조함

⬇

[보충설명]
• 사람에 따라 다르게 말함
• 통치자나 연장자에게 특별한 칭호를 사용함
• '일류'라고 여겨지는 말이나 통용어 사용함

258 정답 ⑤

지문 All in One

1 **Welcome!** (환영합니다)

2 The Pasadena Flea Market features / fascinating antiques and collectibles, thousands of tools,

(패서디나 벼룩시장은 특징으로 합니다 / 매력적인 골동품들과 수집품들, 수천 개의 도구들, — S: The Pasadena Flea Market, V: features)

어휘확인

flea market 벼룩시장 **feature** 특징으로 삼다 **fascinating** 매력적인 **antique** 골동품 **collectibles** 수집품 **tool** 도구 **location** 위치 **parking lot** 주차장 **campus** 캠퍼스,

의류, 장난감들 그리고 훨씬 더 많은 것들을
clothes, toys, and much more.
비교급 강조

위치
³ **Location**

주차장 / 캠퍼스의 동쪽 면을 따라 있는 / 그리고 위치한 우리의 새로운 부지에 있는 캠퍼스의 서쪽 면의 / 힐 거리와 델 마 거리 모퉁이에

⁴ *The parking lots* / [along the east side of campus / and in *our new lot* [located / on the west side of campus / at the corner of Hill and Del Mar]]
전치사구 / 전치사구

개장 시간과 입장
⁵ **Show Time & Admission**

시장은 전통적으로 열립니다 / 그 달의 첫 번째 일요일에 / 오전 8시부터 오후 3시까지 / 그리고 입장료는 무료입니다

⁶ The market is traditionally held / on the first Sunday of the month / from 8:00 a.m. ~ 3:00 p.m., // and admission is FREE.
(S_1, V_1, S_2, V_2, C)

예비 판매인들을 위한 공지
⁷ **Note for Would-be Vendors**

시장의 인기 때문에 / 모든 판매 장소가 다 찼습니다 / 그리고 우리는 대기자 명단을 유지합니다

⁸ Due to the Market's popularity, / all vending spaces are full // and we maintain a waiting list.
(S_1, V_1, C, S_2, V_2)

대기자 명단이 현재 열려 있습니다 / 주목해 주시기 바랍니다 / 일단 대기자 명단에 오르면 / 여러 해가 될 수 있다는 것을 / 공간이 이용할 수 있게 되기 전에

⁹ The waiting list is currently open. ¹⁰ Please note // that once (you are) on the waiting list, / it can be several years / before a space becomes available.
(S, V, C, V, 접속사 접속사, S″, V″, 비인칭주어, V′, C′, 접속사, S‴, V‴, C‴)

주차 요금
¹¹ **Parking Fee**

대학 정책의 변경 때문에 / 벼룩시장의 주차는 / 더 이상 무료가 아닙니다 / 주차는 / 현재 2달러입니다 / 하루에

¹² Due to changes in campus policies, / parking at the Flea Market / is no longer free. ¹³ Parking is now $2.00 / for the day.
(S, V, C, S, V, C)

① 의류와 장난감은 판매되지 않는다.
② 시장은 대학 캠퍼스 운동장에서 열린다.
③ 시장은 매주 일요일마다 열린다.
④ 한 달 정도 대기하면 시장에서 물건을 팔 수 있다.
⑤ 주차장은 유료 이용으로 전환되었다.

해석 한 눈에 보기 ¹ **환영합니다!** ² 패서디나 벼룩시장은 매력적인 골동품과 수집품, 수천 개의 도구, 의류, 장난감 이외에 훨씬 더 많은 것을 특징으로 합니다. ³ **위치** ⁴ 캠퍼스의 동쪽 면을 따라 있는 주차장과 캠퍼스 서쪽 면의 힐 거리와 델 마 거리 모퉁이에 있는 우리의 새로운 부지에 있는 주차장 ⁵ **개장 시간과 입장** ⁶ 시장은 전통적으로 매월 첫 번째 일요일 오전 8시부터 오후 3시까지 열리며 입장료는 무료입니다. ⁷ **예비 판매인들을 위한 공지** ⁸ 시장의 인기로 인해, 모든 판매 공간이 다 차 있고 저희는 대기자 명단을 유지하고 있습니다. ⁹ 대기자 명단이 현재 진행 중입니다. ¹⁰ 일단 대기자 명단에 오르면, 공간이 이용할 수 있기 까지 여러 해가 걸릴 수 있다는 것을 주목해 주시기 바랍니다. ¹¹ **주차 요금** ¹² 대학 정책의 변경으로 인해, 벼룩시장의 주차가 더 이상 무료가 아닙니다. ¹³ 주차는 현재 하루에 2달러입니다.

정답단추 선택지를 먼저 읽고 해당하는 소제목과 내용을 찾아 일치 여부를 확인하면 돼. 안내문의 마지막 부분인 주차 요금 내용을 보면 대학 정책이 바뀌어서 주차가 무료에서 하루에 2달러로 바뀌었다고 하고 있지? 따라서 주차가 유료 이용으로 전환되었다는 ⑤는 안내문과 일치하는 내용이야.

오답단서 ①은 안내문의 앞부분에서 판매되는 항목 중에 의류와 장난감도 언급했기 때문에 일치하지 않아. ②는 Location의 내용을 보면 장터는 운동장이 아니라 주차장(parking lot)임을 알 수 있어서 오답이야. 그리고 시장은 매주 일요일이 아닌 매월 첫째 주 일요일(the first Sunday of the month)에 열린다고 했으니 ③도 잘못된 설명이지. 마지막으로 대기자 명단에 오르면 여러 해를 기다려야 할 수도 있다는 안내문의 내용과 달리 ④에서는 한 달 정도 대기하면 된다고 해서 답이 될 수 없어.

교정; 대학 **lot** (특정 용도용) 부지[지역] **located** ~에 위치한 **admission** 입장; 입장료 **traditionally** 전통적으로 **hold** 열다[개최하다]; 잡고 있다 **note** 공지; ~에 주목하다 **would-be** ~을 지망하는 **vendor** 판매인; 행상인 cf. **vend** 팔다 **due to** ~ 때문에 **popularity** 인기 **maintain** 유지하다 **waiting list** 대기자 명단 **currently** 현재 **once** 일단 ~하면 **several** 몇몇의 **available** 이용할 수 있는 **fee** 요금 **policy** 정책 **no longer** 더 이상 ~ 아닌

지문 Flow

[도입]
패서디나 벼룩시장 안내문

[세부사항1]
• 위치: 주차장
• 개장 시간: 첫 번째 일요일, 오전 8시~오후 3시
• 입장료: 무료

&

[세부사항2]
판매 대기자가 많아 자리가 나기까지 여러 해가 걸릴 수 있음

&

[세부사항3]
주차비 유료 전환: 하루 2달러

259 정답 ④

지문 All in One

Suzanne Collins는 몇몇 소설을 쓴 저자이다 / 더 어린 독자들을 위한 / 베스트셀러 시리즈를 포함하여 / 2008년의 〈헝거 게임〉으로 시작하는 / 연극 전공의 대학 경력으로

¹ Suzanne Collins is the author of several novels / for younger readers, / including *a best-selling series* [that began with 2008's *The Hunger Games*]. ² With a college background in
(S, V, C, 관계대명사)

어휘확인

author 저자, 작가 **several** 몇몇의 **novel** 소설 **including** ~을 포함하여 **best-selling** 베스트셀러의 **series** 시리즈, 연속 **background** 경력, 배경 **career** 경력 **switch** 전환하다, 바꾸다 **publish** 출간하다

그녀는 글쓰기 경력을 시작했다 / 텔레비전 업계에서 / 아이들의 프로그램을 쓰는 데 몇 년을 보낸 후에

theater, / she began her writing career / in television. 3 After spending several years writing
(S V / 분사구문(= After she spent ~))

그녀는 어린 독자들을 위한 소설을 쓰기로 전환했다 / 그리고 5편의 소설을 출간했다

kids' shows, / she switched to writing novels for young readers, / and published five novels
(S V_1 / V_2)

〈언더랜드 연대기〉 시리즈에 / 그녀는 그 다음에 〈헝거 게임〉을 썼다 / 자신의 생명을 위해

/ in *The Underland Chronicles* series. 4 She then wrote *The Hunger Games*, / a tale of *a teen*
(S V)

강제로 싸워야 하는 십대 소녀의 이야기인 / 어둡고 위험한 미래의 미국에서 / Collins는 인정한다

girl [forced to fight for her life / in a dark and dangerous future U.S.A.] 5 Collins admits //
(S V)

그녀의 이야기가 영향을 받았음을 / 그녀의 아버지의 전쟁 경험에 의해 / 베트남 전쟁의 참전

(that) her stories are informed / by the war experiences of her father, / a veteran of the
(접속사 S′ V′)

용사인 / 그리고 군인 가정에서의 그녀의 어린 시절(에 의해) / 흥미진진한 스토리텔링에서의 그녀의 기교가

Vietnam War, / and her childhood in a military family. 6 Her skill at exciting storytelling / is
(S_1 V_1)

〈헝거 게임〉을 인기 있게 만든 것이다 / 그리고 십 대를 위한 소설로 의도된 것은

what made *The Hunger Games* popular, // and what was intended as a novel for teenagers /
(관계대명사 C_1 / 관계대명사 S_2)

큰 인기를 끌었다 / 모든 연령의 독자들에게

became a hit / with readers of all ages.
(V_2)

① 대학에서 연극을 공부하였다.
② 방송 작가로 글쓰기를 시작하였다.
③ 상당 기간 동안, 어린이 프로그램을 썼다.
④ 첫 소설은 *The Hunger Games*이다.
⑤ 아버지의 전쟁 경험을 소설에 반영하기도 했다.

해석 한 눈에 보기 **1** Suzanne Collins는 2008년의 〈헝거 게임〉으로 시작하는 베스트셀러 시리즈를 포함하여, 더 어린 독자들을 위한 몇몇 소설을 쓴 저자이다. **2** 연극 전공의 대학 경력으로, 그녀는 텔레비전 업계에서 글쓰기 경력을 시작했다. **3** 아이들의 프로그램을 쓰는 데 몇 년을 보낸 후에, 그녀는 어린 독자들을 위한 소설을 쓰기로 전환했고, 〈언더랜드 연대기〉 시리즈에 5편의 소설을 출간했다. **4** 그녀는 그 다음에 어둡고 위험한 미래의 미국에서 자신의 생명을 위해 강제로 싸워야 하는 십 대 소녀의 이야기인 〈헝거 게임〉을 썼다. **5** Collins는 자신의 이야기가 베트남 전쟁의 참전 용사인 자신의 아버지의 전쟁 경험, 그리고 군인 가정에서의 어린 시절에 의해 영향을 받았음을 인정한다. **6** 흥미진진한 스토리텔링에서의 그녀의 기교가 〈헝거 게임〉을 인기 있게 만든 것이고, 십 대를 위한 소설로 의도된 것은 모든 연령의 독자들에게 큰 인기를 끌었다.

정답단추 선택지를 먼저 읽고, 순서대로 본문과 대조하면서 일치하지 않는 부분을 찾으면 돼. Suzanne Collins는 〈헝거 게임〉을 쓰기 전에 〈언더랜드 연대기〉 시리즈 5편을 썼다고 했으므로, ④는 글의 내용과 일치하지 않아.

오답단서 ①, ②는 대학에서 연극 전공을 한 경력으로, 텔레비전 업계에서 글쓰기 경력을 시작했다고 했으므로 일치하는 내용이야. ③은 아동 소설을 쓰기 전에 몇 년 간 어린이 프로그램을 썼다고 했으므로 내용과 일치해. ⑤는 자신의 이야기가 아버지의 베트남 전쟁 경험과 군인 가정에서의 어린 시절에 의해 영향을 받았다고 했으므로 일치해.

force 강요하다 **admit** 인정하다 **inform** 영향을 미치다 **veteran** 참전 용사 **childhood** 어린 시절 **military** 군인의, 군대의 **storytelling** 스토리텔링, 이야기하기 **intend** 의도하다

지문 Flow

[인물 소개]
청소년 도서의 베스트셀러 작가 Suzanne Collins

⬇

[세부사항1]
대학에서 연극을 전공하고, 텔레비전에서 글쓰기를 시작하여 몇 년 간 아동용 프로그램에서 글을 씀

&

[세부사항2]
청소년 작가로 전환하여 〈언더랜드 연대기〉 시리즈 5편과 〈헝거 게임〉을 씀

⬇

[추가]
아버지의 전쟁 경험과 군인 가정에서 자란 어린 시절이 작품에 영향을 줌

⬇

[결과]
흥미진진한 스토리텔링으로 〈헝거 게임〉은 전 연령층의 독자에게 인기를 끎

260 정답 ③

지문 All in One

나는 기억난다 / 노르웨이에 처음 도착했을 때가 / 우리가 '유럽 투어'를 시작했을 때

1 I remember / when we first arrived in Norway // when we started our European Tour / last
(S V / 관계부사 / 접속사 S′ V′)

작년에 / 우리가 공항에서 나왔을 때 / 우리는 놀랐다 / 거기에서 공기가 얼마나 깨끗하게 냄새 나는

year. 2 When we got out of the airport, // we were amazed / at how clean the air smelled
(접속사 S′ V′ / S V C / 간접의문문)

지에 / 나는 개와 같았다 / 차 안의 / 창문 밖으로 머리를 내미는 / 흥분해서

there. 3 I was like *a dog* / in a car / [sticking his head out the window and / sniffing
(S V C)

모든 것의 냄새를 맡는 / 그것은 아주 맛있었다 / 그 차이는 / 알아차리기 쉽다 / 여러분 중에

everything excitedly]. 4 It was so delicious. 5 The difference / is easy to notice. 6 For *those of*
(S V C / S V C 부사적 용법(형용사 수식))

깨끗한 공기가 있는 나라에 사는 사람들은 / 그것을 당연한 것으로 생각하지 마라 / 그것은 사랑스럽다 / 나는 좋겠다

you [living in countries with clean air], / don't take it for granted. 7 It's lovely. 8 I wish // I
(V / S V C / I wish+가정법 과거)

그와 같은 공기에서 숨을 쉴 수 있으면 / 항상 / 나는 잠을 거의 잘 수가 없다 / 장기적인 결과가 무엇인지에 대해 생각

could breathe in air like that / all the time. 9 I almost can't sleep / thinking about what the
(S V / 분사구문(= if I think ~))

하면 / 공기 질이 나쁜 장소에 있는 것의 / 우리 인생의 몇 년을

long-term effects are / of being in a place with poor air quality. 10 How many years of our

우리는 포기하고 있는가

lives / are we giving up?
(S V)

어휘확인

arrive in ~에 도착하다 **European** 유럽의 **tour** 여행 **get out of** ~에서 나오다 **be amazed at** ~에 놀라다 **stick out** ~을 내밀다 **sniff** 코를 킁킁거리다, ~의 냄새를 맡다 **excitedly** 흥분해서 **delicious** 맛있는 **difference** 차이 **notice** 알아차리다 **take A for granted** A를 당연시 여기다 **lovely** 사랑스러운 **breathe** 숨을 쉬다 **long-term** 장기적인 **effect** 결과, 영향 **quality** 질 **life** 생활, 삶 **give up** 포기하다

지문 Flow

[도입]
'유럽 투어' 중 노르웨이의 공기의 깨끗함에 놀람

⬇

[보충설명]
차창 밖에서 맡는 공기 냄새가 좋았으며, 차이를 쉽게 알 정도로 공기가 좋음

⬇

① worried → relieved
걱정스러운 안도한

② satisfied → hopeful
만족스러운 희망에 찬

③ delighted → concerned
즐거운 걱정하는

④ anxious → worried
불안한 걱정스러운

⑤ curious → satisfied
호기심 있는 만족스러운

[추가]
항상 그렇게 숨을 쉴 수 있으면 좋겠다고 생각함

해석 한 눈에 보기 **1** 나는 작년에 우리가 '유럽 투어'를 시작했을 때 노르웨이에 처음 도착했을 때가 기억난다. **2** 공항에서 나왔을 때, 우리는 거기에서 공기가 얼마나 깨끗한 냄새가 나는지에 놀랐다. **3** 나는 창문 밖으로 머리를 내밀고 흥분해서 모든 것의 냄새를 맡는 차 안의 개와 같았다. **4** 그것은 아주 맛있었다. **5** 그 차이는 알아차리기 쉽다. **6** 여러분 중에 깨끗한 공기가 있는 나라에 사는 사람들은 그것을 당연한 것으로 생각하지 마라. **7** 그것은 사랑스럽다. **8** 항상 그런 공기에서 숨을 쉴 수 있으면 좋을 텐데. **9** 나는 공기 질이 나쁜 장소에 있는 것의 장기적인 결과가 무엇인지에 대해 생각하면 잠을 거의 잘 수가 없다. **10** 우리는 우리 인생의 몇 년을 포기하고 있는가?

정답단추 필자의 심경 변화를 알려면 자신이 이 글의 주인공이 되어 어떤 상황인지 생각해보는 것도 방법이야. 필자는 유럽 여행 중 노르웨이에 도착했을 때 그곳의 깨끗한 공기에 놀라면서 그것을 만끽하며 즐거워하지만, 이내 현재 자신이 그런 곳에서 지내지 못하고 있음을 생각하며 공기가 나쁜 장소에 장기간 있는 것에 대해 걱정하고 있어. 따라서 필자의 심경 변화로 가장 적절한 것은 ③이야. 글에 특별히 심경을 나타내는 표현이 없으므로, 필자의 생각에서 심경을 파악해야 해.

261 정답 ②

지문 All in One

1 People(S) tend(V) to show / their **self-belief** unconsciously // when(접속사) they(S') are speaking(V'). (사람들은 보여주는 경향이 있다 / 그들의 자기 신념을 무의식적으로 / 그들이 말을 할 때) **2** While(접속사) interviewing applicants (분사구문(= While a university professor interviewed ~)) / for a scholarship, // a university professor(S) noted(V) / that(접속사) students(S') answered(V') questions differently / when (being) asked (분사구문) / about future plans. (지원자들을 인터뷰하는 동안에 / 장학금을 위한 / 한 대학 교수는 주목했다 / 학생들이 질문에 다르게 대답한다는 것을 / 질문을 받았을 때 / 미래 계획에 대해) **3** If(접속사) they(S') had achieved(V') very high grades / at school, // they(S) used(V) the words "I am" [and] "I will." (만약 그들이 매우 높은 성적을 받았다면 / 학교에서 / 그들은 '저는 ~입니다'와 '저는 ~할 것입니다' 라는 말을 사용했다) **4** In contrast, / relatively low-achieving students(S) spoke(V_1) / in qualifiers, / as in "Maybe I...," "But I...," [and] "If I...," // [and] filled(V_2) their sentences / with "Umms" [and] "Errrs." (대조적으로 / 상대적으로 저성취의 학생들은 말했다 / 수식어로 / '어쩌면 저는 …', '하지만 저는 …', '만일 제가 …'에서처럼 / 그리고 그들의 문장을 채웠다 / '음'과 '어'로) **5** *The students*(S) [who(관계대명사) used the words "I am" [and] "I will"] / had(V) a strong belief that they would obtain their goals, // while(접속사) the others(S') merely hoped(V'_1) / to succeed / [but] didn't believe(V'_2) / (that)(접속사) they(S'') would make(V'') it. ('저는 ~ 입니다'와 '저는 ~할 것입니다'라는 말을 사용한 학생들은 / 그들이 자신의 목표를 얻어낼 것이라는 강한 신념을 갖고 있었다 / 반면에 다른 학생들은 단지 희망할 뿐이었다 / 성공하기를 / 그러나 믿지 않았다 / 그들이 해낼 것이라고)

① ambition
야망

② self-belief
자기 신념

③ prejudices
편견

④ sense of competition
경쟁심

⑤ desire for a scholarship
장학금에 대한 욕망

해석 한 눈에 보기 주제문 **1** 사람들은 그들이 말을 할 때 무의식적으로 자기 신념을 보여주는 경향이 있다. **2** 장학금 신청자들을 인터뷰하는 동안에, 한 대학교수는 학생들이 미래 계획에 대해 질문을 받았을 때 질문에 서로 다르게 대답한다는 것에 주목했다. **3** 만약 그들이 학교에서 매우 높은 성적을 받았다면, 그들은 '저는 ~입니다'와 '저는 ~할 것입니다'라는 말을 사용했다. **4** 이와 대조적으로, 상대적으로 저성취의 학생들은 '어쩌면 저는 …', '하지만 저는 …', '만일 제가 …'처럼 수식어를 써서 말했고, 그들의 문장을 '음'과 '어'로 채웠다. **5** '저는 ~ 입니다'와 '저는 ~할 것입니다'라는 말을 사용한 학생들은 그들이 자신의 목표를 얻어낼 것이라는 강한 신념을 갖고 있었던 반면에, 다른 학생들은 단지 성공하기를 희망할 뿐이었지 그들이 해낼 것이라고 믿지는 않았다.

정답단추 빈칸이 포함된 문장을 먼저 읽고, 사람들이 말할 때 '무엇'을 드러내는지 찾으면서 글을 읽어보자. 빈칸 문장 뒤에서 이에 대한 구체적인 예시가 이어지고 있어. 성적이 높은 학생들은 자신 있는 말투를 쓰고 목표 달성에 대한 강한 신념이 있는 반면에 성적이 낮은 학생들은 말투에 자신감이 없고 스스로에 대한 확실한 믿음도 없다고 하고 있어. 즉, 두 그룹 모두 말을 통해 '자기 신념'을 무의식중에 보여주고 있음을 알 수 있어. 따라서 빈칸에 들어갈 적절한 말은 ②야.

어휘확인

tend to-v ~하는 경향이 있다 **self-belief** 자기 신념 **unconsciously** 무의식적으로 **applicant** 지원자 **scholarship** 장학금 **university** 대학 **professor** 교수 **note** 주목하다; 메모 **achieve** 성취하다 **in contrast** 대조적으로 **relatively** 상대적으로; 비교적으로 **low-achieving** 저성취 **speak in** ~으로 말하다 **qualifier** 수식 어구 **belief** 신념 **obtain** 얻다 **merely** 단지, 그저 **succeed** 성공하다 **make it** 해내다, 성공하다
〈선택지 어휘〉
ambition 야망, 포부 **prejudice** 편견 **sense** 의식; 감각 **desire** 욕망, 욕구

지문 Flow

[주제문]
사람들은 말할 때 무의식적으로 자기 신념을 보여줌

⬇

[예시1]
장학금 신청 인터뷰에서, 성적이 높은 학생들은 자신감 있는 말투를 씀

&

[예시2]
성적이 낮은 학생들은 자신감이 없는 말투를 씀

⬇

[결론]
전자는 말투에서 목표 달성에 강한 신념을 보였고, 후자는 말할 때 스스로에 대한 확신이 없었음

262 정답 ③

지문 All in One

당신이 성인이 되었을 때까지 / 당신의 뇌는 개발해왔다 / 수백만 개의 신경 연결
[1] By the time you have reached adulthood, // your brain has developed / *millions of neural*
접속사 S′ V′ / S V

통로를 / 당신이 정보를 신속하게 처리하도록 도와주는 / 친숙한 문제들을 해결하도록 / 그리고
pathways [that help you process information quickly, / solve familiar problems, / and
관계대명사

익숙한 업무를 수행할 수 있도록 / 최소한의 정신적 노력으로 / 그러나 / 당신이 항상 이 흔한 길을 고수하면
execute familiar tasks / with a minimum of mental effort]. [2] But / if you always stick to these
접속사 S′ V′

당신은 당신의 뇌에 자극을 주지 않고 있는 것이다 / 성장과 발전을 유지하는 데 필요한
well-worn paths, // you are not giving your brain *the stimulation* [(which[that]) it needs to
S V IO DO 관계대명사

당신은 생각들을 흔들어야 한다 / 때때로
keep growing and developing]. [3] You have to **shake things up / from time to time!** [4] Try
S V V

새로운 길을 택해 보아라 / 직장이나 식료품점에서 집으로 오는 / 주말에 새로운 장소를 방문해 (보아라)
taking a new route / home from work or the grocery store, / visiting new places on the

또는 다양한 종류의 책을 읽어 (보아라) / 두뇌가 도전을 받도록
weekend, / or reading different kinds of books / to keep your brain challenged / with
부사적 용법(목적)

예기치 못한 정보와 경험으로 / 이러한 활동들은 당신의 일상을 깬다 / 그리고
unexpected information and experiences. [5] These activities break your routine // and
S V_1

당신에게 새로운 뇌의 경로를 사용하고 개발하도록 요구한다
challenge you to use and develop new brain pathways.
V_2 O C

① spare some time for exercise
운동에 시간을 좀 할애해야

② figure out ways to learn more efficiently
보다 효율적으로 학습할 수 있는 방법을 알아내야

③ shake things up from time to time
때때로 생각들을 흔들어야

④ stimulate your brain at a young age
어렸을 때 뇌를 자극해야

⑤ respect your routine in order to develop
개발시키기 위해서 일상을 존중해야

해석 한 눈에 보기 1 당신이 성인이 되었을 때까지, 당신의 뇌는 당신이 정보를 신속하게 처리하고, 친숙한 문제들을 해결하며, 최소한의 정신적 노력으로 익숙한 업무를 수행할 수 있도록 도와주는 수백만 개의 신경 연결 통로를 개발해 왔다. 2 그러나 당신이 항상 이 흔한 길을 고수하면, 당신의 뇌에 성장과 발전을 유지하는 데 필요한 자극을 주지 않고 있는 것이다. 주제문 3 당신은 때때로 생각들을 흔들어야 한다! 4 직장이나 식료품점에서 집으로 오는 새로운 길을 택하거나, 주말에 새로운 장소를 방문하거나, 예기치 못한 정보와 경험으로 두뇌가 도전을 받도록 다양한 종류의 책을 읽어 보아라. 5 이러한 활동들은 당신의 일상을 깨고 당신에게 새로운 뇌의 경로를 사용하고 개발하도록 요구한다.

정답단추 빈칸에 주어와 의무 조동사 have to만 나오므로, 문장의 앞뒤 내용이 어떻게 연결되는지 흐름을 살펴보자. 앞에서는 자신에게 흔한 행동은 뇌에 자극을 주지 않으므로 뇌의 성장과 발전에 도움이 되지 않는다는 내용이 나오고, 뒤에서는 새로운 길로 가거나 새로운 장소에 가거나 다양한 책을 읽으라는, 즉, 뇌에 자극을 줄 수 있는 예들이 나오고 있어. 그러므로 그 예들을 정의하는 문장이 되도록 '때때로 생각들을 흔들다'가 들어가야 해. 따라서 빈칸에 들어갈 말로 가장 적절한 것은 ③이야.

오답단서 ①, ②는 이 글이 운동이나 학습 방법에 대한 것을 다루고 있지 않으므로 답이 될 수 없어. ④는 뇌를 자극한다는 것은 맞지만, 어렸을 때로 국한되어 있지 않으므로 적절하지 않아. ⑤는 일상적 행동에서 벗어난 행동으로 뇌에 자극을 주라는 본문의 내용과 맞지 않으므로 오답이야.

어휘확인

adulthood 성인, 성년 develop 개발하다 millions of 수백만의 neural pathway 신경 연결 통로 process 처리하다 familiar 친숙한 execute 수행하다 minimum 최소한도, 최저(치) mental 정신의 stick to ~을 고수하다 well-worn 흔한, 진부한 path 길 stimulation 자극 cf. stimulate 자극하다 from time to time 때때로 route 길, 경로 grocery store 식료품점 unexpected 예기치 않은 routine 일상 challenge (상대방에게 도전이 될 일을) 요구하다

〈선택지 어휘〉

spare 할애하다, 내어 주다 figure out 알아내다, 이해하다 efficiently 효율적으로 respect 존중하다 in order to ~하기 위해

지문 Flow

[도입]
뇌는 정보를 처리하고 문제를 해결하며 업무를 수행하는 신경 연결 통로를 개발해옴

↓

[대조]
자신에게 흔한 행동을 하면, 뇌가 성장과 발전을 하도록 자극을 주지 않는 것임

↓

[주제]
때때로 생각들을 흔들어라!

↓

[보충설명]
새로운 길, 새로운 장소, 다양한 종류의 책을 경험함

↓

[결과]
자신의 일상을 깨고 새로운 뇌의 경로를 사용하고 개발하게 됨

263 정답 ④

지문 All in One

당신의 식단을 바꾸는 것이 어떻게 영향을 미칠 수 있을까 / 지구의 온도에 / 믿거나 말거나
[1] How can **changing your diet** affect / the temperature of the planet? [2] Believe it or not, //
조동사 S V

연구들은 보여준다 / 그것이 당신이 할 수 있는 가장 큰 일일 수 있다는 것을 / 채식주의자가 되는 것 / 혹은
studies show / that it may be *the biggest thing* [(that) you can do]. [3] Going vegetarian, / or at
S V 접속사 S′ V′ C′ 관계대명사 S_1

적어도 당신의 식단에서 붉은 고기를 제외하는 것은 / 엄청난 손상을 입히고 있는 관습을 멈추는 것에 대한 것이다
least cutting red meat out of your diet, / is about stopping *a practice* [that is doing
S_2 V C 관계대명사

지구 전체에 / 당신이 당신 스스로가 육류를 끊게 할 수 없다면
tremendous damage / to the entire earth]. [4] If you can't bring yourself to quit meat, // try
접속사 S′ V′ O′ C′ V

당신의 동물성 식품을 사도록 해봐라 / 현지의 작은 농장에서 / 많은 작은 농장들은 참여한다
buying your animal products / from local, small farms. [5] Many small farms engage / in
S V

어휘확인

affect 영향을 미치다 planet 지구, 행성 believe it or not 믿거나 말거나 vegetarian 채식주의자 cut A out of B B로부터 A를 제외하다 red meat (소·양·돼지고기 등 살이) 붉은 고기 practice 관습, 관행; 실행 tremendous 엄청난 damage 손상, 피해 entire 전체의 bring oneself to-v (간신히) ~을 하다 quit 끊다, 그만두다 animal product 동물성 식품 local 현지의, 지역의 engage in ~에 참여하다 carbon-offsetting program 탄소 (배출량) 상쇄 프로그램 decrease 줄이다 support 지지하다

탄소 상쇄 프로그램에 / 그 어떤 손상도 줄이기 위해 / 환경에 / 그들이 입히는
carbon-offsetting programs / to decrease *any damage* / to the environment / [(that) they make]. [6] By supporting / *local businesses* [that believe in environmentally friendly programs], / you will be making it known // that these factors matter / and should be encouraged.

부사적 용법(목적) / 관계대명사 / 지지함으로써 / 환경 친화적인 프로그램을 믿는 지역 기업들을 / 관계대명사 / 당신은 알려지게 하고 있을 것이다 / 이러한 요소들이 중요하며 / 장려되어야 한다는 것이 / S V 가목적어 C 진목적어 S′ V'_1 V'_2

① starting small farms
작은 농장을 시작하는 것

② supporting local businesses
지역 기업을 지지하는 것

③ making animal products
동물성 식품을 만드는 것

④ changing your diet
당신의 식단을 바꾸는 것

⑤ protecting the environment
환경을 보호하는 것

해석 한 눈에 보기 **1** 주제문 당신의 식단을 바꾸는 것이 어떻게 지구의 온도에 영향을 미칠 수 있을까? **2** 믿거나 말거나, 연구들은 그것이 당신이 할 수 있는 가장 커다란 일이라는 것을 보여준다. **3** 채식주의자가 되는 것이나 혹은 적어도 당신의 식단에서 붉은 육류를 제거하는 것은 지구 전체에 엄청난 손상을 입히고 있는 관습을 멈추는 것에 대한 것이다. **4** 당신이 당신 스스로가 육류를 끊게 할 수 없다면, 현지의 작은 농장에서 동물성 식품을 사도록 해봐라. **5** 많은 작은 농장들은 그들이 환경에 입히는 그 어떤 손상도 줄이기 위해 탄소 상쇄 프로그램에 참여한다. **6** 환경 친화적인 프로그램을 믿는 지역 기업들을 지지함으로써, 당신은 이러한 요소들이 중요하며 장려되어야 한다는 것이 알려지게 하고 있을 것이다.

정답단추 빈칸을 포함한 문장을 먼저 읽고 무엇에 중점을 두고 읽어야 하는지 파악한 다음 글을 읽으면 시간을 절약할 수 있어. 빈칸 문장을 보면 '무엇'이 어떻게 지구 온도에 영향을 미칠 수 있는지 질문을 하고 있지? 그럼 '무엇'에 들어갈 말에 집중해서 나머지를 읽으면 돼. 이 글은 채식주의자가 되거나 최소한 식단에서 붉은 육류를 없애는 것이 지구에 피해를 주는 관행을 막는 것이고, 육류를 끊지 못하겠다면 환경 친화적인 지역 기업을 지지하라는 내용이야. 다시 말해 지구의 온도 변화를 위해 식단을 바꾸라는 거야. 따라서 빈칸에는 ④가 들어가야 해.

오답단서 ①, ②, ③은 글에서 언급된 어휘를 활용하여 만든 오답으로 전체 내용과는 무관해. 또한, ⑤는 너무 포괄적이라서 글의 핵심으로 보기에는 어려워.

environmentally friendly 환경 친화적인 **factor** 요소, 요인 **matter** 중요하다; 문제 **encourage** 장려하다; 격려하다
〈선택지 어휘〉
protect 보호하다

지문 Flow

[주제문]
식단을 바꾸는 것이 지구의 온도에 영향을 미칠 수 있음

⬇

[보충설명1]
채식주의자가 되거나 식단에서 붉은색 육류를 제거함으로써, 지구에 손상을 주는 관습을 멈출 수 있음

&

[보충설명2]
육류를 끊을 수 없으면, 탄소 상쇄 프로그램에 가담한 지역의 작은 농장에서 구입하면 됨

&

[보충설명3]
환경 친화적인 지역 기업들을 지지함으로써 이것의 중요성을 알림

264 정답 ④

지문 All in One

[1] Mealtimes are more than just eating food; // they are *times* [to sit around the table together and talk]. [2] ① *Children* [who eat meals together with their families] / are able to talk about important things / or ask their parents questions. [3] ② This is an important part of language development // because it helps children improve their vocabularies / to practice / with more experienced speakers. [4] ③ Furthermore, / it's *an opportunity* for children / [to develop a sense / for appropriate dinner conversation], / a valuable social skill. [5] (④ In this way, / the ritual of preparing family meals / fosters feelings of belonging, / as well as teaching the importance of diet.) [6] ⑤ Parents can maximize / the language benefit of family mealtimes / by making it a point to foster interesting dinner conversation / instead of watching TV.

식사 시간은 단순히 음식을 먹는 것 이상이다 (S V C) / 그것은 식탁에 같이 둘러앉아 이야기하는 시간이다 (S V C) / 가족들과 함께 같이 식사를 하는 아이들은 (S, 관계대명사) / 중요한 것들에 관해 이야기할 수 있다 (V_1) / 혹은 부모에게 질문을 (할 수 있다) (V_2 IO DO) / 이것은 언어 발달의 중요한 부분이다 (S V C) / 아이들이 그들의 어휘력을 향상시키도록 도움을 주기 때문이다 (접속사 가주어 V′ O′ C′) / 연습하는 것이 (진주어) / 더 경험 많은 화자들과 / 게다가 / 그것은 아이들에게 기회이다 (S V C, to부정사의 의미상 주어) / 감각을 키울 / 적절한 식사 대화에 대한 / 귀중한 사회적 기술인 / 이런 식으로 / 가족의 식사를 준비하는 의식은 (S) / 소속감을 발전시킨다 (V) / 식습관의 중요성을 가르쳐 줄 뿐만 아니라 / 부모들은 최대화할 수 있다 (S V) / 가족 식사 시간의 언어적 이점을 / 반드시 흥미로운 식사 대화를 조성함으로써 / TV를 보는 대신에

해석 한 눈에 보기 주제문 **1** 식사 시간은 단순히 음식을 먹는 것 이상으로, 그것은 식탁에 같이 둘러앉아 이야기하는 시간이다. **2** ① 가족들과 같이 식사를 하는 아이들은 중요한 것들에 관해 이야기할 수 있고 부모에게 질문할 수 있다. ② **3** 이것은 아이들이 더 경험 많은 화자들과 연습하는 것이 그들의 어휘력을 향상시키도록 도움을 주기 때문에 언어 발달의 중요한 부분이다. **4** ③ 게다가, 그것은 아이들이 귀중한 사회적 기술인 적절한 식사 대화에 대한 감각을 키울 기회이다. **5** (④ 이런 식으로 가족의 식사를 준비하는 의식은 식습관의 중요성을 가르쳐 줄 뿐만 아니라 소속감을 길러 준다.) **6** ⑤ 부모들은 TV를 보는 대신에 반드시 흥미로운 식사 대화를 조성함으로써 가족 식사 시간의 언어적 이점을 최대화할 수 있다.

어휘확인

mealtime 식사 시간 **sit around** ~에 둘러앉다 **development** 발달 **cf. develop** 발달[성장]시키다 **vocabulary** 어휘 **experienced** 경험이 있는 **furthermore** 게다가 **opportunity** 기회 **sense** 감각 **appropriate** 적절한 **conversation** 대화; 회화 **valuable** 귀중한 **in this way** 이런 식으로 **ritual** 의식, 의례 **foster** 발전시키다, 조성하다 **feeling of belonging** 소속감 **as well as** ~뿐만 아니라 **importance** 중요성 **maximize** 최대화하다 **benefit** 이점, 이득 **make it a point to-v** 반드시 ~하다

지문 Flow

[주제문]
식사 시간은 음식을 먹는 시간일 뿐 아니라 대화하는 시간임

⬇

[보충설명1]
부모와의 대화를 통해 어휘력 향상에 도움이 됨

&

[보충설명2]
식사 대화에 대한 감각을 키울 수 있는 기회임

정답단추 글의 흐름에 무관한 문장을 고르는 문제에서는 선택지가 없는 글의 앞부분이 주로 주제문이거나 주제를 소개하는 도입부인 경우가 많아. 이 부분을 잘 활용하여 주제를 추론한 뒤에 그것을 뒷받침하지 않는 문장을 고르면 돼. 이 글의 주제는 가족들과의 식사 시간을 통한 아이들의 언어 학습 효과야. 그러나 ④는 가족 식사 준비의 의의를 설명하고 있어서 글의 주제에서 벗어남을 알 수 있어. 따라서 전체 흐름과 관계없는 문장은 ④야.
오답단서 식탁에 함께 둘러앉아 이야기하는 시간이라는 첫 문장에 이어서 ①은 가족과 함께 하는 식사 시간을 가질 때 아이들이 말할 기회를 가진다는 걸 설명하고 있어. 그리고 ②의 This는 앞 문장의 to talk ~ questions를 받는 대명사로 식사 시간에 말하는 것이 언어 발달에 중요함에 대해 말하고 있지. Furthermore로 시작하여 ③은 언어 발달과 더불어 적절한 식사 대화 감각을 키울 수 있다는 점에 대해서 덧붙이고 있어. 마지막으로 ⑤는 흥미로운 식사 대화를 통해 언어적 이점을 최대화할 수 있다고 앞 내용을 정리하고 있어 자연스러워.

[무관한 문장]
가족의 식사를 준비하는 의식은 식습관의 중요성과 소속감을 길러줌

[결론]
식사 시간 대화를 통해 언어적 이점을 최대화할 수 있음

265 정답 ③

지문 All in One

1 The interesting thing about stress (스트레스에 관해 흥미로운 것은, S) / is (V) its true source (그것의 진짜 근원이다, C). 2 Throughout our lives (우리의 인생 내내), / we (S) receive (V) (우리는 받는다), / in a continuous series (연속적으로), / rewards [and] punishments (보상과 벌을). (①) 3 Through personal experiences (개인적인 경험을 통해) / over time (시간이 흐르면서), / we (S) learn (V) (우리는 배운다) // which of our behaviors will earn rewards (우리 행동 중 어느 것이 보상을 얻는지를, 간접의문문) / [and] which ones will create / *the negative feedback* [associated with punishment] (그리고 어느 것이 만들어 내는지를 벌과 관련된 부정적인 반응을, 간접의문문). (②) 4 We (S) adjust (V) our lives (우리는 우리의 삶을 조정한다) / on the basis of our perceptions (우리의 인지를 기반으로) / of how to maximize rewards [and] minimize punishments (보상을 최대화하고 벌을 최소화하는 방법에 관한). 5 (③ In some cases (어떤 경우에), / however (그러나), / we (S) may not know (V) exactly (우리는 정확히 알지 못할지도 모른다) // what the result of our choice will be (우리의 선택 결과가 무엇일지, 간접의문문).)
6 We (S_1) make (V_1) a decision (우리는 결정한다) / assuming (분사구문) (that) (접속사) it (S′) will have (V′) a positive outcome (그것이 긍정적인 결과를 낼 것으로 추정하면서), // [but] instead it (S_2) may (V_2) turn out badly (하지만 대신에 그것이 안 좋은 것으로 드러날 지도 모른다). (④) 7 When (접속사) this (S′) happens (V′) (이것이 발생할 때), // we (S) must choose (V) (우리는 선택해야 한다) / between the options of fight [or] flight (싸움 혹은 도피라는 선택지 중에). (⑤) 8 At the same time (동시에), / we (S) must attend (V) to *the stress* [we are experiencing] (우리는 우리가 경험하는 스트레스를 돌보아야 한다) // because (접속사) our plans (S′) didn't work out (V′) (우리의 계획이 잘 풀리지 않기 때문에) / as expected (예상된 대로).

해석 한 눈에 보기 **1** 스트레스에 관해 흥미로운 것은 그것의 진짜 근원이다. **2** 우리의 인생 내내, 우리는 연속적으로 보상과 벌을 받는다. **3** 시간이 흐르면서 개인적 경험을 통해, 우리는 행동 중 어느 것이 보상을 얻고 어느 것이 벌과 관련된 부정적인 반응을 만들어 내는지 알게 된다. **4** 우리는 보상을 최대화하고 벌을 최소화하는 방법에 관한 우리의 인지를 기반으로 하여 삶을 조정한다. **5** 그러나 어떤 경우에는 우리의 선택 결과가 무엇일지 우리는 정확히 알지 못할지도 모른다. **6** 우리는 그것이 긍정적인 결과를 낼 거로 추정하면서 결정을 내리지만, 대신에 그것이 안 좋은 것으로 드러날지도 모른다. **7** 이런 일이 발생할 때, 우리는 싸움 혹은 도피라는 선택지 사이에서 선택해야 한다. **8** 동시에 우리는 계획들이 예상된 대로 풀리지 않아서 우리가 경험하게 되는 스트레스도 돌보아야 한다.
정답단추 문장 삽입 문제는 앞뒤 문장 사이의 관계를 잘 파악하면서 읽어야 해. 주어진 문장은 선택의 결과를 정확히 모를 수도 있다는 내용으로 however로 시작하고 있어. ③의 앞에서는 보상을 최대화하고 벌을 최소화하는 것에 초점을 맞춰 삶을 조정한다고 했어. 그런데 ③의 다음 문장에서 긍정적 결과를 바라고 선택을 했지만, 부정적인 결과가 나올 수도 있다고 설명하고 있어서 앞뒤 문장의 흐름이 끊기는 걸 알 수 있어. 따라서 주어진 문장은 ③에 들어가야 가장 자연스러워.
오답단서 ①의 앞뒤 문장을 살펴보면 우리는 평생 보상과 벌을 받는데 이는 행동의 결과로써 경험을 통해 알 수 있다는 내용으로 자연스럽게 이어지고 있음을 알 수 있어. 그리고 ② 다음 문장도 보상을 최대화하고 벌을 최소화할 수 있는 인식을 통해 삶을 조정한다는 내용으로 앞 문장과 유기적으로 연결되어 있지. ④ 다음 문장의 this는 앞 문장의 긍정적인 결과를 바랐던 결정이 좋지 않은 결과를 가져오기도 한다는 내용을 받고 있어. 마지막으로 ⑤의 다음 문장은 At the same time으로 시작해서 스트레스를 돌봐야 한다는 내용이야. 이는 앞 문장의 내용과 동시에 해야 한다는 내용으로 자연스럽게 이어지고 있어서 주어진 문장이 들어가기에는 적절하지 않아.

어휘확인

true 진짜의; 사실인 **source** 근원 **throughout** ~ 내내 **continuous** 연속적인; 계속되는 **series** 일련; 시리즈 **reward** 보상 **punishment** 벌 **personal** 개인적인 **behavior** 행동 **earn** 얻다 **negative** 부정적인 **feedback** 반응, 피드백 **associated with** ~와 관련된 **adjust** 조정하다 **on the basis of** ~을 기반으로 **perception** 인지, 지각 **maximize** 최대화하다(↔ **minimize** 최소화하다) **exactly** 정확히 **make a decision** 결정하다 **assume** 추정하다 **positive** 긍정적인 **outcome** 결과 **turn out** ~인 것으로 드러나다 **option** 선택(지), 옵션 **flight** 도피; 비행 **at the same time** 동시에 **attend to** ~을 돌보다 **work out** (일이) 잘 풀리다 **expect** 예상하다

지문 Flow

[도입]
스트레스의 근원은 인생에서 경험하는 보상과 벌 때문임

[보충설명]
보상을 최대화하고 벌을 최소화하는 방법으로 삶을 조정함

[대조]
우리의 선택 결과를 알지 못해서, 긍정적 추정과는 달리 안 좋은 결과를 얻기도 함

[결과]
그것에 맞설지 피할지 선택해야 하고, 계획대로 풀리지 않아 받게 되는 스트레스도 돌보아야 함

266 정답 ④

지문 All in One

슈퍼마켓의 통로는 채워져 있다 / 도와줄 적은 분량의 '다이어트 포장'의 과자들로

1 Supermarket aisles are loaded / with *small-portion "diet packs" of snacks* [that will help /
S V 관계대명사

당신이 충동을 억제하고 / 바라건대 적게 먹도록 / 그런데 그런 포장을 사는 것이 정말로 도울까

you control your urges / and hopefully eat less]. 2 But will buying such packs really help /
S V

당신이 당신의 음식 섭취를 줄이도록 / 이것을 알아내기 위해 / 연구원들은 참가자들에게 주었다 / 감자 칩 두 봉지

you reduce your consumption? 3 To find out, / researchers gave participants / either two
O C 부사적 용법(목적) S V_1 IO DO

와 다이어트 포장 9개 중 하나를 / 그리고 그들에게 TV를 시청해 달라고 요청했다 / 그들의 간식과 TV에 뛰어들

bags of potato chips or nine diet packs // and asked them to watch TV. 4 Before diving into
V_2 O C 분사구문

기 전에 / 참가자들은 체중이 재어졌다 / 거울 앞에서 / '다이어트의 마음가짐'을 일으

their treats and TV, / participants were weighed / in front of a mirror / to create a "dieting
S V 부사적 용법(목적)

키도록 / 결과는 드러냈다 / 다이어트용 봉지가 주어진 참가자들이 먹었다고 / 커다란 봉지가 주어진

mind-set." 5 The results revealed // that *participants* [given the diet bags] ate / twice as many
S V 접속사 S′ V′ 배수사+as+원급+as

참가자들보다 두 배 더 많은 감자 칩을 / 연구원들은 추측했다 / 다이어트 포장이 주어진 참가자

chips as *those* [given the large bags]. 6 The researchers speculated // that *the participants*
= participants S V 접속사 S′

들은 느꼈다고 / 그들이 발휘할 필요가 없다고 / 그만큼의 자제력을

[given the diet packs] felt / (that) they didn't need to exercise / as much self-control / and
V'_1 접속사 S″ V″

결국 더 많이 먹게 되었다고

thus ended up eating more.
V'_2

⬇

> 다이어트 포장에 대한 실험에 따르면 / 드러난다 / 다이어트 식품이 / 사람들을 조장
>
> 7 According to an experiment on diet packs, / it turns out // that diet foods (A) encourage
> 가주어 V 진주어 S′ V′
>
> 한다는 것이 / 더 많이 먹도록 / 그들이 자신을 통제할 필요를 덜 느끼기 때문에
>
> people / to eat more / because they feel less *need* [to (B) control themselves].
> O C 접속사 S″ V″

	(A)		(B)		(A)		(B)
①	forbid	……	enhance	②	forbid	……	relax
③	urge	……	defend	④	encourage	……	control
⑤	encourage	……	doubt				

해석 한 눈에 보기 1 슈퍼마켓의 통로는 당신이 충동을 억제하고 바라건대 적게 먹도록 도와줄 적은 분량의 '다이어트 포장'의 과자들로 채워져 있다. 2 그런데 그런 포장을 사는 것이 정말로 당신의 음식 섭취를 줄이도록 도와줄까? 3 이것을 알아내기 위해, 연구원들은 참가자들에게 감자 칩 두 봉지와 다이어트 포장 9개 중 하나를 주고 그들이 TV를 시청하도록 요청했다. 4 그들의 간식과 TV에 뛰어들기 전에, 참가자들은 '다이어트의 마음가짐'이 일도록 거울 앞에서 체중이 재어졌다. 5 결과는 다이어트용 봉지가 주어진 참가자들이 커다란 봉지가 주어진 참가자들보다 두 배 더 많은 감자 칩을 먹었음을 드러냈다. 6 연구원들은 다이어트 포장이 주어진 참가자들은 그들이 그만큼의 자제력을 발휘할 필요가 없다고 느꼈고 이리하여 결국 더 많이 먹게 되었다고 추측했다.

> 7 다이어트 포장에 대한 실험에 따르면, 그들이 자신을 (B) 통제할 필요를 덜 느끼기 때문에 다이어트 식품은 사람들을 더 많이 먹도록 (A) 조장한다는 것이 드러난다.

정답단추 요약문은 글의 핵심 내용이니까 글의 요지를 우선 파악하고, 요지를 근거로 빈칸에 들어갈 말을 추론해야 해. 본문을 읽기 전에 요약문과 선택지를 먼저 읽는 게 좋아. 이 글에서는 마지막 두 문장이 요약문의 내용을 추론할 수 있는 직접적인 단서로 다이어트 포장은 사람들이 자제력을 발휘할 필요를 적게 느끼게 함으로써 감자 칩을 두 배 더 많이 먹게 만든다는 내용이야. 이를 요약문에 반영하면 다이어트 식품은 사람들을 더 많이 먹도록 조장하는데 그것은 그들이 자신을 통제할 필요를 덜 느끼기 때문이라고 할 수 있어. 따라서 (A)에는 encourage, (B)에는 control이 들어가야 해.

어휘확인

aisle 통로 **load with** ~으로 채우다 **portion** (음식의) 1인분 **pack** 포장 **urge** 충동, 욕구 **hopefully** 바라건대 **consumption** 음식 섭취[소비]량 **researcher** 연구원 **participant** 참가자 **chip** 감자 칩; 조각 **ask** 요청하다; 묻다 **dive into** ~으로 뛰어들다 **treat** 간식; 대접 **weigh** 체중을 달다 **mirror** 거울 **create** (어떤 느낌을) 불러일으키다; 창조하다 **mind-set** 마음가짐, 태도 **reveal** 드러내다 **speculate** 추측하다 **exercise** 발휘하다; 운동 **self-control** 자제력 **thus** 결국, 따라서 **end up** 결국 ~하게 되다 **according to** ~에 따르면 **experiment** 실험 **turn out** 드러나다 **encourage** 조장하다[부추기다]; 격려하다

〈선택지 어휘〉

forbid 금지하다 **enhance** 향상시키다 **relax** 편히 쉬다 **defend** 방어하다 **doubt** 의심하다

지문 Flow

[도입]
'다이어트 포장'의 과자가 소비를 줄이는 데 도움이 될까?

⬇

[실험]
참가자들에게 감자 칩 두 봉지와 다이어트 포장 9개 중 하나를 주고 TV를 시청하게 함

⬇

[실험 결과]
다이어트 포장이 주어진 참가자들이 두 배 더 많은 감자 칩을 먹었음

⬇

[결론]
다이어트 포장은 자제를 해야 할 필요를 느끼지 못해서 더 많이 먹게 됨

267 정답 ③

지문 All in One

우리의 비교적 안정된 경계(각성) 상태는 / 하루 16시간 동안 / 과학자들이 부르는 것

1 Our relatively steady state of alertness / over the course of a 16-hour day / is due to what
S V 관계대명사

에 기인한다 / 24시간 경계 시스템, 즉 우리의 내부 생체 시계의 기능이라고

scientists call / the circadian alerting system, a function of our internal biological clock.
=

어휘확인

relatively 비교적 **steady** 안정된, 고정된 **state** 상태 **alertness** 경계 태세 **circadian** (24시간을 주기로 변하는 생물체의) 생물학적 주기의 **alerting** 경계, 경보 **function** 기능 **internal** 내부의 **biological clock** 생체 시

그 시계는 / 다수의 일일 주기를 통제하는 데 책임이 있는
(B) [2] *The clock*, / which is responsible for controlling a large number of daily cycles, / is
S / 관계대명사(계속적 용법) / V
발견된다 / 비교적 작은 뉴런 집합체에서 / 뇌 안의 깊숙이 / 정상적인 상태에서
found / in a relatively small collection of neurons / deep within the brain. [3] Under normal
그 시계는 꼭 맞게 일치한다 / 우리의 수면/기상 주기와
conditions, / the clock is closely matched / to our sleep/wake cycle.
S / V
그것이 ~할 때이다 / 그 시계의 경계 신호는 증가한다 / 깨어 있는 매 시간
(C) [4] When it is, // the clock's alerting signal increases / with every hour of wakefulness, /
접속사 S′ V′ / S / V
수면 욕구에 대항하고 있을 때 / 동시에 만들어지고 있는
opposing *the sleep drive* [that is building at the same time].
분사구문(= and it opposes ~) / 관계대명사
내부 시계의 경계 신호가 ~할 때에만 / 줄어들다 / 수면 부하가 이 서로 싸우는 힘을 극복
(A) [5] Only when the internal clock's alerting signal / drops off // does sleep load overcome
접속사 / S′ / V′ / 조동사 / S / V_1
한다 / 그리고 수면의 시작을 고려한다
this opposing force / and allow for the start of sleep.
V_2

① (A) - (B) - (C)　② (B) - (A) - (C)　③ (B) - (C) - (A)
④ (C) - (A) - (B)　⑤ (C) - (B) - (A)

해석 한 눈에 보기 **1** 우리의 비교적 안정된 하루 16시간 동안의 경계(각성) 상태는 과학자들이 24시간 경계 시스템, 즉 우리의 내부 생체 시계의 기능이라고 부르는 것에 기인한다. (B) **2** 다수의 일일 주기를 통제하는 데 책임이 있는 그 시계는 뇌 안의 깊숙이 비교적 작은 뉴런 집합체에서 발견된다. **3** 정상적인 상태에서, 그 시계는 우리의 수면/기상 주기와 꼭 맞게 일치한다. (C) **4** 그 시계의 경계 신호는 깨어 있는 매 시간 증가하는데, 동시에 만들어지고 있는 수면 욕구에 대항하고 있을 때 그렇다. (A) **5** 내부 시계의 경계 신호가 줄어드는 때에만 수면 부하가 이 서로 싸우는 힘을 극복하고 수면의 시작을 고려한다.

정답단추 지시어가 나오는 문장으로 글의 순서를 파악할 수 있어. 주어진 문장은 우리의 생체 시계에 대해 말하고 있는데, (B)에서 생체 시계를 The clock이라는 말로 받고 있고, 그것이 어떤 기능을 하는지 자세히 설명하고 있으므로, 바로 뒤에 이어지는 것이 적절해. 그리고 (C)에서 수면 욕구에 대항할 때 생체 시계의 경계 신호가 증가한다고 했는데, 이것은 (B)의 마지막 문장에 나오는 생체 시계의 수면/기상 주기에 대해 언급하는 내용 뒤에 오는 것이 자연스러워. (A)는 (C)와 반대되는 상황, 즉 수면을 할 수 있는 상황을 언급한 내용이므로 마지막에 오는 것이 적절해. 따라서 글의 순서로 가장 적절한 것은 ③ '(B) – (C) – (A)'야.

계 **responsible** 책임 있는 **neuron** 뉴런, 신경 세포 **normal** 정상적인, 보통의 **closely** 꼭 맞게 **increase** 증가하다 **wakefulness** 잠들지 않음 **oppose** 반대하다 cf. **opposing** 서로 겨루는 **drive** 욕구 **at the same time** 동시에 **drop off** 줄어들다 **load** 부하, 짐 **overcome** 극복하다 **force** 힘 **allow for** ~을 고려하다, ~을 감안하다

지문 Flow

[소재]
우리가 하루 안정되게 깨어 있는 것은 내부 생체 시계의 기능에 기인함

⬇

[개념]
(B) 생체 시계는 뇌 안에서 발견되는데, 우리의 수면/기상 주기와 일치함

⬇

[보충설명1]
(C) 수면 욕구에 대항하고 있을 때, 생체 시계의 경계 신호가 증가함

&

[보충설명2]
(A) 그 경계 신호가 줄어들면 수면이 시작됨

268 정답 ④　269 정답 ⑤　270 정답 ②

지문 All in One

Bette Graham Nesmith는 훌륭한 타이피스트가 아니었다 / 그것은 불행했다 / 비서실장으로서의
(A) [1] Bette Graham Nesmith wasn't a great typist, / which was unfortunate, // because her job
S / V / C / 관계대명사(계속적 용법) / 접속사 / S′
그녀의 직업이 / 텍사스 신탁 은행의 / 그녀(Graham)에게 필요로 했기 (때문이다) / 많은 타이핑
as an executive secretary / at the Texas Bank and Trust / required (a) her / to do a lot of
V′ / O′ / C′
을 할 것을 / 이것은 이 시기에 있었다 / 워드 프로세서 이전의 / 그때는 하나의 타이핑 실수가 필요로 할 수 있었다
typing. [2] This was at *a time* / before word processors, // when a single typing mistake could
S / V / 관계부사
전체 문서를 처음부터 다시 시작하는 것을
require / starting the entire document over.

약간의 초과 근무 수당을 벌고 있는 동안에 / 은행 창문을 장식하면서 / 휴가 때에 / Graham은
(D) [3] While earning some overtime / decorating bank windows / at holiday time, / Graham
분사구문(= While Graham earned ~) / 분사구문(= as Graham decorated ~) / S
주목했다 / 자신이 돕고 있던 화가가 실수들을 고치는 방법을 / 지우는 것이 아니라
noted // how the artist [she was assisting] corrected mistakes / not by erasing / but by
V / 관계부사
덧칠을 함으로써 / 이것은 영감으로 작용했다 / 중대한 아이디어를 위한 / Graham은 결심했다
painting over. [4] This would serve as the inspiration / for a major idea. [5] Graham decided / to
S / V / S / V
약간의 흰색 페인트를 담기로 / 작은 병에 / 아주 작은 붓과 함께 / 타이핑 실수들을 수정하기
put some white paint / in a small bottle / along with a tiny paintbrush / to correct typing
부사적 용법(목적)
위해 / 꼭 그녀(화가)가 했던 것처럼 / 결과는 상당히 성공적이었다
mistakes // just like (e) she had done. [6] The result was quite successful.
접속사 / S′ / V′ / S / V / C
그녀는 노력했다 / 자신의 타이핑 요령을 비밀로 하려고 / 그러나 결국 동료들이 알게 되었다
(B) [7] She tried / to keep her typing trick a secret, // but coworkers eventually caught on.
S_1 / V_1 / S_2 / V_2
사람들은 그녀(Graham)에게 요청하기 시작했다 / 병을 만들어 달라고 / 자신들에게 / 매일 저녁과 주말마다 일하면서
[8] People began asking (b) her / to make bottles / for them. [9] Working nights and weekends, /
S / V / 분사구문(= As she worked ~)

어휘확인

typist 타이피스트, (컴퓨터) 입력 요원 **unfortunate** 불행한 **executive secretary** 비서실장 **trust** 신탁; 신뢰 **require** 필요로 하다 **typing** (타자기·컴퓨터로) 타이핑하기, 타자 치기 **word processor** 워드 프로세서, 문서 처리기 **single** 단 하나의 **start over** 다시 시작하다 **entire** 전체의 **document** 문서, 서류 **earn** (돈을) 벌다 **overtime** 초과 근무 수당 **decorate** 장식하다, 꾸미다 **note** ~에 주목하다; 메모 **assist** 돕다 **erase** (완전히) 지우다 **paint over** ~에 덧칠을 하다 **serve as** ~로 작용하다, ~의 역할을 하다 **inspiration** 영감 **major** 중대한 **paintbrush** (그림 그리는) 붓 **successful** 성공적인, 성공한 **keep a secret** 비밀로 하다 **coworker** 동료, 함께 일하는 사람 **eventually** 결국 **catch on** 알다, 이해하다 **lab**(= **laboratory**) 실험실 **garage** 차고, 주차장 **bottling** 병에 담기; 병에 든 음료 **plant** 공장; 식물 **recruit** 채용하다, 뽑다 **chemistry** 화학 **formula** 제조법; 공식 **then** 그 다음에 **product** 제품 **over the course of** ~ 동안 **venture** 벤처 기업[사업] **major company** 대기업 **buy out** (소유·권리 등을) 매수하다 **nearly** 거의 **dollar** 달러 **plus** ~을 더하여, ~도 또한 **royalty** 로열티, 수익금

그녀는 바꿔 놓았다 / 자신의 부엌을 실험실로 / 그리고 차고를 병에 담는 공장으로

she turned / her kitchen into a lab / and her garage into a bottling plant. 10 She recruited / a *chemistry teacher* [to help perfect the formula]. 11 She began selling / hundreds of bottles a month / — then thousands.

그녀는 채용했다 / 제조법을 완벽하게 하도록 도움을 줄 화학 교사를 / 그녀는 팔기 시작했고 / 한 달에 수백 개의 병을 / 그다음에는 수천 개씩을 (팔았다)

(C) 12 Graham called (c) her product *Mistake Out* // but eventually changed the name / to *Liquid Paper*. 13 Over the course of twenty years, / she turned her one-woman venture / into *a major company* [that sold more than 65,000 bottles of *Liquid Paper*] / every day. 14 (d) She was eventually bought out by Gillette / for nearly 50 million dollars, / plus a royalty / on every bottle sold.

Graham은 자신(Graham)의 제품을 '오류 제거기'라고 불렀다 / 하지만 결국에는 이름을 바꿨다 / '액체 종이'로 / 20년의 기간 동안 / 그녀는 자신의 1인 여성 벤처 기업을 변모시켰다 / 65,000병 이상의 '액체 종이'를 판매하는 대기업으로 (관계대명사) / 매일 / 그녀(Graham)는 질레트에 의해 인수되었다 / 거의 5천만 달러에 / 로열티를 더하여 / 판매되는 병마다

268 ① (B) - (C) - (D) ② (B) - (D) - (C) ③ (C) - (B) - (D)
④ (D) - (B) - (C) ⑤ (D) - (C) - (B)

269 ① (a) ② (b) ③ (c) ④ (d) ⑤ (e)

270 ① 타자를 많이 쳐야 하는 업종에 종사했다. ② 오타 수정법을 알게 되어 동료들에게 널리 알렸다.
③ 더 완벽한 수정액을 만들기 위해 화학 교사를 고용했다. ④ 수정액을 개발한 뒤 5천만 불 이상의 돈을 벌었다.
⑤ 한 화가로부터 수정액에 관한 아이디어를 얻었다.

지문 Flow

[발단]
워드프로세서 이전의 시기에는 하나의 타이핑 실수로 전체 문서를 다시 해야 했음

[전개]
Graham은 화가의 작업에서 힌트를 얻어 타이핑 실수를 흰색 페인트로 덧칠해 수정함

[위기]
동료들이 그 사실을 알게 되었고, 그녀에게 수정용 병을 만들어 달라고 요청함

[절정]
완벽한 제조를 위해 화학 교사를 채용하였고, 더 많은 병을 팔게 됨

[결말]
20년 동안 매일 65,000병 이상의 '액체 종이'를 파는 대기업으로 성장하여, 거액에 질레트에 인수됨

해석 한 눈에 보기 (A) 1 Bette Graham Nesmith는 훌륭한 타이피스트가 아니었는데, 그것은 불행한 일로, 텍사스 신탁 은행의 비서실장으로서의 그녀의 직업이 (a) 그녀(Graham)가 많은 타이핑을 할 것을 필요로 했기 때문이었다. 2 이것은 워드프로세서 이전의 시기에 있었던 일로, 그때는 하나의 타이핑 실수가 전체 문서를 처음부터 다시 하는 것을 필요로 할 수 있었다. (D) 3 휴가 때에 은행 창문을 장식하면서 약간의 초과 근무 수당을 벌고 있는 동안에, Graham은 자신이 돕고 있던 화가가 잘못된 부분들을 지우는 게 아니라 덧칠을 함으로써 고치는 방법을 주목했다. 4 이것은 중대한 아이디어를 위한 영감으로 작용했다. 5 Graham은 약간의 흰색 페인트를 아주 작은 붓과 함께 작은 병에 담아 꼭 (e) 그녀(화가)가 했던 것처럼 타이핑 실수들을 수정하기로 했다. 6 결과는 상당히 성공적이었다. (B) 7 그녀는 자신의 타이핑 요령을 비밀로 유지하려고 애썼지만, 동료들이 결국 알게 되었다. 8 사람들은 (b) 그녀(Graham)에게 자신들에게 병을 만들어 달라고 요청하기 시작했다. 9 매일 저녁과 주말마다 일하면서, 그녀는 자신의 부엌을 실험실로, 그리고 차고를 병에 담는 공장으로 바꿔 놓았다. 10 그녀는 제조법을 완벽하게 하도록 도움을 줄 화학 교사를 채용했다. 11 그녀는 한 달에 수백 개의 병을 팔기 시작했고, 그다음에는 수천 개씩을 팔았다. (C) 12 Graham은 (c) 자신(Graham)의 제품을 '오류 제거기'라고 불렀지만 결국에는 이름을 '액체 종이'로 바꿨다. 13 20년의 기간 동안, 그녀는 자신의 1인 여성 벤처기업을 매일 65,000병 이상의 '액체 종이'를 판매하는 대기업으로 변모시켰다. 14 (d) 그녀(Graham)는 결국 거의 5천만 달러에, 그리고 판매되는 병마다 (받은) 로열티를 더해서 질레트에 의해 인수되었다.

정답단추

268 순서 배열을 해야 하는 지문 중에서는 연결어나 대명사 등의 단서가 거의 없는 글도 있는데, 이럴 때는 내용상의 자연스러운 흐름에 주목해서 읽어야 해. (A)에서 Graham이 훌륭한 타이피스트는 아니었지만, 많은 타이핑을 해야 하는 직업을 가졌다고 했어. 이를 만회하기 위해 한 화가가 사용했던 오류 수정 방식에 착안하여 수정액을 발명하게 되었다는 (D)가 이어져야 자연스러워. 그다음으로는 그것을 알게 된 동료들의 요청으로 제품을 만들기 시작했다는 (B)에 이어 그 결과 큰 수익을 올리는 대기업이 되었다는 (C)의 내용이 오는 게 적절해. 따라서 글의 순서는 ④ '(D) – (B) – (C)'야.

269 대명사는 주로 앞에 나온 명사나 뒤에 나오는 명사를 대신하여 쓰이므로 꼭 명사를 대입해서 해석이 자연스러운지 확인하자. (a)는 앞 문장에서 Graham에 대한 인물 소개가 이어지고 있으므로 Graham을 가리키고 있어. (b), (c), (d)도 마찬가지로 Graham이 *Liquid Paper*를 발견하고부터 대기업으로 성장하는 과정의 내용을 다루고 있으므로 모두 Graham을 대신하고 있어. 그러나 (e)는 앞에 새롭게 등장한 화가를 가리키고 있어. 따라서 가리키는 대상이 다른 것은 ⑤야.

270 선택지를 먼저 읽고 해당 내용이 나오는 곳을 찾아 내용을 확인하는 것이 효율적이야. ②에서 오타 수정법을 알게 되어 동료들에게 널리 알렸다고 했지만, 본문에서는 오타 수정 요령을 처음에는 비밀로 하였는데 동료들이 알게 된 것이므로 내용이 일치하지 않다는 걸 알 수 있어. 따라서 정답은 ②야.

오답단서

270 (A)의 첫 번째 문장에서 Graham은 비서실장으로서 많은 타이핑을 해야 하는 직업에 종사하고 있다는 내용이 나오고 있으므로 ①은 일치해. ③은 (B)에서 그녀는 수정액을 완벽하게 제조하기 위해 화학 교사를 채용했다는 내용에서 알 수 있어. (C)의 마지막 문장을 보면 수정액을 거의 5천만 달러에 질레트가 인수했다고 했으니 ④의 내용도 일치해. 마지막으로 이 수정액에 관한 아이디어는 그녀를 도와주던 화가에게서 받았다고 (D)에 나오고 있으므로 ⑤의 설명도 일치함을 알 수 있어.